COLLINS
POCKET REFERENCE
ENGLISH DICTIONARY

COLLINS
POCKET REFERENCE
ENGLISH
DICTIONARY

COLLINS
London and Glasgow

First Published 1988
Latest Reprint 1989
© William Collins Sons & Co. Ltd. 1988

ISBN 0 00 433197-4

British Library Cataloguing in Publication Data

The Collins pocket reference English
   dictionary.
   1. English language — Dictionaries
   423

Computer typeset by C. R. Barber & Partners,
Wrotham, England.

Printed and bound in Great Britain
by William Collins Sons & Co. Ltd.
P.O. Box, Glasgow G4 0NB.

CONTENTS

EDITORIAL STAFF

Chief Editor
Patrick Hanks

Managing Editor
Marian Makins

Editors
Alice Grandison,
Diana Adams, Danielle McGrath,
Thomas Shearer, Lorna Knight

HOW THE DICTIONARY ENTRIES ARE ARRANGED

All main entries are given in a single alphabetical listing that includes abbreviations, foreign words, and prefixes and suffixes (combining forms). Each such entry consists of a paragraph with the main word printed at the beginning in large bold type.

Within each entry, different meanings of the main word are numbered. After the meanings of the main word come words that are derived from it, printed in smaller bold type, in alphabetical order. These in turn are followed by compounds (if any) formed by the main word with the addition of another word. Derived words and compound words are explained, except when their meaning is obvious from the sense of the main word. Idiomatic phrases associated with the main word come at the end of the entry.

The part of speech is shown by an abbreviation placed after the word (or its pronunciation). When a word can be used as more than one part of speech, the change is indicated by a new part-of-speech label. Spellings of irregular noun plurals and verb parts are shown within brackets, printed in bold type.

In English many easily understood words are formed by adding prefixes such as *non-*, *re-*, *un-*, etc., to existing words. Such words are included, without definition, at the foot of the page on which they would occur in alphabetical sequence.

PRONUNCIATION KEY

The symbols used in the pronunciation transcriptions are those of the International Phonetic Alphabet. The following consonant symbols have their usual English values: *b, d, f, h, k, l, m, n, p, r, s, t, v, w, z.* The remaining symbols and their interpretations are listed below.

English Sounds

ɑː	as in *father* ('fɑːðə), *alms* (ɑːmz)
æ	as in *act* (ækt), *plait* (plæt)
aɪ	as in *dive* (daɪv), *aisle* (aɪl), *guy* (gaɪ)
aɪə	as in *fire* (faɪə), *buyer* ('baɪə), *liar* ('laɪə)
aʊ	as in *out* (aʊt), *bough* (baʊ)
aʊə	as in *flour* (flaʊə), *cower* ('kaʊə)
ɛ	as in *bet* (bɛt), *ate* (ɛt), *bury* ('bɛrɪ)
eɪ	as in *paid* (peɪd), *day* (deɪ), *deign* (deɪn)
ɛə	as in *bear* (bɛə), *dare* (dɛə), *prayer* (prɛə)
g	as in *get* (gɛt), *give* (gɪv), *ghoul* (guːl)
ɪ	as in *pretty* ('prɪtɪ), *build* (bɪld)
iː	as in *see* (siː), *aesthete* ('iːsθiːt)
ɪə	as in *fear* (fɪə), *beer* (bɪə), *mere* (mɪə)
j	as in *yes* (jɛs), *onion* ('ʌnjən)
ɒ	as in *pot* (pɒt), *botch* (bɒtʃ), *sorry* ('sɒrɪ)
əʊ	as in *note* (nəʊt), *beau* (bəʊ), *hoe* (həʊ)
ɔː	as in *thaw* (θɔː), *broad* (brɔːd)

ɔɪ	as in *void* (vɔɪd), *boy* (bɔɪ)
ʊ	as in *pull* (pʊl), *good* (gʊd), *should* (ʃʊd)
uː	as in *zoo* (zuː), *do* (duː), *queue* (kjuː)
ʊə	as in *poor* (pʊə), *skewer* ('skjʊə)
ə	as in *potter* ('pɒtə), *alone* (ə'ləʊn)
ɜː	as in *fern* (fɜːn), *burn* (bɜːn), *fir* (fɜː)
ʌ	as in *cut* (kʌt), *flood* (flʌd), *rough* (rʌf)
ʃ	as in *ship* (ʃɪp), *election* (ɪ'lɛkʃən)
ʒ	as in *treasure* ('trɛʒə), *azure* ('æʒə)
tʃ	as in *chew* (tʃuː), *nature* ('neɪtʃə)
dʒ	as in *jaw* (dʒɔː), *lodge* (lɒdʒ)
θ	as in *thin* (θɪn), *strength* (strɛŋθ)
ð	as in *these* (ðiːz), *bathe* (beɪð)
ŋ	as in *sing* (sɪŋ), *finger* ('fɪŋgə)
ᵊ	indicates that the following consonant (*l* or *n*) is syllabic, as in *bundle* ('bʌndᵊl) and *button* ('bʌtᵊn)

Foreign Sounds

Certain common foreign sounds require additional symbols, as follows:

a	*a* in French *ami*, German *Mann*, Italian *pasta*: a sound between English /æ/ and /ɑː/.
e	*é* in French *été*, *eh* in German *sehr*, *e* in Italian *che*: similar to the Scottish vowel in *day*.
i	*i* in French *il*, German *Idee*, Spanish *filo*, Italian *signor*: similar to English /iː/, but shorter.
ɔ	*o* in Italian *no*, French *bonne*, German *Sonne*: a vowel resembling English /ɒ/, but with a higher tongue position and more rounding of the lips.
y	*u* in French *tu*, *ü* in German *über*: similar to English /iː/ made with closely rounded lips.
ø	*eu* in French *deux*, *ö* in German *schön*: similar to /e/ made with closely rounded lips.

œ	*œ* in French *œuf*, *ö* in German *zwölf*: similar to English /ɛ/ made with open rounded lips.
~	above a vowel indicates nasalization, as in French *un* (œ̃), *bon* (bɔ̃), *vin* (vɛ̃), *blanc* (blã).
x	*ch* in Scottish *loch*, German *Buch*.
ç	*ch* in German *ich*: similar to the first sound in *huge*.
ß	*b* in Spanish *Habana*: similar to /v/ but made by the two lips.
ʎ	*ll* in Spanish *llamar*, *gl* in Italian *consiglio*: similar to the /lj/ sequence in *million*.
ɥ	*u* in French *lui*: a short /y/.
ɲ	*gn* in French *vigne*, Italian *gnocchi*, *ñ* in Spanish *España*: similar to the /nj/ sequence in *onion*.
ɣ	*g* in Spanish *luego*: a weak /g/ made with voiced friction.

Length

The symbol : is shown with certain vowel symbols when the vowels are typically long.

Stress

The main stress is shown by ', immediately *before* the stressed syllable.

Notes

(i) Though words like *castle, path, fast* are shown as pronounced with an /ɑː/ sound, many speakers use an /æ/. Such variations are acceptable and are to be assumed by the reader.

(ii) The letter "r" in some positions is not sounded in the speech of Southern England and elsewhere. However, many speakers in other areas do sound the "r" in such positions. Again, such variations are to be assumed.

(iii) Though the widely received pronunciation of words like *which, why* is with a simple /w/ sound and is so shown in the dictionary, many speakers, in Scotland and elsewhere, preserve an aspirated sound: /hw/. Once again this variation is to be assumed.

ABBREVIATIONS USED IN THE DICTIONARY

a.	adjective	*Gram.*	Grammar
abbrev.	abbreviation	*Her.*	Heraldry
Acc.	Accounting	*Hist.*	History
adv.	adverb	*Hort.*	Horticulture
Aeron.	Aeronautics	*ie*	that is
Afr.	Africa(n)	*impers.*	impersonal
Amer.	America(n)	*ind.*	indicative
Anat.	Anatomy	*inf.*	informal
Archaeol.	Archaeology	*interj.*	interjection
Archit.	Architecture	It.	Italian
Arith.	Arithmetic	k	kilogram(s)
Astrol.	Astrology	km	kilometre(s)
Astron.	Astronomy	l	litre(s)
Aust.	Australia(n)	Lat.	Latin
Biochem.	Biochemistry	*Linguis.*	Linguistics
Biol.	Biology	lit.	literally
Bot.	Botany	*Lit.*	Literary, Literature
Brit.	Britain, British	m	metre(s)
Bus.	Business	*masc.*	masculine
Canad.	Canada, Canadian	*Maths.*	Mathematics
cent.	century	*Mech.*	Mechanics
Ch.	Church	*Med.*	Medicine
Chem.	Chemistry	*Met.*	Meteorology
Cine.	Cinema	*Mil.*	Military
Class. lit.	Classical literature	Min.	Mineralogy
Class. myth.	Classical mythology	mm	millimetre(s)
cm.	centimetre(s)	*Mus.*	Music
Comm.	Commerce	*Myth.*	Mythology
comp.	comparative	*n.*	noun
Comp.	Computers	N	North
conj.	conjunction	*Naut.*	Nautical
cu.	cubic	*N.T.*	New Testament
dial.	dialect	*N.Z.*	New Zealand
dim.	diminutive	*obs.*	obsolete, obsolescent
E	East	*offens.*	offensive
Eccles.	Ecclesiastical	oft.	often
Ecol.	Ecology	orig.	originally
Econ.	Economics	*O.T.*	Old Testament
Educ.	Education	*Pathol.*	Pathology
eg	for example	*pers.*	person
Elec.	Electricity	pert.	pertaining
Electron.	Electronics	*Philos.*	Philosophy
esp.	especially	*Phonet.*	Phonetics
fem.	feminine	*Photog.*	Photography
fig.	figuratively	*Phys.*	Physics
Fin.	Finance	*Phys. Ed.*	Physical Education
Fr.	French	*Physiol.*	Physiology
g	gram(s)	*pl.*	plural
Geog.	Geography	*pl.n.*	plural noun
Ger.	German	*Poet.*	Poetic, Poetry
Gr.	Greek	*Pol.*	Politics

ABBREVIATIONS (*continued*)

poss.	possessive	*sl.*	slang
pp.	past participle	*Sociol.*	Sociology
prep.	preposition	Sp.	Spanish
pres.t.	present tense	sq.	square
Print.	Printing	*St.Ex.*	Stock Exchange
pron.	pronoun	*sup.*	superlative
pr.p.	present participle	*Surg.*	Surgery
Psych.	Psychiatry	*Surv.*	Surveying
Psychoanal.	Psychoanalysis	*Theat.*	Theatre
Psychol.	Psychology	*Trig.*	Trigonometry
pt.	past tense	*T.V.*	Television
Rad.	Radio	usu.	usually
R.C.	Roman Catholic	*v.*	verb
refl.	reflexive	*v.aux.*	auxiliary verb
Rel.	Religion	*Vet.*	Veterinary Medicine
S	South	*vi.*	intransitive verb
Sc.	Science	*vt.*	transitive verb
Scot.	Scottish	W	West
sing.	singular	*Zool.*	Zoology

R	Registered Trade Mark
A	Australian
C	Canadian
NZ	New Zealand
SA	South African
UK	United Kingdom
US	United States

A

a *or* **A** (eɪ) *n.* **1.** first letter of English alphabet **2.** any of several speech sounds represented by this letter, as in *take, calm* **3.** first in series, *esp.* highest mark (*also* **'alpha**) (*pl.* **a's, A's,** *or* **As**) —**from A to Z** from start to finish

a (ə; *emphatic* eɪ) *a.* the indefinite article meaning one; *an* is used before vowel sounds, and sometimes before unaccented syllables beginning with *h* aspirate

A **1.** *Mus.* sixth note of scale of C major; major or minor key having this note as its tonic **2.** human blood type of ABO group **3.** UK major arterial road **4.** UK formerly, (film) certified for viewing by all age groups **5.** ampere —*n.* **6.** absolute (temperature) **7.** area **8.** alto **9.** (*comb. form*) atomic, as in *A-bomb, A-plant*

Å angstrom unit

a. 1. acre **2.** adjective **3.** answer **4.** are

a-[1] *or before vowel* **an-** (*comb. form*) not; without; opposite to, as in *atonal, asocial, anaesthetic*

a-[2] (*comb. form*) **1.** on; in; towards, as in *aground, aback* **2.** in state of, as in *afloat, asleep*

A1, A-1, *or* **A-one** ('eɪ'wʌn) *a.* **1.** physically fit **2.** *inf.* first-class; excellent **3.** (of vessel) in first-class condition

AA 1. Alcoholics Anonymous **2.** anti-aircraft **3.** Automobile Association **4.** UK formerly, (film) that may not be shown to child under fourteen

A.A.A. 1. UK Amateur Athletic Association **2.** US Automobile Association of America

aardvark ('ɑːdvɑːk) *n.* nocturnal Afr. mammal which feeds on termites

A'asia Australasia

AB Alberta

A.B. able-bodied seaman

ab-[1] (*comb. form*) away from; opposite to, as in *abnormal*

ab-[2] (*comb. form*) cgs unit of measurement in electromagnetic system, as in *abampere, abvolt*

aback (ə'bæk) *adv.* —**taken aback** startled

abacus ('æbəkəs) *n.* **1.** counting device of beads on wire frame **2.** flat tablet at top of column

abaft (ə'bɑːft) *Naut. adv./a.* **1.** towards stern of vessel —*prep.* **2.** behind; aft of

abalone (æbə'ləʊnɪ) *n.* edible shellfish, yielding mother-of-pearl

abandon (ə'bændən) *vt.* **1.** desert **2.** give up altogether —*n.* **3.** freedom from inhibitions *etc.* —a'**bandoned** *a.* **1.** deserted, forsaken **2.** uninhibited **3.** wicked —a'**bandonment** *n.*

abase (ə'beɪs) *vt.* humiliate, degrade —a'**basement** *n.*

abash (ə'bæʃ) *vt.* (*usu. passive*) confuse, make ashamed —a'**bashment** *n.*

abate (ə'beɪt) *v.* make or become less, diminish —a'**batement** *n.*

abattoir ('æbətwɑː) *n.* slaughterhouse

abbé ('æbeɪ) *n.* **1.** French abbot **2.** title used in addressing any French cleric

abbess ('æbɪs) *n.* female superior of convent

abbey ('æbɪ) *n.* **1.** dwelling place of community of monks or nuns **2.** church of an abbey

abbot ('æbət) *n.* head of abbey or monastery (**'abbess** *fem.*) —'**abbacy** *n.* office, rights of abbot

abbr., abbrev. abbreviation

abbreviate (ə'briːvɪeɪt) *vt.* shorten, abridge —abbrevi'**ation** *n.* shortened form of word or phrase

ABC *n.* **1.** (*oft. pl. in Amer.*) the alphabet **2.** (*pl. in Amer.*) rudiments of subject **3.** alphabetical guide

abdicate ('æbdɪkeɪt) *v.* formally give up (throne *etc.*) —abdi'**cation** *n.*

abdomen ('æbdəmən) *n.* belly —abdomi-nal (æb'dɒmɪnᵊl) *a.*

abduct (æb'dʌkt) *vt.* carry off, kidnap —ab'**duction** *n.*

abeam (ə'biːm) *adv.* abreast, in line

abele (ə'biːl, 'eɪbᵊl) *n.* white poplar

Aberdeen Angus ('æbədiːn 'æŋgəs) breed of cattle, *orig.* Scottish

aberration (æbə'reɪʃən) *n.* **1.** deviation from what is normal **2.** flaw **3.** lapse —a'**berrant** *a.*

abet (ə'bɛt) *vt.* assist, encourage, *esp.* in doing wrong —a'**better** *or* a'**bettor** *n.*

abeyance (ə'beɪəns) *n.* condition of not being in use or action

abhor (əb'hɔː) *vt.* dislike strongly, loathe —ab'**horrence** *n.* —ab'**horrent** *a.* hateful

abide (ə'baɪd) *vt.* **1.** endure, put up with —*vi.* **2.** *obs.* stay, reside (a'**bode** *or* a'**bided** *pt./pp.*, a'**biding** *pr.p.*) —**abide by** obey

ability (ə'bɪlɪtɪ) *n.* **1.** competence, power **2.** talent

ab initio (æb ɪ'nɪʃɪəʊ) *Lat.* from the start

abject ('æbdʒɛkt) *a.* **1.** humiliated, wretch-ed **2.** despicable —ab'**jection** *or* '**abject-ness** *n.*

abjure (əb'dʒʊə) *vt.* give up by oath, renounce —abju'**ration** *n.*

ablation (æb'leɪʃən) *n.* **1.** surgical removal of organ or part **2.** *Astrophysics* melting or wearing away of part **3.** wearing away of rock or glacier

ablative ('æblətɪv) *n.* case in (*esp.* Latin) nouns indicating source, agent, instrument of action

ablaut ('æblaʊt) *n.* vowel change within word, indicating modification of use, *eg* *sink, sank, sunk*

ablaze (ə'bleɪz) *a.* burning

able ('eɪbᵊl) *a.* capable, competent —'**ably**

adv. —**able-bodied** *a.* —**able-bodied seaman** seaman, *esp.* one in merchant navy, trained in certain skills (*also* **able seaman**)

-able (*a. comb. form*) 1. capable of or deserving of (being acted upon as indicated), as in *enjoyable, washable* 2. inclined to; able to; causing, as in *comfortable, variable* —**ably** (*adv. comb. form*) —**ability** (*n. comb. form*)

ablution (ə'bluːʃən) *n.* (*usu. pl.*) act of washing (oneself)

ABM antiballistic missile

abnegate ('æbnɪgeɪt) *vt.* give up, renounce —**abne'gation** *n.*

abnormal (æb'nɔːməl) *a.* 1. irregular 2. not usual or typical 3. freakish, odd —**abnor'mality** *n.* —**ab'normally** *adv.*

aboard (ə'bɔːd) *adv.* on board, on ship, train or aircraft

abode (ə'bəʊd) *n.* 1. home 2. dwelling —*v.* 3. *pt./pp. of* ABIDE

abolish (ə'bɒlɪʃ) *vt.* do away with —**abo'lition** *n.* —**abo'litionist** *n.* one who wishes to do away with something, *esp.* slavery

A-bomb *n.* atomic bomb

abominate (ə'bɒmɪneɪt) *vt.* detest —**a'bominable** *a.* —**a'bominably** *adv.* —**abomi'nation** *n.* 1. loathing 2. the object loathed —**abominable snowman** large legendary apelike creature said to inhabit the Himalayas

Aboriginal (æbə'rɪdʒɪnəl) *a.* 1. of, relating to the Aborigines of Aust. 2. (**a-**) indigenous, earliest —*n.* 3. Aborigine

Aborigine (æbə'rɪdʒɪnɪ) *n.* 1. one of race of people inhabiting Aust. when European settlers arrived 2. (**a-**) original inhabitant of country *etc.*

abort (ə'bɔːt) *v.* 1. (cause to) end prematurely (*esp.* pregnancy) —*vi.* 2. give birth to dead foetus 3. fail —**a'bortion** *n.* 1. operation to terminate pregnancy 2. something deformed —**a'bortionist** *n.* one who performs abortion, *esp.* illegally —**a'bortive** *a.* unsuccessful —**a'bortively** *adv.*

abound (ə'baʊnd) *vi.* 1. be plentiful 2. overflow —**a'bounding** *a.*

about (ə'baʊt) *adv.* 1. on all sides 2. nearly 3. up and down 4. out, astir —*prep.* 5. round 6. near 7. concerning —**about** to ready to —**about-turn** *n.* reversal, complete change

above (ə'bʌv) *adv.* 1. higher up —*prep.* 2. over 3. higher than, more than 4. beyond

abracadabra (æbrəkə'dæbrə) *n.* supposedly magic word

abrade (ə'breɪd) *vt.* rub off, scrape away

abrasion (ə'breɪʒən) *n.* 1. place scraped or worn by rubbing (*eg* on skin) 2. scraping, rubbing —**a'brasive** *n.* 1. substance for grinding, polishing *etc.* —*a.* 2. causing abrasion 3. grating

abreast (ə'brɛst) *adv.* side by side —**abreast of** keeping up with

abridge (ə'brɪdʒ) *vt.* cut short, abbreviate —**a'bridgment** *or* **a'bridgement** *n.*

abroad (ə'brɔːd) *adv.* 1. to or in a foreign country 2. at large

abrogate ('æbrəʊgeɪt) *vt.* cancel, repeal —**abro'gation** *n.*

abrupt (ə'brʌpt) *a.* 1. sudden 2. blunt 3. hasty 4. steep —**a'bruptly** *adv.* —**a'bruptness** *n.*

abscess ('æbsɛs) *n.* gathering of pus in any part of the body

abscissa (æb'sɪsə) *n. Maths.* distance of point from the axis of coordinates (*pl.* **-s**, **-sae** (-siː))

abscond (əb'skɒnd) *vi.* leave secretly, *esp.* having stolen something

abseil ('æbsaɪl) *vi.* descend vertical slope by means of rope

absent ('æbsənt) *a.* 1. away 2. not attentive —*vt.* (æb'sɛnt) 3. keep away —**'absence** *n.* —**absen'tee** *n.* one who stays away, *esp.* habitually —**absen'teeism** *n.* persistent absence from work *etc.* —**'absently** *adv.* —**absent-minded** *a.*

absinthe *or* **absinth** ('æbsɪnθ) *n.* potent aniseed-flavoured liqueur

absolute ('æbsəluːt) *a.* 1. complete 2. not limited, unconditional 3. pure (as **absolute alcohol**) —*n.* 4. something that is absolute —**abso'lutely** *adv.* 1. completely —*interj.* 2. certainly —**'absoluteness** *n.* —**'absolutism** *n.* political system in which unrestricted power is vested in dictator *etc.*; despotism —**'absolutist** *n.* —**absolute zero** lowest temperature theoretically attainable

absolve (əb'zɒlv) *vt.* free, pardon, acquit —**absolution** (æbsə'luːʃən) *n.*

absorb (əb'sɔːb) *vt.* 1. suck up, drink in 2. engage, occupy (attention *etc.*) 3. receive (impact) —**ab'sorbent** *a.* —**ab'sorption** *n.* —**ab'sorptive** *a.*

abstain (əb'steɪn) *vi.* (*usu. with* from) keep (from), refrain (from drinking alcohol, voting *etc.*) —**ab'stainer** *n.* —**abstention** (əb'stɛnʃən) *n.* —**abstinence** ('æbstɪnəns) *n.* —**abstinent** ('æbstɪnənt) *a.*

abstemious (əb'stiːmɪəs) *a.* sparing in food or *esp.* drink, temperate —**ab'stemiously** *adv.* —**ab'stemiousness** *n.*

abstract ('æbstrækt) *a.* 1. existing only in the mind 2. not concrete 3. not representational —*n.* 4. summary, abridgment —*vt.* (æb'strækt) 5. draw (from), remove 6. deduct —**ab'stracted** *a.* preoccupied —**ab'straction** *n.* —**'abstractly** *adv.*

abstruse (əb'struːs) *a.* obscure, difficult to understand, profound —**ab'strusely** *adv.*

absurd (əb'sɜːd) *a.* contrary to reason —**ab'surdity** *n.* —**ab'surdly** *adv.*

abundance (ə'bʌndəns) *n.* great amount —**a'bundant** *a.* plentiful —**a'bundantly** *adv.*

abuse (ə'bjuːz) *vt.* 1. misuse 2. address rudely —*n.* (ə'bjuːs) 3. improper use 4. insulting speech —**a'busive** *a.* —**a'busively** *adv.* —**a'busiveness** *n.*

abut (ə'bʌt) *vi.* adjoin, border (on) (**-tt-**)

—a'**butment** *n.* support, *esp.* of bridge or arch

abuzz (ə'bʌz) *a.* noisy, busy with activity *etc.*

abysmal (ə'bɪzməl) *a.* 1. immeasurable, very great 2. *inf.* extremely bad —a'**bysmally** *adv.*

abyss (ə'bɪs) *n.* very deep gulf or pit

Ac *Chem.* actinium

AC 1. aircraftman 2. alternating current

a/c account

acacia (ə'keɪʃə) *n.* gum-yielding tree or shrub

academy (ə'kædəmɪ) *n.* 1. society to advance arts or sciences 2. institution for specialized training 3. secondary school —aca'**demic** *a.* 1. of academy 2. belonging to University *etc.* 3. theoretical —aca-'**demically** *adv.* —acade'**mician** *n.*

acanthus (ə'kænθəs) *n.* 1. prickly plant 2. architectural ornament like leaf of acanthus plant (*pl.* -**es**, -**thi** (-θaɪ))

ACAS ('eɪkæs) Advisory Conciliation and Arbitration Service

acc. 1. accompanied 2. account 3. accusative

accede (æk'siːd) *vi.* (*usu. with* to) 1. agree, consent 2. attain (office, right *etc.*)

accelerando (æksɛlə'rændəʊ) *a./adv.* *Mus.* becoming faster

accelerate (æk'sɛləreɪt) *v.* (cause to) increase speed, hasten —acce'**leration** *n.* —ac'**celerative** *a.* —ac'**celerator** *n.* mechanism to increase speed, *esp.* in car

accent ('æksənt) *n.* 1. stress or pitch in speaking 2. mark to show such stress 3. local or national style of pronunciation 4. particular attention or emphasis —*vt.* (æk'sɛnt) 5. stress 6. mark with accent

accentor (æk'sɛntə) *n.* sparrowlike songbird

accentuate (æk'sɛntʃʊeɪt) *vt.* stress, emphasize —ac'**centual** *a.* —accentu'a**tion** *n.*

accept (ək'sɛpt) *vt.* 1. take, receive 2. admit, believe 3. agree to —accepta'**bility** *n.* —ac'**ceptable** *a.* —ac'**ceptably** *adv.* —ac'**ceptance** *n.* —accep'**tation** *n.* common or accepted meaning of word *etc.* —ac'**cepter** *n.* —ac'**ceptor** *n.* 1. *Comm.* person or organization on which bill of exchange is drawn 2. *Electron.* impurity added to semiconductor to increase its p-type conductivity

access ('æksɛs) *n.* 1. act, right or means of entry —*vt. Comp.* 2. obtain or retrieve (information) from storage device 3. place (information) in storage device —acces-**si'bility** *n.* —ac'**cessible** *a.* easy to approach —ac'**cessibly** *adv.* —access **time** *Comp.* time required to retrieve stored information

accessary (ək'sɛsərɪ) *see* ACCESSORY

accession (ək'sɛʃən) *n.* 1. attaining of office, right *etc.* 2. increase, addition

accessory (ək'sɛsərɪ) *n.* 1. additional or supplementary part of motorcar, woman's dress *etc.* 2. person inciting or assisting in crime —a. 3. contributory, assisting

accidence ('æksɪdəns) *n.* the part of grammar dealing with changes in the form of words

accident ('æksɪdənt) *n.* 1. event happening by chance 2. misfortune or mishap, *esp.* causing injury 3. nonessential quality —acci'**dental** *a.* —acci'**dentally** *adv.*

acclaim (ə'kleɪm) *vt.* 1. applaud, praise —*n.* 2. applause —acclamation (æklə-'meɪʃən) *n.* —acclamatory (ə'klæmətərɪ) *a.*

acclimatize *or* -**tise** (ə'klaɪmətaɪz) *vt.* accustom to new climate or environment —acclimati'**zation** *or* -ti'**sation** *n.*

accolade ('ækəleɪd) *n.* 1. praise, public approval 2. award, honour 3. token of award of knighthood

accommodate (ə'kɒmədeɪt) *vt.* 1. supply, *esp.* with board and lodging 2. oblige 3. harmonize, adapt —ac'**commodating** *a.* obliging —accommo'**dation** *n.* 1. lodgings 2. agreement 3. adjustment of lens of eye 4. loan —accommodation **address** address on letters *etc.* that is not permanent or actual address

accompany (ə'kʌmpənɪ) *vt.* 1. go with 2. supplement 3. occur with 4. provide a musical accompaniment for (-**panied**, -**panying**) —ac'**companiment** *n.* that which accompanies, *esp.* in music, part which goes with solos *etc.* —ac'**companist** *n.*

accomplice (ə'kɒmplɪs, ə'kʌm-) *n.* one assisting another in criminal deed

accomplish (ə'kɒmplɪʃ, ə'kʌm-) *vt.* 1. carry out 2. finish —ac'**complished** *a.* 1. complete, perfect 2. proficient —ac'**complishment** *n.* 1. completion 2. personal ability

accord (ə'kɔːd) *n.* 1. agreement, harmony (*esp. in* **in accord with**) —*v.* 2. (cause to) be in accord —*vt.* 3. grant —ac'**cordance** *n.* —ac'**cordant** *a.* —ac'**cordingly** *adv.* 1. as the circumstances suggest 2. therefore —**according to** 1. in proportion to 2. as stated by 3. in conformity with

accordion (ə'kɔːdɪən) *n.* portable musical instrument with keys, metal reeds and a bellows —ac'**cordionist** *n.* —**piano accordion** accordion in which right hand plays piano-like keyboard

accost (ə'kɒst) *vt.* approach and speak to, ask question *etc.*

account (ə'kaʊnt) *n.* 1. report, description 2. importance, value 3. statement of moneys received, paid or owed 4. person's money held in bank 5. credit available to person at store *etc.* —*vt.* 6. reckon 7. judge —*vi.* 8. give reason, answer (for) —ac-**counta'bility** *n.* —ac'**countable** *a.* responsible —ac'**countancy** *n.* keeping, preparation of business accounts, financial records *etc.* —ac'**countant** *n.* one practising accountancy —ac'**counting** *n.* skill or practice of keeping and preparing business accounts

accoutre *or U.S.* **accouter** (ə'ku:tə) *vt.* equip —**accoutrements** *or U.S.* **accouterments** (ə'ku:trəmənts, ə'ku:tər-) *pl.n.* 1. equipment, *esp.* military 2. trappings

accredit (ə'krɛdıt) *vt.* 1. ascribe, attribute 2. give official recognition to 3. certify as meeting required standards 4. (*oft. with* at, to) send (envoy *etc.*) with official credentials; appoint as envoy *etc.* 5. believe —**ac'credited** *a.*

accretion (ə'kri:ʃən) *n.* 1. growth 2. something added on

accrue (ə'kru:) *vi.* 1. be added 2. result

acct. account

acculturate (ə'kʌltʃəreıt) *vi.* assimilate traits of another cultural group —**accultur'ation** *n.*

accumulate (ə'kju:mjʊleıt) *v.* 1. gather, become gathered in increasing quantity 2. collect —**accumu'lation** *n.* —**ac'cumulator** *n.* type of rechargeable battery, as in car

accurate ('ækjərıt) *a.* exact, correct, without errors —**'accuracy** *n.* —**'accurately** *adv.*

accursed (ə'kɜ:sıd, ə'kɜ:st) *or* **accurst** (ə'kɜ:st) *a.* 1. under a curse 2. hateful, detestable

accuse (ə'kju:z) *vt.* 1. charge with wrongdoing 2. blame —**accu'sation** *n.* —**ac'cusative** *n.* grammatical case indicating the direct object —**ac'cusatory** *a.* —**ac'cuser** *n.*

accustom (ə'kʌstəm) *vt.* make used (to), familiarize —**ac'customed** *a.* 1. usual 2. used (to) 3. in the habit (of)

ace (eıs) *n.* 1. the one at dice, cards, dominoes 2. *Tennis* winning serve, *esp.* one untouched by opponent 3. very successful fighter pilot 4. *inf.* person expert at anything —*a.* 5. *inf.* excellent

-aceous (*comb. form*) relating to, having the nature of, or resembling, as in *herbaceous*

acerbate ('æsəbeıt) *vt.* 1. make worse 2. make sour, bitter —**a'cerbity** *n.* 1. severity, sharpness 2. sourness, bitterness

acetaldehyde (æsı'tældıhaıd) *n.* colourless volatile pungent liquid used as solvent

acetate ('æsıteıt) *n.* salt of acetic acid —**acetate rayon** synthetic textile fibre

acetic (ə'si:tık) *a.* derived from or having the nature of vinegar —**acetic acid** colourless pungent liquid used in manufacture of plastics *etc.* (*see also* VINEGAR)

aceto- *or before vowel* **acet-** (*comb. form*) containing acetyl group or derived from acetic acid, as in *acetone*

acetone ('æsıtəʊn) *n.* colourless liquid used as solvent

acetylene (ə'sɛtıli:n) *n.* colourless, flammable gas used *esp.* in welding metals

acetylsalicylic acid (æsıtaılsælı'sılık) *Chem.* aspirin

ache (eık) *n.* 1. continuous pain —*vi.* 2. be painful 3. be in pain —**'aching** *a.*

achieve (ə'tʃi:v) *vt.* 1. accomplish, per-

form successfully 2. gain —**a'chievement** *n.* something accomplished

Achilles heel (ə'kıli:z) small but fatal weakness

Achilles tendon fibrous cord that connects muscles of calf to heelbone

achromatic (ækrə'mætık) *a.* free from or not showing colour, as of a lens, colourless

acid ('æsıd) *a.* 1. sharp, sour —*n.* 2. sour substance 3. *Chem.* one of a class of compounds which combines with bases (alkalis, oxides *etc.*) to form salts —**a'cidic** *a.* —**a'cidify** *v.* (**-fied, -fying**) —**a'cidity** *n.* —**a'cidulate** *vt.* make slightly acid —**a'cidulous** *a.* —**acid rain** rain acidified by atmospheric pollution —**acid test** conclusive test of value

ack-ack ('ækæk) *n.* anti-aircraft guns or gunfire

acknowledge (ək'nɒlıdʒ) *vt.* 1. admit, own, recognize 2. say one has received —**ac'knowledgment** *or* **ac'knowledgement** *n.*

aclinic (ə'klınık) *a.* without inclination, said of the magnetic equator, on which the magnetic needle has no dip

acme ('ækmı) *n.* highest point

acne ('æknı) *n.* pimply skin disease

acolyte ('ækəlaıt) *n.* follower or attendant, *esp.* of priest

aconite ('ækənaıt) *n.* 1. genus of plants related to the buttercup, including monkshood 2. drug, poison obtained from such

acorn ('eıkɔ:n) *n.* nut or fruit of the oak tree

acoustic (ə'ku:stık) *or* **acoustical** *a.* pert. to sound and to hearing —**a'coustics** *pl.n.* 1. (*with sing. v.*) science of sound 2. features of room or building as regards sounds heard within it

acquaint (ə'kweınt) *vt.* make familiar, inform —**ac'quaintance** *n.* 1. person known 2. personal knowledge —**ac'quaintanceship** *n.*

acquiesce (ækwı'ɛs) *vi.* agree, consent without complaint —**acqui'escence** *n.* —**acqui'escent** *a.*

acquire (ə'kwaıə) *vt.* gain, get —**ac'quirement** *n.* —**acquisition** (ækwı'zıʃən) *n.* 1. act of getting 2. material gain —**acquisitive** (ə'kwızıtıv) *a.* desirous of gaining —**acquisitiveness** (ə'kwızıtıvnıs) *n.* —**acquired immuno-deficiency syndrome** disease that breaks down the body's natural immunity, oft. resulting in fatal infection

acquit (ə'kwıt) *vt.* 1. declare innocent 2. settle, discharge, as a debt 3. behave (oneself) (**-tt-**) —**ac'quittal** *n.* declaration of innocence in court —**ac'quittance** *n.* discharge of debts

acre ('eıkə) *n.* 1. measure of land, 4840 square yards —*pl.* 2. lands, estates 3. *inf.* large area or plenty —**'acreage** *n.* extent of land in acres

acrid ('ækrıd) *a.* 1. pungent, sharp 2. irritating —**a'cridity** *n.*

acrimony ('ækrımənı) *n.* bitterness of feeling or language —**acri'monious** *a.*

acrobat ('ækrəbæt) *n.* one skilled in gymnastic feats, *esp.* as entertainer in circus *etc.* —**acro'batic** *a.* —**acro'batics** *pl.n.* (*with sing. v.*) any activity requiring agility

acronym ('ækrənɪm) *n.* word formed from initial letters of other words, *eg* UNESCO, ANZAC, NATO

acrophobia (ækrə'fəʊbɪə) *n.* abnormal fear of being at great height

acropolis (ə'krɒpəlɪs) *n.* citadel, *esp.* in ancient Greece

across (ə'krɒs) *adv./prep.* 1. crosswise 2. from side to side 3. on or to the other side —**get** (*or* **put**) **something across** explain something, make something understood

acrostic (ə'krɒstɪk) *n.* word puzzle in which the first, middle, or last letters of each line spell a word or words

acrylic (ə'krɪlɪk) *n.* variety of synthetic materials, *esp.* textiles, derived from an organic acid —**acrylic resin** any of group of polymers of acrylic acid, its esters or amides, used as paints, plastics *etc.*

act (ækt) *n.* 1. thing done, deed 2. doing 3. law, decree 4. section of a play —*v.* 5. perform, as in a play —*vi.* 6. exert force, work, as mechanism 7. behave —'**acting** *n.* 1. performance of a part —*a.* 2. temporarily performing the duties of another —'**action** *n.* 1. operation 2. deed 3. gesture 4. expenditure of energy 5. battle 6. lawsuit —'**actionable** *a.* subject to lawsuit —'**activate** *vt.* 1. make active, put into operation 2. make radioactive 3. make chemically active —**acti'vation** *n.* —'**activator** *n.* —'**active** *a.* 1. moving, working 2. brisk, energetic —'**actively** *adv.* —'**activism** *n.* —'**activist** *n.* one who takes (direct) action to achieve political or social ends —**ac'tivity** *n.* —'**actor** *n.* one who acts in a play, film *etc.* (-**tress** *fem.*) —**action painting** type of abstract painting characterized by smeared or spattered paint (*also* '**tachisme**) —**action replay** rerunning of section of television film or tape of match *etc.*, oft. in slow motion —**action stations** *pl.n.* 1. *Mil.* positions manned instantly in preparation for battle —*interj.* 2. *Mil.* command to take up such positions 3. *inf.* warning to get ready for something —**activated sludge** aerated sewage added to untreated sewage to hasten bacterial decomposition —**active list** *Mil.* list of officers available for full duty —**Act of God** *Law* unavoidable occurrence, such as earthquake, caused by natural forces

A.C.T. Australian Capital Territory

actinide series ('æktɪnaɪd) series of 15 radioactive elements with increasing atomic numbers from actinium to lawrencium

actinism ('æktɪnɪzəm) *n.* chemical action of sun's rays —**ac'tinic** *a.*

actinium (æk'tɪnɪəm) *n.* radioactive element occurring as decay product of uranium

actual ('æktʃʊəl) *a.* 1. existing in the present 2. real —**actu'ality** *n.* —'**actually** *adv.* really, indeed

actuary ('æktʃʊərɪ) *n.* statistician who calculates insurance risks, premiums *etc.* —**actu'arial** *a.*

actuate ('æktʃʊeɪt) *vt.* 1. activate 2. motivate —**actu'ation** *n.*

acuity (ə'kjuːɪtɪ) *n.* keenness, *esp.* in vision or thought

acumen ('ækjʊmen, ə'kjuːmən) *n.* sharpness of wit, perception, penetration

acupuncture ('ækjʊpʌŋktʃə) *n.* orig. Chinese medical treatment involving insertion of needles at various points on the body —'**acupuncturist** *n.*

acute (ə'kjuːt) *a.* 1. keen, shrewd 2. sharp 3. severe 4. less than 90° —*n.* 5. accent (´) over a letter to indicate the quality or length of its sound, *eg* abbé —**a'cutely** *adv.* —**a'cuteness** *n.*

ad (æd) *n.* advertisement —'**adman** *n. inf.* man who works in advertising

A.D. anno Domini

ad- (*comb. form*) 1. to; towards, as in *adverb* 2. near; next to, as in *adrenal*

adage ('ædɪdʒ) *n.* much-used wise saying, proverb

adagio (ə'dɑːdʒɪəʊ) *a./adv./n. Mus.* leisurely, slow (passage) (*pl.* **-s**)

Adam ('ædəm) *a.* in neoclassical style made popular by Robert Adam, Scottish architect and furniture designer

adamant ('ædəmənt) *a.* very hard, unyielding —**ada'mantine** *a.*

Adam's apple projecting part at front of the throat, the thyroid cartilage

adapt (ə'dæpt) *v.* 1. alter for new use 2. fit, modify 3. change —**adapta'bility** *n.* —**a'daptable** *a.* —**adap'tation** *n.* —**a'dapter** *or* **a'daptor** *n. esp.* appliance for connecting two parts (*eg* electrical)

A.D.C. 1. aide-de-camp 2. analogue-digital converter

add (æd) *v.* 1. join 2. increase by 3. say further —**ad'dition** *n.* —**ad'ditional** *a.* —'**additive** *n.* something added, *esp.* to foodstuffs

addendum (ə'dendəm) *n.* thing to be added (*pl.* **-da** (-də)) —'**addend** *n.* any of set of numbers that form sum

adder ('ædə) *n.* small poisonous snake

addict ('ædɪkt) *n.* 1. one who has become dependent on something, *eg* drugs (*drug addict*) —*vt.* (ə'dɪkt) 2. (*usu. passive*) cause to become dependent on something, *esp.* drug) —**ad'dicted** *a.* —**ad'diction** *n.* —**ad'dictive** *a.* causing addiction

addle ('ædəl) *v.* make or become rotten or muddled

address (ə'dres) *n.* 1. direction on letter 2. place where one lives 3. speech —*pl.* 4. courtship —*vt.* 5. mark destination on 6. speak to 7. direct 8. dispatch —**addres'see** *n.* person addressed

adduce (ə'djuːs) *vt.* 1. offer as proof 2. cite —**ad'ducible** *a.* —**adduction** (ə'dʌkʃən) *n.*

-ade (*comb. form*) sweetened drink made of fruit, as in *lemonade*

adenoids ('ædɪnɔɪdz) *pl.n.* tissue at back of nose —**ade'noidal** *a.*

adept (ə'dɛpt) *a.* 1. skilled —*n.* ('ædɛpt) 2. expert

adequate ('ædɪkwɪt) *a.* 1. sufficient, enough, suitable 2. not outstanding —'**adequacy** *n.* —'**adequately** *adv.*

à deux (a 'dɜ) *Fr.* of or for two persons

adhere (əd'hɪə) *vi.* 1. stick 2. be firm in opinion *etc.* —ad'**herent** *n./a.* —ad'**hesion** *n.* —ad'**hesive** *a./n.*

ad hoc (æd 'hɒk) 1. for a particular occasion only 2. improvised

ad hominem (æd 'hɒmɪnɛm) *Lat.* directed against person rather than his arguments

adieu (ə'djuː) *interj.* 1. farewell —*n.* 2. act of taking leave (*pl.* **-s, adieux** (ə'djuːz))

ad infinitum (æd ɪnfɪ'naɪtəm) *Lat.* endlessly

ad interim (æd 'ɪntərɪm) *Lat.* for the meantime

adipose ('ædɪpəʊs) *a.* of fat, fatty

adit ('ædɪt) *n.* almost horizontal entrance into a mine

adj. 1. adjective 2. adjourned 3. adjutant

adjacent (ə'dʒeɪs'nt) *a.* lying near, next (to) —ad'**jacency** *n.*

adjective ('ædʒɪktɪv) *n.* word which qualifies or limits a noun —**adjectival** (ædʒɪk'taɪv'l) *a.* of adjective

adjoin (ə'dʒɔɪn) *v.* 1. be next (to) 2. join —ad'**joining** *a.* next (to), near

adjourn (ə'dʒɜːn) *vt.* 1. postpone temporarily, as meeting —*vi.* 2. *inf.* move elsewhere —ad'**journment** *n.*

adjudge (ə'dʒʌdʒ) *vt.* 1. declare 2. decide 3. award —ad'**judgment** *or* ad'**judgement** *n.*

adjudicate (ə'dʒuːdɪkeɪt) *v.* 1. try, judge —*vi.* 2. sit in judgment —**adjudi'cation** *n.* —ad'**judicator** *n.*

adjunct ('ædʒʌŋkt) *a.* 1. joined, added —*n.* 2. person or thing added or subordinate —ad'**junctive** *a.*

adjure (ə'dʒʊə) *vt.* beg, entreat earnestly —**adju'ration** *n.*

adjust (ə'dʒʌst) *v.* 1. make suitable, adapt 2. alter slightly, regulate —ad'**justable** *a.* —ad'**juster** *n.* —ad'**justment** *n.*

adjutant ('ædʒətənt) *n.* military officer who assists superiors —'**adjutancy** *n.* his office, rank

ad-lib (æd'lɪb) *v.* 1. improvise, speak *etc.* without previous preparation —*n.* 2. such speech *etc.* —*a.* 3. improvised —**ad lib** without preparation; freely

ad libitum (æd 'lɪbɪtəm) *Mus.* at performer's discretion

Adm. 1. Admiral 2. Admiralty

admin ('ædmɪn) *n. inf.* administration

administer (əd'mɪnɪstə) *vt.* 1. manage, look after 2. dispense, as justice *etc.* 3. apply —ad'**ministrate** *v.* manage (business, institution, government department *etc.*) —admini'**stration** *n.* —ad'**ministrative** *a.* —ad'**ministrator** *n.* (**-atrix** *fem.*)

admiral ('ædmərəl) *n.* naval officer of highest sea rank (*also* **admiral of the fleet**) —**Admiralty (Board)** department in charge of Royal Navy

admire (əd'maɪə) *vt.* 1. look on with wonder and pleasure 2. respect highly —**admirable** ('ædmərəb'l) *a.* —**admirably** ('ædmərəblɪ) *adv.* —**admiration** (ædmə'reɪʃən) *n.* —ad'**mirer** *n.* —ad'**miringly** *adv.*

admit (əd'mɪt) *vt.* 1. confess 2. accept as true 3. allow 4. let in (**-tt-**) —ad'**missible** *a.* —ad'**missibly** *adv.* —ad'**mission** *n.* 1. permission to enter 2. entrance fee 3. confession —ad'**mittance** *n.* permission to enter —ad'**mittedly** *adv.* willingly conceded

admixture (əd'mɪkstʃə) *n.* 1. mixture 2. ingredient —ad'**mix** *vt.*

admonish (əd'mɒnɪʃ) *vt.* 1. reprove 2. advise 3. warn 4. exhort —admo'**nition** *n.* —ad'**monitory** *a.*

ad nauseam (æd 'nɔːzɪæm) *Lat.* to a boring or disgusting extent

ado (ə'duː) *n.* fuss

adobe (ə'dəʊbɪ) *n.* sun-dried brick

adolescence (ædə'lɛsəns) *n.* period of life just before maturity —ado'**lescent** *n.* 1. a youth —*a.* 2. of adolescence 3. immature

Adonis (ə'dəʊnɪs) *n.* a beautiful youth beloved of Venus

adopt (ə'dɒpt) *vt.* 1. take into relationship, *esp.* as one's child 2. take up, as belief, principle, resolution —a'**doption** *n.* —a'**doptive** *a.* due to adoption

adore (ə'dɔː) *vt.* 1. love intensely —*v.* 2. worship —a'**dorable** *a.* —ado'**ration** *n.* —a'**dorer** *n.* lover

adorn (ə'dɔːn) *vt.* beautify, embellish, deck —a'**dornment** *n.* ornament, decoration

A.D.P. automatic data processing

ad rem (æd 'rɛm) *Lat.* to the point

adrenal (ə'driːn'l) *a.* near the kidney —**adrenal gland** —**adrenaline** *or* **adrenalin** (ə'drɛnəlɪn) *n.* 1. hormone secreted by adrenal glands 2. this substance used as drug

adrift (ə'drɪft) *a./adv.* 1. drifting free 2. *inf.* detached 3. *inf.* off course

adroit (ə'drɔɪt) *a.* 1. skilful, expert 2. clever —a'**droitly** *adv.* —a'**droitness** *n.* dexterity

adsorb (əd'sɔːb) *v.* (of gas, vapour) condense and form thin film on surface —ad'**sorbent** *a./n.* —ad'**sorption** *n.*

adulation (ædjʊ'leɪʃən) *n.* flattery —'**adulate** *vt.* flatter —'**adulator** *n.* —'**adulatory** *a.*

adult ('ædʌlt, ə'dʌlt) *a.* 1. grown-up, mature —*n.* 2. grown-up person 3. full-grown animal or plant

adulterate (ə'dʌltəreɪt) *vt.* make impure by addition — a'**dulterant** *n./a.* —a'**dulterated** *a.* —adulter'**ation** *n.* —a'**dultera-tor** *n.*

adultery (ə'dʌltərɪ) *n.* sexual unfaithfulness of a husband or wife —a'**dulterer** *n.* (a'**dulteress** *fem.*) —a'**dulterous** *a.*

adumbrate ('ædʌmbreɪt) *vt.* 1. outline 2.

give indication of —a'dumbrant or a'dumbrative a. —adum'bration n.

adv. 1. adverb(ial) 2. advertisement

ad valorem (æd və'lɔːrəm) Lat. in proportion to the value of goods in question

advance (əd'vɑːns) vt. 1. bring forward 2. suggest 3. encourage 4. pay beforehand —vi. 5. go forward 6. improve in position or value —n. 7. forward movement 8. improvement 9. loan —pl. 10. personal approach(es) to gain favour etc. —a. 11. (with of) ahead in time or position —ad'vanced a. 1. at a late stage 2. not elementary 3. ahead of the times —ad'vancement n. promotion —Advanced level formal name for A LEVEL

advantage (əd'vɑːntɪdʒ) n. 1. superiority 2. more favourable position or state 3. benefit —advan'tageous a. —advan'tageously adv.

advent ('ædvɛnt, -vənt) n. 1. a coming, arrival 2. (A-) the four weeks before Christmas —'Adventist n. one of number of Christian sects believing in imminent return of Christ —the Advent the coming of Christ

adventitious (ædvɛn'tɪʃəs) a. 1. added, artificial 2. accidental, occurring by chance

adventure (əd'vɛntʃə) n. 1. risk 2. bold exploit 3. remarkable happening 4. enterprise 5. commercial speculation —v. 6. (take) risk —ad'venturer n. 1. one who seeks adventures 2. one who lives on his wits (ad'venturess fem.) —ad'venturism n. recklessness, esp. in politics and finance —ad'venturous a. —ad'venturously adv. —ad'venturousness n. —adventure playground UK playground for children that contains building materials etc., used to build with, climb on etc.

adverb ('ædvɜːb) n. word added to verb, adjective or other adverb to modify meaning —ad'verbial a. —ad'verbially adv.

adverse ('ædvɜːs) a. 1. opposed 2. hostile 3. unfavourable, bringing harm —'adversary n. enemy —ad'versative a. —'adversely adv. —ad'versity n. distress, misfortune

advert¹ (əd'vɜːt) vi. 1. turn the mind or attention 2. refer —ad'vertence n. —ad'vertently adv.

advert² ('ædvɜːt) n. inf. advertisement

advertise or U.S. (sometimes) -tize ('ædvətaɪz) vt. 1. publicize 2. make known 3. give notice of, esp. in newspapers etc. —vi. 4. make public request (for) —advertisement or U.S. (sometimes) -tizement (əd'vɜːtɪsmənt) n. —'advertiser or U.S. (sometimes) -tizer n. —'advertising or U.S. (sometimes) -tizing a./n.

advice (əd'vaɪs) n. 1. opinion given 2. counsel 3. information 4. (formal) notification

advise (əd'vaɪz) vt. 1. offer advice 2. recommend a line of conduct 3. give

notice (of) —ad'visable a. expedient —ad'vised a. considered, as in well-advised —advisedly (əd'vaɪzɪdlɪ) adv. —ad'viser or ad'visor n. —ad'visory a.

advocaat ('ædvəʊkɑː) n. liqueur with raw egg base

advocate ('ædvəkɪt) n. 1. one who pleads the cause of another, esp. in court of law 2. barrister —vt. ('ædvəkeɪt) 3. uphold, recommend —'advocacy n. —advo'cation n.

advowson (əd'vaʊz²n) n. English eccles. law right of presentation to vacant benefice

advt. advertisement

adze or U.S. **adz** (ædz) n. carpenter's tool, like axe, but with arched blade set at right angles to handle

A.E.A. Atomic Energy Authority

aegis or U.S. (sometimes) **egis** ('iːdʒɪs) n. sponsorship, protection (orig. shield of Zeus)

aegrotat ('aɪɡrəʊtæt, 'iː-) n. in British university, exemption esp. from final examinations because of illness

-aemia, -haemia, or U.S. **-emia, -hemia** (comb. form) blood, esp. specified condition of blood in diseases, as in leukaemia

Aeolian (iː'əʊlɪən) a. acted on by the wind, as Aeolian harp

aeon or U.S. **eon** ('iːən, 'iːɒn) n. 1. age, very long period of time 2. eternity

aerate ('ɛəreɪt) vt. 1. charge liquid with gas, as effervescent drink 2. expose to air —aer'ation n. —'aerator n. apparatus for charging liquid with gas

aerial ('ɛərɪəl) a. 1. of the air 2. operating in the air 3. pertaining to aircraft —n. 4. part of radio etc. receiving or sending radio waves —'aerialist n. chiefly US trapeze artist

aerie ('ɛərɪ) n. see EYRIE

aero-, aeri-, or before vowel **aer-** (comb. form) air or aircraft, as in aero engine

aerobatics (ɛərəʊ'bætɪks) pl.n. stunt flying

aerobics (ɛə'rəʊbɪks) pl.n. (with sing. v.) exercises designed to increase oxygen in blood

aerodrome ('ɛərədrəʊm) n. UK airfield

aerodynamics (ɛərəʊdaɪ'næmɪks) pl.n. (with sing. v.) study of air flow, esp. round moving solid bodies

aero engine engine for powering aircraft

aerofoil ('ɛərəʊfɔɪl) n. surfaces of wing etc. of aircraft designed to give lift

aerogram or **aerogramme** ('ɛərəɡræm) n. air-mail letter form (also air letter)

aerolite ('ɛərəlaɪt) n. meteoric stone

aerometry (ɛə'rɒmɪtrɪ) n. measurement of weight or density of gases

aeronaut ('ɛərənɔːt) n. pilot or navigator of lighter-than-air craft —aero'nautical a. —aero'nautics pl.n. (with sing. v.) science of air navigation and flying in general

aeroplane ('ɛərəpleɪn) or U.S. **airplane** ('ɛəpleɪn) n. heavier-than-air flying machine

aerosol ('εərɒsɒl) n. (substance dispensed as fine spray from) pressurized can

aerospace ('εərəspeis) n. 1. earth's atmosphere and space beyond —a. 2. of missiles, space vehicles etc.

aerostatics (εərə'stætɪks) pl.n. (with sing. v.) 1. study of gases in equilibrium and bodies held in equilibrium in gases 2. study of lighter-than-air craft

aesthetic (i:s'θetɪk, ɪs-), **aesthetical** or U.S. (sometimes) **esthetic, esthetical** a. relating to principles of beauty, taste and art —aes'thetics or U.S. (sometimes) es'thetics pl.n. (with sing. v.) study of art, taste etc. —aesthete or U.S. esthete ('i:sθi:t) n. one who affects extravagant love of art —aes'thetically or U.S. (sometimes) es'thetically adv. —aes-'theticism or U.S. (sometimes) es'theti-cism n.

aestivate or U.S. **estivate** ('i:stɪveɪt) vi. spend the summer, esp. in dormant condition —aestival or U.S. estival (i:'staɪv'l) a. rare of summer —aesti'va-tion or U.S. esti'vation n.

aether ('i:θə) n. see ETHER

aetiology or U.S. **etiology** (i:tɪ'ɒlədʒɪ) n. study of causes, esp. inquiry into origin of disease —aetio'logical or U.S. etio'logical a.

a.f. audio frequency

afar (ə'fɑː) adv. from, at, or to, a great distance

A.F.C. 1. Air Force Cross 2. Association Football Club 3. automatic frequency control

affable ('æfəb'l) a. easy to speak to, polite and friendly —affa'bility n. —'affably adv.

affair (ə'fεə) n. 1. thing done or attended to 2. business 3. happening 4. sexual liaison —pl. 5. personal or business interests 6. matters of public interest

affect (ə'fεkt) vt. 1. act on, influence 2. move feelings of 3. make show, pretence of 4. assume 5. have liking for —affec'ta-tion n. show, pretence —af'fected a. 1. making a pretence 2. moved 3. acted upon —af'fectedly adv. —af'fecting a. moving the feelings of —af'fectingly adv. —af-'fection n. fondness, love —af'fectionate a. —af'fectionately adv.

afferent ('æfərənt) a. bringing to, esp. describing nerves which carry sensation to the brain

affiance (ə'faɪəns) vt. betroth —af-'fianced a./n. (one) promised in marriage

affidavit (æfɪ'deɪvɪt) n. written statement on oath

affiliate (ə'fɪlɪeɪt) vt. (with to or with) 1. connect, attach (with larger body, organi-zation) 2. adopt —affili'ation n. —affilia-tion order Law order that putative father of illegitimate child contribute towards its maintenance

affinity (ə'fɪnɪtɪ) n. 1. natural liking 2. resemblance 3. relationship by marriage 4. chemical attraction —af'finitive a.

affirm (ə'fɜːm) v. 1. assert positively, declare 2. maintain (statement) —vi. 3. make solemn declaration —affir'mation n. —af'firmative a. 1. asserting —n. 2. word of assent —af'firmatively adv.

affix (ə'fɪks) vt. 1. fasten 2. attach, append —n. ('æfɪks) 3. addition, esp. to word, as suffix, prefix

afflatus (ə'fleɪtəs) n. impulse of creative power or inspiration

afflict (ə'flɪkt) vt. 1. give pain or grief to, distress 2. trouble, vex —af'fliction n. —af'flictive a.

affluent ('æfluənt) a. 1. wealthy 2. abundant —n. 3. tributary stream —'afflu-ence n. wealth, abundance

afford (ə'fɔːd) vt. 1. be able to buy 2. be able to spare (the time etc.) 3. produce, yield, furnish

afforest (ə'fɒrɪst) vt. turn into forest, plant trees on —affores'tation n.

affray (ə'freɪ) n. fight, brawl

affront (ə'frʌnt) vt. 1. insult openly —n. 2. insult 3. offence

aficionado (əfɪʃjə'nɑːdəʊ) n. 1. ardent supporter or devotee 2. devotee of bullfighting (pl. -s)

afield (ə'fiːld) adv. 1. away from home 2. in or on the field

afire (ə'faɪə) adv. on fire

aflame (ə'fleɪm) adv. burning

afloat (ə'fləʊt) adv. 1. floating 2. at sea 3. in circulation

A.F.M. Air Force Medal

afoot (ə'fʊt) adv. 1. astir 2. on foot

afore (ə'fɔː) prep./adv. before, usu. in compounds —a'forementioned a. chiefly in legal documents stated or mentioned before —a'forethought a. premeditated (esp. in malice aforethought)

a fortiori (eɪ fɔːtɪ'ɔːraɪ) adv. for a stronger reason

afoul (ə'faʊl) a./adv. into difficulty

Afr. Africa(n)

afraid (ə'freɪd) a. 1. frightened 2. sorry

afresh (ə'freʃ) adv. again, anew

African ('æfrɪkən) a. 1. belonging to Africa —n. 2. native of Africa —Afri'cana pl.n. objects of cultural or historical interest of southern Afr. origin —African lily S Afr. plant with funnel-shaped flowers —African violet house plant with pink or purple flowers and hairy leaves

Africander (æfrɪ'kændə, æf-) n. breed of humpbacked S Afr. cattle

Afrikaans (æfrɪ'kɑːns, -'kɑːnz, æf-) n. language used in S Afr., derived from 17th-cent. Dutch —Afri'kaner n. White native of S Afr. with Afrikaans as mother tongue

Afro ('æfrəʊ) n. fuzzy, bushy hairstyle

Afro- (comb. form) Africa or African, as in Afro-Asiatic

afrormosia (æfrɔː'məʊzɪə) n. hard teaklike wood obtained from tropical Afr. tree

aft (ɑːft) adv. towards stern of ship

after ('ɑːftə) adv. 1. later 2. behind —prep.

3. behind 4. later than 5. on the model of 6. pursuing —*conj.* 7. at a later time than that at which —*a.* 8. nearer ship's stern —'**afters** *pl.n. inf.* course after main course; dessert —'**afterwards** *or* '**afterward** *adv.* later

afterbirth ('ɑːftəbɜːθ) *n.* membrane expelled after a birth

aftercare ('ɑːftəkɛə) *n.* care, *esp.* medical, bestowed on person after period of treatment, and *esp.* after childbirth

aftereffect ('ɑːftərɪfɛkt) *n.* subsequent effect of deed, event *etc.*

afterglow ('ɑːftəɡləʊ) *n.* light after sunset

afterlife ('ɑːftəlaɪf) *n.* life after death or at later time in person's lifetime

aftermath ('ɑːftəmæθ) *n.* result, consequence, *esp.* difficult one

afternoon (ɑːftə'nuːn) *n.* time from noon to evening

afterpains ('ɑːftəpeɪnz) *pl.n.* pains caused by contraction of uterus after childbirth

aftershave (lotion) ('ɑːftəʃeɪv) *n.* lotion applied to face after shaving

afterthought ('ɑːftəθɔːt) *n.* idea occurring later

Ag *Chem.* silver

again (ə'ɡɛn, ə'ɡeɪn) *adv.* 1. once more 2. in addition 3. back, in return 4. besides

against (ə'ɡɛnst, ə'ɡeɪnst) *prep.* 1. in opposition to 2. in contact with 3. opposite 4. in readiness for

agape (ə'ɡeɪp) *a./adv.* open-mouthed as in wonder *etc.*

agar ('eɪɡɑ) *n.* gelatinous carbohydrate obtained from seaweeds, used as culture medium for bacteria in food *etc.* (*also* **agar-agar**)

agaric ('æɡərɪk) *n.* 1. any of various fungi, *eg* mushroom —*a.* 2. fungoid

agate ('æɡɪt) *n.* coloured, semiprecious, decorative form of quartz

agave (ə'ɡeɪvɪ) *n.* plant native to tropical Amer.

age (eɪdʒ) *n.* 1. length of time person or thing has existed 2. time of life 3. period of history 4. maturity 5. long time —*v.* 6. make or grow old —**aged** ('eɪdʒɪd) *a.* 1. old —*pl.n.* 2. old people —'**ageless** *a.* —**age-old** *a.*

-age (*comb. form*) 1. collection, set or group, as in *baggage* 2. process or action or result of action, as in *breakage* 3. state or relationship, as in *bondage* 4. house or place, as in *orphanage* 5. charge or fee, as in *postage* 6. rate, as in *dosage*

agenda (ə'dʒɛndə) *pl.n.* (*with sing. v.*) 1. things to be done 2. programme of business meeting

agent ('eɪdʒənt) *n.* 1. one authorized to carry on business or affairs for another 2. person or thing producing effect 3. cause 4. natural force —'**agency** *n.* 1. instrumentality 2. business, place of business of agent

agent provocateur (aˈʒɑ̃ prɔvɔkaˈtœːr) *Fr.* police spy who tries to provoke persons to act illegally

agglomerate (ə'ɡlɒməreɪt) *v.* 1. gather into a mass —*n.* (ə'ɡlɒmərɪt, -reɪt) 2. confused mass 3. rock consisting of volcanic fragments —*a.* (ə'ɡlɒmərɪt, -reɪt) 4. formed into a mass —**agglomer'ation** *n.* —**ag'glomerative** *a.*

agglutinate (ə'ɡluːtɪneɪt) *vt.* 1. unite with glue *etc.* 2. form (words) into compounds —*a.* (ə'ɡluːtɪnɪt, -neɪt) 3. united, as by glue —**aggluti'nation** *n.* —**ag'glutinative** *a.*

aggrandize *or* **-dise** (ə'ɡrændaɪz) *vt.* make greater in size, power or rank —**aggrandizement** *or* **-disement** (ə'ɡrændɪzmənt) *n.*

aggravate ('æɡrəveɪt) *vt.* 1. make worse or more severe 2. *inf.* annoy —'**aggravating** *a.* —**aggra'vation** *n.*

aggregate ('æɡrɪɡeɪt) *vt.* 1. gather into mass —*a.* ('æɡrɪɡɪt) 2. gathered thus —*n.* ('æɡrɪɡɪt, -ɡeɪt) 3. mass, sum total 4. rock consisting of mixture of minerals 5. mixture of gravel *etc.* for concrete —**aggre'gation** *n.*

aggression (ə'ɡrɛʃən) *n.* 1. unprovoked attack 2. hostile activity —**ag'gress** *vi.* —**ag'gressive** *a.* —**ag'gressiveness** *n.* —**ag'gressor** *n.*

aggrieve (ə'ɡriːv) *vt.* pain, injure —**ag'grieved** *a.*

aggro ('æɡrəʊ) *n. sl.* aggression

aghast (ə'ɡɑːst) *a.* overcome with horror or amazement

agile ('ædʒaɪl) *a.* 1. nimble 2. active 3. quick —'**agilely** *adv.* —**agility** (ə'dʒɪlɪtɪ) *n.*

agin (ə'ɡɪn) *prep. inf., dial.* against

agitate ('ædʒɪteɪt) *vt.* 1. disturb, excite 2. keep in motion, stir, shake up 3. trouble —*vi.* 4. stir up public opinion (for or against something) —**agi'tation** *n.* —'**agitator** *n.*

agitprop ('ædʒɪtprɒp) *n.* political agitation and propaganda, *esp.* of Communist nature

agley (ə'ɡleɪ, ə'ɡliː, ə'ɡlaɪ) *a. Scot.* awry

aglitter (ə'ɡlɪtə) *a.* sparkling; glittering

aglow (ə'ɡləʊ) *a.* glowing

A.G.M. Annual General Meeting

agnostic (æɡ'nɒstɪk) *n.* 1. one who holds that we know nothing of things outside the material world —*a.* 2. of this theory —**ag'nosticism** *n.*

Agnus Dei ('æɡnʊs 'deɪɪ) 1. figure of a lamb emblematic of Christ 2. part of Mass beginning with these words

ago (ə'ɡəʊ) *adv.* in the past

agog (ə'ɡɒɡ) *a.* eager, astir

agony ('æɡənɪ) *n.* extreme suffering of mind or body, violent struggle —'**agonize** *or* **-ise** *vi.* 1. suffer agony 2. worry greatly —'**agonizing** *or* **-ising** *a.* —**agony column** 1. magazine feature offering advice to readers on personal problems 2. *inf.* newspaper column containing personal messages *etc.*

agoraphobia (æɡərə'fəʊbɪə) *n.* fear of open spaces

AGR advanced gas-cooled reactor

agrarian (ə'ɡrɛərɪən) *a.* of agriculture,

land, or its management —a'**grarian-ism** n.

agree (ə'gri:) v. 1. be of same opinion 2. consent 3. harmonize 4. determine, settle 5. suit (a'**greed**, a'**greeing**) —**agreea'bil-ity** n. —a'**greeable** a. 1. willing 2. pleasant —a'**greeableness** n. —a'**greeably** adv. —a'**greement** n. 1. concord 2. contract

agriculture ('ægrɪkʌltʃə) n. art, practice of cultivating land —**agri'cultural** a. —**agri'culturist** n.

agrimony ('ægrɪmənɪ) n. yellow-flowered plant with bitter taste

agronomy (ə'grɒnəmɪ) n. study of man-agement of land and scientific cultivation of crops —a'**gronomist** n.

aground (ə'graund) adv./a. (of boat) touching bottom

agt. agent

ague ('eɪgju:) n. obs. 1. malarial fever with periodic attacks of chills and sweating 2. fit of shivering

ah (ɑ:) interj. exclamation of pleasure, pain etc.

A.H. (indicating years in Muslim system of dating, numbered from Hegira (622 A.D.)) anno Hegirae

aha (ɑ:'hɑ:) interj. exclamation of tri-umph, surprise etc.

ahead (ə'hɛd) adv. 1. in front 2. onwards

ahem (ə'hɛm) interj. clearing of throat to attract attention etc.

ahoy (ə'hɔɪ) interj. shout used at sea for hailing

A.I. 1. artificial insemination 2. artificial intelligence

aid (eɪd) vt. 1. to help —n. 2. help, support, assistance

A.I.D. artificial insemination by donor

aide (eɪd), **aide-de-camp** or **aid-de-camp** ('eɪd də 'kɒŋ) n. military officer personally assisting superior (pl. **aides** (-de-camp) or **aids-de-camp**)

AIDS (eɪdz) acquired immuno-deficiency syndrome

aigrette or **aigret** ('eɪgrɛt) n. 1. long plume worn on hats or as headdress, esp. one of egret feathers 2. ornament in imitation of plume of feathers

aiguille (eɪ'gwi:l) n. 1. sharp, slender peak 2. blasting drill

A.I.H. artificial insemination by husband

ail (eɪl) vt. 1. trouble, afflict, disturb —vi. 2. be ill —'**ailing** a. sickly —'**ailment** n. illness

aileron ('eɪlərɒn) n. movable section of wing of aircraft which gives lateral control

aim (eɪm) v. 1. give direction to (weapon etc.) 2. direct effort (towards) —n. 3. direction 4. object, purpose —'**aimless** a. without purpose

ain't (eɪnt) nonstandard 1. am not 2. is not 3. are not 4. has not 5. have not

air (ɛə) n. 1. mixture of gases we breathe, the atmosphere 2. breeze 3. tune 4. manner —pl. 5. affected manners —vt. 6. expose to air to dry or ventilate —'**airily**

adv. —'**airiness** n. —'**airing** n. time spent in the open air —'**airless** a. stuffy —'**airy** a. —**air bag** 1. bag in car, that inflates automatically in accident and prevents passengers from being thrown forwards 2. inflatable bag for restraining loads in partly filled containers —**air base** —**air bed** —'**airborne** a. flying, in the air —**air brake** 1. brake worked by compressed air 2. method of slowing down an aircraft —'**airbrick** n. chiefly UK brick with holes in it, for ventilation —'**airbus** n. airliner operated over short distances —**air commodore** —**air-condition** vt. —**air conditioner** —**air conditioning** system for controlling temperature and humidity of air in building —'**aircraft** n. 1. collective name for flying machines 2. aeroplane —**aircraft carrier** —**air curtain** air stream across doorway to exclude draughts etc. —**air cushion** 1. pillow which can be inflated 2. pocket of air supporting hovercraft —'**airfield** n. landing and taking-off area for aircraft —**air force** strength of country in military aircraft —**air gun** gun discharged by force of compressed air —**air hostess** stewardess on aircraft —'**air letter** air-mail letter, aerogram —'**airlift** n. transport of goods etc. by aircraft —'**airline** n. company operating aircraft —'**airliner** n. large passenger aircraft —'**airlock** n. 1. air bubble obstructing flow of liquid in pipe 2. airtight chamber —**air mail** —'**airman** n. —**air pocket** less dense air where aeroplane drops suddenly —'**airport** n. airfield for civilian aircraft —**air pump** machine to extract or supply air —**air raid** attack by aircraft —**air rifle** rifle discharged by compressed air —**air sac** any of air-filled extensions of lungs of birds —'**airscrew** n. propeller of any aircraft —**air shaft** passage for air into a mine etc. —'**airship** n. lighter-than-air flying machine with means of propulsion —'**airsickness** n. nausea caused by motion of aircraft in flight —'**airspeed** n. speed of aircraft relative to air —'**airstrip** n. small airfield with only one runway —'**airtight** a. not allowing passage of air —**air-to-air** a. operating between aircraft in flight —**air trap** device to prevent escape of foul gases —**air valve** —'**airway** n. 1. regular aircraft route 2. passage for ventilation, esp. in mine —'**airworthiness** n. —'**airworthy** a. fit for service in air

Airedale ('ɛədeɪl) n. large rough-coated terrier dog

aisle (aɪl) n. passageway separating seating areas in church, theatre etc.

aitch (eɪtʃ) n. letter h or sound represented by it

aitchbone ('eɪtʃbəʊn) n. 1. rump bone in cattle 2. cut of beef from rump bone

ajar¹ (ə'dʒɑ:) a./adv. partly open

ajar² (ə'dʒɑ:) a. not in harmony

AK Alaska

akimbo (ə'kɪmbəʊ) adv. with hands on hips and elbows outwards

akin (əˈkɪn) a. 1. related by blood 2. alike, having like qualities

Al Chem. aluminium

AL Alabama

-al¹ (a. comb. form) of; related to, as in functional, sectional

-al² (n. comb. form) act or process of, as in renewal

-al³ (n. comb. form) 1. aldehyde, as in salicylal 2. pharmaceutical product, as in phenobarbital

à la (ɑː lɑː) 1. in the manner of 2. as prepared in, by or for

alabaster (ˈæləbɑːstə) n. soft, white, semitransparent stone —**alaˈbastrine** a. of, like this

à la carte (ɑː lɑː ˈkɑːt) Fr. selected freely from menu

alack (əˈlæk) or **alackaday** (əˈlækədeɪ) interj. obs., poet. cry of sorrow

alacrity (əˈlækrɪtɪ) n. quickness, briskness, readiness

à la mode (ɑː lɑː ˈməʊd) Fr. in fashion

alarm (əˈlɑːm) n. 1. sudden fright 2. apprehension 3. notice of danger 4. bell, buzzer 5. call to arms —vt. 6. frighten 7. warn of danger —**aˈlarming** a. —**aˈlarmist** n. one given to prophesying danger or exciting alarm esp. needlessly —**alarm clock** clock which sounds a buzzer or bell at a set time, as to wake someone up

alas (əˈlæs) interj. cry of grief

alate (ˈeɪleɪt) a. having wings

alb (ælb) n. long white priestly vestment, worn at Mass

albacore (ˈælbəkɔː) n. tunny occurring esp. in warm regions of Atlantic and Pacific

albatross (ˈælbətrɒs) n. large oceanic bird of petrel family

albeit (ɔːlˈbiːɪt) conj. although

albert (ˈælbət) n. watch chain usu. attached to waistcoat

albino (ælˈbiːnəʊ) n. person or animal with white skin and hair, and pinkish eyes, due to lack of colouring matter (pl. -s) —**albinism** (ˈælbɪnɪzəm) n.

Albion (ˈælbɪən) n. obs., poet. 1. Britain 2. England

album (ˈælbəm) n. 1. book of blank leaves, for photographs, stamps, autographs etc. 2. one or more longplaying gramophone records

albumen (ˈælbjʊmɪn) n. egg white

albumin or **albumen** (ˈælbjʊmɪn) n. constituent of animal and vegetable matter, found nearly pure in white of egg —**alˈbuminous** a.

alchemy (ˈælkəmɪ) n. medieval chemistry, esp. attempts to turn base metals into gold and find elixir of life —**ˈalchemist** n.

alcohol (ˈælkəhɒl) n. 1. intoxicating fermented liquor 2. class of organic chemical substances —**alcoˈholic** a. 1. of alcohol —n. 2. one addicted to alcoholic drink —**ˈalcoholism** n. (disease caused by) habitual heavy consumption of alcoholic drink

alcove (ˈælkəʊv) n. recess

aldehyde (ˈældɪhaɪd) n. one of a group of organic chemical compounds

alder (ˈɔːldə) n. tree related to the birch

alderman (ˈɔːldəmən) n. formerly, member of governing body of a municipality —**alderˈmanic** a.

ale (eɪl) n. fermented malt liquor, type of beer, orig. without hops —**ˈalehouse** n. obs. public house

aleatory (ˈeɪlɪətərɪ) or **aleatoric** (eɪlɪəˈtɒrɪk) a. 1. dependent on chance 2. Mus. involving elements chosen at random

alembic (əˈlɛmbɪk) n. 1. formerly, retort used for distillation 2. anything that distils or purifies

alert (əˈlɜːt) a. 1. watchful 2. brisk, active —n. 3. warning of sudden attack or surprise —vt. 4. warn, esp. of danger 5. draw (someone's) attention to something —**aˈlertness** n. —**on the alert** watchful

A level UK 1. advanced level of General Certificate of Education 2. pass in subject at A level

Alexandrine (ælɪgˈzændraɪn) n. verse of six iambic feet

alexandrite (ælɪgˈzændraɪt) n. green chrysoberyl used as gemstone

alexia (əˈlɛksɪə) n. impaired ability to read

alfalfa (ælˈfælfə) n. plant of Europe and Asia used as fodder (also **luˈcerne**)

alfresco (ælˈfrɛskəʊ) adv./a. in the open air

alg. algebra

algae (ˈældʒiː) pl.n. various water plants, including seaweed (sing. **alga** (ˈælgə))

algebra (ˈældʒɪbrə) n. method of calculating, using symbols to represent quantities and to show relations between them, making a kind of abstract arithmetic —**algebraic(al)** (ældʒɪˈbreɪk(ˈl)) a. —**algebraist** (ældʒɪˈbreɪɪst) n.

-algia (n. comb. form) pain in part specified, as in neuralgia —**algic** (a. comb. form)

algid (ˈældʒɪd) a. Med. chilly, cold

ALGOL (ˈælgɒl) computer programming language designed for mathematical and scientific purposes

algorism (ˈælgərɪzəm) n. 1. Arabic or decimal system of counting 2. skill of computation 3. algorithm

algorithm (ˈælgərɪðəm) n. procedural model for complicated calculations

alias (ˈeɪlɪəs) adv. 1. otherwise —n. 2. assumed name (pl. -es)

alibi (ˈælɪbaɪ) n. 1. plea of being somewhere else when crime was committed 2. inf. excuse (pl. -s)

alien (ˈeɪlɪən) a. 1. foreign 2. different in nature 3. repugnant —n. 4. foreigner —**alienaˈbility** n. —**ˈalienable** a. able to be transferred to another owner —**ˈalienate** vt. 1. estrange 2. transfer —**alieˈnation** n. —**ˈalienist** n. US psychiatrist who specializes in legal aspects of mental illness

alight¹ (əˈlaɪt) vi. 1. get down 2. land, settle

alight² (ə'laɪt) a. 1. burning 2. lit up

align (ə'laɪn) vt. bring into line or agreement —**a'lignment** n.

alike (ə'laɪk) a. 1. like, similar —adv. 2. in the same way

aliment ('ælɪmənt) n. something that nourishes or sustains body or mind —**ali'mentary** a. of food —**alimentary canal** food passage in body

alimony ('ælɪmənɪ) n. allowance paid under court order to separated or divorced spouse

aline (ə'laɪn) vt. rare see ALIGN —**a'lineament** n.

A-line ('eɪlaɪn) a. (of garments) flaring out slightly from waist or shoulders

aliped ('ælɪpɛd) a. 1. wing-footed —n. 2. animal, like the bat, whose toes are joined by membrane that serves as wing

aliphatic (ælɪ'fætɪk) a. (of organic compound) not aromatic, esp. having open chain structure

aliquant ('ælɪkwənt) a. Maths. (of quantity or number) that is not exact divisor of given quantity or number

aliquot ('ælɪkwɒt) a. Maths. of or signifying an exact divisor of a quantity or number

alive (ə'laɪv) a. 1. living 2. active 3. aware 4. swarming

alizarin (ə'lɪzərɪn) n. brown-to-red crystalline solid used as dye

alkali ('ælkəlaɪ) n. substance which combines with acid and neutralizes it, forming a salt; potash, soda etc. are alkalis (pl. -s, -lies) —**alkaline** a. —**alkalinity** (ælkə'lɪnɪtɪ) n. —**alkalize** or **-ise** vt. —**alkaloid** n./a.

Alkoran or **Alcoran** (ælkɒ'rɑːn) n. see KORAN

all (ɔːl) a. 1. the whole of, every one of —adv. 2. wholly, entirely —n. 3. the whole 4. everything, everyone —**All Black** member of international Rugby Union football team of N.Z. —**all found** (of accommodation charges) inclusive of meals, heating etc. —**all fours** hands and feet —**all in** exhausted —**all-in** a. Wrestling of style of professional wrestling with no internationally agreed set of rules —**all out** inf. to one's maximum capacity —**all-out** a. inf. using one's maximum powers —**all right** a. 1. adequate; satisfactory 2. unharmed; safe —adv. 3. very well 4. satisfactorily 5. without doubt (also (nonstandard) **al'right**) —**all-right** a. US sl. acceptable; reliable (also (nonstandard) **al'right**) —**all-round** a. 1. efficient in all respects, esp. in sport 2. comprehensive; many-sided —**all-rounder** n. person with ability in many fields —**All Saints' Day** Christian festival celebrated on Nov. 1st to honour all saints —**All Souls' Day** R.C.Ch. day of prayer (Nov. 2nd) for the dead in purgatory

alla breve ('ælə 'breɪvɪ) Mus. a./adv. 1. with two beats to the bar —n. 2. formerly, time of two or four minims to the bar

Allah ('ælə) n. Moslem name for the Supreme Deity

allay (ə'leɪ) vt. lighten, relieve, calm, soothe

allege (ə'lɛdʒ) vt. 1. state without or before proof 2. produce as argument —**allegation** (ælɪ'geɪʃən) n. —**al'leged** a. —**allegedly** (ə'lɛdʒɪdlɪ) adv.

allegiance (ə'liːdʒəns) n. duty of a subject to his sovereign or state, loyalty

allegory ('ælɪgərɪ) n. 1. story with a meaning other than literal one 2. description of one thing under image of another —**alle'goric(al)** a. —**alle'gorically** adv. —**'allegorist** n. —**'allegorize** or **-rise** vt.

allegretto (ælɪ'grɛtəʊ) adv./a./n. Mus. lively (passage) but not so quick as allegro

allegro (ə'leɪgrəʊ, -'lɛg-) adv./a./n. Mus. fast (passage)

alleluia (ælɪ'luːjə) interj. praise the Lord

allergy ('ælədʒɪ) n. abnormal sensitivity to some food or substance innocuous to most people —**'allergen** n. substance capable of inducing an allergy —**aller'genic** a. —**al'lergic** a. 1. having or caused by an allergy 2. inf. having an aversion (to)

alleviate (ə'liːvɪeɪt) vt. 1. ease, lessen, mitigate 2. make light —**allevi'ation** n. —**al'leviator** n.

alley ('ælɪ) n. 1. narrow street 2. walk, path 3. enclosure for skittles 4. fine marble (pl. -s)

Allhallows (ɔːl'hæləʊz) n. see **All Saints' Day** at ALL

alliance (ə'laɪəns) n. 1. state of being allied 2. union between families by marriage, and states by treaty 3. confederation

alligator ('ælɪgeɪtə) n. animal of crocodile family found in Amer.

alliteration (əlɪtə'reɪʃən) n. beginning two or more words in close succession with same sound, eg Sing a Song of Sixpence —**al'literate** v. —**al'literative** a.

allocate ('æləkeɪt) vt. 1. assign as a share 2. place —**allo'cation** n.

allocution (ælə'kjuːʃən) n. formal address

allogamy (ə'logəmɪ) n. cross-fertilization

allomorphism (ælə'mɔːfɪzəm) n. 1. variation of form without change in essential nature 2. variation of crystalline form of chemical compound

allopathy (ə'lopəθɪ) n. 1. orthodox practice of medicine 2. opposite of homeopathy

allot (ə'lɒt) vt. 1. distribute as shares 2. give out (-tt-) —**al'lotment** n. 1. distribution 2. portion of land rented for cultivation 3. portion allotted

allotropy (ə'lɒtrəpɪ) or **allotropism** (ə'lɒtrəpɪzəm) n. property of some elements of existing in more than one form, eg carbon in the form of diamond and graphite —**'allotrope** n. —**allo'tropic** a.

allow (ə'laʊ) vt. 1. permit 2. acknowledge 3. set aside —vi. (usu. with for) 4. take into account —**al'lowable** a. —**al'lowably** adv.

—**al'lowance** *n.* —**allowedly** (ə'laʊɪdlɪ) *adv.* 1. by general agreement 2. admittedly

alloy ('ælɔɪ, ə'lɔɪ) *n.* 1. mixture of two or more metals —*vt.* (ə'lɔɪ) 2. mix (metals) to form an alloy 3. debase by mixing with something inferior

allspice ('ɔːlspaɪs) *n.* 1. berry of W Indian tree 2. spice made from this berry

allude (ə'luːd) *vi.* 1. mention lightly, hint (at), make indirect reference (to) 2. refer (to) —**al'lusion** *n.* —**al'lusive** *a.* —**al'lusively** *adv.*

allure (ə'lʊə) *vt.* 1. entice, win over, fascinate —*n.* 2. attractiveness —**al'lurement** *n.* —**al'luring** *a.* charming, seductive —**al'luringly** *adv.*

alluvial (ə'luːvɪəl) *a.* deposited by rivers —**al'luvion** *n.* land formed by washed-up deposit —**al'luvium** *n.* water-borne matter deposited by rivers, floods *etc.* (*pl.* **-s, -via** (-vɪə))

ally (ə'laɪ) *vt.* 1. join in relationship by treaty, marriage or friendship *etc.* (**al'lied, al'lying**) —*n.* ('ælaɪ) 2. state or sovereign bound to another by treaty 3. confederate (*pl.* **'allies**) —**allied** (ə'laɪd, 'ælaɪd) *a.* —**'Allies** *pl.n.* 1. (in World War I) powers of the Triple Entente (France, Russia and Britain) together with nations allied with them 2. (in World War II) countries that fought against the Axis, *esp.* Britain and Commonwealth countries, Amer., Soviet Union and France

alma mater ('ælmə 'mɑːtə, 'meɪtə) *Lat.* one's school, university, or college

almanac ('ɔːlmənæk) *n.* yearly calendar with detailed information on year's tides, events *etc.*

almighty (ɔːl'maɪtɪ) *a.* 1. having all power, omnipotent 2. *inf.* very great —**the** Almighty God

almond ('ɑːmənd) *n.* 1. edible kernel of the fruit of a tree related to the peach 2. tree bearing this fruit

almoner ('ɑːmənə) *n.* UK in hospitals, formerly, trained social worker dealing with patients' welfare

almost ('ɔːlməʊst) *adv.* very nearly, all but

alms (ɑːmz) *pl.n.* gifts to the poor —**'almshouse** *n.* UK privately supported house offering accommodation to the needy

aloe ('æləʊ) *n.* 1. genus of plants of medicinal value —*pl.n.* (*with sing. v.*) 2. bitter drug made from plant

aloft (ə'lɒft) *adv.* 1. on high 2. overhead 3. in ship's rigging

alone (ə'ləʊn) *a.* 1. single, solitary —*adv.* 2. separately, only

along (ə'lɒŋ) *adv.* 1. in a line 2. together with one 3. forward —*prep.* 4. over the length of —**along'side** *adv./prep.* beside (something)

aloof (ə'luːf) *a.* 1. withdrawn 2. distant 3. uninvolved —**a'loofness** *n.*

alopecia (æləʊ'piːʃɪə) *n.* baldness

aloud (ə'laʊd) *adv.* 1. loudly 2. audibly

alp (ælp) *n.* high mountain —**'alpine** *a.* 1.

of the Alps 2. of high mountains —*n.* 3. mountain plant —**'alpinist** *n.* mountain climber —**'alpenstock** *n.* iron-shod staff used by climbers —**the Alps** high mountain range in S central Europe

alpaca (æl'pækə) *n.* 1. Peruvian llama 2. its wool 3. cloth made from this

alpha ('ælfə) *n.* 1. first letter in Greek alphabet (Α, α) 2. UK highest grade or mark, as in examination —*a.* 3. involving helium nuclei; denoting isomeric or allotropic form of substance —**alpha particle** helium nucleus emitted during some radioactive transformations —**alpha ray** ionizing radiation consisting of stream of alpha particles —**alpha and omega** first and last

alphabet ('ælfəbet) *n.* the set of letters used in writing a language —**alpha'betic(al)** *a.* in the standard order of the letters —**alpha'betically** *adv.* —**'alphabetize** *or* **-ise** *vt.* 1. arrange in alphabetical order 2. express by alphabet

alphanumeric (ælfənjuː'merɪk) *or* **alphameric** (ælfə'merɪk) *a.* consisting of alphabetical and numerical symbols

already (ɔːl'redɪ) *adv.* 1. before, previously 2. sooner than expected

alright (ɔːl'raɪt) *adv. nonstandard see* **all right** *at* ALL

Alsatian (æl'seɪʃən) *n.* large dog of wolfhound breed, German shepherd dog

also ('ɔːlsəʊ) *adv.* 1. as well, too 2. besides, moreover —**also-ran** *n.* 1. contestant *etc.* failing to finish among first three 2. *inf.* loser

alt. 1. alternate 2. altitude 3. alto

Alta. Alberta

altar ('ɔːltə) *n.* 1. raised place, stone *etc.*, on which sacrifices are offered 2. in Christian church, table on which priest consecrates the Eucharist —**altar boy** boy serving as an acolyte —**'altarcloth** *n.* —**'altarpiece** *n.*

alter ('ɔːltə) *v.* change, make or become different —**altera'bility** *n.* —**'alterable** *a.* —**'alterably** *adv.* —**alte'ration** *n.* —**'alterative** *a.*

altercation (ɔːltə'keɪʃən) *n.* dispute, wrangling, controversy —**'altercate** *vi.*

alter ego ('æltər 'iːgəʊ, 'egəʊ) *Lat.* 1. second self 2. close friend

alternate ('ɔːltəneɪt) *v.* 1. occur or cause to occur by turns —*a.* 2. one after the other, by turns —**al'ternately** *adv.* —**alter'nation** *n.* —**al'ternative** *n.* 1. one of two choices —*a.* 2. presenting choice, *esp.* between two possibilities only 3. (of two things) mutually exclusive 4. denoting lifestyle *etc.* regarded as preferable to that of contemporary society because it is less conventional, materialistic or institutionalized —**al'ternatively** *adv.* —**'alternator** *n.* electric generator for producing alternating current —**alternating current** electric current that reverses direction with a frequency independent of characteristics of circuit

—**alternative society** group of people who agree in rejecting traditional values of society around them

althorn ('ælthɔːn) n. a tenor saxhorn

although (ɔːl'ðəʊ) conj. despite the fact that

altimeter (æl'tɪmɪtə, 'æltɪmiːtə) n. instrument for measuring height

altitude ('æltɪtjuːd) n. height, eminence, elevation, loftiness

alto ('æltəʊ) n. Mus. 1. male singing voice or instrument above tenor 2. contralto (pl. -s) —**alto clef** clef that establishes middle C as being on third line of staff

altogether (ɔːltə'geðə, 'ɔːltəgeðə) adv. 1. entirely 2. on the whole 3. in total

altruism ('æltruːɪzəm) n. principle of living and acting for good of others —**altru'istic** a. —**altru'istically** adv.

alum ('æləm) n. mineral salt, double sulphate of aluminium and potassium —**aluminous** (ə'luːmɪnəs) a.

aluminium (æljʊ'mɪnɪəm) or U.S. **aluminum** (ə'luːmɪnəm) n. light silvery nonrusting metal —**alumina** (ə'luːmɪnə) n. oxide of aluminium —**aluminize** or **-ise** (ə'luːmɪnaɪz) vt. coat with aluminium —**aluminous** (ə'luːmɪnəs) a.

alumnus (ə'lʌmnəs) or (fem.) **alumna** (ə'lʌmnə) n. US graduate of college (pl. **-ni** (-naɪ) or **-nae** (-niː))

always ('ɔːlweɪz) adv. 1. at all times 2. for ever

alyssum ('ælɪsəm) n. garden plant with small yellow or white flowers

am (æm, unstressed əm) first person sing. pres. ind. of BE

Am Chem. americium

AM or **am** amplitude modulation

Am. America(n)

a.m. or **A.M.** ante meridiem

Amadhlozi or **Amadlozi** (æmæ'hlɒʒiː) pl.n. SA ancestral spirits

amah ('ɑːmə) n. in East, esp. formerly, nurse or maidservant

amain (ə'meɪn) adv. obs., poet. with great strength or haste

amalgam (ə'mælgəm) n. 1. compound of mercury and another metal 2. soft, plastic mixture 3. combination of elements

amalgamate (ə'mælgəmeɪt) v. mix, combine or cause to combine —**amalga'mation** n.

amanuensis (əmænjʊ'ɛnsɪs) n. 1. person employed to take dictation 2. copyist 3. secretary (pl. **-ses** (-siːz))

amaranth ('æmərænθ) n. 1. imaginary purple everlasting flower 2. genus of flowering plants —**ama'ranthine** a. never fading

amaryllis (æmə'rɪlɪs) n. lilylike plant

amass (ə'mæs) vt. collect in quantity —**a'massable** a.

amateur ('æmətə) n. 1. one who carries on an art, study, game etc. for pleasure rather than for financial gain 2. unskilled practitioner —a. 3. not professional or expert —**'amateurish** a. imperfect, un-

trained —**'amateurishly** adv. —**'amateurism** n.

amatol ('æmətɒl) n. high explosive consisting of ammonium nitrate and trinitrotoluene (TNT)

amatory ('æmətərɪ) or **amatorial** (æmə'tɔːrɪəl) a. relating to love

amaze (ə'meɪz) vt. surprise greatly, astound —**a'mazement** n. —**a'mazing** a. —**a'mazingly** adv.

Amazon ('æməz'n) n. 1. female warrior of legend 2. tall, strong woman —**Ama'zonian** a.

ambassador (æm'bæsədə) n. senior diplomatic representative sent by one state to another (**am'bassadress** fem.) —**ambassa'dorial** a. —**am'bassadorship** n.

amber ('æmbə) n. 1. yellowish, translucent fossil resin —a. 2. made of, coloured like amber

ambergris ('æmbəgriːs, -grɪs) n. waxy substance secreted by the sperm whale, used in making perfumes

ambi- (comb. form) both, as in ambidextrous, ambivalence

ambiance ('æmbɪəns) n. see AMBIENCE

ambidextrous (æmbɪ'dekstrəs) a. able to use both hands with equal ease —**ambi'dexterity** n.

ambience or **ambiance** ('æmbɪəns) n. atmosphere of a place

ambient ('æmbɪənt) a. surrounding

ambiguous (æm'bɪgjʊəs) a. 1. having more than one meaning 2. obscure —**ambi'guity** n. —**am'biguously** adv.

ambit ('æmbɪt) n. 1. circuit 2. compass

ambition (æm'bɪʃən) n. 1. desire for power, fame, honour etc. 2. the object of that desire —**am'bitious** a. —**am'bitiously** adv. —**am'bitiousness** n.

ambivalence (æm'bɪvələns) or **ambivalency** n. simultaneous existence of two conflicting desires, opinions etc. —**am'bivalent** a.

amble ('æmb'l) vi. 1. move along easily and gently 2. move at an easy pace —n. 3. this movement or pace —**'ambler** n.

ambrosia (æm'brəʊzɪə) n. 1. Myth. food of the gods 2. anything smelling or tasting particularly good

ambulance ('æmbjʊləns) n. conveyance for sick or injured

ambulatory (æmbjʊ'leɪtərɪ) a. 1. of or for walking 2. not fixed 3. able to walk (also **'ambulant**) —n. 4. place for walking, such as cloister

ambuscade (æmbə'skeɪd) n. 1. act of hiding to launch surprise attack 2. ambush

ambush ('æmbʊʃ) n. 1. act of lying in wait —vt. 2. waylay, attack from hiding, lie in wait for

ameliorate (ə'miːljəreɪt) v. make better, improve —**amelio'ration** n. —**a'meliorative** a.

amen (eɪ'mɛn, ɑː'mɛn) interj. 1. surely 2. so let it be

amenable (ə'miːnəb'l) a. easy to be led or controlled —**amena'bility** or **a'menable-**

ness n. —a'menably adv. —amenable to 1. likely to respond to 2. answerable to

amend (ə'mɛnd) vt. 1. correct 2. improve 3. alter in detail, as bill in parliament etc. —a'mendment n. —a'mends pl.n. reparation

amenity (ə'miːnɪti) n. (oft. pl.) useful or pleasant facility or service

amenorrhoea or esp. U.S. amenorrhea (æmɛnə'rɪə, eɪ-) n. abnormal absence of menstruation

American (ə'mɛrɪkən) n./a. (native or inhabitant) of the American continent or the U.S.A.

americium (æmə'rɪsɪəm) n. white metallic transuranic element artificially produced from plutonium

amethyst ('æmɪθɪst) n. bluish-violet semiprecious stone

Amharic (æm'hærɪk) n. 1. official language of Ethiopia —a. 2. denoting this language

amiable ('eɪmɪəbəl) a. friendly, kindly —amia'bility or 'amiableness n. —'amiably adv.

amicable ('æmɪkəbəl) a. friendly —amica'bility n. —'amicably adv.

amicus curiae (æ'miːkʊs 'kjʊəriːiː) Law person, not directly engaged in case, who advises court (pl. amici curiae (æ'miːkaɪ))

amid (ə'mɪd) or amidst prep. in the middle of, among

amidships (ə'mɪdʃɪps) adv. near, towards middle of ship

amino acid (ə'miːnəʊ) organic compound found in protein

amiss (ə'mɪs) a. 1. wrong —adv. 2. faultily, badly —take amiss be offended by

amity ('æmɪti) n. friendship

ammeter ('æmɪtə) n. instrument for measuring electric current

ammo ('æməʊ) n. inf. ammunition

ammonia (ə'məʊnɪə) n. pungent alkaline gas containing hydrogen and nitrogen —am'moniac or ammoniacal (æmə'naɪəkəl) a. —am'moniated a. —am'monium n.

ammonite ('æmənaɪt) n. whorled fossil shell like ram's horn

ammunition (æmjʊ'nɪʃən) n. 1. any projectiles (bullets, rockets etc.) that can be discharged from a weapon 2. any means of defence or attack, as in argument

amnesia (æm'niːzɪə, -'niːzjə, -'niːʒjə) n. loss of memory

amnesty ('æmnɪsti) n. 1. general pardon —vt. 2. grant amnesty to

amnion ('æmnɪən) n. innermost of two membranes enclosing embryonic reptile, bird or mammal (pl. -s, amnia ('æmnɪə)) —amni'otic a. —amniotic fluid fluid surrounding baby in womb

amoeba or U.S. ameba (ə'miːbə) n. microscopic single-celled animal able to change its shape, found in ponds etc. (pl. -s, -bae (-biː))

amok (ə'mʌk, ə'mɒk) adv. see AMUCK

among (ə'mʌŋ) or amongst prep. mixed with, in the midst of, of the number of, between

amoral (eɪ'mɒrəl) a. nonmoral, having no moral qualities —amo'rality n.

amorous ('æmərəs) a. 1. inclined to love 2. in love —'amorously adv. —'amorousness n.

amorphous (ə'mɔːfəs) a. without distinct shape —a'morphism n.

amortize or -tise (ə'mɔːtaɪz) vt. pay off (a debt) by a sinking fund

amount (ə'maʊnt) vi. 1. come (to), be equal (to) —n. 2. quantity 3. sum total

amour (ə'mʊə) n. (illicit) love affair

amour-propre (amuːr'prɒpr) Fr. self-respect

amp. 1. amperage 2. ampere

ampere ('æmpɛə) n. unit of electric current —amperage ('æmpərɪdʒ) n. strength of electric current measured in amperes

ampersand ('æmpəsænd) n. the sign & (and)

amphetamine (æm'fɛtəmiːn) n. synthetic liquid used medicinally mainly for its stimulant action on central nervous system

amphi- (comb. form) 1. on both sides; at both ends; of both kinds, as in amphipod, amphibious 2. around, as in amphibole

amphibious (æm'fɪbɪəs) a. living or operating both on land and in water —am'phibian n. 1. animal that lives first in water then on land 2. vehicle able to travel on land or water 3. aircraft that can alight on land or water

amphitheatre or U.S. amphitheater ('æmfɪθɪətə) n. building with tiers of seats rising round an arena

amphora ('æmfərə) n. two-handled jar of ancient Greece and Rome (pl. -rae (-riː), -s)

ample ('æmpəl) a. 1. big enough 2. large, spacious —'amply adv.

amplify ('æmplɪfaɪ) vt. 1. increase 2. make bigger, louder etc. (-fied, -fying) —amplifi'cation n. —'amplifier n.

amplitude ('æmplɪtjuːd) n. spaciousness, width, magnitude —amplitude modulation Rad. method of transmitting information in which amplitude of carrier wave is varied

ampoule ('æmpuːl, -pjuːl) or (esp. U.S.) ampule n. container for hypodermic dose

ampulla (æm'pʊlə) n. 1. Anat. dilated end part of duct or canal 2. Christianity vessel for wine and water used at the Eucharist; small flask for consecrated oil 3. Roman two-handled bottle (pl. ampullae (-'pʊliː))

amputate ('æmpjʊteɪt) v. cut off (limb etc.) —ampu'tation n.

amuck (ə'mʌk) or amok adv. —run amuck rush about as in murderous frenzy

amulet ('æmjʊlɪt) n. something carried or worn as a charm

amuse (ə'mjuːz) vt. 1. divert 2. occupy pleasantly 3. cause to laugh or smile

—a'**musement** n. entertainment, pastime —a'**musing** a. —a'**musingly** adv.

amylase ('æmɪleɪz) n. enzyme that hydrolyses starch and glycogen to simple sugar

amylum ('æmɪləm) n. see STARCH

an (æn; unstressed ən) see ʌ

an- or before consonant **a-** (comb. form) not; without, as in anaphrodisiac

-an, -ean, or **-ian** (comb. form) 1. belonging to; coming from; typical of; adhering to, as in European, Elizabethan, Christian 2. person who specializes or is expert in, as in dietician

Anabaptist (ænə'bæptɪst) n. member of Protestant movement that rejected infant baptism and insisted adults be rebaptized

anabolism (ə'næbəlɪzəm) n. metabolic process in which complex molecules are synthesized from simpler ones with storage of energy —ana'**bolic** a. —ana**bolic steroid** any of various hormones that encourage muscle and bone growth

anabranch ('ɑːnəbrɑːntʃ) n. stream that leaves a river and re-enters it further downstream

anachronism (ə'nækrənɪzəm) n. 1. mistake of time, by which something is put in wrong historical period 2. something out of date —anachro'**nistic** a.

anacoluthon (ænəkə'luːθɒn) n. a sentence or words faulty in grammatical sequence (pl. **-tha** (-θə))

anaconda (ænə'kɒndə) n. large snake which kills by constriction

anadromous (ə'nædrəməs) a. (of salmon etc.) migrating up rivers to breed

anaemia or U.S. **anemia** (ə'niːmɪə) n. deficiency in number of red blood cells —a'**naemic** or U.S. a'**nemic** a. 1. suffering from anaemia 2. pale, sickly, lacking vitality

anaerobe (æn'ɛərəʊb) or **anaerobium** (ænɛə'rəʊbɪəm) n. organism that can live without free oxygen (pl. **-obes** or **-obia** (-'əʊbɪə)) —anaer'**obic** a.

anaesthetic or U.S. **anesthetic** (ænɪs-'θetɪk) n./a. (drug) causing loss of sensation —anaesthesia or U.S. anesthesia (ænɪs'θiːzɪə) n. loss of sensation —anaes'**thetically** or U.S. anes'**thetically** adv. —anaesthetist or U.S. anesthetist (ə'niːsθətɪst) n. expert in use of anaesthetics —anaesthetize, anaesthetise, or U.S. anesthetize (ə'niːsθətaɪz) vt.

Anaglypta (ænə'glɪptə) n. R thick, embossed wallpaper

anagram ('ænəgræm) n. word or words made by arranging in different order the letters of another word or words, eg ant from tan —anagram'**matical** a. —ana'**grammatist** n.

anal ('eɪn²l) a. see ANUS

analects ('ænəlɛkts) or **analecta** (ænə-'lɛktə) pl.n. selected literary passages from one or more works

analgesia (ænʲl'dʒiːzɪə) or **analgia** (æn-

'ældʒɪə) n. absence of pain —anal'**gesic** a./n. (drug) relieving pain

analogue or U.S. (sometimes) **analog** ('ænʲlɒg) n. 1. something analogous to something else 2. Biol. analogous part or organ —a. 3. using analogue (such as dial and pointer) to represent data or information —**analogue computer** computer that uses voltages to represent numbers of physical quantities

analogy (ə'nælədʒɪ) n. 1. agreement or likeness in certain respects 2. correspondence —ana'**logical** a. —ana'**logically** adv. —a'**nalogist** n. —a'**nalogize** or **-gise** v. explain by analogy —a'**nalogous** a. 1. similar 2. parallel —a'**nalogously** adv.

analysis (ə'nælɪsɪs) n. separation of something into its elements or components (pl. **-yses** (-ɪsiːz)) —'**analyse** or U.S. **-lyze** vt. 1. examine critically 2. determine the constituent parts of —'**analyst** n. one skilled in analysis, esp. chemical or psychiatric analysis —ana'**lytic(al)** a. 1. relating to analysis 2. capable of or given to analysing —ana'**lytically** adv.

anapaest or **anapest** ('ænəpest, -piːst) n. metrical foot of two short syllables followed by one long

anaphora (ə'næfərə) n. 1. Rhetoric repetition of word or phrase at beginning of successive clauses 2. Gram. use of word such as pronoun to avoid repetition

anarchy ('ænəkɪ) n. 1. lawlessness 2. lack of government in a state 3. confusion —an'**archic(al)** a. —an'**archically** adv. —'**anarchism** n. —'**anarchist** n. one who opposes all forms of government

anastigmat (æ'næstɪgmæt, ænə'stɪgmæt) n. lens corrected for astigmatism —anas**tig'matic** a. (of lens) not astigmatic

anastomosis (ənæstə'məʊsɪs) n. interconnection of veins, arteries etc. (pl. **-ses** (-siːz))

anat. 1. anatomical 2. anatomy

anathema (ə'næθəmə) n. 1. anything detested, hateful 2. ban of the church 3. curse —a'**nathematize** or **-tise** v.

anatomy (ə'nætəmɪ) n. 1. science of structure of the body 2. detailed analysis 3. the body —ana'**tomical** a. —ana'**tomically** adv. —a'**natomist** n. —a'**natomize** or **-mise** vt.

-ance or **-ancy** (comb. form) action, state or condition, or quality, as in utterance, resemblance

ancestor ('ænsɛstə) n. 1. person from whom another is descended 2. early type of later form or product —an'**cestral** a. —'**ancestry** n.

anchor ('æŋkə) n. 1. heavy (usu. hooked) implement dropped on cable, chain etc. to bottom of sea to secure vessel 2. source of stability or security —vt. 3. fasten by or as by anchor —'**anchorage** n. act of, place of anchoring —**anchor man** 1. Sport end member of tug-of-war team; last runner in relay team 2. in broadcasting, compere who links different parts of programme

—**weigh anchor** haul up anchor and set sail

anchorite ('æŋkərait) n. hermit, recluse ('**anchoress** fem.)

anchovy ('æntʃəvɪ) n. small savoury fish of herring family

anchusa (æŋ'kjuːsə) n. plant with hairy leaves and blue flowers

ancien régime (ãsjẽ reˈʒim) Fr. political and social system of France before the Revolution of 1789 (pl. **anciens régimes** (ãsjẽ reˈʒim))

ancient ('einʃənt) a. **1.** belonging to former age **2.** old **3.** timeworn —n. **4.** (oft. pl.) one who lived in an earlier age —'**anciently** adv. —**ancient monument** notable building or site preserved as public property

ancillary (æn'sɪlərɪ) a. subordinate, subservient, auxiliary

-**ancy** (comb. form) condition or quality, as in poignancy (see also -ance)

and (ænd; unstressed ənd, ən) conj. connecting word, used to join words and sentences, to introduce a consequence etc. —**and/or** conj. used to join terms when either one or other or both is indicated

andante (æn'dæntɪ) Mus. a./adv. **1.** at moderately slow tempo —n. **2.** passage or piece performed in this manner

andantino (ændæn'tiːnəu) Mus. a./adv. **1.** slightly faster or slower than andante —n. **2.** passage or piece performed in this manner (pl. -s)

andiron ('ændaɪən) n. iron bar or bracket for supporting logs in fireplace

andro- or before vowel **andr-** (comb. form) **1.** male; masculine **2.** in botany, stamen or anther

androgen ('ændrədʒən) n. steroid that promotes development of male sexual characteristics

androgynous (æn'drɒdʒɪnəs) a. **1.** Bot. having male and female flowers in same inflorescence **2.** hermaphrodite

android ('ændrɔɪd) n. **1.** in science fiction, robot resembling human being —a. **2.** resembling human being

anecdote ('ænɪkdəut) n. very short story dealing with single incident —**anec'dotal** or **anec'dotic** a.

anemia (ə'niːmɪə) n. US see ANAEMIA

anemograph (ə'nɛməugrɑːf) n. self-recording anemometer

anemometer (ænɪ'mɒmɪtə) n. instrument for recording force and direction of wind —**anemo'metric** a. —**ane'mometry** n.

anemone (ə'nɛmənɪ) n. flower related to buttercup —**sea anemone** plantlike sea animal

anent (ə'nɛnt) prep. obs. concerning

aneroid ('ænərɔɪd) a. denoting a barometer which measures atmospheric pressure without the use of mercury or other liquid

aneurysm or **aneurism** ('ænjərɪzəm) n. swelling out of a part of an artery

anew (ə'njuː) adv. afresh, again

angel ('eɪndʒəl) n. **1.** divine messenger **2.**
ministering or attendant spirit **3.** person with the qualities of such a spirit, as gentleness, purity etc. —**angelic** (æn-'dʒɛlɪk) a. —**angelically** (æn'dʒɛlɪkəlɪ) adv. —**angel cake** or esp. U.S. **angel food cake** light sponge cake made without egg yolks —'**angelfish** n. **1.** small tropical marine fish which has brightly coloured body **2.** S Amer. freshwater fish which has large dorsal and anal fins **3.** shark with flattened pectoral fins (pl. **-fish, -fishes**)

angelica (æn'dʒɛlɪkə) n. **1.** aromatic plant **2.** the candied stalks of this plant used in cookery

Angelus ('ændʒɪləs) n. devotional service in R.C. Church in memory of the Incarnation, said at morning, noon and sunset

anger ('æŋgə) n. **1.** strong emotion excited by a real or supposed injury **2.** wrath **3.** rage —vt. **4.** excite to wrath **5.** enrage —'**angrily** adv. —'**angry** a. **1.** full of anger **2.** inflamed

angina pectoris (æn'dʒaɪnə 'pɛktɔrɪs) severe pain accompanying heart disease

angiosperm ('ændʒɪəspɜːm) n. any plant having a seed vessel

angle¹ ('æŋg'l) vi. fish with hook and line —'**angler** n. **1.** fisherman **2.** sea fish with spiny dorsal fin (also **angler fish**) —'**angling** n.

angle² ('æŋg'l) n. **1.** meeting of two lines or surfaces **2.** sharp corner **3.** point of view **4.** inf. devious motive —vt. **5.** bend at an angle —**angle of incidence 1.** angle of line or beam of radiation to line perpendicular to surface at point of incidence **2.** angle between chord line of aircraft wing or tailplane and longitudinal axis

Anglican ('æŋglɪkən) a./n. (member) of the Church of England —'**Anglicanism** n.

anglicize or -**cise** ('æŋglɪsaɪz) vt. express in English, turn into English form —'**Anglicism** n. English idiom or peculiarity

Anglo ('æŋgləu) n. C English-speaking Canadian (pl. **-s**)

Anglo- ('æŋgləu-) (comb. form) English, as in Anglo-American

Anglo-French a. **1.** of England and France **2.** of Anglo-French —n. **3.** Norman-French language of medieval England

Anglo-Norman a. **1.** relating to Norman conquerors of England or their language —n. **2.** Norman inhabitant of England after 1066 **3.** Anglo-French language

Anglophile ('æŋgləufaɪl, -faɪl) or **Anglophil** n. person having admiration for England or the English

Anglophobia (æŋgləu'fəubɪə) n. dislike of England etc.

Anglo-Saxon n. **1.** member of West Germanic tribes that settled in Britain from 5th century A.D. **2.** language of these tribes (see **Old English** at OLD) **3.** White person whose native language is English **4.** inf. plain blunt English —a. **5.** forming part of Germanic element in Modern English **6.**

of Anglo-Saxons or Old English language 7. of White Protestant culture of Britain and Amer.

angora (æŋˈgɔːrə) *n.* (*sometimes* A-) 1. goat with long white silky hair which is used in the making of mohair 2. cloth or wool made from this hair —**angora cat** *or* **rabbit** varieties of cat and rabbit with long, silky fur

angostura bitters (æŋgəˈstjʊərə) R (*oft.* A-) bitter tonic, used as flavouring in alcoholic drinks

angstrom (ˈæŋstrəm) *n.* unit of length for measuring wavelengths of electromagnetic radiation

anguish (ˈæŋgwɪʃ) *n.* great mental or physical pain

angular (ˈæŋgjʊlə) *a.* 1. (of people) bony, awkward 2. having angles 3. measured by an angle —**angu'larity** *n.*

anhydrous (ænˈhaɪdrəs) *a.* (of chemical substances) free from water

anil (ˈænɪl) *n.* leguminous West Indian shrub (*also* **'indigo**)

aniline (ˈænɪlɪn, -liːn) *n.* product of coal tar or indigo, which yields dyes

animadvert (ænɪmædˈvɜːt) *vi.* (*usu.* with on *or* upon) criticize, pass censure —**animad'version** *n.* criticism, censure

animal (ˈænɪməl) *n.* 1. living creature, having sensation and power of voluntary motion 2. beast —*a.* 3. of, pert. to animals 4. sensual —**ani'malcular** *a.* —**ani'malcule** *n.* very small animal, *esp.* one which cannot be seen by naked eye —**'animalism** *n.* —**'animally** *adv.* —**animal husbandry** science of breeding and rearing farm animals —**animal magnetism** 1. quality of being attractive, *esp.* to opposite sex 2. *obs.* hypnotism

animate (ˈænɪmeɪt) *vt.* 1. give life to 2. enliven 3. inspire 4. actuate 5. make cartoon film of —**'animated** *a.* 1. lively 2. in form of cartoons —**ani'mation** *n.* 1. life, vigour 2. cartoon film —**'animator** *n.*

animato (ænɪˈmɑːtəʊ) *a./adv. Mus.* lively; animated

animism (ˈænɪmɪzəm) *n.* belief that natural effects are due to spirits or that inanimate things have spirits —**'animist** *n.* —**ani'mistic** *a.*

animosity (ænɪˈmɒsɪtɪ) *n.* hostility, enmity

animus (ˈænɪməs) *n.* 1. intense dislike; hatred 2. animosity

anion (ˈænaɪən) *n.* ion with negative charge

anise (ˈænɪs) *n.* plant with aromatic seeds, which are used for flavouring

aniseed (ˈænɪsiːd) *n.* liquorice-flavoured seed of anise

ankle (ˈæŋkˀl) *n.* joint between foot and leg —**'anklet** *n.* ornamental chain *etc.* worn around ankle

ankylosis *or* **anchylosis** (æŋkɪˈləʊsɪs) *n.* abnormal adhesion or immobility of bones in joint

anna (ˈænə) *n.* formerly, Indian coin worth one sixteenth of rupee

annals (ˈænˀlz) *pl.n.* historical records of events —**'annalist** *n.*

anneal (əˈniːl) *vt.* 1. toughen (metal or glass) by heating and slow cooling 2. temper (determination, will *etc.*) —**an'nealing** *n.*

annelid (ˈænəlɪd) *n.* one of class of invertebrate animals, including the earthworm *etc.*

annex (əˈnɛks) *vt.* 1. add, append, attach 2. take possession of (*esp.* territory) —**annex'ation** *n.*

annexe *or esp. U.S.* **annex** (ˈænɛks) *n.* 1. supplementary building 2. something added

annihilate (əˈnaɪəleɪt) *vt.* reduce to nothing, destroy utterly —**annihi'lation** *n.* —**an'nihilative** *a.* —**an'nihilator** *n.*

anniversary (ænɪˈvɜːsərɪ) *n.* 1. yearly recurrence of a date of notable event 2. celebration of this

anno Domini (ˈænəʊ ˈdɒmɪnaɪ, -niː) *Lat.* in the year of our Lord

annotate (ˈænəʊteɪt, ˈænə-) *vt.* provide notes for (literary work *etc.*), comment —**anno'tation** *n.* —**'annotator** *n.*

announce (əˈnaʊns) *vt.* make known, proclaim —**an'nouncement** *n.* —**an'nouncer** *n.* broadcaster who announces items in programme, introduces speakers *etc.*

annoy (əˈnɔɪ) *vt.* 1. vex 2. make slightly angry 3. tease —**an'noyance** *n.*

annual (ˈænjʊəl) *a.* 1. yearly 2. of, for a year —*n.* 3. plant which completes its life cycle in a year 4. book published each year —**'annually** *adv.*

annuity (əˈnjuːɪtɪ) *n.* sum or grant paid every year —**an'nuitant** *n.* holder of annuity

annul (əˈnʌl) *vt.* make void, cancel, abolish (-ll-) —**an'nulment** *n.*

annular (ˈænjʊlə) *a.* ring-shaped —**'annulate** *a.* having or marked with rings —**'annulated** *a.* formed in rings —**annu'lation** *n.* —**'annulet** *n.* small ring or fillet

Annunciation (ənʌnsɪˈeɪʃən) *n.* 1. angel's announcement to the Virgin Mary 2. (a-) announcing —**an'nunciate** *vt.* proclaim, announce

anode (ˈænəʊd) *n. Elec.* the positive pole, or point of entry of current —**'anodize** *or* **-dise** *vt.* cover metal object with protective film by using it for anode in electrolysis

anodyne (ˈænədaɪn) *a.* 1. relieving pain, soothing —*n.* 2. pain-relieving drug

anoint (əˈnɔɪnt) *vt.* 1. smear with oil or ointment 2. consecrate with oil —**a'nointment** *n.* —**the Anointed** the Messiah

anomalous (əˈnɒmələs) *a.* irregular, abnormal —**a'nomaly** *n.* 1. irregularity 2. deviation from rule

anomie *or* **anomy** (ˈænəʊmɪ) *n. Sociol.* lack of social or moral standards

anon (əˈnɒn) *adv. obs.* 1. in a short time, soon 2. now and then

anon. anonymous

anonymous (ə'nɒnɪməs) a. nameless, *esp.* without an author's name —**ano'nymity** n. —**a'nonymously** adv.

anopheles (ə'nɒfɪliːz) n. genus of the malarial mosquito

anorak ('ænəræk) n. lightweight, warm, waterproof, *usu.* hooded jacket

anorexia (ænɒ'rɛksɪə) n. loss of appetite —**anorexia nervosa** (nɜː'vəʊsə) psychological condition characterized by refusal to eat

another (ə'nʌðə) pron./a. 1. one other 2. a different (one) 3. one more

ans. answer

anserine ('ænsəraɪn) a. 1. of or like goose 2. silly

answer ('ɑːnsə) v. 1. reply (to) 2. be accountable (for, to) —vt. 3. solve; reply correctly 4. meet 5. match 6. satisfy, suit —n. 7. reply 8. solution —'**answerable** a. accountable

ant (ænt) n. small social insect, proverbial for industry —**ant bear** see AARDVARK —'**anteater** n. animal which feeds on ants by means of long, sticky tongue —**ant hill** mound raised by ants

-ant (*comb. form*) causing or performing action or existing in certain condition, as in *pleasant, deodorant, servant*

antacid (ænt'æsɪd) n. 1. substance used to treat acidity, *esp.* in stomach —a. 2. having properties of this substance

antagonist (æn'tægənɪst) n. opponent, adversary —an'**tagonism** n. —antago'**nistic** a. —antago'**nistically** adv. —an'**tagonize** or -**nise** vt. arouse hostility in

antalkali (ænt'ælkəlaɪ) n. substance that neutralizes alkalis (pl. -**s, -lies**)

Antarctic (ænt'ɑːktɪk) a. 1. of south polar regions —n. 2. region round South Pole —**Antarctic Circle** imaginary circle around earth at latitude 66° 32' S

ante ('æntɪ) n. 1. player's stake in poker —v. 2. place stake

ante- (*comb. form*) before, as in *antechamber*. Such words are not given here where the meaning may easily be inferred from the simple word

antecedent (æntɪ'siːdˀnt) a./n. (event, person or thing) going before

antedate ('æntɪdeɪt) vt. 1. be or occur at earlier date than 2. affix or assign date to (document *etc.*) earlier than actual date 3. cause to occur sooner —n. 4. earlier date

antediluvian (æntɪdɪ'luːvɪən) a. before the Flood 2. ancient

antelope ('æntɪləʊp) n. deerlike ruminant animal, remarkable for grace and speed

ante meridiem (mə'rɪdɪəm) *Lat.* before noon

antenatal (æntɪ'neɪtˀl) a. of care *etc.* during pregnancy

antenna (æn'tɛnə) n. 1. insect's feeler 2. aerial (pl. -**ae** (-iː))

antepenultimate (æntɪpɪ'nʌltɪmɪt) a. 1. third last —n. 2. anything third last

anterior (æn'tɪərɪə) a. 1. to the front 2. earlier

anteroom ('æntɪruːm, -rʊm) n. room giving entrance to larger room, oft. used as waiting room

anthem ('ænθəm) n. 1. song of loyalty, *esp.* to a country 2. Scripture passage set to music 3. piece of sacred music, orig. sung in alternate parts by two choirs

anther ('ænθə) n. sac in flower, containing pollen, at top of stamen —'**antheral** a.

anthology (æn'θɒlədʒɪ) n. collection of poems, literary extracts *etc.* —an'**thologist** n. maker of such —an'**thologize** or -**gise** vt. include (poem *etc.*) in anthology

anthracene ('ænθrəsiːn) n. colourless crystalline solid used in manufacture of chemicals *etc.*

anthracite ('ænθrəsaɪt) n. hard coal that burns slowly almost without flame or smoke

anthrax ('ænθræks) n. 1. malignant disease in cattle, communicable to man 2. sore caused by this

anthropo- (*comb. form*) man, human, as in *anthropology*

anthropocentric (ænθrəpəʊ'sɛntrɪk) a. regarding man as central factor in universe

anthropoid ('ænθrəpɔɪd) a. 1. like man —n. 2. ape resembling man

anthropology (ænθrə'pɒlədʒɪ) n. scientific study of origins, development of human race —anthropo'**logical** a. —anthro'**pologist** n.

anthropomorphize or -**ise** (ænθrəpə-'mɔːfaɪz) vt. ascribe human attributes to (God or an animal) —anthropo'**morphic** a. —anthropo'**morphism** n. —anthropo-'**morphous** a. shaped like human being

anti ('æntɪ) inf. a. 1. opposed to party *etc.* —n. 2. opponent

anti- (*comb. form*) against, as in *antiaircraft, antispasmodic.* Such words are not given here where meaning may easily be inferred from simple word

antibiosis (æntɪbaɪ'əʊsɪs) n. association between two organisms that is harmful to one of them

antibiotic (æntɪbaɪ'ɒtɪk) n. 1. any of various chemical, fungal or synthetic substances, *esp.* penicillin, used against bacterial infection —a. 2. of antibiotics

antibody ('æntɪbɒdɪ) n. substance in, or introduced into, blood serum, which counteracts growth and harmful action of bacteria

Antichrist ('æntɪkraɪst) n. 1. *Bible* the antagonist of Christ 2. (*sometimes* a-) an enemy of Christ or Christianity

anticipate (æn'tɪsɪpeɪt) vt. 1. expect 2. take or consider beforehand 3. foresee 4. enjoy in advance —antici'**pation** n. —an'**ticipative** or an'**ticipatory** a.

anticlerical (æntɪ'klɛrɪkˀl) a. 1. opposed to influence of clergy, *esp.* in politics —n. 2. supporter of anticlerical party

anticlimax (æntɪ'klaɪmæks) n. 1. disappointing conclusion to series of events *etc.*

2. sudden descent to the trivial or ludicrous

anticline ('æntıklaın) *n.* formation of stratified rock folded into broad arch so that strata slope down on both sides from common crest

antics ('æntıks) *pl.n.* absurd or grotesque movements or acts

anticyclone (æntı'saıkloun) *n.* system of winds moving round centre of high barometric pressure

antidote ('æntıdout) *n.* counteracting remedy

antifreeze ('æntıfriːz) *n.* liquid added to water to lower its freezing point, as in car radiators

antigen ('æntıdʒən, -dʒɛn) *n.* substance stimulating production of antibodies in the blood

antihero ('æntıhıərəʊ) *n.* central character in novel *etc.*, who lacks traditional heroic virtues

antihistamine (æntı'hıstəmiːn, -mın) *n.* drug used *esp.* to treat allergies

antiknock (æntı'nɒk) *n.* compound added to petrol to reduce knocking in engine

antilogarithm (æntı'lɒɡərıðəm) *n.* number whose logarithm is the given number (*also* **'antilog**)

antimacassar (æntımə'kæsə) *n.* cover to protect chairs from macassar oil

antimatter ('æntımætə) *n.* hypothetical form of matter composed of antiparticles

antimony ('æntımənı) *n.* brittle, bluish-white metal

antinomy (æn'tınəmı) *n.* **1.** opposition of one law *etc.* to another **2.** *Philos.* contradiction between two apparently indubitable propositions

antinovel ('æntınɒv²l) *n.* prose fiction in which conventional novelistic elements are rejected

antiparticle ('æntıpɑːtık²l) *n.* any of group of elementary particles that have same mass as corresponding particle but have charge of equal magnitude but opposite sign

antipasto (æntı'pɑːstəʊ, -'pæs-) *n.* course of hors d'œuvres in Italian meal (*pl.* -s)

antipathy (æn'tıpəθı) *n.* dislike, aversion —**antipa'thetic** *a.*

antiperspirant (æntı'pɜːspərənt) *n.* substance used to reduce sweating

antiphon ('æntıfən) *n.* **1.** composition in which verses, lines are sung alternately by two choirs **2.** anthem —**an'tiphonal** *a.*

antipodes (æn'tıpədiːz) *pl.n.* countries, peoples on opposite side of the globe (oft. refers to Aust. and N.Z.) —**an'tipodal** *or* **antipo'dean** *a.*

antipope ('æntıpəʊp) *n.* pope elected in opposition to the one regularly chosen

antipyretic (æntıpaı'rɛtık) *n./a.* (remedy) effective against fever

antique (æn'tiːk) *n.* **1.** relic of former times, usu. piece of furniture *etc.* that is collected —*a.* **2.** ancient **3.** old-fashioned —**antiquary** ('æntıkwərı) *or* **antiquarian**

(æntı'kwɛərıən) *n.* student or collector of old things —**antiquated** ('æntıkweıtıd) *a.* out-of-date —**antiquity** (æn'tıkwıtı) *n.* **1.** great age **2.** former times

antirrhinum (æntı'raınəm) *n.* genus of plants including snapdragon

antiscorbutic (æntıskɔː'bjuːtık) *n./a.* (agent) preventing or curing scurvy

anti-Semitic *a.* discriminating against Jews —**anti-Semitism** (-'sɛmıtızəm) *n.*

antiseptic (æntı'sɛptık) *n./a.* **1.** (substance) preventing infection —*a.* **2.** free from infection

antisocial (æntı'səʊʃəl) *a.* **1.** avoiding company of other people; unsociable **2.** contrary to interests of society in general

antistatic (æntı'stætık) *a.* (of textile *etc.*) retaining sufficient moisture to provide conducting path, thus avoiding effects of static electricity

antithesis (æn'tıθısıs) *n.* **1.** direct opposite **2.** contrast **3.** opposition of ideas (*pl.* **-eses** (-ısiːz)) —**anti'thetical** *a.* —**anti'thetically** *adv.*

antitoxin (æntı'tɒksın) *n.* serum used to neutralize disease poisons

antitrades ('æntıtreıdz) *pl.n.* winds blowing in opposite direction from and above trade winds

antitrust (æntı'trʌst) *a. chiefly US* regulating or opposing trusts or similar organizations

antitype ('æntıtaıp) *n.* **1.** person or thing foreshadowed or represented by type or symbol **2.** opposite type

antivenin (æntı'vɛnın) *n.* antitoxin to counteract specific venom, *eg* of snake or spider

antler ('æntlə) *n.* branching horn of certain deer —**'antlered** *a.*

antonym ('æntənım) *n.* word of opposite meaning to another, *eg cold* is an antonym of *hot*

antrum ('æntrəm) *n. Anat.* natural cavity or sinus, *esp.* in bone (*pl.* **-tra** (-trə))

anuresis (ænjʊ'riːsıs) *n.* inability to urinate

anus ('eınəs) *n.* the lower opening of the bowels —**'anal** *a.* of or near the anus

anvil ('ænvıl) *n.* heavy iron block on which a smith hammers metal into shape

anxious ('æŋkʃəs, 'æŋʃəs) *a.* **1.** troubled, uneasy **2.** concerned —**anxiety** (æŋ'zaıtı) *n.* —**'anxiously** *adv.*

any ('ɛnı) *a./pron.* **1.** one indefinitely **2.** some **3.** whatever, whichever —**'anybody** *pron.* —**'anyhow** *adv.* —**any more** *or esp. U.S.* **any'more** *adv.* any longer; still; nowadays —**'anyone** *pron.* —**'anything** *pron.* —**'anyway** *adv.* —**'anywhere** *adv.*

Anzac ('ænzæk) *a.* **1.** of Australian-New Zealand Army Corps in WWI —*n.* **2.** soldier of that corps, Gallipoli veteran —**Anzac Day** Apr. 25th, public holiday in Aust. and N.Z. commemorating Anzac landing at Gallipoli in 1915

ANZUS ('ænzəs) Aust., N.Z. and U.S., with

reference to security alliance between them

a.o.b. or **A.O.B.** any other business

aorist ('eɪɒrɪst, 'ɛɒrɪst) n. Gram. tense of verb, esp. in classical Greek, indicating past action without reference to whether action involved was momentary or continuous.

aorta (eɪ'ɔːtə) n. great artery rising from left ventricle of heart —**a'ortal** a.

apace (ə'peɪs) adv. swiftly

Apache (ə'pætʃɪ) n. 1. member of N Amer. Indian people of SW U.S. and N Mexico (pl. -s, A'pache) 2. language of this people

apart (ə'pɑːt) adv. 1. separately, aside 2. in pieces

apartheid (ə'pɑːthaɪt, -heɪt) n. esp. in S Afr., official government policy of racial segregation

apartment (ə'pɑːtmənt) n. 1. room 2. esp. US a flat —pl. 3. lodgings

apathy ('æpəθɪ) n. 1. indifference 2. lack of emotion —**apa'thetic** a. —**apa'thetically** adv.

apatite ('æpətaɪt) n. common mineral consisting basically of calcium fluorophosphate

ape (eɪp) n. 1. tailless primate (eg chimpanzee, gorilla) 2. coarse, clumsy person 3. imitator —vt. 4. imitate —**'apish** a. —**'apishly** adv. —**'apeman** n. apelike primate thought to have been forerunner of modern man

aperient (ə'pɪərɪənt) a. 1. mildly laxative —n. 2. any mild laxative

aperiodic (eɪpɪərɪ'ɒdɪk) a. Elec. having no natural period or frequency

apéritif (əperɪ'tiːf) n. alcoholic appetizer

aperture ('æpətʃə) n. opening, hole

apex ('eɪpɛks) n. 1. top, peak 2. vertex (pl. -es, 'apices) —'apical a. of, at, or being apex

APEX ('eɪpɛks) 1. Advanced Purchase Excursion (reduced airline fare, paid for at least 30 days before departure) 2. Association of Professional, Executive, Clerical and Computer Staff

aphasia (ə'feɪzɪə) n. dumbness or loss of speech control, due to disease of brain

aphelion (æp'hiːlɪən, ə'fiː-) n. point of planet's orbit farthest from sun (pl. -lia (-lɪə))

aphis ('eɪfɪs) n. any of various sap-sucking insects (pl. **aphides** ('eɪfɪdiːz)) —'aphid n. an aphis

aphorism ('æfərɪzəm) n. maxim, pithy saying —'aphorist n. —apho'ristic a.

aphrodisiac (æfrə'dɪzɪæk) a. 1. exciting sexual desire —n. 2. substance which so excites

apiary ('eɪpɪərɪ) n. place where bees are kept —api'arian or 'apian a. —'apiarist n. beekeeper —'apiculture n. breeding and care of bees

apices ('æpɪsiːz, 'eɪ-) n., pl. of APEX

apiece (ə'piːs) adv. for each

aplomb (ə'plɒm) n. self-possession, coolness, assurance

apo- or **ap-** (comb. form) 1. away from; off, as in apogee 2. separation of, as in apocarpous

apocalypse (ə'pɒkəlɪps) n. 1. prophetic revelation, esp. of St. John 2. (A-) last book of New Testament —apoca'lyptic a. —apoca'lyptically adv.

apocrypha (ə'pɒkrɪfə) n. religious writing of doubtful authenticity —a'pocryphal a. spurious —**the Apocrypha** collective name for 14 books orig. in Old Testament

apodosis (ə'pɒdəsɪs) n. consequent clause in conditional sentence, as distinct from protasis or if clause (pl. -oses (-əsiːz))

apogee ('æpədʒiː) n. 1. point of moon's or satellite's orbit farthest from the earth 2. climax

apolitical (eɪpə'lɪtɪkʰl) a. politically neutral

apologia (æpə'ləʊdʒɪə) n. written defence of one's beliefs, conduct etc.

apologue ('æpəlɒg) n. allegory, moral fable

apology (ə'pɒlədʒɪ) n. 1. acknowledgment of offence and expression of regret 2. written or spoken defence 3. (with for) poor substitute —apolo'getic a. —apolo-'getically adv. —apolo'getics pl.n. (with sing. v.) branch of theology charged with defence of Christianity —a'pologist n. —a'pologize or -gise vi.

apophthegm or **apothegm** ('æpəθɛm) n. terse saying, maxim —**apophthegmatic** or **apothegmatic** (æpəθɛg'mætɪk) a.

apoplexy ('æpəplɛksɪ) n. loss of sense and oft. paralysis caused by broken or blocked blood vessel in brain —apo'plectic a.

apostasy (ə'pɒstəsɪ) n. abandonment of one's religious or other faith —a'postate n./a.

a posteriori (eɪ pɒstɛrɪ'ɔːraɪ, -rɪ, ɑː) 1. denoting form of inductive reasoning which arrives at causes from effects 2. empirical

apostle (ə'pɒsʰl) n. 1. (oft. A-) one sent to preach the Gospel, esp. one of the first disciples of Jesus 2. founder of Christian church in a country 3. leader of reform —a'postleship n. —apostolic(al) (æpə-'stɒlɪk(ʰl)) a. —**Apostles' Creed** concise statement of Christian beliefs —**Apostolic See** see of pope

apostrophe (ə'pɒstrəfɪ) n. 1. mark (') showing omission of letter or letters in word 2. digression to appeal to someone dead or absent —a'postrophize or -phise v.

apothecary (ə'pɒθɪkərɪ) n. old name for one who prepares and sells drugs, now chemist —**apothecaries' measure** system of liquid volume measure used in pharmacy in which 20 fluid ounces equal 1 pint

apothegm ('æpəθɛm) n. see APOPHTHEGM

apothem ('æpəθɛm) n. perpendicular from centre of regular polygon to any of its sides

apotheosis (əpɒθɪ'əʊsɪs) n. deification, act

of raising any person or thing to status of a god (*pl.* **-ses** (-si:z)) —a'**potheosize** *or* -**ise** *vt.* **1.** deify **2.** glorify, idealize

appal *or* U.S. **appall** (ə'pɔːl) *vt.* dismay, terrify (**-ll-**) —**ap'palling** *a.* dreadful, terrible

appanage *or* **apanage** ('æpənɪdʒ) *n.* **1.** land or other provision granted by king for support of *esp.* younger son **2.** customary perquisite

apparatus (æpə'reɪtəs, -'rɑːtəs) *n.* **1.** equipment, instruments, for performing any experiment, operation *etc.* **2.** means by which something operates

apparel (ə'pærəl) *n.* **1.** clothing —*vt.* **2.** clothe (**-ll-**)

apparent (ə'pærənt) *a.* **1.** seeming **2.** obvious **3.** acknowledged, as in *heir apparent* —ap'**parently** *adv.*

apparition (æpə'rɪʃən) *n.* appearance, *esp.* of ghost

appeal (ə'piːl) *vi.* **1.** make earnest request **2.** be attractive **3.** refer, have recourse **4.** apply to higher court —*n.* **5.** request **6.** reference **7.** supplication —ap'**pealable** *a.* —ap'**pealing** *a.* **1.** making appeal **2.** pleasant, attractive —ap'**pealingly** *adv.* —ap'**pellant** *n.* one who appeals to higher court —**appellate** (ə'pɛlɪt) *a.* of appeals

appear (ə'pɪə) *vi.* **1.** become visible or present **2.** seem, be plain **3.** be seen in public —ap'**pearance** *n.* **1.** an appearing **2.** aspect **3.** pretence

appease (ə'piːz) *vt.* pacify, quiet, allay, satisfy —ap'**peasable** *a.* —ap'**peasement** *n.*

appellant (ə'pɛlənt) *n. see* APPEAL

appellation (æpi'leɪʃən) *n.* name —ap'**pellative** *a./n.*

append (ə'pɛnd) *vt.* join on, add —ap'**pendage** *n.*

appendix (ə'pɛndɪks) *n.* **1.** subsidiary addition to book *etc.* **2.** *Anat.* projection, *esp.* small worm-shaped part of intestine (*pl.* **-dices** (-dɪsiːz), **-es**) —**appendi'cectomy** *or* **appen'dectomy** *n.* surgical removal of any appendage, *esp.* vermiform appendix —**appendi'citis** *n.* inflammation of vermiform appendix

apperception (æpə'sɛpʃən) *n.* **1.** perception **2.** apprehension **3.** the mind's perception of itself as a conscious agent —**apper'ceive** *vt.*

appertain (æpə'teɪn) *vi.* belong, relate, be appropriate

appetence ('æpɪtəns) *or* **appetency** *n.* **1.** desire, craving **2.** sexual appetite —**appetent** *a.*

appetite ('æpɪtaɪt) *n.* desire, inclination, *esp.* desire for food —ap'**petitive** *a.* —'**appetizer** *or* -**iser** *n.* something stimulating to appetite —'**appetizing** *or* -**ising** *a.* —'**appetizingly** *or* -**isingly** *adv.*

applaud (ə'plɔːd) *v.* **1.** express approval (of) by hand-clapping —*vt.* **2.** praise; approve —ap'**plauder** *n.* —ap'**plause** *n.* loud approval

apple ('æpļ) *n.* **1.** round, firm, fleshy fruit

2. tree bearing it —**apple-pie bed** UK way of making bed to prevent person from entering it —**apple-pie order** *inf.* perfect order —**apple of one's eye** person or thing very much loved

appliance (ə'plaɪəns) *n.* piece of equipment, *esp.* electrical

appliqué (æ'pliːkeɪ) *n.* **1.** ornaments, embroidery *etc.*, secured to surface of material —*vt.* **2.** ornament thus

apply (ə'plaɪ) *vt.* **1.** utilize, employ **2.** lay or place on **3.** administer, devote —*vi.* **4.** have reference (to) **5.** make request (to) (**-lied, -lying**) —**applicability** (æplɪkə'bɪlɪtɪ) *n.* —**applicable** ('æplɪkəbļ, ə'plɪkə-) *a.* relevant —**applicably** ('æplɪkəblɪ, ə'plɪkə-) *adv.* —**applicant** ('æplɪkənt) *n.* —**application** (æplɪ'keɪʃən) *n.* **1.** applying something for a particular use **2.** relevance **3.** request for job *etc.* **4.** concentration, diligence —**applicator** ('æplɪkeɪtə) *n.* device, such as spatula, for applying medicine, glue *etc.* —ap'**plied** *a.* (of skill, science *etc.*) put to practical use

appoint (ə'pɔɪnt) *vt.* **1.** name for, assign to job or position **2.** fix, settle **3.** equip —ap'**pointment** *n.* **1.** engagement to meet **2.** (selection for a) job —*pl.* **3.** fittings

apportion (ə'pɔːʃən) *vt.* divide out in shares —ap'**portionment** *n.*

appose (ə'pəʊz) *vt.* **1.** place side by side **2.** place (something) near or against another thing

apposite ('æpəzɪt) *a.* suitable, apt —'**appositely** *adv.* —'**appositeness** *n.* —**appo'sition** *n.* **1.** proximity **2.** the placing of one word beside another

appraise (ə'preɪz) *vt.* set price on, estimate value of —ap'**praisable** *a.* —ap'**praisal** *or* ap'**praisement** *n.* —ap'**praiser** *n.*

appreciate (ə'priːʃɪeɪt, -sɪ-) *vt.* **1.** value at true worth **2.** be grateful for **3.** understand **4.** enjoy —*vi.* **5.** rise in value —ap'**preciable** *a.* **1.** estimable **2.** substantial —ap'**preciably** *adv.* —**appreci'ation** *n.* —ap'**preciative** *or* ap'**preciatory** *a.* capable of expressing pleasurable recognition —ap'**preciator** *n.*

apprehend (æprɪ'hɛnd) *vt.* **1.** seize by authority **2.** take hold of **3.** recognize, understand **4.** dread —**apprehensi'bility** *n.* —**appre'hensible** *a.* —**appre'hension** *n.* **1.** dread, anxiety **2.** arrest **3.** conception **4.** ability to understand —**appre'hensive** *a.*

apprentice (ə'prɛntɪs) *n.* **1.** person learning a trade under specified conditions **2.** novice —*vt.* **3.** bind as apprentice —ap'**prenticeship** *n.*

apprise *or* -**ize** (ə'praɪz) *vt.* inform

appro ('æprəʊ) *inf.* approval

approach (ə'prəʊtʃ) *v.* **1.** draw near (to) —*vt.* **2.** set about **3.** address request to **4.** approximate to —*n.* **5.** a drawing near **6.** means of reaching or doing **7.** approximation **8.** (*oft. pl.*) friendly overture(s) —**approacha'bility** *n.* —ap'**proachable** *a.*

approbation (æprə'beɪʃən) *n.* approval

appropriate (ə'prəuprieit) *vt.* 1. take for oneself 2. put aside for particular purpose —*a.* (ə'prəuprit) 3. suitable, fitting —**ap'propriately** *adv.* —**ap'propriateness** *n.* —**appropri'ation** *n.* 1. act of setting apart for purpose 2. parliamentary vote of money —**ap'propriative** *a.* —**ap'propria-tor** *n.*

approve (ə'pruːv) *vt.* 1. think well of, commend 2. authorize, agree to —*vi.* 3. (*usu. with* of) take favourable view —**ap'proval** *n.* —**ap'prover** *n.* —**ap'prov-ingly** *adv.*

approx. approximate(ly)

approximate (ə'prɒksimit) *a.* 1. very near, nearly correct 2. inexact, imprecise —*vt.* (ə'prɒksimeit) 3. bring close 4. be almost the same as —*vi.* (ə'prɒksimeit) 5. come near —**ap'proximately** *adv.* —**ap-proxi'mation** *n.* —**ap'proximative** *a.*

appurtenance (ə'pɜːtinəns) *n.* 1. less significant thing or part 2. accessory

Apr. April

après-ski (æprei'skiː) *n.* social activities after day's skiing

apricot ('eiprikɒt) *n.* 1. orange-coloured stone-fruit related to plum —*a.* 2. of the colour of the fruit

April ('eiprəl) *n.* fourth month —**April fool** victim of practical joke performed on Apr. 1st (**April Fools' Day** *or* **All Fools' Day**)

a priori (ei prai'ɔːrai, ɑː pri'ɔːri) *a.* 1. denoting deductive reasoning from general principle to expected facts or effects 2. denoting knowledge gained independently of experience

apron ('eiprən) *n.* 1. cloth, piece of leather *etc.*, worn in front of body to protect clothes, or as part of official dress 2. in theatre, strip of stage before curtain 3. on airfield, tarmac area where aircraft stand, are loaded *etc.* 4. *fig.* any of a variety of things resembling these —**tied to some-one's apron strings** dominated by one's mother or wife

apropos (æprə'pəʊ) *adv.* 1. to the purpose 2. by the way —*a.* 3. apt, appropriate —**apropos of** concerning

apse (æps) *n.* arched recess, *esp.* in church —**'apsidal** *a.*

apsis ('æpsis) *n.* either of two points lying at extremities of eccentric orbit of satellite *etc.* (*pl.* **apsides** (æp'saidiːz)) (*also* **apse**)

apt (æpt) *a.* 1. suitable 2. likely 3. prompt, quick-witted 4. dexterous —**'aptitude** *n.* capacity, fitness —**'aptly** *adv.* —**'apt-ness** *n.*

APT Advanced Passenger Train

apteryx ('æptəriks) *n. see* KIWI (sense 1)

aqua ('ækwə) *n.* 1. water (*pl.* **aquae** ('ækwiː), **-s**) —*a.* 2. *see* AQUAMARINE (sense 2)

aqualung ('ækwəlʌŋ) *n.* breathing appa-ratus used in underwater swimming

aquamarine (ækwəmə'riːn) *n.* 1. variety of beryl used as gemstone —*a.* 2. greenish-blue, sea-coloured

aquanaut ('ækwənɔːt) *n.* person who works or swims underwater

aquaplane ('ækwəplein) *n.* 1. plank or boat towed by fast motorboat —*vi.* 2. ride on aquaplane 3. (of car) be in contact with water on road, not with road surface —**'aquaplaning** *n.*

aquarium (ə'kweəriəm) *n.* tank or pond for keeping aquatic animals or plants (*pl.* **-s, -ria** (-riə))

Aquarius (ə'kweəriəs) *n.* (the water-bearer) 11th sign of zodiac, operative c. Jan. 20th-Feb. 18th

aquatic (ə'kwætik) *a.* living, growing, done in or on water —**a'quatics** *pl.n.* water sports

aquatint ('ækwətint) *n.* etching, engraving imitating drawings *etc.*

aqua vitae ('viːtai, 'vaitiː) *Lat. obs.* brandy

aqueduct ('ækwidʌkt) *n.* 1. artificial channel for water, *esp.* one like bridge 2. conduit

aqueous ('eikwiəs) *a.* of, like, containing water —**aqueous humour** *Physiol.* fluid between cornea and lens of eye

aquilegia (ækwi'liːdʒiə) *n.* columbine

aquiline ('ækwilain) *a.* 1. relating to eagle 2. hooked like eagle's beak

Ar *Chem.* argon

AR Arkansas

ar. 1. arrival 2. arrive(s)

Ar. 1. Arabic 2. Aramaic

Arab ('ærəb) *n.* 1. native of Arabia 2. general term for inhabitants of Middle Eastern countries 3. Arabian horse (small breed used for riding) —**Arabian** (ə'reibiən) *a.* 1. of Arabia —*n.* 2. Arab —**'Arabic** *n.* 1. language of Arabs —*a.* 2. of Arabia or Arabs —**Arabic numeral** one of numbers 1,2,3,4,5,6,7,8,9,0

arabesque (ærə'bɛsk) *n.* 1. classical ballet position 2. fanciful painted or carved ornament of Arabian origin —*a.* 3. (in style) of arabesque

arabis ('ærəbis) *n.* low-growing garden plant with white, pink or lilac flowers

arable ('ærəb'l) *a.* suitable for ploughing or planting crops

Araby ('ærəbi) *n. obs., poet.* Arabia

arachnid (ə'ræknid) *n.* one of the Arachnida (spiders, scorpions and mites) —**a'rachnoid** *a.* —**arach'nology** *n.*

arak ('ærək) *n. see* ARRACK

Aramaic (ærə'meiik) *n.* 1. ancient Semitic language of Middle East —*a.* 2. of, relating to or using this language

Aran ('ærən) *a.* (of sweaters *etc.*) made with naturally oily, unbleached wool, oft. with complicated pattern

arbiter ('ɑːbitə) *n.* judge, umpire (**-tress** *fem.*) —**ar'bitrament** *n.* —**'arbitrarily** *adv.* —**'arbitrary** *a.* 1. not bound by rules, despotic 2. random —**'arbitrate** *vt.* 1. decide (dispute) 2. submit to, settle by arbitration —*vi.* 3. act as umpire —**arbi-'tration** *n.* hearing, settling of disputes, *esp.* industrial and legal, by impartial referee(s) —**'arbitrator** *n.*

arbor ('ɑːbə) *n.* **1.** rotating shaft in machine on which grinding wheel is fitted **2.** rotating shaft

arboreal (ɑːˈbɔːrɪəl) *a.* relating to trees —**arbo'rescent** *a.* having characteristics of tree —**arbo'retum** *n.* place for cultivating specimens of trees (*pl.* **-s, -ta** (-tə)) —**'arboriculture** *n.* forestry, cultivation of trees

arbour ('ɑːbə) *n.* leafy glade *etc.*, sheltered by trees

arbutus (ɑːˈbjuːtəs) *n.* shrub having evergreen leaves and strawberry-like berries (*pl.* **-es**)

arc (ɑːk) *n.* **1.** part of circumference of circle or similar curve **2.** luminous electric discharge between two conductors —*vi.* **3.** form an arc (**arced, 'arcing** *or* **arcked, 'arcking**) —**arc lamp** —**arc light**

arcade (ɑːˈkeɪd) *n.* **1.** row of arches on pillars **2.** covered walk or avenue, *esp.* lined by shops

Arcadian (ɑːˈkeɪdɪən) *a.* **1.** of idealized Arcadia of pastoral poetry **2.** rustic, bucolic —*n.* **3.** person who leads simple rural life

arcane (ɑːˈkeɪn) *a.* **1.** mysterious **2.** esoteric

arch[1] (ɑːtʃ) *n.* **1.** curved structure in building, supporting itself over open space by pressure of stones one against the other **2.** any similar structure **3.** curved shape **4.** curved part of sole of foot —*v.* **5.** form, make into, an arch —**arched** *a.* —**'archway** *n.*

arch[2] (ɑːtʃ) *a.* **1.** chief **2.** experienced, expert **3.** superior, knowing; coyly playful —**'archly** *adv.* —**'archness** *n.*

arch. **1.** archaic **2.** architecture

arch- *or* **archi-** (*comb. form*) chief, as in *archangel, archenemy.* Such words are not given here where the meaning may easily be inferred from the simple word

-arch (*comb. form*) leader; ruler; chief, as in *patriarch, monarch*

archaeology *or* **archeology** (ɑːkɪˈɒlədʒɪ) *n.* study of ancient times from remains of art, implements *etc.* —**archaeo'logical** *or* **archeo'logical** *a.* —**archae'ologist** *or* **arche'ologist** *n.*

archaeopteryx (ɑːkɪˈɒptərɪks) *n.* extinct bird of Jurassic times, with teeth, long tail and well-developed wings

archaic (ɑːˈkeɪɪk) *a.* old, primitive —**ar'chaically** *adv.* —**'archaism** *n.* obsolete word or phrase

archbishop ('ɑːtʃˈbɪʃəp) *n.* chief bishop —**'arch'bishopric** *n.*

archdeacon ('ɑːtʃˈdiːkən) *n.* chief deacon, clergyman next to bishop —**'arch'deaconry** *n.* —**archidiaconal** (ɑːkɪdaɪˈækənˀl) *a.*

archdiocese (ɑːtʃˈdaɪəsiːs) *n.* diocese of archbishop

archduke ('ɑːtʃˈdjuːk) *n.* duke of specially high rank (**'arch'duchess** *fem.*) —**'arch'ducal** *a.* —**'arch'duchy** *n.*

archery ('ɑːtʃərɪ) *n.* skill, sport of shooting with bow and arrow —**'archer** *n.*

archetype ('ɑːkɪtaɪp) *n.* **1.** prototype **2.** perfect specimen —**'archetypal** *a.*

archfiend (ɑːtʃˈfiːnd) *n.* (*oft.* **A-**) the devil; Satan

archiepiscopal (ɑːkɪˈpɪskəpˀl) *a.* of archbishop —**archie'piscopate** *n.*

archipelago (ɑːkɪˈpɛləgəʊ) *n.* **1.** group of islands **2.** sea full of small islands, *esp.* Aegean (*pl.* **-es**) —**archipelagic** (ɑːkɪpəˈlædʒɪk) *a.*

architect ('ɑːkɪtɛkt) *n.* **1.** one qualified to design and supervise construction of buildings **2.** contriver —**architec'tonic** *a.* of or resembling architecture —**archi'tectural** *a.* —**'architecture** *n.*

architrave ('ɑːkɪtreɪv) *n.* *Archit.* **1.** lowest division of entablature **2.** ornamental band round door or window opening

archives ('ɑːkaɪvz) *pl.n.* **1.** collection of records, documents *etc.* about institution, family *etc.* **2.** place where these are kept —**ar'chival** *a.* —**archivist** ('ɑːkɪvɪst) *n.*

archpriest ('ɑːtʃˈpriːst) *n.* **1.** formerly, chief assistant to bishop **2.** senior priest

Arctic ('ɑːktɪk) *a.* **1.** of northern polar regions **2.** (**a-**) very cold —*n.* **3.** region round North Pole —**Arctic Circle** imaginary circle around earth at latitude 66° 32′ N

ardent ('ɑːdˀnt) *a.* **1.** fiery **2.** passionate —**'ardency** *n.* —**'ardently** *adv.* —**'ardour** *or U.S.* **'ardor** *n.* **1.** enthusiasm **2.** zeal

arduous ('ɑːdjuːəs) *a.* **1.** hard to accomplish, difficult **2.** strenuous; laborious —**'arduously** *adv.* —**'arduousness** *n.*

are[1] (ɑː; *unstressed* ə) *pres. ind. pl. of* BE

are[2] (ɑː) *n.* unit of measure, 100 square metres

area ('ɛərɪə) *n.* **1.** extent, expanse of any surface **2.** two-dimensional expanse enclosed by boundary (area of square, circle *etc.*) **3.** region **4.** part, section **5.** subject, field of activity **6.** small sunken yard

areca ('ærɪkə, əˈriːkə) *n.* genus of palms, including betel palm

arena (əˈriːnə) *n.* **1.** enclosure for sports events *etc.* **2.** space in middle of amphitheatre or stadium **3.** sphere, scene of conflict

arenaceous (ærɪˈneɪʃəs) *a.* **1.** composed of sand **2.** growing in sandy soil

aren't (ɑːnt) **1.** *contraction of* are not **2.** *inf., chiefly UK* (used in interrogative sentences) *contraction of* am not

areola (əˈrɪələ) *n.* **1.** *Biol.* space outlined on surface, such as area between veins on leaf **2.** *Anat.* any small circular area, such as pigmented ring around human nipple (*pl.* **-lae** (-liː), **-s**)

arête (əˈreɪt) *n.* sharp ridge that separates glacial valleys

argent ('ɑːdʒənt) *n.* **1.** silver —*a.* **2.** silver, silvery-white, *esp.* in heraldry

argon ('ɑːgɒn) *n.* a gas, inert constituent of air

argosy ('ɑːgəsɪ) n. Poet. large richly-laden merchant ship

argot ('ɑːgəʊ) n. slang

argue ('ɑːgjuː) vi. 1. quarrel, dispute 2. offer reasons —vt. 3. prove by reasoning 4. discuss —'**arguable** a. —'**arguably** adv. as can be argued —'**arguer** n. —'**argument** n. 1. quarrel 2. reasoning 3. discussion 4. theme —**argumen'tation** n. —**argu'mentative** a.

Argus ('ɑːgəs) n. fabulous being with a hundred eyes —**Argus-eyed** a. watchful

aria ('ɑːrɪə) n. air or rhythmical song in cantata, opera etc.

arid ('ærɪd) a. 1. parched with heat, dry 2. dull —a'**ridity** n.

Aries ('ɛəriːz) n. (the ram) 1st sign of zodiac, operative c. Mar. 21st–Apr. 21st

aright (ə'raɪt) adv. rightly

arise (ə'raɪz) vi. 1. come about 2. get up 3. rise (up), ascend (a'**rose**, **arisen** (ə'rɪzⁿn), a'**rising**)

aristocracy (ærɪ'stɒkrəsɪ) n. 1. nobility 2. upper classes 3. government by the best in birth or fortune —'**aristocrat** n. —**aristo'cratic** a. 1. noble 2. elegant —**aristo'cratically** adv.

arithmetic (ə'rɪθmətɪk) n. 1. science of numbers 2. art of reckoning by figures —**arith'metical** a. —**arith'metically** adv. —**arithme'tician** n. —**arithmetic mean** average value of set of terms or quantities, expressed as their sum divided by their number (also '**average**) —**arithmetic progression** sequence, each term of which differs from succeeding term by constant amount

ark (ɑːk) n. Noah's vessel

Ark (ɑːk) n. Judaism 1. most sacred symbol of God's presence among Hebrew people, carried in their journey from Sinai to Promised Land (also **Ark of the Covenant**) 2. receptacle for the scrolls of the Law (also **Holy Ark**)

arm¹ (ɑːm) n. 1. limb extending from shoulder to wrist 2. anything projecting from main body, as branch of sea, supporting rail of chair etc. 3. sleeve —'**armlet** n. band worn round arm —'**armchair** n. —'**armful** n. —'**armhole** n. —'**armpit** n. hollow under arm at shoulder

arm² (ɑːm) vt. 1. supply with weapons, furnish 2. prepare (bomb etc.) for use —vi. 3. take up arms —n. 4. weapon 5. branch of army —pl. 6. weapons 7. war, military exploits 8. official heraldic symbols —'**armament** n.

armada (ɑː'mɑːdə) n. large number of ships or aircraft

armadillo (ɑːmə'dɪləʊ) n. small Amer. burrowing mammal protected by bands of bony plates (pl. -s)

Armageddon (ɑːmə'gɛdⁿn) n. 1. Bible place designated as scene of final battle at end of world 2. catastrophic and extremely destructive conflict

armature ('ɑːmətjʊə) n. part of electric machine, esp. revolving structure in electric motor, generator

armistice ('ɑːmɪstɪs) n. truce, suspension of fighting —**Armistice Day** anniversary of signing of armistice that ended World War I (see also **Remembrance Day** at REMEMBER)

armoire (ɑːm'wɑː) n. large cabinet, orig. used for storing weapons

armour or U.S. **armor** ('ɑːmə) n. 1. defensive covering or dress 2. plating of tanks, warships etc. 3. armoured fighting vehicles, as tanks —**ar'morial** a. relating to heraldic arms —'**armourer** or U.S. '**armorer** n. —'**armoury** or U.S. '**armory** n. —**armour plate** tough heavy steel oft. hardened on surface, used for protecting warships etc.

army ('ɑːmɪ) n. 1. large body of men armed for warfare and under military command 2. host, great number

arnica ('ɑːnɪkə) n. Bot. genus of hardy perennials. A tincture of Arnica montana is used for sprains and bruises

aroma (ə'rəʊmə) n. 1. sweet smell, fragrance 2. peculiar charm —aro'**matic** a. —a'**romatize** or -**tise** vt.

arose (ə'rəʊz) pt. of ARISE

around (ə'raʊnd) prep. 1. on all sides of 2. somewhere in or near 3. approximately (of time) —adv. 4. on every side 5. in a circle 6. here and there, nowhere in particular 7. inf. present in or at some place

arouse (ə'raʊz) vt. 1. awaken 2. stimulate

arpeggio (ɑː'pɛdʒɪəʊ) n. Mus. 1. notes sounded in quick succession, not together 2. chord so played (pl. -s)

arquebus ('ɑːkwɪbəs) or **harquebus** n. portable gun dating from 15th century

arr. 1. arranged 2. arrival 3. arrive(d)

arrack or **arak** ('ærək) n. coarse spirit distilled from rice etc.

arraign (ə'reɪn) vt. accuse, indict, put on trial —ar'**raigner** n. —ar'**raignment** n.

arrange (ə'reɪndʒ) vt. 1. set in order 2. arrive at agreement about 3. plan 4. adapt, as music 5. settle, as dispute —ar'**rangement** n.

arrant ('ærənt) a. downright, notorious —'**arrantly** adv.

arras ('ærəs) n. tapestry

array (ə'reɪ) n. 1. order, esp. military order 2. dress 3. imposing show, splendour —vt. 4. set in order 5. dress, equip, adorn

arrears (ə'rɪəz) pl.n. amount unpaid or undone

arrest (ə'rɛst) vt. 1. detain by legal authority 2. stop 3. catch (attention) —n. 4. seizure by warrant 5. making prisoner —ar'**resting** a. attracting attention, striking —ar'**restor** n. 1. person who arrests 2. mechanism to stop or slow moving object

arrière-pensée (arjɛrpɑː'se) Fr. hidden meaning or purpose

arris ('ærɪs) n. sharp ridge or edge

arrive (ə'raɪv) vi. 1. reach destination 2.

(*with* at) reach, attain **3.** *inf.* succeed —**ar'rival** *n.*

arrivederci (arrive'dertʃi) *It.* goodbye

arriviste (æriː'viːst) *n.* person who is unscrupulously ambitious

arrogance ('ærəgəns) *n.* aggressive conceit —**'arrogant** *a.* **1.** proud **2.** overbearing —**'arrogantly** *adv.*

arrogate ('ærəgeɪt) *vt.* **1.** claim for oneself without justification **2.** attribute to another without justification

arrow ('ærəʊ) *n.* pointed shaft shot from bow —**'arrowhead** *n.* **1.** head of arrow **2.** any triangular shape

arrowroot ('ærəʊruːt) *n.* nutritious starch from W Indian plant, used as a food

arsenal ('ɑːsənˀl) *n.* magazine of stores for warfare, guns, ammunition

arsenic ('ɑːsnɪk) *n.* **1.** soft, grey, metallic element **2.** its oxide, a powerful poison —**ar'senical** *a.* —**arsenious** (ɑː'siːnɪəs) *a.*

arson ('ɑːsˀn) *n.* crime of intentionally setting property on fire

art (ɑːt) *n.* **1.** skill **2.** human skill as opposed to nature **3.** creative skill in painting, poetry, music *etc.* **4.** any of the works produced thus **5.** profession, craft **6.** knack **7.** contrivance, cunning, trick **8.** system of rules —*pl.* **9.** certain branches of learning, languages, history *etc.*, as distinct from natural science **10.** wiles —**'artful** *a.* wily —**'artfully** *adv.* —**'artfulness** *n.* —**'artist** *n.* **1.** one who practises fine art, *esp.* painting **2.** one who makes his craft a fine art —**ar'tiste** *n.* professional entertainer, singer, dancer *etc.* —**ar'tistic** *a.* —**ar'tistically** *adv.* —**'artistry** *n.* —**'artless** *a.* natural, frank —**'artlessly** *adv.* —**'artlessness** *n.* —**'arty** *a.* ostentatiously artistic

art. 1. article **2.** artificial

artefact *or* **artifact** ('ɑːtɪfækt) *n.* something made by man, *esp.* by hand

arteriosclerosis (ɑːtɪərɪəʊsklɪ'rəʊsɪs) *n.* hardening of the arteries (*pl.* **-ses** (-siːz))

artery ('ɑːtərɪ) *n.* **1.** one of tubes carrying blood from heart **2.** any main channel of communications —**ar'terial** *a.* pert. to an artery **2.** main, important, as in *arterial road*

artesian well (ɑː'tiːzɪən) deep well in which water rises by internal pressure

arthritis (ɑː'θraɪtɪs) *n.* painful inflammation of joint(s) —**arthritic** (ɑː'θrɪtɪk) *a./n.*

arthropod ('ɑːθrəpɒd) *n.* animal with jointed limbs and segmented body, *eg* insect, spider

artic (ɑː'tɪk) *inf.* articulated lorry

artichoke ('ɑːtɪtʃəʊk) *n.* **1.** thistlelike perennial **2.** its edible flower —**Jerusalem artichoke** sunflower with edible tubers like potato

article ('ɑːtɪkˀl) *n.* **1.** item, object **2.** short written piece **3.** paragraph, section **4.** *Gram.* words *the*, *a*, *an* **5.** clause in contract **6.** rule, condition —*vt.* **7.** bind as apprentice

articular (ɑː'tɪkjʊlə) *a.* of joints or structural components in joint

articulate (ɑː'tɪkjʊlɪt) *a.* **1.** able to express oneself fluently **2.** jointed **3.** (of speech) clear, distinct —*vt.* (ɑː'tɪkjʊleɪt) **4.** joint **5.** utter distinctly —*vi.* (ɑː'tɪkjʊleɪt) **6.** speak —**ar'ticulated** *a.* jointed —**ar'ticulately** *adv.* —**ar'ticulateness** *n.* —**articu'lation** *n.*

artifice ('ɑːtɪfɪs) *n.* **1.** contrivance **2.** trick **3.** cunning; skill —**ar'tificer** *n.* craftsman —**arti'ficial** *a.* **1.** manufactured, synthetic **2.** insincere —**artifici'ality** *n.* —**arti'ficially** *adv.* —**artificial respiration** method of restarting person's breathing after it has stopped

artillery (ɑː'tɪlərɪ) *n.* **1.** large guns on wheels **2.** troops who use them

artisan ('ɑːtɪzæn, ɑːtɪ'zæn) *n.* craftsman; skilled mechanic; manual worker

artiste (ɑː'tiːst) *n.* see ARTE

Art Nouveau ('ɑː nuː'vəʊ; *Fr.* ar nu'vo) style of art and architecture of 1890s, characterized by sinuous outlines and stylized natural forms

arum lily ('ɛərəm) plant with large white flower

-ary (*comb. form*) **1.** of; related to; belonging to, as in *cautionary* **2.** person or thing connected with, as in *missionary*, *aviary*

Aryan ('ɛərɪən) *a.* relating to Indo-European family of nations and languages

as (æz; əz) *adv./conj. denoting* **1.** comparison **2.** similarity **3.** equality **4.** identity **5.** concurrence **6.** reason

As *Chem.* arsenic

AS 1. Anglo-Saxon (*also* **A.S.**) **2.** antisubmarine

A.S.A. 1. UK Amateur Swimming Association **2.** US American Standards Association

asafoetida *or* **asafetida** (æsə'fɛtɪdə) *n.* bitter resin with unpleasant smell, obtained from roots of some umbelliferous plants

asap as soon as possible

asbestos (æs'bɛstɒs) *n.* fibrous mineral which does not burn —**asbestosis** (æsbɛs-'təʊsɪs) *n.* lung disease caused by inhalation of asbestos fibre

ascend (ə'sɛnd) *vi.* **1.** climb, rise —*vt.* **2.** walk up, climb, mount —**as'cendancy** *or* **as'cendency** *n.* control, dominance —**as'cendant** *or* **as'cendent** *a.* rising —**as'cension** *n.* —**as'cent** *n.* rise

Ascension Day (ə'sɛnʃən) 40th day after Easter, when Ascension of Christ into heaven is celebrated

ascertain (æsə'teɪn) *vt.* get to know, find out, determine —**ascer'tainable** *a.* —**ascer'tainment** *n.*

ascetic (ə'sɛtɪk) *n.* **1.** one who practises severe self-denial —*a.* **2.** rigidly abstinent, austere —**as'cetically** *adv.* —**as'ceticism** *n.*

ascorbic acid (ə'skɔːbɪk) vitamin C, present in green vegetables, citrus fruits *etc.*

ascribe (ə'skraɪb) *vt.* attribute, impute,

assign —as'cribable a. —ascription (ə'skrɪpʃən) n.

aseptic (ə'sɛptɪk, eɪ-) a. germ-free —a'sepsis n.

asexual (eɪ'sɛksjʊəl) a. without sex

ash¹ (æʃ) n. 1. dust or remains of anything burnt —pl. 2. ruins 3. remains, eg of cremated body —'ashen a. 1. like ashes 2. pale —'ashy a. —ash can US dustbin (also garbage can, ash bin, trash can) —'ashtray n. receptacle for tobacco ash, cigarette butts etc. —Ash Wednesday first day of Lent —the Ashes symbol of victory in cricket test-match series between England and Australia

ash² (æʃ) n. 1. deciduous timber tree 2. its wood —'ashen a.

ashamed (ə'ʃeɪmd) a. affected with shame, abashed

ashlar or ashler ('æʃlə) n. hewn or squared building stone

ashore (ə'ʃɔː) adv. towards or on shore

ashram ('æʃrəm) n. religious retreat or community where Hindu holy man lives

Asian ('eɪʃən, 'eɪʒən) a. 1. pert. to continent of Asia —n. 2. native of Asia or descendant of one —Asi'atic a.

aside (ə'saɪd) adv. 1. to or on one side 2. privately —n. 3. words spoken in an undertone not to be heard by some person present

asinine ('æsɪnaɪn) a. of or like an ass, silly —asininity (æsɪ'nɪnɪtɪ) n.

ask (ɑːsk) vt. 1. request, require, question, invite —vi. 2. make inquiry or request

askance (ə'skæns) or askant (ə'skænt) adv. 1. sideways, awry 2. with a side look or meaning —look askance view with suspicion

askew (ə'skjuː) adv. awry

aslant (ə'slɑːnt) adv. on the slant, obliquely, athwart

asleep (ə'sliːp) a. sleeping, at rest

ASLEF ('æzlɛf) Associated Society of Locomotive Engineers and Firemen

asocial (eɪ'səʊʃəl) a. 1. avoiding contact 2. unconcerned about welfare of others 3. hostile to society

asp (æsp) n. small venomous snake

asparagus (ə'spærəgəs) n. plant whose young shoots are a table delicacy

aspect ('æspɛkt) n. 1. look 2. view 3. appearance 4. expression

aspen ('æspən) n. type of poplar tree

asperity (æ'spɛrɪtɪ) n. 1. roughness 2. harshness 3. coldness

aspersion (ə'spɜːʃən) n. 1. (usu. in pl.) malicious remarks 2. slanderous attack

asphalt ('æsfælt) n. black, hard bituminous substance used for road surfaces etc. —as'phaltic a.

asphodel ('æsfədɛl) n. plant with clusters of yellow or white flowers

asphyxia (æs'fɪksɪə) n. suffocation —as'phyxiate v. —as'phyxiated a. —asphyxi'ation n.

aspic ('æspɪk) n. 1. jelly used to coat meat, eggs, fish etc. 2. Bot. species of lavender

aspidistra (æspɪ'dɪstrə) n. plant with broad tapered leaves

aspire (ə'spaɪə) vi. 1. desire eagerly 2. rise to great height —aspirant ('æspɪrənt) n. 1. one who aspires 2. candidate —aspirate ('æspɪreɪt) vt. pronounce with full breathing, as 'h' —aspiration (æspɪ'reɪʃən) n. —aspirator ('æspɪreɪtə) n. device employing suction, such as jet pump or one for removing fluids from body cavity —as'piring a. —as'piringly adv.

aspirin ('æspərɪn) n. (a tablet of) drug used to allay pain and fever

ass (æs) n. 1. quadruped of horse family 2. stupid person

assagai ('æsəgaɪ) n. see ASSEGAI

assail (ə'seɪl) vt. attack, assault —as'sailable a. —as'sailant n.

assassin (ə'sæsɪn) n. 1. one who kills, esp. prominent person, by treacherous violence 2. murderer —as'sassinate vt. —assassi'nation n.

assault (ə'sɔːlt) n. 1. attack, esp. sudden —vt. 2. attack —assault and battery Law threat of attack to person followed by actual attack

assay (ə'seɪ) v. test (esp. proportions of metals) in alloy or ore —n. (ə'seɪ, 'æseɪ) 2. analysis, esp. of metals 3. trial, test —as'sayer n.

assegai or assagai ('æsəgaɪ) n. slender spear of S Afr. tribes

assemble (ə'sɛmbˀl) v. 1. meet, bring together 2. collect —vt. 3. put together (of machinery etc.) —as'semblage n. —as'sembly n. 1. gathering, meeting 2. assembling —assembly line sequence of machines, workers in factory assembling product

assent (ə'sɛnt) vi. 1. concur, agree —n. 2. acquiescence, agreement, compliance

assert (ə'sɜːt) vt. 1. declare strongly 2. insist upon —as'sertion n. —as'sertive a. —as'sertively adv.

assess (ə'sɛs) vt. 1. fix value of 2. evaluate, estimate, esp. for taxation 3. fix amount of (tax or fine) 4. impose tax or fine on (a person etc.) —as'sessable a. —as'sessment n. —as'sessor n.

asset ('æsɛt) n. 1. valuable or useful person, thing —pl. 2. property available to pay debts, esp. of insolvent debtor —asset-stripping n. Comm. practice of taking over a company at low price and then selling assets piecemeal

asseverate (ə'sɛvəreɪt) vt. assert solemnly —asseve'ration n.

assiduous (ə'sɪdjʊəs) a. persevering, attentive, diligent —assi'duity n. —as'siduously adv.

assign (ə'saɪn) vt. 1. appoint to job etc. 2. allot, apportion, fix 3. ascribe 4. transfer —n. 5. assignee —as'signable a. —assignation (æsɪg'neɪʃən) n. 1. secret meeting 2. appointment to meet —assignee (æsɪ'niː) n. Law person to whom property etc. is transferred —as'signment n. 1. act of assigning 2. allotted duty —**assignor** (æsɪˈnɔː) n.

assimilate (əˈsɪmɪleɪt) vt. 1. learn and understand 2. make similar 3. absorb into the system —**asˈsimilable** a. —**assimiˈlation** n. —**asˈsimilative** a.

assist (əˈsɪst) v. 1. give help 2. work as assistant (to) —**asˈsistance** n. —**asˈsistant** n. helper

assizes (əˈsaɪzɪz) pl.n. formerly, law court held in each area or county of England and Wales

assn. association

assoc. 1. associated 2. association

associate (əˈsəʊʃɪeɪt, -sɪ-) vt. 1. link, connect, esp. as ideas in mind 2. join —vi. 3. keep company 4. combine, unite —n. (əˈsəʊʃɪɪt) 5. companion, partner 6. friend, ally 7. subordinate member of association —a. (əˈsəʊʃɪɪt) 8. affiliated —**associ'ation** n. society, club —**association football** 1. see SOCCER 2. A Australian Rules played in football association rather than league

assonance (ˈæsənəns) n. 1. likeness in sound 2. rhyming of vowels only —**ˈassonant** a.

assort (əˈsɔːt) vt. 1. classify, arrange —vi. 2. match, agree, harmonize —**asˈsorted** a. mixed —**asˈsortment** n.

ASSR Autonomous Soviet Socialist Republic

asst. assistant

assuage (əˈsweɪdʒ) vt. 1. soften, pacify 2. soothe —**asˈsuagement** n.

assume (əˈsjuːm) vt. 1. take for granted 2. pretend to 3. take upon oneself 4. claim —**assumption** (əˈsʌmpʃən) n. —**assumptive** (əˈsʌmptɪv) a.

assure (əˈʃʊə) vt. 1. tell positively, promise 2. make sure 3. insure against loss, esp. of life 4. affirm —**asˈsurance** n. —**asˈsured** a. sure —**asˈsuredly** (əˈʃʊərɪdlɪ) adv.

A.S.T. US, C Atlantic Standard Time

astatic (æˈstætɪk, eɪ-) a. Phys. having no tendency to take fixed position

astatine (ˈæstətiːn) n. radioactive element that occurs naturally in minute amounts and is artificially produced by bombarding bismuth with alpha particles

aster (ˈæstə) n. 1. plant with starlike flowers 2. Michaelmas daisy

asterisk (ˈæstərɪsk) n. 1. star (*) used in printing —vt. 2. mark thus —**ˈasterism** n.

astern (əˈstɜːn) adv. 1. in or towards the stern 2. backwards

asteroid (ˈæstərɔɪd) n. 1. small planet —a. 2. star-shaped

asthma (ˈæsmə) n. illness in which one has difficulty in breathing —**asthˈmatic** a./n. —**asthˈmatically** adv.

astigmatism (əˈstɪgmətɪzəm) or **astigmia** (əˈstɪgmɪə) n. inability of lens (esp. of eye) to focus properly —**astigˈmatic** a.

astilbe (əˈstɪlbɪ) n. plant with ornamental pink or white flowers

astir (əˈstɜː) a. 1. on the move 2. out of bed 3. in excitement

A.S.T.M.S. Association of Scientific, Technical, and Managerial Staffs

astonish (əˈstɒnɪʃ) vt. amaze, surprise —**aˈstonishing** a. —**aˈstonishment** n.

astound (əˈstaʊnd) vt. 1. astonish greatly 2. stun with amazement —**aˈstounding** a. startling

astraddle (əˈstrædˀl) a. 1. with a leg on either side of something —prep. 2. astride

astrakhan (æstrəˈkæn) n. lambskin with curled wool

astral (ˈæstrəl) a. of the stars or spirit world —**astral body**

astray (əˈstreɪ) adv. 1. off the right path 2. in error

astride (əˈstraɪd) adv. 1. with the legs apart —prep. 2. straddling

astringent (əˈstrɪndʒənt) a. 1. severe, harsh 2. sharp 3. constricting (body tissues, blood vessels etc.) —n. 4. astringent substance —**asˈtringency** n.

astro- (comb. form) indicating star or star-shaped structure

astrol. astrology

astrolabe (ˈæstrəleɪb) n. instrument used by early astronomers to measure altitude of stars etc.

astrology (əˈstrɒlədʒɪ) n. 1. foretelling of events by stars 2. medieval astronomy —**asˈtrologer** n. —**astroˈlogical** a.

astrometry (əˈstrɒmɪtrɪ) n. determination of apparent magnitudes of fixed stars

astron. astronomy

astronaut (ˈæstrənɔːt) n. one trained for travel in space —**astroˈnautics** pl.n. (with sing. v.) science and technology of space flight

astronomy (əˈstrɒnəmɪ) n. scientific study of heavenly bodies —**asˈtronomer** n. —**astroˈnomical** a. 1. very large 2. of astronomy —**astronomical unit** unit of distance used in astronomy equal to the mean distance between the earth and the sun

astrophysics (æstrəʊˈfɪzɪks) n. the science of the chemical and physical characteristics of heavenly bodies —**astroˈphysical** a. —**astroˈphysicist** n.

astute (əˈstjuːt) a. perceptive, shrewd —**asˈtutely** adv. —**asˈtuteness** n.

asunder (əˈsʌndə) adv. 1. apart 2. in pieces

asylum (əˈsaɪləm) n. 1. refuge, sanctuary, place of safety 2. old name for home for care of the unfortunate, esp. of mentally ill

asymmetry (æˈsɪmɪtrɪ, eɪ-) n. lack of symmetry —**asymˈmetric(al)** a.

asymptote (ˈæsɪmtəʊt) n. straight line that continually approaches a curve, but never meets it

asyndeton (æˈsɪndɪtən) n. omission of conjunctions between parts of sentence (pl. -**deta** (-dɪtə)) —**asynˈdetic** a. without conjunctions or cross-references

at (æt) prep./adv. denoting 1. location in space or time 2. rate 3. condition or state 4. amount 5. direction 6. cause

At Chem. astatine

at. 1. atmosphere 2. atomic

ataraxia (ætə'ræksɪə) *or* **ataraxy** ('ætə- ræksɪ) *n.* calmness, emotional tranquillity

atavism ('ætəvɪzəm) *n.* appearance of ancestral, not parental, characteristics in human beings, animals or plants —**ata- 'vistic** *a.*

ataxia (ə'tæksɪə) *or* **ataxy** (ə'tæksɪ) *n.* lack of muscular coordination

A.T.C. 1. air traffic control 2. UK Air Training Corps

ate (et, eɪt) *pt. of* EAT

-ate[1] (*comb. form*) 1. having appearance or characteristics of, as in *fortunate* 2. chemical compound, *esp.* salt or ester of acid, as in *carbonate* 3. product of process, as in *condensate* 4. forming verbs from nouns and adjectives, as in *hyphenate*

-ate[2] (*comb. form*) office, rank or group having certain function, as in *episcopate*

atelier ('ætəljeɪ) *n.* workshop, artist's studio

atheism ('eɪθɪɪzəm) *n.* belief that there is no God —'**atheist** *n.* —**athe'istic(al)** *a.*

athenaeum *or U.S.* **atheneum** (æθɪ- 'niːəm) *n.* 1. institution for promotion of learning 2. building containing reading room or library

atherosclerosis (æθərəʊsklɪə'rəʊsɪs) *n.* degenerative disease of arteries charac- terized by thickening of arterial walls, caused by deposits of fatty material (*pl.* **-oses** (-əʊsiːz))

athlete ('æθliːt) *n.* 1. one trained for physical exercises, feats or contests of strength 2. one good at sports —**athletic** (æθ'letɪk) *a.* —**athletically** (æθ'letɪkəlɪ) *adv.* —**athleticism** (æθ'letɪsɪzəm) *n.* —**ath- letics** (æθ'letɪks) *pl.n.* (*with sing. v.*) sports such as running, jumping, throwing *etc.* —**athlete's foot** fungal infection of skin of foot, *esp.* between toes and on soles

at-home *n.* 1. social gathering in person's home 2. occasion when school *etc.* is open for inspection by public (*also* **open day**)

athwart (ə'θwɔːt) *prep.* 1. across —*adv.* 2. across, *esp.* obliquely

Atlantic (ət'læntɪk) *n.* 1. (*short for* **Atlantic Ocean**) world's second largest ocean —*a.* 2. of or bordering Atlantic Ocean 3. of Atlas or Atlas Mountains

Atlantis (ət'læntɪs) *n.* in ancient legend, continent said to have sunk beneath Atlantic west of Gibraltar

atlas ('ætləs) *n.* volume of maps

atm. 1. atmosphere 2. atmospheric

atmosphere ('ætməsfɪə) *n.* 1. mass of gas surrounding heavenly body, *esp.* the earth 2. prevailing tone or mood (of place *etc.*) 3. unit of pressure in cgs system —**atmospheric** (ætməs'ferɪk) *a.* —**atmos- pherics** (ætməs'ferɪks) *pl.n.* noises in radio reception due to electrical disturb- ance in the atmosphere

at. no. atomic number

atoll ('ætɒl) *n.* ring-shaped coral island enclosing lagoon

atom ('ætəm) *n.* 1. smallest unit of an element which can enter into chemical combination 2. any very small particle —**a'tomic** *a.* of, arising from atoms —**ato'micity** *n.* number of atoms in molecule of an element —'**atomize** *or* **-ise** *vt.* reduce to atoms or small particles —'**atomizer** *or* **-iser** *n.* instrument for discharging liquids in fine spray —**atom bomb** *or* **atomic bomb** bomb whose immense power derives from nuclear fission or fusion, nuclear bomb —**atomic energy** nuclear energy —**atomic number** the number of protons in the nucleus of an atom —**atomic pile** *see* reactor *at* REACT —**atomic theory** 1. any theory in which matter is regarded as consisting of atoms 2. current concept of atom as entity with definite structure —**atomic weight** the weight of an atom of an element relative to that of carbon 12

atonality (eɪtəʊ'nælɪtɪ) *n.* 1. absence of or disregard for established musical key in composition 2. principles of composition embodying this

atone (ə'təʊn) *vi.* 1. make reparation, amends 2. give satisfaction —**a'tone- ment** *n.*

atonic (eɪ'tɒnɪk, æ-) *a.* unaccented

atop (ə'tɒp) *adv.* 1. at or on the top —*prep.* 2. above

atrocious (ə'trəʊʃəs) *a.* 1. extremely cruel or wicked 2. horrifying 3. *inf.* very bad —**a'trociously** *adv.* —**atrocity** (ə'trɒsɪtɪ) *n.* wickedness

atrophy ('ætrəfɪ) *n.* 1. wasting away, emaciation —*vi.* 2. waste away, become useless

atropine ('ætrəpiːn) *n.* poisonous alkaloid obtained from deadly nightshade

att. 1. attention 2. attorney

attach (ə'tætʃ) *v.* 1. join, fasten 2. unite 3. be connected 4. attribute 5. appoint 6. seize by law —**at'tached** *a.* (*with* to) fond (of) —**at'tachment** *n.*

attaché (ə'tæʃeɪ) *n.* specialist attached to diplomatic mission (*pl.* **-s**) —**attaché case** small leather hand-case for papers

attack (ə'tæk) *vt.* 1. take action against (in war, sport *etc.*) 2. criticize 3. set about with vigour 4. affect adversely —*n.* 5. attacking action 6. bout

attain (ə'teɪn) *vt.* 1. arrive at 2. reach, gain by effort, accomplish —**attaina'bility** *n.* —**at'tainable** *a.* —**at'tainment** *n. esp.* personal accomplishment

attainder (ə'teɪndə) *n. Hist.* loss of rights through conviction of high treason

attar ('ætə), **otto** ('ɒtəʊ), *or* **ottar** ('ɒtə) *n.* fragrant oil made *esp.* from rose petals

attempt (ə'tempt) *vt.* 1. try, endeavour —*n.* 2. trial, effort

attend (ə'tend) *vt.* 1. be present at 2. accompany —*vi.* (*with* to) 3. take care (of) 4. give the mind (to), pay attention (to) —**at'tendance** *n.* 1. an attending 2. presence 3. persons attending —**at'tend- ant** *n./a.* —**at'tention** *n.* 1. notice 2. heed 3. act of attending 4. care 5. courtesy 6. alert position in military drill —at**'tentive** a. —at**'tentively** adv. —at**'tentiveness** n.

attenuate (ə'tɛnjʊeɪt) v. 1. weaken or become weak 2. make or become thin —at**'tenuated** a. —attenu**'ation** n. reduction of intensity

attest (ə'tɛst) vt. bear witness to, certify —atte**'station** n. formal confirmation by oath etc. —at**'tested** a. UK (of cattle etc.) certified free from disease, esp. tuberculosis

attic ('ætɪk) n. space within roof where ceiling follows line of roof

Attic ('ætɪk) a. 1. of Attica, esp. its dialect 2. classically pure

attire (ə'taɪə) vt. 1. dress, array —n. 2. dress, clothing

attitude ('ætɪtjuːd) n. 1. mental view, opinion 2. posture, pose 3. disposition, behaviour —atti**'tudinize** or **-nise** vi. assume affected attitudes

attorney (ə'tɜːnɪ) n. one legally appointed to act for another, esp. a lawyer (pl. -s)

attract (ə'trækt) vt. 1. draw (attention etc.) 2. arouse interest of 3. cause to come closer (as magnet etc.) —at**'traction** n. 1. power to attract 2. something offered so as to interest, please —at**'tractive** a. —at**'tractively** adv. —at**'tractiveness** n.

attribute (ə'trɪbjuːt) vt. 1. (usu. with to) regard as belonging (to) or produced (by) —n. ('ætrɪbjuːt) 2. quality, property or characteristic of anything —at**'tributable** a. —attri**'bution** n. —at**'tributive** a. —at**'tributively** adv.

attrition (ə'trɪʃən) n. 1. wearing away of strength etc. 2. rubbing away, friction

attune (ə'tjuːn) vt. 1. tune, harmonize 2. make accordant

A.T.V. UK Associated Television

at. wt. atomic weight

atypical (eɪ'tɪpɪk'l) a. not typical

Au Chem. gold

aubergine ('əʊbəʒiːn) n. edible, purple fruit of the eggplant

aubrietia or **aubretia** (ɔː'briːʃə) n. trailing plant with purple flowers

auburn ('ɔːb'n) a. 1. reddish-brown —n. 2. this colour

au courant (o ku'rɑ̃) Fr. 1. up-to-date 2. acquainted

auction ('ɔːkʃən) n. 1. public sale in which bidder offers increase of price over another and what is sold goes to one who bids highest —vt. 2. (oft. with off) sell by auction —auctio**'neer** n. —auction bridge card game —Dutch auction auction in which price starts high and is reduced until purchaser is found

audacious (ɔː'deɪʃəs) a. 1. bold 2. daring, impudent —audacity (ɔː'dæsɪtɪ) n.

audible ('ɔːdɪb'l) a. able to be heard —audi**'bility** n. —'**audibly** adv.

audience ('ɔːdɪəns) n. 1. assembly of hearers 2. act of hearing 3. judicial hearing 4. formal interview

audio- (comb. form) relating to sound or hearing

audio frequency ('ɔːdɪəʊ) frequency in audible range of 50 hertz to 20 000 hertz

audiometer (ɔːdɪ'ɒmɪtə) n. instrument for testing hearing

audiotypist ('ɔːdɪəʊtaɪpɪst) n. typist trained to type from dictating machine

audiovisual (ɔːdɪəʊ'vɪzjʊəl) a. (esp. of teaching aids) involving, directed at, both sight and hearing, as film etc.

audit ('ɔːdɪt) n. 1. formal examination or settlement of accounts —vt. 2. examine (accounts) —'**auditor** n.

audition (ɔː'dɪʃən) n. 1. screen or other test of prospective performer 2. hearing —v. 3. conduct or be tested in such a test —audi**'torium** n. 1. place where audience sits 2. hall (pl. -s, -ia (-ɪə)) —'**auditory** a. pert. to sense of hearing

A.U.E.W. Amalgamated Union of Engineering Workers

au fait (o 'fɛ) Fr. 1. fully informed 2. expert

auf Wiedersehen (auf 'viːdərzeːən) Ger. goodbye

Aug. August

Augean (ɔː'dʒiːən) a. extremely dirty

auger ('ɔːgə) n. carpenter's tool for boring holes, large gimlet

aught or **ought** (ɔːt) Lit., obs. n. 1. anything —adv. 2. UK dial. to any extent

augment (ɔːg'mɛnt) v. increase, enlarge —augmen**'tation** n. —aug**'mentative** a. increasing in force

au gratin (o gra'tɛ̃) Fr. with browned breadcrumbs and sometimes cheese

augur ('ɔːgə) n. 1. among the Romans, soothsayer —v. 2. be a sign of future events, foretell —**augural** ('ɔːgjʊrəl) a. —**augury** ('ɔːgjʊrɪ) n.

august (ɔː'gʌst) a. majestic, dignified

August ('ɔːgəst) n. eighth month

Augustan (ɔː'gʌstən) a. 1. of Augustus, the Roman Emperor 2. classic, distinguished, as applied to a period of literature

auk (ɔːk) n. northern web-footed seabird with short wings used only as paddles

au lait (əʊ 'leɪ) with milk

auld lang syne ('ɔːld læŋ 'saɪn) times past, esp. those remembered with nostalgia

au naturel (o naty'rɛl) Fr. 1. naked; nude 2. uncooked or plainly cooked

aunt (ɑːnt) n. 1. father's or mother's sister 2. uncle's wife —'**auntie** or '**aunty** n. 1. inf. aunt 2. (A-) sl. British Broadcasting Corporation —Aunt Sally UK 1. figure used as target in fairground 2. person who is target for insults or criticism

au pair (əʊ 'pɛə) young foreigner who receives free board and lodging in return for housework etc.

aura ('ɔːrə) n. 1. quality, air, atmosphere considered distinctive of person or thing 2. medical symptom warning of impending epileptic fit etc.

aural ('ɔːrəl) a. of, by ear —'**aurally** adv.

aureate ('ɔːrɪt) a. 1. covered with gold; gilded 2. (of style of writing or speaking) excessively elaborate

aureole (ˈɔːrɪəʊl) *or* **aureola** (ɔːˈriːələ) *n.* 1. gold disc round head in sacred pictures 2. halo

au revoir (o rəˈvwaːr) *Fr.* goodbye

auricle (ˈɔːrɪkˀl) *n.* 1. outside ear 2. upper cavity of heart —**au'ricular** *a.* 1. of the auricle 2. aural

auricula (ɔːˈrɪkjʊlə) *n.* 1. widely cultivated alpine primrose with leaves shaped like bear's ear (*also* **bear's ear**) 2. *Biol.* earshaped part (*also* **'auricle**) (*pl.* **-lae** (-liː), **-s**)

auriferous (ɔːˈrɪfərəs) *a.* gold-bearing

aurochs (ˈɔːrɒks) *n.* species of wild ox, now extinct

aurora (ɔːˈrɔːrə) *n.* 1. lights in the atmosphere seen radiating from regions of the poles. The northern is called **aurora borealis** and the southern, **aurora australis** 2. *Poet.* dawn (*pl.* **-s**)

auscultation (ɔːskəlˈteɪʃən) *n.* listening to movement of heart and lungs with stethoscope —**'auscultator** *n.* —**aus'cultatory** *a.*

auspice (ˈɔːspɪs) *n.* 1. omen, augury —*pl.* 2. patronage —**aus'picious** *a.* of good omen, favourable —**aus'piciously** *adv.*

Aussie (ˈɒzɪ) *n./a. inf.* Australian

austere (ɒˈstɪə) *a.* 1. harsh, strict, severe 2. without luxury —**aus'terely** *adv.* —**austerity** (ɒˈstɛrɪtɪ) *n.*

austral (ˈɔːstrəl) *a.* southern

Australasian (ɒstrəˈleɪzɪən) *a./n.* (native or inhabitant) of Australasia (Australia, New Zealand and adjacent islands)

Australian (ɒˈstreɪlɪən) *n./a.* (native or inhabitant) of Australia —**Australian Rules** game resembling rugby football, played in Aust. between teams of 18 men each on oval pitch, with ball resembling large rugby ball

Austro-¹ (*comb. form*) southern, as in *Austro-Asiatic*

Austro-² (*comb. form*) Austrian, as in *Austro-Hungarian*

autarchy (ˈɔːtɑːkɪ) *n.* despotism, absolute power, dictatorship

autarky (ˈɔːtɑːkɪ) *n.* (*esp.* of political unit) policy of economic self-sufficiency

auth. 1. author 2. authority 3. authorized

authentic (ɔːˈθɛntɪk) *a.* 1. real, genuine, true 2. trustworthy —**au'thentically** *adv.* —**au'thenticate** *vt.* 1. make valid, confirm 2. establish truth, authorship *etc.* of —**authenti'cation** *or* **authenticity** (ɔːθɛnˈtɪsɪtɪ) *n.*

author (ˈɔːθə) *n.* 1. writer of book 2. originator, constructor (**-ess** *fem.*) —**'authorship** *n.*

authority (ɔːˈθɒrɪtɪ) *n.* 1. legal power or right 2. delegated power 3. influence 4. permission 5. expert 6. (*oft. pl.*) body or board in control —**authori'tarian** *a.* 1. favouring or characterized by strict obedience to authority or government by small elite 2. dictatorial —*n.* 3. person who favours or practises authoritarian policies

—**au'thoritative** *a.* —**au'thoritatively** *adv.* —**authori'zation** *or* **-ri'sation** *n.* —**'authorize** *or* **-rise** *vt.* 1. empower 2. permit, sanction —**Authorized Version** English translation of the Bible published in 1611 under James I (*also* **King James Version**)

autistic (ɔːˈtɪstɪk) *a.* withdrawn and divorced from reality

auto- *or sometimes before vowel* **aut-** (*comb. form*) self, as in *autograph, autosuggestion.* Such words are not given here where the meaning may easily be inferred from the simple word

autobahn (ˈɔːtəbɑːn) *n.* German motorway

autobiography (ɔːtəʊbaɪˈɒɡrəfɪ) *n.* life story of person written by himself —**autobi'ographer** *n.* —**autobio'graphical** *a.* —**autobio'graphically** *adv.*

autochthon (ɔːˈtɒkθən) *n.* primitive or original inhabitant —**au'tochthonous** *a.*

autocrat (ˈɔːtəkræt) *n.* 1. absolute ruler 2. despotic person —**au'tocracy** *n.* —**auto'cratic** *a.* —**auto'cratically** *adv.*

autocross (ˈɔːtəʊkrɒs) *n.* motor-racing sport over rough course

auto-da-fé (ɔːtəʊdɑːˈfeɪ) *n.* 1. *Hist.* ceremony of Spanish Inquisition including pronouncement and execution of sentences passed on heretics 2. burning to death of people condemned as heretics by Inquisition (*pl.* **autos-da-fé**)

autoeroticism (ɔːtəʊɪˈrɒtɪsɪzəm) *or* **autoerotism** (ɔːtəʊˈɛrɒtɪzəm) *n.* self-produced sexual arousal

autogamy (ɔːˈtɒɡəmɪ) *n.* self-fertilization

autogenous (ɔːˈtɒdʒɪnəs) *a.* self-generated

autogiro *or* **autogyro** (ɔːtəʊˈdʒaɪrəʊ) *n.* aircraft like helicopter using horizontal airscrew for vertical ascent and descent

autograph (ˈɔːtəɡrɑːf) *n.* 1. handwritten signature 2. person's handwriting —*vt.* 3. sign —**auto'graphic** *a.*

autogyro (ɔːtəʊˈdʒaɪrəʊ) *n. see* AUTOGIRO

autointoxication (ɔːtəʊɪntɒksɪˈkeɪʃən) *n.* poisoning of tissues of the body as a result of the absorption of bodily waste

automat (ˈɔːtəmæt) *n.* vending machine

automate (ˈɔːtəmeɪt) *vt.* make (manufacturing process *etc.*) automatic

automatic (ɔːtəˈmætɪk) *a.* 1. operated or controlled mechanically 2. done without conscious thought —*a./n.* 3. self-loading (weapon) —**auto'matically** *adv.* —**automation** (ɔːtəˈmeɪʃən) *n.* use of automatic devices in industrial production —**au'tomatism** *n.* involuntary action —**au'tomaton** *n.* self-acting machine, *esp.* simulating a human being (*pl.* **-ata** (-ətə)) —**automatic transmission** transmission system in motor vehicle, in which gears change automatically

automobile (ˈɔːtəməbiːl) *n.* motor car —**automo'bilist** *n.* motorist

automotive (ɔːtəˈməʊtɪv) *a.* 1. relating to motor vehicles 2. self-propelling

autonomy (ɔːˈtɒnəmɪ) *n.* self-government —**auˈtonomous** *a.*

autopsy (ˈɔːtɒpsɪ, ˈɔːtəp-) *n.* 1. post-mortem examination to determine cause of death 2. critical analysis —**auˈtoptic(al)** *a.*

autoroute (ˈɔːtəʊruːt) *n.* French motorway

autostrada (ˈɔːtəʊstrɑːdə) *n.* Italian motorway

autosuggestion (ɔːtəʊsəˈdʒɛstʃən) *n.* process of influencing the mind (towards health *etc.*), conducted by the subject himself

autumn (ˈɔːtəm) *n./a.* (typical of) the season after summer —**autumnal** (ɔːˈtʌmnəl) *a.* typical of the onset of winter —**autumnally** (ɔːˈtʌmnəlɪ) *adv.*

aux. auxiliary

auxiliary (ɔːgˈzɪljərɪ, -ˈzɪlə-) *a.* 1. helping, subsidiary —*n.* 2. helper 3. something subsidiary, as troops 4. verb used to form tenses of others

av. average

A.V. Authorized Version (of the Bible)

avail (əˈveɪl) *v.* 1. be of use, advantage, value (to) —*n.* 2. benefit (*esp.* **in of no avail, to little avail**) —**availaˈbility** *n.* —**aˈvailable** *a.* 1. obtainable 2. accessible —**avail oneself of** make use of

avalanche (ˈævəlɑːntʃ) *n.* 1. mass of snow, ice, sliding down mountain 2. sudden overwhelming quantity of anything

avant-garde (ævɒŋˈgɑːd) *a.* markedly experimental or in advance

avarice (ˈævərɪs) *n.* greed for wealth —**avaˈricious** *a.* —**avaˈriciously** *adv.*

avast (əˈvɑːst) *interj.* stop

avatar (ˈævətɑː) *n.* 1. *Hinduism* manifestation of deity in human or animal form 2. visible manifestation of abstract concept

avaunt (əˈvɔːnt) *interj. obs.* go away, depart

avdp. avoirdupois

Ave. *or* **ave.** Avenue

Ave Maria (ˈɑːvɪ məˈriːə) *R.C.Ch.* prayer to Virgin Mary, based on salutations of angel Gabriel and Elisabeth to her

avenge (əˈvɛndʒ) *vt.* take vengeance on behalf of (person) or on account of (thing) —**aˈvenger** *n.*

avenue (ˈævɪnjuː) *n.* 1. wide street, oft. lined with trees 2. approach 3. double row of trees

aver (əˈvɜː) *vt.* affirm, assert (-**rr**-) —**aˈverment** *n.*

average (ˈævərɪdʒ, ˈævrɪdʒ) *n.* 1. the mean value or quantity of a number of values or quantities —*a.* 2. calculated as an average 3. medium, ordinary —*vt.* 4. fix or calculate an average of —*vi.* 5. exist in or form a mean

averse (əˈvɜːs) *a.* disinclined, unwilling —**aˈversion** *n.* (*usu.* with **to** or **for**) dislike, person or thing disliked —**aversion therapy** *Psychiatry* way of suppressing undesirable habit by associating unpleasant effect, such as electric shock, with it

avert (əˈvɜːt) *vt.* 1. turn away 2. ward off

aviary (ˈeɪvjərɪ) *n.* enclosure for birds —**ˈaviarist** *n.*

aviation (eɪvɪˈeɪʃən) *n.* 1. art of flying aircraft 2. design, production and maintenance of aircraft —**ˈaviator** *n.*

avid (ˈævɪd) *a.* 1. keen, enthusiastic 2. (*oft.* with **for**) greedy —**aˈvidity** *n.*

avocado (ævəˈkɑːdəʊ) *n.* 1. tropical tree 2. its green-skinned edible fruit

avocation (ævəˈkeɪʃən) *n.* 1. vocation 2. employment, business

avocet *or* **avoset** (ˈævəsɛt) *n.* wading bird of snipe family with upward-curving bill

avoid (əˈvɔɪd) *vt.* 1. keep away from 2. refrain from 3. not allow to happen —**aˈvoidable** *a.* —**aˈvoidance** *n.*

avoirdupois *or* **avoirdupois weight** (ævədəˈpɔɪz) *n./a.* (of) system of weights used in many English-speaking countries based on pounds and ounces

avouch (əˈvaʊtʃ) *vt. obs.* affirm, maintain, attest, own —**aˈvouchment** *n.*

avow (əˈvaʊ) *vt.* 1. declare 2. admit —**aˈvowable** *a.* —**aˈvowal** *n.* —**aˈvowed** *a.* —**avowedly** (əˈvaʊɪdlɪ) *adv.*

avuncular (əˈvʌŋkjʊlə) *a.* of or resembling an uncle, genial

await (əˈweɪt) *vt.* 1. wait or stay for 2. be in store for

awake (əˈweɪk) *v.* 1. emerge or rouse from sleep 2. become or cause to become alert (**aˈwoke** *or* **aˈwaked, aˈwoken** *or* **aˈwaked, aˈwaking**) —*a.* 3. not sleeping 4. alert —**aˈwakening** *n.*

award (əˈwɔːd) *vt.* 1. give formally (*esp.* prize or punishment) —*n.* 2. prize 3. judicial decision

aware (əˈwɛə) *a.* informed, conscious —**aˈwareness** *n.*

awash (əˈwɒʃ) *a.* 1. level with surface of water 2. filled or overflowing with water

away (əˈweɪ) *a.* 1. absent, apart, at a distance, out of the way —*n.* 2. *Sport* game played on opponent's ground

awe (ɔː) *n.* dread mingled with reverence —**ˈawesome** *a.*

aweigh (əˈweɪ) *a. Naut.* (of anchor) no longer hooked into bottom; hanging by its rope or chain

awful (ˈɔːfʊl) *a.* 1. very bad, unpleasant 2. *obs.* impressive 3. *inf.* very great —**ˈawfully** *adv.* 1. in an unpleasant way 2. *inf.* very much

awhile (əˈwaɪl) *adv.* for a time

awkward (ˈɔːkwəd) *a.* 1. clumsy, ungainly 2. difficult 3. inconvenient 4. embarrassed —**ˈawkwardly** *adv.* —**ˈawkwardness** *n.*

awl (ɔːl) *n.* pointed tool for boring wood, leather *etc.*

awn (ɔːn) *n.* any of bristles growing from flowering parts of certain grasses and cereals

awning (ˈɔːnɪŋ) *n.* (canvas) roof or shelter, to protect from weather

awoke (əˈwəʊk) *pt.* of AWAKE —**aˈwoken** *pp.* of AWAKE

A.W.O.L. *or* **AWOL** (when acronym

'eiwɒl) absent without leave

awry (ə'raɪ) *adv.* **1.** crookedly **2.** amiss **3.** at a slant —*a.* **4.** crooked, distorted **5.** wrong

axe *or U.S.* **ax** (æks) *n.* **1.** tool with sharp blade for chopping **2.** *inf.* dismissal from employment *etc.* —*vt.* **3.** *inf.* dismiss, dispense with

axel ('æksəl) *n. Skating* jump of one and a half turns, taking off from forward outside edge of one skate and landing on backward outside edge of other

axes[1] ('æksiːz) *n., pl. of* AXIS

axes[2] ('æksiz) *n., pl. of* AXE

axil ('æksɪl) *n.* upper angle between branch or leaf stalk and stem

axiom ('æksɪəm) *n.* **1.** received or accepted principle **2.** self-evident truth —**axio'matic** *a.*

axis ('æksɪs) *n.* **1.** (imaginary) line round which body spins **2.** line or column around which parts of thing, system *etc.* are arranged (*pl.* **'axes**) —**'axial** *a.* —**'axially** *adv.* —**'Axis** *n.* coalition of Germany, Italy and Japan, 1936–45

axle ('æksəl) *n.* rod on which wheel turns

axolotl ('æksəlɒt'l) *n.* aquatic salamander of N Amer.

ay *or* **aye** (eɪ) *adv. Poet., obs.* always

ayah ('aɪə) *n.* in parts of former British Empire, native maidservant or nursemaid

ayatollah (aɪə'tɒlə) *n.* one of class of Islamic religious leaders

aye *or* **ay** (aɪ) *adv.* **1.** yes —*n.* **2.** affirmative answer or vote —*pl.* **3.** those voting for motion

AZ Arizona

azalea (ə'zeɪljə) *n.* genus of shrubby flowering plants, allied to rhododendron

azimuth ('æzɪməθ) *n.* **1.** vertical arc from zenith to horizon **2.** angular distance of this from meridian

AZT azidothymidine: drug that prolongs life and alleviates symptoms in AIDS sufferers

Aztec ('æztɛk) *a./n.* (member) of Indian race ruling Mexico before Spanish conquest

azure ('æʒə, 'eɪ-) *n.* **1.** sky-blue colour **2.** sky —*a.* **3.** sky-blue

B

b *or* **B** (biː) *n.* **1.** second letter of English alphabet **2.** speech sound represented by this letter, as in *bell* **3.** second in series, class or rank (*also* **'beta**) (*pl.* **b's, B's,** *or* **Bs**)

B 1. *Mus.* seventh note of scale of C major; major or minor key having this note as its tonic **2.** less important of two things **3.** human blood type of ABO group **4.** *UK* secondary road **5.** *Chem.* boron **6.** magnetic flux density **7.** *Chess* bishop **8.** (of pencils) black **9.** *Phys.* bel (*also* **b**) **10.** *Phys.* baryon number

b. *or* **B. 1.** *Mus.* bass; basso **2.** (on maps *etc.*) bay **3.** (B.) Bible **4.** book **5.** born **6.** (b.) *Cricket* bowled; bye **7.** breadth

Ba *Chem.* barium

B.A. Bachelor of Arts

B.A.A. British Airports Authority

baa (bɑː) *vi.* **1.** make cry of sheep; bleat (**'baaing, baaed**) —*n.* **2.** cry made by sheep

baas (bɑːs) *n. SA* boss

baba ('bɑːbɑː) *n.* small cake, usu. soaked in rum

babble ('bæb'l) *vi.* **1.** speak foolishly, incoherently, or childishly —*n.* **2.** foolish, confused talk —**'babbler** *n.* **1.** one who babbles **2.** tropical bird with incessant song —**'babbling** *n./a.*

babe (beɪb) *n.* **1.** *old-fashioned* baby **2.** guileless person

babel ('beɪb'l) *n.* confused noise or scene, uproar

baboon (bə'buːn) *n.* large monkey of Afr. and Asia —**ba'boonish** *a.*

baby ('beɪbɪ) *n.* very young child, infant —**'babyhood** *n.* —**'babyish** *a.* —**baby grand** small grand piano —**baby-sit** *vi.* —**baby-sitter** *n.* one who cares for children when parents are out

baccarat ('bækərɑː, bækə'rɑː) *n.* gambling card game

bacchanal ('bækən'l) *n.* **1.** follower of Bacchus **2.** (participant in) drunken, riotous celebration

bacchanalia (bækə'neɪlɪə) *pl.n.* **1.** (*oft.* **B-**) orgiastic rites associated with Bacchus **2.** drunken revelry —**baccha'nalian** *a./n.*

bacchant ('bækənt) *or (fem.)* **bacchante** (bə'kæntɪ) *n.* **1.** priest or priestess of Bacchus **2.** drunken reveller

baccy ('bækɪ) *n. UK inf.* tobacco

bachelor ('bætʃələ, 'bætʃlə) *n.* **1.** unmarried man **2.** holder of lowest university degree **3.** *Hist.* young knight —**'bachelorhood** *or* **'bachelorship** *n.* —**bachelor girl** young unmarried woman, *esp.* one who is self-supporting

bacillus (bə'sɪləs) *n.* minute organism sometimes causing disease (*pl.* **-cilli** (-'sɪlaɪ)) —**ba'cilliform** *a.*

back (bæk) *n.* **1.** hinder part of anything, *eg* human body **2.** part opposite front **3.** part or side of something further away or less used **4.** (position of) player in ball games behind other (forward) players —*a.* **5.** situated behind **6.** earlier —*adv.* **7.** at, to the back **8.** in, into the past **9.** in return —*vi.* **10.** move backwards —*vt.* **11.** support **12.** put wager on **13.** provide with back or backing —**'backer** *n.* **1.** one supporting another, *esp.* in contest **2.** one betting on horse, *etc.* in race —**'backing** *n.* **1.** support **2.** material to protect the back of something **3.** musical accompaniment, *esp.* for pop singer —**'backward** *a.* **1.** directed towards the rear **2.** behind in education **3.** reluctant, bashful —*adv.* **4.** backwards —**'backwardness** *n.* —**'backwards** *adv.* **1.** to the rear **2.** to the past **3.** into a worse state (*also* **'backward**) —**'back'bencher** *n.* Brit. or Aust. member of Parliament not holding office in government or opposition —**'backbite** *v.* slander (absent person) —**'backbiter** *n.* —**'backbiting** *n.* —**'backboard** *n.* **1.** board that is placed behind something to form or support its back **2.** board worn to support back, as after surgery **3.** *Basketball* flat upright surface under which basket is attached —**back boiler** tank or series of pipes at back of fireplace for heating water —**'backbone** *n.* **1.** spinal column **2.** strength of character —**'backbreaking** *a.* exhausting —**'backchat** *n. inf.* impudent answer —**'backcloth** *or* **'backdrop** *n.* painted cloth at back of stage —**'backcomb** *v.* comb under layers of hair towards roots to add bulk to hair style (*also* **back tease**) —**back'date** *vt.* make effective from earlier date —**back door 1.** door at rear or side of building **2.** means of entry to job *etc.* that is secret or obtained through influence —**back'fire** *vi.* **1.** ignite at wrong time, as fuel in cylinder of internal-combustion engine **2.** (of plan, scheme *etc.*) fail to work, *esp.* to the cost of the instigator **3.** ignite wrongly, as gas burner *etc.* —**'backgammon** *n.* game played with draughtsmen and dice —**'background** *n.* **1.** space behind chief figures of picture *etc.* **2.** past history of person —**'backhand** *n. Tennis etc.* stroke with hand turned backwards —**back'handed** *a.* (of compliment *etc.*) with second, uncomplimentary meaning —**'backhander** *n.* **1.** blow with back of hand **2.** *inf.* a bribe —**'backlash** *n.* sudden and adverse reaction —**'backlog** *n.* accumulation of work *etc.* to be dealt with —**back marker** competitor who is at back of field in race —**back number 1.** issue of newspaper *etc.* that appeared on a previous date **2.** *inf.* person or thing considered old-fashioned —**back pack** *n.* **1.** type of knapsack —*vi.* **2.** travel with knapsack —**back-pedal** vi. 1. turn pedals of bicycle backwards 2. retract previous opinion etc. —**back room** place where important and usu. secret research is done —**back seat** 1. seat at back, esp. of vehicle 2. inf. subordinate or inconspicuous position (esp. in **take a back seat**) —**back-seat driver** inf. 1. passenger who offers unwanted advice to driver 2. person who offers advice on matters that are not his concern —**back'side** n. rump —**backslide** vi. fall back in faith or morals —**back'stage** adv. 1. behind part of theatre in view of audience —a. 2. situated backstage —**back'stairs** pl.n. 1. secondary staircase in house —a. 2. underhand (also **'back-'stair**) —**'backstroke** n. Swimming stroke performed on the back —**'backtrack** vi. 1. return by same route by which one has come 2. retract or reverse one's opinion etc. —**'backup** n. chiefly US 1. support; reinforcement 2. reserve; substitute —**'backwash** n. 1. water thrown back by ship's propellers etc. 2. a backward current 3. a reaction —**'backwater** n. still water fed by back flow of stream —**'backwoods** pl.n. remote forest areas —**back yard** yard at back of house etc. —**back up** 1. support 2. (of water) accumulate 3. Comp. make copy of (data file) —**in one's own back yard** close at hand

bacon ('beɪkən) n. cured pig's flesh

Baconian (beɪ'kəʊnɪən) a. 1. pert. to English philosopher Francis Bacon or his inductive method of reasoning —n. 2. follower of Bacon's philosophy

bacteria (bæk'tɪərɪə) pl.n. microscopic organisms, some causing disease (sing. **-rium** (-rɪəm)) —**bac'terial** a. —**bacteri-'ologist** n. —**bacteri'ology** n. study of bacteria

Bactrian camel ('bæktrɪən) two-humped camel, used in deserts of central Asia

bad (bæd) a. 1. of poor quality 2. faulty 3. evil 4. immoral 5. offensive 6. severe 7. rotten, decayed (**worse** comp., **worst** sup.) —**'badly** adv. —**'badness** n. —**bad blood** feeling of intense hatred or hostility; enmity —**bad debt** debt which is not collectable

bade (bæd, beɪd) or **bad** pt. of BID

badge (bædʒ) n. distinguishing emblem or sign

badger ('bædʒə) n. 1. carnivorous burrowing mammal, about the size of a fox —vt. 2. pester, worry

badinage ('bædɪnɑːʒ) n. playful talk, banter

badminton ('bædmɪntən) n. game like tennis, played with shuttlecocks over high net

baffle ('bæfʲl) vt. 1. check 2. frustrate 3. bewilder —**'baffler** n. —**'baffling** a. —**baffle plate** device to regulate or divert flow of liquid, gas, soundwaves etc.

bag (bæg) n. 1. sack, pouch 2. measure of quantity 3. woman's handbag 4. offens.

unattractive woman —pl. 5. inf. lots (of) —vi. 6. swell out 7. bulge 8. sag —vt. 9. put in bag 10. kill as game etc. (**-gg-**) —**'bagging** n. cloth —**'baggy** a. loose, drooping —**'bagman** n. commercial traveller

bagasse (bə'gæs) n. sugar cane refuse

bagatelle (bægə'tɛl) n. 1. trifle 2. game like pinball played with nine balls and cue on a board

baggage ('bægɪdʒ) n. 1. suitcases etc., packed for journey 2. offens. woman

bagpipes ('bægpaɪps) pl.n. musical wind instrument, of windbag and pipes —**'bagpiper** n.

bah (bɑː, bæ) interj. expression of contempt or disgust

Bahaism (bə'hɑːɪzəm) n. religious system founded in 1863, emphasizing value of all religions and spiritual unity of mankind —**Ba'haist** or **Ba'haite** a./n.

bail¹ (beɪl) n. 1. Law security given for person's reappearance in court 2. one giving such security —vt. 3. release, or obtain release of, on security —**bail out** inf. help (person, firm etc.) out of trouble

bail² (beɪl) n. 1. Cricket crosspiece on wicket 2. bar separating horses in stable

bail³ or **bale** (beɪl) vt. empty out (water) from boat —**bail out** leave aircraft by parachute

bailey ('beɪlɪ) n. outermost wall of castle

Bailey bridge ('beɪlɪ) bridge composed of prefabricated sections

baillie ('beɪlɪ) n. Scot. municipal magistrate

bailiff ('beɪlɪf) n. 1. land steward, agent 2. sheriff's officer

bailiwick ('beɪlɪwɪk) n. jurisdiction of bailiff

bain-marie (bɛ̃ma'ri) Fr. vessel for holding hot water, in which sauces etc. are gently cooked or kept warm (pl. **bains-marie** (bɛ̃ma'ri))

bairn (bɛən) n. Scot. infant, child

bait (beɪt) n. 1. food to entice fish 2. any lure or enticement —vt. 3. set a lure for 4. annoy, persecute

baize (beɪz) n. smooth woollen cloth

bake (beɪk) vt. 1. cook or harden by dry heat —vi. 2. make bread, cakes etc. 3. be scorched or tanned —**'baker** n. —**'bakery** or **'bakehouse** n. —**'baking** n. —**baked beans** haricot beans, baked and tinned in tomato sauce —**baker's dozen** thirteen —**baking powder** raising agent containing sodium bicarbonate etc. used in cooking

Bakelite ('beɪkəlaɪt) n. R hard nonflammable synthetic resin, used for dishes, trays, electrical insulators etc.

baksheesh or **backsheesh** ('bækʃiːʃ) n. in some Eastern countries, esp. formerly, money given as tip

Balaclava helmet (bælə'klɑːvə) close-fitting woollen helmet covering head and neck

balalaika (bælə'laɪkə) n. Russian musical instrument similar to guitar

balance ('bæləns) n. 1. pair of scales 2.

equilibrium **3.** surplus **4.** sum due on an account **5.** difference between two sums —*vt.* **6.** weigh **7.** bring to equilibrium —**balance of payments** difference over given time between total payments to and receipts from foreign nations —**balance of power** distribution of power among countries so that no nation can seriously threaten another —**balance sheet** tabular statement of assets and liabilities —**balance wheel** regulating wheel of watch

balcony ('bælkənı) *n.* **1.** railed platform outside window **2.** upper seats in theatre

bald (bɔːld) *a.* **1.** hairless **2.** plain **3.** bare —'**balding** *a.* becoming bald —'**baldly** *adv.* —'**baldness** *n.*

balderdash ('bɔːldədæʃ) *n.* idle, senseless talk

baldric ('bɔːldrɪk) *n.* shoulder-belt for sword *etc.*

bale[1] (beɪl) *n.* **1.** bundle or package —*vt.* **2.** make into bundles or pack into cartons —'**baler** *n.* machine which makes bales of hay *etc.*

bale[2] (beɪl) *vt. see* BAIL[1]

baleen (bə'liːn) *n.* whalebone

baleful ('beɪlfʊl) *a.* menacing —'**balefully** *adv.*

balk *or* **baulk** (bɔːk, bɔːlk) *vi.* **1.** swerve, pull up —*vt.* **2.** thwart, hinder —*n.* **3.** hindrance **4.** square timber, beam —**balk at 1.** recoil from **2.** stop short at

Balkan ('bɔːlkən) *a.* of or denoting large peninsula in SE Europe, its inhabitants, countries *etc.*

ball[1] (bɔːl) *n.* **1.** anything round **2.** globe, sphere, *esp.* as used in games **3.** *Cricket* ball as delivered **4.** bullet —*vi.* **5.** clog, gather into a mass —**ball-and-socket joint** *Anat.* joint in which rounded head fits into rounded cavity —**ball bearings** steel balls used to lessen friction on bearings —**ball boy** *esp.* in tennis, person who retrieves balls that go out of play —**ball cock** device for regulating flow of liquid into cistern *etc.*, consisting of floating ball and a valve —**ball game 1.** any game played with a ball **2.** US game of baseball **3.** US *inf.* any activity —**ball-park figure** rough estimate; guess —'**ballpoint** *or* **ballpoint pen** *n.* pen with tiny ball bearing as nib (*also* '**Biro**)

ball[2] (bɔːl) *n.* assembly for dancing —'**ballroom** *n.*

ballad ('bæləd) *n.* **1.** narrative poem **2.** simple song

ballade (bæ'lɑːd) *n.* **1.** short poem with refrain and envoy **2.** piece of music

ballast ('bæləst) *n.* **1.** heavy material put in ship to give steadiness **2.** that which renders anything steady —*vt.* **3.** load with ballast, steady

ballet ('bæleɪ, bæ'leɪ) *n.* theatrical presentation of dancing and miming —**balle'rina** *n.* female ballet dancer

balletomania (bælɪtəʊ'meɪnɪə) *n.* enthusiasm for ballet —**bal'letomane** *n.*

ballista (bə'lɪstə) *n.* ancient catapult for

hurling stones *etc.* (*pl.* **-tae** (-tiː)) —**bal'listic** *a.* moving as, or pertaining to motion of a projectile —**bal'listics** *pl.n.* (*with sing. v.*) scientific study of ballistic motion —**ballistic missile** missile that follows ballistic trajectory when propulsive power is discontinued

balloon (bə'luːn) *n.* **1.** large, airtight bag that rises when filled with air or gas —*vi.* **2.** puff out —**bal'looning** *n.* —**bal'loonist** *n.*

ballot ('bælət) *n.* **1.** method of voting secretly, usu. by marking ballot paper and putting it into box —*v.* **2.** vote or elicit a vote from —**ballot box 1.** sealed receptacle for completed ballot papers **2.** *fig.* the democratic process

ballyhoo (bælɪ'huː) *n.* **1.** noisy confusion or uproar **2.** vulgar, exaggerated publicity or advertisement

balm (bɑːm) *n.* **1.** aromatic substance obtained from certain trees, used for healing or soothing **2.** anything soothing —'**balminess** *n.* —'**balmy** *a.*

baloney *or* **boloney** (bə'ləʊnɪ) *n. inf.* foolish talk; nonsense

BALPA ('bælpə) British Airline Pilots' Association

balsa ('bɔːlsə) *n.* Amer. tree with light but strong wood

balsam ('bɔːlsəm) *n.* **1.** resinous aromatic substance obtained from various trees and shrubs **2.** soothing ointment —**bal'samic** *a.*

Baltic ('bɔːltɪk) *a.* **1.** denoting or relating to the Baltic Sea or the states bordering it **2.** of or characteristic of Baltic as a group of languages

baluster ('bæləstə) *n.* short pillar used as support to rail of staircase *etc.* —'**balustrade** *n.* row of short pillars surmounted by rail

bamboo (bæm'buː) *n.* large tropical treelike reed

bamboozle (bæm'buːz'l) *vt.* **1.** mystify **2.** hoax

ban (bæn) *vt.* **1.** prohibit, forbid, outlaw (**-nn-**) —*n.* **2.** prohibition **3.** proclamation —**bans** *or* **banns** *pl.n.* proclamation of marriage

banal (bə'nɑːl) *a.* commonplace, trivial, trite —**ba'nality** *n.*

banana (bə'nɑːnə) *n.* **1.** tropical treelike plant **2.** its fruit —**banana republic** *inf.* small country, *esp.* in Central Amer., that is politically unstable and has economy dominated by foreign interest

band[1] (bænd) *n.* **1.** strip used to bind **2.** range of values, frequencies *etc.*, between two limits —'**bandage** *n.* strip of cloth for binding wound —**band saw** power-operated saw consisting of endless toothed metal band running over two wheels

band[2] (bænd) *n.* **1.** company, group **2.** company of musicians —*v.* **3.** (*with* together) bind together —'**bandmaster** *n.* —'**bandsman** *n.* —'**bandstand** *n.*

bandanna *or* **bandana** (bæn'dænə) *n.* coloured silk or cotton handkerchief

b. and b. bed and breakfast

bandbox ('bændbɒks) n. light box of cardboard for hats etc.

bandeau ('bændəʊ) n. band, ribbon for the hair (pl. **-deaux** (-dəʊz))

bandicoot ('bændɪkuːt) n. ratlike Aust. marsupial

bandit ('bændɪt) n. 1. outlaw 2. robber, brigand (pl. **-s**, **banditti** (bæn'dɪtɪ))

bandoleer or **bandolier** (bændə'lɪə) n. shoulder belt for cartridges

bandwagon ('bændwægən) n. —**climb, jump, get on the bandwagon** join something that seems assured of success

bandy ('bændɪ) vt. 1. beat to and fro 2. toss from one to another ('**bandied, 'bandying**) —'**bandy** or **bandy-legged** a. having legs curving outwards

bane (beɪn) n. person or thing causing misery or distress —'**baneful** a. —'**banefully** adv.

bang[1] (bæŋ) n. 1. sudden loud noise, explosion 2. heavy blow —vi. 3. make loud noise —vt. 4. beat, strike violently 5. slam —'**banger** n. UK 1. sl. sausage 2. old decrepit car 3. firework that explodes loudly

bang[2] (bæŋ) n. fringe of hair cut straight across forehead

bangle ('bæŋg'l) n. ring worn on arm or leg

banian ('bænjən) n. see BANYAN

banish ('bænɪʃ) vt. 1. condemn to exile 2. drive away 3. dismiss —'**banishment** n. exile

banisters ('bænɪstəz) pl.n. railing and supporting balusters on staircase

banjo ('bændʒəʊ) n. musical instrument like guitar, with circular body (pl. **-s**, **-es**) —'**banjoist** n.

bank[1] (bæŋk) n. 1. establishment for keeping, lending, exchanging etc. money 2. any supply or store for future use, as blood bank —vt. 3. put in bank —vi. 4. transact business with bank —'**banker** n. —'**banking** n. —**bank account** account created by deposit of money at bank by customer —'**bankbook** n. book held by depositor, in which bank enters record of deposits, withdrawals etc. (also '**passbook**) —**bank card** or **banker's card** card guaranteeing payment of cheques by bank up to an agreed amount —**bank holiday** day(s), usu. public holiday(s), when banks are closed by law —**bank note** written promise of payment —**bank rate** (sometimes **B- R-**) minimum rate by which central bank is obliged to rediscount bills of exchange —**bank on** rely on

bank[2] (bæŋk) n. 1. mound or ridge of earth 2. edge of river, lake etc. 3. rising ground in sea —vt. 4. enclose with ridge —v. 5. pile up 6. (of aircraft) tilt inwards in turning

bank[3] (bæŋk) n. 1. tier 2. row of oars

bankrupt ('bæŋkrʌpt, -rəpt) n. 1. one who fails in business, insolvent debtor —a. 2. financially ruined —vt. 3. make, cause to be, bankrupt —'**bankruptcy** n.

banksia ('bæŋksɪə) n. genus of Aust. shrubs with dense, usu. yellow, cylindrical heads of flowers

banner ('bænə) n. 1. long strip with slogan etc. 2. placard 3. flag used as ensign

bannisters ('bænɪstəz) pl.n. see BANISTERS

bannock ('bænək) n. round flat cake orig. in Scotland, made from wheat or barley

banns or **bans** (bænz) pl.n. see BAN

banquet ('bæŋkwɪt) n. 1. feast —vi. 2. hold or take part in banquet —vt. 3. treat with feast —'**banqueter** n.

banquette (bæŋ'kɛt) n. 1. raised firing step behind parapet 2. US upholstered bench

banshee ('bænʃiː, bæn'ʃiː) n. Irish fairy with a wail portending death

bantam ('bæntəm) n. dwarf variety of domestic fowl —'**bantamweight** n. 1. professional boxer weighing 112-118 lbs. (51-53.5 kg); amateur boxer weighing 112-119 lbs. (51-54 kg) 2. wrestler weighing usu. 115-126 lbs. (52-57 kg)

banter ('bæntə) v. 1. speak or tease lightly or jokingly —n. 2. light, teasing language

Bantu ('bɑːntuː) n. 1. collective name for large group of related native tribes in Afr. 2. family of languages spoken by Bantu peoples

bantubeer ('bɑːntuːbɪə) n. SA malted drink made from sorghum

banyan or **banian** ('bænjən) n. Indian fig tree with spreading branches which take root

baobab ('beɪəʊbæb) n. Afr. tree with thick trunk and angular branches

bap (bæp) n. UK soft bread roll

baptise or **-ize** ('bæp'taɪz) vt. 1. immerse in, sprinkle with water ceremoniously 2. christen —'**baptism** n. —**bap'tismal** a. —**bap'tismally** adv. —'**Baptist** n. member of Protestant Christian denomination believing in necessity of baptism by immersion, esp. of adults —'**baptistry** or '**baptistery** n. place where baptism is performed —**baptism of fire** 1. soldier's first experience of battle 2. any initiating ordeal

bar[1] (bɑː) n. 1. rod or block of any substance 2. obstacle 3. bank of sand at mouth of river 4. rail in law court 5. body of lawyers 6. counter where drinks are served, esp. in hotel etc. 7. unit of music —vt. 8. fasten 9. obstruct 10. exclude (**-rr-**) —prep. 11. except —'**barring** prep. excepting —**bar code** arrangement of parallel lines, readable by computer, printed on, and giving details of, merchandise in shop etc. —**bar graph** graph consisting of bars whose lengths are proportional to quantities —'**barmaid** n. —**bar sinister** 1. (not in heraldic usage) see **bend sinister** at BEND 2. condition of being of illegitimate birth —'**bartender** n.

bar[2] (bɑː) n. unit of pressure

bar. 1. barometer 2. barrel 3. barrister

barb (bɑːb) n. 1. sharp point curving backwards behind main point of spear, fish hook *etc.* **2.** cutting remark —**barbed** *a.* —**barbed wire** fencing wire with barbs at close intervals

barbarous ('bɑːbərəs) *a.* **1.** savage, brutal **2.** uncivilized —**barbarian** (bɑː'beəriən) *n.* —**barbaric** (bɑː'bærɪk) *a.* —'**barbarism** *n.* —**barbarity** (bɑː'bærɪtɪ) *n.* —'**barbarously** *adv.*

Barbary ape ('bɑːbərɪ) tailless macaque that inhabits NW Afr. and Gibraltar

barbecue ('bɑːbɪkjuː) *n.* **1.** meal cooked outdoors over open fire **2.** fireplace or grill used for this —*vt.* **3.** cook (meat *etc.*) in this manner (**-cued, -cuing**)

barbel ('bɑːb²l) *n.* **1.** spine or bristle that hangs from jaws of certain fishes **2.** any of several European fishes resembling carp

barbell ('bɑːbel) *n.* metal rod to which heavy discs are attached at each end used for weightlifting exercises

barber ('bɑːbə) *n.* one who shaves beards and cuts hair

barberry ('bɑːbərɪ) *n.* **1.** any spiny Asian shrub, having yellow flowers and orange or red berries **2.** fruit of these plants

barbican ('bɑːbɪkən) *n.* **1.** outwork of fortified place, *esp.* to defend drawbridge **2.** watchtower projecting from fortification

barbiturate (bɑː'bɪtjurɪt, -reɪt) *n.* derivative of barbituric acid used as drug —'**barbitone** *or U.S.* '**barbital** *n.* —**barbituric acid** crystalline solid used in preparation of barbiturate drugs

barcarole *or* **barcarolle** ('bɑːkərəʊl, -rɒl; bɑːkə'rəʊl) *n.* gondolier's song

bard (bɑːd) *n.* **1.** formerly, Celtic poet **2.** wandering minstrel —'**bardic** *a.* —**the Bard** Shakespeare

bare (beə) *a.* **1.** uncovered **2.** naked **3.** plain **4.** scanty —*vt.* **5.** make bare —'**barely** *adv.* only just, scarcely —'**bareness** *n.* —'**barebacked** *a.* on unsaddled horse —'**barefaced** *a.* shameless

bargain ('bɑːgɪn) *n.* **1.** something bought at price favourable to purchaser **2.** contract, agreement —*vi.* **3.** haggle, negotiate **4.** make bargain

barge (bɑːdʒ) *n.* **1.** flat-bottomed freight boat **2.** state or pleasure boat —*vi. inf.* **3.** (*with* into *or* in) interrupt **4.** (*with* into) bump (into), push —**bar'gee** *or U.S.* '**bargeman** *n.* —**bargepole** *n.* long pole used to propel barge —**not touch with a bargepole** *inf.* refuse to have anything to do with

baritone ('bærɪtəʊn) *n.* **1.** (singer with) second lowest adult male voice —*a.* **2.** written for or possessing this vocal range

barium ('beərɪəm) *n.* white metallic element —**barium meal** preparation of barium sulphate, which is opaque to x-rays, swallowed by patient before x-ray of upper part of alimentary canal

bark¹ (bɑːk) *n.* **1.** sharp loud cry of dog *etc.* —*v.* **2.** make, utter with such sound —'**barker** *n.* crier outside fair booth *etc.*

bark² (bɑːk) *n.* **1.** outer layer of trunk, branches of tree —*vt.* **2.** strip bark from **3.** rub off (skin), graze (shins *etc.*)

bark³ (bɑːk) *n. see* BARQUE

barley ('bɑːlɪ) *n.* grain used for food and in making malt —'**barleycorn** *n.* **1.** (grain of) barley **2.** *obs.* unit of length equal to a third of an inch —**barley sugar** sweet originally made with barley —**barley water** drink made from infusion of barley

barm (bɑːm) *n.* **1.** *obs.* yeast **2.** froth —'**barmy** *a. inf.* silly, insane

bar mitzvah (bɑː 'mɪtsvə) (*sometimes* B-M-) *Judaism* **1.** ceremony marking 13th birthday of boy, who then assumes full religious obligations **2.** the boy himself

barn (bɑːn) *n.* farm building, used to store grain, hay *etc.* —**barn dance** (party with) country dancing —**barn owl** owl with pale brown and white plumage —'**barnstorm** *vi. chiefly US* tour rural districts putting on shows or making speeches in political campaign —'**barnstormer** *n.* —'**barnyard** *n.* farmyard

barnacle ('bɑːnək²l) *n.* shellfish which adheres to rocks and ships' bottoms —**barnacle goose** N European goose that has black-and-white head and body

barney ('bɑːnɪ) *inf. n.* **1.** noisy argument **2.** fight —*vi.* **3.** argue or fight

barograph ('bærəgrɑːf, -græf) *n.* recording barometer

barometer (bə'rɒmɪtə) *n.* instrument to measure pressure of atmosphere —**baro'metric** *a.* —**ba'rometry** *n.*

baron ('bærən) *n.* **1.** member of lowest rank of peerage (**-ess** *fem.*) **2.** powerful businessman —'**baronage** *n.* —**ba'ronial** *a.* —'**barony** *n.* —**baron of beef** cut of beef consisting of double sirloin joined at backbone

baronet ('bærənɪt, -nɛt) *n.* lowest British hereditary title, below baron but above knight —'**baronetage** *n.* —'**baronetcy** *n.*

baroque (bə'rɒk, bə'rəʊk) *a.* extravagantly ornamented, *esp.* in architecture and art

baroscope ('bærəskəʊp) *n.* any instrument for measuring atmospheric pressure —**baroscopic** (bærə'skɒpɪk) *a.*

barouche (bə'ruːʃ) *n.* four-wheeled carriage with folding top over rear seat

barque (bɑːk) *n.* sailing ship, *esp.* large, three-masted one —'**barquentine** *n.* small barque

barrack¹ ('bærək) *n.* **1.** (*usu. pl.*) building for lodging soldiers **2.** huge bare building

barrack² ('bærək) *inf. vi.* **1.** (*usu. with* for) encourage by cheering, *esp.* at sporting events —*vt.* **2.** criticize loudly —*v.* **3.** jeer —'**barracking** *n.*

barracouta (bærə'kuːtə) *n.* type of large, elongated, predatory fish, mostly tropical

barrage ('bærɑːʒ) *n.* **1.** heavy artillery fire **2.** continuous and heavy delivery, *esp.* of questions *etc.* **3.** dam across river —**barrage balloon** one of number of tethered balloons with cables or net suspended from them, used to deter low-flying air attack

barratry *or* **barretry** ('bærətrɪ) *n.* 1. fraudulent breach of duty by master of ship 2. stirring up of law suits —'**barrator** *n.* —'**barratrous** *a.*

barre (baːr) *Fr.* rail used for ballet practice

barrel ('bærəl) *n.* 1. round wooden vessel, made of curved staves bound with hoops 2. amount that barrel can hold (*also* '**barrelful**) 3. anything long and hollow, as tube of gun *etc.* —*vt.* 4. put in barrel (**-ll-**) —'**barrelled** *a.* —**barrel organ** instrument consisting of cylinder turned by handle, having pins that interrupt air flow to certain pipes or pluck strings, thereby playing tunes —**barrel vault** *Archit.* vault in form of half cylinder

barren ('bærən) *a.* 1. unfruitful, sterile 2. unprofitable 3. dull —'**barrenness** *n.* —**Barren Grounds** sparsely inhabited tundra region in N Canada

barricade (bærɪ'keɪd, 'bærɪkeɪd) *n.* 1. improvised fortification, barrier —*vt.* 2. protect by building barrier 3. block

barrier ('bærɪə) *n.* fence, obstruction, obstacle, boundary —**barrier cream** cream to protect skin —**barrier reef** coral reef lying parallel to shore

barrister ('bærɪstə) *n.* advocate in the higher law courts

barrow[1] ('bærəʊ) *n.* 1. small wheeled handcart 2. wheelbarrow

barrow[2] ('bærəʊ) *n.* 1. burial mound 2. tumulus

Bart. Baronet

barter ('baːtə) *v.* 1. trade by exchange of goods —*n.* 2. practice of bartering

baryon ('bærɪɒn) *n. Phys.* elementary particle of matter

baryta (bə'raɪtə) *n.* 1. barium oxide 2. barium hydroxide

barytes (bə'raɪtiːz) *n.* barium sulphate

basalt ('bæsɔːlt) *n.* dark-coloured, hard, compact, igneous rock —**ba'saltic** *a.*

bascule ('bæskjuːl) *n.* 1. lever apparatus 2. drawbridge on counterpoise principle

base[1] (beɪs) *n.* 1. bottom, foundation 2. starting point 3. centre of operations 4. fixed point 5. *Chem.* compound that combines with an acid to form a salt 6. medium into which other substances are mixed 7. *Maths.* number that when raised to a certain power has logarithm equal to that power —*vt.* 8. found, establish —'**basal** *a.* of base —'**baseless** *a.* —'**baseline** *n.* 1. *Surv.* measured line through survey area from which triangulations are made 2. line at each end of tennis court that marks limit of play —'**basement** *n.* lowest storey of building

base[2] (beɪs) *a.* 1. low, mean 2. despicable —'**basely** *adv.* —'**baseness** *n.* —'**baseborn** *a.* illegitimate

baseball ('beɪsbɔːl) *n.* game, orig. Amer., played with bat and ball

bases ('beɪsiːz) *n., pl. of* BASIS

bash (bæʃ) *inf. vt.* 1. strike violently —*n.* 2. blow 3. attempt

bashful ('bæʃfʊl) *a.* shy, modest —'**bashfully** *adv.* —'**bashfulness** *n.*

basic ('beɪsɪk; *Austral. also* 'bæsɪk) *a.* 1. relating to, serving as base 2. fundamental 3. necessary —**basic slag** slag produced in steel-making, containing calcium phosphate

BASIC ('beɪsɪk) *Comp.* Beginners' All-purpose Symbolic Instruction Code

basil ('bæz²l) *n.* aromatic herb

basilica (bə'zɪlɪkə) *n.* type of church with long hall and pillars —**ba'silican** *a.*

basilisk ('bæzɪlɪsk) *n.* legendary small fire-breathing dragon

basin ('beɪs²n) *n.* 1. deep circular dish 2. harbour 3. land drained by river

basis ('beɪsɪs) *n.* 1. foundation 2. principal constituent (*pl.* '**bases**)

bask (baːsk) *vi.* lie in warmth and sunshine —**basking shark** large plankton-eating shark

basket ('baːskɪt) *n.* vessel made of woven cane, straw *etc.* —'**basketry** *or* '**basketwork** *n.* —'**basketball** *n.* ball game played by two teams —**basket chair** wickerwork chair —**basket weave** weave of yarns, resembling that of basket

basque (bæsk) *n.* tight-fitting bodice for women

Basque (bæsk, baːsk) *n.* 1. one of race from W Pyrenees 2. their language

bas-relief (baːrɪ'liːf, 'bæsrɪliːf) *n.* sculpture with figures standing out slightly from background

bass[1] (beɪs) *n.* 1. lowest part in music 2. bass singer or voice —*a.* 3. relating to or denoting the bass —**bass clef** clef that establishes F a fifth below middle C on fourth line of staff

bass[2] (bæs) *n.* any of large variety of fish, *esp.* sea perch

basset ('bæsɪt) *n.* type of smooth-haired dog

basset horn obsolete woodwind instrument

bassinet (bæsɪ'nɛt) *n.* wickerwork or wooden cradle or pram, usu. hooded

bassoon (bə'suːn) *n.* woodwind instrument of low tone —**bas'soonist** *n.*

bast (bæst) *n.* fibrous material obtained from phloem of jute, flax *etc.* used for making rope *etc.*

bastard ('baːstəd, 'bæs-) *n.* 1. child born of unmarried parents 2. *inf.* person, as in *lucky bastard* —*a.* 3. illegitimate 4. spurious —'**bastardize** *or* **-ise** *vt.* 1. debase 2. declare illegitimate —'**bastardy** *n.*

baste[1] (beɪst) *vt.* 1. moisten (meat) during cooking with hot fat 2. beat with stick —'**basting** *n.*

baste[2] (beɪst) *vt.* sew loosely, tack

bastinado (bæstɪ'neɪdəʊ) *n.* 1. beating with stick, *esp.* on soles of feet (*pl.* **-es**) —*vt.* 2. inflict a bastinado on (**-doing, -doed**)

bastion ('bæstɪən) *n.* 1. projecting part of

fortification, tower **2.** strong defence or bulwark

bat¹ (bæt) *n.* **1.** any of various types of club used to hit ball in certain sports, *eg* cricket, baseball —*v.* **2.** strike with bat or use bat in sport (-tt-) —'**batting** *n.* performance with bat —'**batsman** *n.*

bat² (bæt) *n.* nocturnal mouselike flying animal

bat³ (bæt) *vt.* flutter (one's eyelids) (-tt-)

batch (bætʃ) *n.* group or set of similar objects, *esp.* cakes *etc.* baked together

bated ('beɪtɪd) *a.* —**with bated breath** anxiously

bath (bɑːθ) *n.* **1.** vessel or place to bathe in **2.** water for bathing **3.** act of bathing —*pl.* **4.** place for swimming —*v.* **5.** wash —**bath cube** cube of soluble scented material for use in bath —'**bathrobe** *n.* loose-fitting garment of towelling, for wear before or after bath or swimming —'**bathroom** *n.* **1.** room containing bath and usu. washbasin and lavatory **2.** US lavatory —**bath salts** soluble scented salts for use in bath

Bath chair (bɑːθ) invalid chair

bathe (beɪð) *vi.* **1.** swim —*vt.* **2.** apply liquid to —*v.* **3.** wash **4.** immerse or be immersed in water (**bathed**, '**bathing**) —*n.* **5.** a swim or paddle —'**bather** *n.*

bathometer (bə'θɒmɪtə) *n.* instrument for measuring depth of water —**batho'metric** *a.*

bathos ('beɪθɒs) *n.* ludicrous descent from the elevated to the ordinary in writing or speech

bathyscaph ('bæθɪskæf), **bathyscaphe** ('bæθɪskeɪf, -skæf), *or* **bathyscape** *n.* vessel for deep-sea observation

bathysphere ('bæθɪsfɪə) *n.* strong steel deep-sea diving sphere, lowered by cable

batik *or* **battik** ('bætɪk) *n.* dyeing process using wax

batiste (bæ'tiːst) *n.* fine plain-weave cotton

batman ('bætmən) *n.* military officer's servant

baton ('bætɒn) *n.* **1.** slender stick used by conductor of an orchestra **2.** policeman's truncheon **3.** staff serving as symbol of office

batrachian (bə'treɪkɪən) *n.* any amphibian, *esp.* frog or toad

battalion (bə'tæljən) *n.* military unit consisting of three or more companies

batten¹ ('bætən) *n.* **1.** narrow piece of board, strip of wood —*vt.* **2.** (*esp.* with down) fasten, make secure

batten² ('bætən) *vi.* (usu. with on) thrive, *esp.* at someone else's expense

batter ('bætə) *vt.* **1.** strike continuously —*n.* **2.** mixture of flour, eggs, milk, used in cooking —**battered baby** young child who has sustained serious injuries through violence of parent or other adult —**battering ram** *esp.* formerly, large beam used to break down fortifications

battery ('bætərɪ) *n.* **1.** connected group of electrical cells **2.** any electrical cell or accumulator **3.** number of similar things occurring together **4.** *Law* assault by beating **5.** number of guns **6.** place where they are mounted **7.** unit of artillery **8.** large number of cages for rearing poultry *etc.*

batting ('bætɪŋ) *n.* cotton fibre, used as stuffing

battle ('bæt°l) *n.* **1.** fight between armies, combat —*vi.* **2.** fight **3.** struggle —'**battlement** *n.* wall, parapet on fortification with openings or embrasures —**battle-axe** *n. inf.* domineering woman —**battle cruiser** high-speed heavily armed warship of battleship size but with light armour —**battle dress** ordinary uniform of soldier —**battle fatigue** mental disorder characterized by anxiety and depression, caused by stress of warfare —'**battlefield** *or* '**battleground** *n.* place where battle is fought —**battle royal 1.** fight involving more than two combatants **2.** long violent argument —'**battleship** *n.* heavily armed and armoured fighting ship

battledore ('bæt°ldɔː) *n.* **1.** ancient racket game **2.** light racket used in this game (*also* **battledore and shuttlecock**)

batty ('bætɪ) *a. inf.* crazy, silly

bauble ('bɔːb°l) *n.* showy trinket

baulk (bɔːk) *see* BALK —**baulk line** *or* **balk line** *Billiards* straight line across table behind which cue balls start game

bauxite ('bɔːksaɪt) *n.* clay yielding aluminium

bawd (bɔːd) *n.* **1.** prostitute **2.** brothel keeper —'**bawdy** *a.* obscene, lewd

bawl (bɔːl) *v.* **1.** cry **2.** shout —*n.* **3.** loud cry or shout

bay¹ (beɪ) *n.* **1.** wide inlet of sea **2.** space between two columns **3.** recess —**bay window** window projecting from wall and forming alcove of a room

bay² (beɪ) *n.* **1.** bark **2.** cry of hounds in pursuit —*vi.* **3.** bark —**at bay 1.** cornered **2.** at a distance

bay³ (beɪ) *n.* **1.** laurel tree —*pl.* **2.** honorary crown of victory —'**bayberry** *n.* tropical Amer. tree that yields oil —**bay rum** aromatic liquid, used in medicines *etc.*, orig. obtained by distilling leaves of bayberry tree with rum

bay⁴ (beɪ) *a.* reddish-brown

bayonet ('beɪənɪt) *n.* **1.** stabbing weapon fixed to rifle —*vt.* **2.** stab with this ('**bayoneted**, '**bayoneting**)

bazaar *or* **bazar** (bə'zɑː) *n.* **1.** market, *esp.* in Orient **2.** sale of goods for charity

bazooka (bə'zuːkə) *n.* antitank rocket launcher

B.B. 1. Boys' Brigade **2.** (of pencils) double black

B.B.C. British Broadcasting Corporation

BC British Columbia

B.C. before Christ

BCG Bacillus Calmette-Guérin (antituberculosis vaccine)

B.Com. *or* **B.Comm.** Bachelor of Commerce

B.D. Bachelor of Divinity

B/D bank draft

B.D.S. Bachelor of Dental Surgery

be (bi:; *unstressed* bɪ) *vi.* 1. live 2. exist 3. have a state or quality (I **am**, he **is**; we, you, they **are**, *pr. ind.* —**was**, *pl.* **were**, *pt.* —**been** *pp.* —'**being** *pr.p.*)

Be *Chem.* beryllium

be- (*comb. form*) 1. surround; cover, as in *befog* 2. affect completely, as in *bedazzle* 3. consider as; cause to be, as in *befriend* 4. at, for, against, on, or over, as in *bewail*, *berate*

B.E. 1. bill of exchange 2. Bachelor of Engineering

beach (bi:tʃ) *n.* 1. shore of sea —*vt.* 2. run (boat) on shore —'**beachcomber** *n.* one who habitually searches shore debris for items of value —'**beachhead** *n.* 1. area on beach captured from enemy 2. base for operations

beacon ('bi:kən) *n.* 1. signal fire 2. lighthouse, buoy 3. (radio) signal used for navigation

bead (bi:d) *n.* 1. little ball pierced for threading on string of necklace, rosary *etc.* 2. drop of liquid 3. narrow moulding —'**beaded** *a.* —'**beading** *n.* —'**beady** *a.* small and bright

beadle ('bi:d³l) *n. Hist.* church or parish officer

beagle ('bi:g³l) *n.* small hound

beak (bi:k) *n.* 1. projecting horny jaws of bird 2. anything pointed or projecting 3. *sl.* magistrate

beaker ('bi:kə) *n.* 1. large drinking cup 2. glass vessel used by chemists

beam (bi:m) *n.* 1. long squared piece of wood 2. ship's cross timber, side, or width 3. ray of light *etc.* 4. broad smile 5. bar of a balance —*vt.* 6. aim (light, radio waves *etc.*) in a certain direction —*vi.* 7. shine 8. smile benignly —**on her beam-ends** (of vessel) heeled over through angle of 90° —**on one's beam-ends** out of resources; destitute

bean (bi:n) *n.* any of various leguminous plants or their seeds —'**beano** *n. inf.* celebration —'**beanbag** *n.* 1. small cloth bag filled with dried beans and thrown in games 2. large cushion filled with foam rubber or polystyrene granules and used as seat —'**beanfeast** *n.* UK *inf.* 1. annual dinner given by employers to employees 2. any festive occasion —**full of beans** *inf.* lively

bear¹ (bɛə) *vt.* 1. carry 2. support 3. produce 4. endure —*vi.* 5. (*with* upon) press (upon) (**bore** *pt.*, **born** *or* **borne** *pp.*, '**bearing** *pr.p.*) —'**bearable** *a.* endurable; tolerable —'**bearer** *n.*

bear² (bɛə) *n.* 1. heavy carnivorous quadruped 2. other bearlike animals, *eg* Aust. koala bear —**bear garden** scene of tumult —**bear hug** 1. wrestling hold in which arms are locked round opponent's chest and arms 2. any similar tight

embrace —'**bearskin** *n.* Guards' tall fur helmet

beard (bɪəd) *n.* 1. hair on chin —*vt.* 2. oppose boldly

bearing ('bɛərɪŋ) *n.* 1. support or guide for mechanical part, *esp.* one reducing friction 2. relevance 3. behaviour 4. direction 5. relative position 6. device on shield

beast (bi:st) *n.* 1. animal 2. four-footed animal 3. brutal man —'**beastliness** *n.* —'**beastly** *a.*

beat (bi:t) *vt.* 1. strike repeatedly 2. overcome 3. surpass 4. stir vigorously with striking action 5. flap (wings) 6. make, wear (path) —*vi.* 7. throb 8. sail against wind (**beat** *pt.*, '**beaten** *pp.*) —*n.* 9. stroke 10. pulsation 11. appointed course 12. basic rhythmic unit in piece of music —*a.* 13. *sl.* exhausted —'**beater** *n.* 1. instrument for beating 2. one who rouses game for shooters

beatify (bɪ'ætɪfaɪ) *vt.* 1. make happy 2. *R.C.Ch.* pronounce in eternal happiness (first step in canonization) (-**fied**, -**fying**) —**bea'tific** *a.* —**beatifi'cation** *n.* —**be'atitude** *n.* blessedness

beatnik ('bi:tnɪk) *n.* 1. member of Beat Generation of 1950s, rebelling against conventional attitudes 2. *inf.* person with long hair and shabby clothes

beau (bəʊ) *n.* suitor (*pl.* -**s**, **beaux** (bəʊ, bəʊz))

Beaufort scale ('bəʊfət) system of indicating wind strength (from 0, calm, to 17, hurricane)

beaujolais ('bəʊʒəleɪ) *n.* (*sometimes* B-) red or white wine from southern Burgundy, France

beauty ('bju:tɪ) *n.* 1. loveliness, grace 2. beautiful person or thing —'**beauteous** *a.* —**beau'tician** *n.* one who works in beauty parlour —'**beautiful** *a.* —'**beautifully** *adv.* —'**beautify** *vt.* —**beauty parlour** *or* **salon** establishment offering hairdressing, manicure *etc.* —**beauty sleep** *inf.* sleep, *esp.* before midnight —**beauty spot** 1. small dark-coloured patch worn on lady's face as adornment 2. mole or similar natural mark on skin 3. place of outstanding beauty

beaver ('bi:və) *n.* 1. amphibious rodent 2. its fur —**beaver away** work hard

bebop ('bi:bɒp) *n. see* BOP (sense 1)

B.Ec. Bachelor of Economics

becalmed (bɪ'kɑ:md) *a.* (of ship) motionless through lack of wind

became (bɪ'keɪm) *pt. of* BECOME

because (bɪ'kɒz, -'kəz) *conj.* since —**because of** on account of

béchamel sauce (beɪʃə'mɛl) thick white sauce

bêche-de-mer (bɛʃdə'mɛə) *n.* edible sea slug

beck¹ (bɛk) *n.* —**at someone's beck and call** subject to someone's slightest whim

beck² (bɛk) *n.* stream

beckon ('bɛkən) v. (*sometimes with* to) summon or lure by silent signal

become (bɪ'kʌm) vi. 1. come to be —vt. 2. suit (be'came pt., be'come pp., be'coming pr.p.) —be'coming a. 1. suitable to 2. proper

becquerel (bɛkə'rɛl) n. SI unit of activity of radioactive source

bed (bɛd) n. 1. piece of furniture for sleeping on 2. garden plot 3. place in which anything rests 4. bottom of river 5. layer, stratum —vt. 6. lay in a bed 7. plant (-dd-) —'bedding n. —'bedbug n. any of several bloodsucking wingless insects infesting dirty houses —'bedclothes pl.n. sheets, blankets, and other bed coverings —bedding plant immature plant that may be planted out in garden bed —bed linen sheets, pillowcases etc. —'bedpan n. container used as lavatory by bedridden people —'bedridden a. confined to bed by age or sickness —'bedrock n. —'bedroom n. —'bedsitter n. one-roomed flat —'bedsore n. chronic ulcer on skin of bedridden person, caused by prolonged pressure —'bedspread n. top cover on bed —'bedstead n. —bed and breakfast chiefly UK in hotel, boarding house etc., overnight accommodation and breakfast

B.Ed. Bachelor of Education

bedaub (bɪ'dɔ:b) vt. 1. smear with something thick, sticky or dirty 2. ornament in gaudy or vulgar fashion

bedeck (bɪ'dɛk) vt. cover with decorations; adorn

bedevil (bɪ'dɛv³l) vt. 1. confuse 2. torment —be'devilment n.

bedew (bɪ'dju:) vt. wet as with dew

bedizen (bɪ'daɪz³n, -'dɪz³n) vt. obs. dress gaudily or tastelessly —be'dizenment n.

bedlam ('bɛdləm) n. noisy confused scene

Bedlington terrier ('bɛdlɪŋtən) woolly-coated terrier with convex head profile

Bedouin or **Beduin** ('bɛduɪn) n. 1. member of nomadic Arab race —a. 2. nomadic

bedraggle (bɪ'dræg³l) vt. dirty by trailing in wet or mud —be'draggled a.

Beds. (bɛdz) Bedfordshire

bee[1] (bi:) n. insect that makes honey —'beeeater n. insect-eating bird —'beehive n. —'beeline n. shortest route —'beeswax n. wax secreted by bees —'beeswing n. filmy crust of tartar that forms in some wines after long keeping in bottle

bee[2] (bi:) n. chiefly US social gathering for specific purpose, as to carry out communal task

Beeb (bi:b) n. inf. the B.B.C.

beech (bi:tʃ) n. 1. European tree with smooth greyish bark and small nuts 2. its wood —'beechen a.

beef (bi:f) n. 1. flesh of cattle raised and killed for eating 2. inf. complaint —vi. 3. inf. complain —'beefy a. fleshy, stolid —beeves pl.n. cattle —'beefburger n. see HAMBURGER —'beefeater n. 1. yeoman of the guard 2. warder of Tower of London

—beef tea drink made by boiling pieces of lean beef

Beelzebub (bɪ'ɛlzɪbʌb) n. Satan or any devil

been (bi:n, bɪn) pp. of BE

beep (bi:p) n. 1. short, loud sound of car horn etc. —vi. 2. make this sound

beer (bɪə) n. fermented alcoholic drink made from hops and malt —'beery a. —beer parlour C licensed place where beer is sold to the public —beer and skittles inf. enjoyment or pleasure

beestings, biestings, or U.S. **beastings** ('bi:stɪŋz) pl.n. (with sing. v.) first milk secreted by cow or similar animal after giving birth

beet (bi:t) n. any of various plants with root used for food or extraction of sugar —'beetroot n. variety of beet that has bulbous dark red root that may be eaten as vegetable

beetle[1] ('bi:t³l) n. class of insect with hard upper-wing cases closed over the back for protection —beetle-browed a. with prominent brows

beetle[2] ('bi:t³l) vi. 1. overhang; jut —a. 2. overhanging; prominent

befall (bɪ'fɔ:l) v. happen (to) (be'fell, be'fallen)

befit (bɪ'fɪt) vt. be suitable to (-tt-) —be'fittingly adv.

befog (bɪ'fɒg) vt. perplex, confuse (-gg-)

before (bɪ'fɔ:) prep. 1. in front of 2. in presence of 3. in preference to 4. earlier than —adv. 5. earlier 6. in front —conj. 7. sooner than —be'forehand adv. previously

befoul (bɪ'faul) vt. make filthy

befriend (bɪ'frɛnd) vt. make friend of

befuddle (bɪ'fʌd³l) vt. 1. confuse 2. make stupid with drink —be'fuddlement n.

beg (bɛg) vt. 1. ask earnestly, beseech —vi. 2. ask for or live on alms (-gg-) —'beggar n. —'beggarly a.

began (bɪ'gæn) pt. of BEGIN

beget (bɪ'gɛt) vt. produce, generate (be'got, be'gat pt., be'gotten, be'got pp., be'getting pr.p.) —be'getter n.

begin (bɪ'gɪn) v. 1. (cause to) start —vt. 2. originate 3. initiate (be'gan, be'gun, be'ginning) —be'ginner n. novice —be'ginning n.

begone (bɪ'gɒn) interj. go away

begonia (bɪ'gəunjə) n. genus of tropical plant

begot (bɪ'gɒt) pt./pp. of BEGET

begrudge (bɪ'grʌdʒ) vt. grudge, envy someone the possession of

beguile (bɪ'gaɪl) vt. 1. charm, fascinate 2. amuse 3. deceive —be'guiler n.

beguine (bɪ'gi:n) n. 1. dance of S Amer. origin 2. music in rhythm of this dance

begum ('beigəm) n. esp. in India, Muslim woman of high rank

begun (bɪ'gʌn) pp. of BEGIN

behalf (bɪ'hɑ:f) n. favour, benefit, interest (esp. in on behalf of)

behave (bɪ'heiv) vi. act, function in

particular way —**be'haviour** or U.S. **be'havior** n. conduct —**be'haviourism** or U.S. **be'haviorism** n. school of psychology that regards observable behaviour as the only valid subject for study —**behave oneself** conduct oneself (well)

behead (bɪ'hɛd) vt. cut off head of

beheld (bɪ'hɛld) pt./pp. of BEHOLD

behemoth (bɪ'hiːmɒθ) n. **1.** Bible gigantic beast described in Job **2.** huge person or thing

behest (bɪ'hɛst) n. charge, command

behind (bɪ'haɪnd) prep. **1.** further back or earlier than **2.** in support of —adv. **3.** in the rear —**be'hindhand** a./adv. **1.** in arrears **2.** tardy

behold (bɪ'həʊld) vt. watch, see (**be'held** pt., **be'held, be'holden** pp.) —**be'holder** n.

beholden (bɪ'həʊld'n) a. bound in gratitude

behove (bɪ'həʊv) vt. (only impers.) be fit, necessary for

beige (beɪʒ) n. **1.** undyed woollen cloth **2.** its colour

being ('biːɪŋ) n. **1.** existence **2.** that which exists **3.** creature —v. **4.** pr.p. of BE

bejewel (bɪ'dʒuːəl) vt. decorate as with jewels (-**ll**-)

bel (bɛl) n. unit for comparing two power levels

belabour or U.S. **belabor** (bɪ'leɪbə) vt. beat soundly

belated (bɪ'leɪtɪd) a. **1.** late **2.** too late

belay (bɪ'leɪ) vt. fasten (rope) to peg, pin etc.

belch (bɛltʃ) vi. **1.** void wind by mouth —vt. **2.** eject violently **3.** cast up —n. **4.** emission of wind etc.

beldam or **beldame** ('bɛldəm) n. obs. old woman

beleaguer (bɪ'liːgə) vt. besiege

belfry ('bɛlfrɪ) n. bell tower

Belial (bɪːlɪəl) n. the devil, Satan

belie (bɪ'laɪ) vt. **1.** contradict **2.** misrepresent (**be'lied** pt./pp., **be'lying** pr.p.)

believe (bɪ'liːv) vt. **1.** regard as true or real —vi. **2.** have faith —**be'lief** n. —**be'lievable** a. credible —**be'liever** n. esp. one of same religious faith

Belisha beacon (bə'liːʃə) flashing light in orange globe marking a pedestrian crossing

belittle (bɪ'lɪt'l) vt. regard, speak of, as having little worth or value —**be'littlement** n.

bell (bɛl) n. **1.** hollow metal instrument giving ringing sound when struck **2.** electrical device emitting ring or buzz as signal —**bell-bottomed** a. —**bell-bottoms** pl.n. trousers that flare from knee —'**bellboy** n. pageboy in hotel —**bell jar** bell-shaped glass cover to protect flower arrangements etc. or to cover apparatus in experiments (also **bell glass**) —**bell metal** alloy of copper and tin, used in casting bells —'**bellwether** n. **1.** sheep that leads flock, oft. bearing bell **2.** leader, esp. one followed blindly

belladonna (bɛlə'dɒnə) n. deadly nightshade

belle (bɛl) n. beautiful woman, reigning beauty

belles-lettres (Fr. bɛl'lɛtr) pl.n. (with sing. v.) literary works, esp. essays and poetry —**bel'letrist** n.

bellicose ('bɛlɪkəʊs, -kəʊz) a. warlike

belligerent (bɪ'lɪdʒərənt) a. **1.** hostile, aggressive **2.** making war —n. **3.** warring person or nation —**bel'ligerence** n.

bellow ('bɛləʊ) v. **1.** roar like bull **2.** shout —n. **3.** roar of bull **4.** any deep cry or shout

bellows ('bɛləʊz) pl.n. instrument for creating stream of air

belly ('bɛlɪ) n. **1.** part of body which contains intestines **2.** stomach —v. **3.** swell out ('**bellied, 'bellying**) —**belly ache** inf. stomachache —'**bellyache** vi. sl. complain repeatedly —'**bellybutton** n. inf. navel (also **tummy button**) —**belly dance** sensuous dance performed by women, with undulating movements of abdomen —**belly-dance** vi. perform belly dance —**belly flop** dive into water in which body lands horizontally —**belly-flop** vi. perform belly flop —'**bellyful** n. **1.** as much as one wants or can eat **2.** sl. more than one can tolerate —**belly laugh** inf. hearty laugh

belong (bɪ'lɒŋ) vi. **1.** (with to) be the property or attribute (of) **2.** (with to) be a member or inhabitant (of) **3.** have an allotted place **4.** pertain —**be'longings** pl.n. personal possessions

beloved (bɪ'lʌvɪd, -'lʌvd) a. much loved —n. **2.** dear one

below (bɪ'ləʊ) adv. **1.** beneath —prep. **2.** lower than

belt (bɛlt) n. **1.** band **2.** girdle **3.** zone or district —vt. **4.** surround, fasten with belt **5.** mark with band **6.** inf. thrash

beluga (bɪ'luːgə) n. large white sturgeon

belvedere ('bɛlvɪdɪə, bɛlvɪ'dɪə) n. building, such as summerhouse, sited to command fine view

B.E.M. British Empire Medal

bemoan (bɪ'məʊn) vt. grieve over (loss etc.)

bemuse (bɪ'mjuːz) vt. confuse, bewilder

ben[1] (bɛn) Scot. n. **1.** inner room in cottage —prep./adv. **2.** in; within; inside

ben[2] (bɛn) n. Scot., Irish mountain peak

bench (bɛntʃ) n. **1.** long seat **2.** seat or body of judges etc. —vt. **3.** provide with benches —**bench mark** fixed point, criterion

bend (bɛnd) v. **1.** (cause to) form a curve (**bent** pt./pp.) —n. **2.** curve —pl. **3.** decompression sickness —'**bender** n. inf. drinking bout —**bend sinister** Her. diagonal line on shield, typically indicating bastard line

beneath (bɪ'niːθ) prep. **1.** under, lower than —adv. **2.** below

Benedictine (bɛnɪ'dɪktiːn, -taɪn) n. **1.** monk or nun of order of Saint Benedict **2.** (bɛnɪ'dɪktiːn) liqueur first made at Benedictine monastery

benediction (bɛnɪ'dɪkʃən) n. invocation of divine blessing

benefit ('bɛnɪfɪt) n. 1. advantage, favour, profit, good 2. money paid by a government etc. to unemployed etc. —vt. 3. do good to —vi. 4. receive good ('benefited, 'benefiting) —bene'faction n. —'benefactor n. 1. one who helps or does good to others 2. patron ('benefactress fem.) —'benefice n. an ecclesiastical living —be'neficence n. —be'neficent a. 1. doing good 2. kind —be'neficently adv. —bene'ficial a. advantageous, helpful —bene'ficially adv. —bene'ficiary n. —benefit society US see friendly society at FRIEND

benevolent (bɪ'nɛvələnt) a. 1. kindly 2. charitable —be'nevolence n. —be'nevolently adv.

Bengali (bɛn'gɔːlɪ, bɛŋ-) n. 1. member of people living chiefly in Bangladesh and West Bengal 2. their language —a. 3. of Bengal, Bengalis or their language

benighted (bɪ'naɪtɪd) a. ignorant, uncultured

benign (bɪ'naɪn) a. 1. kindly 2. mild 3. favourable 4. Pathol. (of tumour etc.) not malignant —benignancy (bɪ'nɪgnənsɪ) n. —benignant (bɪ'nɪgnənt) a. —benignantly (bɪ'nɪgnəntlɪ) adv. —benignity (bɪ'nɪgnɪtɪ) n. —be'nignly adv.

benison ('bɛnɪzˀn, -sˀn) n. obs. blessing

bent (bɛnt) v. 1. pt./pp. of BEND —a. 2. curved 3. resolved (on) 4. inf. corrupt 5. inf. deviant 6. inf. crazy —n. 7. inclination, personal propensity —'bentwood n. wood bent in moulds after being heated by steaming

bent grass low-growing perennial grass which has spreading panicle of tiny flowers

benumb (bɪ'nʌm) vt. make numb, deaden

Benzedrine ('bɛnzɪdriːn, -drɪn) n. R amphetamine

benzene ('bɛnziːn) n. one of group of related flammable liquids used in chemistry and as solvents, cleaning agents etc.

benzoin ('bɛnzɔɪn, -zəʊɪn) n. gum resin obtained from various tropical Asian trees, used in ointments, perfume etc.

bequeath (bɪ'kwiːð, -'kwiːθ) vt. leave (property etc.) by will —bequest (bɪ'kwɛst) n. 1. bequeathing 2. legacy

berate (bɪ'reɪt) vt. scold harshly

Berber ('bɜːbə) n. 1. member of Caucasoid Muslim people of N Afr. 2. language of this people —a. 3. of this people or their language

berberis ('bɜːbərɪs) n. shrub with red berries

berceuse (Fr. bɛr'søːz) n. 1. lullaby 2. instrumental piece suggestive of this

bereave (bɪ'riːv) vt. (usu. with of) deprive (of), esp. by death —'reaved, -'reft pt./pp.) —be'reavement n. loss, esp. by death

beret ('bɛreɪ) n. round, closefitting hat

berg (bɜːg) n. 1. large mass of ice 2. SA mountain

bergamot ('bɜːgəmɒt) n. 1. type of pear with strong flavour 2. type of orange 3. fragrant oil produced from this, used in perfumery

beriberi (bɛrɪ'bɛrɪ) n. tropical disease caused by vitamin B deficiency

berk (bɜːk) n. UK sl. stupid person

berkelium (bɜː'kiːlɪəm, 'bɜːklɪəm) n. radioactive transuranic element

Berks. (bɑːks) Berkshire

Bermuda shorts (bə'mjuːdə) close-fitting shorts that come down to knees

berry ('bɛrɪ) n. 1. small juicy stoneless fruit —vi. 2. look for or pick berries

berserk (bə'zɜːk, -'sɜːk) a. frenzied

berth (bɜːθ) n. 1. ship's mooring place 2. place to sleep in ship or train —vt. 3. moor

beryl ('bɛrɪl) n. variety of crystalline mineral including aquamarine and emerald

beryllium (bɛ'rɪlɪəm) n. corrosion-resistant toxic metallic element

beseech (bɪ'siːtʃ) vt. entreat, implore (be'sought pt./pp.)

beset (bɪ'sɛt) vt. assail, surround with danger, problems (be'set, be'setting)

beside (bɪ'saɪd) prep. 1. by the side of, near 2. distinct from —be'sides adv./prep. in addition (to)

besiege (bɪ'siːdʒ) vt. surround (with armed forces etc.)

besmirch (bɪ'smɜːtʃ) vt. 1. make dirty; soil 2. reduce brightness of 3. sully

besom ('biːzəm) n. broom, esp. one made of bundle of twigs tied to handle

besotted (bɪ'sɒtɪd) a. 1. drunk 2. foolish, infatuated

besought (bɪ'sɔːt) pt./pp. of BESEECH

bespangle (bɪ'spæŋgˀl) vt. cover with or as if with spangles

bespatter (bɪ'spætə) vt. 1. splash, as with dirty water 2. defile; besmirch

bespeak (bɪ'spiːk) vt. engage beforehand (be'spoke pt., be'spoke, be'spoken pp.) —be'spoke a. 1. (of garments) made to order 2. selling such garments

Bessemer process ('bɛsɪmə) process for producing steel by blowing air through molten pig iron in refractory-lined furnace to remove impurities

best (bɛst) a./adv. 1. sup. of GOOD and WELL —vt. 2. defeat —best man (male) attendant of bridegroom at wedding —best seller 1. book or other product that has sold in great numbers 2. author of one or more such books etc.

bestial ('bɛstɪəl) a. like a beast, brutish —besti'ality n.

bestiary ('bɛstɪərɪ) n. moralizing medieval collection of descriptions of real and/or mythical animals

bestir (bɪ'stɜː) vt. rouse to activity

bestow (bɪ'stəʊ) vt. give, confer —be'stowal n.

bestrew (bɪ'struː) vt. scatter over (surface)

bestride (bɪ'straɪd) vt. 1. sit or stand over

bet with legs apart **2.** mount (horse) (be-'strode, be'stridden, be'striding)

bet (bɛt) v. **1.** agree to pay (money *etc.*) if wrong (or win if right) in guessing result of contest *etc.* (**bet** or **'betted** *pt./pp.*, **'betting** *pr.p.*) —n. **2.** money risked in this way

beta ('biːtə) n. **1.** second letter in Gr. alphabet (B or β) **2.** second in group or series

beta-blocker n. drug that decreases activity of heart: used in treatment of high blood pressure and angina pectoris

betake (bɪ'teɪk) vt. —**betake oneself** go; move

beta particle electron or positron emitted by nucleus during radioactive decay

betatron ('biːtətrɒn) n. particle accelerator for producing high-energy beams of electrons by magnetic induction

betel ('biːtˀl) n. species of pepper, chewed in parts of Asia as a narcotic —**betel nut** the nut of the areca palm

bête noire (bɛt 'nwaːr) *Fr.* pet aversion

bethink (bɪ'θɪŋk) *obs., dial.* v. **1.** cause (oneself) to consider or meditate —vt. **2.** (*oft. with* of) remind (oneself)

betide (bɪ'taɪd) v. happen (to)

betimes (bɪ'taɪmz) adv. *obs.* **1.** in good time; early **2.** soon

betoken (bɪ'təʊkən) vt. be a sign of

betony ('bɛtənɪ) n. plant with reddish-purple flower spike

betray (bɪ'treɪ) vt. **1.** be disloyal to, *esp.* by assisting an enemy **2.** reveal, divulge **3.** show signs of —be'trayal n. —be'trayer n.

betroth (bɪ'trəʊð) vt. promise to marry —be'trothal n. —be'trothed n./a.

better ('bɛtə) a./adv. **1.** comp. of GOOD and WELL —v. **2.** improve —'betterment n.

between (bɪ'twiːn) prep./adv. **1.** in the intermediate part, in space or time **2.** indicating reciprocal relation or comparison

betwixt (bɪ'twɪkst) prep./adv. *obs.* between

bevel ('bɛvˀl) n. **1.** surface not at right angle to another **2.** slant —vi. **3.** slope, slant —vt. **4.** cut on slant (**-ll-**) —a. **5.** slanted —**bevel gear** gear having teeth cut into conical surface

beverage ('bɛvərɪdʒ, 'bɛvrɪdʒ) n. drink

bevy ('bɛvɪ) n. flock or group

bewail (bɪ'weɪl) vt. lament

beware (bɪ'wɛə) v. be on one's guard (against), be wary (of)

bewilder (bɪ'wɪldə) vt. puzzle, confuse —be'wildering a. —be'wilderingly adv. —be'wilderment n.

bewitch (bɪ'wɪtʃ) vt. **1.** cast spell over **2.** charm, fascinate —be'witching a. —be'witchingly adv.

bey (beɪ) n. **1.** in Ottoman Empire, title given to provincial governors **2.** in modern Turkey, title of address, corresponding to Mr. (*also* **beg**)

beyond (bɪ'jɒnd) adv. **1.** farther away **2.** besides —prep. **3.** on the farther side of **4.** later than **5.** surpassing, out of reach of

bezel ('bɛzˀl) n. **1.** sloping face adjacent to working edge of cutting tool **2.** oblique faces of cut gem **3.** grooved ring or part holding watch crystal *etc.*

bezique (bɪ'ziːk) n. **1.** card game for two or more players **2.** in this game, queen of spades and jack of diamonds declared together

b.f. 1. UK *inf.* bloody fool **2.** *Print.* bold face

B/F or **b/f** brought forward

BFPO British Forces Post Office

bhang or **bang** (bæŋ) n. preparation of leaves and flower tops of Indian hemp, much used as narcotic in India

b.h.p. brake horsepower

Bi *Chem.* bismuth

bi- or *sometimes before vowel* **bin-** (*comb. form*) **1.** two; having two, as in *bifocal* **2.** occurring every two, as in *biennial* **3.** on both sides *etc.*, as in *bilateral* **4.** occurring twice during, as in *biweekly* **5.** indicating acid salt of dibasic acid, as in *sodium bicarbonate*

biannual (baɪ'ænjʊəl) a. occurring twice a year —bi'annually adv.

bias ('baɪəs) n. **1.** slant **2.** personal inclination or preference **3.** one-sided inclination (pl. **-es**) —vt. **4.** influence, affect (**-s-**, **-ss-**) —'biased a. prejudiced —**bias binding** strip of material cut on bias, used for binding hems or for decoration

biaxial (baɪ'æksɪəl) a. (*esp.* of crystal) having two axes

bib (bɪb) n. **1.** cloth put under child's chin to protect clothes when eating **2.** top of apron or overalls

bibcock ('bɪbkɒk) or **bibb** (bɪb) n. tap with nozzle bent downwards

bibelot ('bɪbləʊ) n. attractive or curious trinket

bibl. 1. bibliographical **2.** bibliography

Bibl. Biblical

Bible ('baɪbˀl) n. the sacred writings of the Christian religion —**biblical** ('bɪblɪkˀl) a. —**biblicist** ('bɪblɪsɪst) n.

biblio- (*comb. form*) book or books, as in *bibliography*

bibliography (bɪblɪ'ɒgrəfɪ) n. **1.** list of books on a subject **2.** history and description of books —**bibli'ographer** n. —**biblio'graphical** a.

bibliomania (bɪblɪəʊ'meɪnɪə) n. extreme fondness for books —**biblio'maniac** n./a.

bibliophile ('bɪblɪəfaɪl) or **bibliophil** ('bɪblɪəfɪl) n. lover, collector of books —**bibli'ophily** n.

bibulous ('bɪbjʊləs) a. given to drinking

bicameral (baɪ'kæmərəl) a. (of legislature) consisting of two chambers —bi'cameralism n.

bicarb ('baɪkɑːb) n. bicarbonate of soda

bicarbonate (baɪ'kɑːbənɪt, -neɪt) n. chemical compound releasing carbon dioxide when mixed with acid —**bicarbonate of soda** sodium bicarbonate, *esp.* as medicine or raising agent

bicentenary (baɪsɛn'tiːnərɪ) *or U.S.* **bicentennial** (baɪsɛn'tɛnɪəl) *n.* **1.** two hundredth anniversary **2.** its celebration

biceps ('baɪsɛps) *n.* two-headed muscle, *esp.* muscle of upper arm

bicker ('bɪkə) *vi./n.* quarrel over petty things —'**bickering** *n.*

bicolour ('baɪkʌlə), **bicoloured** *or U.S.* **bicolor, bicolored** *a.* two-coloured

bicuspid (baɪ'kʌspɪd) *or* **bicuspidate** (baɪ'kʌspɪdeɪt) *a.* **1.** having two points —*n.* **2.** bicuspid tooth; premolar

bicycle ('baɪsɪk²l) *n.* vehicle with two wheels, one in front of other, pedalled by rider —'**bicyclist** *n.*

bid (bɪd) *vt.* **1.** offer **2.** say **3.** command **4.** invite (**bad, bade** *or* **bid,** '**bidden**) —*n.* **5.** offer, *esp.* of price **6.** try **7.** *Cards* call —'**biddable** *a.* **1.** having sufficient value to be bid on **2.** docile; obedient —'**biddableness** *n.* —'**bidder** *n.* —'**bidding** *n.*

biddy ('bɪdɪ) *n. dial.* chicken or hen

bide (baɪd) *vi.* **1.** remain **2.** dwell —*vt.* **3.** await (**bided** *or* **bode,** '**bided**) —'**biding** *n.*

bidet ('biːdeɪ) *n.* low basin for washing genital area

biennial (baɪ'ɛnɪəl) *a.* **1.** happening every two years **2.** lasting two years —*n.* **3.** plant living two years —**bi'ennially** *adv.*

bier (bɪə) *n.* frame for bearing dead to grave

biff (bɪf) *sl. n.* **1.** blow with fist —*vt.* **2.** give (someone) such a blow

bifid ('baɪfɪd) *a.* divided into two lobes by median cleft —**bi'fidity** *n.*

bifocal (baɪ'fəʊk²l) *a.* having two different focal lengths —**bi'focals** *pl.n.* spectacles having bifocal lenses for near and distant vision

bifurcate ('baɪfəkeɪt) *vi.* **1.** divide into two branches —*a.* ('baɪfəkeɪt, -kɪt) **2.** forked or divided into two branches —**bifur'cation** *n.*

big (bɪg) *a.* of great or considerable size, height, number, power *etc.* ('**bigger** *comp.,* '**biggest** *sup.*) —'**bigness** *n.* —**Big Brother** person or organization that exercises total dictatorial control —**big dipper** (in amusement parks) narrow railway with open carriages that run swiftly over route of sharp curves and steep inclines —**big end** *UK* larger end of connecting rod in internal-combustion engine —**big shot** *sl.* important person —**big stick** *inf.* force or threat of force —**big time** *sl.* highest level of profession, *esp.* entertainment —**big-timer** *n.* —**big top** *inf.* **1.** main tent of circus **2.** circus itself —'**bigwig** *n. sl.* important person

bigamy ('bɪgəmɪ) *n.* crime of marrying a person while one is still legally married to someone else —'**bigamist** *n.* —'**bigamous** *a.*

bight (baɪt) *n.* **1.** curve or loop in rope **2.** long curved shoreline or water bounded by it

bigot ('bɪgət) *n.* person intolerant or not

receptive to ideas of others, *esp.* on religion *etc.* —'**bigoted** *a.* —'**bigotry** *n.*

bijou ('biːʒuː) *n.* **1.** something small and delicately worked (*pl.* -**joux** (-ʒuːz)) —*a.* **2.** *oft. ironic* small but tasteful

bike (baɪk) *n.* **1.** bicycle **2.** motor bike

bikini (bɪ'kiːnɪ) *n.* woman's brief two-piece swimming costume

bilateral (baɪ'lætərəl) *a.* two-sided

bilberry ('bɪlbərɪ) *n.* small European moorland plant with edible blue berries

bile (baɪl) *n.* **1.** fluid secreted by the liver **2.** anger, ill-temper —**biliary** ('bɪlɪərɪ) *a.* of bile, ducts that convey bile, or gall bladder —**bilious** ('bɪlɪəs) *a.* nauseous, nauseating —**biliousness** ('bɪlɪəsnɪs) *n.*

bilge (bɪldʒ) *n.* **1.** bottom of ship's hull **2.** dirty water that collects in vessel's bilge (*also* **bilge water**) **3.** *inf.* nonsense —*vi.* **4.** spring a leak

bilingual (baɪ'lɪŋgwəl) *a.* speaking, or written in, two languages —**bi'lingualism** *n.*

bilk (bɪlk) *vt.* **1.** balk; thwart **2.** (*oft. with of*) cheat, deceive **3.** escape from; elude —*n.* **4.** swindle, cheat **5.** person who swindles or cheats —'**bilker** *n.*

bill[1] (bɪl) *n.* **1.** written account of charges **2.** draft of Act of Parliament **3.** poster **4.** commercial document —*vt.* **5.** present account of charges to **6.** announce by advertisement —'**billing** *n.* degree of importance, *esp.* in theatre *etc.* —'**billboard** *n. chiefly US see* HOARDING —'**billposter** *or* '**billsticker** *n.* person who sticks advertising posters to walls *etc.* —'**billposting** *or* '**billsticking** *n.* —**bill of exchange** document instructing third party to pay stated sum at designated future date or on demand —**bill of fare** menu —**bill of lading** document containing full particulars of goods shipped —**clean bill of health** *inf.* **1.** good report of one's physical condition **2.** favourable account of person's or company's financial position

bill[2] (bɪl) *n.* **1.** bird's beak —*vi.* **2.** touch bills, as doves **3.** caress

bill[3] (bɪl) *n.* **1.** tool for pruning **2.** hooked weapon —'**billhook** *n.* hatchet with hook at end of cutting edge

billabong ('bɪləbɒŋ) *n.* **A** pool in intermittent stream

billet[1] ('bɪlɪt) *n.* **1.** civilian quarters for troops **2.** resting place —*vt.* **3.** quarter, as troops

billet[2] ('bɪlɪt) *n.* **1.** chunk of wood, *esp.* for fuel **2.** small bar of iron or steel

billet-doux (bɪl'duː) *Fr.* love letter

billiards ('bɪljədz) *n.* game played on table with balls and cues

billion ('bɪljən) *n.* million millions (*U.S., France* thousand millions)

billow ('bɪləʊ) *n.* **1.** great swelling wave —*pl.* **2.** the sea —*vi.* **3.** surge **4.** swell out

billy ('bɪlɪ) *or* **billycan** ('bɪlɪkæn) *n.* can with wire handle used for boiling water on open fire —**billy goat** male goat

biltong ('bıltɒŋ) *n.* SA thin strips of meat dried in sun

B.I.M. British Institute of Management

bimetallism (baı'metəlızəm) *n.* use of two metals, *esp.* gold and silver, in fixed relative values as standard of value and currency

bimonthly (baı'mʌnθlı) *adv./a.* 1. every two months 2. twice a month

bin (bın) *n.* 1. receptacle for corn, refuse *etc.* 2. one particular bottling of wine

binary ('baınərı) *a.* 1. composed of, characterized by, two 2. dual —**binary star** double star system containing two associated stars revolving around common centre of gravity

bind (baınd) *vt.* 1. tie fast 2. tie round, gird 3. tie together 4. oblige 5. seal 6. constrain 7. bandage 8. unite 9. put (book) into cover —*v.* 10. (cause to) cohere (**bound** *pt./pp.*) —'**binder** *n.* one who, or that which binds —'**bindery** *n.* —'**binding** *n.* 1. cover of book 2. tape for hem *etc.* —'**bindweed** *n.* convolvulus

bine (baın) *n.* climbing or twining stem of any of various plants, such as bindweed

binge (bındʒ) *n. inf.* 1. excessive indulgence in eating or drinking 2. spree

bingo ('bıŋgəʊ) *n.* game of chance in which numbers drawn are matched with those on a card

binnacle ('bınək³l) *n.* box holding ship's compass

binocular (bı'nɒkjʊlə, baı-) *a.* seeing with, made for both eyes —**bi'noculars** *pl.n.* telescope made for both eyes

binomial (baı'nəʊmıəl) *a./n.* (denoting) algebraic expression consisting of two terms —**binomial theorem** general formula that expresses any power of binomial without multiplying out

bio- *or before vowel* **bi-** (*comb. form*) life, living, as in *biochemistry*. Such words are not given here where the meaning may easily be inferred from the simple word

bioastronautics (baıəʊæstrə'nɔːtıks) *pl.n.* (*with sing. v.*) study of effects of space flight on living organisms

biocoenosis (baıəʊsiː'nəʊsıs) *n.* relationships between animals and plants subsisting together

biodegradable (baıəʊdı'greıdəb³l) *a.* capable of decomposition by natural means

bioengineering (baıəʊendʒı'nıərıŋ) *n.* 1. design and manufacture of aids to rectify defective body functions 2. design, manufacture and maintenance of engineering equipment used in biosynthetic processes —**bioengi'neer** *n.*

biog. 1. biographical 2. biography

biogenesis (baıəʊ'dʒenısıs) *n.* principle that living organism must originate from similar parent organism —**bioge'netic(al)** *a.*

biography (baı'ɒgrəfı) *n.* story of one person's life —**bi'ographer** *n.* —**bio'graphical** *a.* —**bio'graphically** *adv.*

biol. 1. biological 2. biology

biology (baı'ɒlədʒı) *n.* study of living organisms —**bio'logical** *a.* —**bio'logically** *adv.* —**bi'ologist** *n.* —**biological control** control of destructive organisms by nonchemical means —**biological warfare** use of living organisms or their toxic products as weapon of war

biomedicine (baıəʊ'medısın) *n.* medical and biological study of effects of unusual environmental stress

bionics (baı'ɒnıks) *pl.n.* (*with sing. v.*) study of relation of biological and electronic processes —**bi'onic** *a.* having physical functions augmented by electronic equipment

biophysics (baıəʊ'fızıks) *pl.n.* (*with sing. v.*) physics of biological processes and application of methods used in physics to biology —**bio'physical** *a.* —**biophysicist** (baıəʊ'fızısıst) *n.*

biopsy ('baıɒpsı) *n.* examination of tissue removed surgically from a living body

biorhythm ('baıəʊrıðəm) *n.* complex repeated pattern of physiological states, believed to affect physical, emotional, or mental states

bioscope ('baıəskəʊp) *n.* SA cinema

bioscopy (baı'ɒskəpı) *n.* examination of body to determine whether it is alive

biosphere ('baıəsfıə) *n.* part of earth's surface and atmosphere inhabited by living things

biosynthesis (baıəʊ'sınθısıs) *n.* formation of chemical compounds by living organisms —**biosynthetic** (baıəʊsın'θetık) *a.*

biotin ('baıətın) *n.* vitamin of B complex, abundant in egg yolk and liver

bipartisan (baıpɑːtı'zæn, baı'pɑːtızæn) *a.* consisting of or supported by two political parties

bipartite (baı'pɑːtaıt) *a.* consisting of two parts or parties

biped ('baıped) *n.* two-footed animal —**bipedal** (baı'piːd³l, -'ped³l) *a.*

biplane ('baıpleın) *n.* aeroplane with two pairs of wings

bipolar (baı'pəʊlə) *a.* 1. having two poles 2. of North and South Poles 3. having two opposed opinions *etc.*—**bipo'larity** *n.*

birch (bɜːtʃ) *n.* 1. tree with silvery bark —*vt.* 2. flog —'**birchen** *a.* —**the birch** rod made of birch twigs used, *esp.* formerly, for punishment

bird (bɜːd) *n.* 1. feathered animal 2. *sl.* young woman or girl —'**birdlime** *n.* 1. sticky substance smeared on twigs to catch small birds —*vt.* 2. smear with birdlime —**bird of paradise** any of various songbirds of New Guinea and neighbouring regions, males having brilliantly coloured plumage —**bird of passage** 1. bird that migrates seasonally 2. transient person —**bird's-eye** *a.* 1. seen from above; summarizing (*esp. in* **bird's-eye view**) 2. having markings resembling birds' eyes

birdie ('bɜːdı) *n.* 1. *Golf* score of one stroke under par for hole 2. *inf.* bird, *esp.* small bird

biretta or **berretta** (bɪ'rɛtə) n. square cap worn by Catholic clergy

Biro ('baɪrəʊ) n. **R** ballpoint pen

birth (bɜːθ) n. **1.** bearing, or the being born, of offspring **2.** parentage, origin **3.** noble descent —**birth control** limitation of childbearing usu. by artificial means —'**birthday** n. —'**birthmark** n. blemish, usu. dark, formed on skin before birth —**birth rate** ratio of live births in specified area etc. to population, usu. expressed per 1000 population per year —'**birthright** n. **1.** privileges that person is entitled to as soon as he is born **2.** privileges of first-born son **3.** inheritance —'**birthstone** n. precious or semiprecious stone associated with month or sign of zodiac and thought to bring luck if worn by person born in that month

biscuit ('bɪskɪt) n. dry, small, thin variety of cake

bisect (baɪ'sɛkt) vt. divide into two equal parts —**bi'sector** n.

bisexual (baɪ'sɛksjʊəl) a. **1.** sexually attracted to both men and women **2.** of both sexes

bishop ('bɪʃəp) n. **1.** clergyman governing diocese **2.** chess piece —'**bishopric** n. diocese or office of a bishop

bismuth ('bɪzməθ) n. reddish-white metal used in medicine etc.

bison ('baɪs'n) n. **1.** large wild ox **2.** Amer. buffalo

bisque[1] (bɪsk) n. thick rich soup made from shellfish

bisque[2] (bɪsk) n. **1.** pink to yellowish tan colour **2.** earthenware or porcelain that has been fired but not glazed

bistre or U.S. **bister** ('bɪstə) n. **1.** transparent water-soluble brownish-yellow pigment made by boiling soot of wood **2.** yellowish-brown to dark brown colour

bistro ('biːstrəʊ) n. small restaurant

bit[1] (bɪt) n. **1.** fragment, piece **2.** biting, cutting part of tool **3.** mouthpiece of horse's bridle —'**bitty** a. **1.** lacking unity; disjointed **2.** containing bits, sediment etc.

bit[2] (bɪt) pt./pp. of BITE

bit[3] (bɪt) n. Comp. smallest unit of information

bitch (bɪtʃ) n. **1.** female dog, fox or wolf **2.** offens. sl. spiteful woman **3.** inf. complaint —vi. **4.** inf. complain —'**bitchy** a.

bite (baɪt) vt. **1.** cut into, esp. with teeth **2.** grip —vi. **3.** rise to bait —v. **4.** (of corrosive material) eat away or into (**bit** pt., **bit**, '**bitten** pp., '**biting** pr.p.) —n. **5.** act of biting **6.** wound so made **7.** mouthful —'**biter** n. —'**biting** a. **1.** piercing; keen **2.** sarcastic; incisive —'**bitingly** adv.

bitter ('bɪtə) a. **1.** sharp, sour tasting **2.** unpleasant **3.** (of person) angry or resentful **4.** sarcastic —'**bitterly** adv. —'**bitterness** n. —'**bitters** pl.n. essence of bitter herbs —**bitter end** final extremity —'**bittersweet** n. **1.** N Amer. climbing plant **2.** woody nightshade —a. **3.** being

mixture of bitterness and sweetness **4.** pleasant but tinged with sadness

bittern ('bɪtən) n. wading bird like heron

bitumen ('bɪtjʊmɪn) n. viscous substance occurring in asphalt, tar etc. —**bi'tuminous** a.

bivalent (baɪ'veɪlənt, 'bɪvə-) a. **1.** Chem. see DIVALENT **2.** (of homologous chromosomes) associated together in pairs —**bi'valency** n.

bivalve ('baɪvælv) a. **1.** having a double shell —n. **2.** mollusc with such shell

bivouac ('bɪvʊæk, 'bɪvwæk) n. **1.** temporary encampment of soldiers, hikers etc. —vi. **2.** pass the night in temporary camp ('**bivouacked**, '**bivouacking**)

biz (bɪz) n. inf. business

bizarre (bɪ'zɑː) a. unusual, weird

Bk Chem. berkelium

bk. 1. bank **2.** book

B.L. 1. Bachelor of Laws **2.** Bachelor of Letters **3.** Barrister-at-Law **4.** British Library

blab (blæb) v. **1.** reveal (secrets) —vi. **2.** chatter idly (-bb-) —n. **3.** telltale **4.** gossip —'**blabber** n. **1.** person who blabs **2.** idle chatter —vi. **3.** talk without thinking; chatter

black (blæk) a. **1.** of the darkest colour **2.** without light **3.** dark **4.** evil **5.** sombre **6.** dishonourable —n. **7.** darkest colour **8.** black dye, clothing etc. **9.** (**B-**) person of dark-skinned race —vt. **10.** boycott (specified goods etc.) in industrial dispute —'**blacken** v. —'**blacking** n. substance used for blacking and cleaning leather etc. —'**blackamoor** n. obs. Negro or other person with dark skin —**black-and-blue** a. **1.** (of skin) discoloured, as from bruise **2.** feeling pain, as from beating —**black-and-white** n. photograph etc. in black, white, and shades of grey rather than in colour —**black art** black magic —'**blackball** vt. vote against, exclude —**black belt** Judo, karate black belt worn by instructor or expert; person entitled to wear this —'**blackberry** n. plant with thorny stems and dark juicy berries, bramble —'**blackbird** n. common European songbird —'**blackboard** n. dark-coloured surface for writing on with chalk —**black book** book containing names of people to be punished, blacklisted etc. —**black box** inf. flight recorder —'**blackcap** n. type of warbler —'**blackcock** n. male of the black grouse —**black'currant** n. **1.** N temperate shrub having edible black berries **2.** its fruit —**black eye** inf. bruising round eye —'**blackhead** n. dark, fatty plug blocking pore in skin —**black hole** Astron. region of space resulting from collapse of star, and surrounded by gravitational field that neither matter nor radiation could escape from —'**blackleg** n. **1.** one who works during strike **2.** disease of cattle —'**blacklist** n. **1.** list of people, organizations considered suspicious, untrustworthy etc. —vt. **2.** put on blacklist —**black magic**

magic used for evil purposes —'**blackmail**
vt. 1. extort money from (a person) by
threats —*n.* 2. act of blackmailing 3.
money extorted thus —'**blackmailer** *n.*
—**Black Maria** (mə'raɪə) police van for
transporting prisoners —**black mark**
indication of disapproval *etc.* —**black
market** illegal buying and selling of goods
—**black mass** travesty of Christian Mass
performed by practitioners of black magic
—'**blackout** *n.* 1. complete failure of
electricity supply 2. sudden cutting off of
all stagelights 3. state of temporary
unconsciousness 4. obscuring of all lights
as precaution against night air attack
—**Black Power** social, economic, and
political movement of Black people to
obtain equality with Whites —**black
pudding** sausage made from minced pork
fat, pig's blood *etc.* (*also* **blood pudding**)
—**black sheep** person regarded as disgrace or failure by his family or group
—'**Blackshirt** *n.* member of fascist
organization, *esp.* It. Fascist party before
and during World War II —'**blacksmith** *n.*
smith who works in iron —**black spot**
dangerous place, *esp.* on a road —'**blackthorn** *n.* shrub with black twigs —**black tie**
n. 1. black bow tie worn with dinner jacket
—*a.* 2. denoting occasion when dinner
jacket should be worn —**black widow**
highly poisonous Amer. spider —**black out**
1. obliterate or extinguish (lights) 2. create
a blackout in (a city *etc.*) 3. lose
consciousness, vision or memory temporarily —**in black and white** in print or
writing; in extremes —**in someone's black
books** *inf.* out of favour with someone
—**the Black Country** heavily industrial-
ized West Midlands of England —**the
Black Death** form of bubonic plague
pandemic in Europe and Asia during 14th
cent. (*see* BUBONIC PLAGUE)

blackguard ('blægɑːd, -gəd) *n.* 1. scoundrel —*a.* 2. unprincipled, wicked —*vt.* 3.
revile —'**blackguardism** *n.* —'**black-
guardly** *a.*

bladder ('blædə) *n.* membranous bag to
contain liquid, *esp.* urinary bladder

blade (bleɪd) *n.* 1. edge, cutting part of
knife or tool 2. leaf of grass *etc.* 3. sword 4.
obs. dashing fellow 5. flat of oar

blain (bleɪn) *n.* 1. inflamed swelling 2.
pimple, blister

blame (bleɪm) *n.* 1. censure 2. culpability
—*vt.* 3. find fault with 4. censure
—'**blamable** *or* '**blameable** *a.* —'**blameless** *a.* —'**blameworthy** *a.*

blanch (blɑːntʃ) *vt.* 1. whiten, bleach, take
colour out of 2. (of foodstuffs) briefly boil
or fry —*v.* 3. turn pale

blancmange (blə'mɒnʒ) *n.* jellylike dessert made with milk

bland (blænd) *a.* 1. devoid of distinctive
characteristics 2. smooth in manner

blandish ('blændɪʃ) *vt.* 1. coax 2. flatter
—'**blandishments** *pl.n.*

blank (blæŋk) *a.* 1. without marks or

writing 2. empty 3. vacant, confused 4. (of
verse) without rhyme —*n.* 5. empty space
6. void 7. cartridge containing no bullet
—'**blankly** *adv.* —**blank cheque** 1. cheque
that has been signed but on which amount
payable has not been specified 2. complete
freedom of action —**blank verse** unrhymed verse, *esp.* in iambic pentameters

blanket ('blæŋkɪt) *n.* 1. thick (woollen)
covering for bed 2. concealing cover —*vt.*
3. cover with blanket 4. cover, stifle
—**blanket stitch** strong reinforcing stitch
for edges of blankets and other thick
material

blare (blɛə) *v.* 1. sound loudly and harshly
—*n.* 2. such sound

blarney ('blɑːnɪ) *n.* flattering talk

blasé ('blɑːzeɪ) *a.* 1. indifferent through
familiarity 2. bored

blaspheme (blæs'fiːm) *v.* show contempt
or disrespect for (God or sacred things,
esp. in speech) —**blas'phemer** *n.* —**blasphemous** ('blæsfɪməs) *a.* —**blasphemous-
ly** ('blæsfɪməslɪ) *adv.* —**blasphemy**
('blæsfɪmɪ) *n.*

blast (blɑːst) *n.* 1. explosion 2. high-
pressure wave of air coming from an
explosion 3. current of air 4. gust of wind
or air 5. loud sound 6. *sl.* reprimand —*vt.* 7.
blow up 8. remove, open *etc.* by explosion
9. blight 10. ruin —'**blasted** *a.* 1. blighted,
withered 2. damned —**blast furnace**
furnace for smelting ore, using preheated
blast of air —'**blastoff** *n.* 1. launching of
rocket 2. time at which this occurs —**blast
off** be launched

blatant ('bleɪt*ə*nt) *a.* obvious —'**blatan-
cy** *n.*

blather ('blæðə) *vi.* 1. speak foolishly —*n.*
2. foolish talk; nonsense

blaze[1] (bleɪz) *n.* 1. strong fire or flame 2.
brightness 3. outburst —*vi.* 4. burn strongly
5. be very angry

blaze[2] (bleɪz) *v.* 1. mark (trees) to establish
trail —*n.* 2. mark on tree 3. white mark on
horse's face

blaze[3] (bleɪz) *vt.* 1. proclaim, publish (as
with trumpet) —*n.* 2. wide publicity

blazer ('bleɪzə) *n.* type of jacket, worn *esp.*
for sports

blazon ('bleɪz*ə*n) *vt.* 1. make public,
proclaim 2. describe, depict (arms) —*n.* 3.
coat of arms

bleach (bliːtʃ) *v.* 1. make or become white
—*n.* 2. bleaching substance —**bleaching
powder** white powder consisting of
chlorinated calcium hydroxide (*also* **chloride of lime, chlorinated lime**)

bleak[1] (bliːk) *a.* 1. cold and cheerless 2.
exposed —'**bleakly** *adv.*

bleak[2] (bliːk) *n.* small, silvery fish

bleary ('blɪərɪ) *a.* with eyes dimmed, as by
tears or tiredness —**bleary-eyed** *or* **blear-
eyed** *a.* having bleary eyes

bleat (bliːt) *vi.* 1. cry, as sheep —*v.* 2. say,
speak plaintively —*n.* 3. sheep's cry

bleed (bliːd) *vi.* 1. lose blood —*vt.* 2. draw

blood or liquid from **3.** extort money from (**bled** *pt./pp.*)

bleep (bliːp) *n.* short high-pitched sound —'**bleeper** *n.* small portable electronic signalling device

blemish ('blɛmɪʃ) *n.* **1.** defect **2.** stain —*vt.* **3.** make (something) defective, dirty *etc.* —'**blemished** *a.*

blench (blɛntʃ) *vi.* start back, flinch

blend (blɛnd) *vt.* **1.** mix —*n.* **2.** mixture —'**blender** *n.* one who, that which blends, *esp.* electrical kitchen appliance for mixing food

blende (blɛnd) *n.* **1.** a zinc ore **2.** any of several sulphide ores

blenny ('blɛnɪ) *n.* small fish with tapering scaleless body

blesbok *or* **blesbuck** ('blɛsbʌk) *n.* S Afr. antelope

bless (blɛs) *vt.* **1.** consecrate **2.** give thanks to **3.** ask God's favour for **4.** (*usu. pass.*) endow (with) **5.** glorify **6.** make happy (**blessed, blest** *pp.*) —**blessed** ('blɛsɪd, blɛst) *a.* **1.** made holy **2.** worthy of deep reverence **3.** *R.C.Ch.* (of person) beatified by pope **4.** characterized by happiness **5.** bringing great happiness **6.** damned —'**blessedness** ('blɛsɪdnɪs) *n.* —'**blessing** *n.* **1.** (ceremony asking for) God's protection, aid **2.** short prayer **3.** approval **4.** welcome event, benefit

blether ('blɛðə) *n.* nonsense, gossip (*also* '**blather**)

blew (bluː) *pt. of* BLOW[1]

blight (blaɪt) *n.* **1.** plant disease **2.** harmful influence —*vt.* **3.** injure as with blight

blighter ('blaɪtə) *n. inf.* fellow, person

Blighty ('blaɪtɪ) *n. UK sl.* **1.** Britain; home **2.** *esp.* in World War I, wound that causes recipient to be sent home to Britain (*also* **blighty one**)

blimey ('blaɪmɪ) *interj. UK sl.* exclamation of surprise or annoyance

blimp (blɪmp) *n.* small, nonrigid airship used for observing

blind (blaɪnd) *a.* **1.** unable to see **2.** heedless, random **3.** dim **4.** closed at one end **5.** *sl.* very drunk —*vt.* **6.** deprive of sight —*n.* **7.** something cutting off light **8.** window screen **9.** pretext —'**blindly** *adv.* —'**blindness** *n.* —**blind alley 1.** alley open at one end only; cul-de-sac **2.** *inf.* situation in which no further progress can be made —**blind date** *inf.* social meeting between man and woman who have not met before —**blind flying** navigation of aircraft by use of instruments alone —'**blindfold** *vt.* **1.** cover the eyes of, so as to prevent vision —*n.* **2.** piece of cloth *etc.* used to cover eyes —**blindman's buff** game in which one player is blindfolded —**blind spot 1.** small area of retina, where optic nerve enters, in which vision is not experienced **2.** area where vision is obscured **3.** subject about which person is ignorant or prejudiced

blink (blɪŋk) *vi.* **1.** wink **2.** twinkle **3.** shine intermittently —*n.* **4.** gleam —'**blinkers**

pl.n. leather flaps to prevent horse from seeing to the side —**blink at** see, know about, but ignore —**on the blink** *inf.* not working (properly)

blip (blɪp) *n.* repetitive sound or visible pulse, *eg* on radar screen

bliss (blɪs) *n.* perfect happiness —'**blissful** *a.* —'**blissfully** *adv.* —'**blissfulness** *n.*

blister ('blɪstə) *n.* **1.** bubble on skin **2.** surface swelling, *eg* on paint —*v.* **3.** form blisters (on) —'**blistering** *a.* (of verbal attack) bitter —**blister pack** package for goods with hard, raised, transparent cover

blithe (blaɪð) *a.* happy, gay —'**blithely** *adv.* —'**blitheness** *n.*

blithering ('blɪðərɪŋ) *a.* **1.** talking foolishly; jabbering **2.** *inf.* stupid; foolish

B.Litt. *or* **B.Lit. 1.** Bachelor of Letters **2.** Bachelor of Literature

blitz (blɪts) *n.* sudden, concentrated attack —**blitzkrieg** ('blɪtskriːg) *n.* intensive military attack designed to defeat opposition quickly

blizzard ('blɪzəd) *n.* blinding storm of wind and snow

bloat (bləʊt) *v.* **1.** puff or swell out —*n.* **2.** distension of stomach of cow *etc.* by gas —'**bloated** *a.* swollen —'**bloater** *n.* smoked herring

blob (blɒb) *n.* **1.** soft mass, *esp.* drop of liquid **2.** shapeless form

bloc (blɒk) *n.* (political) grouping of people or countries

block (blɒk) *n.* **1.** solid (rectangular) piece of wood, stone *etc.*, *esp. Hist.* that on which people were beheaded **2.** obstacle **3.** stoppage **4.** pulley with frame **5.** large building of offices, flats *etc.* **6.** group of buildings **7.** area enclosed by intersecting streets —*vt.* **8.** obstruct, stop up **9.** shape on block —'**blockage** *n.* obstruction —**block and tackle** hoisting device in which rope or chain is passed around pair of blocks containing one or more pulleys —'**blockbuster** *n. inf.* **1.** large bomb used to demolish extensive areas **2.** very forceful person, thing *etc.* —'**blockhead** *n.* derogatory fool, simpleton —'**blockhouse** *n.* **1.** formerly, wooden fortification with ports for defensive fire *etc.* **2.** concrete structure strengthened for protection against enemy fire, with apertures for defensive gunfire **3.** building constructed of logs or squared timber —**block letters** written capital letters —**block release** *UK* release of trainees from work for study at college for several weeks at a time —**block vote** *see* card vote *at* CARD —**block in** sketch in

blockade (blɒ'keɪd) *n.* **1.** physical prevention of access, *esp.* to port *etc.* —*vt.* **2.** subject to blockade

bloke (bləʊk) *n. inf.* fellow, chap

blond (blɒnd) *a.* **1.** (of hair) light-coloured —*n.* **2.** someone with blond hair (**blonde** *fem.*)

blood (blʌd) *n.* **1.** red fluid in veins **2.** race **3.** kindred **4.** parental heritage **5.** temperament **6.** passion —*vt.* **7.** initiate (into hunting, war *etc.*) —'**bloodily** *adv.* —'**bloodless** *a.* —'**bloody** *a.* **1.** covered in blood **2.** slaughterous —*a./adv.* **3.** *sl.* common intensifier —*vt.* **4.** make bloody —**blood bank** (institution managing) store of human blood preserved for transfusion —**blood bath** indiscriminate slaughter; massacre —**blood count** determination of number of red and white blood corpuscles in sample of blood —'**bloodcurdling** *a.* terrifying; horrifying —**blood group** any of various groups into which human blood is classified (*also* **blood type**) —'**bloodhound** *n.* breed of large hound noted for its keen powers of scent —**blood-letting** *n.* **1.** therapeutic removal of blood **2.** bloodshed, *esp.* in feud —**blood money 1.** compensation paid to relatives of murdered person **2.** money paid to hired murderer —**blood poisoning** disease in which blood contains poisonous matter (*also* septi'caemia) —**blood pressure** pressure exerted by blood on inner walls of arteries —**blood relation** *or* **relative** person related by birth —'**bloodshed** *n.* slaughter, killing —'**bloodshot** *a.* (of eyes) inflamed —**blood sport** sport in which animals are killed, *eg* fox-hunting —**blood stream** flow of blood through vessels of living body —'**bloodsucker** *n.* **1.** parasite (*eg* mosquito) living on host's blood **2.** parasitic person —**blood test** examination of sample of blood —'**bloodthirsty** *a.* murderous, cruel —**blood transfusion** transfer of blood from one person to another —**blood vessel** artery, capillary or vein —**bloody-minded** *a.* UK *inf.* deliberately obstructive and unhelpful —**in cold blood** cruelly and ruthlessly; deliberately and calmly —**make one's blood boil** cause to be angry —**make one's blood run cold** fill with horror

bloom[1] (blu:m) *n.* **1.** flower of plant **2.** blossoming **3.** prime, perfection **4.** glow **5.** powdery deposit on fruit —*vi.* **6.** be in flower **7.** flourish —'**blooming** *a.*

bloom[2] (blu:m) *n.* rectangular mass of metal obtained by rolling or forging cast ingot

bloomer ('blu:mə) *n. inf.* ludicrous mistake

bloomers ('blu:məz) *pl.n.* wide, baggy knickers

blossom ('blɒsəm) *n.* **1.** flower **2.** flower bud —*vi.* **3.** flower **4.** develop

blot (blɒt) *n.* **1.** spot, stain **2.** disgrace —*vt.* **3.** spot, stain **4.** obliterate **5.** detract from **6.** soak up (ink *etc.*) from (-**tt-**) —**blotting paper** absorbent paper, used *esp.* for soaking up surplus ink

blotch (blɒtʃ) *n.* **1.** dark spot on skin —*vt.* **2.** make spotted —'**blotchy** *a.*

blotto ('blɒtəʊ) *a. sl.* unconscious, *esp.* through drunkenness

blouse (blaʊz) *n.* light, loose upper garment

blouson ('blu:zɒn) *n.* loosely fitting but tight-waisted jacket

blow[1] (bləʊ) *vi.* **1.** make a current of air **2.** pant **3.** make sound by blowing **4.** (of whale) spout —*vt.* **5.** drive air upon or into **6.** drive by current of air **7.** sound **8.** fan **9.** *sl.* squander (**blew, blown**) —*n.* **10.** blast **11.** gale —'**blower** *n.* —'**blowy** *a.* windy —**blow-by-blow** *a.* explained in great detail —**blow-dry** *vt.* **1.** style (hair) after washing, using hand-held hair dryer —*n.* **2.** this method of drying hair —'**blowfly** *n.* fly which infects food *etc.* (*also* 'blue-bottle) —'**blowhole** *n.* **1.** nostril of whales, situated far back on skull **2.** hole in ice through which seals *etc.* breathe **3.** vent for air or gas —'**blowlamp** *n.* small burner with very hot flame, for removing paint *etc.* (*also* **blow torch**) —**blow-out** *n.* **1.** sudden puncture in tyre **2.** uncontrolled escape of oil or gas from well **3.** *sl.* large meal —'**blowpipe** *n.* dart tube —**blow out 1.** extinguish **2.** (of tyre) puncture suddenly **3.** (of fuse) melt —**blow up 1.** explode **2.** inflate **3.** enlarge (photograph) **4.** *inf.* lose one's temper

blow[2] (bləʊ) *n.* **1.** stroke, knock **2.** sudden misfortune, loss

blown (bləʊn) *pp. of* BLOW[1]

blowzy *or* **blowsy** ('blaʊzɪ) *a.* **1.** slovenly, sluttish **2.** red-faced

blubber ('blʌbə) *vi.* **1.** weep —*n.* **2.** fat of whales **3.** weeping

bludgeon ('blʌdʒən) *n.* **1.** short thick club —*vt.* **2.** strike (as) with bludgeon **3.** coerce

blue (blu:) *a.* **1.** of colour of sky or shades of that colour **2.** depressed **3.** indecent —*n.* **4.** the colour **5.** dye or pigment **6.** indigo powder used in laundering —*vt.* **7.** make blue **8.** dip in blue liquid (**blued** *pt./pp.*) —**blues** *pl.n. inf.* (*oft. with sing. v.*) **1.** depression **2.** form of Amer. Negro folk song in slow tempo, employed in jazz music —'**bluish** *a.* —**blue baby** baby born with bluish skin caused by heart defect —'**bluebell** *n.* wild spring flower —'**blueberry** *n.* N Amer. shrub with blue-black edible berries —**blue blood** royal or aristocratic descent —'**bluebook** *n.* UK government publication bound in blue cover —'**bluebottle** *n.* blowfly —**blue-collar** *a.* denoting manual industrial workers —**blue-eyed boy** *inf.*, *chiefly* UK favourite of person or group —**blue-pencil** *vt.* alter, delete parts of, *esp.* to censor —**blue peter** signal flag of blue with white square at centre, displayed by vessel about to leave port —'**blueprint** *n.* **1.** copy of drawing **2.** original plan —**blue ribbon 1.** UK badge of blue silk worn by members of Order of the Garter **2.** badge awarded as first prize in competition —'**bluestocking** *n.* scholarly, intellectual woman —'**bluetit** *n.* common European tit having blue crown, wings, and tail, and yellow underparts —**blue whale** largest mammal: bluish-grey whalebone whale

bluff[1] (blʌf) *n.* **1.** cliff, steep bank **2.** C

clump of trees —a. **3.** hearty **4.** blunt **5.** steep **6.** abrupt

bluff² (blʌf) v. **1.** deceive (someone) by pretence of strength —n. **2.** pretence

blunder ('blʌndə) n. **1.** clumsy mistake —vi. **2.** make stupid mistake **3.** act clumsily

blunderbuss ('blʌndəbʌs) n. obsolete short gun with wide bore

blunt (blʌnt) a. **1.** not sharp **2.** (of speech) abrupt —vt. **3.** make blunt —'**bluntly** adv. —'**bluntness** n.

blur (blɜː) v. **1.** make, become less distinct (-rr-) —n. **2.** something vague, indistinct —'**blurry** a.

blurb (blɜːb) n. statement, advertising or recommending book etc.

blurt (blɜːt) vt. (oft. with out) utter suddenly or unadvisedly

blush (blʌʃ) vi. **1.** become red in face **2.** be ashamed **3.** redden —n. **4.** this effect —'**blusher** n. cosmetic applied to cheeks to give rosy colour

bluster ('blʌstə) vi./n. (indulge in) noisy, aggressive behaviour —'**blusterer** n. —'**blustering** or '**blustery** a. (of wind etc.) noisy and gusty

B.M. British Museum

B.M.A. British Medical Association

B.Mus. Bachelor of Music

B.O. 1. inf. body odour **2.** box office

boa ('bəʊə) n. **1.** large, nonvenomous snake **2.** long scarf of fur or feathers —**boa constrictor** very large snake of tropical Amer. and W Indies, that kills prey by constriction

boar (bɔː) n. **1.** male pig **2.** wild pig

board (bɔːd) n. **1.** broad, flat piece of wood **2.** sheet of rigid material for specific purpose **3.** table **4.** meals **5.** group of people who administer company **6.** governing body **7.** thick, stiff paper —pl. **8.** theatre, stage **9.** C wooden enclosure where ice hockey, box lacrosse is played —vt. **10.** cover with planks **11.** supply with regular meals **12.** enter (ship etc.) —vi. **13.** take daily meals —'**boarder** n. —**boarding house** lodging house where meals may be had —**boarding school** school providing living accommodation for pupils —'**board-room** n. room where board of company meets —**above board** beyond suspicion —**on board** in or into ship

boast (bəʊst) vi. **1.** speak too much in praise of oneself, one's possessions etc. —n. **2.** something boasted (of) —'**boaster** n. —'**boastful** a. —'**boastfully** adv. —'**boastfulness** n. —**boast of 1.** brag of **2.** have to show

boat (bəʊt) n. **1.** small open vessel **2.** ship —vi. **3.** sail about in boat —'**boater** n. flat straw hat —'**boating** n. —'**boathook** n. —'**boathouse** n. —'**boatman** n. —**boat-swain** ('bəʊs'n) n. ship's officer in charge of boats, sails etc. —**boat train** train scheduled to take passengers to or from particular ship

bob (bɒb) vi. **1.** move up and down —vt. **2.**

move jerkily **3.** cut (hair) short (-bb-) —n. **4.** short, jerking motion **5.** short hair style **6.** weight on pendulum etc. **7.** inf. formerly, shilling —**bobbed** a.

bobbejaan ('bɒbəjɑːn) n. SA baboon

bobbin ('bɒbɪn) n. cylinder on which thread is wound

bobble ('bɒb'l) n. small, tufted ball for decoration

bobby ('bɒbɪ) n. inf. policeman

bobcat ('bɒbkæt) n. Amer. wild cat, bay lynx

bobolink ('bɒbəlɪŋk) n. Amer. songbird

bobsleigh ('bɒbsleɪ) n. **1.** racing sledge for two or more people, with steering mechanism —vi. **2.** ride on bobsleigh (also (esp. US) **bobsled** ('bɒbslɛd))

bobtail ('bɒbteɪl) n. **1.** docked or diminutive tail **2.** animal with such tail —a. **3.** having tail cut short (also '**bobtailed**) —vt. **4.** dock tail of **5.** cut short; curtail

BOC British Oxygen Company

bode¹ (bəʊd) vt. be an omen of

bode² (bəʊd) pt. of BIDE

bodega (bəʊ'diːgə) n. shop selling wine, esp. in Spanish-speaking country

bodge (bɒdʒ) vt. inf. make mess of; botch

bodice ('bɒdɪs) n. upper part of woman's dress

bodkin ('bɒdkɪn) n. **1.** large blunt needle **2.** tool for piercing holes

body ('bɒdɪ) n. **1.** whole frame of man or animal **2.** main part of such frame **3.** corpse **4.** main part of anything **5.** substance **6.** mass **7.** person **8.** number of persons united or organized **9.** matter, opposed to spirit —'**bodiless** a. —'**bodily** a./adv. —'**bodyguard** n. escort to protect important person —**body politic** people of nation or nation itself considered as political entity —**body stocking** one-piece undergarment, usu. of nylon, covering torso —'**bodywork** n. shell of motor vehicle

Boer (bʊə) n. a S Afr. of Dutch or Huguenot descent —**boerbul** ('bʊəbəl) n. SA cross-bred mastiff —**boerewors** ('bʊərəvɔːs) n. SA mincemeat sausage —**boerperd** ('bʊəpɜːt) n. S Afr. breed of horse

boet (but) or **boetie** n. SA inf. friend

boffin ('bɒfɪn) n. inf. scientist, technical research worker

bog (bɒg) n. **1.** wet, soft ground **2.** sl. lavatory —'**boggy** a. marshy —**bog down** stick as in a bog

bogan ('bəʊgən) n. C sluggish side stream

bogey or **bogy** ('bəʊgɪ) n. **1.** evil or mischievous spirit **2.** standard golf score for good player —'**bogeyman** n.

boggle ('bɒg'l) vi. stare, be surprised

bogie or **bogy** ('bəʊgɪ) n. **1.** low truck on four wheels **2.** pivoted undercarriage, as on railway rolling stock

bogus ('bəʊgəs) a. sham, false

Bohemian (bəʊ'hiːmɪən) a. **1.** unconventional —n. **2.** (oft. b-) one who leads an unsettled life —Bo'**hemianism** n.

boil¹ (bɔɪl) vi. **1.** change from liquid to gas,

esp. by heating **2.** become cooked by boiling **3.** bubble **4.** be agitated **5.** seethe **6.** *inf.* be hot **7.** *inf.* be angry —*vt.* **8.** cause to boil **9.** cook by boiling —*n.* **10.** boiling state —**'boiler** *n.* vessel for boiling —**boiler suit** garment covering whole body —**boiling point** temperature at which boiling occurs (100°C for water)

boil² (bɔɪl) *n.* inflamed suppurating swelling on skin

boisterous ('bɔɪstərəs, -strəs) *a.* **1.** wild **2.** noisy **3.** turbulent —**'boisterously** *adv.* —**'boisterousness** *n.*

bold (bəʊld) *a.* **1.** daring, fearless **2.** presumptuous **3.** striking, prominent —**'boldly** *adv.* —**'boldness** *n.*

bole (bəʊl) *n.* trunk of tree

bolero (bə'leərəʊ) *n.* **1.** Spanish dance **2.** short loose jacket

boll (bəʊl) *n.* seed capsule of cotton, flax *etc.*

bollard ('bɒlɑːd, 'bɒləd) *n.* **1.** post on quay or ship to secure mooring lines **2.** short post in road or footpath as barrier or marker

Bolshevik ('bɒlʃɪvɪk) *n.* violent revolutionary —**'bolshie** *or* **'bolshy** *a. inf.* **1.** rebellious, uncooperative **2.** left-wing

bolster ('bəʊlstə) *vt.* **1.** support, uphold —*n.* **2.** long pillow **3.** pad, support

bolt¹ (bəʊlt) *n.* **1.** bar or pin, *esp.* with thread for nut **2.** rush **3.** discharge of lightning **4.** roll of cloth —*vt.* **5.** fasten with bolt **6.** swallow hastily —*vi.* **7.** rush away **8.** break from control

bolt² *or* **boult** (bəʊlt) *vt.* **1.** pass (flour *etc.*) through sieve **2.** examine and separate —**'bolter** *n.*

bomb (bɒm) *n.* **1.** explosive projectile **2.** any explosive device **3.** *sl.* large amount of money —*vt.* **4.** attack with bombs —**bom'bard** *vt.* **1.** shell **2.** attack (verbally) —**bombar'dier** (bɒmbə'dɪə) *n.* artillery noncommissioned officer —**bom'bard-ment** *n.* —**'bomber** *n.* aircraft capable of carrying bombs —**'bombshell** *n.* **1.** shell of bomb **2.** surprise **3.** *inf.* very attractive girl —**the bomb** nuclear bomb

bombast ('bɒmbæst) *n.* **1.** pompous language **2.** pomposity —**bom'bastic** *a.*

Bombay duck (bɒm'beɪ) fish eaten dried with curry dishes as savoury (*also* **'bummalo**)

bombazine *or* **bombasine** (bɒmbə'ziːn, 'bɒmbəziːn) *n.* twilled fabric, *esp.* one of silk and worsted

bona fide ('bəʊnə 'faɪdɪ) *Lat.* **1.** genuine-(ly) **2.** sincere(ly) —**bona fides** ('faɪdiːz) good faith, sincerity

bonanza (bə'nænzə) *n.* sudden good luck or wealth

bonbon ('bɒnbɒn) *n.* sweet

bond (bɒnd) *n.* **1.** that which binds **2.** link, union **3.** written promise to pay money or carry out contract —*vt.* **4.** bind **5.** store (goods) until duty is paid on them —**'bonded** *a.* **1.** placed in bond **2.** mortgaged —**'bonding** *n.* process by

which individuals become emotionally attached to one another —**'bondsman** *n.* **1.** *Law* person bound by bond to act as surety for another **2.** serf, slave (*also* **'bondservant**)

bondage ('bɒndɪdʒ) *n.* slavery

bone (bəʊn) *n.* **1.** hard substance forming animal's skeleton **2.** piece of this —*pl.* **3.** essentials —*vt.* **4.** remove bones from —*vi.* **5.** *inf.* (*with* up) study hard —**'boneless** *a.* —**'bony** *a.* —**bone china** porcelain containing bone ash —**bone-dry** *a. inf.* completely dry —**'bonehead** *n. inf.* stupid person —**bone meal** dried and ground animal bones, used as fertilizer or in stock feeds —**'boneshaker** *n.* **1.** early type of bicycle having solid tyres **2.** *sl.* any rickety vehicle

bonfire ('bɒnfaɪə) *n.* large outdoor fire

bongo ('bɒŋgəʊ) *n.* small drum, usu. one of pair, played with fingers (*pl.* **-s, -es**)

bonhomie ('bɒnəmiː) *Fr.* good humour, geniality

bonk (bɒŋk) *inf. vt.* **1.** hit —*v.* **2.** have sexual intercourse (with) —**'bonking** *n.*

bonkers ('bɒŋkəz) *a. sl.* crazy

bon mot (*Fr.* bɔ̃ 'məʊ) clever and fitting remark (*pl.* **bons mots** (bɔ̃ 'məʊ))

bonnet ('bɒnɪt) *n.* **1.** hat with strings **2.** cap **3.** cover of motor vehicle engine

bonny ('bɒnɪ) *a.* beautiful, handsome —**'bonnily** *adv.*

bonsai ('bɒnsaɪ) *n.* (art of growing) dwarf trees, shrubs

bontebok ('bɒntɪbʌk) *n.* S Afr. antelope

bonus ('bəʊnəs) *n.* extra (unexpected) payment or gift

bon vivant (bɔ̃ viː'vɑ̃) *Fr.* person who enjoys luxuries, *esp.* good food and drink (*pl.* **bons vivants** (bɔ̃ viː'vɑ̃))

bon voyage (*Fr.* bɔ̃ vwa'jaːʒ) phrase used to wish traveller pleasant journey

bonze (bɒnz) *n.* Chinese or Japanese Buddhist priest or monk

boo (buː) *interj.* **1.** expression of disapproval or contempt **2.** exclamation to surprise *esp.* child —*v.* **3.** make this sound (at)

boob (buːb) *n. sl.* **1.** foolish mistake **2.** female breast

booby ('buːbɪ) *n.* **1.** fool **2.** tropical marine bird —**booby prize** mock prize for poor performance —**booby trap** **1.** harmless-looking object which explodes when disturbed **2.** form of practical joke

boodle ('buːdˀl) *n. US sl.* money

boogie-woogie ('buːgɪ'wuːgɪ, 'buːgɪ'wuːgɪ) *n.* kind of jazz piano playing, emphasizing a rolling bass in syncopated eighth notes

book (bʊk) *n.* **1.** collection of sheets of paper bound together **2.** literary work **3.** main division of this —*v.* **4.** reserve (room, ticket *etc.*) —*vt.* **5.** charge with legal offence **6.** enter name in book —**'booking** *n.* reservation —**'bookish** *a.* studious, fond of reading —**'booklet** *n.* —**'bookbinder** *n.* —**'bookcase** *n.* —**book club** club that sells books at low prices to members —**book end** one of pair of ornamental supports for holding row of books upright —**book-keeping** n. systematic recording of business transactions —'**bookmaker** n. person whose work is taking bets (also (inf.) '**bookie**) —'**bookmark** or '**bookmarker** n. strip of material put between pages of book to mark place —'**bookplate** n. label bearing owner's name and design, pasted into book —**book value 1.** value of asset of business according to its books **2.** net capital value of enterprise as shown by excess of book assets over book liabilities —'**bookworm** n. great reader

boom[1] (bu:m) n. **1.** sudden commercial activity **2.** prosperity —vi. **3.** become active, prosperous

boom[2] (bu:m) vi./n. (make) loud, deep sound

boom[3] (bu:m) n. **1.** long spar, as for stretching the bottom of a sail **2.** barrier across harbour **3.** pole carrying overhead microphone etc.

boomerang ('bu:məræŋ) n. **1.** curved wooden missile of Aust. Aborigines, which returns to the thrower —vi. **2.** recoil **3.** return unexpectedly **4.** backfire

boon (bu:n) n. something helpful, favour

boor (buə) n. rude person —'**boorish** a.

boost (bu:st) n. **1.** encouragement, help **2.** upward push **3.** increase —vt. **4.** encourage, assist or improve —'**booster** n. person or thing that supports, increases power etc. —**booster shot** inf. supplementary injection of vaccine given to maintain immunization

boot[1] (bu:t) n. **1.** covering for the foot and ankle **2.** luggage receptacle in car **3.** inf. kick —vt. **4.** inf. kick —'**booted** a. —'**bootee** n. baby's soft shoe

boot[2] (bu:t) n. profit, use —'**bootless** a. fruitless, vain —**to boot** in addition

booth (bu:ð, bu:θ) n. **1.** stall **2.** cubicle

bootleg ('bu:tlɛg) v. **1.** make, carry, sell (illicit goods, esp. alcohol) (-gg-) —a. **2.** produced, distributed or sold illicitly —'**bootlegger** n.

booty ('bu:tɪ) n. plunder, spoil

booze (bu:z) n./vi. inf. (consume) alcoholic drink —'**boozer** n. inf. **1.** person fond of drinking **2.** bar, pub —'**boozy** a. inf. inclined to or involving excessive consumption of alcohol —**booze-up** n. inf. drinking spree

bop (bɒp) n. **1.** form of jazz characterized by rhythmic and harmonic complexity (also '**bebop**) —vi. **2.** inf. dance to pop music (-pp-) —'**bopper** n.

borage ('bɒrɪdʒ, 'bʌrɪdʒ) n. Mediterranean plant with star-shaped blue flowers

borax ('bɔ:ræks) n. white soluble substance, compound of boron —**boracic** (bə-'ræsɪk) a.

Bordeaux (bɔ:'dəʊ) n. any of several red, white or rosé wines produced around Bordeaux in SW France —**Bordeaux mixture** Hort. fungicide consisting of solution of copper sulphate and quicklime

border ('bɔ:də) n. **1.** margin **2.** frontier **3.** limit **4.** strip of garden —vt. **5.** provide with border **6.** adjoin —'**borderline** n. **1.** border; dividing line **2.** indeterminate position between two conditions —a. **3.** on edge of one category and verging on another

bore[1] (bɔ:) vt. **1.** pierce —vi. **2.** make a hole —n. **3.** hole **4.** calibre of gun —'**borer** n. **1.** instrument for making holes **2.** insect which bores holes

bore[2] (bɔ:) vt. **1.** make weary by repetition etc. —n. **2.** tiresome person or thing —'**boredom** n. —'**boring** a.

bore[3] (bɔ:) n. tidal wave which rushes up river estuary

bore[4] (bɔ:) pt. of BEAR[1]

born (bɔ:n) pp. of BEAR[1] —**born again** having undergone a conversion, esp. to new spiritual life

borne (bɔ:n) pp. of BEAR[1] —**be borne in on** or **upon** (of fact etc.) be realized by

boron ('bɔ:rɒn) n. chemical element used in hardening steel etc. —'**boric** a. of or containing boron (also bo'**racic**) —**boric acid** white weakly acid crystalline solid, used as mild antiseptic (also **orthoboric acid**)

borough ('bʌrə) n. town

borrow ('bɒrəʊ) vt. **1.** obtain on loan or trust **2.** appropriate —'**borrower** n.

borsch, borsh (bɔ:ʃ), **borscht** (bɔ:ʃt), or **borshch** (bɔ:ʃtʃ) n. Russian and Polish soup based on beetroot

borstal ('bɔ:stəl) n. reformatory for young criminals

borzoi ('bɔ:zɔɪ) n. breed of tall hound with long, silky coat

bosh (bɒʃ) n. inf. nonsense

bo's'n ('bəʊs'n) n. Naut. see **boatswain** at BOAT

bosom ('bʊzəm) n. **1.** human breast **2.** seat of passions and feelings

boss[1] (bɒs) n. **1.** person in charge of or employing others —vt. **2.** be in charge of **3.** be domineering over —'**bossy** a. overbearing

boss[2] (bɒs) n. **1.** knob or stud **2.** raised ornament —vt. **3.** emboss

bosun ('bəʊs'n) n. Naut. see **boatswain** at BOAT

bot. 1. botanical **2.** botany **3.** bottle

botany ('bɒtənɪ) n. study of plants —bo'**tanic(al)** a. —'**botanist** n.

botch (bɒtʃ) vt. (oft. with up) spoil by clumsiness

botfly ('bɒtflaɪ) n. fly, larvae of which are parasites of man, sheep and horses

both (bəʊθ) a./pron. **1.** the two —adv./conj. **2.** as well

bother ('bɒðə) vt. **1.** pester **2.** perplex —vi./n. **3.** fuss, trouble —**bothe'ration** n. **1.** state of worry, trouble, or confusion —interj. **2.** chiefly UK exclamation of slight annoyance —'**bothersome** a. causing bother; troublesome

bo tree (bəʊ) Indian tree sacred to Buddhists

bottle ('bɒt'l) n. **1.** vessel for holding liquid **2.** its contents **3.** UK sl. courage; nerve;

initiative —*vt.* **4.** put into bottle —**'bottler** *n.* —**'bottlebrush** *n.* cylindrical brush for cleaning bottle —**'bottleneck** *n.* narrow outlet which impedes smooth flow of traffic or production of goods —**bottle party** party to which guests bring drink —**bottle up 1.** restrain (powerful emotion) **2.** *inf.* keep (army or other force) contained or trapped

bottom ('bɒtəm) *n.* **1.** lowest part of anything **2.** bed of sea, river *etc.* **3.** buttocks —*vt.* **4.** put bottom to **5.** base **6.** get to bottom of —**'bottomless** *a.* —**bottom drawer** UK young woman's collection of linen, cutlery *etc.* made in anticipation of marriage —**bottom line** last line of financial statement that shows net profit or loss of company *etc.* —**bottom out** reach lowest point

botulism ('bɒtjulɪzəm) *n.* type of food poisoning

bouclé ('bu:kleɪ) *n.* looped yarn giving knobbly effect

boudoir ('bu:dwɑː, -dwɔː) *n.* **1.** lady's private sitting-room **2.** bedroom

bouffant ('bu:fɒŋ) *a.* **1.** (of hair style) having extra height through backcombing **2.** (of skirts *etc.*) puffed out

bougainvillea (bu:gən'vɪlɪə) *n.* (sub)tropical climbing plant with red or purple bracts

bough (baʊ) *n.* branch of tree

bought (bɔːt) *pt./pp. of* BUY

bouillabaisse (bu:jə'bes) *n.* rich stew or soup of fish and vegetables

bouillon ('bu:jɒn) *n.* plain unclarified broth or stock

boulder ('bəʊldə) *n.* large weatherworn rounded stone —**boulder clay** unstratified glacial deposit consisting of fine clay, boulders, and pebbles

boulevard ('bu:lvɑː, -vɑːd) *n.* broad street or promenade

boult (bəʊlt) *vt. see* BOLT²

bounce (baʊns) *v.* **1.** (cause to) rebound (repeatedly) on impact, as a ball —*n.* **2.** rebounding **3.** quality in object causing this **4.** *inf.* vitality, vigour —**'bouncer** *n. sl.* man, *esp.* one employed at club *etc.* to evict undesirables (forcibly) —**'bouncing** *a.* vigorous, robust —**'bouncy** *a.* lively

bound¹ (baʊnd) *n./vt.* limit —**'boundary** *n.* —**'bounded** *a.* —**'boundless** *a.*

bound² (baʊnd) *vi./n.* spring, leap

bound³ (baʊnd) *a.* on a specified course, as **outward bound**

bound⁴ (baʊnd) *v.* **1.** *pt./pp. of* BIND —*a.* **2.** committed **3.** certain **4.** tied

bounden ('baʊndən) *a.* morally obligatory (*obs. except in* **bounden duty**)

bounder ('baʊndə) *n. old-fashioned* UK *sl.* morally reprehensible person; cad

bounty ('baʊntɪ) *n.* **1.** liberality **2.** gift **3.** premium —**'bounteous** *or* **'bountiful** *a.* liberal, generous

bouquet (bu:'keɪ) *n.* **1.** bunch of flowers **2.** fragrance of wine **3.** compliment —**bouquet garni** ('bu:keɪ gɑː'ni:) bunch of herbs tied together and used for flavouring stews *etc.* (*pl.* **bouquets garnis** ('bu:keɪz gɑː-'ni:))

bourbon ('bɜːbⁿn) *n.* US whiskey made from maize

bourgeois ('bʊəʒwɑː) *n./a. oft. disparaging* **1.** middle class **2.** smugly conventional (person) —**bourgeoi'sie** *n.* **1.** middle classes **2.** in Marxist thought, capitalist ruling class

bourn¹ *or* **bourne** (bɔːn) *n. obs.* **1.** destination; goal **2.** boundary

bourn² (bɔːn) *n. chiefly S Brit.* stream

Bourse (bʊəs) *n.* stock exchange of continental Europe, *esp.* Paris

bout (baʊt) *n.* **1.** period of time spent doing something **2.** contest, fight

boutique (bu:'ti:k) *n.* small shop, *esp.* one selling clothes

bouzouki (bu:'zu:kɪ) *n.* Greek stringed musical instrument

bovine ('bəʊvaɪn) *a.* **1.** of the ox or cow **2.** oxlike **3.** stolid, dull

bow¹ (bəʊ) *n.* **1.** weapon for shooting arrows **2.** implement for playing violin *etc.* **3.** ornamental knot of ribbon *etc.* **4.** bend, bent line **5.** rainbow —*v.* **6.** bend —**bow-legged** *a.* bandy —**bow tie** tie tied in bow —**bow window** window with outward curve

bow² (baʊ) *vi.* **1.** bend body in respect, assent *etc.* **2.** submit —*vt.* **3.** bend downwards **4.** cause to stoop **5.** crush —*n.* **6.** bowing of head or body

bow³ (baʊ) *n.* **1.** fore end of ship **2.** prow **3.** rower nearest bow —**bowline** ('bəʊlɪn) *n. Naut.* **1.** line for controlling weather leech of square sail when vessel is close-hauled **2.** knot for securing loop —**bowsprit** ('bəʊsprɪt) *n.* spar projecting from ship's bow

bowdlerize *or* **-ise** ('baʊdləraɪz) *vt.* expurgate

bowel ('baʊəl) *n.* (*oft. pl.*) **1.** part of intestine (*esp.* with reference to defecation) **2.** inside of anything

bower ('baʊə) *n.* **1.** shady retreat **2.** inner room —**'bowerbird** *n.* Aust. bird that hoards decorative but useless things

bowie knife ('bəʊɪ) stout hunting knife with short hilt and guard for hand

bowl¹ (bəʊl) *n.* **1.** round vessel, deep basin **2.** drinking cup **3.** hollow

bowl² (bəʊl) *n.* **1.** wooden ball —*pl.* **2.** game played with such balls —*v.* **3.** roll or throw (ball) in various ways —**'bowler** *n.* —**'bowling** *n.* **1.** game in which heavy ball is rolled down alley at group of wooden pins **2.** game of bowls **3.** *Cricket* delivering ball to batsman —**bowling alley** —**bowling green**

bowler ('bəʊlə) *n.* man's low-crowned stiff felt hat

bowser ('baʊzə) *n.* fuel tanker

box¹ (bɒks) *n.* **1.** (wooden) container, usu. rectangular with lid **2.** its contents **3.** small enclosure **4.** any boxlike cubicle, shelter or receptacle, *eg* letter box —*vt.* **5.** put in box

box 56 **brass**

6. confine —**box girder** girder that is hollow and square or rectangular in shape —**Boxing Day** UK first weekday after Christmas —**box junction** UK road junction having yellow cross-hatching on road surface —**box lacrosse** C indoor lacrosse —**box number** number given to newspaper advertisements to which replies may be sent —**box office 1.** office at theatre *etc.* where tickets are sold **2.** public appeal of actor or production —**box pleat** double pleat made by folding under fabric on either side of it —**'boxroom** *n.* small room or large cupboard —**the box** UK *inf.* television —**box the compass** make complete turn

box² (boks) *v.* **1.** fight with fists, *esp.* wearing padded gloves —*vt.* **2.** strike —*n.* **3.** blow —**'boxer** *n.* **1.** one who boxes **2.** breed of large dog resembling bulldog —**'boxing** *n.* art or profession of fighting with fists

box³ (boks) *n.* evergreen shrub used for hedges

boy (bɔɪ) *n.* **1.** male child **2.** young man —*interj.* **3.** exclamation of surprise —**'boyhood** *n.* —**'boyfriend** *n.* male friend with whom person is romantically or sexually involved —**boy scout** *see* SCOUT (sense 2)

boycott ('bɔɪkɒt) *vt.* **1.** refuse to deal with or participate in —*n.* **2.** act of boycotting

boysenberry ('bɔɪz*ə*nbərɪ) *n.* **1.** type of bramble, cross of loganberry, various blackberries and raspberries **2.** edible fruit of this plant

B.P. 1. British Petroleum **2.** British Pharmacopoeia

Br *Chem.* bromine

B.R. British Rail

br. 1. branch **2.** bronze **3.** brother

Br. 1. Breton **2.** Britain **3.** British

bra (brɑː) *n. short for* BRASSIERE

brace (breɪs) *n.* **1.** tool for boring **2.** clasp, clamp **3.** pair, couple **4.** strut, support —*pl.* **5.** straps worn over shoulders to hold up trousers —*vt.* **6.** steady (oneself), as before a blow **7.** support, make firm —**'bracelet** *n.* **1.** ornament for the arm —*pl.* **2.** *sl.* handcuffs —**'bracing** *a.* invigorating —**brace and bit** tool for boring holes, consisting of cranked handle and drilling bit

brachiopod ('breɪkɪəpɒd, 'bræk-) *n.* any marine invertebrate animal having ciliated feeding organ and shell consisting of dorsal and ventral valves

bracken ('brækən) *n.* large fern

bracket ('brækɪt) *n.* **1.** support for shelf *etc.* **2.** group —*pl.* **3.** marks [ ], ( ) used to enclose words *etc.* —*vt.* **4.** enclose in brackets **5.** connect

brackish ('brækɪʃ) *a.* (of water) slightly salty

bract (brækt) *n.* small scalelike leaf

brad (bræd) *n.* small nail —**'bradawl** *n.* small boring tool

brae (breɪ) *n. Scot.* hill(side); slope

brag (bræg) *vi.* **1.** boast (-**gg**-) —*n.* **2.** boastful talk —**'braggart** *n.*

braggadocio (brægə'dəʊtʃɪəʊ) *n.* **1.** vain empty boasting **2.** braggart (*pl.* -**s**)

Brahma ('brɑːmə) *n.* **1.** Hindu god, the Creator **2.** *Hinduism* ultimate and impersonal divine reality of universe (*also* **'Brahman**)

Brahman ('brɑːmən) *n.* **1.** member of priestly Hindu caste (*also esp.* (*formerly*) **'Brahmin**) **2.** breed of beef cattle

braid (breɪd) *vt.* **1.** interweave **2.** trim with braid —*n.* **3.** length of anything interwoven or plaited **4.** ornamental tape

Braille (breɪl) *n.* system of printing for blind, with arrangements of raised dots instead of letters

brain (breɪn) *n.* **1.** mass of nerve tissue in head **2.** intellect —*vt.* **3.** kill by hitting on head —**'brainless** *a.* —**'brainy** *a.* —**'brainchild** *n.* invention —**brain death** irreversible cessation of respiration due to irreparable brain damage —**brain drain** *inf.* emigration of scientists, academics *etc.* —**'brainstorm** *n.* sudden mental aberration —**brains trust** group of knowledgeable people who answer questions in panel games, quizzes *etc.* —**'brainwash** *vt.* change, distort ideas or beliefs of —**brain wave** sudden, clever idea

braise (breɪz) *vt.* stew in covered pan

brake¹ (breɪk) *n.* **1.** instrument for retarding motion of wheel on vehicle —*vt.* **2.** apply brake to —**brake horsepower** rate at which engine does work, expressed in horsepower, measured by resistance of applied brake —**brake shoe** curved metal casting to which brake lining is riveted in drum brake

brake² (breɪk) *n.* **1.** fern **2.** bracken **3.** thicket **4.** brushwood

bramble ('bræmb*ə*l) *n.* prickly shrub **2.** blackberry —**'brambly** *a.*

brambling ('bræmblɪŋ) *n.* type of finch

bran (bræn) *n.* sifted husks of corn

branch (brɑːntʃ) *n.* **1.** limb of tree **2.** offshoot or subsidiary part of something larger or primary —*vi.* **3.** bear branches **4.** diverge **5.** spread —**branched** *a.* —**'branchy** *a.*

brand (brænd) *n.* **1.** trademark **2.** class of goods **3.** particular kind, sort **4.** mark made by hot iron **5.** burning piece of wood **6.** sword **7.** mark of infamy —*vt.* **8.** burn with iron **9.** mark **10.** stigmatize —**brand-new** *a.* absolutely new

brandish ('brændɪʃ) *vt.* flourish, wave (weapon *etc.*)

brandy ('brændɪ) *n.* spirit distilled from wine —**brandy snap** crisp, sweet biscuit

brash (bræʃ) *a.* bold, impudent

brass (brɑːs) *n.* **1.** alloy of copper and zinc **2.** group of brass wind instruments forming part of orchestra or band **3.** *inf.* money **4.** *inf.* (army) officers —*a.* **5.** made of brass —**'brassy** *a.* **1.** showy **2.** harsh —**brass hat** UK *inf.* top-ranking official, *esp.* military officer —**brass tacks** *inf.* basic realities; hard facts (*esp. in* **get down to brass tacks**)

brasserie ('bræsərɪ) *n.* restaurant specializing in food and beer

brassica ('bræsɪkə) *n.* plant of cabbage and turnip family

brassiere ('bræsɪə, 'bræz-) *n.* woman's undergarment for supporting the breasts

brat (bræt) *n. disparaging* child

bravado (brə'vɑːdəʊ) *n.* showy display of boldness

brave (breɪv) *a.* **1.** bold, courageous **2.** splendid, fine —*n.* **3.** warrior —*vt.* **4.** defy, meet boldly —'**bravely** *adv.* —'**bravery** *n.*

bravo (brɑː'vəʊ) *interj.* well done

bravura (brə'vjʊərə, -'vʊərə) *n.* **1.** display of boldness or daring **2.** *Mus.* passage requiring great spirit and skill by performer

brawl (brɔːl) *vi.* **1.** fight noisily —*n.* **2.** noisy disagreement or fight —'**brawler** *n.*

brawn (brɔːn) *n.* **1.** muscle **2.** strength **3.** pickled pork —'**brawny** *a.* muscular

bray (breɪ) *n.* **1.** donkey's cry —*vi.* **2.** utter this sound **3.** give out harsh or loud sounds

braze¹ (breɪz) *vt.* decorate with or make of brass

braze² (breɪz) *vt.* make joint between (two metal surfaces) by fusing layer of high-melting solder between them —'**brazer** *n.*

brazen ('breɪz'n) *a.* **1.** of, like brass **2.** impudent, shameless —*vt.* **3.** (*usu. with* out) face, carry through with impudence —'**brazenness** *n.* effrontery

brazier¹ *or* **brasier** ('breɪzɪə) *n.* brassworker

brazier² *or* **brasier** ('breɪzɪə) *n.* pan for burning charcoal or coals

brazil nut (brə'zɪl) **1.** tropical S Amer. tree producing globular capsules, each containing several triangular nuts **2.** its nut

B.R.C.S. British Red Cross Society

breach (briːtʃ) *n.* **1.** break, opening **2.** breaking of rule, duty *etc.* **3.** quarrel —*vt.* **4.** make a gap in —**breach of promise** *Law* formerly, failure to carry out promise to marry

bread (brɛd) *n.* **1.** food made of flour or meal and then baked **2.** food **3.** *sl.* money —'**breadfruit** *n.* breadlike fruit found in Pacific Islands —'**breadline** *n.* queue for free food —'**breadwinner** *n.* person supporting dependants by his earnings —**bread and butter** *inf.* means of support or subsistence; livelihood —**on the breadline** *inf.* living at subsistence level

breadth (brɛdθ, brɛtθ) *n.* **1.** extent across, width **2.** largeness of view, mind

break (breɪk) *vt.* **1.** part by force **2.** shatter **3.** burst, destroy **4.** fail to observe **5.** disclose **6.** interrupt **7.** surpass **8.** make bankrupt **9.** relax **10.** mitigate **11.** accustom (horse) to being ridden **12.** decipher (code) —*vi.* **13.** become broken, shattered, divided **14.** open, appear **15.** come suddenly **16.** crack, give way **17.** part, fall out **18.** (of voice) change in tone, pitch

(broke, 'broken) —*n.* **19.** fracture **20.** gap **21.** opening **22.** separation **23.** interruption **24.** respite **25.** interval **26.** *inf.* opportunity **27.** dawn **28.** *Billiards* consecutive series of successful strokes **29.** *Boxing* separation after a clinch **30.** *Cricket* deviation of a ball on striking the pitch —'**breakable** *a.* —'**breakage** *n.* —'**breaker** *n.* **1.** one that breaks, *eg* electrical circuit breaker **2.** wave beating on rocks or shore —'**breakaway** *n.* loss or withdrawal of group of members from association, club *etc.* —**break dance** acrobatic dance style of 1980s —**break-dance** *vi.* perform break dance —**break dancer** —**break dancing** —'**breakdown** *n.* **1.** collapse, as nervous breakdown **2.** failure to function effectively **3.** analysis —**breakfast** ('brɛkfəst) *n.* first meal of the day —**break-in** *n.* illegal entering of building, *esp.* by thieves —'**breakneck** *a.* dangerous —**break-out** *n.* escape, *esp.* from prison —'**breakthrough** *n.* important advance —**break-up** *n.* **1.** separation or disintegration **2.** in Canad. north, breaking up of ice on body of water that marks beginning of spring **3.** this season —'**breakwater** *n.* barrier to break force of waves —**break away** (*oft. with* from) **1.** leave hastily; escape **2.** withdraw, secede —**break out 1.** begin suddenly **2.** make escape, *esp.* from prison **3.** (*with* in) (of skin) erupt (in rash *etc.*) —**break up 1.** (cause to) separate **2.** put an end to (a relationship) or (of a relationship) to come to an end **3.** dissolve or cause to dissolve **4.** *sl.* lose control of emotions

bream (briːm; *Austral.* brɪm) *or Austral.* **brim** (brɪm) *n.* broad, thin fish

breast (brɛst) *n.* **1.** human chest **2.** milk-secreting gland on chest of human female **3.** seat of the affections **4.** any protuberance —*vt.* **5.** face, oppose **6.** reach summit of —'**breastbone** *n.* thin flat structure of bone to which most of ribs are attached in front of chest (*also* '**sternum**) —**breast-feed** *v.* feed (baby) with milk from breast —'**breastplate** *n.* piece of armour covering chest —'**breaststroke** *n.* stroke in swimming —'**breastwork** *n.* temporary defensive work, usu. breast-high

breath (brɛθ) *n.* **1.** air used by lungs **2.** life **3.** respiration **4.** slight breeze —**breathe** (briːð) *vi.* **1.** inhale and exhale air from lungs **2.** live **3.** pause, rest —*vt.* **4.** inhale and exhale **5.** utter softly, whisper —**breather** ('briːðə) *n.* short rest —**breathing** ('briːðɪŋ) *n.* —'**breathless** *a.* —'**breathtaking** *a.* causing awe or excitement —**breath test** UK chemical test of driver's breath to determine amount of alcohol he has consumed

Breathalyser *or* **-lyzer** ('brɛθəlaɪzə) *n.* **R** device that estimates amount of alcohol in breath —'**breathalyse** *or* **-lyze** *vt.*

bred (brɛd) *pt./pp. of* BREED

breech (briːtʃ) *n.* **1.** buttocks **2.** hinder part of anything, *esp.* gun —**breeches** ('brɪtʃɪz, 'briː-) *pl.n.* trousers —**breech delivery** birth of baby with feet or buttocks appearing first —**breeches buoy** ring-shaped life buoy with support in form of pair of breeches —'**breechloader** n.

breed (briːd) vt. **1.** generate, bring forth, give rise to **2.** rear —vi. **3.** be produced **4.** be with young (**bred** pt./pp.) —n. **5.** offspring produced **6.** race, kind —'**breeder** n. —'**breeding** n. **1.** producing **2.** manners **3.** ancestry —**breeder reactor** nuclear reactor that produces more fissionable material than it consumes

breeze (briːz) n. gentle wind —'**breezily** adv. —'**breezy** a. **1.** windy **2.** jovial, lively **3.** casual

breeze block light building brick made of ashes bonded by cement

Bren gun (brɛn) air-cooled gas-operated submachine gun, used by Brit. in World War II

brent (brɛnt) or esp. U.S. **brant** (brænt) n. small goose that has dark grey plumage and short neck and occurs in most northern coastal regions (also **brent goose**)

brethren ('brɛðrɪn) n., pl. of BROTHER, obs. except in religious contexts

Breton ('brɛt'n) a. **1.** of Brittany, its people or their language —n. **2.** native or inhabitant of Brittany

breve (briːv) n. long musical note

breviary ('brɛvjərɪ, 'briː-) n. book of daily prayers of R.C. Church

brevity ('brɛvɪtɪ) n. **1.** conciseness of expression **2.** short duration

brew (bruː) vt. **1.** prepare (liquor, as beer) from malt etc. **2.** make (drink, as tea) by infusion **3.** plot, contrive —vi. **4.** be in preparation —n. **5.** beverage produced by brewing —'**brewer** n. —'**brewery** n. —'**brewing** n.

briar[1] or **brier** ('braɪə) n. prickly shrub, esp. the wild rose

briar[2] or **brier** ('braɪə) n. European shrub —**briar pipe** tobacco pipe made from its root

bribe (braɪb) n. **1.** anything offered or given to someone to gain favour, influence —vt. **2.** influence by bribe —'**briber** n. —'**bribery** n.

bric-a-brac ('brɪkəbræk) n. miscellaneous small objects, used for ornament

brick (brɪk) n. **1.** oblong mass of hardened clay used in building —vt. **2.** build, block etc. with bricks —'**brickbat** n. **1.** piece of brick etc., esp. used as weapon **2.** inf. blunt criticism —'**bricklayer** n.

bride (braɪd) n. woman about to be, or just, married —'**bridal** a. of, relating to, a bride or wedding —'**bridegroom** n. man about to be, or just, married —'**bridesmaid** n.

bridge[1] (brɪdʒ) n. **1.** structure for crossing river etc. **2.** something joining or supporting other parts **3.** raised narrow platform on ship **4.** upper part of nose **5.** part of violin supporting strings —vt. **6.** make bridge over, span —'**bridgehead** n. advanced position established on enemy territory —**bridging loan** loan to cover

period between two transactions, such as buying of another house before sale of first is completed

bridge[2] (brɪdʒ) n. card game

bridle ('braɪd'l) n. **1.** headgear of horse harness **2.** curb —vt. **3.** put bridle on **4.** restrain —vi. **5.** show resentment —**bridle path** path suitable for riding horses

Brie (briː) n. soft creamy white cheese

brief (briːf) a. **1.** short in duration **2.** concise **3.** scanty —n. **4.** summary of case for counsel's use **5.** papal letter **6.** instructions —pl. **7.** underpants **8.** panties —vt. **9.** give instructions —'**briefly** adv. —'**briefness** n. —'**briefcase** n. hand case for carrying papers

brier ('braɪə) n. see BRIAR[1], BRIAR[2]

brig (brɪg) n. two-masted, square-rigged ship

Brig. 1. Brigade **2.** Brigadier

brigade (brɪ'geɪd) n. **1.** subdivision of army **2.** organized band —**briga'dier** n. high-ranking army officer, usu. in charge of a brigade

brigand ('brɪgənd) n. bandit, esp. member of gang in mountainous areas

brigantine ('brɪgəntiːn, -taɪn) n. two-masted vessel with square-rigged foremast and fore-and-aft mainmast

bright (braɪt) a. **1.** shining **2.** full of light **3.** cheerful **4.** clever —'**brighten** v. —'**brightly** adv. —'**brightness** n.

Bright's disease (braɪts) chronic inflammation of kidneys; chronic nephritis

brill (brɪl) n. European food fish

brilliant ('brɪljənt) a. **1.** shining **2.** sparkling **3.** splendid **4.** very clever **5.** distinguished —'**brilliance** or '**brilliancy** n. —'**brilliantly** adv.

brilliantine ('brɪljəntiːn) n. perfumed hair oil

brim (brɪm) n. margin, edge, esp. of river, cup, hat —**brim'ful** a. —'**brimless** a. —'**brimming** a.

brimstone ('brɪmstəʊn) n. sulphur

brindled ('brɪnd'ld) a. spotted and streaked

brine (braɪn) n. **1.** salt water **2.** pickle —'**briny** a. **1.** very salty —n. **2.** inf. the sea

bring (brɪŋ) vt. **1.** fetch **2.** carry with one **3.** cause to come (**brought** pt./pp.)

brink (brɪŋk) n. **1.** edge of steep place **2.** verge, margin —'**brinkmanship** n. practice of pressing dangerous situation, esp. in international affairs, to limit of safety in order to win advantage

briquette or **briquet** (brɪ'kɛt) n. block of compressed coal dust

brisk (brɪsk) a. active, vigorous —'**briskly** adv. —'**briskness** n.

brisket ('brɪskɪt) n. joint of meat from breast of animal

brisling ('brɪslɪŋ) n. see SPRAT

bristle ('brɪs'l) n. **1.** short stiff hair —vi. **2.** stand erect **3.** show temper —'**bristliness** n. —'**bristly** a.

Brit (brɪt) n. inf. British person

Brit. 1. Britain **2.** Britannia **3.** British

Britannia (brɪ'tænɪə) n. 1. female warrior carrying trident, personifying Great Britain or British Empire 2. in ancient Roman Empire, southern part of Great Britain —**Britannia metal** alloy of tin with antimony and copper, used for decorative purposes and for bearings

Britannic (brɪ'tænɪk) a. of Britain; British (*esp. in* His *or* Her Britannic Majesty)

britches ('brɪtʃɪz) *pl.n.* see breeches at BREECH —**too big for one's britches** *inf.* overconfident; arrogant

British ('brɪtɪʃ) a. 1. of Great Britain or the British Commonwealth 2. relating to English language as spoken in Britain —n. 3. natives or inhabitants of Britain —'Briton n. native or inhabitant of Britain —**British thermal unit** unit of heat equal to 1055 joules

brittle ('brɪtªl) a. 1. easily broken, fragile 2. curt, irritable —'**brittleness** n.

broach (brəʊtʃ) vt. 1. pierce (cask) 2. open, begin —vi. 3. *Naut.* turn beam-on to wind and waves

broad (brɔːd) a. 1. wide, spacious, open 2. plain, obvious 3. coarse 4. general 5. tolerant 6. (of pronunciation) dialectal —'broaden v. —'broadly adv. —'broadness n. —broad bean 1. Eurasian plant cultivated for its large edible seeds 2. its seed —'broadcast v. 1. transmit (broadcast) by radio or television —vt. 2. make widely known 3. scatter, as seed —n. 4. radio or television programme —'broadcaster n. —'broadcloth n. 1. fabric woven on wide loom 2. closely woven fabric of wool *etc.* with lustrous finish —broadminded a. 1. tolerant 2. generous —'broadsheet n. 1. newspaper with large format 2. ballad or popular song printed on one side of sheet of paper, *esp.* in 16thcent. England (*also* broadside (ballad)) —'broadside n. 1. discharge of all guns on one side of ship 2. strong (verbal) attack —'broadsword n. broad-bladed sword for cutting rather than stabbing

B-road n. secondary road in Britain

brocade (brəʊ'keɪd) n. rich woven fabric with raised design

broccoli ('brɒkəlɪ) n. type of cabbage

brochure ('brəʊʃjʊə, -ʃə) n. pamphlet, booklet

broderie anglaise ('brəʊdərɪ: ɑːŋ'gleɪz) open embroidery on white cotton *etc.*

brogue (brəʊg) n. 1. stout shoe 2. dialect, *esp.* Irish accent

broil[1] (brɔɪl) n. noisy quarrel

broil[2] (brɔɪl) vt. 1. cook over hot coals 2. grill —vi. 3. be heated

broke (brəʊk) v. 1. *pt. of* BREAK —a. 2. *inf.* penniless —'**broken** *pp. of* BREAK —broken chord *see* ARPEGGIO —**broken-down** a. 1. worn out, as by age; dilapidated 2. not in working order —**broken'hearted** a. overwhelmed by grief or disappointment

broker ('brəʊkə) n. 1. one employed to buy and sell for others 2. dealer —'**brokerage** n. payment to broker

brolly ('brɒlɪ) n. *inf.* umbrella

bromide ('brəʊmaɪd) n. chemical compound used in medicine and photography —**bromide paper** photographic printing paper, treated with silver bromide

bromine ('brəʊmiːn, -mɪn) n. liquid element used in production of chemicals —'bromic a.

bronchus ('brɒŋkəs) n. either of two main branches of trachea (*pl.* bronchi ('brɒŋkaɪ)) —'bronchial a. —bron'chitis n. inflammation of bronchi

bronco *or* **broncho** ('brɒŋkəʊ) n. halftamed horse (*pl.* -s)

brontosaurus (brɒntə'sɔːrəs) *or* **brontosaur** ('brɒntəsɔː) n. very large herbivorous dinosaur

bronze (brɒnz) n. 1. alloy of copper and tin —a. 2. made of, or coloured like, bronze —vt. 3. give appearance of bronze to —'bronzed a. 1. coated with bronze 2. sunburnt —**Bronze Age** era of bronze implements

brooch (brəʊtʃ) n. ornamental pin or fastening

brood (bruːd) n. 1. family of young, *esp.* of birds 2. tribe, race —vi. 3. sit, as hen on eggs 4. meditate, fret —'broody a. moody, sullen

brook[1] (brʊk) n. small stream —'brooklet n.

brook[2] (brʊk) vt. put up with, endure, tolerate

broom (bruːm, brʊm) n. 1. brush for sweeping 2. yellow-flowered shrub —'broomstick n. handle of broom

bros. *or* **Bros.** brothers

brose (brəʊz) n. *Scot.* porridge made by adding boiling liquid to meal, *esp.* oatmeal

broth (brɒθ) n. thick soup

brothel ('brɒθəl) n. house of prostitution

brother ('brʌðə) n. 1. son of same parents 2. one closely united with another —'brotherhood n. 1. relationship 2. fraternity, company —'brotherliness n. —'brotherly a. —brother-in-law n. 1. brother of husband or wife 2. husband of sister

brougham ('bruːəm, bruːm) n. 1. fourwheeled horse-drawn closed carriage having raised open driver's seat in front 2. *obs.* early electric car

brought (brɔːt) *pt./pp. of* BRING

brouhaha (bruː'hɑːhɑː) n. loud confused noise; uproar

brow (braʊ) n. 1. ridge over eyes 2. forehead 3. eyebrow 4. edge of hill —'browbeat vt. bully

brown (braʊn) a. 1. of dark colour inclining to red or yellow —n. 2. brown colour, pigment, or dye —v. 3. make, become brown —'brownie n. 1. in folklore, elf said to do helpful work at night, *esp.* household chores 2. *chiefly US* flat, nutty, chocolate cake —**Brownie Guide** *or* 'Brownie n. junior Girl Guide —**brown rice** unpolished rice —**brown study** mood of deep absorption; reverie

—**brown sugar** unrefined or partially refined sugar —**browned off** *inf.* bored, depressed

browse (brauz) *vi.* 1. look (through book, articles for sale *etc.*) in a casual manner 2. feed on shoots and leaves

brucellosis (bru:sɪ'ləʊsɪs) *n.* infectious disease of cattle, goats, and pigs, caused by bacteria and transmittable to man (*also* **undulant fever**)

bruin ('bru:ɪn) *n.* name for a bear, used in children's tales *etc.*

bruise (bru:z) *vt.* 1. injure without breaking skin —*n.* 2. contusion, discoloration caused by blow —**'bruiser** *n.* strong, tough person

brumby ('brʌmbɪ) *n.* Aust. wild horse

brunch (brʌntʃ) *n. inf.* breakfast and lunch combined

brunette (bru:'nɛt) *n.* 1. woman of dark complexion and hair —*a.* 2. dark brown

brunt (brʌnt) *n.* 1. shock of attack, chief stress 2. first blow

brush (brʌʃ) *n.* 1. device with bristles, hairs, wires *etc.* used for cleaning, painting *etc.* 2. act, instance of brushing 3. brief contact 4. skirmish, fight 5. bushy tail 6. brushwood 7. (carbon) device taking electric current from moving to stationary parts of generator *etc.* —*vt.* 8. apply, remove, clean, with brush —*v.* 9. touch lightly —**'brushoff** *n. inf.* 1. dismissal 2. refusal 3. snub 4. rebuff —**brush-up** *n.* UK act or instance of tidying one's appearance (*esp. in* **wash and brush-up**) —**'brushwood** *n.* 1. broken-off branches 2. land covered with scrub —**brush up** *inf.* 1. (*oft. with* on) refresh one's knowledge, memory of (subject) 2. make person or oneself clean or neat as after journey

brusque (bru:sk, brʊsk) *a.* rough in manner, curt, blunt

Brussels sprout ('brʌs'lz) 1. variety of cabbage, having stem with heads resembling tiny cabbages 2. head of this plant, eaten as vegetable

brute (bru:t) *n.* 1. any animal except man 2. crude, vicious person —*a.* 3. animal 4. sensual, stupid 5. physical —**'brutal** *a.* —**bru'tality** *n.* —**'brutalize** *or* **-ise** *vt.* —**'brutally** *adv.* —**'brutish** *a.* bestial, gross

bryony *or* **briony** ('braɪənɪ) *n.* wild climbing hedge plant

bryophyte ('braɪəfaɪt) *n.* any moss or liverwort —**bryophytic** (braɪə'fɪtɪk) *a.*

BS British Standard(s)

b.s. 1. balance sheet 2. bill of sale

B.Sc. Bachelor of Science

B.S.C. 1. British Steel Corporation 2. British Sugar Corporation

BSI British Standards Institution

B.S.T. British Summer Time

Bt. Baronet

btu *or* **B.Th.U.** British Thermal Unit

bubble ('bʌb'l) *n.* 1. hollow globe of liquid, blown out with air 2. something insubstantial, not serious 3. transparent dome —*vi.*

4. rise in bubbles 5. make gurgling sound —**'bubbly** *a.* —**bubble and squeak** UK dish of cabbage and potatoes fried together —**bubble gum** chewing gum that can be blown into bubbles

bubonic plague (bju:'bɒnɪk) acute infectious disease characterized by swellings and fever

buccaneer (bʌkə'nɪə) *n.* pirate, searover —**bucca'neering** *n.*

buck¹ (bʌk) *n.* 1. male deer, or other male animal 2. act of bucking 3. US, A *sl.* dollar —*vt.* 4. (of horse) attempt to throw rider by jumping upwards *etc.* 5. resist, oppose —**'buckshot** *n.* lead shot in shotgun shell —**'buckskin** *n.* 1. skin of male deer 2. strong greyish-yellow leather, orig. made from deerskin but now usu. made from sheepskin 3. starched cotton cloth 4. strong satin-woven woollen fabric —**'buckteeth** *pl.n.* projecting upper teeth

buck² (bʌk) *n. Poker* marker in jackpot to remind winner of some obligation when his turn to deal —**pass the buck** *inf.* shift blame or responsibility

buckboard ('bʌkbɔːd) *n.* US open four-wheeled horse-drawn carriage with seat attached to flexible board between front and rear axles

bucket ('bʌkɪt) *n.* 1. vessel, round with arched handle, for water *etc.* 2. anything resembling this —*vt.* 3. put, carry, in bucket —**'bucketful** *n.* —**bucket seat** seat with back shaped to occupier's figure —**bucket shop** *chiefly UK* firm specializing in cheap airline tickets —**bucket down** rain very hard

buckle ('bʌk'l) *n.* 1. metal clasp for fastening belt, strap *etc.* —*vt.* 2. fasten with buckle —*vi.* 3. warp, bend —**'buckler** *n.* shield —**buckle down** start work

buckram ('bʌkrəm) *n.* coarse cloth stiffened with size

Bucks. (bʌks) Buckinghamshire

buckshee (bʌk'ʃi:) *a. sl.* free

bucolic (bju:'kɒlɪk) *a.* rustic

bud (bʌd) *n.* 1. shoot or sprout on plant containing unopened leaf, flower *etc.* —*vi.* 2. begin to grow —*vt.* 3. graft (**-dd-**)

Buddhism ('bʊdɪzəm) *n.* religion founded in India by the Buddha —**'Buddhist** *a./n.*

buddleia ('bʌdlɪə) *n.* shrub with mauve flower spikes

buddy ('bʌdɪ) *n. chiefly US sl.* mate, chum

budge (bʌdʒ) *v.* move, stir

budgerigar ('bʌdʒərɪgɑː) *n.* small Aust. parakeet (*also* **'budgie**)

budget ('bʌdʒɪt) *n.* 1. annual financial statement 2. plan of systematic spending —*vi.* 3. prepare financial statement —*v.* 4. plan financially

buff¹ (bʌf) *n.* 1. leather made from buffalo or ox hide 2. light yellow colour 3. bare skin 4. polishing pad —*vt.* 5. polish

buff² (bʌf) *n. inf.* expert on some subject

buffalo ('bʌfələʊ) *n.* any of several species of large oxen (*pl.* **-es, -s, -lo**)

buffer¹ ('bʌfə) *n.* contrivance to lessen

shock of concussion —**buffer state** small, usu. neutral state between two rival powers

buffer² ('bʌfə) n. UK inf. stupid or bumbling man (esp. in **old buffer**)

buffet¹ ('bufeɪ) n. 1. refreshment bar 2. meal at which guests serve themselves 3. ('bʌfɪt, 'bufeɪ) sideboard —**buffet car** UK railway coach where light refreshments are served

buffet² ('bʌfɪt) n. 1. blow, slap 2. misfortune —vt. 3. strike with blows 4. contend against —**buffeting** n.

buffoon (bə'fuːn) n. 1. clown 2. fool —**buffoonery** n. clowning

bug (bʌg) n. 1. any small insect 2. inf. disease, infection 3. inf. concealed listening device —vt. inf. 4. install secret microphone etc. in 5. irritate (**-gg-**)

bugbear ('bʌgbeə) n. 1. object of needless terror 2. nuisance

bugger ('bʌgə) n. 1. sodomite 2. vulg. sl. unpleasant person or thing —vt. sl. 3. tire 4. (with up) ruin, complicate

buggy ('bʌgɪ) n. light horse-drawn carriage having two or four wheels

bugle ('bjuːgʼl) n. instrument like trumpet —**bugler** n.

bugloss ('bjuːglɒs) n. shrub with blue flower clusters

build (bɪld) v. 1. make, construct, by putting together parts or materials (built pt./pp.) —n. 2. make, form —**builder** n. —**building** n. —**building society** cooperative banking enterprise financed by deposits on which interest is paid and from which mortgage loans are advanced on homes —**build-up** n. 1. progressive increase in number etc. 2. extravagant publicity or praise 3. Mil. process of attaining required strength of forces and equipment —**built-in** a. 1. made as integral part 2. essential; inherent —n. 3. A built-in cupboard —**built-up** a. having many buildings —**build up** 1. construct gradually 2. increase, esp. by degrees 3. improve health of 4. prepare for climax, as in story

bulb (bʌlb) n. 1. modified leaf bud emitting roots from base, eg onion 2. anything resembling this 3. globe surrounding filament of electric light —**bulbous** a.

bulbul ('bulbul) n. tropical songbird

bulge (bʌldʒ) n. 1. swelling, protuberance 2. temporary increase —vi. 3. swell out —**bulginess** n. —**bulgy** a.

bulk (bʌlk) n. 1. size 2. volume 3. greater part 4. cargo —vt. 5. be of weight or importance —**bulkiness** n. —**bulky** a.

bulkhead ('bʌlkhed) n. partition in interior of ship

bull¹ (bul) n. 1. male of cattle 2. male of various other animals —**bullock** n. castrated bull —**bulldog** n. thickset breed of dog —**bulldoze** vt. —**bulldozer** n. powerful tractor with blade for excavating etc. —**bullfight** n. traditional Spanish spectacle in which matador baits and usu.

kills bull in arena —**bullfighter** n. —**bullfighting** n. —**bullfinch** n. 1. European finch, male of which has bright red throat and breast 2. any of similar finches —**bull-headed** a. blindly obstinate; stupid —**bullring** n. arena for bullfighting —**bull's-eye** n. middle part of target —**bull terrier** breed of terrier developed by crossing bulldog with English terrier

bull² (bul) n. papal edict

bull³ (bul) n. sl. nonsense

bullet ('bulɪt) n. projectile discharged from rifle, pistol etc.

bulletin ('bulɪtɪn) n. official report

bullion ('buljən) n. gold or silver in mass

bully ('bulɪ) n. 1. one who hurts, persecutes, or intimidates weaker people —vt. 2. intimidate, overawe 3. ill-treat (**'bullied, 'bullying**) —**bully beef** corned beef

bully-off n. Hockey method of starting play, in which two players strike sticks together and against ground three times before trying to hit ball (also **'bully**) —**bully off** Hockey start play with bully-off (also **'bully**)

bulrush ('bulrʌʃ) n. tall reedlike marsh plant with brown velvety spike

bulwark ('bulwək) n. 1. rampart 2. any defence or means of security 3. raised side of ship 4. breakwater

bum (bʌm) sl. n. 1. buttocks, anus 2. US loafer, scrounger —vt. 3. get by scrounging —a. 4. useless —**bum'bailiff** n. UK derogatory formerly, officer employed to collect debts and arrest debtors

bumble ('bʌmbʼl) vi. speak or proceed clumsily —**bumbler** n.

bumblebee ('bʌmbʼlbiː) or **humblebee** n. large bee

bump (bʌmp) n. 1. heavy blow, dull in sound 2. swelling caused by blow 3. protuberance 4. sudden movement —vt. 5. strike or push against —**bumper** n. 1. horizontal bar at front and rear of motor vehicle to protect against damage 2. full glass —a. 3. full, abundant —**bump off** sl. murder

bumph or **bumf** (bʌmf) n. inf. useless documents, information etc.

bumpkin ('bʌmpkɪn) n. rustic

bumptious ('bʌmpʃəs) a. offensively self-assertive

bun (bʌn) n. 1. small, round cake 2. round knot of hair

bunch (bʌntʃ) n. 1. number of things tied or growing together 2. cluster 3. tuft, knot 4. group, party —vt. 5. put together in bunch —vi. 6. gather together —**bunchy** a.

bundle ('bʌndʼl) n. 1. package 2. number of things tied together 3. sl. lot of money —vt. 4. tie in bundle 5. send (off) without ceremony

bundu ('bundu) n. SA wild uninhabited country

bung (bʌŋ) n. 1. stopper for cask 2. large cork —vt. 3. stop up, seal, close 4. inf. throw, sling —**bunghole** n.

bungalow ('bʌŋgələu) n. one-storeyed house

bungle ('bʌŋg'l) vt. 1. do badly from lack of skill, botch —vi. 2. act clumsily, awkwardly —n. 3. blunder, muddle —'bungled a. —'bungler n. —'bungling a./n.

bunion ('bʌnjən) n. inflamed swelling on foot or toe

bunk' (bʌŋk) n. narrow, shelflike bed —**bunk bed** one of pair of beds constructed one above the other

bunk' (bʌŋk) n. sl. hasty departure

bunk' (bʌŋk) n. see BUNKUM

bunker ('bʌŋkə) n. 1. large storage container for oil, coal etc. 2. sandy hollow on golf course 3. (military) underground defensive position

bunkum or **buncombe** ('bʌŋkəm) n. nonsense

bunny ('bʌnɪ) n. inf. rabbit

Bunsen burner ('bʌns'n) gas burner, producing great heat, used for chemical experiments

bunting' ('bʌntɪŋ) n. material for flags

bunting' ('bʌntɪŋ) n. bird with short, stout bill

buoy (bɔɪ; U.S. 'buːɪ) n. 1. floating marker anchored in sea 2. lifebuoy —vt. 3. mark with buoy 4. keep from sinking 5. support —'buoyancy n. —'buoyant a.

BUPA ('bjuːpə, 'buːpə) British United Provident Association

bur (bɜː) n. head of plant with prickles or hooks (also **burr**)

burble ('bɜːb'l) vi. 1. gurgle, as stream or baby 2. talk idly

burden' ('bɜːd'n) n. 1. load 2. weight, cargo 3. anything difficult to bear —vt. 4. load, encumber —'burdensome a.

burden' ('bɜːd'n) n. 1. chorus of a song 2. chief theme

burdock ('bɜːdɒk) n. plant with prickly burs

bureau ('bjuərəu) n. 1. writing desk 2. office 3. government department (pl. -s, -reaux (-rəuz)) —bureaucracy (bjuə-'rɒkrəsɪ) n. 1. government by officials 2. body of officials —'bureaucrat n. —bureau'cratic a.

burette or **buret** (bjuˈrɛt) n. graduated glass tube with stopcock on one end, for dispensing known volumes of fluids

burgee ('bɜːdʒiː) n. small nautical flag

burgeon or **bourgeon** ('bɜːdʒən) vi. 1. bud 2. develop rapidly

burgess ('bɜːdʒɪs) n. inhabitant of borough, esp. citizen with full municipal rights

burgh ('bʌrə) n. Scottish borough —**burgher** ('bɜːgə) n. citizen

burglar ('bɜːglə) n. one who enters building to commit crime, esp. theft —'burglary n. —'burgle, 'burglarize or -ise vt.

burgundy ('bɜːgəndɪ) n. name of various red or white wines produced in the Burgundy region of France

burin ('bjuərɪn) n. chisel of tempered steel used for engraving metal, wood, or marble

burlap ('bɜːlæp) n. coarse canvas

burlesque (bɜːˈlɛsk) n. 1. (artistic) caricature 2. ludicrous imitation —vt. 3. caricature

burly ('bɜːlɪ) a. sturdy, stout, robust —'burliness n.

burn' (bɜːn) vt. 1. destroy or injure by fire —vi. 2. be on fire (lit. or fig.) 3. be consumed by fire (**burned** or **burnt** pt./pp.) —n. 4. injury, mark caused by fire —'burner n. 1. part of stove etc. that produces flame 2. apparatus for burning fuel, refuse etc. —'burning a. —**burning glass** convex lens for concentrating sun's rays to produce fire

burn' (bɜːn) n. small stream

burnish ('bɜːnɪʃ) vt. 1. make bright by rubbing 2. polish —n. 3. gloss, lustre —'burnisher n.

burnoose, burnous, or **burnouse** (bɜː-'nuːs, -'nuːz) n. long circular cloak with hood, worn esp. by Arabs

burnt (bɜːnt) v. 1. pt./pp. of BURN' —a. 2. affected as if by burning; charred

burp (bɜːp) n./v. inf. (cause to) belch

burr' (bɜː) n. 1. soft trilling sound given to letter r in some dialects

burr' (bɜː) n. rough edge left after cutting, drilling etc.

burro ('burəu) n. donkey (pl. -s)

burrow ('bʌrəu) n. 1. hole dug by rabbit etc. —v. 2. make holes in (ground) —vt. 3. bore 4. conceal

bursar ('bɜːsə) n. official managing finances of college, school etc. —'bursary n. scholarship

burst (bɜːst) vi. 1. fly asunder 2. break into pieces 3. rend 4. break suddenly into some expression of feeling —vt. 5. shatter, break violently (**burst** pt./pp.) —n. 6. bursting 7. explosion 8. outbreak 9. spurt

bury ('bɛrɪ) vt. 1. put underground 2. inter 3. conceal ('buried, 'burying) —'burial n./a.

bus (bʌs) n. 1. large motor vehicle for passengers (orig. omnibus) —v. 2. travel or transport by bus (**bused** or **bussed** pt., 'busing or 'bussing pr.p.) —'busman's holiday inf. holiday spent doing same as one does at work

bus. business

busby ('bʌzbɪ) n. tall fur hat worn by certain soldiers

bush' (buʃ) n. 1. shrub 2. woodland, thicket 3. **A, SA** etc. uncleared country, backwoods, interior —**bushed** a. 1. tired out 2. **A** lost, bewildered —'bushy a. shaggy —'bushbaby n. tree-living, nocturnal Afr. animal —**bush fire** widespread destructive fire in the bush —**bush jacket** SA shirtlike jacket with patch pockets —**bush line** C airline operating in bush country —'Bushman n. member of hunting and gathering people of southern Afr. —**bush pilot** —**bush telegraph** inf. means of spreading rumour *etc.* —**bushveld** (ˈbuʃfelt) *n.* SA bushy countryside

bush² (buʃ) *n.* 1. thin metal sleeve or tubular lining serving as bearing —*v.* 2. fit bush to (casing *etc.*)

bushel (ˈbuʃəl) *n.* dry measure of eight gallons

business (ˈbɪznɪs) *n.* 1. profession, occupation 2. commercial or industrial establishment 3. commerce, trade 4. responsibility, affair, matter 5. work —**businesslike** *a.* —**businessman** *n.* person engaged in business, *esp.* as owner or executive (**businesswoman** *fem.*)

busker (ˈbʌskə) *n.* one who makes money by singing, dancing *etc.* in the street —**busk** *vi.*

buskin (ˈbʌskɪn) *n.* 1. formerly, sandal-like covering for foot and leg, reaching calf 2. thick-soled laced half boot worn *esp.* by actors of ancient Greece 3. (*usu. with* the) tragic drama

bust¹ (bʌst) *n.* 1. sculpture of head and shoulders of human body 2. woman's breasts

bust² (bʌst) *inf. v.* 1. burst 2. make, become bankrupt —*vt.* 3. raid 4. arrest —*a.* 5. broken 6. bankrupt —*n.* 7. police raid or arrest

bustard (ˈbʌstəd) *n.* large swift-running bird

bustle¹ (ˈbʌsˀl) *vi.* 1. be noisily busy, active —*n.* 2. fuss, commotion

bustle² (ˈbʌsˀl) *n. Hist.* pad worn by ladies to support back of skirt

busy (ˈbɪzɪ) *a.* 1. actively employed 2. full of activity —*vt.* 3. occupy (**busied**, **busying**) —**busily** *adv.* —**busybody** *n.* meddler —**busy lizzie** (ˈlɪzɪ) house plant

but (bʌt; *unstressed* bət) *prep./conj.* 1. without 2. except 3. only 4. yet 5. still 6. besides

butane (ˈbjuːteɪn, bjuːˈteɪn) *n.* gas used for fuel

butch (butʃ) *a./n. sl.* markedly or aggressively masculine (person)

butcher (ˈbutʃə) *n.* 1. one who kills animals for food, or sells meat 2. ruthless or brutal murderer —*vt.* 3. slaughter, murder 4. spoil (work) —**butchery** *n.*

butler (ˈbʌtlə) *n.* chief male servant

butt¹ (bʌt) *n.* 1. the thick end 2. target 3. object of ridicule 4. bottom or unused end of anything —*v.* 5. lie, be placed end-on to

butt² (bʌt) *vt.* 1. strike with head 2. push —*n.* 3. blow with head, as of sheep —**butt in** interfere, meddle

butt³ (bʌt) *n.* large cask

butter (ˈbʌtə) *n.* 1. fatty substance made from cream by churning —*vt.* 2. spread with butter 3. flatter —**butter bean** lima bean with large pale edible seeds —**butterfingered** *a.* —**butterfingers** *n. inf.* person who drops things inadvertently —**buttermilk** *n.* milk that remains after churning —**butterscotch** *n.* kind of hard, brittle toffee

buttercup (ˈbʌtəkʌp) *n.* plant with glossy, yellow flowers

butterfly (ˈbʌtəflaɪ) *n.* 1. insect with large wings 2. inconstant person 3. stroke in swimming —**butterfly nut** *see* wing nut *at* WING

buttery (ˈbʌtərɪ) *n.* storeroom for food or wine

buttock (ˈbʌtək) *n.* (*usu. pl.*) rump, protruding hinder part

button (ˈbʌtˀn) *n.* 1. knob, stud for fastening dress 2. knob that operates doorbell, machine *etc.* —*vt.* 3. fasten with buttons —**buttonhole** *n.* 1. slit in garment to pass button through as fastening 2. flower, spray worn on lapel *etc.* —*vt.* 3. detain (reluctant listener) in conversation

buttress (ˈbʌtrɪs) *n.* 1. structure to support wall 2. prop —*vt.* 3. support (wall) with buttress

buxom (ˈbʌksəm) *a.* 1. full of health, plump, gay 2. large-breasted

buy (baɪ) *vt.* 1. get by payment, purchase 2. bribe (**bought** *pt./pp.*) —**buyer** *n.*

buzz (bʌz) *vi.* 1. make humming sound —*n.* 2. humming sound of bees 3. *inf.* telephone call —**buzzer** *n.* any apparatus that makes buzzing sound

buzzard (ˈbʌzəd) *n.* bird of prey of hawk family

B.V.M. Beata Virgo Maria (*Lat.*, Blessed Virgin Mary)

bwana (ˈbwɑːnə) *n.* in E Afr., master, oft. used as form of address corresponding to *sir*

by (baɪ) *prep.* 1. near 2. along 3. across 4. past 5. during 6. not later than 7. through use or agency of 8. in units of —*adv.* 9. near 10. away, aside 11. past —**by and by** soon, in the future —**by and large** 1. on the whole 2. speaking generally —**come by** obtain

by- *or* **bye-** (*comb. form*) subsidiary, incidental, out-of-the-way, near, as in *bypath*, *by-product*, *bystander*

bye (baɪ) *n.* 1. *Sport* situation where player, team, wins by default of opponent 2. *Cricket* run scored off ball not touched by batsman

by-election *or* **bye-election** *n.* parliamentary election caused by death or resignation of member

bygone (ˈbaɪɡɒn) *a.* 1. past, former —*n.* 2. (*oft. pl.*) past occurrence 3. small antique

bylaw *or* **bye-law** (ˈbaɪlɔː) *n.* law, regulation made by local subordinate authority

by-line *n.* 1. line under title of newspaper or magazine article giving author's name 2. *see* **touchline** *at* TOUCH

bypass (ˈbaɪpɑːs) *n.* road for diversion of traffic from crowded centres

by-play *n.* diversion, action apart from main action of play

byre (baɪə) *n.* cowshed

Byronic (baɪˈrɒnɪk) *a.* of, like, or characteristic of Byron, his poetry, or his style

bystander ('baɪstændə) n. person present but not involved; spectator

byte (baɪt) n. Comp. sequence of bits processed as single unit of information

byway ('baɪweɪ) n. 1. secondary or side road 2. area, field of study etc. that is of secondary importance

byword ('baɪwɜːd) n. well-known name, saying

Byzantine (bɪ'zæntaɪn, -tiːn, baɪ-; 'bɪzəntiːn, -taɪn) a. 1. of Byzantium or Byzantine Empire 2. of Orthodox Church 3. of style of architecture developed in Byzantine Empire, characterized by domes, mosaics etc. 4. complicated —n. 5. inhabitant of Byzantium

C

c or **C** (si:) *n.* **1.** third letter of English alphabet **2.** speech sound represented by this letter, usu. either as in *cigar* or as in *case* **3.** third in series, *esp.* third highest grade in examination **4.** something shaped like C (*pl.* **c's, C's** or **Cs**)

C 1. *Mus.* first degree of major scale containing no sharps or flats (**C major**); major or minor key having this note as tonic; time signature denoting four crotchet beats to bar (*see also* ALLA BREVE (sense 2), **common time** *at* COMMON) **2.** *Chem.* carbon **3.** capacitance **4.** heat capacity **5.** cold (water) **6.** *Phys.* compliance **7.** Celsius **8.** centigrade **9.** Conservative **10.** century, as in *C20* **11.** Roman numeral, 100

c. 1. carat **2.** cent **3.** circa **4.** copyright

Ca *Chem.* calcium

CA California

ca. circa

C.A. chartered accountant

C.A.A. UK Civil Aviation Authority

cab (kæb) *n.* **1.** taxi **2.** driver's enclosed compartment on locomotive, lorry *etc.* —'**cabman** or '**cabby** *n.*

cabal (kə'bæl) *n.* **1.** small group of intriguers **2.** secret plot

cabaret ('kæbəreı) *n.* floor show at nightclub or restaurant

cabbage ('kæbıdʒ) *n.* vegetable with large head of green or reddish leaves

cabbala, cabala, kabbala or **kabala** (kə'baːlə) *n.* **1.** ancient Jewish mystical tradition **2.** any secret or occult doctrine —'**cabbalist,** '**cabalist,** '**kabbalist** or '**kabalist** *n.* —cabba'listic, caba'listic, kabba'listic or kaba'listic *a.*

caber ('keıbə) *n.* heavy wooden pole tossed as trial of strength at Highland games

cabin ('kæbın) *n.* **1.** hut, shed **2.** small room, *esp.* in ship —*vt.* **3.** cramp, confine —**cabin boy** boy who waits on officers and passengers of ship —**cabin cruiser** power boat with cabin, bunks *etc.*

cabinet ('kæbınıt) *n.* **1.** piece of furniture with drawers or shelves **2.** outer case of television, radio *etc.* **3.** (*oft.* C-) committee of politicians governing country **4.** *obs.* small room —**cabinet-maker** *n.* craftsman who makes fine furniture

cable ('keıb'l) *n.* **1.** strong rope **2.** wire or bundle of wires conveying electric power, telegraph signals *etc.* **3.** message sent by this **4.** nautical unit of measurement (100–120 fathoms) —*v.* **5.** telegraph by cable —**cable car** passenger car on cable railway, drawn by strong cable operated by motor —'**cablegram** *n.* cabled message

caboodle (kə'buːd'l) *n. inf.* —**the whole caboodle** the whole lot

caboose (kə'buːs) *n.* **1.** ship's galley **2.** US guard's van on train

cabriolet (kæbrıəu'leı) *n.* early type of hansom cab

cacao (kə'kɑːəu, -'keıəu) *n.* tropical tree from the seeds of which chocolate and cocoa are made

cachalot ('kæʃəlɒt) *n.* sperm whale

cache (kæʃ) *n.* **1.** secret hiding place **2.** store of food *etc.*

cachet ('kæʃeı) *n.* **1.** mark, stamp **2.** mark of authenticity **3.** prestige, distinction

cachinnate ('kækıneıt) *vi.* laugh loudly —cachin'nation *n.*

cachou ('kæʃuː, kæ'ʃuː) *n.* **1.** lozenge eaten to sweeten breath **2.** substance obtained from certain tropical plants and used in medicine *etc.* (*also* '**catechu, cutch**)

cack-handed (kæk'hændıd) *a. inf.* **1.** left-handed **2.** clumsy

cackle ('kæk'l) *vi.* **1.** make chattering noise, as hen —*n.* **2.** cackling noise or laughter **3.** empty chatter —'**cackler** *n.*

caco- (*comb. form*) bad, unpleasant, incorrect, as in *cacophony*

cacoethes (kækəu'iːθiːz) *n.* uncontrollable urge or desire

cacophony (kə'kɒfənı) *n.* **1.** disagreeable sound **2.** discord of sounds —ca'cophonous *a.*

cactus ('kæktəs) *n.* spiny succulent plant (*pl.* -es, cacti ('kæktaı))

cad (kæd) *n.* UK *inf., old-fashioned* dishonourable, unchivalrous person —'**caddish** *a.*

cadaver (kə'deıvə, -'dɑ:v-) *n.* corpse —**cadaverous** (kə'dævərəs) *a.* **1.** corpse-like **2.** sickly-looking **3.** gaunt

caddie or **caddy** ('kædı) *n.* **1.** golfer's attendant —*vi.* **2.** act as caddie

caddis fly ('kædıs) small mothlike insect having two pairs of hairy wings —**caddis worm** or '**caddis** *n.* aquatic larva of caddis fly, which constructs protective case around itself made of silk *etc.* (*also* '**caseworm,** '**strawworm**)

caddy ('kædı) *n.* small box for tea

cadence ('keıd'ns) or **cadency** *n.* fall or modulation of voice in music or verse

cadenza (kə'dɛnzə) *n. Mus.* elaborate passage for solo instrument or singer

cadet (kə'dɛt) *n.* youth in training, *esp.* for officer status in armed forces

cadge (kædʒ) *v.* get (food, money *etc.*) by sponging or begging —'**cadger** *n.* sponger

cadi or **kadi** ('kɑːdı, 'keıdı) *n.* judge in Muslim community (*pl.* -s)

cadmium ('kædmıəm) *n.* metallic element

cadre ('kɑːdə) *n.* nucleus or framework, *esp.* skeleton of regiment

caduceus (kə'djuːsıəs) *n.* **1.** *Class. myth.* winged staff entwined with two serpents carried by Hermes (Mercury) **2.** insignia resembling this, used as emblem of medical profession (*pl.* **-cei** (-sɪaɪ))

caecum *or U.S.* **cecum** ('siːkəm) *n. Anat.* pouch, *esp.* at beginning of large intestine (*pl.* **-ca** (-kə))

Caenozoic (siːnəʊ'zəʊɪk) *see* CAINOZOIC

Caerphilly (kɛə'fɪlɪ) *n.* creamy white mild-flavoured cheese

Caesarean, Caesarian, *or U.S.* **Cesarean, Cesarian** (sɪ'zɛərɪən) *a.* **1.** of any of Caesars, *esp.* Julius Caesar —*n.* **2.** (*sometimes* c-) *Surg.* Caesarean section —**Caesarean section** surgical incision through abdominal wall to deliver baby

caesium *or U.S.* **cesium** ('siːzɪəm) *n.* ductile silvery-white element of alkali metal group, used in photocells *etc.*

caesura (sɪ'zjʊərə) *n.* **1.** in modern prosody, pause, *esp.* for sense, usu. near middle of verse line **2.** in classical prosody, break between words within metrical foot (*pl.* **-s, -rae** (-riː))

café ('kæfeɪ, 'kæfɪ) *n.* small or inexpensive restaurant serving light refreshments —**cafe'teria** *n.* restaurant designed for self-service

caff (kæf) *n. sl.* café

caffeine *or* **caffein** ('kæfiːn) *n.* stimulating alkaloid found in tea and coffee plants

caftan ('kæftæn, -tɑːn) *n. see* KAFTAN

cage (keɪdʒ) *n.* **1.** enclosure, box with bars or wires, *esp.* for keeping animals or birds **2.** place of confinement **3.** enclosed platform of lift, *esp.* in mine —*vt.* **4.** put in cage, confine —**'cagey** *or* **'cagy** *a.* wary, not communicative

cagoule (kə'guːl) *n.* lightweight, usu. knee-length type of anorak

cahoots (kə'huːts) *pl.n. sl.* partnership (*esp. in* **in cahoots with**)

caiman ('keɪmən) *n. see* CAYMAN

Cainozoic (kaɪnəʊ'zəʊɪk, keɪ-), **Cenozoic** *or* **Caenozoic** *a.* **1.** of most recent geological era characterized by development and increase of mammals —*n.* **2.** Cainozoic era

cairn (kɛən) *n.* heap of stones, *esp.* as monument or landmark —**cairn terrier** small rough-haired terrier orig. from Scotland

cairngorm ('kɛəngɔːm) *n.* yellow or brownish-coloured gem

caisson (kə'suːn, 'keɪsˈn) *n.* **1.** chamber for working under water **2.** apparatus for lifting vessel out of water **3.** ammunition wagon

caitiff ('keɪtɪf) *obs. n.* **1.** mean, despicable fellow —*a.* **2.** base, mean

cajole (kə'dʒəʊl) *vt.* persuade by flattery, wheedle —**ca'jolement** *n.* —**ca'joler** *n.* —**ca'jolery** *n.*

cake (keɪk) *n.* **1.** baked, sweetened, breadlike food **2.** compact mass —*vt.* **3.** make into cake —*vi.* **4.** harden (as of mud) —**'cakewalk** *n.* **1.** dance orig. performed by Amer. Negroes for prize of cake **2.** piece of music for this dance

cal. 1. calendar **2.** calibre **3.** (small) calorie

Cal. (large) Calorie

calabash ('kæləbæʃ) *n.* **1.** tree with large hard-shelled fruit **2.** this fruit **3.** drinking, cooking vessel made from gourd

calaboose ('kæləbuːs) *n. US inf.* prison

calamine ('kæləmaɪn) *n.* pink powder used medicinally in soothing ointment

calamity (kə'læmɪtɪ) *n.* **1.** great misfortune **2.** deep distress, disaster —**ca'lamitous** *a.*

calceolaria (kælsɪə'lɛərɪə) *n.* Amer. plant with speckled, slipper-shaped flowers

calces ('kælsiːz) *n., pl. of* CALX

calciferol (kæl'sɪfərɒl) *n.* fat-soluble steroid, found *esp.* in fish-liver oils and used in treatment of rickets (*also* **vitamin D₂**)

calcium ('kælsɪəm) *n.* metallic element, the basis of lime —**calcareous** (kæl-'kɛərɪəs) *a.* containing lime —**cal'ciferous** *a.* producing salts of calcium, *esp.* calcium carbonate —**'calcify** *v.* convert, be converted, to lime —**'calcine** *vt.* **1.** reduce to quicklime **2.** burn to ashes —**'calcite** *n.* crystalline calcium carbonate —**calcium carbonate** white crystalline salt occurring in limestone, chalk *etc.*

calculate ('kælkjʊleɪt) *vt.* **1.** estimate **2.** compute —*vi.* **3.** make reckonings —**'calculable** *a.* —**'calculated** *a.* **1.** undertaken after considering likelihood of success **2.** premeditated —**'calculating** *a.* **1.** able to perform calculations **2.** shrewd, designing, scheming —**calcu'lation** *n.* —**'calculator** *n.* electronic device for making calculations —**'calculus** *n.* **1.** branch of mathematics **2.** stone in body (*pl.* **calculi** ('kælkjʊlaɪ))

caldron ('kɔːldrən) *n. see* CAULDRON

calèche (*Fr.* ka'leʃ) *n.* C horse-drawn carriage for taking tourists around

Caledonian (kælɪ'dəʊnɪən) *a.* **1.** relating to Scotland —*n.* **2.** *Lit.* native of Scotland

calendar ('kælɪndə) *n.* **1.** table of months and days in the year **2.** list of events, documents, register —*vt.* **3.** enter in list **4.** index

calender ('kælɪndə) *n.* **1.** machine in which paper or cloth is smoothed by passing between rollers —*vt.* **2.** subject to such process

calends *or* **kalends** ('kælɪndz) *pl.n.* first day of each month in ancient Roman calendar

calendula (kæ'lɛndjʊlə) *n.* marigold

calf¹ (kɑːf) *n.* **1.** young of cow and of other animals **2.** leather made of calf's skin (*pl.* **calves**) —**calve** *vi.* give birth to calf —**calf love** infatuation of adolescent for member of opposite sex

calf² (kɑːf) *n.* fleshy back part of leg below knee (*pl.* **calves**)

calibre *or U.S.* **caliber** ('kælɪbə) *n.* **1.** size of bore of gun **2.** capacity, character —**'calibrate** *vt.* mark (scale of measuring instrument) so that readings can be made in appropriate units —**cali'bration** *n.*

calices ('kælɪsiːz) *n., pl. of* CALIX

calico ('kælɪkəʊ) n. cotton cloth

californium (kælɪ'fɔːnɪəm) n. transuranic element artificially produced from curium

caliper ('kælɪpə) n. US see CALLIPER

caliph, calif or **khalif** ('keɪlɪf, 'kæl-) n. Islam title of successors of Mohammed as rulers of Islamic world —**caliphate, califate** or **khalifate** ('keɪlɪfeɪt) n. office or reign of caliph

calix ('keɪlɪks, 'kæ-) n. cup; chalice (pl. 'calices)

calk¹ (kɔːk) vt. see CAULK

calk² (kɔːk) or **calkin** ('kɔːkɪn, 'kæl-) n. 1. metal projection on horse's shoe to prevent slipping —vt. 2. provide with calks

call (kɔːl) vt. 1. speak loudly to attract attention of 2. summon 3. (oft. with up) telephone 4. name —vi. 5. shout 6. pay visit —n. 7. shout 8. animal's cry 9. visit 10. inner urge, summons, as to be priest etc. 11. need, demand —**caller** n. —**calling** n. vocation, profession —**call box** kiosk for public telephone —**call girl** prostitute with whom appointments are made by telephone —**call up** 1. summon to serve in army 2. imagine

calligraphy (kə'lɪgrəfɪ) n. handwriting, penmanship —**calli'graphic** a.

calliper or U.S. **caliper** ('kælɪpə) n. 1. metal splint for leg —pl. 2. instrument for measuring diameters

callisthenics or **calisthenics** (kælɪs'θenɪks) pl.n. light gymnastic exercises —**callis'thenic** or **calis'thenic** a.

callosity (kə'lɒsɪtɪ) n. 1. hardheartedness 2. callus

callous ('kæləs) a. hardened, unfeeling —'**callously** adv. —'**callousness** n.

callow ('kæləʊ) a. 1. inexperienced 2. immature

callus ('kæləs) n. area of thick, hardened skin

calm (kɑːm) a. 1. still 2. quiet 3. tranquil —n. 4. stillness 5. tranquillity 6. absence of wind —v. 7. become, make, still or quiet —'**calmly** adv. —'**calmness** n.

calomel ('kæləmel, -məl) n. colourless, tasteless powder used medicinally, esp. as cathartic

Calor Gas ('kælə) R butane gas liquefied under pressure in portable containers for domestic use

calorie or **calory** ('kælərɪ) n. 1. unit of heat 2. unit of energy obtained from foods —**ca'loric** a. 1. of heat or calories —n. 2. obs. hypothetical elastic fluid, embodiment of heat —**calo'rific** a. heat-making —**calo'rimeter** n.

calumet ('kæljumet) n. 1. tobacco pipe of N Amer. Indians 2. pipe of peace

calumny ('kæləmnɪ) n. slander, false accusation —**ca'lumniate** vt. —**calumni'ation** n. —**ca'lumniator** n. —**ca'lumnious** a.

Calvary ('kælvərɪ) n. place outside walls of Jerusalem where Jesus was crucified (also Gol'gotha)

calves (kɑːvz) n., pl. of CALF¹, CALF²

Calvinism ('kælvɪnɪzəm) n. theological system of Calvin, characterized by emphasis on predestination and justification by faith —'**Calvinist** n./a. —**Calvin'istic(al)** a.

calx (kælks) n. 1. powdery metallic oxide formed when ore or mineral is roasted 2. calcium oxide (pl. **-es, 'calces**)

calypso (kə'lɪpsəʊ) n. W Indian improvised song on topical subject

calyx ('keɪlɪks, 'kælɪks) n. covering of bud (pl. **-es, calyces** ('kælɪsiːz, 'keɪlɪ-))

cam (kæm) n. device to change rotary to reciprocating motion —'**camshaft** n. in motoring, rotating shaft to which cams are fixed to lift valves

camaraderie (kæmə'rɑːdərɪ) n. spirit of comradeship, trust

camber ('kæmbə) n. 1. convexity on upper surface of road, bridge etc. 2. curvature of aircraft wing

Cambrian ('kæmbrɪən) a. 1. of first 100 million years of Palaeozoic era 2. of Wales —n. 3. Cambrian period or rock system 4. Welshman

cambric ('keɪmbrɪk) n. fine white linen or cotton cloth

Cambs. (kæmbz) Cambridgeshire

came (keɪm) pt. of COME

camel ('kæməl) n. animal of Asia and Afr., with humped back, used as beast of burden —**camel's hair** or '**camelhair** n. 1. hair of camel, used in rugs etc. 2. soft cloth made of this hair, usu. tan in colour —a. 3. (of painter's brush) made from tail hairs of squirrels

camellia (kə'miːlɪə) n. ornamental shrub

camelopard ('kæmɪləpɑːd, kə'mel-) n. obs. giraffe

Camembert ('kæməmbeə) n. soft creamy cheese

cameo ('kæmɪəʊ) n. 1. medallion, brooch etc. with profile head or design carved in relief 2. single brief scene or appearance in film etc. by (well-known) actor

camera ('kæmərə) n. apparatus used to take photographs —'**cameraman** n. photographer, esp. for television or cinema —**camera obscura** (ɒb'skjʊərə) darkened chamber in which views of surrounding country are shown on sheet by means of lenses —**in camera** (of legal proceedings etc.) conducted in private

camiknickers ('kæmɪnɪkəz) pl.n. women's knickers attached to camisole top

camisole ('kæmɪsəʊl) n. underbodice

camomile or **chamomile** ('kæməmaɪl) n. aromatic creeping plant, used medicinally

camouflage ('kæməflɑːʒ) n. 1. disguise, means of deceiving enemy observation, eg by paint, screen —vt. 2. disguise

camp (kæmp) n. 1. (place for) tents of hikers, army etc. 2. cabins etc. for temporary accommodation 3. group supporting political party etc. 4. SA field, pasture —a. inf. 5. homosexual 6. consciously artificial —vi. 7. form or lodge in camp —'**camper** n. 1. person who lives or temporarily stays in tent *etc.* **2.** US vehicle equipped for camping out —'**camping** *n.* —**camp follower 1.** civilian, *esp.* prostitute, who unofficially provides services to military personnel **2.** nonmember who is sympathetic to group *etc.*

campaign (kæm'peɪn) *n.* **1.** series of coordinated activities for some purpose, *eg* political or military campaign —*vi.* **2.** serve in campaign —**cam'paigner** *n.*

campanile (kæmpə'niːlɪ) *n. esp.* in Italy, bell tower, not usu. attached to another building

campanology (kæmpə'nɒlədʒɪ) *n.* art of ringing bells musically

campanula (kæm'pænjʊlə) *n.* plant with blue or white bell-shaped flowers

camphor ('kæmfə) *n.* solid essential oil with aromatic taste and smell —'**camphorated** *a.* —**cam'phoric** *a.* —**camphorated oil** liniment consisting of camphor and peanut oil, used as counterirritant

campion ('kæmpɪən) *n.* white or pink wild flower

campus ('kæmpəs) *n.* grounds of college or university

can[1] (kæn; *unstressed* kən) *vi.* **1.** be able to **2.** have the power to **3.** be allowed to (**could** *pt.*)

can[2] (kæn) *n.* **1.** container, usu. metal, for liquids, foods —*vt.* **2.** put in can (**-nn-**) —**canned** *a.* **1.** preserved in a can **2.** (of music, programmes *etc.*) previously recorded —'**cannery** *n.* factory where food is canned

Can. 1. Canada **2.** Canadian

Canadian (kə'neɪdɪən) *n./a.* (native) of Canada —**Ca'nadianize** *or* **-ise** *v.* make, become Canadian —**Canada balsam** ('kænədə) **1.** yellow transparent resin obtained from balsam fir **2.** balsam fir —**Canada Day** Jul. 1st, anniversary of day in 1867 when Canad. received dominion status —**Canada goose** large greyish-brown N Amer. goose —**Canadian Shield** wide area of rock extending over most of E and Central Canad.: rich in minerals (*also* **Laurentian Shield**)

canaille (ka'nɑːj) *Fr.* masses; mob; rabble

canal (kə'næl) *n.* **1.** artificial watercourse **2.** duct in body —**canali'zation** *or* **-li'sation** *n.* —'**canalize** *or* **-lise** *vt.* **1.** convert into canal **2.** direct (thoughts, energies *etc.*) into one channel

canapé ('kænəpɪ, -peɪ) *n.* small piece of toast *etc.* with savoury topping

canard (kæ'nɑːd) *n.* **1.** false report; rumour, hoax **2.** aircraft in which tailplane is mounted in front of wing

canary (kə'neərɪ) *n.* yellow singing bird

canasta (kə'næstə) *n.* card game played with two packs

cancan ('kænkæn) *n.* high-kicking (orig. Fr. music-hall) dance

cancel ('kænsəl) *vt.* **1.** cross out **2.** annul **3.** call off (**-ll-**) —**cancel'lation** *n.*

cancer ('kænsə) *n.* malignant growth or tumour —'**cancerous** *a.*

Cancer ('kænsə) *n.* **1.** (crab) 4th sign of zodiac, operative c. Jun. 21st–Jul. 21st **2.** constellation —**tropic of Cancer** parallel of latitude 23½° N of the equator

candela (kæn'diːlə, -'deɪlə) *n.* basic SI unit of luminous intensity

candid ('kændɪd) *a.* **1.** frank, open **2.** impartial —'**candidly** *adv.* —'**candidness**, '**candour** *or* U.S. '**candor** *n.* frankness —**candid camera** small camera used to take informal photographs of people

candidate ('kændɪdeɪt) *n.* **1.** one who seeks office, appointment *etc.* **2.** person taking examination or test —'**candidacy** *or* '**candidature** *n.*

candle ('kændˀl) *n.* **1.** stick of wax with wick **2.** light —**candelabrum** (kændɪ'læbrəm) *n.* large, branched candle holder (*pl.* **-bra** (-brə)) —'**candlepower** *n.* unit for measuring light —'**candlestick** *n.* —'**candlewick** *n.* cotton fabric with tufted surface

Candlemas ('kændˀlməs) *n. Christianity* Feb. 2nd, Feast of Purification of Virgin Mary and presentation of Christ in Temple

candy ('kændɪ) *n.* **1.** crystallized sugar **2.** US confectionery in general —*vt.* **3.** preserve with sugar —*vi.* **4.** become encrusted with sugar ('**candied**, '**candying**) —'**candied** *a.* —'**candyfloss** *n.* UK light fluffy confection made from coloured spun sugar, usu. held on stick

candytuft ('kændɪtʌft) *n.* garden plant with clusters of white, pink or purple flowers

cane (keɪn) *n.* **1.** stem of small palm or large grass **2.** walking stick —*vt.* **3.** beat with cane —**cane sugar 1.** sucrose obtained from sugar cane **2.** *see* SUCROSE

canine ('keɪnaɪn, 'kæn-) *a.* like, pert. to, dog —**canine tooth** one of four sharp, pointed teeth, two in each jaw

canister ('kænɪstə) *n.* container, usu. of metal, *esp.* for storing dry food

canker ('kæŋkə) *n.* **1.** eating sore **2.** thing that eats away, destroys, corrupts —*vt.* **3.** infect, corrupt —*vi.* **4.** decay —'**cankered** *or* '**cankerous** *a.* —'**cankerworm** *n.*

canna ('kænə) *n.* tropical flowering plant

cannabis ('kænəbɪs) *n.* **1.** hemp plant **2.** drug derived from this

cannel coal *or* **cannel** ('kænˀl) *n.* dull coal burning with smoky luminous flame

cannelloni *or* **canneloni** (kænɪ'ləʊnɪ) *pl.n.* tubular pieces of pasta filled with meat *etc.*

cannibal ('kænɪbˀl) *n.* **1.** one who eats human flesh —*a.* **2.** relating to this practice —'**cannibalism** *n.* —**cannibal'istic** *a.* —'**cannibalize** *or* **-ise** *vt.* use parts from (one machine *etc.*) to repair another

cannon[1] ('kænən) *n.* large gun (*pl.* **-s**, '**cannon**) —**canno'nade** *n./vt.* attack with cannon —'**cannonball** *n.* —**cannon bone** horse's leg bone —**cannon fodder** men regarded as expendable in war because they are part of huge army

cannon[2] ('kænən) *n.* **1.** billiard stroke,

hitting both object balls with one's own —vi. **2.** make this stroke **3.** rebound, collide

cannot ('kænɒt, kæ'nɒt) *negative form of* CAN[1]

canny ('kænɪ) *a.* **1.** shrewd **2.** cautious **3.** crafty —'**cannily** *adv.*

canoe (kə'nuː) *n.* very light boat propelled with paddle or paddles —ca'**noeist** *n.*

canon[1] ('kænən) *n.* **1.** law or rule, *esp.* of church **2.** standard **3.** body of books accepted as genuine **4.** list of saints —**canoni'zation** *or* **-i'sation** *n.* —'**canon-ize** *or* **-ise** *vt.* enrol in list of saints

canon[2] ('kænən) *n.* church dignitary, member of cathedral chapter —ca'**noni-cal** *a.* —ca'**nonicals** *pl.n.* vestments worn by clergy when officiating —canon'**istic** *a.* —**canonical hour 1.** R.C.Ch. one of seven prayer times appointed for each day by canon law **2.** *Ch. of England* any time at which marriages may lawfully be cel-ebrated —**canon law** body of laws enacted by supreme authorities of Christian Church

canoodle (kə'nuːd'l) *vi.* (*oft. with* with) *sl.* kiss and cuddle

canopy ('kænəpɪ) *n.* **1.** covering over throne, bed *etc.* **2.** any overhanging shelter —*vt.* **3.** cover with canopy (-**opied,** -**opying**)

can't (kɑːnt) *v.* cannot

cant[1] (kænt) *n.* **1.** hypocritical speech **2.** whining **3.** language of a sect **4.** technical jargon **5.** slang, *esp.* of thieves —*vi.* **6.** use cant

cant[2] (kænt) *vt.* **1.** tilt, slope **2.** bevel —*n.* **3.** inclination from vertical or horizontal plane

Cantab. (kæn'tæb) Cantabrigiensis (*Lat.,* of Cambridge)

cantabile (kæn'tɑːbɪlɪ) *Mus. a./adv.* **1.** singing —*n.* **2.** piece or passage performed in this way

Cantabrigian (kæntə'brɪdʒɪən) *a.* **1.** of Cambridge or Cambridge University —*n.* **2.** member or graduate of Cambridge University **3.** inhabitant or native of Cambridge

cantaloupe *or* **cantaloup** ('kæntəluːp) *n.* variety of muskmelon

cantankerous (kæn'tæŋkərəs) *a.* ill-natured, quarrelsome

cantata (kæn'tɑːtə) *n.* choral work like, but shorter than, oratorio

canteen (kæn'tiːn) *n.* **1.** place in factory, school *etc.* where meals are provided **2.** small shop in military camp **3.** case of cutlery **4.** mess tin

canter ('kæntə) *n.* **1.** easy gallop —*v.* **2.** move at, make to canter

Canterbury bell ('kæntəbərɪ) cultivated campanula

cantharides (kæn'θærɪdiːz) *pl.n.* diuretic and urogenital stimulant prepared from dried bodies of Spanish fly (*sing.* '**cantha-ris**) (*also* **Spanish fly**)

canticle ('kæntɪk'l) *n.* short hymn

cantilever ('kæntɪliːvə) *n.* beam, girder *etc.* fixed at one end only

canto ('kæntəʊ) *n.* division of poem (*pl.* -s)

canton ('kæntən, kæn'tɒn) *n.* division of country, *esp.* Swiss federal state

Cantonese (kæntə'niːz) *n.* **1.** Chinese language spoken in Canton *etc.* **2.** native or inhabitant of Canton (*pl.* -ese) —*a.* **3.** of Canton or Chinese language spoken there

cantonment (kən'tuːnmənt) *n.* quarters for troops

cantor ('kæntɔː) *n.* **1.** *Judaism* leading singer in synagogue liturgy **2.** *Christianity* leader of singing in church choir

Canuck (kə'nʌk) *n./a. C inf.* Canadian

canvas ('kænvəs) *n.* **1.** coarse cloth used for sails, painting on *etc.* **2.** sails of ship **3.** picture —**under canvas** in tents

canvass ('kænvəs) *vt.* **1.** solicit votes, contributions *etc.* from **2.** discuss, examine —*n.* **3.** solicitation

canyon *or* **cañon** ('kænjən) *n.* deep gorge

caoutchouc ('kaʊtʃʊk) *n. see* RUBBER[1] (sense 1)

cap (kæp) *n.* **1.** covering for head **2.** lid, top or other covering —*vt.* **3.** put cap on **4.** outdo **5.** select for a team (-**pp-**)

cap. 1. capacity **2.** capital **3.** capitalize **4.** capital letter

capable ('keɪpəb'l) *a.* **1.** able, gifted **2.** competent **3.** having the capacity, power —capa'**bility** *n.*

capacity (kə'pæsɪtɪ) *n.* **1.** power of holding or grasping **2.** room **3.** volume **4.** character **5.** ability, power of mind —**capacious** (kə-'peɪʃəs) *a.* roomy —ca'**pacitance** *n.* (measure of) ability of system to store electric charge —ca'**pacitor** *n.*

caparison (kə'pærɪs'n) *n.* **1.** ornamental covering, equipment for horse —*vt.* **2.** adorn thus

cape[1] (keɪp) *n.* covering for shoulders

cape[2] (keɪp) *n.* point of land running into sea, headland —**Cape Coloured** SA *see* Coloured (sense 2) *at* COLOUR —**Cape pigeon** pied petrel of southern oceans —**Cape salmon** SA geelbek —**Cape sparrow** common S Afr. bird

caper[1] ('keɪpə) *n.* **1.** skip **2.** frolic **3.** escapade —*vi.* **4.** skip, dance

caper[2] ('keɪpə) *n.* pickled flower bud of Sicilian shrub

capercaillie *or* **capercailzie** (kæpə'keɪlɪ) *n.* large black grouse

capillary (kə'pɪlərɪ) *a.* **1.** hairlike **2.** of capillarity —*n.* **3.** tube with very small bore, *esp.* small blood vessel —capil'**larity** *n.* phenomenon caused by surface tension and resulting in elevation or depression of surface of liquid in contact with solid (*also* **capillary action**)

capital ('kæpɪt'l) *n.* **1.** chief town **2.** money, stock, funds **3.** large-sized letter **4.** headpiece of column —*a.* **5.** involving or punishable by death **6.** serious **7.** chief **8.** leading **9.** excellent —'**capitalism** *n.* economic system which is based on private ownership of industry —'**capital-**

ist *n.* **1.** owner of capital **2.** supporter of capitalism —*a.* **3.** run by, possessing, capital —'**capitalize** *or* -**ise** *vt.* **1.** convert into capital —*vi.* **2.** (*with* on) turn to advantage —'**capitally** *adv.* —**capital gain** amount by which selling price of financial asset exceeds cost —**capital levy** tax on capital or property as contrasted with tax on income —**capital punishment** punishment of death for crime; death penalty —**capital stock 1.** par value of total share capital a company is authorized to issue **2.** total physical capital existing in economy at any time —**capital transfer tax** UK tax payable on total of gifts of money or property made during donor's lifetime or after his death

capitation (kæpɪ'teɪʃən) *n.* **1.** tax or grant per head **2.** census

Capitol ('kæpɪtˀl) *n.* **1.** U.S. Congress House **2.** a U.S. state legislature building **3.** temple of Jupiter in Rome

capitulate (kə'pɪtjuleɪt) *vi.* surrender on terms, give in —**capitu'lation** *n.*

capo ('kæpəʊ) *n.* device fitted across all strings of guitar etc. to raise pitch of each string simultaneously (*pl.* -**s**) (*also* **capo tasto** ('tæstəʊ))

capon ('keɪpən) *n.* castrated cock fowl fattened for eating —'**caponize** *or* -**ise** *vt.*

cappuccino (kæpu'tʃiːnəʊ) *n.* coffee with steamed milk

caprice (kə'priːs) *n.* whim —**capricious** (kə'prɪʃəs) *a.* —**capriciousness** (kə-'prɪʃəsnɪs) *n.*

Capricorn ('kæprɪkɔːn) *n.* **1.** (sea-goat) 10th sign of zodiac, operative c. Dec. 21st–Jan. 19th **2.** constellation —**tropic of Capricorn** parallel of latitude 23½° S of the equator

capriole ('kæprɪəʊl) *Dressage n.* **1.** upward but not forward leap made by horse with all four feet off ground —*vi.* **2.** perform capriole

caps. **1.** capital letters **2.** capsule

capsicum ('kæpsɪkəm) *n.* tropical vegetable with mild peppery flavour, sweet pepper

capsize (kæp'saɪz) *vt.* **1.** (of boat) upset —*vi.* **2.** be overturned —**cap'sizal** *n.*

capstan ('kæpstən) *n.* machine to wind cable, *esp.* to hoist anchor

capsule ('kæpsjuːl) *n.* **1.** gelatin case for dose of medicine or drug **2.** any small enclosed area or container **3.** seed vessel of plant —'**capsulize** *or* -**ise** *vt.* **1.** state in highly condensed form **2.** enclose in capsule

Capt. Captain

captain ('kæptɪn) *n.* **1.** commander of vessel or company of soldiers **2.** leader, chief —*vt.* **3.** be captain of

caption ('kæpʃən) *n.* heading, title of article, picture *etc.*

captious ('kæpʃəs) *a.* **1.** ready to find fault **2.** critical **3.** peevish —'**captiously** *adv.* —'**captiousness** *n.*

captive ('kæptɪv) *n.* **1.** prisoner —*a.* **2.**

taken, imprisoned **3.** unable to avoid speeches *etc.* —'**captivate** *vt.* fascinate —'**captivating** *a.* delightful —**cap'tivity** *n.*

capture ('kæptʃə) *vt.* **1.** seize, make prisoner —*n.* **2.** seizure, taking —'**captor** *n.*

Capuchin ('kæpjutʃɪn, -ʃɪn) *n.* friar belonging to branch of Franciscan Order

capybara (kæpɪ'bɑːrə) *n.* largest rodent, found in S Amer.

car (kɑː) *n.* **1.** self-propelled road vehicle **2.** passenger compartment, as in cable car **3.** railway carriage of specified type —**car park** area, building where vehicles may be left for a time —'**carport** *n.* shelter for car usu. consisting of roof supported by posts

carabineer *or* **carabinier** (kærəbɪ'nɪə) *n. see* **carabineer** *at* CARBINE

caracal ('kærəkæl) *n.* **1.** lynxlike feline mammal inhabiting deserts of N Afr. and S Asia, having smooth coat of reddish fur **2.** this fur

caracole ('kærəkəʊl) *or* **caracol** ('kærəkɒl) *Dressage n.* **1.** half turn to right or left —*vi.* **2.** execute half turn

caracul ('kærəkʌl) *n.* **1.** black, loosely curled fur from skins of newly born lambs of caracul sheep (*also* **Persian lamb**) **2.** sheep of Central Asia with coarse dark hair (*also* '**karakul**)

carafe (kə'ræf, -'rɑːf) *n.* glass water bottle for table, decanter

caramel ('kærəməl) *n.* **1.** burnt sugar for cooking **2.** type of confectionery

carapace ('kærəpeɪs) *n.* thick hard shield that covers part of body of tortoise *etc.*

carat ('kærət) *n.* **1.** small weight used for gold, diamonds *etc.* **2.** proportional measure of twenty-fourths used to state fineness of gold

caravan ('kærəvæn) *n.* **1.** large enclosed vehicle for living in, pulled as trailer by car *etc.* **2.** company of merchants travelling together for safety in the East —**caravanserai** (kærə'vænsəraɪ) *or* **caravansary** (kærə'vænsərɪ) *n.* in some Eastern countries, large inn enclosing courtyard, providing accommodation for caravans

caravel ('kærəvɛl) *or* **carvel** *n.* two- or three-masted sailing ship in 15th and 16th centuries

caraway ('kærəweɪ) *n.* plant of which the seeds are used as spice in cakes *etc.*

carbide ('kɑːbaɪd) *n.* compound of carbon with an element, *esp.* calcium carbide

carbine ('kɑːbaɪn) *n.* short rifle —**carbineer** (kɑːbɪ'nɪə), **carabi'neer** *or* **cara-bi'nier** *n.* formerly, soldier equipped with carbine

carbo- *or before vowel* **carb-** (*comb. form*) carbon, as in *carbohydrate, carbonate*

carbohydrate (kɑːbəʊ'haɪdreɪt) *n.* any of large group of compounds containing carbon, hydrogen and oxygen, *esp.* sugars and starches as components of food

carbolic acid (kɑː'bɒlɪk) disinfectant

derived from coal tar —'**carbolated** a. containing carbolic acid

carbon ('kɑːbᵊn) n. nonmetallic element, substance of pure charcoal, found in all organic matter —**carbo'naceous** a. of, resembling or containing carbon —'**carbonate** n. salt of carbonic acid —**car'bonic** a. —**carbo'niferous** a. —'**carbonize** or -**ise** v. —**carbon black** finely divided carbon produced by incomplete combustion of natural gas or petroleum: used in pigments and ink —**carbon dating** technique for determining age of wood etc., based on its content of radioisotope ¹⁴C acquired from atmosphere when it formed part of living plant —**carbon dioxide** colourless gas exhaled in respiration of animals —**carbonic acid** 1. carbon dioxide 2. compound formed by carbon dioxide and water —**carbon monoxide** colourless, odourless poisonous gas formed when carbon compounds burn in insufficient air —**carbon paper** paper coated with a dark, waxy pigment, used for duplicating written or typed matter, producing **carbon copy** —**carbon tetrachloride** colourless volatile nonflammable liquid made from chlorine and used as solvent etc.

Carboniferous (kɑːbə'nıfərəs) a. 1. of fifth period of Palaeozoic era during which coal measures were formed —n. 2. Carboniferous period or rock system divided into **Upper Carboniferous** and **Lower Carboniferous** periods

Carborundum (kɑːbə'rʌndəm) n. R artificial silicate of carbon

carboy ('kɑːbɔɪ) n. large glass jar protected by wicker casing

carbuncle ('kɑːbʌŋkᵊl) n. 1. inflamed ulcer, boil or tumour 2. fiery-red precious stone

carburettor, carburetter (kɑːbju'retə, 'kɑːbjuretə) or U.S. **carburetor** ('kɑːbjureitə) n. device for vaporizing and mixing petrol with air in internal-combustion engine

carcass or **carcase** ('kɑːkəs) n. 1. dead animal body 2. skeleton 3. inf. person's body

carcinoma (kɑːsɪ'nəumə) n. a cancer —**car'cinogen** n. substance producing cancer

card¹ (kɑːd) n. 1. thick, stiff paper 2. piece of this giving identification etc. 3. illustrated card sending greetings etc. 4. one of the 52 playing cards making up a pack 5. inf. a character, eccentric —pl. 6. any card game 7. employee's tax and national insurance documents or information held by employer —'**cardboard** n. thin, stiff board made of paper pulp —**card index** index in which each entry is made on separate card —'**cardsharp** or '**cardsharper** n. professional card player who cheats —**card vote** UK vote by delegates, esp. at trade union conference, in which each delegate's vote counts as vote by all his constituents

card² (kɑːd) n. 1. instrument for combing wool etc. —vt. 2. comb —'**carder** n.

cardamom or **cardamum** ('kɑːdəməm) n. 1. tropical Asian plant with large hairy leaves 2. seeds of this plant, used esp. as spice or condiment

cardiac ('kɑːdɪæk) a. 1. pert. to the heart —n. 2. person with heart disorder —'**cardiogram** n. tracing made by cardiograph —'**cardiograph** n. instrument which records movements of the heart —'**cardioid** a. heart-shaped —**cardi'olo-gist** n. —**cardi'ology** n. branch of medical science concerned with heart and its diseases

cardigan ('kɑːdıgən) n. knitted jacket

cardinal ('kɑːdın³l) a. 1. chief, principal —n. 2. highest rank, next to the Pope in R.C. Church 3. bright red N Amer. bunting (also '**redbird**) —'**cardinalate** n. —**cardinal numbers** 1, 2, 3, etc. —**cardinal points** north, south, east and west

cardio- or before vowel **cardi-** (comb. form) heart, as in cardiogram

care (kɛə) vi. 1. be anxious —n. 2. attention 3. pains, heed 4. charge, protection 5. anxiety 6. caution —'**carefree** a. —'**care-ful** a. —'**carefully** adv. —'**carefulness** n. —'**careless** a. —'**carelessness** n. —'**care-taker** n. 1. person in charge of premises —a. 2. temporary, interim —'**careworn** a. showing signs of care, stress etc. —**care for** 1. have regard or liking for 2. look after 3. be disposed to

careen (kə'riːn) vt. 1. lay (ship) over on her side for cleaning and repair —vi. 2. keel over 3. sway dangerously

career (kə'rıə) n. 1. course through life 2. profession 3. rapid motion —vi. 4. run or move at full speed —**ca'reerist** n. person who seeks to advance his career by any possible means

caress (kə'res) vt. 1. fondle, embrace, treat with affection —n. 2. act or expression of affection

caret ('kærıt) n. mark (⅄) showing where to insert something omitted

cargo ('kɑːgəu) n. load, freight, carried by ship, plane etc. (pl. -es)

Carib ('kærıb) n. 1. member of group of Amer. Indian peoples of NE South Amer. and Lesser Antilles (pl. -s, '**Carib**) 2. family of languages spoken by these peoples

caribou ('kærıbuː) n. N Amer. reindeer

caricature ('kærıkətjuə) n. 1. likeness exaggerated or distorted to appear ridiculous —vt. 2. portray in this way

caries ('kɛəriːz) n. decay of tooth or bone —'**carious** a. (of teeth or bone) affected with caries; decayed

carillon (kə'rıljən) n. 1. set of bells usu. hung in tower and played by set of keys, pedals etc. 2. tune so played

cariole ('kærıəul) n. see CARRIOLE

carl or **carle** (kɑːl) n. obs., Scot. churl

Carlovingian (kɑːləu'vındʒıən) Hist. see CAROLINGIAN

Carmelite ('kɑːməlaɪt) *n. R.C.Ch.* **1.** member of order of mendicant friars **2.** member of corresponding order of nuns

carminative ('kɑːmɪnətɪv) *n.* **1.** medicine to remedy flatulence —*a.* **2.** acting as this

carmine ('kɑːmaɪn) *n.* **1.** brilliant red colour (prepared from cochineal) —*a.* **2.** of this colour

carnage ('kɑːnɪdʒ) *n.* slaughter

carnal ('kɑːnᵊl) *a.* **1.** fleshly, sensual **2.** worldly —'**carnalism** *n.* —**car'nality** *n.* —'**carnally** *adv.* —**carnal knowledge** *chiefly law* sexual intercourse

carnation (kɑː'neɪʃən) *n.* **1.** cultivated flower **2.** flesh colour

carnelian (kɑː'niːljən) *n.* reddish-yellow translucent chalcedony, used as gemstone

carnival ('kɑːnɪvᵊl) *n.* **1.** festive occasion **2.** travelling fair **3.** show or display for amusement

carnivorous (kɑː'nɪvərəs) *a.* flesh-eating —'**carnivore** *n.*

carob ('kærəb) *n.* **1.** evergreen Mediterranean tree with edible pods **2.** long blackish sugary pod of this tree, used for fodder and sometimes human food

carol ('kærəl) *n.* **1.** song or hymn of joy or praise (*esp.* Christmas carol) —*vi.* **2.** sing carols (-**ll**-)

Caroline ('kærəlaɪn) *or* **Carolean** (kærə-'liːən) *a.* of Charles I or Charles II (kings of England, Scotland and Ireland), society over which they ruled or their government (*also* **Caro'linian**)

Carolingian (kærə'lɪndʒɪən) *Hist. a.* **1.** of Frankish dynasty founded by Pepin the Short —*n.* **2.** member of dynasty of Carolingian Franks (*also* **Carlo'vingian**, **Caro'linian**)

carotid (kə'rɒtɪd) *n.* **1.** either of two principal arteries that supply blood to head and neck —*a.* **2.** of either of these arteries

carouse (kə'raʊz) *vi.* **1.** have merry drinking spree —*n.* **2.** merry drinking party (*also* **ca'rousal**) —**ca'rouser** *n.*

carousel (kærə'sɛl, -'zɛl) *n.* US merry-go-round

carp¹ (kɑːp) *n.* freshwater fish

carp² (kɑːp) *vi.* **1.** complain about small faults or errors **2.** nag —'**carper** *n.* —'**carping** *a.* —'**carpingly** *adv.*

carpal ('kɑːpᵊl) *n.* any bone of wrist

carpel ('kɑːpᵊl) *n.* female reproductive organ of flowering plants, consisting of ovary, style and stigma

carpenter ('kɑːpɪntə) *n.* worker in timber as in building *etc.* —'**carpentry** *n.* art of carpenter

carpet ('kɑːpɪt) *n.* **1.** heavy fabric for covering floor —*vt.* **2.** cover (floor) with carpet **3.** *inf.* call up for censure —'**carpetbag** *n.* travelling bag —'**carpetbagger** *n.* political adventurer —**carpet slipper** slipper orig. made with woollen upper resembling carpeting

carpus ('kɑːpəs) *n.* **1.** wrist **2.** eight small bones of human wrist (*pl.* **carpi** ('kɑːpaɪ))

carrageen, carragheen *or* **carageen** ('kærəgiːn) *n.* edible red seaweed of N Amer. and N Europe, used to make jelly *etc.* (*also* **Irish moss**)

carriage ('kærɪdʒ) *n.* **1.** railway coach **2.** bearing, conduct **3.** horse-drawn vehicle **4.** act, cost, of carrying —**carriage clock** portable clock, usu. in rectangular case, orig. used by travellers —**carriage forward** charge for conveying, to be paid by receiver —**carriage paid** charge for conveying, to be paid by sender —'**carriageway** *n.* part of road along which traffic passes in single line

carriole *or* **cariole** ('kærɪəʊl) *n.* small open carriage for one

carrion ('kærɪən) *n.* rotting dead flesh —**carrion crow** scavenging European crow

carrot ('kærət) *n.* **1.** plant with orange-red edible root **2.** inducement —'**carroty** *a.* red, reddish

carry ('kærɪ) *vt.* **1.** convey, transport **2.** capture, win **3.** effect **4.** conduct (oneself) in specified manner —*vi.* **5.** (of projectile, sound) reach or penetrate to distance ('**carried**, '**carrying**) —*n.* **6.** range —'**carrier** *n.* **1.** one that carries goods **2.** one who, himself immune, communicates a disease to others **3.** aircraft carrier —**carrier bag** UK large paper or plastic bag for shopping *etc.* —**carrier pigeon** homing pigeon, *esp.* for carrying messages —**carrier wave** *Rad.* wave of fixed amplitude and frequency, modulated to carry signal in radio transmission *etc.* (*also* '**carrier**) —'**carrycot** *n.* light cot with handles, similar to but smaller than body of pram —**carry-out** *n. chiefly Scot.* **1.** alcohol bought at off-licence *etc.* for consumption elsewhere **2.** shop which sells hot cooked food for consumption away from premises —**carry on 1.** continue **2.** *inf.* fuss unnecessarily **3.** *inf.* have an affair —**carry out 1.** perform; cause to be implemented **2.** accomplish

cart (kɑːt) *n.* **1.** open (two-wheeled) vehicle, *esp.* pulled by horse —*vt.* **2.** convey in cart **3.** carry with effort —'**cartage** *n.* —'**carter** *n.* —'**carthorse** *n.* —'**cartwheel** *n.* **1.** large, spoked wheel **2.** sideways somersault —'**cartwright** *n.* maker of carts

carte blanche ('kɑːt 'blɑːntʃ) *Fr.* complete discretion or authority

cartel (kɑː'tɛl) *n.* **1.** industrial combination for the purpose of fixing prices, output *etc.* **2.** alliance of political parties *etc.* to further common aims

Cartesian (kɑː'tiːzɪən) *a.* **1.** pert. to French philosopher René Descartes (1596-1650) or his system of coordinates —*n.* **2.** adherent of his philosophy —**Cartesian coordinates** system of coordinates that defines location of point in terms of perpendicular distance from each of set of mutually perpendicular axes

Carthusian (kɑː'θjuːzɪən) *n. R.C.Ch.* member of monastic order founded by Saint Bruno

cartilage ('kɑːtɪlɪdʒ) n. 1. firm elastic tissue in the body 2. gristle —**cartilaginous** (kɑːtɪ'lædʒɪnəs) a.

cartogram ('kɑːtəgræm) n. map showing statistical information in diagrammatic form

cartography (kɑː'tɒgrəfɪ) n. mapmaking —**car'tographer** n. —**carto'graphic(al)** a.

carton ('kɑːt²n) n. cardboard or plastic container

cartoon (kɑː'tuːn) n. 1. drawing, esp. humorous or satirical 2. sequence of drawings telling story 3. preliminary design for painting —**car'toonist** n.

cartouche or **cartouch** (kɑː'tuːʃ) n. 1. carved or cast ornamental tablet or panel in form of scroll 2. oblong figure enclosing characters expressing royal or divine names in Egyptian hieroglyphics

cartridge ('kɑːtrɪdʒ) n. 1. case containing charge for gun 2. container for film, magnetic tape etc. 3. unit in head of gramophone pick-up —**cartridge paper** strong, thick paper

carve (kɑːv) vt. 1. cut 2. hew 3. sculpture 4. engrave 5. cut (meat) in pieces or slices —'**carver** n. —'**carving** n.

carvel ('kɑːv²l) n. see CARAVEL

caryatid (kærɪ'ætɪd) n. supporting column in shape of female figure

Casanova (kæsə'nəʊvə) n. any man noted for amorous adventures

casbah ('kæzbɑː) n. (sometimes C-) 1. citadel of various N Afr. cities 2. quarter where casbah is located (also '**kasbah**)

cascade (kæs'keɪd) n. 1. waterfall 2. anything resembling this —vi. 3. fall in cascades

cascara (kæs'kɑːrə) n. 1. dried bark of cascara buckthorn, used as laxative and stimulant (also **cascara sagrada**) 2. shrub or small tree of NW North Amer. (also **cascara buckthorn**)

case¹ (keɪs) n. 1. instance 2. event, circumstance 3. question at issue 4. state of affairs, condition 5. arguments supporting particular action etc. 6. Med. patient under treatment 7. lawsuit 8. grounds for suit 9. grammatical relation of words in sentence —**case history** record of person's background, medical history etc. —**case law** law established by following judicial decisions given in earlier cases

case² (keɪs) n. 1. box, sheath, covering 2. receptacle 3. box and contents —vt. 4. put in a case —'**casing** n. 1. protective cover 2. material for cover 3. frame containing door or window (also **case**) —**case-harden** vt. 1. harden by carbonizing the surface of (esp. iron) by converting into steel 2. make hard, callous

casein ('keɪsiːn, -siːɪn) n. protein in milk and its products —'**caseous** a. like cheese

casement ('keɪsmənt) n. window opening on hinges

cash (kæʃ) n. 1. money, banknotes and coins —vt. 2. turn into or exchange for money —ca'**shier** n. one in charge of receiving and paying of money —**cash-and-carry** a./adv. sold on basis of cash payment for merchandise that is not delivered —'**cashbook** n. —**cash crop** crop grown for sale rather than subsistence —**cash dispenser** computerized device outside bank that supplies cash when user inserts card and keys in number —**cash flow** movement of money into and out of a business —**cash register** till that records amount of money put in —**cash on delivery** service entailing cash payment to carrier on delivery of merchandise

cashew ('kæʃuː, kæ'ʃuː) n. 1. tropical tree bearing kidney-shaped nuts 2. nut of this tree, edible only when roasted (also **cashew nut**)

cashier (kæ'ʃɪə) vt. dismiss from office or service

cashmere ('kæʃmɪə) n. 1. fine soft fabric 2. shawl made from goat's wool

casino (kə'siːnəʊ) n. building, institution for gambling (pl. -s)

cask (kɑːsk) n. 1. barrel 2. container for wine

casket ('kɑːskɪt) n. 1. small case for jewels etc. 2. US coffin

casque (kæsk) n. Zool. helmet or helmetlike structure, as on bill of most hornbills

Cassandra (kə'sændrə) n. 1. Gr. myth. daughter of Priam and Hecuba, endowed with gift of prophecy but fated never to be believed 2. anyone whose prophecies of doom are unheeded

cassata (kə'sɑːtə) n. ice cream, esp. containing fruit and nuts

cassava (kə'sɑːvə) n. 1. any of various tropical plants, esp. Amer. species (**bitter cassava, sweet cassava**) (also '**manioc**) 2. starch derived from root of this plant: source of tapioca

casserole ('kæsərəʊl) n. 1. fireproof cooking and serving dish 2. kind of stew cooked in this dish —v. 3. cook or cooked in casserole

cassette (kæ'sɛt) n. plastic container for film, magnetic tape etc.

cassia ('kæsɪə) n. 1. tropical plant whose pods yield **cassia pulp,** mild laxative (see also SENNA) 2. lauraceous tree of tropical Asia —**cassia bark** cinnamonlike bark of this tree, used as spice

cassis (kɑː'siːs) n. blackcurrant cordial

cassock ('kæsək) n. long tunic worn by clergymen

cassowary ('kæsəwɛərɪ) n. large flightless bird of NE Aust., New Guinea and adjacent islands

cast (kɑːst) v. 1. throw, fling 2. shed 3. throw down 4. deposit (a vote) 5. allot, as parts in play 6. mould, as metal (**cast** pt./pp.) —n. 7. throw 8. distance thrown 9. squint 10. mould 11. that which is shed or ejected 12. set of actors 13. type, quality

—'**casting** *n.* —'**castaway** *n./a.* ship-wrecked (person) —**casting vote** decisive vote —**cast iron** iron containing so much carbon that it must be cast into shape —**cast-iron** *a.* 1. made of cast iron 2. rigid, unyielding —**cast-off** *a.* abandoned —'**castoff** *n.* 1. person or thing discarded or abandoned 2. *Print.* estimate of amount of space a piece of copy will occupy —**cast steel** steel containing varying amounts of carbon *etc.*, that is cast into shape —**cast off** 1. remove (mooring lines) that hold (vessel) to dock 2. knot (row of stitches, *esp.* final row) in finishing off knitted or woven material 3. *Print.* estimate amount of space that will be taken up by (book *etc.*)

castanets (kæstə'nɛts) *pl.n.* in Spanish dancing, two small curved pieces of wood *etc.* clicked together in hand

caste (kɑːst) *n.* 1. section of society in India 2. social rank

castellated ('kæstɪleɪtɪd) *a.* 1. having turrets and battlements, like castle 2. having indentations similar to battlements —**castel'lation** *n.*

caster ('kɑːstə) *n. see* CASTOR

caster sugar ('kɑːstə) finely powdered sugar (*also* **castor sugar**)

castigate ('kæstɪgeɪt) *vt.* 1. punish, rebuke severely, correct 2. chastise —**casti'gation** *n.* —'**castigator** *n.* —**casti'gatory** *a.*

castle ('kɑːs⁰l) *n.* 1. fortress 2. country mansion 3. chess piece —**castle in the air** *or* **in Spain** hope or desire unlikely to be realized; daydream

castor ('kɑːstə) *n.* 1. bottle with perforated top 2. small swivelled wheel on table leg *etc.*

castor oil vegetable medicinal oil

castrate (kæ'streɪt) *vt.* 1. remove testicles of, deprive of power of generation 2. deprive of vigour, masculinity *etc.* —**cas'tration** *n.*

casual ('kæʒjʊəl) *a.* 1. accidental 2. unforeseen 3. occasional 4. unconcerned 5. informal —'**casually** *adv.* —'**casualty** *n.* 1. person killed or injured in accident, war *etc.* 2. thing lost, destroyed, in accident *etc.*

casuarina (kæsjʊə'raɪnə) *n.* tree of Aust. and E Indies, having jointed leafless branches

casuist ('kæzjʊɪst) *n.* 1. one who studies and solves moral problems 2. quibbler —**casu'istical** *a.* —'**casuistry** *n.*

cat (kæt) *n.* any of various feline animals, including small domesticated furred animal, and lions, tigers *etc.* —'**catkin** *n.* drooping flower spike —'**catty** *a.* spiteful —**cat burglar** burglar who enters buildings by climbing through upper windows *etc.* —'**catcall** *n.* derisive cry —'**catfish** *n.* mainly freshwater fish with catlike whiskers —'**catgut** *n.* strong cord made from dried intestines of sheep *etc.*, used for stringing musical instruments and sports rackets —'**catmint** *n.* scented plant

—'**catnap** *vi./n.* doze —**cat-o'-nine-tails** *n.* whip consisting of nine knotted thongs, used formerly to flog prisoners (*pl.* -**tails**) (*also* **cat**) —**cat's cradle** game played by making patterns with loop of string between fingers —**Cats'eye** *n.* R glass reflector set in road to indicate traffic lanes —**cat's-paw** *n.* 1. person used by another as tool; dupe 2. pattern of ripples on surface of water caused by light wind —'**catwalk** *n.* narrow, raised path or plank

C.A.T. UK College of Advanced Technology

catabolism *or* **katabolism** (kə'tæbəlɪzəm) *n.* breaking down of complex molecules, destructive metabolism

cataclysm ('kætəklɪzəm) *n.* 1. (disastrous) upheaval 2. deluge —**cata'clysmal** *a.*

catacomb ('kætəkəʊm) *n.* 1. underground gallery for burial —*pl.* 2. series of underground tunnels and caves

catafalque ('kætəfælk) *n.* temporary raised platform on which body lies in state before or during funeral

Catalan ('kætəlæn) *n.* 1. language of Catalonia, closely related to Provençal 2. native of Catalonia —*a.* 3. of Catalonia

catalepsy ('kætəlɛpsɪ) *n.* condition of unconsciousness with rigidity of muscles —**cata'leptic** *a.*

catalogue *or U.S.* **catalog** ('kætəlɒg) *n.* 1. descriptive list —*vt.* 2. make such list of 3. enter in catalogue

catalyst ('kætəlɪst) *n.* substance causing or assisting a chemical reaction without taking part in it —'**catalyse** *or U.S.* -**lyze** *vt.* —**ca'talysis** *n.*

catamaran (kætəmə'ræn) *n.* 1. type of sailing boat with twin hulls 2. raft of logs

cataplexy ('kætəplɛksɪ) *n.* 1. sudden temporary paralysis, brought on by intense emotion *etc.* 2. state assumed by animals shamming death —**cata'plectic** *a.*

catapult ('kætəpʌlt) *n.* 1. small forked stick with elastic sling used for throwing stones 2. *Hist.* engine of war for hurling arrows, stones *etc.* 3. launching device —*vt.* 4. shoot forth (as) from catapult —*v.* 5. move precipitately

cataract ('kætərækt) *n.* 1. waterfall 2. downpour 3. disease of eye

catarrh (kə'tɑː) *n.* inflammation of a mucous membrane —**ca'tarrhal** *a.*

catastrophe (kə'tæstrəfɪ) *n.* 1. great disaster, calamity 2. culmination of a tragedy —**cata'strophic** *a.*

catatonia (kætə'təʊnɪə) *n.* form of schizophrenia characterized by stupor, with outbreaks of excitement —**catatonic** (kætə'tɒnɪk) *a./n.*

catch (kætʃ) *vt.* 1. take hold of, seize 2. understand 3. hear 4. contract (disease) 5. be in time for 6. surprise, detect —*vi.* 7. be contagious 8. get entangled 9. begin to burn (**caught** *pt./pp.*) —*n.* 10. seizure 11. thing that holds, stops *etc.* 12. what is caught 13. *inf.* snag, disadvantage 14. form of musical composition 15. thing, person

worth catching —'**catcher** *n.* —'**catching**
a. —'**catchy** *a.* **1.** pleasant, memorable **2.**
tricky —**catchment area 1.** area in which
rainfall collects to form the supply of river
etc. **2.** area from which people are
allocated to a particular school, hospital
etc. —'**catchpenny** *a.* **1.** worthless **2.** made
to sell quickly —**catch phrase** frequently
used phrase, *esp.* associated with particular group *etc.* —'**catchword** *n.* popular
phrase or idea —**catch 22** inescapable
dilemma

catechize *or* -**ise** ('kætɪkaɪz) *vt.* **1.** instruct
by question and answer **2.** question
—**cate'chetical** *a.* —'**catechism** *n.* —'**cat-
echist** *n.* —**cate'chumen** *n.* one under
instruction in Christianity

catechu ('kætɪtʃuː), **cachou,** *or* **cutch**
(kʌtʃ) *n.* astringent resinous substance
obtained from certain tropical plants, and
used in dyeing *etc.*

category ('kætɪgərɪ) *n.* class, order,
division —**cate'gorical** *a.* **1.** positive **2.** of
category —**cate'gorically** *adv.* —'**catego-
rize** *or* -**ise** *vt.*

catenary (kə'tiːnərɪ) *n.* **1.** curve formed by
heavy flexible cord hanging from two
points **2.** hanging cable between pylons
along railway track, from which trolley
wire is suspended —*a.* **3.** of catenary or
suspended chain

catenation (kætɪ'neɪʃən) *n.* chain, or
series as links of chain

cater ('keɪtə) *vi.* provide what is required
or desired, *esp.* food *etc.* —'**caterer** *n.*

caterpillar ('kætəpɪlə) *n.* **1.** hairy grub of
moth or butterfly **2.** type of tractor fitted
with caterpillar wheels —**caterpillar
wheel** articulated belt revolving round two
or more wheels to propel heavy vehicle
over difficult ground

caterwaul ('kætəwɔːl) *vi.* wail, howl

catharsis *or* **katharsis** (kə'θɑːsɪs) *n.* **1.**
purging of emotions through evocation of
pity and fear, as in tragedy **2.** *Psychoanal.*
bringing repressed ideas or experiences to
consciousness, by means of free association *etc.* **3.** purgation, *esp.* of bowels
—**ca'thartic** *a.* **1.** purgative **2.** effecting
catharsis —*n.* **3.** purgative drug or agent

Cathay (kæ'θeɪ) *n. Lit., obs.* China

cathedral (kə'θiːdrəl) *n.* **1.** principal
church of diocese —*a.* **2.** pert. to,
containing cathedral

Catherine wheel ('kæθrɪn) **1.** firework
which rotates, producing sparks **2.** circular
window having ribs radiating from centre

catheter ('kæθɪtə) *n. Med.* long slender
flexible tube for inserting into bodily
cavity for introducing or withdrawing fluid

cathode ('kæθəʊd) *n.* negative electrode
—**cathode rays** stream of electrons
—**cathode-ray tube** vacuum tube in which
beam of electrons is focused on to
fluorescent screen to give visible spot of
light

catholic ('kæθəlɪk, 'kæθlɪk) *a.* **1.** universal
2. including whole body of Christians **3.**

(C-) relating to R.C. Church —*n.* **4.** (C-)
adherent of R.C. Church —**Ca'tholicism** *n.*
—**catho'licity** *n.* —**ca'tholicize** *or* -**cise** *v.*

cation ('kætaɪən) *n.* positively charged ion;
ion attracted to cathode during electrolysis —**cati'onic** *a.*

cattle ('kætˀl) *pl.n.* beasts of pasture, *esp.*
oxen, cows —**cattle-grid** *n.* heavy grid
over ditch in road to prevent passage of
livestock —'**cattleman** *n.*

Caucasoid ('kɔːkəzɔɪd) *a.* of, pert. to, light-
complexioned racial group of mankind
—**Cau'casian** *a.* **1.** Caucasoid **2.** of
Caucasus in SW Soviet Union —*n.* **3.**
member of Caucasoid race; White person
4. native of Caucasus

caucus ('kɔːkəs) *n.* group, meeting, *esp.* of
members of political party, with power to
decide policy *etc.*

caudal ('kɔːdˀl) *a.* **1.** *Anat.* of posterior part
of body **2.** *Zool.* resembling or in position
of tail —'**caudate** *or* '**caudated** *a.* having
tail

caudle ('kɔːdˀl) *n.* hot spiced wine drink
made with gruel, formerly used medicinally

caught (kɔːt) *pt./pp.* of CATCH

caul (kɔːl) *n. Anat.* portion of amniotic sac
sometimes covering child's head at birth

cauldron *or* **caldron** ('kɔːldrən) *n.* large
pot used for boiling

cauliflower ('kɒlɪflaʊə) *n.* variety of
cabbage with edible white flowering head
—**cauliflower ear** permanent distortion of
ear as result of ruptures of blood vessels:
usu. caused by blows received in boxing

caulk *or* **calk** (kɔːk) *vt.* stop up (cracks)
with waterproof filler —'**caulker** *n.*
—'**caulking** *n.*

cause (kɔːz) *n.* **1.** that which produces an
effect **2.** reason, origin **3.** motive, purpose
4. charity, movement **5.** lawsuit —*vt.* **6.**
bring about, make happen —'**causal** *a.*
—**cau'sality** *n.* —**cau'sation** *n.* —**causative** *a.* **1.** *Gram.* relating to form or class of
verbs that express causation **2.** (*oft.* with
of) producing effect —*n.* **3.** causative form
or class of verbs —'**causeless** *a.* groundless

cause célèbre ('kɔːz sə'lɛbrə) *Fr.* famous
case

causerie ('kəʊzərɪ) *n.* **1.** informal talk **2.**
conversational piece of writing

causeway ('kɔːzweɪ) *n.* **1.** raised way over
marsh *etc.* **2.** paved street

caustic ('kɔːstɪk) *a.* **1.** burning **2.** bitter,
severe —*n.* **3.** corrosive substance
—'**caustically** *adv.* —**caustic soda** *see*
sodium hydroxide *at* SODIUM

cauterize *or* -**ise** ('kɔːtəraɪz) *vt.* burn with
caustic or hot iron —**cauteri'zation** *or*
-**i'sation** *n.* —'**cautery** *n.*

caution ('kɔːʃən) *n.* **1.** heedfulness, care **2.**
warning —*vt.* **3.** warn —'**cautionary** *a.*
containing warning or precept —'**cautious** *a.* —'**cautiously** *adv.* —'**cautious-
ness** *n.*

cavalcade (kævəl'keɪd) *n.* column or procession of riders

cavalier (kævə'lɪə) *a.* 1. careless, disdainful —*n.* 2. courtly gentleman 3. *obs.* horseman 4. (C-) adherent of Charles I in English Civil War —**cava'lierly** *adv.*

cavalry ('kævəlrɪ) *n.* mounted troops

cave (keɪv) *n.* 1. hollow place in the earth 2. den —**cavern** ('kævᵊn) *n.* deep cave —**cavernous** ('kævənəs) *a.* —**cavernously** ('kævənəslɪ) *adv.* —**caving** *n.* sport of exploring caves —**cavity** ('kævɪtɪ) *n.* hollow —**caveman** *n.* prehistoric cave dweller —**cave in** 1. fall in 2. submit 3. give in

caveat ('keɪvɪæt, 'kæv-) *n.* 1. *Law* formal notice requesting court not to take action without warning person lodging caveat 2. a caution

caviar *or* **caviare** ('kævɪɑː, kævɪ'ɑː) *n.* salted sturgeon roe

cavil ('kævɪl) *vi.* find fault without sufficient reason, make trifling objections (-ll-) —'**caviller** *n.* —'**cavilling** *a.*

cavort (kə'vɔːt) *vi.* prance, frisk

cavy ('keɪvɪ) *n.* small S Amer. rodent

caw (kɔː) *n.* 1. crow's cry —*vi.* 2. cry so

cay (keɪ, kiː) *n.* low island or bank composed of sand and coral fragments

cayenne pepper (keɪ'ɛn) pungent red pepper

cayman *or* **caiman** ('keɪmən) *n.* tropical American crocodilian similar to alligator (*pl.* -s)

Cb *Chem.* columbium

CB Citizens' Band

C.B. Companion of the (Order of the) Bath

CBC Canadian Broadcasting Corporation

C.B.E. Commander of the (Order of the) British Empire

C.B.I. Confederation of British Industry

cc *or* **c.c.** 1. carbon copy or copies 2. cubic centimetre

cc. chapters

C.C. 1. City Council 2. County Council 3. Cricket Club

cd candela

Cd *Chem.* cadmium

C.D. 1. Civil Defence (Corps) 2. compact disc 3. Corps Diplomatique (Diplomatic Corps)

Cdr. *Mil.* Commander

Ce *Chem.* cerium

cease (siːs) *v.* bring or come to an end —'**ceaseless** *a.* —'**ceaselessly** *adv.*

cedar ('siːdə) *n.* 1. large evergreen tree 2. its wood

cede (siːd) *v.* yield, give up, transfer, *esp.* of territory

cedilla (sɪ'dɪlə) *n.* hooklike mark (,) placed under a letter *c* to show the sound of *s*

Ceefax ('siːfæks) *n.* R B.B.C. teletext service

ceilidh ('keɪlɪ) *n.* informal social gathering for singing and dancing, *esp.* in Scotland

ceiling ('siːlɪŋ) *n.* 1. inner, upper surface of a room 2. maximum price, wage *etc.* 3. *Met.* lower level of clouds 4. *Aviation* limit of height to which aircraft can climb —**ceil** *vt.* line (room), *esp.* with plaster

celandine ('sɛləndaɪn) *n.* yellow wild flower

celebrate ('sɛlɪbreɪt) *v.* 1. rejoice or have festivities to mark (happy day, event *etc.*) —*vt.* 2. observe (birthday *etc.*) 3. perform (religious ceremony *etc.*) 4. praise publicly —'**celebrant** *n.* —'**celebrated** *a.* famous —**cele'bration** *n.* —ce'**lebrity** *n.* 1. famous person 2. fame

celeriac (sɪ'lɛrɪæk) *n.* variety of celery with large turniplike root, used as vegetable

celerity (sɪ'lɛrɪtɪ) *n.* swiftness

celery ('sɛlərɪ) *n.* vegetable with long juicy edible stalks

celestial (sɪ'lɛstɪəl) *a.* 1. heavenly, divine 2. of the sky —**celestial equator** great circle lying on celestial sphere, plane of which is perpendicular to line joining north and south celestial poles (*also* **equi'noctial, equinoctial circle**) —**celestial sphere** imaginary sphere of infinitely large radius enclosing universe

celibacy ('sɛlɪbəsɪ) *n.* single life, unmarried state —'**celibate** *n./a.*

cell (sɛl) *n.* 1. small room, *esp.* in prison 2. small cavity 3. minute, basic unit of living matter 4. device converting chemical energy into electrical energy 5. small local group operating as nucleus of larger political or religious organization —'**cellular** *a.* —'**cellule** *n.* small cell

cellar ('sɛlə) *n.* 1. underground room for storage 2. stock of wine —'**cellarage** *n.* —'**cellarer** *n.* monastic official responsible for food *etc.* —**cella'ret** *n.* cabinet for wine

cello ('tʃɛləʊ) *n.* stringed instrument of violin family

cellophane ('sɛləfeɪn) *n.* R transparent wrapping

cellulite ('sɛljʊlaɪt) *n.* subcutaneous fat alleged to resist dieting

Celluloid ('sɛljʊlɔɪd) *n.* 1. R synthetic plastic substance with wide range of uses 2. coating of photographic film 3. cinema film

cellulose ('sɛljʊləʊz, -ləʊs) *n.* 1. substance of vegetable cell wall 2. group of carbohydrates 3. varnish

Celsius ('sɛlsɪəs) *a./n.* (of) scale of temperature from 0° (melting point of ice) to 100° (boiling point of water)

Celtic ('kɛltɪk, 'sɛl-) *or* **Keltic** ('kɛltɪk) *n.* 1. branch of languages including Gaelic and Welsh —*a.* 2. of Celtic peoples or languages —**Celt** *or* **Kelt** *n.* 1. person who speaks a Celtic language 2. member of Indo-European people who in pre-Roman times inhabited Brit., Gaul and Spain

cement (sɪ'mɛnt) *n.* 1. fine mortar 2. adhesive, glue —*vt.* 3. unite with cement 4. join firmly

cemetery ('sɛmɪtrɪ) *n*. burial ground, *esp.* other than churchyard

cenobite ('si:nəʊbaɪt) *n. see* CŒNOBITE

cenotaph ('sɛnətɑːf) *n*. monument to person buried elsewhere

Cenozoic (si:nəʊ'zəʊɪk) *see* CAINOZOIC

censer ('sɛnsə) *n*. pan in which incense is burned

censor ('sɛnsə) *n*. **1.** one authorized to examine films, books *etc*. and suppress all or part if considered morally or otherwise unacceptable —*vt*. **2.** ban or cut portions of (film *etc*.) **3.** act as censor of (behaviour *etc*.) —**cen'sorial** *a*. of censor —**cen'sorious** *a*. fault-finding —**cen'soriousness** *n*. —'**censorship** *n*.

censure ('sɛnʃə) *n*. **1.** blame **2.** harsh criticism —*vt*. **3.** blame **4.** criticize harshly

census ('sɛnsəs) *n*. official counting of people, things *etc*.

cent (sɛnt) *n*. hundredth part of dollar *etc*.

cent. 1. centigrade **2.** central **3.** century

centaur ('sɛntɔː) *n*. mythical creature, half man, half horse

centenary (sɛn'ti:nərɪ) *n*. **1.** 100 years **2.** celebration of hundredth anniversary —*a*. **3.** pert. to a hundred —**cente'narian** *n*. one a hundred years old —**centennial** (sɛn-'tɛnɪəl) *a*. lasting, happening every hundred years

centi- *or before vowel* **cent-** (*comb. form*) **1.** one hundredth, as in *centimetre* **2.** rare hundred, as in *centipede*

centigrade ('sɛntɪɡreɪd) *a*. **1.** Celsius **2.** having one hundred degrees

centigram *or* **centigramme** ('sɛntɪɡræm) *n*. hundredth part of gram

centilitre *or U.S.* **centiliter** ('sɛntɪliːtə) *n*. hundredth part of litre

centime ('sɒntiːm; *Fr.* sɑ̃'tim) *n*. monetary unit of France *etc*., worth one hundredth of standard unit of currency

centimetre *or U.S.* **centimeter** ('sɛntɪmiːtə) *n*. hundredth part of metre —**centimetre-gram-second** *n. see* CGS UNITS

centipede ('sɛntɪpiːd) *n*. small segmented animal with many legs

CENTO ('sɛntəʊ) Central Treaty Organization

centre *or U.S.* **center** ('sɛntə) *n*. **1.** midpoint **2.** pivot, axis **3.** point to or from which things move or are drawn **4.** place for specific organization or activity —'**central** *a*. —**cen'trality** *n*. —**centrali'zation** *or* **-li'sation** *n*. —'**centralize** *or* **-lise** *vt*. **1.** bring to a centre **2.** concentrate under one control —'**centrally** *adv*. —'**centric** *a*. —**cen'trifugal** *a*. tending from centre —**cen'trifuge** *n*. **1.** rotating machine that separates liquids from solids or other liquids by centrifugal force **2.** rotating device for subjecting human beings or animals to varying accelerations —*vt*. **3.** subject to action of centrifuge —**cen'tripetal** *a*. tending towards centre —'**centrist** *n*. person holding moderate political views —**central bank** national

bank that does business mainly with government and other banks —**central heating** method of heating building from one central source —**central processing unit** part of computer that performs logical and arithmetical operations on data —**central reserve** *or* **reservation** *UK* strip that separates two sides of motorway or dual carriageway —'**centreboard** *n*. supplementary keel for sailing vessel —'**centrefold** *or U.S.* '**centerfold** *n*. large coloured illustration folded to form central spread of magazine —**centre forward** *Soccer, hockey etc*. central forward in attack —**centre half** *Soccer* defender in middle of defence —**centre of gravity** point through which resultant of gravitational forces on body always acts —'**centrepiece** *n*. object used as centre of something, *esp*. for decoration

centuplicate (sɛn'tjuːplɪkeɪt) *vt*. **1.** increase 100 times —*a*. (sɛn'tjuːplɪkɪt) **2.** increased hundredfold —*n*. (sɛn'tjuːplɪkɪt) **3.** one hundredfold (*also* '**centuple**)

centurion (sɛn'tjʊərɪən) *n*. Roman commander of 100 men

century ('sɛntʃərɪ) *n*. **1.** 100 years **2.** any set of 100

cephalic (sɪ'fælɪk) *a*. **1.** of head **2.** situated in, on or near head

cephalopod ('sɛfələpɒd) *n*. any of various marine molluscs characterized by well-developed head and eyes and ring of sucker-bearing tentacles, including octopus

ceramic (sɪ'ræmɪk) *n*. **1.** hard brittle material of baked clay **2.** object made of this —*pl*. **3.** (*with sing. v.*) art, techniques of making ceramic objects **4.** such objects —*a*. **5.** of ceramic or ceramics

cere (sɪə) *n*. soft waxy swelling, containing nostrils, at base of upper beak, as in parrot

cereal ('sɪərɪəl) *n*. **1.** any edible grain, *eg* wheat, rice *etc*. **2.** (breakfast) food made from grain —*a*. **3.** of cereal

cerebellum (sɛrɪ'bɛləm) *n*. one of major divisions of vertebrate brain whose function is coordination of voluntary movements (*pl*. **-s, -la** (-lə))

cerebrum ('sɛrɪbrəm) *n*. **1.** anterior portion of brain of vertebrates: dominant part of brain in man, associated with intellectual function *etc*. **2.** brain as whole (*pl*. **-s, -bra** (-brə)) —**cerebral** ('sɛrɪbrəl; *U.S. also* sə'riːbrəl) *a*. pert. to brain —'**cerebrate** *vi. usu. jocular* use the mind; think; ponder; consider —**cere'bration** *n*. —**cerebro'spinal** *a*. of brain and spinal cord —**cerebro'vascular** *a*. of blood vessels and blood supply of brain —**cerebral palsy** impairment of muscular function and weakness of limbs, caused by damage to brain before or during birth

cerecloth ('sɪəklɒθ) *n*. waxed waterproof cloth formerly used for shrouds

ceremony ('sɛrɪmənɪ) *n*. **1.** formal observance **2.** sacred rite **3.** courteous act —**cere'monial** *a./n*. —**cere'monially** *adv*.

—cere'monious a. —cere'moniously adv. —cere'moniousness n.

cerise (sə'riːz, -'riːs) n./a. clear, pinkish red

cerium ('sɪərɪəm) n. steel-grey element of lanthanide series of metals, used in lighter flints

CERN (sɜːn) Conseil Européen pour la Recherche Nucléaire; organization of European states with centre in Geneva, for research in high-energy particle physics

cert (sɜːt) n. inf. something certain (esp. in a dead cert)

cert. 1. certificate 2. certification 3. certified

certain ('sɜːtªn) a. 1. sure 2. settled, inevitable 3. some, one 4. of moderate (quantity, degree etc.) —'certainly adv. —'certainty n. —'certitude n. confidence

certes ('sɜːtiz) adv. obs. with certainty; truly

certify ('sɜːtɪfaɪ) vt. 1. declare formally 2. endorse, guarantee 3. declare legally insane (-fied, -fying) —certificate (sə'tɪfɪkɪt) n. 1. written declaration —vt. (sə'tɪfɪkeɪt) 2. authorize by or present with official document —certifi'cation n. —'certified a. 1. holding or guaranteed by certificate 2. endorsed, guaranteed 3. (of person) declared legally insane —'certifier n. —Certificate of Secondary Education UK examination the first grade pass of which is equivalent to GCE O level

cerulean (sɪ'ruːlɪən) a. sky-blue

cervix ('sɜːvɪks) n. neck, esp. of womb —'cervical a. —cervical smear Med. smear taken from neck of uterus for detection of cancer (see also PAP TEST)

cesium ('siːzɪəm) n. US caesium

cessation (sɛ'seɪʃən) n. ceasing, stopping; pause

cession ('sɛʃən) n. yielding up

cesspool ('sɛspuːl) or cesspit ('sɛspɪt) n. pit in which filthy water collects, receptacle for sewage

cestus or caestus ('sɛstəs) n. in classical Roman boxing, pugilist's gauntlet of bull's hide studded with metal (pl. -tus, -es)

cesura (sɪ'zjʊərə) n. Prosody see CAESURA

cetacean (sɪ'teɪʃən) a. 1. of order of aquatic mammals having no hind limbs and blowhole for breathing: includes toothed and whalebone whales (also ce'taceous) —n. 2. whale

cetane ('siːteɪn) n. colourless liquid hydrocarbon used in determination of cetane number of diesel fuel (also 'hexadecane) —cetane number measure of quality of diesel fuel expressed as percentage of cetane (also cetane rating)

Cf Chem. californium

cf. confer (Lat., compare)

c/f carried forward

CFL Canadian Football League

cg centigram

cgs units metric system of units based on centimetre, gram, second

ch. 1. chapter 2. church

cha-cha-cha (tʃɑːtʃɑː'tʃɑː) or cha-cha n. 1. modern ballroom dance from Latin Amer. 2. music composed for this dance —vi. 3. perform this dance

chafe (tʃeɪf) vt. 1. make sore or worn by rubbing 2. make warm by rubbing 3. vex, irritate —chafing dish vessel with heating apparatus beneath it, for cooking or keeping food warm at table

chafer ('tʃeɪfə) n. any of various beetles, such as cockchafer

chaff (tʃɑːf) n. 1. husks of corn 2. worthless matter 3. banter —vt. 4. tease good-naturedly

chaffer ('tʃæfə) vi. 1. haggle, bargain —n. 2. bargaining

chaffinch ('tʃæfɪntʃ) n. small songbird

chagrin ('ʃægrɪn) n. 1. vexation, disappointment —vt. 2. embarrass 3. annoy 4. disappoint

chain (tʃeɪn) n. 1. series of connected links or rings 2. thing that binds 3. connected series of things or events 4. surveyor's measure —vt. 5. fasten with chain 6. confine 7. restrain —chain armour —chain gang US group of prisoners chained together —chain mail —chain reaction —chain smoker one who smokes cigarettes etc. continuously, esp. lighting one from preceding one —chain stitch —chain store

chair (tʃɛə) n. 1. movable seat, with back, for one person 2. seat of authority 3. professorship 4. iron support for rail on railway —vt. 5. preside over 6. carry in triumph —'chairlift n. series of chairs fixed to cable for conveying people (esp. skiers) up mountain —'chairman n. one who presides over meeting —'chairmanship n.

chaise (ʃeɪz) n. light horse-drawn carriage —chaise longue (lɒŋ) sofa

chalcedony (kæl'sɛdənɪ) n. whitish or bluish-white variety of quartz

chalet ('ʃæleɪ) n. Swiss wooden house

chalice ('tʃælɪs) n. 1. Poet. cup; bowl 2. communion cup

chalk (tʃɔːk) n. 1. white substance, carbonate of lime 2. crayon —v. 3. rub, draw, mark with chalk —'chalkiness n. —'chalky a.

challenge ('tʃælɪndʒ) vt. 1. call to fight or account 2. dispute 3. stimulate 4. object to 5. claim —n. 6. call to engage in fight etc. 7. questioning of statement etc. 8. demanding situation etc. 9. demand by sentry etc. for identification or password —'challenger n. —'challenging a. difficult but stimulating

chamber ('tʃeɪmbə) n. 1. room for assembly 2. assembly, body of men 3. compartment 4. cavity 5. obs. room —pl. 6. office or apartments of barrister 7. lodgings —chamberlain ('tʃeɪmbəlɪn) n. official at court of a monarch having charge of domestic and ceremonial affairs —'chambermaid n. servant with care of bedrooms —**chamber music** music for performance by a few instruments —**chamber of commerce** organization composed mainly of local businessmen to promote and protect their interests —**chamber pot** vessel for urine

chameleon (kə'mi:liən) n. 1. small lizard famous for its power of changing colour 2. changeable person

chamfer ('tʃæmfə) vt. 1. groove 2. bevel 3. flute —n. 4. groove

chamois ('ʃæmwɑː) n. 1. goatlike mountain antelope 2. ('ʃæmɪ) soft pliable leather

champ[1] (tʃæmp) v. 1. munch (food) noisily, as horse 2. be nervous, impatient

champ[2] (tʃæmp) n. inf. champion

champagne (ʃæm'peɪn) n. light, sparkling white wine of several varieties

champers ('ʃæmpəz) n. sl. champagne

champion ('tʃæmpiən) n. 1. one that excels all others 2. defender of a cause 3. one who fights for another 4. hero —vt. 5. fight for, maintain —'**championship** n.

chance (tʃɑːns) n. 1. unpredictable course of events 2. fortune, luck 3. opportunity 4. possibility 5. risk 6. probability —vt. 7. risk —vi. 8. happen —a. 9. casual, unexpected —'**chancy** a. risky

chancel ('tʃɑːnsəl) n. part of church where altar is

chancellor ('tʃɑːnsələ) n. 1. high officer of state 2. head of university —'**chancellorship** n. —'**chancellery** or '**chancellory** n. —**Chancellor of the Exchequer** UK cabinet minister responsible for finance

chancery ('tʃɑːnsərɪ) n. division of British High Court of Justice

chancre ('ʃæŋkə) n. Pathol. small hard growth: first sign of syphilis —'**chancrous** a.

chandelier (ʃændɪ'lɪə) n. hanging frame with branches for holding lights

chandler ('tʃɑːndlə) n. dealer in ropes, ships' supplies etc.

change (tʃeɪndʒ) v. 1. alter, make or become different 2. put on (different clothes, fresh coverings) —vt. 3. put or give for another 4. exchange, interchange —n. 5. alteration, variation 6. variety 7. conversion of money 8. small money, coins 9. balance received on payment —changea'bility n. —'**changeable** a. —'**changeably** adv. —'**changeful** a. —'**changeless** a. —'**changeling** n. child believed substituted for another by fairies —**change of life** menopause

channel ('tʃænəl) n. 1. bed of stream 2. strait 3. deeper part of strait, bay, harbour 4. groove 5. means of passing or conveying 6. band of radio frequencies 7. television broadcasting station —vt. 8. groove, furrow 9. guide, convey

chant (tʃɑːnt) n. 1. simple song or melody 2. rhythmic or repetitious slogan —vi. 3. sing or utter chant 4. speak monotonously or repetitiously

chanticleer (tʃæntɪ'klɪə) or **chantecler** (tʃæntɪ'klɛə) n. cock

chantry ('tʃɑːntrɪ) n. Christianity 1. endowment for singing of Masses for soul of founder 2. chapel or altar so endowed

chanty ('ʃæntɪ, 'tʃæn-) n. see SHANTY[2]

chaos ('keɪɒs) n. 1. disorder, confusion 2. state of universe before Creation —cha·'otic a.

chap[1] (tʃæp) v. (of skin) become dry, raw and cracked, esp. by exposure to cold and wind (-pp-) —**chapped** a.

chap[2] (tʃæp) n. inf. fellow, man

chapatti or **chapati** (tʃə'pætɪ, -'pɑːtɪ) n. in Indian cookery, flat unleavened bread resembling pancake (pl. -ti, -s, -es)

chapel ('tʃæpəl) n. 1. private church 2. subordinate place of worship 3. division of church with its own altar 4. Nonconformist place of worship 5. (meeting of) members of trade union in particular newspaper office, printing house etc.

chaperon or **chaperone** ('ʃæpərəʊn) n. 1. one who attends young unmarried lady in public as protector —vt. 2. attend in this way

chaplain ('tʃæplɪn) n. clergyman attached to chapel, regiment, warship, institution etc. —'**chaplaincy** n. his office

chaplet ('tʃæplɪt) n. 1. ornamental wreath of flowers worn on head 2. string of beads 3. R.C.Ch. string of prayer beads constituting one third of rosary; prayers counted on this string 4. narrow moulding in form of string of beads

chapman ('tʃæpmən) n. obs. trader, esp. itinerant pedlar

chappie ('tʃæpɪ) n. inf. see CHAP[2]

chaps (tʃæps, ʃæps) pl.n. cowboy's leggings of thick leather

chapter ('tʃæptə) n. 1. division of book 2. section, heading 3. assembly of clergy, bishop's council etc. 4. organized branch of society, fraternity —'**chapterhouse** n.

char[1] (tʃɑː) vt. scorch, burn to charcoal (-rr-) —**charred** a.

char[2] (tʃɑː) inf. n. 1. charwoman —vi. 2. do cleaning as job (-rr-)

char[3] or **charr** (tʃɑː) n. troutlike small fish

char[4] (tʃɑː) n. sl. tea

charabanc ('ʃærəbæŋ) n. UK coach, esp. for sightseeing

character ('kærɪktə) n. 1. nature 2. total of qualities making up individuality 3. moral qualities 4. reputation, esp. good one 5. statement of qualities of person 6. an eccentric 7. personality in play or novel 8. letter, sign or any distinctive mark 9. essential feature —character'istic n./a. —character'istically adv. —characteri'zation or -i'sation n. —'**characterize** or -ise vt. 1. mark out, distinguish 2. describe by peculiar qualities —'**characterless** a.

charade (ʃə'rɑːd) n. 1. absurd act 2. travesty —pl. 3. word-guessing parlour game with syllables of word acted

charcoal ('tʃɑːkəʊl) n. 1. black residue of wood, bones etc., produced by smothered burning 2. charred wood —**charcoal-burner** n.

chard (tʃɑːd) *n.* beet with large succulent leaves and thick stalks, used as vegetable (*also* **Swiss chard**)

charge (tʃɑːdʒ) *vt.* 1. ask as price 2. bring accusation against 3. lay task on 4. command 5. attack 6. deliver injunction against 7. fill with electricity 8. fill, load —*vi.* 9. make onrush, attack —*n.* 10. cost, price 11. accusation 12. attack, onrush 13. command, exhortation 14. accumulation of electricity —*pl.* 15. expenses —'**chargeable** *a.* —'**charger** *n.* 1. strong, fast battle horse 2. that which charges, *esp.* electrically

chargé d'affaires ('ʃɑːʒeɪ dæ'feə) 1. temporary head of diplomatic mission in absence of ambassador or minister 2. head of diplomatic mission of lowest level (*pl.* **chargés d'affaires** ('ʃɑːʒeɪ, -ʒeɪz))

chariot ('tʃærɪət) *n.* 1. two-wheeled car used in ancient fighting 2. state carriage —**chario'teer** *n.*

charisma (kə'rɪzmə) *or* **charism** ('kærɪzəm) *n.* special power of individual to inspire fascination, loyalty *etc.* —**char is'matic** *a.*

charity ('tʃærɪtɪ) *n.* 1. the giving of help, money *etc.* to those in need 2. organization for doing this 3. the money *etc.* given 4. love, kindness 5. disposition to think kindly of others —'**charitable** *a.* —'**charitably** *adv.*

charlatan ('ʃɑːlət'n) *n.* quack, impostor —'**charlatanry** *n.*

Charles's Wain ('tʃɑːlzɪz weɪn) the Plough

charleston ('tʃɑːlstən) *n.* fast, rhythmic dance of 1920s

charlie ('tʃɑːlɪ) *n. inf.* fool

charlock ('tʃɑːlɒk) *n.* weedy Eurasian plant with yellow flowers (*also* **wild mustard**)

charlotte ('ʃɑːlət) *n.* 1. dessert made with fruit and bread or cake crumbs, sponge cake *etc.* 2. cold dessert made with sponge fingers, cream *etc.* (*also* **charlotte russe**)

charm (tʃɑːm) *n.* 1. attractiveness 2. anything that fascinates 3. amulet 4. magic spell —*vt.* 5. bewitch 6. delight, attract —**charmed** *a.* —'**charmer** *n.* —'**charming** *a.*

charnel house ('tʃɑːn'l) *esp.* formerly, vault for bones of the dead

chart (tʃɑːt) *n.* 1. map of sea 2. diagram or tabulated statement —*vt.* 3. map 4. represent on chart —**the charts** *inf.* lists produced weekly of best-selling pop records

charter ('tʃɑːtə) *n.* 1. document granting privileges *etc.* 2. patent —*vt.* 3. let or hire 4. establish by charter

Chartism ('tʃɑːtɪzəm) *n. English hist.* movement to achieve certain political reforms, demand for which was embodied in charters presented to Parliament —'**Chartist** *n./a.*

chartreuse (ʃɑː'trɜːz; *Fr.* ʃarˈtrøːz) *n.* 1. either of two liqueurs, green or yellow, made from herbs 2. yellowish-green colour

charwoman ('tʃɑːwumən) *n.* woman paid to clean office, house *etc.*

chary ('tʃeərɪ) *a.* cautious, sparing —'**charily** *adv.* —'**chariness** *n.* caution

Charybdis (kə'rɪbdɪs) *n.* ship-devouring monster in classical mythology, identified with whirlpool off coast of Sicily

chase[1] (tʃeɪs) *vt.* 1. hunt, pursue 2. drive (from, away, into *etc.*) —*n.* 3. pursuit, hunting 4. the hunted 5. hunting ground —'**chaser** *n.* drink of beer, soda *etc.* taken after spirit

chase[2] (tʃeɪs) *vt.* engrave —'**chaser** *n.* —'**chasing** *n.*

chase[3] (tʃeɪs) *n.* 1. *Letterpress print.* rectangular steel frame into which metal type and blocks are locked for printing 2. part of cannon enclosing bore 3. groove or channel, *esp.* to take pipe *etc.* —*vt.* 4. cut groove, furrow or flute in (surface *etc.*) (*also* '**chamfer**)

chasm ('kæzəm) *n.* 1. deep cleft, fissure 2. abyss

chassé ('ʃæseɪ) *n.* 1. rapid gliding step used in dancing —*vi.* 2. perform the step

chassis ('ʃæsɪ) *n.* 1. framework, wheels and machinery of motor vehicle excluding body and coachwork 2. underframe of aircraft (*pl.* **-sis** (-sɪz))

chaste (tʃeɪst) *a.* 1. virginal 2. pure 3. modest 4. virtuous —'**chastely** *adv.* —**chastity** ('tʃæstɪtɪ) *n.*

chasten ('tʃeɪs'n) *vt.* 1. correct by punishment 2. restrain, subdue —'**chastened** *a.* —**chastise** (tʃæs'taɪz) *vt.* inflict punishment on —**chastisement** (tʃæs-'taɪzmənt) *n.*

chasuble ('tʃæzjub'l) *n.* priest's long sleeveless outer vestment

chat[1] (tʃæt) *vi.* 1. talk idly or familiarly (*-tt-*) —*n.* 2. familiar idle talk —'**chattily** *adv.* —'**chatty** *a.*

chat[2] (tʃæt) *n.* any of various European songbirds, Amer. warblers, Aust. wrens

chateau *or* **château** ('ʃætəu) *n. esp.* in France, castle, country house (*pl.* **-teaux** (-təu, -təuz), **-s**)

chatelaine ('ʃætəleɪn; *Fr.* ʃat'lɛn) *n.* 1. *esp.* formerly, mistress of castle or large household 2. chain or clasp worn at waist by women in 16th to 19th century, with handkerchief *etc.* attached

chattel ('tʃæt'l) *n.* (*usu. pl.*) any movable property

chatter ('tʃætə) *vi.* 1. talk idly or rapidly 2. rattle teeth —*n.* 3. idle talk —'**chatterer** *n.* —'**chattering** *n.* —'**chatterbox** *n.* one who chatters incessantly

chauffeur ('ʃəufə, ʃəu'fɜː) *n.* paid driver of motorcar (**chauf'feuse** *fem.*)

chauvinism ('ʃəuvɪnɪzəm) *n.* 1. aggressive patriotism 2. smug sense of superiority

cheap (tʃiːp) *a.* 1. low in price 2. inexpensive 3. easily obtained 4. of little value or estimation 5. mean, inferior —'**cheapen** *vt.* —'**cheaply** *adv.* —'**cheapness** *n.* —**cheap-jack** *inf.* *n.* 1. person who sells cheap and shoddy goods —*a.* 2.

shoddy, inferior —'**cheapskate** n. inf. miserly person

cheat (tʃiːt) vt. 1. deceive, defraud, swindle, impose upon —vi. 2. practise deceit to gain advantage —n. 3. fraud

check (tʃek) vt. 1. stop 2. restrain 3. hinder 4. repress 5. control 6. examine for accuracy, quality etc. —n. 7. repulse 8. stoppage 9. restraint 10. brief examination for correctness or accuracy 11. pattern of squares on fabric 12. threat to king at chess —'**checkmate** n. 1. Chess final winning move 2. any overthrow, defeat —vt. 3. Chess place (opponent's king) in checkmate 4. defeat —'**checkout** n. counter in supermarket where customers pay —'**checkup** n. examination (esp. medical) to see if all is in order

checked (tʃekt) a. having pattern of small squares

checker ('tʃekə) see CHEQUER

Cheddar ('tʃedə) n. (sometimes c-) smooth hard orange or whitish cheese

cheek (tʃiːk) n. 1. side of face below eye 2. inf. impudence —vt. 3. inf. address impudently —'**cheeky** a.

cheep (tʃiːp) vi./n. (utter) high-pitched cry, as of young bird

cheer (tʃiə) vt. 1. comfort 2. gladden 3. encourage by shouts —vi. 4. shout applause —n. 5. shout of approval 6. happiness, good spirits 7. mood 8. obs. rich food —'**cheerful** a. —'**cheerfully** adv. —'**cheerfulness** n. —'**cheerily** adv. —'**cheerless** a. —'**cheerlessness** n. —**cheers** interj. inf., chiefly UK 1. drinking toast 2. goodbye, cheerio 3. thanks —'**cheery** a. —**three cheers** three shouts of hurrah in unison to honour someone or celebrate something

cheerio (tʃɪərɪˈəʊ) inf. interj. 1. chiefly UK farewell greeting 2. chiefly UK drinking toast —n. 3. NZ small sausage

cheese (tʃiːz) n. curd of milk coagulated, separated from whey and pressed —'**cheesiness** n. —'**cheesy** a. —'**cheeseburger** n. hamburger cooked with cheese on top —'**cheesecake** n. 1. tart filled with cheese, esp. cream cheese, cream, sugar etc. 2. sl. women displayed for their sex appeal, as in photographs or films —'**cheesecloth** n. loosely woven cotton cloth —'**cheeseparing** a. mean —**cheesed off** UK sl. bored; disgusted; angry

cheetah or **chetah** ('tʃiːtə) n. large, swift, spotted feline animal

chef (ʃef) n. head cook, esp. in restaurant

chef-d'œuvre (ʃɛ'dœːvr) Fr. masterpiece

chem. 1. chemical 2. chemistry

chemin de fer (ʃəˈmæn də ˈfɛə) gambling game, variation of baccarat

chemise (ʃəˈmiːz) n. loose-fitting dress hanging straight from shoulders; loose shirtlike undergarment (also **shift**)

chemistry ('kemɪstrɪ) n. science concerned with properties of substances and their combinations and reactions —'**chemical** n./a. —'**chemically** adv.

—'**chemist** n. 1. qualified dispenser of prescribed medicines 2. shop that sells medicines etc. 3. one trained in chemistry —**chemical engineer** —**chemical engineering** engineering concerned with design and manufacture of plant used in industrial chemical processes —**chemical warfare** warfare using asphyxiating gases, poisons etc.

chemotherapy (kɛməʊˈθɛrəpɪ) n. treatment of disease by chemical means

chemurgy ('kɛmɜːdʒɪ) n. branch of applied chemistry devoted to the development of agricultural products —che'**murgic(al)** a.

chenille (ʃəˈniːl) n. soft cord, fabric of silk or worsted

cheongsam ('tʃɔːŋˈsæm) n. (Chinese) straight dress with slit in one side of skirt

cheque or U.S. **check** (tʃek) n. 1. written order to banker to pay money from one's account 2. printed slip of paper used for this —'**chequebook** or U.S. '**checkbook** n. book of cheques —**cheque card** banker's card

chequer or U.S. **checker** ('tʃekə) n. 1. marking as on chessboard 2. marble, peg etc. used in games, eg Chinese chequers —pl. 3. squares like those of chessboard 4. (with sing. v.) draughts —vt. 5. mark in squares 6. variegate —'**chequered** or esp. U.S. '**checkered** a. 1. marked in squares 2. uneven, varied

cherish ('tʃerɪʃ) vt. 1. treat with affection 2. protect 3. foster

cheroot (ʃəˈruːt) n. cigar with both ends open

cherry ('tʃerɪ) n. 1. small red fruit with stone 2. tree bearing it —a. 3. ruddy, bright red

cherub ('tʃerəb) n. 1. winged creature with human face 2. angel (pl. '**cherubim, -s**) —che'**rubic** a.

chervil ('tʃɜːvɪl) n. a herb

Ches. Cheshire

chess (tʃes) n. game of skill played by two with 32 pieces on chequered board of 64 squares —'**chessboard** n. —'**chessmen** pl.n. pieces used in chess

chest (tʃest) n. 1. upper part of trunk of body 2. large, strong box —**chest of drawers** piece of furniture containing drawers

chesterfield ('tʃestəfiːld) n. padded sofa

chestnut ('tʃesnʌt) n. 1. large reddish-brown nut growing in prickly husk 2. tree bearing it 3. inf. old joke 4. horse of golden-brown colour —a. 5. reddish-brown

cheval glass (ʃəˈvæl) full-length mirror mounted to swivel within frame

chevalier (ʃevəˈlɪə) n. 1. member of order of merit, such as French Legion of Honour 2. lowest title of rank in old French nobility 3. obs. knight 4. chivalrous man; gallant

Cheviot ('tʃiːvɪɒt, 'tʃev-) n. 1. Brit. sheep reared for its wool 2. (oft. c-) rough woollen fabric

chevron ('ʃɛvrən) n. Mil. V-shaped band of braid worn on sleeve to designate rank

chew (tʃuː) v. 1. grind with teeth —n. 2. act of chewing 3. something that is chewed —'**chewy** a. firm, sticky when chewed —**chewing gum** —**chew the fat** sl. 1. argue over a point 2. talk idly; gossip

chi (kaɪ) n. 22nd letter in Gr. alphabet (χ, X)

chianti (kɪˈæntɪ) n. It. wine

chiaroscuro (kɪɑːrəˈskʊərəʊ) n. 1. artistic distribution of light and dark masses in picture 2. monochrome painting using light and dark only (pl. -s)

chic (ʃiːk, ʃɪk) a. 1. stylish, elegant —n. 2. stylishness, esp. in dress

chicane (ʃɪˈkeɪn) n. 1. bridge or whist hand without trumps 2. Motor racing barrier placed before dangerous corner to reduce speeds 3. rare chicanery —vt. 4. deceive or trick by chicanery —vi. 5. use chicanery —**chi'canery** n. 1. quibbling 2. trick, artifice

chick (tʃɪk) n. 1. young of birds, esp. of hen 2. sl. young woman —'**chicken** n. 1. domestic fowl bred for flesh or eggs 2. its flesh as food 3. sl. cowardly person —a. 4. sl. easily scared; cowardly; timid —**chicken feed** trifling amount (of money) —**chicken-hearted** a. timid, cowardly —'**chickenpox** n. infectious disease, esp. of children —'**chickpea** n. dwarf pea —'**chickweed** n. weed with small white flowers

chicle ('tʃɪkʔl) n. substance obtained from sapodilla; main ingredient of chewing gum

chicory ('tʃɪkərɪ) n. salad plant of which the root is ground and used with, or instead of, coffee

chide (tʃaɪd) vt. scold, reprove, censure (**chid** pt., '**chidden**, **chid** pp., '**chiding** pr.p.)

chief (tʃiːf) n. 1. head or principal person —a. 2. principal, foremost, leading —'**chiefly** adv. —**chieftain** ('tʃiːftən, -tɪn) n. leader, chief of clan or tribe —**chief petty officer** senior naval rank for personnel without commissioned or warrant rank —**chief technician** noncommissioned officer in Royal Air Force, junior to flight sergeant

chiffchaff ('tʃɪftʃæf) n. common European warbler

chiffon (ʃɪˈfɒn, 'ʃɪfɒn) n. thin gauzy material —**chiffo'nier** n. ornamental cupboard

chignon ('ʃiːnjɒn) n. roll, knot of hair worn at back of head

chigoe ('tʃɪgəʊ) n. tropical flea, female of which burrows into skin of man etc. (also '**chigger**)

Chihuahua (tʃɪˈwɑːwɑː, -wə) n. breed of tiny dog, orig. from Mexico

chilblain ('tʃɪlbleɪn) n. inflamed sore on hands, legs etc., due to cold

child (tʃaɪld) n. 1. young human being 2. offspring (pl. **children** ('tʃɪldrən)) —'**childhood** n. period between birth and puberty —'**childish** a. 1. of or like a child 2. silly 3. trifling —'**childishly** adv. —'**childless** a. —'**childlike** a. 1. of or like a child 2. innocent 3. frank 4. docile —'**childbed** n. state of giving birth to child —**child benefit** UK regular government payment to parents of children up to a certain age —'**childbirth** n. —**child minder** person who looks after children, esp. those whose parents are working —**child's play** very easy task

chiliad ('kɪlɪæd) n. 1. group of one thousand 2. thousand years

chill (tʃɪl) n. 1. coldness 2. cold with shivering 3. anything that damps, discourages —v. 4. make, become cold (esp. food, drink) —**chilled** a. —'**chilliness** n. —'**chilly** a.

chilli ('tʃɪlɪ) n. 1. small red hot-tasting seed pod 2. plant producing it

Chiltern Hundreds ('tʃɪltən) UK Stewardship of the Chiltern Hundreds; nominal office that MP applies for to resign seat

chime (tʃaɪm) n. 1. sound of bell 2. harmonious, ringing sound —vi. 3. ring harmoniously 4. agree —vt. 5. strike (bells) —**chime in** come into conversation with agreement

chimera or **chimaera** (kaɪˈmɪərə, kɪ-) n. 1. fabled monster, made up of parts of various animals 2. wild fancy —**chimeric(al)** (kaɪˈmɛrɪk(ʔl), kɪ-) a. fanciful

chimney ('tʃɪmnɪ) n. 1. a passage for smoke 2. narrow vertical cleft in rock (pl. -s)

chimp (tʃɪmp) n. inf. chimpanzee

chimpanzee (tʃɪmpænˈziː) n. gregarious, intelligent ape of Afr.

chin (tʃɪn) n. part of face below mouth —**chinless wonder** UK inf. person, esp. upper-class, lacking strength of character —'**chinwag** n. UK inf. chat

china ('tʃaɪnə) n. 1. fine earthenware, porcelain 2. cups, saucers etc. collectively —**china clay** see KAOLIN

chincherinchee (tʃɪntʃərɪnˈtʃiː, -ˈrɪntʃɪ) n. S Afr. plant with white or yellow flower spikes

chinchilla (tʃɪnˈtʃɪlə) n. S Amer. rodent with soft, grey fur

chine (tʃaɪn) n. 1. backbone 2. joint of meat 3. ridge or crest of land

Chinese (tʃaɪˈniːz) a. 1. of China, its people or their languages —n. 2. native of China or descendant of one (pl. -ese) 3. any of languages of China —**Chinese lantern** Asian plant cultivated for its orange-red inflated calyx

chink[1] (tʃɪŋk) n. cleft, crack

chink[2] (tʃɪŋk) n. 1. light metallic sound —v. 2. (cause to) make this sound

chinoiserie (ʃiːnwɑːzəˈriː, -ˈwɑːzərɪ) n. 1. style of decorative art based on imitations of Chinese motifs 2. object or objects in this style

chinook (tʃɪˈnuːk, -ˈnʊk) n. 1. warm dry wind blowing down eastern slopes of Rocky Mountains 2. warm moist wind blowing on to Washington and Oregon coasts

chintz (tʃɪnts) *n.* cotton cloth printed in coloured designs

chip (tʃɪp) *n.* **1.** splinter **2.** place where piece has been broken off **3.** thin strip of potato, fried **4.** tiny wafer of silicon forming integrated circuit in computer *etc.* —*vt.* **5.** chop into small pieces **6.** break small pieces from **7.** shape by cutting off pieces —*vi.* **8.** break off (**-pp-**) —**chip-based** *a.* using microchips in electronic equipment —**'chipboard** *n.* thin rigid sheet made of compressed wood particles —**chip in 1.** interrupt **2.** contribute

chipmunk ('tʃɪpmʌŋk) *n.* small, striped N Amer. squirrel

chipolata (tʃɪpə'lɑːtə) *n.* small sausage

Chippendale ('tʃɪpˈndeɪl) *a.* (of furniture) in style of Thomas Chippendale, characterized by use of Chinese and Gothic motifs *etc.*

chirography (kaɪ'rɒgrəfɪ) *n.* calligraphy

chiromancy ('kaɪrəmænsɪ) *n.* palmistry —**'chiromancer** *n.*

chiropodist (kɪ'rɒpədɪst) *n.* one who treats disorders of feet —**chi'ropody** *n.*

chiropractor ('kaɪrəpræktə) *n.* one skilled in treating bodily disorders by manipulation, massage *etc.* —**chiro'practic** *n.*

chirp (tʃɜːp) *n.* **1.** short, sharp cry of bird —*vi.* **2.** make this sound —**'chirpy** *a. inf.* happy

chisel ('tʃɪzˈl) *n.* **1.** cutting tool, usu. bar of steel with edge across main axis —*vt.* **2.** cut, carve with chisel **3.** *sl.* cheat (**-ll-**)

chit[1] (tʃɪt) *n.* informal note, memorandum

chit[2] (tʃɪt) *n.* child, young girl

chitchat ('tʃɪttʃæt) *n.* **1.** gossip —*vi.* **2.** gossip

chitin (kaɪtɪn) *n.* polysaccharide that is principal component of outer coverings of arthropods *etc.* —**'chitinous** *a.*

chivalry ('ʃɪvəlrɪ) *n.* **1.** bravery and courtesy **2.** medieval system of knighthood —**'chivalrous** *a.* —**'chivalrously** *adv.*

chive (tʃaɪv) *n.* herb with mild onion flavour

chivy, chivvy ('tʃɪvɪ) *or* **chevy** ('tʃɛvɪ) UK *vt.* **1.** harass; nag **2.** hunt —*vi.* **3.** run about (**'chivied, 'chivying, 'chivvied, 'chivvying** *or* **'chevied, 'chevying**) —*n.* **4.** hunt **5.** *obs.* hunting cry

chloral hydrate ('klɔːrəl) colourless crystalline soluble solid produced by reaction of chloral with water and used as sedative

chlorine ('klɔːriːn) *or* **chlorin** ('klɔːrɪn) *n.* nonmetallic element, yellowish-green poison gas —**'chlorate** *n.* salt of chloric acid —**'chloric** *a.* —**'chloride** *n.* **1.** compound of chlorine **2.** bleaching agent —**'chlorinate** *vt.* **1.** disinfect **2.** purify with chlorine

chloroform ('klɔːrəfɔːm) *n.* **1.** volatile liquid formerly used as anaesthetic —*vt.* **2.** render insensible with it

chlorophyll *or* *U.S.* **chlorophyl** ('klɔːrəfɪl) *n.* green colouring matter in plants; used to colour food

chock (tʃɒk) *n.* block or wedge to prevent heavy object rolling or sliding —**chock-full** *or* **chock-a-block** *a.* packed full

chocolate ('tʃɒkəlɪt, 'tʃɒklɪt, -lət) *n.* **1.** paste from ground cacao seeds **2.** confectionery, drink made from this —*a.* **3.** dark brown —**choc-ice** *n.* chocolate-covered slice of ice cream —**chocolate-box** *a. inf.* sentimentally pretty or appealing

choice (tʃɔɪs) *n.* **1.** act or power of choosing **2.** alternative **3.** thing or person chosen —*a.* **4.** select, fine, worthy of being chosen —**'choicely** *adv.*

choir (kwaɪə) *n.* **1.** band of singers, *esp.* in church **2.** part of church set aside for them

choke (tʃəʊk) *vt.* **1.** hinder, stop the breathing of **2.** smother, stifle **3.** obstruct —*vi.* **4.** suffer choking —*n.* **5.** act, noise of choking **6.** device in carburettor to increase richness of petrol-air mixture —**choked** *a.* —**'choker** *n.* **1.** woman's high collar **2.** neckband or necklace worn tightly around throat **3.** high clerical collar; stock **4.** person or thing that chokes —**'chokebore** *n.* gun with bore narrowed towards muzzle —**'chokedamp** *n.* carbon dioxide gas in coal mines

choler ('kɒlə) *n.* bile, anger —**'choleric** *a.* bad-tempered

cholera ('kɒlərə) *n.* deadly infectious disease marked by vomiting and diarrhoea

cholesterol (kə'lɛstərɒl) *or* **cholesterin** (kə'lɛstərɪn) *n.* substance found in animal tissue and fat

chomp (tʃɒmp) *or* **chump** (tʃʌmp) *v.* chew noisily

choose (tʃuːz) *vt.* **1.** pick out, select **2.** take by preference —*vi.* **3.** decide, think fit (**chose, 'chosen, 'choosing**) —**'chooser** *n.* —**'choosy** *a.* fussy

chop[1] (tʃɒp) *vt.* **1.** cut with blow **2.** hack (**-pp-**) —*n.* **3.** hewing blow **4.** slice of meat containing rib or other bone —**'chopper** *n.* **1.** short axe **2.** *inf.* helicopter **3.** *inf.* large motorbike —**'choppy** *a.* (of sea) having short, broken waves

chop[2] (tʃɒp) *vt.* exchange, bandy (*esp.* in **chop logic, chop and change**) (**-pp-**)

chops (tʃɒps) *pl.n.* jaws, cheeks

chopsticks ('tʃɒpstɪks) *pl.n.* implements used by Chinese for eating food

chop suey ('suːɪ) a kind of rich Chinese stew with rice

choral ('kɔːrəl) *a.* of, for, sung by, a choir

chorale *or* **choral** (kɒ'rɑːl) *n.* slow, stately hymn tune

chord (kɔːd) *n.* **1.** emotional response, *esp.* of sympathy **2.** simultaneous sounding of musical notes **3.** straight line joining ends of arc

chore (tʃɔː) *n.* **1.** (unpleasant) task **2.** odd job

chorea (kɒ'rɪə) *n.* disorder of central nervous system characterized by uncontrollable jerky movements (*also* **Saint Vitus's dance**)

choreography (kɒrɪ'ɒgrəfɪ) *or* **choregraphy** (kɒ'rɛgrəfɪ) *n*. 1. art of arranging dances, *esp*. ballet 2. art, notation of ballet dancing —**chore'ographer** *or* **cho'regrapher** *n*. —**choreo'graphic** *or* **chore'graphic** *a*.

chorography *n*. art of describing and making maps of particular regions —**choro'graphic** *a*.

choroid ('kɔːrɔɪd) *or* **chorioid** ('kɔːrɪɔɪd) *n*. vascular membrane of eyeball between sclera and retina

chorology (kɒ'rɒlədʒɪ) *n*. science of geographical distribution of plants and animals —**cho'rological** *a*.

chortle ('tʃɔːt'l) *vi*. 1. chuckle happily —*n*. 2. gleeful chuckle

chorus ('kɔːrəs) *n*. 1. band of singers 2. combination of voices singing together 3. refrain —*vt*. 4. sing or say together —**choric** ('kɒrɪk) *a*. —**chorister** ('kɒrɪstə) *n*.

chose (tʃəʊz) *pt. of* CHOOSE —**'chosen** *pp. of* CHOOSE

chough (tʃʌf) *n*. black passerine bird of Europe, Asia and Afr., with red bill

choux pastry (ʃuː) very light pastry made with eggs

chow (tʃaʊ) *n. inf*. food

chow-chow *n*. thick-coated dog with curled tail, *orig*. from China (*also* **chow**)

chowder ('tʃaʊdə) *n. chiefly US* thick soup or stew containing clams or fish

chow mein (meɪn) Chinese-American dish, consisting of mushrooms, meat, shrimps *etc*.

chrism *or* **chrisom** ('krɪzəm) *n*. mixture of olive oil and balsam used for sacramental anointing

Christ (kraɪst) *n*. 1. Jesus of Nazareth, regarded by Christians as fulfilling Old Testament prophecies of Messiah 2. Messiah as subject of Old Testament prophecies 3. image of Christ —*interj*. 4. *offens. sl*. oath expressing annoyance *etc*. (*see also* JESUS)

Christian ('krɪstʃən) *n*. 1. follower of Christ —*a*. 2. following Christ 3. relating to Christ or his religion 4. exhibiting kindness or goodness —**christen** ('krɪs'n) *vt*. baptise, give name to —**Christendom** ('krɪs'ndəm) *n*. all the Christian world —**Christi'anity** *n*. religion of Christ —**'christianize** *or* **-ise** *vt*. —**Christian name** name given at baptism —**Christian Science** religious system founded by Mrs. Eddy in U.S.A.

Christmas ('krɪsməs) *n*. festival of birth of Christ —**'Christmassy** *a*. —**Christmas box** tip, present given at Christmas —**Christmas card** —**Christmas rose** evergreen plant of S Europe and W Asia, with white or pinkish winter-blooming flowers (*also* **'hellebore, winter rose**) —**Christmas tree**

Christy *or* **Christie** ('krɪstɪ) *n. Skiing* turn

in which body is swung sharply round with skis parallel

chromatic (krə'mætɪk) *a*. 1. of colour 2. *Mus*. of scale proceeding by semitones

chromatin ('krəʊmətɪn) *n*. part of protoplasmic substance in nucleus of cells which takes colour in staining tests

chromatography (krəʊmə'tɒgrəfɪ) *n*. technique of separating and analysing components of mixture by selective adsorption in column of powder or on strip of paper

chrome (krəʊm) *n*. metal used in alloys and for plating

chromosome ('krəʊməsəʊm) *n*. microscopic gene-carrying body in tissue of a cell

chromosphere ('krəʊməsfɪə) *n*. layer of incandescent gas surrounding the sun

Chron. *Bible* Chronicles

chronic ('krɒnɪk) *a*. 1. lasting a long time 2. habitual 3. *inf*. serious 4. *inf*. of bad quality

chronicle ('krɒnɪk'l) *n*. 1. record of events in order of time 2. account —*vt*. 3. record —**'chronicler** *n*.

chronology (krə'nɒlədʒɪ) *n*. 1. determination of sequence of past events 2. arrangement in order of occurrence —**chrono'logical** *a*. arranged in order of time —**chrono'logically** *adv*. —**chro'nologist** *n*.

chronometer (krə'nɒmɪtə) *n*. 1. instrument for measuring time exactly 2. watch —**chrono'metrical** *a*. —**chro'nometry** *n*.

chrysalis ('krɪsəlɪs) *n*. 1. resting state of insect between grub and butterfly *etc*. 2. case enclosing it (*pl*. **-es, chrysalides** (krɪ'sælɪdiːz))

chrysanthemum (krɪ'sænθəməm) *n*. garden flower of various colours

chub (tʃʌb) *n*. 1. European freshwater fish 2. any of various N Amer. fishes, *esp*. whitefishes and minnows

chubby ('tʃʌbɪ) *a*. plump

chuck[1] (tʃʌk) *vt*. 1. *inf*. throw 2. pat affectionately (under chin) 3. *inf*. give up, reject

chuck[2] (tʃʌk) *n*. 1. cut of beef 2. device for gripping, adjusting bit in power drill *etc*.

chuckle ('tʃʌk'l) *vi*. 1. laugh softly —*n*. 2. such laugh —**'chucklehead** *n. inf*. stupid person; blockhead; dolt

chuff[1] (tʃʌf) *n*. 1. puffing sound as of steam engine —*vi*. 2. move while emitting such sounds

chuff[2] (tʃʌf) *vt*. (*usu. as pp./a*. **chuffed**) *UK sl*. please, delight

chug (tʃʌg) *n*. 1. short dull sound, such as that made by engine —*vi*. 2. (of engine *etc*.) operate while making such sounds (-**gg**-)

chukker *or* **chukka** ('tʃʌkə) *n*. period of play in game of polo

chum (tʃʌm) *n. inf*. close friend —**'chummy** *a*.

chump (tʃʌmp) *n*. 1. *inf*. stupid person 2. heavy block of wood 3. thick blunt end of anything, *esp.* meat 4. UK *sl.* head (*esp. in off one's chump*)

chunk (tʃʌŋk) *n.* thick, solid piece —'**chunky** *a.*

church (tʃɜːtʃ) *n.* 1. building for Christian worship 2. (C-) whole body or sect of Christians 3. clergy —'**churchman** *n.* —**Church of England** reformed state Church in England, with Sovereign as temporal head —**church'warden** *n.* 1. officer who represents interests of parish 2. long clay pipe —'**churchyard** *n.*

churl (tʃɜːl) *n.* 1. rustic 2. ill-bred fellow —'**churlish** *a.* —'**churlishly** *adv.* —'**churlishness** *n.*

churn (tʃɜːn) *n.* 1. large container for milk 2. vessel for making butter —*v.* 3. shake up, stir (liquid) violently

chute (ʃuːt) *n.* 1. slide for sending down parcels, coal *etc.* 2. channel 3. slide into swimming pool 4. narrow passageway, *eg* for spraying, counting cattle, sheep *etc.* 5. *inf.* parachute

chutney ('tʃʌtnɪ) *n.* pickle of fruit, spices *etc.*

chyle (kaɪl) *n.* milky fluid composed of lymph and emulsified fat globules, formed in small intestine during digestion

chyme (kaɪm) *n.* thick fluid mass of partially digested food that leaves stomach

C.I.A. US Central Intelligence Agency

cicada (sɪ'kɑːdə) *or* **cicala** *n.* cricketlike insect

cicatrix ('sɪkətrɪks) *n.* scar of healed wound —**cicatri'zation** *or* **-i'sation** *n.* —'**cicatrize** *or* **-ise** *v.* heal

cicely ('sɪsəlɪ) *n.* perennial plant similar to chervil, used as herb (*also* **sweet cicely**)

cicerone (sɪsə'rəʊnɪ, tʃɪtʃ'ɛ-) *n.* person who conducts and informs sightseers (*pl.* **-s, -ni** (-nɪ))

C.I.D. Criminal Investigation Department

-cide (*n. comb. form*) 1. person or thing that kills, as in *insecticide* 2. killing; murder, as in *homicide* —**-cidal** (*a. comb. form*)

cider *or* **cyder** ('saɪdə) *n.* fermented drink made from apples

c.i.f. *or* **C.I.F.** cost, insurance and freight (included in price quoted)

cigar (sɪ'gɑː) *n.* roll of tobacco leaves for smoking —**ciga'rette** *n.* finely-cut tobacco rolled in paper for smoking —**cigarette card** small picture card, formerly given away with cigarettes, now collected as hobby

cilium ('sɪlɪəm) *n.* 1. short thread projecting from surface of cell *etc.*, whose rhythmic beating causes movement 2. eyelash (*pl.* **cilia** ('sɪlɪə)) —'**ciliary** *a.* of cilia —'**ciliate** *or* '**ciliated** *a.* —**ciliary body** part of eye that joins choroid to iris

C in C *or* **C.-in-C.** Commander-in-Chief

cinch (sɪntʃ) *n. inf.* easy task, certainty

cinchona (sɪŋ'kəʊnə) *n.* 1. tree or shrub of S Amer. having medicinal bark 2. dried bark of this tree, which yields quinine 3. any of drugs derived from cinchona bark

cincture ('sɪŋktʃə) *n.* something that encircles, *esp.* belt or girdle

cinder ('sɪndə) *n.* remains of burned coal

Cinderella (sɪndə'rɛlə) *n.* 1. girl who achieves fame after being obscure 2. poor, neglected or unsuccessful person or thing

cine camera ('sɪnɪ) camera for taking moving pictures —**cine film**

cinema ('sɪnɪmə) *n.* 1. building used for showing of films 2. films generally or collectively —**cine'matograph** *n.* combined camera, printer and projector —**cinema'tography** *n.*

cineraria (sɪnə'rɛərɪə) *n.* garden plant with daisylike flowers

cinerarium (sɪnə'rɛərɪəm) *n.* place for keeping ashes of dead after cremation (*pl.* **-ria** (-rɪə))

cinerary ('sɪnərərɪ) *a.* pert. to ashes

cinnabar ('sɪnəbɑː) *n.* 1. heavy red mineral consisting of mercuric sulphide: chief ore of mercury 2. red form of mercuric sulphide, *esp.* when used as pigment 3. bright red; vermilion 4. large red-and-black European moth

cinnamon ('sɪnəmən) *n.* 1. spice got from bark of Asian tree 2. the tree —*a.* 3. light-brown colour

cinque (sɪŋk) *n.* number five in cards, dice *etc.* —'**cinquefoil** *n.* plant with five-lobed leaves

cipher *or* **cypher** ('saɪfə) *n.* 1. secret writing 2. arithmetical symbol 3. person of no importance 4. monogram —*vt.* 5. write in cipher

circa ('sɜːkə) *Lat.* about, approximately

circadian (sɜː'keɪdɪən) *a.* of biological processes that occur at 24-hourly intervals

circle ('sɜːk'l) *n.* 1. perfectly round figure 2. ring 3. *Theat.* section of seats above main level of auditorium 4. group, society with common interest 5. spiritualist seance 6. class of society —*vt.* 7. surround —*vi.* 8. move round —'**circular** *a.* 1. round 2. moving round —*n.* 3. letter sent to several persons —**circulari'zation** *or* **-i'sation** *n.* —'**circularize** *or* **-ise** *vt.* 1. distribute circulars to 2. canvass or petition, as for votes *etc.* by distributing letters *etc.* 3. make circular —'**circulate** *vi.* 1. move round 2. pass from hand to hand or place to place —*vt.* 3. send round —**circu'lation** *n.* 1. flow of blood from, and back to, heart 2. act of moving round 3. extent of sale of newspaper *etc.* —'**circulatory** *a.* —**circular saw** saw in which circular disc with toothed edge is rotated at high speed —**circulating library** 1. *esp.* US lending library 2. small library circulated in turn to group of institutions

circuit ('sɜːkɪt) *n.* 1. complete round or course 2. area 3. path of electric current 4. round of visitation, *esp.* of judges 5. series of sporting events 6. district —**circuitous** (sə'kjuːɪtəs) *a.* round about, indirect —**circuitously** (sə'kjuːɪtəslɪ) *adv.* —'**cir-**

cuitry n. electrical circuit(s) —**circuit breaker** device that under abnormal conditions stops flow of current in electrical circuit

circum- (comb. form) around; surrounding; on all sides, as in circumlocution, circumpolar. Such compounds are not given here where the meaning may easily be found from the simple word

circumambient (sɜːkəmˈæmbɪənt) a. surrounding

circumcise (ˈsɜːkəmsaɪz) vt. cut off foreskin of —**circum'cision** n.

circumference (səˈkʌmfərəns) n. boundary line, esp. of circle

circumflex (ˈsɜːkəmflɛks) n. 1. mark (ˆ) placed over vowel to show it is pronounced with rising and falling pitch or as long vowel —a. 2. (of nerves etc.) bending or curving around

circumlocution (sɜːkəmləˈkjuːʃən) n. roundabout speech

circumnavigate (sɜːkəmˈnævɪgeɪt) vt. sail or fly right round —**circumnavi'gation** n. —**circum'navigator** n.

circumscribe (sɜːkəmˈskraɪb, ˈsɜːkəmskraɪb) vt. confine, bound, limit, hamper

circumspect (ˈsɜːkəmspɛkt) a. watchful, cautious, prudent —**circum'spection** n. —'**circumspectly** adv.

circumstance (ˈsɜːkəmstəns) n. 1. detail 2. event 3. matter of fact —pl. 4. state of affairs 5. condition in life, esp. financial 6. surroundings or things accompanying an action —**circum'stantial** a. 1. depending on detail or circumstances 2. detailed, minute 3. incidental —**circumstanti'ality** n. —**circum'stantially** adv. —**circum'stantiate** vt. 1. prove by details 2. describe exactly —**circumstantial evidence** indirect evidence that tends to establish conclusion by inference

circumvent (sɜːkəmˈvɛnt) vt. outwit, evade, get round —**circum'vention** n.

circus (ˈsɜːkəs) n. 1. (performance of) travelling group of acrobats, clowns, performing animals etc. 2. circular structure for public shows 3. circular space in town where roads converge

cirque (sɜːk) n. steep-sided semicircular depression found in mountainous regions

cirrhosis (sɪˈrəusɪs) n. any of various chronic progressive diseases of liver —**cirrhotic** (sɪˈrɒtɪk) a.

cirrus (ˈsɪrəs) n. high wispy cloud (pl. **cirri** (ˈsɪraɪ)) —**cirro'cumulus** n. high cloud of ice crystals grouped into small separate globular masses (pl. -**li** (-laɪ)) —**cirro'stratus** n. uniform layer of cloud above about 6000 metres (pl. -**tai** (-taɪ))

cisalpine (sɪsˈælpaɪn) a. on this (southern) side of Alps, as viewed from Rome

cisco (ˈsɪskəu) n. N Amer. whitefish (pl. -**s**, -**es**)

cist (sɪst) or **kist** (kɪst) n. box-shaped burial chamber made from stone slabs or hollowed tree-trunk

Cistercian (sɪˈstɜːʃən) n. member of Christian order of monks and nuns, which follows strict form of Benedictine rule (also **White Monk**)

cistern (ˈsɪstən) n. water tank

cistus (ˈsɪstəs) n. any of various shrubs or herbaceous plants cultivated for yellow-white or reddish roselike flowers (also 'rockrose)

citadel (ˈsɪtədʒl, -dɛl) n. fortress in, near or commanding a city

cite (saɪt) vt. 1. quote 2. bring forward as proof 3. commend (soldier etc.) for outstanding bravery etc. 4. summon to appear before court of law —**ci'tation** n. 1. quoting 2. commendation for bravery etc.

cithara (ˈsɪθərə) or **kithara** (ˈkɪθərə) n. stringed musical instrument of ancient Greece, similar to lyre

citizen (ˈsɪtɪzʰn) n. 1. native, naturalized member of state, nation etc. 2. inhabitant of city —'**citizenry** n. citizens collectively —'**citizenship** n. —**Citizens' Band** range of radio frequencies assigned officially for use by public for private communication

citron (ˈsɪtrən) n. 1. fruit like a lemon 2. the tree —'**citric** a. of the acid of lemon or citron —'**citrus** fruit citrons, lemons, limes, oranges etc.

citronella (sɪtrəˈnɛlə) n. 1. tropical Asian grass with bluish-green lemon-scented leaves 2. aromatic oil obtained from this grass, used in perfumes etc. (also **citronella oil**)

cittern (ˈsɪtɜːn), **cither** (ˈsɪθə), or **cithern** (ˈsɪθən) n. medieval stringed instrument resembling lute but having wire strings and flat back

city (ˈsɪtɪ) n. large town —**city editor** (on newspaper) 1. UK editor in charge of financial and commercial news 2. US editor in charge of local news —**city father** person who is prominent in public affairs of city —**the City** 1. area in central London where United Kingdom's major financial business is transacted 2. financial institutions located in this area

civet (ˈsɪvɪt) n. strong, musky perfume —**civet-cat** n. catlike animal producing it

civic (ˈsɪvɪk) a. pert. to city or citizen —'**civics** pl.n. (with sing. v.) study of the rights and responsibilities of citizenship —**civic centre** UK public buildings of town, including recreational facilities and offices of local administration

civil (ˈsɪvʰl) a. 1. relating to citizens of state 2. not military 3. refined, polite 4. Law not criminal —**ci'vilian** n. nonmilitary person —**ci'vility** n. —'**civilly** adv. —**civil defence** organizing of civilians to deal with enemy attacks —**civil disobedience** refusal to obey laws, pay taxes etc.: nonviolent means of protesting —**civil engineer** person qualified to design and construct roads, bridges etc. —**civil engineering** —**civil law** 1. law of state relating to private affairs 2. body of law in ancient Rome, esp. as applicable to private citizens 3. law based on Roman system —**civil liberty** right of individual to freedom of speech and action —**civil marriage** *Law* marriage performed by official other than clergyman —**civil rights** *pl.n.* 1. personal rights of individual citizen —*a.* 2. of equality in social, economic and political rights —**civil service** service responsible for public administration of government of a country —**civil war** war between factions within same nation

civilize *or* **-ise** ('sɪvɪlaɪz) *vt.* 1. bring out of barbarism 2. refine —**civili'zation** *or* **-i'sation** *n.* —**'civilized** *or* **-ised** *a.*

civvy ('sɪvɪ) *sl. n.* 1. civilian —*pl.* 2. civilian clothing —**civvy street** civilian life

cl centilitre

Cl *Chem.* chlorine

clack (klæk) *n.* 1. sound, as of two pieces of wood striking together —*v.* 2. make such sound 3. jabber

clad (klæd) *pt./pp. of* **clothe** (*see* CLOTH)

cladding ('klædɪŋ) *n.* material used for outside facing of building *etc.*

claim (kleɪm) *vt.* 1. demand as right 2. assert 3. call for —*n.* 4. demand for thing supposed due 5. right 6. thing claimed 7. plot of mining land marked out by stakes as required by law —**'claimant** *n.*

clairvoyance (kleə'vɔɪəns) *n.* power of seeing things not present to senses, second sight —**clair'voyant** *n./a.*

clam (klæm) *n.* edible mollusc

clamber ('klæmbə) *vi.* climb with difficulty or awkwardly

clammy ('klæmɪ) *a.* moist and sticky —**'clamminess** *n.*

clamour *or U.S.* **clamor** ('klæmə) *n.* 1. loud shouting, outcry, noise —*vi.* 2. shout, call noisily —**'clamorous** *a.* —**'clamorously** *adv.*

clamp¹ (klæmp) *n.* 1. tool for holding or compressing —*vt.* 2. fasten, strengthen with or as with clamp

clamp² (klæmp) *n.* 1. mound of harvested root crop, covered with straw and earth to protect it from winter weather —*vt.* 2. enclose in mound

clan (klæn) *n.* 1. tribe or collection of families under chief and of common ancestry 2. faction, group —**'clannish** *a.* —**'clannishly** *adv.* —**'clannishness** *n.*

clandestine (klæn'dɛstɪn) *a.* 1. secret 2. sly

clang (klæŋ) *v.* 1. (cause to) make loud ringing sound —*n.* 2. loud ringing sound —**'clanger** *n.* 1. *inf.* conspicuous mistake 2. that which clangs

clangor *or* **clangour** ('klæŋgə, 'klæŋə) *n.* 1. loud resonant noise 2. uproar —*vi.* 3. make loud resonant noise —**'clangorous** *or* **'clangourous** *a.*

clank (klæŋk) *n.* 1. short sound as of pieces of metal struck together —*v.* 2. cause, move with, such sound

clap¹ (klæp) *v.* 1. (cause to) strike with noise 2. strike (hands) together 3. applaud —*vt.* 4. pat 5. place or put quickly (**-pp-**)

—*n.* 6. hard, explosive sound 7. slap —**'clapper** *n.* —**'clapping** *n.* —**'claptrap** *n. inf.* empty words

clap² (klæp) *n. sl.* gonorrhoea

claque (klæk) *n.* 1. group of people hired to applaud 2. group of fawning admirers

claret ('klærət) *n.* a dry dark red wine of Bordeaux

clarify ('klærɪfaɪ) *v.* make or become clear, pure or more easily understood (**-fied, -fying**) —**clarifi'cation** *n.* —**'clarity** *n.* clearness

clarinet (klærɪ'nɛt) *n.* woodwind musical instrument

clarion ('klærɪən) *n.* 1. clear-sounding trumpet 2. rousing sound

clary ('kleərɪ) *n.* herb

clash (klæʃ) *n.* 1. loud noise, as of weapons striking 2. conflict, collision —*vi.* 3. make clash 4. come into conflict 5. (of events) coincide 6. (of colours) look ugly together —*vt.* 7. strike together to make clash

clasp (klɑːsp) *n.* 1. hook or other means of fastening 2. embrace —*vt.* 3. fasten 4. embrace, grasp —**clasp knife**

class (klɑːs) *n.* 1. any division, order, kind, sort 2. rank 3. group of school pupils *etc.* taught together 4. division by merit 5. quality 6. *inf.* excellence; elegance —*vt.* 7. assign to proper division —**classifi'cation** *n.* —**'classified** *a.* 1. arranged in classes 2. secret 3. (of advertisements) arranged under headings in newspapers —**'classify** *vt.* arrange methodically in classes (**-fied, -fying**) —**'classy** *a. inf.* stylish, elegant —**class-conscious** *a.* aware of belonging to particular social rank —**class-consciousness** *n.*

classic ('klæsɪk) *a.* 1. of first rank 2. of highest rank generally, but *esp.* of art 3. refined 4. typical 5. famous —*n.* 6. (literary) work of recognized excellence —*pl.* 7. ancient Latin and Greek literature —**'classical** *a.* 1. of Greek and Roman literature, art, culture 2. of classic quality 3. *Mus.* of established standards of form, complexity *etc.* —**'classically** *adv.* —**'classicism** *n.* —**'classicist** *n.*

clatter ('klætə) *n.* 1. rattling noise 2. noisy conversation —*v.* 3. (cause to) make clatter

clause (klɔːz) *n.* 1. part of sentence, containing verb 2. article in formal document as treaty, contract *etc.*

claustrophobia (klɔːstrə'fəʊbɪə, klɒs-) *n.* abnormal fear of confined spaces

clavichord ('klævɪkɔːd) *n.* musical instrument with keyboard, forerunner of piano

clavicle ('klævɪk²l) *n.* collarbone —**cla'vicular** *a.* pert. to this

clavier (klə'vɪə, 'klævɪə) *n.* keyboard instrument; keyboard

claw (klɔː) *n.* 1. sharp hooked nail of bird or beast 2. foot of bird of prey 3. clawlike article —*vt.* 4. tear with claws 5. grip

clay (kleɪ) *n.* 1. fine-grained earth, plastic when wet, hardening when baked 2. earth

—**clayey** a. —**clay pigeon** disc of baked clay hurled into air as target to be shot at

claymore ('kleımɔː) n. ancient Highland two-edged sword

CLC Canadian Labour Congress

clean (kliːn) a. 1. free from dirt, stain or defilement 2. pure 3. guiltless 4. trim, shapely —adv. 5. so as to leave no dirt 6. entirely —vt. 7. free from dirt —'**cleaner** n. —**cleanliness** ('klɛnlınıs) n. —**cleanly** ('kliːnlı) adv. 1. in a clean manner —a. ('klɛnlı) 2. clean —'**cleanness** n. —**cleanse** (klɛnz) vt. make clean —**clean-cut** a. 1. clearly outlined; neat 2. definite —**come clean** inf. confess

clear (klıə) a. 1. pure, undimmed, bright 2. free from cloud 3. transparent 4. plain, distinct 5. without defect or drawback 6. unimpeded —adv. 7. brightly 8. wholly, quite —vt. 9. make clear 10. acquit 11. pass over or through 12. make as profit 13. free from obstruction, difficulty 14. free by payment of dues —vi. 15. become clear, bright, free, transparent —'**clearance** n. 1. making clear 2. removal of obstructions, surplus stock etc. 3. certificate that ship has been cleared at custom house 4. space for moving part, vehicle, to pass within, through or past something —'**clearing** n. land cleared of trees —'**clearly** adv. —'**clearness** n. —**clear-cut** a. 1. definite; not vague 2. clearly outlined —**clearing bank** UK bank that makes use of central clearing house in London —**clearing house** 1. Banking institution where cheques etc. drawn on member banks are cancelled against each other 2. central agency for collection and distribution of information —**clear-sighted** a. discerning —'**clearway** n. stretch of road on which motorists may stop only in an emergency

clearstory ('klıəstɔːrı) n. see CLERESTORY

cleat (kliːt) n. 1. wedge 2. piece of wood or iron with two projecting ends round which ropes are made fast

cleave[1] (kliːv) vt. 1. split asunder —vi. 2. crack, part asunder (**clove, cleft** pt., '**cloven, cleft** pp., '**cleaving** pr.p.) —'**cleavage** n. —'**cleaver** n. short chopper

cleave[2] (kliːv) vi. 1. stick, adhere 2. be loyal (**cleaved,** '**cleaving**)

clef (klɛf) n. Mus. mark to show pitch of stave

cleft (klɛft) n. 1. crack, fissure, chasm 2. opening made by cleaving —v. 3. pt./pp. of CLEAVE[1] —**cleft palate** congenital fissure in midline of hard palate, oft. associated with harelip —**cleft stick** situation involving choice between two equally unsatisfactory alternatives

cleg (klɛg) n. horsefly

clematis ('klɛmətıs) n. flowering climbing perennial plant

clement ('klɛmənt) a. 1. merciful 2. gentle 3. mild —'**clemency** n. —'**clemently** adv.

clench (klɛntʃ) vt. 1. set firmly together 2. grasp, close (fist)

clerestory or **clearstory** ('klıəstɔːrı) n. 1. row of windows in upper part of wall of church that divides nave from aisle 2. part of wall in which these windows are set —'**clerestoried** or '**clearstoried** a.

clergy ('klɜːdʒı) n. body of appointed ministers of Christian Church —'**clergyman** n.

clerical ('klɛrık²l) a. 1. of clergy 2. of, connected with, office work —'**cleric** n. clergyman —'**clericalism** n.

clerk (klɑːk, U.S. klɜːrk) n. 1. subordinate who keeps files etc. in an office 2. officer in charge of records, correspondence etc., of department or corporation 3. US shop assistant —'**clerkly** a. —'**clerkship** n. —**clerk of the works** employee who supervises building work

clever ('klɛvə) a. 1. intelligent 2. able, skilful, adroit —'**cleverly** adv. —'**cleverness** n.

clew (kluː) n. 1. ball of thread or yarn 2. Naut. lower corner of sail —vt. 3. coil into ball

cliché ('kliːʃeı) n. stereotyped hackneyed phrase

click[1] (klık) n. 1. short, sharp sound, as of latch in door 2. catch —v. 3. (cause to) make short, sharp sound

click[2] (klık) vi. 1. sl. be a success 2. inf. become clear 3. inf. strike up friendship

client ('klaıənt) n. 1. customer 2. one who employs professional person —**clientele** (kliːɒn'tɛl) n. body of clients

cliff (klıf) n. steep rock face —'**cliffhanger** n. tense situation, esp. in film etc.

climacteric (klaı'mæktərık, klaımæk-'tɛrık) n. 1. critical event or period 2. see MENOPAUSE 3. period in life of man corresponding to menopause, characterized by diminished sexual activity —a. (also **climac'terical**) 4. involving crucial event or period

climate ('klaımıt) n. 1. condition of country with regard to weather 2. prevailing feeling, atmosphere —**cli'matic** a. of climate

climax ('klaımæks) n. 1. highest point, culmination 2. point of greatest excitement, tension in story etc. —**cli'mactic** a.

climb (klaım) v. 1. go up or ascend 2. progress with difficulty 3. creep up, mount 4. slope upwards —'**climber** n. —'**climbing** n.

clime (klaım) n. 1. region, country 2. climate

clinch (klıntʃ) vt. 1. see CLENCH 2. settle, conclude (an agreement) —'**clincher** n. inf. something decisive

cling (klıŋ) vi. 1. adhere 2. be firmly attached 3. be dependent (on) (**clung** pt./pp.)

Clingfilm ('klıŋfılm) n. R thin polythene material having power to adhere closely: used for wrapping food

clinic ('klınık) n. place for medical examination, advice or treatment —'**clinical** a. 1. relating to clinic, care of sick etc.

2. objective, unemotional 3. bare, plain —'**clinically** adv. —**clinical thermometer** thermometer used for taking body temperature

clink[1] (klɪŋk) n. 1. sharp metallic sound —v. 2. (cause to) make this sound

clink[2] (klɪŋk) n. sl. prison

clinker ('klɪŋkə) n. 1. fused coal residues from fire or furnace 2. hard brick

clinker-built or **clincher-built** a. (of boat) with outer boards or plates overlapping

clip[1] (klɪp) vt. 1. cut with scissors 2. cut short (**-pp-**) —n. 3. inf. sharp blow —'**clipper** n. —'**clipping** n. something cut out, esp. article from newspaper; cutting —**clip joint** sl. nightclub etc. in which customers are overcharged

clip[2] (klɪp) n. device for gripping or holding together, esp. hair, clothing etc. —'**clipboard** n. portable writing board with clip at top for holding paper

clipper ('klɪpə) n. fast sailing ship

clippie ('klɪpɪ) n. UK inf. bus conductress

clique (kliːk, klɪk) n. 1. small exclusive set 2. faction, group of people —'**cliquish** a.

clitoris ('klɪtərɪs, 'klaɪ-) n. small erectile part of female genitals

cloak (kləʊk) n. 1. loose outer garment 2. disguise, pretext —vt. 3. cover with cloak 4. disguise, conceal —**cloak-and-dagger** a. concerned with intrigue and espionage —'**cloakroom** n. place for keeping coats, hats, luggage

clobber ('klɒbə) inf. vt. 1. beat, batter 2. defeat utterly —n. 3. belongings

cloche (klɒʃ) n. 1. cover to protect young plants 2. woman's close-fitting hat

clock (klɒk) n. 1. instrument for measuring time 2. device with dial for recording or measuring —'**clockwise** adv./a. in the direction that the hands of a clock rotate —'**clockwork** n. mechanism similar to that of a clock, as in a wind-up toy —**clock in** or **on, out** or **off** record arrival or departure on automatic time recorder

clod (klɒd) n. 1. lump of earth 2. blockhead —'**cloddish** a. —'**clodhopper** n. inf. 1. clumsy person; lout 2. (usu. pl.) large heavy shoe

clog (klɒg) vt. 1. hamper, impede, choke up (**-gg-**) —n. 2. obstruction, impediment 3. wooden-soled shoe —**clog dance**

cloisonné (klwɑːˈzɒneɪ) n. 1. enamel decoration in compartments formed by small fillets of metal —a. 2. of cloisonné

cloister ('klɔɪstə) n. 1. covered pillared arcade 2. monastery or convent —'**cloistered** a. confined, secluded, sheltered

clomp (klɒmp) n. see CLUMP[2]

clone (kləʊn) n. 1. group of organisms, cells of same genetic constitution as another, derived by asexual reproduction, as graft of plant etc. —v. 2. (cause to) produce clone

clop (klɒp) vi. move, sound, as horse's hooves (**-pp-**)

close[1] (kləʊs) a. 1. adjacent, near 2. compact 3. crowded 4. affectionate, intimate 5. almost equal 6. careful, searching 7. confined 8. secret 9. unventilated, stifling 10. reticent 11. niggardly 12. strict, restricted —adv. 13. nearly 14. tightly —n. 15. shut-in place 16. precinct of cathedral —'**closely** adv. —'**closeness** n. —**close-fisted** a. 1. mean 2. avaricious —**close harmony** singing in which all parts except bass lie close together —**close quarters** cramped space or position —**close season** time when it is illegal to kill certain kinds of game and fish —**close shave** inf. narrow escape —'**closeup** n. close view, esp. portion of cinema film —**at close quarters** engaged in hand-to-hand combat; in close proximity; very near together

close[2] (kləʊz) vt. 1. shut 2. stop up 3. prevent access to 4. finish —vi. 5. come together 6. grapple —n. 7. end —**closed circuit** complete electrical circuit through which current can flow —**closed shop** place of work in which all workers must belong to a trade union

closet ('klɒzɪt) n. 1. US cupboard 2. small private room 3. water closet, lavatory —a. 4. US private, secret —vt. 5. shut up in private room, esp. for conference 6. conceal

closure ('kləʊʒə) n. 1. act of closing 2. ending of debate by majority vote or other authority

clot (klɒt) n. 1. mass or lump 2. inf. fool 3. Med. coagulated mass of blood —vt. 4. form into lumps —vi. 5. coagulate (**-tt-**)

cloth (klɒθ) n. woven fabric —**clothe** (kləʊð) vt. put clothes on (**clothed** or **clad** pt./pp.) —**clothes** (kləʊðz) pl.n. 1. dress 2. bed coverings —**clothier** ('kləʊðɪə) n. —**clothing** ('kləʊðɪŋ) n. —**clotheshorse** ('kləʊðhɔːs) n. 1. frame on which to hang laundry for drying or airing 2. inf. excessively fashionable person

cloud (klaʊd) n. 1. condensed water vapour floating in air 2. state of gloom 3. multitude —vt. 4. overshadow, dim, darken —vi. 5. become cloudy —'**cloudless** a. —'**cloudy** a. —'**cloudburst** n. heavy downpour

clout (klaʊt) n. 1. inf. blow 2. short, flat-headed nail 3. influence, power —vt. 4. inf. strike

clove[1] (kləʊv) n. 1. dried flower bud of tropical tree, used as spice 2. one of small bulbs making up compound bulb

clove[2] (kləʊv) pt. of CLEAVE[1] —'**cloven** pp. of CLEAVE[1] —**cloven hoof** or **foot** 1. divided hoof of cow, deer etc. 2. symbol of Satan

clove hitch knot for securing rope to spar, post or larger rope

clover ('kləʊvə) n. low-growing forage plant, trefoil —'**cloverleaf** n. 1. arrangement of connecting roads, resembling four-leaf clover, that joins two intersecting main roads —a. 2. in shape of leaf of clover —**be in clover** be in luxury

clown (klaʊn) n. 1. comic entertainer in

circus 2. jester, fool —*vi.* 3. play jokes or tricks 4. act foolishly —'**clownish** *a.*

cloy (klɔɪ) *vt.* weary by sweetness, sameness *etc.*

club (klʌb) *n.* 1. thick stick 2. bat, stick used in some games 3. association for pursuance of common interest 4. building used by such association 5. one of the suits at cards —*vt.* 6. strike with club —*vi.* 7. join for a common object (-**bb**-) —**club foot** deformed foot —**club root** fungal disease of cabbages *etc.*, in which roots become thickened and distorted

cluck (klʌk) *vi./n.* (make) noise of hen

clue (kluː) *n.* 1. indication, *esp.* of solution of mystery or puzzle —*vt.* 2. (*usu. with* up) provide with helpful information —'**clueless** *a. sl.* helpless; stupid —**not have a clue** be ignorant or incompetent

clump¹ (klʌmp) *n.* 1. cluster of trees or plants 2. compact mass

clump² (klʌmp) *vi.* 1. walk, tread heavily —*n.* 2. dull, heavy tread or similar sound

clumsy ('klʌmzɪ) *a.* 1. awkward, unwieldy, ungainly 2. badly made or arranged —'**clumsily** *adv.* —'**clumsiness** *n.*

clung (klʌŋ) *pt./pp.* of CLING

clunk (klʌŋk) *n.* (sound of) blow or something falling

cluster ('klʌstə) *n.* 1. group, bunch —*v.* 2. gather, grow in cluster

clutch¹ (klʌtʃ) *v.* 1. grasp eagerly 2. snatch (at) —*n.* 3. grasp, tight grip 4. device enabling two revolving shafts to be connected and disconnected at will

clutch² (klʌtʃ) *n.* 1. set of eggs hatched at one time 2. brood of chickens

clutter ('klʌtə) *v.* 1. strew 2. crowd together in disorder —*n.* 3. disordered, obstructive mass of objects

Clydesdale ('klaɪdzdeɪl) *n.* heavy powerful carthorse, orig. from Scotland

cm *or* **cm.** centimetre

Cm *Chem.* curium

Cmdr. *Mil.* Commander

C.N.D. UK Campaign for Nuclear Disarmament

Co *Chem.* cobalt

CO Colorado

Co. *or* **co.** Company

Co. County

C.O. Commanding Officer

co- (*comb. form*) 1. together, as in *coproduction* 2. partnership or equality, as in *costar, copilot* 3. to similar degree, as in *coextend* 4. *Maths., astron.* of complement of angle, as in *cosecant*

c/o 1. care of 2. carried over

coach (kəʊtʃ) *n.* 1. long-distance or touring bus 2. large four-wheeled carriage 3. railway carriage 4. tutor, instructor —*vt.* 5. instruct —**coach-builder** *n.* —'**coachman** *n.* —'**coachwork** *n.* 1. design and manufacture of car bodies 2. body of car

coadjutor (kəʊ'ædʒʊtə) *n.* 1. bishop appointed as assistant to diocesan bishop 2. *rare* assistant

coagulate (kəʊ'ægjʊleɪt) *v.* 1. curdle, clot, form into a mass 2. congeal, solidify —**coagu'lation** *n.*

coal (kəʊl) *n.* 1. mineral consisting of carbonized vegetable matter, used as fuel 2. glowing ember —*v.* 3. supply with or take in coal —'**coalface** *n.* exposed seam of coal in mine —'**coalfield** *n.* district in which coal is found —**coal gas** mixture of gases produced by distillation of bituminous coal and used for heating and lighting —**coal tar** black tar, produced by distillation of bituminous coal, that can be further distilled to yield benzene *etc.* —**coal tit** small songbird having black head with white patch on nape

coalesce (kəʊə'lɛs) *vi.* unite, merge —**coa'lescence** *n.*

coalfish ('kəʊlfɪʃ) *n.* food fish with dark-coloured skin

coalition (kəʊə'lɪʃən) *n.* alliance, *esp.* of political parties

coaming ('kəʊmɪŋ) *n.* raised frame round ship's hatchway for keeping out water

coarse (kɔːs) *a.* 1. rough, harsh 2. unrefined 3. indecent —'**coarsely** *adv.* —'**coarsen** *v.* make or become coarse —'**coarseness** *n.* —**coarse fish** freshwater fish not of salmon family —**coarse fishing**

coast (kəʊst) *n.* 1. sea shore —*v.* 2. move under momentum 3. sail along (coast) —*vi.* 4. proceed without making much effort —'**coaster** *n.* 1. small ship 2. that which, one who, coasts 3. small table mat for glasses *etc.* —'**coastguard** *n.* 1. maritime force which aids shipping, prevents smuggling *etc.* 2. member of such force (*also* '**coastguardsman**)

coat (kəʊt) *n.* 1. sleeved outer garment 2. animal's fur or feathers 3. covering layer —*vt.* 4. cover with layer 5. clothe —**coat of arms** armorial bearings

coax (kəʊks) *vt.* wheedle, cajole, persuade, force gently

coaxial (kəʊ'æksɪəl) *or* **coaxal** (kəʊ'æksⁱl) *a.* having the same axis —**coaxial cable** high-frequency cable with outer conductor tube surrounding insulated central conductor

cob (kɒb) *n.* 1. short-legged stout horse 2. male swan 3. head of corn 4. round loaf of bread

cobalt ('kəʊbɔːlt) *n.* 1. metallic element 2. blue pigment from it —**cobalt bomb** 1. cobalt-60 device used in radiotherapy 2. nuclear weapon consisting of hydrogen bomb encased in cobalt

cobber ('kɒbə) *n. A obs., NZ* friend; mate: used as term of address to males

cobble ('kɒbⁱl) *vt.* 1. patch roughly 2. mend (shoes) —*n.* 3. round stone —'**cobbler** *n.* shoe mender —'**cobblestone** *n.* rounded stone used for paving (*also* '**cobble**)

cobbler ('kɒblə) *n.* 1. sweetened iced drink, usu. made from fruit and wine 2. *chiefly US* hot dessert of fruit covered with cakelike crust

cobblers ('kɒbləz) *pl.n.* UK *vulg. sl.*

testicles —(**a load of old**) **cobblers** rubbish; nonsense

COBOL ('kəʊbɒl) computer programming language for general commercial use

cobra ('kəʊbrə) n. venomous, hooded snake of Asia and Afr.

cobweb ('kɒbwɛb) n. spider's web

coca ('kəʊkə) n. either of two shrubs, native to Andes, whose dried leaves contain cocaine

Coca-Cola (kəʊkə'kəʊlə) n. R carbonated soft drink

cocaine or **cocain** (kə'keɪn) n. addictive narcotic drug used medicinally as anaesthetic

coccus ('kɒkəs) n. spherical or nearly spherical bacterium, such as staphylococcus (pl. **-ci** (-saɪ))

coccyx ('kɒksɪks) n. small triangular bone at end of spinal column (pl. **coccyges** (kɒk'saɪdʒiːz))

cochineal (kɒtʃɪ'niːl, 'kɒtʃɪniːl) n. scarlet dye from Mexican insect

cochlea ('kɒklɪə) n. spiral tube that forms part of internal ear, converting sound vibrations into nerve impulses (pl. **-leae** (-lɪiː))

cock (kɒk) n. 1. male bird, esp. of domestic fowl 2. tap for liquids 3. hammer of gun 4. its position drawn back —vt. 5. draw back (gun hammer) to firing position 6. raise, turn in alert or jaunty manner —'**cockerel** n. young cock —**cock-a-hoop** a. 1. in very high spirits 2. boastful 3. askew; confused —**cock-a-leekie** or **cocky-leeky** n. soup made from fowl boiled with leeks etc. —**cock-and-bull story** inf. obviously improbable story, esp. one used as excuse —'**cockcrow** or '**cockcrowing** n. daybreak —**cocked hat** hat with brims turned up and caught together to give two or three points —'**cockeyed** a. 1. crosseyed 2. with a squint 3. askew —'**cockfight** n. staged fight between roosters —'**cockscomb** or '**coxcomb** n. 1. comb of domestic cock 2. garden plant with flowers in broad spike resembling comb of cock 3. inf. conceited dandy —'**cockshy** n. UK 1. target in throwing games 2. throw itself (also shy) —**cock'sure** a. overconfident; arrogant —**knock into a cocked hat** sl. outdo, defeat

cockade (kɒ'keɪd) n. rosette, badge for hat

cockatoo (kɒkə'tuː, 'kɒkətuː) n. Aust., New Guinea, crested parrot

cockatrice ('kɒkətrɪs, -traɪs) n. fabulous animal similar to basilisk

cockchafer ('kɒktʃeɪfə) n. large, flying beetle

cocker spaniel ('kɒkə) small compact spaniel

cockle¹ ('kɒk'l) n. shellfish —'**cockleshell** n. 1. shell of cockle 2. shell of certain other molluscs 3. small light boat

cockle² ('kɒk'l) v. 1. wrinkle 2. pucker

cockney ('kɒknɪ) n. (oft. C-) native of London, esp. of East End (pl. **-s**)

cockpit ('kɒkpɪt) n. 1. pilot's seat, compartment in small aircraft 2. driver's

seat in racing car 3. orig. enclosure for cockfighting

cockroach ('kɒkrəʊtʃ) n. kind of insect, household pest

cocktail ('kɒkteɪl) n. 1. short drink of spirits with flavourings etc. 2. appetizer

cocky ('kɒkɪ) a. conceited, pert

cocoa ('kəʊkəʊ) or **cacao** n. 1. powder made from seed of cacao (tropical) tree 2. drink made from the powder

coconut or **cocoanut** ('kəʊkənʌt) n. 1. tropical palm 2. very large, hard nut from this palm —**coconut matting** coarse matting made from fibrous husk of coconut

cocoon (kə'kuːn) n. 1. sheath of insect in chrysalis stage 2. any protective covering

cocopan ('kəʊkəʊpæn) n. SA small truck on rails used esp. in mines

cocotte (kəʊ'kɒt, kə-) n. 1. small fireproof dish in which individual portions of food are cooked and served 2. prostitute; promiscuous woman

cod (kɒd) n. large sea fish of northern hemisphere —**cod-liver oil** extracted from livers of cod and related fish, rich in vitamins A and D

C.O.D. cash on delivery

coda ('kəʊdə) n. Mus. final part of musical composition

coddle ('kɒd'l) vt. overprotect, pamper

code (kəʊd) n. 1. system of letters, symbols and rules for their association to transmit messages secretly or briefly 2. scheme of conduct 3. collection of laws —**codifi'cation** n. —'**codify** vt.

codeine ('kəʊdiːn) n. alkaline sedative, analgesic drug

codex ('kəʊdɛks) n. ancient manuscript volume, esp. of Bible etc. (pl. **codices** ('kəʊdɪsiːz, 'kɒdɪ-))

codger ('kɒdʒə) n. inf. old man

codicil ('kɒdɪsɪl) n. addition to will —**codi'cillary** a.

codpiece ('kɒdpiːs) n. bag covering male genitals, attached to breeches: worn in 15th and 16th centuries

coeducation (kəʊɛdjʊ'keɪʃən) n. instruction in schools etc. attended by both sexes —**co-ed** n. 1. coeducational school etc. —a. 2. coeducational —**coedu'cational** a. of education of boys and girls together in mixed classes

coefficient (kəʊɪ'fɪʃənt) n. Maths. numerical or constant factor

coelenterate (sɪ'lɛntəreɪt, -rɪt) n. any of various invertebrates having saclike body with single opening (mouth), such as jellyfishes

coeliac or U.S. **celiac** ('siːlɪæk) a. pert. to belly —**coeliac disease** intestinal disorder caused by inadequate absorption of fats

coenobite or **cenobite** ('siːnəʊbaɪt) n. member of religious order following communal rule of life —**coenobitic(al)** or **cenobitic(al)** (siːnəʊ'bɪtɪk('l)) a.

coequal (kəʊ'iːkwəl) a. 1. of same size,

rank *etc.* —*n.* **2.** person or thing equal with another —**coe'quality** *n.*

coerce (kəʊ'ɜːs) *vt.* compel, force —**co'ercion** *n.* forcible compulsion or restraint —**co'ercive** *or* **co'ercible** *a.*

coeval (kəʊ'iːvəl) *a.* of same age or generation

coexist (kəʊɪg'zɪst) *vi.* exist together —**coex'istence** *n.* —**coex'istent** *a.*

coextend (kəʊɪk'stend) *v.* extend or cause to extend equally in space or time —**coex'tension** *n.* —**coex'tensive** *a.*

C. of E. Church of England

coffee ('kɒfɪ) *n.* **1.** seeds of tropical shrub **2.** drink made from roasting and grinding these —**coffee bar** café; snack bar —**coffee mill** machine for grinding roasted coffee beans —**coffee table** low table on which coffee may be served

coffer ('kɒfə) *n.* **1.** chest for valuables **2.** treasury, funds

cofferdam ('kɒfədæm) *n.* watertight structure enabling construction work to be done under water

coffin ('kɒfɪn) *n.* box in which corpse is buried or cremated

C. of S. Church of Scotland

cog (kɒg) *n.* **1.** one of series of teeth on rim of wheel **2.** person, thing forming small part of big process, organization *etc.* —'**cogwheel** *n.*

cogent ('kəʊdʒənt) *a.* convincing, compelling, persuasive —'**cogency** *n.* —'**cogently** *adv.*

cogitate ('kɒdʒɪteɪt) *vi.* think, reflect, ponder —**cogi'tation** *n.* —'**cogitative** *a.*

Cognac ('kɒnjæk) *n.* French brandy

cognate ('kɒgneɪt) *a.* of same stock, related, kindred —**cog'nation** *n.*

cognition (kɒg'nɪʃən) *n.* act or faculty of knowing —**cog'nitional** *a.*

cognizance *or* **cognisance** ('kɒgnɪzəns, 'kɒnɪ-) *n.* knowledge, perception —'**cognizable** *or* '**cognisable** *a.* —'**cognizant** *or* '**cognisant** *a.*

cognomen (kɒg'nəʊmen) *n.* surname, nickname (*pl.* **-s**, **-nomina** (-'nɒmɪnə, -'nəʊ-))

cognoscenti (kɒnjəʊ'ʃɛntɪ, kɒgnə-) *or* **conoscenti** (kɒnəʊ'ʃɛntɪ) *pl.n.* people with knowledge in particular field, *esp.* arts (*sing.* **-te** (-tiː))

cohabit (kəʊ'hæbɪt) *vi.* live together as husband and wife

coheir (kəʊ'ɛə) *n.* a joint heir (**co'heiress** *fem.*)

cohere (kəʊ'hɪə) *vi.* stick together, be consistent —**co'herence** *n.* —**co'herent** *a.* **1.** capable of logical speech, thought **2.** connected, making sense **3.** sticking together —**co'herently** *adv.* —**co'hesion** *n.* cohering —**co'hesive** *a.*

cohort ('kəʊhɔːt) *n.* **1.** troop **2.** associate

COHSE ('kəʊzɪ) Confederation of Health Service Employees

C.O.I. UK Central Office of Information

coif (kɔɪf) *n.* **1.** close-fitting cap worn under veil in Middle Ages **2.** leather cap worn under chainmail hood **3.** (kwɑːf) *rare* coiffure —*vt.* **4.** cover with or as if with coif **5.** (kwɑːf) arrange (hair) (**-ff-**)

coiffure (kwɑː'fjʊə) *n.* hairstyle —**coiffeur** (kwɑː'fɜː) *n.* hairdresser

coign of vantage (kɔɪn) advantageous position for observation or action

coil (kɔɪl) *vt.* **1.** lay in rings **2.** twist into winding shape —*vi.* **3.** twist, take up a winding shape or spiral —*n.* **4.** series of rings **5.** device in vehicle *etc.* to transform low-tension current to higher voltage for ignition purposes **6.** contraceptive device inserted in womb

coin (kɔɪn) *n.* **1.** piece of money **2.** money —*vt.* **3.** make into money, stamp **4.** invent —'**coinage** *n.* **1.** coining **2.** coins collectively —'**coiner** *n.* maker of counterfeit money

coincide (kəʊɪn'saɪd) *vi.* **1.** happen together **2.** agree exactly —**co'incidence** *n.* —**co'incident** *a.* coinciding —**coinci'dental** *a.*

Cointreau ('kwɑːntrəʊ) *n.* R colourless liqueur with orange flavouring

coir ('kɔɪə) *n.* fibre of coconut husk

coitus ('kɔɪtəs) *or* **coition** (kəʊ'ɪʃən) *n.* sexual intercourse

coke[1] (kəʊk) *n.* residue left from distillation of coal, used as fuel

coke[2] (kəʊk) *n. sl.* cocaine

Coke (kəʊk) *n.* R *short for* COCA-COLA

col (kɒl) *n.* high mountain pass

Col. 1. Colonel **2.** Colossians

cola *or* **kola** ('kəʊlə) *n.* **1.** tropical tree **2.** its nut, used to flavour drink

colander ('kɒləndə, 'kʌl-) *or* **cullender** *n.* culinary strainer perforated with small holes

cold (kəʊld) *a.* **1.** lacking heat **2.** indifferent, unmoved, apathetic **3.** dispiriting **4.** reserved or unfriendly **5.** (of colours) giving an impression of coldness —*n.* **6.** lack of heat **7.** illness, marked by runny nose *etc.* —'**coldly** *adv.* —'**coldness** *n.* —**cold-blooded** *a.* **1.** lacking pity, mercy **2.** having body temperature that varies with that of the surroundings —**cold chisel** toughened steel chisel —**cold cream** emulsion of water and fat for softening and cleansing skin —**cold feet** *sl.* loss of confidence —**cold frame** unheated wooden frame with glass top, used to protect young plants —**cold front** Met. boundary line between warm air mass and cold air pushing it —**cold-hearted** *a.* lacking in feeling or warmth; unkind —**cold-heartedness** *n.* —**cold shoulder** *inf.* show of indifference; slight —**cold-shoulder** *vt. inf.* treat with indifference —**cold sore** cluster of blisters at margin of lips, caused by viral infection (*also* **herpes labialis**) —**cold storage 1.** method of preserving perishable foods *etc.* by keeping them at artificially reduced temperature **2.** *inf.* state of temporary suspension —**cold sweat** *inf.* bodily reaction to fear or nervousness, characterized by chill and moist skin —**cold war** economic, diplomatic but nonmilitary hostility —(**out**) **in the cold** *inf.* neglected; ignored

cole (kəʊl) *n.* any of various plants such as cabbage and rape (*also* '**colewort**)

coleopteran (kɒlɪ'ɒptərən) *n.* **1.** any of order of insects, including beetles, in which forewings form shell-like protective elytra (*also* **cole'opteron**) —*a.* **2.** of this order (*also* **cole'opterous**)

coleslaw ('kəʊlslɔː) *n.* salad dish based on shredded cabbage

coletit ('kəʊltɪt) *n. see* **coal tit** *at* COAL

coleus ('kəʊlɪəs) *n.* plant cultivated for its variegated leaves

coley ('kəʊlɪ, 'kɒlɪ) *n.* **UK** any of various edible fishes, *esp.* coalfish

colic ('kɒlɪk) *n.* severe pains in the intestines —**co'litis** *n.* inflammation of the colon

coliseum (kɒlɪ'sɪəm) *or* **colosseum** (kɒlə'sɪəm) *n.* large building, such as stadium, used for entertainments *etc.*

collaborate (kə'læbəreɪt) *vi.* work with another on a project —**collabo'ration** *n.* —**col'laborator** *n.* one who works with another, *esp.* one who aids an enemy in occupation of his own country

collage (kə'lɑːʒ, kɒ-) *n.* (artistic) composition of bits and pieces stuck together on background

collagen ('kɒlədʒən) *n.* fibrous protein of connective tissue and bones that yields gelatin on boiling

collapse (kə'læps) *vi.* **1.** fall **2.** give way **3.** lose strength, fail —*n.* **4.** act of collapsing **5.** breakdown —**col'lapsible** *or* **col'lapsable** *a.*

collar ('kɒlə) *n.* **1.** band, part of garment, worn round neck —*vt.* **2.** seize by collar **3.** *inf.* capture, seize —'**collarbone** *n.* bone from shoulder to breastbone

collate (kɒ'leɪt, kə-) *vt.* **1.** compare carefully **2.** place in order (as printed sheets for binding) —**col'lation** *n.* **1.** collating **2.** light meal

collateral (kɒ'lætərəl, kə-) *n.* **1.** security pledged for repayment of loan —*a.* **2.** accompanying **3.** side by side **4.** of same stock but different line **5.** subordinate

colleague ('kɒliːg) *n.* associate, companion in office or employment, fellow worker

collect[1] (kə'lɛkt) *vt.* **1.** gather, bring together —*vi.* **2.** come together **3.** *inf.* receive money —*adv./a.* **4.** **US** (of telephone calls *etc.*) on transferred-charge basis —**col'lected** *a.* **1.** calm **2.** gathered —**col'lection** *n.* —**col'lective** *n.* **1.** factory, farm *etc.*, run on principles of collectivism —*a.* **2.** formed or assembled by collection **3.** forming whole or aggregate **4.** of individuals acting in cooperation —**col'lectively** *adv.* —**col'lectivism** *n.* theory that the state should own all means of production —**col'lector** *n.* —**collective bargaining** negotiation between trade union and employer or employers' organi-

zation on incomes and working conditions of employees —**collector's item** any rare or beautiful object thought worthy of collection

collect[2] ('kɒlɛkt) *n.* short prayer

colleen ('kɒliːn, kɒ'liːn) *n. Irish name for* girl

college ('kɒlɪdʒ) *n.* **1.** place of higher education **2.** society of scholars **3.** association —**col'legian** *n.* student —**col'legiate** *a.*

collide (kə'laɪd) *vi.* **1.** strike or dash together **2.** come into conflict —**collision** (kə'lɪʒən) *n.* colliding

collie ('kɒlɪ) *n.* any of several breeds of dog orig. bred to herd sheep

collier ('kɒlɪə) *n.* **1.** coal miner **2.** coal ship —'**colliery** *n.* coal mine

collimate ('kɒlɪmeɪt) *vt.* **1.** adjust line of sight of (optical instrument) **2.** make parallel or bring into line —**colli'mation** *n.*

collocate ('kɒləkeɪt) *vt.* group, place together —**collo'cation** *n.*

collodion (kə'ləʊdɪən) *or* **collodium** (kə-'ləʊdɪəm) *n.* chemical solution used in photography and medicine

colloid ('kɒlɔɪd) *n.* suspension of particles in a solution

collop ('kɒləp) *n. dial.* **1.** slice of meat **2.** small piece of anything

colloquial (kə'ləʊkwɪəl) *a.* pert. to, or used in, informal conversation —**col'loquialism** *n.* —'**colloquy** *n.* **1.** conversation **2.** dialogue

colloquium (kə'ləʊkwɪəm) *n.* **1.** gathering for discussion **2.** academic seminar (*pl.* **-s**, **-quia** (-kwɪə))

collusion (kə'luːʒən) *n.* secret agreement for a fraudulent purpose, *esp.* in legal proceedings —**col'lusive** *a.*

collywobbles ('kɒlɪwɒb'lz) *pl.n. sl.* **1.** upset stomach **2.** intense feeling of nervousness

cologne (kə'ləʊn) *n.* perfumed liquid (*also* **eau de cologne**)

colon[1] ('kəʊlən) *n.* mark (:) indicating break in sentence

colon[2] ('kəʊlən) *n.* part of large intestine from caecum to rectum

colonel ('kɜːn'l) *n.* commander of regiment or battalion —'**colonelcy** *n.*

colonnade (kɒlə'neɪd) *n.* row of columns

colony ('kɒlənɪ) *n.* **1.** body of people who settle in new country but remain subject to parent state **2.** country so settled **3.** distinctive group living together —**co'lonial** *a.* of colony —**co'lonialism** *n.* policy and practice of extending control over weaker peoples or areas (*also* **im'perialism**) —**co'lonialist** *n./a.* —**col'onist** *n.* —**coloni'zation** *or* **-i'sation** *n.* —'**colonize** *or* **-ise** *v.*

colophon ('kɒləfɒn, -fən) *n.* publisher's imprint or device

Colorado beetle (kɒlə'rɑːdəʊ) black-and-yellow beetle that is serious pest of potatoes

coloratura (kɒlərə'tʊərə) *n. Mus.* **1.** florid

virtuoso passage **2.** soprano who specializes in such music (*also* **coloratura soprano**)

colossus (kə'lɒsəs) *n.* **1.** huge statue **2.** something, somebody very large (*pl.* **colossi** (kə'lɒsaɪ), **-es**) —**co'lossal** *a.* huge, gigantic

colostomy (kə'lɒstəmɪ) *n.* surgical formation of opening from colon on to surface of body, which functions as anus

colostrum (kə'lɒstrəm) *n.* thin milky secretion from nipples that precedes and follows true lactation

colour *or U.S.* **color** ('kʌlə) *n.* **1.** hue, tint **2.** complexion **3.** paint **4.** pigment **5.** *fig.* semblance, pretext **6.** *fig.* timbre, quality **7.** *fig.* mood —*pl.* **8.** flag **9.** *Sport* distinguishing badge, symbol —*vt.* **10.** stain, dye, paint, give colour to **11.** *fig.* disguise **12.** *fig.* influence or distort —*vi.* **13.** become coloured **14.** blush —**colo'ration** *n.* —**'colourable** *a.* **1.** capable of being coloured **2.** appearing to be true; plausible **3.** pretended; feigned —**'coloured** *a.* **1.** possessing colour **2.** having strong element of fiction or fantasy; distorted (*esp. in* **highly coloured**) —**'Coloured** *a.* **1.** non-White **2.** in S Afr., of mixed descent —**'colourful** *a.* **1.** with bright or varied colours **2.** distinctive —**'colouring** *n.* **1.** process or art of applying colour **2.** anything used to give colour, such as paint **3.** appearance with regard to shade and colour **4.** arrangements of colours, as in markings of birds **5.** colour of complexion **6.** false appearance —**'colourless** *a.* **1.** without colour **2.** lacking interest **3.** grey; pallid **4.** without prejudice; neutral —**colour bar** discrimination against people of different race, *esp.* as practised by Whites against Blacks —**colour sergeant** sergeant who carries regimental, battalion or national colours

colt (kəʊlt) *n.* young male horse —**'coltish** *a.* **1.** inexperienced; unruly **2.** playful and lively

coltsfoot ('kəʊltsfʊt) *n.* wild plant with heart-shaped leaves and yellow flowers (*pl.* **-s**)

columbine ('kɒləmbaɪn) *n.* flower with five spurred petals

column ('kɒləm) *n.* **1.** long vertical cylinder, pillar **2.** support **3.** division of page **4.** *Journalism* regular feature in paper **5.** body of troops —**columnar** (kə'lʌmnə) *a.* —**'columnist** *n.* journalist writing regular feature for newspaper

com- *or* **con-** (*comb. form*) together; with; jointly, as in *commingle*

coma ('kəʊmə) *n.* state of unconsciousness —**'comatose** *a.*

comb (kəʊm) *n.* **1.** toothed instrument for tidying, arranging, ornamenting hair **2.** cock's crest **3.** mass of honey cells —*vt.* **4.** use comb on **5.** search with great care —**'comber** *n.* **1.** person, tool or machine that combs wool, flax *etc.* **2.** long curling wave; roller

combat ('kɒmbæt, -bət, 'kʌm-) *vt./n.* fight, contest —**'combatant** *n.* —**'combative** *a.* —**combat fatigue** *see* **battle fatigue** *at* BATTLE

combe *or* **comb** (kuːm) *n. see* COOMB

combine (kəm'baɪn) *v.* **1.** join together **2.** ally —*n.* ('kɒmbaɪn) **3.** trust, syndicate, *esp.* of businesses, trade organizations *etc.* —**combination** (kɒmbɪ'neɪʃən) *n.* —**combinative** ('kɒmbɪneɪtɪv) *a.* —**combination lock** lock that can only be opened when set of dials is turned to show specific sequence of numbers —**combine harvester** machine to harvest and thresh grain in one operation —**combining form** linguistic element that occurs only as part of compound word, such as *anthropo-* in *anthropology*

combo ('kɒmbəʊ) *n.* **1.** small group of jazz musicians **2.** *inf.* any combination (*pl.* **-s**)

combustion (kəm'bʌstʃən) *n.* process of burning —**combusti'bility** *n.* —**com'bustible** *a.*

come (kʌm) *vi.* **1.** approach, arrive, move towards something or someone nearer **2.** reach **3.** happen as a result **4.** occur **5.** be available **6.** originate **7.** become, turn out to be (**came, come, 'coming**) —**'coming** *a.* **1.** (of time *etc.*) approaching; next **2.** promising (*esp. in* **up and coming**) —*n.* **3.** arrival; approach —**'comeback** *n. inf.* **1.** return to active life after retirement **2.** retort —**'comedown** *n.* **1.** setback **2.** descent in social status —**come-hither** *a. inf.* alluring; seductive —**come-on** *n. inf.* anything that serves as lure —**come'uppance** *n. sl.* just retribution —**come on 1.** (of power *etc.*) start functioning **2.** progress **3.** advance, *esp.* in battle **4.** begin **5.** make entrance on stage —**come on strong** make forceful or exaggerated impression —**have it coming to one** *inf.* deserve what one is about to suffer

Comecon ('kɒmɪkɒn) *n.* association of Soviet-oriented Communist nations, founded in 1949 to coordinate economic development *etc.*

comedy ('kɒmɪdɪ) *n.* **1.** dramatic or other work of light, amusing character **2.** humour **3.** *Class. lit.* play in which main characters triumph over adversity —**co'median** *n.* **1.** entertainer who tells jokes *etc.* **2.** actor in comedy (**comedi'enne** *fem.*)

comely ('kʌmlɪ) *a.* fair, pretty, good-looking —**'comeliness** *n.*

comestible (kə'mɛstɪb'l) *n.* (*usu. pl.*) food

comet ('kɒmɪt) *n.* luminous heavenly body consisting of diffuse head, nucleus and long tail —**'cometary** *a.*

comfit ('kʌmfɪt, 'kɒm-) *n.* sweet

comfort ('kʌmfət) *n.* **1.** wellbeing **2.** ease **3.** consolation **4.** means of consolation or satisfaction —*vt.* **5.** soothe **6.** cheer, gladden, console —**comfortable** ('kʌmftəb'l) *a.* **1.** free from pain *etc.* **2.** *inf.* well-off financially —**comfortably** ('kʌmftəblɪ) *adv.* —**'comforter** *n.* **1.** a person who comforts **2.** baby's dummy **3.** woollen scarf —'**comfy** a. inf. comfortable

comfrey ('kʌmfrɪ) n. wild plant with hairy leaves

comic ('kɒmɪk) a. **1.** relating to comedy **2.** funny, laughable —n. **3.** comedian **4.** magazine consisting of strip cartoons —'**comical** a. —'**comically** adv. —**comic strip** sequence of drawings in newspaper etc., relating comic or adventurous situation

comity ('kɒmɪtɪ) n. **1.** mutual civility; courtesy **2.** friendly recognition accorded by nation to laws and usages of another (also **comity of nations**)

comm. 1. commonwealth **2.** communist

comma ('kɒmə) n. punctuation mark (,) separating parts of sentence

command (kə'mɑːnd) vt. **1.** order **2.** rule **3.** compel **4.** have in one's power **5.** overlook, dominate **6.** receive as due —vi. **7.** exercise rule —n. **8.** order **9.** power of controlling, ruling, dominating, overlooking **10.** knowledge, mastery **11.** post of one commanding **12.** district commanded, jurisdiction —'**commandant** n. —**com'man'deer** vt. seize for military use, appropriate —**com'mander** n. —**com'manding** a. **1.** in command **2.** with air of authority —**com'mandment** n.

commando (kə'mɑːndəʊ) n. (member of) special military unit trained for airborne, amphibious attack (pl. **-s**)

commedia dell'arte (kɒm'mɛdja del-'lartɛ) It. form of improvised comedy in Italy in 16th to 18th cent., with stock characters such as Punchinello, Harlequin etc.

commemorate (kə'mɛməreɪt) vt. **1.** celebrate, keep in memory by ceremony **2.** be a memorial of —**commemo'ration** n. —**com'memorative** a.

commence (kə'mɛns) v. begin —**com'mencement** n.

commend (kə'mɛnd) vt. **1.** praise **2.** commit, entrust —**com'mendable** a. —**com'mendably** adv. —**commen'dation** n. —**com'mendatory** a.

commensurate (kə'mɛnsərɪt, -ʃə-) a. **1.** equal in size or length of time **2.** in proportion, adequate —**com'mensurable** a. **1.** Maths. having common factor; having units of same dimensions and being related by whole numbers **2.** proportionate

comment ('kɒmɛnt) n. **1.** remark, criticism **2.** gossip **3.** note, explanation —vi. **4.** remark, note **5.** write notes explaining or criticizing a text —'**commentary** n. **1.** explanatory notes or comments **2.** spoken accompaniment to film etc. —'**commentate** vi. —'**commentator** n. author, speaker of commentary

commerce ('kɒmɜːs) n. **1.** buying and selling **2.** dealings **3.** trade —**com'mercial** a. **1.** of, concerning, business, trade, profit etc. —n. **2.** advertisement, esp. on radio or television —**com'mercialize** or **-lise** vt. **1.** make commercial **2.** exploit for profit, esp.

at expense of quality —**commercial traveller** travelling salesman

commie or **commy** ('kɒmɪ) n./a. inf., offens. communist

commination (kɒmɪ'neɪʃən) n. act of threatening punishment or vengeance —**comminatory** ('kɒmɪnətərɪ) a.

commingle (kɒ'mɪŋg'l) v. mix or be mixed

comminute ('kɒmɪnjuːt) vt. **1.** break (bone) into small fragments **2.** divide (property) into small lots —**commi'nution** n.

commis ('kɒmɪs, 'kɒmɪ) n. **1.** agent or deputy **2.** apprentice waiter or chef (pl. **-mis**)

commiserate (kə'mɪzəreɪt) vi. (usu. with with) pity, condole, sympathize —**commis'er'ation** n.

commissar ('kɒmɪsɑː, kɒmɪ'sɑː) n. official of Communist Party responsible for political education

commissariat (kɒmɪ'sɛərɪət) n. military department of food supplies and transport

commissary ('kɒmɪsərɪ) n. **1.** US shop supplying food or equipment, as in military camp **2.** US army officer responsible for supplies **3.** US restaurant in film studio **4.** representative or deputy, esp. of bishop

commission (kə'mɪʃən) n. **1.** something entrusted to be done **2.** delegated authority **3.** body entrusted with some special duty **4.** payment by percentage for doing something **5.** warrant, esp. royal warrant, giving authority **6.** document appointing soldier, sailor or airman to officer's rank **7.** doing, committing —vt. **8.** charge with duty or task **9.** Mil. confer a rank on **10.** give order for —**com'missioner** n. **1.** one empowered to act by commission or warrant **2.** member of commission or government board —**commissioned officer** military officer holding commission, such as Second Lieutenant in British Army, Acting Sub-Lieutenant in Royal Navy, Pilot Officer in Royal Air Force, and officers of all ranks senior to these —**commissioner for oaths** solicitor authorized to authenticate oaths on sworn statements

commissionaire (kəmɪʃə'nɛə) n. messenger, porter, doorkeeper (usu. uniformed)

commit (kə'mɪt) vt. **1.** entrust, give in charge **2.** perpetrate, be guilty of **3.** pledge, promise **4.** compromise, entangle **5.** send for trial (**-tt-**) —**com'mitment** n. —**com'mittal** n.

committee (kə'mɪtɪ) n. body appointed, elected for special business usu. from larger body

commode (kə'məʊd) n. **1.** chest of drawers **2.** stool containing chamber pot

commodious (kə'məʊdɪəs) a. roomy

commodity (kə'mɒdɪtɪ) n. **1.** article of trade **2.** anything useful

commodore ('kɒmədɔː) n. **1.** naval officer, senior to captain **2.** president of yacht club

3. senior captain in convoy of merchant ships

common ('kɒmən) a. **1.** shared by or belonging to all, or to several **2.** public, general **3.** ordinary, usual, frequent **4.** inferior **5.** vulgar —n. **6.** land belonging to community —pl. **7.** ordinary people **8.** (C-) lower House of British Parliament, House of Commons —**commo'nality** n. **1.** fact of being common **2.** commonalty —'**commonalty** n. general body of people —'**commoner** n. one of the common people, ie not of the nobility —'**commonly** adv. —**common fraction** see **simple fraction** at SIMPLE —**common law** body of law based on judicial decisions and custom —**common-law marriage** state of marriage deemed to exist between man and woman after years of cohabitation —**Common Market** European Economic Community —'**commonplace** a. **1.** ordinary, everyday —n. **2.** trite remark **3.** anything occurring frequently —**common room** chiefly UK sitting room in schools etc. —**common sense** sound, practical understanding —**common time** Mus. time signature indicating four crotchet beats to bar; four-four time —'**commonwealth** n. **1.** republic **2.** (C-) federation of self-governing states

commotion (kə'məʊʃən) n. stir, disturbance, tumult

commune[1] (kə'mju:n) vi. converse together intimately —**com'munion** n. **1.** sharing of thoughts, feelings etc. **2.** fellowship **3.** body with common faith **4.** (C-) participation in sacrament of the Lord's Supper **5.** (C-) that sacrament, Eucharist

commune[2] ('kɒmju:n) n. group of families, individuals living together and sharing property, responsibility etc. —'**communal** a. for common use

communicate (kə'mju:nɪkeɪt) vt. **1.** impart, convey **2.** reveal —vi. **3.** give or exchange information **4.** have connecting passage, door **5.** receive Communion —**com'municable** a. —**com'municant** n. one who receives Communion —**communi'cation** n. **1.** act of giving, esp. information **2.** information, message **3.** (usu. pl.) passage (road, railway etc.) or means of exchanging messages (radio, post etc.) between places —pl. **4.** connections between military base and front —**com'municative** a. free with information —**communication cord** UK cord or chain which may be pulled by passenger to stop train in emergency

communiqué (kə'mju:nɪkeɪ) n. official announcement

communism ('kɒmjʊnɪzəm) n. doctrine that all goods, means of production etc. should be property of community —'**communist** n./a. —**commu'nistic** a.

community (kə'mju:nɪtɪ) n. **1.** body of people with something in common, eg district of residence, religion etc. **2.** society, the public **3.** joint ownership **4.**

similarity, agreement —**community centre** building for communal activities

commute (kə'mju:t) vi. **1.** travel daily some distance to work —vt. **2.** exchange **3.** change (punishment etc.) into something less severe **4.** change (duty etc.) for money payment —**commu'tation** n. —**com'mutative** a. relating to or involving substitution —'**commutator** n.

compact[1] (kəm'pækt) a. **1.** neatly arranged or packed **2.** solid, concentrated **3.** terse —v. **4.** make, become compact —vt. **5.** compress —**com'pactly** adv. —**com'pactness** n. —**compact disc** ('kɒmpækt) small audio disc on which sound is recorded as series of metallic pits enclosed in PVC and read by optical laser system

compact[2] ('kɒmpækt) n. small case to hold face powder, powder puff and mirror

compact[3] ('kɒmpækt) n. agreement, covenant, treaty, contract

companion[1] (kəm'pænjən) n. **1.** mate, fellow, comrade, associate **2.** person employed to live with another —**com'panionable** a. —**com'panionship** n.

companion[2] (kəm'pænjən) n. **1.** raised cover over staircase from deck to cabin of ship **2.** deck skylight —**com'panionway** n. staircase from deck to cabin

company ('kʌmpənɪ) n. **1.** gathering of persons **2.** companionship, fellowship **3.** guests **4.** business firm **5.** division of regiment under captain **6.** crew of ship **7.** actors in play —**company sergeant-major** Mil. senior noncommissioned officer in company

compare (kəm'pɛə) vt. **1.** notice or point out likenesses and differences of **2.** liken **3.** make comparative and superlative of (adjective or adverb) —vi. **4.** compete —**comparability** (kɒmpərə'bɪlɪtɪ) n. —**comparable** ('kɒmpərəb'l) a. —**comparative** (kəm'pærətɪv) a. **1.** that may be compared **2.** not absolute **3.** relative, partial **4.** Gram. denoting form of adjective, adverb, indicating 'more' —n. **5.** comparative form of adjective or adverb —**comparatively** (kəm'pærətɪvlɪ) adv. —**comparison** (kəm'pærɪs'n) n. act of comparing —**compare with** be like

compartment (kəm'pɑ:tmənt) n. **1.** division or part divided off, eg in railway carriage **2.** section —**compart'mentalize** or **-lise** vt. put into categories etc., esp. to excessive degree

compass ('kʌmpəs) n. **1.** instrument for showing the north **2.** (usu. pl.) instrument for drawing circles **3.** circumference, measurement round **4.** space, area **5.** scope, reach —vt. **6.** surround **7.** comprehend **8.** attain, accomplish

compassion (kəm'pæʃən) n. pity, sympathy —**com'passionate** a. —**com'passionately** adv.

compatible (kəm'pætəb'l) a. **1.** capable of harmonious existence **2.** consistent, agree-

ing —**compati'bility** *n.* —**com'patibly**
adv.

compatriot (kəm'pætrɪət) *n.* fellow
countryman

compeer ('kɒmpɪə) *n.* equal, associate,
companion

compel (kəm'pɛl) *vt.* 1. force, oblige 2.
bring about by force (-**ll**-)

compendium (kəm'pɛndɪəm) *n.* 1. collection of different games 2. abridgment,
summary (*pl.* -**s**, -**ia** (-ɪə)) —**com'pendious**
a. brief but inclusive —**com'pendiously**
adv.

compensate ('kɒmpɛnseɪt) *vt.* 1. make up
for 2. recompense suitably 3. reward —*vi.*
4. (*with* for) supply an equivalent
—**compen'sation** *n.*

compere ('kɒmpɛə) *n.* 1. one who
presents artists in cabaret, television
shows *etc.* —*v.* 2. act as compere (for)

compete (kəm'piːt) *vi.* (*oft. with* with)
strive in rivalry, contend, vie —**competition** (kɒmpɪ'tɪʃən) *n.* —**competitive** (kəm-
'pɛtɪtɪv) *a.* —**competitor** (kəm'pɛtɪtə) *n.*

competent ('kɒmpɪtənt) *a.* 1. able, skilful
2. properly qualified 3. proper, due,
legitimate 4. suitable, sufficient —'**competence** *n.* efficiency —'**competently** *adv.*

compile (kəm'paɪl) *vt.* 1. make up (eg
book) from various sources or materials 2.
gather, put together —**compilation**
(kɒmpɪ'leɪʃən) *n.* —**com'piler** *n.*

complacent (kəm'pleɪs°nt) *a.* 1. self-
satisfied 2. pleased, gratified —**com'pla-
cence** *or* **com'placency** *n.* —**com'placent-
ly** *adv.*

complain (kəm'pleɪn) *vi.* 1. grumble 2.
bring charge, make known a grievance 3.
(*with* of) make known that one is suffering
from —**com'plainant** *n.* —**com'plaint** *n.* 1.
statement of a wrong, grievance 2.
ailment, illness

complaisant (kəm'pleɪz°nt) *a.* obliging,
willing to please, compliant —**com'plai-
sance** *n.* 1. act of pleasing 2. affability

complement ('kɒmplɪmənt) *n.* 1. person
or thing that completes something 2.
full allowance, equipment *etc.* —*vt.*
('kɒmplɪmɛnt) 3. add to, make complete
—**comple'mentary** *a.*

complete (kəm'pliːt) *a.* 1. full, perfect 2.
finished, ended 3. entire 4. thorough —*vt.*
5. make whole, perfect 6. finish —**com-
'pletely** *adv.* —**com'pleteness** *n.* —**com-
'pletion** *n.*

complex ('kɒmplɛks) *a.* 1. intricate,
compound, involved —*n.* 2. complicated
whole 3. group of related buildings 4.
psychological abnormality, obsession
—**com'plexity** *n.* —**complex fraction**
Maths. fraction in which numerator or
denominator or both contain fractions
(*also* **compound fraction**) —**complex
number** number of form *a* + *bi*, where *a*
and *b* are real numbers and i = $\sqrt{-1}$

complexion (kəm'plɛkʃən) *n.* 1. look,
colour, of skin, *esp.* of face, appearance 2.
aspect, character 3. disposition

compliant (kəm'plaɪənt) *a.* *see* COMPLY

complicate ('kɒmplɪkeɪt) *vt.* make intricate, involved, difficult, mix up —**compli-
'cation** *n.*

complicity (kəm'plɪsɪtɪ) *n.* partnership in
wrongdoing

compliment ('kɒmplɪmənt) *n.* 1. expression of regard, praise 2. flattering speech
—*pl.* 3. expression of courtesy, formal
greetings —*vt.* ('kɒmplɪmɛnt) 4. praise,
congratulate —**compli'mentary** *a.* 1.
expressing praise 2. free of charge

compline ('kɒmplɪn, -plaɪn) *or* **complin**
('kɒmplɪn) *n.* last service of day in R.C.
Church

comply (kəm'plaɪ) *vi.* consent, yield, do as
asked (**com'plied, com'plying**) —**com'pli-
ance** *n.* —**com'pliant** *a.*

component (kəm'pəʊnənt) *n.* 1. part,
element, constituent of whole —*a.* 2.
composing, making up

comport (kəm'pɔːt) *vi.* 1. agree —*vt.* 2.
behave

compose (kəm'pəʊz) *vt.* 1. arrange, put in
order 2. write, invent 3. make up 4. calm 5.
settle, adjust —**com'posed** *a.* calm —**com-
'poser** *n.* one who composes, *esp.* music
—'**composite** *a.* made up of distinct parts
—**compo'sition** *n.* —**compositor** (kəm-
'pɒzɪtə) *n.* typesetter, one who arranges
type for printing —**com'posure** *n.* calmness —**composite school** C one offering
both academic and nonacademic courses

compos mentis ('kɒmpəs 'mɛntɪs) *Lat.* of
sound mind

compost ('kɒmpɒst) *n.* fertilizing mixture
of decayed vegetable matter for soil

compote ('kɒmpəʊt) *n.* fruit stewed or
preserved in syrup

compound[1] ('kɒmpaʊnd) *n.* 1. mixture,
joining 2. substance, word, made up of
parts —*a.* 3. not simple 4. composite,
mixed —*vt.* (kəm'paʊnd) 5. mix, make up,
put together 6. intensify, make worse 7.
Law agree not to prosecute in return for a
consideration —*v.* 8. compromise, settle
(debt) by partial payment —**compound
eye** convex eye of insects and some
crustaceans, consisting of numerous separate units —**compound fracture** fracture
in which broken bone pierces skin
—**compound interest** interest calculated
on both principal and its accrued interest
—**compound sentence** sentence containing at least two coordinate clauses
—**compound time** *Mus.* time in which
number of beats per bar is multiple of
three

compound[2] ('kɒmpaʊnd) *n.* (fenced or
walled) enclosure containing houses *etc.*

comprehend (kɒmprɪ'hɛnd) *vt.* 1. understand, take in 2. include, comprise
—**compre'hensible** *a.* —**compre'hension**
n. —**compre'hensive** *a.* 1. wide, full 2.
taking in much —**compre'hensively** *adv.*
—**compre'hensiveness** *n.* —**comprehensive school** secondary school for children
of all abilities

compress (kəm'prɛs) *vt.* **1.** squeeze together **2.** make smaller in size, bulk —*n.* ('kɒmprɛs) **3.** pad of lint applied to wound, inflamed part *etc.* —**com'pressible** *a.* —**com'pression** *n.* in internal combustion engine, squeezing of explosive charge before ignition, to give additional force —**com'pressor** *n. esp.* machine to compress air, gas

comprise (kəm'praɪz) *vt.* include, contain —**com'prisable** *a.*

compromise ('kɒmprəmaɪz) *n.* **1.** meeting halfway, coming to terms by giving up part of claim **2.** middle course —*v.* **3.** settle (dispute) by making concessions —*vt.* **4.** expose to risk or suspicion

Comptometer (kɒmp'tɒmɪtə) *n.* **R** calculating machine

comptroller (kən'trəʊlə) *n.* controller (in some titles)

compulsion (kəm'pʌlʃən) *n.* **1.** act of compelling **2.** irresistible impulse —**com'pulsive** *a.* —**com'pulsorily** *adv.* —**com'pulsory** *a.* not optional

compunction (kəm'pʌŋkʃən) *n.* regret for wrongdoing

compute (kəm'pjuːt) *v.* reckon, calculate, *esp.* using computer —**compu'tation** *n.* reckoning, estimate —**com'puter** *n.* electronic machine for storing, retrieving information and performing calculations —**com'puterize** *or* **-ise** *v.* equip with, perform by computer

comrade ('kɒmreɪd, -rɪd) *n.* mate, companion, friend —'**comradeship** *n.*

con¹ (kɒn) *inf. n.* **1.** confidence trick —*vt.* **2.** swindle, defraud

con² (kɒn) *n.* contra, against —**pros and cons** (arguments) for and against

con³ *or* (*esp. U.S.*) **conn** (kɒn) *vt.* direct steering of (ship) —'**conner** *n.*

concatenate (kɒn'kætɪneɪt) *vt.* link together —**concate'nation** *n.* connected chain (as of circumstances)

concave ('kɒnkeɪv, kɒn'keɪv) *a.* hollow, rounded inwards —**concavity** (kɒn'kævɪtɪ) *n.*

conceal (kən'siːl) *vt.* hide, keep secret —**con'cealment** *n.*

concede (kən'siːd) *vt.* **1.** admit, admit truth of **2.** grant, allow —*vi.* **3.** yield

conceit (kən'siːt) *n.* **1.** vanity, overweening opinion of oneself **2.** far-fetched comparison —**con'ceited** *a.*

conceive (kən'siːv) *vt.* **1.** believe **2.** form conception of **3.** become pregnant with —*vi.* **4.** become pregnant —**con'ceivable** *a.* —**con'ceivably** *adv.* —**conceive of** have an idea of; imagine; think of

concentrate ('kɒnsəntreɪt) *vt.* **1.** focus (one's efforts *etc.*) **2.** increase in strength **3.** reduce to small space —*vi.* **4.** devote all attention **5.** come together —*n.* **6.** concentrated material or solution —**con'centration** *n.* —**concentration camp** prison camp, *esp.* one in Nazi Germany

concentric (kən'sɛntrɪk) *a.* having the same centre

concept ('kɒnsɛpt) *n.* **1.** abstract idea **2.** mental expression —**con'ceptual** *a.* —**con'ceptualize** *or* **-lise** *v.*

conception (kən'sɛpʃən) *n.* **1.** idea, notion **2.** act of conceiving

concern (kən'sɜːn) *vt.* **1.** relate or apply to **2.** interest, affect, trouble **3.** (*with in or with*) involve (oneself) —*n.* **4.** affair **5.** regard, worry **6.** importance **7.** business enterprise —**con'cerned** *a.* **1.** connected **2.** interested **3.** worried **4.** involved —**con'cerning** *prep.* respecting, about

concert ('kɒnsɜːt) *n.* **1.** musical entertainment **2.** harmony, agreement —*v.* (kən'sɜːt) **3.** arrange, plan together —**con'certed** *a.* **1.** mutually arranged, planned **2.** determined —**concer'tina** *n.* **1.** musical instrument with bellows and keys —*vi.* **2.** fold, collapse, as bellows —**concerto** (kən'tʃɛətəʊ) *n.* musical composition for solo instrument and orchestra (*pl.* **-s**) —**concert pitch 1.** frequency of 440 hertz assigned to A above middle C **2.** *inf.* state of extreme readiness

concession (kən'sɛʃən) *n.* **1.** act of conceding **2.** thing conceded **3.** grant **4.** special privilege **5. C** land division in township survey —**concessio'naire, con'cessioner** *or* **con'cessionary** *n.* someone who holds or operates concession —**con'cessive** *a.*

conch (kɒŋk, kɒntʃ) *n.* seashell —**conchology** (kɒŋ'kɒlədʒɪ) *n.* study, collection of shells and shellfish

concierge (kɒnsɪ'ɛəʒ) *n.* in France, caretaker, doorkeeper

conciliate (kən'sɪlɪeɪt) *vt.* pacify, win over from hostility —**concili'ation** *n.* —**con'ciliator** *n.* —**con'ciliatory** *a.*

concise (kən'saɪs) *a.* brief, terse —**con'cisely** *adv.* —**con'ciseness** *n.* —**concision** (kən'sɪʒən) *n.*

conclave ('kɒnkleɪv) *n.* **1.** private meeting **2.** assembly for election of Pope

conclude (kən'kluːd) *vt.* **1.** end, finish **2.** deduce **3.** settle **4.** decide —*vi.* **5.** come to an end —**con'clusion** *n.* —**con'clusive** *a.* decisive, convincing —**con'clusively** *adv.*

concoct (kən'kɒkt) *vt.* **1.** make (mixture), with various ingredients **2.** make up **3.** contrive, plan —**con'coction** *n.*

concomitant (kən'kɒmɪtənt) *a.* accompanying —**con'comitance** *n.* existence

concord ('kɒnkɔːd) *n.* **1.** agreement **2.** harmony —**con'cordance** *n.* **1.** agreement **2.** index to words of book (*esp.* Bible) —**con'cordant** *a.* —**con'cordat** *n.* pact or treaty, *esp.* between Vatican and another state concerning interests of religion in that state

concourse ('kɒnkɔːs) *n.* **1.** crowd **2.** large, open place in public area

concrete ('kɒnkriːt) *n.* **1.** mixture of sand, cement *etc.*, used in building —*a.* **2.** made of concrete **3.** particular, specific **4.** perceptible, actual **5.** solid —'**concretely** *adv.* —**con'cretion** *n.* **1.** mass of compressed particles **2.** stonelike growth in body

concubine ('kɒŋkjʊbaɪn, 'kɒn-) n. **1.** woman living with man as his wife, but not married to him **2.** 'secondary' wife of inferior legal status —**concubinage** (kɒn-'kjuːbɪnɪdʒ) n.

concupiscence (kən'kjuːpɪsəns) n. lust

concur (kən'kɜː) vi. **1.** agree, express agreement **2.** happen together **3.** coincide (**-rr-**) —**con'currence** n. —**con'current** a. —**con'currently** adv. at the same time

concuss (kən'kʌs) vt. injure (brain) by blow, fall etc. —**con'cussion** n. **1.** brain injury **2.** physical shock

condemn (kən'dɛm) vt. **1.** blame **2.** find guilty **3.** doom **4.** find, declare unfit for use —**condemnation** (kɒndɛm'neɪʃən) n. —**condemnatory** (kɒndɛm'neɪtərɪ) a.

condense (kən'dɛns) vt. **1.** concentrate, make more solid **2.** turn from gas into liquid **3.** pack into few words —vi. **4.** turn from gas to liquid —**conden'sation** n. —**con'denser** n. **1.** Elec. apparatus for storing electrical energy, a capacitor **2.** apparatus for reducing vapours to liquid form **3.** a lens or mirror for focusing light —**condensed milk** milk reduced by evaporation to thick concentration, with sugar added

condescend (kɒndɪ'sɛnd) vi. **1.** treat graciously one regarded as inferior **2.** do something below one's dignity —**conde-'scending** a. —**conde'scension** n.

condign (kən'daɪn) a. (esp. of punishment) fitting; deserved

condiment ('kɒndɪmənt) n. relish, seasoning for food

condition (kən'dɪʃən) n. **1.** state or circumstances of anything **2.** thing on which statement or happening or existing depends **3.** stipulation, prerequisite **4.** health, physical fitness **5.** rank —vt. **6.** accustom **7.** regulate **8.** make fit, healthy **9.** be essential to happening or existence of —**con'ditional** a. **1.** dependent on circumstances or events —n. **2.** Gram. conditional verb form, clause etc. —**conditioned reflex** in psychology and physiology, automatic response induced by stimulus repeatedly applied

condole (kən'dəʊl) vi. **1.** grieve (with), offer sympathy **2.** commiserate (with) —**con'dolence** n.

condom ('kɒndəm) n. sheathlike rubber contraceptive device worn by man

condominium (kɒndə'mɪnɪəm) n. joint rule by two or more states

condone (kən'dəʊn) vt. overlook, forgive, treat as not existing

condor ('kɒndɔː) n. large vulture found in the Andes

conduce (kən'djuːs) vi. (with to) **1.** help, promote **2.** tend (towards) —**con'ducive** a.

conduct ('kɒndʌkt) n. **1.** behaviour **2.** management —vt. (kən'dʌkt) **3.** escort, guide **4.** lead, direct **5.** manage **6.** transmit (heat, electricity) —**con'ductance** n.

ability of system to conduct electricity —**con'duction** n. —**con'ductive** a. —**conduc'tivity** n. —**con'ductor** n. **1.** person in charge of bus etc., who collects fares **2.** director of orchestra **3.** one who leads, guides **4.** substance capable of transmitting heat, electricity etc. **5.** US official in charge of passenger train

conduit ('kɒndɪt, -djʊɪt) n. channel or pipe for conveying water, electric cables etc.

cone (kəʊn) n. **1.** solid figure with circular base, tapering to a point **2.** fruit of pine, fir etc. —'**conic(al)** a. of or like cone —**conic section** one of group of curves formed by intersection of plane and right circular cone

confabulate (kən'fæbjʊleɪt) vi. chat —'**confab** n. inf. shortened form of **confabu'lation** n. confidential conversation

confection (kən'fɛkʃən) n. prepared delicacy, esp. something sweet —**con'fectioner** n. dealer in fancy cakes, pastries, sweets etc. —**con'fectionery** n. sweets, cakes etc.

confederate (kən'fɛdərɪt) n. **1.** ally **2.** accomplice —v. (kən'fɛdəreɪt) **3.** unite —**con'federacy** n. —**confede'ration** n. alliance of political units

confer (kən'fɜː) vt. **1.** grant, give **2.** bestow **3.** award —vi. **4.** consult together (**-rr-**) —'**conference** n. meeting for consultation or deliberation —**con'ferment** n.

confess (kən'fɛs) vt. **1.** admit, own **2.** (of priest) hear sins of —vi. **3.** acknowledge **4.** declare one's sins orally to priest —**con'fession** n. —**con'fessional** n. confessor's stall or box —**con'fessor** n. priest who hears confessions

confetti (kən'fɛtɪ) n. small bits of coloured paper for throwing at weddings

confide (kən'faɪd) vi. **1.** (with in) tell secrets, trust —vt. **2.** entrust —**confidant** (kɒnfɪ'dænt, 'kɒnfɪdænt) n. one entrusted with secrets (**-e** fem.) —**confidence** ('kɒnfɪdəns) n. **1.** trust **2.** boldness, assurance **3.** intimacy **4.** something confided, secret —**confident** ('kɒnfɪdənt) a. **1.** having or showing certainty; sure **2.** sure of oneself **3.** presumptuous —**confidential** (kɒnfɪ'dɛnʃəl) a. **1.** private **2.** secret **3.** entrusted with another's confidences —**confidentially** (kɒnfɪ'dɛnʃəlɪ) adv. —**confidently** ('kɒnfɪdəntlɪ) adv. —**con'fiding** a. unsuspicious; trustful —**confidence trick** swindle in which victim entrusts money etc., to thief, believing him honest

configuration (kənfɪgjʊ'reɪʃən) n. shape, aspect, conformation, arrangement

confine (kən'faɪn) vt. **1.** keep within bounds **2.** keep in house, bed etc. **3.** shut up, imprison —**con'finement** n. **1.** act of confining or state of being confined **2.** period of birth of child —'**confines** pl.n. boundaries, limits

confirm (kən'fɜːm) vt. **1.** make certain of, verify **2.** strengthen, settle **3.** make valid, ratify **4.** administer confirmation to —**confir'mation** *n.* **1.** making strong, certain **2.** rite administered by bishop to confirm vows made at baptism —**con'firmative** *or* **con'firmatory** *a.* **1.** tending to confirm or establish **2.** corroborative —**con'firmed** *a.* (of habit *etc.*) long-established

confiscate ('kɒnfɪskeɪt) *vt.* seize by authority —**confis'cation** *n.* —**con'fiscatory** *a.*

conflagration (kɒnflə'greɪʃən) *n.* great destructive fire

conflate (kən'fleɪt) *vt.* combine, blend to form whole

conflict ('kɒnflɪkt) *n.* **1.** struggle, trial of strength **2.** disagreement —*vi.* (kən'flɪkt) **3.** be at odds (with), be inconsistent (with) **4.** clash

confluence ('kɒnfluəns) *or* **conflux** ('kɒnflʌks) *n.* **1.** union of streams **2.** meeting place —**'confluent** *a.*

conform (kən'fɔːm) *vi.* **1.** comply with accepted standards, conventions *etc.* —*v.* **2.** adapt to rule, pattern, custom *etc.* —**con'formable** *a.* —**con'formably** *adv.* —**confor'mation** *n.* structure, adaptation —**con'formist** *n.* one who conforms, *esp.* excessively —**con'formity** *n.* compliance

confound (kən'faund) *vt.* **1.** baffle, perplex **2.** confuse **3.** defeat —**con'founded** *a. esp. inf.* damned

confrère ('kɒnfreə) *n.* fellow member of profession *etc.*

confront (kən'frʌnt) *vt.* **1.** face **2.** bring face to face (with) —**confron'tation** *n.*

Confucianism (kən'fjuːʃənɪzəm) *n.* ethical system of Confucius, Chinese philosopher, emphasizing devotion to family, peace and justice

confuse (kən'fjuːz) *vt.* **1.** bewilder **2.** jumble **3.** make unclear **4.** mistake (one thing) for another **5.** disconcert —**con'fusion** *n.*

confute (kən'fjuːt) *vt.* **1.** prove wrong **2.** disprove —**confu'tation** *n.*

conga ('kɒŋgə) *n.* Latin American dance performed by number of people in single file

congé ('kɒnʒeɪ) *n.* **1.** permission to depart or dismissal, *esp.* when formal **2.** farewell

congeal (kən'dʒiːl) *v.* solidify by cooling or freezing —**conge'lation** *n.*

congener (kən'dʒiːnə, 'kɒndʒɪnə) *n.* member of class, group *etc. esp.* any animal of specified genus

congenial (kən'dʒiːnjəl) *a.* **1.** pleasant, to one's liking **2.** of similar disposition, tastes *etc.* —**congeni'ality** *n.* —**con'genially** *adv.*

congenital (kən'dʒɛnɪt³l) *a.* **1.** existing at birth **2.** dating from birth

conger ('kɒŋgə) *n.* variety of large, voracious, sea eel

congeries (kɒn'dʒɪəriːz) *n. sing.* and *pl.* collection or mass of small bodies, conglomeration

congest (kən'dʒɛst) *v.* overcrowd or clog

—**con'gested** *a.* —**con'gestion** *n.* abnormal accumulation, overcrowding

conglomerate (kən'glɒmərɪt) *n.* **1.** thing, substance (*esp.* rock) composed of mixture of other, smaller elements or pieces **2.** business organization comprising many companies —*v.* (kən'glɒməreɪt) **3.** gather together —*a.* **4.** made up of heterogeneous elements **5.** (of sedimentary rocks) consisting of rounded fragments within finer matrix —**conglomer'ation** *n.*

congratulate (kən'grætjuleɪt) *vt.* express pleasure at good fortune, success *etc.* —**congratu'lation** *n.* —**con'gratulatory** *a.*

congregate ('kɒŋgrɪgeɪt) *v.* **1.** assemble **2.** collect, flock together —**congre'gation** *n.* assembly, *esp.* for worship —**congre'gational** *a.* —**Congre'gationalism** *n.* system in which each separate church is self-governing —**Congre'gationalist** *n.*

congress ('kɒŋgrɛs) *n.* **1.** meeting **2.** formal assembly for discussion **3.** legislative body —**con'gressional** *a.* —**'congressman** *n.* a member of the U.S. Congress

congruent ('kɒŋgruənt) *a.* **1.** suitable, accordant **2.** fitting together, *esp.* triangles —**'congruence** *n.* —**con'gruity** *n.* —**'con gruous** *a.*

conic(al) ('kɒnɪk(³l)) *a. see* CONE

conifer ('kəunɪfə, 'kɒn-) *n.* cone-bearing tree, as fir, pine *etc.* —**co'niferous** *a.*

conjecture (kən'dʒɛktʃə) *n.* **1.** guess, guesswork —*v.* **2.** guess, surmise —**con'jectural** *a.*

conjoin (kən'dʒɔɪn) *vt.* **1.** combine —*vi.* **2.** come, or act, together —**con'joint** *a.* concerted, united —**con'jointly** *adv.*

conjugal ('kɒndʒug³l) *a.* **1.** relating to marriage **2.** between married persons —**conju'gality** *n.*

conjugate ('kɒndʒugeɪt) *vt.* inflect verb in its various forms (past, present *etc.*) —**conju'gation** *n.*

conjunction (kən'dʒʌŋkʃən) *n.* **1.** union **2.** simultaneous happening **3.** part of speech joining words, phrases *etc.* —**con'junctive** *a.* —**con'juncture** *n.*

conjunctiva (kɒndʒʌŋk'taɪvə) *n.* mucous membrane lining eyelid —**conjuncti'vitis** *n.* inflammation of this

conjure ('kʌndʒə) *vi.* **1.** produce magic effects **2.** perform tricks by jugglery *etc.* **3.** invoke devils —*vt.* (kən'dʒuə) **4.** implore earnestly —**conju'ration** *n.* —**'conjurer** *or* **'conjuror** *n.* —**conjure up 1.** present to the mind **2.** call up (spirit or devil) by incantation

conk (kɒŋk) *inf. vt.* **1.** strike (*esp.* on head) —*n.* **2.** nose —**conk out** *inf.* **1.** break down **2.** tire suddenly; collapse

conker ('kɒŋkə) *n. inf.* horse chestnut

connect (kə'nɛkt) *v.* **1.** join together, unite —*vt.* **2.** associate in the mind —**con'nection** *or* **con'nexion** *n.* **1.** association **2.** train *etc.* timed to enable passengers to transfer from another **3.** family relation —**con'nective** *a.* —**connecting rod** that part of engine which transfers motion from piston to crankshaft

conning tower (ˈkɒnɪŋ) armoured control position in submarine, battleship *etc*. (*see also* CON³)

connive (kəˈnaɪv) *vi*. 1. plot, conspire 2. assent, refrain from preventing or forbidding —**conˈnivance** *n*.

connoisseur (kɒnɪˈsɜː) *n*. 1. critical expert in matters of taste, *esp*. fine arts 2. competent judge

connote (kɒˈnəʊt) *vt*. imply, mean in addition to primary meaning —**connoˈtation** *n*.

connubial (kəˈnjuːbɪəl) *a*. of marriage

conquer (ˈkɒŋkə) *vt*. 1. win by force of arms, overcome 2. defeat —*vi*. 3. be victorious —ˈ**conqueror** *n*. —ˈ**conquest** *n*.

conquistador (kɒnˈkwɪstədɔː) *n*. adventurer or conqueror, *esp*. one of Sp. conquerors of New World in 16th cent. (*pl*. **-s, -dores** (-dɔːrɛs))

Cons. Conservative

consanguinity (kɒnsæŋˈgwɪnɪtɪ) *n*. kinship —**consanˈguineous** *a*.

conscience (ˈkɒnʃəns) *n*. sense of right or wrong governing person's words and actions —**consciˈentious** *a*. scrupulous 2. obedient to the dictates of conscience —**consciˈentiously** *adv*. —**conscience money** money paid voluntarily to compensate for dishonesty, *esp*. for taxes formerly evaded —**conscience-stricken** *a*. feeling anxious or guilty (*also* **conscience-smitten**) —**conscientious objector** one who refuses military service on moral or religious grounds

conscious (ˈkɒnʃəs) *a*. 1. aware 2. awake to one's surroundings and identity 3. deliberate, intentional —ˈ**consciously** *adv*. —ˈ**consciousness** *n*. being conscious

conscript (ˈkɒnskrɪpt) *n*. 1. one compulsorily enlisted for military service —*vt*. (kənˈskrɪpt) 2. enrol for compulsory military service —**conˈscription** *n*.

consecrate (ˈkɒnsɪkreɪt) *vt*. make sacred —**conseˈcration** *n*.

consecutive (kənˈsɛkjʊtɪv) *a*. in unbroken succession —**conˈsecutively** *adv*.

consensus (kənˈsɛnsəs) *n*. widespread agreement, unanimity

consent (kənˈsɛnt) *vi*. 1. agree, comply —*n*. 2. acquiescence 3. permission 4. agreement —**conˈsentient** *a*.

consequence (ˈkɒnsɪkwəns) *n*. 1. result, effect, outcome 2. that which naturally follows 3. significance, importance —ˈ**consequent** *a*. —**conseˈquential** *a*. important —ˈ**consequently** *adv*. therefore, as a result

conservatoire (kənˈsɜːvətwɑː) *n*. school for teaching music

conserve (kənˈsɜːv) *vt*. 1. keep from change or decay 2. preserve 3. maintain —*n*. (ˈkɒnsɜːv, kənˈsɜːv) 4. jam, preserved fruit *etc*. —**conˈservancy** *n*. 1. UK court or commission with jurisdiction over river, port *etc*. 2. conservation —**conserˈvation**

n. protection, careful management of natural resources and environment —**conˈservationist** *n./a*. —**conˈservatism** *n*. —**conˈservative** *a*. 1. tending, or wishing to conserve 2. moderate —*n*. 3. *Pol*. one who desires to preserve institutions of his country against change and innovation 4. one opposed to hasty changes or innovations —**conˈservatory** *n*. greenhouse —**conservation of energy** principle that total energy of isolated system is constant and independent of changes occurring within system —**conservation of mass** principle that total mass of isolated system is constant and independent of chemical and physical changes taking place within system

consider (kənˈsɪdə) *vt*. 1. think over 2. examine 3. make allowance for 4. have as opinion 5. discuss —**conˈsiderable** *a*. 1. important 2. somewhat large —**conˈsiderably** *adv*. —**conˈsiderate** *a*. thoughtful for others' feelings, careful —**conˈsiderately** *adv*. —**consideˈration** *n*. 1. deliberation 2. point of importance 3. thoughtfulness 4. bribe, recompense —**conˈsidered** *a*. 1. presented or thought out with care 2. esteemed —**conˈsidering** *prep*. 1. in view of —*adv*. 2. *inf*. all in all; taking circumstances into account —*conj*. 3. in view of the fact (that)

consign (kənˈsaɪn) *vt*. 1. commit, hand over 2. entrust to carrier —**consignˈee** *n*. —**conˈsignment** *n*. goods consigned —**conˈsignor** *n*.

consist (kənˈsɪst) *vi*. 1. be composed (of) 2. (*with* in) have as basis 3. agree (with), be compatible (with) —**conˈsistency** *or* **conˈsistence** *n*. 1. agreement 2. harmony 3. degree of firmness —**conˈsistent** *a*. 1. unchanging, constant 2. agreeing (with) —**conˈsistently** *adv*.

consistory (kənˈsɪstərɪ) *n*. ecclesiastical court or council, *esp*. of Pope and Cardinals

console¹ (kənˈsəʊl) *vt*. comfort, cheer in distress —**consoˈlation** *n*. —**consolatory** (kənˈsɒlətərɪ) *a*.

console² (ˈkɒnsəʊl) *n*. 1. bracket supporting shelf 2. keyboard, stops *etc*., of organ 3. cabinet for television, radio *etc*.

consolidate (kənˈsɒlɪdeɪt) *vt*. 1. combine into connected whole 2. make firm, secure —**consoliˈdation** *n*.

consols (ˈkɒnsɒlz, kənˈsɒlz) *pl.n*. Brit. government securities

consommé (kənˈsɒmeɪ) *n*. clear meat soup

consonant (ˈkɒnsənənt) *n*. 1. sound making a syllable only with vowel 2. nonvowel —*a*. 3. agreeing, in accord —ˈ**consonance** *n*.

consort (kənˈsɔːt) *vi*. 1. associate, keep company —*n*. (ˈkɒnsɔːt) 2. husband, wife, *esp*. of ruler 3. ship sailing with another —**conˈsortium** *n*. association of banks, companies *etc*.

conspectus (kənˈspɛktəs) *n*. 1. a comprehensive view or survey of subject **2.** synopsis

conspicuous (kən'spɪkjʊəs) a. **1.** striking, noticeable, outstanding **2.** prominent **3.** eminent —**con'spicuously** adv.

conspire (kən'spaɪə) vi. **1.** combine for evil purpose **2.** plot, devise —**conspiracy** (kən'spɪrəsɪ) n. —**conspirator** (kən-'spɪrətə) n. —**conspiratorial** (kənspɪrə-'tɔːrɪəl) a.

constable ('kʌnstəb'l, 'kɒn-) n. **1.** police-man of the lowest rank **2.** Hist. officer of the peace —**con'stabulary** n. police force

constant ('kɒnstənt) a. **1.** fixed, unchang-ing **2.** steadfast **3.** always duly happening or continuing —n. **4.** quantity that does not vary —'**constancy** n. **1.** steadfastness **2.** loyalty —'**constantly** adv.

constellation (kɒnstɪ'leɪʃən) n. group of stars

consternation (kɒnstə'neɪʃən) n. alarm, dismay, panic —'**consternate** vt.

constipation (kɒnstɪ'peɪʃən) n. difficulty in emptying bowels —'**constipate** vt. affect with this disorder

constituent (kən'stɪtjʊənt) a. **1.** going towards making up whole **2.** having power to make, alter constitution of state **3.** electing representative —n. **4.** component part **5.** element **6.** elector —**con'stituency** n. **1.** body of electors **2.** parliamentary division

constitute ('kɒnstɪtjuːt) vt. **1.** compose, set up, establish, form **2.** make into, found, give form to —**consti'tution** n. **1.** structure, composition **2.** health **3.** charac-ter, disposition **4.** principles on which state is governed —**consti'tutional** a. **1.** pert. to constitution **2.** in harmony with political constitution —n. **3.** walk taken for health's sake —**consti'tutionally** adv. —'**constitu-tive** a. **1.** having power to enact or establish **2.** see CONSTITUENT (sense 1)

constrain (kən'streɪn) vt. force, compel —**con'straint** n. **1.** compulsion **2.** restraint **3.** embarrassment, tension

constriction (kən'strɪkʃən) n. compres-sion, squeezing together —**con'strict** vt. —**con'strictive** a. —**con'strictor** n. that which constricts (see also BOA (sense 1))

construct (kən'strʌkt) vt. **1.** make, build, form **2.** put together **3.** compose —n. ('kɒnstrʌkt) **4.** something formulated systematically —**con'struction** n. —**con-'structive** a. **1.** serving to improve **2.** positive —**con'structively** adv.

construe (kən'struː) vt. **1.** interpret **2.** deduce **3.** analyse grammatically

consul ('kɒns'l) n. **1.** officer appointed by a government to represent it in a foreign country **2.** in ancient Rome, one of the chief magistrates —**consular** ('kɒnsjʊlə) a. —**consulate** ('kɒnsjʊlɪt) n. —'**consul-ship** n.

consult (kən'sʌlt) vt. seek counsel, advice, information from —**con'sultant** n. **1.** specialist, expert **2.** senior hospital physi-cian or surgeon —**consul'tation** n. **1.**

consulting **2.** appointment to seek profes-sional advice, esp. of doctor, lawyer —**con'sultative** a. **1.** having privilege of consulting, but not of voting **2.** advisory

consume (kən'sjuːm) vt. **1.** eat or drink **2.** engross, possess **3.** use up **4.** destroy —**con'sumer** n. **1.** buyer or user of commodity **2.** one who consumes —**con'sumerism** n. **1.** protection of interests of consumers **2.** advocacy of high rate of consumption as basis for sound economy —**consumption** (kən'sʌmpʃən) n. **1.** using up **2.** destruction **3.** wasting disease, esp. tuberculosis of the lungs —**consumptive** (kən'sʌmptɪv) a./n. —**con-sumptiveness** (kən'sʌmptɪvnɪs) n.

consummate ('kɒnsəmeɪt) vt. **1.** perfect **2.** fulfil **3.** complete (esp. marriage by sexual intercourse) —a. (kən'sʌmɪt, 'kɒnsəmɪt) **4.** of greatest perfection or completeness —**con'summately** adv. —**consum'ma-tion** n.

cont. continued

contact ('kɒntækt) n. **1.** touching **2.** being in touch **3.** junction of two or more electrical conductors **4.** useful acquaint-ance —vt. ('kɒntækt, kən'tækt) **5.** put, come or be in touch (with) —**contact lens** lens fitting over eyeball to correct defect of vision

contagion (kən'teɪdʒən) n. **1.** passing on of disease by touch, contact **2.** contagious disease **3.** harmful physical or moral influence —**con'tagious** a. communicable by contact, catching

contain (kən'teɪn) vt. **1.** hold **2.** have room for **3.** include, comprise **4.** restrain —**con'tainer** n. **1.** box etc. for holding **2.** large cargo-carrying standard-sized recep-tacle for different modes of transport —**containeri'zation** or **-i'sation** n. —**con-'tainerize** or **-ise** vt. **1.** convey in standard-sized containers **2.** adapt to use of standard-sized containers —**con'tainment** n. act of containing, esp. of restraining power of hostile country or operations of hostile military force

contaminate (kən'tæmɪneɪt) vt. **1.** stain, pollute, infect **2.** make radioactive —**con-tami'nation** n. pollution

contemn (kən'tɛm) vt. regard with contempt; scorn

contemplate ('kɒntɛmpleɪt) vt. **1.** reflect, meditate on **2.** gaze upon **3.** intend —**contem'plation** n. **1.** thoughtful consid-eration **2.** spiritual meditation —'**contem-plative** a./n. (one) given to contemplation

contemporary (kən'tɛmprərɪ) a. **1.** exist-ing or lasting at same time **2.** of same age **3.** present-day —n. **4.** one existing at same time as another —**contempo'raneous** a.

contempt (kən'tɛmpt) n. **1.** feeling that something is worthless, despicable etc. **2.** expression of this feeling **3.** state of being despised, disregarded **4.** wilful disrespect of authority

contend (kən'tɛnd) vi. **1.** strive, fight —v. **2.** dispute —vt. **3.** maintain —**con'tention**

n. **1.** strife **2.** debate **3.** subject matter of dispute —**con'tentious** *a.* **1.** quarrelsome **2.** causing dispute —**con'tentiously** *adv.*

content[1] ('kɒntent) *n.* **1.** that contained **2.** holding capacity —*pl.* **3.** that contained **4.** index of topics in book

content[2] (kən'tent) *a.* **1.** satisfied **2.** willing —*vt.* **3.** satisfy —*n.* **4.** satisfaction —**con'tented** *a.* —**con'tentment** *n.*

conterminous (kən'tɜːmɪnəs) *or* **coterminous** (kəu'tɜːmɪnəs) *a.* **1.** of the same extent (in time *etc.*) **2.** meeting along a common boundary **3.** meeting end to end

contest ('kɒntest) *n.* **1.** competition **2.** conflict —*vt.* (kən'test) **3.** dispute, debate **4.** fight or compete for —**con'testable** *a.* —**con'testant** *n.* —**contes'tation** *n.*

context ('kɒntekst) *n.* **1.** words coming before, after a word or passage **2.** conditions and circumstances of event, fact *etc.* —**con'textual** *a.*

contiguous (kən'tɪgjʊəs) *a.* touching, near —**conti'guity** *n.*

continent[1] ('kɒntɪnənt) *n.* large continuous mass of land —**conti'nental** *a.* —**continental breakfast** light breakfast of coffee and rolls —**continental drift** *Geol.* theory that earth's continents move gradually over surface of planet on substratum of magma —**continental quilt** *UK* quilt, stuffed with down, used as bed cover in place of top sheet and blankets (*also* 'duvet) —**continental shelf** sea bed surrounding continent at depths of up to about 200 metres

continent[2] ('kɒntɪnənt) *a.* **1.** able to control one's urination and defecation **2.** sexually chaste —'**continence** *n.*

contingent (kən'tɪndʒənt) *a.* **1.** depending **2.** possible **3.** accidental —*n.* **4.** group of troops, sportsmen *etc.*) part of or representative of a larger group —**con'tingency** *n.* —**con'tingently** *adv.*

continue (kən'tɪnjuː) *v.* **1.** remain, keep in existence **2.** carry on, last, go on **3.** resume **4.** prolong —**con'tinual** *a.* recurring frequently, *esp.* at regular intervals —**con'tinually** *adv.* —**con'tinuance** *n.* **1.** act of continuing **2.** duration of action *etc.* **3.** *US* adjournment of legal proceeding —**continu'ation** *n.* **1.** extension, extra part **2.** resumption **3.** constant succession, prolongation —**conti'nuity** *n.* **1.** logical sequence **2.** state of being continuous —**con'tinuo** *n.* **1.** *Mus.* bass part underlying piece of concerted music (*also* **basso continuo, thorough bass**) **2.** thorough-bass part as played on keyboard instrument (*pl.* -s) —**con'tinuous** *a.* unceasing —**con'tinuously** *adv.* —**con'tinuum** *n.* continuous series or whole with no part perceptibly different from adjacent parts (*pl.* -'tinua, -s)

contort (kən'tɔːt) *vt.* twist out of normal shape —**con'tortion** *n.* —**con'tortionist** *n.* one who contorts his body to entertain

contour ('kɒntʊə) *n.* outline, shape, *esp.* mountains, coast *etc.* —**contour line** line on map drawn through places of same height —**contour map**

contra- (*comb. form*) against, as in *contraposition.* Such words are omitted where the meaning may easily be inferred from the simple word

contraband ('kɒntrəbænd) *n.* **1.** smuggled goods **2.** illegal traffic in such goods —*a.* **3.** prohibited by law

contraception (kɒntrə'sepʃən) *n.* prevention of conception usu. by artificial means, birth control —**contra'ceptive** *a./n.*

contract (kən'trækt) *v.* **1.** make or become smaller, shorter —*vi.* (kɒn'trækt) **2.** make a contract —*vt.* **3.** become affected by **4.** incur **5.** undertake by contract —*n.* ('kɒntrækt) **6.** bargain, agreement **7.** formal document recording agreement **8.** agreement enforceable by law —**con'tracted** *a.* drawn together —**con'tractile** *a.* tending to contract —**con'traction** *n.* —**con'tractor** *n.* one making contract, *esp.* builder —**con'tractual** *a.*

contradict (kɒntrə'dɪkt) *vt.* **1.** deny **2.** be at variance or inconsistent with —**contra'diction** *n.* —**contra'dictious** *a.* —**contra'dictor** *n.* —**contra'dictory** *a.*

contradistinction (kɒntrədɪ'stɪŋkʃən) *n.* distinction made by contrasting different qualities

contralto (kən'træltəu) *n.* lowest of three female voices (*pl.* -s)

contraption (kən'træpʃən) *n.* **1.** gadget **2.** device **3.** construction, device oft. overelaborate or eccentric

contrapuntal (kɒntrə'pʌnt'l) *a. Mus.* pert. to counterpoint

contrary ('kɒntrərɪ) *a.* **1.** opposed **2.** opposite, other **3.** (kən'treərɪ) perverse, obstinate —*n.* **4.** something the exact opposite of another —*adv.* **5.** in opposition —**contra'riety** *n.* —**con'trarily** *adv.* —'**contrariwise** *adv.* conversely

contrast (kən'trɑːst) *vt.* **1.** distinguish by comparison of unlike or opposite qualities —*vi.* **2.** show great difference —*n.* ('kɒntrɑːst) **3.** striking difference **4.** *T.V.* sharpness of image

contravene (kɒntrə'viːn) *vt.* **1.** transgress, infringe **2.** conflict with **3.** contradict —**contra'vention** *n.*

contretemps ('kɒntrətɑːn) *n.* unexpected and embarrassing situation or mishap

contribute (kən'trɪbjuːt) *v.* **1.** give, pay to common fund **2.** write (articles *etc.*) for the press —*vi.* **3.** help to occur —**contri'bution** *n.* —**con'tributive** *a.* —**con'tributor** *n.* **1.** one who writes articles for newspapers *etc.* **2.** one who donates —**con'tributory** *a.* **1.** partly responsible **2.** giving to pension fund *etc.*

contrite (kən'traɪt, 'kɒntraɪt) *a.* remorseful for wrongdoing, penitent —**con'tritely** *adv.* —**contrition** (kən'trɪʃən) *n.*

contrive (kən'traɪv) *vt.* **1.** manage **2.** devise, invent, design —*v.* **3.** plot, scheme —**con'trivance** *n.* artifice or device

—con'trived a. obviously planned, artificial —con'triver n.

control (kən'trəʊl) vt. 1. command, dominate 2. regulate 3. direct, check, test (-ll-) —n. 4. power to direct or determine 5. curb, check 6. standard of comparison in experiment —pl. 7. system of instruments to control car, aircraft etc. —con'trollable a. —con'troller n. 1. one who controls 2. official controlling expenditure —control tower in airfield from which take-offs and landings are directed

controversy ('kɒntrəvɜːsɪ, kən'trɒv-) n. dispute, debate, esp. over public issues —contro'versial a. —contro'versialist n. —'controvert vt. 1. deny 2. argue about —contro'vertible a.

contumacy ('kɒntjʊməsɪ) n. stubborn disobedience —contu'macious a.

contumely ('kɒntjʊmɪlɪ) n. insulting language or treatment —contumelious (kɒntjʊ'miːlɪəs) a. abusive, insolent

contusion (kən'tjuːʒən) n. bruise —con'tuse vt. bruise

conundrum (kə'nʌndrəm) n. riddle, esp. with punning answer

conurbation (kɒnɜː'beɪʃən) n. densely populated urban sprawl formed by spreading of towns

convalesce (kɒnvə'lɛs) vi. recover health after illness, operation etc. —conva'lescence n. —conva'lescent a./n.

convection (kən'vɛkʃən) n. transmission, esp. of heat, by currents in liquids or gases —con'vector n.

convene (kən'viːn) vt. call together, assemble, convoke —convention (kən-'vɛnʃən) n. 1. assembly 2. treaty, agreement 3. rule 4. practice based on agreement 5. accepted usage —conventional (kən'vɛnʃən'l) a. 1. (slavishly) observing customs of society 2. customary 3. (of weapons, war etc.) not nuclear —conventionality (kənvɛnʃə'nælɪtɪ) n. —conventionally (kən'vɛnʃənəlɪ) adv.

convenient (kən'viːnɪənt) a. 1. handy 2. favourable to needs, comfort 3. well-adapted to one's purpose —con'venience n. 1. ease, comfort, suitability 2. (public) lavatory —a. 3. (of food) quick to prepare —con'veniently adv.

convent ('kɒnvənt) n. 1. religious community, esp. of nuns 2. their building 3. school in which teachers are nuns (also convent school) —con'ventual a.

conventicle (kən'vɛntɪk'l) n. 1. secret or unauthorized assembly for worship 2. small meeting house or chapel, esp. of Dissenters

converge (kən'vɜːdʒ) vi. 1. move towards same point 2. meet, join 3. Maths. (of infinite series) approach finite limit as number of terms increases —con'vergence or con'vergency n. —con'vergent a.

conversant (kən'vɜːs'nt) a. acquainted, familiar, versed (in)

converse¹ (kən'vɜːs) vi. 1. talk —n.

('kɒnvɜːs) 2. talk —conver'sation n. —conver'sational a. —conver'sationalist n.

converse² ('kɒnvɜːs) a. 1. opposite, turned round, reversed —n. 2. the opposite, contrary

convert (kən'vɜːt) vt. 1. apply to another purpose 2. change 3. transform 4. cause to adopt (another) religion, opinion —vi. 5. Rugby make a conversion —n. ('kɒnvɜːt) 6. converted person —con'version n. 1. change of state 2. unauthorized appropriation 3. change of opinion, religion or party 4. Rugby score made after a try by kicking ball over crossbar —con'verter n. 1. one who, that which converts 2. electrical machine for changing alternating current into direct current 3. vessel in which molten metal is refined —con'vertible n. 1. car with folding roof —a. 2. capable of being converted 3. (of car) having folding or removable roof

convex ('kɒnvɛks, kɒn'vɛks) a. 1. curved outwards 2. of a rounded form —con'vexity n.

convey (kən'veɪ) vt. 1. carry, transport 2. impart, communicate 3. Law make over, transfer —con'veyance n. 1. carrying 2. vehicle 3. act by which title to property is transferred —con'veyancer n. one skilled in legal forms of transferring property —con'veyancing n. this work —conveyor belt continuous moving belt for transporting things, esp. in factory

convict (kən'vɪkt) vt. 1. prove or declare guilty —n. ('kɒnvɪkt) 2. person found guilty of crime 3. criminal serving prison sentence —con'viction n. 1. verdict of guilty 2. being convinced, firm belief, state of being sure

convince (kən'vɪns) vt. firmly persuade, satisfy by evidence or argument —con'vincing a. capable of compelling belief, effective

convivial (kən'vɪvɪəl) a. sociable, festive, jovial —convivi'ality n.

convoke (kən'vəʊk) vt. call together —convo'cation n. calling together, assembly, esp. of clergy, university graduates etc.

convolute ('kɒnvəluːt) vt. twist, coil, tangle —'convoluted a. —convo'lution n.

convolvulus (kən'vɒlvjʊləs) n. genus of plants with twining stems

convoy ('kɒnvɔɪ) n. 1. party of ships, troops, lorries etc. travelling together for protection —vt. 2. escort for protection

convulse (kən'vʌls) vt. 1. shake violently 2. affect with violent involuntary contractions of muscles —con'vulsion n. 1. violent upheaval —pl. 2. spasms 3. fits of laughter or hysteria —con'vulsive a. —con'vulsively adv.

cony or **coney** ('kəʊnɪ) n. rabbit

coo (kuː) n. 1. cry of doves —vi. 2. make such cry (cooed, 'cooing)

cooee or **cooey** ('kuːiː) interj. 1. call to attract attention —n. 2. A, NZ inf. calling

distance (*esp. in* **within (a) cooee (of)**)
—*vi.* **3.** utter this call (**'cooeeing, 'cooeed** *or* **'cooeying, 'cooeyed**)

cook (kʊk) *vt.* **1.** prepare (food) for table, *esp.* by heat **2.** *inf.* falsify (accounts *etc.*) —*vi.* **3.** undergo cooking **4.** act as cook —*n.* **5.** one who prepares food for table —**'cooker** *n.* **1.** cooking apparatus **2.** cooking apple —**'cookery** *n.* —**'cookie** *n. esp.* US biscuit —**cook up 1.** *inf.* invent, plan **2.** prepare (meal)

cool (ku:l) *a.* **1.** moderately cold **2.** unexcited, calm **3.** lacking friendliness or interest **4.** *inf.* calmly insolent **5.** *inf.* sophisticated, elegant —*v.* **6.** make, become cool —*n.* **7.** cool time, place *etc.* **8.** *inf.* calmness, composure —**'coolant** *n.* fluid used for cooling tool, machinery *etc.* —**'cooler** *n.* **1.** vessel in which liquids are cooled **2.** *sl.* prison —**'coolly** *adv.* —**cooling tower** structure, designed to permit free passage of air, inside which hot water trickles down, becoming cool as it does so

coolie *or* **cooly** ('ku:lɪ) *n. oft. offens.* cheaply hired oriental unskilled labourer

coomb, combe, coombe, *or* **comb** (ku:m) *n.* valley

coon (ku:n) *n. sl. offens.* coloured person

coop¹ (ku:p) *n.* **1.** cage or pen for fowls —*vt.* (*oft. with* up) **2.** shut up in a coop **3.** confine

coop² *or* **co-op** ('kəʊɒp) *n.* cooperative society or shop run by one

cooper ('ku:pə) *n.* one who makes casks

cooperate *or* **co-operate** (kəʊ'ɒpəreɪt) *vi.* work together —**coope'ration** *or* **co-operation** *n.* —**co'operative** *or* **co-operative** *a.* **1.** willing to cooperate **2.** (of an enterprise) owned collectively and managed for joint economic benefit —*n.* **3.** cooperative organization, such as farm —**co'operator** *or* **co-operator** *n.*

coopt *or* **co-opt** (kəʊ'ɒpt) *vt.* bring on (committee *etc.*) as member, colleague, without election by larger body choosing first members

coordinate *or* **co-ordinate** (kəʊ'ɔ:dɪneɪt) *vt.* **1.** bring into order as parts of whole **2.** place in same rank **3.** put into harmony —*n.* (kəʊ'ɔ:dɪnɪt) **4.** *Maths.* any of set of numbers defining location of point —*pl.* **5.** clothes of matching or harmonious colours and design, suitable for wearing together —*a.* (kəʊ'ɔ:dɪnɪt) **6.** equal in degree, status *etc.* —**coordi'nation** *or* **co-ordination** *n.* —**co'ordinative** *or* **co-ordinative** *a.*

coot (ku:t) *n.* **1.** small black water fowl **2.** *sl.* silly (old) person

cop (kɒp) *sl. vt.* **1.** catch **2.** (*usu. with* it) be punished —*n.* **3.** policeman **4.** a capture —**cop-out** *n. sl.* act of copping out —**cop out** *sl.* fail to assume responsibility, fail to perform

copal ('kəʊpˀl, -pæl) *n.* resin used in varnishes

copartner (kəʊ'pɑ:tnə) *n.* joint partner —**co'partnership** *n.*

cope¹ (kəʊp) *vi.* deal successfully

cope² (kəʊp) *n.* ecclesiastical vestment like long cloak

Copernican (kə'pɜ:nɪkən) *a.* pert. to Copernicus, Polish astronomer (1473-1543), or to his system —**Copernican system** theory published by Copernicus, which stated that earth and planets rotated around sun

copestone ('kəʊpstəʊn) *n.* **1.** stone used to form coping (*also* **coping stone**) **2.** stone at top of wall *etc.*

copier ('kɒpɪə) *n. see* COPY

copilot ('kəʊpaɪlət) *n.* second or relief pilot of aircraft

coping ('kəʊpɪŋ) *n.* top course of wall, usu. sloping to throw off rain

coping saw handsaw with U-shaped frame for cutting curves in material too thick for fret saw

copious ('kəʊpɪəs) *a.* **1.** abundant **2.** plentiful **3.** full, ample —**'copiously** *adv.* —**'copiousness** *n.*

copper¹ ('kɒpə) *n.* **1.** reddish-brown malleable ductile metal **2.** bronze money, coin **3.** large washing vessel —*vt.* **4.** cover with copper —**copper-bottomed** *a.* reliable, *esp.* financially —**'copperplate** *n.* **1.** plate of copper for engraving, etching **2.** print from this **3.** copybook writing **4.** fine handwriting based upon that used on copperplate engravings —**'coppersmith** *n.* one who works with copper

copper² ('kɒpə) *n. sl.* policeman

coppice ('kɒpɪs) *n.* wood of small trees

copra ('kɒprə) *n.* dried coconut kernels

Copt (kɒpt) *n.* **1.** member of Coptic Church **2.** Egyptian descended from ancient Egyptians —**'Coptic** *n.* **1.** Afro-Asiatic language, written in Greek alphabet but descended from ancient Egyptian —*a.* **2.** of this language **3.** of Copts

copula ('kɒpjʊlə) *n.* **1.** word, *esp.* verb acting as connecting link in sentence **2.** connection, tie

copulate ('kɒpjʊleɪt) *vi.* unite sexually —**copu'lation** *n.* —**'copulative** *a.*

copy ('kɒpɪ) *n.* **1.** imitation **2.** single specimen of book **3.** matter for printing **4.** *Journalism inf.* suitable material for an article —*vt.* **5.** make copy of, imitate **6.** transcribe **7.** follow example of (**'copied, 'copying**) —**'copier** *n.* person or device that copies —**'copyist** *n.* —**'copybook** *n.* **1.** book of specimens, *esp.* of penmanship, for imitation **2.** *chiefly* US book for or containing documents —*a.* **3.** trite, unoriginal —**'copycat** *n. inf.* person, *esp.* child, who imitates another —**'copyhold** *n. Law* formerly, tenure less than freehold of land in England evidenced by copy of Court roll —**'copyright** *n.* **1.** legal exclusive right to print and publish book, article, work of art *etc.* —*vt.* **2.** protect by copyright —**'copywriter** *n.* one who composes advertisements —**blot one's copybook** *inf.* sully one's reputation

coquette (kəʊ'kɛt, kɒ'kɛt) *n.* woman who flirts —'**coquetry** *n.* —co'**quettish** *a.*

coracle ('kɒrək²l) *n.* boat of wicker covered with skins

coral ('kɒrəl) *n.* 1. hard substance made by sea polyps and forming growths, islands, reefs 2. ornament of coral —*a.* 3. made of coral 4. of deep pink colour —'**coralline** *a.*

cor anglais ('kɔːr 'ɑːŋgleɪ) oboe set a fifth lower than ordinary oboe

corbel ('kɔːb²l) *n.* stone or timber projection from wall to support something

corbie ('kɔːbɪ) *n. Scot.* 1. raven 2. crow CROW¹

cord (kɔːd) *n.* 1. thin rope or thick string 2. rib on cloth 3. ribbed fabric —*vt.* 4. fasten with cord —'**cordage** *n.*

cordate ('kɔːdeɪt) *a.* heart-shaped

cordial ('kɔːdɪəl) *a.* 1. hearty, sincere, warm —*n.* 2. sweet, fruit-flavoured drink —cordi'**ality** *n.* —'**cordially** *adv.*

cordite ('kɔːdaɪt) *n.* explosive compound

cordon ('kɔːd²n) *n.* 1. chain of troops or police 2. fruit tree grown as single stem —*vt.* 3. (*oft. with* off) form cordon around

cordon bleu (*Fr.* kɔrdɔ̃ 'blø) (*esp.* of food preparation) of highest standard

cordovan ('kɔːdəv²n) *n.* fine leather now made principally from horsehide

corduroy ('kɔːdərɔɪ, kɔːdə'rɔɪ) *n.* cotton fabric with velvety, ribbed surface

cordwainer ('kɔːdweɪnə) *n. obs.* shoe-maker or worker in leather

core (kɔː) *n.* 1. horny seed case of apple and other fruits 2. central or innermost part of anything —*vt.* 3. take out the core of

co-respondent (kəʊrɪ'spɒndənt) *n.* one cited in divorce case, alleged to have committed adultery with the respondent

corgi ('kɔːgɪ) *n.* a small Welsh dog

coriaceous (kɒrɪ'eɪʃəs) *a.* of, like leather

coriander (kɒrɪ'ændə) *n.* herb

Corinthian (kə'rɪnθɪən) *a.* 1. of Corinth 2. of Corinthian order of architecture, ornate Greek

cork (kɔːk) *n.* 1. bark of an evergreen Mediterranean oak tree 2. piece of it or other material, *esp.* used as stopper for bottle *etc.* —*vt.* 3. stop up with cork —'**corkage** *n.* charge for opening wine bottles in restaurant —**corked** *a.* tainted through having cork containing excess tannin —'**corker** *n. sl.* something, someone outstanding —'**corkscrew** *n.* tool for pulling out corks

corm (kɔːm) *n.* underground stem like a bulb, but more solid

cormorant ('kɔːmərənt) *n.* large voracious sea bird

corn¹ (kɔːn) *n.* 1. grain, fruit of cereals 2. grain of all kinds 3. US maize 4. oversentimental, trite quality in play, film *etc.* —*vt.* 5. preserve (meat) with salt —'**corny** *a. inf.* trite, oversentimental,

hackneyed —'**corncrake** *n.* brown bird with harsh call, land rail —'**cornflakes** *pl.n.* breakfast cereal —'**cornflour** *n.* finely ground maize —'**cornflower** *n.* blue flower growing in cornfields

corn² (kɔːn) *n.* painful horny growth on foot or toe

cornea ('kɔːnɪə) *n.* transparent membrane covering front of eye

cornel ('kɔːn²l) *n.* any small tree with very hard wood, as the dogwood *etc.*

cornelian (kɔː'niːlɪən) *n.* precious stone, kind of chalcedony

corner ('kɔːnə) *n.* 1. part of room where two sides meet 2. remote or humble place 3. point where two walls, streets *etc.* meet 4. angle, projection 5. *Business* buying up of whole existing stock of commodity 6. *Sport* free kick or shot from corner of field —*vt.* 7. drive into position of difficulty, or leaving no escape 8. acquire enough of (commodity) to attain control of (commodity) to attain control of market 9. attain control of (market) in such a manner (*also* en'**gross**) —*vi.* 10. move round corner —'**cornered** *a.* —'**cornerstone** *n.* indispensable part, basis

cornet ('kɔːnɪt) *n.* 1. trumpet with valves 2. cone-shaped ice-cream wafer

cornice ('kɔːnɪs) *n.* 1. projection near top of wall 2. ornamental, carved moulding below ceiling

Cornish ('kɔːnɪʃ) *a.* 1. of Cornwall or its inhabitants —*n.* 2. formerly, language of Cornwall: extinct by 1800 —*pl.* 3. natives of Cornwall —'**Cornishman** *n.* —**Cornish pasty** ('pæstɪ) *Cookery* pastry case with filling of meat and vegetables

cornucopia (kɔːnjʊ'kəʊpɪə) *n.* symbol of plenty, consisting of goat's horn, overflowing with fruit and flowers

corolla (kə'rɒlə) *n.* flower's inner envelope of petals

corollary (kə'rɒlərɪ) *n.* 1. inference from a preceding statement 2. deduction 3. result

corona (kə'rəʊnə) *n.* 1. halo around heavenly body 2. flat projecting part of cornice 3. top or crown (*pl.* -**s**, -**nae** (-niː)) —co'**ronal** *a.*

coronary ('kɒrənərɪ) *a.* 1. of blood vessels surrounding heart —*n.* 2. coronary thrombosis —**coronary thrombosis** formation of obstructing clot in coronary artery

coronation (kɒrə'neɪʃən) *n.* ceremony of crowning a sovereign

coroner ('kɒrənə) *n.* officer who holds inquests on bodies of persons supposed killed by violence, accident *etc.* —'**coronership** *n.*

coronet ('kɒrənɪt) *n.* small crown

corporal¹ ('kɔːpərəl) *a.* 1. of the body 2. material, not spiritual —**corporal punishment** punishment (flogging *etc.*) of physical nature

corporal² ('kɔːpərəl, 'kɔːprəl) *n.* 1. non-commissioned officer below sergeant 2. *Navy* petty officer under a master-at-arms —**Corporal of Horse** noncommissioned rank in British army, above that of sergeant and below that of staff sergeant

corporation (kɔːpəˈreɪʃən) n. 1. association, body of persons legally authorized to act as an individual 2. authorities of town or city —ˈcorporate a.

corporeal (kɔːˈpɔːrɪəl) a. 1. of the body, material 2. tangible

corps (kɔː) n. 1. military force, body of troops 2. any organized body of persons (pl. corps (kɔːz)) —corps de ballet members of ballet company who dance together in group —corps diplomatique (dɪplɔʊməˈtiːk) body of diplomats accredited to state (also diplomatic corps)

corpse (kɔːps) n. dead body

corpulent (ˈkɔːpjʊlənt) a. fat —ˈcorpulence n.

corpus (ˈkɔːpəs) n. 1. collection or body of works, esp. by single author 2. main part or body of something (pl. -pora (-pərə))

corpuscle (ˈkɔːpʌsᵊl) n. minute organism or particle, esp. red and white corpuscles of blood

corral (kɒˈrɑːl) n. US enclosure for cattle, or for defence

correct (kəˈrɛkt) vt. 1. set right 2. indicate errors in 3. rebuke, punish 4. counteract, rectify —a. 5. right, exact, accurate 6. in accordance with facts or standards —corˈrection n. —corˈrective n./a. —corˈrectly adv. —corˈrectness n.

correlate (ˈkɒrɪleɪt) vt. 1. bring into reciprocal relation —n. 2. either of two things or words necessarily implying the other —correˈlation n. —corˈrelative a./n.

correspond (kɒrɪˈspɒnd) vi. 1. be in agreement, be consistent (with) 2. be similar (to) 3. exchange letters —correˈspondence n. 1. agreement, corresponding 2. similarity 3. exchange of letters 4. letters received —correˈspondent n. 1. writer of letters 2. one employed by newspaper etc. to report on particular topic, country etc. —correspondence school educational institution that offers tuition by post

corridor (ˈkɒrɪdɔː) n. 1. passage in building, railway train etc. 2. strip of territory (or air route) not under control of state through which it passes —corridors of power higher echelons of government considered as location of power and influence

corrie (ˈkɒrɪ) n. 1. Scot. circular hollow on hillside 2. Geol. see CIRQUE

corrigendum (kɒrɪˈdʒɛndəm) n. thing to be corrected (pl. -da (-də))

corrigible (ˈkɒrɪdʒɪbᵊl) a. 1. capable of being corrected 2. submissive

corroborate (kəˈrɒbəreɪt) vt. confirm, support (statement etc.) —corroboˈration n. —corˈroborative a.

corroboree (kəˈrɒbərɪ) n. A 1. native assembly of sacred, festive or warlike character 2. any noisy gathering

corrode (kəˈrəʊd) vt. eat, wear away, eat into (by chemical action, disease etc.) —corˈrosion n. —corˈrosive a.

corrugate (ˈkɒrʊgeɪt) v. wrinkle, bend into wavy ridges —ˈcorrugated a. —corruˈgation n.

corrupt (kəˈrʌpt) a. 1. lacking integrity 2. open to, or involving, bribery 3. wicked 4. spoilt by mistakes, altered from original (of words, literary passages etc.) —vt. 5. make evil, pervert 6. bribe 7. make rotten —corruptiˈbility n. —corˈruptible a. —corˈruption n. —corˈruptly adv.

corsage (kɔːˈsɑːʒ) n. (flower, spray, worn on) bodice of woman's dress

corsair (ˈkɔːsɛə) n. pirate

corselet (ˈkɔːslɪt) n. 1. piece of armour to cover the trunk 2. one-piece foundation garment

corset (ˈkɔːsɪt) n. close-fitting undergarment stiffened to give support or shape to the body

cortege or **cortège** (kɔːˈteɪʒ) n. formal (funeral) procession

cortex (ˈkɔːtɛks) n. 1. Anat. outer layer 2. bark 3. sheath (pl. cortices (ˈkɔːtɪsiːz)) —ˈcortical a.

cortisone (ˈkɔːtɪzəʊn) n. synthetic hormone used in the treatment of a variety of diseases

corundum (kəˈrʌndəm) n. native crystalline aluminium oxide, used as abrasive

coruscate (ˈkɒrəskeɪt) vi. emit flashes of light; sparkle —corusˈcation n.

corvette (kɔːˈvɛt) n. lightly armed warship for escort and antisubmarine duties

corymb (ˈkɒrɪmb, -rɪm) n. inflorescence in form of flat-topped flower cluster with oldest flowers at periphery

coryza (kəˈraɪzə) n. acute inflammation of mucous membrane of nose, with discharge of mucus; head cold

cos¹ or **cos lettuce** (kɒs) n. lettuce with long slender head and crisp leaves

cos² (kɒz) cosine

cosec (ˈkəʊsɛk) cosecant

cosecant (kəʊˈsiːkənt) n. (of angle) trigonometric function that in right-angled triangle is ratio of length of hypotenuse to that of opposite side

cosh (kɒʃ) n. 1. blunt weapon —vt. 2. strike with one

cosignatory (kəʊˈsɪgnətərɪ, -trɪ) n. 1. person, country etc. that signs document jointly with others —a. 2. signing jointly

cosine (ˈkəʊsaɪn) n. in a right-angled triangle, the ratio of a side adjacent to a given angle and the hypotenuse

cosmetic (kɒzˈmɛtɪk) n. 1. preparation to beautify or improve skin, hair etc. —a. 2. designed to improve appearance only

cosmic (ˈkɒzmɪk) a. 1. relating to the universe 2. of the vastness of the universe —cosmic rays high-energy electromagnetic rays from space

cosmo- or before vowel **cosm-** (comb. form) world; universe, as in cosmology, cosmonaut

cosmopolitan (kɒzməˈpɒlɪtᵊn) n. 1. person

who has lived and travelled in many countries —*a.* **2.** familiar with many countries **3.** sophisticated **4.** free from national prejudice —**cosmo'politanism** *n.* —**cos'mopolite** *n.*

cosmos[1] ('kɒzmɒs) *n.* the world or universe considered as an ordered system —**cos'mogony** *n.* study of origin and development of universe or system in universe —**cos'mographer** *n.* —**cosmo'graphic** *a.* —**cos'mography** *n.* description or mapping of the universe —**cosmo'logical** *a.* —**cos'mology** *n.* the science or study of the universe —**cosmonaut** ('kɒzmənɔːt) *n.* Soviet astronaut

cosmos[2] ('kɒzmɒs) *n.* plant cultivated for brightly coloured flowers (*pl.* **-mos, -es**)

Cossack ('kɒsæk) *n.* member of tribe in SE Russia

cosset ('kɒsɪt) *vt.* pamper, pet

cost (kɒst) *n.* **1.** price **2.** expenditure of time, labour *etc.* —*pl.* **3.** expenses of lawsuit —*vt.* **4.** have as price **5.** entail payment, loss or sacrifice of (*cost pt./pp.*) —**'costing** *n.* system of calculating cost of production —**'costliness** *n.* —**'costly** *a.* **1.** valuable **2.** expensive —**cost of living** basic cost of food, clothing and shelter necessary to maintain life —**cost price** price at which article is bought by one intending to resell it

costal ('kɒst'l) *a.* pert. to side of body or ribs —**'costate** *a.* ribbed

costermonger ('kɒstəmʌŋgə) or **coster** *n.* UK, *rare* person who sells fruit *etc.* from barrow

costive ('kɒstɪv) *a.* **1.** constipated **2.** niggardly

costume ('kɒstjuːm) *n.* **1.** style of dress of particular place or time, or for particular activity **2.** theatrical clothes —**cos'tumier** *n.* dealer in costumes —**costume jewellery** artificial jewellery

cosy or U.S. **cozy** ('kəʊzɪ) *a.* **1.** snug, comfortable, sheltered —*n.* **2.** covering to keep teapot *etc.* hot —**'cosily** or U.S. **'cozily** *adv.*

cot[1] (kɒt) *n.* **1.** child's bed usu. with barred sides **2.** swinging bed on ship —**cot death** unexplained death of baby while asleep

cot[2] (kɒt) *n.* **1.** *Lit., obs.* small cottage **2.** small shelter, *esp.* for pigeons, sheep *etc.* (*also* **cote**)

cot[3] (kɒt) cotangent

cotangent (kəʊ'tændʒənt) *n.* (of angle) trigonometric function that in right-angled triangle is ratio of length of adjacent side to that of opposite side

cote (kəʊt) or **cot** *n.* shelter, shed for animals or birds, *eg* dovecot(e)

coterie ('kəʊtərɪ) *n.* **1.** exclusive group of people with common interests **2.** social clique

cotillion or **cotillon** (kə'tɪljən, kəʊ-) *n.* Hist. lively dance

cotoneaster (kətəʊnɪ'æstə) *n.* garden shrub with red berries

cottage ('kɒtɪdʒ) *n.* small house —**cottage**

cheese mild, soft cheese —**cottage industry** industry in which workers work in their own homes —**cottage pie** UK *see* **shepherd's pie** *at* SHEPHERD

cotter ('kɒtə) *n.* pin, wedge *etc.* to prevent relative motion of two parts of machine *etc.*

cotton ('kɒt'n) *n.* **1.** plant **2.** white downy fibrous covering of its seeds **3.** thread or cloth made of this —**cotton wool 1.** *chiefly* UK bleached sterilized cotton from which impurities have been removed **2.** cotton in natural state **3.** UK *inf.* state of pampered comfort and protection —**cotton to** or **on to** understand (idea *etc.*)

cotyledon (kɒtɪ'liːd'n) *n.* primary leaf of plant embryos

couch (kaʊtʃ) *n.* **1.** piece of furniture for reclining on by day, sofa —*vt.* **2.** express in a particular style of language **3.** cause to lie down —**'couchant** *a. Her.* lying down

couch grass (kaʊtʃ, kuːtʃ) type of creeping grass

cougar ('kuːgə) *n.* puma

cough (kɒf) *vi.* **1.** expel air from lungs with sudden effort and noise, oft. to remove obstruction —*n.* **2.** act of coughing —**cough drop** lozenge to relieve cough —**cough mixture** medicine that relieves coughing

could (kʊd) *pt. of* CAN[1]

coulomb ('kuːlɒm) *n.* unit of quantity of electricity

coulter ('kəʊltə) *n.* sharp blade or disc at front of plough

council ('kaʊnsəl) *n.* **1.** deliberative or administrative body **2.** one of its meetings **3.** local governing authority of town *etc.* —**'councillor** or U.S. **'councilor** *n.* member of council

counsel ('kaʊnsəl) *n.* **1.** advice, deliberation, debate **2.** barrister; barristers **3.** plan, policy —*vt.* **4.** advise, recommend (**-ll-**) —**'counsellor** or U.S. **'counselor** *n.* adviser —**keep one's counsel** keep a secret

count[1] (kaʊnt) *vt.* **1.** reckon, calculate, number **2.** include **3.** consider to be —*vi.* **4.** depend (on) **5.** be of importance —*n.* **6.** reckoning **7.** total number reached by counting **8.** item in list of charges or indictment **9.** act of counting —**'countless** *a.* too many to be counted —**'countdown** *n.* act of counting backwards to time critical operation exactly, such as launching of rocket —**counting house** room or building for book-keeping —**count down** count backwards to time critical operation exactly —**count out 1.** *inf.* leave out; exclude **2.** (of boxing referee) judge (floored boxer) to have failed to recover within specified time

count[2] (kaʊnt) *n.* nobleman corresponding to British earl —**'countess** *n.* wife or widow of count or earl

countenance ('kaʊntɪnəns) *n.* **1.** face or its expression **2.** support, approval **3.** composure; self-control —*vt.* **4.** give support to, approve

counter[1] ('kaʊntə) n. 1. horizontal surface in bank, shop etc., over which business is transacted 2. disc, token used for counting or scoring, esp. in board games

counter[2] ('kaʊntə) adv. 1. in opposite direction 2. contrary —vt. 3. oppose, contradict 4. Fencing parry —n. 5. parry

counter- (comb. form) reversed, opposite, rival, as in counterclaim, counterclockwise, counterirritant, countermarch, countermeasure, countermine, counterrevolution. Such words are not given here where the meaning may be inferred from the simple word

counteract (kaʊntər'ækt) vt. neutralize, hinder —**counter'action** n.

counterattack ('kaʊntərətæk) v./n. attack after enemy's advance

counterbalance ('kaʊntəbæləns) n. weight balancing or neutralizing another

counterfeit ('kaʊntəfɪt) a. 1. sham, forged —n. 2. imitation, forgery —vt. 3. imitate with intent to deceive 4. forge —'**counterfeiter** n. —'**counterfeitly** adv.

counterfoil ('kaʊntəfɔɪl) n. part of cheque, receipt, postal order, kept as record

counterintelligence (kaʊntərɪn'telɪdʒəns) n. activities designed to frustrate enemy espionage

countermand (kaʊntə'mɑːnd) vt. cancel (previous order)

counterpane ('kaʊntəpeɪn) n. top cover for bed

counterpart ('kaʊntəpɑːt) n. 1. thing so like another as to be mistaken for it 2. something complementary to or correlative of another

counterpoint ('kaʊntəpɔɪnt) n. 1. melody added as accompaniment to given melody 2. art of so adding melodies

counterpoise ('kaʊntəpɔɪz) n. 1. force, influence etc. that counterbalances another 2. state of balance; equilibrium 3. weight that balances another —vt. 4. oppose with something of equal effect, weight or force; offset 5. bring into equilibrium

counterproductive (kaʊntəprə'dʌktɪv) a. tending to hinder achievement of aim; having effects contrary to those intended

Counter-Reformation (kaʊntərefə'meɪʃən) n. reform movement in Catholic Church in 16th and early 17th centuries

countersign ('kaʊntəsaɪn, kaʊntə'saɪn) vt. 1. sign document already signed by another 2. ratify

countersink ('kaʊntəsɪŋk) vt. enlarge (upper part of hole drilled in timber etc.) to take head of screw, bolt etc. below surface

countertenor (kaʊntə'tɛnə) n. 1. adult male voice with alto range 2. singer with such voice

countervail (kaʊntə'veɪl, 'kaʊntəveɪl) v. 1. act or act against with equal power or force —vt. 2. make up for; compensate; offset

counterweight ('kaʊntəweɪt) n. counterbalancing weight, influence or force

countess ('kaʊntɪs) n. see COUNT[2]

country ('kʌntrɪ) n. 1. region, district 2. territory of nation 3. land of birth, residence etc. 4. rural districts as opposed to town 5. nation —'**countrified** a. rural in manner or appearance —**country-and-western** n. urban 20th-century White folk music of SE Amer. —**country club** club in the country, having sporting and social facilities —**country dance** folk dance in which couples face one another in line —'**countryman** n. 1. rustic 2. compatriot —'**countryside** n. 1. rural district 2. its inhabitants

county ('kaʊntɪ) n. 1. division of country 2. shire —a. 3. UK inf. upper-class; of or like landed gentry —**county town** town in which county's affairs are or were administered

coup (kuː) n. 1. successful stroke, move or gamble 2. (short for coup d'état) sudden, violent seizure of government

coup de grâce (ku də 'grɑs) Fr. 1. mortal or finishing blow, esp. delivered as act of mercy to sufferer 2. final or decisive stroke (pl. coups de grâce (ku də 'grɑs))

coupé ('kuːpeɪ) n. sporty style of motor car, usu. with two doors

couple ('kʌp'l) n. 1. two, pair 2. indefinite small number 3. two people who regularly associate with each other or live together 4. any two persons —vt. 5. connect, fasten together 6. associate, connect in the mind —vi. 7. join —'**coupler** n. —'**couplet** n. two lines of verse, esp. rhyming and of equal length —'**coupling** n. connection, esp. chain between railway wagons

coupon ('kuːpɒn) n. 1. ticket or voucher entitling holder to discount, gift etc. 2. detachable slip used as order form 3. (in betting etc.) printed form on which to forecast results

courage ('kʌrɪdʒ) n. bravery, boldness —cou'rageous a. —cou'rageously adv.

courgette (kʊə'ʒɛt) n. type of small vegetable marrow

courier ('kʊərɪə) n. 1. express messenger 2. person who looks after, guides travellers

course (kɔːs) n. 1. movement in space or time 2. direction of movement 3. successive development, sequence 4. line of conduct or action 5. series of lectures, exercises etc. 6. any of successive parts of meal 7. continuous line of masonry at particular level in building 8. area where golf is played 9. track or ground on which a race is run —vt. 10. hunt —vi. 11. run swiftly, gallop about 12. (of blood) circulate —'**courser** n. Poet. swift horse —'**coursing** n. 1. (of hounds or dogs) hunting by sight 2. sport in which hounds are matched against one another in pairs for hunting of hares by sight

court (kɔːt) n. 1. space enclosed by buildings, yard 2. area marked off or enclosed for playing various games 3.

retine and establishment of sovereign **4.** body with judicial powers, place where it meets, one of its sittings **5.** attention, homage, flattery —*vt.* **6.** woo, try to win or attract **7.** seek, invite —'**courtier** *n.* one who frequents royal court —'**courtliness** *n.* —'**courtly** *a.* **1.** ceremoniously polite **2.** characteristic of a court —'**courtship** *n.* wooing —**court card** king, queen or jack at cards —'**courthouse** *n.* public building in which courts of law are held —**court martial** court of naval or military officers for trying naval or military offences (*pl.* **court martials, courts martial**) —**court plaster** plaster, composed of isinglass on silk, formerly used to cover superficial wounds —**court shoe** low-cut shoe for women, without laces or straps —'**court-yard** *n.* paved space enclosed by buildings or walls

courtesan *or* **courtezan** (kɔːtɪ'zæn) *n.* *obs.* **1.** court mistress **2.** high-class prostitute

courtesy ('kɜːtɪsɪ) *n.* **1.** politeness, good manners **2.** act of civility —'**courteous** *a.* polite —'**courteously** *adv.* —**courtesy title** title accorded by usage to which one has no valid claim

cousin ('kʌz²n) *n.* **1.** son or daughter of uncle or aunt **2.** formerly, any kinsman —'**cousinly** *a.*

couture (kuː'tʊə) *n.* high-fashion designing and dressmaking —**couturier** (kuː'tʊərɪeɪ) *n.* person who designs, makes and sells fashion clothes for women (**couturière** (kuːtuːrɪ'ɛə) *fem.*)

cove[1] (kəʊv) *n.* small inlet of coast, sheltered bay

cove[2] (kəʊv) *n.* *sl.* fellow, chap

coven ('kʌv²n) *n.* gathering of witches

covenant ('kʌvənənt) *n.* **1.** contract, mutual agreement **2.** compact —*v.* **3.** agree to a covenant (concerning) —'**Covenanter** *n.* *Scot. hist.* person upholding either of two 17th-cent. Presbyterian covenants

Coventry ('kɒvəntrɪ) *n.* —**send to Coventry** ostracize; ignore

cover ('kʌvə) *vt.* **1.** place or spread over **2.** extend over, spread over **3.** bring upon (oneself) **4.** screen, protect **5.** travel over **6.** include **7.** be sufficient to meet **8.** *Journalism* report on **9.** point a gun at —*n.* **10.** lid, wrapper, envelope, binding, screen, anything which covers —'**coverage** *n.* amount, extent covered —'**coverlet** *n.* top covering of bed —**cover charge** fixed charge added to cost of food in restaurant *etc.* —**covering letter** accompanying letter sent as explanation, introduction or record —**cover point** *Cricket* fielding position in covers; fielder in this position —**cover-up** *n.* concealment or attempted concealment of crime *etc.* —**cover up 1.** cover completely **2.** attempt to conceal (mistake or crime)

covert ('kʌvət) *a.* **1.** secret, veiled,

concealed, sly —*n.* **2.** thicket, place sheltering game —'**covertly** *adv.*

covet ('kʌvɪt) *vt.* long to possess, *esp.* what belongs to another —'**covetous** *a.* avaricious —'**covetousness** *n.*

covey ('kʌvɪ) *n.* brood of partridges or quail (*pl.* **-s**)

cow[1] (kaʊ) *n.* **1.** the female of the bovine and of certain other animals, *eg* elephant, whale **2.** *inf.* disagreeable woman —'**cowboy** *n.* **1.** herdsman in charge of cattle on western plains of U.S. **2.** *inf.* ruthless or unscrupulous operator in business *etc.* —**cow parsley** Eurasian umbelliferous hedgerow plant —'**cowpox** *n.* disease of cows, source of vaccine

cow[2] (kaʊ) *vt.* frighten into submission, overawe, subdue

coward ('kaʊəd) *n.* one who lacks courage, shrinks from danger —'**cowardice** *n.* —'**cowardly** *a.*

cower ('kaʊə) *vi.* crouch, shrink in fear

cowl (kaʊl) *n.* **1.** monk's hooded cloak **2.** its hood **3.** hooded top for chimney, ship's funnel *etc.*

cowling ('kaʊlɪŋ) *n.* covering for aircraft engine

co-worker *n.* fellow worker; associate

cowry *or* **cowrie** ('kaʊrɪ) *n.* brightly-marked sea shell

cowslip ('kaʊslɪp) *n.* wild species of primrose

coxcomb ('kɒkskəʊm) *n.* *obs.* one given to showing off

coxswain ('kɒksən, -sweɪn) *n.* steersman of boat —**cox** *n.* **1.** coxswain —*v.* **2.** command or steer

coy (kɔɪ) *a.* (pretending to be) shy, modest —'**coyly** *adv.* —'**coyness** *n.*

coyote ('kɔɪəʊt, kɔɪ'əʊtɪ; *esp.* U.S. 'kaɪəʊt, kaɪ'əʊtɪ) *n.* N Amer. prairie wolf

coypu ('kɔɪpuː) *n.* aquatic rodent, orig. from S Amer., yielding nutria fur

cozen ('kʌz²n) *vt.* flatter in order to cheat, beguile

cp. compare

C.P. 1. Canadian Pacific **2.** Cape Province **3.** Communist Party

cpd. compound

Cpl. Corporal

C.P.U. central processing unit

CQ symbol transmitted by amateur radio operator requesting communication with any other amateur radio operator

Cr *Chem.* chromium

crab[1] (kræb) *n.* **1.** edible crustacean with ten legs, noted for sidelong and backward walk **2.** type of louse —*vi.* **3.** catch crabs **4.** move sideways —**crabbed** ('kræbɪd) *a.* (of handwriting) hard to read —'**crabby** *a.* bad-tempered —**crab louse** parasitic louse that infests pubic region in man —**catch a crab** *Rowing* dig oar too deeply for clean retrieval

crab[2] (kræb) *inf.* *vi.* **1.** find fault; grumble (**-bb-**) —*n.* **2.** irritable person

crab apple wild sour apple

crack (kræk) *vt.* **1.** break, split partially **2.**

break with sharp noise **3.** cause to make sharp noise, as of whip, rifle *etc.* **4.** yield **5.** *inf.* tell (joke) **6.** solve, decipher —*vi.* **7.** make sharp noise **8.** split, fissure **9.** (of the voice) lose clearness when changing from boy's to man's —*n.* **10.** sharp explosive noise **11.** split, fissure **12.** flaw **13.** *inf.* joke, *esp.* sarcastic **14.** *dial.* chat **15.** *sl.* concentrated, highly addictive form of cocaine —*a.* **16.** *inf.* special, smart, of great reputation for skill —**cracked** *a.* **1.** damaged by cracking **2.** *sl.* crazy —'**cracker** *n.* **1.** decorated paper tube, pulled apart with a bang, containing paper hat, motto, toy *etc.* **2.** explosive firework **3.** thin dry biscuit —'**crackers** *a. sl.* unbalanced, crazy —'**cracking** *a.* **1.** *inf.* fast; vigorous (*esp. in a cracking pace*) —*adv./a.* **2.** *UK inf.* first-class; excellent —*n.* **3.** process of breaking down hydrocarbons by heat and pressure, as in producing petrol —'**crackle** *n.* **1.** sound of repeated small cracks —*vi.* **2.** make this sound —'**crackling** *n.* **1.** crackle **2.** crisp skin of roast pork —'**crackbrained** *a.* insane, idiotic, crazy —'**crackpot** *inf. n.* **1.** eccentric person; crank —*a.* **2.** eccentric; crazy —'**cracksman** *n.* burglar, *esp.* safe-breaker —**get cracking** *inf.* start doing something quickly or with increased speed

cradle ('kreɪd'l) *n.* **1.** infant's bed (on rockers) **2.** *fig.* earliest resting-place or home **3.** supporting framework —*vt.* **4.** hold or rock as in a cradle **5.** cherish —'**cradling** *n.*

craft[1] (krɑːft) *n.* **1.** skill, ability, *esp.* manual ability **2.** cunning **3.** skilled trade **4.** members of a trade —'**craftily** *adv.* —'**craftsman** *n.* —'**craftsmanship** *n.* —'**crafty** *a.* cunning, shrewd

craft[2] (krɑːft) *n.* **1.** vessel **2.** ship (*pl.* **craft**)

crag (kræg) *n.* steep rugged rock —'**craggy** *a.* rugged

crake (kreɪk) *n.* any of various birds of rail family

cram (kræm) *vt.* **1.** fill quite full **2.** stuff, force **3.** pack tightly **4.** feed to excess **5.** prepare quickly for examination —*vi.* **6.** study, *esp.* for examination, by hastily memorizing (-**mm**-) —*n.* **7.** act or condition of cramming **8.** crush

cramp (kræmp) *n.* **1.** painful muscular contraction **2.** clamp for holding masonry, timber *etc.* together —*vt.* **3.** restrict, hamper **4.** hem in, keep within too narrow limits

crampon ('kræmpən) *or* **crampoon** (kræm'puːn) *n.* spike in shoe for mountain climbing, *esp.* on ice

cranberry ('krænbərɪ, -brɪ) *n.* edible red berry of dwarf evergreen shrub

crane (kreɪn) *n.* **1.** wading bird with long legs, neck, and bill **2.** machine for moving heavy weights —*v.* **3.** stretch (neck) to see

crane fly insect with long spindly legs (*also* **daddy-longlegs**)

cranesbill ('kreɪnzbɪl) *n.* plant with pink or purple flowers and beaked fruits

craniometry (kreɪnɪ'ɒmɪtrɪ) *n.* the study of the measurements of the human head

cranium ('kreɪnɪəm) *n.* skull (*pl.* **-s, -nia** (-nɪə)) —'**cranial** *a.* —**cranio'logical** *a.* —**crani'ologist** *n.* —**crani'ology** *n.* branch of science concerned with shape and size of human skull

crank (kræŋk) *n.* **1.** arm at right angles to axis, for turning main shaft, changing reciprocal into rotary motion *etc.* **2.** *inf.* eccentric person, faddist —*v.* **3.** start (engine) by turning crank —'**cranky** *a.* **1.** eccentric **2.** bad-tempered **3.** shaky —'**crankpin** *n.* short cylindrical surface fitted between two arms of crank parallel to main shaft of crankshaft —'**crankshaft** *n.* principal shaft of engine

cranny ('krænɪ) *n.* small opening, chink —'**crannied** *a.*

crap (kræp) *n.* gambling game played with two dice (*also* **craps**)

crape (kreɪp) *n.* crepe, *esp.* when used for mourning clothes

crapulent ('kræpjʊlənt) *or* **crapulous** ('kræpjʊləs) *a.* **1.** given to or resulting from intemperance **2.** suffering from intemperance; drunken —'**crapulence** *n.*

crash (kræʃ) *v.* **1.** (cause to) make loud noise **2.** (cause to) fall with crash **3.** cause (aircraft) to hit land or water or (of aircraft) land in this way **4.** (cause to) collide (with another car *etc.*) **5.** move noisily or violently —*vi.* **6.** break, smash **7.** collapse, fail, *esp.* financially —*n.* **8.** loud, violent fall or impact **9.** collision, *esp.* between vehicles **10.** sudden, uncontrolled descent of aircraft to land **11.** sudden collapse or downfall **12.** bankruptcy —*a.* **13.** requiring, using, great effort to achieve results quickly —'**crashing** *a. inf.* thorough (*esp. in crashing bore*) —**crash helmet** helmet worn by motorcyclists *etc.* to protect head —**crash-land** *v.* land (aircraft) in emergency, *esp.* with damage to craft

crass (kræs) *a.* grossly stupid —'**crassly** *adv.* —'**crassness** *n.*

crate (kreɪt) *n.* large (*usu.* wooden) container for packing goods

crater ('kreɪtə) *n.* **1.** mouth of volcano **2.** bowl-shaped cavity, *esp.* one made by explosion of large shell, bomb, mine *etc.*

cravat (krə'væt) *n.* man's neckcloth

crave (kreɪv) *v.* **1.** have very strong desire (for), long (for) —*vt.* **2.** ask humbly **3.** beg —'**craving** *n.*

craven ('kreɪv'n) *a.* **1.** cowardly, abject, spineless —*n.* **2.** coward

craw (krɔː) *n.* **1.** bird's or animal's stomach **2.** bird's crop

crawfish ('krɔːfɪʃ) *n. see* CRAYFISH

crawl (krɔːl) *vi.* **1.** move on belly or on hands and knees **2.** move very slowly **3.** ingratiate oneself, cringe **4.** swim with crawl-stroke **5.** be overrun (with) —*n.* **6.** crawling motion **7.** very slow pace or motion **8.** racing stroke at swimming —'**crawler** *n.*

crayfish ('kreɪfɪʃ) *or esp. U.S.* **crawfish** *n.* edible freshwater crustacean like lobster

crayon ('kreɪən, -ɒn) *n.* stick or pencil of coloured chalk, wax *etc.*

craze (kreɪz) *n.* **1.** short-lived current fashion **2.** strong desire or passion, mania **3.** madness —**crazed** *a.* **1.** demented **2.** (of porcelain) having fine cracks —'**crazy** *a.* **1.** insane **2.** very foolish **3.** (*with* about *or* over) madly eager (for) —**crazy paving** paving made with flat irregularly shaped slabs of stone

creak (kriːk) *n.* **1.** harsh grating noise —*vi.* **2.** make creaking sound

cream (kriːm) *n.* **1.** fatty part of milk **2.** various foods, dishes, resembling cream **3.** cosmetic *etc.* with creamlike consistency **4.** yellowish-white colour **5.** best part of anything —*vt.* **6.** take cream from **7.** take best part from **8.** beat to creamy consistency —'**creamer** *n.* **1.** vessel or device for separating cream from milk **2.** powdered milk substitute for coffee —'**creamery** *n.* **1.** establishment where milk and cream are made into butter and cheese **2.** place where dairy products are sold —'**creamy** *a.* —**cream cheese** soft white cheese made from soured cream or milk —**cream of tartar** potassium hydrogen tartrate, *esp.* when used in baking powders

crease (kriːs) *n.* **1.** line made by folding **2.** wrinkle **3.** *Cricket* line defining bowler's and batsman's positions **4.** superficial bullet wound —*v.* **5.** make, develop creases

create (kriː'eɪt) *vt.* **1.** bring into being **2.** give rise to **3.** make —*vi.* **4.** *inf.* make a fuss —**cre'ation** *n.* —**cre'ative** *a.* —**cre'ator** *n.*

creature ('kriːtʃə) *n.* **1.** living being **2.** thing created **3.** dependant —**creature comforts** bodily comforts

crèche (kreʃ, kreɪʃ) *n.* day nursery for very young children

credence ('kriːd⁽ᵉ⁾ns) *n.* **1.** belief, credit **2.** side-table for elements of the Eucharist before consecration

credentials (krɪ'denʃəlz) *pl.n.* **1.** testimonials **2.** letters of introduction, *esp.* those given to ambassador

credible ('kredɪb⁽ᵊ⁾l) *a.* **1.** worthy of belief **2.** trustworthy —**credi'bility** *n.* —'**credibly** *adv.* —**credibility gap** disparity between claims or statements and facts

credit ('kredɪt) *n.* **1.** commendation, approval **2.** source, cause, of honour **3.** belief, trust **4.** good name **5.** influence, honour or power based on trust of others **6.** system of allowing customers to take goods for later payment **7.** money at one's disposal in bank *etc.* **8.** side of book on which such sums are entered **9.** reputation for financial reliability —*pl.* **10.** list of those responsible for production of film —*vt.* **11.** (*with* with) attribute **12.** believe **13.** put on credit side of account —'**creditable** *a.* bringing honour —'**creditably** *adv.* —'**creditor** *n.* one to whom

debt is due —**credit card** card issued by banks *etc.* enabling holder to obtain goods and services on credit

credo ('kriːdəʊ, 'kreɪ-) *n.* formal statement of beliefs, principles or opinions (*pl.* -s)

credulous ('kredjʊləs) *a.* too easy of belief, easily deceived or imposed on, gullible —**cre'dulity** *n.* —'**credulousness** *n.*

creed (kriːd) *n.* **1.** formal statement of Christian beliefs **2.** statement, system of beliefs or principles

creek (kriːk) *n.* narrow inlet on seacoast

creel (kriːl) *n.* angler's fishing basket

creep (kriːp) *vi.* **1.** make way along ground, as snake **2.** move with stealthy, slow movements **3.** crawl **4.** act in servile way **5.** (of skin or flesh) feel shrinking, shivering sensation, due to fear or repugnance (**crept** *pt./pp.*) —*n.* **6.** creeping **7.** *sl.* repulsive person —*pl.* **8.** *sl.* feeling of fear or repugnance —'**creeper** *n.* creeping or climbing plant, *eg* ivy —'**creepy** *a. inf.* uncanny, unpleasant **2.** causing flesh to creep —**creepy-crawly** *UK inf. n.* **1.** small crawling creature (*pl.* -**crawlies**) —*a.* **2.** feeling or causing sensation as of creatures crawling on skin

cremation (krɪ'meɪʃən) *n.* burning as means of disposing of corpses —**cre'mate** *vt.* —**crema'torium** *n.* place for cremation

crème de la crème (krem də la 'krem) *n. Fr.* the very best

crème de menthe ('krem də 'menθ, 'mɪnt, 'kriːm, 'kreɪm) liqueur flavoured with peppermint

crenate ('kriːneɪt) *or* **crenated** *a.* having scalloped margin, as certain leaves —'**crenation** *n.*

crenellated *or U.S.* **crenelated** ('krenɪleɪtɪd) *a.* having battlements

creole ('kriːəʊl) *n.* **1.** hybrid language **2.** (**C**-) native-born W Indian, Latin American, of European descent

creosote ('krɪəsəʊt) *n.* **1.** oily antiseptic liquid distilled from coal or wood tar, used for preserving wood —*vt.* **2.** coat or impregnate with creosote

crepe *or* **crape** (kreɪp) *n.* **1.** fabric with crimped surface **2.** very thin pancake, oft. folded round filling —**crepe de Chine** (də 'ʃiːn) very thin crepe of silk or similar light fabric —**crepe paper** thin crinkled paper resembling crepe —**crepe rubber** rough-surfaced rubber used for soles of shoes

crepitate ('krepɪteɪt) *vi.* make rattling or crackling sound

crepitus ('krepɪtəs) *n.* **1.** crackling chest sound heard in pneumonia *etc.* **2.** grating sound of two ends of broken bone rubbing together

crept (krept) *pt./pp. of* CREEP

crepuscular (krɪ'pʌskjʊlə) *a.* **1.** of or like twilight; dim **2.** (of creatures) active at twilight

Cres. Crescent

crescendo (krɪ'ʃendəʊ) *n.* **1.** gradual

increase of loudness, *esp.* in music —*adv.*
2. with a crescendo

crescent ('kres²nt, -z²nt) *n.* **1.** (shape of) moon as seen in first or last quarter **2.** any figure of this shape **3.** row of houses built on curve

cress (krɛs) *n.* any of various plants with edible pungent leaves

crest (krɛst) *n.* **1.** comb or tuft on bird's or animal's head **2.** plume on top of helmet **3.** top of mountain, ridge, wave *etc.* **4.** badge above shield of coat of arms, also used separately on seal, plate *etc.* —*vt.* **5.** crown **6.** reach top of —'**crestfallen** *a.* cast down by failure, dejected

cretaceous (krɪ'teɪʃəs) *a.* chalky

Cretaceous (krɪ'teɪʃəs) *a.* **1.** of last period of Mesozoic era, during which chalk deposits were formed —*n.* **2.** Cretaceous period or rock system

cretin ('krɛtɪn) *n.* **1.** person afflicted with cretinism **2.** *inf.* stupid person —'**cretinism** *n.* deficiency in thyroid gland causing physical and mental retardation

cretonne (krɛ'tɒn, 'krɛtɒn) *n.* unglazed cotton cloth printed in coloured patterns

crevasse (krɪ'væs) *n.* deep open chasm, *esp.* in glacier

crevice ('krɛvɪs) *n.* cleft, fissure, chink

crew (kruː) *n.* **1.** ship's, boat's or aircraft's company, excluding passengers **2.** *inf.* gang, set —*v.* **3.** serve as crew (on) —**crew cut** man's closely cropped haircut

crewel ('kruːɪl) *n.* fine worsted yarn, used in fancy work and embroidery

crib (krɪb) *n.* **1.** child's cot **2.** barred rack used for fodder **3.** plagiarism **4.** translation used by students, sometimes illicitly —*vt.* **5.** confine in small space **6.** copy unfairly (**-bb-**)

cribbage ('krɪbɪdʒ) *n.* card game for two, three or four players

crick (krɪk) *n.* spasm or cramp in muscles, *esp.* in neck

cricket¹ ('krɪkɪt) *n.* chirping insect

cricket² ('krɪkɪt) *n.* outdoor game played with bats, ball and wickets by teams of eleven a side —'**cricketer** *n.*

cri de coeur (kri də 'kœːr) *Fr.* heartfelt or impassioned appeal (*pl.* **cris de coeur** (kri də 'kœːr))

cried (kraɪd) *pt./pp. of* CRY

crier ('kraɪə) *n.* **1.** person or animal that cries **2.** formerly, official who made public announcements, *esp.* in town or court

crime (kraɪm) *n.* **1.** violation of law (usu. a serious offence) **2.** wicked or forbidden act **3.** *inf.* something to be regretted —**criminal** ('krɪmɪn²l) *a./n.* —**criminality** (krɪmɪ'nælɪtɪ) *n.* —**criminally** ('krɪmɪnəlɪ) *adv.* —**criminology** (krɪmɪ'nɒlədʒɪ) *n.* study of crime and criminals

crimp (krɪmp) *vt.* **1.** pinch into tiny parallel pleats **2.** wrinkle

Crimplene ('krɪmpliːn) *n.* **R** crease-resistant synthetic material, similar to Terylene

crimson ('krɪmzən) *a./n.* **1.** (of) rich deep red —*v.* **2.** turn crimson

cringe (krɪndʒ) *vi.* **1.** shrink, cower **2.** behave obsequiously

crinkle ('krɪŋk²l) *v./n.* wrinkle

crinoline ('krɪn²lɪn) *n.* hooped petticoat or skirt

cripple ('krɪp²l) *n.* **1.** one not having normal use of limbs, disabled or deformed person —*vt.* **2.** maim, disable, impair **3.** weaken, lessen efficiency of

crisis ('kraɪsɪs) *n.* **1.** turning point or decisive moment, *esp.* in illness **2.** time of acute danger or difficulty (*pl.* **crises** ('kraɪsiːz))

crisp (krɪsp) *a.* **1.** brittle but firm **2.** brisk, decided **3.** clear-cut **4.** fresh, invigorating **5.** (of hair) curly —*n.* **6.** very thin, fried slice of potato, eaten cold —'**crisper** *n.* refrigerator compartment for storing salads *etc.* —'**crispy** *a.* —'**crispbread** *n.* thin, dry biscuit

crisscross ('krɪskrɒs) *v.* **1.** (cause to) move in crosswise pattern **2.** mark with or consist of pattern of crossing lines —*a.* **3.** (*esp.* of lines) crossing one another in different directions —*n.* **4.** pattern made of crossing lines —*adv.* **5.** in crosswise manner or pattern

criterion (kraɪ'tɪərɪən) *n.* standard of judgment (*pl.* **-ria** (-rɪə))

critical ('krɪtɪk²l) *a.* **1.** fault-finding **2.** discerning **3.** skilled in or given to judging **4.** of great importance, crucial, decisive —'**critic** *n.* **1.** one who passes judgment **2.** writer expert in judging works of literature, art *etc.* —'**critically** *adv.* —'**criticism** *n.* —'**criticize** *or* **-ise** *v.* —**critique** (krɪ'tiːk) *n.* critical essay, carefully written criticism —**critical path analysis** technique for planning projects with reference to critical path, which is sequence of stages requiring longest time

croak (krəʊk) *vi.* **1.** utter deep hoarse cry, as raven, frog **2.** talk dismally **3.** *sl.* die —*n.* **4.** deep hoarse cry —'**croaker** *n.* —'**croaky** *a.* hoarse

Croatian (krəʊ'eɪʃən) *a.* **1.** of Croatia, its people or their dialect of Serbo-Croatian —*n.* **2.** dialect of Croatia **3.** native or inhabitant of Croatia

crochet ('krəʊʃeɪ, -ʃɪ) *n.* **1.** kind of handicraft like knitting, done with small hooked needle —*vi.* **2.** do such work —*vt.* **3.** make (garment *etc.*) by such work

crock (krɒk) *n.* **1.** earthenware jar or pot **2.** broken piece of earthenware **3.** *inf.* old broken-down thing or person **4.** *inf.* cripple —'**crockery** *n.* earthenware dishes, utensils *etc.*

crocodile ('krɒkədaɪl) *n.* **1.** large amphibious reptile **2.** line of children walking two by two —**crocodilian** (krɒkə'dɪlɪən) *n.* **1.** large predatory reptile, such as crocodile, alligator *etc.* —*a.* **2.** of crocodiles or crocodilians —**crocodile tears** insincere grief

crocus ('krəʊkəs) *n.* small bulbous plant with yellow, white or purple flowers

Croesus ('kriːsəs) *n.* very rich man

croft (krɒft) *n. Scot.* small piece of arable land, smallholding —**'crofter** *n.* one who works croft

croissant ('krwʌsɒŋ) *n.* crescent-shaped roll of yeast dough like pastry

Cro-Magnon man ('krəʊ'mænjɒn) early type of modern man who lived in Europe during late Palaeolithic times

cromlech ('krɒmlɛx) *n.* prehistoric structure, monument of flat stone resting on two upright ones

crone (krəʊn) *n.* witchlike old woman

crony ('krəʊnɪ) *n.* intimate friend

crook (krʊk) *n.* 1. hooked staff 2. any hook, bend, sharp turn 3. *inf.* swindler, criminal —**crooked** ('krʊkɪd) *a.* 1. bent, twisted 2. deformed 3. *inf.* dishonest

croon (kruːn) *v.* hum, sing in soft, low tone —**'crooner** *n.*

crop (krɒp) *n.* 1. produce of cultivation of any plant or plants 2. harvest (*lit. or fig.*) 3. pouch in bird's gullet 4. stock of whip 5. hunting whip 6. short haircut —*vt.* 7. cut short 8. poll, clip 9. (of animals) bite, eat down —*vi.* 10. raise, produce or occupy land with crop (**-pp-**) —**'cropper** *n. inf.* 1. heavy fall 2. disastrous failure —**cropdusting** *n.* spreading fungicide *etc.* on crops from aircraft —**crop up** *inf.* happen unexpectedly

croquet ('krəʊkeɪ, -kɪ) *n.* lawn game played with balls, wooden mallets and hoops

croquette (krəʊ'kɛt, krɒ-) *n.* fried ball of minced meat, fish *etc.* in breadcrumbs

crosier *or* **crozier** ('krəʊʒə) *n.* bishop's or abbot's staff

cross (krɒs) *n.* 1. structure or symbol of two intersecting lines or pieces (at right angles) 2. such a structure of wood as means of execution by tying or nailing victim to it 3. symbol of Christian faith 4. any thing or mark in the shape of cross 5. misfortune, annoyance, affliction 6. intermixture of breeds, hybrid —*v.* 7. move or go across (something) 8. intersect —*vi.* 9. meet and pass —*vt.* 10. mark with lines across 11. (*with* out) delete 12. place or put in form of cross 13. make sign of cross on or over 14. modify breed of animals or plants by intermixture 15. thwart 16. oppose —*a.* 17. out of temper, angry 18. peevish, perverse 19. transverse 20. intersecting 21. contrary 22. adverse —**'crossing** *n.* 1. intersection of roads, rails *etc.* 2. part of street where pedestrians are expected to cross —**'crossly** *adv.* —**'crosswise** *adv./a.* —**'crossbar** *n.* 1. horizontal bar, line, stripe *etc.* 2. horizontal beam across pair of goal posts 3. horizontal bar on man's bicycle —**cross-bench** *n.* (*usu. pl.*) UK seat in Parliament occupied by neutral or independent member —**cross-bencher** *n.* —**'crossbill** *n.* bird whose mandibles cross

when closed —**'crossbow** *n.* bow fixed across wooden shoulder stock —**'crossbreed** *n.* breed produced from parents of different breeds —**cross'check** *v.* 1. verify (report *etc.*) by consulting other sources —*n.* 2. act of crosschecking —**crosscountry** *n.* long race held over open ground —**cross-examination** *n.* —**crossexamine** *vt.* examine (witness already examined by other side) —**cross-eyed** *a.* having eye(s) turning inward —**crossfertilization** *n.* fertilization of one plant by pollen of another —**'crossfire** *n.* 1. *Mil.* converging fire from one or more positions 2. lively exchange of ideas, opinions *etc.* —**cross-grained** *a.* perverse —**'crosspatch** *n. inf.* bad-tempered person —**cross-ply** *a.* (of tyre) having fabric cords in outer casing running diagonally —**cross-purpose** *n.* contrary aim or purpose —**cross-question** *vt.* 1. crossexamine —*n.* 2. question asked in crossexamination —**cross-refer** *v.* refer from one part to another —**cross-reference** *n.* reference within text to another part of text —**'crossroads** *n.* —**cross section** 1. transverse section 2. group of people fully representative of a nation, community *etc.* —**cross-stitch** *n.* 1. embroidery stitch made by two stitches forming cross —*v.* 2. embroider (piece of needlework) with cross-stitch —**'crosstalk** *n.* 1. *Rad., telephony* unwanted sounds picked up on receiving channel 2. UK rapid or witty talk —**crossword (puzzle)** puzzle built up of intersecting words, of which some letters are common, the words being indicated by clues —**at cross-purposes** conflicting; opposed; disagreeing —**the Cross** 1. cross on which Jesus Christ was executed 2. model or picture of this

crosse (krɒs) *n.* light staff with triangular frame to which network is attached, used in playing lacrosse

crotch (krɒtʃ) *n.* 1. angle between legs, genital area 2. fork

crotchet ('krɒtʃɪt) *n.* musical note, equal to half the length of a minim

crotchety ('krɒtʃɪtɪ) *a.* 1. peevish 2. irritable

croton ('krəʊtʰn) *n.* any chiefly tropical shrub or tree, seeds of which yield croton oil, formerly used as purgative

crouch (krautʃ) *vi.* 1. bend low 2. huddle down close to ground 3. stoop servilely, cringe —*n.* 4. act of stooping or bending

croup[1] (kruːp) *n.* throat disease of children, with cough

croup[2] (kruːp) *n.* 1. hindquarters of horse 2. place behind saddle

croupier ('kruːpɪə) *n.* person dealing cards, collecting money *etc.* at gambling table

crouton ('kruːtɒn) *n.* small piece of fried or toasted bread, usu. served in soup

crow[1] (krəʊ) *n.* large black carrion-eating bird —**'crowfoot** *n.* any of several plants that have yellow or white flowers and leaves resembling foot of crow (*pl.* **-s**) —**crow's-foot** *n.* wrinkle at corner of eye —**crow's-nest** *n.* lookout platform high on ship's mast

crow² (krəʊ) *vi.* 1. utter cock's cry 2. boast one's happiness or superiority —*n.* 3. cock's cry

crowbar ('krəʊbɑː) *n.* iron bar, usu. beaked, for levering

crowd (kraʊd) *n.* 1. throng, mass —*vi.* 2. flock together —*vt.* 3. cram, force, thrust, pack 4. fill with people —**crowd out** exclude by excess already in

crown (kraʊn) *n.* 1. monarch's headdress 2. wreath for head 3. monarch 4. monarchy 5. royal power 6. formerly, British coin of five shillings 7. various foreign coins 8. top of head 9. summit, top 10. completion or perfection of thing —*vt.* 11. put crown on 12. confer title upon 13. occur as culmination of series of events 14. *inf.* hit on head —**crown court** *English law* court of criminal jurisdiction holding sessions throughout England and Wales —**crown green** bowling green in which sides are lower than middle —**crown jewels** jewellery, including regalia, used by sovereign on state occasion —**crown land** public land —**crown prince** heir to throne

crozier ('krəʊʒə) *n. see* CROSIER

CRT cathode-ray tube

crucial ('kruːʃəl) *a.* 1. decisive, critical 2. *inf.* very important

cruciate ('kruːʃɪt, -eɪt) *a.* cross-shaped

crucible ('kruːsɪbˀl) *n.* small melting pot

crucify ('kruːsɪfaɪ) *vt.* 1. put to death on cross 2. treat cruelly 3. *inf.* ridicule ('crucified, 'crucifying) —**crucifix** *n.* 1. cross 2. image of (Christ on the) Cross —**cruci'fixion** *n.* —**cruciform** *a.*

crude (kruːd) *a.* 1. lacking taste, vulgar 2. in natural or raw state, unrefined 3. rough, unfinished —**'crudely** *adv.* —**'crudity** *n.*

cruel ('kruːəl) *a.* 1. delighting in others' pain 2. causing pain or suffering —**'cruelly** *adv.* —**'cruelty** *n.*

cruet ('kruːɪt) *n.* 1. small container for salt, pepper, vinegar, oil *etc.* 2. stand holding such containers

cruise (kruːz) *vi.* 1. travel about in a ship for pleasure *etc.* 2. (of vehicle, aircraft) travel at safe, average speed —*n.* 3. cruising voyage, *esp.* organized for holiday purposes —**'cruiser** *n.* 1. ship that cruises 2. warship lighter and faster than battleship —**'cruiserweight** *n. Boxing* light-heavyweight

crumb (krʌm) *n.* 1. small particle, fragment, *esp.* of bread —*vt.* 2. reduce to, break into, cover with crumbs —**'crumby** *a.*

crumble ('krʌmbˀl) *v.* 1. break into small fragments, disintegrate, crush 2. perish, decay —*vi.* 3. fall apart or away —*n.* 4. pudding covered with crumbly mixture —**'crumbly** *a.*

crummy ('krʌmɪ) *a. sl.* inferior, contemptible

crump (krʌmp) *vi.* 1. thud, explode with dull sound —*n.* 2. crunching sound 3. *inf.* shell, bomb

crumpet ('krʌmpɪt) *n.* 1. flat, soft cake eaten with butter 2. *sl.* sexually desirable woman or women

crumple ('krʌmpˀl) *v.* 1. (cause to) collapse 2. make or become crushed, wrinkled, creased —**'crumpled** *a.*

crunch (krʌntʃ) *n.* 1. sound made by chewing crisp food, treading on gravel, hard snow *etc.* 2. *inf.* critical moment or situation —*v.* 3. (cause to) make crunching sound

crupper ('krʌpə) *n.* 1. strap holding back saddle in place by passing round horse's tail 2. horse's hindquarters

crusade (kruː'seɪd) *n.* 1. medieval Christian war to recover Holy Land 2. campaign against something believed to be evil 3. concerted action to further a cause —*vi.* 4. campaign vigorously for something 5. go on crusade —**cru'sader** *n.*

cruse (kruːz) *n.* small earthenware jug or pot

crush¹ (krʌʃ) *vt.* 1. compress so as to break, bruise, crumple 2. break to small pieces 3. defeat utterly, overthrow —*n.* 4. act of crushing 5. crowd of people *etc.* 6. drink prepared by or as if by crushing fruit

crush² (krʌʃ) *n. inf.* infatuation

crust (krʌst) *n.* 1. hard outer part of bread 2. similar hard outer casing on anything —*v.* 3. cover with, form, crust —**'crustily** *adv.* —**'crusty** *a.* 1. having, or like, crust 2. short-tempered

crustacean (krʌ'steɪʃən) *n.* hard-shelled animal, *eg* crab, lobster —**crus'taceous** *a.*

crutch (krʌtʃ) *n.* 1. staff with crosspiece to go under armpit of lame person 2. support 3. groin, crotch

crux (krʌks) *n.* 1. that on which a decision turns 2. anything that puzzles very much (*pl.* **-es, cruces** ('kruːsiːz))

cry (kraɪ) *vi.* 1. weep 2. wail 3. utter call 4. shout 5. clamour or beg (for) —*vt.* 6. utter loudly, proclaim (**cried, 'crying**) —*n.* 7. loud utterance 8. scream, wail, shout 9. call of animal 10. fit of weeping 11. watchword —**'crying** *a.* notorious; lamentable (*esp.* in **crying shame**)

cryogenics (kraɪə'dʒɛnɪks) *n.* branch of physics concerned with phenomena at very low temperatures —**cryo'genic** *a.*

crypt (krɪpt) *n.* vault, *esp.* under church —**'cryptic** *a.* secret, mysterious —**'cryptically** *adv.* —**'cryptograph** *n.* piece of writing in code —**cryp'tography** *n.* art of writing, decoding ciphers

cryptogam ('krɪptəʊgæm) *n.* nonflowering plant, *eg* fern, moss *etc.*

crystal ('krɪstˀl) *n.* 1. clear transparent mineral 2. very clear glass 3. cut-glass ware 4. characteristic form assumed by many substances, with definite internal structure and external shape of symmetrically arranged plane surfaces —'**crystalline** or '**crystalloid** a. —**crystalli'zation** or **-i'sation** n. —'**crystallize** or **-ise** v. 1. (cause to) form into crystals 2. (cause to) become definite —**crystal'lographer** n. —**crystal'lography** n. science of the structure, forms and properties of crystals —**crystal gazer** —**crystal gazing** 1. act of staring into crystal ball supposedly to arouse visual perceptions of future etc. 2. act of trying to foresee or predict

Cs Chem. caesium

CSE Certificate of Secondary Education

CS gas gas causing tears, salivation and painful breathing, used in chemical warfare and civil disturbances

CST US, C Central Standard Time

CT Connecticut

ct. 1. cent 2. carat 3. court

ctenophore ('tɛnəfɔː, 'tiːnə-) n. marine invertebrate whose body bears eight rows of fused cilia for locomotion

CTV Canadian Television (Network Ltd.)

cu or **cu.** cubic

Cu Chem. copper

cub (kʌb) n. 1. young of fox and other animals 2. (C-) Cub Scout —v. 3. give birth to (cubs) (-bb-) —**Cub Scout** member of junior branch of the Scout Association

cubbyhole ('kʌbɪhəʊl) n. small, enclosed space or room

cube (kjuːb) n. 1. regular solid figure contained by six equal square sides 2. cube-shaped block 3. product obtained by multiplying number by itself twice —vt. 4. multiply thus —'**cubic(al)** a. —'**cubism** n. style of art in which objects are presented as assemblage of geometrical shapes —'**cubist** n./a. —**cube root** number or quantity whose cube is a given number or quantity —**cubic measure** system of units for measurement of volumes

cubicle ('kjuːbɪkʰl) n. partially or totally enclosed section of room, as in dormitory

cubit ('kjuːbɪt) n. old measure of length, about 18 inches

cuckold ('kʌkəld) n. 1. man whose wife has committed adultery —vt. 2. make cuckold of

cuckoo ('kukuː) n. 1. migratory bird which deposits its eggs in nests of other birds 2. its call —a. 3. sl. crazy —'**cuckoopint** n. European plant with arrow-shaped leaves, pale purple spadix and scarlet berries (also **lords-and-ladies**) —**cuckoo spit** white frothy mass on plants, produced by froghopper larvae

cucumber ('kjuːkʌmbə) n. 1. plant with long fleshy green fruit 2. the fruit, used in salad

cud (kʌd) n. food which ruminant animal brings back into mouth to chew again —**chew the cud** reflect, meditate

cuddle ('kʌdʰl) vt. 1. hug —vi. 2. lie close and snug, nestle —n. 3. close embrace, esp. when prolonged

cuddy ('kʌdɪ) n. small cabin in boat

cudgel ('kʌdʒəl) n. 1. short thick stick —vt. 2. beat with cudgel (-ll-)

cue[1] (kjuː) n. 1. last words of actor's speech etc. as signal to another to act or speak 2. signal, hint, example for action

cue[2] (kjuː) n. 1. long tapering rod used in billiards 2. pigtail

cuff[1] (kʌf) n. 1. ending of sleeve 2. wristband —**cuff link** one pair of linked buttons to join buttonholes on shirt cuffs —**off the cuff** inf. without preparation

cuff[2] (kʌf) vt. strike with open hand —n. 2. blow of this kind

cuirass (kwɪ'ræs) n. metal or leather armour of breastplate and backplate

Cuisenaire rod (kwɪzə'neə) R one of set of rods of various colours and lengths representing different numbers, used to teach arithmetic to young children

cuisine (kwɪ'ziːn) n. 1. style of cooking 2. menu, food offered by restaurant etc.

cul-de-sac ('kʌldəsæk, 'kʊl-) n. 1. street, lane open only at one end 2. blind alley (pl. **culs-de-sac**)

culinary ('kʌlɪnərɪ) a. of, for, suitable for, cooking or kitchen

cull (kʌl) vt. 1. gather, select 2. take out (selected animals) from herd —n. 3. act of culling

culminate ('kʌlmɪneɪt) vi. 1. reach highest point 2. come to climax, to a head —culmi'nation n.

culottes (kjuː'lɒts) pl.n. flared trousers (esp. for women) cut to look like skirt

culpable ('kʌlpəbʰl) a. blameworthy —**culpa'bility** n. —'**culpably** adv.

culprit ('kʌlprɪt) n. one guilty of usu. minor offence

cult (kʌlt) n. 1. system of religious worship 2. pursuit of, devotion to, some person, thing, or activity

cultivate ('kʌltɪveɪt) vt. 1. till and prepare (ground) to raise crops 2. develop, improve, refine 3. devote attention to, cherish 4. practise 5. foster —'**cultivable** or '**cultivatable** a. (of land) capable of being cultivated —culti'vation n. —'**cultivator** n.

culture ('kʌltʃə) n. 1. state of manners, taste and intellectual development at a time or place 2. cultivating 3. artificial rearing 4. set of bacteria so reared —'**cultural** a. —'**cultured** a. refined, showing culture —**cultured pearl** pearl artificially induced to grow in oyster shell

culvert ('kʌlvət) n. tunnelled drain for passage of water under road, railway etc.

cum (kʌm) Lat. with

cumbersome ('kʌmbəsəm) or **cumbrous** ('kʌmbrəs) a. awkward, unwieldy —'**cumber** vt. 1. obstruct; hinder 2. obs. inconvenience —'**cumbrance** n. 1. burden; obstacle; hindrance 2. trouble; bother

Cumbrian ('kʌmbrɪən) a./n. (native or inhabitant) of Cumbria, county of NW England

cumin or **cummin** ('kʌmɪn) n. herb

cummerbund or **kummerbund** ('kʌmə-bʌnd) n. broad sash worn round waist

cumquat ('kʌmkwɒt) n. see KUMQUAT

cumulative ('kju:mjulətiv) a. 1. becoming greater by successive additions 2. representing the sum of many items

cumulus ('kju:mjuləs) n. cloud shaped in rounded white woolly masses (pl. **cumuli** ('kju:mjulai))

cuneiform ('kju:nifɔ:m) a. wedge-shaped, esp. of ancient Babylonian writing

cunning ('kʌnɪŋ) a. 1. crafty, sly 2. ingenious —n. 3. skill in deceit or evasion 4. skill, ingenuity —'**cunningly** adv.

cup (kʌp) n. 1. small drinking vessel with handle at one side 2. any small drinking vessel 3. contents of cup 4. various cup-shaped formations, cavities, sockets etc. 5. cup-shaped trophy as prize 6. portion, lot 7. iced drink of wine and other ingredients 8. either of two cup-shaped parts of brassiere etc. —vt. 9. shape as cup (hands etc.) —'**cupful** n. (pl. '**cupfuls**) —'**cupping** n. Med. formerly, use of evacuated glass cup to draw blood to surface of skin for bloodletting —**cupboard** ('kʌbəd) n. piece of furniture, recess in room, with door, for storage —**cupboard love** show of love inspired by selfish or greedy motive —**Cup Final** 1. annual final of F.A. Cup soccer competition 2. final of any cup competition —**cup tie** Sport eliminating match between two teams in cup competition

cupel ('kju:pʌl, kju:'pɛl) n. small vessel used in refining metals

Cupid ('kju:pɪd) n. god of love

cupidity (kju:'pɪdɪtɪ) n. 1. greed for possessions 2. covetousness

cupola ('kju:pələ) n. dome

cupreous ('kju:priəs) a. of, containing, copper

cupronickel (kju:prəu'nɪkʎl) n. copper alloy containing up to 40 per cent nickel

cur (kɜ:) n. 1. dog of mixed breed 2. surly, contemptible or mean person

curaçao (kjuərə'səu) n. liqueur flavoured with bitter orange peel

curare or **curari** (kju'rɑ:rɪ) n. poisonous resin of S Amer. tree, now used as muscle relaxant in medicine

curate ('kjuərɪt) n. parish priest's appointed assistant —'**curacy** n. his office

curative ('kjuərətɪv) a. 1. tending to cure disease —n. 2. anything able to heal or cure

curator (kjuə'reɪtə) n. custodian, esp. of museum, library etc. —**cura'torial** a. —**cu'ratorship** n.

curb (kɜ:b) n. 1. check, restraint 2. chain or strap passing under horse's lower jaw and giving powerful control with reins —vt. 3. restrain 4. apply curb to

curd (kɜ:d) n. coagulated milk —'**curdle** v. turn into curd, coagulate —'**curdy** a.

cure (kjuə) vt. 1. heal, restore to health 2. remedy 3. preserve (fish, skins etc.) —n. 4. remedy 5. course of medical treatment 6. successful treatment, restoration to health

—**cura'bility** n. —'**curable** a. —**cure of souls** care of parish or congregation

curet or **curette** (kjuə'rɛt) n. surgical instrument for removing dead tissue etc. from some body cavities —**curettage** (kjuəri'tɑ:ʒ, kjuə'rɛtɪdʒ) n.

curfew ('kɜ:fju:) n. 1. official regulation restricting or prohibiting movement of people, esp. at night 2. time set as deadline by such regulation

curia ('kjuərɪə) n. 1. papal court and government of Roman Catholic Church 2. (in Middle Ages) court held in king's name (pl. **curiae** ('kjuərɪi:))

curie ('kjuərɪ, -ri:) n. standard unit of radium emanation

curio ('kjuərɪəu) n. rare or curious thing of the kind sought for collections (pl. **-s**)

curious ('kjuərɪəs) a. 1. eager to know, inquisitive 2. prying 3. puzzling, strange, odd —**curi'osity** n. 1. eagerness to know 2. inquisitiveness 3. strange or rare thing —'**curiously** adv.

curium ('kjuərɪəm) n. element produced from plutonium

curl (kɜ:l) vi. 1. take spiral or curved shape or path —vt. 2. bend into spiral or curved shape —n. 3. spiral lock of hair 4. spiral, curved state, form or motion —'**curler** n. 1. pin, clasp or roller for curling hair 2. person or thing that curls 3. person who plays curling —'**curling** n. game like bowls, played with large rounded stones on ice —'**curly** a. —**curling tongs** heated, metal, scissor-like device for curling hair

curlew ('kɜ:lju:) n. large long-billed wading bird

curlicue or **curlycue** ('kɜ:lɪkju:) n. intricate ornamental curl or twist

curmudgeon (kɜ:'mʌdʒən) n. surly or miserly person

currach or **curragh** ('kʌrəx, 'kʌrə) n. Scot., Irish coracle

currant ('kʌrənt) n. 1. dried type of grape 2. fruit of various plants allied to gooseberry 3. any of these plants

current ('kʌrənt) a. 1. of immediate present, going on 2. up-to-date, not yet superseded 3. in circulation or general use —n. 4. body of water or air in motion 5. tendency, drift 6. transmission of electricity through conductor —'**currency** n. 1. money in use 2. state of being in use 3. time during which thing is current —'**currently** adv. —**current account** bank account against which cheques may be drawn at any time

curricle ('kʌrɪkʎl) n. two-wheeled open carriage drawn by two horses side by side

curriculum (kə'rɪkjuləm) n. specified course of study (pl. **-s**, **-la** (-lə)) —**curriculum vitae** ('vi:taɪ, 'vaɪtɪ) outline of person's educational and professional history, usu. for job applications (pl. **curricula vitae**)

curry[1] ('kʌrɪ) n. 1. highly-flavoured, pungent condiment, preparation of turmeric **2.** dish flavoured with it —*vt.* **3.** prepare, flavour dish with curry (**'curried, 'currying**)

curry² ('kʌrɪ) *vt.* **1.** groom (horse) with comb **2.** dress (leather) (**'curried, 'currying**) —**curry comb** metal comb for grooming horse —**curry favour** try to win favour unworthily, ingratiate oneself

curse (kɜːs) *n.* **1.** profane or obscene expression of anger *etc.* **2.** utterance expressing extreme ill will towards some person or thing **3.** affliction, misfortune, scourge —*v.* **4.** utter curse, swear (at) —*vt.* **5.** afflict —**cursed** ('kɜːsɪd, kɜːst) *a.* **1.** hateful **2.** wicked **3.** deserving of, or under, a curse —**cursedly** ('kɜːsɪdlɪ) *adv.* —**cursedness** ('kɜːsɪdnɪs) *n.*

cursive ('kɜːsɪv) *a.* written in running script, with letters joined

cursor ('kɜːsə) *n.* **1.** sliding part of measuring instrument, *esp.* on slide rule **2.** movable point of light *etc.* that identifies specific position on visual display unit

cursory ('kɜːsərɪ) *a.* rapid, hasty, not detailed, superficial —**'cursorily** *adv.*

curt (kɜːt) *a.* short, rudely brief, abrupt —**'curtly** *adv.* —**'curtness** *n.*

curtail (kɜː'teɪl) *vt.* cut short, diminish —**cur'tailment** *n.*

curtain ('kɜːt'n) *n.* **1.** hanging drapery at window *etc.* **2.** cloth hung as screen **3.** screen separating audience and stage in theatre **4.** end to act or scene *etc.* —*pl.* **5.** *inf.* death or ruin: the end —*vt.* **6.** provide, cover with curtain —**curtain call** return to stage by performers to acknowledge applause —**curtain-raiser** *n.* **1.** short play coming before main one **2.** any preliminary event'

curtsy *or* **curtsey** ('kɜːtsɪ) *n.* **1.** woman's bow or respectful gesture made by bending knees and lowering body —*vi.* **2.** make a curtsy

curve (kɜːv) *n.* **1.** line of which no part is straight **2.** bent line or part —*v.* **3.** bend into curve —**cur'vaceous** *a.* *inf.* shapely —**'curvature** *n.* **1.** a bending **2.** bent shape —**curvi'linear** *a.* of bent lines

curvet (kɜː'vɛt) *n.* **1.** *Dressage* low leap with all four feet off the ground —*vi.* **2.** prance or frisk about

cushion ('kʊʃən) *n.* **1.** bag filled with soft stuffing or air, to support or ease body **2.** any soft pad or support **3.** resilient rim of billiard table —*vt.* **4.** provide, protect with cushion **5.** lessen effects of

cushy ('kʊʃɪ) *a.* *inf.* soft, comfortable, pleasant, light, well-paid

cusp (kʌsp) *n.* pointed end, *esp.* of tooth —**'cuspid** *n.* pointed tooth —**'cuspidal** *a.* **1.** ending in point **2.** of, or like, cusp

cuspidor ('kʌspɪdɔː) *n.* spittoon

cuss (kʌs) *inf. n.* **1.** curse; oath **2.** person or animal, *esp.* annoying one —*v.* **3.** *see* CURSE (sense 4) —**cussed** ('kʌsɪd) *a.* *inf.* **1.** *see* **cursed** *at* CURSE **2.** obstinate **3.** annoying —**'cussedness** *n.*

custard ('kʌstəd) *n.* **1.** dish made of eggs

and milk **2.** sweet sauce of milk and cornflour

custody ('kʌstədɪ) *n.* safekeeping, guardianship, imprisonment —**cus'todian** *n.* keeper, caretaker, curator

custom ('kʌstəm) *n.* **1.** habit **2.** practice **3.** fashion, usage **4.** business patronage **5.** toll, tax —*pl.* **6.** duties levied on imports **7.** government department which collects these **8.** area in airport *etc.* where customs officials examine baggage for dutiable goods —**'customarily** *adv.* —**'customary** *a.* usual, habitual —**'customer** *n.* **1.** one who enters shop to buy, *esp.* regularly **2.** purchaser —**custom-built** *a.* *chiefly US* (of cars, houses *etc.*) made to specifications of buyer —**custom-made** *a.* *chiefly US* (of suits *etc.*) made to specifications of buyer —**customs duties** taxes laid on imported or exported goods —**customs house** building where customs are collected

cut (kʌt) *vt.* **1.** sever, penetrate, wound, divide, or separate with pressure of edge or edged instrument **2.** pare, detach, trim, or shape by cutting **3.** divide **4.** intersect **5.** reduce, decrease **6.** abridge **7.** *inf.* ignore (person) **8.** strike (with whip *etc.*) **9.** hit (cricket ball) to point's left **10.** *inf.* stay deliberately away from —*vi.* *Cine.* **11.** call a halt to shooting sequence **12.** (*with to*) move quickly to another scene (**cut, 'cutting**) —*n.* **13.** act of cutting **14.** stroke **15.** blow, wound (of knife, whip *etc.*) **16.** reduction, decrease **17.** fashion, shape **18.** incision **19.** engraving **20.** piece cut off **21.** division **22.** *inf.* share, *esp.* of profits —**'cutter** *n.* **1.** one who, that which, cuts **2.** warship's rowing and sailing boat **3.** small sloop-rigged vessel with straight running bowsprit —**'cutting** *n.* **1.** act of cutting, thing cut off or out, *esp.* excavation (for road, canal *etc.*) through high ground **2.** shoot, twig of plant **3.** piece cut from newspaper *etc.* —*a.* **4.** sarcastic, unkind —**'cutaway** *n.* **1.** man's coat cut diagonally from front waist to back of knees **2.** drawing or model of machine *etc.* in which part of casing is omitted to reveal workings —**'cutback** *n.* decrease; reduction —**cut glass** glass, *esp.* vases *etc.*, decorated by facet-cutting or grinding —**cut-price** *or esp. U.S.* **cut-rate** *a.* **1.** available at prices or rates below standard price or rate **2.** offering goods or services at prices below standard price —**'cutthroat** *a.* **1.** merciless —*n.* **2.** murderer **3.** UK razor with long blade that usu. folds into handle (*also* **cutthroat razor**) —**cut back 1.** shorten by cutting off end; prune **2.** reduce or make reduction (in) —**cut dead** refuse to recognize an acquaintance —**cut in 1.** drive in front of another's vehicle so as to affect his driving **2.** interrupt (in conversation) **3.** intrude

cutaneous (kjuː'teɪnɪəs) *a.* of skin

cute (kjuːt) *a.* appealing, attractive, pretty

cuticle ('kjuːtɪk'l) *n.* dead skin, *esp.* at base of fingernail

cutis ('kjuːtɪs) *n. Anat.* skin (*pl.* **-tes** (-tiːz), **-es**)

cutlass ('kʌtləs) *n.* short broad-bladed sword

cutlery ('kʌtlərɪ) *n.* knives, forks, spoons *etc.* —'**cutler** *n.* one who makes, repairs, deals in knives and cutting implements

cutlet ('kʌtlɪt) *n.* small piece of meat grilled or fried

cuttlefish ('kʌt'lfɪʃ) *n.* sea mollusc like squid (*also* '**cuttle**) —'**cuttlebone** *n.* internal shell of cuttlefish, used as mineral supplement to diet of cagebirds and as polishing agent

Cwlth. Commonwealth

cwm (kuːm) *n.* 1. in Wales, valley 2. *Geol.* *see* CIRQUE

c.w.o. *or* **C.W.O.** cash with order

cwt. hundredweight

-cy (*comb. form*) 1. state, quality, condition, as in *plutocracy, lunacy* 2. rank, office, as in *captaincy*

cyan ('saɪæn, 'saɪən) *n.* 1. green-blue colour —*a.* 2. of this colour

cyanide ('saɪənaɪd) *or* **cyanid** ('saɪənɪd) *n.* extremely poisonous chemical compound —**cy'anogen** *n.* poisonous gas composed of nitrogen and carbon

cyanosis (saɪə'nəʊsɪs) *n.* blueness of the skin

cybernetics (saɪbə'netɪks) *pl.n.* (*with sing. v.*) comparative study of control mechanisms of electronic and biological systems

cyclamate ('saɪkləmeɪt, 'sɪkləmeɪt) *n.* compound formerly used as food additive and sugar substitute

cyclamen ('sɪkləmən, -mɛn) *n.* plant with flowers having turned-back petals

cycle ('saɪk'l) *n.* 1. recurrent series or period 2. rotation of events 3. complete series or period 4. development following course of stages 5. series of poems *etc.* 6. bicycle —*vi.* 7. move in cycles 8. ride bicycle —'**cyclic(al)** *a.* —'**cyclist** *n.* bicycle rider —**cy'clometer** *n.* instrument for measuring circles or recording distance travelled by wheel, *esp.* of bicycle

cyclo- *or before vowel* **cycl-** (*comb. form*) 1. indicating circle or ring, as in *cyclotron* 2. denoting cyclic compound, as in *cyclopropane*

cyclone ('saɪkləʊn) *n.* 1. system of winds moving round centre of low pressure 2. circular storm —**cyclonic** (saɪ'klɒnɪk) *a.*

cyclopedia *or* **cyclopaedia** (saɪkləʊ-'piːdɪə) *n. see* ENCYCLOPEDIA

cyclopropane (saɪkləʊ'prəʊpeɪn) *n.* colourless gaseous hydrocarbon, used as anaesthetic

Cyclops ('saɪklɒps) *n. Class. myth.* one of race of giants having single eye in middle of forehead (*pl.* **Cyclopes** (saɪ'kləʊpiːz), **-es**)

cyclorama (saɪkləʊ'rɑːmə) *n.* 1. picture on interior wall of cylindrical room, designed to appear in natural perspective to spectator 2. *Theat.* curtain or wall curving along back of stage —**cycloramic** (saɪkləʊ-'ræmɪk) *a.*

cyclostyle ('saɪkləstaɪl) *vt.* 1. produce (pamphlets *etc.*) in large numbers for distribution —*a./n.* 2. (of) machine, method for doing this

cyclotron ('saɪklətrɒn) *n.* powerful apparatus which accelerates the circular movement of subatomic particles in a magnetic field, used for work in nuclear disintegration *etc.*

cygnet ('sɪgnɪt) *n.* young swan

cylinder ('sɪlɪndə) *n.* 1. roller-shaped solid or hollow body, of uniform diameter 2. piston chamber of engine —**cy'lindrical** *a.* —'**cylindroid** *a.*

cymbal ('sɪmb'l) *n.* one of pair of two brass plates struck together to produce ringing or clashing sound in music

cyme (saɪm) *n.* inflorescence in which first flower is terminal bud of main stem and subsequent flowers develop as terminal buds of lateral stems —**cy'miferous** *a.*

Cymric *or* **Kymric** ('kɪmrɪk) *a.* Welsh

cynic ('sɪnɪk) *n.* one who expects, believes, the worst about people, their motives, or outcome of events —'**cynical** *a.* —'**cynicism** *n.* being cynical

cynosure ('sɪnəzjʊə, -ʃʊə) *n.* centre of attraction

cypher ('saɪfə) *see* CIPHER

cypress ('saɪprəs) *n.* coniferous tree with very dark foliage

Cypriot ('sɪprɪət) *or* **Cypriote** ('sɪprɪəʊt) *n.* 1. native of Cyprus 2. dialect of Greek spoken in Cyprus —*a.* 3. relating to Cyprus

Cyrillic (sɪ'rɪlɪk) *a.* 1. relating to alphabet devised supposedly by Saint Cyril, for Slavonic languages —*n.* 2. this alphabet

cyst (sɪst) *n.* sac containing liquid secretion or pus —'**cystic** *a.* 1. of cysts 2. of the bladder —**cys'titis** *n.* inflammation of bladder —**cystic fibrosis** congenital disease, usu. affecting children, characterized by chronic infection of respiratory tract and pancreatic insufficiency

cytology (saɪ'tɒlədʒɪ) *n.* study of plant and animal cells

cytoplasm ('saɪtəʊplæzəm) *n.* protoplasm of cell excluding nucleus

czar (zɑː) *n.* emperor, king, *esp.* of Russia 1547–1917 —**Cza'rina, Cza'ritsa, Tsa'ritsa** *or* **Tza'ritsa** *n.* wife of Czar

czardas ('tʃɑːdæʃ) *n.* 1. Hungarian national dance of alternating slow and fast sections 2. music for this dance

Czech (tʃɛk) *n.* member of western branch of Slavs —**Czechoslovak** (tʃɛkəʊ'sləʊvæk) *or* **Czechoslovakian** (tʃɛkəʊsləʊ'vækɪən) *a.* 1. of Czechoslovakia, its peoples or languages —*n.* 2. (loosely) either of two languages of Czechoslovakia: Czech or Slovak

D

d *or* **D** (diː) *n.* **1.** fourth letter of English alphabet **2.** speech sound represented by this letter (*pl.* **d's, D's** *or* **Ds**)

d *Phys.* density

D 1. *Mus.* second note of scale of C major; major or minor key having this note as its tonic **2.** *Chem.* deuterium **3.** Roman numeral, 500

d. 1. day **2.** denarius (*Lat.*, penny) **3.** departs **4.** diameter **5.** died

D. Democratic

dab¹ (dæb) *vt.* **1.** apply with momentary pressure (*esp.* anything wet and soft) **2.** strike feebly (**-bb-**) —*n.* **3.** smear **4.** slight blow or tap **5.** small mass —**'dabchick** *n.* small grebe —**dab hand** *inf.* someone good at something

dab² (dæb) *n.* small flatfish

dabble (ˈdæbʰl) *vi.* **1.** splash about **2.** be desultory student or amateur —**'dabbler** *n.*

da capo (dɑː ˈkɑːpəʊ) *Mus.* repeat from beginning

dace (deɪs) *n.* small freshwater fish (*pl.* **dace, -s**)

dachshund (ˈdækshʊnd) *n.* short-legged long-bodied dog

Dacron (ˈdeɪkrɒn, ˈdæk-) *n.* US R Terylene

dactyl (ˈdæktɪl) *n.* metrical foot of one long followed by two short syllables

dad (dæd) *or* **daddy** (ˈdædɪ) *n. inf.* father —**daddy-longlegs** *n. inf.* crane fly

Dada (ˈdɑːdɑː) *or* **Dadaism** (ˈdɑːdɑːɪzəm) *n.* artistic movement of early 20th century, founded on principles of incongruity and irreverence towards accepted aesthetic criteria —**'Dadaist** *n./a.*

dado (ˈdeɪdəʊ) *n.* lower part of room wall when lined or painted separately (*pl.* **-es, -s**)

daemon (ˈdiːmən) *or* **daimon** (ˈdaɪmɒn) *n.* **1.** demigod **2.** guardian spirit of place or person

daff (dæf) *inf.* daffodil

daffodil (ˈdæfədɪl) *n.* spring flower, yellow narcissus (*also* **Lent lily**)

daft (dɑːft) *a.* foolish, crazy

dag (dæg) *n.* **1.** daglock **2. A, NZ** *sl.* eccentric character —**'daglock** *n.* dung-caked locks of wool around hindquarters of sheep

dagga (ˈdaxə, ˈdɑːgə) *n.* SA hemp, smoked as narcotic

dagger (ˈdægə) *n.* short, edged stabbing weapon

dago (ˈdeɪgəʊ) *n. offens.* Spaniard or other Latin (*pl.* **-s, -es**)

daguerreotype (dəˈgɛrəʊtaɪp) *n.* **1.** early photographic process **2.** photograph formed by this process

dahlia (ˈdeɪljə) *n.* garden plant of various colours

Dáil Eireann (ˈdɔɪl ˈɛərən) *or* **Dáil** *n.* lower chamber of parliament in the Irish Republic

daily (ˈdeɪlɪ) *a.* **1.** done, occurring, published every day —*adv.* **2.** every day —*n.* **3.** daily newspaper **4.** charwoman

dainty (ˈdeɪntɪ) *a.* **1.** delicate **2.** elegant, choice **3.** pretty and neat **4.** fastidious —*n.* **5.** delicacy —**'daintily** *adv.* —**'daintiness** *n.*

daiquiri (ˈdaɪkɪrɪ, ˈdæk-) *n.* iced drink containing rum, lime juice and sugar (*pl.* **-s**)

dairy (ˈdɛərɪ) *n.* place for processing milk and its products —**'dairying** *n.* —**dairy cattle** cows raised mainly for milk —**dairy farm** farm specializing in producing milk —**'dairymaid** *n.* —**'dairyman** *n.* —**dairy products** milk, cheese, butter *etc.*

dais (ˈdeɪs, deɪs) *n.* raised platform, usu. at end of hall

daisy (ˈdeɪzɪ) *n.* flower with yellow centre and white petals —**daisy-wheel** *n.* flat, wheel-shaped device with printing characters at end of spokes

Dalai Lama (ˈdælaɪ ˈlɑːmə) head of Buddhist hierarchy in Tibet

dale (deɪl) *n.* valley —**'dalesman** *n.* native of dale, *esp.* in N England

dalles (dælz) *pl.n.* **C** river rapids flowing between high rock walls

dally (ˈdælɪ) *vi.* **1.** trifle, spend time in idleness or amusement **2.** loiter (**'dallied, 'dallying**) —**'dalliance** *n.*

Dalmatian (dælˈmeɪʃən) *n.* large dog, white with black spots

dal segno (ˈdæl ˈsɛnjəʊ) *Mus.* repeat from point marked with sign to word *fine*

dam¹ (dæm) *n.* **1.** barrier to hold back flow of waters **2.** water so collected —*vt.* **3.** hold with or as with dam (**-mm-**)

dam² (dæm) *n.* female parent (used of animals)

damage (ˈdæmɪdʒ) *n.* **1.** injury, harm, loss —*pl.* **2.** sum claimed or adjudged in compensation for injury —*vt.* **3.** harm

damask (ˈdæməsk) *n.* **1.** figured woven material of silk or linen, *esp.* white table linen with design shown up by light **2.** colour of damask rose, velvety red —**damascene** (ˈdæməsiːn) *vt.* decorate (steel *etc.*) with inlaid gold or silver —**damask rose** fragrant rose used to make the perfume attar

dame (deɪm) *n.* **1.** *obs.* lady **2.** (**D-**) title of lady in Order of the British Empire **3.** *sl. chiefly* US woman

damn (dæm) *vt.* **1.** condemn to hell **2.** be the ruin of **3.** give hostile reception to —*vi.* **4.** curse (**damned, 'damning**) —*interj.* **5.** expression of annoyance, impatience *etc.*

—**damnable** ('dæmnəb'l) a. 1. deserving damnation 2. hateful, annoying —**dam'nation** n. —**damnatory** ('dæmnətəri) a.

damp (dæmp) a. 1. moist 2. slightly moist —n. 3. diffused moisture 4. in coal mines, dangerous gas —vt. 5. make damp 6. (oft. with down) deaden, discourage —'**dampen** v. 1. make, become damp —vt. 2. stifle, deaden —'**damper** n. 1. anything that discourages or depresses 2. plate in flue to control draught —'**dampcourse** n. layer of impervious material in wall, to stop moisture rising (also **damp-proof course**)

damsel ('dæmz'l) n. obs. girl

damson ('dæmzən) n. 1. small dark purple plum 2. tree bearing it 3. its colour

dan (dæn) n. Judo 1. any one of 12 black-belt grades of proficiency 2. competitor entitled to dan grading

Dan. Bible Daniel

dance (dɑːns) vi. 1. move with measured rhythmic steps, usu. to music 2. be in lively movement 3. bob up and down —vt. 4. perform (dance) 5. cause to dance —n. 6. lively, rhythmical movement 7. arrangement of such movements 8. tune for them 9. social gathering for the purpose of dancing —'**dancer** n.

D and C dilation and curettage (of womb)

dandelion ('dændɪlaɪən) n. yellow-flowered wild plant

dander ('dændə) n. inf. temper, fighting spirit

dandle ('dænd'l) vt. 1. move (young child) up and down (on knee or in arms) 2. pet; fondle

dandruff ('dændrəf) or **dandriff** ('dændrɪf) n. dead skin in small scales among the hair

dandy ('dændɪ) n. 1. man excessively concerned with smartness of dress —a. 2. inf. excellent —'**dandify** vt. dress like or cause to resemble a dandy —'**dandyism** n.

Dane (deɪn) n. 1. native of Denmark 2. Viking who invaded England from late 8th to 11th cent. A.D. —'**Danish** a. 1. of Denmark —n. 2. official language of Denmark 3. people of Denmark collectively

danger ('deɪndʒə) n. 1. liability or exposure to harm 2. risk, peril —'**dangerous** a. —'**dangerously** adv. —**danger money** extra money paid to compensate for risks involved in certain dangerous jobs

dangle ('dæŋg'l) vi. 1. hang loosely and swaying —vt. 2. hold suspended 3. tempt with

dank (dæŋk) a. unpleasantly damp and chilly —'**dankness** n.

danseuse (dãˈsɜːz) n. female dancer

daphne ('dæfnɪ) n. ornamental shrub with bell-shaped flowers

dapper ('dæpə) a. neat and precise, esp. in dress, spruce

dapple ('dæp'l) v. mark or become marked with spots —'**dappled** a. spotted

2. mottled 3. variegated —**dapple-grey** a. (of horse) grey marked with darker spots

Darby and Joan ('dɑːbɪ, dʒəʊn) elderly married couple living in domestic harmony —**Darby and Joan Club** club for elderly people

dare (dɛə) v. 1. venture, have courage (to) —vt. 2. challenge —n. 3. challenge —'**daring** a. 1. bold —n. 2. adventurous courage —'**daredevil** a./n. reckless (person)

dark (dɑːk) a. 1. without light 2. gloomy 3. deep in tint 4. secret 5. unenlightened 6. wicked —n. 7. absence of light, colour or knowledge —'**darken** v. —'**darkly** adv. —'**darkness** n. —**Dark Ages** Hist. period from about late 5th cent. A.D. to about 1000 A.D. —**Dark Continent** Africa when relatively unexplored —**dark horse** somebody, esp. competitor in race, about whom little is known —'**darkroom** n. darkened room for processing film

darling ('dɑːlɪŋ) a./n. much loved or very lovable (person)

darn¹ (dɑːn) vt. 1. mend by filling (hole) with interwoven yarn —n. 2. place so mended —'**darning** n.

darn² (dɑːn) interj. mild expletive

darnel ('dɑːn'l) n. grass that grows as weed in grain fields

dart (dɑːt) n. 1. small light pointed missile 2. darting motion 3. small seam or intake in garment —pl. 4. indoor game played with numbered target and miniature darts —vt. 5. cast, throw rapidly (glance etc.) —vi. 6. go rapidly or abruptly —'**dartboard** n. circular piece of wood etc. used as target in darts

Darwinian (dɑːˈwɪnɪən) a. pert. to Charles Darwin or his theory of evolution

dash (dæʃ) vt. 1. smash, throw, thrust, send with violence 2. cast down 3. tinge, flavour, mix —vi. 4. move, go with great speed or violence —n. 5. rush 6. vigour 7. smartness 8. small quantity, tinge 9. stroke (-) between words —'**dasher** n. C ledge along top of boards at ice-hockey rink —'**dashing** a. spirited, showy —'**dashboard** n. in car etc., instrument panel in front of driver

dassie ('dæsɪ) n. SA hyrax

dastard ('dæstəd) n. obs. contemptible, sneaking coward —'**dastardly** a.

dasyure ('dæsɪjʊə) n. 1. small carnivorous marsupial of Aust., New Guinea and adjacent islands 2. ursine dasyure (see TASMANIAN DEVIL)

data ('deɪtə, 'dɑːtə) pl.n. (oft. with sing. v.) 1. series of observations, measurements or facts 2. information —**data bank** or **base** store of information, esp. in form that can be handled by computer —**data processing** sequence of operations performed on data, esp. by computer, to extract information etc.

date¹ (deɪt) n. 1. day of the month 2. statement on document of its time of writing 3. time of occurrence 4. period of work of art *etc*. **5.** engagement, appointment —*vt*. **6.** mark with date **7.** refer to date of **8.** reveal age of **9.** *inf*. accompany on social outing —*vi*. **10.** exist (from) **11.** betray time or period of origin, become old-fashioned —'**dateless** *a*. **1.** without date **2.** immemorial —**date line** (*oft*. D- L-) line (approx. 180° meridian) E of which is one day earlier than W of it —'**dateline** *n*. *Journalism* date and location of story, placed at top of article —**date stamp 1.** adjustable rubber stamp for recording date **2.** inked impression made by this

date² (deɪt) *n*. **1.** sweet, single-stone fruit of palm **2.** the palm

dative ('deɪtɪv) *n*. noun case indicating indirect object *etc*.

datum ('deɪtəm, 'dɑːtəm) *n*. thing given, known, or assumed as basis for reckoning, reasoning *etc*. (*pl*. '**data**)

daub (dɔːb) *vt*. **1.** coat, plaster, paint coarsely or roughly —*n*. **2.** rough picture **3.** smear —'**dauber** *n*.

daughter ('dɔːtə) *n*. one's female child —'**daughterly** *a*. —**daughter-in-law** *n*. son's wife

daunt (dɔːnt) *vt*. frighten, *esp*. into giving up purpose —'**dauntless** *a*. intrepid, fearless

dauphin ('dɔːfɪn; *Fr*. do'fɛ̃) *n*. formerly, eldest son of French king

davenport ('dævənpɔːt) *n*. **1.** small writing table with drawers **2. US** large couch or settee

davit ('dævɪt, 'deɪ-) *n*. crane, usu. one of pair, at ship's side for lowering and hoisting boats

Davy Jones's locker ('deɪvɪ 'dʒəʊnzɪz) sea, considered as sailors' grave

Davy lamp miner's safety lamp

daw (dɔː) *n*. *obs*. jackdaw

dawdle ('dɔːdˀl) *vi*. idle, waste time, loiter —'**dawdler** *n*.

dawn (dɔːn) *n*. **1.** first light, daybreak **2.** first gleam or beginning of anything —*vi*. **3.** begin to grow light **4.** appear, begin **5.** (begin to) be understood —'**dawning** *n*. —**dawn chorus** singing of birds at dawn

day (deɪ) *n*. **1.** period of 24 hours **2.** time when sun is above horizon **3.** point or unit of time **4.** daylight **5.** part of day occupied by certain activity, time period **6.** special or designated day —**day bed** couch intended for use as seat and as bed —'**daybook** *n*. *Book-keeping* book in which day's sales *etc*. are entered for later transfer to ledger —'**dayboy** *n*. **UK** boy who attends boarding school daily, but returns home each evening ('**daygirl** *fem*.) —'**daybreak** *n*. dawn —**day centre** place providing meals *etc*. where the elderly, handicapped *etc*. may spend the day —'**daydream** *n*. **1.** idle fancy —*vi*. **2.** indulge in idle fantasy —'**daylight** *n*. **1.** natural light **2.** dawn —*pl*. **3.** consciousness, wits —**daylight robbery** *inf*. blatant overcharging —**daylight saving** in summer, time set one hour ahead of local

standard time, giving extra daylight in evenings —**day release UK** system of releasing employees for part-time education —**day room** communal living room in residential institution —'**dayspring** *n*. dawn —'**daystar** *n*. morning star —'**daytime** *n*. time between sunrise and sunset —**day-to-day** *a*. routine; everyday

Dayak ('daɪæk) *n*. *see* DYAK

daze (deɪz) *vt*. **1.** stupefy, stun, bewilder —*n*. **2.** stupefied or bewildered state —**dazed** *a*.

dazzle ('dæzˀl) *vt*. **1.** blind, confuse or overpower with brightness, light, brilliant display or prospects —*n*. **2.** brightness that dazzles the vision —'**dazzlement** *n*.

dB *or* **db** decibel(s)

D.B.E. Dame Commander of the British Empire

DBS Direct Broadcasting by Satellite

DC direct current

D.C. District of Columbia

D.C.B. Dame Commander of the Order of the Bath

D.C.M. Distinguished Conduct Medal

DD Doctor of Divinity

D-day *n*. day selected for start of something, *esp*. Allied invasion of Europe in 1944

DDT dichlorodiphenyltrichloroethane, hydrocarbon compound used as an insecticide

DE Delaware

de- (*comb. form*) removal of, from, reversal of, as in *delouse, desegregate*. Such words are not given here where the meaning may be inferred from the simple word

deacon ('diːkən) *n*. **1.** one in lowest degree of holy orders **2.** one who superintends secular affairs of presbyterian church ('**deaconess** *fem*.)

deactivate (diː'æktɪveɪt) *vt*. **1.** make (bomb *etc*.) harmless or inoperative **2.** make less radioactive

dead (dɛd) *a*. **1.** no longer alive **2.** obsolete **3.** numb, without sensation **4.** no longer functioning, extinguished **5.** lacking lustre, movement or vigour **6.** sure, complete —*n*. **7.** dead person or persons (*oft*. in *pl*., **the dead**) —*adv*. **8.** utterly —'**deaden** *vt*. —'**deadly** *a*. **1.** fatal **2.** deathlike —*adv*. **3.** as if dead —**dead-and-alive** *a*. dull —'**deadbeat** *a./n. inf*. lazy, useless (person) —**dead duck** *sl*. person or thing doomed to death, failure *etc*., *esp*. because of mistake —**dead end 1.** cul-de-sac **2.** situation in which further progress is impossible —'**deadhead** *n*. **US, C** log sticking out of water as hindrance to navigation —**dead heat** race in which competitors finish exactly even —**dead letter 1.** law no longer observed **2.** letter which post office cannot deliver —'**deadline** *n*. limit of time allowed —'**deadlock** *n*. standstill —**dead loss 1.** complete loss for which no compensation is paid **2.** *inf*. useless person or thing —**deadly night-**

shade plant with poisonous black berries —**dead man's handle** or **pedal** safety switch on piece of machinery that allows operation only while depressed by operator —**dead march** solemn funeral music to accompany procession —**'deadpan** a. expressionless —**dead reckoning** calculation of ship's position from log and compass, when observations cannot be taken —**dead set** adv. 1. absolutely —n. 2. resolute attack —**dead weight** 1. heavy weight or load 2. oppressive burden 3. difference between loaded and unloaded weights of ship 4. intrinsic invariable weight of structure —**'deadwood** n. 1. dead trees or branches 2. inf. useless person; encumbrance —**dead of night** time of greatest stillness and darkness

deaf (dɛf) a. 1. wholly or partly without hearing 2. unwilling to listen —**'deafen** vt. make deaf —**'deafness** n. —**deaf aid** hearing aid —**deaf-and-dumb** a. 1. unable to hear or speak 2. for use of deaf-mutes —**deaf-mute** n. 1. person unable to hear or speak —a. 2. unable to hear or speak

deal¹ (diːl) vt. 1. distribute, give out 2. inflict —vi. 3. act 4. treat 5. do business (with, in) (dealt pt./pp.) —n. 6. agreement 7. treatment 8. share 9. business transaction —**'dealer** n. 1. one who deals (esp. cards) 2. trader —**'dealings** pl.n. transactions or relations with others —**deal with** handle, act towards

deal² (diːl) n. (plank of) fir or pine wood

dealt (dɛlt) pt./pp. of DEAL¹

dean¹ (diːn) n. 1. university or college official 2. head of cathedral chapter —**'deanery** n. cathedral dean's house or appointment

dean² (diːn) n. see DENE

dear (dɪə) a. 1. beloved 2. precious 3. costly, expensive —n. 4. beloved one —adv. 5. at a high price —**'dearly** adv. —**'dearness** n.

dearth (dɜːθ) n. scarcity

death (dɛθ) n. 1. dying 2. end of life 3. end, extinction 4. annihilation 5. (**D-**) personification of death, as skeleton —**'deathless** a. immortal —**'deathly** a./adv. like death —**'deathbed** n. bed in which person is about to die —**'deathblow** n. thing or event that destroys life or hope, esp. suddenly —**death certificate** legal document issued by doctor, certifying death of person and stating cause if known —**death duty** tax on property left at death —**death mask** cast of person's face taken after death —**death penalty** capital punishment —**death rate** ratio of deaths in specified area etc. to population of that area etc. (also **mortality rate**) —**death's-head** n. human skull or representation of one —**'deathtrap** n. building etc. considered unsafe —**death warrant** official authorization for carrying out sentence of death —**deathwatch beetle** beetle that bores into wood —**sign one's (own) death warrant** cause one's own destruction

debacle (deɪˈbɑːkʲl, dɪ-) n. utter collapse, rout, disaster

debar (dɪˈbɑː) vt. 1. shut out 2. stop 3. prohibit 4. preclude (**-rr-**)

debark (dɪˈbɑːk) v. disembark

debase (dɪˈbeɪs) vt. 1. lower in value, quality or character 2. adulterate —**de'basement** n.

debate (dɪˈbeɪt) v. 1. argue, discuss, esp. in a formal assembly 2. consider (something) —n. 3. discussion 4. controversy —**de'batable** a. —**de'bater** n.

debauch (dɪˈbɔːtʃ) vt. 1. lead into a life of depraved self-indulgence —n. 2. bout of sensual indulgence —**debau'chee** n. dissipated person —**de'bauchery** n.

debenture (dɪˈbɛntʃə) n. bond of company or corporation —**debenture stock** shares issued by company, which guarantee fixed return at regular intervals

debility (dɪˈbɪlɪtɪ) n. 1. feebleness, esp. of health 2. languor —**de'bilitate** vt. weaken, enervate

debit ('dɛbɪt) Accounting n. 1. entry in account of sum owed 2. side of book in which such sums are entered —vt. 3. charge, enter as due

debonair or **debonnaire** (dɛbəˈnɛə) a. 1. suave 2. genial 3. affable

debouch (dɪˈbaʊtʃ) vi. move out from narrow place to wider one —**de'bouchment** n.

debrief (diːˈbriːf) v. (of soldier etc.) report to superior on result of mission

debris or **débris** ('deɪbrɪ, 'dɛbrɪ) n. fragments, rubbish

debt (dɛt) n. 1. what is owed 2. state of owing —**'debtor** n. —**debt of honour** debt that is morally but not legally binding

debug (diːˈbʌɡ) vt. inf. 1. remove concealed microphones from (room etc.) 2. remove defects in (device etc.) 3. remove insects from (**-gg-**)

debunk (diːˈbʌŋk) vt. expose falseness, pretentiousness of, esp. by ridicule

debut ('deɪbjuː, 'dɛbjuː) n. first appearance in public —**debutante** ('dɛbjʊtɑːnt, -tænt) n. girl making official debut into society

Dec. December

deca-, deka- or before vowel **dec-, dek-** (comb. form) ten, as in decalitre

decade ('dɛkeɪd, dɪˈkeɪd) n. 1. period of ten years 2. set of ten

decadent ('dɛkədənt) a. 1. declining, deteriorating 2. morally corrupt —**'decadence** or **'decadency** n.

decaffeinated (dɪˈkæfɪneɪtɪd) a. (of coffee) with caffeine removed

decagon ('dɛkəɡɒn) n. figure of 10 angles —**de'cagonal** a.

decagram or **decagramme** ('dɛkəɡræm) n. measure of weight equal to 10 grams

decahedron (dɛkəˈhiːdrən) n. solid of 10 faces —**deca'hedral** a.

decalcify (diːˈkælsɪfaɪ) vt. deprive of lime, as bones or teeth of their calcareous matter (**-fied, -fying**)

decalitre or *U.S.* **decaliter** ('dɛkəli:tə) *n.* 10 litres

Decalogue ('dɛkəlɒg) *n.* the Ten Commandments

decametre or *U.S.* **decameter** ('dɛkəmi:tə) *n.* 10 metres

decamp (dɪ'kæmp) *vi.* 1. make off 2. break camp 3. abscond

decanal (dɪ'keɪn³l) *a.* of dean, deanery

decant (dɪ'kænt) *vt.* pour off (liquid, as wine) without disturbing sediment —**de'canter** *n.* stoppered bottle for wine or spirits

decapitate (dɪ'kæpɪteɪt) *vt.* behead —**de capi'tation** *n.* —**de'capitator** *n.*

decapod ('dɛkəpɒd) *n.* 1. crustacean having five pairs of walking limbs, as crab *etc.* 2. cephalopod mollusc having eight short tentacles and two longer ones, as squid *etc.*

decarbonize or **-ise** (di:'kɑːbənaɪz) *vt.* remove deposit of carbon, as from motor cylinder —**decarboni'zation** or **-i'sation** *n.*

decasyllable ('dɛkəsɪləb³l) *n.* ten-syllabled line —**decasyl'labic** *a.*

decathlon (dɪ'kæθlɒn) *n.* athletic contest with ten events

decay (dɪ'keɪ) *v.* 1. rot, decompose 2. (cause to) fall off, decline —*n.* 3. rotting 4. a falling away, break up

decease (dɪ'siːs) *n.* 1. death —*vi.* 2. die —**de'ceased** *n./a.*

deceive (dɪ'siːv) *vt.* 1. mislead 2. delude 3. cheat —**de'ceit** *n.* 1. fraud 2. duplicity —**de'ceitful** *a.* —**de'ceiver** *n.*

decelerate (di:'sɛləreɪt) *vi.* slow down

December (dɪ'sɛmbə) *n.* twelfth and last month of year

decennial (dɪ'sɛnɪəl) *a.* of period of ten years —**de'cennially** *adv.*

decent ('diːs³nt) *a.* 1. respectable 2. fitting, seemly 3. not obscene 4. adequate 5. *inf.* kind —**'decency** *n.* —**'decently** *adv.*

decentralize or **-ise** (di:'sɛntrəlaɪz) *vt.* divide (government, organization) among local centres

deception (dɪ'sɛpʃən) *n.* 1. deceiving 2. illusion 3. fraud 4. trick —**de'ceptive** *a.* 1. misleading 2. apt to mislead

deci- (*comb. form*) one tenth, as in *decimetre*

decibel ('dɛsɪbɛl) *n.* unit for measuring intensity of a sound

decide (dɪ'saɪd) *vt.* 1. settle, determine, bring to resolution 2. give judgment on —*vi.* 3. come to a decision, conclusion —**de'cided** *a.* 1. unmistakable 2. settled 3. resolute —**de'cidedly** *adv.* certainly, undoubtedly —**decision** (dɪ'sɪʒən) *n.* —**de'cisive** *a.* —**de'cisively** *adv.*

deciduous (dɪ'sɪdjʊəs) *a.* 1. (of trees) losing leaves annually 2. (of antlers, teeth *etc.*) being shed at the end of a period of growth

decigram ('dɛsɪgræm) *n.* tenth of gram

decilitre or *U.S.* **deciliter** ('dɛsɪliːtə) *n.* tenth of litre

decimal ('dɛsɪməl) *a.* 1. relating to tenths 2. proceeding by tens —*n.* 3. decimal fraction —**decimali'zation** or **-i'sation** *n.* —**'decimalize** or **-ise** *vt.* convert into decimal fractions or system —**decimal system** system of weights and measures or coinage, in which value of each denomination is ten times the one below it

decimate ('dɛsɪmeɪt) *vt.* kill a tenth or large proportion of —**deci'mation** *n.* —**'decimator** *n.*

decimetre or *U.S.* **decimeter** ('dɛsɪmiːtə) *n.* tenth of metre

decipher (dɪ'saɪfə) *vt.* 1. make out meaning of 2. decode —**de'cipherable** *a.*

deck (dɛk) *n.* 1. platform or floor, *esp.* one covering whole or part of ship's hull 2. turntable of record-player 3. part of tape recorder supporting tapes —*vt.* 4. array, decorate —**deck chair** folding chair made of canvas suspended in wooden frame —**deck hand** 1. seaman assigned duties on deck of ship 2. *UK* seaman who has seen sea duty for at least one year 3. helper aboard yacht

deckle edge ('dɛk³l) 1. rough edge of paper oft. left as ornamentation 2. imitation of this

declaim (dɪ'kleɪm) *vi.* 1. speak dramatically, rhetorically or passionately 2. protest loudly —**declamation** (dɛklə'meɪʃən) *n.* —**declamatory** (dɪ'klæmətərɪ) *a.*

declare (dɪ'klɛə) *vt.* 1. announce formally 2. state emphatically 3. show 4. name (as liable to customs duty) —*vi.* 5. take sides (for) 6. *Cricket* bring innings to an end before last wicket has fallen —**declaration** (dɛklə'reɪʃən) *n.* —**declarative** (dɪ'klærətɪv) or **declaratory** (dɪ'klærətərɪ) *a.* —**de'clarer** *n.* *Bridge* person who names trumps or calls 'No trumps'

declassify (di:'klæsɪfaɪ) *vt.* release (document *etc.*) from security list (**-fying, -fied**) —**declassifi'cation** *n.*

decline (dɪ'klaɪn) *v.* 1. refuse 2. list case endings of (nouns) —*vi.* 3. slope, bend or sink downwards 4. deteriorate gradually 5. grow smaller, diminish —*n.* 6. gradual deterioration 7. movement downwards 8. diminution 9. downward slope —**declension** (dɪ'klɛnʃən) *n.* 1. group of nouns 2. falling off 3. declining —**de'clinable** *a.* —**decli'nation** (dɛklɪ'neɪʃən) *n.* 1. sloping away, deviation 2. angle

declivity (dɪ'klɪvɪtɪ) *n.* downward slope

declutch (dɪ'klʌtʃ) *vi.* disengage clutch of car *etc.*

decoction (dɪ'kɒkʃən) *n.* 1. extraction of essence by boiling down 2. such essence —**de'coct** *vt.* boil down

decode (di:'kəʊd) *vt.* convert from code into intelligible language

decoke (di:'kəʊk) *vt. see* DECARBONIZE

décolleté (deɪ'kɒlteɪ) *a.* (of women's garment) having a low-cut neckline —**décolletage** (deɪkɒl'tɑːʒ) *n.* low-cut dress or neckline

decommission (di:kə'mɪʃən) *vt.* dismantle

(industrial plant or nuclear reactor) to an extent such that it can be safely abandoned

decompose (di:kəm'pəuz) v. 1. separate into elements 2. rot —**decompo'sition** n. decay

decompress (di:kəm'prɛs) vt. 1. free from pressure 2. return to condition of normal atmospheric pressure —**decom'pression** n. —**decompression sickness** or **illness** disorder characterized by severe pain etc., caused by sudden change in atmospheric pressure

decongestant (di:kən'dʒɛstənt) a./n. (drug) relieving (esp. nasal) congestion

decontaminate (di:kən'tæmɪneɪt) vt. free from contamination, eg from poisons, radioactive substances etc. —**decontami'nation** n.

decontrol (di:kən'trəul) vt. release from state control (-ll-)

décor or **decor** ('deɪkɔ:) n. 1. decorative scheme of room etc. 2. stage decoration, scenery

decorate ('dɛkəreɪt) vt. 1. beautify by additions 2. paint or wallpaper room etc. 3. invest (with an order, medal etc.) —**deco'ration** n. —**decorative** a. —**decorator** n. —**Decorated style** 14th-century style of English architecture characterized by geometrical tracery etc.

decorum (dɪ'kɔ:rəm) n. seemly behaviour, propriety, decency —**'decorous** a. —**'decorously** adv.

decoy ('di:kɔɪ, dɪ'kɔɪ) n. 1. something used to entrap others or to distract their attention 2. bait, lure —v. (dɪ'kɔɪ) 3. lure, be lured as with decoy

decrease (dɪ'kri:s) v. 1. diminish, lessen —n. ('di:kri:s, dɪ'kri:s) 2. lessening

decree (dɪ'kri:) n. 1. order having the force of law 2. edict —vt. 3. determine judicially 4. order —**decree absolute** final decree in divorce proceedings, which leaves parties free to remarry —**decree nisi** decree coming into effect within a certain time, unless cause is shown for rescinding it (esp. in divorce cases)

decrement ('dɛkrɪmənt) n. 1. act or state of decreasing 2. quantity lost by decrease

decrepit (dɪ'krɛpɪt) a. 1. old and feeble 2. broken down, worn out —**de'crepitude** n.

decrescendo (di:krɪ'ʃɛndəu) a. diminuendo

decretal (dɪ'kri:t'l) n. 1. R.C.Ch. papal decree; edict on doctrine or church law —a. 2. of decree

decry (dɪ'kraɪ) vt. disparage (**de'cried**, **de'crying**)

dedicate ('dɛdɪkeɪt) vt. 1. commit wholly to special purpose or cause 2. inscribe or address (book etc.) 3. devote to God's service —**'dedicated** a. 1. devoted to particular purpose or cause 2. Comp. designed to fulfil one function 3. manufactured for specific purpose —**dedi'cation** n. —**'dedicator** n. —**'dedicatory** a.

deduce (dɪ'dju:s) vt. draw as conclusion

from facts —**de'duct** vt. take away, subtract —**de'ductible** a. 1. capable of being deducted 2. US tax-deductible —**de'duction** n. 1. deducting 2. amount subtracted 3. conclusion deduced 4. inference from general to particular —**de'ductive** a. —**de'ductively** adv.

deed (di:d) n. 1. action 2. exploit 3. legal document —**deed box** strong box in which deeds and other documents are kept —**deed poll** Law deed made by one party only, esp. one by which person changes his name

deejay ('di:dʒeɪ) inf. disc jockey

deem (di:m) vt. judge, consider, regard —**'deemster** n. title of either of two justices in Isle of Man (also **'dempster**)

deep (di:p) a. 1. extending far down, in or back 2. at, of given depth 3. profound 4. heartfelt 5. hard to fathom 6. cunning 7. engrossed, immersed 8. (of colour) dark and rich 9. (of sound) low and full —n. 10. deep place 11. the sea —adv. 12. far down etc. —**'deepen** v. —**'deeply** adv. —**deep field** Cricket position behind bowler, near boundary —**deep'freeze** n. refrigerator storing frozen food —**deep-laid** a. (of plot or plan) carefully worked out and kept secret —**deep-rooted** or **deep-seated** a. (of ideas etc.) firmly fixed or held; ingrained

deer (dɪə) n. family of ruminant animals typically with antlers in male (pl. **deer**, **-s**) —**'deerhound** n. large rough-coated dog —**'deerskin** n. hide of deer —**'deerstalker** n. 1. one who stalks deer 2. kind of cloth hat with peaks

def (dɛf) a. sl. (esp. of hip-hop) very good

deface (dɪ'feɪs) vt. 1. spoil or mar surface of 2. disfigure —**de'facement** n.

de facto (deɪ 'fæktəu) Lat. existing in fact, whether legally recognized or not

defalcate ('di:fælkeɪt) vi. Law misuse or misappropriate property or funds entrusted to one

defame (dɪ'feɪm) vt. speak ill of, dishonour by slander or rumour —**defamation** (dɛfə'meɪʃən) n. —**defamatory** (dɪ'fæmətərɪ) a.

default (dɪ'fɔ:lt) n. 1. failure to act, appear or pay —vi. 2. fail (to pay) —**de'faulter** n. esp. soldier guilty of military offence —**in default of** in the absence of

defeat (dɪ'fi:t) vt. 1. overcome, vanquish 2. thwart —n. 3. overthrow 4. lost battle or encounter 5. frustration —**de'featism** n. attitude tending to accept defeat —**de'featist** n./a.

defecate ('dɛfɪkeɪt) vi. 1. empty the bowels —vt. 2. clear of impurities —**defe'cation** n.

defect (dɪ'fɛkt, 'di:fɛkt) n. 1. lack 2. blemish, failing —vi. (dɪ'fɛkt) 3. desert one's country, cause etc., esp. to join opponents —**de'fection** n. abandonment of duty or allegiance —**de'fective** a. 1. incomplete 2. faulty

defend (dɪ'fɛnd) vt. 1. protect 2. support by argument, evidence 3. (try to) maintain (title etc.) against challenger —**de'fence** or U.S. **de'fense** n. —**de'fendant** n. person

accused in court —de'**fender** n. —**defen-**
si'bility n. —de'**fensible** a. —de'**fensive**
a. **1.** serving for defence —n. **2.** position or
attitude of defence

defer[1] (dɪ'fɜː) vt. put off, postpone (-**rr**-)
—de'**ferment** n.

defer[2] (dɪ'fɜː) vi. submit to opinion or
judgment of another (-**rr**-) —**deference**
('dɛfərəns) n. respect for another inclining one to accept his views etc.
—**deferential** (dɛfə'rɛnʃəl) a. —**deferen-**
tially (dɛfə'rɛnʃəlɪ) adv.

defiance (dɪ'faɪəns) n. see DEFY

deficient (dɪ'fɪʃənt) a. lacking or falling
short in something, insufficient —de'**fi-**
ciency n. —**deficit** ('dɛfɪsɪt, dɪ'fɪsɪt) n.
amount by which sum of money is too
small —**deficiency disease** any condition,
such as pellagra, produced by lack of
vitamins etc.

defile[1] (dɪ'faɪl) vt. **1.** make dirty, pollute,
soil **2.** sully **3.** desecrate —de'**filement** n.

defile[2] ('diːfaɪl, dɪ'faɪl) n. **1.** narrow pass or
valley —vi. **2.** march in file

define (dɪ'faɪn) vt. **1.** state contents or
meaning of **2.** show clearly the form or
outline of **3.** lay down clearly, fix **4.** mark
out —de'**finable** a. —**definite** ('dɛfɪnɪt) a.
1. exact, defined **2.** clear, specific **3.**
certain, sure —**definitely** ('dɛfɪnɪtlɪ) adv.
—**definition** (dɛfɪ'nɪʃən) n. —**definitive**
(dɪ'fɪnɪtɪv) a. conclusive, to be looked on as
final —**definitively** (dɪ'fɪnɪtɪvlɪ) adv.

deflate (diː'fleɪt) v. **1.** (cause to) collapse
by release of gas **2.** Econ. cause deflation
of (an economy etc.) —vt. **3.** take away
self-esteem from —de'**flation** n. **1.** deflat-
ing **2.** Econ. reduction of economic and
industrial activity —de'**flationary** a.

deflect (dɪ'flɛkt) v. (cause to) turn from
straight course —de'**flection** or
de'**flexion** n.

deflower (diː'flaʊə) vt. deprive of virginity, innocence etc. —**defloration** (diːflɔː-
'reɪʃən) n.

defoliate (diː'fəʊlɪeɪt) v. (cause to) lose
leaves, esp. by action of chemicals
—de'**foliant** n. —**defoli'ation** n.

deforest (diː'fɒrɪst) vt. clear of trees
—**deforest'ation** n.

deform (dɪ'fɔːm) vt. **1.** spoil shape of **2.**
make ugly **3.** disfigure —**defor'mation** n.
—de'**formed** a. —de'**formity** n.

defraud (dɪ'frɔːd) vt. cheat, swindle

defray (dɪ'freɪ) vt. provide money for
(expenses etc.)

defrock (diː'frɒk) vt. deprive (priest,
minister) of ecclesiastical status

defrost (diː'frɒst) v. **1.** make, become free
of frost, ice **2.** thaw

deft (dɛft) a. skilful, adroit —'**deftly** adv.
—'**deftness** n.

defunct (dɪ'fʌŋkt) a. **1.** dead **2.** obsolete

defuse or U.S. (sometimes) **defuze** (diː-
'fjuːz) vt. **1.** remove fuse of (bomb etc.) **2.**
remove tension from (situation etc.)

defy (dɪ'faɪ) vt. **1.** challenge, resist
successfully **2.** disregard (de'**fied**, de'**fy-**

ing) —de'**fiance** n. resistance —de'**fiant**
a. **1.** openly and aggressively hostile **2.**
insolent —de'**fiantly** adv.

degauss (diː'gaʊs) vt. equip (ship) with
apparatus which prevents it detonating
magnetic mines

degenerate (dɪ'dʒɛnəreɪt) vi. **1.** deteriorate to lower mental, moral or physical
level —a. (dɪ'dʒɛnərɪt) **2.** fallen away in
quality —n.. (dɪ'dʒɛnərɪt) **3.** degenerate
person —de'**generacy** n. —**degene'ration**
n. —de'**generative** a.

degrade (dɪ'greɪd) vt. **1.** dishonour **2.**
debase **3.** reduce to lower rank —vi. **4.**
decompose chemically —de'**gradable** a.
capable of chemical, biological decomposition —**degradation** (dɛgrə'deɪʃən) n.
—de'**graded** a. shamed, humiliated

degree (dɪ'griː) n. **1.** step, stage in process,
scale, relative rank, order, condition,
manner, way **2.** university rank **3.** unit of
measurement of temperature or angle
—**third degree** severe, lengthy examination, esp. of accused person by police, to
extract information, confession

dehiscent (dɪ'hɪsənt) a. opening, as capsule
of plant —de'**hisce** vi. burst open
—de'**hiscence** n.

dehumanize or -**ise** (diː'hjuːmənaɪz) vt. **1.**
deprive of human qualities **2.** render
mechanical, artificial or routine

dehumidify (diːhjuː'mɪdɪfaɪ) vt. extract
moisture from

dehydrate (diː'haɪdreɪt) vt. remove moisture from —**dehy'dration** n.

de-ice (diː'aɪs) vt. dislodge ice from (eg
windscreen) or prevent its forming

deify ('diːɪfaɪ, 'deɪ-) vt. make god of, treat,
worship as god ('**deified,** '**deifying**)
—**deifi'cation** n. —'**deiform** a. godlike in
form

deign (deɪn) vi. **1.** condescend, stoop **2.**
think fit

deism ('diːɪzəm, 'deɪ-) n. belief in god but
not in revelation —'**deist** n. —de'**istic** a.
—'**deity** n. **1.** divine status or attributes **2.**
a god

déjà vu ('deɪʒæ 'vuː) Fr. experience of
perceiving new situation as if it had
occurred before

deject (dɪ'dʒɛkt) vt. dishearten, cast down,
depress —de'**jected** a. —de'**jection** n.

de jure (deɪ 'dʒʊəreɪ) Lat. in law, by right

dekko ('dɛkəʊ) n. sl. look

delay (dɪ'leɪ) vt. postpone, hold back
—vi. **2.** be tardy, linger (de'**layed,**
de'**laying**) —n. **3.** act or instance of
delaying **4.** interval of time between
events

delectable (dɪ'lɛktəbʔl) a. delightful —de-
lec'**tation** n. pleasure

delegate ('dɛlɪgeɪt, -gɪt) n. **1.** person
chosen to represent another —vt.
('dɛlɪgeɪt) **2.** send as deputy **3.** commit
(authority, business etc.) to a deputy
—'**delegacy** n. —dele'**gation** n.

delete (dɪ'liːt) vt. remove, cancel, erase
—de'**letion** n.

deleterious (dɛlɪˈtɪərɪəs) a. harmful, injurious

Delft (dɛlft) n. 1. town in Netherlands 2. tin-glazed earthenware orig. from Delft, usu. with blue decoration on white ground (also **'delftware**)

deliberate (dɪˈlɪbərɪt) a. 1. intentional 2. well-considered 3. without haste, slow —vt. (dɪˈlɪbəreɪt) 4. consider, debate —de'liberately adv. —delibe'ration n. —de'liberative a.

delicate ('dɛlɪkɪt) a. 1. exquisite 2. not robust, fragile 3. sensitive 4. requiring tact 5. deft —'delicacy n. —'delicately adv.

delicatessen (dɛlɪkəˈtɛsᵊn) n. shop selling esp. imported or unusual foods

delicious (dɪˈlɪʃəs) a. delightful, pleasing to senses, esp. taste —de'liciously adv.

delight (dɪˈlaɪt) vt. 1. please greatly —vi. 2. take great pleasure (in) —n. 3. great pleasure —de'lightful a. charming

delimitation (diːlɪmɪˈteɪʃən) n. assigning of boundaries —de'limit vt.

delineate (dɪˈlɪnɪeɪt) vt. portray by drawing or description —deline'ation n. —de'lineator n.

delinquent (dɪˈlɪŋkwənt) n. someone, esp. young person, guilty of delinquency —de'linquency n. (minor) offence or misdeed

deliquesce (dɛlɪˈkwɛs) vi. become liquid —deli'quescence n. —deli'quescent a.

delirium (dɪˈlɪrɪəm) n. 1. disorder of the mind, esp. in feverish illness 2. violent excitement (pl. -s, -liria (-'lɪrɪə)) —de'lirious a. 1. raving 2. light-headed, wildly excited —delirium tremens ('trɛmɛnz, 'triː-) disordered mental state produced by advanced alcoholism (also **D.T.'s**)

deliver (dɪˈlɪvə) vt. 1. carry (goods etc.) to destination 2. hand over 3. release 4. give birth (to) or assist in birth (of) 5. utter or present (speech etc.) —de'liverance n. rescue —de'liverer n. —de'livery n.

dell (dɛl) n. wooded hollow

Delphic ('dɛlfɪk) or **Delphian** a. pert. to Delphi or to the oracle of Apollo

delphinium (dɛlˈfɪnɪəm) n. garden plant with tall spikes of usu. blue flowers (pl. -s, -ia (-ɪə))

delta ('dɛltə) n. 1. alluvial tract where river at mouth breaks into several streams 2. fourth letter in Gr. alphabet (Δ or δ) 3. shape of this letter —delta wing triangular swept-back aircraft wing

delude (dɪˈluːd) vt. 1. deceive 2. mislead —de'lusion n. —de'lusive a.

deluge ('dɛljuːdʒ) n. 1. flood, great flow 2. rush 3. downpour, cloudburst —vt. 4. flood 5. overwhelm

de luxe (də ˈlʌks, ˈlʊks) 1. rich, sumptuous 2. superior in quality

delve (dɛlv) v. 1. (with into) search intensively 2. dig

demagnetize or **-ise** (diːˈmægnətaɪz) vt. deprive of magnetic polarity

demagogue or U.S. (sometimes) **demagog** ('dɛməgɒg) n. mob leader or agitator —demagogic (dɛməˈgɒgɪk) a. —demagogy ('dɛməgɒgɪ) n.

deman (diːˈmæn) vt. UK reduce the manpower of (plant, industry etc.)

demand (dɪˈmɑːnd) vt. 1. ask as giving an order 2. ask as by right 3. call for as due, right or necessary —n. 4. urgent request, claim, requirement 5. call (for specific commodity) —de'manding a. requiring great skill, patience etc.

demarcate ('diːmɑːkeɪt) vt. mark boundaries or limits of —demar'cation or demar'kation n.

demean (dɪˈmiːn) vt. degrade, lower, humiliate

demeanour or U.S. **demeanor** (dɪˈmiːnə) n. 1. conduct, behaviour 2. bearing

demented (dɪˈmɛntɪd) a. 1. mad, crazy 2. beside oneself —dementia (dɪˈmɛnʃə, -ʃɪə) n. form of insanity

demerara (dɛməˈrɛərə, -ˈrɑːrə) n. kind of brown cane sugar

demerge (dɪˈmɜːdʒ) v. 1. split (business concern) into two or more independent companies —vi. 2. (of companies) be so split 3. undo previous merger —de'merger n.

demerit (diːˈmɛrɪt) n. 1. bad point 2. undesirable quality

demesne (dɪˈmeɪn, -ˈmiːn) n. 1. estate, territory 2. sphere of action —hold in demesne have unrestricted possession of

demi- (comb. form) half, as in demigod. Such words are not given here where the meaning may be inferred from the simple word

demijohn ('dɛmɪdʒɒn) n. large wicker-cased bottle

demilitarize or **-ise** (diːˈmɪlɪtəraɪz) vt. prohibit military presence or function in (an area) —demilitari'zation or -i'sation n.

demimonde (dɛmɪˈmɒnd) n. class of women of doubtful reputation

demise (dɪˈmaɪz) n. 1. death 2. conveyance by will or lease 3. transfer of sovereignty on death or abdication —vt. 4. convey to another by will 5. lease

demisemiquaver ('dɛmɪsɛmɪkweɪvə) n. Mus. note having time value of one thirty-second of semibreve

demist (diːˈmɪst) v. free or become free of condensation —de'mister n.

demiurge ('dɛmɪɜːdʒ) n. name given in some philosophies (esp. Platonic) to the creator of the world and man

demo ('dɛməʊ) inf. demonstration

demob (diːˈmɒb) vt. inf. demobilize (-bb-)

demobilize or **-ise** (diːˈməʊbɪlaɪz) vt. 1. disband (troops) 2. discharge (soldier) —demobili'zation or -i'sation n.

democracy (dɪˈmɒkrəsɪ) n. 1. government by the people or their elected representatives 2. state so governed —'democrat n. advocate of democracy —demo'cratic a. 1. connected with democracy 2. favouring popular rights —demo'cratically adv.

—**democrati'zation** or **-i'sation** n. —**de-'mocratize** or **-ise** vt.

demodulation (diːmɒdjuˈleɪʃən) n. Electron. process by which output wave or signal is obtained having characteristics of original modulating wave or signal

demography (dɪˈmɒgrəfɪ) n. study of population statistics, as births, deaths, diseases —**de'mographer** n. —**demo-'graphic** a.

demolish (dɪˈmɒlɪʃ) vt. 1. knock down (buildings etc.) 2. destroy utterly 3. overthrow —**demo'lition** n.

demon (ˈdiːmən) n. 1. devil, evil spirit 2. very cruel or malignant person 3. person very good at or devoted to a given activity —**demoniac** (dɪˈməʊnɪæk) n. one possessed with a devil —**demo'niacal** a. —**de'monic** a. of the nature of a devil —**demo'nology** n. study of demons

demonetize or **-ise** (diːˈmʌnɪtaɪz) vt. 1. deprive (metal) of its capacity as monetary standard 2. withdraw from use as currency —**demoneti'zation** or **-i'sation** n.

demonstrate (ˈdɛmənstreɪt) vt. 1. show by reasoning, prove 2. describe, explain by specimens or experiments —vi. 3. make exhibition of support, protest etc. by public parade, rally 4. make show of armed force —**de'monstrable** a. —**de'monstrably** adv. —**demon'stration** n. 1. making clear, proving by evidence 2. exhibition and description 3. organized expression of public opinion 4. display of armed force —**de'monstrative** a. 1. expressing feelings, emotions easily and unreservedly 2. pointing out 3. conclusive —**'demonstrator** n. 1. one who demonstrates equipment, products etc. 2. one who takes part in a public demonstration 3. professor's assistant in laboratory etc.

demoralize or **-ise** (dɪˈmɒrəlaɪz) vt. 1. deprive of courage and discipline 2. undermine morally —**demorali'zation** or **-i'sation** n.

demote (dɪˈməʊt) vt. reduce in status or rank —**de'motion** n.

demotic (dɪˈmɒtɪk) a. 1. of common people; popular 2. of simplified form of hieroglyphics used in ancient Egypt —n. 3. demotic script of ancient Egypt

demur (dɪˈmɜː) vi. 1. make difficulties, object (-rr-) —n. 2. raising of objection 3. objection raised —**de'murrer** n. Law exception taken to opponent's point

demure (dɪˈmjʊə) a. reserved, quiet —**de'murely** adv.

demurrage (dɪˈmʌrɪdʒ) n. charge for keeping ship etc. beyond time agreed for unloading

demystify (diːˈmɪstɪfaɪ) vt. remove mystery from; make clear —**demystifi'cation** n.

den (dɛn) n. 1. cave or hole of wild beast 2. lair 3. small room, esp. study 4. site, haunt

denarius (dɪˈnɛərɪəs) n. 1. ancient Roman silver coin, oft. called penny in translation 2. gold coin worth 25 silver denarii (pl. -narii (-ˈnɛərɪaɪ))

denary (ˈdiːnərɪ) a. 1. calculated by tens; decimal 2. containing ten parts; tenfold

denationalize or **-ise** (diːˈnæʃənˀlaɪz) vt. return (an industry) from public to private ownership —**denationali'zation** or **-i'sation** n.

denature (diːˈneɪtʃə) or **denaturize, -ise** (diːˈneɪtʃəraɪz) vt. deprive of essential qualities, adulterate —**denatured alcohol** spirit made undrinkable

dendrology (dɛnˈdrɒlədʒɪ) n. natural history of trees

dene or **dean** (diːn) n. valley

dengue (ˈdɛŋgɪ) or **dandy** n. infectious tropical fever

denial (dɪˈnaɪəl) n. see DENY

denier (ˈdɛnɪə, ˈdɛnjə) n. unit of weight of silk, rayon and nylon yarn

denigrate (ˈdɛnɪgreɪt) vt. belittle or disparage character of

denim (ˈdɛnɪm) n. strong cotton drill for trousers, overalls etc.

denizen (ˈdɛnɪzən) n. inhabitant

denominate (dɪˈnɒmɪneɪt) vt. give name to —**denomi'nation** n. 1. distinctly named church or sect 2. name, esp. of class or group —**denomi'national** a. —**de'nominator** n. divisor in vulgar fraction

denote (dɪˈnəʊt) vt. 1. stand for, be the name of 2. mark, indicate, show —**deno-'tation** n.

denouement (deɪˈnuːmɒn) or **dénouement** (Fr. denuˈmã) n. 1. unravelling of dramatic plot 2. final solution of mystery

denounce (dɪˈnaʊns) vt. 1. speak violently against 2. accuse 3. terminate (treaty) —**denunci'ation** n. denouncing —**denunciatory** (dɪˈnʌnsɪətərɪ) a.

dense (dɛns) a. 1. thick, compact 2. stupid —**'densely** adv. —**'density** n. mass per unit of volume

dent (dɛnt) n. 1. hollow or mark left by blow or pressure —vt. 2. make dent in 3. mark with dent

dental (ˈdɛntˀl) a. 1. of, pert. to teeth or dentistry 2. pronounced by applying tongue to teeth —**'dentate** a. toothed —**dentifrice** (ˈdɛntɪfrɪs) n. powder, paste or wash for cleaning teeth —**'dentist** n. surgeon who attends to teeth —**'dentistry** n. art of dentist —**den'tition** n. 1. teething 2. arrangement of teeth —**'denture** n. (usu. pl.) set of false teeth —**dental floss** soft thread for cleaning between teeth —**dental surgeon** dentist

dentine (ˈdɛntiːn) or **dentin** (ˈdɛntɪn) n. the hard bonelike part of a tooth

denude (dɪˈnjuːd) vt. 1. strip, make bare 2. expose (rock) by erosion of plants, soil etc. —**denudation** (dɛnjuˈdeɪʃən) n.

denumerable (dɪˈnjuːmərəbˀl) a. Maths. capable of being counted by correspondence with positive integers; countable

denunciation (dɪnʌnsɪˈeɪʃən) n. see DENOUNCE

deny (dɪˈnaɪ) vt. 1. declare untrue 2.

contradict **3.** reject, disown **4.** refuse to give **5.** refuse **6.** (*refl.*) abstain from (**de'nied, de'nying**) —**de'niable** *a.* —**de'nial** *n.*

deodar ('diːəʊdɑː) *n.* **1.** Himalayan cedar with drooping branches **2.** fragrant wood of this tree

deodorize *or* **-ise** (diːˈəʊdəraɪz) *vt.* rid of smell or mask smell of —**de'odorant** *n.* —**deodori'zation** *or* **-i'sation** *n.* —**de'odorizer** *or* **-iser** *n.*

deontology (diːɒnˈtɒlədʒɪ) *n.* science of ethics and moral obligations —**deon'tologist** *n.*

Deo volente ('deɪəʊ vɒˈlɛntɪ) *Lat.* God willing

deoxidize *or* **-ise** (diːˈɒksɪdaɪz) *vt.* deprive of oxygen —**deoxidi'zation** *or* **-i'sation** *n.*

dep. **1.** depart(s) **2.** departure **3.** deposed **4.** deposit **5.** deputy

depart (dɪˈpɑːt) *vi.* **1.** go away **2.** start out, set forth **3.** deviate, vary **4.** die —**de'parture** *n.*

department (dɪˈpɑːtmənt) *n.* **1.** division **2.** branch **3.** province —**depart'mental** *a.* —**depart'mentally** *adv.* —**department store** large shop selling all kinds of goods

depend (dɪˈpɛnd) *vi.* **1.** (*usu. with* on) rely entirely **2.** be contingent, await settlement or decision —**de'pendable** *a.* reliable —**de'pendant** *n.* one for whose maintenance another is responsible —**de'pendence** *n.* —**de'pendency** *n.* subject territory —**de'pendent** *a.* depending

depict (dɪˈpɪkt) *vt.* **1.** give picture of **2.** describe in words —**de'piction** *n.* —**de'pictor** *n.*

depilatory (dɪˈpɪlətərɪ, -trɪ) *n.* **1.** substance that removes hair —*a.* **2.** serving to remove hair

deplete (dɪˈpliːt) *vt.* **1.** empty **2.** reduce **3.** exhaust —**de'pletion** *n.*

deplore (dɪˈplɔː) *vt.* **1.** lament, regret **2.** deprecate, complain of —**de'plorable** *a.* **1.** lamentable **2.** disgraceful

deploy (dɪˈplɔɪ) *v.* **1.** (of troops, ships) (cause to) adopt battle formation —*vt.* ·**2.** arrange —**de'ployment** *n.*

depolarize *or* **-ise** (diːˈpəʊləraɪz) *vt.* deprive of polarity —**depolari'zation** *or* **-i'sation** *n.*

deponent (dɪˈpəʊnənt) *a.* **1.** (of verb) having passive form but active meaning —*n.* **2.** deponent verb **3.** one who makes statement on oath **4.** deposition

depopulate (dɪˈpɒpjʊleɪt) *v.* (cause to) be reduced in population —**depopu'lation** *n.*

deport (dɪˈpɔːt) *vt.* expel from a country, banish —**depor'tation** *n.*

deportment (dɪˈpɔːtmənt) *n.* behaviour, conduct, bearing —**de'port** *vt.* behave, carry (oneself)

depose (dɪˈpəʊz) *vt.* **1.** remove from office, *esp.* of sovereign —*vi.* **2.** make statement on oath, give evidence —**de'posable** *a.* —**de'posal** *n.* **1.** removal from office **2.** statement made on oath

deposit (dɪˈpɒzɪt) *vt.* **1.** set down, *esp.*

carefully **2.** give into safekeeping, *esp.* in bank **3.** let fall (as sediment) —*n.* **4.** thing deposited **5.** money given in part payment or as security **6.** sediment —**de'positary** *n.* person with whom thing is deposited —**deposition** (dɛpəˈzɪʃən) *n.* **1.** statement written and attested **2.** act of deposing or depositing —**de'positor** *n.* —**de'pository** *n.* place for safekeeping —**deposit account** UK bank account that earns interest and usu. requires notice of withdrawal

depot ('dɛpəʊ) *n.* **1.** storehouse **2.** building for storage and servicing of buses, railway engines *etc.* **3.** US railway station

deprave (dɪˈpreɪv) *vt.* make bad, corrupt, pervert —**depravity** (dɪˈprævɪtɪ) *n.* wickedness, viciousness

deprecate ('dɛprɪkeɪt) *vt.* **1.** express disapproval of **2.** advise against —**depre'cation** *n.* —**depre'catory** *a.*

depreciate (dɪˈpriːʃɪeɪt) *vt.* **1.** lower price, value or purchasing power of **2.** belittle —*vi.* **3.** fall in value —**depreci'ation** *n.* —**de'preciator** *n.* —**de'preciatory** *a.*

depredation (dɛprɪˈdeɪʃən) *n.* plundering, pillage —**'depredate** *vt.* plunder, despoil —**'depredator** *n.*

depress (dɪˈprɛs) *vt.* **1.** affect with low spirits **2.** lower in level or activity —**de'pressant** *n.* —**de'pressed** *a.* **1.** low in spirits; downcast **2.** lower than surrounding surface **3.** pressed down; flattened **4.** characterized by economic hardship (*also* **dis'tressed**) **5.** lowered in force *etc.* **6.** *Bot., zool.* flattened —**de'pression** *n.* **1.** hollow **2.** low spirits, dejection, despondency **3.** low state of trade, slump —**de'pressive** *a.*

deprive (dɪˈpraɪv) *vt.* strip, dispossess —**deprivation** (dɛprɪˈveɪʃən) *n.* —**de'prived** *a.* lacking adequate food, care, amenities *etc.*

dept. department

depth (dɛpθ) *n.* **1.** (degree of) deepness **2.** deep place, abyss **3.** intensity (of colour, feeling) **4.** profundity (of mind) —**depth charge** *or* **bomb** bomb for use against submarines

depute (dɪˈpjuːt) *vt.* **1.** allot **2.** appoint as agent or substitute —*a./n.* ('dɛpjʊt) **3.** in Scotland, assistant —**depu'tation** *n.* persons sent to speak for others —**'deputize** *or* **-ise** *vi.* **1.** act for another —*vt.* **2.** depute —**'deputy** *n.* **1.** assistant **2.** substitute, delegate

derail (dɪˈreɪl) *v.* (cause to) go off the rails, as train *etc.* —**de'railment** *n.*

derailleur (dəˈreɪljə) *a./n.* (of) gearchange mechanism for bicycles

derange (dɪˈreɪndʒ) *vt.* **1.** put out of place, out of order **2.** upset **3.** make insane —**de'rangement** *n.*

derby ('dɜːbɪ) *n.* US bowler hat

Derby ('dɑːbɪ, *U.S.* 'dɜːbɪ) *n.* **1.** horserace, *esp.* famous one at Epsom, England **2.** contest between local teams

deregulate (dɪˈrɛgjʊleɪt) *v.* **1.** cancel

regulations (concerning an activity or process) —vt. 2. exempt (an activity) from regulations —**deregu'lation** n.

derelict ('dɛrɪlɪkt) a. 1. abandoned, forsaken 2. falling into ruins, dilapidated —n. 3. social outcast, vagrant 4. abandoned property, ship etc. —**dere'liction** n. 1. neglect (of duty) 2. abandoning

derestrict (di:rɪ'strɪkt) vt. render or leave free from restriction, esp. road from speed limits

deride (dɪ'raɪd) vt. speak of or treat with contempt, ridicule —**derision** (dɪ'rɪʒən) n. ridicule —**de'risive** a. —**de'risory** a. mocking, ridiculing

de rigueur (də ri'gœːr) Fr. required by etiquette or fashion

derive (dɪ'raɪv) vt. 1. deduce, get (from) 2. show origin of —vi. 3. issue, be descended (from) —**derivation** (dɛrɪ'veɪʃən) n. —**derivative** (dɪ'rɪvətɪv) a./n.

derma ('dɜːmə) or **dermis** ('dɜːmɪs) n. the fine skin, below the epidermis, containing blood vessels

dermatitis (dɜːmə'taɪtɪs) n. inflammation of skin

dermato-, derma- or before vowel **dermat-, derm-** (comb. form) skin, as in *dermatitis*

dermatology (dɜːmə'tɒlədʒɪ) n. science of skin —**derma'tologist** n. physician specializing in skin diseases

derogate ('dɛrəgeɪt) vi. 1. (with from) cause to seem inferior; detract 2. (with from) deviate in standard or quality —vt. 3. cause to seem inferior etc.; disparage —**dero'gation** n.

derogatory (dɪ'rɒgətərɪ) a. disparaging, belittling, intentionally offensive

derrick ('dɛrɪk) n. 1. hoisting machine 2. framework over oil well etc.

derring-do ('dɛrɪŋ'duː) n. (act of) spirited bravery, boldness

derringer or **deringer** ('dɛrɪndʒə) n. small pistol with large bore

derv (dɜːv) n. diesel oil for road vehicles (*d*iesel *e*ngine *r*oad *v*ehicle)

dervish ('dɜːvɪʃ) n. member of Muslim ascetic order, noted for frenzied, whirling dance

desalination (diːsælɪ'neɪʃən) or **desalinization, -isation** n. process of removing salt, esp. from sea water

descant ('dɛskænt) n. 1. Mus. decorative variation sung as accompaniment to basic melody —vi. (with on or upon) 2. talk in detail (about) 3. dwell (on) at length

descend (dɪ'sɛnd) vi. 1. come or go down 2. slope down 3. stoop, condescend 4. spring (from ancestor etc.) 5. pass to heir, be transmitted 6. swoop on, attack —vt. 7. go or come down —**des'cendant** n. person descended from an ancestor —**des'cendent** a. 1. descending —n. 2. descendant —**des'cent** n.

describe (dɪ'skraɪb) vt. 1. give detailed account of 2. pronounce, label 3. trace out (geometrical figure etc.) —**description**

(dɪ'skrɪpʃən) n. 1. detailed account 2. marking out 3. kind, sort, species —**descriptive** (dɪ'skrɪptɪv) a.

descry (dɪ'skraɪ) vt. make out, catch sight of, esp. at a distance, espy (**de'scried, de'scrying**)

desecrate ('dɛsɪkreɪt) vt. 1. violate sanctity of 2. profane 3. convert to evil use —**dese'cration** n.

desert¹ ('dɛzət) n. 1. uninhabited and barren region —a. 2. barren, uninhabited, desolate —**desert boots** ankle-high boots with soft soles

desert² (dɪ'zɜːt) vt. 1. abandon, forsake, leave —vi. 2. (esp. of soldiers etc.) run away from service —**de'serter** n. —**de'sertion** n.

desert³ (dɪ'zɜːt) n. 1. (usu. pl.) what is due as reward or punishment 2. merit, virtue

deserve (dɪ'zɜːv) vt. 1. show oneself worthy of 2. have by conduct a claim to —**de'served** a. rightfully earned; justified; warranted —**deservedly** (dɪ'zɜːvɪdlɪ) adv. —**deservedness** (dɪ'zɜːvɪdnɪs) n. —**de'serving** a. worthy (of reward etc.)

deshabille (deɪzæ'biːl) n. see DISHABILLE

desiccate ('dɛsɪkeɪt) vt. 1. dry 2. dry up —**desic'cation** n.

desideratum (dɪzɪdə'rɑːtəm) n. something lacked and wanted (pl. **-ta** (-tə))

design (dɪ'zaɪn) vt. 1. make working drawings for 2. sketch 3. plan out 4. intend, select for —n. 5. outline sketch 6. working plan 7. art of making decorative patterns etc. 8. project, purpose, mental plan —**designedly** (dɪ'zaɪnɪdlɪ) adv. on purpose —**de'signer** n. 1. esp. one who draws designs for manufacturers —a. 2. designed by and having label of well-known fashion designer —**de'signing** a. crafty, scheming

designate ('dɛzɪgneɪt) vt. 1. name 2. pick out 3. appoint to office —a. ('dɛzɪgnɪt, -neɪt) 4. appointed but not yet installed —**desig'nation** n. name, appellation

desire (dɪ'zaɪə) vt. 1. wish, long for 2. ask for, entreat —n. 3. longing, craving 4. expressed wish, request 5. sexual appetite 6. something wished for or requested —**desira'bility** n. —**de'sirable** a. worth desiring —**de'sirous** a. filled with desire

desist (dɪ'zɪst) vi. cease, stop

desk (dɛsk) n. 1. table or other piece of furniture designed for reading or writing at 2. counter 3. editorial section of newspaper etc. covering specific subject —**desk-top** a. of computer system, small enough to use at desk, that can produce print-quality documents

desolate ('dɛsəlɪt) a. 1. uninhabited 2. neglected, barren, ruinous 3. solitary 4. dreary, dismal, forlorn —vt. ('dɛsəleɪt) 5. depopulate, lay waste 6. overwhelm with grief —**deso'lation** n.

despair (dɪ'spɛə) vi. 1. (oft. with of) lose hope —n. 2. loss of all hope 3. cause of this 4. despondency

despatch (dɪ'spætʃ) see DISPATCH

desperate ('dɛspərɪt, -prɪt) a. 1. reckless

from despair **2.** difficult; dangerous **3.** frantic **4.** hopelessly bad **5.** leaving no room for hope **—desperado** (despə-'rɑːdəu) *n.* reckless, lawless person (*pl.* **-es, -s**) **—'desperately** *adv.* **—despe'ration** *n.*

despise (dɪ'spaɪz) *vt.* look down on as contemptible, inferior **—despicable** ('despɪkəbʰl, dɪ'spɪk-) *a.* base, contemptible, vile **—despicably** (dɪ'spɪkəblɪ) *adv.*

despite (dɪ'spaɪt) *prep.* in spite of

despoil (dɪ'spɔɪl) *vt.* plunder, rob, strip **—despoliation** (dɪspəʊlɪ'eɪʃən) *n.*

despondent (dɪ'spɒndənt) *a.* dejected, depressed **—de'spond** *vi.* **—de'spondency** *n.* **—de'spondently** *adv.*

despot ('despɒt) *n.* tyrant, oppressor **—des'potic** *a.* **—des'potically** *adv.* **—'despotism** *n.* autocratic government, tyranny

despumate (dɪ'spjuːmeɪt, 'despjumeɪt) *vi.* **1.** throw off impurities **2.** form scum

desquamate ('deskwəmeɪt) *vi.* (of skin) come off in scales **—desqua'mation** *n.*

dessert (dɪ'zɜːt) *n.* sweet course, or fruit, served at end of meal **—des'sertspoon** *n.* spoon intermediate in size between tablespoon and teaspoon

destination (dɛstɪ'neɪʃən) *n.* **1.** place a person or thing is bound for **2.** goal **3.** purpose

destine ('dɛstɪn) *vt.* **1.** ordain or fix beforehand **2.** set apart, devote

destiny ('dɛstɪnɪ) *n.* **1.** course of events; person's fate **2.** the power which foreordains

destitute ('dɛstɪtjuːt) *a.* **1.** in absolute want **2.** in great need, devoid (of) **3.** penniless **—desti'tution** *n.*

destroy (dɪ'strɔɪ) *vt.* **1.** ruin **2.** pull to pieces **3.** undo **4.** put an end to **5.** demolish **6.** annihilate **—de'stroyer** *n.* **1.** one who destroys **2.** small, swift, heavily armed warship **—de'struct** *vt.* destroy (one's own missile *etc.*) for safety **—de'structible** *a.* **—de'struction** *n.* **1.** ruin, overthrow **2.** death **—de'structive** *a.* **1.** destroying **2.** negative, not constructive **—de'structively** *adv.* **—de'structor** *n.* that which destroys, *esp.* incinerator

desuetude (dɪ'sjuːɪtjuːd, 'dɛswɪtjuːd) *n.* disuse, discontinuance

desultory ('dɛsəltərɪ, -trɪ) *a.* **1.** passing, changing fitfully from one thing to another **2.** aimless **3.** unmethodical

detach (dɪ'tætʃ) *vt.* unfasten, disconnect, separate **—de'tachable** *a.* **—de'tached** *a.* **1.** standing apart, isolated **2.** impersonal, disinterested **—de'tachment** *n.* **1.** aloofness **2.** detaching **3.** a body of troops detached for special duty

detail ('diːteɪl) *n.* **1.** particular **2.** small or unimportant part **3.** treatment of anything item by item **4.** party or man assigned for duty in army **—***vt.* **5.** relate in full **6.** appoint for duty

detain (dɪ'teɪn) *vt.* **1.** keep under restraint **2.** hinder **3.** keep waiting **—de'tention** *n.* **1.** confinement **2.** arrest **3.** detaining

detect (dɪ'tɛkt). *vt.* find out or discover existence, presence, nature or identity of **—de'tection** *n.* **—de'tective** *n.* **1.** policeman or private agent employed in detecting crime **—***a.* **2.** employed in detection **—de'tector** *n. esp.* mechanical sensing device or device for detecting radio signals

détente (deɪ'tɑːnt; *Fr.* de'tãt) *n.* lessening of tension in political or international affairs

detention (dɪ'tɛnʃən) *n. see* DETAIN

deter (dɪ'tɜː) *vt.* **1.** discourage, frighten **2.** hinder, prevent **(-rr-)** **—de'terrent** *a./n.*

detergent (dɪ'tɜːdʒənt) *n.* **1.** cleansing, purifying substance **—***a.* **2.** having cleansing power **—de'terge** *vt.*

deteriorate (dɪ'tɪərɪəreɪt) *v.* become or make worse **—deterio'ration** *n.*

determine (dɪ'tɜːmɪn) *vt.* **1.** make up one's mind on, decide **2.** fix as known **3.** bring to a decision **4.** be deciding factor in **5.** *Law* end **—***vi.* **6.** come to an end **7.** come to decision **—de'terminable** *a.* **—de'terminant** *a./n.* **—de'terminate** *a.* fixed in scope or nature **—determi'nation** *n.* **1.** determining **2.** firm or resolute conduct or purpose **3.** resolve **—de'termined** *a.* resolute **—de'terminism** *n.* theory that human action is settled by factors independent of will **—de'terminist** *n./a.*

detest (dɪ'tɛst) *vt.* hate, loathe **—de'testable** *a.* **—de'testably** *adv.* **—detes'tation** *n.*

dethrone (dɪ'θrəun) *vt.* remove from throne, depose **—de'thronement** *n.*

detonate ('dɛtəneɪt) *vt.* **1.** cause (bomb, mine *etc.*) to explode **—***vi.* **2.** (of bomb, mine *etc.*) explode **—deto'nation** *n.* **—'detonator** *n.* mechanical, electrical device, or small amount of explosive, used to set off main explosive charge

detour ('diːtuə) *n.* **1.** course which leaves main route to rejoin it later **2.** roundabout way **—***vi.* **3.** make detour

detoxify (diː'tɒksɪfaɪ) *vt.* remove poison from **(-fying, -fied)** **—detoxifi'cation** *n.*

detract (dɪ'trækt) *v.* take away (a part) from, diminish **—de'traction** *n.* **—de'tractive** *a.* **—de'tractor** *n.*

detriment ('dɛtrɪmənt) *n.* harm done, loss, damage **—detri'mental** *a.* damaging, injurious **—detri'mentally** *adv.*

detritus (dɪ'traɪtəs) *n.* worn-down matter, such as gravel or rock debris **—de'trital** *a.* **—detrition** (dɪ'trɪʃən) *n.* wearing away from solid bodies by friction

de trop (də 'tro) *Fr.* not wanted, superfluous

detrude (dɪ'truːd) *vt.* thrust down **—de'trusion** *n.*

detumescence (diːtjuː'mɛsəns) *n.* subsidence of swelling

deuce (djuːs) *n.* **1.** two **2.** card with two spots **3.** *Tennis* forty all **4.** in exclamatory phrases, the devil **—deuced** ('djuːsɪd, djuːst) *a. inf.* excessive

Deut. Deuteronomy

deuterium (djuː'tɪərɪəm) *n.* form of hydrogen twice as heavy as normal gas —'**deuteron** *n.* nucleus of this gas

Deutsche Mark ('dɔɪtʃə) *or* **Deutschmark** *n.* monetary unit of W Germany

deutzia ('djuːtsɪə, 'dɔɪtsɪə) *n.* shrub with white or pink flower clusters

devalue (diː'væljuː) *or* **devaluate** (diː'væljueɪt) *v.* 1. (of currency) reduce or be reduced in value —*vt.* 2. reduce the value or worth of —**devalu'ation** *n.*

devastate ('dɛvəsteɪt) *vt.* 1. lay waste 2. ravage 3. *inf.* overwhelm —**devas'tation** *n.*

develop (dɪ'vɛləp) *vt.* 1. bring to maturity 2. elaborate 3. bring forth, bring out 4. evolve 5. treat (photographic plate or film) to bring out image 6. improve value or change use of (land) by building *etc.* —*vi.* 7. grow to maturer state (**de'veloped, de'veloping**) —**de'veloper** *n.* 1. one who develops land 2. chemical for developing film —**de'velopment** *n.* —**developing country** poor country seeking to develop its resources by industrialization —**development area** UK depressed area which is given government assistance to establish new industry

deviate ('diːvɪeɪt) *vi.* leave the way, turn aside, diverge —'**deviant** *n./a.* (person) deviating from normal, *esp.* in sexual practices —**devi'ation** *n.* —'**deviator** *n.* —'**devious** *a.* 1. deceitful, underhand 2. roundabout, rambling 3. erring

device (dɪ'vaɪs) *n.* 1. contrivance, invention 2. apparatus 3. stratagem 4. scheme, plot 5. heraldic or emblematic figure or design

devil ('dɛvˀl) *n.* 1. personified spirit of evil 2. superhuman evil being 3. person of great wickedness, cruelty *etc.* 4. *inf.* fellow 5. *inf.* something difficult or annoying 6. energy, dash, unconquerable spirit 7. *inf.* rogue, rascal 8. *English law* junior barrister working without payment to gain experience —*vi.* 9. do work that passes for employer's, as for lawyer or author —*vt.* 10. grill with hot condiments (**-ll-**) —'**devilish** *a.* 1. like, of the devil 2. evil —*adv.* 3. *inf.* very, extremely —'**deviliment** *n.* 1. wickedness 2. wild and reckless mischief, revelry, high spirits —'**devilry** *n.* —**devil-may-care** *a.* happy-go-lucky —**devil's advocate** 1. one who advocates opposing, unpopular view, *usu.* for sake of argument 2. *R.C.Ch.* one appointed to state disqualifications of person whom it is proposed to make a saint

devious ('diːvɪəs) *a. see* DEVIATE

devise (dɪ'vaɪz) *vt.* 1. plan, contrive 2. invent 3. plot 4. leave by will —**devi'see** *n.* —**de'visor** *n.*

devitrification (diːvɪtrɪfɪ'keɪʃən) *n.* loss of glassy or vitreous condition —**de'vitrify** *vt.* deprive of character or appearance of glass (**-fied, -fying**)

devoid (dɪ'vɔɪd) *a.* (*usu. with* of) empty, lacking, free (from)

devolve (dɪ'vɒlv) *vi.* 1. pass or fall (to, upon) —*vt.* 2. throw (duty *etc.*) on to another —**devo'lution** *n.* devolving, *esp.* transfer of authority from central to regional government

Devonian (də'vəʊnɪən) *a.* 1. of fourth period of Palaeozoic era, between Silurian and Carboniferous periods 2. of Devon —*n.* 3. Devonian period or rock system

devote (dɪ'vəʊt) *vt.* set apart, give up exclusively (to person, purpose *etc.*) —**de'voted** *a.* loving, attached —**devotee** (dɛvə'tiː) *n.* 1. ardent enthusiast 2. zealous worshipper —**de'votion** *n.* 1. deep affection, loyalty 2. dedication 3. religious earnestness —*pl.* 4. prayers, religious exercises —**de'votional** *a.*

devour (dɪ'vaʊə) *vt.* 1. eat greedily 2. consume, destroy 3. read, gaze at eagerly —**de'vourer** *n.*

devout (dɪ'vaʊt) *a.* 1. earnestly religious, pious 2. sincere, heartfelt —**de'voutly** *adv.*

dew (djuː) *n.* 1. moisture from air deposited as small drops on cool surface between nightfall and morning 2. any beaded moisture —*vt.* 3. wet with or as with dew —'**dewiness** *n.* —'**dewy** *a.* —'**dewclaw** *n.* partly developed inner toe of dogs —'**dewlap** *n.* fold of loose skin hanging from neck —**dew point** temperature at which dew begins to form —**dew pond** small natural pond —**dew-worm** *n.* C large earthworm used as bait —**dewy-eyed** *a.* naive, innocent

dewberry ('djuːbərɪ, -brɪ) *n.* bramble with blue-black fruits

Dewey Decimal System ('djuːɪ) system of library book classification with ten main subject classes (*also* **decimal classification**)

DEW line (djuː) distant early warning line, network of sensors situated in Arctic regions of N Amer.

dexterity (dɛk'stɛrɪtɪ) *n.* 1. manual skill 2. neatness 3. deftness 4. adroitness —'**dexter** *a. Her.* on the bearer's right-hand side of a shield —'**dexterous** *a.* showing dexterity, skilful

dextrin ('dɛkstrɪn) *or* **dextrine** ('dɛkstrɪn, -triːn) *n.* sticky substance obtained from starch, used as thickening agent in foods and as gum

dextrose ('dɛkstrəʊz, -trəʊs) *n.* white, soluble, sweet-tasting crystalline solid, occurring naturally in fruit, honey, animal tissue

D.F. Defender of the Faith

D.F.C. Distinguished Flying Cross

D.F.M. Distinguished Flying Medal

dg *or* **dg.** decigram

dharma ('dɑːmə) *n.* 1. *Hinduism* social custom regarded as religious and moral duty 2. *Hinduism* essential principle of cosmos; natural law; conduct that conforms with this 3. *Buddhism* ideal truth

dhow (daʊ) *n.* lateen-rigged Arab sailing vessel

DHSS Department of Health and Social Security

di-¹ (*comb. form*) **1.** twice; two; double, as in *dicotyledon* **2.** containing two specified atoms or groups of atoms, as in *carbon dioxide*

di-² (*comb. form*) see DIA-

dia- *or before vowel* **di-** (*comb. form*) through

diabetes (daɪə'biːtɪs, -tiːz) *n.* any of various disorders characterized by excretion of abnormal amount of urine, *esp.* diabetes mellitus, in which body fails to store and utilize glucose —**diabetic** (daɪə'bɛtɪk) *n./a.*

diabolic (daɪə'bɒlɪk) *a.* devilish —**dia'bolical** *a. inf.* very bad —**dia'bolically** *adv.* —**di'abolism** *n.* devil-worship

diabolo (dɪ'æbələʊ) *n.* game in which top is spun into air from string attached to two sticks

diaconal (daɪ'ækən°l) *a.* pert. to deacon —**di'aconate** *n.* **1.** office, rank of deacon **2.** body of deacons

diacritic (daɪə'krɪtɪk) *n.* **1.** sign above letter or character indicating special phonetic value *etc.* —*a.* **2.** diacritical —**dia'critical** *a.* **1.** of a diacritic **2.** showing a distinction (*also* **dia'critic**)

diadem ('daɪədɛm) *n.* a crown

diaeresis *or* (*esp. U.S.*) **dieresis** (daɪ'ɛrɪsɪs) *n.* mark (¨) placed over vowel to show that it is sounded separately from preceding one, as in Noël (*pl.* **-ses** (-siːz))

diagnosis (daɪəg'nəʊsɪs) *n.* identification of disease from symptoms (*pl.* **-ses** (-siːz)) —'**diagnose** *v.* —**diag'nostic** *a.*

diagonal (daɪ'ægən°l) *a.* **1.** from corner to corner **2.** oblique —*n.* **3.** line from corner to corner —**di'agonally** *adv.*

diagram ('daɪəgræm) *n.* drawing, figure in lines, to illustrate something being expounded —**diagram'matic** *a.* —**diagram'matically** *adv.*

dial ('daɪəl) *n.* **1.** face of clock *etc.* **2.** plate marked with graduations on which pointer moves (as on meter, weighing machine *etc.*) **3.** numbered disc on front of telephone **4.** *sl.* face —*vt.* **5.** operate (telephone) **6.** indicate on dial (**-ll-**) —**dialling tone** *or U.S.* **dial tone** continuous purring heard over telephone indicating that number can be dialled

dialect ('daɪəlɛkt) *n.* **1.** characteristic speech of district **2.** local variety of a language —**dia'lectal** *a.*

dialectic (daɪə'lɛktɪk) *n.* art of arguing —**dia'lectical** *a.* —**dia'lectically** *adv.* —**dialec'tician** *n.* **1.** logician **2.** reasoner

dialogue *or U.S.* (*oft.*) **dialog** ('daɪəlɒg) *n.* **1.** conversation between two or more (persons) **2.** representation of such conversation in drama, novel *etc.* **3.** discussion between representatives of two states, countries *etc.*

dialysis (daɪ'ælɪsɪs) *n. Med.* filtering of blood through membrane to remove waste products

diamagnetism (daɪə'mægnɪtɪzəm) *n.* phenomenon exhibited by substances that are repelled by both poles of magnet

diamanté (daɪə'mæntɪ) *n.* (fabric covered with) glittering particles —**dia'mantine** *a.* like diamond

diameter (daɪ'æmɪtə) *n.* **1.** (length of) straight line from side to side of figure or body (*esp.* circle) through centre **2.** thickness —**dia'metrical** *a.* opposite —**dia'metrically** *adv.*

diamond ('daɪəmənd) *n.* **1.** very hard and brilliant precious stone, also used in industry as an abrasive **2.** rhomboid figure **3.** suit at cards **4.** playing field in baseball —**diamond jubilee** *or* **wedding** 60th (sometimes 75th) anniversary

dianthus (daɪ'ænθʊs) *n.* genus of herbaceous flowers, *eg* pinks and carnations

diapason (daɪə'peɪz°n) *n.* **1.** fundamental organ stop **2.** compass of voice or instrument

diaper ('daɪəpə) *n.* **1.** US baby's napkin **2.** fabric with small diamond pattern **3.** pattern of that kind —'**diapered** *a.*

diaphanous (daɪ'æfənəs) *a.* transparent

diaphoretic (daɪəfə'rɛtɪk) *n.* **1.** diaphoretic drug —*a.* **2.** relating to or causing perspiration

diaphragm ('daɪəfræm) *n.* **1.** muscular partition dividing two cavities of body, midriff **2.** plate or disc wholly or partly closing tube or opening **3.** any thin dividing or covering membrane —**diaphragmatic** (daɪəfræg'mætɪk) *a.*

diapositive (daɪə'pɒzɪtɪv) *n.* positive transparency; slide

diarrhoea *or esp. U.S.* **diarrhea** (daɪə'rɪə) *n.* excessive looseness of the bowels —**diar'rhoeal** *or esp. U.S.* **diar'rheal** *a.*

diary ('daɪərɪ) *n.* **1.** daily record of events, engagements, thoughts *etc.* **2.** book for this —'**diarist** *n.* writer of diary

Diaspora (daɪ'æspərə) *n.* **1.** dispersion of Jews from Palestine after Babylonian captivity; Jewish communities that arose after this **2.** (*oft.* **d-**) dispersion, as of people orig. of one nation

diastase ('daɪəsteɪs, -steɪz) *n.* enzyme that converts starch into sugar

diastole (daɪ'æstəlɪ) *n.* dilation of chambers of heart

diathermy ('daɪəθɜːmɪ) *or* **diathermia** (daɪə'θɜːmɪə) *n.* heating of body tissues with electric current for medical or surgical purposes

diatom ('daɪətəm) *n.* one of order of microscopic algae —**dia'tomic** *a.* of two atoms

diatonic (daɪə'tɒnɪk) *a. Mus.* **1.** pert. to regular major and minor scales **2.** (of melody) composed in such a scale

diatribe ('daɪətraɪb) *n.* violently bitter verbal attack, invective, denunciation

dibble ('dɪb°l) *n.* **1.** small tool used to make holes in ground for bulbs *etc.* (*also* '**dibber**) —*v.* **2.** make hole in (ground) with dibble **3.** plant (seeds *etc.*) with dibble

dice (daɪs) *pl.n.* **1.** (*also* functions as *sing.*, *orig. sing.* die) cubes each with six sides marked one to six for games of chance —*vi.* 2. gamble with dice —*vt.* 3. cut into small cubes —**'dicer** *n.* —**'dicey** *a. inf.* dangerous, risky

dicephalous (daɪ'sɛfələs) *a.* two-headed

dichotomy (daɪ'kɒtəmɪ) *n.* division into two parts

dichroism ('daɪkrəʊɪzəm) *n.* property possessed by some crystals of exhibiting different colours when viewed from different directions —**di'chroic** *a.*

dichromatic (daɪkrəʊ'mætɪk) *a.* 1. having two colours (*also* **di'chroic**) 2. (of animal species) having two different colour varieties 3. able to perceive only two colours

dick (dɪk) *n. sl.* 1. fellow, person 2. detective

Dickensian (dɪ'kɛnzɪən) *a.* 1. of Charles Dickens or his novels 2. denoting poverty, distress and exploitation as depicted in Dickens's novels 3. grotesquely comic, as some Dickens characters

dicker ('dɪkə) *chiefly US v.* 1. trade (goods) by bargaining; barter —*n.* 2. petty bargain or barter

dicky[1] *or* **dickey** ('dɪkɪ) *n.* detachable false shirt front (*pl.* **'dickies, 'dickeys**) —**'dickybird** *n. inf.* child's word for small bird

dicky[2] *or* **dickey** ('dɪkɪ) *a. sl.* shaky, unsound

dicotyledon (daɪkɒtɪ'liːd²n) *n.* flowering plant having two embryonic seed leaves

Dictaphone ('dɪktəfəʊn) *n.* R tape recorder, used *esp.* for dictation

dictate (dɪk'teɪt) *v.* 1. say or read for another to transcribe —*vt.* 2. prescribe, lay down —*vi.* 3. seek to impose one's will on others —*n.* ('dɪkteɪt) 4. bidding —**dic'tation** *n.* —**dic'tator** *n.* absolute ruler —**dicta'torial** *a.* 1. despotic 2. overbearing —**dicta'torially** *adv.* —**dic'tatorship** *n.*

diction ('dɪkʃən) *n.* 1. choice and use of words 2. enunciation

dictionary ('dɪkʃənərɪ) *n.* 1. book setting forth, alphabetically, words of language with meanings *etc.* 2. reference book with items in alphabetical order

dictum ('dɪktəm) *n.* 1. pronouncement 2. saying, maxim (*pl.* **-s, -ta** (-tə))

did (dɪd) *pt. of* DO[1]

didactic (dɪ'dæktɪk) *a.* 1. designed to instruct 2. (of people) opinionated, dictatorial —**di'dacticism** *n.*

diddle ('dɪd²l) *vt. inf.* cheat

didgeridoo (dɪdʒərɪ'duː) *n. Mus.* native Aust. wind instrument

die[1] (daɪ) *vi.* 1. cease to live 2. come to an end 3. stop functioning 4. *inf.* be nearly overcome (with laughter *etc.*) (**died, 'dying**) —**'diehard** *n.* one who resists (reform *etc.*) to the end —**be dying for** be looking eagerly forward to

die[2] (daɪ) *n. see* DICE

die[3] (daɪ) *n.* 1. shaped block of hard

material to form metal in forge, press *etc.* 2. tool for cutting thread on pipe *etc.* —**die-cast** *vt.* shape or form (object) by introducing molten metal or plastic into reusable mould —**die-casting** *n.*

dieldrin ('diːldrɪn) *n.* highly toxic crystalline insecticide

dielectric (daɪɪ'lɛktrɪk) *n.* 1. substance through or across which electric induction takes place 2. nonconductor 3. insulator

dieresis (daɪ'ɛrɪsɪs) *n. see* DIAERESIS

diesel ('diːz²l) *a.* 1. pert. to internal-combustion engine using oil as fuel —*n.* 2. this engine 3. diesel oil or fuel —**diesel-electric** *n.* 1. locomotive fitted with diesel engine driving electric generator —*a.* 2. of such locomotive or system —**diesel oil** *or* **fuel** fuel, distilled from petroleum, used in diesel engines

diet[1] ('daɪət) *n.* 1. restricted or regulated course of feeding 2. kind of food lived on 3. food —*vi.* 4. follow a dietary regimen, as to lose weight —**'dietary** *a.* 1. relating to diet —*n.* 2. a regulated diet 3. system of dieting —**die'tetic** *a.* —**die'tetics** *pl.n.* (with sing. v.) science of diet —**die'titian** *or* **die'tician** *n.* one skilled in dietetics

diet[2] ('daɪət) *n.* 1. parliament of some countries 2. formal assembly

differ ('dɪfə) *vi.* 1. be unlike 2. disagree —**'difference** *n.* 1. unlikeness 2. degree or point of unlikeness 3. disagreement 4. remainder left after subtraction —**'different** *a.* unlike —**'differently** *adv.*

differentia (dɪfə'rɛnʃɪə) *n. Logic* feature by which subclasses of same class of named objects can be distinguished (*pl.* **-tiae** (-ʃiːiː))

differential (dɪfə'rɛnʃəl) *a.* 1. varying with circumstances 2. special 3. *Maths.* pert. to an infinitesimal change in variable quantity 4. *Phys. etc.* relating to difference between sets of motions acting in the same direction or between pressures *etc.* —*n.* 5. *Maths.* infinitesimal difference between two consecutive states of variable quantity 6. differential gear 7. difference between rates of pay for different types of labour —**differ'entially** *adv.* —**differ'entiate** *vt.* 1. serve to distinguish between, make different —*vi.* 2. discriminate —**differenti'ation** *n.* —**differential calculus** method of calculating relative rate of change for continuously varying quantities —**differential gear** epicyclic gear mounted in driving axle of vehicle, that permits one driving wheel to rotate faster than the other, as when cornering

difficult ('dɪfɪk²lt) *a.* 1. requiring effort, skill *etc.* to do or understand, not easy 2. obscure —**'difficulty** *n.* 1. being difficult 2. difficult task, problem 3. embarrassment 4. hindrance 5. obscurity 6. trouble

diffident ('dɪfɪdənt) *a.* lacking confidence, timid, shy —**'diffidence** *n.* shyness —**'diffidently** *adv.*

diffract (dɪ'frækt) *vi.* break up, *esp.* of

rays of light, sound-waves —**dif'fraction** n. deflection of ray of light, electromagnetic wave caused by obstacle

diffuse (dɪ'fjuːz) vt. 1. spread abroad —a. (dɪ'fjuːs) 2. widely spread 3. loose, verbose, wordy —**diffusely** (dɪ'fjuːslɪ) adv. 1. loosely 2. wordily —**dif'fusible** a. —**dif'fusion** n. —**diffusive** (dɪ'fjuːsɪv) a. —**diffusively** (dɪ'fjuːsɪvlɪ) adv.

dig (dɪg) vi. 1. work with spade 2. search, investigate —vt. 3. turn up with spade 4. hollow out, make hole in 5. excavate 6. thrust 7. (oft. with out or up) discover by searching (**dug**, **'digging**) —n. 8. piece of digging 9. archaeological excavation 10. thrust 11. jibe, taunt —pl. 12. inf. lodgings —**'digger** n. 1. one who digs 2. goldminer 3. Aust. or N.Z. soldier

digest (dɪ'dʒɛst, dai-) vt. 1. prepare (food) in stomach etc. for assimilation 2. bring into handy form by sorting, tabulating, summarizing 3. reflect on 4. absorb —vi. 5. (of food) undergo digestion —n. ('daɪdʒɛst) 6. methodical summary, esp. of laws 7. magazine containing condensed version of articles etc. already published elsewhere —**di'gestible** a. —**di'gestion** n. digesting —**di'gestive** a. 1. relating to digestion —n. 2. substance that aids digestion —**digestive biscuit** round semi-sweet biscuit made from wholemeal flour

digit ('dɪdʒɪt) n. 1. finger or toe 2. any of the numbers 0 to 9 —**'digital** a. 1. of, resembling digits 2. performed with fingers 3. displaying information (time etc.) by numbers rather than by pointer on dial —**'digitate** or **'digitated** a. having separate fingers, toes —**digital clock** or **watch** clock or watch in which time is indicated by digits rather than by hands on dial —**digital computer** electronic computer consisting of numbers, letters etc. that are represented internally in binary notation

digitalis (dɪdʒɪ'teɪlɪs) n. drug made from foxglove

dignity ('dɪgnɪtɪ) n. 1. stateliness, gravity 2. worthiness, excellence, repute 3. honourable office or title —**'dignified** a. stately, majestic —**'dignify** vt. give dignity to (**-fied**, **-fying**) —**'dignitary** n. holder of high office

digraph ('daɪgrɑːf) n. combination of two letters used to represent single sound such as gh in tough

digress (dai'grɛs) vi. turn from main course, esp. to deviate from subject in speaking or writing —**di'gression** n. —**di'gressive** a.

dihedral (dai'hiːdrəl) a. having two plane faces or sides

dik-dik ('dɪkdɪk) n. small Afr. antelope

dike (daik) n. see DYKE

diktat ('dɪktɑːt) n. arbitrary decree

dilapidate (dɪ'læpɪdeɪt) v. (cause to) fall into ruin —**di'lapidated** a. 1. in ruins 2. decayed —**dilapi'dation** n.

dilate (dai'leɪt, dɪ-) vt. 1. widen, expand

—vi. 2. expand 3. talk or write at length (on) —**di'lation** or **dilatation** (daɪlə-'teɪʃən) n.

dilatory ('dɪlətərɪ) a. tardy, slow, belated —'dilatorily adv. —'dilatoriness n. delay

dilemma (dɪ'lɛmə, dai-) n. 1. position in fact or argument offering choice only between unwelcome alternatives 2. predicament

dilettante (dɪlɪ'tɑːntɪ) n. 1. person with taste and knowledge of fine arts as pastime 2. dabbler (pl. dilettanti (dɪlɪ-'tɑːntɪ)) —a. 3. amateur, desultory —dilet'tantism n.

diligent ('dɪlɪdʒənt) a. unremitting in effort, industrious, hard-working —'diligence n.

dill (dɪl) n. yellow-flowered herb with medicinal seeds

dilly ('dɪlɪ) n. sl., chiefly US remarkable person or thing

dilly-dally ('dɪlɪdælɪ) vi. inf. 1. loiter 2. vacillate

dilute (dai'luːt) vt. 1. reduce (liquid) in strength, esp. by adding water 2. thin 3. reduce in force, effect etc. —a. 4. weakened thus —**diluent** ('dɪljuənt) a./n. —di'lution n.

diluvial (dai'luːvɪəl, dɪ-) or **diluvian** a. of, connected with, a deluge or flood, esp. the Flood of the Book of Genesis

dim (dɪm) a. 1. indistinct, faint, not bright 2. mentally dull 3. unfavourable ('dimmer comp., 'dimmest sup.) —v. 4. make, grow dim (**-mm-**) —'dimly adv. —'dimmer n. device for dimming electric lights —'dimness n. —'dimwit n. inf. stupid or silly person —dim-witted a.

dime (daim) n. 10-cent piece, coin of U.S. and Canad.

dimension (dɪ'mɛnʃən) n. 1. measurement, size 2. aspect —di'mensional a. —**fourth dimension** Phys. 1. time 2. supranatural, fictional dimension additional to those of length, breadth, thickness

diminish (dɪ'mɪnɪʃ) v. lessen —dimi'nution n. —di'minutive a. 1. very small —n. 2. derivative word, affix implying smallness —diminished responsibility Law plea under which mental derangement is submitted as demonstrating lack of criminal responsibility

diminuendo (dɪmɪnju'ɛndəʊ) a. Mus. (of sound) dying away

dimity ('dɪmɪtɪ) n. strong cotton fabric

dimple ('dɪmp'l) n. 1. small hollow in surface of skin, esp. of cheek 2. any small hollow —v. 3. mark with, show dimples

din (dɪn) n. continuous roar of confused noises —din into instil into by constant repetition

dinar ('diːnɑː) n. 1. standard monetary unit of Iraq, Jordan, Libya, Yugoslavia etc. 2. an Iranian monetary unit

dine (daɪn) vi. 1. eat dinner —vt. 2. give dinner to —'diner n. 1. one who dines 2. chiefly US small cheap restaurant 3. railway restaurant car —dining car railway coach in which meals are served (*also* **restaurant car**) —**dining room** room where meals are eaten

ding (dɪŋ) *v.* 1. ring (*esp.* with tedious repetition) —*vi.* 2. make (imitation of) sound of bell —*n.* 3. this sound —**ding-dong** *n.* 1. sound of bell 2. imitation of sound of bell 3. violent exchange of blows or words —*a.* 4. sounding or ringing repeatedly

dinghy, dingy, *or* **dingey** ('dɪŋɪ) *n.* 1. small open boat 2. collapsible rubber boat

dingle ('dɪŋg'l) *n.* dell

dingo ('dɪŋgəʊ) *n.* Aust. wild dog

dingy ('dɪndʒɪ) *a.* dirty-looking, dull —**'dinginess** *n.*

dinkum ('dɪŋkəm) *a.* **A, NZ** *inf.* genuine; right —**dinkum oil** truth

dinky ('dɪŋkɪ) *a. inf.* 1. **UK** small and neat; dainty 2. **US** inconsequential; insignificant

dinner ('dɪnə) *n.* 1. chief meal of the day 2. official banquet —**dinner jacket** man's semiformal evening jacket without tails, usu. black

dinosaur ('daɪnɔːsɔː) *n.* extinct reptile, oft. of gigantic size —**dino'saurian** *a.*

dint (dɪnt) *n.* dent, mark —**by dint of** by means of

diocese ('daɪəsɪs) *n.* district, jurisdiction of bishop —**diocesan** (daɪ'ɒsɪs'n) *a.* 1. of diocese —*n.* 2. bishop, clergyman, people of diocese

diode ('daɪəʊd) *n.* 1. semiconductor device for converting alternating current to direct current 2. electronic valve having two electrodes between which current can flow in only one direction

dioecious (daɪ'iːʃəs) *a.* (of plants) having male and female reproductive organs on separate plants

Dionysus (daɪə'naɪziən) *n.* 1. of Dionysus, Gr. god of wine and revelry 2. (*oft.* **d-**) wild; orgiastic

dioptre *or* **U.S. diopter** (daɪ'ɒptə) *n.* unit for measuring refractive power of lens —**di'optrics** *pl.n.* (*with sing. v.*) that part of the science of optics which deals with refraction of light

diorama (daɪə'rɑːmə) *n.* miniature three-dimensional scene, *esp.* as museum exhibit

dioxide (daɪ'ɒksaɪd) *n.* oxide with two parts of oxygen to one of the other constituents

dioxin (daɪ'ɒksɪn) *n.* any of various by-products of manufacture of certain herbicides and bactericides

dip (dɪp) *vt.* 1. put partly or briefly into liquid, *esp.* to coat 2. immerse 3. lower and raise again 4. take up in ladle, bucket *etc.* 5. direct (headlights of vehicle) downwards —*vi.* 6. plunge partially or temporarily 7. go down, sink 8. slope downwards (-**pp-**) —*n.* 9. act of dipping 10. bathe 11. liquid chemical in which livestock are immersed to treat insect pests *etc.* 12. downward slope 13. hollow 14. creamy (savoury) mixture in which crisps *etc.* are dipped before being eaten

15. lottery —**'dipstick** *n.* graduated rod dipped into container to indicate fluid level —**dip switch** device for dipping car headlights —**dip into** 1. glance at 2. make inroads into for funds

Dip. A. D. Diploma in Art and Design

Dip. Ed. UK Diploma in Education

diphtheria (dɪp'θɪərɪə) *n.* infectious disease of throat with membranous growth —**diphtheritic** (dɪpθə'rɪtɪk) *a.*

diphthong ('dɪfθɒŋ) *n.* union of two vowel sounds in single compound sound

diploma (dɪ'pləʊmə) *n.* 1. document vouching for person's proficiency 2. title to degree, honour *etc.*

diplomacy (dɪ'pləʊməsɪ) *n.* 1. management of international relations 2. skill in negotiation 3. tactful, adroit dealing —**'diplomat** *n.* one engaged in official diplomacy —**diplo'matic** *a.* —**diplo'matically** *adv.* —**di'plomatist** *n.* 1. diplomat 2. tactful person —**diplomatic immunity** immunity from local jurisdiction *etc.* afforded to diplomatic staff abroad

diplopia (dɪ'pləʊpɪə) *n.* double vision

dipolar (daɪ'pəʊlə) *a.* having two poles

dipole ('daɪpəʊl) *n.* type of radio and television aerial

dipper ('dɪpə) *n.* 1. ladle, bucket, scoop 2. diving bird (*also* **water ouzel**)

dipsomania (dɪpsəʊ'meɪnɪə) *n.* uncontrollable craving for alcohol —**dipso'maniac** *n.* victim of this

dipterous ('dɪptərəs) *a.* 1. of order of insects having single pair of wings and sucking or piercing mouthparts (*also* **'dipteran**) 2. *Bot.* having two winglike parts

diptych ('dɪptɪk) *n.* 1. ancient tablet hinged in centre, folding together like a book 2. painting, carving on two hinged panels

dire (daɪə) *a.* 1. terrible 2. urgent

direct (dɪ'rɛkt, daɪ-) *vt.* 1. control, manage, order 2. tell or show the way 3. aim, point, turn 4. address (letter *etc.*) 5. supervise (actors *etc.*) in play or film —*a.* 6. frank, straightforward 7. straight 8. going straight to the point 9. immediate 10. lineal —**di'rection** *n.* 1. directing 2. aim, course of movement 3. address, instruction —**di'rectional** *a.* 1. of or relating to spatial direction 2. *Electron.* having or relating to increased sensitivity to radio waves *etc.* coming from particular direction; (of aerial) transmitting or receiving radio waves more effectively in some directions than in others 3. *Phys., electron.* concentrated in, following or producing motion in particular direction —**di'rective** *a./n.* —**di'rectly** *adv.* —**di'rectness** *n.* —**di'rector** *n.* 1. one who directs, *esp.* a film 2. member of board managing company (**di'rectress** *fem.*) —**di'rectorate** *n.* 1. body of directors 2. office of director —**di'rectorship** *n.* —**di'rectory** *n.* 1. alphabetical book of names, addresses, streets *etc.* 2. (**D-**) French revolutionary government 1795-9 —**direct current**

continuous electric current that flows in one direction —**direct-grant school** *UK* formerly, school financed by endowment, fees and state grant conditional upon admittance of percentage of nonpaying pupils —**direction finder** radio receiver that determines the direction of incoming waves —**direct object** *Gram.* noun, pronoun or noun phrase whose referent receives direct action of verb —**direct speech** *or esp. U.S.* **direct discourse** reporting of what someone has said or written by quoting exact words —**direct tax** tax paid by person or organization on which it is levied

dirge (dɜːdʒ) *n.* song of mourning

dirigible (dɪˈrɪdʒɪbʲl) *a.* 1. steerable —*n.* 2. balloon; airship

dirk (dɜːk) *n.* short dagger orig. carried by Scottish clansmen

dirndl (ˈdɜːndʲl) *n.* full, gathered skirt

dirt (dɜːt) *n.* 1. filth 2. soil, earth 3. obscene or pornographic material 4. contamination —**'dirtiness** *n.* —**'dirty** *a.* 1. unclean, filthy 2. obscene 3. unfair 4. dishonest —**dirt-cheap** *a./adv. inf.* at extremely low price —**dirt track** loose-surfaced track, *eg* for motorcycle racing

dis- (*comb. form*) negation, opposition, deprivation; in many verbs indicates undoing of the action of simple verb. In the list below, the meaning may be inferred from the word to which *dis-* is prefixed

disable (dɪsˈeɪbʲl) *vt.* 1. make unable 2. cripple, maim —**disaˈbility** *n.* 1. incapacity 2. drawback

disabuse (dɪsəˈbjuːz) *vt.* 1. undeceive, disillusion 2. free from error

disadvantage (dɪsədˈvɑːntɪdʒ) *n.* 1. drawback 2. hindrance 3. detriment —*vt.* 4. handicap —**disadˈvantaged** *a.* deprived, discriminated against, underprivileged —**disadvanˈtageous** *a.*

disaffected (dɪsəˈfɛktɪd) *a.* ill-disposed, alienated, estranged —**disafˈfection** *n.*

disagree (dɪsəˈgriː) *vi.* (*oft. with* with) 1. be at variance 2. conflict 3. (of food *etc.*) have bad effect (on) —**disaˈgreeable** *a.* unpleasant —**disaˈgreement** *n.* 1. difference of opinion 2. discord 3. discrepancy

disallow (dɪsəˈlaʊ) *vt.* reject as untrue or invalid —**disalˈlowance** *n.*

disappear (dɪsəˈpɪə) *vi.* 1. vanish 2. cease to exist 3. be lost —**disapˈpearance** *n.*

disappoint (dɪsəˈpɔɪnt) *vt.* fail to fulfil (hope), frustrate —**disapˈpointment** *n.*

disarm (dɪsˈɑːm) *vt.* 1. deprive of arms or weapons 2. reduce war weapons of (a country) 3. win over —**disˈarmament** *n.* —**disˈarming** *a.* removing hostility, suspicion

disarray (dɪsəˈreɪ) *vt.* 1. throw into disorder, derange —*n.* 2. disorderliness, *esp.* of clothing

disassociate (dɪsəˈsəʊʃɪeɪt) *v. see* DISSOCIATE

disaster (dɪˈzɑːstə) *n.* calamity, sudden or great misfortune —**disˈastrous** *a.* calamitous

disbar (dɪsˈbɑː) *vt. Law* expel from the bar

disbud (dɪsˈbʌd) *vt.* remove superfluous buds, shoots from

disburse (dɪsˈbɜːs) *vt.* pay out —**disˈbursement** *n.*

disc (dɪsk) *n.* 1. thin, flat, circular object like a coin 2. gramophone record —**disc brake** brake in which two pads rub against flat disc attached to wheel hub when brake is applied —**disc harrow** *or* **plough** harrow or plough which cuts soil with inclined discs —**disc jockey** announcer playing records, oft. on radio

discard (dɪsˈkɑːd) *vt.* 1. reject 2. give up 3. cast off, dismiss

discern (dɪˈsɜːn) *vt.* 1. make out 2. distinguish —**disˈcernible** *a.* —**disˈcerning** *a.* 1. discriminating 2. penetrating —**disˈcernment** *n.* insight

discharge (dɪsˈtʃɑːdʒ) *vt.* 1. release 2. dismiss 3. emit 4. perform (duties), fulfil (obligations) 5. let go 6. fire off 7. unload 8. pay —*n.* (ˈdɪstʃɑːdʒ, dɪsˈtʃɑːdʒ) 9. discharging 10. being discharged 11. release 12. matter emitted 13. document certifying release, payment *etc.*

disciple (dɪˈsaɪpʲl) *n.* follower, one who takes another as teacher and model —**disˈcipleship** *n.*

discipline (ˈdɪsɪplɪn) *n.* 1. training that produces orderliness, obedience, self-control 2. result of such training in order, conduct *etc.* 3. system of rules *etc.* —*vt.* 4. train 5. punish —**discipliˈnarian** *n.* one who enforces rigid discipline —**'disciplinary** *a.*

disclaim (dɪsˈkleɪm) *vt.* deny, renounce —**disˈclaimer** *n.* repudiation, denial

disclose (dɪsˈkləʊz) *vt.* 1. allow to be seen 2. make known —**disˈclosure** *n.* revelation

disco (ˈdɪskəʊ) discotheque

discobolus (dɪsˈkɒbələs) *n.* discus thrower (*pl.* **-li** (-laɪ))

discolour *or U.S.* **discolor** (dɪsˈkʌlə) *vt.* alter colour of, stain —**discolorˈation** *n.*

discomfit (dɪsˈkʌmfɪt) *vt.* embarrass, disconcert, baffle —**disˈcomfiture** *n.*

discomfort (dɪsˈkʌmfət) *n.* 1. inconvenience, distress or mild pain 2. something that disturbs or deprives of ease —*vt.* 3. make uncomfortable or uneasy

discommode (dɪskəˈməʊd) *vt.* 1. put to inconvenience 2. disturb —**discomˈmodious** *a.*

disappro'bation	disa'vow	discom'pose
disap'proval	dis'band	discom'posure
disap'prove	disbe'lief	
disar'range	disbe'lieve	

disconcert (dɪskən'sɜːt) vt. 1. ruffle, confuse 2. upset, embarrass

disconsolate (dɪs'kɒnsəlɪt) a. unhappy, downcast, forlorn

discord ('dɪskɔːd) n. 1. strife 2. difference, dissension 3. disagreement of sounds —**dis'cordance** n. —**dis'cordant** a. —**dis'cordantly** adv.

discotheque ('dɪskətɛk) n. 1. club etc. for dancing to recorded music 2. mobile equipment for providing music for dancing

discount (dɪs'kaʊnt, 'dɪskaʊnt) vt. 1. consider as possibility but reject as unsuitable, inappropriate etc. 2. deduct (amount, percentage) from usual price 3. sell at reduced price —n. ('dɪskaʊnt) 4. amount deducted from cost, expressed as cash amount or percentage

discountenance (dɪs'kaʊntɪnəns) vt. 1. abash 2. discourage 3. frown upon

discourage (dɪs'kʌrɪdʒ) vt. 1. reduce confidence of 2. deter 3. show disapproval of —**dis'couragement** n.

discourse ('dɪskɔːs, dɪs'kɔːs) n. 1. conversation 2. speech, treatise, sermon —vi. (dɪs'kɔːs) 3. speak, converse, lecture

discover (dɪ'skʌvə) vt. 1. (be the first to) find out, light upon 2. make known —**dis'coverable** a. —**dis'coverer** n. —**dis'covery** n.

discredit (dɪs'krɛdɪt) vt. 1. damage reputation of 2. cast doubt on 3. reject as untrue —n. 4. disgrace 5. doubt —**dis'creditable** a.

discreet (dɪ'skriːt) a. prudent, circumspect —**dis'creetly** adv. —**dis'creetness** n.

discrepancy (dɪ'skrɛpənsɪ) n. conflict, variation, as between figures —**dis'crepant** a.

discrete (dɪ'skriːt) a. separate, disunited, discontinuous

discretion (dɪ'skrɛʃən) n. 1. quality of being discreet 2. prudence 3. freedom to act as one chooses —**dis'cretionary** or **dis'cretional** a.

discriminate (dɪ'skrɪmɪneɪt) vi. 1. single out particular person, group etc. for special favour or disfavour 2. distinguish (between) 3. be discerning —**discrimi'nation** n. —**dis'criminatory** or **dis'criminative** a. 1. based on prejudice; biased 2. capable of making fine distinctions

discursive (dɪs'kɜːsɪv) a. passing from subject to subject, rambling

discus ('dɪskəs) n. disc-shaped object thrown in athletic competition (pl. **-es**, **disci** ('dɪskaɪ))

discuss (dɪ'skʌs) vt. 1. exchange opinions about 2. debate —**dis'cussion** n.

disdain (dɪs'deɪn) n. 1. scorn, contempt —vt. 2. scorn —**dis'dainful** a. —**dis'dainfully** adv.

disease (dɪ'ziːz) n. 1. illness 2. disorder of health —**dis'eased** a.

disembodied (dɪsɪm'bɒdɪd) a. (of spirit) released from bodily form

disembowel (dɪsɪm'baʊəl) vt. take out entrails of (**-ll-**)

disenchanted (dɪsɪn'tʃɑːntɪd) a. disillusioned

disengage (dɪsɪn'geɪdʒ) v. 1. release or become released from connection etc. 2. Mil. withdraw (forces) from close action 3. Fencing move (one's blade) from one side of opponent's blade to another in circular motion —**disen'gaged** a. —**disen'gagement** n.

disfavour or U.S. **disfavor** (dɪs'feɪvə) n. 1. disapproval; dislike 2. state of being disapproved of or disliked 3. unkind act —vt. 4. treat with disapproval or dislike

disfigure (dɪs'fɪgə) vt. mar appearance of —**disfigu'ration** n. —**dis'figurement** n. blemish, defect

disgorge (dɪs'gɔːdʒ) vt. 1. vomit 2. give up —**dis'gorgement** n.

disgrace (dɪs'greɪs) n. 1. shame, loss of reputation, dishonour —vt. 2. bring shame or discredit upon —**dis'graceful** a. shameful —**dis'gracefully** adv.

disgruntled (dɪs'grʌnt³ld) a. 1. vexed 2. put out

disguise (dɪs'gaɪz) vt. 1. change appearance of, make unrecognizable 2. conceal, cloak 3. misrepresent —n. 4. false appearance 5. costume, mask etc. to conceal identity

disgust (dɪs'gʌst) n. 1. violent distaste, loathing, repugnance —vt. 2. affect with loathing

dish (dɪʃ) n. 1. shallow vessel for food 2. portion or variety of food 3. contents of dish 4. sl. attractive person —vt. 5. put in dish —'**dishy** a. sl., chiefly UK good-looking, attractive —**dish aerial** microwave aerial, used in satellite broadcasting etc., consisting of parabolic reflector —'**dishcloth** n. cloth or rag for washing or drying dishes —**dish up** 1. serve (meal etc.) 2. inf. prepare or present, esp. attractively

dishabille (dɪsæ'biːl) or **deshabille** n. state of being partly or carelessly dressed

---

dishevelled (dɪˈʃɛvˀld) *a.* 1. with disordered hair 2. ruffled, untidy, unkempt

dishonour *or U.S.* **dishonor** (dɪsˈɒnə) *vt.* 1. treat with disrespect 2. fail or refuse to pay 3. cause disgrace of (woman) by seduction or rape —*n.* 4. lack of honour or respect 5. state of shame or disgrace 6. person or thing that causes loss of honour 7. insult; affront 8. refusal or failure to accept or pay a commercial paper —**disˈhonourable** *or U.S.* **disˈhonorable** *a.* 1. characterized by or causing dishonour or discredit 2. having little or no integrity; unprincipled

disillusion (dɪsɪˈluːʒən) *vt.* 1. destroy ideals, illusions, or false ideas of —*n.* 2. act of disillusioning or being disillusioned (*also* **disilˈlusionment**)

disincentive (dɪsɪnˈsɛntɪv) *n.* 1. something that acts as deterrent —*a.* 2. acting as deterrent

disincline (dɪsɪnˈklaɪn) *v.* make or be unwilling, reluctant or averse —**disinclination** (dɪsɪnklɪˈneɪʃən) *n.*

disinfectant (dɪsɪnˈfɛktənt) *n.* substance that prevents or removes infection —**disinˈfect** *vt.*

disinformation (dɪsɪnfəˈmeɪʃən) *n.* deliberately leaked false information intended to mislead foreign agents

disingenuous (dɪsɪnˈdʒɛnjʊəs) *a.* not sincere or frank

disinherit (dɪsɪnˈhɛrɪt) *vt.* deprive of inheritance

disintegrate (dɪsˈɪntɪɡreɪt) *vi.* break up, fall to pieces —**disinteˈgration** *n.*

disinterest (dɪsˈɪntrɪst) *n.* 1. freedom from bias or involvement —**disˈinterested** *a.*

disjoint (dɪsˈdʒɔɪnt) *vt.* 1. put out of joint 2. break the natural order or logical arrangement of —**disˈjointed** *a.* 1. (of discourse) incoherent 2. disconnected

disjunctive (dɪsˈdʒʌŋktɪv) *a.* 1. serving to disconnect or separate 2. *Gram.* denoting word, *esp.* conjunction, that serves to express opposition or contrast 3. *Logic* characterizing, containing or included in disjunction —*n.* 4. *Gram.* disjunctive word, *esp.* conjunction 5. *Logic* disjunctive proposition

disk (dɪsk) *n.* 1. *see* DISC 2. *Comp.* direct-access storage device, consisting of stack of plates coated with magnetic layer, that rotates rapidly as single unit

dislike (dɪsˈlaɪk) *vt.* 1. consider unpleasant or disagreeable —*n.* 2. aversion; antipathy —**disˈlikable** *or* **disˈlikeable** *a.*

dislocate (ˈdɪsləkeɪt) *vt.* 1. put out of joint 2. disrupt, displace —**disloˈcation** *n.*

dislodge (dɪsˈlɒdʒ) *vt.* drive out or remove from hiding place or previous position —**disˈlodgement** *or* **disˈlodgment** *n.*

dismal (ˈdɪzməl) *a.* 1. depressing 2. depressed 3. cheerless, dreary, gloomy —**ˈdismally** *adv.*

dismantle (dɪsˈmæntˀl) *vt.* take apart —**disˈmantlement** *n.*

dismay (dɪsˈmeɪ) *vt.* 1. dishearten, daunt —*n.* 2. consternation, horrified amazement 3. apprehension

dismember (dɪsˈmɛmbə) *vt.* 1. remove limbs or members of 2. divide, partition —**disˈmemberment** *n.*

dismiss (dɪsˈmɪs) *vt.* 1. remove, discharge from employment 2. send away 3. reject —**disˈmissal** *n.*

disobey (dɪsəˈbeɪ) *v.* refuse or fail to obey —**disobedience** (dɪsəˈbiːdɪəns) *n.* —**disobedient** (dɪsəˈbiːdɪənt) *a.*

disoblige (dɪsəˈblaɪdʒ) *vt.* disregard the wishes, preferences of

disorder (dɪsˈɔːdə) *n.* 1. disarray, confusion, disturbance 2. upset of health, ailment —*vt.* 3. upset order of 4. disturb health of —**disˈorderly** *a.* 1. untidy 2. unruly

disorientate (dɪsˈɔːrɪenteɪt) *or* **disorient** *vt.* cause (someone) to lose his bearings, confuse

disown (dɪsˈəʊn) *vt.* refuse to acknowledge

disparage (dɪˈspærɪdʒ) *vt.* 1. speak slightingly of 2. belittle —**disˈparagement** *n.*

disparate (ˈdɪspərɪt) *a.* essentially different, unrelated —**disˈparity** *n.* 1. inequality 2. incongruity

dispassionate (dɪsˈpæʃənɪt) *a.* 1. unswayed by passion 2. calm, impartial

dispatch *or* **despatch** (dɪˈspætʃ) *vt.* 1. send off to destination or on an errand 2. send off 3. finish off, get done with speed 4. *inf.* eat up 5. kill —*n.* 6. sending off 7. efficient speed 8. official message, report —**dispatch rider** horseman *or* motorcyclist who carries dispatches

dispel (dɪˈspɛl) *vt.* clear, drive away, scatter (**-ll-**)

dispense (dɪˈspɛns) *vt.* 1. deal out 2. make up (medicine) 3. administer (justice) 4. grant exemption from —**disˈpensable** *a.* —**disˈpensary** *n.* place where medicine is made up —**dispenˈsation** *n.* 1. act of dispensing 2. licence; exemption 3. provision of nature or providence —**disˈpenser** *n.* —**dispense with** 1. do away with 2. manage without

disperse (dɪˈspɜːs) *v.* scatter —**disˈpersal** *or* **disˈpersion** *n.* —**disˈpersed** *a.* 1. scattered 2. placed here and there

dispirited (dɪˈspɪrɪtɪd) *a.* dejected, disheartened —**disˈpiritedly** *adv.* —**disˈpiriting** *a.*

displace (dɪsˈpleɪs) *vt.* 1. move from the usual place 2. remove from office 3. take place of —**disˈplacement** *n.* 1. displacing 2. weight of liquid displaced by a solid in a

---

dis'honest
dis'honesty
disin'ter

disin'terment
dis'loyal
dis'loyalty

dis'mount
disorgani'zation
dis'organize

fluid —**displaced person** person forced from his home country, *esp.* by war *etc.*

display (dɪˈspleɪ) *vt.* **1.** spread out for show **2.** show, expose to view **3.** (of visual display unit *etc.*) represent (data) visually, as on cathode-ray tube screen —*n.* **4.** displaying **5.** parade **6.** show, exhibition **7.** ostentation **8.** *Electron.* device capable of representing data visually, as on cathode-ray tube screen

displease (dɪsˈpliːz) *v.* **1.** offend **2.** annoy —**displeasure** (dɪsˈplɛʒə) *n.* anger, vexation

disport (dɪˈspɔːt) *v.refl.* **1.** amuse oneself **2.** frolic, gambol

dispose (dɪˈspəʊz) *vt.* **1.** arrange **2.** distribute **3.** incline **4.** adjust —*vi.* **5.** determine —**disˈposable** *a.* designed to be thrown away after use —**disˈposal** *n.* —**disˈposed** *a.* having inclination as specified (towards something) —**dispoˈsition** *n.* **1.** inclination **2.** temperament **3.** arrangement **4.** plan —**dispose of 1.** sell, get rid of **2.** have authority over **3.** deal with

dispossess (dɪspəˈzɛs) *vt.* cause to give up possession (of)

disprove (dɪsˈpruːv) *vt.* to show (assertion, claim *etc.*) to be incorrect

dispute (dɪˈspjuːt) *vi.* **1.** debate, discuss —*vt.* **2.** call in question **3.** debate, argue **4.** oppose, contest —**disˈputable** *a.* —**disˈputant** *n.* —**dispuˈtation** *n.* —**dispuˈtatious** *a.* **1.** argumentative **2.** quarrelsome

disqualify (dɪsˈkwɒlɪfaɪ) *vt.* make ineligible, unfit for some special purpose

disquiet (dɪsˈkwaɪət) *n.* **1.** anxiety, uneasiness —*vt.* **2.** cause (someone) to feel this —**disˈquietude** *n.* feeling of anxiety

disquisition (dɪskwɪˈzɪʃən) *n.* learned or elaborate treatise, discourse or essay

disrepair (dɪsrɪˈpɛə) *n.* state of bad repair, neglect

disrobe (dɪsˈrəʊb) *v.* **1.** undress —*vt.* **2.** divest of robes

disrupt (dɪsˈrʌpt) *vt.* **1.** interrupt **2.** throw into turmoil or disorder —**disˈruption** *n.* —**disˈruptive** *a.*

dissect (dɪˈsɛkt, daɪ-) *vt.* **1.** cut up (body, organism) for detailed examination **2.** examine or criticize in detail —**disˈsection** *n.* —**disˈsector** *n.* anatomist

dissemble (dɪˈsɛmbˀl) *v.* **1.** conceal, disguise (feelings *etc.*) —*vt.* **2.** simulate —**disˈsembler** *n.*

disseminate (dɪˈsɛmɪneɪt) *vt.* spread abroad, scatter —**dissemiˈnation** *n.* —**disˈseminator** *n.*

dissent (dɪˈsɛnt) *vi.* **1.** differ in opinion **2.** express such difference **3.** disagree with doctrine *etc.* of established church —*n.* **4.**

such disagreement —**disˈsension** *n.* —**disˈsenter** *n.* —**disˈsentient** *a./n.*

dissertation (dɪsəˈteɪʃən) *n.* **1.** written thesis **2.** formal discourse —**ˈdissertate** *vi.* hold forth

disservice (dɪsˈsɜːvɪs) *n.* ill turn, wrong, injury

dissident (ˈdɪsɪdənt) *n./a.* (one) not in agreement, *esp.* with government —**ˈdissidence** *n.* **1.** dissent **2.** disagreement

dissimulate (dɪˈsɪmjʊleɪt) *v.* dissemble, practise deceit —**dissimuˈlation** *n.* —**disˈsimulator** *n.*

dissipate (ˈdɪsɪpeɪt) *vt.* **1.** scatter **2.** waste, squander —**ˈdissipated** *a.* **1.** indulging in pleasure without restraint, dissolute **2.** scattered, wasted —**dissiˈpation** *n.* **1.** scattering **2.** frivolous, dissolute way of life

dissociate (dɪˈsəʊʃɪeɪt, -sɪ-) *v.* **1.** separate —*vt.* **2.** disconnect, sever —**dissociˈation** *n.*

dissolute (ˈdɪsəluːt) *a.* lax in morals

dissolution (dɪsəˈluːʃən) *n.* **1.** break-up **2.** termination of parliament, meeting or legal relationship **3.** destruction **4.** death

dissolve (dɪˈzɒlv) *vt.* **1.** absorb or melt in fluid **2.** break up, put an end to, annul —*vi.* **3.** melt in fluid **4.** disappear, vanish **5.** break up, scatter —**disˈsolvable** *or* **dissoluble** (dɪˈsɒljʊbˀl) *a.* capable of being dissolved —**disˈsolvent** *n.* thing with power to dissolve

dissonant (ˈdɪsənənt) *a.* jarring, discordant —**ˈdissonance** *n.*

dissuade (dɪˈsweɪd) *vt.* advise to refrain, persuade not to do something —**disˈsuasion** *n.* —**disˈsuasive** *a.*

dissyllable (dɪˈsɪləbˀl) *or* **disyllable** (ˈdaɪsɪləbˀl) *n.* word or metrical foot having two syllables —**dissylˈlabic** *or* **disylˈlabic** *a.*

distaff (ˈdɪstɑːf) *n.* cleft stick to hold wool *etc.* for spinning —**distaff side 1.** maternal side **2.** female line of family

distance (ˈdɪstəns) *n.* **1.** amount of space between two things **2.** remoteness **3.** aloofness, reserve —*vt.* **4.** hold or place at distance —**ˈdistant** *a.* **1.** far off, remote **2.** haughty, cold —**ˈdistantly** *adv.*

distaste (dɪsˈteɪst) *n.* **1.** dislike of food or drink **2.** aversion, disgust —**disˈtasteful** *a.* unpleasant, displeasing to feelings —**disˈtastefully** *adv.* —**disˈtastefulness** *n.*

distemper (dɪsˈtɛmpə) *n.* **1.** disease of dogs **2.** method of painting on plaster without oil **3.** paint used for this —*vt.* **4.** paint with distemper

distend (dɪˈstɛnd) *v.* swell out by pressure from within, inflate —**disˈtensible** *a.* —**disˈtension** *n.*

distich (ˈdɪstɪk) *n.* couplet

distil *or U.S.* **distill** (dɪsˈtɪl) *vt.* **1.** vaporize

dispro'portion	disre'pute
dispro'portionate	disre'spect
disre'gard	disre'spectful
dis'reputable	dissatis'faction

dis'satisfy
dis'similar
dissimi'larity
dis'symmetry

and recondense (a liquid) **2.** purify, separate, concentrate (liquids) by this method **3.** *fig.* extract quality of —*vi.* **4.** trickle down (-**ll**-) —'**distillate** *n.* distilled liquid, *esp.* as fuel for some engines —**distil'lation** *n.* **1.** distilling **2.** process of evaporating or boiling liquid and condensing its vapour **3.** purification or separation of mixture by using different evaporation rates or boiling points of their components **4.** process of obtaining essence or extract of substance, usu. by heating in solvent **5.** distillate **6.** concentrated essence —**dis'tiller** *n.* one who distils, *esp.* manufacturer of alcoholic spirits —**dis'tillery** *n.*

distinct (dɪ'stɪŋkt) *a.* **1.** clear, easily seen **2.** definite **3.** separate, different —**dis'tinction** *n.* **1.** point of difference **2.** act of distinguishing **3.** eminence, repute, high honour, high quality —**dis'tinctive** *a.* characteristic —**dis'tinctly** *adv.* —**dis'tinctness** *n.*

distingué (distɛ̃'ge) *Fr.* distinguished; noble

distinguish (dɪ'stɪŋgwɪʃ) *vt.* **1.** make difference in **2.** recognize, make out **3.** honour **4.** make prominent or honoured (*usu. refl.*) **5.** class —*vi.* **6.** (*usu.* with *between* or *among*) draw distinction, grasp difference —**dis'tinguishable** *a.* —**dis'tinguished** *a.* **1.** noble, dignified **2.** famous, eminent

distort (dɪ'stɔːt) *vt.* **1.** put out of shape, deform **2.** misrepresent **3.** garble, falsify —**dis'tortion** *n.*

distract (dɪ'strækt) *vt.* **1.** draw attention of (someone) away from work *etc.* or divert **2.** perplex, bewilder **4.** drive mad —**dis'traction** *n.*

distraint (dɪ'streɪnt) *n.* legal seizure of goods to enforce payment —**dis'train** *vt.* —**dis'trainment** *n.*

distrait (dɪ'streɪ; *Fr.* di'stre) *a.* **1.** absent-minded **2.** abstracted

distraught (dɪ'strɔːt) *a.* **1.** bewildered, crazed with grief **2.** frantic, distracted

distress (dɪ'strɛs) *n.* **1.** severe trouble, mental pain **2.** severe pressure of hunger, fatigue or want **3.** *Law* distraint —*vt.* **4.** afflict, give mental pain —**dis'tressed** *a.* **1.** much troubled; upset; afflicted **2.** in financial straits; poor **3.** *Econ. see* depressed (sense 4) *at* DEPRESS —**dis'tressful** *a.*

distribute (dɪ'strɪbjuːt) *vt.* **1.** deal out, dispense **2.** spread, dispose at intervals **3.** classify —**distri'bution** *n.* —**dis'tributive** *a.* —**dis'tributor** *n.* rotary switch distributing electricity in car engine

district ('dɪstrɪkt) *n.* **1.** region, locality **2.** portion of territory —**district nurse** UK nurse appointed to attend patients within particular district, usu. in patients' homes

disturb (dɪ'stɜːb) *vt.* trouble, agitate,

unsettle, derange —**dis'turbance** *n.* —**dis'turbed** *a.* *Psych.* emotionally or mentally unstable —**dis'turber** *n.*

disuse (dɪs'juːs) *n.* state of being no longer used —**disused** (dɪs'juːzd) *a.*

disyllable ('daɪsɪləb²l) *n. see* DISSYLLABLE

ditch (dɪtʃ) *n.* **1.** long narrow hollow dug in ground for drainage *etc.* —*v.* **2.** make ditch in **3.** run (car *etc.*) into ditch —*vt.* **4.** *sl.* abandon, discard

dither ('dɪðə) *vi.* **1.** be uncertain or indecisive —*n.* **2.** this state

dithyramb ('dɪθɪræm, -ræmb) *n.* ancient Gr. hymn sung in honour of Dionysus —**dithy'rambic** *a.*

dittany ('dɪtənɪ) *n.* aromatic plant native to Greece

ditto ('dɪtəʊ) *n.* **1.** the aforementioned; the above; the same: used in lists *etc.* to avoid repetition, and symbolized by two small marks (,,) placed under thing to be repeated **2.** *inf.* duplicate (*pl.* **-s**) —*adv.* **3.** in same way —*interj.* **4.** *inf.* used to avoid repeating or confirm agreement with preceding sentence —*vt.* **5.** copy; repeat (**-toing, -toed**)

ditty ('dɪtɪ) *n.* simple song

diuretic (daɪjʊ'rɛtɪk) *a.* **1.** increasing the discharge of urine —*n.* **2.** substance with this property

diurnal (daɪ'ɜːn²l) *a.* **1.** daily **2.** in or of daytime **3.** taking a day

divalent (daɪ'veɪlənt, 'daɪveɪ-) *a.* capable of combining with two atoms of hydrogen or their equivalent —**di'valency** *n.*

divan (dɪ'væn) *n.* **1.** bed, couch without back or head **2.** backless low cushioned seat

dive (daɪv) *vi.* **1.** plunge under surface of water **2.** descend suddenly **3.** disappear **4.** go deep down **5.** rush or go quickly (*dived* or *U.S.* **dove** (dəʊv), **dived, 'diving**) —*n.* **6.** act of diving **7.** *sl.* disreputable bar or club —'**diver** *n.* **1.** one who descends into deep water **2.** any of various kinds of diving bird —**dive bomber** aircraft which attacks after diving steeply —**diving bell** early diving submersible having open bottom and being supplied with compressed air —**diving board** platform or springboard from which swimmers may dive —**diving suit** or **dress** waterproof suit used by divers, having heavy detachable helmet and air supply

diverge (daɪ'vɜːdʒ) *vi.* **1.** get farther apart **2.** separate —**di'vergence** or **di'vergency** *n.* —**di'vergent** *a.*

divers ('daɪvəz) *a. obs.* some, various

diverse (daɪ'vɜːs, 'daɪvɜːs) *a.* different, varied —**di'versely** *adv.* —**diversifi'cation** *n.* —**di'versify** *vt.* make diverse or varied **2.** give variety to (**-ified, -ifying**) —**di'versity** *n.*

divert (daɪ'vɜːt) *vt.* **1.** turn aside, ward off **2.** amuse, entertain —**di'version** *n.* **1.** a diverting **2.** official detour for traffic when main route is closed **3.** amusement —**di'verting** a.

divertissement (dɪˈvɜːtɪsmənt) n. brief entertainment or diversion, usu. between acts of play

divest (daɪˈvɛst) vt. **1.** unclothe, strip **2.** dispossess, deprive

divide (dɪˈvaɪd) vt. **1.** make into two or more parts, split up, separate **2.** distribute, share **3.** classify —v. **4.** diverge in opinion —vi. **5.** become separated **6.** part into two groups for voting —n. **7.** watershed —**dividend** (ˈdɪvɪdɛnd) n. **1.** share of profits, of money divided among creditors etc. **2.** number to be divided by another —**di'viders** pl.n. measuring compasses

divine (dɪˈvaɪn) a. **1.** of, pert. to, proceeding from, God **2.** sacred **3.** heavenly —n. **4.** theologian **5.** clergyman —vt. **6.** guess **7.** predict, foresee, tell by inspiration or magic —**divination** (dɪvɪˈneɪʃən) n. divining —**di'vinely** adv. —**di'viner** n. —**divinity** (dɪˈvɪnɪtɪ) n. **1.** quality of being divine **2.** god **3.** theology —**divining rod** (forked) stick said to move when held over ground where water is present (also **dowsing rod**)

division (dɪˈvɪʒən) n. **1.** act of dividing **2.** part of whole **3.** barrier **4.** section **5.** political constituency **6.** difference in opinion etc. **7.** Maths. method of finding how many times one number is contained in another **8.** army unit **9.** separation, disunion —**di'visible** a. capable of division —**di'visional** a. —**divisive** (dɪˈvaɪsɪv) a. causing disagreement —**divisor** (dɪˈvaɪzə) n. Maths. number which divides dividend —**division sign** symbol ÷, placed between dividend and divisor to indicate division, as in $12 ÷ 6 = 2$

divorce (dɪˈvɔːs) n. **1.** legal dissolution of marriage **2.** complete separation, disunion —v. **3.** separate or be separated by divorce —vt. **4.** separate **5.** sunder —**divorcee** (dɪvɔːˈsiː) or (masc.) **divorcé** (dɪˈvɔːseɪ) n.

divot (ˈdɪvət) n. piece of turf

divulge (daɪˈvʌldʒ) vt. reveal, let out (secret) —**di'vulgence** n.

divvy (ˈdɪvɪ) inf. vt. **1.** esp. US (esp. with up) divide and share —n. **2.** dividend

dixie (ˈdɪksɪ) n. **1.** inf. (military) cooking utensil or mess tin **2.** (**D-**) southern states of U.S.A. (also **'Dixieland**) —**'Dixieland** n. **1.** jazz derived from New Orleans tradition of playing, but with more emphasis on melody, regular rhythms etc. **2.** Dixie

D.I.Y. or **d.i.y.** do-it-yourself

dizzy (ˈdɪzɪ) a. **1.** feeling dazed, unsteady, as if about to fall **2.** causing or fit to cause dizziness, as speed etc. **3.** inf. silly —vt. **4.** make dizzy (**'dizzied, 'dizzying**) —**'dizzily** adv. —**'dizziness** n.

D.J. or **d.j. 1.** dinner jacket **2.** disc jockey

djellaba (ˈdʒɛləbə) n. see JELLABA

djinni or **djinny** (dʒɪˈniː, ˈdʒɪnɪ) n. see JINNI (pl. **djinn** (dʒɪn))

dl decilitre

D.Litt. or **D.Lit. 1.** Doctor of Letters **2.** Doctor of Literature

dm decimetre

D.Mus. or **DMus** Doctor of Music

DNA deoxyribonucleic acid, main constituent of the chromosomes of all organisms

D-notice n. UK official notice sent to newspapers etc. prohibiting publication of certain security information

do¹ (duː; unstressed dʊ, də) vt. **1.** perform, effect, transact, bring about, finish **2.** work at **3.** work out, solve **4.** suit **5.** cover (distance) **6.** provide, prepare **7.** sl. cheat, swindle **8.** frustrate —vi. **9.** (oft. with for) look after **10.** act **11.** manage **12.** work **13.** fare **14.** serve, suffice **15.** happen —v. aux. **16.** makes negative and interrogative sentences and expresses emphasis (**did, done, 'doing**) —n. **17.** inf. celebration, festivity —**'doer** n. active or energetic person —**do-gooder** n. inf. well-intentioned person, esp. naive or impractical one —**do-it-yourself** n. hobby of constructing and repairing things oneself —**do away with** destroy —**do up 1.** fasten **2.** renovate —**do with 1.** need **2.** make use of —**do without** deny oneself

do² (dəʊ) n. see DOH (pl. **-s**)

do. ditto (It., the same)

dobbin (ˈdɒbɪn) n. name for horse, esp. workhorse

Doberman pinscher (ˈdəʊbəmən ˈpɪnʃə) breed of large dog with glossy black-and-tan coat

doc (dɒk) n. inf. doctor

docile (ˈdəʊsaɪl) a. willing to obey, submissive —**docility** (dəʊˈsɪlɪtɪ) n.

dock¹ (dɒk) n. **1.** artificial enclosure near harbour for loading or repairing ships —v. **2.** (of vessel) put or go into dock **3.** (of spacecraft) link or be linked together in space —**'docker** n. one who works at docks, esp. loading etc. cargoes —**'dockyard** n. enclosure with docks, for building or repairing ships

dock² (dɒk) n. **1.** solid part of tail **2.** cut end, stump —vt. **3.** cut short, esp. tail **4.** curtail, deduct (an amount) from

dock³ (dɒk) n. enclosure in criminal court for prisoner

dock⁴ (dɒk) n. coarse weed

docket (ˈdɒkɪt) n. **1.** piece of paper sent with package etc. with details of contents, delivery instructions etc. —vt. **2.** fix docket to

doctor (ˈdɒktə) n. **1.** medical practitioner **2.** one holding university's highest degree in any faculty —vt. **3.** treat medically **4.** repair, mend **5.** falsify (accounts etc.) **6.** inf. castrate, spay —**'doctoral** a. —**'doctorate** n.

doctrine (ˈdɒktrɪn) n. **1.** what is taught **2.** teaching of church, school or person **3.** belief, opinion, dogma —**doctri'naire** n. **1.** person who stubbornly applies theory without regard for circumstances —a. **2.** adhering to a doctrine in a stubborn, dogmatic way —**doctrinal** (dɒkˈtraɪnˀl) a.

document ('dɒkjumənt) n. 1. piece of paper etc. providing information or evidence —vt. ('dɒkjumɛnt) 2. furnish with proofs, illustrations, certificates —docu'mentary a./n. esp. (of) type of film dealing with real life, not fiction —docu men'tation n.

dodder ('dɒdə) vi. totter or tremble, as with age —'dodderer n. feeble or inefficient person

doddle ('dɒd'l) n. UK sl. something easily accomplished

dodecagon (dəʊ'dɛkəgɒn) n. polygon having twelve sides

dodecahedron (dəʊdɛkə'hiːdrən) n. solid figure having twelve plane faces

dodge (dɒdʒ) v. 1. avoid or attempt to avoid (blow, discovery etc.) as by moving quickly 2. evade (questions) by cleverness —n. 3. trick, artifice 4. ingenious method 5. act of dodging —'dodger n. shifty person —'dodgy a. inf. 1. dangerous 2. unreliable 3. tricky

Dodgem ('dɒdʒəm) n. R car used for bumping other cars in rink at funfair

dodo ('dəʊdəʊ) n. large extinct bird (pl. -s, -es)

doe (dəʊ) n. female of deer, hare, rabbit —'doeskin n. 1. skin of deer, lamb or sheep 2. very supple leather made from this 3. heavy smooth cloth

Doe (dəʊ) n. Law formerly, name of fictitious plaintiff in action of ejectment

D.O.E. UK Department of the Environment

doek (dʊk) n. SA inf. head cloth worn esp. by Afr. women

doer ('duːə) n. see DO[1]

does (dʌz) third pers. sing., pres. ind. active of DO[1]

doff (dɒf) vt. 1. take off (hat, clothing) 2. discard, lay aside

dog (dɒg) n. 1. domesticated carnivorous four-legged mammal 2. male of wolf, fox and other animals 3. person (in contempt, abuse or playfully) 4. name given to various mechanical contrivances acting as holdfasts 5. device with tooth which penetrates or grips object and detains it 6. firedog —vt. 7. follow steadily or closely (-gg-) —dogged ('dɒgɪd) a. persistent, resolute, tenacious —'doggy a. —'doglike a. —'dogcart n. open vehicle with crosswise back-to-back seats —dog collar 1. collar for dog 2. inf. clerical collar 3. inf. tight-fitting necklace —dog days 1. hot season of the rising of Dog Star 2. period of inactivity —dog-ear n. 1. turned-down corner of page in book —vt. 2. turn down corners of (pages) —dog-end n. inf. 1. cigarette end 2. rejected piece of anything —'dogfight n. 1. skirmish between fighter planes 2. savage contest characterized by disregard of rules —'dogfish n. very small species of shark —'doghouse n. 1. US kennel 2. inf. disfavour (esp. in in the doghouse) —'dogleg n. sharp bend or angle —dog paddle swimming stroke in

which swimmer paddles his hands in imitation of swimming dog —dog-paddle vi. swim using dog paddle —dog rose wild rose —'dogsbody n. inf. drudge —Dog Star star Sirius —dog-tired a. inf. exhausted —dog train C sleigh drawn by dog team —'dogwatch n. in ships, short half-watch, 4-6, 6-8 p.m. —'dogwood n. any of various shrubs and trees —go to the dogs degenerate —the dogs greyhound race meeting

doge (dəʊdʒ) n. formerly, chief magistrate in Venice

doggerel ('dɒgərəl) or **dogrel** ('dɒgrəl) n. slipshod, unpoetic or trivial verse

doggo ('dɒgəʊ) adv. —lie doggo inf. keep quiet, still, hidden

dogie, dogy, or **dogey** ('dəʊgɪ) n. US, C motherless calf (pl. -gies or -geys)

dogma ('dɒgmə) n. 1. article of belief, esp. one laid down authoritatively by church 2. body of beliefs (pl. -s, -ata (-ətə)) —dog'matic(al) a. 1. asserting opinions with arrogance 2. relating to dogma —dog'matically adv. —'dogmatism n. arrogant assertion of opinion —'dogmatist n. —'dogmatize or -ise v.

doh (dəʊ) n. Mus. in tonic sol-fa, first degree of any major scale (pl. -s)

doily or **doyley** ('dɔɪlɪ) n. small cloth, paper, piece of lace to place under cake, dish etc.

Dolby ('dɒlbɪ) n. R system used in tape recorders which reduces noise level on recorded or broadcast sound

dolce ('dɒltʃɪ) a. Mus. sweet

doldrums ('dɒldrəmz) pl.n. 1. state of depression, dumps 2. region of light winds and calms near the equator

dole (dəʊl) n. 1. charitable gift 2. (usu. with the) inf. payment under unemployment insurance —vt. 3. (usu. with out) deal out sparingly

doleful ('dəʊlfʊl) a. dreary, mournful —'dolefully adv.

doll (dɒl) n. 1. child's toy image of human being 2. sl. attractive girl or woman —doll up dress up in latest fashion or smartly

dollar ('dɒlə) n. standard monetary unit of many countries, esp. U.S.A. and (since 1966) Aust.

dollop ('dɒləp) n. inf. semisolid lump

dolly ('dɒlɪ) n. 1. child's word for doll 2. wheeled support for film, TV camera 3. any of various metal devices used as aids in hammering, riveting —dolly bird sl., chiefly UK attractive, fashionable girl

dolman sleeve ('dɒlmən) sleeve that is wide at armhole and tapers to tight wrist

dolmen ('dɒlmɛn) n. kind of cromlech 2. stone table

dolomite ('dɒləmaɪt) n. type of limestone

dolour or U.S. **dolor** ('dɒlə) n. grief, sadness, distress —'dolorous a. —'dolorously adv.

dolphin ('dɒlfɪn) n. sea mammal, smaller than whale, with beaklike snout

—**dolphi'narium** n. pool or aquarium for dolphins

dolt (dǝult) n. stupid fellow —'**doltish** a.

-**dom** (comb. form) 1. state, condition, as in freedom 2. rank, office or domain of, as in earldom 3. collection of persons, as in officialdom

domain (dǝ'meɪn) n. 1. lands held or ruled over 2. sphere, field of influence 3. province

dome (dǝum) n. 1. rounded vault forming a roof 2. something of this shape

Domesday Book or **Doomsday Book** ('du:mzdeɪ) record of survey of England in 1086

domestic (dǝ'mestɪk) a. 1. of, in the home 2. home-loving 3. (of animals) tamed, kept by man 4. of, in one's own country, not foreign —n. 5. house servant —**do'mesti-cate** vt. 1. tame (animals) 2. accustom to home life 3. adapt to an environment —**domesti'cation** n. —**domes'ticity** n. —**domestic science** study of cooking and other subjects concerned with household skills

domicile ('dɒmɪsaɪl) or **domicil** ('dɒmɪsɪl) n. person's regular place of abode —'**domiciled** a. living —**domicili-ary** (dɒmɪ'sɪlɪǝrɪ) a. of a dwelling place

dominate ('dɒmɪneɪt) vt. 1. rule, control, sway 2. (of heights) overlook —vi. 3. control, be the most powerful or influen-tial member or part of something —'**dominant** a./n. —**domi'nation** n. —**domi'neer** vi. act imperiously, tyrannize

dominee ('du:mɪnɪ, 'dʊǝ-) n. SA minister of Dutch Reformed Church

Dominican (dǝ'mɪnɪkǝn) n. 1. friar or nun of the order of St. Dominic —a. 2. pert. to this order

dominion (dǝ'mɪnjǝn) n. 1. sovereignty, rule 2. territory of government

Dominion Day see Canada Day at CANADIAN

dominoes ('dɒmɪnǝuz) pl.n. 1. game played with 28 oblong flat pieces marked on one side with 0 to 6 spots on each half of the face —sing. 2. one of these pieces 3. cloak with eye mask for masquerading —**domino theory** theory that event in one place, esp. political takeover, will influ-ence occurrence of similar events else-where

don[1] (dɒn) vt. put on (clothes) (-nn-)

don[2] (dɒn) n. 1. fellow or tutor of college 2. Sp. title, Sir —'**donnish** a. of or resembling university don, esp. denoting pedantry or fussiness

Doña ('dɒnjǝ) n. Sp. title of address equivalent to Mrs. or Madam

donate (dǝu'neɪt) v. give —**do'nation** n. gift to fund —'**donor** n.

done (dʌn) pp. of DO[1]

dong (dɒŋ) n. 1. imitation of sound of bell —vi. 2. make such sound

donga ('dɒŋgǝ) n. SA, A deep gully

donjon ('dʌndʒǝn, 'dɒn-) n. see DUNGEON

Don Juan ('dɒn 'dʒu:ǝn) 1. legendary Sp.

nobleman and philanderer 2. successful seducer of women

donkey ('dɒŋkɪ) n. ass (pl. -s) —**donkey engine** auxiliary engine —**donkey jacket** short, thick jacket, oft. worn by workmen —**donkey's years** inf. a long time —**donkey-work** n. drudgery

Donna ('dɒnǝ) n. It. title of address equivalent to Madam

Don Quixote ('dɒn ki:'hǝutɪ:, 'kwɪksǝt) impractical idealist

doodle ('du:d³l) v. 1. scribble absent-mindedly —n. 2. picture etc. drawn aimlessly —'**doodlebug** n. 1. see V-1 2. diviner's rod

doom (du:m) n. 1. fate, destiny 2. ruin 3. judicial sentence, condemnation 4. the Last Judgment —vt. 5. sentence, condemn 6. destine to destruction or suffering —'**doomsday** or '**domesday** n. the day of the Last Judgment

door (dɔ:) n. hinged or sliding barrier to close any entrance —'**doorjamb** n. one of two vertical members forming sides of doorframe (also '**doorpost**) —'**doorman** n. man employed to attend doors of certain buildings —'**doormat** n. 1. mat at entrance for wiping shoes on 2. sl. person who offers little resistance to ill-treatment —'**door-stop** n. any device which prevents open door from moving —'**doorway** n. entrance with or without door —**door to door** 1. (of selling etc.) from one house to next 2. (of journeys etc.) direct

dope (dǝup) n. 1. kind of varnish 2. drug, esp. illegal, narcotic drug 3. inf. informa-tion 4. inf. stupid person —vt. 5. drug (esp. of racehorses) —'**dopey** or '**dopy** a. inf. 1. foolish 2. drugged 3. half asleep

Doppelgänger ('dɒp³lgeŋǝ) n. Legend ghostly duplicate of living person

Doppler effect ('dɒplǝ) change in apparent frequency of sound or light wave etc. as result of relative motion between observer and source (also **Doppler shift**)

Doric ('dɒrɪk) a. 1. of the inhabitants of Doris, in ancient Greece, or their dialect —n. 2. dialect of Dorians 3. style of Gr. architecture 4. rustic dialect —**Dorian** ('dɔ:rɪǝn) a./n. (member) of early Gr. race

dormant ('dɔ:mǝnt) a. 1. not active, in state of suspension 2. sleeping —'**dorman-cy** n.

dormer ('dɔ:mǝ) n. upright window set in sloping roof

dormitory ('dɔ:mɪtǝrɪ, -trɪ) n. sleeping room with many beds —**dormitory town** town whose inhabitants travel elsewhere to work

Dormobile ('dɔ:mǝubi:l) n. R vanlike vehicle specially equipped for living in while travelling

dormouse ('dɔ:maus) n. small hibernating mouselike rodent

dorp (dɔ:p) n. SA small town

dorsal ('dɔ:s³l) a. Anat., zool. of, on back

dory ('dɔ:rɪ) n. deep-bodied type of fish, esp. John Dory

dose (dəʊs) n. 1. amount (of drug etc.) administered at one time 2. inf. instance or period of something unpleasant, esp. disease —vt. 3. give doses to —'**dosage** n.

doss (dɒs) inf. n. 1. temporary bed —vi. 2. sleep in dosshouse 3. sleep —'**dosshouse** n. cheap lodging house

dossier ('dɒsɪeɪ) n. set of papers on some particular subject or event

dot[1] (dɒt) n. 1. small spot, mark —vt. 2. mark with dots 3. sprinkle 4. sl. hit —'**dotty** a. 1. sl. crazy 2. sl. (with about) extremely fond (of) 3. marked with dots

dot[2] (dɒt) n. dowry

dote (dəʊt) vi. 1. (with on or upon) be passionately fond (of) 2. be silly or weak-minded —'**dotage** n. senility —'**dotard** n. —'**doting** a. blindly affectionate

dotterel or **dottrel** ('dɒtrəl) n. kind of plover

dottle ('dɒt'l) n. plug of tobacco left in pipe after smoking

double ('dʌb'l) a. 1. of two parts, layers etc., folded 2. twice as much or as many 3. of two kinds 4. designed for two users 5. ambiguous 6. deceitful —adv. 7. twice 8. to twice the amount or extent 9. in a pair —n. 10. person or thing exactly like, or mistakable for, another 11. quantity twice as much as another 12. sharp turn 13. running pace —pl. 14. game between 2 pairs of players —v. 15. make, become double 16. increase twofold 17. fold in two 18. get round, sail round (headland etc.) —vi. 19. turn sharply —'**doubly** adv. —**double agent** spy employed simultaneously by two opposing sides —**double-barrelled** or U.S. **-barreled** a. 1. (of gun) having two barrels 2. extremely forceful 3. UK (of surnames) having two hyphenated parts 4. serving two purposes; ambiguous —**double bass** largest and lowest-toned instrument in violin form —**double-breasted** a. (of garment) having overlapping fronts —**double-check** v. check again; verify —**double check** 1. second examination or verification 2. Chess simultaneous check from two pieces —**double chin** fold of fat under chin —**double cream** thick cream with high fat content —**double-cross** vt. cheat; betray —**double-crosser** n. —**double dagger** character (‡) used in printing to indicate cross-reference —**double-dealing** n. artifice, duplicity —**double-decker** n. 1. chiefly UK bus with two passenger decks 2. inf., chiefly US thing or structure having two decks, layers etc. —**double Dutch** inf. incomprehensible talk, gibberish —**double-edged** a. 1. acting in two ways 2. (of remark etc.) having two possible interpretations 3. (of knife etc.) having cutting edge on either side of blade —**double entry** book-keeping system in which transaction is entered as debit in one account and as credit in another —**double glazing** two panes of glass in window to insulate against cold, sound etc. —**double-jointed** a. having

unusually flexible joints permitting abnormal degree of motion —**double pneumonia** pneumonia affecting both lungs —**double-quick** a./adv. very fast —**double standard** set of principles that allows greater freedom to one person or group than another —**double take** delayed reaction to a remark, situation etc. —**double talk** 1. rapid speech with mixture of nonsense syllables and real words; gibberish 2. empty, deceptive or ambiguous talk —**double time** 1. doubled wage rate for working on public holidays etc. 2. Mus. two beats per bar 3. U.S. Army fast march; slow running pace, keeping in step

double entendre (uːn'tɑːndrə) word or phrase with two meanings, one usu. indelicate

doublet ('dʌblɪt) n. 1. close-fitting body garment formerly worn by men 2. one of two words from same root but differing in form and usu. in meaning, as warden and guardian 3. false gem of thin layer of gemstone fused on to base of glass etc.

doubloon (dʌ'bluːn) n. ancient Sp. gold coin

doubt (daʊt) vt. 1. hesitate to believe 2. call into question 3. suspect —vi. 4. be wavering or uncertain in belief or opinion —n. 5. uncertainty, wavering in belief 6. state of affairs giving cause for uncertainty —'**doubter** n. —'**doubtful** a. —'**doubtfully** adv. —'**doubtless** adv./a.

douche (duːʃ) n. 1. jet or spray of water applied to (part of) body —vt. 2. give douche to

dough (dəʊ) n. 1. flour or meal kneaded with water 2. sl. money —'**doughy** a. —'**doughnut** n. sweetened and fried ball or ring-shaped piece of dough

doughty ('daʊtɪ) a. valiant —'**doughtily** adv. —'**doughtiness** n. boldness

dour (dʊə) a. grim, stubborn, severe

douse or **dowse** (daʊs) vt. 1. thrust into water 2. extinguish (light)

dove (dʌv) n. bird of pigeon family —**dovecot** ('dʌvkɒt) or **dovecote** ('dʌvkəʊt) n. house for doves —**dovetail** n. 1. joint made with fan-shaped tenon —v. 2. fit closely, neatly, firmly together

dowager ('daʊədʒə) n. widow with title or property derived from deceased husband

dowdy ('daʊdɪ) a. 1. unattractively or shabbily dressed —n. 2. woman so dressed

dowel ('daʊəl) n. wooden, metal peg, esp. joining two adjacent parts

dower ('daʊə) n. 1. widow's share for life of husband's estate —vt. 2. endow —'**dowry** n. 1. property wife brings to husband at marriage 2. any endowment —**dower house** house for use of widow, oft. on her deceased husband's estate

down[1] (daʊn) adv. 1. to, in, or towards, lower position 2. below the horizon 3. (of payment) on the spot, immediate —prep. 4. from higher to lower part of 5. at lower part of 6. along —a. 7. depressed, miserable —vt. 8. knock, pull, push down 9.

inf. drink, *esp.* quickly —'**downward** *a./adv.* —'**downwards** *adv.* —'**downcast** *a.* **1.** dejected **2.** looking down —'**downfall** *n.* **1.** sudden loss of health, reputation *etc.* **2.** fall of rain, snow *etc.*, *esp.* sudden heavy one —'**downgrade** *vt.* **1.** reduce in importance or value, *esp.* to demote (person) to poorer job **2.** speak of disparagingly —*n.* **3.** *chiefly US* downward slope —**down'hearted** *a.* discouraged; dejected —'**down'hill** *a.* **1.** going or sloping down —*adv.* **2.** towards bottom of hill; downwards —*n.* **3.** downward slope of hill; descent **4.** skiing race downhill —**down payment** deposit paid on item purchased on hire-purchase *etc.* —'**down-pour** *n.* heavy fall of rain —'**downright** *a.* **1.** plain, straightforward —*adv.* **2.** quite, thoroughly —'**down'stage** *a./adv.* at, to front of stage —'**down'stairs** *adv.* **1.** down the stairs; to or on lower floor —*n.* **2.** lower or ground floor **3.** *UK inf.* servants of household collectively —'**down'stream** *adv./a.* in or towards lower part of stream; with current —**down time** time during which computer *etc.* is not working because incapable of production, as when under repair —**down-to-earth** *a.* sensible; practical; realistic —'**downtrodden** *a.* **1.** subjugated; oppressed **2.** trodden down —'**down'wind** *adv./a.* in same direction towards which wind is blowing; with wind from behind —**down and out** finished, defeated —**down under** *inf.* Australia and New Zealand —**go downhill** *inf.* decline; deteriorate —**have a down on** *inf.* have grudge against —**on the downgrade** waning in importance *etc.*

down² (daʊn) *n.* **1.** soft underfeathers, hair or fibre **2.** fluff —'**downy** *a.*

down³ (daʊn) *n. obs.* hill, *esp.* sand dune (*also* **downs**) —'**downland** *n.* open high land (*also* **downs**)

Downing Street ('daʊnɪŋ) **1.** street in London: official residences of prime minister of Great Britain and chancellor of the exchequer **2.** *inf.* prime minister; British Government

Down's syndrome (daʊnz) *Pathol.* chromosomal abnormality resulting in flat face and nose, short stubby fingers, vertical fold of skin at inner edge of eye and mental retardation

dowry ('daʊərɪ) *n. see* DOWER

dowse (daʊz) *vi.* use divining rod —'**dowser** *n.* water diviner

doxology (dɒk'sɒlədʒɪ) *n.* short hymn of praise to God

doyen ('dɔɪən) *n.* senior member of a body or profession (**doyenne** (dɔɪ'ɛn) *fem.*)

doyley ('dɔɪlɪ) *n. see* DOILY

doz. dozen

doze (dəʊz) *vi.* **1.** sleep drowsily, be half-asleep —*n.* **2.** nap —'**dozy** *a.* **1.** drowsy **2.** *inf.* stupid

dozen ('dʌz°n) *n.* (set of) twelve

D.Phil., D.Ph., *or* **DPh** Doctor of Philosophy (*also* **Ph.D., PhD**)

DPP *or* **D.P.P.** Director of Public Prosecutions

Dr. **1.** Doctor **2.** Drive

drab¹ (dræb) *a.* **1.** dull, monotonous **2.** of a dingy brown colour —*n.* **3.** mud colour

drab² (dræb) *obs. n.* **1.** slatternly woman **2.** whore —*vi.* **3.** consort with prostitutes (**-bb-**)

drachm (dræm) *n.* unit of weight, 1/8 of fluid ounce, 1/16 of avoirdupois ounce (*also* **fluid dram**)

drachma ('drækmə) *n.* monetary unit of Greece (*pl.* **-s, -mae** (-miː))

Draconian (dreɪ'kəʊnɪən) *or* **Draconic** (dreɪ'kɒnɪk) *a.* (*oft.* **d-**) **1.** like the laws of Draco **2.** very harsh, cruel

draft¹ (drɑːft) *n.* **1.** design, sketch **2.** rough copy of document **3.** order for money **4.** detachment of men, *esp.* troops, reinforcements —*vt.* **5.** make sketch, plan or rough design of **6.** make rough copy of (writing *etc.*) —*v.* **7.** detach (military personnel) from one unit to another

draft² (drɑːft) *vt. US* select for compulsory military service

drag (dræg) *vt.* **1.** pull along with difficulty or friction **2.** trail on ground **3.** sweep with net or grapnels **4.** protract —*vi.* **5.** lag, trail **6.** (*oft.* **with** *on* or *out*) be tediously protracted (**-gg-**) —*n.* **7.** check on progress **8.** checked motion **9.** iron shoe to check wheel **10.** type of carriage **11.** lure for hounds to hunt **12.** kind of harrow **13.** sledge, net, grapnel, rake **14.** *inf.* tedious person or thing **15.** *sl.* women's clothes worn by man (*esp.* **in** in **drag**) —'**dragnet** *n.* **1.** fishing net to be dragged along sea floor **2.** comprehensive search, *esp.* by police for criminal *etc.* —'**dragster** *n.* car designed, modified for drag racing —**drag race** motor car race where cars are timed over measured distance

dragée (dræ'ʒeɪ) *n.* sugar-coated sweet, nut or pill

draggle ('dræg°l) *v.* **1.** make or become wet or dirty by trailing on ground —*vi.* **2.** lag; dawdle

dragoman ('drægəʊmən) *n.* in some Middle Eastern countries, *esp.* formerly, professional interpreter or guide (*pl.* **-s, -men**)

dragon ('drægən) *n.* **1.** mythical fire-breathing monster, like winged crocodile **2.** type of large lizard —'**dragonfly** *n.* long-bodied insect with gauzy wings

dragoon (drə'guːn) *n.* **1.** cavalryman of certain regiments —*vt.* **2.** oppress **3.** coerce

drain (dreɪn) *vt.* **1.** draw off (liquid) by pipes, ditches *etc.* **2.** dry **3.** drink to dregs **4.** empty, exhaust —*vi.* **5.** flow off or away **6.** become rid of liquid —*n.* **7.** channel for removing liquid **8.** sewer **9.** depletion, strain —'**drainage** *n.* —**draining board** sloping grooved surface at side of sink for draining washed dishes *etc.* (*also* '**drainer**) —'**drainpipe** *n.* pipe for carrying off rainwater *etc.* —**drainpipe trousers** *or*

'drainpipes *pl.n.* trousers with narrow legs

drake (dreɪk) *n.* male duck

dram (dræm) *n.* 1. small draught of strong drink 2. drachm

drama ('drɑːmə) *n.* 1. stage play 2. art or literature of plays 3. playlike series of events —**dra'matic** *a.* 1. pert. to drama 2. suitable for stage representation 3. with force and vividness of drama 4. striking 5. tense 6. exciting —**'dramatist** *n.* writer of plays —**dramati'zation** or -**i'sation** *n.* —**'dramatize** or -**ise** *vt.* adapt novel for acting

dramatis personae ('drɑːmətɪs pɔː'səʊnaɪ) characters in play

dramaturgy ('dræmətɜːdʒɪ) *n.* technique of writing and producing plays —**drama-'turgic(al)** *a.* —**'dramaturgist** or '**dramaturge** *n.* playwright

drank (dræŋk) *pt. of* DRINK

drape (dreɪp) *vt.* 1. cover, adorn with cloth 2. arrange in graceful folds —**'draper** *n.* dealer in cloth, linen *etc.* —**'drapery** *n.*

drastic ('dræstɪk) *a.* 1. extreme, forceful 2. severe

draught or *U.S.* **draft** (drɑːft) *n.* 1. current of air between apertures in room *etc.* 2. act or action of drawing 3. dose of medicine 4. act of drinking 5. quantity drunk at once 6. inhaling 7. depth of ship in water 8. the drawing in of, or fish taken in, net 9. (*now usu.* draft) preliminary plan or layout for work to be executed —*pl.* 10. game played on chessboard with flat round 'men' —*a.* 11. for drawing 12. drawn —*vt.* 13. *see* DRAFT² —**'draughty** or *U.S.* '**drafty** *a.* full of air currents —**'draughtboard** *n.* board with 64 squares of alternating colours, for playing draughts or chess on —**draught horse** horse for vehicles carrying heavy loads —**'draughtsman** or *U.S.* '**draftsman** *n.* one who makes drawings, plans *etc.* —**'draughtsmanship** or *U.S.* '**draftsmanship** *n.*

draw (drɔː) *vt.* 1. pull, pull along, haul 2. inhale 3. entice, attract 4. delineate, portray with pencil *etc.* 5. frame, compose, draft, write 6. bring (upon, out *etc.*) 7. get by lot 8. (of ship) require (depth of water) 9. take from (well, barrel *etc.*) 10. receive (money) 11. bend (bow) —*vi.* 12. pull, shrink 13. make, admit current of air 14. make pictures with pencil *etc.* 15. finish game with equal points, goals *etc.*, tie 16. write orders for money 17. come, approach (near) (**drew** *pt.*, **drawn** *pp.*) —*n.* 18. act of drawing 19. casting of lots 20. game or contest ending in a tie —**'drawable** *a.* —**drawer** ('drɔːə) *n.* 1. one who or that which draws 2. (drɔː) sliding box in table or chest —*pl.* (drɔːz) 3. two-legged undergarment —**'drawing** *n.* 1. art of depicting in line 2. sketch so done 3. action of verb —**'drawback** *n.* 1. anything that takes away from satisfaction 2. snag —**'drawbridge** *n.* hinged bridge that can

be raised or lowered —**drawing pin** UK short tack with broad head, for fastening papers to drawing board *etc.* —**drawing room** living room, sitting room —**'drawstring** *n.* cord *etc.* run through hem around opening, so that when it is pulled tighter, the opening closes —**draw near** approach —**draw out** lengthen —**draw up** 1. arrange 2. stop

drawl (drɔːl) *v.* 1. speak or utter (words) slowly —*n.* 2. such speech —**'drawlingly** *adv.*

drawn (drɔːn) *v.* 1. *pp. of* DRAW —*a.* 2. haggard, tired or tense in appearance

dray (dreɪ) *n.* low cart without sides for heavy loads

dread (drɛd) *vt.* 1. fear greatly —*n.* 2. awe, terror —*a.* 3. feared, awful —**'dreadful** *a.* disagreeable, shocking, bad —**'dreadnought** *n.* large battleship mounting heavy guns

dream (driːm) *n.* 1. vision during sleep 2. fancy 3. reverie 4. aspiration 5. very pleasant idea, person, thing —*vi.* 6. have dreams —*vt.* 7. see, imagine in dreams 8. think of as possible (**dreamt** (drɛmt) or **dreamed** *pt./pp.*) —**'dreamer** *n.* —**'dreamless** *a.* —**'dreamy** *a.* 1. given to daydreams, unpractical, vague 2. *inf.* wonderful

dreary ('drɪərɪ) *a.* dismal, dull —**drear** *a.* *Lit.* dreary —**'drearily** *adv.* —**'dreariness** *n.* gloom

dredge¹ (drɛdʒ) *v.* 1. bring up (mud *etc.*) from sea bottom 2. deepen (channel) by dredge —*vt.* 3. search for, produce (obscure, remote, unlikely material) —*n.* 4. form of scoop or grab —**'dredger** *n.* ship for dredging

dredge² (drɛdʒ) *vt.* sprinkle with flour *etc.* —**'dredger** *n.*

dregs (drɛgz) *pl.n.* 1. sediment, grounds 2. worthless part

drench (drɛntʃ) *vt.* 1. wet thoroughly, soak 2. make (animal) take dose of medicine —*n.* 3. soaking 4. dose for animal

Dresden ('drɛzdᵊn) *n.* 1. city in East Germany 2. delicate and decorative porcelain ware made near Dresden (*also* **Dresden china**) —*a.* 3. of Dresden china

dress (drɛs) *vt.* 1. clothe 2. array for show 3. trim, smooth, prepare surface of 4. prepare (food) for table 5. put dressing on (wound) 6. align (troops) —*vi.* 7. put on one's clothes 8. form in proper line —*n.* 9. one-piece garment for woman 10. clothing 11. clothing for ceremonial evening wear —**'dresser** *n.* 1. one who dresses, *esp.* actors or actresses 2. surgeon's assistant 3. kitchen sideboard —**'dressing** *n.* 1. something applied to something else, as sauce to food, ointment to wound, manure to land *etc.* 2. *inf.* scolding, as in *dressing down* —**'dressy** *a.* 1. stylish 2. fond of dress —**dress circle** first gallery in theatre —**dress coat** cutaway coat worn by men as evening dress —**dressing gown** loose robe worn while one is resting or before dressing —**dressing room** room, *esp.* one in theatre for changing costumes and make-up —**dressing station** *Mil.* first-aid post close to combat area —**dressing table** —'**dressmaker** *n.* —**dress rehearsal** 1. last rehearsal of play *etc.* using costumes *etc.* as for first night 2. any full-scale practice —**dress suit** man's evening suit, *esp.* tails

dressage ('drɛsɑːʒ) *n.* method of training horse in special manoeuvres to show obedience

drew (druː) *pt. of* DRAW

drey *or* **dray** (dreɪ) *n.* squirrel's nest

dribble ('drɪb'l) *v.* 1. (allow to) flow in drops, trickle 2. *Football* work (ball) forward with short kicks —*vi.* 3. run at the mouth —*n.* 4. trickle, drop —'**driblet** *n.* small portion or instalment

dried (draɪd) *pt./pp. of* DRY

drier ('draɪə) *comp. of* DRY

driest ('draɪɪst) *sup. of* DRY

drift (drɪft) *vi.* 1. be carried as by current of air, water 2. move aimlessly or passively —*n.* 3. process of being driven by current 4. slow current or course 5. deviation from course 6. tendency 7. meaning 8. wind-heaped mass of snow, sand *etc.* 9. material driven or carried by water —'**drifter** *n.* 1. one who, that which drifts 2. *inf.* aimless person with no fixed job *etc.* —'**driftwood** *n.* wood washed ashore by sea

drill¹ (drɪl) *n.* 1. boring tool or machine 2. exercise of soldiers or others in handling of arms and manoeuvres 3. routine teaching —*v.* 4. bore, pierce (hole) in (material) (as if) with drill 5. exercise in military and other routine —*vi.* 6. practise routine

drill² (drɪl) *n.* 1. machine for sowing seed 2. small furrow for seed 3. row of plants —*v.* 4. sow (seed) in drills or furrows

drill³ (drɪl) *n.* coarsely woven twilled fabric

drill⁴ (drɪl) *n.* W Afr. monkey

drink (drɪŋk) *v.* 1. swallow (liquid) 2. take (intoxicating liquor), *esp.* to excess —*vt.* 3. absorb (**drank** *pt.*, **drunk** *pp.*) —*n.* 4. liquid for drinking 5. portion of this 6. act of drinking 7. intoxicating liquor or excessive consumption of it —'**drinkable** *a.* —'**drinker** *n.* —**drink to** *or* **drink the health of** express good wishes *etc.* by drinking a toast to

drip (drɪp) *v.* 1. fall or let fall in drops (-**pp**-) —*n.* 2. act of dripping 3. drop 4. *Med.* intravenous administration of solution 5. *inf.* dull, insipid person —'**dripping** *n.* 1. melted fat that drips from roasting meat —*a.* 2. very wet —**drip-dry** *a.* (of fabric) drying free of creases if hung up while wet —'**dripstone** *n.* projection over window or door to stop dripping of water

drive (draɪv) *vt.* 1. urge in some direction 2. make move and steer (vehicle, animal *etc.*) 3. urge, impel 4. fix by blows, as nail 5. chase 6. convey in vehicle 7. hit ball with force as in golf, tennis —*vi.* 8. keep

machine, animal going, steer it 9. be conveyed in vehicle 10. rush, dash, drift fast (**drove**, **driven** ('drɪv'n), '**driving**) —*n.* 11. act, action of driving 12. journey in vehicle 13. private road leading to house 14. capacity for getting things done 15. united effort, campaign 16. energy 17. forceful stroke in cricket, golf, tennis —'**driver** *n.* 1. one that drives 2. *Golf* club used for tee shots —**drive-in** *a.* 1. denoting public facility or service designed for use by patrons in cars —*n.* 2. *chiefly US* cinema designed to be used in such a manner —'**driveway** *n.* path for vehicles, oft. connecting house with public road —**driving belt** belt that communicates motion to machinery —**driving licence** official document authorizing person to drive motor vehicle

drivel ('drɪv'l) *vi.* 1. run at mouth or nose 2. talk nonsense (-**ll**-) —*n.* 3. silly or senseless talk —'**driveller** *n.*

drizzle ('drɪz'l) *vi.* 1. rain in fine drops —*n.* 2. fine, light rain

drogue (drəʊg) *n.* 1. any funnel-like device, *esp.* of canvas, used as sea anchor 2. small parachute 3. wind indicator 4. windsock towed behind target aircraft 5. funnel-shaped device on end of refuelling hose of tanker aircraft to receive probe of aircraft being refuelled

droll (drəʊl) *a.* funny, odd, comical —'**drollery** *n.* —'**drolly** *adv.*

dromedary ('drʌmədərɪ) *n.* one-humped camel bred *esp.* for racing

drone (drəʊn) *n.* 1. male of honey bee 2. lazy idler 3. deep humming 4. bass pipe of bagpipe 5. its note —*vi.* 6. hum 7. talk in monotonous tone

drongo ('drɒŋgəʊ) *n.* black tropical bird

drool (druːl) *vi.* slaver, drivel

droop (druːp) *vi.* 1. hang down 2. wilt, flag —*vt.* 3. let hang down —*n.* 4. drooping condition —'**droopy** *a.*

drop (drɒp) *n.* 1. globule of liquid 2. very small quantity 3. fall, descent 4. distance through which thing falls 5. thing that falls, as gallows platform —*vt.* 6. let fall 7. let fall in drops 8. utter casually 9. set down, unload 10. discontinue —*vi.* 11. fall 12. fall in drops 13. lapse 14. come or go casually (-**pp**-) —'**droplet** *n.* —'**dropper** *n.* 1. small tube having rubber bulb at one end for dispensing drops of liquid 2. person or thing that drops —'**droppings** *pl.n.* dung of rabbits, sheep, birds *etc.* —'**dropout** *n.* person who fails to complete course of study or one who rejects conventional society —**drop scone** scone made by dropping spoonful of batter on hot griddle

dropsy ('drɒpsɪ) *n.* disease causing watery fluid to collect in the body —'**dropsical** *a.*

droshky ('drɒʃkɪ) *or* **drosky** ('drɒskɪ) *n.* open four-wheeled carriage, formerly used in Russia

dross (drɒs) *n.* 1. scum of molten metal 2. impurity, refuse 3. anything of little or no value

drought 149 duct

drought (draut) *n.* long spell of dry weather

drove¹ (drəuv) *pt. of* DRIVE

drove² (drəuv) *n.* 1. herd, flock, crowd, *esp.* in motion —*v.* 2. drive (cattle *etc.*) *esp.* a long distance —**'drover** *n.* driver of cattle

drown (draun) *v.* 1. die or kill by immersion in liquid —*vt.* 2. get rid of as by submerging in liquid 3. (*sometimes* with out) make (sound) inaudible by louder sound

drowsy ('drauzı) *a.* 1. half asleep 2. lulling 3. dull —**drowse** *v.* —**'drowsily** *adv.* —**'drowsiness** *n.*

drub (drʌb) *vt.* thrash, beat (**-bb-**) —**'drubbing** *n.* beating

drudge (drʌdʒ) *vi.* 1. work at menial or distasteful tasks, slave —*n.* 2. one who drudges, hack —**'drudgery** *n.*

drug (drʌg) *n.* 1. medical substance 2. narcotic 3. commodity which is unsaleable because of overproduction —*vt.* 4. mix drugs with 5. administer drug to, *esp.* one inducing unconsciousness (**-gg-**) —**drug addict** person abnormally dependent on narcotic drugs —**'drugstore** *n.* US pharmacy where wide variety of goods is available

drugget ('drʌgıt) *n.* coarse woollen fabric, *esp.* used for carpeting

druid ('druːıd) *n.* (*sometimes* D-) 1. member of ancient order of Celtic priests 2. Eisteddfod official —**dru'idic(al)** *a.* —**'druidism** *n.*

drum (drʌm) *n.* 1. percussion instrument of skin stretched over round hollow frame, played by beating with sticks 2. various things shaped like drum 3. *see* eardrum *at* EAR¹ —*vi.* 4. play drum —*v.* 5. tap, thump continuously (**-mm-**) —**'drummer** *n.* one who plays drum —**'drumfire** *n.* heavy continuous rapid artillery fire —**drumhead court-martial** summary court-martial held at war front —**drum major** leader of military band —**'drumstick** *n.* 1. stick for beating drum 2. lower joint of cooked fowl's leg —**drum out** expel (from club *etc.*) —**drum up** obtain (support *etc.*) by solicitation or canvassing

drunk (drʌŋk) *a.* 1. overcome by strong drink 2. *fig.* overwhelmed by strong emotion —*v.* 3. *pp. of* DRINK —**'drunkard** *n.* one given to excessive drinking —**'drunken** *a.* 1. intoxicated 2. habitually drunk 3. caused by, showing intoxication —**'drunkenness** *n.*

drupe (druːp) *n.* fruit that has fleshy or fibrous part around stone that encloses seed, as peach *etc.*

dry (draı) *a.* 1. without moisture 2. rainless 3. not yielding milk or other liquid 4. cold, unfriendly 5. caustically witty 6. having prohibition of alcoholic drink 7. uninteresting 8. needing effort to study 9. lacking sweetness (as wines) —*vt.* 10. remove water, moisture —*vi.* 11. become dry 12. evaporate (**dried**, **'drying**) —**'dryer** *or* **'drier** *n.* 1. person or thing that dries 2.

apparatus for removing moisture —**'dryly** *or* **'drily** *adv.* —**'dryness** *n.* —**dry battery** electric battery without liquid —**dry cell** primary cell in which electrolyte is in form of paste or is treated in some way to prevent spilling —**dry-clean** *vt.* clean (clothes) with solvent other than water —**dry-cleaner** *n.* —**dry dock** dock that can be pumped dry for work on ship's bottom —**dry farming** methods of producing crops in areas of low rainfall —**dry fly** *Angling* artificial fly designed to be floated on surface of water —**dry ice** solid carbon dioxide —**dry measure** unit or system of units for measuring dry goods, such as grains *etc.* —**dry point** 1. needle for engraving without acid 2. engraving so made —**dry rot** fungoid decay in wood —**dry run** practice, rehearsal in simulated conditions —**dry-stone** *a.* (of wall) made without mortar —**dry out** 1. make or become dry 2. *inf.* (cause to) undergo treatment for alcoholism or drug addiction

dryad ('draıəd, -æd) *n.* wood nymph

dryly ('draılı) *adv. see* DRY

D.Sc. Doctor of Science

D.S.C. Distinguished Service Cross

D.S.M. *Mil.* Distinguished Service Medal

D.S.O. Distinguished Service Order

D.T.'s *inf.* delirium tremens

dual ('djuːəl) *a.* 1. twofold 2. of two, double, forming pair —**'dualism** *n.* recognition of two independent powers or principles, *eg* good and evil, mind and matter —**du'ality** *n.* —**dual carriageway** UK road on which traffic travelling in opposite directions is separated by central strip of turf *etc.*

dub (dʌb) *vt.* 1. confer knighthood on 2. give title to 3. provide (film) with soundtrack not in original language 4. smear with grease, dubbin (**-bb-**) —**'dubbin** *or* **'dubbing** *n.* grease for making leather supple

dubious ('djuːbıəs) *a.* 1. causing doubt, not clear or decided 2. of suspect character —**du'biety** *n.* uncertainty, doubt

ducal ('djuːkʔl) *a.* of duke or duchy

ducat ('dʌkət) *n.* former gold coin of Italy *etc.*

duchess ('dʌtʃıs) *n.* duke's wife or widow

duchy ('dʌtʃı) *n.* territory of duke, dukedom

duck¹ (dʌk) *n.* 1. common swimming bird (**drake** *masc.*) 2. *Cricket* batsman's score of nothing 3. UK *inf.* dear, darling (as term of address) (*also* **ducks**) —*v.* 4. plunge (someone) under water 5. bob down —**'duckling** *n.* —**'ducky** *or* **'duckie** *inf. n.* 1. UK darling, dear —*a.* 2. delightful; fine —**duck-billed platypus** *see* PLATYPUS —**'duckweed** *n.* plant that floats on ponds *etc.*

duck² (dʌk) *n.* 1. strong linen or cotton fabric —*pl.* 2. trousers made of this fabric

duck³ (dʌk) *n.* amphibious vehicle used in World War II

duct (dʌkt) *n.* channel, tube —**'ductile** *a.* 1.

capable of being drawn into wire **2.** flexible and tough **3.** docile —**ductility** (dʌk'tɪlɪtɪ) *n.* —'**ductless** *a.* (of glands) secreting directly certain substances essential to health

dud (dʌd) *n.* **1.** futile, worthless person or thing **2.** shell that fails to explode —*a.* **3.** worthless

dude (dju:d) *n.* tourist, *esp.* in ranch district —**dude ranch** ranch serving as guesthouse and showplace

dudgeon ('dʌdʒən) *n.* anger, indignation, resentment

duds (dʌdz) *pl.n. inf.* clothes

due (dju:) *a.* **1.** owing **2.** proper to be given, inflicted *etc.* **3.** adequate, fitting **4.** under engagement to arrive, be present **5.** timed (for) —*adv.* **6.** (with points of compass) exactly —*n.* **7.** person's right **8.** (*usu. pl.*) charge, fee *etc.* —'**duly** *adv.* **1.** properly **2.** fitly **3.** rightly **4.** punctually —**due to 1.** attributable to **2.** caused by

duel ('dju:əl) *n.* **1.** arranged fight with deadly weapons, between two persons **2.** keen two-sided contest —*vi.* **3.** fight in duel (-**ll**-) —'**duellist** *n.*

duenna (dju:'enə) *n.* **1.** Sp. lady-in-waiting **2.** elderly governess, guardian, chaperon

duet (dju:'et) *n.* piece of music for two performers —**du'ettist** *n.*

duff¹ (dʌf) *n.* kind of boiled pudding

duff² (dʌf) *vt.* **1.** manipulate, alter (article) so as to make it look like new **2.** mishit, *esp.* at golf —*a.* **3.** *sl.* bad, useless

duffel *or* **duffle** ('dʌfᵊl) *n.* **1.** coarse woollen cloth **2.** coat made of this —**duffel bag** large cylindrical cloth bag for clothing *etc.*

duffer ('dʌfə) *n.* stupid inefficient person

dug¹ (dʌg) *pt./pp. of* DIG

dug² (dʌg) *n.* udder, teat of animal

dugong ('du:gɒŋ) *n.* whalelike mammal of tropical seas

dugout ('dʌgaʊt) *n.* **1.** covered excavation to provide shelter for troops *etc.* **2.** canoe of hollowed-out tree **3.** *Sport* covered enclosure where players wait when not on the field

duiker *or* **duyker** ('daɪkə) *n.* small Afr. antelope (*also* '**duikerbok**)

duke (dju:k) *n.* **1.** peer of rank next below prince **2.** sovereign of small state called duchy ('**duchess** *fem.*) —'**dukedom** *n.*

dukes (dju:ks) *pl.n. sl.* fists

dulcet ('dʌlsɪt) *a.* (of sounds) sweet, melodious

dulcimer ('dʌlsɪmə) *n.* percussion instrument consisting of set of strings stretched over sounding board, played with two hammers

dull (dʌl) *a.* **1.** stupid **2.** insensible **3.** sluggish **4.** tedious **5.** lacking liveliness or variety **6.** gloomy, overcast —*v.* **7.** make or become dull —'**dullard** *n.* —'**dully** *adv.*

duly ('dju:lɪ) *adv. see* DUE

dumb (dʌm) *a.* **1.** incapable of speech **2.** silent **3.** *inf.* stupid —'**dumbly** *adv.* —'**dumbness** *n.* —'**dumbbell** *n.* weight for

exercises —**dumb'found** *vt.* confound into silence —**dumb show** acting without words —'**dumbwaiter** *n.* **1.** UK stand placed near dining table to hold food; revolving circular tray placed on table to hold food **2.** lift for carrying rubbish *etc.* between floors

dumdum ('dʌmdʌm) *n.* soft-nosed expanding bullet

dummy ('dʌmɪ) *n.* **1.** tailor's or dressmaker's model **2.** imitation object **3.** *Cards* hand exposed on table and played by partner **4.** *Sports* feigned move or pass **5.** baby's dummy teat **6.** prototype of book, indicating appearance of finished product; designer's layout of page —*a.* **7.** sham, bogus —**dummy run** experimental run; practice; rehearsal

dump (dʌmp) *vt.* **1.** throw down in mass **2.** deposit **3.** unload **4.** send (low-priced goods) for sale abroad —*n.* **5.** rubbish heap **6.** *inf.* dirty, unpleasant place **7.** temporary depot of stores or munitions —*pl.* **8.** low spirits, dejection

dumpling ('dʌmplɪŋ) *n.* small round pudding of dough, oft. fruity —'**dumpy** *a.* short, stout —**dumpy level** surveyor's levelling instrument

dun¹ (dʌn) *vt.* **1.** persistently press (debtor) for payment of debts (-**nn**-) —*n.* **2.** one who duns

dun² (dʌn) *a.* **1.** of dull greyish-brown —*n.* **2.** this colour **3.** horse of this colour

dunce (dʌns) *n.* slow learner, stupid pupil

dunderhead ('dʌndəhed) *n.* blockhead —'**dunderheaded** *a.*

dune (dju:n) *n.* sandhill on coast or desert

dung (dʌŋ) *n.* **1.** excrement of animals **2.** manure —*vt.* **3.** manure (ground) —'**dunghill** *n.* **1.** heap of dung **2.** foul place, condition or person

dungaree (dʌŋgə'ri:) *n.* **1.** coarse cotton fabric —*pl.* **2.** overalls made of this material

dungeon ('dʌndʒən) *n.* **1.** underground cell or vault for prisoners, donjon **2.** formerly, tower or keep of castle

dunk (dʌŋk) *vt.* **1.** dip (bread *etc.*) in liquid before eating it **2.** submerge

dunlin ('dʌnlɪn) *n.* small sandpiper

dunnage ('dʌnɪdʒ) *n.* material for packing cargo

dunnock ('dʌnək) *n.* hedge sparrow

duo ('dju:əʊ) *n.* pair of performers (*pl.* **-s, dui** ('dju:i:))

duodecimo (dju:əʊ'desɪməʊ) *n.* **1.** size of book in which each sheet is folded into 12 leaves **2.** book of this size (*pl.* **-s**) —*a.* **3.** of this size —**duo'decimal** *a.* **1.** computed by twelves **2.** twelfth

duodenum (dju:əʊ'di:nəm) *n.* upper part of small intestine —**duo'denal** *a.*

duologue *or* U.S. (*sometimes*) **duolog** ('dju:əlɒg) *n.* **1.** part or all of play in which speaking roles are limited to two actors **2.** *rare* dialogue

dupe (dju:p) *n.* **1.** victim of delusion or

sharp practice —*vt.* **2.** deceive for advantage, impose upon

duple ('dju:p⁰l) *a.* **1.** *rare* double **2.** *Mus.* (of time or music) having two beats in bar

duplex ('dju:plɛks) *a.* twofold

duplicate ('dju:plɪkeɪt) *vt.* **1.** make exact copy of **2.** double —*a.* ('dju:plɪkɪt) **3.** double **4.** exactly the same as something else —*n.* ('dju:plɪkɪt) **5.** exact copy —**dupli'cation** *n.* —**'duplicator** *n.* machine for making copies —**du'plicity** *n.* deceitfulness, double-dealing, bad faith

Dur. Durham

durable ('djuərəb⁰l) *a.* lasting, resisting wear —**dura'bility** *n.* —**'durably** *adv.* —**durable goods** goods that require infrequent replacement (*also* **'durables**)

dura mater ('djuərə 'meɪtə) outermost and toughest of three membranes covering brain and spinal cord (*also* **'dura**)

durance ('djuərəns) *n. obs.* imprisonment

duration (dju'reɪʃən) *n.* length of time something lasts

durbar ('dɜ:bɑ:, dɜ:'bɑ:) *n.* formerly, court of native ruler or governor in India or levée at such court

duress (dju'rɛs, djuə-) *n.* compulsion by use of force or threats

during ('djuərɪŋ) *prep.* throughout, in the time of, in the course of

durst (dɜ:st) *obs. pt. of* DARE

dusk (dʌsk) *n.* **1.** darker stage of twilight **2.** partial darkness —**'duskily** *adv.* —**'dusky** *a.* **1.** dark **2.** dark-coloured

dust (dʌst) *n.* **1.** fine particles, powder of earth or other matter, lying on surface or blown along by wind **2.** ashes of the dead —*vt.* **3.** sprinkle with powder **4.** rid of dust —**'duster** *n.* cloth for removing dust —**'dusty** *a.* covered with dust —**'dustbin** *n.* large, *usu.* cylindrical container for household rubbish —**'dustbowl** *n.* area in which dust storms have carried away the top soil —**'dustcart** *n.* road vehicle for collecting refuse —**dust cover 1.** large cloth used to protect furniture from dust (*also* **'dustsheet**) **2.** removable paper cover to protect bound book (*also* **dust jacket**) **3.** Perspex cover for gramophone turntable —**'dustman** *n.* UK man whose job is to collect domestic refuse —**'dustpan** *n.* short-handled hooded shovel into which dust is swept —**dust-up** *n. inf.* fight; argument —**dust up** attack

Dutch (dʌtʃ) *a.* pert. to the Netherlands, its inhabitants or its language —**Dutch barn** UK farm building consisting of steel frame and curved roof —**Dutch cap** contraceptive diaphragm (*also* **cap**) —**Dutch courage** drunken bravado —**Dutch elm disease** fungal disease of elm trees characterized by withering of foliage and stems —**Dutch oven 1.** iron or earthenware container with cover, used for stews *etc.* **2.** metal box, open in front, for cooking in front of open fire —**Dutch treat** meal *etc.* where each person pays his own share —**Dutch uncle** *inf.* person who criticizes or reproves frankly and severely

duty ('dju:tɪ) *n.* **1.** moral or legal obligation **2.** that which is due **3.** tax on goods **4.** military service **5.** one's proper employment —**'duteous** *a.* —**'dutiable** *a.* liable to customs duty —**'dutiful** *a.* —**duty-bound** *a.* morally obliged —**duty-free** *a./adv.* with exemption from customs or excise duties

duvet ('du:veɪ) *n.* quilt filled with down or artificial fibre (*also* **continental quilt**)

dux (dʌks) *n.* head pupil of school or class, leader

D.V. *Deo volente*

dwarf (dwɔ:f) *n.* **1.** very undersized person **2.** mythological, small, manlike creature (*pl.* **-s, dwarves**) —*a.* **3.** unusually small, stunted —*vt.* **4.** make seem small by contrast **5.** make stunted —**'dwarfish** *a.*

dwell (dwɛl) *vi.* **1.** live, make one's abode (in) **2.** fix one's attention, write or speak at length (on) (**dwelt** *pt./pp.*) —**'dweller** *n.* —**'dwelling** *n.* house

dwindle ('dwɪnd⁰l) *vi.* grow less, waste away, decline

Dy *Chem.* dysprosium

Dyak *or* **Dayak** ('daɪæk) *n.* member of Malaysian people of Borneo (*pl.* **-s, -ak**)

dye (daɪ) *vt.* **1.** impregnate (cloth *etc.*) with colouring matter **2.** colour thus (**dyed, 'dyeing**) —*n.* **3.** colouring matter in solution or which may be dissolved for dyeing **4.** tinge, colour —**'dyeing** *n.* process or industry of colouring yarns *etc.* —**'dyer** *n.* —**dyed-in-the-wool** *a.* **1.** extreme or unchanging in opinion *etc.* **2.** (of fabric) made of dyed yarn

dying ('daɪɪŋ) *v.* **1.** *pr.p.* of DIE¹ —*a.* **2.** relating to or occurring at moment of death

dyke *or esp. U.S.* **dike** (daɪk) *n.* **1.** embankment to prevent flooding **2.** ditch

dynamics (daɪ'næmɪks) *pl.n.* **1.** (*with sing. v.*) branch of physics dealing with force as producing or affecting motion **2.** physical forces —**dy'namic** *a.* **1.** of, relating to motive force, force in operation **2.** energetic and forceful —**dy'namical** *a.* —**dy'namically** *adv.* —**'dynamism** *n.* **1.** *Philos.* theory that attempts to explain phenomena in terms of immanent force or energy **2.** forcefulness of energetic personality

dynamite ('daɪnəmaɪt) *n.* **1.** high explosive mixture —*vt.* **2.** blow up with this —**'dynamiter** *n.*

dynamo ('daɪnəməʊ) *n.* **1.** machine to convert mechanical into electrical energy, generator of electricity (*pl.* **-s**) **2.** *inf.* energetic, hard-working person —**dyna'mometer** *n.* instrument to measure energy expended

dynasty ('dɪnəstɪ) *n.* line, family, succession of hereditary rulers —**'dynast** *n.* —**dy'nastic** *a.* of dynasty

dyne (daɪn) *n.* cgs unit of force

dys- (*comb. form*) **1.** diseased; abnormal **2.** difficult; painful **3.** bad

dysentery ('dɪsᵊntrɪ) *n.* infection of intestine causing severe diarrhoea

dysfunction (dɪs'fʌŋkʃən) *n.* abnormal, impaired functioning, *esp.* of bodily organ

dyslexia (dɪs'lɛksɪə) *n.* impaired ability to read, caused by brain disorder —**dys'lexic** *a.*

dysmenorrhoea *or esp. U.S.* **dysmenor-** **rhea** (dɪsmɛnə'rɪə) *n.* abnormally difficult or painful menstruation

dyspepsia (dɪs'pɛpsɪə) *n.* indigestion —**dys'peptic** *a./n.*

dysprosium (dɪs'prəʊsɪəm) *n.* metallic element of lanthanide series

dystrophy ('dɪstrəfɪ) *n.* wasting of body tissues, *esp.* muscles

dz. dozen

E

e *or* **E** (i:) *n.* **1.** fifth letter of English alphabet **2.** any of several speech sounds represented by this letter, as in *he, bet* (*pl.* **e's, E's** *or* **Es**)

e 1. *Maths.* transcendental number used as base of natural logarithms **2.** electron

E 1. *Mus.* third note of scale of C major; major or minor key having this note as its tonic **2.** *Phys.* energy; electromotive force **3.** East **4.** Eastern **5.** English **6.** Egypt(ian)

E. engineer(ing)

E. Earl

ea. each

each (i:tʃ) *a./pron.* every (one) taken separately

eager ('i:gə) *a.* **1.** having a strong wish (for something) **2.** keen, impatient —**'eagerly** *adv.* —**'eagerness** *n.* —**eager beaver** *inf.* person who displays conspicuous diligence

eagle ('i:g'l) *n.* **1.** large bird with keen sight which preys on small birds and animals **2.** *Golf* score of two strokes under par for a hole —**'eaglet** *n.* young eagle —**eagle-eyed** *a.* having keen eyesight

ear¹ (ɪə) *n.* **1.** organ of hearing, *esp.* external part of it **2.** sense of hearing **3.** sensitiveness to sounds **4.** attention —**'earache** *n.* acute pain in ear —**'eardrum** *n. see* **tympanic membrane** *at* TYMPANUM —**'earmark** *vt.* **1.** assign, reserve for definite purpose **2.** make identification mark on ear of (sheep *etc.*) —*n.* **3.** this mark —**'earmuffs** *pl.n.* pads of fur *etc.* for keeping ears warm —**'earphone** *n.* receiver for radio *etc.* held to or put in ear —**ear-piercing** *a.* deafening —**'earring** *n.* ornament for lobe of ear —**'earshot** *n.* hearing distance —**ear trumpet** trumpet-shaped instrument formerly used as hearing aid —**'earwig** *n.* small insect with pincerlike tail

ear² (ɪə) *n.* spike, head of corn

earl (ɜːl) *n.* Brit. nobleman ranking next below marquis —**'earldom** *n.* his domain, title

early ('ɜːlɪ) *a./adv.* **1.** before expected or usual time **2.** in first part, near or nearer beginning of some portion of time —**early bird** *inf.* one who arrives or rises early

earn (ɜːn) *vt.* **1.** obtain by work or merit **2.** gain —**'earnings** *pl.n.*

earnest¹ ('ɜːnɪst) *a.* **1.** serious, ardent **2.** sincere —**'earnestly** *adv.* —**in earnest** serious, determined

earnest² ('ɜːnɪst) *n.* **1.** money paid over in token to bind bargain, pledge **2.** foretaste

earth (ɜːθ) *n.* **1.** planet or world we live on **2.** ground, dry land **3.** mould, soil, mineral **4.** fox's hole **5.** wire connecting electrical apparatus to earth —*vt.* **6.** cover with earth **7.** connect electrically with earth —**'earthen** *a.* made of clay or earth —**'earthly** *a.* possible, feasible —**'earthy** *a.* **1.** of earth **2.** uninhibited **3.** vulgar —**earth closet** lavatory in which earth is used to cover excreta —**'earthenware** *n.* (vessels of) baked clay —**'earthnut** *n.* **1.** plant of Europe and Asia, having edible dark brown tubers **2.** any of various plants having edible root, tuber or underground pod, such as peanut —**'earthquake** *n.* convulsion of earth's surface —**earth science** any of various sciences, such as geology, concerned with structure *etc.* of the earth —**'earthwork** *n.* bank of earth in fortification —**'earthworm** *n.* —**come back** *or* **down to earth** return to reality from fantasy

ease (i:z) *n.* **1.** comfort **2.** freedom from constraint, annoyance, awkwardness, pain or trouble **3.** idleness —*v.* **4.** make or become less burdensome **5.** give bodily or mental ease to **6.** (cause to) move carefully or gradually —*vt.* **7.** slacken **8.** relieve of pain —**'easement** *n. Law* right of way *etc.* over another's land —**'easily** *adv.* —**'easiness** *n.* **1.** quality or condition of being easy to accomplish *etc.* **2.** ease or relaxation of manner —**'easy** *a.* **1.** not difficult **2.** free from pain, care, constraint or anxiety **3.** compliant **4.** characterized by low demand **5.** fitting loosely **6.** *inf.* having no preference for any particular course of action —**easy chair** comfortable upholstered armchair —**easy-going** *a.* **1.** not fussy **2.** indolent

easel ('i:z'l) *n.* frame to support artist's canvas *etc.*

east (i:st) *n.* **1.** part of horizon where sun rises **2.** eastern lands, orient —*a.* **3.** on, in or near east **4.** coming from east —*adv.* **5.** from or to east —**'easterly** *a./adv.* from or to east —**'eastern** *a.* of, dwelling in, east —**'easterner** *n.* —**'easting** *n.* distance eastwards of a point from a given meridian —**'eastward** *a./n.* —**'eastwards** *or* **'eastward** *adv.* —**Eastern Church 1.** any of Christian Churches of former Byzantine Empire **2.** any Church owing allegiance to Orthodox Church —**eastern hemisphere** (*oft.* E- H-) **1.** that half of the globe containing Europe, Asia, Afr. and Aust. **2.** lands in this, *esp.* Asia

Easter ('i:stə) *n.* movable festival of the Resurrection of Christ —**Easter egg** chocolate egg or hen's egg with its shell painted, given as gift at Easter —**'Eastertide** *n.* Easter season

easy ('i:zɪ) *a. see* EASE

eat (i:t) *v.* **1.** chew and swallow **2.** gnaw —*vt.* **3.** consume, destroy **4.** wear away (**ate** *pt.,* **'eaten** *pp.*) —**'eatable** *a.* —**'eating** *n.* **1.** food, *esp.* in relation to quality or taste —*a.* **2.** suitable for eating —**eats** *pl.n. sl.* articles of food —**eat one's words** take back something said

eau de Cologne (ɔʊ də kəˈləʊn) *Fr.* light perfume

eau de vie (ɔʊ də ˈviː) brandy

eaves (iːvz) *pl.n.* overhanging edges of roof —ˈ**eavesdrop** *vi.* listen secretly —ˈ**eavesdropper** *n.* —ˈ**eavesdropping** *n.*

ebb (ɛb) *vi.* 1. flow back 2. decay —*n.* 3. flowing back of tide 4. decline, decay —**ebb tide**

ebony (ˈɛbənɪ) *n.* 1. hard black wood —*a.* 2. made of, black as ebony —ˈ**ebonite** *n.* vulcanite —ˈ**ebonize** or **-ise** *vt.* make colour of ebony

ebullient (ɪˈbʌljənt, ɪˈbʊl-) *a.* 1. exuberant 2. boiling —e'**bullience** *n.* —**ebullition** (ɛbəˈlɪʃən) *n.* 1. boiling 2. effervescence 3. outburst

EC East Central

eccentric (ɪkˈsɛntrɪk) *a.* 1. odd, unconventional 2. irregular 3. not placed, or not having axis placed, centrally 4. not circular (in orbit) —*n.* 5. odd, unconventional person 6. mechanical contrivance to change circular into to-and-fro movement —ec'**centrically** *adv.* —**eccen'tricity** *n.*

Eccles. *or* **Eccl.** *Bible* Ecclesiastes

ecclesiastic (ɪkliːzɪˈæstɪk) *n.* 1. clergyman —*a.* 2. of, relating to the Christian Church —**ecclesi'astical** *a.* —**ecclesi'ology** *n.* science of church building and decoration

eccrinology (ɛkrɪˈnɒlədʒɪ) *n.* branch of physiology that relates to bodily secretions

E.C.G. 1. electrocardiogram 2. electrocardiograph

echelon (ˈɛʃəlɒn) *n.* 1. level, grade, of responsibility or command 2. formation of troops, planes *etc.* in parallel divisions, each slightly to left or right of the one in front

echidna (ɪˈkɪdnə) *n.* spine-covered mammal of Aust. and New Guinea (*pl.* -s, -nae (-niː)) *also* **spiny anteater**)

echinoderm (ɪˈkaɪnəʊdɜːm) *n.* marine invertebrate characterized by tube feet, calcite body-covering, and five-part symmetrical body

echo (ˈɛkəʊ) *n.* 1. repetition of sounds by reflection 2. close imitation (*pl.* -es) —*vt.* 3. repeat as echo, send back the sound of 4. imitate closely —*vi.* 5. resound 6. be repeated (ˈechoed, ˈechoing) —**echoic** (ɛˈkəʊɪk) *a.* 1. characteristic of or resembling echo 2. onomatopoeic —**echo chamber** room with walls that reflect sound, used to make acoustic measurements and in recording (*also* **reverberation chamber**) —**echolo'cation** *n.* determination of position of object by measuring reflected sound —**echo sounder** —**echo sounding** system of ascertaining depth of water by measuring time required to receive echo from sea bottom or submerged object

éclair (eɪˈklɛə, ɪˈklɛə) *n.* finger-shaped, iced cake filled with cream

éclat (eɪˈklɑː) *n.* 1. splendour 2. renown 3. acclamation

eclectic (ɪˈklɛktɪk, ɛˈklɛk-) *a.* 1. selecting 2. borrowing one's philosophy from various sources 3. catholic in views or taste —*n.* 4. person who favours eclectic approach —e'**clecticism** *n.*

eclipse (ɪˈklɪps) *n.* 1. blotting out of sun, moon *etc.* by another heavenly body 2. obscurity —*vt.* 3. obscure, hide 4. surpass —e'**cliptic** *a.* 1. of eclipse —*n.* 2. apparent path of sun

eclogue (ˈɛklɒg) *n.* short poem, *esp.* pastoral dialogue

eco- (*comb. form*) ecology; ecological, as in *ecosphere*

ecology (ɪˈkɒlədʒɪ) *n.* science of plants and animals in relation to their environment —eco'**logical** *a.* —e'**cologist** *n.* specialist in or advocate of ecological studies

econ. 1. economical 2. economics 3. economy

economy (ɪˈkɒnəmɪ) *n.* 1. careful management of resources to avoid unnecessary expenditure or waste 2. sparing, restrained or efficient use 3. system of interrelationship of money, industry and employment in a country —eco'**nomic** *a.* 1. of economics 2. profitable 3. economical —eco'**nomical** *a.* 1. not wasteful of money, time, effort *etc.* 2. frugal —eco'**nomically** *adv.* —eco'**nomics** *pl.n.* 1. (*with sing.* v.) study of economies of nations 2. (*with pl.* v.) financial aspects —e'**conomist** *n.* specialist in economics —e'**conomize** or **-ise** *v.* limit or reduce (expense, waste *etc.*)

ecosystem (ˈiːkəʊsɪstəm, ˈɛkəʊ-) *n. Ecol.* system involving interactions between community and its non-living environment

ecru (ˈɛkruː, ˈeɪkruː) *n./a.* (of) colour of unbleached linen

ecstasy (ˈɛkstəsɪ) *n.* 1. exalted state of feeling, mystic trance 2. frenzy —ec'**static** *a.* —ec'**statically** *adv.*

E.C.T. electroconvulsive therapy

ecto- (*comb. form*) outer, outside, as in *ectoplasm*

-ectomy (*comb. form*) surgical excision of part, as in *appendectomy*

ectoplasm (ˈɛktəʊplæzəm) *n.* in spiritualism, supposedly a semiluminous plastic substance which exudes from medium's body

ecumenical, oecumenical (iːkjuˈmɛnɪkˌl, ɛk-) *or* **ecumenic, oecumenic** *a.* of the Christian Church throughout the world, *esp.* with regard to its unity —ecu'**menicalism**, ecu'**menicism** *or* ecu'**menism** *n.*

eczema (ˈɛksɪmə) *n.* skin disease

ed. 1. edited 2. edition (*pl.* eds.) 3. editor (*pl.* eds.) 4. education

-ed¹ (*comb. form*) forming past tense of most English verbs

-ed² (*comb. form*) forming past participle of most English verbs

-ed³ (*comb. form*) possessing or having characteristics of, as in *salaried, redblooded*

Edam ('i:dæm) *n.* round yellow cheese with red outside covering

E.D.C. European Defence Community

Edda ('ɛdə) *n.* collection of old Icelandic myths

eddy ('ɛdɪ) *n.* 1. small whirl in water, smoke *etc.* —*vi.* 2. move in whirls ('**eddied**, '**eddying**)

edelweiss ('eɪd'lvaɪs) *n.* white-flowered alpine plant

Eden ('i:d'n) *n.* 1. garden in which Adam and Eve were placed at the Creation 2. any delightful, happy place or state

edentate (i:'dɛnteɪt) *n.* 1. any mammal of the order *Edentata,* which have few or no teeth, such as anteater —*a.* 2. of the order *Edentata*

edge (ɛdʒ) *n.* 1. border, boundary 2. cutting side of blade 3. sharpness 4. advantage 5. acrimony, bitterness —*vt.* 6. give edge or border to 7. move gradually —*vi.* 8. advance sideways or gradually —'**edge-ways** *or* '**edgewise** *adv.* —'**edging** *n.* —'**edgy** *a.* irritable, sharp or keen in temper —**on edge** 1. nervy, irritable 2. excited

edible ('ɛdɪb'l) *a.* eatable, fit for eating —**edi'bility** *n.*

edict ('i:dɪkt) *n.* order proclaimed by authority, decree

edifice ('ɛdɪfɪs) *n.* building, *esp.* big one

edify ('ɛdɪfaɪ) *vt.* improve morally, instruct (-**fied**, -**fying**) —**edifi'cation** *n.* improvement of mind or morals

edit ('ɛdɪt) *vt.* prepare (book, film, tape *etc.*) for publication or broadcast —**e'dition** *n.* 1. form in which something is published 2. number of copies of new publication printed at one time —'**editor** *n.* —**edi'torial** *a.* 1. of editor —*n.* 2. article stating opinion of newspaper *etc.*

edit. 1. edited 2. edition 3. editor

E.D.P. electronic data processing

educate ('ɛdjʊkeɪt) *vt.* 1. provide schooling for 2. teach 3. train mentally and morally 4. train 5. improve, develop —**educa'bility** *or* **educa'bility** *n.* —'**educable** *or* '**educatable** *a.* capable of being trained or educated —'**educated** *a.* 1. having education, *esp.* a good one 2. cultivated —**edu'cation** *n.* —**edu'cational** *a.* —**edu-'cationalist** *or* **edu'cationist** *n.* one versed in theory and practice of education —**edu'cationally** *adv.* —'**educative** *a.* —'**educator** *n.* —**educated guess** guess based on experience or information

educe (ɪ'dju:s) *vt.* 1. bring out, elicit, develop 2. infer, deduce —**e'ducible** *a.* —**eduction** (ɪ'dʌkʃən) *n.*

Edwardian (ɛd'wɔːdɪən) *a.* of reign of Edward VII, king of Great Britain and Ireland —**Ed'wardianism** *n.*

-ee (*comb. form*) 1. recipient of action, as in *assignee* 2. person in specified state or condition, as in *absentee*

EEC European Economic Community

EEG electroencephalogram

eel (i:l) *n.* snakelike fish

e'en (i:n) *adv./n. Poet., obs.* even, evening

-eer *or* **-ier** (*comb. form*) 1. person who is concerned with something specified, as in *auctioneer, engineer, profiteer* 2. be concerned with something specified, as in *electioneer*

e'er (ɛə) *adv. Poet., obs.* ever

eerie ('ɪərɪ) *a.* 1. weird, uncanny 2. causing superstitious fear

efface (ɪ'feɪs) *vt.* wipe or rub out —**ef'faceable** *a.* —**ef'facement** *n.*

effect (ɪ'fɛkt) *n.* 1. result, consequence 2. efficacy 3. impression 4. condition of being operative —*pl.* 5. property 6. lighting, sounds *etc.* to accompany film, broadcast *etc.* —*vt.* 7. bring about, accomplish —**ef'fective** *a.* 1. having power to produce effects 2. in effect, operative 3. serviceable 4. powerful 5. striking —**ef'fectively** *adv.* —**ef'fectual** *a.* 1. successful in producing desired effect 2. satisfactory 3. efficacious —**ef'fectually** *adv.* —**ef'fectuate** *vt.*

effeminate (ɪ'fɛmɪnɪt) *a.* (of man or boy) womanish, unmanly —**ef'feminacy** *n.*

efferent ('ɛfərənt) *a.* conveying outward or away

effervesce (ɛfə'vɛs) *vi.* 1. give off bubbles 2. be in high spirits —**effer'vescence** *n.* —**effer'vescent** *a.*

effete (ɪ'fi:t) *a.* worn-out, feeble

efficacious (ɛfɪ'keɪʃəs) *a.* 1. producing or sure to produce desired effect 2. effective 3. powerful 4. adequate —'**efficacy** *n.* 1. potency 2. force 3. efficiency

efficient (ɪ'fɪʃənt) *a.* capable, competent, producing effect —**ef'ficiency** *n.* —**ef'ficiently** *adv.*

effigy ('ɛfɪdʒɪ) *n.* image, likeness

effloresce (ɛflɔː'rɛs) *vi.* burst into flower —**efflo'rescence** *n.* —**efflo'rescent** *a.*

effluent ('ɛflʊənt) *n.* 1. liquid discharged as waste 2. stream flowing from larger stream, lake *etc.* —*a.* 3. flowing out —'**effluence** *or* **efflux** ('ɛflʌks) *n.* —**ef'fluvium** *n.* something flowing out invisibly, *esp.* affecting lungs or sense of smell (*pl.* **-ia** (-ɪə))

effort ('ɛfət) *n.* 1. exertion 2. endeavour, attempt 3. something achieved —'**effortless** *a.*

effrontery (ɪ'frʌntərɪ) *n.* brazen impudence

effulgent (ɪ'fʌldʒənt) *a.* radiant, shining brightly —**ef'fulgence** *n.*

effusion (ɪ'fju:ʒən) *n.* (unrestrained) outpouring —**ef'fuse** *v.* pour out, shed —**ef'fusive** *a.* gushing, demonstrative —**ef'fusively** *adv.* —**ef'fusiveness** *n.*

eft (ɛft) *n. dial., obs.* newt

EFT electronic funds transfer

EFTA ('ɛftə) European Free Trade Association

e.g. exempli gratia (*Lat.,* for example)

egalitarian (ɪgælɪ'tɛərɪən) *a.* 1. believing that all people should be equal 2. promoting this ideal —*n.* 3. adherent of egalitarian principles —**egali'tarianism** *n.*

egg[1] (ɛg) *n.* oval or round object produced

by female of bird *etc.*, from which young emerge, *esp.* egg of domestic hen, used as food **—egg cup** or **—egghead** *n. inf.* intellectual **—egg'nog** or **egg-noggin** *n.* drink made of eggs, milk, sugar, spice, and brandy, rum *etc.* (*also* **egg flip**) **—'egg-plant** *n. esp.* US aubergine **—'eggshell** *n.* 1. outer layer of bird's egg **—***a.* 2. (of paint) having matt finish

egg² (ɛg) *vt.* **—egg on** 1. encourage, urge 2. incite

eglantine ('ɛglantaɪn) *n.* sweet brier

ego ('iːɡəʊ, 'ɛɡəʊ) *n.* 1. the self 2. the conscious thinking subject 3. one's image of oneself 4. morale **—'egoism** *n.* 1. systematic selfishness 2. theory that bases morality on self-interest **—'egoist** *n.* **—ego'istic(al)** *a.* **—'egotism** *n.* 1. selfishness 2. self-conceit **—'egotist** *n.* **—ego'tistic(al)** *a.* **—ego'centric** *a.* 1. self-centred 2. egoistic 3. centred in the ego **—ego trip** *inf.* something undertaken to boost person's own image or appraisal of himself

egregious (ɪ'griːdʒəs, -dʒɪəs) *a.* 1. outstandingly bad, blatant 2. (*esp.* of mistake *etc.*) absurdly obvious

egress ('iːgrɛs) *n.* 1. way out 2. departure

egret ('iːgrɪt) *n.* 1. lesser white heron 2. down of dandelion

Egyptian (ɪ'dʒɪpʃən) *a.* 1. of Egypt **—***n.* 2. native or inhabitant of Egypt **—Egyp'tolo-gist** *n.* **—Egyp'tology** *n.* study of archaeology and language of ancient Egypt

eh (eɪ) *interj.* exclamation expressing surprise or inquiry, or to seek confirmation of statement or question

EHF extremely high frequency

eider or **eider duck** ('aɪdə) *n.* Arctic duck **—'eiderdown** *n.* 1. its breast feathers 2. quilt (stuffed with feathers)

eight (eɪt) *n.* 1. cardinal number one above seven 2. eight-oared boat 3. its crew **—***a.* 4. amounting to eight **—'eigh'teen** *a./n.* eight more than ten **—'eigh'teenth** *a./n.* **—'eigh'teenthly** *adv.* **—eighth** *a./n.* ordinal number of eight **—'eighthly** *adv.* **—'eightieth** *a./n.* **—'eighty** *a./n.* ten times eight **—eightsome reel** Scottish dance for eight people **—figure of eight** 1. a skating figure 2. any figure shaped as 8

einsteinium (aɪn'staɪnɪəm) *n.* radioactive element artificially produced from plutonium

Eire ('ɛərə) *n.* the Republic of Ireland

E.I.S. Educational Institute of Scotland

eisteddfod (aɪ'stɛdfəd) *n.* 1. annual congress of Welsh bards 2. local gathering for competition in music and other performing arts

either ('aɪðə, 'iːðə) *a./pron.* 1. one or the other 2. one of two 3. each **—***adv./conj.* 4. bringing in first of alternatives or strengthening an added negation

ejaculate (ɪ'dʒækjʊleɪt) *v.* 1. eject (semen) 2. exclaim, utter suddenly **—ejacu'lation** *n.* **—e'jaculatory** *a.*

eject (ɪ'dʒɛkt) *vt.* 1. throw out 2. expel,

drive out **—e'jection** *n.* **—e'jectment** *n.* **—e'jector** *n.* **—ejection seat** or **ejector seat** seat, *esp.* in military aircraft, that ejects occupant in emergency

eke out (iːk) 1. make (supply) last, *esp.* by frugal use 2. supply deficiencies of 3. make with difficulty (a living *etc.*)

elaborate (ɪ'læbərɪt) *a.* 1. carefully worked out, detailed 2. complicated **—***vi.* (ɪ'læbəreɪt) 3. expand **—***vt.* (ɪ'læbəreɪt) 4. work out in detail 5. take pains with **—elabo'ration** *n.*

élan (eɪ'lɑːn) *n.* 1. dash 2. ardour 3. impetuosity

eland ('iːlənd) *n.* largest S Afr. antelope, resembling elk

elapse (ɪ'læps) *vi.* (of time) pass

elastic (ɪ'læstɪk) *a.* 1. resuming normal shape after distortion, springy 2. flexible **—***n.* 3. tape, fabric, containing interwoven strands of flexible rubber **—e'lasticated** *a.* **—elas'ticity** *n.* **—elastic band** *see* **rubber band** *at* RUBBER¹

elation (ɪ'leɪʃən) *n.* 1. high spirits 2. pride **—e'late** *vt.* (*usu. passive*) 1. raise the spirits of 2. make happy 3. exhilarate

elbow ('ɛlbəʊ) *n.* 1. joint between fore and upper parts of arm (*esp.* outer part of it) 2. part of sleeve covering this **—***vt.* 3. shove, strike with elbow **—elbow grease** hard work **—'elbowroom** *n.* sufficient room to move or function

elder¹ ('ɛldə) *a. comp. of* OLD 1. older, senior **—***n.* 2. person of greater age 3. old person 4. official of certain churches **—'elderly** *a.* growing old **—'eldest** *a. sup. of* OLD oldest

elder² ('ɛldə) *n.* white-flowered tree **—'elderberry** *n.* 1. fruit of elder 2. elder (tree)

El Dorado (ɛl dɒ'rɑːdəʊ) fictitious country rich in gold

eldritch or **eldrich** ('ɛldrɪtʃ) *a.* 1. hideous 2. weird 3. uncanny 4. haggish

elect (ɪ'lɛkt) *vt.* 1. choose by vote 2. choose **—***a.* 3. appointed but not yet in office 4. chosen, select, choice **—e'lection** *n.* choosing, *esp.* by voting **—election'eer** *vi.* busy oneself in political elections **—e'lective** *a.* appointed, filled or chosen by election **—e'lector** *n.* one who elects **—e'lectoral** *a.* **—e'lectorate** *n.* body of electors **—e'lectorship** *n.*

elect. or **elec.** 1. electric(al) 2. electricity

electricity (ɪlɛk'trɪsɪtɪ, iːlɛk-) *n.* 1. form of energy associated with stationary or moving electrons or other charged particles 2. electric current or charge 3. science dealing with electricity **—e'lectric** *a.* 1. derived from, produced by, producing, transmitting or powered by electricity 2. excited, emotionally charged **—e'lectrical** *a.* **—elec'trician** *n.* one trained in installation *etc.* of electrical devices **—electrifi'cation** *n.* **—e'lectrify** *vt.* **—electric blanket** blanket containing electric heating element **—electric chair** US chair in which criminals sentenced to death are electrocuted —**electric eel** eel-like freshwater fish of N South Amer., having electric organs in body —**electric eye** *see* PHOTOCELL —**electric fire** appliance that supplies heat by means of electrically operated metal coil —**electric organ** *Mus.* organ in which sound is produced by electric devices instead of wind —**electric shock** effect of an electric current passing through body

electro- *or sometimes before vowel* **electr-** (*comb. form*) by, caused by electricity, as in *electrotherapy*. Such words are not given here where the meaning may easily be inferred from the simple word

electrocardiograph (ɪlɛktrəʊˈkɑːdɪəʊgrɑːf, -græf) *n.* instrument for recording electrical activity of heart —**electro'cardiogram** *n.* tracing produced by this instrument

electroconvulsive therapy (ɪlɛktrəʊkənˈvʌlsɪv) *see* **shock therapy** *at* SHOCK¹

electrocute (ɪˈlɛktrəkjuːt) *vt.* execute, kill by electricity —**electro'cution** *n.*

electrode (ɪˈlɛktrəʊd) *n.* conductor by which electric current enters or leaves battery, vacuum tube *etc.*

electrodynamics (ɪlɛktrəʊdaɪˈnæmɪks) *pl.n.* (*with sing. v.*) dynamics of electricity

electroencephalograph (ɪlɛktrəʊɛnˈsɛfələgrɑːf, -græf) *n.* instrument for recording electrical activity of brain —**electroen'cephalogram** *n.* tracing produced by this

electrolyse *or U.S.* **-yze** (ɪˈlɛktrəʊlaɪz) *vt.* decompose by electricity —**elec'trolysis** *n.*

electrolyte (ɪˈlɛktrəʊlaɪt) *n.* solution, molten substance that conducts electricity

electromagnet (ɪlɛktrəʊˈmægnɪt) *n.* magnet containing coil of wire through which electric current is passed —**electromag'netic** *a.* —**electro'magnetism** *n.* 1. magnetism produced by electric current 2. branch of physics concerned with interaction of electric and magnetic fields

electromotive (ɪlɛktrəʊˈməʊtɪv) *a.* of, concerned with or producing electric current —**electromotive force** *Phys.* 1. source of energy that can cause current to flow in electrical circuit 2. rate at which energy is drawn from this source

electron (ɪˈlɛktrɒn) *n.* one of fundamental particles of matter identified with unit of charge of negative electricity and essential component of the atom —**elec'tronic** *a.* 1. of electrons or electronics 2. using devices, such as semiconductors, transistors or valves, dependent on action of electrons —**elec'tronics** *pl.n.* 1. (*with sing. v.*) technology concerned with development of electronic devices and circuits 2. science of behaviour and control of electrons —**electronic brain** *inf.* electronic computer —**electronic data processing** data processing largely performed by electronic equipment —**electronic music**

music consisting of sounds produced by electric currents prerecorded on magnetic tape —**electronic organ** *Mus.* keyboard instrument in which sounds are produced by electronic or electrical means —**electron microscope** microscope that uses electrons and electron lenses to produce magnified image —**electron tube** electrical device, such as valve, in which flow of electrons between electrodes takes place —**electron volt** unit of energy used in nuclear physics

electroplate (ɪˈlɛktrəʊpleɪt) *vt.* 1. coat with silver *etc.* by electrolysis —*n.* 2. articles electroplated

electroscope (ɪˈlɛktrəʊskəʊp) *n.* instrument to show presence or kind of electricity

electroshock therapy (ɪˈlɛktrəʊʃɒk) *see* **shock therapy** *at* SHOCK¹

electrostatics (ɪlɛktrəʊˈstætɪks) *n.* branch of physics concerned with static electricity —**electro'static** *a.*

electrotype (ɪˈlɛktrəʊtaɪp) *n.* 1. art of producing copies of type *etc.* by electric deposition of copper upon mould 2. copy so produced

electrum (ɪˈlɛktrəm) *n.* alloy of gold and silver used in jewellery *etc.*

eleemosynary (ɛliːˈmɒsɪnərɪ) *a.* 1. charitable 2. dependent on charity

elegant (ˈɛlɪgənt) *a.* 1. graceful, tasteful 2. refined —**'elegance** *n.*

elegy (ˈɛlɪdʒɪ) *n.* lament for the dead in poem or song —**elegiac** (ɛlɪˈdʒaɪək) *a.* 1. suited to elegies 2. plaintive —**elegiacs** (ɛlɪˈdʒaɪəks) *pl.n.* elegiac verses

element (ˈɛlɪmənt) *n.* 1. substance which cannot be separated into other substances by ordinary chemical techniques 2. component part 3. small amount, trace 4. heating wire in electric kettle, stove *etc.* 5. proper abode or sphere 6. situation in which person is happiest or most effective (*esp. in* **in** *or* **out of one's element**) —*pl.* 7. powers of atmosphere 8. rudiments, first principles —**ele'mental** *a.* 1. fundamental 2. of powers of nature —**ele'mentary** *a.* rudimentary, simple —**elementary particle** any of several entities, such as electrons *etc.*, that are less complex than atoms —**elementary school** *UK former name for* primary school

elephant (ˈɛlɪfənt) *n.* huge four-footed, thick-skinned animal with ivory tusks and long trunk —**elephan'tiasis** *n.* disease with hardening of skin and enlargement of legs *etc.* —**ele'phantine** *a.* unwieldy, clumsy, heavily big

elevate (ˈɛlɪveɪt) *vt.* raise, lift up, exalt —**ele'vation** *n.* 1. raising 2. height, *esp.* above sea level 3. angle above horizon, as of gun 4. drawing of one side of building *etc.* —**'elevator** *n.* US lift

eleven (ɪˈlɛvən) *n.* 1. number next above 10 2. team of 11 persons —*a.* 3. amounting to eleven —**e'levenfold** *a./adv.* —**e'levenses** *pl.n. inf.* light mid-morning snack —**e'lev-**

enth *a.* ordinal number of eleven —**eleven-plus** *n. esp.* formerly, examination taken by children aged 11 or 12, that selects suitable candidates for grammar schools —**eleventh hour** latest possible time

elf (ɛlf) *n.* 1. fairy 2. woodland sprite (*pl.* **elves**) —**'elfin, 'elfish, 'elvish** *or* **'elflike** *a.* roguish, mischievous

elicit (ɪ'lɪsɪt) *vt.* 1. draw out, evoke 2. bring to light

elide (ɪ'laɪd) *v.* omit (a vowel or syllable) at beginning or end of word—**e'lision** *n.*

eligible ('ɛlɪdʒəb'l) *a.* 1. fit or qualified to be chosen 2. suitable, desirable —**eligi'bility** *n.*

eliminate (ɪ'lɪmɪneɪt) *vt.* remove, get rid of, set aside —**elimi'nation** *n.* —**e'liminator** *n.* one who, that which, eliminates

elision (ɪ'lɪʒən) *n. see* ELIDE

elite *or* **élite** (ɪ'liːt, eɪ-) *n.* 1. choice or select body 2. the pick or best part of society 3. typewriter typesize (12 letters to inch) —*a.* 4. of or suitable for an elite —**e'litism** *n.* 1. belief that society should be governed by an elite 2. pride in being one of an elite group

elixir (ɪ'lɪksə) *n.* 1. preparation sought by alchemists to change base metals into gold, or to prolong life 2. sovereign remedy

Elizabethan (ɪlɪzə'biːθən) *a.* 1. of reigns of Elizabeth I (queen of England, 1558-1603) or Elizabeth II (queen of Great Britain and N Ireland since 1952) 2. of style of architecture used in England during reign of Elizabeth I —*n.* 3. person who lived in England during reign of Elizabeth I

elk (ɛlk) *n.* large deer

ell (ɛl) *n.* obsolete unit of length, approximately 45 inches

ellipse (ɪ'lɪps) *n.* oval —**el'lipsoid** *n.* 1. geometric surface whose plane sections are ellipses or circles 2. solid having this shape —**ellip'soidal** *a.* —**el'liptical** *a.* 1. relating to or having the shape of an ellipse 2. relating to or resulting from ellipsis 3. (of speech *etc.*) very concise, obscure; circumlocutory (*also* **el'liptic**) —**el'liptically** *adv.*

ellipsis (ɪ'lɪpsɪs) *n. Gram.* omission of parts of word or sentence (*pl.* **ellipses** (ɪ'lɪpsiːz))

elm (ɛlm) *n.* 1. tree with serrated leaves 2. its wood

elocution (ɛlə'kjuːʃən) *n.* art of public speaking, voice management —**elo'cutionist** *n.* 1. teacher of this 2. specialist in verse speaking

elongate ('iːlɒŋgeɪt) *vt.* lengthen, extend, prolong —**elon'gation** *n.*

elope (ɪ'ləup) *vi.* run away from home with lover —**e'lopement** *n.*

eloquence ('ɛləkwəns) *n.* fluent, powerful use of language —**'eloquent** *a.* —**'eloquently** *adv.*

Elsan ('ɛlsæn) *n.* **R** type of portable chemical lavatory

else (ɛls) *adv.* 1. besides, instead 2. otherwise —**else'where** *adv.* in or to some other place

elucidate (ɪ'luːsɪdeɪt) *vt.* throw light upon, explain —**eluci'dation** *n.* —**e'lucidatory** *a.*

elude (ɪ'luːd) *vt.* 1. escape, slip away from, dodge 2. baffle —**e'lusion** *n.* 1. act of eluding 2. evasion —**e'lusive** *a.* difficult to catch hold of, deceptive —**e'lusively** *adv.* —**e'lusory** *a.*

elver ('ɛlvə) *n.* young eel

elves (ɛlvz) *n., pl. of* ELF

Elysium (ɪ'lɪzɪəm) *n.* 1. *Gr. myth.* dwelling place of blessed after death (*also* **Elysian fields**) 2. state or place of perfect bliss

em (ɛm) *n. Print.* the square of any size of type

em- (*comb. form*) *see* EN-

'em (əm) *pron. inf.* them

emaciate (ɪ'meɪsɪeɪt) *v.* make or become abnormally thin —**emaci'ation** *n.*

emanate ('ɛməneɪt) *vi.* issue, proceed, originate —**ema'nation** *n.* —**emanative** ('ɛmənətɪv) *a.*

emancipate (ɪ'mænsɪpeɪt) *vt.* set free —**emanci'pation** *n.* 1. act of setting free, *esp.* from social, legal restraint 2. state of being set free —**emanci'pationist** *n.* advocate of emancipation of slaves, women *etc.* —**e'mancipator** *n.* —**emancipatory** (ɪ'mænsɪpətərɪ, -trɪ) *a.*

emasculate (ɪ'mæskjuleɪt) *vt.* 1. castrate 2. enfeeble, weaken —**emascu'lation** *n.* —**e'masculative** *a.*

embalm (ɪm'bɑːm) *vt.* preserve (corpse) from decay by use of chemicals, herbs *etc.* —**em'balmment** *n.*

embankment (ɪm'bæŋkmənt) *n.* artificial mound carrying road, railway, or serving to dam water

embargo (ɛm'bɑːgəu) *n.* 1. order stopping movement of ships 2. suspension of commerce 3. ban (*pl.* **-es**) —*vt.* 4. put under embargo 5. requisition

embark (ɛm'bɑːk) *v.* 1. put, go, on board ship, aircraft *etc.* 2. (*with on or upon*) commence (new project, venture *etc.*) —**embar'kation** *n.*

embarrass (ɪm'bærəs) *vt.* 1. perplex, disconcert 2. abash 3. confuse 4. encumber 5. involve in financial difficulties —**em'barrassment** *n.*

embassy ('ɛmbəsɪ) *n.* 1. office, work or official residence of ambassador 2. deputation

embattle (ɪm'bæt'l) *vt.* 1. deploy (troops) for battle 2. fortify (position *etc.*)

embed *or* **imbed** (ɪm'bɛd) *vt.* fix fast in something solid

embellish (ɪm'bɛlɪʃ) *vt.* adorn, enrich —**em'bellishment** *n.*

ember ('ɛmbə) *n.* 1. glowing cinder —*pl.* 2. red-hot ashes

Ember days appointed by Church for fasting in each quarter

embezzle (ɪm'bɛz'l) *vt.* divert fraudulently, misappropriate (money in trust *etc.*) —**em'bezzlement** *n.* —**em'bezzler** *n.*

embitter (ım'bıtə) vt. make bitter —em-'**bitterment** n.

emblazon (ım'bleız'n) vt. adorn richly, esp. heraldically

emblem ('embləm) n. 1. symbol 2. badge, device —**emblem'atic** a. —**emblem'ati-cally** adv.

embody (ım'bɒdı) vt. 1. give body, concrete expression to 2. represent, include, be expression of (em'**bodied,** em'**bodying**) —em'**bodiment** n.

embolden (ım'bəuld'n) vt. make bold

embolism ('embəlızəm) n. Med. obstruction of artery by blood clot or air bubble

embolus ('embələs) n. material, such as blood clot, that impedes circulation (pl. **-li** (-laı))

emboss (ım'bɒs) vt. mould, stamp or carve in relief

embrace (ım'breıs) vt. 1. clasp in arms, hug 2. seize, avail oneself of, accept 3. comprise —n. 4. act of embracing

embrasure (ım'breıʒə) n. 1. opening in wall for cannon 2. bevelling of wall at sides of window

embrocation (embrəu'keıʃən) n. lotion for rubbing limbs etc. to relieve pain —'**embrocate** vt.

embroider (ım'brɔıdə) vt. 1. ornament with needlework 2. embellish, exaggerate (story) —em'**broidery** n.

embroil (ım'brɔıl) vt. 1. bring into confusion 2. involve in hostility —em-'**broilment** n.

embryo ('embrıəu) n. 1. unborn or undeveloped offspring, germ 2. undeveloped thing (pl. **-s**) —embry'**ologist** n. —embry'**ology** n. —embry'**onic** a.

embus (ım'bʌs) v. (esp. of troops) put into, mount bus (**-ss-**)

emend (ı'mend) vt. remove errors from, correct —emen'**dation** n. —'**emendator** n. —e'**mendatory** a.

emerald ('emərəld, 'emrəld) n. 1. bright green precious stone —a. 2. of the colour of emerald —**Emerald Isle** Poet. Ireland

emerge (ı'mɜːdʒ) vi. 1. come up, out 2. rise to notice 3. come into view 4. come out on inquiry —e'**mergence** n. —e'**mergent** a. —e'**mersion** n. 1. act or instance of emerging 2. Astron. reappearance of celestial body after eclipse or occultation

emergency (ı'mɜːdʒənsı) n. 1. sudden unforeseen thing or event needing prompt action 2. difficult situation 3. exigency, crisis

emeritus (ı'merıtəs) a. retired, honourably discharged but retaining one's title (eg professor) on honorary basis

emery ('emərı) n. hard mineral used for polishing —**emery board** nailfile of cardboard or wood coated with crushed emery —**emery paper** stiff paper coated with finely powdered emery

emetic (ı'metık) n./a. (medicine) causing vomiting

emf or **EMF** electromotive force

emigrate ('emıgreıt) vi. go and settle in another country —'**emigrant** n. —emi-'**gration** n. —'**emigratory** a.

émigré ('emıgreı) n. emigrant, esp. one forced to leave his country for political reasons

éminence grise (eminãs 'griːz) Fr. person who wields power and influence unofficially (pl. **éminences grises** (eminãs 'griːz))

eminent ('emınənt) a. distinguished, notable —'**eminence** n. 1. distinction 2. height 3. rank 4. fame 5. rising ground 6. (E-) title of cardinal —'**eminently** adv.

emir (ε'mıə) n. (in Islamic world) 1. independent ruler or chieftain 2. military commander or governor 3. male descendant of Mohammed —e'**mirate** n.

emissary ('emısərı, -ısrı) n. agent, representative (esp. of government) sent on mission

emit (ı'mıt) vt. give out, put forth (**-tt-**) —e'**mission** n. —e'**mitter** n.

Emmenthal ('eməntɑːl) or **Emmenthal-er** n. hard Swiss cheese with many holes

emollient (ı'mɒljənt) a. 1. softening, soothing —n. 2. ointment or other softening application

emolument (ı'mɒljumənt) n. salary, pay, profit from work

emotion (ı'məuʃən) n. mental agitation, excited state of feeling, as joy, fear etc. —e'**mote** vi. inf. display exaggerated emotion, as in acting —e'**moter** n. —e'**motional** a. 1. given to emotion 2. appealing to the emotions —e'**motive** a. tending to arouse emotion

Emp. 1. Emperor 2. Empire 3. Empress

empanel or **impanel** (ım'pæn'l) vt. Law 1. enter on list (names of persons to be summoned for jury service) 2. select (jury) from such list (**-ll-**) —em'**panelment** or im'**panelment** n.

empathy ('empəθı) n. power of understanding, imaginatively entering into, another's feelings —em'**pathic** or empa-'**thetic** a.

emperor ('empərə) n. ruler of an empire ('**empress** fem.) —**emperor penguin** Antarctic penguin, the largest known, reaching a height of 1.3 m (4 ft.)

emphasis ('emfəsıs) n. 1. importance attached 2. stress on words 3. vigour of speech, expression (pl. **-ses** (-siːz)) —'**emphasize** or **-ise** vt. —em'**phatic** a. 1. forceful, decided 2. stressed —em'**phatically** adv.

empire ('empaıə) n. large territory, esp. aggregate of states under supreme ruler, supreme control —**empire-builder** n. inf. person who seeks extra power, esp. by increasing his staff —**empire-building** n./a.

empirical (εm'pırık'l) a. relying on experiment or experience, not on theory —em'**piric** a. 1. empirical —n. 2. one who relies solely on experience and observation —em'**pirically** adv. —**empiricism** (εm'pırısızəm) n.

emplacement (ɪmˈpleɪsmənt) n. 1. putting in position 2. gun platform

emplane (ɪmˈpleɪn) v. board or put on board aeroplane

employ (ɪmˈplɔɪ) vt. 1. provide work for (a person) in return for money, hire 2. keep busy 3. use (**em'ployed, em'ploying**) —**em'ployee** n. —**em'ployer** n. —**em'ployment** n. 1. an employing, being employed 2. work, trade 3. occupation

emporium (ɛmˈpɔːrɪəm) n. 1. large general shop 2. centre of commerce (pl. **-s, -ria** (-rɪə))

empower (ɪmˈpaʊə) vt. 1. enable 2. authorize

empress (ˈɛmprɪs) n. see EMPEROR

empty (ˈɛmptɪ) a. 1. containing nothing 2. unoccupied 3. senseless 4. vain, foolish —v. 5. make, become devoid of content 6. discharge (contents) (into) (**'emptied, 'emptying**) —**'empties** pl.n. empty boxes, bottles etc. —**'emptiness** n. —**empty-handed** a. 1. carrying nothing in hands 2. having gained nothing —**empty-headed** a. lacking sense

empyrean (ɛmpaɪˈriːən) n. 1. obs. in ancient cosmology, highest part of the heavens 2. Poet. heavens; sky —a., also **empy'real** 3. of sky 4. heavenly, sublime

EMS European Monetary System

emu (ˈiːmjuː) n. large Aust. flightless bird like ostrich

emulate (ˈɛmjʊleɪt) vt. 1. strive to equal or excel 2. imitate —**emu'lation** n. 1. rivalry 2. competition —**'emulative** a. —**'emulator** n. —**'emulous** a. eager to equal or surpass another or his deeds

emulsion (ɪˈmʌlʃən) n. 1. light-sensitive coating of film 2. milky liquid with oily or resinous particles in suspension 3. paint etc. in this form —**e'mulsify** v. (**e'mulsified, e'mulsifying**) —**e'mulsive** a.

en (ɛn) n. Print. unit of measurement, half an em

en- or **em-** (comb. form) put in, into, on, as in enrage. Such words are not given here where the meaning may easily be inferred from the simple word

-en[1] (comb. form) cause to be; become; cause to have, as in blacken, heighten

-en[2] (comb. form) of; made of; resembling, as in ashen, wooden

enable (ɪnˈeɪb⁽ə⁾l) vt. make able, authorize, empower, supply with means (to do something) —**enabling act** legislative act conferring certain powers on person or organization

enact (ɪnˈækt) vt. 1. make law 2. represent or perform as in a play —**en'actment** n.

enamel (ɪˈnæməl) n. 1. glasslike coating applied to metal etc. to preserve surface 2. coating of teeth 3. any hard outer coating —vt. 4. decorate with enamel 5. ornament with glossy variegated colours, as if with enamel 6. portray in enamel (**-ll-**)

enamour or U.S. **enamor** (ɪnˈæmə) vt. 1. inspire with love 2. charm 3. bewitch

en bloc (ɑ̃ ˈblɔk) Fr. 1. in a lump or block 2. all together

enc. 1. enclosed 2. enclosure

encamp (ɪnˈkæmp) v. set up (in) camp —**en'campment** n. camp

encapsulate or **incapsulate** (ɪnˈkæpsjʊleɪt) vt. 1. enclose in capsule 2. put in concise or abridged form

encase or **incase** (ɪnˈkeɪs) vt. place or enclose as in case —**en'casement** or **in'casement** n.

encaustic (ɪnˈkɒstɪk) a. 1. with colours burnt in —n. 2. art of ornament by burnt-in colours

-ence or **-ency** (comb. form) action, state, condition, quality, as in benevolence, residence, patience, fluency, permanency

enceinte (ɒnˈsænt) a. pregnant

encephalitis (ɛnsɛfəˈlaɪtɪs) n. inflammation of brain —**encephalitic** (ɛnsɛfəˈlɪtɪk) a.

encephalo- or before vowel **encephal-** (comb. form) brain, as in encephalogram, encephalitis

encephalogram (ɛnˈsɛfələɡræm) n. x-ray photograph of brain

enchain (ɪnˈtʃeɪn) vt. 1. bind with chains 2. hold fast or captivate (attention etc.) —**en'chainment** n.

enchant (ɪnˈtʃɑːnt) vt. 1. bewitch 2. delight —**en'chanter** n. (**-tress** fem.) —**en'chantment** n.

enchilada (ɛntʃɪˈlɑːdə) n. Mexican dish of tortilla filled with meat, served with chilli sauce

encircle (ɪnˈsɜːk⁽ə⁾l) vt. 1. surround 2. enfold 3. go round so as to encompass —**en'circlement** n.

enclave (ˈɛnkleɪv) n. portion of territory entirely surrounded by foreign land

enclitic (ɪnˈklɪtɪk) a. 1. pronounced as part of another word —n. 2. enclitic word or form

enclose or **inclose** (ɪnˈkləʊz) vt. 1. shut in 2. surround 3. envelop 4. place in with something else (in letter etc.) —**en'closure** or **in'closure** n. —**enclosed order** Christian religious order whose members do not go into the outside world

encomium (ɛnˈkəʊmɪəm) n. 1. formal praise 2. eulogy —**en'comiast** n. one who composes encomiums —**encomi'astic** a. —**encomi'astically** adv.

encompass (ɪnˈkʌmpəs) vt. 1. surround, encircle 2. contain

encore (ˈɒŋkɔː) interj. 1. again, once more —n. 2. call for repetition of song etc. 3. the repetition —vt. 4. ask to repeat

encounter (ɪnˈkaʊntə) vt. 1. meet unexpectedly 2. meet in conflict 3. be faced with (difficulty) —n. 4. casual or unexpected meeting 5. hostile meeting; contest —**encounter group** group of people who meet to develop self-awareness and mutual understanding by openly expressing feelings etc.

encourage (ɪnˈkʌrɪdʒ) vt. 1. hearten,

animate, inspire with hope **2.** embolden —**en'couragement** n.

encroach (ɪn'krəʊtʃ) vi. **1.** intrude (on) as usurper **2.** trespass —**en'croachment** n.

encrust or **incrust** (ɪn'krʌst) v. cover with or form a crust or hard covering

encumber or **incumber** (ɪn'kʌmbə) vt. **1.** hamper **2.** burden —**en'cumbrance** or **in'cumbrance** n. impediment, burden

-ency (comb. form) see -ENCE

encyclical (ɛn'sɪklɪk*ə*l) a. **1.** sent to many persons or places —n. **2.** circular letter, esp. from Pope

encyclopedia or **encyclopaedia** (ɛnsaɪˌkləʊ'piːdɪə) n. book, set of books of information on all subjects, or on every branch of subject, usu. arranged alphabetically —**encyclo'pedic** or **encyclo'paedic** a. —**encyclo'pedist** or **encyclo'paedist** n.

end (ɛnd) n. **1.** limit **2.** extremity **3.** conclusion, finishing **4.** fragment **5.** latter part **6.** death **7.** event, issue **8.** purpose, aim **9.** Sport either of the defended areas of a playing field etc. —vt. **10.** put an end to —vi. **11.** come to an end, finish —**ending** n. —**'endless** a. —**'endmost** a. nearest end; most distant —**'endways** adv. —**'endpapers** pl.n. blank pages at beginning and end of book —**end product** final result of process etc., esp. in manufacturing —**end of steel** C (town at) point to which railway tracks have been laid —**end it all** inf. commit suicide

endanger (ɪn'deɪndʒə) vt. put in danger or peril —**en'dangerment** n.

endear (ɪn'dɪə) vt. make dear or beloved —**en'dearing** adv. —**en'dearingly** adv. —**en'dearment** n. **1.** loving word **2.** tender affection

endeavour or U.S. **endeavor** (ɪn'dɛvə) vi. **1.** try, strive —n. **2.** attempt, effort

endemic (ɛn'dɛmɪk) a. **1.** regularly occurring in a country or district —n. **2.** endemic disease

endive ('ɛndaɪv) n. curly-leaved chicory used as salad

endo- or before vowel **end-** (comb. form) within, as in endocardium, endocrine. Such words are not given here where the meaning may easily be inferred from the simple word

endocardium (ɛndəʊ'kɑːdɪəm) n. lining membrane of the heart

endocrine ('ɛndəʊkraɪn, -krɪn) a. of those glands (thyroid, pituitary etc.) which secrete hormones directly into bloodstream

endogenous (ɛn'dɒdʒɪnəs) a. Biol. developing or originating within an organism —**en'dogeny** n.

endorphin (ɛn'dɔːfɪn) n. chemical occurring in brain, which has similar effect to morphine

endorse or **indorse** (ɪn'dɔːs) vt. **1.** sanction **2.** confirm **3.** write (esp. sign name) on back of **4.** record (conviction) on (driving licence) —**endor'sation** n. C

approval, support —**en'dorsement** or **in'dorsement** n.

endow (ɪn'daʊ) vt. **1.** provide permanent income for **2.** furnish (with) —**en'dowment** n. —**endowment assurance** or **insurance** life insurance that provides for payment of specified sum to policyholder at specified date or to his beneficiary should he die before this date

endue or **indue** (ɪn'djuː) vt. invest, furnish (with quality etc.)

endure (ɪn'djʊə) vt. **1.** undergo **2.** tolerate, bear —vi. **3.** last —**en'durable** a. —**en'durance** n. act or power of enduring —**en'during** a. **1.** permanent **2.** having forbearance —**en'duringness** n.

enema ('ɛnɪmə) n. medicine, liquid injected into rectum

enemy ('ɛnəmɪ) n. **1.** hostile person **2.** opponent **3.** armed foe **4.** hostile force

energy ('ɛnədʒɪ) n. **1.** vigour, force, activity **2.** source(s) of power, as oil, coal etc. **3.** capacity of machine, battery etc. for work or output of power —**ener'getic** a. —**ener'getically** adv. —**'energize** or **-ise** vt. give vigour to

enervate ('ɛnəveɪt) vt. weaken, deprive of vigour —**ener'vation** n. lassitude, weakness

enfant terrible (ãfã tɛ'riːbl) Fr. person given to unconventional conduct or indiscreet remarks (pl. **enfants terribles** (ãfã tɛ'riːbl))

enfeeble (ɪn'fiːb*ə*l) vt. weaken, debilitate —**en'feeblement** n.

enfilade (ɛnfɪ'leɪd) n. fire from artillery, sweeping line from end to end

enfold or **infold** (ɪn'fəʊld) vt. **1.** cover by enclosing **2.** embrace —**en'folder** or **in'folder** n.

enforce (ɪn'fɔːs) vt. **1.** compel obedience to **2.** impose (action) upon **3.** drive home —**en'forceable** a. —**en'forcement** n.

enfranchise (ɪn'fræntʃaɪz) vt. **1.** give right of voting to **2.** give parliamentary representation to **3.** set free —**en'franchisement** n.

Eng. 1. England **2.** English

eng. 1. engine **2.** engineer **3.** engineering **4.** engraved **5.** engraver **6.** engraving

engage (ɪn'geɪdʒ) vt. **1.** employ **2.** reserve, hire **3.** bind by contract or promise **4.** order **5.** pledge oneself **6.** betroth **7.** undertake **8.** attract **9.** occupy **10.** bring into conflict **11.** interlock —vi. **12.** employ oneself (in) **13.** promise **14.** begin to fight —**en'gaged** a. **1.** betrothed **2.** in use **3.** occupied, busy —**en'gagement** n. —**en'gaging** a. charming

engender (ɪn'dʒɛndə) vt. **1.** give rise to **2.** beget **3.** rouse

engine ('ɛndʒɪn) n. **1.** any machine to convert energy into mechanical work, as steam or petrol engine **2.** railway locomotive **3.** fire engine —**engi'neer** n. **1.** one who is in charge of engines, machinery etc. or construction work (eg roads, bridges) or installation of plant **2.**

one who originates, organizes something 3. US driver of railway locomotive —vt. 4. construct as engineer 5. contrive —**engi'neering** n.

English ('ɪŋglɪʃ) n. 1. the language of Britain, the U.S.A., most parts of the Commonwealth and certain other countries 2. the people of England —a. 3. relating to England

engorge (ɪn'gɔːdʒ) vt. 1. Pathol. congest with blood 2. eat (food) greedily 3. gorge (oneself) —**en'gorgement** n.

engraft or **ingraft** (ɪn'grɑːft) vt. 1. graft on 2. plant deeply 3. incorporate

engrain (ɪn'greɪn) vt. see INGRAIN

engrave (ɪn'greɪv) vt. 1. cut in lines on metal for printing 2. carve, incise 3. impress deeply —**en'graver** n. —**en'graving** n. copy of picture printed from engraved plate

engross (ɪn'grəʊs) vt. 1. absorb (attention) 2. occupy wholly 3. write out in large letters or in legal form 4. corner —**en'grossment** n.

engulf or **ingulf** (ɪn'gʌlf) vt. swallow up

enhance (ɪn'hɑːns) vt. heighten, intensify, increase value or attractiveness —**en'hancement** n.

enigma (ɪ'nɪgmə) n. 1. puzzling thing or person 2. riddle —**enig'matic(al)** a. —**enig'matically** adv.

enjambment or **enjambement** (ɪn'dʒæmmənt) n. in verse, continuation of sentence beyond end of line

enjoin (ɪn'dʒɔɪn) vt. 1. command 2. impose, prescribe

enjoy (ɪn'dʒɔɪ) vt. 1. delight in 2. take pleasure in 3. have use or benefit of —v. refl. 4. be happy —**en'joyable** a. —**en'joyment** n.

enkindle (ɪn'kɪnd'l) vt. 1. set on fire; kindle 2. excite to activity or ardour; arouse

enlarge (ɪn'lɑːdʒ) vt. 1. make bigger 2. reproduce on larger scale, as photograph —vi. 3. grow bigger 4. talk, write in greater detail 5. be capable of reproduction on larger scale —**en'largeable** a. —**en'largement** n. —**en'larger** n. optical instrument for enlarging photographs

enlighten (ɪn'laɪt'n) vt. 1. give information to 2. instruct, inform 3. Poet. shed light on —**en'lightenment** n.

enlist (ɪn'lɪst) v. (persuade to) enter armed forces —**en'listment** n.

enliven (ɪn'laɪv'n) vt. brighten, make more lively, animate

en masse (Fr. ã 'mas) 1. in a group, body 2. all together

enmesh, inmesh (ɪn'mɛʃ) or **immesh** (ɪ'mɛʃ) vt. entangle

enmity ('ɛnmɪtɪ) n. ill will, hostility

ennoble (ɪ'nəʊb'l) vt. make noble, elevate —**en'noblement** n.

ennui ('ɒnwiː) n. boredom —'**ennuied** or **ennuyé** ('ɒnwiːjeɪ) a.

enormous (ɪ'nɔːməs) a. very big, vast —**e'normity** n. 1. a gross offence 2. great wickedness 3. inf. great size

enough (ɪ'nʌf) a. 1. as much or as many as need be 2. sufficient —n. 3. sufficient quantity —adv. 4. (just) sufficiently

enounce (ɪ'naʊns) vt. 1. state 2. enunciate, proclaim —**e'nouncement** n.

en passant (ɒn pæ'sɑːnt) Fr. in passing, by the way

enplane (ɛn'pleɪn) vi. board aircraft

enquire (ɪn'kwaɪə) vi. see INQUIRE

enrapture (ɪn'ræptʃə) vt. 1. delight excessively 2. charm —**en'rapt** or **en'raptured** a. entranced

enrich (ɪn'rɪtʃ) vt. 1. make rich 2. add to —**en'richment** n.

enrol or U.S. **enroll** (ɪn'rəʊl) vt. 1. write name of on roll or list 2. engage, enlist, take in as member 3. enter, record —vi. 4. become member (-ll-) —**en'rolment** or U.S. **en'rollment** n.

en route (ɒn 'ruːt) Fr. on the way

ensconce (ɪn'skɒns) vt. 1. place snugly 2. establish in safety

ensemble (ɒn'sɒmb'l) n. 1. whole 2. all parts taken together 3. woman's complete outfit 4. company of actors, dancers etc. 5. Mus. group of soloists performing together 6. Mus. concerted passage 7. general effect —adv. 8. all together or at once

enshrine or **inshrine** (ɪn'ʃraɪn) vt. 1. set in shrine 2. preserve with great care and sacred affection

enshroud (ɪn'ʃraʊd) vt. cover or hide as with shroud

ensign ('ensaɪn) n. 1. (also 'ɛnsən) naval or military flag 2. badge 3. (in U.S. Navy) commissioned officer of lowest rank

ensilage ('ensɪlɪdʒ) n. see SILAGE

enslave (ɪn'sleɪv) vt. make into slave —**en'slavement** n. bondage —**en'slaver** n.

ensnare or **insnare** (ɪn'snɛə) vt. 1. capture in snare or trap 2. trick into false position 3. entangle

ensue (ɪn'sjuː) vi. follow, happen after

en suite (ã 'sɥit) forming a set or single unit

ensure (ɛn'ʃʊə, -'ʃɔː) or (esp. U.S.) **insure** vt. 1. make safe or sure 2. make certain to happen 3. secure

E.N.T. Med. ear, nose and throat

-ent (comb. form) causing or performing action or existing in certain condition; agent that performs action, as in astringent, dependent

entablature (ɛn'tæblətʃə) n. Archit. part of classical temple above columns, having architrave, frieze and cornice

entail (ɪn'teɪl) vt. 1. involve as result, necessitate 2. Law restrict (ownership of property) to designated line of heirs

entangle (ɪn'tæŋg'l) vt. 1. ensnare 2. perplex —**en'tanglement** n.

entente (Fr. ã'tãːt) n. friendly understanding between nations —**entente cordiale** (kɔr'djal) 1. friendly understanding between political powers 2. (oft. E- C-) understanding reached by France and Britain in April 1904 over colonial disputes

enter ('ɛntə) vt. 1. go, come into 2.

penetrate **3.** join **4.** write in, register —*vi.*
5. go, come in **6.** join a party *etc.* **7.** begin
—'**entrance** *n.* **1.** going, coming in **2.** door,
passage to enter **3.** right to enter **4.** fee
paid for this —'**entrant** *n.* one who enters,
esp. contest —'**entry** *n.* **1.** entrance **2.**
entering **3.** item entered, *eg* in account, list

enteric (ɛn'tɛrɪk) *or* **enteral** ('ɛntərəl) *a.*
of intestines —**ente'ritis** *n.* bowel inflammation

enterprise ('ɛntəpraɪz) *n.* **1.** bold or
difficult undertaking **2.** bold spirit **3.** force
of character in launching out **4.** business,
company —'**enterprising** *a.*

entertain (ɛntə'teɪn) *vt.* **1.** amuse, divert **2.**
receive as guest **3.** maintain **4.** consider
favourable **5.** take into consideration
—**enter'tainer** *n.* —**enter'taining** *a.* serving to entertain; amusing —**enter'tainment** *n.*

enthral *or* *U.S.* **enthrall** (ɪn'θrɔːl) *vt.*
captivate, thrill, hold spellbound (-**ll**-)
—**en'thralment** *or* *U.S.* **en'thrallment** *n.*

enthrone (ɛn'θrəʊn) *vt.* **1.** place on throne
2. honour; exalt **3.** assign authority to
—**en'thronement** *n.*

enthusiasm (ɪn'θjuːzɪæzəm) *n.* ardent
eagerness, zeal —**en'thuse** *v.* (cause to)
show enthusiasm —**en'thusiast** *n.* ardent
supporter —**enthusi'astic** *a.* —**enthusi'astically** *adv.*

entice (ɪn'taɪs) *vt.* allure, attract, inveigle,
tempt —**en'ticement** *n.* —**en'ticing** *a.*
alluring

entire (ɪn'taɪə) *a.* **1.** whole, complete **2.**
unbroken —**en'tirely** *adv.* —**entirety**
(ɪn'taɪərɪtɪ) *n.*

entitle (ɪn'taɪt'l) *vt.* **1.** give claim to **2.**
qualify **3.** give title to **4.** style

entity ('ɛntɪtɪ) *n.* **1.** thing's being or
existence **2.** reality **3.** thing having real
existence

entomb (ɪn'tuːm) *vt.* **1.** place in or as if in
tomb; bury **2.** serve as tomb for
—**en'tombment** *n.*

entomology (ɛntə'mɒlədʒɪ) *n.* study of
insects —**entomo'logical** *a.* —**ento'mologist** *n.* —**ento'mologize** *or* **-ise** *vi.*

entourage (ɒntʊ'rɑːʒ) *n.* **1.** associates,
retinue **2.** surroundings

entozoon (ɛntəʊ'zəʊɒn) *n.* internal parasite (*pl.* **-zoa** (-'zəʊə)) —**entozoic** (ɛntəʊ-
'zəʊɪk) *a.*

entr'acte (ɒn'trækt) *n.* **1.** interval between
acts of play *etc.* **2.** *esp.* formerly,
entertainment during such interval

entrails ('ɛntreɪlz) *pl.n.* **1.** bowels, intestines **2.** inner parts

entrain (ɪn'treɪn) *v.* board or put aboard
train —**en'trainment** *n.*

entrance¹ ('ɛntrəns) *n. see* ENTER

entrance² (ɪn'trɑːns) *vt.* **1.** delight **2.** throw
into a trance

entrap (ɪn'træp) *vt.* **1.** catch or snare as in
trap **2.** trick into difficulty *etc.* (-**pp**-)
—**en'trapment** *n.*

entreat *or* **intreat** (ɪn'triːt) *vt.* **1.** ask

earnestly **2.** beg, implore —**en'treaty** *n.*
earnest request

entrecôte (*Fr.* ɑ̃trə'koːt) *n.* beefsteak cut
from between ribs

entrée ('ɒntreɪ) *n.* **1.** (dish served before)
main course of meal **2.** right of access,
admission

entrench *or* **intrench** (ɪn'trɛntʃ) *vt.* **1.**
establish in fortified position with trenches
2. establish firmly —**en'trenchment** *or*
in'trenchment *n.*

entrepreneur (ɒntrəprə'nɜː) *n.* person
who attempts to profit by risk and
initiative

entropy ('ɛntrəpɪ) *n.* **1.** unavailability of
the heat energy of a system for
mechanical work **2.** measurement of this

entrust *or* **intrust** (ɪn'trʌst) *vt.* **1.** commit,
charge (with) **2.** (*oft. with* to) put into care
or protection of

entwine *or* **intwine** (ɪn'twaɪn) *vt.* **1.** plait,
interweave **2.** wreathe **3.** embrace

E number any of series of numbers with
prefix E indicating specific food additive
recognized by EEC

enumerate (ɪ'njuːməreɪt) *vt.* **1.** mention
one by one **2.** count —**enumer'ation** *n.*
—**e'numerative** *a.* —**e'numerator** *n.*

enunciate (ɪ'nʌnsɪeɪt) *vt.* **1.** state clearly **2.**
proclaim **3.** pronounce —**enunci'ation** *n.*
—**e'nunciative** *a.* —**e'nunciator** *n.*

enuresis (ɛnjʊ'riːsɪs) *n.* involuntary discharge of urine, *esp.* during sleep
—**enuretic** (ɛnjʊ'rɛtɪk) *n.*

envelop (ɪn'vɛləp) *vt.* **1.** wrap up, enclose
2. surround **3.** encircle —**en'velopment** *n.*

envelope ('ɛnvələʊp, 'ɒn-) *n.* **1.** folded,
gummed cover of letter **2.** covering,
wrapper

envenom (ɪn'vɛnəm) *vt.* **1.** put poison,
venom in **2.** embitter

environ (ɪn'vaɪrən) *vt.* surround —**en'vi-
ronment** *n.* **1.** surroundings **2.** conditions of
life or growth —**environ'mental** *a.*
—**environ'mentalist** *n.* ecologist —**en'vi-
rons** *pl.n.* districts round town *etc.*,
outskirts

envisage (ɪn'vɪzɪdʒ) *vt.* **1.** conceive of as
possibility **2.** visualize

envoy¹ ('ɛnvɔɪ) *n.* **1.** messenger **2.**
diplomatic minister of rank below ambassador

envoy² *or* **envoi** ('ɛnvɔɪ) *n.* **1.** concluding
stanza, notably in ballades **2.** postscript in
other forms of verse or prose

envy ('ɛnvɪ) *vt.* **1.** grudge (another's good
fortune, success or qualities) **2.** feel jealous
of ('**envied,** '**envying**) —*n.* **3.** bitter
contemplation of another's good fortune **4.**
jealousy **5.** object of this feeling —'**envi-
able** *a.* arousing envy —'**envious** *a.* full of
envy

enzyme ('ɛnzaɪm) *n.* any of group of
complex proteins produced by living cells
and acting as catalysts in biochemical
reactions

Eocene ('iːəʊsiːn) *a.* **1.** of second epoch of
Tertiary period, during which hooved

mammals appeared —n. **2.** Eocene epoch or rock series

eolith ('iːəʊlɪθ) n. early flint implement —**Eo'lithic** a. of the period before Stone Age

-eous (comb. form) relating to or having nature of, as in gaseous

EP 1. extended-play **2.** electroplate

epaulet or **epaulette** ('ɛpəlɛt, -lɪt) n. shoulder ornament on uniform

épée ('ɛpeɪ) n. sword similar to foil but with heavier blade —**'épéeist** n.

epergne (ɪ'pɜːn) n. ornamental centrepiece for table, holding flowers etc.

Eph. or **Ephes.** Bible Ephesians

ephedrine or **ephedrin** (ɪ'fɛdrɪn, 'ɛfɪdriːn, -drɪn) n. alkaloid used for treatment of asthma and hay fever

ephemeral (ɪ'fɛmərəl) a. short-lived, transient —**e'phemeron** n. ephemeral thing (pl. **-s, -ra** (-rə)) (also **e'phemera** (pl. **-s, -rae** (-riː))) —**e'phemerous** a.

epi-, eph-, or before vowel **ep-** (comb. form) **1.** upon; above, as in epidermis **2.** in addition to, as in epiphenomenon **3.** after, as in epilogue **4.** near, as in epicalyx

epic ('ɛpɪk) n. **1.** long poem or story telling of achievements of hero or heroes **2.** film etc. about heroic deeds —a. **3.** of, like, an epic **4.** impressive, grand

epicene ('ɛpisiːn) a. common to both sexes

epicentre or U.S. **epicenter** ('ɛpɪsɛntə) n. focus of earthquake —**epi'central** a.

epicure ('ɛpɪkjʊə) n. one delighting in eating and drinking —**epicu'rean** a. **1.** of Epicurus, who taught that pleasure, in the shape of practice of virtue, was highest good **2.** given to refined sensuous enjoyment —n. **3.** such person or philosopher —**epicu'reanism** n. —**'epicurism** n.

epicycle ('ɛpɪsaɪk²l) n. circle whose centre moves on circumference of greater circle

epidemic (ɛpɪ'dɛmɪk) a. **1.** (esp. of disease) prevalent and spreading rapidly **2.** widespread —n. **3.** widespread occurrence of a disease **4.** rapid development, spread or growth of something —**epi-'demical** a. —**epidemiological** (ɛpɪdiːmɪə-'lɒdʒɪk²l) a. —**epidemiologist** (ɛpɪdiːmɪ-'ɒlədʒɪst) n. —**epidemiology** (ɛpɪdiːmɪ'ɒl-ədʒɪ) n. branch of medical science concerned with epidemic diseases

epidermis (ɛpɪ'dɜːmɪs) n. outer skin

epidiascope (ɛpɪ'daɪəskəʊp) n. optical device for projecting magnified image on to screen

epidural (ɛpɪ'djʊərəl) n./a. (of) spinal anaesthetic used for relief of pain during childbirth

epiglottis (ɛpɪ'glɒtɪs) n. cartilage that covers opening of larynx in swallowing —**epi'glottic** a.

epigram ('ɛpɪgræm) n. concise, witty poem or saying —**epigram'matic(al)** a. —**epigram'matically** adv. —**epi'grammatist** n.

epigraph ('ɛpɪgrɑːf, -græf) n. inscription

epilepsy ('ɛpɪlɛpsɪ) n. disorder of nervous system causing fits and convulsions —**epi'leptic** n. **1.** sufferer from this —a. **2.** of, subject to, this

epilogue ('ɛpɪlɒg) n. short speech or poem at end, esp. of play

Epiphany (ɪ'pɪfənɪ) n. festival of the announcement of Christ to the Magi, celebrated Jan. 6th

Epis. 1. Episcopal; Episcopalian (also **Episc.**) **2.** Epistle

episcopal (ɪ'pɪskəp²l) a. **1.** of bishop **2.** ruled by bishops —**e'piscopacy** n. government by body of bishops —**Episco'palian** a. **1.** of branch of Anglican church —n. **2.** member, adherent of Episcopalian church —**e'piscopate** n. **1.** bishop's office, see, or duration of office **2.** body of bishops

episode ('ɛpɪsəʊd) n. **1.** incident **2.** section of (serialized) book, television programme etc. —**episodic(al)** (ɛpɪ'sɒdɪk(²l)) a.

epistemology (ɪpɪstɪ'mɒlədʒɪ) n. study of source, nature and limitations of knowledge —**epistemo'logical** a. —**episte'mologist** n.

epistle (ɪ'pɪs²l) n. **1.** letter, esp. of apostle **2.** poem in letter form —**epistolary** (ɪ'pɪstələrɪ) a. —**epistoler** (ɪ'pɪst²lə) n.

epitaph ('ɛpɪtɑːf, -tæf) n. memorial inscription on tomb

epithelium (ɛpɪ'θiːlɪəm) n. tissue covering external and internal surfaces of body (pl. **-s, -lia** (-lɪə)) —**epi'thelial** or **epi'thelioid** a.

epithet ('ɛpɪθɛt) n. additional, descriptive word or name —**epi'thetic(al)** a.

epitome (ɪ'pɪtəmɪ) n. **1.** typical example **2.** summary —**e'pitomist** n. —**e'pitomize** or **-ise** vt. typify

E.P.N.S. electroplated nickel silver

epoch ('iːpɒk) n. **1.** beginning of period **2.** period, era, esp. one of notable events —**epochal** ('ɛpɒk²l) a.

epode ('ɛpəʊd) n. third, or last, part of lyric ode

eponym ('ɛpənɪm) n. **1.** name, esp. place name, derived from name of real or mythical person **2.** name of person from which such name is derived —**e'pony-mous** a. —**e'ponymously** adv. —**e'pony-my** n.

epoxy (ɪ'pɒksɪ) a. Chem. of, consisting of, or containing oxygen atom joined to two different groups that are themselves joined to other groups —**epoxy** or **epoxide resin** any of various thermosetting synthetic resins containing epoxy groups: used in surface coatings, adhesives etc.

epsilon ('ɛpsɪlɒn) n. fifth letter of Gr. alphabet (E, ε)

Epsom salts ('ɛpsəm) medicinal preparation of hydrated magnesium sulphate, used as purgative etc.

equable ('ɛkwəb²l) a. **1.** even-tempered, placid **2.** uniform —**equa'bility** n. —**'equably** adv.

equal ('iːkwəl) a. **1.** the same in number,

size, merit *etc.* **2.** identical **3.** fit or qualified **4.** evenly balanced —*n.* **5.** one equal to another —*vt.* **6.** be equal to (-**ll**-) —**equality** (ɪ'kwɒlɪtɪ) *n.* **1.** state of being equal **2.** uniformity —**equali'zation** *or* **-i'sation** *n.* —**'equalize** *or* **-ise** *v.* make, become, equal —**'equally** *adv.*

equanimity (i:kwə'nɪmɪtɪ, ɛkwə-) *n.* calmness, composure, steadiness

equate (ɪ'kweɪt) *vt.* **1.** make equal **2.** bring to a common standard —**equation** (ɪ'kweɪʒən, -ʃən) *n.* **1.** equating of two mathematical expressions **2.** balancing

equator (ɪ'kweɪtə) *n.* imaginary circle round earth equidistant from the poles —**equa'torial** *a.*

equerry (ɪ'kwɛrɪ) *n.* **1.** officer in attendance on sovereign **2.** officer in royal household in charge of horses

equestrian (ɪ'kwɛstrɪən) *a.* **1.** of, skilled in, horse-riding **2.** mounted on horse —*n.* **3.** rider

equi- (*comb. form*) equal, at equal, as in *equidistant.* Such words are not given here where the meaning can easily be inferred from the simple word

equiangular (i:kwɪ'æŋɡjulə) *a.* having equal angles

equilateral (i:kwɪ'lætərəl) *a.* having equal sides

equilibrium (i:kwɪ'lɪbrɪəm) *n.* state of steadiness, equipoise or stability (*pl.* **-s, -ria** (-rɪə))

equine ('ɛkwaɪn) *a.* of, like a horse

equinox ('i:kwɪnɒks) *n.* **1.** time when sun crosses equator and day and night are equal —*pl.* **2.** points at which sun crosses equator —**equinoctial** (i:kwɪ'nɒkʃəl) *a.*

equip (ɪ'kwɪp) *vt.* supply, fit out, array (-**pp**-) —**equipage** ('ɛkwɪpɪdʒ) *n.* **1.** carriage, horses and attendants **2.** *obs.* outfit, requisites —**e'quipment** *n.*

equipoise ('ɛkwɪpɔɪz) *n.* **1.** perfect balance **2.** counterpoise **3.** equanimity —*vt.* **4.** counterbalance

equitation (ɛkwɪ'teɪʃən) *n.* study and practice of riding and horsemanship

equity ('ɛkwɪtɪ) *n.* **1.** fairness **2.** use of principles of justice to supplement law **3.** system of law so made —**'equitable** *a.* fair, reasonable, just —**'equitably** *adv.*

equiv. equivalent

equivalent (ɪ'kwɪvələnt) *a.* **1.** equal in value **2.** having the same meaning or result **3.** tantamount **4.** corresponding —**e'quivalence** *or* **e'quivalency** *n.*

equivocal (ɪ'kwɪvək'l) *a.* **1.** of double or doubtful meaning **2.** questionable **3.** liable to suspicion —**equivo'cality** *n.* —**e'quivocate** *vi.* use equivocal words to mislead —**equivo'cation** *n.* —**e'quivocator** *n.*

er (ə, ɜ:) *interj.* sound made when hesitating in speech

Er *Chem.* erbium

E.R. Elizabeth Regina (*Lat.,* Queen Elizabeth)

-er[1] (*comb. form*) **1.** person or thing that performs specified action, as in *reader* **2.**

person engaged in profession *etc.,* as in *writer* **3.** native or inhabitant of, as in *Londoner* **4.** person or thing having certain characteristic, as in *newcomer*

-er[2] (*comb. form*) forming comparative degree of adjective or adverb, as in *deeper, faster*

era ('ɪərə) *n.* **1.** system of time in which years are numbered from particular event **2.** time of the event **3.** memorable date, period

eradicate (ɪ'rædɪkeɪt) *vt.* **1.** wipe out, exterminate **2.** root out —**e'radicable** *a.* —**eradi'cation** *n.* —**e'radicative** *a./n.* —**e'radicator** *n.*

erase (ɪ'reɪz) *vt.* **1.** rub out **2.** remove, *eg* recording from magnetic tape —**e'raser** *n.* —**e'rasure** *n.*

erbium ('ɜ:bɪəm) *n.* metallic element of the lanthanide series

ere (ɛə) *prep./conj.* **1.** *Poet.* before **2.** sooner than —**ere'long** *adv. obs., poet.* before long; soon

erect (ɪ'rɛkt) *a.* **1.** upright —*vt.* **2.** set up **3.** build —**e'rectile** *a.* —**e'rection** *n. esp.* an erect penis —**e'rector** *n.*

eremite ('ɛrɪmaɪt) *n.* Christian hermit or recluse —**eremitic(al)** (ɛrɪ'mɪtɪk('l)) *a.* —**'eremitism** *n.*

erg (ɜ:ɡ) *n.* cgs unit of work or energy

ergo ('ɜ:ɡəʊ) *adv.* therefore

ergonomics (ɜ:ɡə'nɒmɪks) *pl.n.* (*with sing. v.*) study of relationship between workers and their environment

ergot ('ɜ:ɡət, -ɡɒt) *n.* **1.** disease of grain **2.** diseased seed used as drug —**'ergotism** *n.* disease caused by eating ergot-infested bread

erica ('ɛrɪkə) *n.* genus of plants including heathers

Erin ('ɪərɪn, 'ɛərɪn) *n. obs., poet.* Ireland

ermine ('ɜ:mɪn) *n.* **1.** stoat in northern regions, *esp.* in winter **2.** its white winter fur

erne *or* **ern** (ɜːn) *n.* fish-eating sea eagle

Ernie ('ɜːnɪ) *n.* UK computer that randomly selects winning numbers of Premium Bonds (*Electronic Random Number Indicating Equipment*)

erode (ɪ'rəʊd) *v.* **1.** wear away —*vt.* **2.** eat into —**e'rosion** *n.* —**e'rosive** *a.*

erogenous (ɪ'rɒdʒɪnəs) *or* **erogenic** (ɛrə-'dʒɛnɪk) *a.* sensitive to sexual stimulation

erotic (ɪ'rɒtɪk) *a.* relating to, or treating of, sexual pleasure —**e'rotica** *n.* sexual literature or art —**e'roticism** *n.*

err (ɜː) *vi.* **1.** make mistakes **2.** be wrong **3.** sin —**er'ratic** *a.* irregular in movement, conduct *etc.* —**er'ratically** *adv.* —**erratum** (ɪ'rɑːtəm) *n.* printing mistake noted for correction (*pl.* **-ta** (-tə)) —**er'roneous** *a.* mistaken, wrong —**'error** *n.* **1.** mistake **2.** wrong opinion **3.** sin

errand ('ɛrənd) *n.* **1.** short journey for simple business **2.** purpose of such journey **3.** the business, mission of messenger —**errand boy**

errant ('ɛrənt) *a.* **1.** wandering in search

of adventure **2.** erring —**'errancy** *n.*
erring state or conduct —**'errantry** *n.*
state or conduct of knight errant

ersatz ('eəzæts, 'ɜː-) *a.* substitute, imitation

Erse (ɜːs) *n.* **1.** *see* Gaelic *at* GAEL —*a.* **2.** of or relating to Gaelic language

erst (ɜːst) *adv.* of old, formerly

eruct (ɪ'rʌkt) *or* **eructate** *v.* **1.** belch **2.** (of volcano) pour out (fumes or volcanic matter) —**eruc'tation** *n.*

erudite ('erʊdaɪt) *a.* learned —**erudition** (erʊ'dɪʃən) *n.* learning

erupt (ɪ'rʌpt) *vi.* burst out —**e'ruption** *n.* **1.** bursting out, *esp.* volcanic outbreak **2.** rash on the skin —**e'ruptive** *a.*

-ery *or* **-ry** (*comb. form*) **1.** place of business or activity, as in *bakery, refinery* **2.** class or collection of things, as in *cutlery* **3.** qualities, actions, as in *snobbery, trickery* **4.** practice, occupation, as in *husbandry* **5.** state, condition, as in *slavery*

erysipelas (erɪ'sɪpɪləs) *n.* acute skin infection

erythema (erɪ'θiːmə) *n.* patchy inflammation of skin —**erythematic** (erɪθɪ'mætɪk) *or* **ery'thematous** *a.*

erythrocyte (ɪ'rɪθrəʊsaɪt) *n.* red blood cell of vertebrates that transports oxygen and carbon dioxide —**erythrocytic** (ɪrɪθrəʊ'sɪtɪk) *a.*

Es *Chem.* einsteinium

escalate ('eskəleɪt) *v.* increase, be increased, in extent, intensity *etc.*

escalator ('eskəleɪtə) *n.* moving staircase —**escalator clause** clause in contract stipulating adjustment in wages *etc.* in event of large rise in cost of living *etc.*

escallop (ɛ'skɒlǝp, ɛ'skæl-) *see* SCALLOP

escalope ('eskəlɒp) *n.* thin slice of meat, usu. veal

escape (ɪ'skeɪp) *vi.* **1.** get free **2.** get off safely **3.** go unpunished **4.** find way out —*vt.* **5.** elude **6.** be forgotten by —*n.* **7.** escaping —**escapade** ('eskəpeɪd, eskə'peɪd) *n.* wild (mischievous) adventure —**es'capement** *n.* **1.** mechanism consisting of toothed wheel and anchor, used in timepieces to provide periodic impulses to pendulum or balance **2.** any similar mechanism that regulates movement —**es'capism** *n.* taking refuge in fantasy to avoid facing disagreeable facts —**escapologist** (eskə'pɒlədʒɪst) *n.* entertainer specializing in freeing himself from confinement —**escape road** road provided on hill for driver to drive into if his brakes fail —**escape velocity** minimum velocity necessary for a body to escape from the gravitational field of the earth *etc.*

escarp (ɪ'skɑːp) *n.* steep bank under rampart —**es'carpment** *n.* **1.** steep hillside **2.** escarp

-escent (*a. comb. form*) beginning to be, do, show *etc.,* as in *convalescent, luminescent* —**-escence** (*n. comb. form*)

eschatology (eskə'tɒlədʒɪ) *n.* study of

death, judgment and last things —**eschato-'logical** *a.*

escheat (ɪs'tʃiːt) *Law n.* **1.** before 1926, reversion of property to Crown in absence of legal heirs **2.** property so reverting —*v.* **3.** take (land) by escheat or (of land) revert by escheat —**es'cheatable** *a.* —**es'cheatage** *n.*

eschew (ɪs'tʃuː) *vt.* avoid, abstain from, shun

eschscholtzia (ɪs'kɒlʃǝ) *n.* garden plant with bright flowers, California poppy

escort ('eskɔːt) *n.* **1.** armed guard for traveller *etc.* **2.** person or persons accompanying another —*vt.* (ɪs'kɔːt) **3.** accompany or attend as escort

escritoire (eskrɪ'twɑː) *n.* type of writing desk

esculent ('eskjʊlənt) *a.* edible

escutcheon (ɪ'skʌtʃǝn) *n.* **1.** shield with coat of arms **2.** ornamental plate round keyhole *etc.* —**blot on one's escutcheon** stain on one's honour

-ese (*comb. form*) place of origin, language, style, as in *Cantonese, Japanese, journalese*

Eskimo ('eskɪməʊ) *n.* **1.** one of aboriginal race inhabiting N Amer., Greenland *etc.* (*pl.* **-s**) **2.** their language

E.S.N. educationally subnormal

esoteric (esəʊ'terɪk) *a.* **1.** abstruse, obscure **2.** secret **3.** restricted to initiates

E.S.P. extrasensory perception

esp. especially

espadrille (espə'drɪl) *n.* canvas shoe, *esp.* with braided cord sole

espalier (ɪ'spæljə) *n.* **1.** shrub, (fruit) tree trained to grow flat, as against wall *etc.* **2.** trellis for this

esparto *or* **esparto grass** (ɛ'spɑːtəʊ) *n.* kind of grass yielding fibre used for making rope *etc.*

especial (ɪ'speʃəl) *a.* **1.** pre-eminent, more than ordinary **2.** particular —**es'pecially** *adv.*

Esperanto (espə'ræntəʊ) *n.* artificial language designed for universal use —**Espe'rantist** *n.* one who uses Esperanto

espionage ('espɪɒnɑːʒ) *n.* **1.** spying **2.** use of secret agents

esplanade (esplə'neɪd) *n.* level space, *esp.* one used as public promenade

espouse (ɪ'spaʊz) *vt.* **1.** support, embrace (cause *etc.*) **2.** *obs.* marry —**es'pousal** *n.*

espresso (ɛ'spresəʊ) *n.* strong coffee made by forcing steam through ground coffee beans

esprit (ɛ'spriː) *n.* **1.** spirit **2.** animation —**esprit de corps** (də 'kɔː) attachment, loyalty to the society *etc.* one belongs to

espy (ɪ'spaɪ) *vt.* catch sight of (**es'pied, es'pying**) —**es'pial** *n.* observation

Esq. Esquire

-esque (*comb. form*) specified character, manner, style or resemblance, as in *picturesque, Romanesque, statuesque*

esquire (ɪ'skwaɪə) *n.* **1.** gentleman's

courtesy title used on letters **2.** formerly, squire

ESRO ('ɛzrəʊ) European Space Research Organization

-ess (*comb. form*) female, as in *actress*

essay ('ɛseɪ; *def. 3 also* ɛ'seɪ) *n.* **1.** prose composition **2.** short treatise **3.** attempt —*vt.* (ɛ'seɪ) **4.** try, attempt **5.** test (es'sayed, es'saying) —'**essayist** *n.*

essence ('ɛs²ns) *n.* **1.** all that makes thing what it is **2.** existence, being **3.** entity, reality **4.** extract got by distillation —**es'sential** *a.* **1.** necessary, indispensable **2.** inherent **3.** of, constituting essence of thing —*n.* **4.** indispensable element **5.** chief point —**essenti'ality** *n.* —**essential oil** any of various volatile oils in plants, having odour *etc.* of plant from which they are extracted

E.S.T. *C*, *US* Eastern Standard Time

est. **1.** established **2.** estimate(d)

-est (*comb. form*) forming superlative degree of adjective or adverb, as in *fastest*

establish (ɪ'stæblɪʃ) *vt.* **1.** make secure **2.** set up **3.** settle **4.** prove —**es'tablishment** *n.* **1.** permanent organized body, full number of regiment *etc.* **2.** household **3.** business **4.** public institution —**Established Church** church officially recognized as national institution —**the Establishment** group, class of people holding authority within a society

estate (ɪ'steɪt) *n.* **1.** landed property **2.** person's property **3.** area of property development, *esp.* of houses or factories **4.** class as part of nation **5.** rank, state, condition of life —**estate agent** one who sells houses *etc.* for others —**estate car** car with rear door and luggage space behind rear seats —**estate duty** *see* **death duty** *at* DEATH

esteem (ɪ'stiːm) *vt.* **1.** think highly of **2.** consider —*n.* **3.** favourable opinion, regard, respect

ester ('ɛstə) *n. Chem.* organic compound produced by reaction between acid and alcohol

estimate ('ɛstɪmeɪt) *vt.* **1.** form approximate idea of (amounts, measurements *etc.*) **2.** form opinion of **3.** quote probable price for —*n.* ('ɛstɪmɪt) **4.** approximate judgment of amounts *etc.* **5.** amount *etc.* arrived at **6.** opinion **7.** price quoted by contractor —**'estimable** *a.* worthy of regard —**esti'mation** *n.* **1.** opinion, judgment **2.** esteem

estrange (ɪ'streɪndʒ) *vt.* **1.** lose affection of **2.** alienate —**es'trangement** *n.*

estuary ('ɛstjʊərɪ) *n.* tidal mouth of river, inlet —'**estuarine** *a.*

-et (*comb. form*) small, lesser, as in *islet*, *baronet*

eta ('iːtə) *n.* seventh letter in Gr. alphabet (H, η)

E.T.A. estimated time of arrival

et al. **1.** et alibi (*Lat.*, and elsewhere) **2.** et alii (*Lat.*, and others)

etc. et cetera

et cetera (ɪt 'sɛtrə) *Lat.* and the rest, and others, and so on —**et'ceteras** *pl.n.* miscellaneous extras

etch (ɛtʃ) *v.* **1.** make (engraving) by eating away surface of metal plate with acids *etc.* —*vt.* **2.** imprint vividly —'**etcher** *n.* —'**etching** *n.*

eternal (ɪ'tɜːn²l) *a.* **1.** without beginning or end **2.** everlasting **3.** changeless —e'**ternally** *adv.* —e'**ternity** *n.* —**eternal triangle** emotional relationship in which there are conflicts involving a man and two women or a woman and two men —**eternity ring** ring, *esp.* one set all around with stones to symbolize continuity

ethane ('iːθeɪn, 'ɛθ-) *n.* odourless flammable gaseous alkane obtained from natural gas and petroleum

ether ('iːθə) *n.* **1.** colourless volatile liquid used as anaesthetic **2.** intangible fluid formerly supposed to fill all space **3.** the clear sky, region above clouds —**ethereal** (ɪ'θɪərɪəl) *a.* **1.** light, airy **2.** heavenly, spiritlike —**ethereality** (ɪθɪərɪ'ælɪtɪ) *n.* —**ethereali'zation** *or* **-i'sation** *n.* —**etherealize** *or* **-ise** (ɪ'θɪərɪəlaɪz) *vt.* **1.** make or regard as being ethereal **2.** add ether to or make into ether

ethic ('ɛθɪk) *or* **ethical** *a.* relating to morals —'**ethically** *adv.* —'**ethics** *pl.n.* **1.** (*with sing. v.*) science of morals **2.** moral principles, rules of conduct

Ethiopian (iːθɪ'əʊpɪən) *a.* **1.** of Ethiopia (state in NE Afr.) —*n.* **2.** native of Ethiopia **3.** any of languages of Ethiopia, *esp.* Amharic —*n./a.* **4.** *obs.* Negro

ethnic ('ɛθnɪk) *or* **ethnical** *a.* of race or relating to classification of humans into social, cultural *etc.*, groups —**ethno'graphic** *a.* —**eth'nography** *n.* description of races of men —**ethno'logical** *a.* —**eth'nology** *n.* the study of human races

ethos ('iːθɒs) *n.* distinctive character, spirit *etc.* of people, culture *etc.*

ethyl ('iːθaɪl, 'ɛθɪl) *n.* (C₂H₅) radical of ordinary alcohol and ether —'**ethylene** ('ɛθɪliːn) *n.* poisonous gas used as anaesthetic and fuel —**ethyl alcohol** *see* ALCOHOL (sense 1)

etiolate ('iːtɪəʊleɪt) *v.* **1.** *Bot.* whiten (green plant) through lack of sunlight **2.** (cause to) become pale and weak —**etio'lation** *n.*

etiquette ('ɛtɪkɛt, ɛtɪ'kɛt) *n.* conventional code of conduct or behaviour

Eton collar ('iːt²n) broad stiff white collar worn outside Eton jacket

Eton crop short mannish hair style worn by women in 1920s

Eton jacket waist-length jacket, open in front, formerly worn by pupils of Eton College, public school for boys in S England

Etruscan (ɪ'trʌskən) *or* **Etrurian** (ɪ'trʊərɪən) *n.* **1.** member of ancient people of Etruria in central Italy **2.** language of ancient Etruscans —*a.* **3.** of Etruria, Etruscans, their culture or their language

et seq. **1.** et sequens (*Lat.*, and the

following) **2.** (*also* **et seqq.**) et sequentia (*Lat.*, and those that follow)

-ette (*comb. form*) **1.** small, as in *cigarette* **2.** female, as in *majorette* **3.** imitation, as in *Leatherette*

étude ('eɪtjuːd) *n.* short musical composition, study, intended often as technical exercise

ety., etym., *or* **etymol. 1.** etymological **2.** etymology

etymology (ɛtɪ'mɒlədʒɪ) *n.* **1.** tracing, account of, formation of word's origin, development **2.** science of this —**etymo-'logical** *a.* —**etymo'logically** *adv.* —**ety'mologist** *n.*

Eu *Chem.* europium

eu- (*comb. form*) well, as in *eugenic, euphony*

eucalyptus (juːkə'lɪptəs) *or* **eucalypt** ('juːkəlɪpt) *n.* mostly Aust. genus of tree, the gum tree, yielding timber and oil, used medicinally from leaves

Eucharist ('juːkərɪst) *n.* **1.** Christian sacrament of the Lord's Supper **2.** the consecrated elements —**Eucha'ristic** *a.*

Euclidean *or* **Euclidian** (juː'klɪdɪən) *a.* denoting system of geometry based on axioms of Gr. mathematician Euclid

eugenic (juː'dʒɛnɪk) *a.* relating to, or tending towards, production of fine offspring —**eu'genicist** *n.* —**eu'genics** *pl.n.* (*with sing. v.*) this science

eulogy ('juːlədʒɪ) *n.* **1.** speech or writing in praise of person **2.** praise —**eulogist** *n.* —**eulo'gistic** *a.* —**eulo'gistically** *adv.* —**'eulogize** *or* **-ise** *v.*

eunuch ('juːnək) *n.* castrated man, *esp.* formerly one employed in harem

euphemism ('juːfɪmɪzəm) *n.* **1.** substitution of mild term for offensive or hurtful one **2.** instance of this —**'euphemist** *n.* —**euphe'mistic** *a.* —**euphe'mistically** *adv.* —**'euphemize** *or* **-ise** *v.*

euphony ('juːfənɪ) *n.* pleasantness of sound —**euphonic** (juː'fɒnɪk) *or* **euphonious** (juː-'fəʊnɪəs) *a.* pleasing to ear —**euphonium** (juː'fəʊnɪəm) *n.* brass musical instrument, bass-tenor tuba

euphoria (juː'fɔːrɪə) *n.* sense of wellbeing or elation —**euphoric** (juː'fɒrɪk) *a.*

euphuism ('juːfjuːɪzəm) *n.* affected high-flown manner of writing, *esp.* in imitation of Lyly's *Euphues* (1580) —**euphu'istic** *a.*

Eur. Europe(an)

Eurasian (jʊə'reɪʃən, -ʒən) *a.* **1.** of mixed European and Asiatic descent **2.** of Europe and Asia —*n.* **3.** one of this descent

Euratom (jʊə'rætəm) *n.* European Atomic Energy Commission

eureka (jʊ'riːkə) *interj.* exclamation of triumph at finding something

eurhythmics *or esp. U.S.* **eurythmics** (juː'rɪðmɪks) *pl.n.* (*with sing. v.*) system of training through physical movement to music —**eu'rhythmy** *or* **eu'rythmy** *n.*

Euro- ('jʊərəʊ-) *or before vowel* **Eur-** (*comb. form*) Europe; European

Eurodollar ('jʊərəʊdɒlə) *n.* U.S. dollar as part of European holding

European (jʊərə'pɪən) *n./a.* (native) of Europe —**European Atomic Energy Commission** authority established by Common Market to develop peaceful uses of nuclear energy —**European Economic Community** association of a number of European nations for trade

europium (jʊ'rəʊpɪəm) *n.* silvery-white element of the lanthanide series

eurythmics (juː'rɪðmɪks) *n. esp. US see* EURHYTHMICS

Eustachian tube (juː'steɪʃən) passage leading from pharynx to middle ear

euthanasia (juːθə'neɪzɪə) *n.* **1.** gentle, painless death **2.** putting to death in this way, *esp.* to relieve suffering

euthenics (juː'θɛnɪks) *pl.n.* (*with sing. v.*) science of the relation of environment to human beings

eV electronvolt

evacuate (ɪ'vækjʊeɪt) *vt.* **1.** empty **2.** cause to withdraw **3.** discharge —**evacu'ation** *n.* —**evacu'ee** *n.* person moved from danger area, *esp.* in time of war

evade (ɪ'veɪd) *vt.* **1.** avoid, escape from **2.** elude —**e'vasion** *n.* **1.** subterfuge **2.** excuse **3.** equivocation —**e'vasive** *a.* elusive, not straightforward —**e'vasively** *adv.*

evaluate (ɪ'væljʊeɪt) *vt.* find or judge value of —**evalu'ation** *n.*

evanesce (ɛvə'nɛs) *vi.* fade away —**eva'nescence** *n.* —**eva'nescent** *a.* fleeting, transient

evangelical (iːvæn'dʒɛlɪkˀl) *a.* **1.** of, or according to, gospel teaching **2.** of Protestant sect which maintains salvation by faith —*n.* **3.** member of evangelical sect —**evan'gelicalism** *n.* —**e'vangelism** *n.* —**e'vangelist** *n.* **1.** writer of one of the four gospels **2.** ardent, zealous preacher of the gospel **3.** revivalist —**evangeli'zation** *or* **-i'sation** *n.* —**e'vangelize** *or* **-ise** *vt.* **1.** preach gospel to **2.** convert

evaporate (ɪ'væpəreɪt) *vi.* **1.** turn into, pass off in, vapour —*vt.* **2.** turn into vapour —**evapo'ration** *n.* —**e'vaporative** *a.* —**e'vaporator** *n.* —**evaporated milk** thick unsweetened tinned milk from which some of the water has been evaporated

evasion (ɪ'veɪʒən) *n. see* EVADE

eve (iːv) *n.* **1.** evening before (festival *etc.*) **2.** time just before (event *etc.*) **3.** *obs.* evening

even[1] ('iːvˀn) *a.* **1.** flat, smooth **2.** uniform in quality, equal in amount, balanced **3.** divisible by two **4.** impartial —*vt.* **5.** make even **6.** smooth **7.** equalize —*adv.* **8.** equally **9.** simply **10.** notwithstanding —**'evens** *a./adv.* **1.** (of bet) winning identical sum if successful **2.** (of runner) offered at such odds —**even-handed** *a.* fair; impartial —**even-handedly** *adv.* —**even-handedness** *n.*

even[2] ('iːvˀn) *n. obs.* eve; evening —**'evensong** *n.* evening prayer

evening ('iːvnɪŋ) *n.* **1.** the close of day or

early part of night **2.** decline, end —**evening dress** attire for formal occasion during evening —**evening star** planet, usu. Venus, seen in west just after sunset

event (ɪ'vɛnt) n. **1.** happening **2.** notable occurrence **3.** issue, result **4.** any one contest in series in sporting programme —**e'ventful** a. full of exciting events —**e'venting** n. chiefly UK sport of taking part in equestrian competitions, usu. involving cross-country riding, jumping and dressage —**e'ventual** a. **1.** resulting in the end **2.** ultimate **3.** final —**eventu'ality** n. possible event —**e'ventually** adv. —**e'ventuate** vi. **1.** turn out **2.** happen **3.** end —**in the event that** if it should happen that

ever ('ɛvə) adv. **1.** always **2.** constantly **3.** at any time —**ever'more** adv. —**ever'green** n./a. (tree or shrub) bearing foliage throughout year —**ever'lasting** a. **1.** eternal **2.** lasting for an indefinitely long period —**ever'lastingly** adv.

every ('ɛvrɪ) a. **1.** each of all **2.** all possible —**'everybody** pron. —**'everyday** a. usual, ordinary —**'Everyman** n. (oft. e-) ordinary person; common man —**'everyone** pron. —**'everything** pron. —**'everywhere** adv. to or in all places

evict (ɪ'vɪkt) vt. expel by legal process, turn out —**e'viction** n. —**e'victor** n.

evident ('ɛvɪdənt) a. plain, obvious —**'evidence** n. **1.** ground of belief **2.** sign, indication **3.** testimony —vt. **4.** indicate, prove —**evi'dential** a. —**'evidently** adv. —**in evidence** conspicuous

evil ('iːv'l) a. **1.** bad, harmful —n. **2.** what is bad or harmful **3.** sin —**'evilly** adv. —**'evildoer** n. sinner —**evil-eyed** a. —**the evil eye** **1.** look superstitiously supposed to have power of inflicting harm etc. **2.** power to inflict harm etc. by such a look

evince (ɪ'vɪns) vt. show, indicate

eviscerate (ɪ'vɪsəreɪt) vt. **1.** remove internal organs of **2.** deprive of meaning or significance —**eviscer'ation** n. —**e'viscerator** n.

evoke (ɪ'vəʊk) vt. **1.** draw forth **2.** call to mind —**evocation** (ɛvə'keɪʃən) n. —**evocative** (ɪ'vɒkətɪv) a.

evolve (ɪ'vɒlv) v. **1.** develop or cause to develop gradually —vi. **2.** undergo slow changes in process of growth —**evolution** (iːvə'luːʃən) n. **1.** evolving **2.** development of species from earlier forms —**evolutional** (iːvə'luːʃən'l) a. —**evolutionary** (iːvə'luːʃənərɪ) a. —**evolutionist** (iːvə'luːʃənɪst) n.

ewe (juː) n. female sheep

ewer ('juːə) n. pitcher, water jug for washstand

ex¹ (ɛks) prep. **1.** Fin. excluding; without **2.** Comm. without charge to buyer until removed from —**ex cathedra** (kə'θiːdrə) **1.** with authority **2.** (of papal pronouncements) defined as infallibly true —**ex gratia** ('greɪʃə) given as favour, esp. where no legal obligation exists —**ex**

hypothesi (haɪ'pɒθəsɪ) in accordance with hypothesis stated —**ex libris** ('liːbrɪs) from the library of —**ex officio** (ə'fɪʃɪəʊ, ə'fɪsɪəʊ) by right of position or office —**ex post facto** ('fæktəʊ) having retrospective effect

ex² (ɛks) n. inf. ex-wife, ex-husband etc.

ex-, e-, or **ef-** (comb. form) out from, from, out of, formerly, as in exclaim, evade, effusive, exodus. Such words are not given here where the meaning may easily be inferred from the simple word

Ex. Exodus

ex. **1.** example **2.** except(ed) **3.** extra

exacerbate (ɪg'zæsəbeɪt, ɪk'sæs-) vt. **1.** aggravate, make worse **2.** embitter —**exacer'bation** n.

exact (ɪg'zækt) a. **1.** precise, accurate, strictly correct —vt. **2.** demand, extort **3.** insist upon **4.** enforce —**ex'acting** a. making rigorous or excessive demands —**ex'action** n. **1.** act of exacting **2.** that which is exacted, as excessive work etc. **3.** oppressive demand —**ex'actitude** n. —**ex'actly** adv. —**ex'actness** n. **1.** accuracy **2.** precision —**ex'actor** n.

exaggerate (ɪg'zædʒəreɪt) vt. **1.** magnify beyond truth, overstate **2.** enlarge **3.** overestimate —**exagger'ation** n. —**ex'aggerative** a. —**ex'aggerator** n.

exalt (ɪg'zɔːlt) vt. **1.** raise up **2.** praise **3.** make noble, dignify —**exal'tation** n. **1.** an exalting **2.** elevation in rank, dignity or position **3.** rapture

exam (ɪg'zæm) examination

examine (ɪg'zæmɪn) vt. **1.** investigate **2.** look at closely **3.** ask questions of **4.** test knowledge or proficiency of **5.** inquire into —**exami'nation** n. —**exami'nee** n. —**ex'aminer** n.

example (ɪg'zɑːmp'l) n. **1.** thing illustrating general rule **2.** specimen **3.** model **4.** warning **5.** precedent **6.** instance

exasperate (ɪg'zɑːspəreɪt) vt. **1.** irritate, enrage **2.** intensify, make worse —**exasper'ation** n.

excavate ('ɛkskəveɪt) vt. **1.** hollow out **2.** unearth **3.** make (hole) by digging —**exca'vation** n. —**'excavator** n.

exceed (ɪk'siːd) vt. **1.** be greater than **2.** go beyond **3.** surpass —**ex'ceeding** a. **1.** very great; exceptional; excessive —adv. **2.** obs. to a great or unusual degree —**ex'ceedingly** adv. **1.** very **2.** greatly

excel (ɪk'sɛl) vt. surpass, be better than —vi. **2.** be very good, pre-eminent (-**ll**-) —**'excellence** n. —**'Excellency** n. title borne by viceroys, ambassadors —**'excellent** a. very good

except (ɪk'sɛpt) prep. **1.** not including **2.** but —conj. **3.** obs. unless —vt. **4.** leave or take out **5.** exclude —**ex'cepting** prep. not including —**ex'ception** n. **1.** thing excepted, not included in a rule **2.** objection —**ex'ceptionable** a. open to objection —**ex'ceptional** a. not ordinary, esp. much above average —**ex'ceptionally** adv.

excerpt ('ɛksɜːpt) n. **1.** quoted or

extracted passage from book *etc.* —*vt.* (ɛk'sɜ:pt) 2. extract, quote (passage from book *etc.*) —ex'cerption *n.*

excess (ɪk'sɛs, 'ɛksɛs) *n.* 1. an exceeding 2. amount by which thing exceeds 3. too great amount 4. intemperance, immoderate conduct —ex'cessive *a.* —ex'cessively *adv.* —excess luggage *or* baggage luggage that is more in weight or number of items than airline *etc.* will carry free

exchange (ɪks'tʃeɪndʒ) *vt.* 1. give (something) in return for something else 2. barter —*n.* 3. giving one thing and receiving another 4. thing given for another 5. building where merchants meet for business 6. central telephone office where connections are made *etc.* —exchangea'bility *n.* —ex'changeable *a.* —exchange rate rate at which currency unit of one country may be exchanged for that of another

exchequer (ɪks'tʃɛkə) *n.* government department in charge of revenue

excise[1] ('ɛksaɪz, ɛk'saɪz) *n.* duty charged on home goods during manufacture or before sale

excise[2] (ɪk'saɪz) *vt.* cut out, cut away —excision (ɛk'sɪʒən) *n.*

excite (ɪk'saɪt) *vt.* 1. arouse to strong emotion, stimulate 2. rouse up, set in motion 3. *Elec.* magnetize poles of —excita'bility *n.* —ex'citable *a.* —ex'citably *adv.* —exci'tation *n.* —ex'cited *a.* emotionally or sexually aroused —ex'citedness *n.* —ex'citement *n.* —ex'citing *a.* 1. thrilling 2. rousing to action

exclaim (ɪk'skleɪm) *vi.* 1. speak suddenly —*v.* 2. cry out —exclamation (ɛksklə-'meɪʃən) *n.* —exclamatory (ɪks-'klæmətərɪ) *a.* —exclamation mark *or* U.S. point punctuation mark ! used after exclamations and vehement commands

exclude (ɪk'sklu:d) *vt.* 1. shut out 2. debar 3. reject, not consider —ex'clusion *n.* —ex'clusive *a.* 1. excluding 2. inclined to keep out (from society *etc.*) 3. sole, only 4. select —*n.* 5. something exclusive, *esp.* story appearing only in one newspaper —ex'clusively *adv.*

excommunicate (ɛkskə'mju:nɪkeɪt) *vt.* cut off from the sacraments of the Church —excommuni'cation *n.*

excoriate (ɪk'skɔ:rɪeɪt) *vt.* 1. strip (skin) from (person or animal) 2. denounce vehemently —excori'ation *n.*

excrement ('ɛkskrɪmənt) *n.* 1. waste matter from body, *esp.* from bowels 2. dung —excreta (ɪk'skri:tə) *pl.n.* excrement —excrete (ɪk'skri:t) *vt.* discharge from the system —excretion (ɪk'skri:ʃən) *n.* —excretory (ɪk'skri:tərɪ) *a.*

excrescent (ɪk'skrɛs°nt) *a.* 1. growing out of something 2. redundant —ex'crescence *n.* unnatural outgrowth

excruciate (ɪk'skru:ʃɪeɪt) *vt.* torment acutely, torture in body or mind —ex'cruciating *a.* —excruci'ation *n.*

exculpate ('ɛkskʌlpeɪt, ɪk'skʌlpeɪt) *vt.* free

from blame, acquit —excul'pation *n.* —ex'culpatory *a.*

excursion (ɪk'skɜ:ʃən, -ʒən) *n.* 1. journey, ramble, trip for pleasure 2. digression —ex'cursive *a.* 1. tending to digress 2. involving detours —ex'cursiveness *n.* —ex'cursus *n.* digression (*pl.* -es, -sus (*rare*))

excuse (ɪk'skju:z) *vt.* 1. forgive, overlook 2. try to clear from blame 3. seek exemption for 4. set free, remit —*n.* (ɪk'skju:s) 5. that which serves to excuse 6. apology —ex'cusable *a.*

exeat ('ɛksɪət) *n.* UK 1. leave of absence from school 2. bishop's permission for priest to leave diocese to take up appointment elsewhere

exec. 1. executive 2. executor

execrate ('ɛksɪkreɪt) *vt.* 1. loathe, detest 2. denounce, deplore 3. curse —'execrable *a.* abominable, hatefully bad —exe'cration *n.* —'execrative *or* 'execratory *a.*

execute ('ɛksɪkju:t) *vt.* 1. inflict capital punishment on, kill 2. carry out, perform 3. make, produce 4. sign (document) —ex'ecutant *n.* performer, *esp.* of music —exe'cution *n.* —exe'cutioner *n.* one employed to execute criminals —ex'ecutive *n.* 1. person in administrative position 2. executive body 3. committee carrying on business of society *etc.* —*a.* 4. carrying into effect, *esp.* of branch of government enforcing laws —ex'ecutor *n.* person appointed to carry out provisions of a will (ex'ecutrix *fem.*)

exegesis (ɛksɪ'dʒi:sɪs) *n.* explanation, *esp.* of Scripture (*pl.* -geses (-'dʒi:si:z)) —exegetic(al) (ɛksɪ'dʒɛtɪk(°l)) *a.*

exemplar (ɪg'zɛmplə, -plɑ:) *n.* model type —ex'emplarily *adv.* —ex'emplary *a.* 1. fit to be imitated, serving as example 2. commendable 3. typical —exemplifi'cation *n.* —ex'emplify *vt.* 1. serve as example of 2. illustrate 3. exhibit 4. make attested copy of (-fied, -fying)

exempt (ɪg'zɛmpt) *vt.* 1. free 2. excuse —*a.* 3. freed (from), not liable (for) 4. not affected (by) —ex'emption *n.*

exequies ('ɛksɪkwɪz) *pl.n.* funeral rites or procession

exercise ('ɛksəsaɪz) *vt.* 1. use, employ 2. give exercise to 3. carry out, discharge 4. trouble, harass —*vi.* 5. take exercise —*n.* 6. use of limbs for health 7. practice for training 8. task for training 9. lesson 10. employment 11. use (of limbs, faculty *etc.*)

exert (ɪg'zɜ:t) *vt.* 1. apply (oneself) diligently, make effort 2. bring to bear —ex'ertion *n.* effort, physical activity

exeunt ('ɛksɪʌnt) *Lat. Theat.* they leave the stage: stage direction —exeunt omnes ('ɒmneɪz) they all go out

exfoliate (ɛks'fəʊlɪeɪt) *v.* peel in scales, layers

exhale (ɛks'heɪl, ɪg'zeɪl) *v.* 1. breathe out 2. give, pass off as vapour

exhaust (ɪg'zɔ:st) *vt.* 1. tire out 2. use up 3. empty 4. draw off 5. treat, discuss

exhibit 171 **expend**

thoroughly —*n.* **6.** used steam or fluid from engine **7.** waste gases from internal-combustion engine **8.** passage for, or coming out of this —**exhausti'bility** *n.* —**ex'haustible** *a.* —**ex'haustion** *n.* **1.** state of extreme fatigue **2.** limit of endurance —**ex'haustive** *a.* comprehensive

exhibit (ɪgˈzɪbɪt) *vt.* **1.** show, display **2.** manifest **3.** show publicly (oft. in competition) —*n.* **4.** thing shown, *esp.* in competition or as evidence in court —**exhi'bition** *n.* **1.** display, act of displaying **2.** public show (of works of art *etc.*) —**exhi'bitionism** *n.* —**exhi'bitionist** *n.* one with compulsive desire to draw attention to himself or to expose genitals publicly —**exhibition'istic** *a.* —**ex'hibitor** *n.* one who exhibits, *esp.* in show —**ex'hibitory** *a.*

exhilarate (ɪgˈzɪləreɪt) *vt.* enliven, gladden —**exhila'ration** *n.* high spirits, enlivenment

exhort (ɪgˈzɔːt) *vt.* urge, admonish earnestly —**exhor'tation** *n.* —**ex'horter** *n.*

exhume (ɛksˈhjuːm) *vt.* unearth (what has been buried), disinter —**exhu'mation** *n.*

exigent ('ɛksɪdʒənt) *a.* **1.** exacting **2.** urgent, pressing —**'exigence** *or* **'exigency** *n.* **1.** pressing need **2.** emergency —**'exigible** *a.* liable to be exacted or demanded

exiguous (ɪgˈzɪgjʊəs, ɪkˈsɪg-) *a.* scanty, meagre

exile ('ɛgzaɪl, 'ɛksaɪl) *n.* **1.** banishment, expulsion from one's own country **2.** long absence abroad **3.** one banished or permanently living away from his home or country —*vt.* **4.** banish, expel

exist (ɪgˈzɪst) *vi.* be, have being, live —**ex'istence** *n.* —**ex'istent** *a.*

existential (ɛgzɪˈstɛnʃəl) *a.* **1.** of existence **2.** *Philos.* based on personal experience **3.** of existentialism —**exis'tentialism** *n.* theory which holds that man is free and responsible for his own acts

exit ('ɛgzɪt, 'ɛksɪt) *n.* **1.** way out **2.** going out **3.** death **4.** actor's departure from stage —*vi.* **5.** go out

exo- (*comb. form*) external, outside, or beyond, as in *exothermal*

exocrine ('ɛksəʊkraɪn) *a.* of gland (*eg* salivary, sweat) secreting its products through ducts

Exod. *Bible* Exodus

exodus ('ɛksədəs) *n.* **1.** departure, *esp.* of crowd **2.** (E-) second book of Old Testament

exonerate (ɪgˈzɒnəreɪt) *vt.* **1.** free, declare free, from blame **2.** exculpate **3.** acquit —**exoner'ation** *n.* —**ex'onerative** *a.*

exorbitant (ɪgˈzɔːbɪtənt) *a.* very excessive, inordinate, immoderate —**ex'orbitance** *n.* —**ex'orbitantly** *adv.*

exorcise *or* **-ize** ('ɛksɔːsaɪz) *vt.* cast out (evil spirits) by invocation **2.** free (person) of evil spirits —**exorcism** ('ɛksɔːsɪzəm) *n.* —**exorcist** ('ɛksɔːsɪst) *n.*

exordium (ɛkˈsɔːdɪəm) *n.* introductory part of a speech or treatise (*pl.* **-s, -ia** (-ɪə)) —**ex'ordial** *a.*

exoteric (ɛksəʊˈtɛrɪk) *a.* **1.** understandable by the many **2.** ordinary, popular

exotic (ɪgˈzɒtɪk) *a.* **1.** brought in from abroad, foreign **2.** rare, unusual, having strange or bizarre allure —*n.* **3.** exotic plant *etc.* —**ex'otica** *pl.n.* (collection of) exotic objects —**ex'oticism** *n.* —**exotic dancer** striptease or belly dancer

expand (ɪkˈspænd) *v.* **1.** increase **2.** spread out **3.** dilate **4.** develop —**ex'pandable** *or* **ex'pandible** *a.* —**ex'panse** *n.* **1.** wide space **2.** open stretch of land —**expansi'bility** *n.* —**ex'pansible** *a.* —**ex'pansion** *n.* —**ex-'pansionism** *n.* practice of expanding economy or territory of country —**ex'pansionist** *n./a.* —**expansion'istic** *a.* —**ex-'pansive** *a.* **1.** wide **2.** extensive **3.** friendly, talkative

expatiate (ɪkˈspeɪʃɪeɪt) *vi.* **1.** speak or write at great length **2.** enlarge —**expati'a-tion** *n.*

expatriate (ɛksˈpætrɪeɪt) *vt.* **1.** banish, exile **2.** withdraw (oneself) from one's native land —*a./n.* (ɛksˈpætrɪɪt, -eɪt) **3.** (person) exiled or banished from his native country —**expatri'ation** *n.*

expect (ɪkˈspɛkt) *vt.* **1.** regard as probable **2.** look forward to **3.** await **4.** hope for —**ex'pectancy** *n.* **1.** state or act of expecting **2.** that which is expected **3.** hope —**ex'pectant** *a.* looking or waiting for, *esp.* for birth of child —**ex'pectantly** *adv.* —**expec'tation** *n.* **1.** act or state of expecting **2.** prospect of future good **3.** what is expected **4.** promise **5.** value of something expected —*pl.* **6.** prospect of fortune or profit by will

expectorate (ɪkˈspɛktəreɪt) *v.* spit out (phlegm *etc.*) —**ex'pectorant** *Med. a.* **1.** promoting secretion, liquefaction or expulsion of sputum from respiratory passages —*n.* **2.** expectorant drug or agent —**expecto'ration** *n.*

expedient (ɪkˈspiːdɪənt) *a.* **1.** fitting, advisable, politic, suitable, convenient —*n.* **2.** something suitable, useful, *esp.* in emergency —**ex'pediency** *n.* —**ex'pediently** *adv.*

expedite ('ɛkspɪdaɪt) *vt.* **1.** help on, hasten **2.** dispatch —**expedition** (ɛkspɪˈdɪʃən) *n.* **1.** journey for definite (oft. scientific or military) purpose **2.** people, equipment comprising expedition **3.** excursion **4.** promptness —**expeditionary** ('ɛkspɪ-'dɪʃənərɪ) *a.* —**expeditious** (ɛkspɪˈdɪʃəs) *a.* prompt, speedy

expel (ɪkˈspɛl) *vt.* **1.** drive, cast out **2.** exclude **3.** discharge (**-ll-**) —**expulsion** (ɪkˈspʌlʃən) *n.* —**expulsive** (ɪkˈspʌlsɪv) *a.*

expend (ɪkˈspɛnd) *vt.* **1.** spend, pay out **2.** use up —**ex'pendable** *a.* likely, or meant, to be used up or destroyed —**ex'penditure** *n.* —**ex'pense** *n.* **1.** cost **2.** (cause of) spending —*pl.* **3.** charges, outlay incurred —**ex'pensive** *a.* high-priced, costly, dear —**expense account 1.** arrangement by which expenses are refunded to employee by employer 2. record of such expenses

experience (ɪk'spɪərɪəns) n. 1. observation of facts as source of knowledge 2. being affected consciously by event 3. the event 4. knowledge, skill, gained from life, by contact with facts and events —vt. 5. undergo, suffer, meet with —**ex'perienced** a. skilled, expert, capable —**experi'ential** a.

experiment (ɪk'sperɪmənt) n. 1. test, trial, something done in the hope that it may succeed, or to test theory —vi. (ɪk'sperɪment) 2. make experiment —**experi'mental** a. —**experi'mentalist** n. —**experi'mentally** adv.

expert ('ekspɜːt) n. 1. one skilful, knowledgeable, in something 2. authority —a. 3. practised, skilful —**expertise** (ekspɜː'tiːz) n.

expiate ('ekspɪeɪt) vt. 1. pay penalty for 2. make amends for —**expi'ation** n. —'**expiator** n. —'**expiatory** a.

expire (ɪk'spaɪə) vi. 1. come to an end 2. give out breath 3. die —vt. 4. breathe out —**expiration** (ekspɪ'reɪʃən) n. —**ex'piratory** a. —**ex'piry** n. end

explain (ɪk'spleɪn) vt. 1. make clear, intelligible 2. interpret 3. elucidate 4. give details of 5. account for —**explanation** (eksplə'neɪʃən) n. —**explanatory** (ɪks-'plænətərɪ, -trɪ) or **explanative** (ɪks-'plænətɪv) a.

expletive (ɪk'spliːtɪv) n. 1. exclamation 2. oath —a. 3. serving only to fill out sentence etc.

explicable ('eksplɪkəb'l, ɪk'splɪk-) a. explainable —**'explicate** vt. develop, explain —**ex'plicative** or **ex'plicatory** a.

explicit (ɪk'splɪsɪt) a. 1. stated in detail 2. stated, not merely implied 3. outspoken 4. clear, plain 5. unequivocal

explode (ɪk'spləʊd) vi. 1. go off with bang 2. burst violently 3. (of population) increase rapidly —vt. 4. make explode 5. discredit, expose (a theory etc.) —**ex'plosion** n. —**ex'plosive** a./n.

exploit ('eksplɔɪt) n. 1. brilliant feat, deed —vt. (ɪk'splɔɪt) 2. turn to advantage 3. make use of for one's own ends —**exploi'tation** n. —**ex'ploiter** n.

explore (ɪk'splɔː) vt. 1. investigate 2. examine 3. scrutinize 4. examine (country etc.) by going through it —**exploration** (ɪk'splɔːrətərɪ, -trɪ) a. —**ex'plorer** n.

explosion (ɪk'spləʊʒən) n. see EXPLODE

expo ('ekspəʊ) n. inf. exposition, large international exhibition

exponent (ɪk'spəʊnənt) n. see EXPOUND

export (ɪk'spɔːt, 'ekspɔːt) vt. 1. send (goods) out of the country —n./a. ('ekspɔːt) 2. (of) goods or services sold to foreign country or countries —**expor'tation** n. —**ex'porter** n.

expose (ɪk'spəʊz) vt. 1. exhibit 2. disclose, reveal 3. lay open 4. leave unprotected 5. subject (photographic plate or film) to light —**ex'posed** a. 1. not concealed 2. without shelter from the elements 3. vulnerable —**exposedness** (ɪk'spəʊzɪdnɪs) n. —**ex'posure** n. 1. act of exposing or condition of being exposed 2. position or outlook of building 3. lack of shelter from weather, esp. cold 4. exposed surface 5. Photog. act of exposing film or plate to light etc.; area on film or plate that has been exposed 6. Photog. intensity of light falling on film or plate multiplied by time of exposure; combination of lens aperture and shutter speed used in taking photograph 7. appearance before public, as on TV

exposé (eks'pəʊzeɪ) n. newspaper article etc. disclosing scandal, crime etc.

exposition (ekspə'zɪʃən) n. see EXPOUND

expostulate (ɪk'spɒstjuleɪt) vi. 1. remonstrate 2. reason (in a kindly manner) —**expostu'lation** n. —**ex'postulatory** a.

expound (ɪk'spaʊnd) vt. explain, interpret —**exponent** (ɪk'spəʊnənt) n. 1. one who expounds or promotes (idea, cause etc.) 2. performer, executant 3. Maths. small, raised number showing the power of a factor —**expo'nential** a. —**expo'sition** n. 1. explanation, description 2. exhibition of goods etc. —**expositor** (ɪk'spɒzɪtə) n. one who explains, interpreter —**expository** (ɪk'spɒzɪtərɪ, -trɪ) a. explanatory

express (ɪk'spres) vt. 1. put into words 2. make known or understood by words, behaviour etc. 3. squeeze out —a. 4. definitely stated 5. specially designed 6. clear 7. positive 8. speedy 9. (of messenger) specially sent off 10. (of train) fast and making few stops —adv. 11. specially 12. on purpose 13. with speed —n. 14. express train or messenger 15. rapid parcel delivery service —**ex'pressible** a. —**ex'pression** n. 1. expressing 2. word, phrase 3. look, aspect 4. feeling 5. utterance —**ex'pressionism** n. theory that art depends on expression of artist's creative self, not on mere reproduction —**ex'pressive** a. —**ex'pressly** adv. —**ex'pressway** n. esp. US urban motorway

expresso (ɪk'spresəʊ) n. see ESPRESSO

expropriate (eks'prəʊprɪeɪt) vt. 1. dispossess 2. take out of owner's hands —**expropri'ation** n.

expulsion (ɪk'spʌlʃən) n. see EXPEL

expunge (ɪk'spʌndʒ) vt. strike out, erase —**ex'punction** n.

expurgate ('ekspəgeɪt) vt. remove objectionable parts from (book etc.), purge —**expur'gation** n. —'**expurgator** n. —**ex'purgatory** a.

exquisite (ɪk'skwɪzɪt, 'ekskwɪzɪt) a. 1. of extreme beauty or delicacy 2. keen, acute 3. keenly sensitive —**ex'quisitely** adv.

ex-serviceman n. man who has served in the armed forces

extant (ek'stænt, 'ekstənt) a. still existing

extempore (ɪk'stempərɪ) a./adv. without previous thought or preparation —**extem-**

po'raneous a. —ex'temporary a. —extempori'zation or -i'sation n. —ex'temporize or -ise vi. 1. speak without preparation —vt. 2. devise for the occasion

extend (ik'stɛnd) vt. 1. stretch out, lengthen 2. prolong in duration 3. widen in area, scope 4. accord, grant —vi. 5. reach 6. cover a certain area 7. have a certain range or scope 8. become larger or wider —ex'tendible, ex'tendable, ex'tensible or ex'tensile a. that can be extended —ex'tension n. 1. stretching out, prolongation, enlargement 2. expansion 3. continuation, additional part, as of telephone etc. —ex'tensive a. wide, large, comprehensive —ex'tensor n. straightening muscle —ex'tent n. 1. space or degree to which thing is extended 2. size 3. compass 4. volume —extended family nuclear family together with blood relatives, oft. spanning three or more generations —extended-play a. denoting gramophone record same size as a single but with longer playing time

extenuate (ik'stɛnjueit) vt. make less blameworthy, mitigate —extenu'ation n. —ex'tenuatory a.

exterior (ik'stiəriə) n. 1. the outside 2. outward appearance —a. 3. outer, outward, external —exterior angle 1. angle of polygon contained between one side extended and adjacent side 2. any of four angles made by transversal that are outside region between two intersected lines

exterminate (ik'stɜːmineit) vt. destroy utterly, annihilate, root out, eliminate —extermi'nation n. —ex'terminator n. destroyer

external (ik'stɜːn³l) a. outside, outward —externali'zation, exteriorization or -isation (ikstiəriərai'zeiʃən) n. —ex'ternalize, ex'teriorize or -ise vt. 1. make external 2. Psychol. attribute (one's feelings) to one's surroundings —ex'ternally adv.

extinct (ik'stiŋkt) a. 1. having died out or come to an end 2. no longer existing 3. quenched, no longer burning —ex'tinction n.

extinguish (ik'stiŋgwiʃ) vt. 1. put out, quench 2. wipe out —ex'tinguishable a. —ex'tinguisher n. device, esp. spraying liquid or foam, used to put out fires

extirpate ('ɛkstəpeit) vt. 1. root out 2. destroy utterly —extir'pation n. —'extirpator n.

extol or U.S. extoll (ik'stəul) vt. praise highly (-ll-)

extort (ik'stɔːt) vt. 1. get by force or threats 2. wring out 3. exact —ex'tortion n. —ex'tortionate a. (of prices etc.) excessive, exorbitant —ex'tortioner n.

extra ('ɛkstrə) a. 1. additional 2. larger, better, than usual —adv. 3. additionally 4. more than usually —n. 5. extra thing 6. something charged as additional 7. Cricket run not scored off bat 8. Cine. actor hired for crowd scenes

extra- (comb. form) beyond, as in extradition, extramural, extraterritorial. Such words are not given here where the meaning may easily be inferred from the simple word

extract (ik'strækt) vt. 1. take out, esp. by force 2. obtain against person's will 3. get by pressure, distillation etc. 4. deduce 5. derive 6. copy out, quote —n. ('ɛkstrækt) 7. passage from book, film etc. 8. matter got by distillation 9. concentrated solution —ex'traction n. 1. extracting, esp. of tooth 2. ancestry —ex'tractor n. —extractor fan device for extracting stale air, fumes etc.

extracurricular (ɛkstrəkə'rikjulə) a. 1. taking place outside normal school timetable 2. beyond regular duties etc.

extradition (ɛkstrə'diʃən) n. delivery, under treaty, of foreign fugitive from justice to authorities concerned —extraditable ('ɛkstrədaitəb³l) a. —extradite ('ɛkstrədait) vt. 1. surrender (alleged offender) for trial to foreign state 2. procure extradition of

extramural (ɛkstrə'mjuərəl) a. 1. connected with but outside normal courses etc. of university or college 2. situated outside walls or boundaries of a place

extraneous (ik'streiniəs) a. 1. not essential 2. irrelevant 3. added from without, not belonging

extraordinary (ik'strɔːd³nri) a. 1. out of the usual course 2. additional 3. unusual, surprising, exceptional —ex'traordinarily adv.

extrapolate (ik'stræpəleit) v. 1. infer (something not known) from known facts 2. Maths. estimate (a value) beyond known values

extrasensory (ɛkstrə'sɛnsəri) a. of perception apparently gained without use of known senses

extraterrestrial (ɛkstrəti'rɛstriəl) a. of, or from outside the earth's atmosphere

extravagant (ik'strævigənt) a. 1. wasteful 2. exorbitant 3. wild, absurd —ex'travagance n. —ex'travagantly adv. —extrava-'ganza n. elaborate, lavish, entertainment, display etc.

extravert ('ɛkstrəvɜːt) n. see EXTROVERT

extreme (ik'striːm) a. 1. of high or highest degree 2. severe 3. going beyond moderation 4. at the end 5. outermost —n. 6. utmost degree 7. thing at one end or the other, first and last of series —ex'tremely adv. —ex'tremism n. —ex'tremist n. 1. advocate of extreme measures —a. 2. of immoderate or excessive actions, opinions etc. —extremity (ik'strɛmiti) n. 1. end —pl. 2. hands and feet 3. utmost distress 4. extreme measures —extreme unction sacrament in which dying person is anointed by priest

extricate ('ɛkstrikeit) vt. disentangle,

unravel, set free —**'extricable** a. —**extri-
'cation** n.

extrinsic (εk'strɪnsɪk) a. accessory, not
belonging, not intrinsic —**ex'trinsically**
adv.

extrovert or **extravert** ('εkstrəvɜːt) n.
one who is interested in other people and
things rather than his own feelings
—**extro'version** or **extra'version** n.

extrude (ɪk'struːd) vt. 1. squeeze, force out
2. (esp. of molten metal or plastic etc.)
shape by squeezing through suitable
nozzle or die

exuberant (ɪg'zjuːbərənt) a. 1. high-
spirited, vivacious 2. prolific, abundant,
luxurious —**ex'uberance** n. —**ex'uberant-
ly** adv.

exude (ɪg'zjuːd) vi. 1. ooze out —vt. 2. give
off (moisture) —**exu'dation** n. —**ex'uda-
tive** a.

exult (ɪg'zʌlt) vi. 1. rejoice 2. triumph
—**ex'ultancy** n. —**ex'ultant** a. triumphant
—**exul'tation** n.

-ey (comb. form) see -Y¹, -Y²

eye (aɪ) n. 1. organ of sight 2. look, glance
3. attention 4. aperture 5. view 6. judgment
7. watch, vigilance 8. thing, mark
resembling eye 9. slit in needle for thread
—vt. 10. look at 11. observe —**'eyeless** a.
—**'eyelet** n. small hole for rope etc. to
pass through —**'eyeball** n. ball of eye
—**'eyebrow** n. fringe of hair above eye
—**eye-catcher** n. —**eye-catching** a. striking —**'eyeful** n. inf. 1. view, glance etc. 2.
beautiful sight, esp. a woman —**'eyeglass**
n. 1. glass to assist sight 2. monocle —pl. 3.
chiefly US spectacles —**'eyehole** n. 1. hole
through which rope etc. is passed 2. inf.
cavity containing eyeball 3. peephole
—**'eyelash** n. hair fringing eyelid —**'eyelid** n. either of two muscular folds of skin
that can be moved to cover exposed
portion of eyeball —**'eyeliner** n. cosmetic
used to outline eyes —**eye-opener** n. inf. 1.
surprising news 2. revealing statement
—**'eyepiece** n. lens or lenses in optical
instrument nearest eye of observer —**eye
shadow** coloured cosmetic put on around
the eyes —**'eyeshot** n. range of vision
—**'eyesight** n. ability to see —**'eyesore** n.
1. ugly object 2. thing that annoys one to
see —**'eyestrain** n. fatigue of eyes,
resulting from excessive use or uncorrect-
ed defects of vision —**'eyetooth** n. canine
tooth —**'eyewash** n. inf. deceptive talk
etc., nonsense —**'eyewitness** n. one who
saw something for himself —**an eye for an
eye** retributive justice; retaliation

eyrie ('ɪərɪ, 'εərɪ, 'aɪərɪ) or **aerie** n. 1. nest
of bird of prey, esp. eagle 2. high dwelling
place

F

f or **F** (ɛf) *n*. **1.** sixth letter of English alphabet **2.** speech sound represented by this letter, as in *fat* (*pl*. **f's, F's** or **Fs**)

f, f/, or **f**: f number

f. *Mus*. forte

f. or **F. 1.** female **2.** *Gram*. feminine **3.** folio (*pl*. **ff.** or **FF.**) **4.** following (page) (*pl*. **ff.**) **5.** franc **6.** furlong

F 1. *Mus*. fourth note of scale of C major; major or minor key having this note as tonic **2.** Fahrenheit **3.** *Chem*. fluorine **4.** *Phys*. force **5.** farad **6.** *Genetics* generation of filial offspring, F₁ being first generation **7.** Fellow

fa (fɑː) *n. see* FAH

FA Football Association

Fabian ('feɪbɪən) *a*. **1.** of or resembling delaying tactics of Q. Fabius Maximus, Roman general; cautious —*n*. **2.** member of Fabian Society, socialist organization advocating gradual reforms

fable ('feɪbʰl) *n*. **1.** short story with moral, *esp*. one with animals as characters **2.** tale **3.** legend **4.** fiction; lie —*v*. **5.** tell (fables) —*vi*. **6.** tell lies —*vt*. **7.** talk of in manner of fable —**fabulist** ('fæbjʊlɪst) *n*. writer of fables —**fabulous** ('fæbjʊləs) *a*. **1.** amazing **2.** *inf*. extremely good **3.** told of in fables

fabric ('fæbrɪk) *n*. **1.** cloth **2.** texture **3.** frame, structure —**fabricate** *vt*. **1.** build **2.** frame **3.** construct **4.** invent (lie *etc*.) **5.** forge (document) —**fabri'cation** *n*. —**'fabricator** *n*.

façade or **facade** (fə'sɑːd, fæ-) *n*. **1.** front of building **2.** *fig*. outward appearance

face (feɪs) *n*. **1.** front of head **2.** distorted expression **3.** outward appearance **4.** front, upper surface or chief side of anything **5.** dial of a clock *etc*. **6.** dignity **7.** *inf*. make-up (*esp*. in **put one's face on**) **8.** *Print*. printing surface of type character; style or design of character on type (*also* **'typeface**) —*vt*. **9.** look or front towards **10.** meet (boldly) **11.** give a covering surface to —*vi*. **12.** turn —**'faceless** *a*. **1.** without a face **2.** anonymous —**'facer** *n*. **1.** person or thing that faces **2.** UK *inf*. difficulty, problem —**facet** ('fæsɪt) *n*. **1.** one side of many-sided body, *esp*. cut gem **2.** one aspect —**facial** ('feɪʃəl) *a*. **1.** pert. to face —*n*. **2.** cosmetic treatment for face —**'facing** *n*. **1.** piece of material used *esp*. to conceal seam and prevent fraying **2.** (*usu. pl*.) collar, cuffs *etc*. of military uniform jacket **3.** outer layer or coat of material applied to surface of wall —**face card** US court card —**face-lift** *n*. **1.** operation to tighten skin of face to remove wrinkles **2.** improvement, renovation —**face-saving** *a*. maintaining dignity —**face value 1.** value on face of commercial paper or coin **2.** apparent value —**face up to** accept (unpleasant fact *etc*.) —**on the face of it** to all appearances

facetious (fə'siːʃəs) *a*. **1.** (sarcastically) witty **2.** humorous, given to jesting, *esp*. at inappropriate time

facia ('feɪʃɪə) *n. see* FASCIA

-facient (*comb. form*) state; quality, as in *absorbefacient*

facile ('fæsaɪl) *a*. **1.** easy **2.** working easily **3.** easy-going **4.** superficial, silly —**facilitate** (fə'sɪlɪteɪt) *vt*. make easy, help progress of —**facilitation** (fəsɪlɪ'teɪʃən) *n*. —**facility** (fə'sɪlɪtɪ) *n*. **1.** easiness **2.** dexterity —*pl*. **3.** opportunities, good conditions **4.** means, equipment for doing something

facsimile (fæk'sɪmɪlɪ) *n*. **1.** exact copy **2.** telegraphic system in which document is scanned by photoelectricity, signals being transmitted and reproduced photographically **3.** image produced by this means

fact (fækt) *n*. **1.** thing known to be true **2.** deed **3.** reality —**'factual** *a*. —**as a matter of fact, in (point of) fact** in reality or actuality —**fact of life** (*esp*. unpleasant) inescapable truth

faction¹ ('fækʃən) *n*. **1.** (dissenting) minority group within larger body **2.** dissension —**'factious** *a*. of or producing factions

faction² ('fækʃən) *n*. dramatization of factual event

factitious (fæk'tɪʃəs) *a*. **1.** artificial **2.** specially made up **3.** unreal

factor ('fæktə) *n*. **1.** something contributing to a result **2.** one of numbers which multiplied together give a given number **3.** agent, dealer —**fac'torial** *Maths*. *n*. **1.** product of all positive integers from one up to and including given integer —*a*. **2.** of factorials or factors —**fac'totum** *n*. man-of-all-work —**factor 8** protein that participates in clotting of blood: used in treatment of haemophilia

factory ('fæktərɪ) *n*. building where things are manufactured —**factory farm** farm where animals are intensively reared using modern industrial methods —**factory ship** vessel that processes fish supplied by fleet

faculty ('fækʰltɪ) *n*. **1.** inherent power **2.** power of the mind **3.** ability, aptitude **4.** department of university **5.** members of profession **6.** authorization —**'facultative** *a*. optional **2.** contingent

fad (fæd) *n*. **1.** short-lived fashion **2.** whim —**'faddish** or **'faddy** *a*.

fade (feɪd) *vi*. **1.** lose colour, strength **2.** wither **3.** grow dim **4.** disappear gradually —*vt*. **5.** cause to fade —**'fader** *n*. —**fade-in, fade-out** *n*. **1.** *Rad*. variation in strength of signals **2.** *T.V., cine*. gradual appearance and disappearance of picture

faeces or esp. U.S. **feces** ('fiːsiːz) pl.n. excrement, waste matter —**faecal** or esp. U.S. **fecal** ('fiːkʰl) a.

faerie or **faery** ('feɪərɪ, 'fɛərɪ) obs., poet. n. 1. fairyland —a./n. 2. see FAIRY

Faeroese or **Faroese** (fɛərəʊ'iːz) a. 1. of Faeroes, islands in N Atlantic —n. 2. language of Faeroes 3. native of Faeroes (pl. **-ese**)

faff (fæf) vi. (oft. with about) UK inf. dither; fuss

fag (fæg) n. 1. inf. boring task 2. sl. cigarette 3. US sl. male homosexual 4. UK esp. formerly, young public school boy who performs menial chores for older boy or prefect —v. 5. inf. (esp. with out) tire —vi. 6. do menial tasks for a senior boy in school (**-gg-**) —**fag end** 1. last part, inferior remnant 2. UK inf. stub of cigarette

faggot¹ or esp. U.S. **fagot** ('fægət) n. 1. bundle of sticks for fuel etc. 2. ball of chopped liver etc.

faggot² ('fægət) n. US sl. male homosexual

fah or **fa** (fɑː) n. Mus. 1. in fixed system of solmization, note F 2. in tonic sol-fa, fourth degree of major scale

Fah. or **Fahr.** Fahrenheit

Fahrenheit ('færənhaɪt) a. measured by thermometric scale with freezing point of water 32°, boiling point 212°

faïence (faɪ'ɑːns, feɪ-) n. glazed earthenware or china

fail (feɪl) vi. 1. be unsuccessful 2. stop operating or working 3. be below the required standard 4. be insufficient 5. run short 6. be wanting when in need 7. lose power 8. die away 9. become bankrupt —vt. 10. disappoint, give no help to 11. neglect 12. judge (candidate) to be below required standard —**failing** n. 1. deficiency 2. fault —prep. 3. in default of —**failure** n. —**fail-safe** a. (of device) ensuring safety or remedy of malfunction in machine, weapon etc. —**without fail** certainly

fain (feɪn) obs. a. 1. glad, willing; constrained —adv. 2. gladly

faint (feɪnt) a. 1. feeble, dim, pale 2. weak 3. dizzy, about to lose consciousness —vi. 4. lose consciousness temporarily —**faint-hearted** a. timid

fair¹ (fɛə) a. 1. just, impartial 2. according to rules, legitimate 3. blond 4. beautiful 5. ample 6. of moderate quality or amount 7. unblemished 8. plausible 9. middling 10. (of weather) favourable —adv. 11. honestly 12. absolutely; quite —**fairing** n. Aviation streamlined casing, or any part so shaped that it provides streamline form —**fairish** a. —**fairly** adv. 1. moderately 2. as deserved; justly 3. positively —**fairness** n. —**Fair Isle** intricate multicoloured pattern knitted with Shetland wool —**fair play** (abidance by) established standard of decency —**fairway** n. 1. navigable channel 2. Golf trimmed turf between rough —**fair-weather** a. 1. suitable for use

in fair weather only 2. unreliable in difficult situations —**the fair sex** women collectively

fair² (fɛə) n. 1. travelling entertainment with sideshows, amusements etc. 2. large exhibition of commercial or industrial products 3. periodical market often with amusements —**fairground** n.

fairy ('fɛərɪ) n. 1. imaginary small creature with powers of magic 2. sl. male homosexual —a. 3. of fairies 4. like fairy, beautiful and delicate —**fairy godmother** benefactress, esp. unknown —**fairy lamp** small coloured lamp for decorations —**fairyland** n. —**fairy lights** small, coloured, decorative lights, esp. on Christmas tree —**fairy ring** circle of darker colour in grass —**fairy tale** 1. story of imaginary beings and happenings, esp. as told to children 2. highly improbable account

fait accompli (fɛ takɔ'pli) Fr. something already done that cannot be altered

faith (feɪθ) n. 1. trust 2. belief (without proof) 3. religion 4. promise 5. loyalty, constancy —**faithful** a. constant, true —**faithfully** adv. —**faithless** a. —**faith healing** method of treating illness by religious faith

fake (feɪk) vt. 1. conceal defects by artifice 2. touch up 3. counterfeit 4. sham —n. 5. fraudulent object, person, act —a. 6. not genuine —**faker** n. 1. one who deals in fakes 2. swindler

fakir (fə'kɪə, 'feɪkə) n. 1. member of Islamic religious order 2. Hindu ascetic

Falange ('fælændʒ) n. Fascist movement in Spain —**Fa'langist** n./a.

falchion ('fɔːltʃən, 'fɔːlʃən) n. broad curved medieval sword

falcon ('fɔːlkən, 'fɔːkən) n. small bird of prey, esp. trained in hawking for sport —**falconer** n. one who keeps, trains or hunts with falcons —**falconry** n. hawking

falderal ('fældɪræl) or **folderol** n. 1. showy but worthless trifle 2. nonsense 3. nonsensical refrain in old songs

fall (fɔːl) vi. 1. drop, come down freely 2. become lower 3. decrease 4. hang down 5. come to the ground, cease to stand 6. perish 7. collapse 8. be captured 9. revert 10. lapse 11. be uttered 12. become 13. happen (**fell** pt., '**fallen** pp.) —n. 14. falling 15. amount that falls 16. amount of descent 17. decrease 18. collapse, ruin 19. drop 20. (oft. pl.) cascade 21. cadence 22. yielding to temptation 23. US autumn 24. rope of hoisting tackle —**fall guy** inf., chiefly US victim of confidence trick —**falling sickness** or **evil** former name for epilepsy —**falling star** inf. meteor —**fallout** n. radioactive particles spread as result of nuclear explosion —**fall for** inf. 1. fall in love with 2. be taken in by —**fall out** disagree

fallacy ('fæləsɪ) n. 1. incorrect, misleading opinion or argument 2. flaw in logic 3. illusion —**fallacious** (fə'leɪʃəs) a. —**fal-**

li'bility n. —'fallible a. liable to error —'fallibly adv.

fallen ('fɔːlən) v. 1. pp. of FALL —a. 2. having sunk in reputation or honour 3. killed in battle with glory —fallen arch collapse of arch formed by instep of foot, resulting in flat feet

Fallopian tube (fə'ləupiən) either of pair of tubes through which egg cells pass from ovary to womb

fallow¹ ('fæləu) a. 1. ploughed and harrowed but left without crop 2. uncultivated 3. neglected

fallow² ('fæləu) a. brown or reddish-yellow —fallow deer deer of this colour

false (fɔːls) a. 1. wrong, erroneous 2. deceptive 3. faithless 4. sham, artificial —'falsehood n. lie —'falsely adv. —'falseness n. faithlessness —falsifi'ca-tion n. —'falsify vt. 1. alter fraudulently 2. misrepresent 3. disappoint (hopes etc.) ('falsified, 'falsifying) —'falsity n. —false pretences misrepresentation of facts to gain advantage (esp. in under false pretences)

falsetto (fɔːl'sɛtəu) n. forced voice above natural range (pl. -s)

Falstaffian (fɔːl'stɑːfiən) a. like Shake-speare's Falstaff, fat, convivial and boasting

falter ('fɔːltə) vi. 1. hesitate 2. waver 3. stumble —'falteringly adv.

fame (feim) n. 1. reputation 2. renown —famed a. —'famous a. 1. widely known 2. inf. excellent

familiar (fə'miliə) a. 1. well-known 2. frequent, customary 3. intimate 4. closely acquainted 5. unceremonious 6. imperti-nent, too friendly —n. 7. familiar friend 8. familiar demon —famili'arity n. —famili-iari'zation or -ri'sation n. —fa'miliarize or -rise vt. —fa'miliarly adv.

family ('fæmili, 'fæmli) n. 1. group of parents and children, or near relatives 2. person's children 3. all descendants of common ancestor 4. household 5. group of allied objects —fa'milial a. —family man married man who has children, esp. one who is devoted to his family —family name surname, esp. representing family honour —family planning control of number of children in family, esp. by contraception —family tree chart show-ing relationships and lines of descent of family (also genealogical tree)

famine ('fæmin) n. 1. extreme scarcity of food 2. starvation 3. acute shortage of anything —'famished a. very hungry

famous ('feiməs) a. see FAME

fan¹ (fæn) n. 1. instrument for producing current of air, esp. for ventilating or cooling 2. folding object of paper etc. used, esp. formerly, for cooling the face 3. outspread feathers of a bird's tail —vt. 4. blow or cool with fan —v. 5. spread out like fan (-nn-) —fan belt belt that drives cooling fan in car engine —fanjet n. see TURBOFAN —'fanlight n. (fan-shaped) win-

dow over door —'fantail n. kind of bird (esp. pigeon) with fan-shaped tail —fan vaulting Archit. vaulting having ribs that radiate, like those of fan, from top of capital (also palm vaulting)

fan² (fæn) n. inf. 1. devoted admirer 2. enthusiast, particularly for sport etc.

Fanagalo ('fænəgələu) or Fanakalo n. SA pidgin language of Zulu, English and Afrikaans

fanatic (fə'nætik) a. 1. filled with abnormal enthusiasm, esp. in religion —n. 2. fanatic person —fa'natical a. —fa'nati-cally adv. —fa'naticism n.

fancy ('fænsi) a. 1. ornamental, not plain 2. of whimsical or arbitrary kind —n. 3. whim, caprice 4. liking, inclination 5. imagination 6. mental image —vt. 7. imagine 8. be inclined to believe 9. inf. have a liking for ('fancied, 'fancying) —interj. 10. exclamation of surprise (also fancy that) —'fancier n. one with liking and expert knowledge (respecting some specific thing) —'fanciful a. —'fancifully adv. —fancy dress costume worn at masquerades etc. representing historical figure etc. —fancy-free a. having no commitments —fancy goods small deco-rative gifts —fancy man sl. 1. woman's lover 2. pimp —fancy woman sl. 1. mistress 2. prostitute

fandango (fæn'dæŋgəu) n. 1. lively Sp. dance with castanets 2. music for this dance (pl. -s)

fanfare ('fænfɛə) n. 1. a flourish of trumpets or bugles 2. ostentatious display

fang (fæŋ) n. 1. snake's poison tooth 2. long, pointed tooth

fantasy or phantasy ('fæntəsi) n. 1. power of imagination, esp. extravagant 2. mental image 3. fanciful invention or design —fantasia (fæn'teiziə) n. fanciful musical composition —'fantasize or -sise v. —fan'tastic a. 1. quaint 2. grotesque 3. extremely fanciful, wild 4. inf. very good 5. inf. very large —fan'tastically adv.

FAO Food and Agriculture Organization (of the United Nations)

far (fɑː) adv. 1. at or to a great distance or advanced point 2. at or to a remote time 3. by very much —a. 4. distant 5. more distant ('farther, 'further comp., 'far-thest, 'furthest sup.) —'faraway a. 1. distant 2. absent-minded —Far East countries of E Asia, including China, Japan etc. —Far Eastern —far-fetched a. incredible —far-flung a. 1. widely distrib-uted 2. far distant; remote —Far North Arctic and sub-Arctic regions —far-off a. remote; distant —far-out a. sl. 1. bizarre, avant-garde 2. wonderful —far-sighted a. 1. possessing prudence and foresight 2. Med. of or suffering from hyperopia 3. long-sighted —far and away by a very great margin —far out sl. expression of amazement or delight

farad ('færəd) n. unit of electrical capacity —faradaic (færə'deiik) a.

farce (fɑːs) *n.* **1.** comedy of boisterous humour **2.** absurd and futile proceeding —'**farcical** *a.* ludicrous —'**farcically** *adv.*

fare (fɛə) *n.* **1.** charge for passenger's transport **2.** passenger **3.** food —*vi.* **4.** get on **5.** happen **6.** travel, progress —**fare stage 1.** section of bus journey for which set charge is made **2.** bus stop marking end of such section —**fare'well** *interj.* **1.** goodbye —*n.* **2.** leave-taking

farina (fə'riːnə) *n.* **1.** flour or meal made from cereal grain **2.** *chiefly UK* starch —**farinaceous** (færɪ'neɪʃəs) *a.* **1.** mealy **2.** starchy

farm (fɑːm) *n.* **1.** tract of land for cultivation or rearing livestock **2.** unit of land, water, for growing or rearing a particular crop, animal *etc.* —*v.* **3.** cultivate (land) **4.** rear (livestock) on farm —'**farmer** *n.* —**farm hand** person hired to work on farm —'**farmhouse** *n.* —'**farmstead** *n.* farm or part of farm consisting of main buildings together with adjacent grounds —'**farmyard** *n.* —**farm out 1.** send (work) to be done by others **2.** put into care of others

faro ('fɛərəʊ) *n.* card game

farrago (fə'rɑːgəʊ) *n.* medley, hotchpotch (*pl.* **-s**)

farrier ('færɪə) *n.* one who shoes, cares for horses —'**farriery** *n.* his art

farrow ('færəʊ) *n.* **1.** litter of pigs —*v.* **2.** give birth to (litter)

fart (fɑːt) *vulg. n.* **1.** (audible) emission of gas from anus —*vi.* **2.** break wind

farther ('fɑːðə) *adv./a. comp. of* FAR further —'**farthermost** *a.* most distant —'**farthest** *adv./a. sup. of* FAR furthest

farthing ('fɑːðɪŋ) *n.* formerly, coin worth quarter of penny

farthingale ('fɑːðɪŋgeɪl) *n. Hist.* hoop worn under skirts

fasces ('fæsiːz) *pl.n.* **1.** bundle of rods bound together round axe, forming Roman badge of authority **2.** emblem of It. fascists

fascia *or* **facia** ('feɪʃɪə) *n.* **1.** flat surface above shop window **2.** *Archit.* long flat surface between mouldings under eaves **3.** face of wood or stone in a building **4.** dashboard (*pl.* **-ciae** (-ʃiː))

fascinate ('fæsɪneɪt) *vt.* **1.** attract and delight by rousing interest and curiosity **2.** render motionless, as with a fixed stare —**fasci'nation** *n.*

Fascism ('fæʃɪzəm) *n.* **1.** authoritarian political system opposed to democracy and liberalism **2.** (*oft.* f-) behaviour (*esp.* by those in authority) supposedly typical of this system —'**Fascist** *a./n.*

fashion ('fæʃən) *n.* **1.** (latest) style, *esp.* of dress *etc.* **2.** manner, mode **3.** form, type —*vt.* **4.** shape, make —'**fashionable** *a.* —'**fashionably** *adv.*

fast[1] (fɑːst) *a.* **1.** (capable of) moving quickly **2.** permitting, providing, rapid progress **3.** ahead of true time **4.** *obs.* dissipated **5.** firm, steady **6.** permanent

—*adv.* **7.** rapidly **8.** tightly —'**fastness** *n.* **1.** fast state **2.** fortress, stronghold —'**fastback** *n.* car with back forming continuous slope from roof to rear —**fast-breeder reactor** nuclear reactor that uses little or no moderator and produces more fissionable material than it consumes —**fast food** food, *esp.* hamburgers *etc.*, prepared and served very quickly

fast[2] (fɑːst) *vi.* **1.** go without food, or some kinds of food —*n.* **2.** act or period of fasting —'**fasting** *n.*

fasten ('fɑːs°n) *vt.* **1.** attach, fix, secure —*vi.* **2.** become joined **3.** (*usu. with* on) seize (upon) —'**fastening** *n.* something that fastens, such as clasp

fastidious (fæ'stɪdɪəs) *a.* **1.** hard to please **2.** discriminating, particular

fat (fæt) *n.* **1.** oily animal substance **2.** fat part —*a.* **3.** having too much fat **4.** containing fat, greasy **5.** profitable **6.** fertile ('**fatter** *comp.,* '**fattest** *sup.*) —*vt.* **7.** feed (animals) for slaughter (**-tt-**) —'**fatness** *n.* —'**fatten** *v.* —'**fatty** *a./n.* —'**fathead** *n. inf.* dolt, idiot —**fat stock** livestock fattened and ready for market —**fatty acid** any of class of aliphatic carboxylic acids, such as palmitic acid

fate (feɪt) *n.* **1.** power supposed to predetermine events **2.** goddess of destiny **3.** destiny **4.** person's appointed lot or condition **5.** death; destruction —*vt.* **6.** preordain —'**fatal** *a.* **1.** deadly, ending in death **2.** destructive **3.** disastrous **4.** inevitable —'**fatalism** *n.* **1.** belief that everything is predetermined **2.** submission to fate —'**fatalist** *n.* —**fatal'istic** *a.* —**fatal'istically** *adv.* —**fatality** (fə'tælɪtɪ) *n.* **1.** accident resulting in death **2.** person killed in war, accident —'**fatally** *adv.* —'**fateful** *a.* **1.** fraught with destiny **2.** prophetic

father ('fɑːðə) *n.* **1.** male parent **2.** forefather, ancestor **3.** (F-) God **4.** originator, early leader **5.** priest, confessor **6.** oldest member of a society —*vt.* **7.** beget **8.** originate **9.** pass as father or author of **10.** act as father to —'**fatherhood** *n.* —'**fatherless** *a.* —'**fatherly** *a.* —**father-in-law** *n.* husband's or wife's father —'**fatherland** *n.* **1.** person's native country **2.** country of person's ancestors

fathom ('fæðəm) *n.* **1.** measure of six feet of water —*vt.* **2.** sound (water) **3.** get to bottom of, understand —'**fathomable** *a.* —'**fathomless** *a.* too deep to fathom

fatigue (fə'tiːg) *n.* **1.** weariness **2.** toil **3.** weakness of metals *etc.* subjected to stress **4.** soldier's nonmilitary duty —*pl.* **5.** special clothing worn by military personnel to carry out such duties —*vt.* **6.** weary

fatuous ('fætjʊəs) *a.* very silly, idiotic —**fa'tuity** *n.*

faucet ('fɔːsɪt) *n.* US tap

fault (fɔːlt) *n.* **1.** defect **2.** flaw **3.** misdeed **4.** blame, culpability **5.** blunder, mistake **6.** *Tennis* ball wrongly served **7.** *Geol.* break in strata —*vt.* **8.** find fault in —*v.* **9.** (cause to) undergo fault —*vi.* 10. commit a fault —'**faultily** *adv.* —'**faultless** *a.* —'**faultlessly** *adv.* —'**faulty** *a.* —**to a fault** excessively

faun (fɔ:n) *n.* mythological woodland being with tail and horns

fauna ('fɔ:nə) *n.* animals of region or period collectively (*pl.* **-s, -ae** (-i:))

faux pas (fəʊ 'pɑ:) social blunder or indiscretion (*pl.* **faux pas** (fəʊ 'pɑ:z))

favour *or U.S.* **favor** ('feɪvə) *n.* 1. goodwill 2. approval 3. especial kindness 4. partiality 5. small gift or toy given to guest at party *etc.* 6 *Hist.* badge or knot of ribbons —*vt.* 7. regard or treat with favour 8. oblige 9. treat with partiality 10. aid 11. support 12. resemble —'**favourable** *or U.S.* '**favorable** *a.* 1. advantageous, encouraging, promising 2. giving consent —'**favourably** *or U.S.* '**favorably** *adv.* —'**favoured** *or U.S.* '**favored** *a.* 1. treated with favour 2. having appearance (as specified), as in *ill-favoured* —**favourite** *or U.S.* **favorite** ('feɪvərɪt) *n.* 1. favoured person or thing 2. horse *etc.* expected to win race —*a.* 3. chosen, preferred —**favouritism** *or U.S.* **favoritism** ('feɪvərɪtɪzəm) *n.* practice of showing undue preference

fax (fæks) *n.* 1. *see* FACSIMILE (senses 2, 3) —*vt.* 2. send (document) by facsimile

fawn[1] (fɔ:n) *n.* 1. young deer —*a.* 2. light yellowish-brown

fawn[2] (fɔ:n) *vi.* 1. (of person) cringe, court favour servilely 2. (*esp.* of dog) show affection by wagging tail and grovelling

fay (feɪ) *n.* fairy, sprite

F.B.I. US Federal Bureau of Investigation

F.C. Football Club

F.D. Fidei Defensor

Fe *Chem.* iron

fealty ('fi:əltɪ) *n.* 1. fidelity of vassal to his lord 2. loyalty

fear (fɪə) *n.* 1. dread, alarm, anxiety, unpleasant emotion caused by coming evil or danger —*vi.* 2. have this feeling, be afraid —*vt.* 3. regard with fear 4. shrink from 5. revere —'**fearful** *a.* 1. afraid 2. causing fear 3. *inf.* very unpleasant —'**fearfully** *adv.* —'**fearless** *a.* intrepid —'**fearlessly** *adv.* —'**fearsome** *a.*

feasible ('fi:zəb'l) *a.* 1. able to be done 2. likely —**feasi'bility** *n.* —'**feasibly** *adv.*

feast (fi:st) *n.* 1. banquet, lavish meal 2. religious anniversary 3. something very pleasant, sumptuous —*vi.* 4. partake of banquet; fare sumptuously —*vt.* 5. regale with feast 6. provide delight for —'**feaster** *n.*

feat (fi:t) *n.* 1. notable deed 2. surprising or striking trick

feather ('feðə) *n.* 1. one of the barbed shafts which form covering of birds 2. anything resembling this —*vt.* 3. provide, line with feathers —*vi.* 4. grow feathers —*v.* 5. turn (oar) edgeways —'**feathery** *a.* —**feather bed** mattress filled with feathers —**feather'bed** *vt.* pamper, spoil —'**featherbrain** *or* '**featherhead** *n.* frivolous or forgetful person —'**featherbrained** *or* '**featherheaded** *a.* —'**featherweight** *n.* very light person or thing —**feather one's nest** enrich oneself —**the white feather** cowardice

feature ('fi:tʃə) *n.* 1. (*usu. pl.*) part of face 2. characteristic or notable part of anything 3. main or special item —*vt.* 4. portray 5. *Cine.* present in leading role in a film 6. give prominence to —*vi.* 7. be prominent —'**featureless** *a.* without striking features

Feb. February

febrile ('fi:braɪl) *a.* of fever

February ('fɛbrʊərɪ) *n.* second month of year (normally containing 28 days; in leap year, 29)

feckless ('fɛklɪs) *a.* spiritless; weak; irresponsible

feculent ('fɛkjʊlənt) *a.* full of sediment, turbid —'**feculence** *n.*

fecund ('fi:kənd, 'fɛk-) *a.* fertile, fruitful, fertilizing —'**fecundate** *vt.* fertilize, impregnate —**fecun'dation** *n.* —**fecundity** (fɪ'kʌndɪtɪ) *n.*

Fed. *or* **fed.** 1. Federal 2. Federation 3. Federated

fed (fɛd) *pt./pp.* of FEED —**fed up** bored, dissatisfied

federal ('fɛdərəl) *a.* of or like the government of states which are united but retain internal independence —'**federalism** *n.* —'**federalist** *n./a.* —'**federate** *v.* form into, become, a federation —**fede'ration** *n.* 1. league 2. federal union

fee (fi:) *n.* payment for professional and other services

feeble ('fi:b'l) *a.* 1. weak 2. lacking strength or effectiveness, insipid —'**feebly** *adv.* —**feeble-minded** *a.* 1. lacking in intelligence 2. mentally defective

feed (fi:d) *vt.* 1. give food to 2. supply, support —*vi.* 3. take food (**fed** *pt./pp.*) —*n.* 4. feeding 5. fodder, pasturage 6. allowance of fodder 7. material supplied to machine 8. part of machine taking in material —'**feeder** *n.* 1. one who or that which feeds 2. child's bib 3. tributary channel —'**feedback** *n.* 1. return of part of output of electrical circuit or loudspeakers. In **negative feedback** rise in output energy reduces input energy; in **positive feedback** increase in output energy reinforces input energy 2. information received in response to enquiry *etc.* —'**feedlot** *n.* area, building where cattle are fattened for market

feel (fi:l) *vt.* 1. perceive, examine by touch 2. experience 3. find (one's way) cautiously 4. be sensitive to 5. believe, consider —*vi.* 6. have physical or emotional sensation of (something) (**felt** *pt./pp.*) —*n.* 7. act or instance of feeling 8. quality or impression of something perceived by feeling 9. sense of touch —'**feeler** *n.* 1. special organ of touch in some animals 2. proposal put forward to test others' opinion 3. that which feels —'**feeling** *n.* 1.

sense of touch **2.** ability to feel **3.** physical sensation **4.** emotion **5.** sympathy, tenderness **6.** conviction or opinion not solely based on reason —*pl.* **7.** susceptibilities —*a.* **8.** sensitive, sympathetic, heartfelt —**feel for** show sympathy or compassion towards —**feel like** have an inclination for

feet (fiːt) *n., pl. of* FOOT

feign (feɪn) *v.* pretend, sham

feint[1] (feɪnt) *n.* **1.** sham attack or blow meant to deceive opponent **2.** semblance, pretence —*vi.* **3.** make feint

feint[2] (feɪnt) *n. Print.* narrowest rule used in production of ruled paper

feldspar ('feldspɑː, 'felspɑː) *or* **felspar** *n.* crystalline mineral found in granite *etc.* —**feldspathic** (feld'spæθɪk, fel'spæθ-) *or* **fel'spathic** *a.*

felicity (fɪ'lɪsɪtɪ) *n.* **1.** great happiness, bliss **2.** appropriate expression or style —**fe'licitate** *vt.* congratulate —**felici'tation** *n.* (*usu. in pl.*) —**fe'licitous** *a.* **1.** apt, well-chosen **2.** happy

feline ('fiːlaɪn) *a.* **1.** of cats **2.** catlike —**felinity** (fɪ'lɪnɪtɪ) *n.*

fell[1] (fel) *pt. of* FALL

fell[2] (fel) *vt.* **1.** knock down **2.** cut down (tree) —**'feller** *n.*

fell[3] (fel) *a. obs.* fierce, terrible —**one fell swoop** a single hasty action or occurrence

fell[4] (fel) *n.* skin or hide with hair

fell[5] (fel) *n.* mountain, stretch of moorland, *esp.* in N of England

fellatio (fɪ'leɪʃɪəʊ) *n.* sexual activity in which penis is stimulated by partner's mouth

felloe ('feləʊ) *or* **felly** *n.* outer part (or section) of wheel

fellow ('feləʊ) *n.* **1.** man, boy **2.** person **3.** comrade, associate **4.** counterpart, like thing **5.** member of (society, college *etc.*) —*a.* **6.** of the same class, associated —**'fellowship** *n.* **1.** fraternity **2.** friendship **3.** in university *etc.*, research post; special scholarship —**fellow traveller 1.** companion on journey **2.** non-Communist who sympathizes with Communism

felon ('felən) *n.* one guilty of felony —**fe'lonious** *a.* —**'felony** *n.* serious crime

felspar ('felspɑː) *n. see* FELDSPAR

felt[1] (felt) *pt./pp. of* FEEL

felt[2] (felt) *n.* **1.** soft, matted fabric made by bonding fibres chemically and by pressure **2.** thing made of this —*vt.* **3.** make into, or cover with, felt —*vi.* **4.** become matted like felt —**felt-tip pen** pen whose writing point is made from pressed fibres (*also* **fibre-tip pen**)

fem. feminine

female ('fiːmeɪl) *a.* **1.** of sex which bears offspring **2.** relating to this sex —*n.* **3.** one of this sex

feminine ('femɪnɪn) *a.* **1.** of women **2.** womanly **3.** denoting class or type of grammatical inflection in some languages —**femi'ninity** *n.* —**'feminism** *n.* advocacy of equal rights for women —**'feminist** *n./a.*

femur ('fiːmə) *n.* thigh-bone —**'femoral** *a.* of the thigh

fen (fen) *n.* tract of marshy land, swamp —**'fenny** *a.*

fence (fens) *n.* **1.** structure of wire, wood *etc.* enclosing an area **2.** *Machinery* guard, guide **3.** *sl.* dealer in stolen property —*vt.* **4.** erect fence on or around **5.** (*with* in) enclose —*vi.* **6.** fight (as sport) with swords **7.** avoid question *etc.* **8.** *sl.* deal in stolen property —**'fencing** *n.* art of swordplay

fend (fend) *vt.* **1.** (*usu. with* off) ward off, repel —*vi.* **2.** provide (for oneself *etc.*) —**'fender** *n.* **1.** low metal frame in front of fireplace **2.** name for various protective devices **3.** frame **4.** edge **5.** buffer **6.** US mudguard of car

fenestration (fenɪ'streɪʃən) *n.* arrangement of windows in a building

Fenian ('fiːnɪən, 'fiːnjən) *n.* **1.** formerly, member of Irish revolutionary organization founded in U.S.A. in 19th century to fight for independent Ireland —*a.* **2.** of Fenians

fennel ('fen'l) *n.* yellow-flowered fragrant herb

fenugreek ('fenjugriːk) *n.* heavily scented leguminous plant

feoff (fiːf) *Hist. n.* **1.** *see* FIEF —*vt.* **2.** invest with benefice or fief

-fer (*n. comb. form*) person or thing that bears something specified, as in *crucifer, conifer* —**-ferous** (*a. comb. form*) bearing, producing, as in *coniferous*

feral[1] ('fɪərəl) *a.* wild, uncultivated

feral[2] ('fɪərəl) *a. obs.* funereal, gloomy

feria ('fɪərɪə) *n. Eccles.* ordinary weekday, not festival or fast day

fermata (fə'mɑːtə) *n. Mus.* pause (*pl.* **-s, -te** (-tɪ))

ferment ('fɜːment) *n.* **1.** leaven, substance causing thing to ferment **2.** excitement, tumult —*v.* (fə'ment) **3.** (cause to) undergo chemical change with effervescence, liberation of heat and alteration of properties, *eg* process set up in dough by yeast **4.** (cause to) become excited —**fermen'tation** *n.*

fermium ('fɜːmɪəm) *n.* transuranic element artificially produced by neutron bombardment of plutonium

fern (fɜːn) *n.* plant with feathery fronds —**'fernery** *n.* place for growing ferns —**'ferny** *a.* full of ferns

ferocious (fə'rəʊʃəs) *a.* fierce, savage, cruel —**ferocity** (fə'rɒsɪtɪ) *n.*

ferret ('ferɪt) *n.* **1.** tamed animal like weasel, used to catch rabbits, rats *etc.* —*vt.* (*usu. with* out) **2.** drive out with ferrets **3.** search out —*vi.* **4.** search about, rummage

ferric ('ferɪk) *a.* pert. to, containing, iron —**fer'riferous** *a.* yielding iron —**'ferrous** *a.* of or containing iron in divalent state —**ferruginous** (fe'ruːdʒɪnəs) *a.* **1.** containing iron **2.** reddish-brown —**ferro'concrete** *n.* concrete strengthened by framework of metal

Ferris wheel ('fɛrɪs) in fairground, large, vertical wheel with seats for riding

ferro- (*comb. form*) 1. property or presence of iron, as in *ferromagnetism* 2. presence of iron in divalent state, as in *ferrocyanide*

ferrule ('fɛruːl) *n.* metal cap to strengthen end of stick *etc.*

ferry ('fɛrɪ) *n.* 1. boat *etc.* for transporting people, vehicles, across body of water, *esp.* as repeated or regular service 2. place for ferrying —*v.* 3. carry, travel, by ferry —*vt.* 4. convey (passengers *etc.*) ('**ferried, 'ferrying**) —'**ferryman** *n.*

fertile ('fɜːtaɪl) *a.* 1. (capable of) producing offspring, bearing crops *etc.* 2. fruitful, producing abundantly 3. inventive —**fertility** (fɜː'tɪlɪtɪ) *n.* —**fertilization** or **-lisation** (fɜːtɪlaɪ'zeɪʃən) *n.* —'**fertilize** or **-lise** ('fɜːtɪlaɪz) *vt.* make fertile —**fertilizer** or **-liser** ('fɜːtɪlaɪzə) *n.*

ferule ('fɛruːl) *n.* 1. flat piece of wood, such as ruler, formerly used in some schools to cane children on hand —*vt.* 2. punish with ferule

fervent ('fɜːvənt) or **fervid** ('fɜːvɪd) *a.* ardent, vehement, intense —'**fervency** *n.* —'**fervently** or '**fervidly** *adv.* —'**fervour** or *U.S.* '**fervor** *n.*

fescue ('fɛskjuː) or **fescue grass** *n.* grass used as pasture, with stiff narrow leaves

fesse or **fess** (fɛs) *n. Her.* horizontal band across shield

festal ('fɛstl) *a.* 1. of feast or holiday 2. merry, gay —'**festally** *adv.*

fester ('fɛstə) *v.* 1. (cause to) form pus —*vi.* 2. rankle 3. become embittered

festival ('fɛstɪvl) *n.* 1. day, period set aside for celebration, *esp.* of religious feast 2. organized series of events, performances *etc.*, usu. in one place —'**festive** *a.* 1. joyous, merry 2. of feast —**fes'tivity** *n.* 1. gaiety, mirth 2. rejoicing —*pl.* 3. festive proceedings

festoon (fɛ'stuːn) *n.* 1. chain of flowers, ribbons *etc.* hung in curve between two points —*vt.* 2. form into, adorn with festoons

fetch[1] (fɛtʃ) *vt.* 1. go and bring 2. draw forth 3. be sold for —*n.* 4. trick —'**fetching** *a.* attractive —**fetch up** 1. *inf.* arrive 2. *sl.* vomit (food *etc.*)

fetch[2] (fɛtʃ) *n.* ghost or apparition of living person

fête or **fete** (feɪt) *n.* 1. gala, bazaar *etc.*, *esp.* one held out of doors 2. festival, holiday, celebration —*vt.* 3. feast 4. honour with festive entertainment

fetid or **foetid** ('fɛtɪd, 'fiː-) *a.* stinking

fetish or **fetich** ('fɛtɪʃ, 'fiːtɪʃ) *n.* 1. (inanimate) object believed to have magical powers 2. excessive attention to something 3. object, activity, to which excessive devotion is paid

fetlock ('fɛtlɒk) *n.* projection behind and above horse's hoof, or tuft of hair on this

fetter ('fɛtə) *n.* 1. chain or shackle for feet

2. check, restraint —*pl.* 3. captivity —*vt.* 4. chain up 5. restrain, hamper

fettle ('fɛtl) *n.* condition, state of health

fetus ('fiːtəs) *n. see* FOETUS

feu (fjuː) *n.* in Scotland, tenure of land in return for fixed annual payment

feud (fjuːd) *n.* 1. bitter, lasting, mutual hostility, *esp.* between two families or tribes 2. vendetta —*vi.* 3. carry on feud

feudal ('fjuːdl) *a.* 1. of, like, medieval social and economic system based on holding land from superior in return for service 2. *inf.* very old-fashioned —'**feudalism** *n.*

fever ('fiːvə) *n.* 1. condition of illness with high body temperature 2. intense nervous excitement —'**fevered** *a.* —'**feverish** *a.* 1. having fever 2. accompanied by, caused by, fever 3. in a state of restless excitement —'**feverishly** *adv.* —'**fever-few** *n.* bushy plant with white flower heads —**fever pitch** 1. very fast pace 2. intense excitement

few (fjuː) *a.* 1. not many —*n.* 2. small number —**a good few, quite a few** several

fey (feɪ) *a.* 1. clairvoyant, visionary 2. *esp. Scot.* fated to die

fez (fɛz) *n.* red, brimless, orig. Turkish tasselled cap (*pl.* '**fezzes**)

ff *Mus.* fortissimo

ff. 1. folios 2. and the following (pages *etc.*)

fiancé (fɪ'ɒnseɪ) *n.* person engaged to be married (**fi'ancée** *fem.*)

fiasco (fɪ'æskəʊ) *n.* breakdown, total failure (*pl.* **-s, -es**)

fiat ('faɪət) *n.* 1. decree 2. official permission

fib (fɪb) *n.* 1. trivial lie, falsehood —*vi.* 2. tell fib (**-bb-**) —'**fibber** *n.*

fibre or *U.S.* **fiber** ('faɪbə) *n.* 1. filament forming part of animal or plant tissue 2. substance that can be spun (*eg* wool, cotton) —'**fibril** or **fi'brilla** *n.* 1. small fibre or part of fibre 2. *Biol.* root hair (*pl.* **-s** or **-brillae** (-'brɪliː)) —'**fibroid** *a.* 1. *Anat.* (of structures or tissues) containing or resembling fibres —*n.* 2. benign tumour derived from fibrous connective tissue (*also* **fi'broma**) —**fi'brosis** *n.* formation of abnormal amount of fibrous tissue in organ *etc.* —**fibro'sitis** *n.* inflammation of tissues of muscle sheaths —'**fibrous** *a.* made of fibre —'**fibreboard** *n.* building material of compressed plant fibres —'**fibreglass** *n.* material made of fine glass fibres —**fibre optics** use of bundles of long transparent glass fibres in transmitting light

fibrin ('faɪbrɪn) *n.* insoluble protein in blood, causing coagulation

fibula ('fɪbjʊlə) *n.* slender outer bone of lower leg (*pl.* **-lae** (-liː), **-s**) —'**fibular** *a.*

fickle ('fɪkl) *a.* changeable, inconstant —'**fickleness** *n.*

fiction ('fɪkʃən) *n.* 1. prose, literary works of the imagination 2. invented statement or story —'**fictional** *a.* —'**fictionalize** or

-lise *vt.* make into fiction —**fic'titious** *a.* 1. not genuine, false 2. imaginary 3. assumed

fiddle ('fɪdˀl) *n.* 1. violin 2. triviality 3. *inf.* illegal, fraudulent arrangement —*vi.* 4. play fiddle 5. make idle movements, fidget, trifle —*v.* 6. *sl.* cheat, contrive —**'fiddling** *a.* trivial —**'fiddly** *a.* small, awkward to handle —**fiddler crab** burrowing crab of Amer. coastal regions, male of which has one pincerlike claw enlarged —**'fiddle-sticks** *interj.* nonsense

Fidei Defensor ('faɪdɪaɪ dɪ'fɛnsɔː) *Lat.* Defender of the Faith

fidelity (fɪ'dɛlɪtɪ) *n.* 1. faithfulness 2. quality of sound reproduction

fidget ('fɪdʒɪt) *vi.* 1. move restlessly 2. be uneasy —*n.* 3. (*oft. pl.*) nervous restlessness, restless mood 4. one who fidgets —**'fidgety** *a.*

fiduciary (fɪ'duːʃɪərɪ) *a.* 1. held, given in trust 2. relating to trustee —*n.* 3. trustee

fie (faɪ) *interj. obs., jocular* exclamation of distaste or mock dismay

fief *or* **feoff** (fiːf) *n. Hist.* land held of a superior in return for service

field (fiːld) *n.* 1. area of (farming) land 2. enclosed piece of land 3. tract of land rich in specified product (*eg* goldfield) 4. players in a game or sport collectively 5. all competitors but the favourite 6. battlefield 7. area over which electric, gravitational, magnetic force can be exerted 8. surface of shield, coin *etc.* 9. sphere of knowledge 10. range, area of operation —*vt.* 11. *Sport* stop or return (ball) 12. send (player, team) on to sportsfield —*vi.* 13. *Sport* (of player or team) act or take turn as fielder(s) —**'fielder** *n.* —**field day** 1. day of manoeuvres, outdoor activities 2. important occasion —**field events** throwing and jumping events in athletics —**'fieldfare** *n.* type of thrush with pale grey head and rump —**field glasses** binoculars —**field hockey** US, C hockey played on field, as distinct from ice hockey —**field marshal** army officer of highest rank —**field officer** officer holding rank of major, lieutenant colonel or colonel —**'fieldsman** *n. Cricket* player in field; member of fielding side (*also* **'fielder**) —**field sports** outdoor sports, such as hunting or fishing —**'fieldwork** *n.* research, practical work, conducted away from classroom, laboratory *etc.* —**field of view** area covered in telescope, camera *etc.*

fiend (fiːnd) *n.* 1. demon, devil 2. wicked person 3. person very fond of or addicted to something, *eg* fresh-air fiend, drug fiend —**'fiendish** *a.* 1. wicked 2. *inf.* difficult; unpleasant

fierce (fɪəs) *a.* 1. savage, wild, violent 2. rough 3. severe 4. intense —**'fiercely** *adv.* —**'fierceness** *n.*

fiery ('faɪərɪ) *a.* 1. consisting of fire 2. blazing, glowing, flashing 3. irritable 4. spirited (**'fierier** *comp.*, **'fieriest** *sup.*) —**'fierily** *adv.*

fiesta (fɪ'ɛstə) *n.* (*esp.* in Spain and Latin America) 1. (religious) celebration 2. carnival

FIFA ('fiːfə) Fédération Internationale de Football Association

fife (faɪf) *n.* 1. high-pitched flute —*v.* 2. play (music) on fife —**'fifer** *n.*

fifteen ('fɪf'tiːn) *see* FIVE

fig (fɪg) *n.* 1. soft, pear-shaped fruit 2. tree bearing it 3. something of negligible value

fig. 1. figurative(ly) 2. figure

fight (faɪt) *v.* 1. contend (with) in battle or in single combat 2. maintain (cause *etc.*) against opponent —*vt.* 3. resolve by combat (**fought** *pt./pp.*) —*n.* 4. battle, struggle or physical combat 5. quarrel, dispute, contest 6. resistance 7. boxing match —**'fighter** *n.* 1. one who fights 2. *Mil.* aircraft designed for destroying other aircraft —**fighting chance** chance of success dependent on struggle

figment ('fɪgmənt) *n.* invention, purely imaginary thing

figure ('fɪgə) *n.* 1. numerical symbol 2. amount, number 3. form, shape 4. bodily shape 5. appearance, *esp.* conspicuous appearance 6. character, personage 7. space enclosed by lines, or surfaces 8. diagram, illustration 9. likeness, image 10. pattern, movement in dancing, skating, *etc.* 11. abnormal form of expression for effect in speech, *eg* metaphor —*vt.* 12. calculate, estimate 13. *inf., US, NZ* consider 14. represent by picture or diagram 15. ornament —*vi.* 16. (*oft. with* in) show, appear, be conspicuous, be included —**figu'ration** *n.* 1. *Mus.* florid ornamentation of musical passage 2. instance of representing figuratively, as by allegory 3. figurative representation 4. decorating with design —**'figurative** *a.* 1. metaphorical 2. full of figures of speech —**'figuratively** *adv.* —**figurine** (fɪgə'riːn) *n.* statuette —**'figurehead** *n.* 1. nominal leader 2. ornamental figure under bowsprit of ship —**figure of speech** expression of language by which literal meaning of word is not employed

figwort ('fɪgwɜːt) *n.* plant related to foxglove, having small greenish flowers

filament ('fɪləmənt) *n.* 1. fine wire in electric light bulb and radio valve which is heated by electric current 2. threadlike body

filbert ('fɪlbət) *n.* 1. N temperate shrub with edible nuts 2. this nut (*also* **'hazelnut, 'cobnut**)

filch (fɪltʃ) *vt.* steal, pilfer

file¹ (faɪl) *n.* 1. box, folder, clip *etc.* holding papers for reference 2. papers so kept 3. information about specific person, subject 4. orderly line, as of soldiers, one behind the other —*vt.* 5. arrange (papers *etc.*) and put them away for reference 6. *Law* place on records of a court 7. bring (suit) in lawcourt —*vi.* 8. march in file —**'filing** *n.* —**single** (*or* **Indian**) **file** single line of people one behind the other

file² (faɪl) n. 1. roughened tool for smoothing or shaping —vt. 2. apply file to, smooth, polish —**'filing** n. 1. action of using file 2. scrap of metal removed by file

filial ('fɪljəl) a. of, befitting, son or daughter —**'filially** adv.

filibuster ('fɪlɪbʌstə) US n. 1. process of obstructing legislation by using delaying tactics —v. 2. obstruct (legislation) with delaying tactics —vi. 3. engage in unlawful military action

filigree ('fɪlɪgriː) or **filagree** ('fɪlɪgriː) n. fine tracery or openwork of metal, usu. gold or silver wire

Filipino (fɪlɪ'piːnəʊ) n. 1. native of the Philippines —a. 2. of the Philippines

fill (fɪl) vt. 1. make full 2. occupy completely 3. hold, discharge duties of 4. stop up 5. satisfy, fulfil —vi. 6. become full —n. 7. full supply 8. as much as desired 9. soil etc. to bring area of ground up to required level —**'filler** n. 1. person or thing that fills 2. object or substance used to add weight etc. or to fill in gap 3. paste used for filling in cracks etc. before painting 4. inner portion of cigar 5. Journalism space-filling item in newspaper etc. —**'filling** n. —**filling station** garage selling oil, petrol etc. —**fill the bill** inf. supply all that is wanted

fillet ('fɪlɪt) n. 1. boneless slice of meat, fish 2. narrow strip —vt. 3. cut into fillets, bone —**'filleted** a.

fillip ('fɪlɪp) n. 1. stimulus 2. sudden release of finger bent against thumb 3. snap so produced —vt. 4. stimulate 5. give fillip to

filly ('fɪlɪ) n. female horse under four years old

film (fɪlm) n. 1. sequence of images projected on screen, creating illusion of movement 2. story etc. presented thus, and shown in cinema or on television 3. sensitized celluloid roll used in photography, cinematography 4. thin skin or layer 5. dimness on eyes 6. slight haze —a. 7. connected with cinema —vt. 8. photograph with cine camera 9. make cine film of (scene, story etc.) —v. 10. cover, become covered, with film —**'filmy** a. 1. membranous 2. gauzy —**film star** popular cinema actor or actress —**film strip** strip of film composed of images projected separately as slides

Filofax ('faɪləʊfæks) n. R loose-leaf ring binder with sets of different-coloured paper, used as portable personal filing system

filter ('fɪltə) n. 1. cloth or other material, or a device, permitting fluid to pass but retaining solid particles 2. anything performing similar function —v. 3. (oft. with out) remove or separate (suspended particles etc.) from (liquid, gas etc.) by action of filter —vi. 4. pass slowly (as if) through filter —**'filtrate** n. filtered gas or liquid —**filter paper** porous paper for filtering liquids —**filter tip** 1. attachment to mouth end of cigarette for trapping

impurities 2. cigarette having such attachment —**filter-tipped** a.

filth (fɪlθ) n. 1. disgusting dirt 2. pollution 3. obscenity —**'filthily** adv. —**'filthiness** n. —**'filthy** a. 1. unclean 2. foul

fin (fɪn) n. 1. propelling or steering organ of fish 2. anything like this, eg stabilizing plane of aeroplane

fin. 1. finance 2. financial

finagle (fɪ'neɪg'l) inf. vt. 1. get or achieve by craftiness —v. 2. use trickery on (person) —**fi'nagler** n.

final ('faɪn'l) a. 1. at the end 2. conclusive —n. 3. game, heat, examination etc. coming at end of series —**finale** (fɪ'nɑːlɪ) n. 1. closing part of musical composition, opera etc. 2. termination —**'finalist** n. contestant who has reached last stage of competition —**fi'nality** n. —**'finalize** or **-lise** v. —**'finally** adv.

finance (fɪ'næns, 'faɪnæns) n. 1. management of money 2. (also pl.) money resources —vt. 3. find capital for —**fi'nancial** a. of finance —**fi'nancially** adv. —**fi'nancier** n. —**financial year** UK 1. annual period at end of which firm's accounts are made up 2. annual period ending Apr. 5th, over which Budget estimates are made by British Government

finch (fɪntʃ) n. one of family of small singing birds

find (faɪnd) vt. 1. come across, light upon 2. obtain 3. realize 4. experience, discover 5. discover by searching 6. supply (as funds) 7. Law give a verdict (upon) (**found** pt./pp.) —n. 8. finding 9. (valuable) thing found —**'finder** n. —**'finding** n. judicial verdict —**find out** 1. gain knowledge of (something); learn 2. detect crime, deception etc. of (someone)

fine¹ (faɪn) a. 1. choice, of high quality, excellent 2. delicate 3. subtle 4. pure 5. in small particles 6. slender 7. handsome 8. showy 9. inf. healthy, at ease, comfortable 10. free from rain —vt. 11. make clear or pure 12. refine 13. thin —**'finely** adv. —**'fineness** n. —**'finery** n. showy dress —**finesse** (fɪ'nɛs) n. elegant, skilful management —**fine art** art produced for its aesthetic value —**fine-drawn** a. 1. (of distinctions etc.) precise; subtle 2. (of wire etc.) drawn out until very fine —**'fine-'spun** a. 1. spun out to fine thread 2. excessively subtle or refined —**fine-tooth comb** or **fine-toothed comb** comb with fine, closely set teeth —**go over** or **through with a fine-tooth(ed) comb** examine very thoroughly

fine² (faɪn) n. 1. sum fixed as penalty —vt. 2. punish by fine —**in fine** 1. in conclusion 2. in brief

fines herbes (Fr. fin 'zɛrb) mixture of finely chopped herbs, used to flavour omelettes etc.

finger ('fɪŋgə) n. 1. one of the jointed branches of the hand 2. any of various things like this —vt. 3. touch or handle with fingers —**'fingering** n. 1. *Mus.* technique of using one's fingers 2. *Mus.* numerals in musical part indicating this 3. fine wool yarn for manufacture of stockings *etc.* —**'fingerboard** n. part of musical instrument on which fingers are placed —**finger bowl** small bowl filled with water for rinsing fingers at table after meal —**finger plate** ornamental plate above door handle to prevent finger marks —**'fingerprint** n. impression of tip of finger, *esp.* as used for identifying criminals —**'fingerstall** n. cover to protect finger

finial ('fɪnɪəl) n. *Archit.* ornament at apex of pinnacles, gables, spires *etc.*

finicky ('fɪnɪkɪ) or **finicking** a. 1. fastidious, fussy 2. too fine

finis ('fɪnɪs) *Lat.* end, *esp.* of book

finish ('fɪnɪʃ) v. 1. bring, come to an end, conclude —vt. 2. complete 3. perfect 4. kill —n. 5. end 6. way in which thing is finished, as an *oak finish* of furniture 7. final appearance —**'finisher** n. —**'finishing school** private school for girls, that teaches social graces

finite ('faɪnaɪt) a. bounded, limited

Finn (fɪn) n. native of Finland —**'Finnish** a. 1. of Finland —n. 2. official language of Finland

finnan haddock ('fɪnən) or **haddie** ('hædɪ) smoked haddock

fiord (fjɔːd) n. see FJORD

fipple ('fɪp'l) n. wooden plug forming flue in end of pipe —**fipple flute** end-blown flute with fipple, such as recorder

fir (fɜː) n. 1. kind of coniferous resinous tree 2. its wood

fire (faɪə) n. 1. state of burning, combustion, flame, glow 2. mass of burning fuel 3. destructive burning, conflagration 4. device for heating a room *etc.* 5. ardour, keenness, spirit 6. shooting of firearms —vt. 7. discharge (firearm) 8. propel from firearm 9. *inf.* dismiss from employment 10. bake 11. make burn 12. supply with fuel 13. inspire 14. explode —vi. 15. discharge firearm 16. begin to burn —**'firing** n. 1. process of baking ceramics *etc.* in kiln 2. act of stoking fire or furnace 3. discharge of firearm 4. something used as fuel —**fire alarm** device to give warning of fire —**'firearm** n. gun, rifle, pistol *etc.* —**'fireball** n. 1. ball-shaped discharge of lightning 2. region of hot ionized gas at centre of nuclear explosion 3. *Astron.* large bright meteor 4. *sl.* energetic person —**'firebomb** n. see INCENDIARY (sense 6) —**'firebrand** n. 1. burning piece of wood 2. energetic (troublesome) person —**'firebreak** n. strip of cleared land to arrest progress of bush or grass fire —**'firebrick** n. refractory brick made of fire clay, for lining furnaces *etc.* —**fire brigade** organized body of men and appliances to put out fires and rescue those in danger —**'firebug** n. *inf.* person who intentionally sets fire to buildings *etc.*

—**fire clay** heat-resistant clay used in making of firebricks *etc.* —**'firecracker** n. small cardboard container filled with explosive powder —**'firecrest** n. small European warbler —**'firedamp** n. explosive hydrocarbon gas forming in mines —**'firedog** n. either of pair of metal stands used to support logs in open fire —**fire drill** rehearsal of procedures for escape from fire —**fire-eater** n. 1. performer who simulates swallowing of fire 2. belligerent person —**fire engine** vehicle with apparatus for extinguishing fires —**fire escape** means, *esp.* stairs, for escaping from burning buildings —**'firefly** n. insect giving off phosphorescent glow —**'fireguard** or **fire screen** n. protective grating in front of fire —**fire hall** C fire station —**fire irons** tongs, poker and shovel —**'firelighter** n. composition of highly combustible material for kindling domestic fire —**'fireman** n. 1. member of fire brigade 2. stoker 3. assistant to locomotive driver —**'fireplace** n. recess in room for fire —**fire raiser** person who deliberately sets fire to property *etc.* —**fire ship** burning vessel sent drifting against enemy ships —**fire station** building housing fire brigade —**'firetrap** n. building unsafe in case of fire —**'firework** n. 1. (*oft. pl.*) device to give spectacular effects by explosions and coloured sparks —pl. 2. outburst of temper, anger —**firing line** 1. *Mil.* positions from which fire is delivered 2. leading position in an activity —**firing party** or **squad** detachment sent to fire volleys at military funeral, or to shoot criminal

firkin ('fɜːkɪn) n. 1. small cask 2. UK measure of 9 gallons

firm[1] (fɜːm) a. 1. solid 2. fixed, stable 3. steadfast 4. resolute 5. settled —v. 6. make, become firm

firm[2] (fɜːm) n. 1. commercial enterprise 2. partnership

firmament ('fɜːməmənt) n. expanse of sky, heavens

first (fɜːst) a. 1. earliest in time or order 2. foremost in rank or position 3. most excellent 4. highest, chief —n. 5. beginning 6. first occurrence of something 7. first-class honours degree at university —adv. 8. before others in time, order *etc.* —**'firstly** adv. —**first aid** help given to injured person before arrival of doctor —**first class** n. 1. class of highest value, quality *etc.* —a. 2. of highest class 3. excellent 4. of most comfortable class of accommodation in hotel, train *etc.* 5. UK of letters handled faster than second-class letters —**first-class** adv. by first-class mail, means of transportation *etc.* —**first cousin** son or daughter of one's aunt or uncle —**first-day cover** *Philately* envelope post-marked on first day of issue of its stamps —**first finger** finger next to thumb —**first-foot** *chiefly Scot.* n. 1. first person to enter household in New Year (*also* **first-footer**) —v. 2. enter the house

of (someone) as first-foot —**first-footing** n.
—**first fruits** 1. first results or profits of
undertaking 2. fruit that ripens first
—**first-hand** a. obtained directly from the
first source —**first lady** (*oft.* F- L-) US
wife or official hostess of state governor
or president —**first mate** *or* **officer** officer
of merchant vessel immediately below
captain —**first offender** person convicted
of criminal offence for first time —**first
person** grammatical category of pronouns
and verbs used by speaker to refer to
himself —**first-rate** a. of highest class or
quality —**first-strike** a. (of nuclear
missile) intended for use in opening attack
calculated to destroy enemy's nuclear
weapons —**first water** 1. finest quality of
precious stone 2. best quality

firth (fɜːθ) *or* **frith** n. *esp.* in Scotland, arm
of the sea, river estuary

fiscal ('fɪskˌl) a. of government finances
—**fiscal year** US financial year

fish (fɪʃ) n. 1. vertebrate cold-blooded
animal with gills, living in water 2. its flesh
as food (*pl.* **fish, -es**) —*vi.* 3. (attempt to)
catch fish 4. search (for something) 5.
(*with* for) try to get information indirectly
—**'fisher** n. —**'fishery** n. 1. business of
fishing 2. fishing ground —**'fishy** a. 1. of,
like, or full of fish 2. dubious, open to
suspicion —**fish cake** fried flattened ball
of flaked fish mixed with mashed potatoes
—**'fisherman** n. one who catches fish for a
living or for pleasure —**fish-eye lens**
Photog. lens of small focal length, that
covers almost 180° —**'fish'finger** n. small
piece of fish covered in breadcrumbs
—**fish-kettle** n. oval pot for cooking fish
—**fish meal** ground dried fish used as
fertilizer *etc.* —**'fishmonger** n. seller of
fish —**fish slice** 1. fish carver 2. flat-bladed
utensil for turning or lifting food in frying
—**'fishwife** n. coarse, scolding woman
—**fish out** find, extract

fishplate ('fɪʃpleɪt) n. piece of metal
holding rails together

fissure ('fɪʃə) n. cleft, split, cleavage
—**fissile** ('fɪsaɪl) a. 1. capable of splitting 2.
tending to split —**'fission** n. 1. splitting 2.
reproduction by division of living cells
with two parts, each of which becomes
complete organism 3. splitting of atomic
nucleus with release of large amount of
energy —**'fissionable** a. capable of
undergoing nuclear fission —**fissiparous**
(fɪ'sɪpərəs) a. reproducing by fission

fist (fɪst) n. clenched hand —**'fisticuffs**
pl.n. fighting

fistula ('fɪstjʊlə) n. pipelike ulcer (*pl.* **-s,
-lae** (-liː))

fit' (fɪt) *vt.* 1. be suited to 2. be properly
adjusted to 3. arrange, adjust, apply, insert
4. supply, furnish —*vi.* 5. be correctly
adjusted or adapted 6. be of right size (**-tt-**)
—a. 7. well-suited, worthy 8. qualified 9.
proper, becoming 10. ready 11. in good
condition or health ('**fitter** *comp.,* '**fittest**
sup.) —n. 12. way anything fits, its style 13.
adjustment —'**fitly** *adv.* —'**fitment** n.

piece of furniture —'**fitness** n. —'**fitted** a.
1. designed for excellent fit 2. (of carpet)
cut to cover floor completely 3. (of
furniture) built to fit particular space
—'**fitter** n. 1. one who, that which, makes
fit 2. one who supervises making and
fitting of garments 3. mechanic skilled in
fitting up metalwork —'**fitting** a. 1.
appropriate, suitable, proper —n. 2. fixture
3. apparatus 4. action of fitting —**fit in** 1.
give place or time to 2. belong or conform,
esp. after adjustment

fit² (fɪt) n. 1. seizure with convulsions,
spasms, loss of consciousness *etc.,* of
epilepsy, hysteria *etc.* 2. sudden passing
attack of illness 3. passing state, mood
—'**fitful** a. spasmodic, capricious —'**fitfully** *adv.* —**have** *or* **throw a fit** *inf.* become
very angry

five (faɪv) a./n. cardinal number after four
—'**fif'teen** a./n. ten plus five —'**fif'teenth**
a./n. —**fifth** (fɪfθ) a./n. ordinal number of
five —'**fifthly** ('fɪfθlɪ) *adv.* —'**fiftieth**
('fɪftɪɪθ) a./n. —**fifty** ('fɪftɪ) a./n. five tens
—'**fiver** n. UK *inf.* five-pound note —**fives**
pl.n. (*with* sing. v.) ball game played with
hand or bat in a court —**fifth column**
organization spying for enemy within
country at war —**fifty-fifty** a./*adv. inf.* in
equal parts —**five-a-side** n. football with
teams of five —**five-o'clock shadow** beard
growth visible late in day on man's shaven
face —'**fivepins** *pl.n.* bowling game
played *esp.* in Canada —**Five-Year Plan**
in socialist economies, government plan
for economic development over five-year
period

fix (fɪks) *vt.* 1. fasten, make firm or stable
2. set, establish 3. appoint, assign,
determine 4. make fast 5. repair 6. *inf.*
influence the outcome of unfairly or by
deception 7. *inf.* bribe 8. *inf.* give
(someone) his just deserts —*vi.* 9. become
firm or solidified 10. determine —n. 11.
difficult situation 12. position of ship,
aircraft ascertained by radar, observation
etc. 13. *sl.* dose of narcotic drug
—**fix'ation** n. 1. act of fixing 2. preoccupation, obsession 3. situation of being set in
some way of acting or thinking —'**fixative**
a. 1. capable of, or tending to fix —n. 2.
fluid sprayed over drawings to prevent
smudging *etc.* 3. substance added to liquid
to make it less volatile —**fixed** a. 1.
attached so as to be immovable 2. stable 3.
steadily directed 4. established as to
relative position 5. always at same time 6.
(of ideas *etc.*) firmly maintained 7. (of
element) held in chemical combination 8.
(of substance) nonvolatile 9. arranged 10.
inf. equipped; provided for 11. *inf.* illegally
arranged —**fixedly** ('fɪksɪdlɪ) *adv.* intently
—'**fixity** n. —'**fixture** n. 1. thing fixed in
position 2. thing attached to house 3. date
for sporting event 4. the event —**fixed star**
star whose position appears to be
stationary over long period of time —**fix
(someone) up** attend to (someone's) needs
—**fix up** arrange

fizz (fɪz) *vi.* 1. hiss, splutter —*n.* 2. hissing noise 3. effervescent liquid, such as soda water, champagne —**'fizzle** *vi.* 1. splutter weakly —*n.* 2. fizzling noise 3. fiasco —**'fizzy** *a.* effervescent —**fizzle out** *inf.* come to nothing, fail

fjord *or* **fiord** (fjɔːd) *n. esp.* in Norway, long, narrow inlet of sea

FL Florida

fl. 1. floor 2. *floruit* (*Lat.*, (he or she) flourished) 3. fluid

flabbergast ('flæbəgɑːst) *vt.* overwhelm with astonishment

flabby ('flæbɪ) *a.* 1. hanging loose, limp 2. out of condition, too fat 3. feeble 4. yielding —**flab** *n. inf.* unsightly fat on the body —**'flabbiness** *n.*

flaccid ('flæksɪd) *a.* flabby, lacking firmness —**flac'cidity** *n.*

flag¹ (flæg) *n.* 1. banner, piece of bunting attached to staff or halyard as standard or signal 2. small paper emblem sold on flag days —*vt.* 3. decorate or mark with flag(s) 4. send or communicate (messages *etc.*) by flag signals (**-gg-**) —**flag day** day on which small flags or emblems are sold in streets for charity —**'flagpole** *or* **'flagstaff** *n.* pole on which flag is hoisted and displayed (*pl.* **-poles** *or* **-staffs, -staves** (-steɪvz)) —**'flagship** *n.* admiral's ship 2. most important ship of fleet —**flag down** warn or signal (vehicle) to stop —**flag of convenience** national flag flown by ship registered in that country to gain financial or legal advantage —**flag of truce** white flag indicating invitation to enemy to negotiate

flag² (flæg) *n.* water plant with sword-shaped leaves, *esp.* the iris —**'flaggy** *a.*

flag³ (flæg) *n.* 1. flat slab of stone —*pl.* 2. pavement of flags —*vt.* 3. furnish (floor *etc.*) with flagstones (**-gg-**) —**'flagstone** *n.*

flag⁴ (flæg) *vi.* 1. droop, fade 2. lose vigour (**-gg-**)

flagellate ('flædʒɪleɪt) *vt.* scourge, flog —**'flagellant** *n.* one who scourges himself, *esp.* in religious penance —**flagel'lation** *n.* —**'flagellator** *n.*

flagellum (flə'dʒɛləm) *n.* 1. *Biol.* whiplike outgrowth from cell that acts as organ of locomotion 2. *Bot.* long thin shoot (*pl.* **-la** (-lə), **-s**)

flageolet (flædʒə'lɛt) *n.* small flutelike instrument

flagon ('flægən) *n.* large bottle of wine *etc.*

flagrant ('fleɪgrənt) *a.* glaring, scandalous, blatant —**'flagrancy** *n.* —**'flagrantly** *adv.*

flail (fleɪl) *n.* 1. instrument for threshing corn by hand —*v.* 2. beat with, move as, flail

flair (fleə) *n.* 1. natural ability 2. elegance

flak *or* **flack** (flæk) *n.* 1. anti-aircraft fire 2. *inf.* adverse criticism

flake (fleɪk) *n.* 1. small, thin piece, *esp.* particle of snow 2. piece chipped off —*v.* 3. (cause to) peel off in flakes —**'flaky** *a.* —**flake out** *inf.* collapse, sleep from exhaustion

flambé ('flɑːmbeɪ) *a.* (of food) served in flaming brandy *etc.*

flamboyant (flæm'bɔɪənt) *a.* 1. florid, gorgeous, showy 2. exuberant, ostentatious

flame (fleɪm) *n.* 1. burning gas, *esp.* above fire 2. visible burning 3. passion, *esp.* love 4. *inf.* sweetheart —*vi.* 5. give out flames, blaze 6. shine 7. burst out —**'flaming** *a.* 1. burning with flames 2. glowing brightly 3. ardent 4. *inf.* a common intensifier —**flame-thrower** *n.* weapon that ejects stream of burning fluid

flamenco (flə'mɛnkəʊ) *n.* Sp. dance to guitar

flamingo (flə'mɪŋgəʊ) *n.* large pink bird with long neck and legs (*pl.* **-s, -es**)

flammable ('flæməb³l) *a.* liable to catch fire

flan (flæn) *n.* open sweet or savoury tart

flange (flændʒ) *n.* 1. projecting flat rim, collar or rib —*v.* 2. provide with or take form of flange

flank (flæŋk) *n.* 1. part of side between hips and ribs 2. side of anything, *eg* body of troops —*vt.* 3. guard or strengthen on flank 4. attack flank of 5. be at, move along either side of

flannel ('flæn³l) *n.* 1. soft woollen fabric for clothing, *esp.* trousers 2. small piece of cloth for washing face and hands 3. *inf.* insincere talk —*pl.* 4. trousers *etc.* made of flannel —*vt.* 5. UK *inf.* flatter (**-ll-**) —**flanne'lette** *n.* cotton fabric imitating flannel —**'flannelly** *a.*

flap (flæp) *v.* 1. move (wings, arms *etc.*) as bird flying 2. (cause to) sway —*vt.* 3. strike with flat object —*vi.* 4. *inf.* be agitated, flustered (**-pp-**) —*n.* 5. act of flapping 6. broad piece of anything hanging from hinge or loosely from one side 7. movable part of aircraft wing 8. *inf.* state of excitement or panic —**'flapper** *n.* in 1920s, young woman, *esp.* one flaunting unconventional behaviour —**'flapjack** *n.* 1. chewy biscuit made with rolled oats 2. *chiefly* US pancake

flare (fleə) *vi.* 1. blaze with unsteady flame 2. *inf.* (*with* up) suddenly burst into anger 3. spread outwards, as bottom of skirt —*n.* 4. instance of flaring 5. signal light —**flarepath** *n.* area lit up to facilitate landing or takeoff of aircraft —**flare-up** *n.* 1. sudden burst of fire 2. *inf.* sudden burst of emotion —**flare up** 1. burst suddenly into fire 2. *inf.* burst into anger

flash (flæʃ) *n.* 1. sudden burst of light or flame 2. sudden short blaze 3. very short time 4. brief news item 5. ribbon; badge 6. display —*vi.* 7. break into sudden flame 8. gleam 9. burst into view 10. move very fast 11. appear suddenly 12. *sl.* expose oneself indecently —*vt.* 13. cause to gleam 14. emit (light *etc.*) suddenly —*a.* 15. showy 16. sham (*also* **'flashy**) —**'flasher** *n.* 1. something which flashes 2. *sl.* someone who indecently exposes himself —**'flashing** *n.* weatherproof material used to cover valleys between slopes of roof *etc.*

—'**flashback** n. break in continuity of book, play or film, to introduce what has taken place previously —'**flashbulb** n. Photog. small light bulb triggered, usu. electrically, to produce bright flash of light —'**flashcube** n. boxlike camera attachment, holding four flashbulbs, that turns so that each flashbulb can be used —'**flashlight** n. 1. esp. US torch 2. Photog. brief bright light emitted by electronic flash (also flash) —**flash point** temperature at which a vapour ignites —**flash in the pan** person etc. that enjoys only short-lived success

flask (flɑːsk) n. 1. long-necked bottle for scientific use 2. pocket bottle 3. vacuum flask

flat¹ (flæt) a. 1. level 2. spread out 3. at full length 4. smooth 5. downright 6. dull, lifeless 7. Mus. below true pitch 8. (of tyre) deflated, punctured 9. (of battery) fully discharged, dead ('**flatter** comp., '**flattest** sup.) —adv. 10. completely, utterly; absolutely —n. 11. flat object, surface or part 12. Mus. note half tone below natural pitch —'**flatly** adv. —'**flatness** n. —'**flatten** v. —'**flatfish** n. type of fish which swims along sea floor on one side of body with both eyes on uppermost side —'**flatfoot** n. 1. condition in which instep arch of foot is flattened 2. sl. policeman (pl. -s, -feet) —'**flatiron** n. formerly, iron for pressing clothes —**flat race** race over level ground with no jumps —**flat rate** the same rate in all cases —**flat spin** 1. aircraft spin in which longitudinal axis is more nearly horizontal than vertical 2. inf. state of confusion —'**flatworm** n. parasitic or free-living invertebrate, such as fluke or tapeworm, having flattened body —**flat out** at, with maximum speed or effort

flat² (flæt) n. suite of rooms comprising a residence entirely on one floor of building —'**flatlet** n. small flat

flatter ('flætə) vt. 1. fawn on 2. praise insincerely 3. gratify vanity of 4. represent too favourably —'**flatterer** n. —'**flattery** n.

flatulent ('flætjʊlənt) a. 1. suffering from, generating (excess) gases in intestines 2. pretentious —'**flatulence** n. 1. flatulent condition 2. verbosity, emptiness

flaunt (flɔːnt) v. 1. show off 2. wave proudly

flautist ('flɔːtɪst) or U.S. **flutist** ('fluːtɪst) n. flute player

flavescent (fləˈvɛsˀnt) a. yellowish; turning yellow

flavour or U.S. **flavor** ('fleɪvə) n. 1. mixed sensation of smell and taste 2. distinctive taste, savour 3. undefinable characteristic, quality of anything —vt. 4. give flavour to 5. season —'**flavouring** or U.S. '**flavoring** n.

flaw¹ (flɔː) n. 1. crack 2. defect, blemish —vt. 3. make flaw in —'**flawless** a. perfect

flaw² (flɔː) n. sudden gust of wind; squall

flax (flæks) n. 1. plant grown for its textile

fibre and seeds 2. its fibres, spun into linen thread —'**flaxen** a. 1. of flax 2. light yellow, straw-coloured

flay (fleɪ) vt. 1. strip skin off 2. criticize severely

flea (fliː) n. small, wingless, jumping, blood-sucking insect —'**fleabag** n. unkempt person, horse etc. —'**fleabite** n. 1. insect's bite 2. trifling injury 3. trifle —**flea-bitten** a. 1. bitten by flea 2. mean, worthless 3. scruffy —**flea market** market for cheap goods —'**fleapit** n. inf. shabby cinema or theatre

fleck (flɛk) n. 1. small mark, streak or particle —vt. 2. mark with flecks

fled (flɛd) pt./pp. of FLEE

fledged (flɛdʒd) a. 1. (of birds) able to fly 2. experienced, trained —'**fledgling** or '**fledgeling** n. 1. young bird 2. inexperienced person

flee (fliː) v. run away (from) (**fled**, '**fleeing**)

fleece (fliːs) n. 1. sheep's wool —vt. 2. rob —'**fleecy** a.

fleet¹ (fliːt) n. 1. number of warships organized as unit 2. number of ships, cars etc. operating together —**fleet chief petty officer** noncommissioned officer in Royal Navy comparable in rank to warrant officer in army or Royal Air Force

fleet² (fliːt) a. swift, nimble —'**fleeting** a. passing, transient —'**fleetingly** adv.

Fleet Street (fliːt) 1. street in London where many newspaper offices are situated 2. Brit. journalism or journalists collectively

Flemish ('flɛmɪʃ) n. 1. one of two official languages of Belgium —a. 2. of Flanders —'**Fleming** n. native of Flanders, medieval principality in the Low Countries, or of Flemish-speaking Belgium —**the Flemish** Flemings collectively

flense (flɛns), **flench** (flɛntʃ), or **flinch** (flɪntʃ) vt. strip (esp. whale) of flesh

flesh (flɛʃ) n. 1. soft part, muscular substance, between skin and bone 2. in plants, pulp 3. fat 4. sensual appetites —'**fleshly** adv. —'**fleshly** a. 1. carnal 2. material —'**fleshy** a. 1. plump 2. pulpy —'**fleshpots** pl.n. (places catering for) self-indulgent living —**flesh wound** wound affecting superficial tissues —**in the flesh** in person; actually present

fleur-de-lis or **fleur-de-lys** (flɜːdəˈliː) n. 1. heraldic lily with three petals 2. iris (pl. **fleurs-de-lis** or **fleurs-de-lys** (flɜːdəˈliːz))

flew (fluː) pt. of FLY¹

flews (fluːz) pl.n. fleshy hanging lip of bloodhound or similar dog

flex (flɛks) n. 1. flexible insulated electric cable —v. 2. bend, be bent —**flexi'bility** n. —'**flexible** a. 1. easily bent 2. manageable 3. adaptable —'**flexibly** adv. —'**flexion** or '**flection** n. 1. bending 2. bent state —'**flexitime** n. system permitting variation in starting and finishing times of work, providing an agreed number of hours is worked over a specified period

flibbertigibbet (ˈflɪbətɪdʒɪbɪt) *n.* flighty, gossiping person

flick (flɪk) *vt.* 1. strike lightly, jerk —*n.* 2. light blow 3. jerk —*pl.* 4. *sl.* cinema —**flick knife** knife with retractable blade that springs out when button is pressed

flicker (ˈflɪkə) *vi.* 1. burn, shine, unsteadily 2. waver, quiver —*n.* 3. unsteady light or movement

flight (flaɪt) *n.* 1. act or manner of flying through air 2. number flying together, as birds 3. journey in aircraft 4. Air Force unit of command 5. power of flying 6. swift movement or passage 7. sally 8. distance flown 9. feather *etc.* fitted to arrow or dart to give it stability in flight 10. stairs between two landings 11. running away —**flight deck** 1. crew compartment in airliner 2. upper deck of aircraft carrier where aircraft take off —**flight lieutenant** officer holding commissioned rank senior to flying officer and junior to squadron leader in Royal Air Force —**flight recorder** electronic device in aircraft storing information about its flight —**flight sergeant** noncommissioned officer in Royal Air Force, junior in rank to master aircrew

flighty (ˈflaɪtɪ) *a.* 1. frivolous 2. erratic

flimsy (ˈflɪmzɪ) *a.* 1. frail, weak 2. thin 3. easily destroyed —**flimsily** *adv.*

flinch (flɪntʃ) *vi.* shrink, draw back, wince

fling (flɪŋ) *v.* 1. throw, send, move, with force (**flung** *pt./pp.*) —*n.* 2. throw 3. hasty attempt 4. spell of indulgence 5. vigorous dance

flint (flɪnt) *n.* 1. hard steel-grey stone 2. piece of this 3. hard substance used (as flint) for striking fire —**flintily** *adv.* —**flinty** *a.* 1. like or consisting of flint 2. hard, cruel —**flintlock** *n.* 1. gunlock in which charge is ignited by spark produced by flint in hammer 2. firearm having such lock

flip (flɪp) *vt.* 1. throw or flick lightly 2. turn over —*vi.* 3. *sl.,* chiefly US fly into rage or emotional outburst (*also* **flip one's lid** *or* **top**) (**-pp-**) —*n.* 4. instance, act, of flipping 5. drink with beaten egg —*a.* 6. US *inf.* flippant; pert —**flippancy** *n.* —**flippant** *a.* treating serious things lightly —**flippantly** *adv.* —**flipper** *n.* 1. limb, fin for swimming —*pl.* 2. fin-shaped rubber devices worn on feet to help in swimming —**flip side** less important side of pop record

flirt (flɜːt) *vi.* 1. toy, play with another's affections 2. trifle, toy (with) —*n.* 3. person who flirts —**flir'tation** *n.* —**flir'tatious** *a.*

flit (flɪt) *vi.* 1. pass lightly and rapidly 2. dart 3. *dial.* move house 4. *inf.* go away hastily, secretly (**-tt-**)

flitch (flɪtʃ) *n.* side of bacon

flittermouse (ˈflɪtəmaʊs) *n. dial.* bat (the animal)

float (fləʊt) *vi.* 1. rest, drift on surface of liquid 2. be suspended freely 3. move aimlessly —*vt.* 4. (of liquid) support, bear

alone 5. in commerce, get (company) started 6. *Fin.* allow (currency) to fluctuate against other currencies in accordance with market forces —*n.* 7. anything small that floats (*esp.* to support something else, *eg* fishing net) 8. small delivery vehicle, *esp.* powered by batteries 9. motor vehicle carrying tableau *etc.* in parade 10. sum of money used to provide change —**floating** *a.* 1. having little or no attachment 2. (of organ *etc.*) displaced and abnormally movable 3. uncommitted, unfixed 4. *Fin.* (of capital) available for current use; (of debt) short-term and unfunded; (of currency) free to fluctuate against other currencies in accordance with market forces —**flo'tation** *or* **floa'tation** *n.* act of floating, *esp.* floating of company —**floating rib** any rib of lower two pairs of ribs, which are not attached to breastbone —**floating voter** voter of no fixed political allegiance

flocculent (ˈflɒkjʊlənt) *a.* like tufts of wool

flock¹ (flɒk) *n.* 1. number of animals of one kind together 2. body of people 3. religious congregation —*vi.* 4. gather in a crowd

flock² (flɒk) *n.* 1. lock, tuft of wool *etc.* 2. wool refuse for stuffing cushions *etc.* —**flocky** *a.*

floe (fləʊ) *n.* sheet of floating ice

flog (flɒg) *vt.* 1. beat with whip, stick *etc.* 2. *sl.* sell (**-gg-**) —**flog a dead horse** pursue line of attack or argument from which no results can come

flood (flʌd) *n.* 1. inundation, overflow of water 2. rising of tide 3. outpouring 4. flowing water —*vt.* 5. inundate 6. cover, fill with water —*vi.* 7. arrive, move *etc.* in great numbers —**floodgate** *n.* gate, sluice for letting water in or out —**floodlight** *n.* broad, intense beam of artificial light —**floodlit** *a.* —**flood tide** 1. the rising tide 2. *fig.* peak of prosperity

floor (flɔː) *n.* 1. lower surface of room 2. set of rooms on one level, storey 3. flat space 4. (right to speak in) legislative hall —*vt.* 5. supply with floor 6. knock down 7. confound —**flooring** *n.* material for floors —**floor plan** drawing to scale of arrangement of rooms on one floor of building —**floor show** entertainment in nightclub *etc.*

floozy, floozie, *or* **floosie** (ˈfluːzɪ) *n. sl.* disreputable woman

flop (flɒp) *vi.* 1. bend, fall, collapse loosely, carelessly 2. fall flat on floor, on water *etc.* 3. *inf.* go to sleep 4. *inf.* fail (**-pp-**) —*n.* 5. flopping movement or sound 6. *inf.* failure —**floppily** *adv.* —**floppiness** *n.* —**floppy** *a.* limp, unsteady —**floppy disk** flexible magnetic disk that stores information and can be used to store data in memory of digital computer

flora (ˈflɔːrə) *n.* 1. plants of a region 2. list of them (*pl.* **-s, -rae** (-riː)) —**floral** *a.* of flowers —**flo'rescence** *n.* state or time of flowering —**floret** *n.* small flower forming part of composite flower —**flori'bunda**

n. type of rose whose flowers grow in large clusters —**flori'cultural** *a.* —**'floriculture** *n.* cultivation of flowers —**flori'culturist** *n.* —**florist** ('florɪst) *n.* dealer in flowers

Florentine ('florəntaɪn) *a.* 1. of Florence in Italy —*n.* 2. native of Florence

florid ('florɪd) *a.* 1. with red, flushed complexion 2. ornate

florin ('florɪn) *n.* formerly, Brit. silver two-shilling piece

floss (flos) *n.* 1. mass of fine, silky fibres, *eg* of cotton, silk 2. fluff —**'flossy** *a.* light and downy

flotation *or* **floatation** (fləʊ'teɪʃən) *n.* *see* FLOAT

flotilla (flə'tɪlə) *n.* 1. fleet of small vessels 2. group of destroyers

flotsam ('flotsəm) *n.* 1. floating wreckage 2. discarded waste objects

flounce[1] (flaʊns) *vi.* 1. go, move abruptly and impatiently —*n.* 2. fling, jerk of body or limb

flounce[2] (flaʊns) *n.* ornamental gathered strip on woman's garment

flounder[1] ('flaʊndə) *vi.* 1. plunge and struggle, *esp.* in water or mud 2. proceed in bungling, hesitating manner —*n.* 3. act of floundering

flounder[2] ('flaʊndə) *n.* flatfish

flour (flaʊə) *n.* 1. powder prepared by sifting and grinding wheat *etc.* 2. fine soft powder —*vt.* 3. sprinkle with flour —**'flouriness** *n.* —**'floury** *a.*

flourish ('flʌrɪʃ) *vi.* 1. thrive 2. be in the prime —*vt.* 3. brandish, wave about 4. display —*n.* 5. ornamental curve 6. showy gesture in speech *etc.* 7. waving of hand, weapon *etc.* 8. fanfare (of trumpets)

flout (flaʊt) *vt.* 1. show contempt for, mock 2. defy

flow (fləʊ) *vi.* 1. glide along as stream 2. circulate, as the blood 3. move easily 4. move in waves 5. hang loose 6. be present in abundance —*n.* 7. act, instance of flowing 8. quantity that flows 9. rise of tide 10. ample supply —**flow chart** diagram showing sequence of operations in industrial *etc.* process

flower ('flaʊə) *n.* 1. coloured (not green) part of plant from which fruit is developed 2. bloom, blossom 3. ornamentation 4. choicest part, pick —*pl.* 5. chemical sublimate —*vi.* 6. produce flowers 7. bloom 8. come to prime condition —*vt.* 9. ornament with flowers —**'flowered** *a.* 1. having flowers 2. decorated with floral design —**'floweret** *n.* small flower —**'flowery** *a.* 1. abounding in flowers 2. full of fine words, ornamented with figures of speech —**flower girl** girl selling flowers

flown (fləʊn) *pp.* of FLY[1]

fl. oz. fluid ounce(s)

flu (fluː) influenza

fluctuate ('flʌktjʊeɪt) *v.* 1. vary —*vi.* 2. rise and fall, undulate —**fluctu'ation** *n.*

flue (fluː) *n.* passage or pipe for smoke or hot air, chimney

fluent ('fluːənt) *a.* 1. speaking, writing a given language easily and well 2. easy, graceful

fluff (flʌf) *n.* 1. soft, feathery stuff 2. down 3. *inf.* mistake —*v.* 4. make or become soft, light 5. *inf.* make mistake (in) —**'fluffy** *a.*

fluid ('fluːɪd) *a.* 1. flowing easily 2. not solid —*n.* 3. gas or liquid —**flu'idity** *n.* —**fluid ounce** unit of capacity 1/20 of pint

fluke[1] (fluːk) *n.* 1. flat triangular point of anchor —*pl.* 2. whale's tail

fluke[2] (fluːk) *n.* 1. stroke of luck, accident —*vt.* 2. gain, make, hit by accident or by luck —**'fluky** *a.* 1. uncertain 2. got by luck

fluke[3] (fluːk) *n.* 1. flatfish 2. parasitic worm

flume (fluːm) *n.* narrow (artificial) channel for water

flummery ('flʌmərɪ) *n.* 1. nonsense, idle talk, humbug 2. dish of milk, flour, eggs *etc.*

flummox ('flʌməks) *vt.* bewilder, perplex

flung (flʌŋ) *pt./pp.* of FLING

flunk (flʌŋk) *US, NZ inf. v.* 1. (cause to) fail to reach required standard (in) —*vi.* 2. (*with* out) be dismissed from school

flunky *or* **flunkey** ('flʌŋkɪ) *n.* 1. servant, *esp.* liveried manservant 2. servile person

fluorescence (flʊə'resəns) *n.* emission of light or other radiation from substance when bombarded by particles (electrons *etc.*) or other radiation, as in fluorescent lamp —**fluo'resce** *vi.* —**fluo'rescent** *a.* —**fluorescent lamp** lamp in which ultraviolet radiation from electrical gas discharge causes layer of phosphor on tube's inside surface to fluoresce —**'fluoroscope** *n.* device consisting of fluorescent screen and x-ray source that enables x-ray image of person *etc.* to be observed directly —**fluo'roscopy** *n.* examination of person *etc.* by means of fluoroscope

fluorspar ('flʊəspɑː), *or* **fluor** ('fluːɔː), *or U.S.* **fluorite** *n.* mineral containing fluorine —**'fluoridate** *vt.* —**fluori'dation** *n.* —**'fluoride** *n.* salt containing fluorine, *esp.* as added to domestic water supply as protection against tooth decay —**'fluorinate** *vt.* treat or cause to combine with fluorine —**'fluorine** *n.* nonmetallic element, yellowish gas

flurry ('flʌrɪ) *n.* 1. squall, gust 2. bustle, commotion 3. death struggle of whale 4. fluttering (as of snowflakes) —*vt.* 5. agitate, bewilder, fluster (**'flurried, 'flurrying**)

flush[1] (flʌʃ) *vi.* 1. blush 2. (of skin) redden 3. flow suddenly or violently —*vt.* 4. cleanse (*eg* toilet) by rush of water 5. excite —*n.* 6. reddening, blush 7. rush of water 8. excitement 9. elation 10. glow of colour 11. freshness, vigour —*a.* 12. full 13. *inf.* having plenty of money 14. *inf.* well supplied 15. level with surrounding surface

flush[2] (flʌʃ) *vt.* cause to leave cover and take flight

flush[3] (flʌʃ) *n.* set of cards all of one suit

fluster ('flʌstə) *v.* 1. make or become

nervous, agitated —n. 2. state of confusion or agitation

flute (fluːt) n. 1. wind instrument of tube with holes stopped by fingers or keys and blowhole in side 2. groove, channel —vi. 3. play on flute —vt. 4. make grooves in —'**fluted** a. —'**fluting** n.

flutter ('flʌtə) v. 1. flap (as wings) rapidly without flight or in short flights 2. be or make excited, agitated —vi. 3. quiver —n. 4. flapping movement 5. nervous agitation 6. inf. modest wager

fluvial ('fluːvɪəl) a. of rivers

flux (flʌks) n. 1. discharge 2. constant succession of changes 3. substance mixed with metal to clean, aid adhesion in soldering etc. 4. measure of strength in magnetic field

fly¹ (flaɪ) vi. 1. move through air on wings or in aircraft 2. pass quickly 3. rush 4. flee, run away —vt. 5. operate (aircraft) 6. cause to fly 7. set flying —v. 8. float loosely (**flew** pt., **flown** pp.) —n. 9. (zip or buttons fastening) opening in trousers 10. flap in garment or tent 11. flying —'**flier** or '**flyer** n. 1. person or thing that flies 2. aviator, pilot 3. inf. long, flying leap 4. rectangular step in straight flight of stairs 5. Athletics inf. flying start —'**flying** a. hurried, brief —'**flyaway** a. 1. (of hair etc.) loose and fluttering 2. frivolous, flighty; giddy —**fly-by-night** inf. a. 1. untrustworthy, esp. in finance —n. 2. untrustworthy person —**flyfish** vi. fish with artificial fly as lure —**flying boat** aeroplane fitted with floats instead of landing wheels —**flying buttress** Archit. arched or slanting structure attached at only one point to a mass of masonry —**flying colours** conspicuous success —**flying doctor** (esp. Aust.) doctor visiting patients in outback areas by aircraft —**flying fish** fish with winglike fins used for gliding above the sea —**flying fox** large fruit-eating bat —**flying officer** officer holding commissioned rank senior to pilot officer but junior to flight lieutenant in Brit. and certain other air forces —**flying picket** (in industrial disputes) member of group of pickets organized to be able to move quickly from place to place —**flying saucer** unidentified (disc-shaped) flying object, supposedly from outer space —**flying squad** special detachment of police, soldiers etc., ready to act quickly —**flying start 1.** in sprinting, start by competitor anticipating starting signal 2. start to race in which competitor is already travelling at speed as he passes starting line 3. any promising beginning 4. initial advantage —'**flyleaf** n. blank leaf at beginning or end of book —'**flyover** n. road passing over another by bridge —'**flypaper** n. paper with sticky and poisonous coating, usu. hung from ceiling to trap flies —**fly sheet 1.** fly (in tent) 2. short handbill —**fly spray** liquid sprayed from aerosol to destroy flies —'**flytrap** n. 1. insectivorous plant 2. device for catching flies —'**flyweight** n. 1. profes-

sional boxer weighing not more than 112 lbs. (51 kg); amateur boxer weighing 106-112 lbs. (48-51 kg) 2. in Olympic wrestling, wrestler weighing not more than 115 lbs. (52 kg) —'**flywheel** n. heavy wheel regulating speed of machine

fly² (flaɪ) n. two-winged insect, esp. common housefly —'**flyblown** a. infested with larvae of blowfly —'**flycatcher** n. small insect-eating songbird

fly³ (flaɪ) a. sl. sharp and knowing

Fm Chem. fermium

FM frequency modulation

fm. 1. fathom (also **fm**) 2. from

F.M. Field Marshal

f-number or **f number** n. Photog. numerical value of relative aperture

fo. folio

F.O. Flying Officer

foal (fəʊl) n. 1. young of horse, ass etc. —v. 2. bear (foal)

foam (fəʊm) n. 1. collection of small bubbles on liquid 2. froth of saliva or sweat 3. light cellular solid used for insulation, packing etc. —v. 4. (cause to) produce foam —vi. 5. be very angry (esp. in **foam at the mouth**) —'**foamy** a. —**foam rubber** rubber treated to form firm, spongy foam

fob (fɒb) n. 1. short watch chain 2. small pocket in waistband of trousers or waistcoat

f.o.b. or **F.O.B.** Comm. free on board

fob off 1. ignore, dismiss (someone or something) in offhand (insulting) manner 2. dispose of (-**bb**-)

fo'c's'le or **fo'c'sle** ('fəʊksʲl) n. see FORECASTLE

focus ('fəʊkəs) n. 1. point at which rays meet after being reflected or refracted (also **focal point**) 2. state of optical image when it is clearly defined 3. state of instrument producing such image 4. point of convergence 5. point on which interest, activity is centred (pl. **-es**, **foci** ('fəʊsaɪ)) —vt. 6. bring to focus, adjust 7. concentrate —vi. 8. come to focus 9. converge ('**focused**, '**focusing**) —'**focal** a. of, at focus —**focal length** or **distance** distance from focal point of lens to reflecting surface

fodder ('fɒdə) n. bulk food for livestock

foe (fəʊ) n. enemy

foetid ('fɛtɪd, 'fiː-) a. see FETID

foetus or **fetus** ('fiːtəs) n. fully-developed young in womb or egg —'**foetal** or '**fetal** a.

fog (fɒg) n. 1. thick mist 2. dense watery vapour in lower atmosphere 3. cloud of anything reducing visibility —vt. 4. cover in fog 5. puzzle (-**gg**-) —'**foggy** a. —'**fogbound** a. prevented from operation by fog —'**foghorn** n. instrument to warn ships in fog

fogy or **fogey** ('fəʊgɪ) n. old-fashioned person

foible ('fɔɪbʲl) n. minor weakness; idiosyncrasy

foil[1] (fɔıl) vt. baffle, defeat, frustrate —**'foilable** a.

foil[2] (fɔıl) n. 1. metal in thin sheet 2. anything which sets off another thing to advantage 3. Archit. small arc between cusps

foil[3] (fɔıl) n. light, slender, flexible sword tipped by button

foist (fɔıst) vt. (usu. with off or on) sell, pass off (inferior or unwanted thing) as valuable

fold[1] (fəʊld) vt. 1. double up, bend part of 2. interlace (arms) 3. wrap up 4. clasp (in arms) 5. Cooking mix gently —vi. 6. become folded 7. admit of being folded 8. inf. fail —n. 9. folding 10. coil 11. winding 12. line made by folding 13. crease 14. foldlike geological formation —**'folder** n. binder, file for loose papers —**'foldaway** a. (of bed etc.) able to be folded away when not in use —**folding door** door in form of hinged leaves that can be folded one against another

fold[2] (fəʊld) n. 1. enclosure for sheep 2. body of believers, church

-**fold** (comb. form) having so many parts; being so many times as much or as many, as in hundredfold

folderol ('fɒldərɒl) n. see FALDERAL

foliage ('fəʊlııdʒ) n. leaves collectively, leafage —**foli'aceous** a. of or like leaf —**'foliate** a. leaflike, having leaves —**foli'ation** n. 1. Bot. process of producing leaves; state of being in leaf; arrangement of leaves in leaf bud 2. Archit. ornamentation consisting of cusps and foils 3. consecutive numbering of leaves of book 4. Geol. arrangement of constituents of rock in leaflike layers

folio ('fəʊlıəʊ) n. 1. sheet of paper folded in half to make two leaves of book 2. book of largest common size made up of such sheets 3. page numbered on one side only 4. page number (pl. -s)

folk (fəʊk) n. 1. (with pl. v.) people in general family, relatives 2. race of people —**'folksy** a. inf., chiefly US 1. of or like ordinary people 2. friendly; affable 3. affectedly simple —**folk dance** —**folk etymology** gradual change in form of word through influence of more familiar word with which it becomes associated —**'folklore** n. tradition, customs, beliefs popularly held —**folk music** 1. music passed on from generation to generation 2. any music composed in this idiom —**folk song** 1. song handed down among common people 2. modern song in folk idiom

follicle ('fɒlık'l) n. 1. small sac 2. seed vessel —**fol'licular** a.

follow ('fɒləʊ) v. 1. go or come after —vt. 2. accompany, attend on 3. keep to (path etc.) 4. take as guide, conform to 5. engage in 6. have a keen interest in 7. be consequent on 8. grasp meaning of —vi. 9. come next 10. result —**'follower** n. 1. disciple 2. supporter —**'following** a. 1. about to be mentioned —n. 2. body of

supporters —**follow-on** n. Cricket immediate second innings forced on team scoring prescribed number of runs fewer than its opponents in first innings —**follow-through** n. in ball games, continuation of stroke after impact with ball —**follow-up** n. something done to reinforce initial action —**follow on** (of team) play follow-on

folly ('fɒlı) n. 1. foolishness 2. foolish action, idea etc. 3. useless, extravagant structure

foment (fə'mɛnt) vt. 1. foster, stir up 2. bathe with hot lotions —**fomen'tation** n.

fond (fɒnd) a. 1. tender, loving 2. obs. credulous 3. obs. foolish —**'fondly** adv. —**'fondness** n. —**fond of** having liking for

fondant ('fɒndənt) n. 1. soft sugar mixture for sweets 2. sweet made of this

fondle ('fɒnd'l) vt. caress

fondue ('fɒndjuː; Fr. fɔ̃'dy) n. Swiss dish of sauce (esp. cheese) into which pieces of bread etc. are dipped

font (fɒnt) n. bowl for baptismal water, usu. on pedestal

fontanelle or **fontanel** (fɒntə'nɛl) n. soft, membranous gap between bones of baby's skull

food (fuːd) n. 1. solid nourishment 2. what one eats 3. mental or spiritual nourishment —**'foodie** or **'foody** n. person with enthusiastic interest in preparation and consumption of good food —**food poisoning** acute illness caused by food that is naturally poisonous or contaminated by bacteria —**'foodstuff** n. food

fool (fuːl) n. 1. silly, empty-headed person 2. dupe 3. simpleton 4. Hist. jester, clown 5. dessert of puréed fruit mixed with cream etc. —vt. 6. delude, dupe —vi. 7. act as fool —**'foolery** n. 1. habitual folly 2. act of playing the fool 3. absurdity —**'foolish** a. 1. ill-considered, silly 2. stupid —**'foolishly** adv. —**'foolhardiness** n. —**'foolhardy** a. foolishly adventurous —**'foolproof** a. proof against failure —**fool's cap** 1. jester's or dunce's cap 2. this as watermark —**'foolscap** n. size of paper which formerly had this mark —**fool's errand** fruitless undertaking —**fool's paradise** illusory happiness

foot (fʊt) n. 1. lowest part of leg, from ankle down 2. lowest part of anything, base, stand 3. end of bed etc. 4. infantry 5. measure of twelve inches 6. division of verse (pl. feet) —v. 7. dance (also foot it) —vt. 8. walk over (esp. in foot it) 9. pay cost of (esp. in foot the bill) —**'footage** n. 1. length in feet 2. length, extent, of film used —**'footie** or **'footy** n. sl. football —**'footing** n. 1. basis, foundation 2. firm standing, relations, conditions —pl. 3. (concrete) foundations for walls of buildings —**foot-and-mouth disease** infectious viral disease in sheep, cattle etc. —**'football** n. 1. game played with large blown-up ball 2. the ball —**'footballer** n. —**football pools** form of gambling on

results of football matches —**'footboard** n.
1. treadle or foot-operated lever on machine 2. vertical board at foot of bed —**foot brake** brake operated by pressure on foot pedal —**'footbridge** n. narrow bridge for pedestrians —**'footfall** n. sound of footstep —**foot fault** Tennis fault of overstepping baseline while serving —**'foothill** n. (oft. pl.) low hill at foot of mountain —**'foothold** n. 1. place affording secure grip for the foot 2. secure position from which progress may be made —**'footlights** pl.n. lights across front of stage —**'footloose** a. free from any ties —**'footman** n. liveried servant —**'footnote** n. note of reference or explanation printed at foot of page —**'footpad** n. obs. robber, highwayman —**'footpath** n. narrow path for pedestrians —**'footplate** n. platform for driver and fireman of locomotive —**foot-pound** n. unit of measurement of work in f.p.s. system —**'footprint** n. mark left by foot —**'footrest** n. something that provides support for feet —**'footslog** vi. walk, go on foot —**'footslogger** n. —**'footsore** a. having sore feet, esp. from walking —**'footwear** n. anything worn to cover feet —**'footwork** n. skilful use of feet, as in sports etc.

footle ('fu:t'l) vi. inf. (oft. with around or about) loiter aimlessly

fop (fɒp) n. man excessively concerned with fashion —**'foppery** n. —**'foppish** a. —**'foppishly** adv.

for (fɔ:; unstressed fə) prep. 1. intended to reach 2. directed or belonging to 3. because of 4. instead of 5. towards 6. on account of 7. in favour of 8. respecting 9. during 10. in search of 11. in payment of 12. in the character of 13. in spite of —conj. 14. because —**for it** inf. liable for punishment or blame

for- (comb. form) from, away, against, as in forswear, forbid. Such words are not given here where the meaning may easily be inferred from the simple word

forage ('fɒrɪdʒ) n. 1. food for cattle and horses —vi. 2. collect forage 3. make roving search —**forage cap** soldier's undress cap

foramen (fɒ'reɪmɛn) n. natural hole, esp. in bone (pl. **-ramina** (-'ræmɪnə), -s)

forasmuch as (fərəz'mʌtʃ) conj. seeing that

foray ('fɒreɪ) n. 1. raid, inroad —vi. 2. make one —**'forayer** n.

forbear¹ ('fɔ:bɛə) n. see FOREBEAR

forbear² (fɔ:'bɛə) v. 1. (esp. with from) cease; refrain (from) —vi. 2. be patient (for'**bore** pt., for'**borne** pp.) —**for'bearance** n. self-control; patience —**for'bearing** a.

forbid (fə'bɪd) vt. prohibit, refuse to allow (for'**bade** (fə'bæd, -'beɪd) pt., for'**bidden** pp., for'**bidding** pr.p.) —**for'bidding** a. 1. uninviting 2. threatening

force (fɔ:s) n. 1. strength, power 2. compulsion 3. that which tends to produce

a change in a physical system 4. mental or moral strength 5. body of troops, police etc. 6. group of people organized for particular task or duty 7. effectiveness, operative state 8. violence —vt. 9. constrain, compel 10. produce by effort, strength 11. break open 12. urge, strain 13. drive 14. hasten maturity of —**forced** a. 1. accomplished by great effort 2. compulsory 3. unnatural 4. strained —**'forceful** a. 1. powerful 2. persuasive —**'forcible** a. 1. done by force 2. efficacious, compelling, impressive 3. strong —**'forcibly** adv. —**force-feed** vt. force (person or animal) to eat or swallow (food)

forcemeat ('fɔ:smi:t) n. mixture of chopped ingredients used for stuffing (also **farce**)

forceps ('fɔ:sɪps) pl.n. surgical pincers

ford (fɔ:d) n. 1. shallow place where river may be crossed —vt. 2. cross (river etc.) over shallow area —**'fordable** a.

fore¹ (fɔ:) a. 1. in front ('**former, 'further** comp., '**foremost, first, 'furthest** sup.) —n. 2. front part

fore² (fɔ:) interj. golfer's warning

fore- (comb. form) previous, before, front

fore-and-aft a. placed in line from bow to stern of ship

forearm ('fɔ:rɑ:m) n. 1. arm between wrist and elbow —vt. (fɔ:r'ɑ:m) 2. arm beforehand

forebear or **forebear** ('fɔ:bɛə) n. ancestor

forebode (fɔ:'bəʊd) vt. indicate in advance —**fore'boding** n. anticipation of evil

forecast ('fɔ:kɑ:st) vt. 1. estimate beforehand (esp. weather); prophesy —n. 2. prediction

forecastle, fo'c's'le, or **fo'c's'le** ('fəʊks'l) n. 1. forward raised part of ship 2. sailors' quarters

foreclose (fɔ:'kləʊz) vt. 1. take away power of redeeming (mortgage) 2. prevent 3. shut out, bar —**fore'closure** n.

forecourt ('fɔ:kɔ:t) n. courtyard, open space, in front of building

forefather ('fɔ:fɑ:ðə) n. ancestor

forefinger ('fɔ:fɪŋgə) n. finger next to thumb

forefoot ('fɔ:fʊt) n. either of front feet of quadruped

forefront ('fɔ:frʌnt) n. 1. extreme front 2. position of most prominence or action

foregather (fɔ:'gæðə) vi. see FORGATHER

forego¹ (fɔ:'gəʊ) vt. precede in time, place (-'**went** pt., -'**gone** pp., -'**going** pr.p.) —**fore'going** a. going before, preceding —**fore'gone** a. 1. determined beforehand 2. preceding —**foregone conclusion** result that might have been foreseen

forego² (fɔ:'gəʊ) vt. see FORGO

foreground ('fɔ:graʊnd) n. part of view, esp. in picture, nearest observer

forehand ('fɔ:hænd) a. (of stroke in racket games) made with inner side of wrist leading

forehead ('fɒrɪd) n. part of face above eyebrows and between temples

foreign ('forin) a. 1. not of, or in, one's own country 2. relating to, or connected with other countries 3. irrelevant 4. coming from outside 5. unfamiliar, strange —'**foreigner** n. —**foreign minister** or **secretary** (oft. F- M- or S-) cabinet minister responsible for country's dealings with other countries —**foreign office** ministry of country or state that is concerned with dealings with other states

foreknow (fɔː'nəʊ) vt. know in advance —**foreknowledge** (fɔː'nɒlɪdʒ) n.

foreland ('fɔːlənd) n. 1. headland, promontory 2. land lying in front of something, such as water

foreleg ('fɔːlɛg) n. either of front legs of horse or other quadruped

forelimb ('fɔːlɪm) n. either of front limbs of four-limbed vertebrate

forelock ('fɔːlɒk) n. lock of hair above forehead

foreman ('fɔːmən) n. 1. one in charge of work 2. leader of jury

foremast ('fɔːmɑːst; Naut. 'fɔːməst) n. mast nearest bow

foremost ('fɔːməʊst) a./adv. first in time, place, importance etc.

forenoon ('fɔːnuːn) n. morning

forensic (fə'rɛnsɪk) a. of courts of law —**forensic medicine** application of medical knowledge in legal matters

foreordain (fɔːrɔː'deɪn) vt. determine (events etc.) in future —**foreordination** (fɔːrɔːdɪ'neɪʃən) n.

forepaw ('fɔːpɔː) n. either of front feet of most land mammals that do not have hooves

foreplay ('fɔːpleɪ) n. sexual stimulation before intercourse

forerunner ('fɔːrʌnə) n. one who goes before, precursor

foresail ('fɔːseɪl; Naut. 'fɔːsəl) n. Naut. 1. aftermost headsail of fore-and-aft rigged vessel 2. lowest sail set on foremast of square-rigged vessel

foresee (fɔː'siː) vt. see beforehand (-'saw pt., -'seen pp.)

foreshadow (fɔː'ʃædəʊ) vt. show, suggest beforehand

foreshore ('fɔːʃɔː) n. part of shore between high and low tide marks

foreshorten (fɔː'ʃɔːt'n) vt. 1. draw (object) so that it appears shortened 2. make shorter

foresight ('fɔːsaɪt) n. 1. foreseeing 2. care for future

foreskin ('fɔːskɪn) n. skin that covers the glans penis

forest ('fɒrɪst) n. 1. area with heavy growth of trees and plants 2. these trees 3. fig. something resembling forest —vt. 4. plant, create forest in (an area) —**fores'tation** n. planting of trees over wide area —'**forester** n. one skilled in forestry —'**forestry** n. study, management of forest planting and maintenance

forestall (fɔː'stɔːl) vt. 1. anticipate 2. prevent, guard against in advance

foretaste ('fɔːteɪst) n. 1. anticipation 2. taste beforehand

foretell (fɔː'tɛl) vt. prophesy (**fore'told** pt./pp.)

forethought ('fɔːθɔːt) n. thoughtful consideration of future events

foretoken ('fɔːtəʊkən) n. 1. sign of future event —vt. (fɔː'təʊkən) 2. foreshadow

foretop ('fɔːtɒp; Naut. 'fɔːtəp) n. platform at top of foremast

for ever or **forever** (fɔː'rɛvə, fə-) adv. 1. always 2. eternally 3. inf. for a long time

forewarn (fɔː'wɔːn) vt. warn, caution in advance

forewent (fɔː'wɛnt) pt. of FOREGO[1], FOREGO[2]

foreword ('fɔːwɜːd) n. preface

forfeit ('fɔːfɪt) n. 1. thing lost by crime or fault 2. penalty, fine —a. 3. lost by crime or fault —vt. 4. lose by penalty —'**forfeiture** n.

forgather or **foregather** (fɔː'gæðə) vi. 1. meet together, assemble 2. associate

forgave (fə'geɪv) pt. of FORGIVE

forge[1] (fɔːdʒ) n. 1. place where metal is worked, smithy 2. furnace, workshop for melting or refining metal —vt. 3. shape (metal) by heating in fire and hammering 4. make, shape 5. invent 6. make a fraudulent imitation of, counterfeit —'**forger** n. —'**forgery** n. 1. forged document, banknote etc. 2. the making of it

forge[2] (fɔːdʒ) vi. advance steadily

forget (fə'gɛt) vt. 1. lose memory of 2. neglect, overlook (**for'got** pt., **for'gotten** or (US, obs.) **for'got** pp., **for'getting** pr.p.) —**for'getful** a. liable to forget —**for'getfully** adv. —**forget-me-not** n. plant with small blue flower

forgive (fə'gɪv) v. 1. cease to blame or hold resentment (against) —vt. 2. pardon —**for'giveness** n. —**for'giving** a. willing to forgive

forgo or **forego** (fɔː'gəʊ) vt. go without, give up (-'**went** pt., -'**gone** pp., -'**going** pr.p.)

forgot (fə'gɒt) pt./(US, obs.) pp. of FORGET

fork (fɔːk) n. 1. pronged instrument for eating food 2. pronged tool for digging or lifting 3. division into branches 4. point of this division 5. one of the branches —vi. 6. branch —vt. 7. dig, lift, throw with fork 8. make fork-shaped —**forked** a. 1. having fork or forklike parts 2. zigzag —**fork-lift truck** vehicle having two power-operated horizontal prongs that can be raised and lowered —**fork out** inf. pay (reluctantly)

forlorn (fə'lɔːn) a. 1. forsaken 2. desperate —**forlorn hope** anything undertaken with little hope of success

form (fɔːm) n. 1. shape 2. visible appearance 3. visible person or animal 4. structure 5. nature 6. species, kind 7. regularly drawn up document, esp. printed one with blanks for particulars 8. condition, esp. good condition 9. class in school 10. customary way of doing things 11. set order of words 12. long seat without back, bench **13.** hare's nest **14.** *esp.* US *see* FORME —*vt.* **15.** shape, mould **16.** arrange, organize **17.** train **18.** shape in the mind, conceive **19.** go to make up, make part of —*vi.* **20.** come into existence or shape —**for'mation** *n.* **1.** forming **2.** thing formed **3.** structure, shape, arrangement **4.** military order —**'formative** *a.* **1.** of, relating to, development **2.** serving or tending to form **3.** used in forming —**'formless** *a.*

-form (*comb. form*) having shape or form of; resembling, as in *cruciform, vermiform*

formal ('fɔːməl) *a.* **1.** ceremonial **2.** according to rule **3.** of outward form or routine **4.** of, for, formal occasions **5.** according to rule that does not matter **6.** precise; stiff —**'formalism** *n.* **1.** quality of being formal **2.** exclusive concern for form, structure, technique in an activity, eg art —**'formalist** *n.* —**for'mality** *n.* **1.** observance required by custom or etiquette **2.** condition or quality of being formal **3.** conformity to custom, conventionality, mere form **4.** in art, precision, stiffness, as opposed to originality —**formali'zation** *or* **-li'sation** *n.* —**'formalize** *or* **-lise** *vt.* **1.** make formal **2.** make official or valid **3.** give definite form to —**'formally** *adv.*

formaldehyde (fɔː'mældɪhaɪd) *n.* colourless, poisonous, pungent gas, used in making antiseptics and in chemistry —**'formalin** *n.* solution of formaldehyde in water, used as disinfectant, preservative *etc.*

format ('fɔːmæt) *n.* **1.** size and shape of book **2.** organization of television show *etc.*

forme *or* U.S. **form** (fɔːm) *n. Print.* frame for type

former ('fɔːmə) *a.* **1.** earlier in time **2.** of past times **3.** first named —*n.* **4.** first named thing, person or fact —**'formerly** *adv.* previously

Formica (fɔː'maɪkə) *n.* **R** type of laminated sheet used to make heat-resistant surfaces

formic acid ('fɔːmɪk) acid found in insects (*esp.* ants) and some plants

formidable ('fɔːmɪdəb'l) *a.* **1.** to be feared **2.** overwhelming, terrible, redoubtable **3.** likely to be difficult, serious —**'formidably** *adv.*

formula ('fɔːmjʊlə) *n.* **1.** set form of words setting forth principle, method or rule for doing, producing something **2.** substance so prepared **3.** specific category of car in motor racing **4.** recipe **5.** *Science, maths.* rule, fact expressed in symbols and figures (*pl.* **-ulae** (-juːliː), **-s**) —**'formulary** *n.* collection of formulas —**'formulate** *vt.* **1.** reduce to, express in formula, or in definite form **2.** devise —**formu'lation** *n.* —**'formulator** *n.*

fornication (fɔːnɪ'keɪʃən) *n.* sexual intercourse outside marriage —**'fornicate** *vi.*

forsake (fə'seɪk) *vt.* **1.** abandon, desert **2.** give up (**for'sook, for'saken, for'saking**)

forsooth (fə'suːθ) *adv. obs.* in truth

forswear (fɔː'swɛə) *vt.* **1.** renounce **2.** deny —*v. refl.* **3.** perjure (-**'swore** *pt.,* -**'sworn** *pp.*)

forsythia (fɔː'saɪθɪə) *n.* widely cultivated shrub with yellow flowers

fort (fɔːt) *n.* fortified place, stronghold —**hold the fort** *inf.* guard something temporarily

forte¹ (fɔːt, 'fɔːteɪ) *n.* one's strong point, that in which one excels

forte² ('fɔːtɪ) *adv. Mus.* loudly (**for'tissimo** *sup.*)

forth (fɔːθ) *adv.* **1.** onwards **2.** into view —**'forth'coming** *a.* **1.** about to come **2.** ready when wanted **3.** willing to trade, communicative —**forth'with** *adv.* at once, immediately

forthright ('fɔːθraɪt) *a.* direct, outspoken

fortieth ('fɔːtɪɪθ) *see* FOUR

fortify ('fɔːtɪfaɪ) *vt.* **1.** strengthen **2.** provide with defensive works (**'fortified, 'fortifying**) —**fortifi'cation** *n.*

fortitude ('fɔːtɪtjuːd) *n.* courage in adversity or pain, endurance

fortnight ('fɔːtnaɪt) *n.* two weeks —**'fortnightly** *a./adv.*

FORTRAN ('fɔːtræn) high-level computer programming language for mathematical and scientific purposes

fortress ('fɔːtrɪs) *n.* fortified place, eg castle, stronghold

fortuitous (fɔː'tjuːɪtəs) *a.* accidental, by chance —**for'tuitously** *adv.* —**for'tuity** *n.*

fortune ('fɔːtʃən) *n.* **1.** good luck **2.** prosperity, wealth **3.** chance, luck —**'fortunate** *a.* —**'fortunately** *adv.* —**fortune-hunter** *n.* person seeking fortune, *esp.* by marriage —**fortune-teller** *n.* one who predicts a person's future

forty ('fɔːtɪ) *see* FOUR —**forty winks** short sleep, nap

forum ('fɔːrəm) *n.* (place or medium for) meeting, assembly for open discussion or debate

forward ('fɔːwəd) *a.* **1.** lying in front of something **2.** onward **3.** presumptuous, impudent **4.** advanced, progressive **5.** relating to the future —*n.* **6.** player placed in forward position in various team games, eg football —*adv.* **7.** towards the future **8.** towards the front, to the front **9.** into view **10.** ('fɔːwəd; *Naut.* 'forəd) at, in fore part of ship **11.** onwards, so as to make progress —*vt.* **12.** help forward **13.** send, dispatch —**'forwardly** *adv.* pertly —**'forwardness** *n.* —**'forwards** *adv.*

forwent (fɔː'wɛnt) *pt.* of FORGO

fosse *or* **foss** (fɒs) *n.* ditch; moat

fossil ('fɒs'l) *n.* **1.** remnant or impression of animal or plant, *esp.* prehistoric one, preserved in earth **2.** *inf.* person, idea *etc.* that is outdated and incapable of change —*a.* **3.** of, like or forming fossil **4.** dug from earth **5.** *inf.* antiquated —**'fossilize** *or* **-ise** *v.* **1.** turn into fossil —*vt.* **2.** petrify

foster ('fɒstə) *vt.* **1.** promote growth or development **2.** bring up (child) *esp.* not one's own —**foster brother, sister, father, mother, parent, child** one related by upbringing, not blood

fought (fɔːt) *pt./pp. of* FIGHT

foul (faʊl) *a.* 1. loathsome, offensive 2. stinking 3. dirty 4. unfair 5. (of weather) wet, rough 6. obscene, disgustingly abusive 7. charged with harmful matter, clogged, choked —*n.* 8. act of unfair play 9. the breaking of a rule —*adv.* 10. unfairly —*v.* 11. make, become foul 12. jam —*vt.* 13. collide with —**'foully** *adv.* —**foul play** 1. unfair conduct, *esp.* with violence 2. violation of rules in game —**fall foul of** 1. get into trouble with 2. (of ships) collide with

foulard (fuːˈlɑːd) *n.* soft light fabric of silk or rayon

found[1] (faʊnd) *pt./pp. of* FIND

found[2] (faʊnd) *vt.* 1. establish, institute 2. lay base of 3. base, ground —**foun'dation** *n.* 1. basis 2. base, lowest part of building 3. founding 4. endowed institution *etc.* 5. cosmetic used as base for make-up —**'founder** *n.* (**'foundress** *fem.*) —**foundation garment** woman's undergarment worn to shape and support figure (*also* **foun'dation**) —**foundation stone** one of stones forming foundation of building, *esp.* stone laid with public ceremony

found[3] (faʊnd) *vt.* 1. melt and run into mould 2. cast —**'founder** *n.* —**'foundry** *n.* 1. place for casting 2. art of this

founder (ˈfaʊndə) *vi.* 1. collapse 2. sink 3. become stuck as in mud *etc.*

foundling (ˈfaʊndlɪŋ) *n.* deserted infant

fount[1] (faʊnt) *n.* 1. fountain 2. assortment of printing type of one size

fountain (ˈfaʊntɪn) *n.* 1. jet of water, *esp.* ornamental one 2. spring 3. source —**'fountainhead** *n.* source —**fountain pen** pen with ink reservoir

four (fɔː) *n./a.* cardinal number next after three —**'fortieth** *a./n.* —**'forty** *n./a.* four tens —**'fourteen** *n./a.* four plus ten —**'four'teenth** *a.* —**fourth** *a.* ordinal number of four —**'fourthly** *adv.* —**four-in-hand** *n.* 1. road vehicle drawn by four horses and driven by one driver 2. four-horse team 3. US long narrow tie tied in flat slipknot with ends dangling —**four-leaf clover** *or* **four-leaved clover** clover with four leaves rather than three, supposed to bring good luck —**four-letter word** any of several short English words referring to sex or excrement: regarded generally as offensive —**four-poster** *n.* bed with four posts for curtains *etc.* —**four'score** *a./n. obs.* eighty —**'foursome** *n.* 1. group of four people 2. game or dance for four people —**four'square** *a.* firm, steady —**four-stroke** *n.* internal-combustion engine firing once every four strokes of piston —**fourth estate** (*sometimes* F- E-) journalists; journalism —**on all fours** on hands and knees

fowl (faʊl) *n.* 1. domestic cock or hen 2.

bird, its flesh —*vi.* 3. hunt wild birds —**'fowler** *n.* —**fowling piece** light gun

fox (fɒks) *n.* 1. red bushy-tailed animal 2. its fur 3. cunning person —*vt.* 4. perplex 5. discolour (paper) with brown spots 6. mislead —*vi.* 7. act craftily —**'foxy** *a.* 1. of or resembling fox, *esp.* in craftiness 2. of reddish-brown colour 3. (of paper *etc.*) spotted, *esp.* by mildew 4. US physically attractive —**'foxglove** *n.* tall flowering plant —**'foxhole** *n. sl.* in war, small trench giving protection —**'foxhound** *n.* dog bred for hunting foxes —**fox hunt** 1. hunting of foxes with hounds 2. instance of this 3. organization for fox-hunting within area —**fox-hunting** *n.* —**fox terrier** small dog now mainly kept as pet —**'foxtrot** *n.* 1. (music for) ballroom dance —*vi.* 2. perform this dance

foyer (ˈfɔɪeɪ, ˈfɔɪə) *n.* entrance hall in theatres, hotels *etc.*

F.P. *or* **f.p.** 1. freezing point (*also* fp) 2. fully paid

F.P.A. Family Planning Association

f.p.s. 1. feet per second 2. foot-pound-second

Fr *Chem.* francium

fr. 1. fragment 2. franc 3. from

Fr. 1. Father 2. Frater (*Lat.* brother) 3. French 4. Friday

fracas (ˈfrækɑː) *n.* noisy quarrel; uproar; brawl

fraction (ˈfrækʃən) *n.* 1. numerical quantity not an integer 2. fragment, piece —**'fractional** *a.* 1. constituting a fraction 2. forming but a small part 3. insignificant

fractious (ˈfrækʃəs) *a.* 1. unruly 2. irritable

fracture (ˈfræktʃə) *n.* 1. breakage, part broken 2. breaking of bone 3. breach, rupture —*v.* 4. break

fragile (ˈfrædʒaɪl) *a.* 1. breakable 2. frail, delicate —**fragility** (frəˈdʒɪlɪtɪ) *n.*

fragment (ˈfrægmənt) *n.* 1. piece broken off 2. small portion 3. incomplete part —*v.* (frægˈment) 4. (cause to) break into fragments —**'fragmentary** *a.*

fragrant (ˈfreɪɡrənt) *a.* sweet-smelling —**'fragrance** *n.* scent —**'fragrantly** *adv.*

frail (freɪl) *a.* 1. fragile, delicate 2. infirm, in weak health 3. morally weak —**'frailly** *adv.* —**'frailty** *n.*

frame (freɪm) *n.* 1. that in which thing is set, as square of wood round picture *etc.* 2. structure 3. build of body 4. constitution 5. mood 6. individual exposure on strip of film 7. *Snooker etc.* wooden triangle used to set up balls, balls when set up or single game finished when all balls have been potted —*vt.* 8. put together, make 9. adapt 10. put into words 11. put into frame 12. *sl.* conspire to incriminate on false charge —**frame-up** *n. sl.* 1. plot 2. manufactured evidence —**'framework** *n.* 1. structure into which completing parts can be fitted 2. supporting work

franc (fræŋk; *Fr.* frɑ̃) *n.* monetary unit of France, Switzerland and other countries

franchise (ˈfræntʃaɪz) *n.* 1. right of voting

2. citizenship 3. privilege or right, *esp.* right to sell certain goods

Franciscan (fræn'sɪskən) *n.* monk or nun of the order founded by St. Francis of Assisi

francium ('frænsɪəm) *n.* radioactive element of alkali-metal group

Franco- ('fræŋkəʊ-) (*comb. form*) France; French, as in *Franco-Prussian*

francolin ('fræŋkəʊlɪn) *n.* Afr. or Asian partridge

frangipani (frændʒɪ'pɑːnɪ) *n.* tropical Amer. shrub (*pl.* **-s, -'pani**)

frank (fræŋk) *a.* 1. candid, outspoken 2. sincere —*n.* 3. official mark on letter either cancelling stamp or ensuring delivery without stamp —*vt.* 4. mark letter thus —**'frankly** *adv.* candidly —**'frankness** *n.* —**franking machine** machine that prints marks on letters *etc.* indicating that postage has been paid

Frank (fræŋk) *n.* member of group of W Germanic peoples who gradually conquered most of Gaul and Germany in late 4th century A.D.—**'Frankish** *n.* 1. ancient W Germanic language of Franks —*a.* 2. of Franks or their language

Frankenstein's monster ('fræŋkɪnstaɪnz) creation or monster that brings disaster and is beyond the control of its creator

frankfurter ('fræŋkfɜːtə) *n.* smoked sausage

frankincense ('fræŋkɪnsɛns) *n.* aromatic gum resin burned as incense

frantic ('fræntɪk) *a.* 1. distracted with rage, grief, joy *etc.* 2. frenzied —**'frantically** *adv.*

frappé ('fræpeɪ) *n.* 1. drink consisting of liqueur *etc.* poured over crushed ice —*a.* 2. (*esp.* of drinks) chilled

fraternal (frə'tɜːn°l) *a.* of brother; brotherly —**fra'ternally** *adv.* —**fra'ternity** *n.* 1. brotherliness 2. brotherhood 3. US college society —**fraterni'zation** *or* **-ni'sation** *n.* —**'fraternize** *or* **-nise** *vi.* associate, make friends —**fratri'cidal** *a.* —**'fratricide** *n.* killing, killer of brother or sister

Frau (fraʊ) *n.* married German woman: usu. used as title equivalent to *Mrs.* (*pl.* **Frauen** ('fraʊən), **-s**)

fraud (frɔːd) *n.* 1. criminal deception 2. swindle, imposture 3. *inf.* person who acts in false or deceitful way —**'fraudulence** *n.* —**'fraudulent** *a.*

fraught (frɔːt) *a.* —**fraught with** filled with, involving

Fräulein (*Ger.* 'frɔɪlaɪn) *n.* unmarried German woman: oft. used as title equivalent to *Miss* (*pl.* **-lein** *or English* **-s**)

fray[1] (freɪ) *n.* 1. fight 2. noisy quarrel

fray[2] (freɪ) *v.* 1. wear through by rubbing 2. make, become ragged at edge

frazil ('freɪzɪl) *n.* C broken spikes of ice formed in turbulent water

frazzle ('fræz°l) *inf.* *v.* 1. make or become exhausted 2. make or become irritated —*n.* 3. exhausted state

freak (friːk) *n.* 1. abnormal person, animal, thing —*a.* 2. oddly different from what is normal —**'freakish** *or* (*inf.*) **'freaky** *a.* —**freak out** *inf.* (cause to) hallucinate, be wildly excited *etc.*

freckle ('frɛk°l) *n.* 1. light brown spot on skin, *esp.* caused by sun 2. any small spot —*v.* 3. mark or become marked in freckles —**'freckled** *a.*

free (friː) *a.* 1. able to act at will, not under compulsion or restraint 2. (*with* from) not restricted or affected by 3. not subject to cost or tax 4. independent 5. not exact or literal 6. generous 7. not in use 8. (of person) not occupied, having no engagement 9. loose, not fixed —*vt.* 10. set at liberty 11. (*with* of *or* from) remove (obstacles, pain *etc.*), rid (of) (**freed, 'freeing**) —**'freebie** *n.* *sl.* something provided without charge —**'freedom** *n.* —**'freely** *adv.* —**'freeboard** *n.* space between deck of vessel and waterline —**Free Church** *chiefly* UK any Protestant Church, *esp.* Presbyterian, other than Established Church —**free enterprise** economic system in which commercial organizations compete for profit with little state control —**free flight** flight of rocket *etc.* when engine has ceased to produce thrust —**free-for-all** *n.* brawl —**'freehand** *a.* drawn without guiding instruments —**'freehold** *n.* 1. tenure of land without obligation of service or rent 2. land so held —**free house** public house not bound to sell only one brewer's products —**free kick** *Soccer* place kick awarded for foul or infringement —**'freelance** *a./n.* 1. (of) self-employed, unattached person —*vi.* 2. work as freelance —*adv.* 3. as freelance —**free-living** *a.* 1. given to indulgence of appetites 2. (of animals *etc.*) not parasitic —**free love** practice of sexual relationships without fidelity to single partner —**'Freemason** *n.* member of secret fraternity for mutual help —**free-range** *a.* kept, produced in natural, nonintensive conditions —**free speech** right to express opinions publicly —**free'standing** *a.* not attached to or supported by another object —**'freestyle** *n.* 1. race, as in swimming, in which each participant may use style of his or her choice 2. style of professional wrestling with no internationally agreed set of rules (*also* **all-in wrestling**) —**free'thinker** *n.* sceptic who forms his own opinions, *esp.* in religion —**free trade** international trade free of protective tariffs —**free verse** unrhymed verse without metrical pattern —**'freeway** *n.* US major road —**free'wheel** *n.* 1. device in rear hub of bicycle wheel that permits wheel to rotate while pedals are stationary —*vi.* 2. coast —**free will** 1. apparent human ability to make choices not externally determined 2. doctrine that human beings have such freedom of choice 3. ability to make choice without coercion —**free-will** *a.* voluntary; spontaneous —**free and easy** casual, tolerant;

easy-going —**free on board** (of shipment of goods) delivered on board ship *etc.* without charge to buyer —**International freestyle** amateur style of wrestling with agreed set of rules —**the Free World** non-Communist countries collectively

freesia ('fri:zɪə) *n.* plant with fragrant, tubular flowers

freeze (fri:z) *v.* **1.** change (by reduction of temperature) from liquid to solid, as water to ice —*vt.* **2.** preserve (food *etc.*) by extreme cold, as in freezer **3.** fix (prices *etc.*) —*vi.* **4.** feel very cold **5.** become rigid as with fear **6.** stop (**froze, 'frozen, 'freezing**) —**'freezer** *n.* insulated cabinet for long-term storage of perishable foodstuffs —**frozen** ('frəʊz²n) *a.* (of credits *etc.*) unrealizable —**freeze-dry** *vt.* preserve (substance) by rapid freezing and subsequently drying in vacuum —**freezing point** temperature at which liquid becomes solid

freight (freɪt) *n.* **1.** commercial transport (*esp.* by railway, ship) **2.** cost of this **3.** goods so carried —*vt.* **4.** send as or by freight —**'freightage** *n.* money paid for freight —**'freighter** *n.* —**'freightliner** *n.* goods train, lorry carrying containers

French (frentʃ) *n.* **1.** language spoken by people of France —*a.* **2.** of France —**French bread** crisp white bread in long slender loaf —**French Canadian** Canadian citizen whose native language is French —**French-Canadian** *a.* of French Canadians —**French chalk** variety of talc used to mark cloth or remove grease stains —**French dressing** salad dressing —**French fried potatoes** chips (*also* (US) **French fries**) —**French horn** musical wind instrument —**French knickers** women's underpants with wide legs —**French leave** unauthorized leave —**French letter** UK *sl.* condom —**French polish** varnish for wood made from shellac dissolved in alcohol —**French window** window extended to floor level and used as door

frenetic (frɪ'nɛtɪk) *a.* frenzied

frenzy ('frɛnzɪ) *n.* **1.** violent mental derangement **2.** wild excitement —**'frenzied** *a.*

frequent ('fri:kwənt) *a.* **1.** happening often **2.** common **3.** numerous —*vt.* (frɪ'kwɛnt) **4.** go often to —**'frequency** *n.* **1.** rate of occurrence **2.** in radio *etc.*, cycles per second of alternating current —**fre'quentative** *a.* expressing repetition —**'frequently** *adv.* —**frequency modulation** *Rad.* method of transmitting information in which frequency of carrier wave is varied

fresco ('frɛskəʊ) *n.* **1.** method of painting in watercolour on plaster of wall before it dries **2.** painting done thus (*pl.* **-es, -s**)

fresh (frɛʃ) *a.* **1.** not stale **2.** new **3.** additional **4.** different **5.** recent **6.** inexperienced **7.** pure **8.** not pickled, frozen *etc.* **9.** not faded or dimmed **10.** not tired **11.** (of wind) strong **12.** *inf.* impudent

13. *inf.* arrogant —**'freshen** *v.* —**'freshet** *n.* **1.** rush of water at river mouth **2.** flood of river water —**'freshly** *adv.* —**'freshman** *or* **'fresher** *n.* first-year student —**'freshness** *n.* —**'freshwater** *a.* **1.** of or living in fresh water **2.** (*esp.* of sailor who has not sailed on sea) inexperienced **3.** US little known

fret[1] (frɛt) *v.* **1.** irritate or be irritated **2.** worry (**-tt-**) —*n.* **3.** irritation —**'fretful** *a.* irritable, (easily) upset

fret[2] (frɛt) *n.* **1.** repetitive geometrical pattern **2.** small bar on fingerboard of guitar *etc.* —*vt.* **3.** ornament with carved pattern (**-tt-**) —**fret saw** saw with narrow blade and fine teeth, used for fretwork —**'fretwork** *n.* carved or open woodwork in ornamental patterns and devices

Freudian ('frɔɪdɪən) *a.* pert. to Austrian psychologist Sigmund Freud, or his theories —**Freudian slip** any action, such as slip of tongue, that may reveal unconscious thought

Fri. Friday

friable ('fraɪəb²l) *a.* easily crumbled —**fria'bility** *or* **'friableness** *n.*

friar ('fraɪə) *n.* member of mendicant religious order —**'friary** *n.* house of friars —**friar's balsam** compound containing benzoin, used as inhalant

fricassee (frɪkə'si:, 'frɪkəsɪ) *n.* **1.** dish of pieces of chicken or meat, fried or stewed and served with rich sauce —*vt.* **2.** cook thus

fricative ('frɪkətɪv) *n.* **1.** consonant produced by partial occlusion of air stream, such as (f) or (z) —*a.* **2.** relating to fricative

friction ('frɪkʃən) *n.* **1.** rubbing **2.** resistance met with by body moving over another **3.** clash of wills *etc.*, disagreement —**'frictional** *a.*

Friday ('fraɪdɪ) *n.* sixth day of week —**Good Friday** the Friday before Easter

fridge (frɪdʒ) *inf.* refrigerator

fried (fraɪd) *pt./pp.* of FRY[1]

friend (frɛnd) *n.* **1.** one well known to another and regarded with affection and loyalty **2.** intimate associate **3.** supporter **4.** (**F-**) Quaker —**'friendless** *a.* —**'friendliness** *n.* —**'friendly** *a.* **1.** having disposition of a friend, kind **2.** favourable —**'friendship** *n.* —**friendly society** UK association of people who pay regular dues in return for sickness benefits *etc.* —**Friends of the Earth** organization of environmentalists and conservationists

frier ('fraɪə) *n. see* **fryer** *at* FRY[1]

frieze[1] (fri:z) *n.* ornamental band, strip (on wall)

frieze[2] (fri:z) *n.* kind of coarse woollen cloth

frigate ('frɪgɪt) *n.* **1.** old (sailing) warship corresponding to modern cruiser **2.** fast destroyerlike warship equipped for escort and antisubmarine duties —**frigate bird** bird of tropical and subtropical seas, with wide wingspan

fright (frait) *n.* 1. sudden fear 2. shock 3. alarm 4. grotesque or ludicrous person or thing —*vt.* 5. *obs.* frighten —**'frighten** *vt.* cause fear, fright in —**'frightful** *a.* 1. terrible, calamitous 2. shocking 3. *inf.* very great, very large —**'frightfully** *adv. inf.* 1. terribly 2. very —**'frightfulness** *n.*

frigid ('fridʒid) *a.* 1. formal, dull 2. (sexually) unfeeling 3. cold —**fri'gidity** *n.* —**'frigidly** *adv.* —**Frigid Zone** cold region inside Arctic or Antarctic Circle where sun's rays are very oblique

frill (fril) *n.* 1. fluted strip of fabric gathered at one edge 2. ruff of hair, feathers around neck of dog, bird *etc.* 3. fringe 4. (*oft. pl.*) unnecessary words, politeness; superfluous thing; adornment —*vt.* 5. make into, decorate with frill

fringe (frindʒ) *n.* 1. ornamental edge of hanging threads, tassels *etc.* 2. anything like this 3. hair cut in front and falling over brow 4. edge, limit —*vt.* 5. adorn with fringe 6. be fringe for —*a.* 7. (of theatre *etc.*) unofficial, unconventional, extra —**fringe benefit** benefit provided by employer to supplement employee's regular pay

frippery ('fripəri) *n.* 1. finery 2. trivia

Frisbee ('frizbiː) *n.* **R** plastic disc thrown with spinning motion for recreation

Frisian ('friʒən) *or* **Friesian** ('friːʒən) *n.* 1. language spoken in NW Netherlands and adjacent islands 2. speaker of this language —*a.* 3. of this language or its speakers

frisk (frisk) *vi.* 1. move, leap playfully —*vt.* 2. wave briskly 3. *inf.* search (person) for concealed weapons *etc.* —*n.* 4. playful antic or movement 5. *inf.* instance of frisking a person —**'friskily** *adv.* —**'frisky** *a.*

fritillary (fri'tiləri) *n.* plant with purple or white bell-shaped flowers

fritter¹ ('fritə) *vt.* (*usu. with* away) waste

fritter² ('fritə) *n.* piece of food fried in batter

frivolous ('frivələs) *a.* 1. not serious, flippant 2. unimportant —**fri'volity** *n.*

frizz (friz) *vt.* 1. crisp, curl into small curls —*n.* 2. frizzed hair —**'frizzy** *a.* crimped

frizzle ('friz'l) *v.* fry, toast or grill with sizzling sound

fro (frəu) *adv.* away, from (*only in* **to and fro**)

frock (frɒk) *n.* 1. woman's dress 2. various similar garments —*vt.* 3. invest with office of priest —**frock coat** man's double-breasted skirted coat, as worn in 19th century

frog¹ (frɒg) *n.* tailless amphibious animal developed from tadpole —**'frogman** *n.* swimmer equipped for swimming, working underwater —**'frogmarch** *n.* any method of moving person against his will

frog² (frɒg) *n.* 1. military-style coat fastening of button and loop 2. attachment to belt to carry sword

frolic ('frɒlik) *n.* 1. merrymaking —*vi.* 2. behave playfully (**'frolicked**, **'frolicking**) —**'frolicsome** *a.*

from (frɒm; *unstressed* frəm) *prep.* expressing point of departure, source, distance, cause, change of state *etc.*

frond (frɒnd) *n.* plant organ consisting of stem and foliage, usually with fruit forms, *esp.* in ferns

front (frʌnt) *n.* 1. fore part 2. position directly before or ahead 3. seaside promenade 4. battle line or area 5. *Met.* dividing line between two air masses of different characteristics 6. outward aspect, bearing 7. *inf.* something serving as a respectable cover for another, *usu.* criminal activity 8. field of activity 9. group with common goal —*v.* 10. look, face (on to) —*vt.* 11. *inf.* be a cover for —*a.* 12. of, at the front —**'frontage** *n.* 1. façade of building 2. extent of front —**'frontal** *a.* —**'frontier** *n.* part of country which borders on another —**front bench** 1. UK foremost bench of either Government or Opposition in House of Commons 2. leadership (**frontbenchers**) of either group, who occupy this bench 3. leadership of government or opposition in various legislative assemblies —**'frontispiece** *n.* illustration facing title page of book —**'frontrunner** *n. inf.* leader in race *etc.*

frost (frɒst) *n.* 1. frozen dew or mist 2. act or state of freezing 3. weather in which temperature falls below point at which water turns to ice —*v.* 4. cover, be covered with frost or something similar in appearance —*vt.* 5. give slightly roughened surface to —**'frostily** *adv.* —**'frosting** *n.* 1. *esp.* US icing 2. rough or matt finish on glass *etc.* —**'frosty** *a.* 1. accompanied by frost 2. chilly, cold 3. unfriendly —**'frostbite** *n.* destruction by cold of tissue, *esp.* of fingers, ears *etc.*

froth (frɒθ) *n.* 1. collection of small bubbles, foam 2. scum 3. idle talk —*v.* 4. (cause to) foam —**'frothily** *adv.* —**'frothy** *a.*

froward ('frəuəd) *a.* obstinate; contrary

frown (fraun) *vi.* 1. wrinkle brows —*n.* 2. act of frowning 3. show of dislike or displeasure

frowsty ('frausti) *a.* stale, musty

frowzy *or* **frowsy** ('frauzi) *a.* 1. dirty 2. unkempt

froze (frəuz) *pt. of* FREEZE —**'frozen** *pp. of* FREEZE

F.R.S. Fellow of the Royal Society

fructify ('frʌktifai) *v.* (cause to) bear fruit (**'fructified**, **'fructifying**) —**fructifi'cation** *n.*

fructose ('frʌktəus) *n.* crystalline sugar occurring in many fruits

frugal ('fruːg'l) *a.* 1. sparing, thrifty, economical 2. meagre —**fru'gality** *n.* —**'frugally** *adv.*

fruit (fruːt) *n.* 1. seed and its envelope, *esp.* edible one 2. vegetable products 3. (*usu. in pl.*) result, benefit —*vi.* 4. bear fruit

—'**fruiterer** n. dealer in fruit —'**fruitful** a. 1. bearing fruit in abundance 2. productive, prolific 3. producing results or profits —**fruition** (fruːˈɪʃən) n. 1. enjoyment 2. realization of hopes —'**fruitless** a. 1. unproductive 2. without fruit —'**fruity** a. 1. of or resembling fruit 2. (of voice) mellow, rich 3. inf., chiefly UK erotically stimulating; salacious —**fruit machine** gambling machine operated by coins

frump (frʌmp) n. dowdy woman —'**frump-ish** or '**frumpy** a.

frustrate (frʌˈstreɪt) vt. 1. thwart, balk 2. disappoint —**frus'tration** n.

frustum ('frʌstəm) n. Geom. 1. part of cone or pyramid contained between base and plane parallel to base that intersects solid 2. part of such solid contained between two parallel planes intersecting solid (pl. -s, -ta (-tə))

fry[1] (fraɪ) vt. 1. cook with fat —vi. 2. be cooked thus (**fried, 'frying**) —n. 3. fried meat 4. dish of anything fried —'**fryer** or '**frier** n. 1. one that fries 2. utensil for deep-frying foods —**frying pan** shallow pan for frying —**fry-up** n. UK inf. 1. act of preparing mixed fried dish 2. dish itself —**out of the frying pan into the fire** from bad situation to worse one

fry[2] (fraɪ) n. young fishes —**small fry** young or insignificant beings

f-stop n. any of settings for f-number of camera

ft. 1. feet 2. foot 3. fort

fth. or **fthm.** fathom

fuchsia ('fjuːʃə) n. ornamental shrub with purple-red flowers

fuddle ('fʌdˀl) v. 1. (cause to) be intoxicated, confused —n. 2. this state

fuddy-duddy ('fʌdɪdʌdɪ) n. inf. (elderly) dull person

fudge[1] ('fʌdʒ) n. soft, variously flavoured sweet

fudge[2] (fʌdʒ) vt. 1. make, do carelessly or dishonestly 2. fake

fuel (fjʊəl) n. 1. material for burning as source of heat or power 2. something which nourishes —vt. 3. provide with fuel —**fuel cell** cell in which chemical energy is converted directly into electrical energy —**fuel injection** system for introducing fuel directly into combustion chambers of internal-combustion engine without use of carburettor

fug (fʌg) n. stuffy indoor atmosphere —'**fuggy** a.

fugitive ('fjuːdʒɪtɪv) n. 1. one who flees, esp. from arrest or pursuit —a. 2. fleeing, elusive

fugue (fjuːg) n. musical composition in which themes are repeated in different parts

Führer or **Fuehrer** ('fyːrər) n. leader, title of Ger. dictator, esp. Hitler

-ful (comb. form) 1. full of; characterized by, as in painful, restful 2. able or tending to, as in useful 3. as much as will fill thing specified, as in mouthful

fulcrum ('fʊlkrəm, 'fʌl-) n. point on which lever is placed for support (pl. -cra (-krə))

fulfil or U.S. **fulfill** (fʊlˈfɪl) vt. 1. satisfy 2. carry out 3. obey (-ll-) —ful'filment or U.S. ful'fillment n.

full[1] (fʊl) a. 1. containing as much as possible 2. abundant 3. complete 4. ample 5. plump 6. (of garment) of ample cut —adv. 7. very 8. quite 9. exactly —'**fully** adv. —'**fullness** or esp. U.S. '**fulness** n. —'**fulsome** a. excessive —'**fullback** n. Soccer etc. defensive player or position held by this player —**full-blooded** a. 1. (esp. of horses) of unmixed ancestry 2. having great vigour —**full-blown** a. 1. characterized by fullest or best development 2. in full bloom —**full-bodied** a. having full rich flavour or quality —**full house** 1. Poker hand with three cards of same value and another pair 2. theatre etc. filled to capacity 3. in bingo etc., set of numbers needed to win —**full-scale** a. 1. (of plan etc.) of actual size 2. using all resources —**full stop** punctuation mark (.) at end of sentence —**full-time** a. for entire time appropriate to activity —**full time** adv. 1. on full-time basis —n. 2. end of match —**fully fashioned** a. (of stockings etc.) shaped so as to fit closely —**fully fledged** or **full-fledged** a. 1. (of bird) having acquired adult feathers and being able to fly 2. completely developed 3. of full rank or status

full[2] (fʊl) v. become or make (cloth etc.) more compact during manufacture through shrinking and pressing —**fuller's earth** absorbent clay used for clarifying oils and fats, fulling cloth etc.

fulmar ('fʊlmə) n. Arctic sea bird

fulminate ('fʌlmɪneɪt) vi. 1. (esp. with against) criticize harshly —n. 2. chemical compound exploding readily —fulmi'na-tion n.

fulsome ('fʊlsəm) a. see FULL[1]

fumble ('fʌmbˀl) vi. 1. grope about —vt. 2. handle awkwardly —n. 3. awkward attempt

fume (fjuːm) vi. 1. be angry 2. emit smoke or vapour —n. 3. smoke 4. vapour —'**fumigate** vt. apply fumes or smoke to, esp. for disinfection —fumi'gation n. —'**fumigator** n.

fumitory ('fjuːmɪtərɪ) n. plant with spurred flowers

fun (fʌn) n. anything enjoyable, amusing etc. —'**funnily** adv. —'**funny** a. 1. comical 2. odd 3. difficult to explain —'**funfair** n. UK amusement park, fairground

function ('fʌŋkʃən) n. 1. work a thing is designed to do 2. (large) social event 3. duty 4. profession 5. Maths. quantity whose value depends on varying value of another —vi. 6. operate, work —'**functional** a. 1. having a special purpose 2. practical, necessary 3. capable of operating —'**functionary** n. official

fund (fʌnd) n. 1. stock or sum of money 2. supply, store —pl. 3. money resources

—*vt.* **4.** in financial, business dealings, furnish money to in form of fund

fundamental (ˌfʌndəˈmentˀl) *a.* **1.** of, affecting, or serving as the base **2.** essential, primary —*n.* **3.** basic rule or fact —**'fundament** *n.* **1.** buttocks **2.** foundation —**funda'mentalism** *n.* —**funda'mentalist** *n.* one laying stress on belief in literal and verbal inspiration of Bible and other traditional creeds —**fundamental particle** *see* **elementary particle** *at* ELEMENT

funeral (ˈfjuːnərəl) *n.* (ceremony associated with) burial or cremation of dead —**funereal** (fjuːˈnɪərɪəl) *a.* **1.** like a funeral **2.** dark **3.** gloomy —**funeral director** undertaker —**funeral parlour** place where dead are prepared for burial or cremation

fungus (ˈfʌŋgəs) *n.* plant without leaves, flowers or roots, as mushroom, mould (*pl.* **fungi** (ˈfʌndʒaɪ, ˈfʌŋgaɪ), **-es**) —**'fungal** *or* **'fungous** *a.* —**fungicide** (ˈfʌndʒɪsaɪd) *n.* fungus destroyer —**fungoid** *a.* resembling fungus

funicular (fjuːˈnɪkjʊlə) *n.* cable railway on mountainside with two counterbalanced cars

funk (fʌŋk) *n.* panic (*esp. in* **blue funk**)

funky (ˈfʌŋkɪ) *a. inf.* (of jazz, pop *etc.*) passionate and soulful, reminiscent of early blues

funnel (ˈfʌnˀl) *n.* **1.** cone-shaped vessel or tube **2.** chimney of locomotive or ship **3.** ventilating shaft —*vt.* **4.** (cause to) move as through funnel —*v.* **5.** concentrate, focus (**-ll-**)

funny (ˈfʌnɪ) *a. see* FUN —**funny bone** area near elbow where sharp tingling sensation is experienced when struck

fur (fɜː) *n.* **1.** soft hair of animal **2.** garment *etc.* of dressed skins with such hair **3.** furlike coating —*vt.* **4.** cover with fur (**-rr-**) —**'furrier** *n.* dealer in furs —**'furry** *a.* of, like fur

fur. furlong

furbelow (ˈfɜːbɪləʊ) *n.* **1.** flounce, ruffle **2.** (*oft. pl.*) showy ornamentation —*vt.* **3.** put furbelow on (garment *etc.*)

furbish (ˈfɜːbɪʃ) *vt.* clean up

furcate (ˈfɜːkeɪt) *a.* forked, branching

furious (ˈfjʊərɪəs) *a.* **1.** extremely angry **2.** violent —**'furiously** *adv.* —**'furiousness** *n.*

furl (fɜːl) *vt.* roll up and bind (sail, umbrella *etc.*)

furlong (ˈfɜːlɒŋ) *n.* eighth of mile

furlough (ˈfɜːləʊ) *n.* US leave of absence, *esp.* to soldier

furnace (ˈfɜːnɪs) *n.* **1.** apparatus for applying great heat to metals **2.** closed fireplace for heating boiler *etc.* **3.** hot place

furnish (ˈfɜːnɪʃ) *vt.* **1.** fit up (house) with furniture **2.** equip **3.** supply, yield —**'furnishings** *pl.n.* furniture, carpets *etc.* with which room is furnished —**'furniture** *n.* movable contents of a house or room

furore (fjʊˈrɔːrɪ) *or esp. U.S.* **furor**

(ˈfjʊərɔː) *n.* **1.** public outburst, *esp.* of protest **2.** sudden enthusiasm

furrow (ˈfʌrəʊ) *n.* **1.** trench as made by plough **2.** groove —*vt.* **3.** make furrows in

further (ˈfɜːðə) *adv. comp. of* FAR *and* FORE¹ **1.** more **2.** in addition **3.** at or to a greater distance or extent —*a. comp. of* FAR *and* FORE¹ **4.** more distant **5.** additional —*vt.* **6.** help forward, promote —**'furtherance** *n.* —**'furtherer** *n.* —**'furthermore** *adv.* besides —**'furthermost** *a.* —**'furthest** *a./adv. sup. of* FAR, FORE¹ —**further education** UK formal education beyond school other than at university or polytechnic

furtive (ˈfɜːtɪv) *a.* stealthy, sly, secretive —**'furtively** *adv.*

fury (ˈfjʊərɪ) *n.* **1.** wild rage, violent anger **2.** violence of storm *etc.* **3.** (*usu. pl.*) snake-haired avenging deity

furze (fɜːz) *n.* prickly shrub, gorse

fuscous (ˈfʌskəs) *a.* dark-coloured

fuse (fjuːz) *v.* **1.** blend by melting **2.** melt with heat **3.** amalgamate **4.** (cause to) fail as a result of blown fuse —*n.* **5.** soft wire, with low melting point, used as safety device in electrical systems **6.** device (*orig.* combustible cord) for igniting bomb *etc.* —**'fusible** *a.* —**'fusion** *n.* **1.** melting **2.** state of being melted **3.** union of things, as atomic nuclei, as if melted together

fuselage (ˈfjuːzɪlɑːʒ) *n.* body of aircraft

fusil (ˈfjuːzɪl) *n.* light flintlock musket —**fusi'lier** *n.* soldier of certain regiments —**fusil'lade** *n.* continuous discharge of firearms

fuss (fʌs) *n.* **1.** needless bustle or concern **2.** complaint, objection —*vi.* **3.** make fuss —**'fussily** *adv.* —**'fussiness** *n.* —**'fussy** *a.* **1.** particular **2.** faddy **3.** overmeticulous **4.** overelaborate —**'fusspot** *n.* UK *inf.* person who fusses unnecessarily

fustian (ˈfʌstɪən) *n.* **1.** thick cotton cloth **2.** inflated language

fusty (ˈfʌstɪ) *a.* **1.** mouldy **2.** smelling of damp **3.** old-fashioned —**'fustily** *adv.* —**'fustiness** *n.*

futile (ˈfjuːtaɪl) *a.* **1.** useless, ineffectual **2.** trifling —**futility** (fjuːˈtɪlɪtɪ) *n.*

future (ˈfjuːtʃə) *n.* **1.** time to come **2.** what will happen **3.** tense of verb indicating this **4.** likelihood of development —*a.* **5.** that will be **6.** of, relating to, time to come —**'futurism** *n.* movement in art marked by revolt against tradition —**'futurist** *n./a.* —**futur'istic** *a.* ultramodern —**fu'turity** *n.* —**future perfect** *Gram. a.* **1.** denoting tense of verbs describing action that will have been performed by certain time —*n.* **2.** future perfect tense; verb in this tense

fuze (fjuːz) *n.* US *see* FUSE (sense 6)

fuzz (fʌz) *n.* **1.** fluff **2.** fluffy or frizzed hair **3.** blur **4.** *sl.* police(man) —**'fuzzy** *a.* **1.** fluffy **2.** frizzy **3.** blurred, indistinct

fwd. forward

-fy (*comb. form*) make; become, as in *beautify*

G

g or **G** (dʒiː) n. 1. seventh letter of English alphabet 2. speech sound represented by this letter, usu. as in *grass*, or as in *page* (pl. **g's, G's** or **Gs**)

g 1. gram(s) 2. (acceleration due to) gravity

G 1. *Mus.* fifth note of scale of C major; major or minor key having this note as its tonic 2. gravitational constant 3. *Phys.* conductance 4. German 5. giga 6. good 7. *sl., chiefly US* grand (thousand dollars or pounds)

Ga *Chem.* gallium

GA Georgia

gabble ('gæbḷ) v. 1. talk, utter inarticulately or too fast ('gabbled, 'gabbling) —n. 2. such talk —**gab** vi. 1. talk excessively; chatter (**-bb-**) —n. 2. idle or trivial talk —**gabby** a. *inf.* talkative —**gift of the gab** eloquence, loquacity

gaberdine ('gæbədiːn, gæbə'diːn) n. 1. fine twill cloth like serge used *esp.* for raincoats 2. *Hist.* loose upper garment worn by Jews

gable ('geɪbḷ) n. triangular upper part of wall at end of ridged roof (*also* **gable end**)

gad (gæd) vi. (*esp. with* about) go around in search of pleasure (**-dd-**) —'**gadabout** n. pleasure-seeker

gadfly ('gædflaɪ) n. 1. cattle-biting fly 2. worrying person

gadget ('gædʒɪt) n. 1. small mechanical device 2. object valued for its novelty or ingenuity —'**gadgetry** n.

gadoid ('geɪdɔɪd) a. 1. of order of marine fishes typically having pectoral and pelvic fins close together and small cycloid scales —n. 2. gadoid fish

gadolinium (gædə'lɪnɪəm) n. malleable ferromagnetic element of lanthanide series of metals

gadwall ('gædwɔːl) n. duck related to mallard

Gael (geɪl) n. one who speaks Gaelic —**Gaelic** ('geɪlɪk, 'gæ-) n. 1. language of Ireland and Scottish Highlands —a. 2. of Gaels, their language or customs

gaff¹ (gæf) n. 1. stick with iron hook for landing fish 2. spar for top of fore-and-aft sail —vt. 3. seize (fish) with gaff

gaff² (gæf) n. *sl.* nonsense —**blow the gaff** UK *sl.* divulge a secret

gaffe (gæf) n. social blunder, *esp.* tactless remark

gaffer ('gæfə) n. 1. old man 2. *inf.* foreman, boss

gag¹ (gæg) vt. 1. stop up (person's mouth) with cloth *etc.* —vi. 2. *sl.* retch, choke (**-gg-**) —n. 3. cloth *etc.* put into, tied across mouth

gag² (gæg) n. 1. joke, funny story, gimmick

gaga ('gɑːgɑː) a. *sl.* 1. senile 2. crazy

gage¹ (geɪdʒ) n. 1. pledge, thing given as security 2. challenge, or something symbolizing one

gage² (geɪdʒ) *see* GAUGE

gaggle ('gægḷ) n. 1. flock of geese 2. *inf.* disorderly crowd

gaiety ('geɪətɪ) n. *see* GAY

gain (geɪn) vt. 1. obtain, secure 2. obtain as profit 3. win 4. earn 5. reach —v. 6. increase, improve —vi. 7. (usu. with on or upon) get nearer 8. (of watch, machine *etc.*) operate too fast —n. 9. profit 10. increase, improvement —'**gainful** a. profitable; lucrative —'**gainfully** adv.

gainsay (geɪn'seɪ) vt. deny; contradict (**gain'said, gain'saying**)

gait (geɪt) n. 1. manner of walking 2. pace

gaiter ('geɪtə) n. covering of leather, cloth *etc.* for lower leg

gal or **gal.** gallon

Gal. *Bible* Galatians

gala ('gɑːlə, 'geɪlə) n. 1. festive occasion 2. show 3. competitive sporting event

galah (gə'lɑː) n. Aust. grey cockatoo with reddish breast

galantine ('gæləntiːn) n. cold dish of meat or poultry, boned, cooked, then pressed and glazed

galaxy ('gæləksɪ) n. 1. system of stars bound by gravitational forces 2. splendid gathering, *esp.* of famous people —**ga'lactic** a.

gale (geɪl) n. 1. strong wind 2. *inf.* loud outburst, *esp.* of laughter

galena (gə'liːnə) or **galenite** (gə'liːnaɪt) n. bluish-grey or black mineral consisting of lead sulphide: principal ore of lead

gall¹ (gɔːl) n. 1. *inf.* impudence 2. bitterness —**gall bladder** sac attached to liver, reservoir for bile —'**gallstone** n. hard secretion in gall bladder or ducts leading from it

gall² (gɔːl) n. 1. painful swelling, *esp.* on horse 2. sore caused by chafing —vt. 3. make sore by rubbing 4. vex, irritate —'**galling** a. irritating, exasperating, humiliating

gall³ (gɔːl) n. abnormal outgrowth on trees *etc.*

gallant ('gælənt) a. 1. fine, stately, brave 2. (gə'lænt, 'gælənt) (of man) very attentive to women; chivalrous —n. (gə'lænt, gə'lænt) 3. lover, suitor 4. fashionable young man —'**gallantly** adv. —'**gallantry** n.

galleon ('gælɪən) n. large, high-built sailing ship of war

gallery ('gælərɪ) n. 1. covered walk with side openings, colonnade 2. platform or projecting upper floor in church, theatre *etc.* 3. group of spectators 4. long, narrow platform on outside of building 5. room or rooms for special purposes, *eg* showing works of art 6. passage in wall, open to interior of building **7.** horizontal passage, as in mine *etc.*

galley ('gælɪ) *n.* **1.** one-decked vessel with sails and oars, usu. rowed by slaves or criminals **2.** kitchen of ship or aircraft **3.** large rowing boat **4.** *Print.* tray for holding composed type —**galley proof** printer's proof in long slip form —**galley slave 1.** one condemned to row in galley **2.** drudge

galliard ('gælɪəd) *n.* **1.** dance in triple time for two persons **2.** music for this dance

Gallic ('gælɪk) *a.* **1.** of ancient Gaul **2.** French —'**Gallicism** *n.* French word or idiom

gallinaceous (gælɪ'neɪʃəs) *a.* of order of birds, including domestic fowl, pheasants *etc.*, having heavy rounded body and strong legs

gallium ('gælɪəm) *n.* soft, grey metal of great fusibility

gallivant ('gælɪvænt) *vi.* gad about

Gallo- ('gæləʊ-) (*comb. form*) Gaul; France, as in *Gallo-Roman*

gallon ('gælən) *n.* liquid measure of eight pints (4.55 litres)

gallop ('gæləp) *v.* **1.** go, ride at gallop —*vi.* **2.** move fast —*n.* **3.** horse's fastest pace with all four feet off the ground at once in each stride **4.** ride at this pace —'**galloper** *n.* —'**galloping** *a.* **1.** at a gallop **2.** speedy, swift

gallows ('gæləʊz) *n.* structure, usu. of two upright beams and crossbar, *esp.* for hanging criminals

Gallup Poll ('gæləp) method of finding out public opinion by questioning a cross section of the population

galoot *or* **galloot** (gə'luːt) *n. inf.* silly, clumsy person

galore (gə'lɔː) *adv.* in plenty

galoshes *or* **goloshes** (gə'lɒʃɪz) *pl.n.* waterproof overshoes

galumph (gə'lʌmpf, -'lʌmf) *vi. inf.* leap or move about clumsily or joyfully

galvanic (gæl'vænɪk) *a.* **1.** of, producing, concerning electric current, *esp.* when produced chemically **2.** *inf.* resembling effect of electric shock; startling —'**galvanize** *or* -**ise** *vt.* **1.** stimulate to action; excite; startle **2.** cover (iron *etc.*) with protective zinc coating —**galva'nometer** *n.* instrument for detecting or measuring small electric currents

gambit ('gæmbɪt) *n.* **1.** *Chess* opening involving offer of a pawn **2.** any opening manoeuvre, comment *etc.* intended to secure an advantage

gamble ('gæmbl) *vi.* **1.** play games of chance to win money **2.** act on expectation of something —*n.* **3.** risky undertaking **4.** bet, wager —'**gambler** *n.*

gamboge (gæm'bəʊdʒ, -'buːʒ) *n.* gum resin used as yellow pigment

gambol ('gæmbl) *vi.* **1.** skip, jump playfully (-**ll**-) —*n.* **2.** playful antic

game[1] (geɪm) *n.* **1.** diversion, pastime **2.** jest **3.** contest for amusement **4.** scheme, strategy **5.** animals or birds hunted **6.** their

flesh —*a.* **7.** brave **8.** willing —*vi.* **9.** gamble —'**gamester** *n.* gambler —'**gaming** *n.* gambling —'**gamy** *or* '**gamey** *a.* **1.** having smell or flavour of game **2.** *inf.* spirited; plucky; brave —'**gamecock** *n.* fowl bred for fighting —'**gamekeeper** *n.* man employed to breed and take care of game —**game laws** laws governing hunting and preservation of game —'**gamesmanship** *n. inf.* art of winning games or defeating opponents by cunning practices without actually cheating

game[2] (geɪm) *a.* lame, crippled

gamete ('gæmiːt, gə'miːt) *n. Biol.* sexual cell that unites with another for reproduction or the formation of a new individual

gamin ('gæmɪn) *n.* street urchin

gamine ('gæmiːn) *n.* slim, boyish girl; elfish tomboy

gamma ('gæmə) *n.* third letter of Gr. alphabet (Γ, γ) —**gamma ray** very penetrative electromagnetic ray

gammon[1] ('gæmən) *n.* **1.** cured or smoked ham **2.** bottom piece of flitch of bacon

gammon[2] ('gæmən) *n.* **1.** double victory in backgammon in which player throws off all his pieces before his opponent throws any —*vt.* **2.** score such a victory over

gammy ('gæmɪ) *a.* UK *sl. see* GAME[2]

gamp (gæmp) *n. inf.* large umbrella, usu. clumsy or very worn

gamut ('gæmət) *n.* whole range or scale (*orig.* of musical notes)

gander ('gændə) *n.* **1.** male goose **2.** *inf.* a quick look (*esp. in* take (*or* have) a **gander**)

gang[1] (gæŋ) *n.* **1.** (criminal) group **2.** organized group of workmen —*vi.* **3.** (*esp. with* together) form gang —'**ganger** *n.* foreman of a gang of labourers —**gang up** on *inf.* combine against

gang[2] (gæŋ) *n. see* GANGUE

gangling ('gæŋglɪŋ) *or* **gangly** *a.* lanky, awkward in movement

ganglion ('gæŋglɪən) *n.* nerve nucleus (*pl.* -**glia** (-glɪə), -**s**)

gangplank ('gæŋplæŋk) *or* **gangway** *n.* portable bridge for boarding or leaving vessel

gangrene ('gæŋgriːn) *n.* death or decay of body tissue as result of disease or injury —'**gangrenous** ('gæŋgrɪnəs) *a.*

gangster ('gæŋstə) *n.* **1.** member of criminal gang **2.** notorious or hardened criminal

gangue *or* **gang** (gæŋ) *n.* valueless and undesirable material in ore

gangway ('gæŋweɪ) *n.* **1.** *see* GANGPLANK **2.** passage between row of seats —*interj.* **3.** clear a path

gannet ('gænɪt) *n.* predatory sea bird

ganoid ('gænɔɪd) *a./n.* (fish) with smooth, hard, enamelled, bony scales, *eg* sturgeon

gantry ('gæntrɪ) *or* **gauntry** *n.* **1.** structure to support crane, railway signals *etc.* **2.** framework beside rocket on launching pad (*also* **gantry scaffold**)

gaol (dʒeɪl) *see* JAIL

gap (gæp) *n.* **1.** breach, opening, interval **2.** cleft **3.** empty space

gape (geɪp) *vi.* **1.** stare in wonder **2.** open mouth wide, as in yawning **3.** be, become wide open —*n.* **4.** act of gaping

garage ('gærɑːʒ, -rɪdʒ) *n.* **1.** (part of) building to house cars **2.** refuelling and repair centre for cars —*vt.* **3.** leave (car) in garage

garb (gɑːb) *n.* **1.** dress **2.** fashion of dress —*vt.* **3.** dress, clothe

garbage ('gɑːbɪdʒ) *n.* rubbish

garble ('gɑːbʰl) *vt.* jumble or distort (story, account *etc.*)

garçon (*Fr.* gar'sɔ̃) *n.* waiter, *esp.* French

garden ('gɑːdʰn) *n.* **1.** ground for growing flowers, fruit, or vegetables —*vi.* **2.** cultivate garden —'**gardener** *n.* —'**gardening** *n.* —**garden centre** place selling gardening tools, plants *etc.* —**garden city** UK planned town of limited size surrounded by rural belt

gardenia (gɑː'diːnɪə) *n.* (sub)tropical shrub with fragrant white or yellow flowers

garfish ('gɑːfɪʃ) *n.* elongated bony fish

garganey ('gɑːgənɪ) *n.* small Eurasian duck related to mallard

gargantuan (gɑː'gæntjʊən) *a.* (*sometimes* G-) immense, enormous, huge

gargle ('gɑːgʰl) *vi.* **1.** wash throat with liquid kept moving by the breath —*vt.* **2.** wash (throat) thus —*n.* **3.** gargling **4.** preparation for this purpose

gargoyle ('gɑːgɔɪl) *n.* carved (grotesque) face on waterspout, *esp.* on Gothic church

garish ('gɛərɪʃ) *a.* **1.** showy **2.** gaudy

garland ('gɑːlənd) *n.* **1.** wreath of flowers worn or hung as decoration —*vt.* **2.** decorate with garlands

garlic ('gɑːlɪk) *n.* (bulb of) plant with strong smell and taste, used in cooking and seasoning

garment ('gɑːmənt) *n.* **1.** article of clothing —*pl.* **2.** clothes

garner ('gɑːnə) *vt.* store up, collect, as if in granary

garnet ('gɑːnɪt) *n.* red semiprecious stone

garnish ('gɑːnɪʃ) *vt.* **1.** adorn, decorate (*esp.* food) —*n.* **2.** material for this

garret ('gærɪt) *n.* room on top floor, attic

garrison ('gærɪsʰn) *n.* **1.** troops stationed in town, fort *etc.* **2.** fortified place —*vt.* **3.** station (troops) in (fort *etc.*)

garrotte *or* **garotte** (gə'rɒt) *n.* **1.** Spanish capital punishment by strangling **2.** apparatus for this —*vt.* **3.** execute, kill thus —**gar'rotter** *or* **ga'rotter** *n.*

garrulous ('gærʊləs) *a.* (frivolously) talkative —**gar'rulity** *n.* loquacity

garter ('gɑːtə) *n.* band worn round leg to hold up sock or stocking —**garter stitch** knitting with all rows in plain stitch

gas (gæs) *n.* **1.** air-like substance, *esp.* one that does not liquefy or solidify at ordinary temperatures **2.** fossil fuel in form of gas, used for heating or lighting **3.** gaseous anaesthetic **4.** poisonous or irritant

substance dispersed through atmosphere in warfare *etc.* **5.** *inf., esp.* US petrol **6.** *inf.* idle, boastful talk (*pl.* **-es, 'gasses**) —*vt.* **7.** project gas over **8.** poison with gas —*vi.* **9.** *inf.* talk idly, boastfully (**-ss-**) —'**gaseous** *a.* of, like gas —'**gassy** *a.* —'**gasbag** *n. sl.* person who talks idly —**gas chamber** *or* **oven** airtight room into which poison gas is introduced to kill people —**gas gangrene** gangrene resulting from infection of wound by anaerobic bacteria —'**gasholder** *n.* gasometer; vessel for storing or measuring gas —'**gasman** *n.* man employed to read household gas meters, supervise gas fittings *etc.* —**gas mask** mask with chemical filter to guard against poisoning by gas —**gas meter** apparatus for measuring amount of gas passed through it —**ga'someter** *n.* tank for storing coal gas *etc.* (*also* '**gasholder**) —**gas ring** circular assembly of gas jets used for cooking —'**gasworks** *pl.n.* (*with sing. v.*) plant where gas, *esp.* coal gas, is made

gash (gæʃ) *n.* **1.** gaping wound, slash —*vt.* **2.** cut deeply

gasket ('gæskɪt) *n.* rubber, asbestos *etc.* used as seal between metal faces, *esp.* in engines

gasoline *or* **gasolene** ('gæsəliːn) *n.* US petrol

gasp (gɑːsp) *vi.* **1.** catch breath with open mouth, as in exhaustion or surprise —*n.* **2.** convulsive catching of breath

gasteropod ('gæstərəpɒd) *n. see* GASTROPOD

gastric ('gæstrɪk) *a.* of stomach —**gastroente'ritis** *n.* inflammation of stomach and intestines —'**gastronome, gas'tronomer** *or* **gas'tronomist** *n.* gourmet —**gastro-'nomical** *a.* —**ga'stronomy** *n.* art of good eating —**gastric juice** digestive fluid secreted by stomach, containing hydrochloric acid *etc.* —**gastric ulcer** ulcer of stomach lining

gastro- *or oft. before vowel* **gastr-** (*comb. form*) stomach, as in *gastroenteritis, gastritis*

gastropod ('gæstrəpɒd) *or* **gasteropod** *n.* mollusc, *eg* snail, with disclike organ of locomotion on ventral surface

gate (geɪt) *n.* **1.** opening in wall, fence *etc.* **2.** barrier for closing it **3.** sluice **4.** any entrance or way out **5.** (entrance money paid by) those attending sporting event —**gate-crash** *v.* enter (meeting, social function *etc.*) uninvited —'**gatehouse** *n.* house built at or over gateway —**gate-leg table** *or* **gate-legged table** table with leaves supported by hinged leg swung out from frame

gâteau ('gætəʊ) *n.* elaborate, rich cake (*pl.* **-teaux** (-təʊz))

gather ('gæðə) *v.* **1.** (cause to) assemble **2.** increase gradually **3.** draw together —*vt.* **4.** collect **5.** learn, understand **6.** draw (material) into small tucks or folds —'**gathering** *n.* assembly

GATT (gæt) General Agreement on Tariffs and Trade

gauche (gəʊʃ) a. tactless, blundering —**gaucherie** (gəʊʃə'riː, 'gəʊʃəri) n. awkwardness, clumsiness

gaucho ('gautʃəʊ) n. S Amer. cowboy (pl. -s)

gaud (gɔːd) n. showy ornament —**'gaudily** adv. —**'gaudiness** n. —**'gaudy** a. showy in tasteless way

gauge or **gage** (geidʒ) n. 1. standard measure, as of diameter of wire, thickness of sheet metal etc. 2. distance between rails of railway 3. capacity, extent 4. instrument for measuring such things as wire, rainfall, height of water in boiler etc. —vt. 5. measure 6. estimate

Gaul (gɔːl) n. 1. native of Gaul, region in Roman times stretching from N Italy to S Netherlands 2. Frenchman

gaunt (gɔːnt) a. lean, haggard

gauntlet ('gɔːntlit) n. 1. armoured glove 2. glove covering part of arm —**run the gauntlet** 1. formerly, run as punishment between two lines of men striking at runner with sticks etc. 2. be exposed to criticism or unpleasant treatment 3. undergo ordeal —**throw down the gauntlet** offer challenge

gauntry ('gɔːntri) n. see GANTRY

gauss (gaus) n. unit of density of magnetic field (pl. **gauss**)

gauze (gɔːz) n. thin transparent fabric of silk, wire etc. —**'gauzy** a.

gave (geiv) pt. of GIVE

gavel ('gæv'l) n. mallet of presiding officer or auctioneer

gavotte or **gavot** (gə'vɒt) n. 1. lively dance 2. music for it

gawk (gɔːk) vi. stare stupidly —**'gawky** a. clumsy, awkward

gawp or **gaup** (gɔːp) vi. sl. 1. stare stupidly 2. gape

gay (gei) a. 1. merry 2. lively 3. cheerful 4. bright 5. light-hearted 6. showy 7. given to pleasure 8. inf. homosexual —**'gaiety** n. 1. state or condition of being gay 2. festivity; merrymaking —**'gaily** adv.

gaze (geiz) vi. 1. look fixedly —n. 2. fixed look

gazebo (gə'ziːbəʊ) n. summer-house, turret on roof, with extensive view (pl. -s, -es)

gazelle (gə'zɛl) n. small graceful antelope

gazette (gə'zɛt) n. 1. official newspaper for announcements of government appointments etc. 2. newspaper title —vt. 3. publish in gazette —**gazetteer** (gæzi'tiə) n. geographical dictionary

gazump (gə'zʌmp) v. raise (price of something, esp. house) after agreeing it with prospective buyer

G.B. Great Britain

G.B.E. (Knight or Dame) Grand Cross of the British Empire

g.b.h. grievous bodily harm

G.C. George Cross

G.C.B. (Knight) Grand Cross of the Bath (Brit. title)

G.C.E. or **GCE** General Certificate of Education

G clef see treble clef at TREBLE

G.C.M.G. (Knight or Dame) Grand Cross of the Order of St. Michael and St. George

G.C.V.O. or **GCVO** (Knight or Dame) Grand Cross of the Royal Victorian Order

Gd Chem. gadolinium

Gdns. Gardens

G.D.P. gross domestic product

GDR German Democratic Republic

Ge Chem. germanium

gean (giːn) n. 1. white-flowered tree with round, edible red fruit 2. its fruit

gear (giə) n. 1. set of wheels working together, esp. by engaging cogs 2. connection by which engine, motor etc. is brought into work 3. arrangement by which driving wheel of cycle, car etc. performs more or fewer revolutions relative to pedals, pistons etc. 4. equipment 5. clothing 6. goods, utensils 7. apparatus, tackle, tools 8. rigging 9. harness —vt. 10. adapt (one thing) so as to conform with another 11. provide with gear 12. put in gear —**'gearing** n. 1. assembly of gears for transmitting motion 2. act or technique of providing gears to transmit motion 3. Acc., UK ratio of company's debt capital to its equity capital —**'gearbox** n. case protecting gearing of bicycle, car etc. —**gear lever** or U.S. **'gearshift** n. lever used to move gear wheels relative to each other in motor vehicle etc. —**'gearwheel** n. toothed wheel in system of gears (also **gear**) —**in gear** connected up and ready for work —**out of gear** 1. disconnected, out of working order 2. upset

gecko ('gɛkəʊ) n. insectivorous lizard of warm regions (pl. -s, -es)

gee (dʒiː) interj. 1. exclamation to horse etc. to encourage it to turn to right, go on or go faster (also **gee up**) —vt. 2. (usu. with up) move (horse etc.) ahead; urge on

geelbek ('xiːlbɛk) n. edible S Afr. marine fish

geese (giːs) n., pl. of GOOSE

geezer ('giːzə) n. inf. old (eccentric) man

Geiger counter ('gaigə) or **Geiger-Müller counter** ('mʊlə) instrument for detecting radioactivity, cosmic radiation and charged atomic particles

geisha ('geiʃə) n. in Japan, professional female companion for men

gel (dʒɛl) n. 1. jellylike substance —vi. 2. form a gel (-ll-) (also **jell**)

gelatin ('dʒɛlətin) or **gelatine** ('dʒɛlətiːn) n. 1. substance prepared from animal bones etc., producing edible jelly 2. anything resembling this —**ge'latinous** a. like gelatin or jelly

geld (gɛld) vt. castrate —**'gelding** n. castrated horse

gelid ('dʒɛlid) a. very cold

gelignite ('dʒɛlignait) n. powerful explosive consisting of dynamite in gelatin form

gem (dʒɛm) n. 1. precious stone, esp. when

cut and polished **2.** treasure —*vt.* **3.** adorn with gems (**-mm-**)

geminate ('dʒɛmɪneɪt) *v.* double, pair, repeat —**gemi'nation** *n.*

Gemini ('dʒɛmɪnaɪ, -niː) *n.* (twins) 3rd sign of zodiac, operative May 21st–June 20th

gemma ('dʒɛmə) *n.* asexual reproductive structure in mosses *etc.* that becomes detached from parent and develops into new individual (*pl.* **-mae** (-miː))

gemsbok *or* **gemsbuck** ('gɛmzbʌk) *n.* S Afr. oryx

gen (dʒɛn) *n. inf.* information —**gen someone up** UK *inf.* brief someone in detail

gen. 1. gender **2.** general **3.** genitive **4.** genus

Gen. 1. General **2.** *Bible* Genesis

-gen (*comb. form*) **1.** producing; that which produces, as in *hydrogen* **2.** something produced, as in *antigen*

gendarme ('ʒɒndɑːm) *n.* policeman in France

gender ('dʒɛndə) *n.* **1.** sex, male or female **2.** grammatical classification of nouns, according to sex (actual or attributed)

gene (dʒiːn) *n.* biological factor determining inherited characteristics

genealogy (dʒiːnɪ'ælədʒɪ) *n.* **1.** account of descent from ancestors **2.** pedigree **3.** study of pedigrees —**genea'logical** *a.* —**gene'alogist** *n.*

genera ('dʒɛnərə) *n., pl. of* GENUS

general ('dʒɛnərəl, 'dʒɛnrəl) *a.* **1.** common, widespread **2.** not particular or specific **3.** applicable to all or most **4.** not restricted to one department **5.** usual, prevalent **6.** miscellaneous **7.** dealing with main element only **8.** vague, indefinite —*n.* **9.** army officer of rank above colonel —**gene'rality** *n.* **1.** general principle **2.** vague statement **3.** indefiniteness —**generali'zation** *or* **-i'sation** *n.* **1.** general conclusion from particular instance **2.** inference —**'generalize** *or* **-ise** *vt.* **1.** reduce to general laws —*vi.* **2.** draw general conclusions —**'generally** *adv.* —**General Certificate of Education** public examination for which certificates are awarded at ordinary, advanced or scholarship level —**general election 1.** election in which representatives are chosen in all constituencies of a state **2.** US final election from which successful candidates are sent to legislative body **3. US, C** national, state or provincial election —**general practitioner** nonspecialist doctor with practice serving particular local area —**general-purpose** *a.* having a variety of uses —**general strike** strike by all or most of workers of country *etc.*

generalissimo (dʒɛnərə'lɪsɪməʊ, dʒɛnrə-) *n.* supreme commander of combined military, naval and air forces (*pl.* **-s**)

generate ('dʒɛnəreɪt) *vt.* **1.** bring into being **2.** produce —**gene'ration** *n.* **1.** bringing into being **2.** all persons born about same time **3.** average time between

two such generations (about 30 years) —**'generative** *a.* —**'generator** *n.* **1.** apparatus for producing steam, electricity *etc.* **2.** begetter —**generation gap** years separating one generation from next, *esp.* regarded as representing difference in outlook and lack of understanding between them

generic (dʒɪ'nɛrɪk) *a.* belonging to, characteristic of class or genus —**ge'nerically** *adv.*

generous ('dʒɛnərəs, 'dʒɛnrəs) *a.* **1.** liberal, free in giving **2.** abundant —**gene'rosity** *n.* —**'generously** *adv.*

genesis ('dʒɛnɪsɪs) *n.* **1.** origin **2.** mode of formation **3. (G-)** first book of Bible (*pl.* **-eses** (-ɪsiːz))

-genesis (*comb. form*) genesis, development, generation, as in *biogenesis, parthenogenesis*

genet ('dʒɛnɪt) *or* **genette** (dʒɪ'nɛt) *n.* catlike mammal of Afr. and S Europe

genetics (dʒɪ'nɛtɪks) *pl.n.* (*with sing. v.*) scientific study of heredity and variation in organisms —**ge'netic** *a.* —**genetic code** *Biochem.* order in which four nitrogenous bases of DNA are arranged in molecule, which determines type and amount of protein synthesized in cell —**genetic engineering** alteration of structure of chromosomes in living organisms to produce effects beneficial to man in medicine, agriculture *etc.* —**genetic fingerprinting** pattern of DNA unique to each individual, which can be analysed in sample of blood, saliva or tissue: used as means of identification

Geneva Convention (dʒɪ'niːvə) international agreement, formulated in 1864, establishing code for wartime treatment of sick or wounded: revised to cover maritime warfare and prisoners of war

genial ('dʒiːnjəl, -nɪəl) *a.* **1.** cheerful, warm in behaviour **2.** mild, conducive to growth —**geni'ality** *n.* —**'genially** *adv.*

genie ('dʒiːnɪ) *n.* in fairy tales, servant appearing by, and working, magic

genital ('dʒɛnɪt'l) *a.* relating to sexual organs or reproduction —**'genitals** *pl.n.* the sexual organs

genitive ('dʒɛnɪtɪv) *a./n.* possessive (case) —**genitival** (dʒɛnɪ'taɪv'l) *a.*

genius ('dʒiːnɪəs, -njəs) *n.* **1.** (person with) exceptional power or ability, *esp.* of mind **2.** distinctive spirit or nature (of nation *etc.*)

genocide ('dʒɛnəʊsaɪd) *n.* murder of a nationality or ethnic group

-genous (*comb. form*) **1.** yielding; generating, as in *erogenous* **2.** generated by; issuing from, as in *endogenous*

genre ('ʒɑːnrə) *n.* **1.** kind **2.** sort **3.** style **4.** painting of homely scene

gent (dʒɛnt) *inf. n.* **1.** gentleman —*pl.* **2.** men's public lavatory

genteel (dʒɛn'tiːl) *a.* **1.** well-bred **2.** stylish **3.** affectedly proper —**gen'teelly** *adv.*

gentian ('dʒɛnʃən) *n.* plant, usu. with blue

flowers **—gentian violet** violet dye used as antiseptic *etc.*

Gentile ('dʒɛntaɪl) *a.* **1.** of race other than Jewish **2.** heathen **—n. 3.** person, *esp.* Christian, who is not a Jew

gentle ('dʒɛntˈl) *a.* **1.** mild, quiet, not rough or severe **2.** soft and soothing **3.** courteous **4.** moderate **5.** gradual **6.** noble **7.** well-born **—gen'tility** *n.* **1.** noble birth **2.** respectability, politeness **—'gentleness** *n.* **1.** quality of being gentle **2.** tenderness **—'gently** *adv.* **—'gentry** *n.* people of social standing next below nobility **—'gentlefolk** or **'gentlefolks** *pl.n.* persons regarded as being of good breeding **—'gentleman** *n.* **1.** chivalrous well-bred man **2.** man of good social position **3.** man (used as a mark of politeness) **—'gentlemanly** or **'gentlemanlike** *a.* **—gentlemen's agreement** agreement binding by honour but not valid in law **—'gentlewoman** *n.*

genuflect ('dʒɛnjʊflɛkt) *vi.* bend knee, *esp.* in worship **—genu'flection** or **genu'flexion** *n.*

genuine ('dʒɛnjuɪn) *a.* **1.** real, true, not fake; authentic **2.** sincere **3.** pure

genus ('dʒiːnəs) *n.* class, order, group (*esp.* of insects, animals *etc.*) with common characteristics, usu. comprising several species (*pl.* **-es, 'genera**)

geo- (*comb. form*) earth, as in *geomorphology*

geocentric (dʒiːəʊ'sɛntrɪk) *a. Astron.* **1.** measured, seen from the earth **2.** having the earth as centre **—geo'centrically** *adv.*

geode ('dʒiːəʊd) *n.* **1.** cavity lined with crystals **2.** stone containing these

geodesic (dʒiːəʊ'dɛsɪk, -'diː-) *a.* of geometry of curved surfaces (*also* **geo'detic**) **—geodesic dome** light but strong hemispherical construction formed from set of polygons

geodesy (dʒɪ'ɒdɪsɪ) *n.* science of measuring the earth's surface

geog. 1. geographer **2.** geographic(al) **3.** geography

geography (dʒɪ'ɒɡrəfɪ) *n.* science of earth's form, physical features, climate, population *etc.* **—ge'ographer** *n.* **—geo'graphic(al)** *a.* **—geo'graphically** *adv.* **—geographical mile** *see* **nautical mile** *at* NAUTICAL

geoid ('dʒiːɔɪd) *n.* **1.** hypothetical surface that corresponds to mean sea level, extending under continents **2.** shape of the earth

geol. 1. geologic(al) **2.** geologist **3.** geology

geology (dʒɪ'ɒlədʒɪ) *n.* science of earth's crust, rocks, strata *etc.* **—geo'logical** *a.* **—geo'logically** *adv.* **—ge'ologist** *n.*

geometry (dʒɪ'ɒmɪtrɪ) *n.* science of properties and relations of lines, surfaces *etc.* **—geo'metric(al)** *a.* **—geo'metrically** *adv.* **—geome'trician** *n.* **—geometric progression** sequence of numbers, each of which differs from succeeding one by constant ratio, as 1, 2, 4, 8 **—geometric series** such numbers written as sum

geophysics (dʒiːəʊ'fɪzɪks) *pl.n.* (*with sing. v.*) science dealing with the physics of the earth **—geo'physical** *a.* **—geo'physicist** *n.*

Geordie ('dʒɔːdɪ) *n.* native of Tyneside

George Cross (dʒɔːdʒ) British award for bravery

georgette or **georgette crepe** (dʒɔː'dʒɛt) *n.* fine, silky, semitransparent fabric

Georgian ('dʒɔːdʒən) *a.* of the times of the four Georges (1714-1830) or of George V (1910-36)

georgic ('dʒɔːdʒɪk) *n.* poem on rural life, *esp.* one by Virgil

geostationary (dʒiːəʊ'steɪʃənərɪ) *a.* (of satellite) in orbit around earth so it remains over same point on surface

geotropism (dʒɪ'ɒtrəpɪzəm) *n.* response of plant part to stimulus of gravity

Ger. 1. German **2.** Germany

geranium (dʒɪ'reɪnɪəm) *n.* **1.** common cultivated plant with red, pink or white flowers, pelargonium **2.** strong pink colour

gerbil or **gerbille** ('dʒɜːbɪl) *n.* burrowing desert rodent of Asia and Afr.

gerent ('dʒɛrənt) *n.* ruler, governor, director

gerfalcon ('dʒɜːfɔːlkən, -fɔːkən) *n.* see GYRFALCON

geriatrics (dʒɛrɪ'ætrɪks) *pl.n.* (*with sing. v.*) branch of science dealing with old age and its diseases **—geri'atric** *a./n.* old (person)

germ (dʒɜːm) *n.* **1.** microbe, *esp.* causing disease **2.** elementary thing **3.** rudiment of new organism, of animal or plant **—germi'cidal** *a.* **—'germicide** *n.* substance for destroying disease germs **—germ cell** sexual reproductive cell **—germ warfare** use of bacteria against enemy

german ('dʒɜːmən) *a.* **1.** of the same parents **2.** closely akin (*only in* **brother-, sister-, cousin-german**)

German ('dʒɜːmən) *n./a.* (language or native) of Germany **—Ger'manic** *n.* **1.** branch of Indo-European family of languages including Dutch, German *etc.* **2.** unrecorded language from which these languages developed (*also* **Proto-Germanic**) **—a. 3.** of this group of languages **4.** of Germany, German language or any people that speaks Germanic language **—German measles** *see* RUBELLA

germander (dʒɜː'mændə) *n.* European plant having two-lipped flowers with very small upper lip

germane (dʒɜː'meɪn) *a.* relevant, pertinent

germanium (dʒɜː'meɪnɪəm) *n.* grey element that is semiconducting metalloid

germinate ('dʒɜːmɪneɪt) *v.* (cause to) sprout or begin to grow **—germi'nation** *n.* **—'germinative** *a.*

gerontology (dʒɛrɒn'tɒlədʒɪ) *n.* scientific study of ageing and problems of elderly people **—geron'tologist** *n.*

gerrymander ('dʒɛrɪmændə) vt. 1. divide constituencies of (voting area) so as to give one party unfair advantage 2. manipulate or adapt to one's advantage —n. 3. act or result of gerrymandering

gerund ('dʒɛrənd) n. noun formed from verb, eg living

gerundive (dʒɪ'rʌndɪv) n. 1. in Latin grammar, adjective formed from verb, expressing desirability etc. of activity denoted by verb —a. 2. of gerund or gerundive

gesso ('dʒɛsəʊ) n. 1. white ground of plaster and size, used to prepare panels etc. for painting etc. 2. any white substance, esp. plaster of Paris, that forms ground when mixed with water

Gestapo (gɛ'stɑːpəʊ) n. secret state police in Nazi Germany

gestate ('dʒɛsteɪt) v. carry (developing young) in uterus during pregnancy —ges'tation n.

gesticulate (dʒɛ'stɪkjʊleɪt) vi. use expressive movements of hands and arms when speaking —gesticu'lation n.

gesture ('dʒɛstʃə) n. 1. movement to convey meaning 2. indication of state of mind —vi. 3. make such a movement

get (gɛt) vt. 1. obtain, procure 2. contract 3. catch 4. earn 5. cause to go or come 6. bring into position or state 7. induce 8. engender 9. inf. understand —vi. 10. succeed in coming or going 11. (oft. with to) reach, attain 12. become (got, 'getting) —'getaway n. escape —get-together n. inf. small informal social gathering —get-up n. inf. 1. costume, outfit 2. arrangement of book etc. —get-up-and-go n. inf. energy, drive —get across (cause to) be understood —get at 1. gain access to 2. mean, intend 3. annoy 4. criticize 5. influence —get by inf. manage, esp. in spite of difficulties —get on 1. grow late 2. (of person) grow old 3. make progress, manage, fare 4. (oft. with with) establish friendly relationship 5. (with with) continue to do —get (one's) goat sl. make (one) angry, annoyed —get one's own back inf. obtain one's revenge —have got possess —have got to must, have to

geum ('dʒiːəm) n. garden plant with orange, yellow or white flowers

geyser ('giːzə; U.S. 'gaɪzər) n. 1. hot spring throwing up spout of water from time to time 2. apparatus for heating water and delivering it from a tap

ghastly ('gɑːstlɪ) a. 1. inf. unpleasant 2. deathlike, pallid 3. inf. unwell 4. horrible —adv. 5. sickly

ghat (gɔːt) n. (in India) 1. stairs leading down to river 2. mountain pass

ghee (giː) n. clarified butter used in Indian cookery

gherkin ('gɜːkɪn) n. small cucumber used in pickling

ghetto ('gɛtəʊ) n. densely populated (esp. by one racial group) slum area (pl. -s, -es)

—**ghetto blaster** inf. portable cassette recorder with built-in speakers

ghost (gəʊst) n. 1. spirit, dead person appearing again 2. spectre 3. semblance 4. faint trace 5. one who writes work to appear under another's name —v. 6. ghostwrite —vt. 7. haunt —'ghostly a. —ghost town deserted town, esp. one in western U.S.A. that was formerly a boom town —'ghostwrite v. write (article etc.) on behalf of person who is then credited as author (also ghost) —'ghostwriter n.

ghoul (guːl) n. 1. malevolent spirit 2. person with morbid interests 3. fiend —'ghoulish a. 1. of or like ghoul 2. horrible

G.H.Q. Mil. General Headquarters

ghyll (gɪl) n. see GILL³

GI (short for Government Issue, stamped on U.S. military equipment) inf. U.S. soldier

giant ('dʒaɪənt) n. 1. mythical being of superhuman size 2. very tall person, plant etc. —a. 3. huge —gi'gantic a. enormous, huge

giaour ('dʒaʊə) n. derogatory non-Muslim, esp. Christian

gib (gɪb) n. 1. metal wedge, pad or thrust bearing let into steam engine crosshead —vt. 2. fasten or supply with gib (-bb-)

Gib (dʒɪb) n. inf. Gibraltar

gibber ('dʒɪbə) vi. 1. make meaningless sounds with mouth 2. jabber, chatter —'gibberish n. meaningless speech or words

gibbet ('dʒɪbɪt) n. 1. gallows 2. post with arm on which executed criminals were formerly hung 3. death by hanging —vt. 4. hang on gibbet 5. hold up to scorn

gibbon ('gɪbᵊn) n. type of ape

gibbous ('gɪbəs) or **gibbose** ('gɪbəʊs) a. 1. (of moon etc.) more than half illuminated 2. hunchbacked 3. bulging —'gibbousness or gibbosity (gɪ'bɒsɪtɪ) n.

gibe or **jibe** (dʒaɪb) v. 1. utter taunts (at) 2. mock 3. jeer —n. 4. provoking remark

giblets ('dʒɪblɪts) pl.n. internal edible parts of fowl, as liver, gizzard etc.

giddy ('gɪdɪ) a. 1. dizzy, feeling as if about to fall 2. liable to cause this feeling 3. flighty, frivolous —'giddily adv. —'giddiness n.

gift (gɪft) n. 1. thing given, present 2. faculty, power —vt. 3. present, endow, bestow —'gifted a. talented —gift token voucher given as present which recipient can exchange for gift

gig (gɪg) n. 1. light, two-wheeled carriage 2. inf. single booking of musicians to play at concert etc. 3. cluster of fish-hooks

giga- ('gɪgə, 'gaɪgə) (comb. form) 10⁹, as in gigavolt

gigantic (dʒaɪ'gæntɪk) a. see GIANT

giggle ('gɪgᵊl) vi. 1. laugh nervously, foolishly —n. 2. such a laugh 3. joke

gigolo ('ʒɪgələʊ) n. 1. man kept by (older) woman 2. man paid to escort women

gigot ('dʒɪgət) n. 1. leg of lamb or mutton 2. leg-of-mutton sleeve

gild¹ (gɪld) vt. 1. put thin layer of gold on 2. make falsely attractive ('**gilded** pt., **gilt** or '**gilded** pp.) —**gilt** a. 1. gilded —n. 2. thin layer of gold applied in gilding 3. superficial appearance —**gilt-edged** a. 1. (of securities) dated over short, medium, or long term, and characterized by minimum risk and usu. issued by Government 2. (of books etc.) having gilded edges

gild² (gɪld) n. see GUILD

gill¹ (gɪl) n. (usu. pl.) breathing organ in fish

gill² (dʒɪl) n. liquid measure, quarter of pint (0.142 litres)

gill³ or **ghyll** (gɪl) n. UK dial. 1. narrow stream; rivulet 2. wooded ravine

gillie, ghillie, or **gilly** ('gɪlɪ) n. in Scotland, attendant for hunting or fishing

gillyflower or **gilliflower** ('dʒɪlɪˌflaʊə) n. fragrant flower

gilt (gɪlt) n. young female pig

gimbals ('dʒɪmbˡz, 'gɪm-) pl.n. pivoted rings, for keeping things, eg compass, horizontal at sea

gimcrack ('dʒɪmkræk) a. 1. cheap; shoddy —n. 2. cheap showy trifle

gimlet ('gɪmlɪt) n. boring tool, usu. with screw point —**gimlet-eyed** a. having a piercing glance

gimmick ('gɪmɪk) n. clever device, stratagem etc., esp. designed to attract attention or publicity

gimp or **guimpe** (gɪmp) n. narrow fabric or braid used as edging or trimming

gin¹ (dʒɪn) n. spirit flavoured with juniper berries —**gin rummy** version of rummy in which player may go out if odd cards outside his sequences total less than ten points

gin² (dʒɪn) n. 1. primitive engine in which vertical shaft is turned to drive horizontal beam in a circle 2. machine for separating cotton from seeds 3. snare, trap

ginger ('dʒɪndʒə) n. 1. plant with hot-tasting spicy root used in cooking etc. 2. the root 3. inf. spirit, mettle 4. light reddish-yellow colour —'**gingery** a. 1. of, like ginger 2. hot 3. high-spirited 4. reddish —**ginger ale** ginger-flavoured soft drink —**ginger beer** effervescing beverage made by fermenting ginger —'**gingerbread** n. cake flavoured with ginger —**ginger group** group within a party, association etc. that enlivens or radicalizes its parent body —**ginger snap** or **nut** crisp biscuit flavoured with ginger —**ginger up** stimulate

gingerly ('dʒɪndʒəlɪ) adv. 1. cautiously, warily, reluctantly —a. 2. cautious, reluctant or timid

gingham ('gɪŋəm) n. cotton cloth, usu. checked, woven from dyed yarn

gingivitis (dʒɪndʒɪ'vaɪtɪs) n. inflammation of gums

ginkgo ('gɪŋkgəʊ) or **gingko** ('gɪŋkəʊ) n. ornamental Chinese tree (pl. -es)

ginseng ('dʒɪnsɛŋ) n. 1. plant of China or of N Amer., whose roots are used medicinally in China 2. root of this plant or substance obtained from root

gip (dʒɪp) vt./n. 1. see GYP¹ —n. 2. see GYP²

Gipsy ('dʒɪpsɪ) n. see GYPSY

giraffe (dʒɪ'rɑːf, -'ræf) n. Afr. ruminant animal, with spotted coat and very long neck and legs

gird¹ (gɜːd) vt. 1. put belt round 2. fasten (clothes) thus 3. equip with sword 4. prepare (oneself) 5. encircle (**girt**, '**girded** pt./pp.) —'**girder** n. large beam, esp. of steel

gird² (gɜːd) dial. v. 1. jeer (at); mock —n. 2. taunt; gibe

girdle¹ ('gɜːdˡl) n. 1. corset 2. waistband 3. anything that surrounds, encircles —vt. 4. surround, encircle

girdle² ('gɜːdˡl) n. griddle

girl (gɜːl) n. 1. female child 2. young (unmarried) woman —'**girlhood** n. —'**girlie** a. inf. (of magazine) featuring nude or scantily dressed women —'**girlish** a. —**girl Friday** female employee with wide range of secretarial and clerical duties —'**girlfriend** n. 1. female friend with whom male is romantically or sexually involved 2. any female friend —**Girl Guide** see GUIDE (sense 5)

giro ('dʒaɪrəʊ) n. system operated by banks and post offices which provides for the transfer of money between accounts or by giro cheque (pl. -s)

girt¹ (gɜːt) pt./pp. of GIRD¹

girt² (gɜːt) vt. 1. bind; encircle; gird 2. measure girth of

girth (gɜːθ) n. 1. measurement around something 2. leather or cloth band put around horse's belly to hold saddle etc. —vt. 3. surround, secure with girth

gist (dʒɪst) n. substance, main point (of remarks etc.)

give (gɪv) vt. 1. bestow, confer ownership of, make present of 2. deliver 3. impart 4. assign 5. yield, supply 6. utter, emit 7. be host of (party etc.) 8. make over 9. cause to have —vi. 10. yield, give way, move (**gave, 'given, 'giving**) —n. 11. yielding, elasticity —**give-and-take** n. 1. mutual concessions, shared benefits and cooperation 2. smoothly flowing exchange of ideas and talk —'**giveaway** n. 1. betrayal or disclosure, esp. when unintentional —a. 2. very cheap (esp. in **giveaway prices**) —**give and take** make mutual concessions —**give away** 1. donate or bestow as gift etc. 2. sell very cheaply 3. reveal, betray 4. fail to use (opportunity) through neglect 5. present (bride) formally to her husband in marriage ceremony —**give or take** plus or minus —**give up** 1. acknowledge defeat 2. abandon

gizzard ('gɪzəd) n. part of bird's stomach

glabrous ('gleɪbrəs) a. Biol. without hairs or any unevenness; smooth

glacé ('glæsɪ) a. 1. crystallized, candied, iced 2. glossy

glacier ('glæsɪə, 'gleɪs-) n. river of ice,

slow-moving mass of ice formed by accumulated snow in mountain valleys —**glacial** ('gleisiəl, -ʃəl) a. 1. of ice, or of glaciers 2. very cold —**glaciated** ('gleisieitid) a. —**glaciation** (gleisi'eiʃən) n. —**glacial period** time when large part of earth's surface was covered by ice

glad (glæd) a. 1. pleased 2. happy, joyous 3. giving joy —**'gladden** vt. make glad —**'gladly** adv. —**'gladness** n. —**glad eye** inf. inviting or seductive glance (esp. in **give (someone) the glad eye**) —**'gladrags** pl.n. sl. clothes for special occasions

glade (gleid) n. clear, grassy space in wood or forest

gladiator ('glædieitə) n. trained fighter in Roman arena

gladiolus (glædi'əuləs) n. kind of iris, with sword-shaped leaves (pl. **-lus, -li** (-lai))

Gladstone bag ('glædstən) travelling bag

glair (glɛə) n. 1. white of egg 2. sticky substance —vt. 3. smear with white of egg —**'glairy** a.

Glam. (glæm) Glamorgan

glamour or U.S. (sometimes) **glamor** ('glæmə) n. alluring charm, fascination —**'glamorize, -ise,** or U.S. (sometimes) **'glamourize** vt. make appear glamorous —**'glamorous** a.

glance (glɑ:ns) vi. 1. look rapidly or briefly 2. allude briefly to or touch on subject 3. (usu. with off) glide off (something struck) —n. 4. brief look 5. flash 6. gleam 7. sudden (deflected) blow

gland (glænd) n. one of various small organs controlling different bodily functions by chemical means —**'glanders** n. contagious horse disease —**'glandular** a. —**glandular fever** acute disease characterized by fever, swollen lymph nodes etc. (also **infectious mononucleosis**)

glare (glɛə) vi. 1. look fiercely 2. shine brightly, intensely 3. be conspicuous —n. 4. angry stare —**'glaring** a.

glasnost ('glæsnɒst) n. policy of public frankness and accountability developed in U.S.S.R. under Mikhail Gorbachov's leadership

glass (glɑ:s) n. 1. hard transparent substance made by fusing sand, soda, potash etc. 2. things made of it 3. tumbler 4. its contents 5. lens 6. mirror 7. telescope 8. barometer 9. microscope —pl. 10. spectacles —**'glassily** adv. —**'glassiness** n. —**'glassy** a. 1. like glass 2. expressionless —**glass-blower** n. —**glass-blowing** n. process of shaping molten glass by blowing air into it through tube —**'glasshouse** n. 1. greenhouse 2. inf. army prison —**glass-paper** n. paper coated with pulverized glass for smoothing and polishing —**glass wool** insulating fabric

Glaswegian (glæz'wi:dʒən) a. 1. of Glasgow, city in Scotland —n. 2. native or inhabitant of Glasgow

glaucoma (glɔ:'kəumə) n. eye disease —**glau'comatous** a.

glaucous ('glɔ:kəs) a. 1. Bot. covered with waxy or powdery bloom 2. bluish-green

glaze (gleiz) vt. 1. furnish with glass 2. cover with glassy substance —vi. 3. become glassy —n. 4. transparent coating 5. substance used for this 6. glossy surface —**'glazier** n. person who glazes windows

G.L.C. Greater London Council

gleam (gli:m) n. 1. slight or passing beam of light 2. faint or momentary show —vi. 3. give out gleams

glean (gli:n) v. 1. pick up (facts etc.) 2. gather (useful remnants of crop) in cornfields after harvesting —**'gleaner** n.

glebe (gli:b) n. land belonging to parish church or benefice

glee (gli:) n. 1. mirth, merriment 2. musical composition for three or more voices —**'gleeful** a. —**'gleefully** adv.

glen (glen) n. narrow valley, usu. wooded and with a stream, esp. in Scotland

glengarry (glen'gæri) n. Scottish woollen boat-shaped cap with ribbons hanging down back

glib (glib) a. 1. fluent but insincere or superficial 2. plausible —**'glibly** adv. —**'glibness** n.

glide (glaid) vi. 1. pass smoothly and continuously 2. (of aeroplane) move without use of engines —n. 3. smooth, silent movement 4. Mus. sounds made in passing from tone to tone —**'glider** n. aircraft without engine which moves in air currents —**'gliding** n. sport of flying gliders

glimmer ('glimə) vi. 1. shine faintly, flicker —n. 2. glow or twinkle of light —**'glimmering** n. 1. faint gleam of light 2. faint idea, notion

glimpse (glimps) n. 1. brief or incomplete view —vt. 2. catch glimpse of

glint (glint) v. 1. flash —vi. 2. glance, glitter 3. reflect —n. 4. bright gleam; flash

glissade (gli'sɑ:d, -'seid) n. 1. gliding dance step 2. slide, usu. on feet down slope of ice —vi. 3. perform glissade

glisten ('glis'n) vi. gleam by reflecting light

glister ('glistə) vi./n. obs. glitter

glitch (glitʃ) n. sudden instance of malfunctioning in electronic system

glitter ('glitə) vi. 1. shine with bright quivering light, sparkle 2. be showy —n. 3. lustre 4. sparkle —**glitterati** (glitə'rɑ:ti) pl.n. inf. leaders of society, esp. the rich and beautiful —**glitter ice** C ice formed from freezing rain

glitzy ('glitsi) a. sl. showily attractive; flashy; glittery

gloaming ('gləumiŋ) n. Scot., poet. evening twilight

gloat (gləut) vi. regard, dwell (on) with smugness or malicious satisfaction

glob (glob) n. inf. soft lump or mass

globe (gləub) n. 1. sphere with map of earth or stars 2. heavenly sphere, esp. the earth 3. ball, sphere —**'global** a. —**globular** ('globjulə) a. globe-shaped —**globule**

('glɒbjuːl) n. 1. small round particle 2. drop —'**globetrotter** n. (habitual) world-wide traveller —**the globe** the world; the earth

globulin ('glɒbjulɪn) n. kind of simple protein

glockenspiel ('glɒkənspiːl, -ʃpiːl) n. percussion instrument of metal bars which are struck with hammers

glomerate ('glɒmərɪt) a. 1. gathered into rounded mass 2. Anat. (esp. of glands) conglomerate in structure

gloom (gluːm) n. 1. darkness 2. melancholy, depression —'**gloomily** adv. —'**gloomy** a.

glory ('glɔːrɪ) n. 1. renown, honourable fame 2. splendour 3. exalted or prosperous state 4. heavenly bliss —vi. 5. take pride ('**gloried**, '**glorying**) —**glorifi'cation** n. —'**glorify** vt. 1. make glorious 2. invest with glory (-**ified**, -**ifying**) —'**glorious** a. 1. illustrious 2. splendid 3. excellent 4. delightful —'**gloriously** adv. —**glory hole** inf. untidy cupboard, room or receptacle for storage

Glos. (glɒs) Gloucestershire

gloss[1] (glɒs) n. 1. surface shine, lustre —vt. 2. put gloss on 3. (esp. with over) (try to) cover up, pass over (fault, error) —'**glossiness** n. —'**glossy** a. 1. smooth, shiny —n. 2. magazine printed on shiny paper

gloss[2] (glɒs) n. 1. marginal interpretation of word 2. comment, explanation —vt. 3. interpret 4. comment 5. (oft. with over) explain away —'**glossary** n. list of items peculiar to a field of knowledge with explanations

glottis ('glɒtɪs) n. human vocal apparatus, larynx (pl. **-es**, **-tides** (-tɪdiːz)) —'**glottal** or '**glottic** a.

glove (glʌv) n. 1. (oft. pl.) covering for the hand —vt. 2. cover with, or as with glove —**glove box** or **compartment** small storage area in dashboard of car —**the gloves** 1. boxing gloves 2. boxing

glow (gləʊ) vi. 1. give out light and heat without flames 2. shine 3. experience feeling of wellbeing or satisfaction 4. be or look hot 5. burn with emotion —n. 6. shining heat 7. warmth of colour 8. feeling of wellbeing 9. ardour —**glow-worm** n. female insect giving out green light

glower ('glaʊə) vi. 1. scowl —n. 2. sullen or angry stare

gloxinia (glɒk'sɪnɪə) n. tropical plant with large bell-shaped flowers

glucose ('gluːkəʊz, -kəʊs) n. type of sugar found in fruit etc.

glue (gluː) n. 1. any natural or synthetic adhesive 2. any sticky substance —vt. 3. fasten with glue —'**gluey** a.

glum (glʌm) a. sullen, moody, gloomy

glut (glʌt) n. 1. surfeit, excessive amount —vt. 2. feed, gratify to the full or to excess 3. overstock (market etc.) with commodity (**-tt-**)

gluten ('gluːtən) n. protein present in cereal grain —'**glutinous** a. sticky, gluey

glutton[1] ('glʌtən) n. 1. greedy person 2. one with great liking or capacity for something —'**gluttonous** a. like glutton, greedy —'**gluttony** n.

glutton[2] ('glʌtən) n. wolverine

glycerin ('glɪsərɪn), **glycerine** ('glɪsərɪn, glɪsə'riːn), or **glycerol** ('glɪsərɒl) n. colourless sweet liquid with wide application in chemistry and industry

glycogen ('glaɪkəʊdʒən) n. polysaccharide consisting of glucose units: form in which carbohydrate is stored in animals —**glyco'genesis** n. —**glyco'genic** a.

glyptic ('glɪptɪk) a. pert. to carving, esp. on precious stones

gm. gram

G.M. George Medal

G-man n. 1. US sl. FBI agent 2. Irish political detective

GMT Greenwich Mean Time

gnarled (nɑːld) or **gnarly** a. 1. knobby, rugged 2. (esp. of hands) twisted

gnash (næʃ) vt. grind (teeth) together as in anger or pain

gnat (næt) n. small, biting, two-winged fly

gnaw (nɔː) v. 1. bite or chew steadily 2. (esp. with at) cause distress (to)

gneiss (naɪs) n. coarse-grained metamorphic rock

gnome (nəʊm) n. 1. legendary creature like small old man 2. Facetious, derogatory international financier

gnomic ('nəʊmɪk, 'nɒm-) a. of or like an aphorism

gnomon ('nəʊmɒn) n. 1. stationary arm that projects shadow on sundial 2. geometric figure remaining after parallelogram has been removed from corner of larger parallelogram

gnostic ('nɒstɪk) a. 1. of, relating to knowledge, esp. spiritual knowledge —n. 2. (**G-**) adherent of Gnosticism —'**Gnosticism** n. religious movement characterized by belief in intuitive spiritual knowledge: regarded as heresy by Christian Church

GNP Gross National Product

gnu (nuː) n. S Afr. antelope somewhat like ox (pl. **-s**, **gnu**)

go (gəʊ) vi. 1. move along, make way 2. be moving 3. depart 4. function 5. make specified sound 6. fail, give way, break down 7. elapse 8. be kept, put 9. be able to be put 10. result 11. (with towards) contribute to (result) 12. (with towards) tend to 13. be accepted, have force 14. become (**went** pt., **gone** pp.) —n. 15. going 16. energy, vigour 17. attempt 18. turn —'**goer** n. 1. person who attends something regularly, as in filmgoer 2. person or thing that goes, esp. very fast 3. A inf. acceptable idea etc. 4. A, NZ energetic person —'**going** n. 1. departure; farewell 2. condition of road surface with regard to walking etc. 3. inf. speed, progress etc. —a. 4. thriving (esp. in **a going concern**) 5. current; accepted 6. available —**goner**

('gɒnə) n. person beyond help or recovery, esp. person about to die —**go-ahead** n. 1. inf. permission to proceed —a. 2. enterprising, ambitious —**go-between** n. person who acts as intermediary for two people or groups —**go-by** n. sl. deliberate snub or slight (esp. in **give (a person) the go-by**) —**go-getter** n. inf. ambitious person —**go-go dancer** dancer, usu. scantily dressed, who performs rhythmic and oft. erotic modern dance routines in nightclubs etc. —**going-over** n. inf. 1. check; examination; investigation 2. castigation; thrashing (pl. **goings-over**) —**goings-on** pl.n. inf. 1. actions or conduct, esp. regarded with disapproval 2. happenings or events, esp. mysterious or suspicious —**go-kart** or **go-cart** n. see KART —**go-slow** n. deliberate slackening of the rate of production as form of industrial protest —**go down** 1. move to lower place or level; sink, decline, decrease etc. 2. be defeated; lose 3. be remembered or recorded (esp. in **go down in history**) 4. (usu. with **with**) UK fall ill; be infected

goad (gəʊd) n. 1. spiked stick for driving cattle 2. anything that urges to action 3. incentive —vt. 4. urge on 5. torment

goal (gəʊl) n. 1. end of race 2. object of effort 3. posts through which ball is to be driven in football etc. 4. the score so made —**goalkeeper** n. Sport player in goal whose duty is to prevent ball from entering it

goat (gəʊt) n. four-footed animal with long hair, horns and beard —**goa'tee** n. pointed tuftlike beard growing on chin —**goatherd** n. —**goatsucker** n. US nightjar —**get (someone's) goat** sl. annoy (someone)

gob (gɒb) n. 1. lump 2. sl. mouth —**gobbet** n. lump (of food) —**gobble** v. eat hastily, noisily or greedily

gobble ('gɒb'l) n. 1. throaty, gurgling cry of the turkey-cock —vi. 2. make this sound —**gobbler** n. male turkey

gobbledegook or **gobbledygook** ('gɒb'l-dɪgu:k) n. pretentious language, esp. as used by officials

goblet ('gɒblɪt) n. drinking cup

goblin ('gɒblɪn) n. Folklore small, usu. malevolent being

goby ('gəʊbɪ) n. small spiny-finned fish having ventral fins modified as sucker

god (gɒd) n. 1. superhuman being worshipped as having supernatural power 2. object of worship, idol 3. (G-) in monotheistic religions, the Supreme Being, creator and ruler of the universe ('**goddess** fem.) —'**godlike** a. —'**godliness** n. —'**godly** a. devout, pious —'**godchild** n. person sponsored by adults at baptism ('**godson** or '**goddaughter**) —**god-fearing** a. religious, good —'**godforsaken** a. hopeless, dismal —'**godhead** n. divine nature or deity —'**godparent** n. sponsor at baptism ('**godfather** or '**godmother**) —'**godsend** n. something unexpected but welcome —'**God'speed** interj./n. expression of good wishes for person's success and safety

godetia (gə'di:ʃə) n. annual garden plant

godwit ('gɒdwɪt) n. large shore bird of N regions

goffer ('gəʊfə) vt. 1. press pleats into (frill) 2. decorate (edges of book) —n. 3. ornamental frill made by pressing pleats 4. decoration formed by goffering books

gogga ('xɒxə) n. SA inf. insect, creepy-crawly

goggle ('gɒg'l) vi. 1. (of eyes) bulge 2. stare —pl.n. 3. protective spectacles —'**gogglebox** n. UK sl. television set

Goidelic (gɔɪ'delɪk) n. 1. N group of Celtic languages, consisting of Irish Gaelic, Scottish Gaelic and Manx —a. 2. of or characteristic of this group of languages

goitre or U.S. **goiter** ('gɔɪtə) n. enlargement of thyroid gland, in some cases nearly doubling size of neck

gold (gəʊld) n. 1. yellow precious metal 2. coins made of this 3. wealth 4. beautiful or precious thing 5. colour of gold —a. 6. of, like gold —'**golden** a. —'**goldcrest** n. small bird with yellow crown —**gold-digger** n. woman skilful in extracting money from men —**golden age** 1. Class. myth. first and best age of mankind, when existence was happy, prosperous and innocent 2. most flourishing period, esp. in history of art or nation —**golden eagle** large eagle of mountainous regions of N hemisphere —**Golden Fleece** Gr. myth. fleece of winged ram stolen by Jason and Argonauts —**golden handshake** inf. money given to employee on retirement or for loss of employment —**golden mean** middle course between extremes —**golden'rod** n. tall plant with golden flower spikes —**golden rule** important principle —**golden wedding** fiftieth wedding anniversary —'**goldfield** n. place where gold deposits are known to exist —'**goldfinch** n. bird with yellow feathers —'**goldfish** n. any of various ornamental pond or aquarium fish —**gold plate** 1. thin coating of gold, usu. produced by electroplating 2. vessels or utensils made of gold —**gold-plate** vt. —**gold rush** large-scale migration of people to territory where gold has been found —'**goldsmith** n. 1. dealer in articles made of gold 2. artisan who makes such articles —**gold standard** financial arrangement whereby currencies of countries accepting it are expressed in fixed terms of gold

golf (gɒlf) n. 1. outdoor game in which small hard ball is struck with clubs into a succession of holes —vi. 2. play this game —'**golfer** n. —**golf club** 1. long-shafted club with wood or metal head used to strike golf ball 2. (premises of) association of golf players, usu. having its own course and facilities —**golf course** or **links** area of open land on which golf is played

Goliath (gə'laɪəθ) n. Bible Philistine giant killed by David with stone from sling

golliwog ('gɒlɪwɒg) n. black-faced doll

golly ('gɒlɪ) interj. exclamation of mild surprise

goloshes (gə'lɒʃɪz) pl.n. see GALOSHES

-gon (comb. form) figure having specified number of angles, as in pentagon

gonad ('gɒnæd) n. gland producing gametes

gondola ('gɒndələ) n. Venetian canal boat —**gondo'lier** n. rower of gondola

gone (gɒn) pp. of GO

gonfalon ('gɒnfələn) n. 1. banner hanging from crossbar, used esp. by certain medieval Italian republics 2. battle flag suspended crosswise on staff, usu. having serrated edge

gong (gɒŋ) n. 1. metal plate with turned rim which resounds as bell when struck with soft mallet 2. anything used thus

gonorrhoea or esp. U.S. **gonorrhea** (gɒnə'rɪə) n. a venereal disease

good (gʊd) a. 1. commendable 2. right 3. proper 4. excellent 5. beneficial 6. well-behaved 7. virtuous 8. kind 9. financially safe or secure 10. adequate 11. sound 12. valid (**'better** comp., **best** sup.) —n. 13. benefit 14. wellbeing 15. profit —pl. 16. property 17. wares —**'goodly** a. large, considerable —**'goodness** n. —**Good Book** the Bible —**good-hearted** a. kind and generous —**Good Samaritan** 1. N.T. figure in one of Christ's parables who is example of compassion towards those in distress 2. kindly person who helps another in difficulty —**good sort** inf. agreeable person —**good turn** helpful, friendly act; good deed; favour —**good will** 1. kindly feeling, heartiness 2. value of a business in reputation etc. over and above its tangible assets —**goody-goody** n. 1. inf. smugly virtuous or sanctimonious person —a. 2. smug and sanctimonious

goodbye (gʊd'baɪ) interj./n. form of address on parting

gooey ('guːɪ) a. inf. sticky, soft —**goo** n. inf. 1. sticky substance 2. coy or sentimental language or ideas

goof (guːf) inf. n. 1. mistake 2. stupid person —vi. 3. make mistake —**'goofy** a. silly, sloppy

googly ('guːglɪ) n. Cricket ball which changes direction unexpectedly on the bounce

goon (guːn) n. inf. stupid fellow

goosander (guː'sændə) n. type of duck

goose (guːs) n. 1. web-footed bird 2. its flesh 3. simpleton (pl. **geese**) —**goose flesh** bristling of skin due to cold, fright —**goose step** formal parade step

gooseberry ('gʊzbərɪ, -brɪ) n. 1. thorny shrub 2. its hairy fruit 3. inf. unwelcome third party (oft. in **play gooseberry**)

gopher ('gəʊfə) n. various species of Amer. burrowing rodents

Gordian knot ('gɔːdɪən) 1. in Greek legend, complicated knot, tied by King Gordius, that Alexander the Great cut with

sword 2. intricate problem (esp. in **cut the Gordian knot**)

gore¹ (gɔː) n. (dried) blood from wound —**'gorily** adv. —**'gory** a. 1. horrific; bloodthirsty 2. involving bloodshed and killing 3. covered in gore

gore² (gɔː) vt. pierce with horns

gore³ (gɔː) n. 1. triangular piece inserted to shape garment —vt. 2. shape thus

gorge (gɔːdʒ) n. 1. ravine 2. disgust, resentment —vi. 3. eat greedily —**'gorget** n. armour, ornamentation or clothing for throat —**gorge oneself** stuff oneself with food

gorgeous ('gɔːdʒəs) a. 1. splendid, showy, dazzling 2. inf. extremely pleasing

Gorgon ('gɔːgən) n. terrifying or repulsive woman

Gorgonzola (gɔːgən'zəʊlə) n. blue-veined Italian cheese

gorilla (gə'rɪlə) n. largest anthropoid ape, found in Afr.

gormandize or **-dise** ('gɔːməndaɪz) v. eat (food) hurriedly or like a glutton

gormless ('gɔːmlɪs) a. inf. stupid

gorse (gɔːs) n. prickly shrub

gory ('gɔːrɪ) a. see GORE¹

gosh (gɒʃ) interj. exclamation of mild surprise or wonder

goshawk ('gɒshɔːk) n. large hawk

gosling ('gɒzlɪŋ) n. young goose

gospel ('gɒspˀl) n. 1. unquestionable truth 2. (G-) any of first four books of New Testament

gossamer ('gɒsəmə) n. 1. filmy substance like spider's web 2. thin gauze or silk fabric

gossip ('gɒsɪp) n. 1. idle (malicious) talk about other persons, esp. regardless of facts 2. one who talks thus (also **'gossipmonger**) —vi. 3. engage in gossip 4. chatter —**gossip column** part of newspaper devoted to gossip about well-known people

got (gɒt) pt./pp. of GET

Goth (gɒθ) n. 1. member of East Germanic people who invaded Roman Empire from 3rd to 5th cent. 2. rude or barbaric person —**'Gothic** a. 1. Archit. of the pointed arch style common in Europe from 12th–16th centuries 2. of Goths 3. (sometimes g-) barbarous 4. (sometimes g-) of literary style characterized by gloom, the grotesque, and the supernatural —n. 5. (of type) German black letter

gotten ('gɒtˀn) US pp. of GET

gouache (gʊ'ɑːʃ) n. 1. painting technique using opaque watercolour in which pigments are bound with glue (also **body colour**) 2. paint used in this technique 3. painting done by this method

Gouda ('gaʊdə) n. large, flat, round Dutch cheese with mild flavour

gouge (gaʊdʒ) vt. (usu. with out) 1. scoop out 2. force out —n. 3. chisel with curved cutting edge

goulash ('guːlæʃ) n. stew of meat and

vegetables seasoned with paprika (*also* **Hungarian goulash**)

gourd (guəd) *n.* 1. trailing or climbing plant 2. its large fleshy fruit 3. its rind as vessel

gourmand ('guəmənd) *or* **gormand** ('gɔːmənd) *n.* glutton

gourmet ('guəmeɪ) *n.* 1. connoisseur of wine, food 2. epicure

gout (gaut) *n.* disease characterized by inflammation, *esp.* of joints —**'gouty** *a.*

Gov. *or* **gov.** 1. government 2. governor

govern ('gʌv'n) *vt.* 1. rule, direct, guide, control 2. decide, determine 3. be followed by (grammatical case *etc.*) —**'governable** *a.* —**'governance** *n.* act of governing —**'governess** *n.* woman teacher, *esp.* in private household —**'government** *n.* 1. exercise of political authority in directing a people, state *etc.* 2. system by which community is ruled 3. body of people in charge of government of state 4. ministry 5. executive power 6. control 7. direction 8. exercise of authority —**govern'mental** *a.* —**'governor** *n.* 1. one who governs, *esp.* one invested with supreme authority in state *etc.* 2. chief administrator of an institution 3. member of committee responsible for an organization or institution 4. regulator for speed of engine —**governor general** 1. representative of Crown in dominion of commonwealth 2. UK governor with jurisdiction over other governors (*pl.* **governors general, governor generals**)

Govt. *or* **govt.** government

gown (gaun) *n.* 1. loose flowing outer garment 2. woman's (long) dress 3. official robe, as in university *etc.*

goy (gɔɪ) *n. sl.* derogatory word used by Jews for non-Jew (*pl.* **goyim** ('gɔɪm), **-s**)

G.P. General Practitioner

G.P.O. General Post Office

Gr. 1. Grecian 2. Greece 3. Greek

gr. 1. grain(s) 2. gram(me)(s) 3. gross

grab (græb) *vt.* 1. grasp suddenly 2. snatch (**-bb-**) —*n.* 3. sudden clutch 4. quick attempt to seize 5. device or implement for clutching

grace (greɪs) *n.* 1. charm, elegance 2. accomplishment 3. good will, favour 4. sense of propriety 5. postponement granted 6. short thanksgiving before or after meal 7. title of duke or archbishop —*pl.* 8. affectation of manner (*esp. in* **airs and graces**) —*vt.* 9. add grace to, honour —**'graceful** *a.* —**'gracefully** *adv.* —**'graceless** *a.* shameless, depraved —**'gracious** *a.* 1. favourable 2. kind 3. pleasing 4. indulgent, beneficent, condescending —**'graciously** *adv.* —**grace note** *Mus.* melodic ornament

Graces ('greɪsɪz) *pl.n. Gr. myth.* three sister goddesses, givers of charm and beauty

grade (greɪd) *n.* 1. step, stage 2. degree of rank *etc.* 3. class 4. mark, rating 5. slope —*vt.* 6. arrange in classes 7. assign grade to 8. level (ground), move (earth) with grader —**gradation** (grə'deɪʃən) *n.* 1. series of degrees or steps 2. each of them 3. arrangement in steps 4. in painting, gradual passing from one shade *etc.* to another —**'grader** *n.* 1. person or thing that grades 2. machine with wide blade used in road making —**make the grade** succeed

gradient ('greɪdɪənt) *n.* (degree of) slope

gradual ('grædjuəl) *a.* 1. taking place by degrees 2. slow and steady 3. not steep —**'gradually** *adv.*

graduate ('grædjueɪt) *vi.* 1. take university degree —*vt.* 2. divide into degrees 3. mark, arrange according to scale —*n.* ('grædjuɪt) 4. holder of university degree —**gradu'ation** *n.* —**graduated pension** UK national pension scheme in which employees' contributions are scaled in accordance with their wage rate

Graeco- *or esp. U.S.* **Greco-** ('griːkəʊ-, 'grekəʊ-) (*comb. form*) Greek, as in *Graeco-Roman*

graffiti (græ'fiːtiː) *pl.n.* (*oft.* obscene) writing, drawing on walls (*sing.* **graf'fito**)

graft¹ (grɑːft) *n.* 1. shoot of plant set in stalk of another 2. the process 3. surgical transplant of skin to an area of body in need of tissue —*vt.* 4. insert (shoot) in another stalk 5. transplant (living tissue in surgery)

graft² (grɑːft) *n.* 1. *inf.* hard work 2. self-advancement, profit by unfair means, *esp.* through official or political privilege 3. bribe 4. swindle —**'grafter** *n.*

Grail (greɪl) *n. see* **Holy Grail** *at* HOLY

grain (greɪn) *n.* 1. seed, fruit of cereal plant 2. wheat and allied plants 3. small hard particle 4. unit of weight, 1/7000 of pound avoirdupois (0.0648 gram) 5. texture 6. arrangement of fibres 7. any very small amount 8. natural temperament or disposition —**'grainy** *a.*

gram *or* **gramme** (græm) *n.* unit of weight in metric system, one thousandth of a kilogram

-gram (*comb. form*) drawing; something written or recorded, as in *hexagram*, *telegram*

gramineous (grə'mɪnɪəs) *a.* 1. of or belonging to grass family 2. resembling grass; grasslike (*also* **graminaceous** (græmɪ'neɪʃəs))

graminivorous (græmɪ'nɪvərəs) *a.* (of animals) feeding on grass

grammar ('græmə) *n.* 1. science of structure and usages of language 2. book on this 3. correct use of words —**grammarian** (grə'mɛərɪən) *n.* —**gram'matical** *a.* according to grammar —**gram'matically** *adv.* —**grammar school** *esp.* formerly, state-maintained secondary school providing education with strong academic bias

gramophone ('græməfəʊn) *n.* instrument for reproducing sounds on discs, record-player

grampus ('græmpəs) n. 1. type of dolphin 2. person who huffs, breathes heavily

gran (græn) or **granny** ('grænɪ) n. inf. grandmother —**granny flat** flat in or added to house (for elderly parent) —**granny knot** or **granny's knot** reef knot with ends crossed wrong way

granary ('grænərɪ; U.S. 'greɪnərɪ) n. 1. storehouse for grain 2. rich grain growing region

grand (grænd) a. 1. imposing 2. magnificent 3. majestic 4. noble 5. splendid 6. eminent 7. lofty 8. chief, of chief importance 9. final (total) —**grandeur** ('grændʒə) n. 1. nobility 2. magnificence 3. dignity —**gran'diloquence** n. —**gran'diloquent** a. pompous in speech —**gran'diloquently** adv. —'**grandiose** a. 1. imposing 2. affectedly grand 3. striking —**grandchild** ('græntʃaɪld) n. child of one's child (**grandson** ('grænsʌn, 'grænd-) or **granddaughter** ('grændɔːtə)) —**grand duke** 1. prince or nobleman who rules territory, state or principality 2. son or male descendant in male line of Russian tsar —**grandfather clock** long-pendulum clock in tall standing wooden case —**grand jury** Law esp. in U.S.A., jury summoned to inquire into accusations of crime and ascertain whether evidence is adequate to found indictment —**Grand National** annual steeplechase run at Aintree, Liverpool —**grand opera** opera with serious plot and fully composed text —**grandparent** ('grænpɛərənt, 'grænd-) n. parent of parent (**grandfather** ('grænfɑːðə, 'grænd-) or **grandmother** ('grænmʌðə, 'grænd-)) —**grand piano** large harpshaped piano with horizontal strings —**grandstand** ('grænstænd, 'grænd-) n. structure with tiered seats for spectators

grande dame (grãd 'dam) Fr. woman regarded as most experienced or prominent member of her profession etc.

grandee (græn'diː) n. Spanish nobleman of highest rank

grand mal ('grɒn 'mæl) form of epilepsy characterized by convulsions and loss of consciousness

Grand Prix (Fr. grã 'pri) any of series of international formula motor races

grange (greɪndʒ) n. country house with farm buildings

granite ('grænɪt) n. hard crystalline igneous rock —**gra'nitic** a.

granivorous (græ'nɪvərəs) a. feeding on grain or seeds

grant (grɑːnt) vt. 1. consent to fulfil (request) 2. permit 3. bestow 4. admit —n. 5. sum of money provided by government for specific purpose, as education 6. gift 7. allowance, concession —**gran'tee** n. —'**granter** or (Law) '**grantor** n. —**grant-in-aid** n. money granted by central to local government for programme etc. (pl. **grants-in-aid**)

granule ('grænjuːl) n. small grain —'**granular** a. of or like grains —'**granu-**

late vt. 1. form into grains —vi. 2. take form of grains —**granu'lation** n. —**granulated sugar** coarsely ground white sugar

grape (greɪp) n. fruit of vine —**grape hyacinth** plant with clusters of small, rounded blue flowers —'**grapeshot** n. bullets scattering when fired —'**grapevine** n. 1. grape-bearing vine 2. inf. unofficial means of conveying information

grapefruit ('greɪpfruːt) n. subtropical citrus fruit

graph (grɑːf, græf) n. drawing depicting relation of different numbers, quantities etc. (also **chart**)

-**graph** (n. comb. form) 1. instrument that writes or records, as in telegraph 2. writing, record; drawing, as in autograph, lithograph —**grapher** (n. comb. form) 1. person skilled in subject, as in geographer, photographer 2. person who writes or draws in specified way, as in stenographer, lithographer —**graphic(al)** (a. comb. form) —**graphy** (n. comb. form) 1. form of writing, representing etc., as in calligraphy, photography 2. art; descriptive science, as in choreography, oceanography

graphic ('græfɪk) or **graphical** a. 1. vividly descriptive 2. of, in, relating to, writing, drawing, painting etc. —'**graphically** adv. —'**graphics** pl.n. 1. (with sing. v.) art of drawing in accordance with mathematical principles 2. (with sing. v.) study of writing systems 3. (with pl. v.) drawings etc. in layout of magazine or book —'**graphite** n. form of carbon (used in pencils) —**gra'phology** n. study of handwriting —**graphic arts** fine or applied visual arts based on drawing or use of line, esp. illustration and print-making —**graphic equalizer** electronic device for cutting or boosting selected frequencies, using small linear faders —**graph paper** paper with intersecting lines for drawing graphs etc.

grapnel ('græpnˈl) n. 1. hooked iron instrument for seizing anything 2. small anchor with several flukes

grapple ('græpˈl) v. 1. come to grips, wrestle 2. cope, contend —n. 3. grappling 4. grapnel —**grappling iron** or **hook** grapnel, esp. for securing ships

grasp (grɑːsp) v. 1. (try, struggle to) seize hold (of) —vt. 2. understand —n. 3. act of grasping 4. grip 5. comprehension —'**grasping** a. greedy, avaricious

grass (grɑːs) n. 1. common type of plant with jointed stems and long narrow leaves (including cereals, bamboo etc.) 2. such plants grown as lawn 3. pasture 4. sl. marijuana 5. sl. informer, esp. criminal who betrays others to police —vt. 6. cover with grass —vi. 7. sl. (with on) inform —**grass hockey** C hockey played on field —'**grasshopper** n. jumping, chirping insect —**grass roots** fundamentals —'**grassroots** a. coming from ordinary people, the rank and file —**grass widow** wife whose husband is absent

grate¹ (greɪt) vt. 1. rub into small bits on rough surface —vi. 2. rub with harsh noise 3. have irritating effect —**'grater** n. utensil with rough surface for reducing substance to small particles

grate² (greɪt) n. framework of metal bars for holding fuel in fireplace —**'grating** n. framework of parallel or latticed bars covering opening

grateful ('greɪtful) a. 1. thankful 2. appreciative 3. pleasing —**'gratefully** adv. —**'gratefulness** n. —**gratitude** ('grætɪtjuːd) n. sense of being thankful for favour

gratify ('grætɪfaɪ) vt. 1. satisfy 2. please 3. indulge —**gratifi'cation** n.

gratin (Fr. gra'tɛ̃) n. 1. method of cooking with covering of breadcrumbs to form light crust 2. dish so cooked

gratis ('greɪtɪs, 'grætɪs, 'grɑːtɪs) adv./a. free, for nothing

gratuitous (grə'tjuːɪtəs) a. 1. given free 2. uncalled for —**gra'tuitously** adv. —**gra'tuity** n. 1. gift of money for services rendered 2. donation

gravamen (grə'veɪmɛn) n. 1. Law part of accusation weighing most heavily against accused 2. Law substance of complaint 3. rare grievance (pl. -**vamina** (-'væmɪnə))

grave¹ (greɪv) n. 1. hole dug to bury corpse 2. Poet. death —**'gravestone** n. monument on grave —**'graveyard** n.

grave² (greɪv) a. 1. serious, weighty 2. dignified, solemn 3. plain, dark in colour 4. deep in note —**'gravely** adv.

grave³ (greɪv) vt. clean (ship's bottom) by scraping —**graving dock** dry dock

grave⁴ (grɑːv) n. Phonet. accent (`) used to indicate quality of vowel, full pronunciation of syllable etc.

gravel ('grævˀl) n. 1. small stones 2. coarse sand —vt. 3. cover with gravel (-**ll**-) —**'gravelly** a.

graven ('greɪvˀn) a. carved, engraved

Graves (grɑːv) n. 1. (sometimes g-) white or red wine from district around Bordeaux, France 2. dry or medium sweet white wine from any country

gravid ('grævɪd) a. pregnant

gravimetric (grævɪ'mɛtrɪk) a. 1. of measurement by weight 2. Chem. of analysis of quantities by weight

gravitate ('grævɪteɪt) vi. 1. move by gravity 2. tend (towards centre of attraction) 3. sink, settle down —**gravi'tation** n.

gravity ('grævɪtɪ) n. 1. force of attraction of one body for another, esp. of objects to the earth 2. heaviness 3. importance 4. seriousness 5. staidness

gravy ('greɪvɪ) n. 1. juices from meat in cooking 2. sauce for food made from these —**gravy boat** small boat-shaped vessel for serving gravy

gray (greɪ) see GREY —**'grayling** n. fish of salmon family

graze¹ (greɪz) v. feed on (grass, pasture)

—**'grazier** n. one who raises cattle for market —**'grazing** n. 1. vegetation on ranges or pastures that is available for livestock to feed upon 2. land on which this is growing

graze² (greɪz) vt. 1. touch lightly in passing, scratch, scrape —n. 2. grazing 3. abrasion

grease (griːs) n. 1. soft melted fat of animals 2. thick oil as lubricant —vt. (griːs, griːz) 3. apply grease to —**'greaser** n. 1. one who greases 2. inf. mechanic 3. sl. unpleasant, dirty person —**'greasiness** n. —**'greasy** a. —**grease gun** appliance for injecting oil or grease into machinery —**grease monkey** inf. mechanic —**'greasepaint** n. theatrical make-up —**grease the palm** (or **hand**) **of** bribe

great (greɪt) a. 1. large, big 2. important 3. pre-eminent, distinguished 4. inf. excellent —**'greatly** adv. —**'greatness** n. —**Great Bear** see URSA MAJOR —**great circle** circular section of sphere with radius equal to that of sphere —**'greatcoat** n. overcoat, esp. military —**Great Dane** breed of very large dog —**Great Russian** n. 1. Linguis. Russian 2. member of chief East Slavonic people of Russia —a. 3. of this people or their language —**great seal** (oft. G- S-) principal seal of nation etc. used to authenticate documents of highest importance —**Great War** World War I

great- (comb. form) indicates a degree further removed in relationship, as in great-grandfather

greave (griːv) n. (oft. pl.) armour for leg below knee

grebe (griːb) n. aquatic bird

Grecian ('griːʃən) a. of (ancient) Greece —**Grecian profile** profile in which nose and forehead form almost straight line

Greco- (comb. form) esp. US see GRAECO-

greed (griːd) n. excessive consumption of, desire for, food, wealth —**'greedily** adv. —**'greediness** n. voracity of appetite —**'greedy** a. 1. gluttonous 2. eagerly desirous 3. voracious 4. covetous

Greek (griːk) n. 1. native language of Greece —a. 2. of Greece, the Greeks or the Greek language —**Greek cross** cross with four arms of same length —**Greek Orthodox Church** 1. established Church of Greece, in which Metropolitan of Athens has primacy of honour (also **Greek Church**) 2. see Orthodox Church at ORTHODOX

green (griːn) a. 1. of colour between blue and yellow 2. grass-coloured 3. emerald 4. unripe 5. (of bacon) unsmoked 6. inexperienced 7. gullible 8. envious 9. (oft. G-) concerned with preserving the environment —n. 10. colour 11. area of grass, esp. for playing bowls etc. 12. (oft. G-) member of political movement whose main concern is preserving the environment —pl. 13. green vegetables —**'greenery** n. vegetation —**green bean** any bean plant, such as French bean, having narrow green edible pods —**green belt** area of farms, open country around a town —**Green Cross Code** UK code for children giving rules for road safety —**green-eyed** a. jealous, envious —**green-eyed monster** jealousy, envy —'**greenfinch** n. European finch with dull green plumage in male —**green fingers** talent for gardening —'**greenfly** n. aphid, small green garden pest —'**greengage** n. kind of plum —'**greengrocer** n. dealer in vegetables and fruit —'**greengrocery** n. —'**greenhorn** n. inexperienced person, newcomer —'**greenhouse** n. glasshouse for rearing plants —'**greenkeeper** n. person responsible for maintaining golf course etc. —**green light** 1. signal to go, esp. green traffic light 2. permission to proceed with project etc. —**green paper** (oft. G- P-) UK government document containing policy proposals to be discussed, esp. by Parliament —**green pepper** green unripe fruit of sweet pepper, eaten raw or cooked —**green pound** unit of account used in calculating Britain's contributions to and payments from Community Agricultural Fund of EEC —'**greenroom** n. room for actors when offstage —'**greenshank** n. large European sandpiper —'**greenstick fracture** fracture in children in which bone is partly bent and splinters only on convex side of bend —'**greenstone** n. New Zealand jade —'**greensward** n. turf

Greenwich Mean Time or **Greenwich Time** ('grɪnɪdʒ) local time of 0° meridian passing through Greenwich, England: standard time for Britain and basis for calculating times throughout world

greet (griːt) vt. 1. meet with expressions of welcome 2. accost, salute 3. receive —'**greeting** n.

gregarious (grɪ'gɛərɪəs) a. 1. fond of company, sociable 2. living in flocks —gre'**gariousness** n.

Gregorian calendar (grɪ'gɔːrɪən) calendar introduced by Pope Gregory XIII, whereby ordinary year is made to consist of 365 days

Gregorian chant see PLAINSONG

gremlin ('grɛmlɪn) n. imaginary being blamed for mechanical and other troubles

grenade (grɪ'neɪd) n. explosive shell or bomb, thrown by hand or shot from rifle —**grenadier** (grɛnə'dɪə) n. 1. soldier of Grenadier Guards 2. formerly, grenade thrower

grenadine (grɛnə'diːn, 'grɛnədiːn) n. syrup made from pomegranate juice, for sweetening and colouring drinks

grew (gruː) pt. of GROW

grey or U.S. **gray** (greɪ) a. 1. between black and white, as ashes or lead 2. clouded 3. dismal 4. turning white 5. aged 6. intermediate, indeterminate —n. 7. grey colour 8. grey or whitish horse —**Grey Friar** Franciscan friar —'**greyhen** n. female of black grouse —'**greyhound** n. swift slender dog used in coursing and

racing —'**greylag** or **greylag goose** n. large grey Eurasian goose —**grey matter** 1. greyish tissue of brain and spinal cord, containing nerve cell bodies and fibres 2. inf. brains; intellect

grid (grɪd) n. 1. network of horizontal and vertical lines, bars etc. 2. any interconnecting system of links 3. national network of electricity supply

griddle ('grɪdl) n. flat iron plate for cooking (also '**girdle**)

gridiron ('grɪdaɪən) n. 1. frame of metal bars for grilling 2. (field of play for) American football

grief (griːf) n. deep sorrow —'**grievance** n. real or imaginary grounds for complaint —**grieve** vi. 1. feel grief —vt. 2. cause grief to —'**grievous** a. 1. painful, oppressive 2. very serious —**grief-stricken** a. stricken with grief; sorrowful

griffin ('grɪfɪn), **griffon**, or **gryphon** n. fabulous monster with eagle's head and wings and lion's body

grill (grɪl) n. 1. device on cooker to radiate heat downwards 2. food cooked under grill 3. gridiron —v. 4. cook (food) under grill —vt. 5. subject to severe questioning —'**grilling** a. 1. very hot —n. 2. severe cross-examination —'**grillroom** n. restaurant where grilled food is served

grille or **grill** (grɪl) n. grating, crosswork of bars over opening

grilse (grɪls) n. salmon at stage when it returns for first time from sea (pl. -s, **grilse**)

grim (grɪm) a. 1. stern 2. of stern or forbidding aspect, relentless 3. joyless —'**grimly** adv.

grimace (grɪ'meɪs) n. 1. wry face —vi. 2. pull wry face

grimalkin (grɪ'mælkɪn, -'mɔːl-) n. 1. old cat, esp. female cat 2. crotchety or shrewish old woman

grime (graɪm) n. 1. ingrained dirt, soot —vt. 2. soil, dirty, blacken —'**grimy** a.

grin (grɪn) vi. 1. show teeth, as in laughter (-nn-) —n. 2. grinning smile

grind (graɪnd) vt. 1. crush to powder 2. oppress 3. make sharp, smooth 4. grate —vi. 5. perform action of grinding 6. inf. work, esp. study hard 7. grate (ground pt./pp.) —n. 8. inf. hard work 9. act of grinding —'**grinder** n. —'**grindstone** n. stone used for grinding

gringo ('grɪŋgəʊ) n. in Mexico, contemptuous name for foreigner, esp. Englishman or American (pl. -s)

grip (grɪp) n. 1. firm hold, grasp 2. grasping power 3. mastery 4. handle 5. suitcase or travelling bag (also '**handgrip**) —vt. 6. grasp or hold tightly 7. hold interest or attention of (-pp-)

gripe (graɪp) vi. 1. inf. complain (persistently) —n. 2. intestinal pain (esp. in infants) 3. inf. complaint

grippe or **grip** (grɪp) n. influenza

grisly ('grɪzlɪ) a. grim, causing terror, ghastly

grist (grɪst) *n.* corn to be ground —**grist to** (*or* **for**) **the** (*or* **one's**) **mill** something which can be turned to advantage

gristle ('grɪs'l) *n.* cartilage, tough flexible tissue

grit (grɪt) *n.* **1.** rough particles of sand **2.** coarse sandstone **3.** courage —*n./a.* **4.** (**G**-) **C** *inf.* Liberal —*pl.* **5.** wheat *etc.* coarsely ground —*vt.* **6.** clench, grind (teeth) (**-tt-**) —'**grittiness** *n.* —'**gritty** *a.*

grizzle[1] ('grɪz'l) *v.* make, become grey —'**grizzled** *a.* —'**grizzly** *a.* —**grizzly bear** large Amer. bear

grizzle[2] ('grɪz'l) *vi. inf.* grumble, whine, complain

groan (grəʊn) *vi.* **1.** make low, deep sound of grief or pain **2.** be in pain or overburdened —*n.* **3.** groaning sound

groat (grəʊt) *n.* formerly, silver coin worth four pennies

groats (grəʊts) *pl.n.* hulled and crushed grain of oats, wheat or certain other cereals

grocer ('grəʊsə) *n.* dealer in foodstuffs —'**groceries** *pl.n.* commodities sold by grocer —'**grocery** *n.* trade, premises of grocer

grog (grɒg) *n.* spirit (*esp.* rum) and water —'**groggy** *a. inf.* unsteady, shaky, weak

grogram ('grɒgrəm) *n.* coarse fabric of silk, wool, or silk mixed with wool or mohair, formerly used for clothing

groin (grɔɪn) *n.* **1.** fold where legs meet abdomen **2.** euphemism for genitals **3.** *Archit.* edge made by intersection of two vaults —*vt.* **4.** build with groins

groom (gru:m, grʊm) *n.* **1.** person caring for horses **2.** *see* **bridegroom** *at* BRIDE **3.** officer in royal household —*vt.* **4.** tend or look after **5.** brush or clean (*esp.* horse) **6.** train (someone for something) —'**grooms- man** *n.* friend attending bridegroom —**well-groomed** *a.* neat, smart

groove (gru:v) *n.* **1.** narrow channel, hollow, *esp.* cut by tool **2.** rut, routine —*vt.* **3.** cut groove in —'**groovy** *a. sl.* fashionable, exciting

grope (grəʊp) *vi.* feel about, search blindly

groper ('grəʊpə) *or* **grouper** *n.* large marine fish of warm and tropical seas

grosbeak ('grəʊsbiːk, 'grɒs-) *n.* finch with large powerful bill

grosgrain ('grəʊgreɪn) *n.* heavy ribbed silk or rayon fabric used for trimming clothes *etc.*

gros point (grəʊ) **1.** needlepoint stitch covering two horizontal and two vertical threads **2.** work done in this stitch

gross (grəʊs) *a.* **1.** very fat **2.** total, not net **3.** coarse **4.** indecent **5.** flagrant **6.** thick, rank —*n.* **7.** twelve dozen —'**grossly** *adv.* —**gross national product** total value of final goods and services produced annually by nation

grotesque (grəʊ'tɛsk) *a.* **1.** (horribly) distorted **2.** absurd —*n.* **3.** 16th-cent. decorative style using distorted human, animal and plant forms **4.** grotesque person, thing —**gro'tesquely** *adv.*

grotto ('grɒtəʊ) *n.* cave

grotty ('grɒtɪ) *a. inf.* dirty, untidy, unpleasant

grouch (graʊtʃ) *inf. n.* **1.** persistent grumbler **2.** discontented mood —*vi.* **3.** grumble, be peevish

ground[1] (graʊnd) *n.* **1.** surface of earth **2.** soil, earth **3.** (*oft. pl.*) reason, motive **4.** coating to work on with paint **5.** background, main surface worked on in painting, embroidery *etc.* **6.** special area **7.** bottom of sea —*pl.* **8.** dregs, *esp.* from coffee **9.** enclosed land round house —*vt.* **10.** establish **11.** instruct (in elements) **12.** place on ground —*vi.* **13.** run ashore —'**grounded** *a.* (of aircraft) unable or not permitted to fly —'**grounding** *n.* basic general knowledge of a subject —'**ground- less** *a.* without reason —**ground crew** group of people in charge of maintenance and repair of aircraft —**ground floor** floor of building level or almost level with ground —'**groundnut** *n.* **1.** earthnut **2.** peanut —'**groundsheet** *n.* waterproof sheet on ground under tent *etc.* —'**groundsman** *n.* person employed to maintain sports ground *etc.* —'**ground- speed** *n.* aircraft's speed in relation to ground —**ground swell 1.** considerable swell of sea, oft. caused by distant storm **2.** rapidly developing general opinion —'**groundwork** *n.* **1.** preliminary work as foundation or basis **2.** ground or back- ground of painting *etc.* —**get in on the ground floor** *inf.* be in project *etc.* from its inception

ground[2] (graʊnd) *pt./pp.* of GRIND

groundsel ('graʊnsəl) *n.* yellow flowered plant

group (gru:p) *n.* **1.** number of persons or things considered as collective unit **2.** number of persons bound together by common interests *etc.* **3.** small musical band of players or singers **4.** class **5.** two or more figures forming one artistic design —*v.* **6.** place, fall into group —**group captain** officer holding commissioned rank senior to squadron leader but junior to air commodore in British R.A.F. and certain other air forces —**group therapy** *Psych.* simultaneous treatment of number of individuals brought together to share their problems in group discussion

grouper ('gru:pə) *n. see* GROPER

grouse[1] (graʊs) *n.* **1.** game bird **2.** its flesh (*pl.* **grouse**)

grouse[2] (graʊs) *vi.* **1.** grumble, complain —*n.* **2.** complaint —'**grouser** *n.* grumbler

grout (graʊt) *n.* **1.** thin fluid mortar —*vt.* **2.** fill up with grout

grove (grəʊv) *n.* **1.** small group of trees **2.** road lined with trees

grovel ('grɒv'l) *vi.* **1.** abase oneself **2.** lie face down (**-ll-**)

grow (grəʊ) *vi.* **1.** develop naturally **2.** increase in size, height *etc.* **3.** be produced

4. become by degrees —vt. 5. produce by cultivation (**grew** pt., **grown** pp.) —**growth** n. 1. growing 2. increase 3. what has grown or is growing —**growing pains** 1. pains in joints sometimes experienced by growing children 2. difficulties besetting new enterprise in early stages —**grown-up** a./n. adult

growl (graʊl) vi. 1. make low guttural sound of anger 2. rumble 3. murmur, complain —n. 4. act or sound of growling

groyne or esp. U.S. **groin** (grɔɪn) n. wall or jetty built out from riverbank or shore to control erosion

grub (grʌb) vt. 1. (oft. with up or out) dig superficially 2. root up —vi. 3. dig, rummage 4. plod (**-bb-**) —n. 5. larva of insect 6. sl. food —**grubby** a. dirty

grudge (grʌdʒ) vt. 1. be unwilling to give, allow —n. 2. ill will

gruel ('gru:əl) n. food of oatmeal etc., boiled in milk or water —**gruelling** or U.S. **grueling** a./n. exhausting, severe (experience)

gruesome ('gru:səm) a. fearful, horrible, grisly —**gruesomeness** n.

gruff (grʌf) a. rough in manner or voice, surly —**gruffly** adv.

grumble ('grʌmb'l) vi. 1. complain 2. rumble, murmur 3. make growling sounds —n. 4. complaint 5. low growl —**grumbler** n.

grumpy ('grʌmpɪ) or **grumpish** a. ill-tempered, surly —**grumpily** or **grumpishly** adv.

grunt (grʌnt) vi. 1. make sound characteristic of pig —n. 2. deep, hoarse sound of pig 3. gruff noise

Gruyère or **Gruyère cheese** ('gru:jɛə) n. pale yellow whole milk cheese with holes

gryphon ('grɪf'n) n. see GRIFFIN

grysbok ('graɪsbɒk) n. small Afr. antelope

G.S. 1. General Secretary 2. General Staff

G-string n. 1. very small covering for genitals 2. Mus. string tuned to G

G-suit n. close-fitting garment worn by crew of high-speed aircraft, pressurized to prevent blackout during manoeuvres

GT gran turismo (touring car, used of (sports) car capable of high speed)

guanaco (gwɑːˈnɑːkəʊ) n. cud-chewing S Amer. mammal closely related to domesticated llama (pl. **-s**)

guano ('gwɑːnəʊ) n. sea bird manure (pl. **-s**)

guarantee (gærənˈtiː) n. 1. formal assurance, esp. in writing, that product etc. will meet certain standards, last for given time etc. —vt. 2. give guarantee of, for something 3. secure (against risk etc.) (**guaran'teed, guaran'teeing**) —**guaran'tor** n. one who undertakes fulfilment of another's promises —**guaranty** n. 1. pledge of responsibility for fulfilling another person's obligations in case of default 2. thing given or taken as security for guaranty 3. act of providing security 4. guarantor —v. 5. guarantee

guard (gɑːd) vt. 1. protect, defend —vi. 2. be careful, take precautions —n. 3. person, group that protects, supervises, keeps watch 4. sentry 5. soldiers protecting anything 6. official in charge of train 7. protection 8. screen for enclosing anything dangerous 9. protector 10. posture of defence —pl. 11. (G-) any of certain British regiments —**guarded** a. 1. kept under surveillance 2. prudent, restrained or noncommittal —**guardedly** adv. —**guardian** n. 1. keeper, protector 2. person having custody of infant etc. —**guardianship** n. care —**guardhouse** or **guardroom** n. place for stationing those on guard or for prisoners —**guardsman** n. soldier in Guards

guava ('gwɑːvə) n. tropical tree with fruit used to make jelly

gubernatorial (gjuːbənəˈtɔːrɪəl, guː-) a. chiefly US of or relating to governor

gudgeon[1] ('gʌdʒən) n. small freshwater fish

gudgeon[2] ('gʌdʒən) n. 1. pivot bearing 2. socket for rudder 3. kind of connecting pin

guelder-rose ('gɛldərəʊz) n. shrub with clusters of white flowers

guerdon ('gɜːd'n) n. reward

Guernsey ('gɜːnzɪ) n. 1. breed of cattle 2. close-fitting knitted jumper

guerrilla or **guerilla** (gəˈrɪlə) n. member of irregular armed force, esp. fighting established force, government etc.

guess (gɛs) vt. 1. estimate without calculation 2. conjecture, suppose 3. US consider, think —vi. 4. form conjectures —n. 5. estimate —**guesswork** n. 1. set of conclusions etc. arrived at by guessing 2. process of making guesses

guest (gɛst) n. 1. one entertained at another's house 2. one living in hotel —**guesthouse** n. boarding house, usu. without alcoholic licence

guff (gʌf) n. sl. silly talk

guffaw (gʌˈfɔː) n. 1. burst of boisterous laughter —vi. 2. laugh in this way

guide (gaɪd) n. 1. one who shows the way 2. adviser 3. book of instruction or information 4. contrivance for directing motion 5. (usu. G-) member of organization for girls equivalent to Scouts —vt. 6. lead, act as guide to 7. arrange —**guidance** n. —**guider** n. adult leader of company of Guides —**guided missile** missile whose flight path is controlled by radio or preprogrammed homing mechanism —**guide dog** dog trained to lead blind person —**guideline** n. principle put forward to determine course of action

guidon ('gaɪd'n) n. 1. pennant, used as marker, esp. by cavalry regiments 2. man or vehicle that carries this

guild or **gild** (gɪld) n. 1. organization, club 2. society for mutual help, or with common object 3. Hist. society of merchants or tradesmen —**guildhall** n. meeting place of guild or corporation

guilder ('gɪldə) or **gulden** ('gʊld'n) n. 1.

standard monetary unit of Netherlands (*also* **'gilder**) **2.** former gold or silver coin of Germany, Austria or Netherlands (*pl.* **-s, -der** *or* **-s, -den**)

guile (gaɪl) *n.* cunning, deceit —**'guileful** *a.* —**'guilefully** *adv.* —**'guileless** *a.*

guillemot (ˈgɪlɪmɒt) *n.* species of sea bird

guillotine (ˈgɪlətiːn) *n.* **1.** device for beheading **2.** machine for cutting paper **3.** in parliament *etc.*, method of restricting length of debate by fixing time for taking vote —*vt.* (gɪləˈtiːn) **4.** behead **5.** use guillotine on **6.** limit (debate) by guillotine

guilt (gɪlt) *n.* **1.** fact, state of having done wrong **2.** responsibility for criminal or moral offence —**'guiltily** *adv.* —**'guiltiness** *n.* —**'guiltless** *a.* innocent —**'guilty** *a.* having committed an offence

guinea (ˈgɪnɪ) *n.* formerly, gold coin worth 21 shillings —**guinea fowl** bird allied to pheasant —**guinea pig 1.** rodent originating in S Amer. **2.** *inf.* person or animal used in experiments

guipure (gɪˈpjʊə) *n.* **1.** any of many types of lace that have their pattern connected by threads, rather than supported on net mesh (*also* **guipure lace**) **2.** heavy corded trimming; gimp

guise (gaɪz) *n.* external appearance, *esp.* one assumed —**'guiser** *n.* —**'guising** *n.* in Scotland and N England, custom of disguising oneself in fancy dress and visiting people's houses at Hallowe'en

guitar (gɪˈtɑː) *n.* usu. 6-stringed instrument played by plucking or strumming —**gui-'tarist** *n.* player of guitar

Gulag (ˈguːlæg) *n.* central administrative department of Soviet security service, responsible for prisons, labour camps *etc.*

gulch (gʌltʃ) *n.* **1.** ravine **2.** gully

gulf (gʌlf) *n.* **1.** large inlet of the sea **2.** chasm **3.** large gap —**Gulf Stream** warm ocean current flowing from Gulf of Mexico towards NW Europe (*also* **North Atlantic Drift**) —**'gulfweed** *n.* seaweed forming dense floating masses in tropical Atlantic waters, *esp.* Gulf Stream (*also* **sar'gasso, sargasso weed**)

gull[1] (gʌl) *n.* long-winged web-footed sea bird

gull[2] (gʌl) *n.* **1.** dupe, fool —*vt.* **2.** dupe, cheat —**gulli'bility** *n.* —**'gullible** *a.* easily imposed on, credulous

gullet (ˈgʌlɪt) *n.* food passage from mouth to stomach

gully (ˈgʌlɪ) *n.* channel or ravine worn by water

gulp (gʌlp) *vt.* **1.** swallow eagerly —*vi.* **2.** gasp, choke —*n.* **3.** act of gulping

gum[1] (gʌm) *n.* firm flesh in which teeth are set —**'gummy** *a.* toothless —**'gumboil** *n.* abscess on gum

gum[2] (gʌm) *n.* **1.** sticky substance issuing from certain trees **2.** an adhesive **3.** chewing gum —*vt.* **4.** stick with gum (**-mm-**) —**'gummy** *a.* —**'gumboots** *pl.n.* boots of rubber —**gum resin** mixture of resin and gum obtained from various plants and trees —**'gumtree** *n.* any species of eucalypt —**gum up the works** *inf.* impede progress —**up a gumtree** *sl.* in a difficult position

gumption (ˈgʌmpʃən) *n.* **1.** resourcefulness **2.** shrewdness, sense

gun (gʌn) *n.* **1.** weapon with metal tube from which missiles are discharged by explosion **2.** cannon, pistol *etc.* —*vt.* **3.** (*oft.* *with* down) shoot **4.** race (engine of car) —*vi.* **5.** hunt with gun (**-nn-**) —**'gunner** *n.* —**'gunnery** *n.* use or science of large guns —**'gunboat** *n.* small warship —**gunboat diplomacy** diplomacy conducted by threats of military intervention —**'gun-cotton** *n.* cellulose nitrate containing large amount of nitrogen: used as explosive —**gun dog** (breed of) dog used to find or retrieve game —**'gunman** *n.* armed criminal —**'gunmetal** *n.* alloy of copper and tin or zinc, formerly used for guns —**'gunpoint** *n.* muzzle of gun —**'gunpowder** *n.* explosive mixture of saltpetre, sulphur and charcoal —**'gunroom** *n.* in warship, mess room of junior officers —**'gunrunner** *n.* —**'gunrunning** *n.* smuggling of guns and ammunition into country —**'gunshot** *n.* **1.** shot or range of gun —*a.* **2.** caused by missile from gun —**'gunstock** *n.* wooden handle or support to which is attached barrel of rifle —**gunwale** *or* **gunnel** (ˈgʌnˀl) *n.* upper edge of ship's side —**at gunpoint** under threat of being shot

gunge (gʌndʒ) *n.* *inf.* any sticky, unpleasant substance

gunk (gʌŋk) *n.* *inf.* any dirty, oily matter

gunny (ˈgʌnɪ) *n.* strong, coarse sacking made from jute

guppy (ˈgʌpɪ) *n.* small colourful aquarium fish

gurgle (ˈgɜːgˀl) *n.* **1.** bubbling noise —*vi.* **2.** utter, flow with gurgle

Gurkha (ˈgɜːkə) *n.* **1.** any of a warlike people in Nepal **2.** member of this people serving as soldier in British army

gurnard (ˈgɜːnəd) *or* **gurnet** (ˈgɜːnɪt) *n.* spiny armour-headed sea fish

guru (ˈgʊruː, ˈguːruː) *n.* spiritual teacher, *esp.* in India

gush (gʌʃ) *vi.* **1.** flow out suddenly and copiously, spurt **2.** act effusively —*n.* **3.** sudden and copious flow **4.** effusiveness —**'gusher** *n.* **1.** gushing person **2.** something, such as oil well, that gushes

gusset (ˈgʌsɪt) *n.* triangle or diamond-shaped piece of material let into garment —**'gusseted** *a.*

gust (gʌst) *n.* **1.** sudden blast of wind **2.** burst of rain, anger, passion *etc.* —**'gusty** *a.*

gustation (gʌˈsteɪʃən) *n.* act of tasting or faculty of taste —**'gustatory** *a.*

gusto (ˈgʌstəʊ) *n.* enjoyment, zest

gut (gʌt) *n.* **1.** (*oft.* *pl.*) entrails, intestines **2.** material made from guts of animals, *eg* for violin strings *etc.* —*pl.* **3.** *inf.* essential, fundamental part **4.** courage —*vt.* **5.** remove guts from (fish *etc.*) **6.** remove, destroy contents of (house) (-tt-) —'**gut-less** a. inf. lacking courage —'**gutsy** a. inf. 1. greedy 2. courageous

gutta-percha ('gʌtə'pɜːtʃə) n. (tropical tree producing) whitish rubber substance

gutter ('gʌtə) n. 1. shallow trough for carrying off water from roof or side of street —vt. 2. make channels in —vi. 3. flow in streams 4. (of candle) melt away by wax forming channels and running down —**gutter press** journalism that relies on sensationalism —'**guttersnipe** n. 1. neglected slum child 2. mean vindictive person

guttural ('gʌtərəl) a. 1. of, relating to, or produced in, the throat —n. 2. guttural sound or letter

guy[1] (gaɪ) n. 1. effigy of Guy Fawkes burnt on Nov. 5th 2. inf. person (usu. male) —vt. 3. make fun of, ridicule —**wise guy** inf., usu. disparaging clever person

guy[2] (gaɪ) n. 1. rope, chain to steady, secure something (eg tent) —vt. 2. keep in position by guy —'**guyrope** n.

guzzle ('gʌz³l) v. eat or drink greedily

gybe or **jibe** (dʒaɪb) vi. 1. (of boom of fore-and-aft sail) swing over to other side with following wind 2. alter course thus

gym (dʒɪm) n. 1. gymnasium 2. gymnastics —**gym shoes** see PLIMSOLLS —'**gymslip** n. tunic or pinafore dress worn by school-girls, oft. part of school uniform

gymkhana (dʒɪm'kɑːnə) n. competition or display of horse riding

gymnasium (dʒɪm'neɪzɪəm) n. place equipped for muscular exercises, athletic training (pl. -s, -**nasia** (-'neɪzɪə)) —'**gym-nast** n. expert in gymnastics —**gym'nas-tics** pl.n. muscular exercises, with or without apparatus, eg parallel bars

gymnosperm ('dʒɪmnəʊspɜːm, 'gɪm-) n. seed-bearing plant in which ovules are borne naked on open scales, oft. in cones; any conifer or related plant

gynaecology or U.S. **gynecology** (gaɪnɪ-'kɒlədʒɪ) n. branch of medicine dealing with diseases in women —**gynaeco'logi-cal, gynaeco'logic** or U.S. **gyneco'logical, gyneco'logic** a. —**gynae'cologist** or U.S. **gyne'cologist** n.

gyp[1] (dʒɪp) sl. vt. 1. swindle, cheat, defraud —n. 2. act of cheating 3. person who gyps

gyp[2] (dʒɪp) n. UK, NZ sl. severe pain

gypsophila (dʒɪp'sɒfɪlə) n. garden plant with small white or pink flowers

gypsum ('dʒɪpsəm) n. crystalline sulphate of lime: source of plaster

Gypsy or **Gipsy** ('dʒɪpsɪ) n. one of wandering race originally from NW India, Romany

gyrate (dʒaɪ'reɪt) vi. move in circle, spirally, revolve —**gy'ration** n. —**gy'ra-tional** a. —**gyratory** ('dʒaɪrətərɪ) a. revolving, spinning

gyrfalcon or **gerfalcon** ('dʒɜːfɔːlkən, -fɔːkən) n. large, rare falcon

gyro ('dʒaɪrəʊ) n. 1. see GYROCOMPASS 2. see GYROSCOPE (pl. -**s**)

gyro- or before vowel **gyr-** (comb. form) 1. rotating or gyrating motion, as in gyroscope 2. gyroscope, as in gyrocom-pass

gyrocompass ('dʒaɪrəʊkʌmpəs) n. com-pass using gyroscope to indicate true north

gyroscope ('dʒaɪrəskəʊp) n. disc or wheel so mounted as to be able to rotate about any axis, esp. to keep disc (with compass etc.) level despite movement of ship etc. —**gyroscopic** (dʒaɪrə'skɒpɪk) a.

gyrostabilizer or **-liser** (dʒaɪrəʊ-'steɪbɪlaɪzə) n. gyroscopic device to prevent rolling of ship or aeroplane

gyve (dʒaɪv) obs. vt. 1. shackle, fetter —n. 2. (usu. pl.) fetter

H

h *or* **H** (eɪtʃ) 1. eighth letter of English alphabet 2. speech sound represented by this letter 3. something shaped like an H

H 1. (of pencils) hard 2. *Chem.* hydrogen

ha hectare

habeas corpus ('heɪbɪəs 'kɔːpəs) writ issued to produce prisoner in court

haberdasher ('hæbədæʃə) *n.* dealer in articles of dress, ribbons, pins, needles *etc.* —**'haberdashery** *n.*

habiliments (hə'bɪlɪmənts) *pl.n.* dress

habit ('hæbɪt) *n.* 1. settled tendency or practice 2. constitution 3. customary apparel, *esp.* of nun or monk 4. woman's riding dress —**ha'bitual** *a.* 1. formed or acquired by habit 2. usual, customary —**ha'bitually** *adv.* —**ha'bituate** *vt.* accustom —**habitu'ation** *n.* —**habitué** (hə-'bɪtjʊeɪ) *n.* constant visitor

habitable ('hæbɪtəb'l) *a.* fit to live in —**'habitant** *n.* C (descendant of) original French settler —**'habitat** *n.* natural home (of animal *etc.*) —**habi'tation** *n.* dwelling place

hachure (hæ'ʃjʊə) *n.* shading of short lines drawn on relief map to indicate gradients

hacienda (hæsɪ'ɛndə) *n.* ranch or large estate in Spanish Amer.

hack¹ (hæk) *vt.* 1. cut, chop (at) violently 2. *Sport* foul by kicking the shins —*vi.* 3. *inf.* utter harsh, dry cough —*n.* 4. cut or gash 5. any tool used for shallow digging —**'hacker** *n.* 1. one who hacks 2. *sl.* computer fanatic, *esp.* one who, through personal computer, breaks into computer system of a company *etc.* —**'hackery** *n.* *inf.* practice of gaining illegal access to computer system

hack² (hæk) *n.* 1. horse for ordinary riding 2. drudge, *esp.* writer of inferior literary works —**hack work** dull, repetitive work

hackle ('hæk'l) *n.* 1. neck feathers of turkey *etc.* —*pl.* 2. hairs on back of neck of dog and other animals, which are raised in anger

hackney ('hæknɪ) *n.* carriage or coach kept for hire

hackneyed ('hæknɪd) *a.* (of words *etc.*) stale, trite because of overuse

hacksaw ('hæksɔː) *n.* handsaw for cutting metal

had (hæd) *pt./pp.* of HAVE

haddock ('hædək) *n.* large, edible seafish

hadedah ('hɑːdɪdə) *n.* S Afr. ibis

Hades ('heɪdiːz) *n.* 1. abode of the dead 2. underworld 3. hell

hadj (hædʒ) *n.* see HAJJ

haematite *or U.S.* **hematite** ('hiːmətaɪt, 'hɛm-) *n.* ore of iron

haematology *or U.S.* **hematology** (hiːmə-'tɒlədʒɪ) *n.* branch of medicine concerned with diseases of blood

haemo-, haema-, *or before vowel* **haem-** (*comb. form*) blood

haemoglobin *or U.S.* **hemoglobin** (hiːməʊ'ɡləʊbɪn) *n.* colouring and oxygen-bearing matter of red blood corpuscles

haemophilia *or U.S.* **hemophilia** (hiːməʊ-'fɪlɪə) *n.* hereditary tendency to intensive bleeding as blood fails to clot —**haemo-'philiac** *or U.S.* **hemo'philiac** *n.*

haemorrhage *or U.S.* **hemorrhage** ('hɛmərɪdʒ) *n.* profuse bleeding

haemorrhoids *or U.S.* **hemorrhoids** ('hɛmərɔɪdz) *pl.n.* swollen veins in rectum (*also* **piles**)

hafnium ('hæfnɪəm) *n.* metallic element found in zirconium ores

haft (hɑːft) *n.* 1. handle (of knife *etc.*) —*vt.* 2. provide with haft

hag (hæg) *n.* 1. ugly old woman 2. witch —**hag-ridden** *a.* troubled, careworn

haggard ('hægəd) *a.* 1. wild-looking 2. anxious, careworn —*n.* 3. *Falconry* untamed hawk

haggis ('hægɪs) *n.* Scottish dish made from sheep's heart, lungs, liver, chopped with oatmeal, suet, onion *etc.* and boiled in stomach-bag

haggle ('hæg'l) *vi.* (*oft. with* over) bargain, wrangle (over price, terms *etc.*)

hagiology (hægɪ'ɒlədʒɪ) *n.* literature of the lives and legends of saints —**hagi'ographer** *n.* —**hagi'ography** *n.* writing of this

ha-ha¹ ('hɑː'hɑː) *or* **haw-haw** ('hɔː'hɔː) *interj.* 1. representation of the sound of laughter 2. exclamation expressing derision, mockery *etc.*

ha-ha² ('hɑːhɑː) *or* **haw-haw** ('hɔːhɔː) *n.* sunken fence bordering garden *etc.*, that allows uninterrupted views from within

haiku ('haɪkuː) *or* **hokku** ('hɒkuː) *n.* epigrammatic Japanese verse form in 17 syllables (*pl.* **-ku**)

hail¹ (heɪl) *n.* 1. (shower of) pellets of ice 2. intense shower, barrage —*v.* 3. pour down as shower of hail —**'hailstone** *n.*

hail² (heɪl) *vt.* 1. greet, *esp.* enthusiastically 2. acclaim, acknowledge 3. call —**hail from** come from —**Hail Mary** *see* AVE MARIA

hair (heə) *n.* 1. filament growing from skin of animal, as covering of man's head 2. such filaments collectively —**'hairiness** *n.* —**'hairy** *a.* —**'hairdo** *n.* way of dressing hair —**'hairdresser** *n.* one who attends to and cuts hair, *esp.* women's hair —**'hairgrip** *n.* chiefly UK tightly bent metal hair clip (*also esp. US* **bobby pin**) —**'hairline** *a./n.* very fine (line) —**'hairpiece** *n.* 1. wig or toupee 2. false hair attached to one's real hair to give it greater bulk or length —**'hairpin** *n.* pin for keeping hair in place —**hairpin bend** U-shaped turn of road —**hair-raising** *a.* terrifying —**hair's-**

breadth n. very short margin or distance —**hair shirt** rough shirt worn as penance by religious ascetics —**hair slide** ornamental hinged clip for the hair —'**hairsplitting** n. making of overfine distinctions —'**hairspring** n. very fine, delicate spring in timepiece —**hair trigger** trigger operated by light touch

hajj or **hadj** (hædʒ) n. pilgrimage to Mecca that every Muslim is required to make (pl. '**hajjes** or '**hadjes**) —'**hajji**, '**hadji**, or '**haji** n. Muslim who has made pilgrimage to Mecca (pl. '**hajjis**, '**hadjis**, or '**hajis**)

hake (heɪk) n. edible fish of the cod family

halberd ('hælbəd) or **halbert** n. combined spear and battleaxe

halcyon ('hælsɪən) n. bird fabled to calm the sea and to breed on floating nest, kingfisher —**halcyon days** time of peace and happiness

hale[1] (heɪl) a. robust, healthy (esp. in **hale and hearty**)

hale[2] (heɪl) vt. pull; drag —'**haler** n.

half (hɑːf) n. 1. either of two equal parts of something (pl. **halves**) —a. 2. forming half —adv. 3. to the extent of half —**half-and-half** n. mixture of half one thing and half another thing —'**halfback** n. Football man behind forwards —**half-baked** a. 1. underdone 2. inf. immature, silly —**half-blood** n. 1. relationship between individuals having only one parent in common; individual having such relationship 2. half-breed —**half-breed** or **half-caste** n. person with parents of different races —**half-brother**, **-sister** n. brother (sister) by one parent only —**half-cock** n. halfway position of firearm's hammer when trigger is locked —**half-cocked** a. ill-prepared —**half-crown** n. formerly, British coin worth 12½ (new) pence —**half-hearted** a. unenthusiastic —**half-hitch** n. knot made by passing end of piece of rope around itself and through loop thus made —**half-life** n. time taken for half the atoms in radioactive material to decay —**half-mast** n. (of flag) halfway position to which flag is lowered as mark to mourn dead —**half measures** inadequate measures or actions —**half-nelson** n. hold in wrestling —**halfpenny** ('heɪpnɪ) n. 1. British coin worth half a new penny (also (inf.) **half**) 2. formerly, coin worth half an old penny —**half-size** n. any size, esp. in clothing, halfway between two sizes —**half term** UK short holiday midway through academic term —**half-timbered** or **half-timber** a. (of building) having exposed timber framework filled with brick —**half-time** n. Sport rest period between two halves of game —**half-title** n. 1. title of book as printed on right-hand page preceding title page 2. title on separate page preceding section of book —'**halftone** n. illustration printed from relief plate, showing light and shadow by means of minute dots —**half-track** n. vehicle with caterpillar tracks on wheels that supply motive power only —**half-true**

a. —**half-truth** n. partially true statement intended to mislead —**half volley** striking of ball the moment it bounces —**half'way** adv./a. at or to half distance —**halfway house** 1. place to rest midway on journey 2. halfway point in any progression 3. centre or hostel to facilitate readjustment to private life of released prisoners etc. —'**halfwit** n. 1. mentally-retarded person 2. stupid person —**by halves** imperfectly —**go halves** share expenses etc. equally —**half seas over** inf. drunk —**meet halfway** compromise with

halibut ('hælɪbət) n. large edible flatfish

halitosis (hælɪ'təʊsɪs) n. bad-smelling breath

hall (hɔːl) n. 1. (entrance) passage 2. large room or building belonging to particular group or used for particular purpose, esp. public assembly —'**hallway** n. hall or corridor

hallelujah, halleluiah (hælɪ'luːjə), or **alleluia** (ælɪ'luːjə) n./interj. exclamation of praise to God

hallmark ('hɔːlmɑːk) n. 1. mark used to indicate standard of tested gold and silver 2. mark of excellence 3. distinguishing feature

hallo (hə'ləʊ) interj. see HELLO

halloo (hə'luː), **hallo,** or **halloa** (hə'ləʊ) n. 1. call to spur on hunting dogs —vi. 2. shout loudly

hallow ('hæləʊ) vt. make or honour as holy —**Hallowe'en** or **Halloween** (hæləʊ'iːn) n. the evening of Oct. 31st, the day before Allhallows or All Saints' Day

hallucinate (hə'luːsɪneɪt) vi. suffer illusions —**halluci'nation** n. illusion —**hal'lucinatory** a. —**hal'lucinogen** n. drug inducing hallucinations

halm (hɔːm) n. see HAULM

halo ('heɪləʊ) n. 1. circle of light round moon, sun etc. 2. disc of light round saint's head in picture 3. aura surrounding admired person, thing etc. (pl. **-es, -s**) —vt. 4. surround with halo

halogen ('hælədʒɛn) n. any of the chemical elements fluorine, chlorine, bromine, iodine, and astatine —**halogenous** (hə'lɒdʒɪnəs) a.

halt[1] (hɔːlt) n. 1. interruption or end to progress etc., esp. as command to stop marching 2. minor railway station without station buildings —v. 3. (cause to) stop

halt[2] (hɔːlt) vi. falter, fail —'**halting** a. hesitant, lame

halter ('hɔːltə) n. 1. rope or strap with headgear to fasten horses or cattle 2. low-cut dress style with strap passing behind neck 3. noose for hanging a person —vt. 4. put halter on

halve (hɑːv) vt. 1. cut in half 2. reduce to half 3. share

halyard or **halliard** ('hæljəd) n. rope for raising sail, signal flags etc.

ham (hæm) n. 1. meat, esp. salted or smoked, from thigh of pig 2. actor adopting exaggerated, unconvincing style

3. amateur radio enthusiast —*v.* **4.** overact (-mm-) —'**hammy** *a. inf.* **1.** (of actor) tending to overact **2.** (of play, performance *etc.*) overacted —**ham-fisted** *or* **ham-handed** *a.* clumsy —'**hamstring** *n.* **1.** tendon at back of knee —*vt.* **2.** cripple by cutting this

hamadryad (hæmə'draɪəd) *n. Class. myth.* nymph which inhabits tree and dies with it

hamburger ('hæmbɜːgə) *n.* fried cake of minced beef, *esp.* served in bread roll

Hamitic (hæ'mɪtɪk, hə-) *n.* **1.** group of N Afr. languages related to Semitic —*a.* **2.** denoting this group of languages **3.** denoting Hamites, group of peoples of N Afr., including ancient Egyptians, supposedly descended from Noah's son Ham

hamlet ('hæmlɪt) *n.* small village

hammer ('hæmə) *n.* **1.** tool usu. with heavy head at end of handle, for beating, driving nails *etc.* **2.** machine with similar function **3.** contrivance for exploding charge of gun **4.** auctioneer's mallet **5.** metal ball on wire thrown in sports —*v.* **6.** strike (blows) with, or as with, hammer —'**hammerhead** *n.* shark with wide, flattened head —'**hammertoe** *n.* deformed toe —**hammer and sickle** emblem on flag of Soviet Union, representing industrial workers and peasants respectively —**hammer out** solve problem by full investigation of difficulties

hammock ('hæmək) *n.* bed of canvas *etc.*, hung on cords

hamper[1] ('hæmpə) *n.* **1.** large covered basket **2.** large parcel, box *etc.* of food, wines *etc.*, *esp.* one sent as Christmas gift

hamper[2] ('hæmpə) *vt.* impede, obstruct movements of

hamster ('hæmstə) *n.* type of rodent, sometimes kept as pet

hamstrung ('hæmstrʌŋ) *a.* **1.** crippled **2.** thwarted

hand (hænd) *n.* **1.** extremity of arm beyond wrist **2.** side, quarter, direction **3.** style of writing **4.** cards dealt to player **5.** measure of four inches **6.** manual worker **7.** sailor **8.** help, aid **9.** pointer on dial **10.** applause —*vt.* **11.** pass **12.** deliver **13.** hold out —'**handful** *n.* **1.** small quantity or number **2.** *inf.* person or thing causing problems (*pl.* -s) —'**handily** *adv.* —'**handiness** *n.* **1.** dexterity **2.** state of being near, available —'**handy** *a.* **1.** convenient **2.** clever with the hands —'**handbag** *n.* **1.** woman's bag for personal articles **2.** bag for carrying in hand —'**handbill** *n.* small printed notice —'**handbook** *n.* small reference or instruction book —'**handcuff** *n.* **1.** fetter for wrist, usu. joined in pair —*vt.* **2.** secure thus —'**handicraft** *n.* manual occupation or skill —'**handiwork** *n.* thing done by particular person —**handkerchief** ('hæŋkətʃɪf, -tʃiːf) *n.* **1.** small square of fabric carried in pocket for wiping nose *etc.* **2.** neckerchief —**hand-me-down** *n. inf.* **1.** something, *esp.* outgrown garment, passed down from one person to another **2.**

anything already used by another —**handout** *n.* **1.** money, food *etc.* given free **2.** pamphlet giving news, information *etc.* —**hand-pick** *vt.* select with great care —**hand-picked** *a.* —'**handset** *n.* telephone mouthpiece and earpiece mounted as single unit —**hands-on** *a.* involving active participation and operating experience —'**handspring** *n.* gymnastic feat in which person leaps forwards or backwards into handstand and then on to his feet —'**handstand** *n.* act of supporting body in upside-down position by hands alone —**hand-to-hand** *a./adv.* at close quarters —**hand-to-mouth** *a./adv.* with barely enough money or food to satisfy immediate needs —'**handwriting** *n.* way person writes —'**handyman** *n.* **1.** man employed to do various tasks **2.** man skilled in odd jobs —**hand in glove** very intimate

h & c hot and cold (water)

handicap ('hændɪkæp) *n.* **1.** something that hampers or hinders **2.** race, contest in which chances are equalized by starts, weights carried *etc.* **3.** condition so imposed **4.** any physical disability —*vt.* **5.** hamper **6.** impose handicaps on (-pp-) —'**handicapped** *a.* physically or mentally disabled

handle ('hænd°l) *n.* **1.** part of utensil *etc.* which is to be held —*vt.* **2.** touch, feel with hands **3.** manage **4.** deal with **5.** trade —'**handler** *n.* **1.** person who trains and controls animals **2.** trainer or second of boxer —'**handlebars** *pl.n.* curved metal bar used to steer bicycle, motorbike *etc.*

handsome ('hændsəm) *a.* **1.** of fine appearance **2.** generous **3.** ample —'**handsomely** *adv.*

hanepoot ('hɑːnəpɔːt) *n. SA* type of grape

hang (hæŋ) *vt.* **1.** suspend **2.** kill by suspension by neck (**hanged** *pt./pp.*) **3.** attach, set up (wallpaper, doors *etc.*) —*vi.* **4.** be suspended (**hung** *pt./pp.*) —'**hanger** *n.* frame on which clothes *etc.* can be hung —'**hangdog** *a.* sullen, dejected —**hanger-on** *n.* sycophantic follower or dependant (*pl.* **hangers-on**) —**hang-glider** *n.* glider like large kite, with pilot hanging in frame below —**hang-gliding** *n.* —'**hangman** *n.* executioner —'**hangnail** *n.* piece of skin hanging loose at base or side of fingernail —'**hangover** *n.* after-effects of too much drinking —**hang-up** *n. inf.* persistent emotional problem —**hang out** *inf.* reside, frequent

hangar ('hæŋə) *n.* large shed for aircraft

hank (hæŋk) *n.* coil, skein, length, *esp.* as measure of yarn

hanker ('hæŋkə) *vi.* (with **for** *or* **after**) have a yearning

hanky *or* **hankie** ('hæŋkɪ) *n. inf.* handkerchief

hanky-panky ('hæŋkɪ'pæŋkɪ) *n. inf.* **1.** trickery **2.** illicit sexual relations

Hansard ('hænsɑːd) *n.* official printed record of speeches, debates *etc.* in Brit., Aust. and other parliaments

Hanseatic League (hænsɪˈætɪk) commercial organization of towns in N Germany formed to protect and control trade

hansom (ˈhænsəm) n. (*sometimes* H-) two-wheeled horse-drawn cab for two to ride inside with driver mounted up behind

Hants. (hænts) Hampshire

haphazard (hæpˈhæzəd) a. 1. random 2. careless

hapless (ˈhæplɪs) a. unlucky

happen (ˈhæpˀn) vi. 1. come about, occur 2. chance (to do) —**'happening** n. occurrence, event

happy (ˈhæpɪ) a. 1. glad 2. content 3. lucky, fortunate 4. apt —**'happily** adv. —**'happiness** n. —**happy-go-lucky** a. casual, lighthearted

harakiri (hærəˈkɪrɪ) or **harikari** n. formerly, in Japan, ritual suicide by disembowelling

harangue (həˈræŋ) n. 1. vehement speech 2. tirade —v. 3. address (person or crowd) in angry, forceful or persuasive way

harass (ˈhærəs) vt. worry, trouble, torment —**'harassment** n.

harbinger (ˈhɑːbɪndʒə) n. 1. one who announces another's approach 2. forerunner, herald

harbour or U.S. **harbor** (ˈhɑːbə) n. 1. shelter for ships 2. shelter —vt. 3. give shelter or protection to 4. maintain (secretly) (*esp.* grudge *etc.*)

hard (hɑːd) a. 1. firm, resisting pressure 2. solid 3. difficult to understand 4. harsh, unfeeling 5. difficult to bear 6. practical, shrewd 7. heavy 8. strenuous 9. (of water) not making lather well with soap 10. (of drugs) highly addictive —adv. 11. vigorously 12. with difficulty 13. close —**'harden** v. —**'hardly** adv. 1. unkindly, harshly 2. scarcely, not quite 3. only just —**'hardness** n. —**'hardship** n. 1. ill luck 2. severe toil, suffering 3. instance of this —**'hardback** n. 1. book bound in stiff covers —a. 2. of or denoting hardback or publication of hardbacks (*also* **'casebound, 'hardbound, 'hardcover**) —**hard-bitten** a. *inf.* tough and realistic —**'hardboard** n. thin stiff sheet made of compressed sawdust and woodchips —**hard-boiled** a. boiled so long as to be hard 2. *inf.* (of person) experienced, unemotional, unsympathetic —**hard copy** Comp. output that can be read by eye —**hard core** 1. members of group who form intransigent nucleus resisting change 2. material, such as broken stones, used to form foundation for road *etc.* —**hard-core** a. 1. (of pornography) depicting sexual acts in explicit detail 2. completely established in belief *etc.* —**hard court** tennis court made of asphalt, concrete *etc.* —**hard disk** Comp. inflexible disk in sealed container, usu. with storage capacity of several megabytes —**hard-headed** a. shrewd —**hard'hearted** a. unkind or intolerant —**hard'heartedness** n. —**hard labour** formerly, penalty of compulsory labour in addition to imprisonment —**hard line** uncompromising course or policy —**hard'liner** n. —**hard palate** anterior bony portion of roof of mouth —**hard-pressed** a. 1. in difficulties 2. closely pursued —**hard sell** aggressive technique of selling or advertising —**hard shoulder** surfaced verge at motorway edge for emergency stops —**'hardware** n. 1. tools, implements 2. necessary (parts of) machinery 3. Comp. mechanical and electronic parts —**'hardwood** n. wood from deciduous trees —**hard of hearing** rather deaf —**hard up** very short of money

hardy (ˈhɑːdɪ) a. 1. robust, vigorous 2. bold 3. (of plants) able to grow in the open all year round —**'hardihood** n. extreme boldness, audacity —**'hardily** adv. —**'hardiness** n.

hare (hɛə) n. animal like large rabbit, with longer legs and ears, noted for speed —**'harebell** n. round-leaved bell-flower —**'harebrained** a. rash, wild —**'harelip** n. fissure of upper lip —**hare and hounds** paper chase

harem (ˈhɛərəm, hɑːˈriːm) or **hareem** (hɑːˈriːm) n. 1. women's part of Mohammedan dwelling 2. one man's wives collectively

haricot (ˈhærɪkəʊ) n. type of French bean that can be dried and stored

harikari (hærɪˈkɑːrɪ) n. see HARAKIRI

hark (hɑːk) vi. listen —**hark back** return (to previous subject of discussion)

harlequin (ˈhɑːlɪkwɪn) n. stock comic character, esp. masked clown in diamond-patterned costume —**harlequi'nade** n. 1. scene in pantomime 2. buffoonery

Harley Street (ˈhɑːlɪ) street in central London famous for its large number of medical specialists' consulting rooms

harlot (ˈhɑːlət) n. whore, prostitute —**'harlotry** n.

harm (hɑːm) n. 1. damage, injury —vt. 2. cause harm to —**'harmful** a. —**'harmfully** adv. —**'harmless** a. unable or unlikely to hurt —**'harmlessly** adv.

harmony (ˈhɑːmənɪ) n. 1. agreement 2. concord 3. peace 4. Mus. combination of notes to make chords 5. melodious sound —**harmonic** (hɑːˈmɒnɪk) a. 1. of harmony —n. 2. tone or note whose frequency is a multiple of its pitch —**harmonica** (hɑːˈmɒnɪkə) n. any of various musical instruments, esp. mouth organ —**harmonics** (hɑːˈmɒnɪks) pl.n. 1. science of musical sounds 2. harmonious sounds —**har'monious** a. —**har'moniously** adv. —**'harmonist** n. —**har'monium** n. small organ —**harmoni'zation** or **-ni'sation** n. —**'harmonize** or **-nise** vt. 1. bring into harmony 2. cause to agree 3. reconcile —vi. 4. be in harmony 5. sing in harmony, as with other singers

harness (ˈhɑːnɪs) n. 1. equipment for attaching horse to cart, plough *etc.* 2. any such equipment —vt. 3. put on, in harness 4. utilize energy or power of (waterfall *etc.*) —**in harness** in or at one's routine work

harp (hɑːp) *n.* 1. musical instrument of strings played by hand —*vi.* 2. play on harp 3. (*with* on *or* upon) dwell (on) continuously —**'harper** *or* **'harpist** *n.* —**'harpsichord** *n.* stringed instrument like piano

harpoon (hɑː'puːn) *n.* 1. barbed spear with rope attached for catching whales —*vt.* 2. catch, kill with or as if with a harpoon —**har'pooner** *n.* —**harpoon gun** gun for firing harpoon in whaling

harpy ('hɑːpɪ) *n.* 1. monster with body of woman and wings and claws of bird 2. cruel, grasping person

harridan ('hærɪd²n) *n.* shrewish old woman, hag

harrier ('hærɪə) *n.* 1. hound used in hunting hares 2. falcon 3. cross-country runner

harrow ('hærəʊ) *n.* 1. implement for smoothing, levelling, or stirring up soil —*vt.* 2. draw harrow over 3. distress greatly —**'harrowing** *a.* 1. heart-rending 2. distressful

harry ('hærɪ) *vt.* 1. harass 2. ravage (**-ried, -rying**)

harsh (hɑːʃ) *a.* 1. rough, discordant 2. severe 3. unfeeling —**'harshly** *adv.*

hart (hɑːt) *n.* male deer —**hartshorn** ('hɑːtshɔːn) *n.* material made from harts' horns, formerly chief source of ammonia

hartal (hɑː'tɑːl) *n.* in India, act of suspending work, *esp.* in political protest

hartebeest ('hɑːtɪbiːst) *or* **hartbeest** ('hɑːtbiːst) *n.* Afr. antelope

harum-scarum ('hɛərəm'skɛərəm) *a.* 1. reckless, wild 2. giddy

harvest ('hɑːvɪst) *n.* 1. (season for) gathering in grain 2. gathering 3. crop 4. product of action —*v.* 5. reap and gather in (crop) —**'harvester** *n.*

has (hæz) *third person sing. pres. indicative of* HAVE —**has-been** *n. inf.* person or thing that is no longer popular, successful *etc.*

hash (hæʃ) *n.* 1. dish of hashed meat *etc.* 2. *inf.* hashish —*vt.* 3. cut up small, chop 4. mix up

hashish ('hæʃiːʃ, -ɪʃ) *or* **hasheesh** *n.* resinous extract of Indian hemp, *esp.* used as hallucinogen

haslet ('hæzlɪt) *or* **harslet** ('hɑːzlɪt, 'hɑːs-) *n.* loaf of cooked minced pig's offal, eaten cold

hasp (hɑːsp) *n.* 1. clasp passing over staple for fastening door *etc.* —*vt.* 2. fasten, secure with hasp

hassle ('hæs²l) *inf. n.* 1. quarrel 2. great deal of bother or trouble —*vi.* 3. quarrel, fight —*vt.* 4. harass (persistently)

hassock ('hæsɔk) *n.* 1. kneeling-cushion 2. tuft of grass

hast (hæst) *obs. second person sing. pres. indicative of* HAVE

haste (heɪst) *n.* 1. speed, quickness, hurry —*vi.* 2. *Poet.* hasten —**hasten** ('heɪs²n) *v.*

(cause to) hurry, increase speed —**'hastily** *adv.* —**'hasty** *a.*

hat (hæt) *n.* head-covering, usu. with brim —**'hatter** *n.* dealer in, maker of hats —**hat trick** any three successive achievements, *esp.* in sport

hatch¹ (hætʃ) *v.* 1. (of young, *esp.* of birds) (cause to) emerge from egg —*vt.* 2. contrive, devise —**'hatchery** *n.*

hatch² (hætʃ) *n.* 1. hatchway 2. trapdoor over it 3. opening in wall or door, as service hatch, to facilitate service of meals *etc.* between two rooms 4. lower half of divided door —**'hatchback** *n.* car with single lifting door in rear —**'hatchway** *n.* opening in deck of ship *etc.*

hatch³ (hætʃ) *vt.* 1. engrave or draw lines on for shading 2. shade with parallel lines

hatchet ('hætʃɪt) *n.* small axe —**hatchet job** *inf.* malicious verbal or written attack —**hatchet man** *inf.* person carrying out unpleasant assignments for another —**bury the hatchet** make peace

hate (heɪt) *vt.* 1. dislike strongly, bear malice towards —*n.* 2. intense dislike 3. that which is hated —**'hateful** *a.* detestable —**'hatefully** *adv.* —**'hatred** ('heɪtrɪd) *n.* extreme dislike, active ill-will

hauberk ('hɔːbɜːk) *n.* long coat of mail

haughty ('hɔːtɪ) *a.* proud, arrogant —**'haughtily** *adv.* —**'haughtiness** *n.*

haul (hɔːl) *vt.* 1. pull, drag with effort —*vi.* 2. (of wind) shift —*n.* 3. hauling 4. something that is hauled 5. catch of fish 6. acquisition 7. distance (to be) covered —**'haulage** *n.* 1. carrying of loads 2. charge for this —**'haulier** *n.* firm, person that transports goods by road

haulm *or* **halm** (hɔːm) *n.* 1. stalks of beans, potatoes, grasses *etc.* collectively 2. single stem of such plant

haunch (hɔːntʃ) *n.* 1. human hip or fleshy hindquarter of animal 2. leg and loin of venison

haunt (hɔːnt) *vt.* 1. visit regularly 2. visit in form of ghost 3. recur to —*n.* 4. place frequently visited —**'haunted** *a.* 1. frequented by ghosts 2. worried —**'haunting** *a.* 1. (of memories) poignant or persistent 2. poignantly sentimental —**'hauntingly** *adv.*

hautboy ('əʊbɔɪ) *n.* 1. strawberry with large fruit 2. *obs.* oboe

haute couture (ot ku'tyːr) *Fr.* high fashion

hauteur (əʊ'tɜː) *n.* haughty spirit

Havana cigar (hə'vænə) fine quality of cigar (*also* **Ha'vana**)

have (hæv) *vt.* 1. hold, possess 2. be possessed, affected with 3. cheat, outwit 4. engage in 5. obtain 6. contain 7. allow 8. cause to be (done) 9. give birth to 10. as auxiliary, forms perfect and other tenses (*pres. tense:* I *have,* thou *hast,* he *has,* we, you, they *have*) (**had, 'having**) —**have to** be obliged to

haven ('heɪv²n) *n.* place of safety

haver ('heɪvə) *vi. UK* 1. *dial.* babble; talk

nonsense 2. dither —*n.* 3. (*usu. pl.*) *Scot.* nonsense

haversack ('hævəsæk) *n.* canvas bag for provisions *etc.*, carried on back or shoulder when hiking

havoc ('hævək) *n.* 1. devastation, ruin 2. *inf.* confusion, chaos

haw (hɔː) *n.* 1. fruit of hawthorn 2. hawthorn

hawfinch ('hɔːfɪntʃ) *n.* uncommon European finch

hawk[1] (hɔːk) *n.* 1. bird of prey smaller than eagle 2. supporter, advocate of warlike policies —*vi.* 3. hunt with hawks 4. soar and swoop like hawk —**hawk-eyed** *a.* 1. having extremely keen sight 2. vigilant or observant

hawk[2] (hɔːk) *vt.* offer (goods) for sale, as in street —**'hawker** *n.*

hawk[3] (hɔːk) *vi.* clear throat noisily

hawse (hɔːz) *n.* part of ship's bows with holes for cables

hawser ('hɔːzə) *n.* large rope or cable

hawthorn ('hɔːθɔːn) *n.* thorny shrub or tree having pink or white flowers and reddish fruits (*also* (UK) **may, may tree,** 'mayflower)

hay (heɪ) *n.* grass mown and dried —**'haybox** *n.* box filled with hay in which heated food is left to finish cooking —**hay fever** allergic reaction to pollen, dust *etc.* —**'haymaker** *n.* 1. person who cuts or turns hay 2. either of two machines, one designed to crush stems of hay, the other to break and bend them, in order to cause more rapid and even drying 3. *Boxing sl.* wild swinging punch —**'haymaking** *a./n.* —**'haystack** *n.* large pile of hay —**'haywire** *a.* 1. crazy 2. disorganized

hazard ('hæzəd) *n.* 1. chance 2. risk, danger —*vt.* 3. expose to risk 4. run risk of —**'hazardous** *a.* risky

haze (heɪz) *n.* 1. mist, oft. due to heat 2. obscurity —**'hazy** *a.* 1. misty 2. obscured 3. vague

hazel ('heɪz'l) *n.* 1. bush bearing nuts 2. yellowish-brown colour of the nuts —*a.* 3. light yellowish brown

Hb haemoglobin

HB UK (on pencils) hard-black

H.B.C. Hudson's Bay Company

H-bomb hydrogen bomb

H.C.F. *or* **h.c.f.** highest common factor

he (hiː; *unstressed* i:) *pron.* 1. (*third person masculine pronoun*) person, animal already referred to 2. (*comb. form*) male, as in *he-goat* —**he-man** *n. inf.* strongly built muscular man

He *Chem.* helium

HE *or* **H.E.** 1. high explosive 2. His Eminence 3. His (*or* Her) Excellency

head (hɛd) *n.* 1. upper part of person's or animal's body, containing mouth, sense organs and brain 2. upper part of anything 3. chief of organization, school *etc.* 4. chief part 5. aptitude, capacity 6. culmination or crisis (*esp.* in **bring** *or* **come to a head**) 7. leader 8. section of chapter 9. title 10.

headland 11. person, animal considered as unit 12. white froth on beer *etc.* 13. *inf.* headache —*a.* 14. chief, principal 15. (of wind) contrary —*vt.* 16. be at the top, head of 17. lead, direct 18. provide with head 19. hit (ball) with head —*vi.* 20. (*with* for) make (for) 21. form a head —**'header** *n.* 1. *inf.* headlong fall or dive 2. brick laid with end in face of wall 3. action of striking ball with head —**'heading** *n.* title —**heads** *adv. inf.* with obverse side (of coin) uppermost —**'heady** *a.* apt to intoxicate or excite —**'headache** *n.* 1. continuous pain in head 2. *inf.* worrying circumstance —**'headboard** *n.* vertical board at head of bed —**'headdress** *n.* any head covering, *esp.* ornate one —**'headgear** *n.* 1. hat, headdress *etc.* 2. any part of horse's harness worn on head 3. hoisting mechanism at pithead of mine —**head-hunter** *n.* —**head-hunting** *n.* 1. practice among certain peoples of removing heads of slain enemies and preserving them as trophies 2. (of company or corporation) recruitment of, or drive to recruit, new high-level personnel —**'headland** *n.* promontory —**'headlight** *n.* powerful lamp carried on front of locomotive, motor vehicle *etc.* —**'headline** *n.* news summary, *usu.* in large type in newspaper —**'headlong** *adv.* 1. with head foremost 2. with great haste —**head-on** *adv./a.* 1. (of collision *etc.*) front foremost 2. with directness —**'headphones** *pl.n.* electrical device consisting of two earphones held in position by strap over head (*also* (*inf.*) **cans**) —**'headquarters** *pl.n.* 1. residence of commander-in-chief 2. centre of operations —**'headroom** *or* **'headway** *n.* height of bridge *etc.*; clearance —**'headshrinker** *n.* 1. *sl.* psychiatrist (*also* **shrink**) 2. headhunter who shrinks heads of his victims —**'headstall** *n.* part of bridle that fits round horse's head —**head start** initial advantage in competitive situation —**'headstone** *n.* gravestone —**'headstrong** *a.* self-willed —**'headwaters** *pl.n.* tributary streams of river —**'headway** *n.* advance, progress —**'headwind** *n.* wind blowing directly against course of aircraft or ship —**'headword** *n.* key word placed at beginning of line *etc.* as in dictionary entry

heal (hiːl) *v.* make or become well —**health** (hɛlθ) *n.* 1. soundness of body 2. condition of body 3. toast drunk in person's honour —**healthily** ('hɛlθɪlɪ) *adv.* —**healthiness** ('hɛlθɪnɪs) *n.* —**healthy** ('hɛlθɪ) *a.* 1. of strong constitution 2. of or producing good health, wellbeing *etc.* 3. vigorous —**health centre** surgery and offices of group medical practice —**health visitor** UK nurse who visits and gives advice to old and sick in their homes

heap (hiːp) *n.* 1. pile of things lying one on another 2. great quantity —*vt.* 3. pile 4. load (with)

hear (hɪə) *vt.* 1. perceive by ear 2. listen to 3. *Law* try (case) 4. heed —*vi.* 5. perceive sound **6.** (*with* of or about) learn (**heard** (hɜːd) *pt./pp.*) —'**hearer** *n.* —'**hearing** *n.* **1.** ability to hear **2.** earshot **3.** judicial examination —'**hearsay** *n.* **1.** rumour —*a.* **2.** based on hearsay —**hear! hear!** exclamation of approval, agreement

hearken or U.S. (*sometimes*) **harken** ('hɑːkən) *vi.* listen

hearse (hɜːs) *n.* funeral carriage for carrying coffin to grave

heart (hɑːt) *n.* **1.** organ which makes blood circulate **2.** seat of emotions and affections **3.** mind, soul, courage **4.** central part **5.** playing card marked with symbol of heart **6.** one of these marks —'**hearten** *v.* make, become cheerful —'**heartily** *adv.* —'**heartless** *a.* unfeeling —'**hearty** *a.* **1.** friendly **2.** vigorous **3.** in good health **4.** satisfying the appetite —'**heartache** *n.* intense anguish or mental suffering —**heart attack** sudden severe malfunction of heart —'**heartbreak** *n.* intense and overwhelming grief or disappointment —'**heartbreaking** *a.* —'**heartburn** *n.* pain in higher intestine —**heart failure 1.** inability of heart to pump adequate amount of blood to tissues **2.** sudden cessation of heartbeat, resulting in death —'**heartfelt** *a.* sincerely and strongly felt —'**heartfree** *a.* with the affections free or disengaged —**heart-rending** *a.* **1.** overwhelming with grief **2.** agonizing —**heart-searching** *n.* examination of one's feelings or conscience —'**heartsease** *n.* wild pansy —**heart-throb** *n. sl.* object of infatuation —**heart-to-heart** *a.* **1.** (*esp.* of conversation) concerned with personal problems —*n.* **2.** intimate conversation —**heart-warming** *a.* **1.** pleasing; gratifying **2.** emotionally moving —'**heartwood** *n.* central core of dark hard wood in tree trunks —**by heart** by memory

hearth (hɑːθ) *n.* **1.** part of room where fire is made **2.** home

heat (hiːt) *n.* **1.** hotness **2.** sensation of this **3.** hot weather or climate **4.** warmth of feeling, anger *etc.* **5.** sexual excitement caused by readiness to mate in female animals **6.** one of many races *etc.* to decide persons to compete in finals —*v.* **7.** make, become hot —'**heated** *a.* angry —'**heatedly** *adv.* —'**heater** *n.* any device for supplying heat, such as a convector —**heat pump** device for extracting heat from substance that is at slightly higher temperature than its surroundings and delivering it to factory *etc.* at much higher temperature —'**heatstroke** *n.* condition resulting from prolonged exposure to intense heat, characterized by fever —**heat wave** continuous spell of abnormally hot weather

heath (hiːθ) *n.* **1.** tract of wasteland **2.** low-growing evergreen shrub

heathen ('hiːðən) *a.* **1.** not adhering to a religious system **2.** pagan **3.** barbarous **4.** unenlightened —*n.* **5.** heathen person (*pl.* -**s**, '**heathen**) —'**heathendom** *n.* —'**hea-**

thenish *a.* **1.** of or like heathen **2.** rough **3.** barbarous —'**heathenism** *n.*

heather ('hɛðə) *n.* shrub growing on heaths and mountains —'**heathery** *a.*

Heath Robinson (hiːθ 'rɒbɪnsʰn) (of mechanical device) absurdly complicated in design

heave (hiːv) *vt.* **1.** lift with effort **2.** throw (something heavy) **3.** utter (sigh) —*vi.* **4.** swell, rise **5.** feel nausea —*n.* **6.** act or effort of heaving

heaven ('hɛvʰn) *n.* **1.** abode of God **2.** place of bliss **3.** (*also pl.*) sky —'**heavenly** *a.* **1.** lovely, delightful, divine **2.** beautiful **3.** of or like heaven

heavy ('hɛvɪ) *a.* **1.** weighty, striking, falling with force **2.** dense **3.** sluggish **4.** difficult, severe **5.** sorrowful **6.** serious **7.** dull —'**heavily** *adv.* —'**heaviness** *n.* —**heavy-duty** *a.* made to withstand hard wear, bad weather *etc.* —**heavy-handed** *a.* **1.** clumsy **2.** harsh and oppressive —**heavy-hearted** *a.* sad; melancholy —**heavy industry** basic, large-scale industry producing metal, machinery *etc.* —**heavy-metal** *a.* of type of rock music characterized by strong beat and amplified instrumental effects —**heavy water** deuterium oxide, water in which normal hydrogen content has been replaced by deuterium

Heb. or **Hebr. 1.** Hebrew **2.** *Bible* Hebrews

hebdomadal (hɛb'dɒmədʰl) *a.* weekly

Hebrew ('hiːbruː) *n.* **1.** member of an ancient Semitic people **2.** their language **3.** its modern form, used in Israel —**He'braic(al)** *a.* of or characteristic of Hebrews, their language or culture

heckle ('hɛkʰl) *v.* interrupt or try to annoy (speaker) by questions, taunts *etc.*

hectare ('hɛktɑː) *n.* one hundred ares or 10 000 square metres (2.471 acres)

hectic ('hɛktɪk) *a.* rushed, busy

hecto- or before vowel **hect-** (*comb. form*) one hundred, *esp.* in metric system, as in *hectolitre, hectometre*

hector ('hɛktə) *vt.* **1.** bully —*vi.* **2.** bluster —*n.* **3.** blusterer

heddle ('hɛdʰl) *n. Weaving* one of set of frames of vertical wires

hedge (hɛdʒ) *n.* **1.** fence of bushes —*vt.* **2.** surround with hedge **3.** obstruct **4.** hem in **5.** guard against risk of loss in (bet *etc.*), *esp.* by laying bets with other bookmakers —*vi.* **6.** make or trim hedges **7.** be evasive **8.** secure against loss —'**hedgehog** *n.* small animal covered with spines —'**hedgerow** *n.* bushes forming hedge —**hedge sparrow** small brownish songbird

hedonism ('hiːdʰnɪzəm, 'hɛd-) *n.* **1.** doctrine that pleasure is the chief good **2.** indulgence in sensual pleasure —**he'donics** *pl.n.* (*with sing. v.*) **1.** branch of psychology concerned with the study of pleasant and unpleasant sensations **2.** in philosophy, study of pleasures —'**hedonist** *n.* —**hedo'nistic** *a.*

heed (hiːd) *vt.* take notice of —'**heedful** *a.* —'**heedless** *a.* careless

heehaw (hi:'hɔ:) *interj.* imitation or representation of braying sound of donkey

heel[1] (hi:l) *n.* 1. hinder part of foot 2. part of shoe supporting this 3. *sl.* undesirable person —*vt.* 4. supply with heel 5. touch (ground, ball) with heel —**'heelball** *n.* mixture of beeswax and lampblack used by shoemakers and in taking rubbings, *esp.* brass rubbings

heel[2] (hi:l) *v.* 1. (of ship) (cause to) lean to one side —*n.* 2. heeling, list

hefty ('hɛftɪ) *a.* 1. bulky 2. weighty 3. strong

hegemony (hɪ'gɛmənɪ) *n.* leadership, political domination —**hegemonic** (hɛgə'mɒnɪk) *a.*

Hegira *or* **Hejira** ('hɛdʒɪrə) *n.* 1. flight of Mohammed from Mecca to Medina in 622 A.D. 2. (*oft.* **h-**) escape or flight

heifer ('hɛfə) *n.* young cow

height (haɪt) *n.* 1. measure from base to top 2. quality of being high 3. elevation 4. highest degree 5. (*oft.* *pl.*) hilltop —**'heighten** *vt.* 1. make higher 2. intensify —**height of land** US, C watershed

heinous ('heɪnəs, 'hi:-) *a.* atrocious, extremely wicked, detestable

heir (ɛə) *n.* person entitled to inherit property or rank (**'heiress** *fem.*) —**'heirloom** *n.* thing that has been in family for generations

held (hɛld) *pt./pp. of* HOLD[1]

helical ('hɛlɪk[ə]l) *a.* spiral

helicopter ('hɛlɪkɒptə) *n.* aircraft made to rise vertically by pull of airscrew revolving horizontally —**'heliport** *n.* airport for helicopters

helio- *or before vowel* **heli-** (*comb. form*) sun, as in *heliocentric*

heliocentric (hi:lɪəʊ'sɛntrɪk) *a.* 1. having sun at its centre 2. measured in relation to sun —**helio'centrically** *adv.*

heliograph ('hi:lɪəʊɡrɑːf) *n.* signalling apparatus employing mirror to reflect sun's rays

heliostat ('hi:lɪəʊstæt) *n.* astronomical instrument used to reflect light of sun in constant direction

heliotherapy (hi:lɪəʊ'θɛrəpɪ) *n.* therapeutic use of sunlight

heliotrope ('hi:lɪətrəʊp, 'hɛljə-) *n.* 1. plant with purple flowers 2. bluish-violet to purple colour —**heliotropic** (hi:lɪəʊ'trɒpɪk) *a.* growing, turning towards source of light

helium ('hi:lɪəm) *n.* very light nonflammable gaseous element

helix ('hi:lɪks) *n.* 1. spiral 2. incurving fold that forms margin of external ear (*pl.* **helices** ('hɛlɪsi:z), **-es**)

hell (hɛl) *n.* 1. abode of the damned 2. abode of the dead generally 3. place or state of wickedness, misery or torture —**'hellish** *a./adv.* —**hell'bent** *a.* (*with on*) *inf.* strongly or rashly intent —**'hellfire** *n.* 1. torment of hell, envisaged as eternal fire —*a.* 2. characterizing sermons that emphasize this —**Hell's Angel** member of

motorcycle gang who typically dress in leather clothing, noted for their lawless behaviour

hellebore ('hɛlɪbɔ:) *n.* plant with white flowers that bloom in winter, Christmas rose

Hellenic (hɛ'lɛnɪk, -'li:-) *a.* pert. to inhabitants of Greece —**'Hellenist** *n.*

hello, hallo, *or* **hullo** (hɛ'ləʊ, hə-; 'hɛləʊ) *interj.* expression of greeting or surprise

helm (hɛlm) *n.* tiller, wheel for turning ship's rudder

helmet ('hɛlmɪt) *n.* defensive or protective covering for head (*also* **helm**)

helminth ('hɛlmɪnθ) *n.* parasitic worm, *esp.* nematode or fluke —**hel'minthic** *or* **helminthoid** ('hɛlmɪnθɔɪd, hɛl'mɪnθɔɪd) *a.*

Helot ('hɛlət, 'hi:-) *n.* 1. in ancient Sparta, member of class of serfs owned by state 2. (*usu.* **h-**) serf or slave —**'Helotism** *n.* —**'Helotry** *n.*

help (hɛlp) *vt.* 1. aid, assist 2. support 3. succour 4. remedy, prevent —*n.* 5. act of helping or being helped 6. person or thing that helps —**'helper** *n.* —**'helpful** *a.* —**'helping** *n.* single portion of food taken at meal —**'helpless** *a.* 1. useless, incompetent 2. unaided 3. unable to help —**'helplessly** *adv.* —**'helpmate** *or* **'help-meet** *n.* 1. helpful companion 2. husband or wife

helter-skelter ('hɛltə'skɛltə) *adv./a./n.* 1. (in) hurry and confusion —*n.* 2. high spiral slide at fairground

helve (hɛlv) *n.* handle of hand tool such as axe or pick

hem[1] (hɛm) *n.* 1. border of cloth, *esp.* one made by turning over edge and sewing it down —*vt.* 2. sew thus 3. (*usu.* *with in*) confine, shut in (-**mm**-) —**'hemstitch** *n.* 1. ornamental stitch —*v.* 2. decorate (hem *etc.*) with hemstitches

hem[2] (hɛm) *n./interj.* 1. representation of sound of clearing throat, used to gain attention *etc.* —*vi.* 2. utter this sound (-**mm**-) —**hem** (*or* **hum**) **and haw** hesitate in speaking

hemi- (*comb. form*) half, as in *hemisphere*

hemisphere ('hɛmɪsfɪə) *n.* 1. half sphere 2. half of celestial sphere 3. half of the earth —**hemispheric(al)** (hɛmɪ'sfɛrɪk([ə])l) *a.*

hemistich ('hɛmɪstɪk) *n.* half line of verse

hemlock ('hɛmlɒk) *n.* 1. poisonous plant 2. poison extracted from it 3. US evergreen of pine family

hemo- (*comb. form*) US *see* HAEMO-

hemp (hɛmp) *n.* 1. Indian plant 2. its fibre used for rope *etc.* 3. any of several narcotic drugs made from varieties of hemp —**'hempen** *a.* made of hemp or rope

hen (hɛn) *n.* female of domestic fowl and others —**'henpeck** *vt.* (of woman) harass (a man, *esp.* husband) by nagging

henbane ('hɛnbeɪn) *n.* poisonous plant with sticky hairy leaves

hence (hɛns) *adv.* 1. from this point 2. for this reason —**'hence'forward** *or* **'hence'forth** *adv.* from now onwards

henchman ('hɛntʃmən) n. trusty follower

henge (hɛndʒ) n. circular monument, oft. containing circle of stones

henna ('hɛnə) n. 1. flowering shrub 2. reddish dye made from it

henotheism ('hɛnəʊθiːɪzəm) n. belief in one god (of several) as special god of one's family, tribe etc.

henry ('hɛnrɪ) n. SI unit of electrical inductance

hepatic (hɪ'pætɪk) a. pert. to the liver —**hepa'titis** n. inflammation of the liver

hepta- or before vowel **hept-** (comb. form) seven, as in heptameter

heptagon ('hɛptəgən) n. figure with seven angles —**hep'tagonal** a.

heptarchy ('hɛptɑːkɪ) n. rule by seven

her (hɜː; unstressed hə, ə) a. objective and possessive case of SHE —**hers** pron. of her —**her'self** pron.

herald ('hɛrəld) n. 1. messenger, envoy 2. officer who makes royal proclamations, arranges ceremonies, regulates armorial bearings etc. —vt. 3. announce 4. proclaim approach of —**he'raldic** a. —**'heraldry** n. study of (right to have) heraldic bearings

herb (hɜːb; U.S. ɜːrb) n. 1. plant with soft stem which dies down after flowering 2. plant, such as rosemary, used in cookery or medicine —**her'baceous** a. 1. of, like herbs 2. flowering perennially —**'herbage** n. 1. herbs 2. grass 3. pasture —**'herbal** a. 1. of herbs —n. 2. book on herbs —**'herbalist** n. 1. writer on herbs 2. dealer in medicinal herbs —**her'barium** n. collection of dried plants (pl. **-s, -ia** (-ɪə)) —**'herbicide** n. chemical which destroys plants —**her'bivorous** a. feeding on plants

Hercules ('hɜːkjuːliːz) n. mythical hero noted for strength —**herculean** (hɜːkjʊ-'liːən) a. requiring great strength, courage etc.

herd (hɜːd) n. 1. company of animals, usu. of same species, feeding or travelling together 2. herdsman —v. 3. collect or be collected together —vt. 4. tend (livestock) —**herd instinct** Psychol. inborn tendency to associate with others and follow group's behaviour —**'herdsman** n.

here (hɪə) adv. 1. in this place 2. at or to this point —**here'after** adv. 1. in time to come —n. 2. future existence —**here'by** adv. by means of or as result of this —**hereto'fore** adv. before —**here'with** adv. together with this

heredity (hɪ'rɛdɪtɪ) n. tendency of organism to transmit its nature to its descendants —**here'ditament** n. Law property that can be inherited —**he'reditarily** adv. —**he'reditary** a. 1. descending by inheritance 2. holding office by inheritance 3. that can be transmitted from one generation to another

heresy ('hɛrəsɪ) n. opinion contrary to orthodox opinion or belief —**'heretic** n. one holding opinions contrary to orthodox faith —**he'retical** a. —**he'retically** adv.

heritage ('hɛrɪtɪdʒ) n. 1. what may be or is

inherited 2. anything from past, esp. owned or handed down by tradition —**'heritable** a. that can be inherited

hermaphrodite (hɜː'mæfrədaɪt) n. 1. animal or flower that has both male and female reproductive organs 2. person having both male and female characteristics

hermetic (hɜː'mɛtɪk) or **hermetical** a. sealed so as to be airtight —**her'metically** adv.

hermit ('hɜːmɪt) n. one living in solitude, esp. from religious motives —**'hermitage** n. his abode —**hermit crab** soft-bodied crustacean living in and carrying about empty shells of molluscs

hernia ('hɜːnɪə) n. projection of (part of) organ through lining encasing it (pl. **-s, -iae** (-iiː)) —**'hernial** a.

hero ('hɪərəʊ) n. 1. one greatly regarded for achievements or qualities 2. principal character in play etc. 3. illustrious warrior 4. demigod (pl. **-es**) (**heroine** ('hɛrəʊɪn) fem.) —**heroic** (hɪ'rəʊɪk) a. 1. of, like hero 2. courageous, daring —**heroically** (hɪ'rəʊɪkəlɪ) adv. —**heroics** (hɪ'rəʊɪks) pl.n. extravagant behaviour —**heroism** ('hɛrəʊɪzəm) n. 1. qualities of hero 2. courage, boldness —**heroic verse** type of verse suitable for epic or heroic subjects —**hero worship** 1. admiration of heroes or of great men 2. excessive admiration of others —**hero-worship** vt. feel admiration or adulation for

heroin ('hɛrəʊɪn) n. white crystalline derivative of morphine, a highly addictive narcotic

heron ('hɛrən) n. long-legged wading bird —**'heronry** n. place where herons breed

herpes ('hɜːpiːz) n. any of several skin diseases, including shingles (**herpes zoster**) and cold sores (**herpes simplex**)

Herr (German hɛr) n. German man: used before name as title equivalent to Mr (pl. **Herren** ('hɛrən))

herring ('hɛrɪŋ) n. important food fish of northern hemisphere —**'herringbone** n. stitch or pattern of zigzag lines —**herring gull** common gull that has white plumage with black-tipped wings

Herts. (hɑːts) Hertfordshire

hertz (hɜːts) n. SI unit of frequency (pl. **hertz**)

hesitate ('hɛzɪteɪt) vi. 1. hold back 2. feel or show indecision 3. be reluctant —**'hesitancy** or **hesi'tation** n. 1. wavering 2. doubt 3. stammering —**'hesitant** a. undecided, pausing —**'hesitantly** adv.

Hesperus ('hɛspərəs) n. evening star, esp. Venus

hessian ('hɛsɪən) n. coarse jute cloth

hest (hɛst) n. behest, command

hetaera (hɪ'tɪərə) or **hetaira** (hɪ'taɪrə) n. esp. in ancient Greece, prostitute, esp. educated courtesan (pl. **-taerae** (-'tɪəriː) or **-tairai** (-'taɪraɪ))

hetero- (comb. form) other; different, as in heterosexual

heterodox ('hɛtərəʊdɒks) a. not orthodox —'**heterodoxy** n.

heterodyne ('hɛtərəʊdaɪn) v. 1. Electron. mix (two alternating signals) to produce two signals having frequencies corresponding to sum and difference of original frequencies —a. 2. produced by, operating by, or involved in heterodyning two signals

heterogeneous (hɛtərəʊ'dʒiːnɪəs) a. composed of diverse elements —**hetero-ge'neity** n.

heteromorphic (hɛtərəʊ'mɔːfɪk) or **heteromorphous** a. Biol. 1. differing from normal form 2. (esp. of insects) having different forms at different stages of life cycle —**hetero'morphism** n.

heterosexual (hɛtərəʊ'sɛksjʊəl) n. person sexually attracted to members of the opposite sex —**heterosexu'ality** n.

het up (hɛt) inf. angry; excited

heuchera ('hɔɪkərə) n. plant with ornamental foliage

heuristic (hjʊə'rɪstɪk) a. serving to find out or to stimulate investigation

hew (hjuː) v. chop, cut with axe (**hewn, hewed** pp.) —'**hewer** n.

hexa- or before vowel **hex-** (comb. form) six, as in hexachord

hexagon ('hɛksəgən) n. figure with six angles —**hex'agonal** a.

hexagram ('hɛksəgræm) n. star-shaped figure formed by extending sides of regular hexagon to meet at six points

hexameter (hɛk'sæmɪtə) n. line of verse of six feet

hexapod ('hɛksəpɒd) n. insect

hey (heɪ) interj. expression indicating surprise, dismay, discovery etc.—'**heyday** n. bloom, prime —**hey presto** exclamation used by conjurors to herald climax of trick

Hf Chem. hafnium

HF, H.F., hf, or **h.f.** high frequency

hf. half

Hg Chem. mercury

HGV UK heavy goods vehicle

H.H. 1. His (or Her) Highness 2. His Holiness (title of Pope)

HI Hawaii

hiatus (haɪ'eɪtəs) n. break or gap where something is missing (pl. **-es, hi'atus**)

hibernate ('haɪbəneɪt) vi. pass the winter, esp. in a torpid state —**hiber'nation** n. —'**hibernator** n.

Hibernian (haɪ'bɜːnɪən) a./n. Irish (person)

hibiscus (hɪ'bɪskəs) n. flowering (sub)-tropical shrub

hiccup ('hɪkʌp) n. 1. spasm of the breathing organs with an abrupt cough-like sound —vi. 2. make a hiccup or hiccups (also '**hiccough**)

hick (hɪk) inf. a. 1. rustic 2. unsophisticated —n. 3. person like this

hickory ('hɪkərɪ) n. 1. N Amer. nut-bearing tree 2. its tough wood

hide¹ (haɪd) vt. 1. put, keep out of sight 2. conceal, keep secret —vi. 3. conceal oneself (**hid** (hɪd) pt., **hidden** ('hɪd'n) or **hid** pp., '**hiding** pr.p.) —n. 4. place of concealment, eg for birdwatcher —'**hide-away** n. hiding place or secluded spot —'**hide-out** n. hiding place

hide² (haɪd) n. skin of animal —'**hiding** n. sl. thrashing —'**hidebound** a. 1. restricted, esp. by petty rules etc. 2. narrow-minded 3. (of tree) having bark so close that it impedes growth

hideous ('hɪdɪəs) a. repulsive, revolting —'**hideously** adv.

hie (haɪ) v. obs. hasten (**hied** pt./pp., '**hying** or '**hieing** pr.p.)

hierarchy ('haɪərɑːkɪ) n. system of persons or things arranged in graded order —**hier'archic(al)** a.

hieratic (haɪə'rætɪk) a. 1. of priests 2. of cursive form of hieroglyphics used by priests in ancient Egypt —n. 3. hieratic script of ancient Egypt —**hier'atically** adv.

hieroglyphic (haɪərə'glɪfɪk) a. 1. of a system of picture writing, esp. as used in ancient Egypt —n. 2. symbol representing object, concept, or sound 3. symbol, picture, difficult to decipher —'**hieroglyph** n.

hi-fi ('haɪ'faɪ) inf. a. 1. see **high-fidelity** at HIGH —n. 2. high-fidelity equipment

higgledy-piggledy ('hɪg'ldɪ'pɪg'ldɪ) adv./ a. inf. in confusion

high (haɪ) a. 1. tall, lofty 2. far up 3. (of roads) main 4. (of meat) tainted 5. (of season) well advanced 6. (of sound) acute in pitch 7. expensive 8. of great importance, quality, or rank 9. inf. in state of euphoria, esp. induced by drugs 10. inf. bad-smelling —adv. 11. far up 12. strongly, to a great extent 13. at, to a high pitch 14. at a high rate —'**highly** adv. —'**highness** n. 1. quality of being high 2. (H-) title of prince or princess —'**highball** n. US long iced drink consisting of spirit base with soda water etc. —'**highbrow** sl. n. 1. intellectual, esp. intellectual snob —a. 2. intellectual 3. difficult 4. serious —'**high-chair** n. long-legged chair for child, esp. one with table-like tray —**High Church** party within Church of England emphasizing authority of bishops and importance of sacraments, rituals and ceremonies —**high commissioner** senior diplomatic representative sent by one Commonwealth country to another —**higher education** education and training at colleges, universities etc. —**high explosive** extremely powerful chemical explosive —**highfa'lutin** or **highfa'luting** a. inf. pompous or pretentious —**high-fidelity** a. of high-quality sound-reproducing equipment —**high-flier** or **high-flyer** n. 1. person extreme in aims, ambition etc. 2. person of great ability, esp. in career —**high-flown** a. extravagant, bombastic —**high frequency** radio frequency lying between 30 and 3 megahertz —**High**

German standard German language, historically developed from the form of W Germanic spoken in S Germany —**high-handed** a. domineering, dogmatic —**high jump** athletic event in which competitor has to jump over high bar —**Highland** ('haɪlənd) a. of, from the Highlands of Scotland —**highland(s)** ('haɪlənd(z)) (pl.)n. relatively high ground —**high-level language** Comp. programming language closer to human language or mathematical notation than to machine language —'**highlight** n. 1. lightest or brightest area in painting, photograph etc. 2. outstanding feature —vt. 3. bring into prominence —**highly strung** excitable, nervous —**High Mass** solemn and elaborate sung Mass —**high-minded** a. having or characterized by high moral principles —**high-mindedness** n. —**high-powered** a. 1. (of optical instrument or lens) having high magnification 2. dynamic and energetic —**high-pressure** a. 1. having, using, or designed to withstand pressure above normal 2. inf. (of selling) persuasive in aggressive and persistent manner —**high priest** 1. Judaism priest of highest rank 2. head of cult —**high-rise** a. of building that has many storeys —**high school** 1. UK see **grammar school** at GRAMMAR 2. US, NZ secondary school —**high seas** open seas, outside jurisdiction of any one nation —**high-sounding** a. pompous, imposing —**high-spirited** a. vivacious, bold or lively —**high tea** early evening meal usu. with cooked course followed by cakes etc., accompanied by tea —**high tech** 1. high technology 2. style of interior design using features of industrial equipment —**high-tech** a. —**high technology** highly sophisticated, oft. electronic, techniques used in manufacturing etc. —**high-technology** a. —**high-tension** a. carrying or operating at relatively high voltage —**high tide** 1. tide at its highest level 2. culminating point —**high time** latest possible time —**high treason** act of treason directly affecting sovereign or state —**high water** 1. high tide 2. state of any stretch of water at its highest level —'**highway** n. 1. main road 2. ordinary route —**Highway Code** UK regulations and recommendations applying to all road users —'**highwayman** n. formerly, robber on road, esp. mounted —**the high jump** UK inf. severe reprimand or punishment

hijack or **highjack** ('haɪdʒæk) vt. 1. divert or wrongfully take command of (vehicle or its contents) while in transit 2. rob —'**hijacker** or '**highjacker** n.

hike (haɪk) vi. 1. walk a long way (for pleasure) in country —vt. 2. pull (up), hitch —n. 3. long walk —'**hiker** n.

hilarity (hɪ'lærɪtɪ) n. cheerfulness, gaiety —**hilarious** (hɪ'lɛərɪəs) a.

hill (hɪl) n. 1. natural elevation, small mountain 2. mound —'**hillock** n. little hill —'**hilly** a. —'**hillbilly** n. unsophisticated (country) person

hilt (hɪlt) n. handle of sword etc. —**to the hilt** to the full

hilum ('haɪləm) n. Bot. scar on seed marking its point of attachment to seed stalk (pl. -la (-lə))

him (hɪm; unstressed ɪm) pron. objective case of HE —**him'self** pron. emphatic form of HE

hind¹ (haɪnd) or **hinder** ('haɪndə) a. at the back, posterior —'**hindquarter** n. 1. one of two back quarters of carcass of beef etc. —pl. 2. rear, esp. of four-legged animal —'**hindsight** n. 1. ability to understand, after something has happened, what should have been done 2. firearm's rear sight

hind² (haɪnd) n. female of deer

hinder ('hɪndə) vt. obstruct, impede, delay —'**hindrance** n.

Hindi ('hɪndɪ) n. language of N central India —'**Hindu** or '**Hindoo** n. person who adheres to **Hinduism**, the dominant religion of India —**Hindustani, Hindoostani** (hɪndʊ'stɑːnɪ), or **Hindo'stani** n. 1. dialect of Hindi spoken in Delhi 2. all spoken forms of Hindi and Urdu considered together —a. 3. of or relating to these languages or Hindustan

hinge (hɪndʒ) n. 1. movable joint, as that on which door hangs —vt. 2. attach with, or as with, hinge —vi. 3. turn, depend (on)

hinny ('hɪnɪ) n. sterile hybrid offspring of male horse and female donkey

hint (hɪnt) n. 1. slight indication or suggestion —v. 2. (sometimes with at) suggest indirectly

hinterland ('hɪntəlænd) n. district lying behind coast, or near city, port etc.

hip¹ (hɪp) n. 1. (oft. pl.) either side of body below waist and above thigh 2. angle formed where sloping sides of roof meet 3. fruit of rose, esp. wild

hip² (hɪp) a. sl. 1. aware of or following latest trends 2. informed

hip-hop n. U.S. pop culture movement of 1980s comprising rap music, graffiti and break dancing

hippie or **hippy** ('hɪpɪ) n. (young) person whose behaviour, dress etc. implies rejection of conventional values

hippo ('hɪpəʊ) n. inf. hippopotamus (pl. -s)

Hippocratic oath (hɪpəʊ'krætɪk) oath taken by doctor to observe code of medical ethics

hippodrome ('hɪpədrəʊm) n. 1. music hall 2. variety theatre 3. circus

hippogriff or **hippogryph** ('hɪpəʊgrɪf) n. griffinlike creature with horse's body

hippopotamus (hɪpə'pɒtəməs) n. large Afr. animal living in rivers (pl. -es, -mi (-maɪ))

hire (haɪə) vt. 1. obtain temporary use of by payment 2. engage for wage —n. 3. hiring or being hired 4. payment for use of something —'**hireling** n. one who serves for wages —**hire-purchase** n. system by which something becomes hirer's after stipulated number of payments

hirsute ('hɜːsjuːt) *a.* hairy

his (hɪz; *unstressed* ɪz) *pron./a.* belonging to him

Hispanic (hɪ'spænɪk) *a.* of or derived from Spain or the Spanish —**His'panicism** *n.*

hispid ('hɪspɪd) *a.* **1.** rough with bristles or minute spines **2.** bristly, shaggy —**his'pidity** *n.*

hiss (hɪs) *vi.* **1.** make sharp sound of letter *s, esp.* in disapproval —*vt.* **2.** express disapproval of, deride thus —*n.* **3.** sound like that of prolonged *s* —**'hissing** *n.*

hist. 1. historian **2.** historical **3.** history

histamine ('hɪstəmiːn) *n.* substance released by body tissues, sometimes creating allergic reactions

histogeny (hɪ'stɒdʒənɪ) *n.* formation and development of organic tissues

histogram ('hɪstəgræm) *n.* graph using vertical columns to illustrate frequency distribution

histology (hɪ'stɒlədʒɪ) *n.* branch of biology concerned with the structure of organic tissues —**his'tologist** *n.*

history ('hɪstərɪ) *n.* **1.** record of past events **2.** study of these **3.** past events **4.** train of events, public or private **5.** course of life or existence **6.** systematic account of phenomena —**his'torian** *n.* writer of history —**historic** (hɪ'stɒrɪk) *a.* noted in history —**historical** (hɪ'stɒrɪkᵊl) *a.* **1.** of, based on, history **2.** belonging to the past —**historically** (hɪ'stɒrɪkəlɪ) *adv.* —**histo'ricity** *n.* historical authenticity —**histori'ographer** *n.* **1.** official historian **2.** one who studies historical method

histrionic (hɪstrɪ'ɒnɪk) *a.* excessively theatrical, insincere, artificial in manner —**histri'onics** *pl.n.* behaviour like this

hit (hɪt) *vt.* **1.** strike with blow or missile **2.** affect injuriously **3.** reach —*vi.* **4.** strike a blow **5.** (*with* upon) light (upon) (**hit, 'hitting**) —*n.* **6.** blow **7.** *inf.* success —**'hitter** *n.* —**hit-and-run** *a.* **1.** denoting motor-vehicle accident in which driver leaves scene without stopping **2.** (of attack *etc.*) relying on surprise allied to rapid departure from scene of operations —**hit man US** hired assassin —**hit parade** list of currently most popular songs, ranked in order of sales per record —**hit it off** get along (with person) —**hit or miss** casual; haphazard —**hit the hay** *sl.* go to bed —**hit the trail** *or* **road** *inf.* **1.** proceed on journey **2.** leave

hitch (hɪtʃ) *vt.* **1.** fasten with loop *etc.* **2.** raise, move with jerk —*vi.* **3.** be caught or fastened —*n.* **4.** difficulty **5.** knot, fastening **6.** jerk —**'hitchhike** *or* **hitch** *vi.* travel by begging free rides

hither ('hɪðə) *adv.* **1.** to or towards this place (*esp. in* **come hither**) —*a.* **2.** *obs.* situated on this side —**'hither'to** *adv.* up to now or to this time

HIV human immunodeficiency virus: the virus that causes AIDS

hive (haɪv) *n.* **1.** structure in which bees live or are housed **2.** *fig.* place swarming with busy occupants —*v.* **3.** gather, place bees, in hive —**hive away** store, keep —**hive off 1.** transfer **2.** dispose of

hives (haɪvz) *pl.n.* eruptive skin disease

H.M. His (*or* Her) Majesty

H.M.C.S. His (*or* Her) Majesty's Canadian Ship

H.M.I. UK His (*or* Her) Majesty's Inspector (of schools)

H.M.S. His (*or* Her) Majesty's Service *or* Ship

H.M.S.O. UK His (*or* Her) Majesty's Stationery Office

H.N.C. UK Higher National Certificate

H.N.D. UK Higher National Diploma

ho (həʊ) *interj.* **1.** imitation or representation of sound of deep laugh (*also* **ho-ho**) **2.** exclamation used to attract attention *etc.*

Ho *Chem.* holmium

hoard (hɔːd) *n.* **1.** stock, store, *esp.* hidden away —*vt.* **2.** amass and hide away **3.** store

hoarding ('hɔːdɪŋ) *n.* **1.** large board for displaying advertisements **2.** temporary wooden fence round building or piece of ground

hoarse (hɔːs) *a.* rough, harsh-sounding, husky —**'hoarsely** *adv.* —**'hoarseness** *n.*

hoary ('hɔːrɪ) *a.* **1.** grey with age **2.** greyish-white **3.** of great antiquity **4.** venerable —**'hoarfrost** *n.* frozen dew

hoax (həʊks) *n.* **1.** practical joke **2.** deceptive trick —*vt.* **3.** play trick upon **4.** deceive —**'hoaxer** *n.*

hob (hɒb) *n.* **1.** flat-topped casing of fireplace **2.** top area of cooking stove —**'hobnail** *n.* large-headed nail for boot soles

hobble ('hɒbᵊl) *vi.* **1.** walk lamely —*vt.* **2.** tie legs of (horse *etc.*) together —*n.* **3.** straps or ropes put on an animal's legs to prevent it straying **4.** limping gait

hobbledehoy (hɒbᵊldɪ'hɔɪ) *n. obs.* rough, ill-mannered clumsy youth

hobby ('hɒbɪ) *n.* **1.** favourite occupation as pastime **2.** small falcon —**'hobbyhorse** *n.* **1.** toy horse **2.** favourite topic, preoccupation

hobgoblin (hɒb'gɒblɪn) *n.* mischievous fairy

hobnob ('hɒbnɒb) *vi.* (*oft. with* with) **1.** be familiar **2.** *obs.* drink (**-bb-**)

hobo ('həʊbəʊ) *n.* shiftless, wandering person (*pl.* **-s, -es**)

Hobson's choice ('hɒbsᵊnz) choice of taking what is offered or nothing at all

hock[1] (hɒk) *n.* **1.** backward-pointing joint on leg of horse *etc.*, corresponding to human ankle —*vt.* **2.** disable by cutting tendons of hock

hock[2] (hɒk) *n.* dry white wine

hock[3] (hɒk) *inf., chiefly* **US** *vt.* **1.** pawn, pledge —*n.* **2.** state of being in pawn —**'hocker** *n.* —**in hock 1.** in prison **2.** in debt **3.** in pawn

hockey ('hɒkɪ) *n.* **1.** team game played on field with ball and curved sticks **2. US, C** ice hockey

hocus-pocus ('həʊkəs'pəʊkəs) n. 1. trickery 2. mystifying jargon

hod (hɒd) n. 1. small trough on a staff for carrying mortar, bricks etc. 2. tall, narrow coal scuttle

hoe (həʊ) n. 1. tool for weeding, breaking ground etc. —v. 2. dig, weed or till (surface soil) with hoe (**hoed, 'hoeing**)

hog (hɒg) n. 1. pig, esp. castrated male for fattening 2. greedy, dirty person —vt. 3. inf. eat, use selfishly (**-gg-**) —'**hogback** n. 1. narrow ridge with steep sides (also **hog's back**) 2. Archaeol. tomb with sloping sides —'**hogshead** n. 1. large cask 2. liquid measure, having several values, used esp. for alcoholic beverages —'**hogwash** n. 1. nonsense 2. pig food

Hogmanay (hɒgmə'neɪ) n. in Scotland, last day of year

hoick (hɔɪk) vt. raise abruptly and sharply

hoi polloi ('hɔɪ pə'lɔɪ) 1. the common mass of people 2. the masses

hoist (hɔɪst) vt. raise aloft, raise with tackle etc.

hoity-toity (hɔɪtɪ'tɔɪtɪ) a. inf. arrogant, haughty

hokum ('həʊkəm) n. US sl. 1. claptrap; bunk 2. obvious or hackneyed material of a sentimental nature in film etc.

hold[1] (həʊld) vt. 1. keep fast, grasp 2. support in or with hands etc. 3. maintain in position 4. have capacity for 5. own, occupy 6. carry on 7. detain 8. celebrate 9. keep back 10. believe —vi. 11. cling 12. remain fast or unbroken 13. (with to) abide (by) 14. keep 15. remain relevant, valid or true (**held** pt./pp.) —n. 16. grasp 17. influence —'**holder** n. —'**holding** n. (oft. pl.) property, such as land or stocks and shares —'**holdall** n. valise or case for carrying clothes etc. —'**holdfast** n. clamp —**holding company** company with controlling shareholdings in other companies —'**holdup** n. 1. armed robbery 2. delay

hold[2] (həʊld) n. space in ship or aircraft for cargo

hole (həʊl) n. 1. hollow place, cavity 2. perforation 3. opening 4. inf. unattractive place 5. inf. difficult situation —vt. 6. make holes in 7. drive into a hole —vi. 8. go into a hole —'**holey** a. —**hole-and-corner** a. inf. furtive or secretive

holiday ('hɒlɪdeɪ) n. day or other period of rest from work etc., esp. spent away from home

holland ('hɒlənd) n. linen fabric —'**Hollands** n. spirit, gin

holler ('hɒlə) inf. v. 1. shout or yell (something) —n. 2. shout; call

hollo ('hɒləʊ) or **holla** ('hɒlə) n./interj. 1. cry for attention, or of encouragement (pl. **-s**) —vi. 2. shout

hollow ('hɒləʊ) a. 1. having a cavity, not solid 2. empty 3. false 4. insincere 5. not full-toned —n. 6. cavity, hole, valley —vt. 7. make hollow, make hole in 8. excavate

holly ('hɒlɪ) n. evergreen shrub with prickly leaves and red berries

hollyhock ('hɒlɪhɒk) n. tall plant bearing many large flowers

holmium ('hɒlmɪəm) n. silver-white metallic element of lanthanide series

holm oak (həʊm) evergreen Mediterranean oak tree

holocaust ('hɒləkɔːst) n. great destruction of life, esp. by fire

holograph ('hɒləgræf, -grɑːf) n. document wholly written by the signer

holography (hɒ'lɒgrəfɪ) n. science of using lasers to produce photographic record (**hologram**) which can reproduce a three-dimensional image

holster ('həʊlstə) n. leather case for pistol, hung from belt etc.

holt (həʊlt) n. Poet. wood, wooded hill

holy ('həʊlɪ) a. 1. belonging, devoted to God 2. free from sin 3. divine 4. consecrated —'**holily** adv. —'**holiness** n. 1. sanctity 2. (**H-**) Pope's title —**holier-than-thou** a. offensively sanctimonious or self-righteous —**Holy Communion** service of the Eucharist —**holy day** day of religious festival —**Holy Ghost** or **Spirit** third person of Trinity —**Holy Grail** cup or dish used by Christ at the Last Supper —**holy orders** 1. sacrament whereby person is admitted to Christian ministry 2. grades of Christian ministry 3. status of ordained Christian minister —**Holy See** R.C.Ch. 1. the see of the pope as bishop of Rome 2. Roman curia —**Holy Week** week before Easter —**the Holy Land** Palestine

homage ('hɒmɪdʒ) n. 1. tribute, respect, reverence 2. formal acknowledgment of allegiance

homburg ('hɒmbɜːg) n. man's hat of soft felt with dented crown and stiff upturned brim

home (həʊm) n. 1. dwelling-place 2. residence 3. native place 4. institution for the elderly, infirm etc. —a. 5. of one's home, country etc. —adv. 6. to, at one's home 7. to the point —v. 8. direct or be directed on to a point or target —'**homeless** a. —'**homely** a. plain —'**homeward** a./adv. —'**homewards** adv. —**home-brew** n. alcoholic drink made at home —**Home Counties** counties surrounding London —**home economics** study of diet, budgeting and other subjects concerned with running a home —**home help** UK woman employed, esp. by local authority, to do housework in person's home —**Home Office** UK government department responsible for internal affairs —**home rule** 1. self-government 2. partial autonomy sometimes granted to national minority or colony —**Home Secretary** UK head of Home Office —'**homesick** a. depressed by absence from home —'**homesickness** n. —'**homespun** a. 1. domestic 2. simple —n. 3. cloth made of homespun yarn —'**homestead** n. 1. house with outbuildings, esp. on farm 2. US, C house and land occupied by owner and exempt from seizure and forced sale for debt —**'homesteader** n. —**'homework** n. school work to be done at home —**'homing** a. Zool. of ability to return home after travelling great distances —**homing pigeon** domestic pigeon developed for its homing instinct, used for racing (also **'homer**) —**bring home to** impress deeply upon —**home and dry** safe or successful

homeo-, homoeo-, or **homoio-** (comb. form) like, similar, as in homeomorphism

homeopathy or **homoeopathy** (hǝʊmɪ-'ɒpǝθɪ) n. treatment of disease by small doses of drug that produces, in healthy person, symptoms similar to those of disease being treated —**'homeopath** or **'homoeopath** n. one who believes in or practises homeopathy —**homeo'pathic** or **homoeo'pathic** a. —**homeo'pathically** or **homoeo'pathically** adv.

homicide ('hɒmɪsaɪd) n. 1. killing of human being 2. killer —**homi'cidal** a.

homily ('hɒmɪlɪ) n. 1. sermon 2. religious discourse —**homi'letic** a. —**homi'letics** pl.n. (with sing. v.) art of preaching

hominid ('hɒmɪnɪd) n. 1. member of mammal family, extinct or living —a. 2. of or belonging to mammal family

hominoid ('hɒmɪnɔɪd) a. 1. manlike 2. of or belonging to primate family, which includes anthropoid apes and man —n. 3. hominoid animal

Homo ('hǝʊmǝʊ) n. genus to which modern man belongs —**Homo sapiens** ('sæpɪɛnz) specific name of modern man

homo- (comb. form) same, as in homosexual. Such words are not given here where the meaning may easily be inferred from the simple word

homogeneous (hǝʊmǝ'dʒiːnɪǝs, hɒm-) a. 1. formed of uniform parts 2. similar, uniform 3. of the same nature —**homoge'neity** n. —**homogenize** or **-nise** (hɒ-'mɒdʒɪnaɪz) vt. break up fat globules in (milk and cream) to distribute them evenly

homograph ('hɒmǝgrɑːf) n. one of group of words spelt in the same way but having different meanings —**homo'graphic** a.

homologous (hǝʊ'mɒlǝgǝs, hɒ-), **homological** (hǝʊmǝ'lɒdʒɪk'l, hɒm-), or **homologic** a. having the same relation, relative position etc. —**'homologue** n. homologous thing

homonym ('hɒmǝnɪm) n. word of same form as another, but having different meaning —**homo'nymic** or **ho'monymous** a.

homosexual (hǝʊmǝʊ'sɛksjʊǝl, hɒm-) n. 1. person sexually attracted to members of the same sex —a. 2. of or relating to homosexuals or homosexuality —**homo'sexu'ality** n.

Hon or **Hon.** 1. Honourable 2. (also **h-**) honorary

hone (hǝʊn) n. 1. whetstone —vt. 2. sharpen with hone

honest ('ɒnɪst) a. 1. not cheating, lying, stealing etc. 2. genuine 3. without pretension —**'honestly** adv. —**'honesty** n. 1. quality of being honest 2. plant with silvery seed pods

honey ('hʌnɪ) n. sweet fluid made by bees —**'honeyed** or **'honied** a. Poet. 1. flattering or soothing 2. made sweet or agreeable 3. full of honey —**'honeybee** n. any of various social bees widely domesticated as source of honey and beeswax (also **hive bee**) —**'honeycomb** n. 1. wax structure in hexagonal cells in which bees place honey, eggs etc. —vt. 2. fill with cells or perforations —**'honeydew** n. 1. sweet sticky substance found on plants 2. type of sweet melon —**'honeymoon** n. holiday taken by newly-wedded pair —**'honeysuckle** n. climbing plant

honk (hɒŋk) n. 1. call of wild goose 2. any sound like this, esp. sound of motor horn —vi. 3. make this sound

honky-tonk ('hɒŋkɪtɒŋk) n. 1. US sl. cheap disreputable nightclub etc. 2. style of ragtime piano-playing

honour or U.S. **honor** ('ɒnǝ) n. 1. personal integrity 2. renown 3. reputation 4. sense of what is right or due 5. chastity 6. high rank or position 7. source, cause of honour 8. pleasure, privilege —pl. 9. mark of respect 10. distinction in examination —vt. 11. respect highly 12. confer honour on 13. accept or pay (bill etc.) when due —**hono'rarium** n. a fee (pl. **-s, -ia** (-ɪǝ)) —**'honorary** a. 1. conferred for the sake of honour only 2. holding position without pay or usual requirements 3. giving services without pay —**hono'rific** a. conferring honour —**'honourable** or U.S. **'honorable** a. —**'honourably** or U.S. **'honorably** adv.

hooch or **hootch** (huːtʃ) n. US sl. alcoholic drink, esp. illicitly distilled spirits

hood (hʊd) n. 1. covering for head and neck, oft. part of cloak or gown 2. hoodlike thing as (adjustable) top of motorcar, perambulator etc. 3. esp. US car bonnet —**'hooded** a. covered with or shaped like hood —**hooded crow** crow that has grey body and black head, wings, and tail (also (Scot.) **'hoodie, hoodie crow**) —**'hoodwink** vt. deceive

hoodlum ('huːdlǝm) n. gangster, bully —**hood** n. US sl. hoodlum

hoodoo ('huːduː) n. cause of bad luck

hooey ('huːɪ) n./interj. sl. nonsense

hoof (huːf) n. horny casing of foot of horse etc. (pl. **-s, hooves**) —**on the hoof** (of livestock) alive

hoo-ha ('huːhɑː) n. needless fuss, bother etc.

hook (hʊk) n. 1. bent piece of metal used to suspend, hold, or pull something 2. something resembling hook in shape or function 3. curved cutting tool 4. Boxing blow delivered with bent elbow —vt. 5. grasp, catch, hold, as with hook 6. fasten with hook 7. Golf drive (ball) widely to the left 8. Cricket hit off (ball) to leg —**hooked**

a. **1.** shaped like hook **2.** caught **3.** *sl.* addicted —**'hooker** *n.* **1.** US *sl.* prostitute **2.** *Rugby* player who uses feet to get ball in scrum —**hook-up** *n.* linking of radio, television stations —**'hookworm** *n.* parasitic worm infesting humans and animals

hookah or **hooka** ('hukə) *n.* oriental pipe in which smoke is drawn through water and long tube

hooligan ('hu:lɪgən) *n.* violent, irresponsible (young) person —**'hooliganism** *n.*

hoop (hu:p) *n.* **1.** rigid circular band of metal, wood *etc.* **2.** such a band used for binding barrel *etc.,* for use as toy, or for jumping through as in circus acts —*vt.* **3.** bind with hoops **4.** encircle —**go through the hoop(s)** *inf.* go through an ordeal or test

hoopla ('hu:plɑ:) *n.* game played at fairgrounds *etc.,* by throwing rings at objects for prizes

hoopoe ('hu:pu:) *n.* bird with large crest

hooray (huː'reɪ) or **hoorah** (huː'rɑ:) *interj.* **1.** see HURRAH **2.** (hu:'ru:) A, NZ cheerio (*also* **hoo'roo**)

hoot (hu:t) *n.* **1.** owl's cry or similar sound **2.** cry of disapproval or derision **3.** *inf.* funny person or thing —*vi.* **4.** utter hoot, *esp.* in derision **5.** sound motor horn **6.** *inf.* laugh —**'hooter** *n.* **1.** device (eg horn) to emit hooting sound **2.** *sl.* nose

Hoover ('hu:və) *n.* **1.** R vacuum cleaner —*v.* **2.** (h-) vacuum

hooves (hu:vz) *n., pl. of* HOOF

hop[1] (hɒp) *vi.* **1.** spring on one foot **2.** *inf.* move quickly (**-pp-**) —*n.* **3.** leap, skip **4.** one stage of journey —**'hopscotch** *n.* children's game of hopping in pattern drawn on ground

hop[2] (hɒp) *n.* **1.** climbing plant with bitter cones used to flavour beer *etc.* —*pl.* **2.** the cones

hope (həʊp) *n.* **1.** expectation of something desired **2.** thing that gives, or object of, this feeling —*v.* **3.** feel hope —**'hopeful** *a.* —**'hopefully** *adv. inf.* it is hoped —**'hopeless** *a.* —**young hopeful** promising boy or girl

hopper ('hɒpə) *n.* **1.** one who hops **2.** device for feeding material into mill or machine, or grain into railway truck *etc.* **3.** mechanical hop-picker **4.** SA *see* COCOPAN

horal ('hɔ:rəl) or **horary** ('hɔ:rərɪ) *a. obs.* **1.** pert. to an hour **2.** hourly

horde (hɔ:d) *n.* large crowd, *esp.* moving together

horehound or **hoarhound** ('hɔ:haʊnd) *n.* plant with bitter juice formerly used medicinally

horizon (hə'raɪz²n) *n.* **1.** boundary of part of the earth seen from any given point **2.** line where earth and sky seem to meet **3.** boundary of mental outlook —**horizontal** (hɒrɪ'zɒnt²l) *a.* parallel with horizon, level —**horizontally** (hɒrɪ'zɒntəlɪ) *adv.*

hormone ('hɔ:məʊn) *n.* **1.** substance secreted by certain glands which stimu-

lates organs of the body **2.** synthetic substance with same effect

horn (hɔ:n) *n.* **1.** hard projection on heads of certain animals, *eg* cows **2.** substance of horns **3.** various things made of, or resembling it **4.** wind instrument *orig.* made of horn **5.** device, *esp.* in car, emitting sound as warning *etc.* —**horned** *a.* having horns —**'horny** *a.* **1.** of, like or hard as horn **2.** having horn(s) **3.** *sl.* sexually aroused —**'hornbeam** *n.* tree with smooth grey bark —**'hornbill** *n.* type of bird with horny growth on large bill —**'hornbook** *n.* page bearing religious text or alphabet, held in frame with thin window of horn over it —**horn of plenty** *see* CORNUCOPIA —**'hornpipe** *n.* lively dance, *esp.* associated with sailors

hornblende ('hɔ:nblɛnd) *n.* mineral consisting of silica, with magnesia, lime, or iron

hornet ('hɔ:nɪt) *n.* large insect of wasp family

horologe ('hɒrəlɒdʒ) *n. rare* any timepiece —**ho'rology** *n.* art or science of clock-making and measuring time

horoscope ('hɒrəskəʊp) *n.* **1.** observation of, or scheme showing disposition of planets *etc.,* at given moment, *esp.* birth, by which character and abilities of individual are predicted **2.** telling of person's fortune by this method

horror ('hɒrə) *n.* **1.** terror **2.** loathing, fear **3.** its cause —**hor'rendous** *a.* horrific —**'horrible** *a.* exciting horror, hideous, shocking —**'horribly** *adv.* —**'horrid** *a.* **1.** unpleasant, repulsive **2.** *inf.* unkind —**hor'rific** *a.* particularly horrible —**'horrify** *vt.* move to horror (**-ified, -ifying**)

hors d'oeuvre (ɔ: 'dɜ:vr) small dish served before main meal

horse (hɔ:s) *n.* **1.** four-footed animal used for riding and draught **2.** cavalry **3.** vaulting-block **4.** frame for support *etc.,* *esp.* for drying clothes —*vt.* **5.** provide with horse or horses —**'horsy** or **'horsey** *a.* **1.** having to do with horses **2.** devoted to horses or horse racing —**horse brass** decorative brass ornament, *orig.* attached to horse's harness —**horse chestnut** tree with conical clusters of white or pink flowers and large nuts —**'horseflesh** *n.* **1.** horses collectively **2.** flesh of horse, *esp.* edible horse meat —**'horsefly** *n.* large, bloodsucking fly —**horse laugh** harsh boisterous laugh —**'horseman** *n.* rider on horse (**'horsewoman** *fem.*) —**'horseplay** *n.* rough or rowdy play —**'horsepower** *n.* unit of power of engine *etc.* 550 footpounds per second —**'horseradish** *n.* plant with pungent root —**horse sense** *see* **common sense** *at* COMMON —**'horseshoe** *n.* **1.** protective U-shaped piece of iron nailed to horse's hoof **2.** thing so shaped —**'horsetail** *n.* green flowerless plant with erect, jointed stem —**horse about** or **around** *inf.* play roughly, boisterously

hortatory ('hɔ:tətərɪ) or **hortative** ('hɔ:-

tətɪv) *a.* tending to exhort; encouraging —**hor'tation** *n.*

horticulture ('hɔːtɪkʌltʃə) *n.* art or science of gardening —**horti'cultural** *a.* —**horti'culturist** *n.*

Hos. *Bible* Hosea

hosanna (həʊ'zænə) *n./interj.* cry of praise, adoration

hose (həʊz) *n.* **1.** flexible tube for conveying liquid or gas **2.** stockings —*vt.* **3.** water with hose —**'hosier** *n.* dealer in stockings *etc.* —**'hosiery** *n.* stockings *etc.*

hospice ('hɒspɪs) *n. obs.* traveller's house of rest kept by religious order

hospital ('hɒspɪt'l) *n.* institution for care of sick —**hospitali'zation** *or* -**li'sation** *n.* —**'hospitalize** *or* -**lise** *vt.* place for care in hospital

hospitality (hɒspɪ'tælɪtɪ) *n.* friendly and liberal reception of strangers or guests —**'hospitable** *a.* welcoming, kindly —**'hospitably** *adv.*

host¹ (həʊst) *n.* **1.** one who entertains another (**'hostess** *fem.*) **2.** innkeeper **3.** compere of show **4.** animal, plant on which parasite lives —*v.* **5.** be host of (party, programme *etc.*)

host² (həʊst) *n.* large number

Host (həʊst) *n.* consecrated bread of the Eucharist

hosta ('hɒstə) *n.* garden plant with large ornamental leaves

hostage ('hɒstɪdʒ) *n.* person taken or given as pledge or security

hostel ('hɒst'l) *n.* building providing accommodation at low cost for particular category of people, as students or the homeless —**'hostelry** *n. obs.* inn

hostile ('hɒstaɪl) *a.* **1.** opposed, antagonistic **2.** warlike **3.** of or relating to an enemy **4.** unfriendly —**hostility** (hɒ'stɪlɪtɪ) *n.* **1.** enmity —*pl.* **2.** acts of warfare

hot (hɒt) *a.* **1.** of high temperature, very warm, giving or feeling heat **2.** angry **3.** severe **4.** recent, new **5.** much favoured **6.** spicy **7.** *sl.* good, quick, smart **8.** *sl.* stolen (**'hotter** *comp.*, **'hottest** *sup.*) —**'hotly** *adv.* —**'hotness** *n.* —**hot air** *inf.* boastful, empty talk —**'hotbed** *n.* **1.** bed of earth heated by manure and grass for young plants **2.** any place encouraging growth —**hot-blooded** *a.* passionate, excitable —**hot dog** hot sausage, *esp.* frankfurter, in split bread roll —**'hotfoot** *vi./adv.* (go) quickly —**'hothead** *n.* hasty, intemperate person —**hot-headed** *a.* impetuous, rash or hot-tempered —**hot-headedness** *n.* —**'hothouse** *n.* **1.** forcing house for plants **2.** heated building for cultivating tropical plants in cold or temperate climates —**hot line** direct communication link between heads of government *etc.* —**hot money** capital that is transferred from one commercial centre to another seeking best opportunity for short-term gain —**'hotplate** *n.* **1.** heated plate on electric cooker **2.** portable device for keeping food warm —**'hotpot** *n.* UK casserole covered with layer of potatoes —**hot rod** car with engine that has been modified to produce increased power —**hot seat 1.** *inf.* difficult or dangerous position **2.** US *sl.* electric chair —**hot-foot it** go quickly —**in hot water** *inf.* in trouble

hotchpotch ('hɒtʃpɒtʃ) *or esp. U.S.* **hodgepodge** ('hɒdʒpɒdʒ) *n.* **1.** medley **2.** dish of many ingredients

hotel (həʊ'tɛl) *n.* commercial establishment providing lodging and meals —**hotel keeper** *or* **ho'telier** *n.*

Hottentot ('hɒt'ntɒt) *n.* member of a native S Afr. race, now nearly extinct (*pl.* -**tot, -s**)

hough (hɒx) *see* HOCK¹

hound (haʊnd) *n.* **1.** hunting dog —*vt.* **2.** chase, pursue **3.** urge on

hour (aʊə) *n.* **1.** twenty-fourth part of day **2.** sixty minutes **3.** time of day **4.** appointed time —*pl.* **5.** fixed periods for work, prayers *etc.* **6.** book of prayers —**'hourly** *adv.* **1.** every hour **2.** frequently —*a.* **3.** frequent **4.** happening every hour —**'hourglass** *n.* **1.** device consisting of two transparent chambers linked by narrow channel, containing quantity of sand that takes specified time to trickle from one chamber to the other —*a.* **2.** wellproportioned with small waist

houri ('hʊərɪ) *n.* beautiful nymph of the Muslim paradise (*pl.* -**s**)

house (haʊs) *n.* **1.** building for human habitation **2.** building for other specified purpose **3.** legislative or other assembly **4.** family **5.** business firm **6.** theatre audience —*v.* (haʊz) **7.** give or receive shelter, lodging or storage —*vt.* **8.** cover; contain —**housing** ('haʊzɪŋ) *n.* **1.** (providing of) houses **2.** part or structure designed to cover, protect, contain —**house arrest** confinement to one's own home rather than in prison —**'houseboat** *n.* boat for living in on river *etc.* —**'housebound** *a.* unable to leave one's house because of illness *etc.* —**'housebreaker** *n.* burglar —**'housecoat** *n.* woman's long loose garment for casual wear at home —**'household** *n.* inmates of house collectively —**'householder** *n.* **1.** occupier of house as his dwelling **2.** head of household —**household name** *or* **word** person or thing that is very well known —**'housekeeper** *n.* person managing affairs of household —**'housekeeping** *n.* (money for) running household —**'housemaid** *n.* maidservant who cleans rooms *etc.* —**housemaid's knee** inflammation and swelling of bursa in front of kneecap —**'houseman** *n.* junior doctor who is member of medical staff of hospital —**House of Commons** UK, C lower chamber of Parliament —**House of Lords** UK upper chamber of Parliament, composed of the peers of the realm —**house-proud** *a.* preoccupied with appearance of one's house —**'housetop** *n.* roof of house —**house-train** *vt.* UK train (pets) to urinate and defecate outdoors

—**house-warming** n. party to celebrate entry into new house —**housewife** n. woman who runs a household —**house-work** n. work of running home, such as cleaning etc. —**housey-housey** n. gambling game, bingo —**proclaim from the housetops** announce publicly

hove (həʊv) chiefly Naut. pt./pp. of HEAVE

hovel ('hɒvˀl) n. mean dwelling

hover ('hɒvə) vi. 1. (of bird etc.) hang in the air 2. loiter 3. be in state of indecision —**'hovercraft** n. type of craft which can travel over both land and sea on a cushion of air

how (haʊ) adv. 1. in what way 2. by what means 3. in what condition 4. to what degree —**howbeit** (haʊ'biːɪt) adv. obs. nevertheless —**how'ever** adv. 1. nevertheless 2. in whatever way, degree 3. all the same

howdah ('haʊdə) n. (canopied) seat on elephant's back

howitzer ('haʊɪtsə) n. short gun firing shells at high elevation

howl (haʊl) vi. 1. utter long loud cry —n. 2. such cry —**'howler** n. 1. one that howls 2. inf. stupid mistake —**'howling** a. inf. great

hoyden or **hoiden** ('hɔɪdˀn) n. wild, boisterous girl, tomboy —**'hoydenish** or **'hoidenish** a.

H.P. 1. high pressure 2. horsepower (also **hp**) 3. UK hire purchase (also **h.p.**)

H.Q. or **h.q.** headquarters

hr. or **hr** hour

H.R.H. His (or Her) Royal Highness

HT Phys. high tension

hub (hʌb) n. 1. middle part of wheel, from which spokes radiate 2. central point of activity

hubble-bubble ('hʌbˀl'bʌbˀl) n. 1. see HOOKAH 2. turmoil 3. gargling sound

hubbub ('hʌbʌb) n. 1. confused noise of many voices 2. uproar

hubris ('hjuːbrɪs) or **hybris** ('haɪbrɪs) n. pride or arrogance —**hu'bristic** or **hy'bristic** a.

huckaback ('hʌkəbæk) n. coarse absorbent linen or cotton fabric used for towels etc. (also **huck**)

huckster ('hʌkstə) n. 1. person using aggressive or questionable methods of selling —vt. 2. sell (goods) thus

huddle ('hʌdˀl) n. 1. crowded mass 2. inf. impromptu conference —v. 3. heap, crowd together 4. hunch (oneself)

hue (hjuː) n. colour, complexion

hue and cry 1. public uproar, outcry 2. formerly, loud outcry usu. in pursuit of wrongdoer

huff (hʌf) n. 1. passing mood of anger —v. 2. make or become angry, resentful —n. 3. blow, puff heavily —**'huffily** adv. —**'huffy** a.

hug (hʌg) vt. 1. clasp tightly in the arms 2. cling to 3. keep close to (-**gg**-) —n. 4. fond embrace

huge (hjuːdʒ) a. very big —**'hugely** adv. very much

huggermugger ('hʌgəmʌgə) n. 1. confusion 2. rare secrecy —a./adv. obs. 3. with secrecy 4. in confusion —vt. 5. obs. keep secret —vi. 6. obs. act secretly

Huguenot ('hjuːgənəʊ, -nɒt) n. 1. French Calvinist, esp. of 16th or 17th century —a. 2. designating French Protestant Church

huh (spelling pron. hʌ) interj. exclamation of derision, bewilderment, inquiry etc.

hula ('huːlə) or **hula-hula** n. native dance of Hawaii

Hula-Hoop n. R hoop of plastic etc. swung round body by wriggling hips

hulk (hʌlk) n. 1. body of abandoned vessel 2. offens. large, unwieldy person or thing —**'hulking** a. unwieldy, bulky

hull (hʌl) n. 1. frame, body of ship 2. calyx of strawberry, raspberry, or similar fruit 3. shell, husk —vt. 4. remove shell, hull from 5. pierce hull of (vessel etc.)

hullabaloo or **hullaballoo** (hʌləbə'luː) n. uproar, clamour, row

hullo (hʌ'ləʊ) interj. see HELLO

hum (hʌm) vi. 1. make low continuous sound as bee 2. sl. smell unpleasantly 3. sl. be very active —vt. 4. sing with closed lips (-**mm**-) —n. 5. humming sound 6. sl. smell 7. sl. great activity 8. in radio, disturbance affecting reception —**'hummingbird** n. very small bird whose wings make humming noise

human ('hjuːmən) a. of, relating to, or characteristic of mankind —**humane** (hjuː-'meɪn) a. 1. benevolent, kind 2. merciful —**'humanism** n. 1. belief in human effort rather than religion 2. interest in human welfare and affairs 3. classical literary culture —**'humanist** n. —**humani'tarian** n. 1. philanthropist —a. 2. having the welfare of mankind at heart —**hu'manity** n. 1. human nature 2. human race 3. kindliness —pl. 4. study of literature, philosophy, the arts —**'humanize** or **-ise** vt. 1. make human 2. civilize —**'humanly** adv. —**'humanoid** a. 1. like human being in appearance —n. 2. being with human rather than anthropoid characteristics 3. in science fiction, robot or creature resembling human being —**human'kind** n. whole race of man

humble ('hʌmbˀl) a. 1. lowly, modest —vt. 2. bring low, abase, humiliate —**'humbly** adv. —**humble pie** formerly, pie made from heart, entrails etc. of deer —**eat humble pie** be forced to behave humbly

humbug ('hʌmbʌg) n. 1. impostor 2. sham, nonsense, deception 3. sweet of boiled sugar —vt. 4. deceive; defraud (-**gg**-)

humdinger ('hʌmdɪŋə) n. sl. excellent person or thing

humdrum ('hʌmdrʌm) a. commonplace, dull, monotonous

humeral ('hjuːmərəl) a. of shoulder —**'humerus** n. long bone of upper arm (pl. **-meri** (-məraɪ))

humid ('hjuːmɪd) a. moist, damp —**hu-'midifier** n. device for increasing amount

of water vapour in air in room *etc.*
—**hu'midify** *vt.* —**hu'midity** *n.*

humiliate (hju:'mɪlɪeɪt) *vt.* lower dignity of, abase, mortify —**humili'ation** *n.*

humility (hju:'mɪlɪtɪ) *n.* 1. state of being humble 2. meekness

hummock ('hʌmək) *n.* 1. low knoll, hillock 2. ridge of ice

humour *or U.S.* **humor** ('hju:mə) *n.* 1. faculty of saying or perceiving what excites amusement 2. state of mind, mood 3. temperament 4. *obs.* any of various fluids of body —*vt.* 5. gratify, indulge —**'humorist** *n.* person who acts, speaks, writes humorously —**'humorous** *a.* 1. funny 2. amusing —**'humorously** *adv.*

hump (hʌmp) *n.* 1. normal or deforming lump, *esp.* on back 2. hillock 3. *inf.* dejection —*vt.* 4. make hump-shaped 5. *sl.* carry, heave —**'humpback** *n.* person with hump —**'humpbacked** *a.* having a hump

humph (*spelling pron.* hʌmf) *interj.* exclamation of annoyance, indecision *etc.*

humus ('hju:məs) *n.* decayed vegetable and animal mould

Hun (hʌn) *n.* 1. member of Asiatic nomadic peoples who invaded Europe in 4th and 5th centuries A.D. 2. *inf. derog.* German 3. *inf.* vandal —**'Hunlike** *a.* —**'Hunnish** *a.*

hunch (hʌntʃ) *n.* 1. intuition or premonition 2. hump —*vt.* 3. thrust, bend into hump —**'hunchback** *n.* humpback

hundred ('hʌndrəd) *n./a.* cardinal number, ten times ten —**'hundredfold** *a./adv.* —**'hundredth** *a./n.* ordinal number of a hundred —**hundreds and thousands** tiny beads of coloured sugar, used in decorating cakes *etc.* —**'hundredweight** *n.* weight of 112 lbs. (50.8 kg), 20th part of ton

hung (hʌŋ) *v.* 1. *pt./pp. of* HANG —*a.* 2. (of jury *etc.*) unable to decide 3. not having majority —**hung-over** *a. inf.* suffering from aftereffects of excessive drinking —**hung parliament** parliament in which no party has absolute majority —**hung up** *inf.* 1. delayed 2. emotionally disturbed

hunger ('hʌŋgə) *n.* 1. discomfort, exhaustion from lack of food 2. strong desire —*vi.* 3. (*usu. with* for *or* after) have great desire (for) —**'hungrily** *adv.* —**'hungry** *a.* having keen appetite —**hunger strike** refusal of all food, as protest

hunk (hʌŋk) *n.* 1. thick piece 2. *sl., chiefly US* sexually attractive man

hunkers ('hʌŋkəz) *pl.n. dial.* haunches

hunt (hʌnt) *v.* 1. (seek out to) kill or capture for sport or food 2. search (for) —*n.* 3. chase, search 4. track of country hunted over 5. (party organized for) hunting 6. pack of hounds 7. hunting district or society —**'hunter** *n.* 1. one who hunts (**'huntress** *fem.*) 2. horse, dog bred for hunting —**'huntsman** *n.* man in charge of pack of hounds

hurdle ('hɜːd²l) *n.* 1. portable frame of bars for temporary fences or for jumping over 2. obstacle —*pl.* 3. race over hurdles

—*vi.* 4. race over hurdles —**'hurdler** *n.* one who races over hurdles

hurdy-gurdy ('hɜːdɪ'gɜːdɪ) *n.* mechanical (musical) instrument (*eg* barrel organ)

hurl (hɜːl) *vt.* throw violently —**hurly-burly** *n.* loud confusion

hurling ('hɜːlɪŋ) *or* **hurley** *n.* Irish game like hockey

hurrah (hʊ'rɑː), **hooray** (hu:'reɪ), *or* **hoorah** (hu:'rɑː) *interj.* exclamation of joy or applause

hurricane ('hʌrɪk²n) *n.* very strong, potentially destructive wind or storm —**hurricane lamp** lamp with glass covering round flame

hurry ('hʌrɪ) *v.* 1. (cause to) move or act in great haste ('**hurried**, '**hurrying**) —*n.* 2. undue haste 3. eagerness —**'hurriedly** *adv.*

hurst (hɜːst) *n. obs.* 1. wood 2. sandbank

hurt (hɜːt) *vt.* 1. injure, damage, give pain to 2. wound feelings of, distress —*vi.* 3. *inf.* feel pain (**hurt** *pt./pp.*) —*n.* 4. wound, injury, harm —**'hurtful** *a.*

hurtle ('hɜːt²l) *vi.* 1. move rapidly 2. rush violently 3. whirl

husband ('hʌzbənd) *n.* 1. married man —*v.* 2. economize, manage or use to best advantage —**'husbandry** *n.* 1. farming 2. economy

hush (hʌʃ) *v.* 1. make or be silent —*n.* 2. stillness 3. quietness —**hush-hush** *a. inf.* secret —**hush up** suppress (rumours, information), make secret

husk (hʌsk) *n.* 1. dry covering of certain seeds and fruits 2. worthless outside part —*vt.* 3. remove husk from —**'husky** *a.* 1. rough in tone 2. hoarse 3. dry as husk, dry in the throat 4. of, full of, husks 5. *inf.* big and strong

husky ('hʌskɪ) *n.* 1. Arctic sledgedog 2. C *sl.* Inuit

hussar (hʊ'zɑː) *n.* lightly armed cavalry soldier

hussy ('hʌsɪ, -zɪ) *n.* cheeky girl or young woman

hustings ('hʌstɪŋz) *pl.n.* 1. platform from which parliamentary candidates were nominated 2. political campaigning

hustle ('hʌs²l) *v.* 1. push about, jostle, hurry —*vi.* 2. *sl.* solicit —*n.* 3. instance of hustling —**'hustler** *n.*

hut (hʌt) *n.* any small house or shelter, usu. of wood or metal

hutch (hʌtʃ) *n.* box-like pen for rabbits *etc.*

hyacinth ('haɪəsɪnθ) *n.* 1. bulbous plant with bell-shaped flowers, *esp.* purple-blue 2. this blue 3. orange gem jacinth

hyaena (haɪ'iːnə) *n. see* HYENA

hyaline ('haɪəlɪn) *a.* clear, translucent

hybrid ('haɪbrɪd) *n.* 1. offspring of two plants or animals of different species 2. mongrel —*a.* 3. crossbred —**'hybridism** *n.* —**'hybridize** *or* **-ise** *v.* (cause to) produce hybrids; cross-breed

hydatid ('haɪdətɪd) *a./n.* (of) watery cyst, resulting from development of tapeworm larva causing serious disease (in man)

hydra ('haɪdrə) n. 1. fabulous many-headed water serpent 2. any persistent problem 3. freshwater polyp (pl. **-s, -drae** (-driː)) —**hydra-headed** a. hard to root out

hydrangea (haɪ'dreɪndʒə) n. ornamental shrub with pink, blue, or white flowers

hydrant ('haɪdrənt) n. water-pipe with nozzle for hose

hydrate ('haɪdreɪt) n. 1. chemical compound containing water that is chemically combined with substance —v. 2. (cause to) undergo treatment or impregnation with water —**hy'dration** n. —'**hydrator** n.

hydraulic (haɪ'drɔlɪk) a. concerned with, operated by, pressure transmitted through liquid in pipe —**hy'draulics** pl.n. (with sing. v.) science of mechanical properties of liquid in motion

hydro ('haɪdrəʊ) n. UK (esp. formerly) hotel or resort offering facilities for hydropathic treatment (pl. **-s**)

Hydro ('haɪdrəʊ) n. C hydroelectric power company

hydro- or before vowel **hydr-** (comb. form) 1. water, as in hydroelectric 2. presence of hydrogen, as in hydrocarbon

hydrocarbon (haɪdrəʊ'kɑːbˀn) n. compound of hydrogen and carbon

hydrocephalus (haɪdrəʊ'sefələs) or **hydrocephaly** (haɪdrəʊ'sefəlɪ) n. accumulation of cerebrospinal fluid within ventricles of brain —**hydrocephalic** (haɪdrəʊse'fælɪk) or **hydro'cephalous** a.

hydrochloric acid (haɪdrə'klɒrɪk) strong colourless acid used in many industrial and laboratory processes

hydrocyanic acid (haɪdrəʊsaɪ'ænɪk) see hydrogen cyanide at HYDROGEN

hydrodynamics (haɪdrəʊdaɪ'næmɪks, -dɪ-) pl.n. (with sing. v.) science of the motions of system wholly or partly fluid

hydroelectric (haɪdrəʊɪ'lektrɪk) a. pert. to generation of electricity by use of water

hydrofoil ('haɪdrəfɔɪl) n. fast, light vessel with hull raised out of water at speed by vanes in water

hydrogen ('haɪdrɪdʒən) n. colourless gas which combines with oxygen to form water —'**hydrogenate** v. (cause to) undergo reaction with hydrogen —**hydrogen'ation** n. —**hydrogen bomb** atom bomb of enormous power in which hydrogen nuclei are converted into helium nuclei —**hydrogen cyanide** colourless poisonous liquid with faint odour of bitter almonds, used for making plastics and as war gas —**hydrogen peroxide** colourless liquid used as antiseptic and bleach

hydrography (haɪ'drɒgrəfɪ) n. description of waters of the earth —**hy'drographer** n. —**hydro'graphic** a.

hydrology (haɪ'drɒlədʒɪ) n. study of distribution, use etc. of the water of the earth and its atmosphere —**hydrologic** (haɪdrə'lɒdʒɪk) a. —**hy'drologist** n.

hydrolysis (haɪ'drɒlɪsɪs) n. decomposition of chemical compound reacting with water

hydrometer (haɪ'drɒmɪtə) n. device for measuring relative density of liquid

hydrophilic (haɪdrəʊ'fɪlɪk) a. Chem. tending to dissolve in, mix with, or be wetted by water —'**hydrophile** n.

hydrophobia (haɪdrə'fəʊbɪə) n. aversion to water, esp. as symptom of rabies

hydrophone ('haɪdrəfəʊn) n. instrument for detecting sound through water

hydroplane ('haɪdrəʊpleɪn) n. 1. light skimming motorboat 2. seaplane 3. vane controlling motion of submarine etc.

hydroponics (haɪdrəʊ'pɒnɪks) pl.n. (with sing. v.) science of cultivating plants in water without using soil

hydrosphere ('haɪdrəsfɪə) n. watery part of earth's surface, including oceans, lakes, water vapour in atmosphere etc.

hydrostatics (haɪdrəʊ'stætɪks) pl.n. (with sing. v.) branch of science concerned with mechanical properties and behaviour of fluids that are not in motion —**hydro'static** a.

hydrotherapy (haɪdrəʊ'θerəpɪ) n. Med. treatment of disease by external application of water

hydrotropism (haɪ'drɒtrəpɪzəm) n. directional growth of plants in response to water

hydrous ('haɪdrəs) a. containing water

hydroxide (haɪ'drɒksaɪd) n. 1. base or alkali containing ion OH⁻ 2. any compound containing -OH group

hydrozoan (haɪdrəʊ'zəʊən) n. 1. any coelenterate of the class Hydrozoa, which includes hydra and Portuguese man-of-war —a. 2. of Hydrozoa

hyena or **hyaena** (haɪ'iːnə) n. wild animal related to dog

hygiene ('haɪdʒiːn) n. 1. principles and practice of health and cleanliness 2. study of these principles —**hy'gienic** a. —**hy'gienically** adv. —'**hygienist** n.

hygrometer (haɪ'grɒmɪtə) n. instrument for measuring humidity of air

hygroscopic (haɪgrə'skɒpɪk) a. readily absorbing moisture from the atmosphere

hymen ('haɪmen) n. 1. membrane partly covering vagina of virgin 2. (H-) Greek god of marriage

hymenopterous (haɪmɪ'nɒptərəs) a. of large order of insects having two pairs of membranous wings —**hyme'nopteran** or **hyme'nopteron** n. any hymenopterous insect (pl. **-terans, -tera** (-tərə) or **-terons**)

hymn (hɪm) n. 1. song of praise, esp. to God —vt. 2. praise in song —**hymnal** ('hɪmnˀl) a. 1. of hymns —n. 2. book of hymns (also **hymn book**) —**hymnodist** ('hɪmnədɪst) n. —**hymnody** ('hɪmnədɪ) n. singing or composition of hymns

hyoscyamine (haɪə'saɪəmiːn) n. poisonous alkaloid occurring in henbane and related plants and used in medicine

hype¹ (haɪp) sl. n. 1. hypodermic syringe 2. drug addict —vi. 3. (with up) inject oneself with drug

hype² (haɪp) sl. n. 1. deception; racket 2.

intensive or exaggerated publicity or sales promotion —*vt.* **3.** market or promote, using exaggerated or intensive publicity

hyper- (*comb. form*) over, above, excessively, as in *hyperactive*. Such words are not given here where the meaning may easily be inferred from the simple word

hyperbola (haɪˈpɜːbələ) *n.* curve produced when cone is cut by plane making larger angle with the base than the side makes (*pl.* **-s, -le** (-liː))

hyperbole (haɪˈpɜːbəlɪ) *n.* rhetorical exaggeration —**hyperbolic(al)** (haɪpəˈbɒlɪk(ˀl)) *a.*

Hyperborean (haɪpəˈbɔːrɪən) *a./n.* (inhabitant) of extreme north

hypercritical (haɪpəˈkrɪtɪkˀl) *a.* too critical —**hyper'criticism** *n.*

hyperglycaemia *or U.S.* **hyperglycemia** (haɪpəɡlaɪˈsiːmɪə) *n. Pathol.* abnormally large amount of sugar in blood —**hypergly'caemic** *or U.S.* **hypergly'cemic** *a.*

hypermarket (ˈhaɪpəmɑːkɪt) *n. UK* huge self-service store

hyperon (ˈhaɪpərɒn) *n. Phys.* any baryon that is not a nucleon

hyperopia (haɪpəˈrəʊpɪə) *n.* inability to see near objects clearly because images received by eye are focused behind retina —**hyperopic** (haɪpəˈrɒpɪk) *a.*

hypersensitive (haɪpəˈsɛnsɪtɪv) *a.* unduly vulnerable emotionally or physically

hypersonic (haɪpəˈsɒnɪk) *a.* concerned with or having velocity of at least five times that of sound in same medium under the same conditions —**hyper'sonics** *n.*

hypertension (haɪpəˈtɛnʃən) *n.* abnormally high blood pressure

hypertrophy (haɪˈpɜːtrəfɪ) *n.* **1.** enlargement of organ or part resulting from increase in size of cells —*v.* **2.** (cause to) undergo this condition

hyperventilation (haɪpəvɛntɪˈleɪʃən) *n.* increase in rate of breathing, sometimes resulting in cramp and dizziness

hyphen (ˈhaɪfˀn) *n.* short line (-) indicating that two words or syllables are to be connected —**'hyphenate** *vt.* —**'hyphenated** *a.* joined by hyphen

hypno- *or before vowel* **hypn-** (*comb. form*) **1.** sleep, as in *hypnopaedia* **2.** hypnosis, as in *hypnotherapy*

hypnosis (hɪpˈnəʊsɪs) *n.* induced state like deep sleep in which subject acts on external suggestion (*pl.* **-ses** (-siːz)) —**hypnotic** (hɪpˈnɒtɪk) *a.* of hypnosis or of the person or thing producing it —**'hypnotism** *n.* —**'hypnotist** *n.* —**'hypnotize** *or* **-tise** *vt.* affect with hypnosis —**hypno'therapy** *n.* use of hypnosis in treatment of physical or mental disorders

hypo (ˈhaɪpəʊ) *n.* sodium thiosulphate, used as fixer in developing photographs

hypo- *or before vowel* **hyp-** (*comb. form*) under, below, less, as in *hypocrite, hyphen*. Such words are not given here where

meaning may easily be inferred from simple word

hypocaust (ˈhaɪpəkɔːst) *n.* ancient Roman underfloor heating system

hypochondria (haɪpəˈkɒndrɪə) *n.* morbid depression, without cause, about one's own health —**hypo'chondriac** *a./n.* —**hypochondriacal** (haɪpəʊkɒnˈdraɪəkˀl) *a.*

hypocrisy (hɪˈpɒkrəsɪ) *n.* **1.** assuming of false appearance of virtue **2.** insincerity —**'hypocrite** *n.* —**hypo'critical** *a.* —**hypo'critically** *adv.*

hypodermic (haɪpəˈdɜːmɪk) *a.* **1.** introduced, injected beneath the skin —*n.* **2.** hypodermic syringe or needle

hypogastric (haɪpəˈɡæstrɪk) *a.* relating to, situated in, lower part of abdomen

hypostasis (haɪˈpɒstəsɪs) *n.* **1.** *Metaphys.* essential nature of anything **2.** *Christianity* any of the three persons of the Godhead **3.** accumulation of blood in organ or part as result of poor circulation (*pl.* **-ses** (-siːz)) —**hypostatic** (haɪpəˈstætɪk) *or* **hypo'statical** *a.*

hypotension (haɪpəʊˈtɛnʃən) *n. Pathol.* abnormally low blood pressure —**hypo'tensive** *a.*

hypotenuse (haɪˈpɒtɪnjuːz) *n.* side of a right-angled triangle opposite the right angle

hypothecate (haɪˈpɒθɪkeɪt) *vt. Law* pledge (personal property) as security for debt without transferring possession —**hypoth-e'cation** *n.* —**hy'pothecator** *n.*

hypothermia (haɪpəʊˈθɜːmɪə) *n.* condition of having body temperature reduced to dangerously low level

hypothesis (haɪˈpɒθɪsɪs) *n.* **1.** suggested explanation of something **2.** assumption as basis of reasoning (*pl.* **-eses** (-ɪsiːz)) —**hy'pothesize** *or* **-ise** *v.* —**hypo'thetical** *a.* —**hypo'thetically** *adv.*

hypso- *or before vowel* **hyps-** (*comb. form*) height, as in *hypsometry*

hypsography (hɪpˈsɒɡrəfɪ) *n.* branch of geography dealing with altitudes

hypsometer (hɪpˈsɒmɪtə) *n.* instrument for measuring altitudes —**hyp'sometry** *n.* science of measuring altitudes

hyrax (ˈhaɪræks) *n.* genus of hoofed but rodent-like animals (*pl.* **-es, hyraces** (ˈhaɪrəsiːz))

hyssop (ˈhɪsəp) *n.* small aromatic herb

hysterectomy (hɪstəˈrɛktəmɪ) *n.* surgical operation for removing the uterus

hysteresis (hɪstəˈriːsɪs) *n. Phys.* lag or delay in changes in variable property of a system

hysteria (hɪˈstɪərɪə) *n.* **1.** mental disorder with emotional outbursts **2.** any frenzied emotional state **3.** fit of crying or laughing —**hysterical** (hɪˈstɛrɪkˀl) *a.* —**hysterically** (hɪˈstɛrɪkəlɪ) *adv.* —**hysterics** (hɪˈstɛrɪks) *pl.n.* fits of hysteria

Hz hertz

I

i *or* **I** (aɪ) *n.* **1.** ninth letter of English alphabet **2.** any of several speech sounds represented by this letter **3.** something shaped like I (*pl.* **i's, I's** *or* **Is**) —**dot one's i's and cross one's t's** pay attention to detail

I (aɪ) *pron.* the pronoun of the first person singular

I 1. *Chem.* iodine **2.** *Phys.* current **3.** *Phys.* isospin **4.** Roman numeral, one

IA Iowa

-ia (*comb. form*) **1.** in place names, as in *Columbia* **2.** in names of diseases, as in *pneumonia* **3.** in words denoting condition or quality, as in *utopia* **4.** in names of botanical genera and zoological classes, as in *Reptilia* **5.** in collective nouns borrowed from Latin, as in *regalia*

IAEA International Atomic Energy Agency

-ial (*comb. form*) of or relating to, as in *managerial*

iamb (ˈaɪæm, ˈaɪæmb) *or* **iambus** (aɪˈæmbəs) *n.* metrical foot of short and long syllable (*pl.* **iambs** *or* **-buses, -bi** (-baɪ)) —**iˈambic** *a.*

IATA (aɪˈɑːtə, iːˈɑːtə) International Air Transport Association

iatric (aɪˈætrɪk) *or* **iatrical** *a.* of medicine or physicians, *esp.* as suffix **-iatrics, -iatry,** as in *paediatrics, psychiatry*

I.B.A. Independent Broadcasting Authority

Iberian (aɪˈbɪərɪən) *a.* of Iberia, *ie* Spain and Portugal

ibex (ˈaɪbɛks) *n.* wild goat with large horns (*pl.* **-es, ibices** (ˈɪbɪsiːz, ˈaɪ-), **ˈibex**)

ibid. *or* **ib.** ibidem (*Lat.,* in the same place)

ibis (ˈaɪbɪs) *n.* storklike bird

-ible (*a. comb. form*) see **-ABLE** —**-ibility** (*n. comb. form*) —**-ibly** (*adv. comb. form*)

IBM International Business Machines Corporation

i/c 1. in charge (of) **2.** internal combustion

-ic (*comb. form*) **1.** of, relating to or resembling, as in *periodic* (*also* **-ical**) **2.** *Chem.* indicating that element is chemically combined in higher of two possible valence states, as in *ferric*

I.C.A. 1. UK Institute of Contemporary Arts **2.** Institute of Chartered Accountants

-ical (*a. comb. form*) see **-IC** (sense 1) —**-ically** (*adv. comb. form*)

ICBM intercontinental ballistic missile

ice (aɪs) *n.* **1.** frozen water **2.** frozen confection, ice cream —*v.* **3.** (*oft. with up,* over *etc.*) cover, become covered with ice —*vt.* **4.** cool with ice **5.** cover with icing —**ˈicicle** *n.* tapering spike of ice hanging where water has dripped —**ˈicily** *adv.* —**ˈiciness** *n.* —**ˈicing** *n.* mixture of sugar and water *etc.* used to decorate cakes —**ˈicy** *a.* **1.** covered with ice **2.** cold **3.** chilling —**ice age** see **glacial period** at GLACIER —**ˈiceberg** *n.* large floating mass of ice —**ˈicebox** *n.* **1.** compartment in refrigerator for storing or making ice **2.** insulated cabinet packed with ice for storing food —**ˈicebreaker** *n.* **1.** vessel for breaking up ice in bodies of water (*also* **ˈiceboat**) **2.** device for breaking ice into smaller pieces —**ˈicecap** *n.* mass of glacial ice that permanently covers polar regions *etc.* —**ice cream** sweetened frozen dessert made from cream, eggs *etc.* —**ice floe** sheet of floating ice —**ice hockey** team game played on ice with puck —**ice lolly** ice cream, flavoured ice on stick —**ice pack 1.** bag *etc.* containing ice, applied to part of body to reduce swelling *etc.* **2.** see **pack ice** at PACK —**ice skate** boot having steel blade fitted to sole to enable wearer to glide over ice —**ice-skate** *vi.* glide over ice on ice skates —**ice-skater** *n.* —**on thin ice** unsafe; vulnerable

I.C.E. UK Institution of Civil Engineers

Icelandic (aɪsˈlændɪk) *a.* **1.** of Iceland —*n.* **2.** official language of Iceland

I.Chem.E. Institution of Chemical Engineers

ichneumon (ɪkˈnjuːmən) *n.* greyish-brown mongoose

ichor (ˈaɪkɔː) *n.* **1.** *Gr. myth.* fluid said to flow in veins of gods **2.** *Pathol.* foul-smelling watery discharge from wound or ulcer —**ˈichorous** *a.*

ichthyology (ɪkθɪˈɒlədʒɪ) *n.* scientific study of fish —**ichthyosaurus** (ɪkθɪəˈsɔːrəs) *n.* prehistoric marine animal (*pl.* **-i** (-aɪ))

I.C.I. Imperial Chemical Industries

icicle (ˈaɪsɪkˈl) *n.* see ICE

icon *or* **ikon** (ˈaɪkɒn) *n.* image, representation, *esp.* of religious figure —**iˈconoclasm** *n.* —**iˈconoclast** *n.* **1.** one who attacks established principles *etc.* **2.** breaker of icons —**iconoˈclastic** *a.* —**icoˈnography** *n.* **1.** icons collectively **2.** study of icons

icono- *or before vowel* **icon-** (*comb. form*) image; likeness, as in *iconology*

ictus (ˈɪktəs) *n.* **1.** *Prosody* metrical or rhythmical stress in verse feet, as contrasted with stress accent on words **2.** *Med.* sudden attack or stroke (*pl.* **-es, -tus**) —**ˈictal** *a.*

id (ɪd) *n. Psychoanal.* the mind's instinctive energies

ID 1. identification **2.** Idaho

-id (*comb. form*) member of zoological family, as in *cyprinid*

-idae (*comb. form*) name of zoological family, as in *Felidae*

idea (aɪˈdɪə) *n.* **1.** notion in the mind **2.** conception **3.** vague belief **4.** plan, aim —**iˈdeal** *n.* **1.** conception of something that is perfect **2.** perfect person or thing —*a.* **3.**

perfect 4. visionary 5. existing only in idea —**i'dealism** n. 1. tendency to seek perfection in everything 2. philosophy that mind is the only reality —**i'dealist** n. 1. one who holds doctrine of idealism 2. one who strives after the ideal 3. impractical person —**ideal'istic** a. —**ideali'zation** or **-i'sation** n. —**i'dealize** or **-ise** vt. portray as ideal —**i'deally** adv.

idée fixe (ide 'fiks) Fr. fixed idea; obsession (pl. **idées fixes** (ide 'fiks))

idem ('aɪdɛm, 'ɪdɛm) Lat., the same

identity (aɪ'dɛntɪtɪ) n. 1. individuality 2. being the same, exactly alike —**i'dentical** a. very same —**i'dentically** adv. —**i'dentifiable** a. —**identifi'cation** n. —**i'dentify** vt. 1. establish identity of 2. treat as identical —v. 3. associate (oneself) (**i'dentified, i'dentifying**) —**identification parade** group of persons assembled for purpose of discovering whether witness can identify suspect —**I'dentikit** n. R set of pictures of parts of faces that can be built up to form likeness of person sought by police etc.

ideo- (comb. form) idea; ideas, as in ideology

ideogram ('ɪdɪəʊgræm) or **ideograph** ('ɪdɪəʊgrɑːf) n. picture, symbol, figure etc. suggesting an object without naming it —**ide'ography** n. representation of things by ideographs

ideology (aɪdɪ'ɒlədʒɪ) n. body of ideas, beliefs of group, nation etc. —**ideo'logical** a.

ides (aɪdz) n. the 15th of March, May, July and Oct. and the 13th of other months of the Ancient Roman calendar

id est (ɪd ɛst) Lat., that is

idiocy ('ɪdɪəsɪ) n. see IDIOT

idiom ('ɪdɪəm) n. 1. way of expression natural or peculiar to a language or group 2. characteristic style of expression —**idio'matic** a. 1. using idioms 2. colloquial

idiosyncrasy (ɪdɪəʊ'sɪŋkrəsɪ) n. peculiarity of mind, temper or disposition in a person

idiot ('ɪdɪət) n. 1. mentally deficient person 2. foolish, senseless person —**'idiocy** n. 1. state of being an idiot 2. foolish act or remark —**idi'otic** a. utterly senseless or stupid —**idi'otically** adv. —**idiot board** sl. autocue

idle ('aɪd'l) a. 1. unemployed 2. lazy 3. useless; vain 4. groundless —vi. 5. be idle 6. (of engine) run slowly with gears disengaged —vt. 7. (esp. with away) waste —''idleness n. —**'idler** n. —**'idly** adv.

idol ('aɪd'l) n. 1. image of deity as object of worship 2. object of excessive devotion —**i'dolater** n. worshipper of idols (**i'dolatress** fem.) —**i'dolatrous** a. —**i'dolatry** n. —**'idolize** or **-ise** vt. 1. love or venerate to excess 2. make an idol of

idyll or U.S. (sometimes) **idyl** ('ɪdɪl) n. 1. short descriptive poem of picturesque or charming scene or episode, esp. of rustic

life 2. charming or picturesque scene or event —**i'dyllic** a. 1. of, like, idyll 2. delightful —**i'dyllically** adv.

i.e. id est

I.E.E. Institution of Electrical Engineers

if (ɪf) conj. 1. on condition or supposition that 2. whether 3. although —n. 4. uncertainty, doubt (esp. in **ifs and buts**)

-iferous (comb. form) containing, yielding, as in carboniferous

igloo or **iglu** ('ɪgluː) n. dome-shaped Eskimo house of snow and ice

igneous ('ɪgnɪəs) a. (esp. of rocks) formed as molten rock cools and hardens

ignis fatuus ('ɪgnɪs 'fætjʊəs) will-o'-the-wisp (pl. **ignes fatui** ('ɪgniːz 'fætjʊaɪ))

ignite (ɪg'naɪt) v. (cause to) burn —**ignition** (ɪg'nɪʃən) n. 1. act of kindling or setting on fire 2. in internal-combustion engine, means of firing explosive mixture, usu. electric spark

ignoble (ɪg'nəʊb'l) a. 1. mean, base 2. of low birth —**ig'nobly** adv.

ignominy ('ɪgnəmɪnɪ) n. 1. dishonour, disgrace 2. shameful act —**igno'minious** a.

ignore (ɪg'nɔː) vt. disregard; leave out of account —**ignoramus** (ɪgnə'reɪməs) n. ignorant person (pl. **-es**) —**'ignorance** n. lack of knowledge —**'ignorant** a. 1. lacking knowledge 2. uneducated 3. unaware —**'ignorantly** adv.

iguana (ɪ'gwɑːnə) n. large tropical American lizard

ikebana (iːkə'bɑːnə) n. Japanese decorative art of flower arrangement

ikon ('aɪkɒn) n. see ICON

il- (comb. form) see IN-¹, IN-²

ileum ('ɪlɪəm) n. lower part of small intestine —**'ileac** a.

ilex ('aɪlɛks) n. any of genus of trees or shrubs such as holly and inkberry

ilium ('ɪlɪəm) n. uppermost and widest of three sections of hipbone (pl. **-ia** (-ɪə)) —**'iliac** a.

ilk (ɪlk) a. same —**of that ilk** 1. of the same type or class 2. Scot. of the place of the same name

ill (ɪl) a. 1. not in good health 2. bad, evil 3. faulty 4. unfavourable —n. 5. evil, harm 6. mild disease —adv. 7. badly 8. hardly, with difficulty —**'illness** n. —**ill-advised** a. imprudent, injudicious —**ill-bred** a. badly brought up; lacking good manners —**ill-considered** a. done without due consideration; not thought out —**ill-disposed** a. (oft. with towards) not kindly disposed —**ill fame** bad reputation —**ill-fated** a. unfortunate —**ill-favoured** a. ugly, deformed —**ill-founded** a. not founded on true or reliable premises; unsubstantiated —**ill-gotten** a. obtained dishonestly —**ill-mannered** a. boorish, uncivil —**ill-natured** a. naturally unpleasant and mean —**ill-omened** a. unlucky, inauspicious —**ill-starred** a. unlucky, ill-fated —**ill-timed** a. inopportune —**ill-treat** vt. treat cruelly —**ill-use** ('ɪl'juːz) vt. 1. use badly or cruelly; abuse —n. ('ɪl'juːs), also **ill-usage** 2. harsh or cruel treatment; abuse —**ill will** unkind feeling, hostility —**house of ill fame** brothel

illegal (ɪ'liːgᵊl) a. 1. forbidden by law; unlawful; illicit 2. unauthorized or prohibited by code of official or accepted rules —**ille'gality** n. —**il'legally** adv.

illegible (ɪ'lɛdʒɪbᵊl) a. unable to be read or deciphered —**illegi'bility** or **il'legibleness** n.

illegitimate (ɪlɪ'dʒɪtɪmɪt) a. 1. born out of wedlock 2. unlawful 3. not regular —**ille'gitimacy** n.

illiberal (ɪ'lɪbərəl) a. 1. narrow-minded; prejudiced; intolerant 2. not generous; mean 3. lacking in culture or refinement —**illiber'ality** n.

illicit (ɪ'lɪsɪt) a. 1. illegal 2. prohibited, forbidden

illimitable (ɪ'lɪmɪtəbᵊl) a. that cannot be limited, boundless, unrestricted, infinite —**il'limitableness** n.

illiterate (ɪ'lɪtərɪt) a. 1. not literate, unable to read or write 2. violating accepted standards in reading and writing 3. uneducated, ignorant, uncultured —n. 4. illiterate person —**il'literacy** n.

illogical (ɪ'lɒdʒɪkᵊl) a. 1. characterized by lack of logic; senseless; unreasonable 2. disregarding logical principles —**illogi'cality** or **il'logicalness** n. —**il'logically** adv.

illuminate (ɪ'luːmɪneɪt) vt. 1. light up 2. clarify 3. decorate with lights 4. decorate with gold and colours —**il'luminant** n. agent of lighting —**illumi'nation** n. —**il'luminative** a.

illusion (ɪ'luːʒən) n. deceptive appearance or belief —**il'lusionist** n. conjuror —**il'lusory** or **il'lusive** a. false

illust. or **illus.** 1. illustrated 2. illustration

illustrate ('ɪləstreɪt) vt. 1. provide with pictures or examples 2. exemplify —**illus'tration** n. 1. picture, diagram 2. example 3. act of illustrating —**'illustrative** a. providing explanation —**'illustrator** n.

illustrious (ɪ'lʌstrɪəs) a. famous, distinguished, exalted

I.L.O. International Labour Organization

I.L.P. Independent Labour Party

im- (comb. form) see IN-¹, IN-²

image ('ɪmɪdʒ) n. 1. representation or likeness of person or thing 2. optical counterpart, as in mirror 3. double, copy 4. general impression 5. mental picture created by words, esp. in literature 6. personality presented to the public by a person —vt. rare 7. make image of 8. reflect —**'imagery** n. images collectively, esp. in literature

imagine (ɪ'mædʒɪn) vt. 1. picture to oneself 2. think 3. conjecture —**i'maginable** a. —**i'maginary** a. existing only in fancy —**imagi'nation** n. 1. faculty of making mental images of things not present 2. fancy —**im'aginative** a. —**im'aginatively** adv.

imago (ɪ'meɪgəʊ) n. 1. last, perfected state of insect life 2. image (pl. **-s, imagines** (ɪ'mædʒəniːz))

imam (ɪ'mɑːm) n. Islamic minister or priest

imbalance (ɪm'bæləns) n. lack of balance, proportion

imbecile ('ɪmbɪsiːl, -saɪl) n. 1. idiot —a. 2. idiotic —**imbecility** (ɪmbɪ'sɪlɪtɪ) n.

imbed (ɪm'bɛd) vt. see EMBED

imbibe (ɪm'baɪb) vt. 1. drink in 2. absorb —vi. 3. drink

imbricate ('ɪmbrɪkɪt, -keɪt) a. lying over each other in regular order, like tiles or shingles on roof (also **'imbricated**) —**imbri'cation** n.

imbroglio (ɪm'brəʊlɪəʊ) n. complicated situation, plot (pl. **-s**)

imbue (ɪm'bjuː) vt. inspire

I. Mech. E. Institution of Mechanical Engineers

IMF International Monetary Fund

imitate ('ɪmɪteɪt) vt. 1. take as model 2. mimic, copy —**'imitable** a. —**imi'tation** n. 1. act of imitating 2. copy of original 3. likeness 4. counterfeit —**'imitative** a. —**'imitator** n.

immaculate (ɪ'mækjʊlɪt) a. 1. spotless 2. pure 3. unsullied

immanent ('ɪmənənt) a. existing within, inherent —**'immanence** n.

immaterial (ɪmə'tɪərɪəl) a. 1. unimportant, trifling 2. not consisting of matter 3. spiritual

immeasurable (ɪ'mɛʒərəbᵊl) a. incapable of being measured, esp. by virtue of great size; limitless —**immeasura'bility** or **im'measurableness** n. —**im'measurably** adv.

immediate (ɪ'miːdɪət) a. 1. occurring at once 2. direct, not separated by others —**im'mediacy** n. —**im'mediately** adv.

immemorial (ɪmɪ'mɔːrɪəl) a. beyond memory

immense (ɪ'mɛns) a. huge, vast —**im'mensely** adv. —**im'mensity** n. vastness

immerse (ɪ'mɜːs) vt. 1. dip, plunge into liquid 2. involve, engross —**im'mersion** n. immersing —**immersion heater** or **im'merser** n. electric appliance for heating liquid in which it is immersed

immigrate ('ɪmɪgreɪt) vi. come into country as settler —**'immigrant** n./a. —**immi'gration** n.

imminent ('ɪmɪnənt) a. 1. liable to happen soon 2. close at hand —**'imminence** n. —**'imminently** adv.

immobilize or **-ise** (ɪ'məʊbɪlaɪz) vt. 1. make immobile 2. Fin. convert (circulating capital) into fixed capital —**immobili-**

---

imma'ture   im'mobile   im'modest
im'miscible   im'moderate

'**zation** or -**i'sation** n. —**im'mobilizer** or -**iser** n.

immolate ('ɪməʊleɪt) vt. kill, sacrifice —**immo'lation** n.

immoral (ɪ'mɒrəl) a. 1. corrupt 2. promiscuous 3. indecent 4. unethical —**immo'rality** n.

immortal (ɪ'mɔːtᵊl) a. 1. deathless 2. famed for all time —n. 3. immortal being 4. god 5. one whose fame will last —**immor'tality** n. —**im'mortalize** or -**ise** vt.

immune (ɪ'mjuːn) a. 1. proof (against a disease etc.) 2. secure 3. exempt —**im'munity** n. 1. state of being immune 2. freedom from prosecution, tax etc. —**immuni'zation** or -**ni'sation** n. process of making immune to disease —**'immunize** or -**nise** vt. make immune —**immu-'nology** n. branch of biology concerned with study of immunity

immure (ɪ'mjʊə) vt. imprison, wall up

immutable (ɪ'mjuːtəbᵊl) a. unchangeable

imp (ɪmp) n. 1. little devil 2. mischievous child —'**impish** a. of or like an imp; mischievous

imp. 1. imperative 2. imperfect

impact ('ɪmpækt) n. 1. collision 2. profound effect —vt. (ɪm'pækt) 3. drive, press —**im'pacted** a. 1. (of tooth) wedged against another tooth below gum 2. (of fracture) having jagged broken ends wedged into each other

impair (ɪm'pɛə) vt. weaken, damage —**im'pairment** n.

impala (ɪm'pɑːlə) n. antelope of S Afr.

impale or **empale** (ɪm'peɪl) vt. 1. pierce with sharp instrument 2. combine (two coats of arms) by placing them side by side with line between —**im'palement** or **em'palement** n.

impanel (ɪm'pænᵊl) vt. esp. US see EMPANEL

impart (ɪm'pɑːt) vt. 1. communicate (information etc.) 2. give

impartial (ɪm'pɑːʃəl) a. 1. not biased or prejudiced 2. fair —**imparti'ality** n.

impassable (ɪm'pɑːsəbᵊl) a. 1. not capable of being passed 2. blocked, as mountain pass

impasse (ɪm'pɑːs, æm'pɑːs) n. 1. deadlock 2. place, situation, from which there is no outlet

impassible (ɪm'pæsəbᵊl) a. rare 1. not susceptible to pain or injury 2. impassive; unmoved —**impassi'bility** or **im'passible-ness** n.

impassioned (ɪm'pæʃənd) a. deeply moved, ardent

impassive (ɪm'pæsɪv) a. 1. showing no emotion 2. calm —**impas'sivity** n.

impasto (ɪm'pæstəʊ) n. 1. paint applied thickly, so that brush marks are evident 2. technique of painting in this way

impeach (ɪm'piːtʃ) vt. 1. charge with crime 2. call to account 3. denounce —**im'peachable** a. —**im'peachment** n.

impeccable (ɪm'pɛkəbᵊl) a. without flaw or error —**impecca'bility** n.

impecunious (ɪmpɪ'kjuːnɪəs) a. poor —**im-pecuni'osity** n.

impede (ɪm'piːd) vt. hinder —**im'pedance** n. Elec. measure of opposition offered to flow of alternating current —**impediment** (ɪm'pɛdɪmənt) n. 1. obstruction 2. defect —**impedimenta** (ɪmpɛdɪ'mɛntə) pl.n. 1. any objects that impede progress, esp. baggage and equipment carried by army 2. Law obstructions to making of contract, esp. of marriage

impel (ɪm'pɛl) vt. 1. induce, incite 2. drive, force (-**ll**-) —**im'peller** n.

impend (ɪm'pɛnd) vi. 1. threaten, be imminent 2. (with over) rare hang —**im'pending** a.

impenitent (ɪm'pɛnɪtənt) a. not sorry or penitent; unrepentant —**im'penitence** n.

imperative (ɪm'pɛrətɪv) a. 1. necessary 2. peremptory 3. expressing command —n. 4. imperative mood —**im'peratively** adv.

imperceptible (ɪmpə'sɛptɪbᵊl) a. too slight, subtle, gradual etc. to be perceived —**impercepti'bility** n. —**imper'ceptibly** adv.

imperfect (ɪm'pɜːfɪkt) a. 1. exhibiting or characterized by faults, mistakes etc.; defective 2. not complete or finished; deficient 3. Gram. denoting tense of verbs usu. used to describe continuous or repeated past actions or events 4. Law legally unenforceable 5. Mus. proceeding to dominant from tonic, subdominant or any chord other than dominant 6. Mus. of or relating to all intervals other than fourth, fifth and octave —n. 7. Gram. (verb in) imperfect tense —**imper'fection** n. 1. condition or quality of being imperfect 2. fault, defect

imperial (ɪm'pɪərɪəl) a. 1. of empire or emperor 2. majestic 3. denoting weights and measures established by law in Brit. —**im'perialism** n. extension of empire 2. belief in colonial empire —**im'perialist** a./n. —**imperial'istic** a.

imperil (ɪm'pɛrɪl) vt. bring into peril, endanger (-**ll**-)

imperious (ɪm'pɪərɪəs) a. domineering; haughty; dictatorial

impermeable (ɪm'pɜːmɪəbᵊl) a. (of substance) not allowing passage of fluid through interstices —**impermea'bility** n.

impersonal (ɪm'pɜːsənᵊl) a. 1. objective, having no personal significance 2. devoid of human warmth, personality etc. 3. (of verb) without personal subject —**imper-son'ality** n.

impersonate (ɪm'pɜːsəneɪt) vt. 1. pretend

---

im'mov(e)able   im'patient   imper'missible
im'palpable   im'penetrable
im'patience   im'permanent

to be (another person) 2. imitate 3. play the part of —**imperson'ation** n. —**im'personator** n.

impertinent (ɪm'pɜːtɪnənt) a. insolent, rude —**imper'tinence** n. —**im'pertinently** adv.

imperturbable (ɪmpɜː'tɜːbəb'l) a. calm, not excitable —**imper'turbably** adv.

impervious (ɪm'pɜːvɪəs) or **imperviable** a. 1. not affording passage 2. (oft. with to) not receptive (to feeling, argument etc.) —**im'perviously** adv. —**im'perviousness** n.

impetigo (ɪmpɪ'taɪgəʊ) n. contagious skin disease

impetuous (ɪm'pɛtjʊəs) a. likely to act without consideration, rash —**impetu'osity** n. —**im'petuously** adv.

impetus ('ɪmpɪtəs) n. 1. force with which body moves 2. impulse

impinge (ɪm'pɪndʒ) vi. 1. (usu. with on or upon) encroach 2. (usu. with on, against or upon) collide (with) —**im'pingement** n.

impious ('ɪmpɪəs) a. irreverent, profane, wicked —**impiety** (ɪm'paɪtɪ) n. 1. lack of reverence or proper respect for a god 2. any lack of proper respect 3. impious act

implacable (ɪm'plækəb'l) a. 1. not to be appeased 2. unyielding —**implaca'bility** n.

implant (ɪm'plɑːnt) vt. 1. insert, fix —n. ('ɪmplɑːnt) 2. anything implanted, esp. surgically, such as tissue graft

implement ('ɪmplɪmənt) n. 1. tool, instrument, utensil —vt. ('ɪmplɪmɛnt) 2. carry out (instructions etc.); put into effect

implicate ('ɪmplɪkeɪt) vt. 1. involve, include 2. imply 3. rare entangle —**impli'cation** n. something implied —**im'plicit** a. 1. implied but not expressed 2. absolute and unreserved

implode (ɪm'pləʊd) v. collapse inwards

implore (ɪm'plɔː) vt. entreat earnestly

imply (ɪm'plaɪ) vt. 1. indicate by hint, suggest 2. mean (**im'plied, im'plying**)

impolitic (ɪm'pɒlɪtɪk) a. not politic or expedient —**im'politicly** adv.

imponderable (ɪm'pɒndərəb'l, -drəb'l) a. 1. unable to be weighed or assessed —n. 2. something difficult or impossible to assess —**impondera'bility** n. —**im'ponderably** adv.

import (ɪm'pɔːt, 'ɪmpɔːt) vt. 1. bring in, introduce (esp. goods from foreign country) 2. imply —n. ('ɪmpɔːt) 3. thing imported 4. meaning 5. importance 6. C sl. sportsman not native to area where he plays —**im'portable** a. —**impor'tation** n. —**im'porter** n.

important (ɪm'pɔːt'nt) a. 1. of great consequence 2. momentous 3. pompous —**im'portance** n. —**im'portantly** adv.

importune (ɪm'pɔːtjuːn) vt. request, demand of (someone) persistently —**im'portunate** a. persistent —**im'portunately** adv. —**impor'tunity** n.

impose (ɪm'pəʊz) vt. 1. levy (tax, duty etc.) —vi. 2. (usu. with on or upon) take advantage (of), practise deceit (on) —**im'posing** a. impressive —**impo'sition** n. 1. that which is imposed 2. tax 3. burden 4. deception —'**impost** n. duty, tax on imports

impossible (ɪm'pɒsəb'l) a. 1. incapable of being done or experienced 2. absurd 3. unreasonable —**impossi'bility** n. —**im'possibly** adv.

impost ('ɪmpəʊst) n. Archit. member at top of column that supports arch

impostor or **imposter** (ɪm'pɒstə) n. deceiver, one who assumes false identity —**im'posture** n.

impotent ('ɪmpətənt) a. 1. powerless 2. (of males) incapable of sexual intercourse —'**impotence** n. —'**impotently** adv.

impound (ɪm'paʊnd) vt. 1. take legal possession of and, oft., place in a pound (cars, animals etc.) 2. confiscate

impoverish or **empoverish** (ɪm'pɒvərɪʃ) vt. make poor or weak —**im'poverishment** or em'**poverishment** n.

impracticable (ɪm'præktɪkəb'l) a. 1. incapable of being put into practice or accomplished 2. unsuitable for desired use —**impractica'bility** n. —**im'practicably** adv.

impractical (ɪm'præktɪk'l) a. 1. not practical or workable 2. not gifted with practical skills —**impracti'cality** n. —**im'practically** adv.

imprecation (ɪmprɪ'keɪʃən) n. 1. invoking of evil 2. curse —'**imprecate** v.

impregnable (ɪm'prɛgnəb'l) a. 1. proof against attack 2. unassailable 3. unable to be broken into —**impregna'bility** n. —**im'pregnably** adv.

impregnate ('ɪmprɛgneɪt) vt. 1. saturate, infuse 2. make pregnant —**impreg'nation** n.

impresario (ɪmprə'sɑːrɪəʊ) n. organizer of public entertainment; manager of opera, ballet etc. (pl. -s)

impress[1] (ɪm'prɛs) vt. 1. affect deeply, usu. favourably 2. imprint, stamp 3. fix —n. ('ɪmprɛs) 4. act of impressing 5. mark impressed —**impressi'bility** n. —**im'pressible** a. —**im'pression** n. 1. effect produced, esp. on mind 2. notion, belief 3. imprint 4. a printing 5. total of copies printed at once 6. printed copy —**impression'bility** n. —**im'pressionable** a. susceptible to external influences —**im'pressionism** n. art style that renders general effect without detail —**im'pressionist** n. —**impression'istic** a. —**im'pressive** a. making deep impression

impress[2] (ɪm'prɛs) vt. press into service

imprest (ɪm'prɛst) vt. 1. advance on loan by government —n. 2. money advanced by government

---

imprimatur (ımprı'meıtə, -'mɑː-) n. licence to print book etc.

imprint ('ımprınt) n. 1. mark made by pressure 2. characteristic mark 3. publisher's or printer's name and address in book etc. —vt. (ım'prınt) 4. produce (mark) on (surface) by pressure, printing or stamping 5. fix in mind

imprison (ım'prızən) vt. put in prison —im'prisonment n.

improbity (ım'prəubıtı) n. dishonesty, wickedness, unscrupulousness

impromptu (ım'promptjuː) adv./a. 1. extempore; unrehearsed —n. 2. improvisation

improper (ım'propə) a. 1. lacking propriety; not seemly or fitting 2. unsuitable for certain use or occasion; inappropriate 3. irregular; abnormal —**impropriety** (ımprə'praıətı) n. 1. lack of propriety; indecency 2. improper act or use 3. state of being improper —**improper fraction** fraction in which numerator is greater than denominator, as 7/6

improve (ım'pruːv) v. make or become better in quality, standard, value etc. —im'provable a. —im'provement n. —im'prover n.

improvident (ım'provıdənt) a. 1. thriftless; imprudent 2. negligent —im'providence n.

improvise ('ımprəvaız) v. 1. perform or make quickly from materials at hand 2. perform (poem, piece of music etc.), composing as one goes along —improvi-'sation n.

impudent ('ımpjudənt) a. disrespectful, impertinent —'impudence n. —'impudently adv.

impugn (ım'pjuːn) vt. call in question, challenge

impulse ('ımpʌls) n. 1. sudden inclination to act 2. sudden application of force 3. motion caused by it 4. stimulation of nerve moving muscle —im'pulsion n. impulse —im'pulsive a. given to acting without reflection, rash

impunity (ım'pjuːnıtı) n. freedom, exemption from injurious consequences or punishment

impurity (ım'pjuərıtı) n. 1. quality of being impure 2. impure thing or element 3. Electron. small quantity of element added to pure semiconductor crystal to control its electrical conductivity

impute (ım'pjuːt) vt. ascribe, attribute —imputa'bility n. —impu'tation n. 1. that which is imputed as a charge or fault 2. reproach, censure

in (ın) prep. 1. expresses inclusion within limits of space, time, circumstance, sphere etc. —adv. 2. in or into some state, place etc. 3. inf. in vogue etc. —a. 4. inf. fashionable —**in for** about to be affected by —**ins and outs** intricacies, complications; details

In Chem. indium

IN Indiana

in. inch(es)

in-[1], **il-**, **im-**, or **ir-** (comb. form) 1. not; non-, as in incredible, illegal, imperfect, irregular 2. lack of, as in inexperience. See words listed at foot of relevant pages

in-[2], **il-**, **im-**, or **ir-** (comb. form) 1. in; into; towards; within; on, as in infiltrate, immigrate 2. having intensive or causative function, as in inflame, imperil

in absentia (ın æb'sɛntıə) Lat. in absence of (someone indicated)

inadvertent (ınəd'vɜːt[n]t) a. 1. not attentive 2. negligent 3. unintentional —inad-'vertence or inad'vertency n. —inad-'vertently adv.

inalienable (ın'eıljənəb[l]) a. not able to be transferred to another —inaliena'bility n.

inamorata (ınæmə'rɑːtə) or (masc.) **inamorato** (ınæmə'rɑːtəu) n. person with whom one is in love; lover (pl. -s)

inane (ı'neın) a. foolish, silly, vacant —**inanition** (ınə'nıʃən) n. 1. exhaustion 2. silliness —**inanity** (ı'nænıtı) n.

inanimate (ın'ænımıt) a. 1. lacking qualities of living beings 2. appearing dead 3. lacking vitality

inapposite (ın'æpəzıt) a. not appropriate or pertinent

inapt (ın'æpt) a. 1. not apt or fitting 2. lacking skill; inept —in'aptitude or in'aptness n.

inasmuch as (ınəz'mʌtʃ) seeing that

inaugurate (ın'ɔːgjureıt) vt. 1. begin, initiate the use of, esp. with ceremony 2. admit to office —in'augural a. —in'augurally adv. —inaugu'ration n. 1. act of inaugurating 2. ceremony to celebrate the initiation or admittance of

inauspicious (ınɔː'spıʃəs) a. not auspicious; unlucky; unfavourable —inaus'piciously adv.

inboard ('ınbɔːd) a. inside hull or bulwarks

inborn ('ın'bɔːn) a. existing from birth; inherent

inbreed ('ın'briːd) v. breed from union of closely related individuals ('in'bred pt./pp.) —'in'bred a. 1. produced as result of inbreeding 2. inborn, ingrained —'in'breeding n.

inc. 1. inclusive 2. incorporated 3. increase

incalculable (ın'kælkjuləb[l]) a. beyond calculation; very great

in camera in secret or private session

incandescent (ınkæn'dɛs[n]t) a. 1. glowing

---

im'probable	in'accurate	inap'propriate
im'prudent	in'adequate	inar'ticulate
im'pure	inad'missible	inar'tistic
ina'bility	inad'visable	inat'tentive
inac'cessible	in'applicable	in'audible

with heat, shining **2.** (of artificial light) produced by glowing filament —**incan'desce** vi. glow —**incan'descence** n.

incantation (ɪnkæn'teɪʃən) n. magic spell or formula, charm

incapacitate (ɪnkə'pæsɪteɪt) vt. **1.** disable; make unfit **2.** disqualify —**inca'pacity** n.

incarcerate (ɪn'kɑːsəreɪt) vt. imprison —**incarce'ration** n. —**in'carcerator** n.

incarnate (ɪn'kɑːneɪt) vt. **1.** embody in flesh, esp. in human form —a. (ɪn'kɑːnɪt, -neɪt) **2.** embodied in flesh, in human form **3.** typified —**incar'nation** n.

incendiary (ɪn'sɛndɪərɪ) a. **1.** of malicious setting on fire of property **2.** creating strife, violence etc. **3.** designed to cause fires —n. **4.** fire raiser **5.** agitator **6.** bomb filled with inflammatory substance —**in'cendiarism** n.

incense¹ ('ɪnsɛns) n. **1.** gum, spice giving perfume when burned **2.** its smoke —vt. **3.** burn incense to **4.** perfume with it

incense² (ɪn'sɛns) vt. enrage

incentive (ɪn'sɛntɪv) n. **1.** something that arouses to effort or action **2.** stimulus

inception (ɪn'sɛpʃən) n. beginning

incessant (ɪn'sɛs²nt) a. unceasing

incest ('ɪnsɛst) n. sexual intercourse between two people too closely related to marry —**in'cestuous** a.

inch¹ (ɪntʃ) n. **1.** one twelfth of foot, or 0.0254 metre —v. **2.** move very slowly

inch² (ɪntʃ) n. Scot., Irish small island

inchoate (ɪn'kəʊeɪt, -'kəʊɪt) a. **1.** just begun **2.** undeveloped

incident ('ɪnsɪdənt) n. **1.** event, occurrence —a. (usu. with to) **2.** naturally attaching (to) **3.** striking, falling (upon) —**'incidence** n. **1.** degree, extent or frequency of occurrence **2.** a falling on, or affecting —**inci'dental** a. occurring as a minor part or an inevitable accompaniment or by chance —**inci'dentally** adv. **1.** by chance **2.** by the way —**inci'dentals** pl.n. accompanying items —**incidental music** background music for film etc.

incinerate (ɪn'sɪnəreɪt) vt. burn up completely; reduce to ashes —**inciner'ation** n. —**in'cinerator** n. furnace or apparatus for incinerating something, esp. refuse

incipient (ɪn'sɪpɪənt) a. beginning

incise (ɪn'saɪz) vt. produce (lines etc.) by cutting into surface of (something) with sharp tool —**incision** (ɪn'sɪʒən) n. **1.** act of incising **2.** cut, gash, notch **3.** cut made with knife during surgical operation —**incisive** (ɪn'saɪsɪv) a. **1.** (of remark etc.) keen, biting **2.** sharp —**in'cisor** n. cutting tooth

incite (ɪn'saɪt) vt. stir up or provoke to action —**inci'tation** or **in'citement** n.

incl. 1. including **2.** inclusive

inclement (ɪn'klɛmənt) a. (of weather) stormy, severe, cold —**in'clemency** n.

incline (ɪn'klaɪn) v. **1.** lean, slope **2.** (cause to) be disposed —vt. **3.** bend or lower (head etc.) —n. ('ɪnklaɪn, ɪn'klaɪn) **4.** slope —**inclination** (ɪnklɪ'neɪʃən) n. **1.** liking, tendency, preference **2.** sloping surface **3.** degree of deviation —**inclined plane** plane whose angle to horizontal is less than right angle

inclose (ɪn'kləʊz) vt. see ENCLOSE

include (ɪn'kluːd) vt. **1.** have as (part of) contents **2.** comprise **3.** add in **4.** take in —**in'clusion** n. —**in'clusive** a. including (everything) —**in'clusively** adv.

incognito (ɪnkɒg'niːtəʊ) or (fem.) **incognita** adv./a. **1.** under assumed identity —n. **2.** assumed identity (pl. -s)

incognizant (ɪn'kɒgnɪzənt) a. unaware —**in'cognizance** n.

incoherent (ɪnkəʊ'hɪərənt) a. **1.** lacking clarity, disorganized **2.** inarticulate —**inco'herence** n. —**inco'herently** adv.

income ('ɪnkʌm, 'ɪnkəm) n. **1.** amount of money, esp. annual, from salary, investments etc. **2.** receipts —**income tax** personal tax levied on annual income

incoming ('ɪnkʌmɪŋ) a. **1.** coming in **2.** about to come into office; next **3.** (of interest etc.) being received; accruing

incommensurable (ɪnkə'mɛnʃərəbʰl) a. **1.** incapable of being measured comparatively **2.** incommensurate **3.** Maths. having no common factor other than 1 —n. **4.** something incommensurable —**incommensura'bility** n.

incommensurate (ɪnkə'mɛnʃərɪt) a. **1.** disproportionate **2.** incommensurable

incommode (ɪnkə'məʊd) vt. trouble, inconvenience, disturb —**incom'modious** a. **1.** cramped **2.** inconvenient

incommunicado (ɪnkəmjuːnɪ'kɑːdəʊ) a./adv. deprived (by force or by choice) of communication with others

incomparable (ɪn'kɒmpərəbʰl, -prəbʰl) a. **1.** beyond or above comparison; matchless; unequalled **2.** lacking basis for comparison; not having qualities or features that can be compared —**incompara'bility** or **in'comparableness** n. —**in'comparably** adv.

incompetent (ɪn'kɒmpɪtənt) a. **1.** not possessing necessary ability, skill etc. to do or carry out task; incapable **2.** marked by lack of ability, skill etc. **3.** Law not legally qualified —n. **4.** incompetent person —**in'competence** or **in'competency** n.

incongruous (ɪn'kɒŋgruəs) or **incongruent** a. **1.** not appropriate **2.** inconsistent, absurd —**incon'gruity** n. —**in'congruously** adv.

inconsequential (ɪnkɒnsɪ'kwɛnʃəl) or **inconsequent** (ɪn'kɒnsɪkwənt) a. **1.** illogical **2.** irrelevant; trivial

---

in'capable
in'comparable
incom'patible

incom'plete
incompre'hensible
incon'clusive

incon'siderable
incon'siderate

incontrovertible (ɪnkɒntrə'vɜːtəb'l) *a.* undeniable; indisputable

incorporate (ɪn'kɔːpəreɪt) *v.* 1. include 2. unite into one body 3. form into corporation —**incorpo'ration** *n.*

incorporeal (ɪnkɔː'pɔːrɪəl) *a.* 1. without material form, body or substance 2. spiritual, metaphysical 3. *Law* having no material existence —**incorpo'reity** *or* **incorpore'ality** *n.*

incorrigible (ɪn'kɒrɪdʒəb'l) *a.* 1. beyond correction or reform 2. firmly rooted —**incorrigi'bility** *n.*

increase (ɪn'kriːs) *v.* 1. make or become greater in size, number *etc.* —*n.* ('ɪnkriːs) 2. growth, enlargement —**in'creasingly** *adv.* more and more

incredible (ɪn'krɛdəb'l) *a.* 1. unbelievable 2. *inf.* marvellous; amazing

incredulous (ɪn'krɛdʒʊləs) *a.* unbelieving —**incre'dulity** *n.*

increment ('ɪnkrɪmənt) *n.* increase, esp. one of a series

incriminate (ɪn'krɪmɪneɪt) *vt.* 1. imply guilt of 2. charge with crime —**in'criminatory** *a.*

incrust (ɪn'krʌst) *v. see* ENCRUST

incubate ('ɪnkjʊbeɪt) *vt.* 1. provide (eggs, embryos, bacteria *etc.*) with heat or other favourable condition for development —*vi.* 2. develop in this way —**incu'bation** *n.* —'**incubator** *n.* apparatus for artificially hatching eggs, for rearing premature babies

incubus ('ɪnkjʊbəs) *n.* 1. nightmare; obsession 2. (*orig.*) demon believed to afflict sleeping person (*pl.* **-bi** (-baɪ), **-es**)

inculcate ('ɪnkʌlkeɪt, ɪn'kʌlkeɪt) *vt.* impress on the mind —**incul'cation** *n.* —'**inculcator** *n.*

inculpate ('ɪnkʌlpeɪt, ɪn'kʌlpeɪt) *vt.* incriminate; cause blame to be imputed to —**incul'pation** *n.* —**in'culpative** *or* **in'culpatory** *a.*

incumbent (ɪn'kʌmbənt) *a.* 1. lying, resting —*n.* 2. holder of office, esp. church benefice —**in'cumbency** *n.* 1. obligation 2. office or tenure of incumbent —**it is incumbent on** it is the duty of

incur (ɪn'kɜː) *vt.* 1. fall into 2. bring upon oneself (**-rr-**) —**in'cursion** *n.* 1. invasion 2. penetration

incuse (ɪn'kjuːz) *vt.* 1. impress by striking or stamping —*a.* 2. hammered —*n.* 3. impression made by stamping

ind. 1. independent 2. index 3. indicative

Ind. 1. Independent 2. India 3. Indian 4. Indies

indaba (ɪn'dɑːbə) *n.* **SA** 1. meeting, discussion 2. problem

indebted (ɪn'dɛtɪd) *a.* 1. owing gratitude (for help, favours *etc.*) 2. owing money —**in'debtedness** *n.*

indecent (ɪn'diːs'nt) *a.* 1. offensive to standards of decency, *esp.* in sexual matters 2. unseemly, improper (*esp. in* **indecent haste**) —**in'decency** *n.* 1. state or quality of being indecent 2. indecent act *etc.* —**indecent exposure** offence of indecently exposing one's body, esp. genitals, in public

indeed (ɪn'diːd) *adv.* 1. in truth, really, in fact, certainly —*interj.* 2. denoting surprise, doubt *etc.*

indefatigable (ɪndɪ'fætɪgəb'l) *a.* untiring —**inde'fatigably** *adv.*

indefeasible (ɪndɪ'fiːzəb'l) *a.* that cannot be lost or annulled —**indefeasi'bility** *n.*

indefensible (ɪndɪ'fɛnsəb'l) *a.* not justifiable or defensible —**inde'fensibly** *adv.*

indelible (ɪn'dɛlɪb'l) *a.* 1. that cannot be blotted out, effaced or erased 2. producing such a mark —**indeli'bility** *n.* —**in'delibly** *adv.*

indelicate (ɪn'dɛlɪkɪt) *a.* 1. coarse 2. embarrassing, tasteless

indemnity (ɪn'dɛmnɪtɪ) *n.* 1. compensation for loss 2. security against loss —**indemnifi'cation** *n.* —**in'demnify** *vt.* 1. give indemnity to 2. compensate (**in'demnified, in'demnifying**)

indent (ɪn'dɛnt) *v.* 1. set (written matter *etc.*) in from margin *etc.* 2. notch (edge, border *etc.*); make (something) jagged 3. cut (document in duplicate) so that irregular lines may be matched 4. make an order upon (someone) or for (something) —*n.* ('ɪndɛnt) 5. notch 6. order, requisition —**inden'tation** *n.* 1. hollowed, notched or cut place, as an edge or coastline 2. series of hollows, notches or cuts 3. act of indenting; condition of being indented 4. leaving of space or amount of space left between margin and start of indented line (*also* **in'dention, 'indent**) —**in'dention** *n.* indentation (on page) —**in'denture** *n.* 1. indented document 2. contract, esp. one binding apprentice to master —*vt.* 3. bind thus

independent (ɪndɪ'pɛndənt) *a.* 1. not subject to others 2. self-reliant 3. free 4. valid in itself 5. politically of no party —**inde'pendence** *or* **inde'pendency** *n.* 1. being independent 2. self-reliance 3. self-support —**inde'pendently** *adv.* —**independent clause** *Gram.* main or coordinate clause —**independent school UK** school that is neither financed nor controlled by government or local authorities

---

in-depth a. carefully worked out, detailed, thorough

indescribable (ɪndɪˈskraɪbəbˀl) a. 1. beyond description 2. too intense etc. for words —**indeˈscribably** adv.

indeterminate (ɪndɪˈtɜːmɪnɪt) a. 1. uncertain 2. inconclusive 3. incalculable 4. Maths. having no numerical meaning; (of an equation) having more than one variable and an unlimited number of solutions

index (ˈɪndɛks) n. 1. alphabetical list of references, usu. at end of book 2. pointer, indicator 3. Maths. exponent (pl. -es, 'indices) —vt. 4. provide (book) with index 5. insert in index —**index finger** finger next to thumb (also 'forefinger) —**index-linked** a. (of wages, interest rates etc.) directly related to cost-of-living index and rising accordingly

Indian (ˈɪndɪən) n. 1. native of India 2. aboriginal American —a. 3. of India 4. of Amer. Indians or any of their languages —'**Indic** a. 1. denoting, belonging to or relating to Indian branch of Indo-European languages —n. 2. this group of languages (also Indo-Aryan) —'**Indiaman** n. formerly, merchant ship engaged in trade with India —**Indian club** bottle-shaped club, usu. used by gymnasts etc. —**Indian corn** see MAIZE —**Indian file** single file —**Indian hemp** cannabis —**Indian ink** very dark black (drawing) ink —**Indian list** C inf. list of people to whom spirits may not be sold —**Indian summer** period of unusually warm weather, esp. in autumn —**India paper** thin soft opaque printing paper —**India rubber** rubber, eraser

indicate (ˈɪndɪkeɪt) vt. 1. point out 2. state briefly 3. signify —**indiˈcation** n. 1. sign 2. token 3. explanation —**inˈdicative** a. 1. (with of) pointing (to) 2. Gram. stating fact —n. 3. Gram. (verb in) indicative mood —'**indicator** n. 1. one who, that which, indicates 2. on vehicle, flashing light showing driver's intention to turn

indices (ˈɪndɪsiːz) n., pl. of INDEX

indict (ɪnˈdaɪt) vt. accuse, esp. by legal process —**inˈdictable** a. —**inˈdictment** n.

indifferent (ɪnˈdɪfrənt, -fərənt) a. 1. uninterested 2. unimportant 3. neither good nor bad 4. inferior 5. neutral —**inˈdifference** n.

indigenous (ɪnˈdɪdʒɪnəs) a. born in or natural to a country —**indigene** (ˈɪndɪdʒiːn) n. 1. aborigine 2. native

indigent (ˈɪndɪdʒənt) a. poor; needy —'**indigence** n. poverty

indigestion (ɪndɪˈdʒɛstʃən) n. (discomfort, pain caused by) difficulty in digesting food —**indiˈgestible** a.

indignant (ɪnˈdɪgnənt) a. 1. moved by anger and scorn 2. angered by sense of injury or injustice —**inˈdignantly** adv. —**indigˈnation** n. —**inˈdignity** n. humiliation; insult, slight

indigo (ˈɪndɪgəʊ) n. 1. blue dye obtained from plant 2. the plant (pl. -s, -es) —a. 3. deep blue

indirect (ɪndɪˈrɛkt) a. 1. deviating from direct course or line 2. not coming as direct effect or consequence 3. not straightforward, open or fair —**indiˈrectly** adv. —**indiˈrectness** n. —**indirect object** Gram. noun, pronoun or noun phrase indicating recipient or beneficiary of action of verb and its direct object —**indirect speech** or esp. U.S. **indirect discourse** reporting of something said by conveying what was meant rather than repeating exact words (also **reported speech**) —**indirect tax** tax levied on goods or services rather than on individuals or companies

indiscreet (ɪndɪˈskriːt) a. not discreet; imprudent; tactless —**indiscretion** (ɪndɪˈskrɛʃən) n. 1. characteristic or state of being indiscreet 2. indiscreet act, remark etc.

indiscrete (ɪndɪˈskriːt) a. not divisible or divided into parts

indiscriminate (ɪndɪˈskrɪmɪnɪt) a. 1. lacking discrimination 2. jumbled

indispensable (ɪndɪˈspɛnsəbˀl) a. necessary; essential

indisposition (ɪndɪspəˈzɪʃən) n. 1. sickness 2. disinclination —**indisˈpose** vt. —**indisˈposed** a. 1. unwell, not fit 2. disinclined

indissoluble (ɪndɪˈsɒljʊbˀl) a. permanent

indium (ˈɪndɪəm) n. soft silver-white metallic element

individual (ɪndɪˈvɪdjʊəl) a. 1. single 2. characteristic of single person or thing 3. distinctive —n. 4. single person or thing, esp. when regarded as distinct from others —**indiˈvidualism** n. principle of asserting one's independence —**indiˈvidualist** n. —**indiˈvidualˈistic** a. —**individuˈality** n. distinctive character 2. personality —**indiˈvidualize** or -**lise** vt. make (or treat as) individual —**indiˈvidually** adv. singly

Indo- (ˈɪndəʊ-) (comb. form) India; Indian, as in Indo-European

indoctrinate (ɪnˈdɒktrɪneɪt) vt. implant beliefs in the mind of

Indo-European a. 1. denoting or belonging to family of languages that includes English 2. denoting or belonging to any of the peoples speaking these languages —n. 3. Indo-European family of languages

indolent (ˈɪndələnt) a. lazy —**indolence** n.

indomitable (ɪnˈdɒmɪtəbˀl) a. unyielding

indoor (ˈɪndɔː) a. 1. within doors 2. under cover —**inˈdoors** adv. inside or into house or other building

indorse (ɪnˈdɔːs) vt. see ENDORSE

---

indubitable (ɪn'djuːbɪtəbˀl) *a.* beyond doubt; certain —**in'dubitably** *adv.*

induce (ɪn'djuːs) *vt.* 1. persuade 2. bring on 3. cause 4. produce by induction —**in'ducement** *n.* incentive, attraction

induct (ɪn'dʌkt) *vt.* install in office —**in'ductance** *n.* —**in'duction** *n.* 1. an inducting 2. general inference from particular instances 3. production of electric or magnetic state in body by its being near (not touching) electrified or magnetized body 4. in internal combustion engine, part of the piston's action which draws gas from carburettor —**in'ductive** *a.* —**in'ductively** *adv.* —**in'ductor** *n.* —**induction coil** transformer for producing high voltage from low voltage

indue (ɪn'djuː) *vt. see* ENDUE

indulge (ɪn'dʌldʒ) *vt.* 1. gratify 2. give free course to 3. pamper 4. spoil —**in'dulgence** *n.* 1. an indulging 2. extravagance 3. something granted as a favour or privilege 4. *R.C.Ch.* remission of temporal punishment due after absolution —**in'dulgent** *a.* —**in'dulgently** *adv.*

induna (ɪn'duːnə) *n. SA* headman, overseer

indurate ('ɪndjʊreɪt) *v.* 1. make or become hard or callous 2. make or become hardy —*a.* ('ɪndjʊrɪt) 3. hardened, callous, or unfeeling —'**indurative** *a.*

industry ('ɪndəstrɪ) *n.* 1. manufacture, processing *etc.* of goods 2. branch of this 3. diligence, habitual hard work —**in'dustrial** *a.* of industries, trades —**in'dustrialist** *n.* person engaged in control of industrial enterprise —**in'dustrialize** *or* **-lise** *v.* —**in'dustrious** *a.* diligent —**industrial estate** *UK* area of land set aside for industry and business —**Industrial Revolution** transformation in 18th and 19th centuries of Brit. and other countries into industrial nations

-ine (*comb. form*) 1. of, relating to or belonging to, as in *saturnine* 2. consisting of; resembling, as in *crystalline* 3. indicating any of various classes of chemical compounds, as in *chlorine, nicotine, glycerine* (*also* **-in**) 4. indicating feminine form, as in *heroine*

inebriate (ɪn'iːbrɪeɪt) *vt.* 1. make drunk; intoxicate —*a.* (ɪn'iːbrɪt) 2. drunken —*n.* (ɪn'iːbrɪt) 3. habitual drunkard —**inebri'ation** *or* **inebriety** (ɪnɪ'braɪɪtɪ) *n.* drunkenness

inedible (ɪn'ɛdɪbˀl) *a.* 1. not eatable 2. unfit for food —**inedi'bility** *n.*

ineducable (ɪn'ɛdjʊkəbˀl) *a.* incapable of being educated, *esp.* through mental retardation

ineffable (ɪn'ɛfəbˀl) *a.* 1. too great or

sacred for words 2. unutterable —**ineffa'bility** *n.* —**in'effably** *adv.*

ineligible (ɪn'ɛlɪdʒəbəl) *a.* not fit or qualified (for something) —**ineligi'bility** *n.*

ineluctable (ɪnɪ'lʌktəbˀl) *a.* (*esp.* of fate) incapable of being avoided; inescapable

inept (ɪn'ɛpt) *a.* 1. absurd 2. out of place 3. clumsy —**in'eptitude** *n.*

inequality (ɪnɪ'kwɒlɪtɪ) *n.* 1. state or quality of being unequal 2. lack of smoothness or regularity 3. *Maths.* statement indicating that value of one quantity or expression is not equal to another; relation of being unequal

inert (ɪn'ɜːt) *a.* 1. without power of action or resistance 2. slow, sluggish 3. chemically unreactive —**inertia** (ɪn'ɜːʃə, -ʃɪə) *n.* 1. inactivity 2. property by which matter continues in its existing state of rest or motion in straight line, unless that state is changed by external force —**in'ertly** *adv.* —**in'ertness** *n.* —**inertia-reel seat belt** car seat belt in which belt is free to unwind from metal drum except when rapid deceleration occurs —**inertia selling** practice of sending unrequested goods to householders, followed by bill if goods are not returned

inescapable (ɪnɪ'skeɪpəbˀl) *a.* incapable of being escaped or avoided

inestimable (ɪn'ɛstɪməbˀl) *a.* too good, too great to be estimated

inevitable (ɪn'ɛvɪtəbˀl) *a.* 1. unavoidable 2. sure to happen —**inevita'bility** *n.* —**in'evitably** *adv.*

inexorable (ɪn'ɛksərəbˀl) *a.* relentless —**in'exorably** *adv.*

inexpiable (ɪn'ɛkspɪəbˀl) *a.* 1. incapable of being expiated 2. *obs.* implacable

inexplicable (ɪnɪk'splɪkəbˀl) *a.* impossible to explain

in extenso (ɪn ɪk'stɛnsəʊ) *Lat.* at full length

in extremis (ɪn ɪk'striːmɪs) *Lat.* at the point of death

inextricable (ɪnɛks'trɪkəbˀl) *a.* 1. not able to be escaped from 2. not able to be disentangled *etc.* 3. extremely involved or intricate —**inextrica'bility** *or* **inex'tricableness** *n.* —**inex'tricably** *adv.*

inf. 1. infinitive 2. informal 3. information

infallible (ɪn'fælɪbˀl) *a.* 1. unerring 2. not liable to fail 3. certain, sure —**infalli'bility** *n.* —**in'fallibly** *adv.*

infamous ('ɪnfəməs) *a.* 1. notorious 2. shocking —**'infamously** *adv.* —**'infamy** *n.*

infant ('ɪnfənt) *n.* very young child —**'infancy** *n.* —**in'fanticide** *n.* 1. murder of newborn child 2. person guilty of this —**'infantile** *a.* childish —**infantile paraly-**

---

inef'ficient	ines'sential	inex'perience
ine'lastic	inex'act	inex'perienced
in'elegant	inex'cusable	inex'pert
in'equable	inex'pedient	inex'tinguishable
in'equitable	inex'pensive	

sis see POLIOMYELITIS —**infant school** UK school for children aged between 5 and 7

infante (ın'fæntı) n. formerly, son of king of Spain or Portugal, esp. one not heir to throne —**infanta** (ın'fæntə) n. 1. formerly, daughter of king of Spain or Portugal 2. wife of infante

infantry ('ınfəntrı) n. foot soldiers

infatuate (ın'fætjʊeıt) vt. inspire with folly or foolish passion —**infatuated** a. foolishly enamoured —**infatu'ation** n.

infect (ın'fɛkt) vt. 1. affect (with disease) 2. contaminate —**in'fection** n. —**in'fectious** a. catching, spreading, pestilential —**infectious hepatitis** acute infectious viral disease characterized by inflammation of liver, fever and jaundice —**infectious mononucleosis** acute infectious disease characterized by fever, sore throat, swollen lymph nodes etc. (also **glandular fever**)

infelicitous (ınfı'lısıtəs) a. unfortunate; unsuitable —**infe'licity** n. 1. being infelicitous 2. unsuitable or inapt remark etc.

infer (ın'fɜ:) vt. deduce, conclude (-rr-) —**'inference** n. —**infer'ential** a. deduced

inferior (ın'fıərıə) a. 1. of poor quality 2. lower —n. 3. one lower (in rank etc.) —**inferi'ority** n. —**inferiority complex** Psychoanal. repressed sense of inferiority

infernal (ın'fɜ:n²l) a. 1. devilish 2. hellish 3. inf. irritating, confounded —**in'fernally** adv.

inferno (ın'fɜ:nəʊ) n. 1. region of hell 2. conflagration (pl. -s)

infest (ın'fɛst) vt. inhabit or overrun in dangerously or unpleasantly large numbers —**infes'tation** n.

infidelity (ınfı'dɛlıtı) n. 1. unfaithfulness 2. religious disbelief 3. disloyalty 4. treachery —**'infidel** n. 1. unbeliever —a. 2. rejecting a specific religion, esp. Christianity or Islam 3. of unbelievers or unbelief

infield ('ınfi:ld) n. 1. Cricket area of field near pitch 2. Baseball area of playing field enclosed by base lines —**'infielder** n.

infighting ('ınfaıtıŋ) n. 1. Boxing combat at close quarters 2. intense conflict, as between members of same organization —**'infighter** n.

infiltrate ('ınfıltreıt) v. 1. trickle through —vt. 2. (cause to) gain access surreptitiously 3. cause to pass through pores —**infil'tration** n.

infin. infinitive

infinite ('ınfınıt) a. boundless —**'infinitely** adv. exceedingly —**infini'tesimal** a. extremely, infinitely small —**in'finitude** n. state or quality of being infinite —**in'finity** n. unlimited and endless extent

infinitive (ın'fınıtıv) a. 1. Gram. in mood expressing notion of verb without limitation of tense, person or number —n. 2. verb in this mood 3. the mood

infirm (ın'fɜ:m) a. 1. physically weak 2.

mentally weak 3. irresolute —**in'firmary** n. hospital; sick quarters —**in'firmity** n.

infix (ın'fıks, 'ınfıks) vt. 1. fix firmly in 2. instil, inculcate 3. Gram. insert (affix) into middle of word —n. ('ınfıks) 4. Gram. affix inserted into middle of word

in flagrante delicto (ın flə'græntı dı'lıktəʊ) while committing the offence

inflame (ın'fleım) vt. 1. rouse to anger, excitement 2. cause inflammation in —vi. 3. become inflamed —**inflammability** (ınflæmə'bılıtı) n. —**inflammable** (ın'flæmə-b²l) a. 1. easily set on fire 2. excitable —**inflammation** (ınflə'meıʃən) n. infection of part of the body, with pain, heat, swelling and redness —**inflammatory** (ın'flæmətərı, -trı) a.

inflate (ın'fleıt) v. 1. blow up with air, gas 2. swell —vt. 3. cause economic inflation of (prices etc.) —vi. 4. undergo economic inflation —**in'flatable** a. —**in'flation** n. increase in prices and fall in value of money —**in'flationary** a.

inflect (ın'flɛkt) vt. 1. modify (words) to show grammatical relationships 2. bend inwards —**in'flection** or **in'flexion** n. 1. modification of word 2. modulation of voice

inflexible (ın'flɛksəb²l) a. 1. incapable of being bent 2. stern —**inflexi'bility** n.

inflict (ın'flıkt) vt. 1. impose 2. deliver forcibly —**in'fliction** n. 1. inflicting 2. punishment

in-flight a. provided during flight in aircraft

inflorescence (ınflɔ:'rɛsəns) n. 1. the unfolding of blossoms 2. Bot. arrangement of flowers on stem

inflow ('ınfləʊ) n. 1. something, such as liquid or gas, that flows in 2. act of flowing in; influx

influence ('ınflʊəns) n. 1. effect of one person or thing on another 2. power of person or thing having an effect 3. thing, person exercising this —vt. 4. sway 5. induce 6. affect —**influ'ential** a.

influenza (ınflʊ'ɛnzə) n. contagious feverish catarrhal virus disease

influx ('ınflʌks) n. 1. a flowing in 2. inflow

info ('ınfəʊ) inf. information

infold (ın'fəʊld) vt. see ENFOLD

inform (ın'fɔ:m) vt. 1. tell 2. animate —vi. 3. (oft. with on or against) give information (about) —**in'formant** n. one who tells —**infor'mation** n. 1. knowledge acquired through experience or study 2. knowledge of specific and timely events or situations; news 3. act of informing; condition of being informed 4. office, agency etc. providing information 5. charge or complaint made before justices of peace, usu. on oath, to institute summary criminal proceedings 6. Comp. results derived from processing of data according to programmed instructions 7.

Comp. information operated on by computer program (*also* '**data**) —**infor'mational** *a.* —**in'formative** *a.* —**in'formed** *a.* having much knowledge or education; learned, cultured —**in'former** *n.* 1. person who informs against someone, *esp.* criminal 2. person who provides information —**information technology** technology concerned with collecting and storing information, *esp.* by computer or electronically —**information theory** collection of mathematical theories concerned with coding, transmitting, storing, retrieving and decoding information

infra ('ɪnfrə) *adv.* 1. below 2. under 3. after —**infra dig** *inf.* beneath one's dignity —**infra'red** *a.* denoting rays below red end of visible spectrum —**infra'sonic** *a.* having frequency below that of sound

infraction (ɪn'frækʃən) *n. see* INFRINGE

infrangible (ɪn'frændʒɪb'l) *a.* 1. incapable of being broken 2. not capable of being violated or infringed —**infrangi'bility** *or* **in'frangibleness** *n.*

infrastructure ('ɪnfrəstrʌktʃə) *n.* basic structure or fixed capital items of an organization or economic system

infringe (ɪn'frɪndʒ) *vt.* transgress, break —**in'fraction** *n.* breach, violation —**in'fringement** *n.*

infuriate (ɪn'fjʊərɪeɪt) *vt.* enrage

infuse (ɪn'fjuːz) *v.* 1. soak to extract flavour *etc.* —*vt.* 2. instil, charge —**in'fusible** *a.* capable of being infused —**in'fusion** *n.* 1. an infusing 2. liquid extract obtained

infusible (ɪn'fjuːzəb'l) *a.* not fusible; not easily melted; having high melting point —**infusi'bility** *or* **in'fusibleness** *n.*

-ing[1] (*comb. form*) 1. action of, process of, result of or something connected with verb, as in *meeting, wedding, winnings* 2. something used in, consisting of, involving *etc.*, as in *tubing, soldiering*

-ing[2] (*comb. form*) 1. forming present participle of verbs, as in *walking, believing* 2. forming participial adjectives, as in *growing boy, sinking ship* 3. forming adjectives not derived from verbs, as in *swashbuckling*

ingenious (ɪn'dʒiːnjəs, -nɪəs) *a.* 1. clever at contriving 2. cleverly contrived —**in'geniously** *adv.* —**inge'nuity** *n.*

ingénue (ænʒeɪ'njuː) *n.* 1. artless girl or young woman 2. actress playing such a part

ingenuous (ɪn'dʒɛnjʊəs) *a.* 1. frank 2. naive, innocent —**in'genuously** *adv.*

ingest (ɪn'dʒɛst) *vt.* take (food or liquid) into the body —**in'gestible** *a.* —**in'gestion** *n.*

inglenook ('ɪŋg'lnʊk) *n.* corner by a fireplace

inglorious (ɪn'glɔːrɪəs) *a.* dishonourable, shameful, disgraceful

ingot ('ɪŋgət) *n.* brick of cast metal, *esp.* gold

ingrain *or* **engrain** (ɪn'greɪn) *vt.* 1. implant deeply 2. *obs.* dye, infuse deeply —**in'grained** *or* **en'grained** *a.* 1. deep-rooted 2. inveterate 3. (*esp.* of dirt) worked into or through fibre, grain, pores *etc.*

ingratiate (ɪn'greɪʃɪeɪt) *v. refl.* get (oneself) into favour —**in'gratiatingly** *adv.*

ingredient (ɪn'griːdɪənt) *n.* component part of a mixture

ingress ('ɪngrɛs) *n.* 1. entry 2. means or right of entrance

ingrown ('ɪngrəʊn, ɪn'grəʊn) *a.* 1. (*esp.* of toenail) grown abnormally into flesh 2. grown within; native; innate

inhabit (ɪn'hæbɪt) *vt.* dwell in —**in'habitable** *a.* —**in'habitant** *n.* —**inhabi'tation** *n.*

inhale (ɪn'heɪl) *v.* breathe in (air *etc.*) —**in'halant** *a.* 1. (*esp.* of medicinal preparation) inhaled for its therapeutic effect 2. inhaling —*n.* 3. inhalant medicinal preparation —**inha'lation** *n.* —**in'haler** *n.* device producing and assisting inhalation of therapeutic vapours

inhere (ɪn'hɪə) *vi.* 1. (of qualities) exist 2. (of rights) be vested —**in'herence** *or* **in'herency** *n.* —**in'herent** *a.* existing as an inseparable part

inherit (ɪn'hɛrɪt) *vt.* 1. receive as heir 2. derive from parents —*vi.* 3. succeed as heir —**inheri'bility** *or* **in'heritableness** *n.* —**in'heritable** *a.* 1. capable of being transmitted by heredity 2. capable of being inherited —**in'heritance** *n.*

inhesion (ɪn'hiːʒən) *n.* inherence

inhibit (ɪn'hɪbɪt) *vt.* 1. restrain (impulse, desire *etc.*) 2. hinder (action) 3. forbid —**inhibition** (ɪnɪ'bɪʃən, ɪnhɪ-) *n.* 1. repression of emotion, instinct 2. a stopping or retarding —**in'hibitory** *a.*

inhuman (ɪn'hjuːmən) *a.* 1. cruel, brutal 2. not human —**inhu'manity** *n.*

inhume (ɪn'hjuːm) *vt.* bury, inter —**inhu'mation** *n.*

inimical (ɪ'nɪmɪk'l) *a.* 1. unfavourable 2. unfriendly; hostile

inimitable (ɪ'nɪmɪtəb'l) *a.* defying imitation

iniquity (ɪ'nɪkwɪtɪ) *n.* 1. gross injustice 2. wickedness, sin —**in'iquitous** *a.* 1. unfair, unjust 2. sinful 3. *inf.* outrageous

initial (ɪ'nɪʃəl) *a.* 1. of, occurring at the beginning —*n.* 2. initial letter, *esp.* of person's name —*vt.* 3. mark, sign with one's initials (-ll-) —**in'itially** *adv.* —**initial teaching alphabet** alphabet of 44 characters for teaching beginners to read English

initiate (ɪ'nɪʃɪeɪt) *vt.* 1. originate, begin 2. admit into closed society 3. instruct in elements of something —*n.* (ɪ'nɪʃɪɪt, -eɪt) 4.

initiated person —**initi'ation** n. —**in'itia-tive** n. 1. first step, lead 2. ability to act independently —a. 3. originating —**in'itia-tory** a.

inject (in'dʒekt) vt. introduce (esp. fluid, medicine etc. with syringe) —**in'jection** n.

injunction (in'dʒʌŋkʃən) n. 1. judicial order to restrain 2. authoritative order

injury ('indʒərɪ) n. 1. physical damage or harm 2. wrong —**'injurable** a. —**'injure** vt. 1. do harm or damage to 2. offend, esp. by injustice —**'injured** a. —**in'jurious** a. —**in'juriously** adv. —**injury time** Soccer extra time added on to compensate for time spent attending to injured players during match

injustice (in'dʒʌstɪs) n. 1. want of justice 2. wrong 3. injury 4. unjust act

ink (iŋk) n. 1. fluid used for writing or printing —vt. 2. mark with ink 3. cover, smear with ink —**'inker** n. —**'inky** a. 1. resembling ink, esp. in colour; dark; black 2. of, containing or stained with ink —**'inkstand** n. —**'inkwell** n. vessel for holding ink

inkling ('iŋklɪŋ) n. hint, slight knowledge or suspicion

inkosi (iŋ'kɔːsɪ) n. SA chief, leader

inlaid ('inleɪd, in'leɪd) pt./pp. of INLAY

inland ('inlænd, -lənd) n. 1. interior of country —a. ('inlənd) 2. in interior of country 3. away from the sea 4. within a country —adv. 5. in or towards the inland

in-law n. relative by marriage

inlay (in'leɪ) vt. 1. embed 2. decorate with inset pattern (**'inlaid** pt./pp.) —n. ('inleɪ) 3. inlaid piece or pattern

inlet ('inlet) n. 1. entrance 2. mouth of creek 3. piece inserted

in loco parentis (in 'ləʊkəʊ pə'rentɪs) Lat. in place of a parent

inmate ('inmeɪt) n. occupant, esp. of prison, hospital etc.

inmost ('inməʊst) a. sup. of IN most inward, deepest

inn (in) n. 1. public house providing food and accommodation 2. hotel —**'innkeeper** n. —**Inns of Court** 1. four societies admitting to English Bar 2. their buildings

innards ('inədz) pl.n. inf. internal organs or working parts (orig. **'inwards**)

innate (ɪ'neɪt, 'ineɪt) a. 1. inborn 2. inherent

inner ('inə) a. 1. lying within —n. 2. ring next to bull's-eye on target —**'innermost** a. —**inner city** sections of a large city in or near its centre —**inner man** 1. mind; soul 2. jocular stomach; appetite (**inner woman** fem.) —**inner tube** rubber air tube of pneumatic tyre

innings ('inɪŋz) n. 1. (with sing. v.) Sport player's or side's turn of batting 2. (sometimes with sing. v.) spell, turn

innocent ('inəsənt) a. 1. pure 2. guiltless 3. harmless —n. 4. innocent person, esp. young child —**'innocence** n. —**'innocently** adv.

innocuous (ɪ'nɒkjʊəs) a. harmless

innovate ('inəveɪt) vt. introduce (changes, new things) —**inno'vation** n. —**'innova-tor** n.

innuendo (inju'endəʊ) n. 1. allusive remark, hint 2. indirect accusation (pl. -es)

innumerable (ɪ'njuːmərəbʰl, ɪ'njuːmrəbʰl) or **innumerous** a. countless; very numer-ous

innumerate (ɪ'njuːmərɪt) a. 1. having neither knowledge nor understanding of mathematics or science —n. 2. innumer-ate person —**in'numeracy** n.

inoculate (ɪ'nɒkjʊleɪt) vt. immunize by injecting vaccine —**inocu'lation** n.

inoperable (in'ɒpərəbʰl, -'ɒprə-) a. 1. unworkable 2. Med. that cannot be operated on —**in'operative** a. 1. not operative 2. ineffective

inopportune (in'ɒpətjuːn) a. badly timed

inordinate (in'ɔːdɪnɪt) a. excessive

inorganic (inɔː'gænɪk) a. 1. not having structure or characteristics of living organisms 2. of substances without carbon

inpatient ('inpeɪʃənt) n. patient that stays in hospital

in perpetuum (in pɜː'petjʊəm) Lat. for ever

input ('inpʊt) n. 1. act of putting in 2. that which is put in, as resource needed for industrial production etc. 3. data etc. fed into a computer

inquest ('inkwest) n. 1. legal or judicial inquiry presided over by a coroner 2. detailed inquiry or discussion

inquietude (in'kwaɪtjuːd) n. restlessness, uneasiness, anxiety —**in'quiet** a.

inquire (in'kwaɪə) vi. seek information —**in'quirer** n. —**in'quiry** n. 1. question 2. investigation

inquisition (inkwɪ'zɪʃən) n. 1. searching investigation, official inquiry 2. Hist. (I-) tribunal for suppression of heresy —**in-'quisitor** n. —**inquisi'torial** a.

inquisitive (in'kwɪzɪtɪv) a. 1. curious 2. prying

in re (in 'reɪ) in the matter of: used esp. in bankruptcy proceedings

inroad ('inrəʊd) n. incursion

inrush ('inrʌʃ) n. sudden, usu. overwhelm-ing, inward flow or rush; influx

ins. 1. inches 2. insurance

insane (in'seɪn) a. 1. mentally deranged; crazy 2. senseless —**in'sanely** adv. 1. like a lunatic, madly 2. excessively —**insanity** (in'sænɪtɪ) n.

insatiable (in'seɪʃəbʰl, -ʃɪə-) or **insatiate** (in'seɪʃɪt) a. incapable of being satisfied

inscribe (in'skraɪb) vt. 1. write, engrave (in or on something) 2. mark 3. dedicate 4. trace (figure) within another —**inscrip-**

tion (in'skripʃən) n. 1. inscribing 2. words inscribed on monument etc.

inscrutable (in'skruːtəbˀl) a. 1. mysterious, impenetrable 2. affording no explanation —**inscruta'bility** n. —**in'scrutably** adv.

insect ('insekt) n. small invertebrate animal with six legs, usu. segmented body and two or four wings —**in'secticide** n. preparation for killing insects —**insec-'tivorous** a. insect-eating

insecure (insi'kjuə) a. 1. not safe or firm 2. anxious, not confident

inseminate (in'semineit) vt. implant semen into —**artificial insemination** impregnation of the female by artificial means

insensate (in'senseit, -sit) a. 1. without sensation, unconscious 2. unfeeling

insensible (in'sensəbˀl) a. 1. unconscious 2. without feeling 3. not aware 4. not perceptible —**insensi'bility** n. —**in'sensibly** adv. imperceptibly

insert (in'sɜːt) vt. 1. introduce 2. place or put in, into or between —n. ('insɜːt) 3. something inserted —**in'sertion** n.

in-service a. denoting training that is given to employees during the course of employment

inset ('inset) n. 1. something extra inserted, esp. as decoration —vt. (in'set) 2. set or place in or within; insert

inshore ('in'ʃɔː) adv./a. near shore

inside ('in'said) n. 1. inner side, surface or part —a. ('insaid) 2. of, in, or on inside —adv. (in'said) 3. in or into the inside 4. sl. in prison —prep. (in'said) 5. within, on inner side of

insidious (in'sidiəs) a. 1. stealthy, treacherous 2. unseen but deadly —**in'sidiously** adv.

insight ('insait) n. mental penetration, discernment

insignia (in'signiə) pl.n. badges, emblems of honour or office (sing. in'signia)

insinuate (in'sinjueit) vt. 1. hint 2. work (oneself) into favour 3. introduce gradually or subtly —**insinu'ation** n.

insipid (in'sipid) a. 1. dull, spiritless 2. tasteless —**insi'pidity** n.

insist (in'sist) vi. (oft. with on or upon) 1. demand persistently 2. maintain 3. emphasize —**in'sistence** n. —**in'sistent** a.

in situ (in 'sitjuː) Lat. in its original position

in so far or U.S. **insofar** adv. (usu. with as or that) to the degree or extent (that)

insole ('insəul) n. 1. inner sole of shoe or boot 2. loose additional inner sole to give extra warmth or make shoe fit

insolent ('insələnt) a. arrogantly impudent —'**insolence** n. —'**insolently** adv.

insomnia (in'somniə) n. sleeplessness —**in'somniac** a./n.

insomuch (insəu'mʌtʃ) adv. to such an extent

insouciant (in'suːsiənt) a. indifferent, careless, unconcerned —**in'souciance** n.

inspan (in'spæn) vt. SA harness, yoke (-nn-)

inspect (in'spekt) vt. examine closely or officially —**in'spection** n. —**in'spector** n. 1. one who inspects 2. high-ranking police officer —**in'spectorate** n. 1. office, rank or duties of inspector 2. body of inspectors 3. district under inspector —**inspec'torial** a.

inspire (in'spaiə) vt. 1. animate, invigorate 2. arouse, create feeling, thought in 3. give rise to —vi. 4. breathe in, inhale —**inspiration** (inspi'reiʃən) n. 1. good idea 2. creative influence or stimulus

inspirit (in'spirit) vt. animate, put spirit into, encourage

inst. (instant) of the current month

install or **instal** (in'stɔːl) vt. 1. have (apparatus) put in 2. establish 3. place (person in office etc.) with ceremony —**installation** (instə'leiʃən) n. 1. act of installing 2. that which is installed

instalment or U.S. **installment** (in'stɔːlmənt) n. 1. payment of part of debt 2. any of parts of a whole delivered in succession —**installment plan** US hire-purchase

instance ('instəns) n. 1. example, particular case 2. request 3. stage in proceedings —vt. 4. cite —**for instance** for or as an example

instant ('instənt) n. 1. moment, point of time —a. 2. immediate 3. urgent 4. (of foods) requiring little preparation —**instan'taneous** a. happening in an instant —**instan'taneously** adv. —**in'stanter** adv. Law at once —'**instantly** adv. at once

instead (in'sted) adv. 1. in place 2. as a substitute

instep ('instep) n. top of foot between toes and ankle

instigate ('instigeit) vt. 1. incite, urge 2. bring about —**insti'gation** n. —'**instigator** n.

instil or (esp. U.S.) **instill** (in'stil) vt. implant; inculcate —**instil'lation** n. —**in'stilment** n.

instinct ('instiŋkt) n. 1. inborn impulse or propensity 2. unconscious skill 3. intuition —**in'stinctive** a. —**in'stinctively** adv.

institute ('institjuːt) vt. 1. establish, found 2. appoint 3. set going —n. 4. society for promoting some public object, esp. scientific 5. its building —**insti'tution** n. 1. an instituting 2. establishment for care or education, hospital, college etc. 3. an established custom or law or (inf.) figure —**insti'tutional** a. 1. of institutions 2. routine —**insti'tutionalize** or **-ise** vt. 1.

in'sensitive   insin'cere   insta'bility
in'separable   in'soluble
insig'nificant   in'solvent

subject to (adverse) effects of confinement in institution 2. place in an institution —v. 3. make or become an institution —'institutor or 'instituter n.

instruct (ın'strʌkt) vt. 1. teach 2. inform 3. order 4. brief (solicitor, barrister) —in'struction n. 1. teaching 2. order —pl. 3. directions —in'structive a. 1. informative 2. useful —in'structively adv. —in'structor n. (in'structress fem.)

instrument ('ınstrəmənt) n. 1. tool, implement, means, person, thing used to make, do, measure etc. 2. mechanism for producing musical sound 3. legal document —instru'mental a. 1. acting as instrument or means 2. helpful 3. belonging to, produced by musical instruments —instru'mentalist n. player of musical instrument —instrumen'tality n. agency, means —instru'mentally adv. —instrumen'tation n. arrangement of music for instruments

insubordinate (ınsə'bɔːdınıt) a. 1. not submissive 2. mutinous, rebellious —insubordi'nation n.

insufferable (ın'sʌfərəb'l) a. intolerable; unendurable —in'sufferably adv.

insular ('ınsjulə) a. 1. of an island 2. remote, detached 3. narrow-minded; prejudiced —insu'larity n.

insulate ('ınsjuleıt) vt. 1. prevent or reduce transfer of electricity, heat, sound etc. to or from (body or device) by surrounding with nonconducting material 2. isolate, detach —insu'lation n. —'insulator n.

insulin ('ınsjulın) n. pancreatic hormone used in treating diabetes

insult (ın'sʌlt) vt. 1. behave rudely to 2. offend —n. ('ınsʌlt) 3. offensive remark 4. affront —in'sulting a. —in'sultingly adv.

insuperable (ın'suːpərəb'l, -prəb'l, -'sjuː-) a. 1. that cannot be got over or surmounted 2. unconquerable —insupera'bility n. —in'superably adv.

insupportable (ınsə'pɔːtəb'l) a. 1. incapable of being endured; intolerable; insufferable 2. incapable of being supported or justified; indefensible

insure (ın'ʃuə, -'ʃɔː) vi. 1. contract for payment in event of loss, death etc. by payment of premiums —vt. 2. make such contract about 3. (with against) make safe (against) —in'surable a. —in'surance n. —in'surer n. —insurance policy contract of insurance

insurgent (ın'sɜːdʒənt) a. 1. in revolt —n. 2. rebel —in'surgence or insur'rection n. revolt

int. 1. interest 2. interior 3. internal 4. international

intact (ın'tækt) a. 1. untouched 2. uninjured

intaglio (ın'tɑːlıəu) n. 1. engraved design

2. gem so cut (pl. -s, -gli (-ljiː)) —in'tagliated a.

intake ('ınteık) n. 1. what is taken in 2. quantity taken in 3. opening for taking in 4. in car, air passage into carburettor

integer ('ıntıdʒə) n. 1. whole number 2. whole of anything

integral ('ıntıgrəl) a. constituting an essential part of a whole —'integrate v. 1. combine into one whole 2. unify diverse elements (of community etc.) —inte'gration n. —integral calculus branch of mathematics of changing quantities, which calculates total effects of the change —integrated circuit tiny electronic circuit, usu. on silicon chip

integrity (ın'tegrıtı) n. 1. honesty 2. original perfect state

integument (ın'tegjumənt) n. natural covering, skin, rind, husk

intellect ('ıntılekt) n. power of thinking and reasoning —intel'lectual a. 1. of, appealing to intellect 2. having good intellect —n. 3. one endowed with intellect and attracted to intellectual things —intellectu'ality n.

intelligent (ın'telıdʒənt) a. 1. having, showing good intellect 2. quick at understanding 3. informed 4. of or employing advanced technology, esp. involving computers —in'telligence n. 1. quickness of understanding 2. mental power or ability 3. intellect 4. information, news, esp. military information —in'telligently adv. —intelli'gentsia n. intellectual or cultured classes —intelligi'bility n. —in'telligible a. understandable —in'telligibly adv. —intelligence quotient measure of intelligence of individual, derived by dividing individual's mental age by his actual age and multiplying result by 100

intemperate (ın'tempərıt, -prıt) a. 1. drinking alcohol to excess 2. immoderate 3. unrestrained —in'temperance n.

intend (ın'tend) v. propose, mean (to do, say etc.) —in'tended a. 1. planned, future —n. 2. inf. proposed spouse

intense (ın'tens) a. 1. very strong or acute 2. emotional —intensifi'cation n. —in'tensify v. 1. make or become stronger 2. increase (in'tensified, in'tensifying) —in'tensity n. 1. intense quality 2. strength —in'tensive a. characterized by intensity or emphasis on specified factor —in'tensively adv.

intent (ın'tent) n. 1. purpose —a. 2. concentrating 3. resolved, bent 4. preoccupied, absorbed —in'tention n. purpose, aim —in'tentional a. —in'tently adv. —in'tentness n.

inter (ın'tɜː) vt. bury (-rr-) —in'terment n.

inter- (comb. form) between, among, mutually, as in interglacial, interrelation.

Such words are not given here where the meaning may easily be inferred from the simple word

interact (ɪntərˈækt) vi. act on each other —interˈaction n.

inter alia (ˈɪntər ˈeɪlɪə) Lat. among other things

interbreed (ɪntəˈbriːd) v. breed within a related group

intercede (ɪntəˈsiːd) vi. plead (in favour of), mediate —interˈcession (ɪntəˈsɛʃən) n. —interˈcessor (ɪntəˈsɛsə) n.

intercept (ɪntəˈsɛpt) vt. 1. cut off 2. seize, stop in transit —interˈception n. —interˈceptor or interˈcepter n. 1. one who, that which intercepts 2. fast fighter plane, missile etc.

interchange (ɪntəˈtʃeɪndʒ) v. 1. (cause to) exchange places —n. (ˈɪntətʃeɪndʒ) 2. motorway junction —interˈchangeable a. able to be exchanged in position or use

intercity (ɪntəˈsɪtɪ) a. linking cities directly

intercom (ˈɪntəkɒm) n. internal telephonic system

intercommunion (ɪntəkəˈmjuːnjən) n. association between Churches, involving esp. mutual reception of Holy Communion

intercontinental (ɪntəkɒntɪˈnɛntəl) a. 1. connecting continents 2. (of missile) able to reach one continent from another

intercourse (ˈɪntəkɔːs) n. 1. mutual dealings; communication 2. sexual joining of two people; copulation

interdict (ˈɪntədɪkt) n. 1. decree of Pope restraining clergy from performing divine service 2. formal prohibition —vt. (ɪntəˈdɪkt) 3. prohibit, forbid 4. restrain —interˈdiction n.

interdisciplinary (ɪntəˈdɪsɪplɪnərɪ) a. involving two or more academic disciplines

interest (ˈɪntrɪst, -tərɪst) n. 1. concern, curiosity 2. thing exciting this 3. sum paid for use of borrowed money 4. (oft. pl.) benefit, advantage 5. (oft. pl.) right, share —vt. 6. excite curiosity or concern of 7. cause to become involved in something; concern —ˈinterested a. 1. showing or having interest 2. personally involved or implicated —ˈinteresting a. —ˈinterestingly adv.

interface (ˈɪntəfeɪs) n. area, surface, boundary linking two systems

interfere (ɪntəˈfɪə) vi. 1. meddle, intervene 2. clash 3. (with with) euphemistic assault sexually —interˈference n. 1. act of interfering 2. Rad. interruption of reception by atmospherics or by unwanted signals

interferon (ɪntəˈfɪərɒn) n. a cellular

protein that stops the development of an invading virus

interim (ˈɪntərɪm) n. 1. meantime —a. 2. temporary, intervening

interior (ɪnˈtɪərɪə) a. 1. inner 2. inland 3. indoors —n. 4. inside 5. inland region —interior angle angle of polygon contained between two adjacent sides —interior decoration colours, furniture etc. of interior of house etc.

interject (ɪntəˈdʒɛkt) vt. interpose (remark etc.) —interˈjection n. 1. exclamation 2. interjected remark

interlace (ɪntəˈleɪs) vt. unite, as by lacing together —interˈlacement n.

interlard (ɪntəˈlɑːd) vt. intersperse

interleave (ɪntəˈliːv) vt. insert, as blank leaves in book, between other leaves —ˈinterleaf n. extra leaf

interlining (ˈɪntəlaɪnɪŋ) n. material used to interline parts of garments

interlock (ɪntəˈlɒk) v. 1. lock together firmly —a. (ˈɪntəlɒk) 2. knitted with close, small stitches

interlocutor (ɪntəˈlɒkjutə) n. one who takes part in conversation —interloˈcution n. dialogue —interˈlocutory a.

interloper (ˈɪntələupə) n. one intruding in another's affairs

interlude (ˈɪntəluːd) n. 1. interval (in play etc.) 2. something filling an interval

intermarry (ɪntəˈmærɪ) vi. 1. (of families, races, religions) become linked by marriage 2. marry within one's family —interˈmarriage n.

intermediate (ɪntəˈmiːdɪət) a. coming between; interposed —interˈmediary n./a.

intermezzo (ɪntəˈmɛtsəʊ) n. short performance between acts of play or opera (pl. -s, -mezzi (-ˈmɛtsiː))

interminable (ɪnˈtɜːmɪnəbəl) a. endless

intermit (ɪntəˈmɪt) v. stop for a time (-tt-) —interˈmission n. 1. interval, as between parts of film etc. 2. period between events or activities; pause 3. act of intermitting; state of being intermitted —interˈmittent a. occurring at intervals

intern (ɪnˈtɜːn) vt. 1. confine to special area or camp —n. (ˈɪntɜːn) 2. internee 3. US houseman (also ˈinterne) —interˈnee n. person who is interned, esp. enemy citizen in wartime or terrorism suspect —inˈternment n.

internal (ɪnˈtɜːnəl) a. 1. inward 2. interior 3. of a nation's domestic as opposed to foreign affairs —n. 4. euphemistic medical examination of vagina or uterus —inˈternally adv. —internal combustion process of exploding mixture of air and fuel in piston-fitted cylinder

international (ɪntəˈnæʃənᵉl) a. 1. of relations between nations —n. 2. game or match between teams of different countries —**inter'nationalism** n. ideal or practice of cooperation and understanding between nations —**inter'nationalist** n. —**inter'nationally** adv. —**International Phonetic Alphabet** series of signs and letters for representation of human speech sounds

Internationale (ĕtɛrnasjɔˈnal) Fr. socialistic hymn

internecine (ɪntəˈniːsaɪn) a. 1. mutually destructive 2. deadly

interpellate (ɪnˈtɜːpɛleɪt) vt. interrupt business of the day to demand explanation from (minister) —**interpel'lation** n.

interplanetary (ɪntəˈplænɪtərɪ, -trɪ) a. of, linking planets

interplay (ˈɪntəpleɪ) n. 1. action and reaction of two things, sides etc. upon each other 2. interaction 3. reciprocation

Interpol (ˈɪntəpɒl) International Criminal Police Organization

interpolate (ɪnˈtɜːpəleɪt) vt. 1. insert (new, esp. misleading matter) in (book etc.) 2. interject (remark) 3. Maths. estimate (a value) between known values —**interpo'lation** n.

interpose (ɪntəˈpəʊz) vt. 1. insert 2. say as interruption 3. put in the way —vi. 4. intervene —**interpo'sition** n.

interpret (ɪnˈtɜːprɪt) vt. 1. explain 2. Art render, represent —vi. 3. translate, esp. orally —**interpre'tation** n. —**in'terpreter** n.

interregnum (ɪntəˈrɛgnəm) n. 1. interval between reigns 2. gap in continuity (pl. -na (-nə), -s)

interrelate (ɪntərɪˈleɪt) v. place in or come into mutual or reciprocal relationship —**interre'lation** n.

interrogate (ɪnˈtɛrəgeɪt) vt. question, esp. closely or officially —**interro'gation** n. —**inter'rogative** a. 1. questioning —n. 2. word used in asking question —**in'terrogator** n. —**inter'rogatory** a. 1. of inquiry —n. 2. question, set of questions —**interrogation mark** see **question mark** at QUESTION

interrupt (ɪntəˈrʌpt) v. 1. break in (upon) —vt. 2. stop the course of 3. block —**inter'ruption** n.

interscholastic (ɪntəskəˈlæstɪk) a. 1. (of sports events, competitions etc.) occurring between two or more schools 2. representative of various schools

intersect (ɪntəˈsɛkt) vt. 1. divide by passing across or through —vi. 2. meet and cross —**inter'section** n. point where lines, roads cross

interspace (ɪntəˈspeɪs) vt. 1. make or occupy space between —n. (ˈɪntəspeɪs) 2.

space between or among things —**interspatial** (ɪntəˈspeɪʃəl) a.

intersperse (ɪntəˈspɜːs) vt. sprinkle (something) with or (something) among or in —**inter'spersion** n.

interstate (ˈɪntəsteɪt) a. US between, involving two or more states

interstellar (ɪntəˈstɛlə) a. (of the space) between stars

interstice (ɪnˈtɜːstɪs) n. chink, gap, crevice —**inter'stitial** a.

intertwine (ɪntəˈtwaɪn) v. twist together, entwine

interval (ˈɪntəvəl) n. 1. intervening time or space 2. pause, break 3. short period between parts of play, concert etc. 4. difference (of pitch)

intervene (ɪntəˈviːn) vi. 1. come into a situation in order to change it 2. (with on or between) be, come (between or among) 3. occur in meantime 4. interpose —**intervention** (ɪntəˈvɛnʃən) n.

interview (ˈɪntəvjuː) n. 1. meeting, esp. formally arranged and involving questioning of a person —vt. 2. have interview with —**interview'ee** n. —**'interviewer** n.

intestate (ɪnˈtɛsteɪt, -tɪt) a. 1. not having made a will —n. 2. person dying intestate —**in'testacy** n.

intestine (ɪnˈtɛstɪn) n. (usu. pl.) lower part of alimentary canal between stomach and anus —**in'testinal** a. of bowels

intimate¹ (ˈɪntɪmɪt) a. 1. closely acquainted, familiar 2. private 3. extensive 4. having sexual relations —n. 5. intimate friend —**'intimacy** n.

intimate² (ˈɪntɪmeɪt) vt. 1. announce 2. imply —**inti'mation** n. notice

intimidate (ɪnˈtɪmɪdeɪt) vt. 1. frighten into submission 2. deter by threats —**intimi'dation** n. —**in'timidator** n.

into (ˈɪntuː; unstressed ˈɪntə) prep. 1. expresses motion to a point within 2. indicates change of state 3. indicates coming up against, encountering 4. indicates arithmetical division

intone (ɪnˈtəʊn) or **intonate** vt. 1. chant 2. recite in monotone —**into'nation** n. 1. modulation of voice 2. intoning 3. accent

in toto (ɪn ˈtəʊtəʊ) Lat. totally, entirely, completely

intoxicate (ɪnˈtɒksɪkeɪt) vt. 1. make drunk 2. excite to excess —**in'toxicant** a./n. (anything) causing intoxication —**intoxi'cation** n.

intr. intransitive

intra- (comb. form) within, as in intrastate

intractable (ɪnˈtræktəbᵉl) a. 1. difficult to influence 2. hard to control

intramural (ɪntrəˈmjʊərəl) a. chiefly US Education operating within or involving those in single establishment

intransigent (ɪnˈtrænsɪdʒənt) a. uncompromising, obstinate

---

inter'racial
interuni'versity

inter'war
inter'weave

in'tolerable
in'tolerant

intransitive (ɪn'trænsɪtɪv) a. denoting a verb that does not require direct object —**intransi'tivity** or **in'transitiveness** n.

intrauterine (ɪntrə'juːtəraɪn) a. within the womb (see also IUD)

intravenous (ɪntrə'viːnəs) a. into a vein

in-tray n. tray for incoming papers etc. requiring attention

intrepid (ɪn'trɛpɪd) a. fearless, undaunted —**intre'pidity** n.

intricate ('ɪntrɪkɪt) a. involved, puzzlingly entangled —**'intricacy** n. —**'intricately** adv.

intrigue (ɪn'triːg, 'ɪntriːg) n. 1. underhand plot 2. secret love affair —vi. (ɪn'triːg) 3. carry on intrigue —vt. (ɪn'triːg) 4. interest, puzzle

intrinsic (ɪn'trɪnsɪk) or **intrinsical** a. inherent; essential —**in'trinsically** adv.

intro. or **introd.** 1. introduction 2. introductory

intro- (comb. form) into, within, as in introduce, introvert

introduce (ɪntrə'djuːs) vt. 1. make acquainted 2. present 3. bring in 4. bring forward 5. bring into practice 6. insert —**intro'duction** n. 1. an introducing 2. presentation of one person to another 3. preliminary section or treatment 4. Mus. opening passage in movement or composition, that precedes main material —**intro'ductory** a. preliminary

introit ('ɪntrɔɪt) n. Eccles. anthem sung as priest approaches altar

introspection (ɪntrə'spɛkʃən) n. examination of one's own thoughts —**intro'spective** a.

introvert ('ɪntrəvɜːt) n. Psychoanal. one who looks inwards rather than at the external world —**intro'versible** a. —**intro'version** n. —**intro'versive** a. —**intro'verted** a.

intrude (ɪn'truːd) v. thrust (oneself) in uninvited —**in'truder** n. —**in'trusion** n. —**in'trusive** a.

intrust (ɪn'trʌst) vt. see ENTRUST

intuition (ɪntjuː'ɪʃən) n. 1. immediate mental apprehension without reasoning 2. immediate insight —**in'tuit** vt. —**in'tuitive** a.

Inuit ('ɪnjuːɪt) n. C Eskimo of N Amer. or Greenland

inundate ('ɪnʌndeɪt) vt. 1. flood 2. overwhelm —**inun'dation** n.

inure or **enure** (ɪ'njʊə) vt. accustom, esp. to hardship, danger etc.

in vacuo (ɪn 'vækjʊəʊ) Lat. in vacuum

invade (ɪn'veɪd) v. 1. enter (a country etc.) by force with hostile intent —vt. 2. overrun 3. pervade —**in'vader** n. —**in'vasion** n. 1. act of invading with armed forces 2. any encroachment or intrusion 3. onset of something harmful, esp. disease

invalid[1] ('ɪnvəliːd, -lɪd) n. 1. one suffering from chronic ill health —a. 2. ill, suffering from sickness or injury —vt. 3. cause to become an invalid 4. (usu. with out) chiefly UK require (member of armed forces) to retire from active service because of illness etc.

invalid[2] (ɪn'vælɪd) a. 1. not valid; having no cogency or legal force 2. Logic having conclusion that does not necessarily follow from its premises; not valid —**in'validate** vt. 1. render weak or ineffective, as argument 2. take away legal force or effectiveness of; annul —**invali'dation** n. —**in'validator** n.

invaluable (ɪn'væljʊəb[ə]l) a. priceless

Invar (ɪn'vɑː) n. R steel containing 30 per cent nickel, with low coefficient of expansion

invasion (ɪn'veɪʒən) n. see INVADE

inveigh (ɪn'veɪ) vi. speak violently —**invective** (ɪn'vɛktɪv) n. abusive speech or writing, vituperation

inveigle (ɪn'viːg[ə]l, -'veɪ-) vt. entice, seduce, wheedle —**in'veiglement** n.

invent (ɪn'vɛnt) vt. 1. devise, originate 2. fabricate (falsehoods etc.) —**in'vention** n. 1. that which is invented 2. ability to invent 3. contrivance 4. deceit; lie —**in'ventive** a. resourceful; creative —**in'ventively** adv. —**in'ventor** n.

inventory ('ɪnvəntərɪ, -trɪ) n. 1. detailed list of goods etc. —vt. 2. make list of

invert (ɪn'vɜːt) vt. 1. turn upside down 2. reverse position, relations of —**inverse** (ɪn'vɜːs, 'ɪnvɜːs) a. 1. inverted 2. opposite —**in'versely** adv. —**in'version** n. —**inverted comma** or **turned comma** see **quotation mark** at QUOTE

invertebrate (ɪn'vɜːtɪbrɪt, -breɪt) n. 1. animal having no vertebral column —a. 2. spineless

invest (ɪn'vɛst) vt. 1. lay out (money, time, effort etc.) for profit or advantage 2. install 3. endow 4. obs. clothe 5. Poet. cover, as with garment —**in'vestiture** n. formal installation of person in office or rank —**in'vestment** n. 1. investing 2. money invested 3. stocks and shares bought —**in'vestor** n. —**investment trust** financial enterprise that invests its subscribed capital in securities for its investors' benefit

investigate (ɪn'vɛstɪgeɪt) vt. inquire into; examine —**investi'gation** n. —**in'vestigator** n.

inveterate (ɪn'vɛtərɪt) a. 1. deep-rooted; long-established 2. confirmed —**in'veteracy** n.

invidious (ɪn'vɪdɪəs) a. likely to cause ill will or envy —**in'vidiously** adv.

invigilate (ɪn'vɪdʒɪleɪt) vi. supervise examination candidates —**in'vigilator** n.

invigorate (ɪn'vɪgəreɪt) vt. give vigour to, strengthen

invincible (ɪn'vɪnsəb[ə]l) a. unconquerable —**invinci'bility** n.

---

in'variable

inviolable (ɪn'vaɪələb'l) *a.* 1. not to be profaned; sacred 2. unalterable —**in'violate** *a.* 1. unhurt 2. unprofaned 3. unbroken

invisible (ɪn'vɪzəb'l) *a.* 1. not visible; not able to be perceived by eye 2. concealed from sight; hidden 3. not easily seen or noticed 4. kept hidden from public view; secret; clandestine 5. *Econ.* of services, such as insurance and freight, rather than goods —*n.* 6. *Econ.* invisible item of trade; service —**invisi'bility** *or* **in'visibleness** *n.* —**in'visibly** *adv.*

invite (ɪn'vaɪt) *vt.* 1. request the company of 2. ask courteously 3. ask for 4. attract, call forth —*n.* ('ɪnvaɪt) 5. *inf.* invitation —**invitation** (ɪnvɪ'teɪʃən) *n.* —**in'viting** *a.* tempting; alluring; attractive

invoice ('ɪnvɔɪs) *n.* 1. a list of goods or services sold, with prices —*vt.* 2. present with an invoice 3. make an invoice of

invoke (ɪn'vəʊk) *vt.* 1. call on 2. appeal to 3. ask earnestly for 4. summon —**invo'cation** *n.*

involuntary (ɪn'vɒləntərɪ, -trɪ) *a.* 1. not done voluntarily 2. unintentional 3. instinctive

involute ('ɪnvəluːt) *a.* 1. complex 2. coiled spirally 3. rolled inwards (*also* **invo'luted**) —*n.* 4. *Maths.* a type of curve —**invo'lution** *n.*

involve (ɪn'vɒlv) *vt.* 1. include 2. entail 3. implicate (person) 4. concern 5. entangle —**in'volved** *a.* 1. complicated 2. concerned —**in'volvement** *n.*

inward ('ɪnwəd) *a.* 1. internal 2. situated within 3. spiritual, mental —*adv.* 4. towards the inside 5. into the mind (*also* '**inwards**) —*pl.n.* 6. *see* INNARDS —'**inwardly** *adv.* 1. in the mind 2. internally

iodine ('aɪədiːn) *n.* nonmetallic element found in seaweed and used in antiseptic tincture, photography and dyeing —**iodide** ('aɪədaɪd) *n.* 1. salt of hydriodic acid, containing the iodide ion 2. compound containing an iodine atom —'**iodize** *or* **-dise** *vt.* treat with iodine or iodide —**iodoform** (aɪ'ɒdəfɔːm) *n.* antiseptic

I.O.M. Isle of Man

ion ('aɪən, -ɒn) *n.* electrically charged atom or group of atoms —**i'onic** *a.* —**ioni'zation** *or* **-i'sation** *n.* —**ionize** *or* **-ise** *v.* change or become changed into ions —**i'onosphere** *n.* region of atmosphere 60 to 100 km above earth's surface

-ion (*comb. form*) action, process, state, as in *creation, objection*

Ionic (aɪ'ɒnɪk) *a. Archit.* distinguished by scroll-like decoration on columns

iota (aɪ'əʊtə) *n.* 1. ninth letter in Gr. alphabet (I, ι) 2. (*usu. with* not one *or* an) very small amount

IOU *n.* signed paper acknowledging debt

-ious (*comb. form*) characterized by; full of, as in *ambitious, suspicious*

I.O.W. Isle of Wight

IPA International Phonetic Alphabet

ipecac ('ɪpɪkæk) *or* **ipecacuanha** (ɪp-ɪkækjuː'ænə) *n.* S Amer. plant yielding an emetic

ipso facto ('ɪpsəʊ 'fæktəʊ) *Lat.* by that very fact

I.Q. intelligence quotient

Ir *Chem.* iridium

Ir. 1. Ireland 2. Irish

ir- (*comb. form*) *see* IN-[1], IN-[2]

I.R.A. Irish Republican Army

Iranian (ɪ'reɪnɪən) *n.* 1. native or inhabitant of Iran —*a.* 2. of Iran

irascible (ɪ'ræsɪb'l) *a.* hot-tempered —**irasci'bility** *n.* —**i'rascibly** *adv.*

ire (aɪə) *n.* anger, wrath —**i'rate** *a.* angry

iridaceous (ɪrɪ'deɪʃəs, aɪ-) *a.* belonging to iris family

iridescent (ɪrɪ'des'nt) *a.* exhibiting changing colours like those of the rainbow —**iri'descence** *n.*

iridium (aɪ'rɪdɪəm, ɪ'rɪd-) *n.* very hard, corrosion-resistant metal

iris ('aɪrɪs) *n.* 1. circular membrane of eye containing pupil 2. plant with sword-shaped leaves and showy flowers (*pl.* **-es**, **irides** ('aɪrɪdiːz, 'ɪrɪ-))

Irish ('aɪrɪʃ) *a.* 1. of Ireland, its people or their language —*n.* 2. Irish Gaelic —**Irish coffee** coffee mixed with whiskey and topped with cream —**Irish Gaelic** Goidelic language of the Celts of Ireland; official language of the Republic of Ireland since 1921 —**Irish stew** stew made of mutton, potatoes, onions *etc.*

irk (ɜːk) *vt.* irritate, vex —'**irksome** *a.* tiresome

iron ('aɪən) *n.* 1. metallic element, much used for tools *etc.*, and the raw material of steel 2. tool *etc.* of this metal 3. appliance used, when heated, to smooth cloth 4. metal-headed golf club 5. splintlike support for malformed leg 6. great hardness, strength or resolve —*pl.* 7. fetters —*a.* 8. of, like iron 9. inflexible, unyielding 10. robust —*v.* 11. smooth, cover, fetter *etc.* with iron or an iron —'**irony** *a.* of, resembling, or containing iron —**Iron Age** era of iron implements —'**iron'clad** *a.* protected with or as with iron —**Iron Curtain** 1. guarded border between countries of Soviet bloc and the rest of Europe 2. (**i- c-**) any barrier that separates communities or ideologies —**iron hand** harsh or rigorous control —**ironing board** board, usu. on legs, with suitable covering on which to iron clothes —**iron lung** apparatus for administering artificial respiration —**iron maiden** medieval instrument of torture, consisting of enclosed space lined with iron spikes —'**ironmaster** *n.* UK manufacturer of iron —'**ironmonger** *n.* dealer in hardware —'**ironmongery** *n.* his wares —**iron pyrites** *see* PYRITES —**iron rations** emergency food supplies, *esp.* for military personnel in action —'**ironstone** *n.* 1. any rock consisting mainly of iron-bearing ore 2. tough durable earthenware —'**ironwood** *n.* various S Afr. trees —'**ironwork** *n.* work done in iron, *esp.* decorative work —**'ironworks** *pl.n.* (*sometimes with sing. v.*) building in which iron is smelted, cast or wrought

irony ('aɪrənɪ) *n.* **1.** (*usu.* humorous or mildly sarcastic) use of words to mean the opposite of what is said **2.** event, situation opposite of that expected —**i'ronic(al)** *a.* of, using irony

irradiate (ɪ'reɪdɪeɪt) *vt.* **1.** treat by irradiation **2.** shine upon, throw light upon, light up —**irradi'ation** *n.* impregnation by x-rays, light rays

irrational (ɪ'ræʃənˀl) *a.* **1.** inconsistent with reason or logic **2.** incapable of reasoning **3.** *Maths.* (of equation *etc.*) containing one or more variables in irreducible radical form or raised to fractional power —**irration'ality** *n.*

irreconcilable (ɪ'rɛkˀnsaɪləbˀl, ɪrɛkˀn'saɪ-) *a.* **1.** not able to be reconciled; incompatible —*n.* **2.** person or thing that is implacably hostile **3.** (*usu. pl.*) one of various principles *etc.* that are incapable of being brought into agreement —**irreconcila'bility** *n.* —**ir'reconcilably** *adv.*

irrecoverable (ɪrɪ'kʌvərəbˀl, -'kʌvrə-) *a.* **1.** not able to be recovered or regained **2.** not able to be remedied or rectified

irredeemable (ɪrɪ'diːməbˀl) *a.* **1.** (of bonds *etc.*) without date of redemption of capital; incapable of being bought back directly or paid off **2.** (of paper money) not convertible into specie **3.** (of loss) not able to be recovered; irretrievable **4.** not able to be improved or rectified; irreparable —**irre'deemably** *adv.*

irredentist (ɪrɪ'dɛntɪst) *n.* **1.** (*sometimes* I-) person, *esp.* member of 19th-century It. association, who favoured acquisition of territory that had once been part of his country —*a.* **2.** of irredentism —**irre'dentism** *n.*

irreducible (ɪrɪ'djuːsɪbˀl) *a.* **1.** not able to be reduced or lessened **2.** not able to be brought to simpler or reduced form **3.** *Maths.* (of polynomial) unable to be factorized into polynomials of lower degree —**irreduci'bility** *n.*

irrefutable (ɪ'rɛfjʊtəbˀl, ɪrɪ'fjuːtəbˀl) *a.* that cannot be refuted, disproved

irreg. irregular(ly)

irregular (ɪ'rɛgjʊlə) *a.* **1.** lacking uniformity or symmetry; uneven in shape, arrangement *etc.* **2.** not occurring at expected or equal intervals **3.** differing from normal or accepted practice or routine **4.** (of formation, inflections or derivations of word) not following usual pattern of formation in language **5.** (of troops) not belonging to regular forces —*n.* **6.** soldier not in regular army —**irregu'larity** *n.*

irrelevant (ɪ'rɛləvənt) *a.* not relating or pertinent to matter at hand; not important —**ir'relevance** or **ir'relevancy** *n.*

irreparable (ɪ'rɛpərəbˀl, ɪ'rɛprəbˀl) *a.* not able to be repaired or remedied

irreplaceable (ɪrɪ'pleɪsəbˀl) *a.* not able to be replaced

irrepressible (ɪrɪ'prɛsəbˀl) *a.* not capable of being repressed, controlled or restrained —**irrepressi'bility** *n.* —**irre'pressibly** *adv.*

irreproachable (ɪrɪ'prəʊtʃəbˀl) *a.* not deserving reproach; blameless

irresistible (ɪrɪ'zɪstəbˀl) *a.* **1.** not able to be resisted or refused; overpowering **2.** very fascinating or alluring —**irre'sistibly** *adv.*

irresolute (ɪ'rɛzəluːt) *a.* lacking resolution; wavering; hesitating —**ir'resolutely** *adv.* —**ir'resoluteness** or **irreso'lution** *n.*

irrespective (ɪrɪ'spɛktɪv) *a.* —**irrespective of** without taking account of

irresponsible (ɪrɪ'spɒnsəbˀl) *a.* **1.** not showing or done with due care for consequences of one's actions or attitudes; reckless **2.** not capable of bearing responsibility —**irresponsi'bility** or **irre'sponsibleness** *n.* —**irre'sponsibly** *adv.*

irretrievable (ɪrɪ'triːvəbˀl) *a.* not able to be retrieved, recovered or repaired —**irretrieva'bility** *n.* —**irre'trievably** *adv.*

irreverence (ɪ'rɛvərəns, ɪ'rɛvrəns) *n.* **1.** lack of due respect or veneration **2.** disrespectful remark or act —**ir'reverent** *a.*

irreversible (ɪrɪ'vɜːsəbˀl) *a.* **1.** not able to be reversed **2.** not able to be revoked or repealed **3.** *Chem., phys.* capable of changing or producing change in one direction only —**irreversi'bility** *n.* —**irre'versibly** *adv.*

irrevocable (ɪ'rɛvəkəbˀl) *a.* not able to be changed, undone, altered

irrigate ('ɪrɪgeɪt) *vt.* water by artificial channels, pipes *etc.* —**irri'gation** *n.* —**'irrigator** *n.*

irritate ('ɪrɪteɪt) *vt.* **1.** annoy **2.** inflame **3.** stimulate —**'irritable** *a.* easily annoyed —**'irritably** *adv.* —**'irritant** *a./n.* (person or thing) causing irritation —**irri'tation** *n.*

irrupt (ɪ'rʌpt) *vi.* **1.** enter forcibly **2.** increase suddenly —**ir'ruption** *n.*

is (ɪz) third person singular, *present indicative of* BE

Is. 1. *Bible* Isaiah (*also* **Isa.**) **2.** Island(s); Isle(s)

I.S.B.N. *or* **ISBN** International Standard Book Number

-ise (*comb. form*) *see* -IZE

isinglass ('aɪzɪŋɡlɑːs) *n.* kind of gelatin obtained from some freshwater fishes

Islam ('ɪzlɑːm) *n.* Mohammedan faith or world —**Is'lamic** *a.*

island ('aɪlənd) *n.* **1.** piece of land surrounded by water **2.** anything like this, as raised piece for pedestrians in middle of road —**'islander** *n.* inhabitant of island

isle (aɪl) *n.* island —**'islet** *n.* little island

ism ('ɪzəm) *n.* *inf.*, *oft.* derogatory unspecified doctrine, system or practice

-ism (*comb. form*) **1.** action, process, result, as in *criticism* **2.** state; condition, as in *paganism* **3.** doctrine, system, body of principles and practices, as in *Leninism, spiritualism* 4. behaviour; characteristic quality, as in *heroism* 5. characteristic usage, *esp.* of language, as in *Scotticism*

isobar ('aɪsəʊbɑː) *n.* line on map connecting places of equal mean barometric pressure —**iso'baric** *a.*

isochronal (aɪ'sɒkrən'l) *or* **isochronous** *a.* 1. having same duration; equal in time 2. occurring at equal time intervals; having uniform period of vibration —**i'sochronism** *n.*

isolate ('aɪsəleɪt) *vt.* place apart or alone —**iso'lation** *n.* —**iso'lationism** *n.* policy of not participating in international affairs —**iso'lationist** *n./a.*

isomer ('aɪsəmə) *n.* substance with same molecules as another but different atomic arrangement —**iso'meric** *a.* —**i'somerism** *n.*

isometric (aɪsəʊ'metrɪk) *a.* 1. having equal dimensions 2. relating to muscular contraction without movement —**iso'metrics** *pl.n.* (*with sing. v.*) system of isometric exercises

isomorphism (aɪsəʊ'mɔːfɪzəm) *n.* 1. *Biol.* similarity of form 2. *Chem.* existence of two or more substances of different composition in similar crystalline form 3. *Maths.* one-to-one correspondence between elements of two or more sets —**iso'morphic** *or* **iso'morphous** *a.*

isosceles (aɪ'sɒsɪliːz) *a.* (of triangle) having two sides equal

isotherm ('aɪsəʊθɜːm) *n.* line on map connecting points of equal mean temperature

isotope ('aɪsətəʊp) *n.* atom of element having a different nuclear mass and atomic weight from other atoms in same element —**isotopic** (aɪsə'tɒpɪk) *a.*

isotropic (aɪsəʊ'trɒpɪk) *or* **isotropous** (aɪ'sɒtrəpəs) *a.* 1. having uniform physical properties in all directions 2. *Biol.* not having predetermined axes —**i'sotropy** *n.*

Israel ('ɪzreɪəl, -rɪəl) *n.* 1. republic in SW Asia, established as modern state of Israel 2. ancient kingdom of Jews in this region —**'Israelite** *n. Bible* member of ethnic group claiming descent from Jacob; Hebrew —**Children of Israel** the Jewish people or nation

issue ('ɪʃjuː) *n.* 1. sending or giving out officially or publicly 2. number or amount so given out 3. discharge 4. offspring, children 5. topic of discussion 6. question, dispute 7. outcome, result —*vi.* 8. go out 9. result (in) 10. arise (from) —*vt.* 11. emit, give out, send out 12. distribute 13. publish —**take issue** disagree

-ist (*comb. form*) 1. person who performs certain action or is concerned with something specified, as in *motorist, soloist* 2. person who practises in specific field, as in *physicist* 3. person who advocates

particular doctrine, system *etc.;* of doctrine advocated, as in *socialist* 4. person characterized by specified trait, tendency *etc.;* of such a trait, as in *purist* —**-istic** (*a. comb. form*)

isthmus ('ɪsməs) *n.* neck of land between two seas

it (ɪt) *pron.* neuter pronoun of the third person —**its** *a.* belonging to it —**it'self** *pron.* emphatic form of IT

It. 1. Italian 2. Italy

i.t.a. *or* **I.T.A.** initial teaching alphabet

ital. italic (type)

Italian (ɪ'tæljən) *n.* 1. language of Italy 2. native of Italy —*a.* 3. of Italy —**I'talianate** *or* **Italia'nesque** *a.* Italian in style or character

italic (ɪ'tælɪk) *a.* (of type) sloping —**i'talicize** *or* **-ise** *vt.* put in italics —**i'talics** *pl.n.* italic type, now used for emphasis *etc.*

itch (ɪtʃ) *n.* 1. irritation in the skin 2. restless desire —*vi.* 3. feel or produce irritating or tickling sensation 4. have a restless desire (to do something) —**'itchy** *a.*

item ('aɪtəm) *n.* 1. single thing in list, collection *etc.* 2. piece of information 3. entry in account *etc.* —*adv.* ('aɪtem) 4. also —**'itemize** *or* **-ise** *vt.*

iterate ('ɪtəreɪt) *vt.* repeat —**iter'ation** *n.* —**iterative** ('ɪtərətɪv) *a.*

itinerant (ɪ'tɪnərənt, aɪ-) *a.* 1. travelling from place to place 2. working for a short time in various places 3. travelling on circuit —**i'tineracy** *n.* —**i'tinerary** *n.* 1. record, line of travel 2. route 3. guidebook

-itis (*comb. form*) inflammation of specified part, as in *tonsillitis*

ITV Independent Television

-ity (*comb. form*) state; condition, as in *technicality*

IUD intrauterine device (for contraception)

-ive (*comb. form*) tendency, inclination, character, quality, as in *divisive, festive, massive*

IVF in-vitro fertilization: fertilization made to occur outside of body, *esp.* in test tube

ivory ('aɪvərɪ, -vrɪ) *n.* 1. hard white substance of the tusks of elephants *etc.* 2. yellowish-white colour; cream —*a.* 3. yellowish-white; cream —**'ivories** *pl.n. sl.* 1. piano keys 2. billiard balls 3. teeth 4. dice —**ivory tower** seclusion, remoteness

ivy ('aɪvɪ) *n.* climbing evergreen plant —**'ivied** *a.* covered with ivy

-ize *or* **-ise** (*comb. form*) 1. cause to become, resemble or agree with, as in *legalize* 2. become; change into, as in *crystallize* 3. affect in specified way; subject to, as in *hypnotize* 4. act according to some principle, policy *etc.*, as in *economize*

J

j or **J** (dʒeɪ) *n*. **1.** tenth letter of English alphabet **2.** speech sound represented by this letter (*pl*. **j's, J's** or **Js**)

jab (dʒæb) *vt*. **1.** poke roughly **2.** thrust, stab abruptly (**-bb-**) —*n*. **3.** poke **4.** *inf*. injection

jabber ('dʒæbə) *vi*. **1.** chatter **2.** talk rapidly, incoherently —'**jabberwocky** *n*. nonsense, *esp*. in verse

jabot ('ʒæbəʊ) *n*. frill, ruffle at throat or breast of garment

jacaranda (dʒækə'rændə) *n*. S Amer. tree with fernlike leaves and pale purple flowers

jacinth ('dʒæsɪnθ) *n*. reddish-orange precious stone

jack (dʒæk) *n*. **1.** fellow, man **2.** *inf*. sailor **3.** male of some animals **4.** device for lifting heavy weight, *esp*. motor car **5.** various mechanical appliances **6.** lowest court card, with picture of pageboy **7.** *Bowls* ball aimed at **8.** socket and plug connection in electronic equipment **9.** small flag, *esp*. national, at sea —*vt*. **10.** (*usu. with* up) lift (an object) with a jack —**Jack Frost** personification of frost —**jack-in-office** *n*. self-important petty official —**jack-in-the-box** *n*. toy consisting of figure on tight spring in box, which springs out when lid is opened (*pl*. **jack-in-the-boxes, jacks-in-the-box**) —**jack of all trades** person who undertakes many kinds of work (*pl*. **jacks of all trades**) —**jack-o'-lantern** *n*. lantern made from hollowed pumpkin, cut to represent human face **2.** will-o'-the-wisp —**Jack Tar** *chiefly lit.* sailor

jackal ('dʒækɔːl) *n*. wild, gregarious animal of Asia and Afr. closely allied to dog

jackanapes ('dʒækəneɪps) *n*. **1.** conceited impertinent person **2.** mischievous child **3.** *obs*. monkey

jackass ('dʒækæs) *n*. **1.** the male of the ass **2.** blockhead —**laughing jackass** the Aust. kookaburra

jackboot ('dʒækbuːt) *n*. large riding boot coming above knee

jackdaw ('dʒækdɔː) *n*. small kind of crow

jacket ('dʒækɪt) *n*. **1.** outer garment, short coat **2.** outer casing, cover —'**jacketed** *a*.

jackhammer ('dʒækhæmə) *n*. hand-held hammer drill

jackknife ('dʒæknaɪf) *n*. **1.** clasp knife **2.** dive with sharp bend at waist in midair —*vi*. **3.** (of articulated lorry) go out of control in such a way that trailer forms right angle to tractor

jackpot ('dʒækpɒt) *n*. large prize, accumulated stake, as pool in poker —**hit the jackpot** win a jackpot; achieve great success, *esp*. through luck

jack rabbit US hare

jacks (dʒæks) *pl.n*. game in which bone or metal pieces (**jackstones**) are thrown and picked up between bounces of small ball

Jacobean (dʒækə'bɪən) *a*. of the reign of James I

Jacobite ('dʒækəbaɪt) *n*. adherent of Stuarts after overthrow of James II

Jacquard ('dʒækɑːd, dʒə'kɑːd) *n*. fabric in which design is incorporated into the weave

Jacuzzi (dʒə'kuːzɪ) *n*. **1.** R device which swirls water in bath **2.** bath containing such a device

jade¹ (dʒeɪd) *n*. **1.** ornamental semiprecious stone, usu. dark green **2.** this colour

jade² (dʒeɪd) *n*. **1.** old worn-out horse **2.** *obs., offens.* woman considered to be disreputable —'**jaded** *a*. **1.** tired **2.** off colour

Jaffa ('dʒæfə, 'dʒɑː-) *n*. **1.** port in W Israel **2.** large orange with thick skin

jag¹ (dʒæg) *n*. sharp or ragged projection —'**jagged** ('dʒægɪd) *a*.

jag² (dʒæg) *n. sl.* **1.** intoxication from drugs or alcohol **2.** bout of drinking or drug taking

jaguar ('dʒægjʊə) *n*. large S Amer. spotted animal of cat family

jail or **gaol** (dʒeɪl) *n*. **1.** building for confinement of criminals or suspects —*vt*. **2.** send to, confine in prison —'**jailer, 'jailor** or '**gaoler** *n*. —'**jailbird** or '**gaolbird** *n*. hardened criminal

jalopy or **jaloppy** (dʒə'lɒpɪ) *n. inf.* old car

jalousie ('ʒæluːzɪ) *n*. **1.** blind or shutter constructed from angled slats of wood *etc*. **2.** window made of angled slats of glass

jam (dʒæm) *vt*. **1.** pack together **2.** (*oft. with* on) apply fiercely **3.** squeeze **4.** *Rad.* block (another station) with impulses of equal wavelength —*v*. **5.** (cause to) stick together and become unworkable —*vi*. **6.** *sl.* play in jam session (**-mm-**) —*n*. **7.** fruit preserved by boiling with sugar **8.** crush **9.** hold-up of traffic **10.** awkward situation —**jam-packed** *a*. filled to capacity —**jam session** (improvised) jazz or pop music session

jamb or **jambe** (dʒæm) *n*. side post of door, window *etc*.

jamboree (dʒæmbə'riː) *n*. **1.** large gathering or rally of Scouts **2.** spree, celebration

jammy ('dʒæmɪ) *a. UK sl.* **1.** pleasant; desirable **2.** lucky

Jan. January

jangle ('dʒæŋg³l) *v*. **1.** (cause to) sound harshly, as bell —*vt*. **2.** produce jarring effect on —*n*. **3.** harsh sound

janitor ('dʒænɪtə) *n*. **1.** caretaker **2.** doorkeeper ('**janitress** *fem.*)

January ('dʒænjʊərɪ) *n*. first month

japan (dʒə'pæn) *n*. **1.** very hard, *usu*. black varnish —*vt*. **2.** cover with this (**-nn-**)

Japanese (dʒæpə'niːz) *a*. **1.** of Japan —*n*.

2. native of Japan (*pl.* **-nese**) 3. official language of Japan

jape (dʒeɪp) *n./vi.* joke

japonica (dʒə'pɒnɪkə) *n.* shrub with red flowers (*also* **Japanese quince**)

jar¹ (dʒɑː) *n.* 1. usu. round vessel of glass, earthenware *etc.* 2. *inf.* glass of beer

jar² (dʒɑː) *v.* 1. (cause to) vibrate suddenly, violently —*vt.* 2. have disturbing, painful effect on (**-rr-**) —*n.* 3. jarring sound 4. shock *etc.*

jardinière (ʒɑːdɪ'njɛə) *n.* ornamental pot for growing plants

jargon ('dʒɑːgən) *n.* 1. specialized language concerned with particular subject 2. pretentious or nonsensical language

Jas. James

jasmine ('dʒæsmɪn, 'dʒæz-) *n.* flowering shrub

jasper ('dʒæspə) *n.* red, yellow, dark green or brown quartz

jaundice ('dʒɔːndɪs) *n.* 1. disease marked by yellowness of skin (*also* '**icterus**) 2. bitterness, ill humour 3. prejudice —*vt.* 4. make prejudiced, bitter *etc.*

jaunt (dʒɔːnt) *n.* 1. short pleasurable excursion —*vi.* 2. go on such an excursion —'**jaunting car** formerly, light, two-wheeled, one-horse car used in Ireland

jaunty ('dʒɔːntɪ) *a.* 1. sprightly 2. brisk 3. smart, trim —'**jauntily** *adv.*

Javanese (dʒɑːvə'niːz) *a.* 1. of island of Java, in Indonesia —*n.* 2. native or inhabitant of Java (*pl.* **-ese**) 3. Malayan language of Java

javelin ('dʒævlɪn) *n.* spear, *esp.* for throwing in sporting events

jaw (dʒɔː) *n.* 1. one of bones in which teeth are set —*pl.* 2. mouth 3. gripping part of vice *etc.* 4. *fig.* narrow opening of gorge or valley —*vi.* 5. *sl.* talk lengthily

jay (dʒeɪ) *n.* noisy bird with brilliant plumage —'**jaywalk** *vi.* walk in or across street carelessly or illegally —'**jaywalker** *n.*

jazz (dʒæz) *n.* syncopated music and dance —'**jazzy** *a.* flashy, showy —**jazz up** 1. play as jazz 2. make more lively, appealing

jealous ('dʒɛləs) *a.* 1. distrustful of the faithfulness (of) 2. envious 3. suspiciously watchful —'**jealously** *adv.* —'**jealousy** *n.*

jeans (dʒiːnz) *pl.n.* casual trousers, *esp.* made of denim

Jeep (dʒiːp) *n.* R light four-wheel drive motor utility vehicle

jeer (dʒɪə) *v.* 1. scoff —*n.* 2. scoff, taunt, gibe

Jehovah (dʒɪ'həʊvə) *n.* O.T. God —**Jehovah's Witness** member of Christian sect who believes end of world is near

jejune (dʒɪ'dʒuːn) *a.* 1. simple, naive 2. meagre

Jekyll and Hyde ('dʒɛk²l; haɪd) person with two distinct personalities, one good, the other evil

jell *or* **gel** (dʒɛl) *v.* 1. congeal —*vi.* 2. *inf.* assume definite form

jellaba *or* **jellabah** ('dʒɛləbə) *n.* loose cloak with hood, worn *esp.* in N Afr.

jelly ('dʒɛlɪ) *n.* 1. semitransparent food made with gelatin, becoming softly stiff as it cools 2. anything of the consistency of this —'**jellyfish** *n.* jellylike small sea animal

jemmy ('dʒɛmɪ) *or U.S.* **jimmy** ('dʒɪmɪ) *n.* short steel crowbar, pinchbar

jenny ('dʒɛnɪ) *n.* 1. female ass 2. female wren

jeopardy ('dʒɛpədɪ) *n.* (*usu. with* in) danger —'**jeopardize** *or* **-ise** *vt.* endanger

Jer. *Bible* Jeremiah

jerboa (dʒɜː'bəʊə) *n.* 1. small Afr. burrowing rodent resembling a mouse 2. desert rat

jeremiad (dʒɛrɪ'maɪəd) *n.* lamentation; complaint

jerk¹ (dʒɜːk) *n.* 1. sharp, abruptly stopped movement 2. twitch 3. sharp pull 4. *sl.* stupid person —*v.* 5. move or throw with a jerk —'**jerkily** *adv.* —'**jerkiness** *n.* —'**jerky** *a.* uneven, spasmodic

jerk² (dʒɜːk) *vt.* 1. preserve (beef *etc.*) by cutting into strips and drying in sun —*n.* 2. jerked meat (*also* '**jerky**)

jerkin ('dʒɜːkɪn) *n.* sleeveless jacket, *esp.* of leather

Jerry ('dʒɛrɪ) *n.* UK *sl.* 1. German, *esp.* German soldier 2. Germans collectively

jerry-built ('dʒɛrɪ) *a.* of flimsy construction with cheap materials —'**jerry-builder** *n.*

jerry can flat-sided can for storing or transporting motor fuel *etc.*

jersey ('dʒɜːzɪ) *n.* 1. knitted jumper 2. machine-knitted fabric 3. (J-) breed of cow

jessamine ('dʒɛsəmɪn) *n. see* JASMINE

jest (dʒɛst) *n./vi.* joke —'**jester** *n.* joker, *esp.* employed by medieval ruler

Jesuit ('dʒɛzjʊɪt) *n.* member of Society of Jesus, order founded by Ignatius Loyola in 1534 —**Jesu'itical** *a.* of Jesuits

Jesus ('dʒiːzəs) *n.* 1. ?4 B.C.-?29 A.D., founder of Christianity, believed by Christians to be the Son of God (*also* **Jesus Christ, Jesus of Nazareth**) —*interj.* 2. used to express intense surprise, dismay *etc.* (*also* **Jesus wept**)

jet¹ (dʒɛt) *n.* 1. stream of liquid, gas *etc.*, *esp.* shot from small hole 2. the small hole 3. spout, nozzle 4. aircraft driven by jet propulsion —*vt.* 5. throw out —*vi.* 6. shoot forth —*v.* 7. transport or be transported by jet (**-tt-**) —**jet lag** fatigue caused by crossing time zones in jet aircraft —**jet-propelled** *a.* driven by jet propulsion —**jet propulsion** propulsion by thrust provided by jet of gas or liquid —**jet set** rich, fashionable social set, members of which travel widely for pleasure —'**jetsetter** *n.*

jet² (dʒɛt) *n.* hard black mineral capable of brilliant polish —**jet-black** *a.* glossy black

jetsam ('dʒɛtsəm) *n.* cargo thrown overboard to lighten ship and later washed ashore —'**jettison** *vt.* 1. abandon 2. throw overboard

jetty ('dʒetɪ) n. small pier, wharf

Jew (dʒuː) n. 1. person of Hebrew religion or ancestry 2. inf., offens. miser ('Jewess fem.) —'Jewish a. —'Jewry n. Jews collectively —jew's-harp n. small musical instrument held between teeth and played by finger

jewel ('dʒuːəl) n. 1. precious stone 2. ornament containing one 3. precious thing —'jeweller or U.S. 'jeweler n. dealer in jewels —'jewellery or U.S. jewelry ('dʒuːəlrɪ) n.

jewfish ('dʒuːfɪʃ) n. large fish of tropical and temperate waters

Jezebel ('dʒezəbel) n. 1. O.T. wife of Ahab, king of Israel 2. (sometimes j-) shameless or scheming woman

jib (dʒɪb) n. 1. triangular sail set forward of mast 2. projecting arm of crane or derrick —vi. 3. object to proceeding 4. (of horse, person) stop and refuse to go on (-bb-) —'jibber n. —jib boom spar from end of bowsprit

jibe¹ (dʒaɪb) or **jib** (dʒɪb) see GYBE, GIBE

jibe² (dʒaɪb) vi. inf. agree; accord; harmonize

jiffy ('dʒɪfɪ) or **jiff** n. inf. very short period of time

Jiffy bag ('dʒɪfɪ) R large padded envelope

jig (dʒɪg) n. 1. lively dance 2. music for it 3. small mechanical device 4. mechanical device used as guide for cutting etc. 5. Angling any of various lures —vi. 6. dance jig 7. make jerky up-and-down movements (-gg-) —'jigger n. —'jigsaw n. machine fretsaw —jigsaw (puzzle) picture stuck on board and cut into interlocking pieces with jigsaw

jigger ('dʒɪgə) n. small glass for spirits

jiggery-pokery ('dʒɪgərɪ'pəʊkərɪ) n. inf. trickery, nonsense

jiggle ('dʒɪg⁰l) v. move (up and down etc.) with short jerky movements

jilt (dʒɪlt) vt. cast off (lover)

jim crow ('dʒɪm 'krəʊ) (oft. J- C-) US 1. policy or practice of segregating Negroes 2. derogatory Negro 3. implement for bending iron bars or rails

jimjams ('dʒɪmdʒæmz) pl.n. 1. sl. delirium tremens 2. state of nervous tension or anxiety

jingle ('dʒɪŋg⁰l) n. 1. mixed metallic noise, as of shaken chain 2. catchy, rhythmic verse, song etc. —v. 3. (cause to) make jingling sound

jingo ('dʒɪŋgəʊ) n. 1. loud, bellicose patriot 2. jingoism (pl. -es) —'jingoism n. chauvinism —jingo'istic a. —by jingo exclamation of surprise

jinks (dʒɪŋks) pl.n. boisterous merry-making (esp. in high jinks)

jinni, jinnee or **djinni** (dʒɪ'niː) n. spirit in Muslim mythology who could assume human or animal form (pl. jinn or djinn (dʒɪn))

jinx (dʒɪŋks) n. 1. force, person, thing bringing bad luck —vt. 2. be or put a jinx on

jitters ('dʒɪtəz) pl.n. worried nervousness, anxiety —'jittery a. nervous —'jitterbug n. 1. fast jerky Amer. dance popular in 1940s 2. person who dances jitterbug —vi. 3. perform such dance

jiujitsu or **jiujutsu** (dʒuː'dʒɪtsuː) n. see JUJITSU

jive (dʒaɪv) n. 1. (dance performed to) rock and roll music, esp. of 1950s —vi. 2. dance the jive

job (dʒɒb) n. 1. piece of work, task 2. post, office 3. inf. difficult task 4. inf. crime, esp. robbery —'jobber n. stockjobber —'jobbing a. doing single, particular jobs for payment —'jobless a./pl.n. unemployed (people) —job centre government office in town centre providing information about vacant jobs —job lot 1. assortment sold together 2. miscellaneous collection

Job's comforter (dʒəʊbz) person who adds to distress while purporting to give sympathy

jockey ('dʒɒkɪ) n. 1. professional rider in horse races (pl. -s) —v. 2. (esp. with for) manoeuvre ('jockeyed, 'jockeying)

jockstrap ('dʒɒkstræp) n. piece of elasticated material worn by men, esp. athletes, to support genitals (also athletic support)

jocose (dʒə'kəʊs) a. waggish, humorous —jo'cosely adv. —jocosity (dʒə'kɒsɪtɪ) n. —jocular ('dʒɒkjʊlə) a. 1. joking 2. given to joking —jocularity (dʒɒkjʊ'lærɪtɪ) n.

jocund ('dʒɒkənd) a. merry, cheerful —jo'cundity n.

jodhpurs ('dʒɒdpəz) pl.n. tight-legged riding breeches

jog (dʒɒg) vi. 1. run slowly or move at a trot, esp. for physical exercise —vt. 2. jar, nudge 3. remind, stimulate (-gg-) —n. 4. jogging —'jogger n. —'jogging n. —jog trot slow regular trot

joggle ('dʒɒg⁰l) v. 1. move to and fro in jerks 2. shake —n. 3. act of joggling

john (dʒɒn) n. US sl. lavatory

John Bull typical Englishman

joie de vivre (ʒwad 'vivr) Fr. enjoyment of life, ebullience

join (dʒɔɪn) vt. 1. put together, fasten, unite 2. become member of —vi. 3. become united, connected 4. (with up) enlist 5. (usu. with in) take part —n. 6. joining 7. place of joining —'joiner n. 1. maker of finished woodwork 2. one who joins —'joinery n. joiner's work

joint (dʒɔɪnt) n. 1. arrangement by which two things fit together, rigidly or loosely 2. place of this 3. meat for roasting, oft. with bone 4. inf. house, place etc. 5. sl. disreputable bar or nightclub 6. sl. marijuana cigarette —a. 7. common 8. shared by two or more —vt. 9. connect by joints 10. divide at the joints —'jointly adv. —joint-stock company 1. UK business enterprise characterized by sharing of ownership between shareholders, whose liability is limited 2. US business enterprise whose owners are issued shares of transferable stock but do not enjoy limited liability —**out of joint 1.** dislocated **2.** disorganized

jointure ('dʒɔɪntʃə) *n. Law* property settled on wife for her use after husband's death

joist (dʒɔɪst) *n.* one of the parallel beams stretched from wall to wall on which to fix floor or ceiling —**joisted** a.

joke (dʒəʊk) *n.* **1.** thing said or done to cause laughter **2.** something said or done merely in fun **3.** ridiculous or humorous circumstance —*vi.* **4.** make jokes —'**joker** *n.* **1.** one who jokes **2.** *sl.* fellow **3.** extra card in pack, counting as highest card in some games

jolly ('dʒɒlɪ) a. **1.** jovial **2.** festive, merry —*vt.* **3.** (*esp. with* along) (try to) make (person, occasion *etc.*) happier ('**jollied, 'jollying**) —**jollifi'cation** *n.* merrymaking —'**jollity** *n.*

Jolly Roger pirates' flag with white skull and crossbones on black field

jolt (dʒəʊlt) *n.* **1.** sudden jerk **2.** bump **3.** shock —*v.* **4.** move, shake with jolts —'**jolty** a.

Jonah ('dʒəʊnə) *or* **Jonas** ('dʒəʊnəs) *n.* **1.** *O.T.* Hebrew prophet who was swallowed by whale **2.** person believed to bring bad luck to those around him

jonquil ('dʒɒŋkwɪl) *n.* **1.** fragrant yellow or white narcissus —*a.* **2.** pale yellow

Josh. *Bible* Joshua

joss (dʒɒs) *n.* Chinese idol —**joss house** Chinese temple —**joss stick** stick of Chinese incense

jostle ('dʒɒsˀl) *or* **justle** ('dʒʌsˀl) *v.* knock or push against (someone)

jot (dʒɒt) *n.* **1.** small amount, whit —*vt.* **2.** write briefly; make note of (-**tt**-) —'**jotter** *n.* notebook

joule (dʒuːl) *n. Elec.* unit of work or energy

journal ('dʒɜːnˀl) *n.* **1.** daily newspaper or other periodical **2.** daily record **3.** logbook **4.** part of axle or shaft resting on the bearings —'**journa'lese** *n.* journalists' jargon **2.** high-flown style, full of clichés —'**journalism** *n.* editing, writing in periodicals —'**journalist** *n.* —**journa'listic** a.

journey ('dʒɜːnɪ) *n.* **1.** travelling from one place to another; excursion **2.** distance travelled —*vi.* **3.** travel

journeyman ('dʒɜːnɪmən) *n.* craftsman or artisan employed by another

joust (dʒaʊst) *Hist.* —*n.* **1.** encounter with lances between two mounted knights —*vi.* **2.** engage in joust

Jove (dʒəʊv) *n. see* JUPITER (sense 1) —'**Jovian** a. —**by Jove** exclamation of surprise

jovial ('dʒəʊvɪəl) a. convivial, merry, gay

jowl (dʒaʊl) *n.* **1.** cheek, jaw **2.** outside of throat when prominent

joy (dʒɔɪ) *n.* **1.** gladness, pleasure, delight **2.** cause of this —'**joyful** a. —'**joyless** a. —'**joyous** a. **1.** having happy nature or mood **2.** joyful —'**joyously** adv. —**joy ride**

trip, *esp.* in stolen car —'**joystick** *n. inf.* control column of aircraft

J.P. Justice of the Peace

Jr. *or* **jr.** Junior

jubilate ('dʒuːbɪleɪt) *vi.* rejoice —'**jubilant** a. exultant —'**jubilantly** adv. —**jubi'lation** *n.*

jubilee ('dʒuːbɪliː) *n.* time of rejoicing, *esp.* 25th or 50th anniversary

Jud. *Bible* Judges

Judaic (dʒuː'deɪɪk) a. of the Jews or Judaism —'**Judaism** *n.* **1.** religion of the Jews **2.** religious and cultural traditions of the Jews **3.** the Jews collectively —'**Judaize** *or* -**ise** *vt.* **1.** make Jewish —*v.* **2.** conform or bring into conformity with Judaism

Judas ('dʒuːdəs) *n.* **1.** *N.T.* apostle who betrayed Jesus to his enemies for 30 pieces of silver **2.** person who betrays a friend; traitor

judder ('dʒʌdə) *inf. vi.* **1.** shake, vibrate —*n.* **2.** a vibrating motion

judge (dʒʌdʒ) *n.* **1.** officer appointed to try cases in court of law **2.** one who decides in dispute, contest *etc.* **3.** one able to form reliable opinion, arbiter **4.** umpire **5.** in Jewish history, ruler —*vi.* **6.** act as judge —*vt.* **7.** act as judge of **8.** try, estimate **9.** decide —'**judgment** *or* '**judgement** *n.* **1.** faculty of judging **2.** sentence of court **3.** opinion **4.** misfortune regarded as sign of divine displeasure —**Judgment Day** occasion of Last Judgment by God at end of world

judicature ('dʒuːdɪkətʃə) *n.* **1.** administration of justice **2.** body of judges —**ju'dicial** a. **1.** of, or by, a court or judge **2.** having qualities proper to a judge **3.** discriminating —**ju'dicially** adv. —**ju'diciary** *n.* system of courts and judges —**ju'dicious** a. well-judged, sensible, prudent

judo ('dʒuːdəʊ) *n.* modern sport derived from jujitsu

jug (dʒʌg) *n.* **1.** vessel for liquids, with handle and small spout **2.** its contents **3.** *sl.* prison —*vt.* **4.** stew (*esp.* hare) in jug (-**gg**-)

juggernaut ('dʒʌgənɔːt) *n.* **1.** large heavy lorry **2.** any irresistible, destructive force

juggle ('dʒʌgˀl) *v.* **1.** throw and catch (several objects) so most are in the air simultaneously **2.** manage, manipulate (accounts *etc.*) to deceive —*n.* **3.** act of juggling —'**juggler** *n.*

jugular vein ('dʒʌgjʊlə) one of three large veins of the neck returning blood from the head

juice (dʒuːs) *n.* **1.** liquid part of vegetable, fruit or meat **2.** *inf.* electric current **3.** *inf.* petrol **4.** vigour, vitality —'**juicy** a. succulent

jujitsu, jujutsu, *or* **jiujutsu** (dʒuː'dʒɪtsuː) *n.* the Japanese art of wrestling and self-defence

juju ('dʒuːdʒuː) *n.* **1.** object superstitiously revered by certain W Afr. peoples and used as charm or fetish **2.** power associated with juju

jujube ('dʒuːdʒuːb) n. 1. any of several spiny trees that have yellowish flowers and dark red edible fruits 2. fruit of any of these trees 3. lozenge of gelatin, sugar etc.

jukebox ('dʒuːkbɒks) n. automatic, coin-operated record-player

Jul. July

julep ('dʒuːlɪp) n. 1. sweet drink 2. medicated drink

Julian ('dʒuːljən) a. of Julius Caesar —**Julian calendar** calendar as adjusted by Julius Caesar in 46 B.C., in which the year was made to consist of 365 days, 6 hours, instead of 365 days

julienne (dʒuːlɪ'ɛn) n. kind of clear soup

July (dʒuː'laɪ) n. seventh month

jumble ('dʒʌmb'l) v. 1. mingle, mix in confusion 2. remember in confused form —n. 3. confused heap, muddle 4. articles for jumble sale —**jumble sale** sale of miscellaneous, usu. second-hand, items

jumbo ('dʒʌmbəʊ) n. inf. 1. elephant 2. anything very large (pl. -s) —**jumbo jet** inf. large jet-propelled airliner

jump (dʒʌmp) v. 1. (cause to) spring, leap (over) 2. pass or skip (over) —vi. 3. move hastily 4. rise steeply 5. parachute from aircraft 6. start, jerk (with astonishment etc.) 7. (of faulty film etc.) make abrupt movements —vt. 8. come off (tracks, rails etc.) 9. inf. attack without warning —n. 10. act of jumping 11. obstacle to be jumped 12. distance, height jumped 13. sudden nervous jerk or start 14. sudden rise in prices —**'jumper** n. 1. one who, that which jumps 2. sweater, pullover —**'jumpy** a. nervous —**jumped-up** a. inf. suddenly risen in significance, esp. when appearing arrogant —**jump jet** inf. fixed-wing jet aircraft that can land and take off vertically —**jump leads** electric cables to connect discharged car battery to external battery to aid starting of engine —**jump suit** one-piece garment of trousers and top

Jun. 1. June 2. junior (also **jun.**)

junction ('dʒʌŋkʃən) n. 1. railway station etc. where lines, routes join 2. place of joining 3. joining

juncture ('dʒʌŋktʃə) n. state of affairs

June (dʒuːn) n. sixth month

jungle ('dʒʌŋg'l) n. 1. tangled vegetation of equatorial forest 2. land covered with it 3. tangled mass 4. condition of intense competition, struggle for survival —**'jungly** a.

junior ('dʒuːnjə) a. 1. younger 2. of lower standing —n. 3. junior person —**junior school** UK school for children aged between 7 and 11 —**junior technician** rank in Royal Air Force comparable to that of private in army

juniper ('dʒuːnɪpə) n. evergreen shrub with berries yielding oil of juniper, used for medicine and gin making

junk¹ (dʒʌŋk) n. 1. discarded, useless objects 2. inf. nonsense 3. sl. narcotic drug —**'junkie** or **'junky** n. sl. drug addict —**junk food** food eaten in addition to or instead of regular meals, oft. with low nutritional value

junk² (dʒʌŋk) n. Chinese sailing vessel

junket ('dʒʌŋkɪt) n. 1. curdled milk flavoured and sweetened —vi. 2. feast, picnic

junta ('dʒʊntə) n. group of military officers holding power in a country

Jupiter ('dʒuːpɪtə) n. 1. Roman chief of gods 2. largest of the planets

Jurassic (dʒʊ'ræsɪk) a. 1. of second period of Mesozoic era —n. 2. Jurassic period or rock system

juridical (dʒʊ'rɪdɪk'l) a. of law or administration of justice; legal

jurisdiction (dʒʊərɪs'dɪkʃən) n. 1. administration of justice 2. authority 3. territory covered by it —**juris'prudence** n. science of, skill in, law —**'jurist** n. one skilled in law —ju'ristic(al) a.

jury ('dʒʊərɪ) n. 1. body of persons sworn to render verdict in court of law 2. body of judges of competition —**'juror** or **'jury-man** n. one of jury —**jury box** enclosure in court where jury sit

jury- (comb. form) chiefly naut. makeshift, as in jury-rigged

just (dʒʌst) a. 1. fair 2. upright, honest 3. proper, right, equitable —adv. 4. exactly 5. barely 6. at this instant 7. merely, only 8. really —**'justice** n. 1. quality of being just 2. fairness 3. judicial proceedings 4. judge, magistrate —**jus'ticiary** a. 1. of administration of justice —n. 2. officer or administrator of justice; judge —**'justifi-able** a. —**'justifiably** adv. —**justifi'cation** n. —**'justify** vt. 1. prove right, true or innocent 2. vindicate 3. excuse (-ified, -ifying) —**'justly** adv. —**justice of the peace** lay magistrate whose function is to preserve peace in his area and try summarily minor cases

jut (dʒʌt) vi. 1. (oft. with out) project, stick out (-tt-) —n. 2. projection

jute (dʒuːt) n. fibre of certain plants, used for rope, canvas etc.

juvenile ('dʒuːvɪnaɪl) a. 1. young 2. of, for young children 3. immature —n. 4. young person, child —**juve'nescence** n. —**juve'nescent** a. becoming young —**juvenilia** (dʒuːvɪ'nɪlɪə) pl.n. works produced in author's youth —**juve'nility** (dʒuːvɪ'nɪlɪtɪ) n. —**juvenile court** court dealing with young offenders or children in need of care —**juvenile delinquent** young person guilty of some offence, antisocial behaviour etc.

juxtapose (dʒʌkstə'pəʊz) vt. put side by side —**juxtapo'sition** n. contiguity, being side by side

K

k *or* **K** (keɪ) *n.* **1.** 11th letter of English alphabet **2.** speech sound represented by this letter, as in *kitten* (*pl.* **k's, K's** *or* **Ks**)

k 1. kilo **2.** *Maths.* unit vector along *z*-axis **3.** knit

K 1. kelvin **2.** *Chess* king **3.** *Chem.* potassium **4.** *Phys.* kaon **5.** one thousand **6.** *Comp.* unit of 1024 words, bytes or bits

Kaffir *or* **Kafir** ('kæfə) *n.* SA *obs., offens.* any black African —**kaffirboom** ('kæfə-buəm) *n.* S Afr. flowering tree —**kaffir corn** S Afr. variety of sorghum

kaftan *or* **caftan** ('kæftæn) *n.* **1.** long coatlike Eastern garment **2.** imitation of it, *esp.* as woman's long, loose dress with sleeves

Kaiser ('kaɪzə) *n.* (*sometimes* **k-**) *Hist.* **1.** any of three German emperors **2.** any Austro-Hungarian emperor

kale *or* **kail** (keɪl) *n.* type of cabbage

kaleidoscope (kə'laɪdəskəup) *n.* **1.** optical toy for producing changing symmetrical patterns by multiple reflections of coloured glass chips *etc.*, in inclined mirrors enclosed in tube **2.** any complex, frequently changing pattern —**kaleidoscopic** (kəlaɪdə'skɒpɪk) *a.* swiftly changing

Kamasutra (kɑːməˈsuːtrə) *n.* ancient Hindu text on erotic pleasure

kamikaze (kæmɪ'kɑːzɪ) *n.* (*oft.* **K-**) suicidal attack, *esp.* as in World War II, by Japanese pilots

kangaroo (kæŋgə'ruː) *n.* **1.** Aust. marsupial with very strongly developed hind legs for jumping —*vi.* **2.** *inf.* (of car) move forward with sudden jerks —**kangaroo court** irregular, illegal court

kaolin ('keɪəlɪn) *n.* fine white clay used for porcelain and medicinally

kaon ('keɪɒn) *n.* meson that has rest mass of about 996 or 964 electron masses (*also* **K-meson**)

kapok ('keɪpɒk) *n.* **1.** tropical tree **2.** fibre from its seed pods used to stuff cushions *etc.*

kappa ('kæpə) *n.* tenth letter in Gr. alphabet (K, κ)

kaput (kæ'put) *a.* *inf.* ruined, broken, no good

karakul *or* **caracul** ('kærək^əl) *n.* **1.** breed of sheep of central Asia having coarse black, grey or brown hair; lambs have soft curled hair **2.** fur prepared from these lambs

karate (kə'rɑːtɪ) *n.* Japanese system of unarmed combat using feet, hands, elbows *etc.* as weapons in a variety of ways

karoo *or* **karroo** (kə'ruː) *n.* SA high, arid plateau

kaross (kə'rɒs) *n.* SA cloak made of skins

kart (kɑːt) *n.* light low-framed vehicle with small wheels and engine for recreational racing (**karting**) (*also* **go-cart, go-kart**)

katabolism (kə'tæbəlɪzəm) *n.* *see* CATABOLISM

katydid ('keɪtɪdɪd) *n.* green long-horned grasshopper living in trees in N Amer.

kauri ('kaurɪ) *n.* large N.Z. pine giving valuable timber (*pl.* **-s**)

kava ('kɑːvə) *n.* **1.** Polynesian shrub **2.** beverage prepared from the aromatic roots of this shrub

kayak *or* **kaiak** ('kaɪæk) *n.* **1.** Eskimo canoe made of sealskins stretched over frame **2.** any canoe of this design

kazoo (kə'zuː) *n.* cigar-shaped musical instrument producing nasal sound

K.B. Knight of the Bath

kc kilocycle

K.C. King's Counsel

kcal kilocalorie

kea ('keɪə) *n.* large New Zealand parrot with brownish-green plumage

kebab (kə'bæb) *n.* dish of small pieces of meat, tomatoes *etc.* grilled on skewers (*also* **shish kebab**)

kedge (kɛdʒ) *n.* **1.** small anchor —*vt.* **2.** move (ship) by cable attached to kedge

kedgeree (kɛdʒə'riː) *n.* dish of fish cooked with rice, eggs *etc.*

keek (kiːk) *n./vi.* *Scot.* peep

keel (kiːl) *n.* lowest longitudinal support on which ship is built —**'keelhaul** *vt.* **1.** formerly, punish by hauling under keel of ship **2.** rebuke severely —**keelson** ('kɛlsən, 'kiːl-) *or* **kelson** ('kɛlsən) *n.* line of timbers or plates bolted to keel —**keel over 1.** turn upside down **2.** *inf.* collapse suddenly —**on an even keel** well-balanced; steady

keen¹ (kiːn) *a.* **1.** sharp **2.** acute **3.** eager **4.** shrewd **5.** (of price) competitive —**'keenly** *adv.* —**'keenness** *n.*

keen² (kiːn) *n.* **1.** funeral lament —*vi.* **2.** wail over the dead

keep (kiːp) *vt.* **1.** retain possession of, not lose **2.** store **3.** cause to continue **4.** take charge of **5.** maintain **6.** detain **7.** provide upkeep of **8.** reserve —*vi.* **9.** remain good **10.** remain **11.** continue (**kept** *pt./pp.*) —*n.* **12.** living or support **13.** charge or care **14.** central tower of castle, stronghold —**'keeper** *n.* —**'keeping** *n.* **1.** harmony, agreement **2.** care, charge, possession —**'keepsake** *n.* gift that evokes memories of person or event

keg (kɛg) *n.* **1.** small barrel **2.** metal container for beer

kelp (kɛlp) *n.* **1.** large seaweed **2.** its ashes, yielding iodine

kelt (kɛlt) *n.* salmon that has recently spawned

kelvin ('kɛlvɪn) *a.* **1.** of thermometric scale starting at absolute zero (−273.15° Celsius) —*n.* **2.** SI unit of temperature

ken (kɛn) *n.* 1. range of knowledge —*v.* 2. in Scotland, know (**kenned** or **kent** *pt./pp.*)

kendo ('kɛndəʊ) *n.* Japanese form of fencing using wooden staves

kennel ('kɛn³l) *n.* 1. house, shelter for dog —*pl.* 2. place for breeding, boarding dogs —*vt.* 3. put into kennel (**-ll-**)

kentledge ('kɛntlɪdʒ) *n. Naut.* scrap metal used as ballast

kepi ('keɪpiː) *n.* military cap with circular top and horizontal peak (*pl.* **-s**)

kept (kɛpt) *pt./pp. of* KEEP

kerb or *U.S.* **curb** (kɜːb) *n.* stone edging to footpath —**kerb crawler** —**kerb crawling** driving slowly beside pavement and seeking to entice someone into car for sexual purposes

kerchief ('kɜːtʃɪf) *n.* 1. head-cloth 2. handkerchief

kerfuffle (kə'fʌf³l) *n. inf.* commotion, disorder

kermes ('kɜːmɪz) *n.* insect used for red dyestuff

kernel ('kɜːn³l) *n.* 1. inner seed of nut or fruit stone 2. central, essential part

kerosene or **kerosine** ('kɛrəsiːn) *n.* paraffin oil distilled from petroleum or coal and shale

kestrel ('kɛstrəl) *n.* small falcon

ketch (kɛtʃ) *n.* two-masted sailing vessel

ketchup ('kɛtʃəp), **catchup** ('kætʃəp, 'kɛtʃ-), or **catsup** ('kætsəp) *n.* sauce of vinegar, tomatoes *etc.*

ketone ('kiːtəʊn) *n.* chemical compound with general formula R′COR, where R and R′ are usu. alkyl or aryl groups —**ketonic** (kɪ'tɒnɪk) *a.*

kettle ('kɛt³l) *n.* metal vessel with spout and handle, *esp.* for boiling water —'**kettledrum** *n.* musical instrument made of membrane stretched over copper hemisphere —**a fine kettle of fish** awkward situation, mess

key[1] (kiː) *n.* 1. instrument for operating lock, winding clock *etc.* 2. something providing control, explanation, means of achieving an end *etc.* 3. *Mus.* set of related notes 4. operating lever of typewriter, piano, organ *etc.* 5. spanner 6. mode of thought —*vt.* 7. provide symbols on (map *etc.*) to assist identification of positions on it 8. scratch (plaster surface) to provide bond for plaster or paint 9. insert (copy, information) by keystroke —*a.* 10. vital 11. most important —'**keyboard** *n.* set of keys on piano *etc.* —'**keyhole** *n.* aperture in lock case into which key is inserted —**key money** fee, payment required from new tenant of house *etc.* before he moves in —'**keynote** *n.* 1. dominant idea 2. basic note of musical key —**key punch** device having keyboard operated manually to transfer data onto punched cards *etc.* (*also* **card 'punch**) —**key-punch** *vt.* transfer (data) by key punch —**key signature** *Mus.* sharps or flats at beginning of each stave line to indicate key —'**keystone** *n.* 1. central stone of arch 2. something

necessary to connect other related things —'**keystroke** *n.* depression of single key on keyboard of typewriter, computer *etc.* —**key in** enter (information or instructions) in computer *etc.* by means of keyboard *etc.*

key[2] (kiː) *n. see* CAY

kg or **kg.** kilogram

K.G. Knight of the Order of the Garter

K.G.B. Soviet secret police

khaki ('kɑːkɪ) *a.* 1. dull yellowish-brown —*n.* 2. dull yellowish-brown colour 3. hard-wearing fabric of this colour, used *esp.* for military uniforms (*pl.* **-s**)

khan (kɑːn) *n.* 1. formerly, (title borne by) medieval Chinese emperors and Mongol and Turkic rulers 2. title of respect borne by important personages in Afghanistan and central Asia

Khmer (kmɛə) *n.* member of a people of Kampuchea

kHz kilohertz

kibble ('kɪb³l) *vt.* grind into small pieces

kibbutz (kɪ'bʊts) *n.* Jewish communal agricultural settlement in Israel (*pl.* **kibbutzim** (kɪbʊt'siːm))

kibosh ('kaɪbɒʃ) *n. sl.* —**put the kibosh on** 1. silence 2. get rid of 3. defeat

kick (kɪk) *vi.* 1. strike out with foot 2. (*sometimes with* against) be recalcitrant 3. recoil —*vt.* 4. strike or hit with foot 5. score (goal) with a kick 6. *inf.* free oneself of (habit *etc.*) —*n.* 7. foot blow 8. recoil 9. excitement, thrill —'**kickback** *n.* 1. strong reaction 2. money paid illegally for favours done *etc.* —'**kickoff** *n.* 1. place kick from centre of field in football 2. time at which first such kick is due to take place —'**kickstand** *n.* short metal bar which when kicked into vertical position holds stationary cycle upright —**kick-start** *vt.* start (motorcycle engine) by pedal that is kicked downwards —**kick-starter** *n.* this pedal —**kick off** 1. start game of football 2. *inf.* begin (discussion *etc.*)

kid (kɪd) *n.* 1. young goat 2. leather of its skin 3. *inf.* child —*vt.* 4. tease; deceive —*vi.* 5. behave, speak in fun (**-dd-**) —**kid glove** glove made of kidskin —**kid'glove** *a.* 1. overdelicate 2. diplomatic; tactful —**handle with kid gloves** treat with great tact or caution

kidnap ('kɪdnæp) *vt.* seize and hold to ransom (**-pp-**) —'**kidnapper** *n.*

kidney ('kɪdnɪ) *n.* 1. either of the pair of organs which secrete urine 2. animal kidney used as food 3. nature, kind (*esp.* in **of the same** or **a different kidney**) (*pl.* **-s**) —**kidney bean** 1. dwarf French bean 2. scarlet runner —**kidney machine** machine carrying out functions of kidney

kill (kɪl) *vt.* 1. deprive of life 2. destroy 3. neutralize 4. pass (time) 5. weaken; dilute 6. *inf.* exhaust 7. *inf.* cause to suffer pain 8. *inf.* quash, defeat, veto —*n.* 9. act or time of killing 10. animals *etc.* killed in hunt —'**killer** *n.* one who, that which, kills —'**killing** *inf.* a. 1. very tiring 2. very funny

—*n.* **3.** sudden success, *esp.* on stock market —**killer whale** ferocious toothed whale most common in cold seas —**kill-joy** *n.* person who spoils other people's pleasure

kiln (kıln) *n.* furnace, oven

kilo ('kiːləʊ) *n.* kilogram (*pl.* -**s**)

kilo- (*comb. form*) one thousand, as in *kilolitre, kilometre*

kilocycle ('kıləʊsaık*ə*l) *n. short for* kilocycle per second: former unit of frequency equal to 1 kilohertz

kilogram or **kilogramme** ('kıləʊgræm) *n.* weight of 1000 grams

kilohertz ('kıləʊhɜːts) *n.* one thousand cycles per second

kiloton ('kıləʊtʌn) *n.* **1.** one thousand tons **2.** explosive power, *esp.* of nuclear weapon, equal to power of 1000 tons of TNT

kilowatt ('kıləʊwɒt) *n. Elec.* one thousand watts —**kilowatt-hour** *n.* unit of energy equal to work done by power of 1000 watts in one hour

kilt (kılt) *n. usu.* tartan knee-length skirt, deeply pleated, worn orig. by Scottish Highlanders

kimono (kı'məʊnəʊ) *n.* **1.** loose, wide-sleeved Japanese robe, fastened with sash **2.** European garment like this (*pl.* -**s**)

kin (kın) *n.* **1.** family, relatives —*a.* **2.** related by blood —**kindred** ('kındrıd) *n.* **1.** relationship by blood **2.** relatives collectively —*a.* **3.** similar **4.** related —'**kinsfolk** *pl.n.* —'**kinship** *n.*

-kin (*comb. form*) small, as in *lambkin*

kind (kaınd) *n.* **1.** genus, sort, class —*a.* **2.** sympathetic, considerate **3.** good, benevolent **4.** gentle —'**kindliness** *n.* —'**kindly** *a.* **1.** kind, genial —*adv.* **2.** in a considerate or humane way —'**kindness** *n.* —**kind-hearted** *a.* kindly, readily sympathetic —**in kind 1.** (of payment) in goods rather than money **2.** with something similar

kindergarten ('kındəgɑːt*ə*n) *n.* class, school for children of about four to six years old

kindle ('kınd*ə*l) *vt.* **1.** set on fire **2.** inspire, excite —*vi.* **3.** catch fire —'**kindling** *n.* wood, straw *etc.* to kindle fire

kinematic (kını'mætık) *a.* of motion without reference to mass or force —**kine'matics** *pl.n.* (*with sing. v.*) science of this —**kine'matograph** *n. see* cinematograph *at* CINEMA

kinetic (kı'nɛtık) *a.* of motion in relation to force —**ki'netics** *pl.n.* (*with sing. v.*) science of this —**kinetic art** art, *esp.* sculpture, that moves or has moving parts

king (kıŋ) *n.* **1.** male sovereign ruler of independent state, monarch **2.** piece in game of chess **3.** highest court card, with picture of a king **4.** *Draughts* two pieces on top of one another, allowed freedom of movement —'**kingdom** *n.* **1.** state ruled by king **2.** realm **3.** sphere —'**kingly** *a.* **1.** royal **2.** appropriate to a king —'**kingship** *n.* —**King Charles spaniel** toy breed of spaniel with very long ears —'**kingcup** *n.* UK any of several yellow-flowered plants, *esp.* marsh marigold —'**kingfisher** *n.* small bird with bright plumage, which dives for fish —'**kingpin** *n.* **1.** swivel pin **2.** central or front pin in bowling **3.** *inf.* chief person or thing —**king post** beam in roof framework rising from tie beam to the ridge —**King's Bench** (when sovereign is male) *another name for* **Queen's Bench** (*see* QUEEN) —**King's Counsel** (when sovereign is male) *another name for* **Queen's Counsel** (*see* QUEEN) —**King's English** (*esp.* when British sovereign is male) standard Southern British English —**king's evidence** (when sovereign is male) *another name for* **queen's evidence** (*see* QUEEN) —**king's highway** (in Britain, *esp.* when sovereign is male) public road or right of way —**king-size** or **king-sized** *a.* **1.** large **2.** larger than standard size

kingklip ('kıŋklıp) *n.* S Afr. marine fish

kink (kıŋk) *n.* **1.** tight twist in rope, wire, hair *etc.* **2.** crick, as of neck **3.** *inf.* eccentricity —*v.* **4.** make, become kinked —'**kinky** *a.* **1.** full of kinks **2.** *inf.* eccentric, *esp.* given to deviant (sexual) practices

kiosk ('kiːɒsk) *n.* **1.** small, sometimes movable booth selling drinks, cigarettes, newspapers *etc.* **2.** public telephone box

kipper ('kıpə) *vt.* **1.** cure (fish) by splitting open, rubbing with salt and drying or smoking —*n.* **2.** kippered fish

kirk (kɜːk) *n.* in Scotland, church

Kirsch (kıəʃ) or **Kirschwasser** ('kıəʃ-vɑːsə) *n.* brandy made from cherries

kismet ('kızmɛt, 'kıs-) *n.* fate, destiny

kiss (kıs) *n.* **1.** touch or caress with lips **2.** light touch —*vt.* **3.** touch with the lips as an expression of love, greeting *etc.* —*vi.* **4.** join lips with another person in act of love or desire —'**kisser** *n.* **1.** one who kisses **2.** *sl.* mouth; face —**kiss curl** UK circular curl of hair pressed flat against cheek or forehead —**kiss of life** mouth-to-mouth resuscitation

kist (kıst) *n.* large wooden chest

kit (kıt) *n.* **1.** outfit, equipment **2.** personal effects, *esp.* of traveller **3.** set of pieces of equipment sold ready to be assembled —'**kitbag** *n.* bag for holding soldier's or traveller's kit —**kit out** or **up** *chiefly* UK provide with kit of personal effects and necessities

kitchen ('kıtʃın) *n.* room used for preparing and cooking food —**kitchen-'ette** *n.* small room (or part of larger room) used for cooking —**kitchen garden** garden for raising vegetables, herbs *etc.* —**kitchen sink** *n.* **1.** sink in kitchen —*a.* **2.** sordidly domestic

kite (kaıt) *n.* **1.** light papered frame flown in wind **2.** *sl.* aeroplane **3.** large hawk —**Kite mark** official mark on articles approved by British Standards Institution

kith (kıθ) *n.* acquaintance, kindred (*only in* **kith and kin**)

kitsch (kıtʃ) *n.* vulgarized, pretentious art,

literature *etc.*, usu. with popular, sentimental appeal

kitten ('kit'n) *n.* young cat —'**kittenish** *a.* 1. like kitten; lively 2. (of woman) flirtatious, *esp.* coyly

kittiwake ('kitiweik) *n.* type of seagull

kitty ('kiti) *n.* 1. kitten or cat 2. in some gambling games, pool 3. communal fund

kiwi ('ki:wi) *n.* 1. N.Z. flightless bird having long beak, stout legs and weakly barbed feathers 2. *inf.* New Zealander (*pl.* -s)

kl. kilolitre

klaxon ('klæks'n) *n.* formerly, powerful electric motor horn

kleptomania (kleptəʊ'meiniə) *n.* compulsive tendency to steal *esp.* when there is no obvious motivation —**klepto'maniac** *n.*

klipspringer ('klipsprinə) *n.* small agile Afr. antelope

kloof (klu:f) *n.* SA mountain pass

km *or* **km.** kilometre

knack (næk) *n.* 1. acquired facility or dexterity 2. trick 3. habit

knacker ('nækə) *n.* buyer of worn-out horses *etc.*, for killing —'**knackered** *a. sl.* exhausted

knapsack ('næpsæk) *n.* soldier's or traveller's bag to strap to the back, rucksack

knapweed ('næpwi:d) *n.* plant having purplish thistlelike flowers

knave (neiv) *n.* 1. jack at cards 2. *obs.* rogue —'**knavery** *n.* villainy —'**knavish** *a.*

knead (ni:d) *vt.* 1. work (flour) into dough 2. work, massage —'**kneader** *n.*

knee (ni:) *n.* 1. joint between thigh and lower leg 2. part of garment covering knee 3. lap —*vt.* 4. strike, push with knee —'**kneecap** *n.* bone in front of knee —**knees-up** *n. inf.* party, oft. with dancing

kneel (ni:l) *vi.* fall, rest on knees (**knelt** *pt./pp.*)

knell (nel) *n.* 1. sound of a bell, *esp.* at funeral or death 2. portent of doom

knelt (nelt) *pt./pp. of* KNEEL

knew (nju:) *pt. of* KNOW

knickerbockers ('nikəbokəz) *pl.n.* loose-fitting breeches gathered at knees

knickers ('nikəz) *pl.n.* woman's undergarment for lower half of body

knick-knack ('niknæk) *n.* trifle, trinket

knife (naif) *n.* 1. cutting blade, *esp.* one in handle, used as implement or weapon (*pl.* **knives**) —*vt.* 2. cut or stab with knife —**knife edge** critical, possibly dangerous situation

knight (nait) *n.* 1. man of rank below baronet, having right to prefix *Sir* to his name 2. member of medieval order of chivalry 3. champion 4. piece in chess —*vt.* 5. confer knighthood on —'**knighthood** *n.* —'**knightly** *a.*

knit (nit) *v.* 1. form (garment *etc.*) by putting together series of loops in wool or other yarn 2. draw together 3. unite ('**knitted, knit** *pt./pp.*, '**knitting** *pr.p.*) —'**knitter** *n.* —'**knitting** *n.* 1. knitted work

2. act of knitting —'**knitwear** *n.* knitted clothes, *esp.* sweaters

knives (naivz) *n., pl. of* KNIFE

knob (nob) *n.* rounded lump, *esp.* at end or on surface of anything —'**knobby** *or* '**knobbly** *a.*

knock (nok) *vt.* 1. strike, hit 2. *inf.* disparage —*vi.* 3. rap audibly 4. (of engine) make metallic noise, pink —*n.* 5. blow, rap —'**knocker** *n.* 1. metal appliance for knocking on door 2. person or thing that knocks —**knocking copy** publicity material designed to denigrate competing product —**knock-kneed** *a.* having incurved legs —'**knockout** *n.* 1. blow *etc.* that renders unconscious 2. *inf.* person or thing overwhelmingly attractive —**knock down** 1. strike to ground with blow, as in boxing 2. in auctions, declare (article) sold 3. demolish 4. dismantle for ease of transport 5. *inf.* reduce (price *etc.*) —**knocked up** *inf.* exhausted, tired, worn out —**knock off** *inf.* 1. cease work 2. make hurriedly 3. kill 4. steal —**knock out** 1. render unconscious 2. *inf.* overwhelm, amaze

knoll (nəʊl) *n.* small rounded hill, mound

knot (not) *n.* 1. fastening of strands by looping and pulling tight 2. cockade, cluster 3. small closely knit group 4. tie, bond 5. hard lump, *esp.* of wood where branch joins or has joined 6. unit of speed of one nautical mile (1852m) per hour 7. difficulty —*vt.* 8. tie with knot, in knots (**-tt-**) —'**knotty** *a.* 1. full of knots 2. puzzling, difficult —'**knothole** *n.* hole in wood where knot has been

knot² (not) *n.* small northern sandpiper with grey plumage

know (nəʊ) *vt.* 1. be aware of 2. have information about 3. be acquainted with 4. recognize 5. have experience of, understand —*vi.* 6. have information or understanding (**knew** *pt.*, **known** *pp.*) —'**knowable** *a.* —'**knowing** *a.* cunning, shrewd —'**knowingly** *adv.* 1. shrewdly 2. deliberately —**knowledge** ('nolidʒ) *n.* 1. knowing 2. what one knows 3. learning —**knowledgeable** *or* **knowledgable** ('nolidʒəb'l) *a.* well-informed —**known** *a.* identified —**know-how** *n. inf.* practical knowledge, experience, aptitude —**in the know** *inf.* informed

knuckle ('nʌk'l) *n.* 1. bone at finger joint 2. knee joint of calf or pig —*vt.* 3. strike with knuckles —**knuckle-duster** *n.* metal appliance worn on knuckles to add force to blow —**knuckle down** *inf.* get down (to work) —**knuckle under** yield, submit —**near the knuckle** *inf.* approaching indecency

knur, knurr (nɜ:), *or* **knar** (nɑ:) *n.* 1. knot in wood 2. hard lump

knurl *or* **nurl** (nɜ:l) *vt.* 1. impress with series of fine ridges or serrations —*n.* 2. small ridge, *esp.* one of series —**knurled** *or* **nurled** *a.* 1. serrated 2. gnarled

koala *or* **koala bear** (kəʊ'ɑ:lə) *n.* marsupial Aust. animal, native bear

kohl (kəul) *n.* powdered antimony used *esp.* in Eastern countries for darkening the eyelids

kohlrabi (kəul'rɑːbɪ) *n.* type of cabbage with edible stem (*also* **turnip cabbage**)

kokanee (kəu'kænɪ) *n.* salmon of N Amer. lakes

kola ('kəulə) *n. see* COLA

kolinsky (kə'lɪnskɪ) *n.* 1. any of various Asian minks 2. rich tawny fur of this animal

komatik ('kəumætɪk) *n.* C Eskimo sledge with wooden runners

kook (kuːk) *n. US inf.* eccentric or foolish person —**'kooky** *or* **'kookie** *a.*

kookaburra ('kukəbʌrə) *n.* large Aust. kingfisher with cackling cry (*also* **laughing jackass**)

kopeck *or* **copeck** ('kəupɛk) *n.* Soviet monetary unit, one hundredth of rouble

koppie *or* **kopje** ('kɒpɪ) *n.* SA small hill

Koran (kɔː'rɑːn) *n.* sacred book of Muslims

kosher ('kəuʃə) *a.* 1. permitted, clean, good, as of food *etc.*, conforming to the Jewish dietary law 2. *inf.* legitimate, authentic —*n.* 3. kosher food

kowtow ('kautau) *n.* 1. former Chinese custom of touching ground with head in respect 2. submission —*vi.* (*esp. with* to) 3. prostrate oneself 4. be obsequious, fawn (on)

Kr *Chem.* krypton

kraal (krɑːl) *n.* SA 1. hut village, *esp.* one surrounded by fence 2. corral

kraken ('krɑːkən) *n.* mythical Norwegian sea monster

krans (krɑːns) *n.* SA cliff

Kraut (kraut) *a./n. sl., offens.* German

Kremlin ('krɛmlɪn) *n.* central government of Soviet Union

krill (krɪl) *n.* small shrimplike marine animal

kris (krɪs) *n.* Malayan and Indonesian knife with scalloped edge (*also* **crease, creese**)

krona ('krəunə) *n.* standard monetary unit of Sweden (*pl.* **-nor** (-nə))

krone ('krəunə) *n.* standard monetary unit of Norway and Denmark (*pl.* **-ner** (-nə))

krypton ('krɪptɒn) *n.* rare gaseous element present in atmosphere

KS Kansas

Kt *Chess* knight (*also* **N**)

kudos ('kjuːdɒs) *n.* 1. fame 2. credit

kudu *or* **koodoo** ('kuːduː) *n.* Afr. antelope with spiral horns

Ku Klux Klan ('kuː 'klʌks 'klæn) 1. secret organization of White Southerners formed after U.S. Civil War to fight Black emancipation 2. secret organization of White Protestant Americans, mainly in South, who use violence against Blacks, Jews *etc.*

kukri ('kukrɪ) *n.* heavy, curved Gurkha knife

kulak ('kuːlæk) *n.* independent well-to-do Russian peasant

kumara *or* **kumera** ('kuːmərə) *n.* NZ sweet potato

kümmel ('kuməl) *n.* cumin-flavoured German liqueur

kumquat *or* **cumquat** ('kʌmkwɒt) *n.* 1. small Chinese tree 2. its round orange fruit

kung fu ('kʌŋ 'fuː) Chinese martial art combining techniques of judo and karate

kW *or* **kw** kilowatt

kwashiorkor (kwæʃɪ'ɔːkə) *n.* severe malnutrition of young children, resulting from dietary deficiency of protein

kWh, kwh, *or* **kw-h** kilowatt-hour

KWIC (kwɪk) key word in context (*esp. in* **KWIC index**)

KWOC (kwɒk) key word out of context

KY Kentucky

kyle (kaɪl) *n. Scot.* narrow strait or channel

kymograph ('kaɪməgrɑːf) *n.* instrument for recording on graph pressure, oscillations, sound waves

L

l *or* **L** (ɛl) *n.* **1.** 12th letter of English alphabet **2.** speech sound represented by this letter **3.** something shaped like L (*pl.* **l's, L's** *or* **Ls**)

L 1. lambert **2.** large **3.** Latin **4.** (on Brit. motor vehicles) learner driver **5.** *Phys.* length **6.** pound (*usually written:* £) **7.** longitude **8.** *Electron.* inductor (in circuit diagrams) **9.** *Phys.* latent heat **10.** *Phys.* self-inductance **11.** Roman numeral, 50

L. *or* **l. l.** lake **2.** left **3.** line (*pl.* **LL.** *or* **ll.**) **4.** litre

la (lɑː) *n. Mus. see* LAH

La *Chem.* lanthanum

LA Louisiana

laager ('lɑːgə) *n.* **SA** encampment surrounded by wagons

lab (læb) *inf.* laboratory

Lab. 1. *Pol.* Labour **2.** Labrador

label ('leɪb'l) *n.* **1.** slip of paper, metal *etc.*, fixed to object to give information about it **2.** brief, descriptive phrase or term —*vt.* **3.** fasten label to **4.** mark with label **5.** describe or classify in a word or phrase (**-ll-**)

labiate ('leɪbɪeɪt, -ɪt) *n.* **1.** plant of family *Labiatae*, having square stems, aromatic leaves and two-lipped corolla —*a.* **2.** of family *Labiatae*

labium ('leɪbɪəm) *n.* **1.** lip; liplike structure **2.** any of four lip-shaped folds of vulva, comprising outer pair (**labia majora**) and inner pair (**labia minora**) (*pl.* **-bia** (-bɪə)) —**'labial** *a.* **1.** of the lips **2.** pronounced with the lips —*n.* **3.** speech sound pronounced thus

laboratory (lə'bɒrətərɪ, -trɪ; *U.S.* 'læbrətɔːrɪ) *n.* place for scientific investigations or for manufacture of chemicals

labour *or U.S.* **labor** ('leɪbə) *n.* **1.** exertion of body or mind **2.** task **3.** workers collectively **4.** effort, pain of childbirth or time taken for this —*vi.* **5.** work hard **6.** strive **7.** maintain normal motion with difficulty **8.** (*esp.* of ship) be tossed heavily —*vt.* **9.** stress to excess —**la'borious** *a.* tedious —**la'boriously** *adv.* —**'laboured** *or U.S.* **'labored** *a.* uttered, done, with difficulty —**'labourer** *or U.S.* **'laborer** *n.* one who labours, *esp.* man doing manual work for wages —**labour exchange UK** *old name for* Employment Service Agency —**Labour Party 1.** Brit. political party, generally supporting interests of organized labour **2.** similar party in various other countries —**labour-saving** *a.* eliminating or lessening physical labour

Labrador ('læbrədɔː) *n.* breed of large, smooth-coated retriever dog (*also* **Labrador retriever**)

laburnum (lə'bɜːnəm) *n.* tree with yellow hanging flowers

labyrinth ('læbərɪnθ) *n.* **1.** network of tortuous passages, maze **2.** inexplicable difficulty **3.** perplexity —**laby'rinthine** *a.*

lac¹ (læk) *n.* resinous substance secreted by some insects

lac² (lɑːk) *n.* one hundred thousand (of rupees)

lace (leɪs) *n.* **1.** fine patterned openwork fabric **2.** cord, usu. one of pair, to draw edges together, *eg* to tighten shoes *etc.* **3.** ornamental braid —*vt.* **4.** fasten with laces **5.** flavour with spirit —**'lacy** *a.* fine, like lace

lacerate ('læsəreɪt) *vt.* **1.** tear, mangle **2.** distress —**'lacerable** *a.* —**lacer'ation** *n.*

lachrymal, lacrimal, *or* **lacrymal** ('lækrɪməl) *a.* of tears —**'lachrymatory, 'lacrimatory,** *or* **'lacrymatory** *a.* causing tears or inflammation of eyes —**'lachrymose** *a.* tearful

lack (læk) *n.* **1.** deficiency, need —*vt.* **2.** need, be short of —**'lacklustre** *or U.S.* **'lackluster** *a.* lacking brilliance or vitality

lackadaisical (lækə'deɪzɪk'l) *a.* **1.** languid, listless **2.** lazy, careless

lackey ('lækɪ) *n.* **1.** servile follower **2.** footman (*pl.* **-s**) —*vi.* **3.** be or play, the lackey **4.** (*with* for) wait (upon)

laconic (lə'kɒnɪk) *a.* **1.** using, expressed in few words **2.** brief, terse **3.** offhand, not caring —**la'conically** *adv.* —**la'conicism** *n.*

lacquer ('lækə) *n.* **1.** hard varnish —*vt.* **2.** coat with this

lacrimal ('lækrɪməl) *a. see* LACHRYMAL

lacrosse (lə'krɒs) *n.* ball game played with long-handled racket or crosse

lacrymal ('lækrɪməl) *a. see* LACHRYMAL

lactic ('læktɪk) *a.* of milk —**'lactate** *vi.* secrete milk —**lac'tation** *n.* —**lac'tometer** *n.* instrument for measuring purity and density of milk —**'lactose** *n.* white crystalline substance occurring in milk —**lactic acid** colourless syrupy acid found in sour milk *etc.*

lacuna (lə'kjuːnə) *n.* gap, missing part, *esp.* in document or series (*pl.* **-nae** (-niː), **-s**)

lad (læd) *n.* boy, young fellow

ladder ('lædə) *n.* **1.** frame of two poles connected by rungs, used for climbing **2.** flaw in stockings, jumpers *etc.*, caused by running of torn stitch —**ladder back** type of chair in which back is constructed of horizontal slats between two uprights

lade (leɪd) *vt.* **1.** load **2.** ship **3.** burden, weigh down (**'laden** *pp.*) —**'lading** *n.* cargo, freight

la-di-da, lah-di-dah, *or* **la-de-da** (lɑːdiː'dɑː) *a. inf.* affecting exaggeratedly genteel manners or speech

ladle ('leɪd'l) *n.* **1.** spoon with long handle and large bowl —*vt.* **2.** (*oft. with* out) serve out (as) with ladle

lady ('leidi) *n.* **1.** female counterpart of gentleman **2.** *polite term for* a woman **3.** title of some women of rank —'**ladies** *or* **ladies' room** *n. inf.* women's public lavatory —'**ladyship** *n.* title of a lady —'**ladybird** *n.* small beetle, usu. red with black spots —**Lady Day** Feast of the Annunciation, 25th March —**lady-in-waiting** *n.* lady who attends queen or princess (*pl.* **ladies-in-waiting**) —'**lady-killer** *n. inf.* man who believes he is irresistible to women —'**ladylike** *a.* **1.** gracious **2.** well-mannered —**lady's finger** species of small banana —**lady's-slipper** *n.* orchid with reddish or purple flowers —**Our Lady** the Virgin Mary

lag¹ (læg) *vi.* **1.** (*oft. with* behind) go too slowly, fall behind (-**gg**-) —*n.* **2.** lagging, interval of time between events —'**laggard** *n.* one who lags —'**lagging** *a.* loitering, slow

lag² (læg) *vt.* wrap (boiler, pipes *etc.*) with insulating material (-**gg**-) —'**lagging** *n.* this material

lag³ (læg) *n. sl.* convict (*esp. in* old lag)

lager ('lɑːgə) *n.* light-bodied type of beer

lagoon (lə'guːn) *n.* saltwater lake, enclosed by atoll, or separated by sandbank from sea

lah *or* **la** (lɑː) *n. Mus.* in tonic solfa, sixth note of any major scale; submediant

laic ('leiik) *a.* secular, lay —**laici'zation** *or* **-ci'sation** *n.* —'**laicize** *or* **-cise** *vt.* render secular or lay

laid (leid) *pt./pp. of* LAY² —**laid-back** *a.* relaxed in style or character; easy-going and unhurried —**laid paper** paper with regular mesh impressed upon it

lain (lein) *pp. of* LIE¹

lair (leə) *n.* resting place, den of animal

laird (leəd) *n.* Scottish landowner —'**laird-ship** *n.* estate

laissez faire *or* **laisser faire** (lɛsei 'fɛə) *Fr.* **1.** principle of nonintervention, *esp.* by government in commercial affairs **2.** indifference

laity ('leiti) *n.* laymen, the people as opposed to clergy

lake¹ (leik) *n.* expanse of inland water —'**lakelet** *n.*

lake² (leik) *n.* red pigment

lam¹ (læm) *vt. sl.* beat, hit (-**mm**-) —'**lamming** *n.* beating, thrashing

lam² (læm) *n.* US *sl.* —**on the lam** making an escape

Lam. *Bible* Lamentations

lama ('lɑːmə) *n.* Buddhist priest in Tibet or Mongolia —'**Lamaism** *n.* form of Buddhism of Tibet and Mongolia —'**Lamaist** *n./a.* —'**lamasery** *n.* monastery of lamas

lamb (læm) *n.* **1.** young of the sheep **2.** its meat **3.** innocent or helpless creature —*vi.* **4.** (of sheep) give birth —'**lambkin** *n.* **1.** small lamb **2.** term of affection for child —'**lamblike** *a.* meek, gentle —'**lambskin** *n.* skin of lamb, *esp.* with wool still on **2.** material or garment prepared from this

—**lamb's tails** pendulous catkins of hazel tree —**lamb's wool** soft, fine wool (*also* '**lambswool**)

lambaste *or* **lambast** (læm'beist) *vt.* **1.** beat **2.** reprimand

lambda ('læmdə) *n.* 11th letter in Gr. alphabet (Λ, λ)

lambent ('læmbənt) *a.* **1.** (of flame) flickering softly **2.** glowing

lambert ('læmbət) *n.* cgs unit of illumination

lame (leim) *a.* **1.** crippled in a limb, *esp.* leg **2.** limping **3.** (of excuse *etc.*) unconvincing —*vt.* **4.** cripple —**lame duck** disabled, weak person or thing

lamé ('lɑːmei) *n./a.* (fabric) interwoven with gold or silver thread

lamella (lə'mɛlə) *n.* thin plate or scale (*pl.* -**lae** (-liː), -**s**) —**la'mellar** *or* **lamellate** ('læmileit, -lit) *a.*

lament (lə'mɛnt) *v.* **1.** feel, express sorrow (for) —*n.* **2.** passionate expression of grief **3.** song of grief —'**lamentable** *a.* deplorable —**lamen'tation** *n.*

lamina ('læminə) *n.* thin plate, scale, flake (*pl.* -**nae** (-niː), -**s**) —**laminate** ('læmineit) —*vt.* **1.** make (sheet of material) by bonding together two or more thin sheets **2.** split, beat, form into thin sheets **3.** cover with thin sheet of material —*n.* ('læmineit, -nit) **4.** laminated sheet —**lami'nation** *n.*

Lammas ('læmɔs) *n.* Aug. 1st, formerly a harvest festival

lammergeier *or* **lammergeyer** ('læmɔgaiɔ) *n.* type of rare vulture

lamp (læmp) *n.* **1.** any of various appliances (*esp.* electrical) that produce light, heat, radiation *etc.* **2.** formerly, vessel holding oil burned by wick for lighting —'**lampblack** *n.* pigment made from soot —'**lamplight** *n.* —'**lamppost** *n.* post supporting lamp in street —'**lampshade** *n.*

lampoon (læm'puːn) *n.* **1.** satire ridiculing person, literary work *etc.* —*vt.* **2.** satirize, ridicule —**lam'pooner** *or* **lam'poonist** *n.*

lamprey ('læmpri) *n.* fish like an eel with a sucker mouth

lance (lɑːns) *n.* **1.** horseman's spear —*vt.* **2.** pierce with lance or lancet —**lanceolate** ('lɑːnsiəleit, -lit) *a.* lance-shaped, tapering —'**lancer** *n.* formerly, cavalry soldier armed with lance —'**lancers** *pl.n.* (*with sing. v.*) **1.** quadrille for eight or sixteen couples **2.** music for this dance —'**lancet** *n.* pointed two-edged surgical knife —**lance corporal** *or* **sergeant** noncommissioned officer in army

Lancs. (læŋks) Lancashire

land (lænd) *n.* **1.** solid part of earth's surface **2.** ground, soil **3.** country **4.** property consisting of land —*pl.* **5.** estates —*vi.* **6.** come to land, disembark **7.** bring an aircraft (or of aircraft) come from air to land or water **8.** alight, step down **9.** arrive on ground **10.** C be legally admitted as immigrant —*vt.* **11.** bring to land **12.** bring to some point or condition **13.** *inf.*

obtain **14.** catch **15.** *inf.* strike —**'landed** *a.* possessing, consisting of lands —**'landing** *n.* **1.** act of landing **2.** platform between flights of stairs **3.** a landing stage —**'landward** *a./adv.* —**'landwards** *adv.* —**land agent 1.** person who administers landed estate and its tenancies **2.** person who acts as agent for sale of land —**'landfall** *n.* ship's approach to land at end of voyage —**'landgrave** *n.* German *hist.* **1.** (from 13th century to 1806) count who ruled over specified territory **2.** (after 1806) title of various sovereign princes —**landing gear** US undercarriage —**landing stage** platform for embarkation and disembarkation —**'landlocked** *a.* enclosed by land —**'landlord** or **'landlady** *n.* **1.** person who lets land, houses *etc.* **2.** master or mistress of inn, boarding house *etc.* —**'landlubber** *n.* person ignorant of the sea and ships —**'landmark** *n.* **1.** boundary mark, conspicuous object, as guide for direction *etc.* **2.** event, decision *etc.* considered as important stage in development of something —**'landmass** *n.* large continuous area of land —**land mine** *Mil.* explosive charge placed in ground, usu. detonated by stepping or driving on it —**'landowner** *n.* person who owns land —**'landscape** *n.* **1.** piece of inland scenery **2.** picture of it **3.** prospect —*v.* **4.** create, arrange, (garden, park *etc.*) —**landscape gardening** —**landscape painter** —**'landslide** or **'landslip** *n.* **1.** falling of soil, rock *etc.* down mountainside **2.** overwhelming electoral victory —**land of milk and honey 1.** land of natural fertility promised to Israelites by God **2.** any fertile land *etc.*

landau ('lændɔː) *n.* four-wheeled carriage with folding top

lane (leɪn) *n.* **1.** narrow road or street **2.** specified route followed by shipping or aircraft **3.** area of road for one stream of traffic

lang. language

language ('læŋgwɪdʒ) *n.* **1.** system of sounds, symbols *etc.* for communicating thought **2.** specialized vocabulary used by a particular group **3.** style of speech or expression —**language laboratory** room equipped with tape recorders *etc.* for learning foreign languages

languish ('læŋgwɪʃ) *vi.* **1.** be or become weak or faint **2.** be in depressing or painful conditions **3.** droop, pine —**'languid** *a.* **1.** lacking energy, interest **2.** spiritless, dull —**'languidly** *adv.* —**languor** ('læŋgə) *n.* **1.** want of energy or interest **2.** faintness **3.** tender mood **4.** softness of atmosphere —**languorous** ('læŋgərəs) *a.*

lank (læŋk) *a.* **1.** lean and tall **2.** greasy and limp —**'lanky** *a.* tall, thin and ungainly

lanolin ('lænəlɪn) or **lanoline** ('lænəlɪn, -liːn) *n.* grease from wool used in ointments *etc.*

lantern ('læntən) *n.* **1.** transparent case for lamp or candle **2.** erection on dome or roof to admit light —**lantern jaw** long hollow jaw that gives face drawn

appearance —**lantern-jawed** *a.* —**'lanthorn** *n. obs.* lantern

lanthanum ('lænθənəm) *n.* silvery-white ductile metallic element —**lanthanide series** class of 15 chemically related elements (**lanthanides**) with atomic numbers from 57 (lanthanum) to 71 (lutetium)

lanyard or **laniard** ('lænjəd) *n.* **1.** short cord for securing knife or whistle **2.** short nautical rope **3.** cord for firing cannon

lap¹ (læp) *n.* **1.** the part between waist and knees of a person when sitting **2.** *fig.* place where anything lies securely **3.** single circuit of racecourse, track **4.** stage or part of journey **5.** single turn of wound thread *etc.* —*vt.* **6.** enfold, wrap round **7.** overtake (opponent) to be one or more circuits ahead (**-pp-**) —**'lappet** *n.* flap, fold —**'lapdog** *n.* small pet dog —**lap joint** joint made by placing one member over another and fastening together (*also* **lapped joint**) —**lap of honour** ceremonial circuit of racing track *etc.* by winner of race

lap² (læp) *v.* **1.** (*oft. with* up) drink by scooping up with tongue **2.** (of waves *etc.*) beat softly (**-pp-**)

lapel (lə'pɛl) *n.* part of front of coat *etc.* folded back towards shoulders

lapidary ('læpɪdərɪ) *a.* **1.** of stones **2.** engraved on stone —*n.* **3.** cutter, engraver of stones

lapis lazuli ('læpɪs 'læzjʊlaɪ) bright blue stone or pigment

lapse (læps) *n.* **1.** fall (in standard, condition, virtue *etc.*) **2.** slip **3.** mistake **4.** passing (of time *etc.*) —*vi.* **5.** fall away **6.** end, *esp.* through disuse

lapwing ('læpwɪŋ) *n.* type of plover

larboard ('lɑːbəd) *n./a. obs.* port (side of ship)

larceny ('lɑːsɪnɪ) *n.* theft

larch (lɑːtʃ) *n.* deciduous coniferous tree

lard (lɑːd) *n.* **1.** prepared pig's fat —*vt.* **2.** insert strips of bacon in (meat) **3.** intersperse, decorate (speech) (with strange words *etc.*) —**'lardy** *a.* —**lardy cake** UK rich sweet cake made of bread dough, lard, sugar and dried fruit

larder ('lɑːdə) *n.* storeroom or cupboard for food

large (lɑːdʒ) *a.* **1.** broad in range or area **2.** great in size, number *etc.* **3.** liberal **4.** generous —*adv.* **5.** in a big way —**'largely** *adv.* —**lar'gess** or **lar'gesse** *n.* **1.** bounty **2.** gift **3.** donation —**'largish** *a.* fairly large —**large-scale** *a.* **1.** wide-ranging, extensive **2.** (of maps and models) constructed or drawn to big scale —**at large 1.** free, not confined **2.** in general **3.** fully

largo ('lɑːgəʊ) *a./adv. Mus.* to be performed moderately slowly

lariat ('lærɪət) *n.* lasso

lark¹ (lɑːk) *n.* small, brown singing bird, skylark —**'larkspur** *n.* plant with spikes of blue, pink or white flowers

lark² (lɑːk) *n.* **1.** frolic, spree —*vi.* **2.** indulge in lark —**'larky** *a.*

larrigan ('lærɪgən) n. knee-high moccasin boot worn by trappers etc.

larva ('lɑːvə) n. insect in immature but active stage (pl. **-ae** (-iː)) —**'larval** a. —**'larviform** a.

larynx ('lærɪŋks) n. part of throat containing vocal cords (pl. **larynges** (ləˈrɪndʒiːz), **-es**) —**laryn'geal** or **la'ryngal** a. 1. of larynx 2. Phonet. articulated at larynx; glottal —**laryn'gitis** n. inflammation of larynx

lasagne or **lasagna** (ləˈzænjə, -ˈsæn-) n. pasta formed in wide, flat sheets

lascar ('læskə) n. E Indian seaman

lascivious (ləˈsɪvɪəs) a. lustful

laser ('leɪzə) n. device for concentrating electromagnetic radiation or light of mixed frequencies into an intense, narrow, concentrated beam

lash[1] (læʃ) n. 1. stroke with whip 2. flexible part of whip 3. eyelash —vt. 4. strike with whip, thong etc. 5. dash against (as waves) 6. attack verbally, ridicule 7. flick, wave sharply to and fro —**'lashing** n. 1. whipping, flogging 2. scolding —pl. 3. (usu. with of) UK inf. large amounts; lots —**lash out** 1. burst into or resort to verbal or physical attack 2. inf. be extravagant, as in spending

lash[2] (læʃ) vt. fasten or bind tightly with cord etc. —**'lashing** n. rope etc. used for binding or securing —**lash-up** n. temporary connection of equipment for experimental or emergency use

lass (læs) n. girl —**'lassie** n. inf. little lass; girl

Lassa fever ('læsə) serious viral disease of Central W Afr., characterized by high fever etc.

lassitude ('læsɪtjuːd) n. weariness

lasso (læˈsuː, 'læsəʊ) n. 1. rope with noose for catching cattle etc. (pl. **-s**, **-es**) —vt. 2. catch (as) with lasso (**las'soed, las'soing**)

last[1] (lɑːst) a./adv. 1. after all others, coming at the end 2. most recent(ly) —a. 3. sup. of LATE 4. only remaining —n. 5. last person or thing —**'lastly** adv. finally —**last-ditch** a. made or done as last desperate effort in face of opposition —**last name** see SURNAME —**last rites** Christianity religious rites prescribed for those close to death —**the Last Judgment** religious occasion, after resurrection of dead at end of world, when, according to Bible, God will decree final destinies of all men according to good and evil in earthly lives (also **the Last Day**, **'Doomsday, Judgment Day**) —**the last straw** final irritation or problem that stretches one's endurance or patience beyond limit

last[2] (lɑːst) vi. continue, hold out, remain alive or unexhausted, endure —**'lasting** a. permanent; enduring —**'lastingly** adv.

last[3] (lɑːst) n. model of foot on which shoes are made, repaired

lat. latitude

latch (lætʃ) n. 1. fastening for door, consisting of bar, catch for it, and lever to lift it 2. small lock with spring action —vt. 3. fasten with latch —**latchkey child** child who has to let himself in at home after school as his parents are out at work

late (leɪt) a. 1. coming after the appointed time 2. delayed 3. that was recently but now is not 4. recently dead 5. recent in date 6. of late stage of development ('**later** comp., '**latest, last** sup.) —adv. 7. after proper time 8. recently 9. at, till late hour —**'lately** adv. not long since —**'latish** a. rather late —**Late Greek** Greek language from about 3rd to 8th century A.D. —**Late Latin** form of written Latin used from 3rd to 7th century A.D.

lateen sail (ləˈtiːn) triangular sail on long yard hoisted to head of mast

latent ('leɪtᵊnt) a. 1. existing but not developed 2. hidden

lateral ('lætərəl) a. of, at, from the side —**'laterally** adv. —**lateral thinking** way of solving problems by employing unorthodox means

laterite ('lætəraɪt) n. brick-coloured rock or clay formed by weathering of rock in tropical regions

latex ('leɪtɛks) n. sap or fluid of plants, esp. of rubber tree (pl. **-es, latices** ('lætɪsiːz)) —**laticiferous** (lætɪˈsɪfərəs) a. bearing or containing latex or sap

lath (lɑːθ) n. thin strip of wood (pl. **laths** (lɑːðz, lɑːθs)) —**'lathing** n. —**'lathy** a. 1. like a lath 2. tall and thin

lathe (leɪð) n. machine for turning object while it is being shaped

lather ('lɑːðə) n. 1. froth of soap and water 2. frothy sweat —vi. 3. form lather —vt. 4. inf. beat

Latin ('lætɪn) n. 1. language of ancient Romans —a. 2. of ancient Romans 3. of, in their language 4. speaking a language descended from Latin —**'Latinism** n. word, idiom imitating Latin —**La'tinity** n. 1. manner of writing Latin 2. Latin style —**Latin America** those areas of Amer. whose official languages are Spanish and Portuguese, derived from Latin: S Amer., Central Amer., Mexico and certain islands in the Caribbean —**Latin American** n./a.

latitude ('lætɪtjuːd) n. 1. angular distance on meridian reckoned N or S from equator 2. deviation from a standard 3. freedom from restriction 4. scope —pl. 5. regions —**lati'tudinal** a. —**latitudi'narian** a. claiming, showing latitude of thought, esp. in religion —**latitudi'narianism** n.

latrine (ləˈtriːn) n. in army etc., lavatory

latter ('lætə) a. 1. second of two 2. later 3. more recent —n. 4. second or last-mentioned person or thing —**'latterly** adv.

lattice ('lætɪs) n. 1. structure of strips of wood, metal etc. crossing with spaces between 2. window so made —**'latticed** a.

laud (lɔːd) Lit. n. 1. praise, song of praise —vt. 2. praise, glorify —**lauda'bility** n. —**'laudable** a. praiseworthy —**'laudably** adv. —**lau'dation** n. 1. praise 2. honour paid —**'laudatory** a. expressing, containing praise

laudanum ('lɔːdʰnəm) n. tincture of opium

laugh (lɑːf) vi. 1. make sounds instinctively expressing amusement, merriment or scorn —n. 2. such sound —**'laughable** a. ludicrous —**'laughably** adv. —**'laughter** n. —**laughing gas** nitrous oxide as anaesthetic —**laughing hyena** spotted hyena, so called from its cry —**laughing jackass** see KOOKABURRA —**laughing stock** object of general derision

launch[1] (lɔːntʃ) vt. 1. set afloat 2. set in motion 3. begin 4. propel (missile, spacecraft) into space 5. hurl, send —vi. 6. enter on course —**'launcher** n. installation, vehicle, device for launching rockets, missiles etc. —**launching pad** or **launch pad** platform from which spacecraft etc. is launched

launch[2] (lɔːntʃ) n. large power-driven boat

laundry ('lɔːndrɪ) n. 1. place for washing clothes, esp. as a business 2. clothes etc. for washing —**'launder** vt. wash and iron —**Launder'ette** n. R shop with coin-operated washing, drying machines

laureate ('lɔːrɪət) a. crowned with laurels —**'laureateship** n. post of poet laureate —**poet laureate** poet with appointment to Royal Household, nominally to compose verses on occasions of national importance

laurel ('lɒrəl) n. 1. glossy-leaved shrub, bay tree —pl. 2. its leaves, emblem of victory or merit

lava ('lɑːvə) n. molten matter thrown out by volcanoes, solidifying as it cools

lavatory ('lævətərɪ, -trɪ) n. toilet, water closet

lave (leɪv) vt. obs. wash, bathe

lavender ('lævəndə) n. 1. shrub with fragrant flowers 2. colour of the flowers, pale lilac —**lavender water** perfume or toilet water made from flowers of lavender plant

lavish ('lævɪʃ) a. 1. giving or spending profusely 2. very, too abundant —vt. 3. spend, bestow profusely

law (lɔː) n. 1. rule binding on community 2. system of such rules 3. legal science 4. knowledge, administration of it 5. inf. (member of) police force 6. general principle deduced from facts 7. invariable sequence of events in nature —**'lawful** a. allowed by law —**'lawfully** adv. —**'lawless** a. 1. ignoring laws 2. violent —**'lawlessly** adv. —**'lawyer** n. professional expert in law —**law-abiding** a. 1. obedient to laws 2. well-behaved —**law agent** in Scotland, solicitor entitled to appear for client in any Sheriff Court —**'lawgiver** n. one who makes laws —**Law Lord** member of House of Lords who sits as highest court of appeal —**'lawsuit** n. prosecution of claim in court

lawn[1] (lɔːn) n. stretch of carefully tended turf in garden etc. —**lawn mower** hand- or power-operated machine for cutting grass —**lawn tennis** tennis played on grass court

lawn[2] (lɔːn) n. fine linen

lawrencium (lɒ'rɛnsɪəm) n. element artificially produced from californium

lawyer ('lɔːjə, 'lɔɪə) n. see LAW

lax (læks) a. 1. not strict 2. lacking precision 3. loose, slack —**'laxative** a. 1. having loosening effect on bowels —n. 2. agent stimulating evacuation of faeces —**'laxity** or **'laxness** n. 1. slackness 2. looseness of (moral) standards —**'laxly** adv.

lay[1] (leɪ) pt. of LIE[1] —**'layabout** n. lazy person

lay[2] (leɪ) vt. 1. deposit, set, cause to lie 2. taboo sl. have sexual intercourse with (laid, 'laying) —n. taboo sl. 3. act of sexual intercourse 4. sexual partner —**'layer** n. 1. single thickness of some substance, as stratum or coating on surface 2. laying hen 3. shoot of plant pegged down or partly covered with earth to encourage root growth —vt. 4. propagate (plants) by making layers —**lay-by** n. stopping place for traffic beside road —**lay-off** n. —**'layout** n. arrangement, esp. of matter for printing —**lay off** dismiss (staff) during slack period —**lay on** 1. provide, supply 2. apply 3. strike —**lay out** 1. display 2. expend 3. prepare for burial 4. sl. knock out —**lay waste** devastate

lay[3] (leɪ) n. minstrel's song

lay[4] (leɪ) a. 1. not clerical or professional 2. of or done by persons not clergymen —**Lay Lord** peer in House of Lords other than a Law Lord —**'layman** n. ordinary person —**lay reader** 1. Ch. of England person licensed by bishop to conduct religious services other than Eucharist 2. R.C.Ch. layman chosen to read epistle at Mass

layette (leɪ'ɛt) n. clothes, accessories etc. for newborn child

lay figure 1. jointed figure of the body used by artists 2. nonentity

lazy ('leɪzɪ) a. averse to work, indolent —**laze** vi. indulge in laziness —**'lazily** adv. —**'laziness** n.

lb or **lb.** pound

l.b.w. leg before wicket

l.c. 1. left centre (of stage etc.) 2. loco citato 3. Print. lower case

l.c.d., lcd, L.C.D., or **LCD** lowest common denominator

LCD liquid crystal display

L.C.J. UK Lord Chief Justice

l.c.m. or **L.C.M.** lowest common multiple

L/Cpl. lance corporal

L.D.S. 1. Latter-day Saints 2. laus Deo semper (Lat., praise be to God for ever) 3. UK Licentiate in Dental Surgery (also LDS)

lea (liː) n. Poet. piece of meadow or open ground

leach (liːtʃ) v. 1. remove or be removed from substance by percolating liquid 2. (cause to) lose soluble substances by action of percolating liquid —*n.* **3.** act or process of leaching **4.** substance that is leached or constituents removed by leaching **5.** porous vessel for leaching

lead' (liːd) *vt.* **1.** guide, conduct **2.** persuade **3.** direct —*vi.* **5.** be, go, play first **6.** (*with* to) result (in) **7.** give access (**led** (lɛd), **'leading**) —*n.* **8.** leading **9.** that which leads or is used to lead **10.** example **11.** front or principal place, role *etc.* **12.** cable bringing current to electric instrument —**'leader** *n.* **1.** one who leads **2.** article in newspaper expressing editorial views (*also* **leading article**) —**'leadership** *n.* —**leading aircraftman** *Brit.* Air Force rank above aircraftman (**leading aircraftwoman** *fem.*) —**leading case** legal decision used as precedent —**leading light** *inf.* important or outstanding person, *esp.* in organization —**leading note** *Mus.* **1.** seventh degree of major or minor scale (*also* **sub'tonic**) **2.** *esp.* in cadences, note that tends most naturally to resolve to note lying one semitone above —**leading question** question worded to prompt answer desired —**leading rating** rank in Royal Navy comparable but junior to that of corporal in army —**lead time** time between design of product and its production

lead² (lɛd) *n.* **1.** soft heavy grey metal **2.** plummet, used for sounding depths of water **3.** graphite —*pl.* **4.** lead-covered piece of roof **5.** strips of lead used to widen spaces in printing *etc.* —*vt.* **6.** cover, weight or space with lead (**'leaded**, **'leading**) —**'leaden** *a.* **1.** of, like lead **2.** heavy **3.** dull —**leaded windows** windows made of small panes framed in lead —**lead poisoning** **1.** acute or chronic poisoning by lead, characterized by abdominal pain *etc.* **2.** *US sl.* death or injury resulting from being shot with bullets —**'leadsman** *n.* sailor who heaves the lead

leaf (liːf) *n.* **1.** organ of photosynthesis in plants, consisting of a flat, usu. green blade on stem **2.** two pages of book *etc.* **3.** thin sheet **4.** flap, movable part of table *etc.* (*pl.* **leaves** (liːvz)) —*v.* **5.** (*oft. with* through) turn through (pages *etc.*) cursorily —**'leafless** *a.* —**'leaflet** *n.* **1.** small leaf **2.** single sheet, often folded, of printed matter for distribution, handbill —**'leafy** *a.*

league' (liːg) *n.* **1.** agreement for mutual help **2.** parties to it **3.** federation of clubs *etc.* **4.** *inf.* class, level —*vi.* **5.** form an alliance; combine in an association —**'leaguer** *n.* member of league —**league football** **1.** *chiefly A* rugby league football (*also* **league**) **2.** A Australian Rules competition conducted within league

league² (liːg) *n. obs.* measure of distance, about three miles

leak (liːk) *n.* **1.** hole, defect, that allows escape or entrance of liquid, gas, radiation *etc.* **2.** disclosure **3.** *sl.* act of urinating —*vi.* **4.** let fluid *etc.* in or out **5.** (of fluid *etc.*) find its way through leak —*vt.* **6.** let

escape —*v.* **7.** (*oft. with* out) (allow to) become known little by little —**'leakage** *n.* **1.** leaking **2.** gradual escape or loss —**'leaky** *a.*

lean' (liːn) *a.* **1.** lacking fat **2.** thin **3.** meagre **4.** (of mixture of fuel and air) with too little fuel —*n.* **5.** lean part of meat, mainly muscular tissue

lean² (liːn) *v.* **1.** rest (against) **2.** bend, incline —*vi.* **3.** (*with* to *or* towards) tend (towards) **4.** (*with* on *or* upon) depend, rely (on) (**leaned** *or* **leant** (lɛnt) *pt./pp.*) —**'leaning** *n.* tendency —**lean-to** *n.* room, shed built against existing wall

leap (liːp) *vi.* **1.** spring, jump —*vt.* **2.** spring over (**leaped** *or* **leapt** (lɛpt) *pt./pp.*) —*n.* **3.** jump —**'leapfrog** *n.* **1.** game in which player vaults over another bending down —*v.* **2.** (cause to) advance by jumps or stages (**-gg-**) —**leap year** year with Feb. 29th as extra day, occurring every fourth year

learn (lɜːn) *vt.* **1.** gain knowledge of or acquire skill in (something) by study, practice or teaching —*vi.* **2.** gain knowledge **3.** be taught **4.** (*oft. with* of *or* about) find out (**learnt** *or* **learned** *pt./pp.*) —**learned** ('lɜːnɪd) *a.* **1.** erudite, deeply read **2.** showing much learning —**learnedly** ('lɜːnɪdlɪ) *adv.* —**'learner** *n.* —**'learning** *n.* knowledge got by study

lease (liːs) *n.* **1.** contract by which land or property is rented for stated time by owner to tenant —*vt.* **2.** let, rent by, take on lease —**'leasehold** *a.* held on lease

leash (liːʃ) *n.* **1.** thong for holding a dog **2.** set of three animals held in leash —*vt.* **3.** hold in, secure by leash

least (liːst) *sup. of* LITTLE *a.* **1.** smallest —*n.* **2.** smallest one —*adv.* **3.** in smallest degree

leather ('lɛðə) *n.* prepared skin of animal —**'leathery** *a.* like leather, tough —**'leatherjacket** *n.* crane fly grub —**'leatherwood** *n.* N Amer. tree with tough, leathery bark

leave' (liːv) *vt.* **1.** go away from **2.** deposit **3.** allow to remain **4.** entrust **5.** bequeath —*vi.* **6.** go away, set out (**left**, **'leaving**)

leave² (liːv) *n.* **1.** permission **2.** permission to be absent from work, duty **3.** period of such absence **4.** formal parting —**leave of absence** **1.** leave from work or duty, *esp.* for a long time **2.** this period of time —**leave-taking** *n.* act of departing; farewell —**by** *or* **with your leave** with your permission

leave³ (liːv) *vi.* produce or grow leaves (**leaved**, **'leaving**)

leaven ('lɛv²n) *n.* **1.** yeast **2.** *fig.* transforming influence —*vt.* **3.** raise with leaven **4.** taint; modify

lecher ('lɛtʃə) *n.* man given to lewdness —**lech** *vi. inf.* (*usu. with* after) behave lecherously (towards) —**'lecherous** *a.* **1.** lewd **2.** provoking lust **3.** lascivious —**'lecherously** *adv.* —**'lecherousness** *n.* —**'lechery** *n.*

lectern ('lɛktən) *n.* reading desk, *esp.* in church

lection ('lɛkʃən) *n.* 1. difference in copies of manuscript or book 2. reading —'**lectionary** *n.* book, list of scripture lessons for particular days —'**lector** *n.* reader

lecture ('lɛktʃə) *n.* 1. instructive discourse 2. speech of reproof —*vi.* 3. deliver discourse —*vt.* 4. reprove —'**lecturer** *n.* —'**lectureship** *n.* appointment as lecturer

LED light-emitting diode

ledge (lɛdʒ) *n.* 1. narrow shelf sticking out from wall, cliff *etc.* 2. ridge, rock below surface of sea

ledger ('lɛdʒə) *n.* 1. book of debit and credit accounts, chief account book of firm 2. flat stone —**ledger line** *Mus.* short line, above or below stave

lee (liː) *n.* 1. shelter 2. side of anything, *esp.* ship, away from wind —'**leeward** *a./n.* 1. (on) lee side —*adv.* 2. towards this side —**lee shore** shore towards which wind is blowing —'**leeway** *n.* 1. leeward drift of ship 2. room for free movement within limits 3. loss of progress

leech¹ (liːtʃ) *n.* 1. species of bloodsucking worm 2. *Hist.* physician —'**leechcraft** *n.*

leech² (liːtʃ) *n.* edge of a sail

leek (liːk) *n.* 1. plant like onion with long bulb and thick stem 2. this as Welsh emblem

leer (lɪə) *vi.* 1. glance with malign, sly or lascivious expression —*n.* 2. such glance —'**leery** *a.* 1. *chiefly dial.* knowing, sly 2. *sl.* (*with* of) suspicious, wary

lees (liːz) *pl.n.* 1. sediment of wine *etc.* 2. dregs of liquor

leet (liːt) *n.* in Scotland, selected list of candidates for office

left¹ (lɛft) *a.* 1. denotes the side that faces west when the front faces north 2. opposite to the right —*n.* 3. the left hand or part 4. *Pol.* reforming or radical party (*also* **left wing**) —*adv.* 5. on or towards the left —'**leftist** *n./a.* (person) of the political left —**left-handed** *a.* 1. using left hand with greater ease than right 2. performed with left hand 3. designed for use by left hand 4. awkward, clumsy 5. ironically ambiguous 6. turning from right to left; anticlockwise —*adv.* 7. with left hand —**left-hander** *n.*

left² (lɛft) *pt./pp. of* LEAVE¹

leg (lɛg) *n.* 1. one of limbs on which person or animal walks, runs, stands 2. part of garment covering leg 3. anything which supports, as leg of table 4. stage of journey 5. *Cricket* part of field away from the striker's bat —'**leggings** *pl.n.* covering of leather or other material for legs —'**leggy** *a.* 1. long-legged 2. (of plants) straggling —'**legless** *a.* 1. without legs 2. *inf.* very drunk —**leg-pull** *n.* UK *inf.* practical joke, mild deception —'**legroom** *n.* room to move legs comfortably, as in car —**leg before wicket** *Cricket* manner of dismissal on grounds that batsman has been struck on leg by bowled ball that otherwise would have hit wicket

legacy ('lɛgəsɪ) *n.* 1. anything left by will, bequest 2. thing handed down to successor —**lega'tee** *n.* recipient of legacy

legal ('liːg'l) *a.* of, appointed or permitted by, or based on, law —**legal'ese** *n.* conventional language in which legal documents are written —'**legalism** *n.* strict adherence to law, *esp.* letter of law rather than its spirit —**legal'istic** *a.* —**le'gality** *n.* —'**legalize** *or* **-ise** *vt.* make legal —'**legally** *adv.* —**legal aid** financial assistance available to persons unable to meet full cost of legal proceedings —**legal tender** currency that creditor must by law accept in redemption of debt

legate ('lɛgɪt) *n.* ambassador, *esp.* papal —'**legateship** *n.* —**le'gation** *n.* 1. diplomatic minister and his staff 2. his residence

legato (lɪ'gɑːtəʊ) *adv. Mus.* smoothly

legend ('lɛdʒənd) *n.* 1. traditional story or myth 2. traditional literature 3. famous, renowned, person or event 4. inscription —'**legendary** *a.*

legerdemain (lɛdʒədə'meɪn) *n.* 1. juggling, conjuring, sleight of hand 2. trickery

leger line ('lɛdʒə) *see* **ledger line** *at* LEDGER

leghorn ('lɛghɔːn) *n.* 1. kind of straw 2. hat made of it 3. (L-) (lɛ'gɔːn) breed of fowls

legible ('lɛdʒəb'l) *a.* easily read —**legi'bility** *n.* —'**legibly** *adv.*

legion ('liːdʒən) *n.* 1. body of infantry in Roman army 2. various modern military bodies 3. association of veterans 4. large number —*a.* 5. very numerous —'**legionary** *a./n.* —**legion'naire** *n.* (*oft.* L-) member of military force or association —**Legionnaire's disease** sometimes fatal bacterial infection which has symptoms similar to those of pneumonia

legislator ('lɛdʒɪsleɪtə) *n.* maker of laws —'**legislate** *vi.* make laws —**legis'lation** *n.* 1. act of legislating 2. laws which are made —'**legislative** *a.* —'**legislature** *n.* body that makes laws of a state —**legislative assembly** (*oft.* L- A-) single-chamber legislature in most Canad. provinces

legitimate (lɪ'dʒɪtɪmɪt) *a.* 1. born in wedlock 2. lawful, regular 3. fairly deduced —*vt.* (lɪ'dʒɪtɪmeɪt) 4. make legitimate —**le'gitimacy** *n.* —**le'gitimateness** *n.* —**legiti'mation** *n.* —**le'gitimism** *n.* —**le'gitimist** *n.* supporter of hereditary title to monarchy —**le'gitimize** *or* **-mise** *vt.* legitimate

leguan ('lɛgʊɑːn) *n.* large S Afr. lizard

legume ('lɛgjuːm, lɪ'gjuːm) *n.* 1. long dry fruit produced by leguminous plants; pod 2. any of various table vegetables, *esp.* beans or peas 3. any leguminous plant —**le'guminous** *a.* (of plants) pod-bearing

lei (leɪ) *n.* garland of flowers

Leics. ('lɛstəʃə) Leicestershire

leisure ('lɛʒə) *n.* 1. freedom from

occupation **2.** spare time —'**leisured** *a.* with plenty of spare time —'**leisurely** *a.* **1.** deliberate, unhurried —*adv.* **2.** slowly —**leisure centre** a building that provides facilities for a range of leisure pursuits, such as library, sports hall, café *etc.*

leitmotiv *or* **leitmotif** ('laɪtməʊtiːf) *n. Mus.* recurring theme associated with some person, situation, thought

L.E.M. (lɛm) lunar excursion module

lemming ('lɛmɪŋ) *n.* rodent of arctic regions

lemon ('lɛmən) *n.* **1.** pale yellow acid fruit **2.** tree bearing it **3.** its colour **4.** *sl.* useless or defective person or thing —**lemon'ade** *n.* drink made from lemon juice —**lemon curd** creamy spread made of lemons, butter *etc.* —**lemon sole** European flatfish highly valued as food

lemur ('liːmə) *n.* nocturnal animal like monkey

lend (lɛnd) *vt.* **1.** give temporary use of **2.** let out for hire or interest **3.** give, bestow (**lent**, '**lending**) —'**lender** *n.* —**lends itself to** is suitable for

length (lɛŋkθ, lɛŋθ) *n.* **1.** quality of being long **2.** measurement from end to end **3.** duration **4.** extent **5.** piece of a certain length —'**lengthen** *v.* **1.** make, become longer **2.** draw out —'**lengthily** *adv.* —'**lengthways** *or U.S.* '**lengthwise** *adv./a.* in direction of length —'**lengthy** *a.* (over)long —**at length 1.** in full detail **2.** at last

lenient ('liːnɪənt) *a.* mild, tolerant, not strict —'**lenience** *or* '**leniency** *n.* —'**leniently** *adv.*

lenity ('lɛnɪtɪ) *n.* **1.** mercy **2.** clemency

lens (lɛnz) *n.* piece of glass or similar material with one or both sides curved, used to converge or diverge light rays in cameras, spectacles, telescopes *etc.* (*pl.* **-es**)

lent (lɛnt) *pt./pp. of* LEND

Lent (lɛnt) *n.* period of fasting from Ash Wednesday to Easter Eve —'**Lenten** *a.* of, in or suitable to Lent

lentil ('lɛntɪl) *n.* edible seed of leguminous plant —**len'ticular** *a.* like lentil

lento ('lɛntəʊ) *adv. Mus.* slowly

Leo ('liːəʊ) *n.* (lion) 5th sign of zodiac, operative *c.* Jul. 22nd–Aug. 21st

leonine ('liːənaɪn) *a.* like a lion

leopard ('lɛpəd) *n.* large, spotted, carnivorous animal of cat family, like panther ('**leopardess** *fem.*)

leotard ('lɪətɑːd) *n.* tight-fitting garment covering most of body, worn by acrobats, dancers *etc.*

leper ('lɛpə) *n.* **1.** one suffering from leprosy **2.** person ignored or despised —'**leprosy** *n.* disease forming silvery scales on the skin and eating away the parts affected —'**leprous** *a.*

Lepidoptera (lɛpɪ'dɒptərə) *pl.n.* order of insects with four wings covered with fine gossamer scales, as moths, butterflies —**lepi'dopterist** *n.* person who studies or

collects moths and butterflies —**lepi'dopterous** *a.*

leprechaun ('lɛprəkɔːn) *n.* mischievous elf of Irish folklore

lepton ('lɛptɒn) *n. Phys.* any of group of elementary particles and their antiparticles, that participate in weak interactions

lesbian ('lɛzbɪən) *n.* homosexual woman —'**lesbianism** *n.*

lese-majesty ('liːz'mædʒɪstɪ) *n.* **1.** treason **2.** taking of liberties

lesion ('liːʒən) *n.* **1.** injury **2.** injurious change in texture or action of an organ of the body

less (lɛs) *comp. of* LITTLE *a.* **1.** not so much —*n.* **2.** smaller part, quantity **3.** a lesser amount —*adv.* **4.** to a smaller extent or degree —*prep.* **5.** after deducting, minus —'**lessen** *v.* diminish, reduce —'**lesser** *a.* **1.** less **2.** smaller **3.** minor

-less (*comb. form*) **1.** without; lacking, as in *speechless* **2.** not able to (do something) or not able to be (done, performed *etc.*), as in *countless*

lessee (lɛ'siː) *n.* one to whom lease is granted

lesson ('lɛsən) *n.* **1.** instalment of course of instruction **2.** content of this **3.** experience that teaches **4.** portion of Scripture read in church

lessor ('lɛsɔː, lɛ'sɔː) *n.* grantor of a lease

lest (lɛst) *conj.* **1.** in order that not **2.** for fear that

let¹ (lɛt) *vt.* **1.** allow, enable, cause to **2.** allow to escape **3.** grant use of for rent, lease —*vi.* **4.** be leased —*v. aux.* **5.** used to express a proposal, command, threat, assumption (**let**, '**letting**) —'**letdown** *n.* disappointment —**let-up** *n. inf.* lessening, abatement —**let down 1.** lower **2.** disappoint **3.** undo, shorten and resew (hem) **4.** untie (long hair that is bound up) and allow to fall loose **5.** deflate —**let off 1.** allow to disembark or leave **2.** explode or fire (bomb *etc.*) **3.** excuse from (work *etc*) **4.** *inf.* allow to get away without expected punishment *etc.* —**let's** let us: used to express suggestion *etc.* by speaker to himself and hearers

let² (lɛt) *n.* **1.** hindrance **2.** in some games, minor infringement or obstruction of ball requiring replaying of point

lethal ('liːθəl) *a.* deadly

lethargy ('lɛθədʒɪ) *n.* **1.** apathy, want of energy or interest **2.** unnatural drowsiness —le'**thargic** *a.* —le'**thargically** *adv.*

letter ('lɛtə) *n.* **1.** alphabetical symbol **2.** written message **3.** strict meaning, interpretation —*pl.* **4.** literature **5.** knowledge of books —*vt.* **6.** mark with, in, letters —'**lettered** *a.* learned —**letter bomb** explosive device in envelope, detonated when envelope is opened —'**letterhead** *n.* sheet of writing paper printed with one's address, name *etc.* —'**letterpress** *n.* printed matter as distinct from illustrations *etc.* —**letter of credit** letter issued by bank entitling bearer to draw funds from that bank or its agencies —**letters patent** document under seal of state, granting exclusive right, privilege

lettuce ('lɛtɪs) n. plant grown for use in salad

leucocyte or esp. U.S. **leukocyte** ('luːkəsaɪt) n. one of white blood corpuscles

leucoma (luːˈkəʊmə) n. disorder of the eye, characterized by opacity of the cornea

leukaemia or esp. U.S. **leukemia** (luːˈkiːmɪə) n. a progressive blood disease

Lev. Bible Leviticus

Levant (lɪˈvænt) n. old name for area of E. Mediterranean now occupied by Lebanon, Syria and Israel —**le'vanter** n. (sometimes L-) 1. easterly wind in W Mediterranean area 2. inhabitant of the Levant —**Levantine** ('lɛvəntaɪn) a./n.

levee[1] ('lɛvɪ, 'lɛveɪ) n. 1. Brit. sovereign's reception for men only 2. Hist. reception held by sovereign on rising

levee[2] ('lɛvɪ) n. 1. natural or artificial river embankment 2. landing place

level ('lɛvˀl) a. 1. horizontal 2. even in surface 3. consistent in style, quality etc. —n. 4. horizontal line or surface 5. instrument for showing, testing horizontal plane 6. position on scale 7. standard, grade 8. horizontal passage in mine —vt. 9. make level 10. bring to same level 11. knock down 12. aim (gun or accusation etc.) —vi. 13. inf. (esp. with with) be honest, frank (-**ll**-) —**'leveller** or U.S. **'leveler** n. advocate of social equality —**level crossing** point where railway line and road intersect —**level-headed** a. not apt to be carried away by emotion

lever ('liːvə) n. 1. rigid bar pivoted about a fulcrum to transfer a force with mechanical advantage 2. handle pressed, pulled etc. to operate something —vt. 3. prise, move with lever —**'leverage** n. 1. action, power of lever 2. influence 3. power to accomplish something 4. advantage

leveret ('lɛvərɪt, -vrɪt) n. young hare

leviathan (lɪˈvaɪəθən) n. 1. sea monster 2. anything huge or formidable

levitation (lɛvɪˈteɪʃən) n. the power of raising a solid body into the air supernaturally —**'levitate** v. (cause to) do this

levity ('lɛvɪtɪ) n. 1. inclination to make a joke of serious matters, frivolity 2. facetiousness

levy ('lɛvɪ) vt. 1. impose (tax) 2. raise (troops) (**'levied**, **'levying**) —n. 3. imposition or collection of taxes 4. enrolling of troops 5. amount, number levied

lewd (luːd) a. 1. lustful 2. indecent —**'lewdly** adv. —**'lewdness** n.

lexicon ('lɛksɪkən) n. dictionary —**'lexical** a. —**lexi'cographer** n. writer of dictionaries —**lexi'cography** n.

ley (leɪ, liː) n. 1. arable land temporarily under grass 2. line joining two prominent points in landscape, thought to be line of prehistoric track (also **ley line**)

Leyden jar ('laɪdˀn) Phys. early type of capacitor consisting of glass jar with lower part of inside and outside coated with tinfoil

L.F. Rad. low frequency

LG or **L.G.** Low German

Li Chem. lithium

liable ('laɪəbˀl) a. 1. answerable 2. exposed 3. subject 4. likely —**lia'bility** n. 1. state of being liable, obligation 2. hindrance, disadvantage —pl. 3. debts

liaison (lɪˈeɪzɒn) n. 1. union 2. connection 3. intimacy, esp. secret —**li'aise** vi. communicate and maintain contact —**liaison officer** officer who keeps units of troops in touch

liana (lɪˈɑːnə) or **liane** (lɪˈɑːn) n. climbing plant of tropical forests

liar ('laɪə) n. one who tells lies

lib (lɪb) inf. liberation

lib. 1. liber (Lat., book) 2. librarian 3. library

Lib. Liberal

libation (laɪˈbeɪʃən) n. drink poured as offering to the gods

libel ('laɪbˀl) n. 1. published statement falsely damaging person's reputation —vt. 2. defame falsely (-**ll**-) —**'libellous** or **'libelous** a. defamatory

liberal ('lɪbərəl, 'lɪbrəl) a. 1. (also L-) of political party favouring democratic reforms or favouring individual freedom 2. generous 3. tolerant 4. abundant 5. (of education) designed to develop general cultural interests —n. 6. one who has liberal ideas or opinions —**'liberalism** n. principles of Liberal Party —**libe'rality** n. munificence —**'liberalize** or **-ise** v. —**'liberally** adv.

liberate ('lɪbəreɪt) vt. set free —**libe'ration** n. —**'liberator** n.

libertarian (lɪbəˈtɛərɪən) n. 1. believer in freedom of thought etc., or in free will —a. 2. of, like a libertarian —**liber'tarianism** n.

libertine ('lɪbətiːn, -taɪn) n. 1. morally dissolute person —a. 2. dissolute —**'libertinism** n.

liberty ('lɪbətɪ) n. 1. freedom —pl. 2. rights, privileges —**at liberty** 1. free 2. having the right —**take liberties** be presumptuous

libido (lɪˈbiːdəʊ) n. 1. life force 2. emotional craving, esp. of sexual origin (pl. -**s**) —**libidinous** (lɪˈbɪdɪnəs) a. lustful

Libra ('liːbrə) n. 1. (balance) 7th sign of zodiac, operative c. Sept. 22nd–Oct. 22nd 2. ('laɪbrə) (L-) Hist. a pound weight (pl. -**brae** (-briː))

library ('laɪbrərɪ) n. 1. room, building where books are kept 2. collection of books, gramophone records etc. 3. reading, writing room in house —**li'brarian** n. keeper of library —**li'brarianship** n.

libretto (lɪˈbretəʊ) n. words of an opera (pl. -**s**, -**ti** (-tiː)) —**li'brettist** n.

lice (laɪs) n., pl. of LOUSE

licence or U.S. **license** ('laɪsəns) n. 1. (document, certificate giving) leave, permission 2. excessive liberty 3. dissoluteness 4. writer's, artist's transgression of rules of his art (oft. **poetic licence**) —'**license** vt. grant licence to —licen'see n. holder of licence —li'centiate n. one licensed to practise art, profession

licentious (laɪ'sɛnʃəs) a. 1. dissolute 2. sexually immoral —li'centiously adv.

lichee (laɪ'tʃiː) n. see LITCHI

lichen ('laɪkən, 'lɪtʃən) n. small flowerless plants forming crust on rocks, trees etc. —'lichened a. —liche'nology n.

lich gate or **lych gate** (lɪtʃ) roofed gate of churchyard

licit ('lɪsɪt) a. rare lawful

lick (lɪk) vt. 1. pass the tongue over 2. touch lightly 3. sl. defeat 4. sl. flog, beat —n. 5. act of licking 6. small amount (esp. of paint etc.) 7. block or natural deposit of salt or other chemical licked by cattle etc. 8. inf. speed —'licking n. sl. beating

licorice ('lɪkərɪs) n. see LIQUORICE

lid (lɪd) n. 1. movable cover 2. cover of the eye 3. sl. hat

lido ('liːdəʊ) n. pleasure centre with swimming and boating (pl. -s)

lie[1] (laɪ) vi. 1. be horizontal, at rest 2. be situated 3. remain, be in certain state or position 4. exist, be found 5. recline (**lay, lain, 'lying**) —n. 6. state (of affairs etc.) 7. direction

lie[2] (laɪ) vi. 1. make false statement (**lied, 'lying**) —n. 2. deliberate falsehood —'liar n. person who tells lies —**white lie** untruth said without evil intent —**give the lie to** disprove

lief (liːf) adv. 1. rare gladly, willingly —a. obs. 2. ready; glad 3. dear, beloved

liege (liːdʒ) a. 1. bound to render or receive feudal service 2. faithful —n. 3. lord 4. vassal, subject

lien (lɪən, 'liːən) n. right to hold another's property until claim is met

lieu (ljuː, luː) n. place —**in lieu (of)** instead (of)

lieutenant (lɛf'tɛnənt; in Navy, lə'tɛnənt; U.S. luː'tɛnənt) n. 1. deputy 2. Army rank below captain 3. Navy rank below commander 4. US police officer —**lieutenant colonel** officer holding commissioned rank immediately junior to colonel in certain armies, air forces and marine corps —**lieutenant commander** officer holding commissioned rank immediately junior to commander in certain navies —**lieutenant general** officer holding commissioned rank immediately junior to general in certain armies, air forces and marine corps —**lieutenant governor** 1. deputy governor 2. US elected official who acts as deputy to state governor 3. C representative of Crown in province: appointed by federal government

life (laɪf) n. 1. active principle of existence of animals and plants, animate existence 2. time of its lasting 3. history of such

existence 4. way of living 5. vigour, vivacity (pl. **lives**) —'**lifeless** a. 1. dead 2. inert 3. dull —**life assurance** insurance providing for payment of specified sum to named beneficiary on death of policyholder (also **life insurance**) —**life belt** buoyant device to keep afloat person in danger of drowning —'**lifeblood** n. 1. blood, considered as vital to life 2. essential or animating force —**life buoy** buoyant device for keeping people afloat in emergency —'**lifeguard** n. person at beach or pool to guard people against risk of drowning —**life jacket** inflatable sleeveless jacket worn to keep person afloat when in danger of drowning —'**lifelike** a. closely resembling life —'**lifeline** n. 1. line thrown or fired aboard vessel for hauling in hawser for breeches buoy 2. line by which deep-sea diver is raised or lowered 3. vital line of access or communication —'**lifelong** a. lasting a lifetime —**life preserver** 1. UK club kept for self-defence 2. US life belt; life jacket —**life-size** or **life-sized** a. representing actual size —**life style** particular attitudes, habits etc. of person or group —'**lifetime** n. length of time person, animal or object lives or functions

lift (lɪft) vt. 1. raise in position, status, mood, volume etc. 2. take up and remove 3. exalt spiritually 4. inf. steal —vi. 5. rise —n. 6. raising apparatus 7. cage raised and lowered in vertical shaft to transport people or goods 8. act of lifting 9. ride in car etc. as passenger 10. air force acting at right angles on aircraft wing, so lifting it 11. inf. feeling of cheerfulness, uplift —'**liftoff** n. 1. initial movement of rocket from launching pad 2. instant at which this occurs —**lift off** (of rocket) leave launching pad

ligament ('lɪgəmənt) n. band of tissue joining bones —'**ligature** n. 1. anything which binds 2. thread for tying up artery 3. Print. character of two or more joined letters

light[1] (laɪt) a. 1. of, or bearing little weight 2. not severe 3. gentle 4. easy, requiring little effort 5. trivial 6. (of industry) producing small, usu. consumer goods, using light machinery —adv. 7. in light manner —vi. 8. alight (from vehicle etc.) 9. (with on or upon) come by chance (upon) ('**lighted, lit** pt./pp.) —'**lighten** vt. reduce, remove (load etc.) —'**lightly** adv. —'**lightness** n. —**lights** pl.n. lungs of animals —**light-fingered** a. having nimble fingers, esp. for thieving or picking pockets —**light flyweight** amateur boxer weighing not more than 48 kg (106 lbs) —**light-headed** a. 1. dizzy, inclined to faint 2. delirious —**light-hearted** a. carefree —**light heavyweight** 1. professional boxer weighing 72.5–79.5 kg (160–175 lbs) 2. amateur boxer weighing 75–81 kg (165–179 lbs) (also (UK) '**cruiserweight**) 3. wrestler weighing usu. 87–97 kg (192–214 lbs) —**light middleweight** amateur boxer weighing 67–71 kg (148–157 lbs) —**light-minded** a. frivolous —**'lightweight** n./a. (person) of little weight or importance —**light welterweight** amateur boxer weighing 60–63.5 kg (132–140 lbs)

light² (laɪt) n. 1. electromagnetic radiation by which things are visible 2. source of this, lamp 3. window 4. mental vision 5. light part of anything 6. means or act of setting fire to something 7. understanding —pl. 8. traffic lights —a. 9. bright 10. pale, not dark —vt. 11. set burning 12. give light to —vi. 13. take fire 14. brighten (**'lighted, lit** pt./pp.) —**'lighten** vt. give light to —**'lighting** n. apparatus for supplying artificial light —**'lightning** n. visible discharge of electricity in atmosphere —**'lighthouse** n. tower with a light to guide ships —**light year** Astron. distance light travels in one year, about six million million miles

lighter (**'laɪtə**) n. 1. device for lighting cigarettes etc. 2. flat-bottomed boat for unloading ships

ligneous (**'lɪgnɪəs**) a. of, or of the nature of, wood —**'lignite** n. woody or brown coal

lignin (**'lɪgnɪn**) n. organic substance which forms characteristic part of all woody fibres

lignum vitae (**'lɪgnəm 'vaɪtɪ**) Lat. 1. tropical tree 2. its extremely hard wood

like¹ (laɪk) a. 1. resembling 2. similar to 3. characteristic of —adv. 4. in the manner of —pron. 5. similar thing —**'likelihood** n. probability —**'likely** a. 1. probable 2. hopeful, promising —adv. 3. probably —**'liken** vt. compare —**'likeness** n. 1. resemblance 2. portrait —**'likewise** adv. 1. in addition; moreover; also 2. in like manner

like² (laɪk) vt. find agreeable, enjoy, love —**'likable** or **'likeable** a. —**'liking** n. 1. fondness 2. inclination, taste

-like (comb. form) 1. resembling, similar to, as in lifelike 2. having characteristics of, as in childlike

lilac (**'laɪlək**) n. 1. shrub bearing pale mauve or white flowers 2. pale mauve colour —a. 3. of lilac colour

Lilliputian (lɪlɪ'pjuːʃɪən) a. 1. diminutive —n. 2. midget, pygmy

Lilo (**'laɪləʊ**) n. R inflatable rubber mattress (pl. -s)

lilt (lɪlt) vi. 1. (of melody) have a lilt 2. move lightly —n. 3. rhythmical effect in music, swing —**'lilting** a.

lily (**'lɪlɪ**) n. bulbous flowering plant —**lily-livered** a. cowardly; timid —**lily-white** a. 1. of a pure white 2. inf. pure; irreproachable —**lily of the valley** small garden plant with fragrant, white bell-like flowers

limb¹ (lɪm) n. 1. arm or leg 2. wing 3. branch of tree —**limbed** a. 1. having limbs 2. having specified number or kind of limbs

limb² (lɪm) n. 1. edge of sun or moon 2. edge of sextant

limber¹ (**'lɪmbə**) n. detachable front of gun carriage

limber² (**'lɪmbə**) a. pliant, lithe —**limber up** loosen stiff muscles by exercises

limbo¹ (**'lɪmbəʊ**) n. 1. (oft. L-) supposed region intermediate between Heaven and Hell for the unbaptised 2. intermediate, indeterminate place or state (pl. -s)

limbo² (**'lɪmbəʊ**) n. W Indian dance in which dancers pass under a bar (pl. -s)

lime¹ (laɪm) n. 1. any of certain calcium compounds used in making fertilizer, cement —vt. 2. treat (land) with lime —**'limy** a. of, like or smeared with birdlime —**'limekiln** n. kiln in which calcium carbonate is calcined to produce quicklime —**'limelight** n. 1. formerly, intense white light obtained by heating lime 2. glare of publicity —**'limestone** n. sedimentary rock used in building

lime² (laɪm) n. small acid fruit like lemon —**'limy** a. —**lime juice** juice of lime prepared as drink

lime³ (laɪm) n. tree, the linden

limerick (**'lɪmərɪk**) n. self-contained, non-sensical, humorous verse of five lines

limey (**'laɪmɪ**) n. US sl. British person

limit (**'lɪmɪt**) n. 1. utmost extent or duration 2. boundary —vt. 3. restrict, restrain, bound —**'limitable** a. —**limi'tation** n. —**'limited** a. 1. restricted; confined 2. without scope; narrow 3. (of governing powers etc.) restricted or checked, by or as if by constitution, laws or assembly 4. chiefly UK (of business enterprise) owned by shareholders whose liability for enterprise's debts is restricted —**'limitless** a. —**limited company** —**limited liability** principle whereby liability of shareholder is in proportion to amount of his stock

limn (lɪm) vt. paint; depict; draw —**limner** (**'lɪmnə**) n.

limousine (**'lɪməziːn, lɪmə'ziːn**) n. large, luxurious car

limp¹ (lɪmp) a. without firmness or stiffness —**'limply** adv.

limp² (lɪmp) vi. 1. walk lamely —n. 2. limping gait

limpet (**'lɪmpɪt**) n. shellfish which sticks tightly to rocks

limpid (**'lɪmpɪd**) a. 1. clear 2. translucent —**lim'pidity** n. —**'limpidly** adv.

linchpin (**'lɪntʃpɪn**) n. 1. pin to hold wheel on its axle 2. essential person or thing

Lincs. (lɪŋks) Lincolnshire

linctus (**'lɪŋktəs**) n. syrupy cough medicine

linden (**'lɪndən**) n. deciduous tree with fragrant flowers, the lime

line (laɪn) n. 1. long narrow mark 2. stroke made with pen etc. 3. continuous length without breadth 4. row 5. series, course 6. telephone connection 7. progeny 8. province of activity 9. shipping company 10. railway track 11. any class of goods 12. cord 13. string 14. wire 15. advice, guidance 16. inf. medical certificate —vt.

17. cover inside of 18. mark with lines 19. bring into line 20. be, form border, edge of —'linage n. 1. number of lines in piece of written or printed matter 2. payment for written material according to number of lines —lineage ('lɪnɪɪdʒ) n. descent from, descendants of an ancestor —lineal ('lɪnɪəl) a. 1. of lines 2. in direct line of descent —lineament ('lɪnɪəmənt) n. feature —linear ('lɪnɪə) a. of, in lines. —lineation (lɪnɪ'eɪʃən) n. 1. marking with lines 2. arrangement or division into lines —'liner n. large ship or aircraft of passenger line —'lining n. covering for inside of garment etc. —linear measure system of units for measurement of length —line drawing drawing made with lines only —line printer electromechanical device that prints a line of characters at a time —'linesman n. in some sports, official who helps referee, umpire —line-up n. 1. row or arrangement of people or things assembled for particular purpose 2. members of such row or arrangement —get a line on obtain all relevant information about —line of fire flight path of missile discharged from firearm —line up 1. form, put into or organize line-up 2. produce, organize and assemble 3. align

linen ('lɪnɪn) a. 1. made of flax —n. 2. cloth made of flax 3. linen articles collectively 4. sheets, tablecloths etc.; shirts (orig. made of linen)

ling¹ (lɪŋ) n. slender food fish

ling² (lɪŋ) n. heather

-ling (comb. form) 1. oft. disparaging person or thing associated with group, activity or quality specified, as in nestling, underling 2. diminutive, as in duckling

linger ('lɪŋgə) vi. delay, loiter, remain long

lingerie ('læn3ərɪ) n. women's underwear or nightwear

lingo ('lɪŋgəʊ) n. inf. language, speech, esp. applied to dialects (pl. -es)

lingua franca ('lɪŋgwə 'fræŋkə) It. language used for communication between people of different mother tongues (pl. lingua francas, linguae francae ('lɪŋgwiː 'frænsiː))

lingual ('lɪŋgwəl) a. 1. of the tongue or language —n. 2. sound made by the tongue, as d, l, t —'linguist n. one skilled in languages or language study —lin'guistic a. of languages or their study —lin'guistics pl.n. (with sing. v.) study, science of language

liniment ('lɪnɪmənt) n. embrocation

link (lɪŋk) n. 1. ring of a chain 2. connection 3. measure, 1-100th part of chain —vt. 4. join with, as with, link 5. intertwine —vi. 6. be so joined —'linkage n. —'linkman n. presenter of television or radio programme consisting of number of outside broadcasts from different locations

links (lɪŋks) pl.n. golf course

linnet ('lɪnɪt) n. songbird of finch family

lino ('laɪnəʊ) linoleum

linocut ('laɪnəʊkʌt) n. 1. design cut in relief on block of linoleum 2. print from this

linoleum (lɪ'nəʊlɪəm) n. floor covering of hessian with smooth, hard, decorative coating of powdered cork, linseed oil etc.

linseed ('lɪnsiːd) n. seed of flax plant —linseed oil yellow oil extracted from it

linsey-woolsey ('lɪnzɪ'wʊlzɪ) n. rough fabric of linen warp and coarse wool or cotton filling

lint (lɪnt) n. soft material for dressing wounds

lintel ('lɪntˀl) n. top piece of door or window

lion ('laɪən) n. large animal of cat family ('lioness fem.) —'lionize or -ise vt. treat as celebrity —lion-hearted a. brave —the lion's share largest portion

lip (lɪp) n. 1. either edge of the mouth 2. edge or margin 3. sl. impudence —lip-reading n. method of understanding spoken words by interpreting movements of speaker's lips —lip salve ointment for the lips —lip service insincere tribute or respect —'lipstick n. cosmetic preparation in stick form, for colouring lips

liqueur (lɪ'kjʊə; Fr. li'kœːr) n. alcoholic liquor flavoured and sweetened

liquid ('lɪkwɪd) a. 1. fluid, not solid or gaseous 2. flowing smoothly 3. (of assets) in form of money or easily converted into money —n. 4. substance in liquid form —lique'faction or liqui'faction n. —'liquefy or 'liquify v. make or become liquid —li'quescence n. —li'quescent a. tending to become liquid —'liquidize or -dise v. —'liquidizer or -diser n. kitchen appliance with blades for puréeing vegetables, blending liquids etc. (also 'blender) —liquid air or gas air or gas reduced to liquid state on application of increased pressure at low temperature —liquid crystal display display of numbers, esp. in electronic calculator, using cells containing a liquid with crystalline properties, that change their reflectivity when an electric field is applied to them —liquid fuel petrol, paraffin oil etc., carried in liquid form and vaporized for combustion —liquid measure system of units for measuring volumes of liquids or their containers

liquidate ('lɪkwɪdeɪt) vt. 1. pay (debt) 2. arrange affairs of and dissolve (company) 3. wipe out, kill —liqui'dation n. 1. process of clearing up financial affairs 2. state of being bankrupt —'liquidator n. official appointed to liquidate business —li'quidity n. state of being able to meet financial obligations

liquor ('lɪkə) n. liquid, esp. an alcoholic one

liquorice or U.S. **licorice** ('lɪkərɪs, -ərɪʃ) n. 1. black substance used in medicine and as a sweet 2. plant or its root from which liquorice is obtained

lira ('lɪərə; It. 'liːra) n. monetary unit of

Italy and Turkey (*pl.* **lire** ('lıərı; *It.* 'liːre), -s)

lisle (laıl) *n.* fine hand-twisted cotton thread

lisp (lısp) *vi.* 1. speak with faulty pronunciation of 's' and 'z' 2. speak falteringly —*n.* 3. such pronunciation or speech

lissom *or* **lissome** ('lısəm) *a.* 1. supple 2. agile

list[1] (lıst) *n.* 1. inventory, register 2. catalogue 3. edge of cloth —*pl.* 4. field for combat —*vt.* 5. place on list —**listed building** UK building officially recognized as having historical or architectural interest and therefore protected from demolition or alteration —**list price** selling price of merchandise as quoted in catalogue or advertisement

list[2] (lıst) *vi.* 1. (of ship) lean to one side —*n.* 2. inclination of ship

listen ('lıs'n) *vi.* try to hear, attend (to) —'**listener** *n.*

listless ('lıstlıs) *a.* indifferent, languid —'**listlessly** *adv.*

lit (lıt) *pt./pp.* of LIGHT[1], LIGHT[2]

litany ('lıtənı) *n.* prayer with responses from congregation

litchi, lichee, *or* **lychee** (laı'tʃiː) *n.* 1. Chinese tree with red edible fruits 2. fruit of this tree, which has whitish juicy pulp and is usu. eaten dried or as preserve —**litchi nut** dried fruit of this tree

literal ('lıtərəl) *a.* 1. according to sense of actual words, not figurative 2. exact in wording 3. of letters —'**literalism** *n.* 1. disposition to take words and statements in literal sense 2. literal or realistic portrayal in art or literature —'**literally** *adv.*

literate ('lıtərıt) *a.* 1. able to read and write 2. educated —*n.* 3. literate person —'**literacy** *n.* —**literati** (lıtə'rɑːtiː) *pl.n.* scholarly, literary people

literature ('lıtərıtʃə, 'lıtrı-) *n.* 1. books and writings, *esp.* of particular country, period or subject 2. *inf.* printed material —'**literarily** *adv.* —'**literary** *a.* of or learned in literature

lithe (laıð) *a.* supple, pliant —'**lithesome** *a.* lissom, supple

lithium ('lıθıəm) *n.* one of the lightest alkaline metals

litho ('laıθəʊ) *n.* 1. lithography 2. lithograph (*pl.* -s) —*a.* 3. lithographic —*adv.* 4. lithographically

litho- *or before vowel* **lith-** (*comb. form*) stone, as in *lithograph*

lithography (lı'θɒgrəfı) *n.* method of printing from metal or stone block using the antipathy of grease and water —'**lithograph** *n.* 1. print so produced —*vt.* 2. print thus —li'**thographer** *n.* —**litho**-'**graphic** *a.*

litigate ('lıtıgeıt) *vt.* 1. contest in law —*vi.* 2. carry on a lawsuit —'**litigant** *n./a.* (person) conducting a lawsuit —**liti**'**gation**

n. lawsuit —**litigious** (lı'tıdʒəs) *a.* 1. given to engaging in lawsuits 2. disputatious

litmus ('lıtməs) *n.* blue dye turned red by acids and restored to blue by alkali —**litmus paper**

litotes ('laıtəʊtiːz) *n.* ironical understatement for rhetorical effect (*pl.* -tes)

litre *or U.S.* **liter** ('liːtə) *n.* measure of volume of fluid, one cubic decimetre, about 1.75 pints

Litt.D. *or* **Lit.D.** 1. Doctor of Letters 2. Doctor of Literature

litter ('lıtə) *n.* 1. untidy refuse 2. odds and ends 3. young of animal produced at one birth 4. straw *etc.* as bedding for animals 5. portable couch 6. kind of stretcher for wounded —*v.* 7. strew (with) litter 8. give birth to (young) —**litter lout** *or U.S.* '**litterbug** *n. sl.* person who drops refuse in public places

little ('lıt'l) *a.* 1. small, not much (**less**, **least**) —*n.* 2. small quantity —*adv.* 3. to a small extent 4. not much or often 5. not at all (**less**, **least**) —**little people** *Folklore* small supernatural beings, such as leprechauns —**the Little Bear** Ursa Minor

littoral ('lıtərəl) *a.* 1. pert. to the seashore —*n.* 2. coastal district

liturgy ('lıtədʒı) *n.* prescribed form of public worship —li'**turgical** *a.*

live[1] (lıv) *v.* 1. have life 2. pass one's life 3. continue in life 4. continue, last 5. dwell 6. feed —'**livable** *or* '**liveable** *a.* 1. suitable for living in 2. tolerable —'**liver** *n.* person who lives in specified way —'**living** *n.* 1. action of being in life 2. people now alive 3. way of life 4. means of living 5. church benefice —**living room** room in house used for relaxation and entertainment —**living wage** wage adequate to maintain person and his family in reasonable comfort

live[2] (laıv) *a.* 1. living, alive 2. active, vital 3. flaming 4. (of rail *etc.*) carrying electric current 5. (of broadcast) transmitted during the actual performance —'**liveliness** *n.* —'**lively** *a.* brisk, active, vivid —'**liven** *vt.* (*esp. with* up) make (more) lively —'**livestock** *n.* domestic animals —**live wire** 1. wire carrying electric current 2. able, very energetic person

livelihood ('laıvlıhʊd) *n.* 1. means of living 2. subsistence, support

livelong ('lıvlɒŋ) *a.* lasting throughout the whole day

liver ('lıvə) *n.* 1. organ secreting bile 2. animal liver as food —'**liverish** *a.* 1. unwell, as from liver upset 2. cross, touchy, irritable

liverwort ('lıvəwɜːt) *n.* plant growing in wet places and resembling green seaweed or leafy moss

livery ('lıvərı) *n.* 1. distinctive dress of person or group, *esp.* servant(s) 2. allowance of food for horses 3. US a livery stable —'**liveried** *a.* (*esp.* of servants *etc.*) wearing livery —'**liveryman** *n.* member of a London guild —**livery stable** stable where horses are kept at a charge or hired out

lives (laivz) *n., pl. of* LIFE

livid ('livid) *a.* 1. of a bluish pale colour 2. discoloured, as by bruising 3. *inf.* angry, furious

lizard ('lizəd) *n.* four-footed reptile

L.J. Lord Justice

L.L. 1. Late Latin 2. Low Latin 3. Lord Lieutenant

llama ('lɑːmə) *n.* woolly animal used as beast of burden in S Amer.

LL.B. Bachelor of Laws

LL.D. Doctor of Laws

Lloyd's ('loidz) *n.* association of London underwriters originally concerned with marine insurance and shipping information and now subscribing a variety of insurance policies and publishing daily list (**Lloyd's List**) of shipping data and news

loach (ləutʃ) *n.* carplike freshwater fish

load (ləud) *n.* 1. burden 2. amount usu. carried at once 3. actual load carried by vehicle 4. resistance against which engine has to work 5. amount of electrical energy drawn from a source —*vt.* 6. put load on or into 7. charge (gun) 8. weigh down —'**loaded** *a.* 1. carrying a load 2. (of dice) dishonestly weighted 3. biased 4. (of question) containing hidden trap or implication 5. *sl.* wealthy 6. *sl.* drunk

loadstar ('ləudstɑː) *n. see* lodestar *at* LODE

loaf¹ (ləuf) *n.* 1. mass of bread as baked 2. shaped mass of food (*pl.* **loaves**)

loaf² (ləuf) *vi.* idle, loiter —'**loafer** *n.* idler

loam (ləum) *n.* fertile soil

loan (ləun) *n.* 1. act of lending 2. thing lent 3. money borrowed at interest 4. permission to use —*vt.* 5. lend, grant loan of

loath *or* **loth** (ləuθ) *a.* unwilling, reluctant —**loathe** (ləuð) *vt.* hate, abhor —**loathing** ('ləuðiŋ) *n.* 1. disgust 2. repulsion —**loathsome** ('ləuðsəm) *a.* disgusting

loaves (ləuvz) *n., pl. of* LOAF¹

lob (lɒb) *n.* 1. in tennis *etc.*, shot pitched high in air —*v.* 2. throw, pitch (shot) thus (**-bb-**)

lobby ('lɒbi) *n.* 1. corridor into which rooms open 2. passage or room in legislative building, *esp.* houses of parliament of Britain and Aust., to which the public has access 3. group which tries to influence members of lawmaking assembly —'**lobbying** *n.* frequenting lobby to collect news or influence members —'**lobbyist** *n. chiefly US* person employed by particular interest to lobby —**lobby correspondent** reporter who frequents the lobby (in House of Commons) to gain parliamentary news

lobe (ləub) *n.* 1. any rounded projection 2. subdivision of body organ 3. soft, hanging part of ear —'**lobar** *a.* of lobe —'**lobate** *a.* 1. having or resembling lobes 2. (of birds) having separate toes each fringed with weblike lobe —**lobed** *a.* —**lo'botomy** *n.* surgical incision into lobe of organ, *esp.* brain

lobelia (ləu'biːliə) *n.* garden plant with blue, red or white flowers

lobster ('lɒbstə) *n.* shellfish with long tail and claws, turning red when boiled

lobworm ('lɒbwɜːm) *n.* lugworm

local ('ləukˀl) *a.* 1. of, existing in particular place 2. confined to a definite spot, district or part of the body 3. of place —*n.* 4. person belonging to a district 5. *inf.* (nearby) pub —**locale** (ləu'kɑːl) *n.* scene of event —**lo'cality** *n.* 1. place, situation 2. district —'**localize** *or* -**ise** *vt.* assign, restrict to definite place —'**locally** *adv.* —**local anaesthetic** anaesthetic which produces insensibility in one part of body —**local authority** *UK* governing body of county *etc.* —**local colour** behaviour *etc.* characteristic of a certain region or time, introduced into novel *etc.* to supply realism

locate (ləu'keit) *vt.* 1. attribute to a place 2. find the place of 3. situate —**lo'cation** *n.* 1. placing 2. situation 3. site of film production away from studio 4. *SA* black Afr. or coloured township —**locative** ('lɒkətiv) *a./n.* (of) grammatical case denoting 'place where'

loch (lɒx) *n.* Scottish lake or long narrow bay

loci ('ləusai) *n., pl. of* LOCUS

lock¹ (lɒk) *n.* 1. appliance for fastening door, lid *etc.* 2. mechanism for firing gun 3. enclosure in river or canal for moving boats from one level to another 4. extent to which vehicle's front wheels will turn 5. appliance to check the revolution of a wheel 6. interlocking 7. block, jam —*vt.* 8. fasten, make secure with lock 9. join firmly 10. cause to become immovable 11. embrace closely —*vi.* 12. become fixed or united 13. become immovable —'**locker** *n.* small cupboard with lock —'**lockjaw** *n.* tetanus —'**locknut** *n.* second nut used on top of first on bolt to prevent it shaking loose —'**lockout** *n.* exclusion of workmen by employers as means of coercion —'**locksmith** *n.* one who makes and mends locks —'**lockup** *n.* 1. prison 2. garage, storage area away from main premises

lock² (lɒk) *n.* tress of hair

locket ('lɒkit) *n.* small hinged pendant for portrait *etc.*

loco¹ ('ləukəu) *inf.* locomotive

loco² ('ləukəu) *a.* 1. *sl., chiefly US* insane —*vt.* 2. *US sl.* make insane

locomotive (ləukə'məutiv) *n.* 1. engine for pulling carriages on railway tracks —*a.* 2. having power of moving from place to place —**loco'motion** *n.* action, power of moving

locum tenens ('ləukəm 'tiːnenz) *Lat.* substitute, *esp.* for doctor or clergyman during absence (*pl.* **locum tenentes** (tə'nentiːz)) (*also* '**locum**) —**locum tenency**

locus ('ləukəs) *n.* 1. exact place or locality 2. curve made by all points satisfying certain mathematical condition, or by point, line or surface moving under such condition (*pl.* **'loci**)

locust ('ləukəst) *n.* destructive winged insect —**locust bean** bean-shaped fruit of locust tree —**locust tree** 1. N. Amer. leguminous tree having prickly branches, white flowers and reddish-brown seed pods 2. the carob

locution (ləu'kju:ʃən) *n.* 1. a phrase 2. speech 3. mode or style of speaking

lode (ləud) *n.* a vein of ore —**'lodestar** or **'loadstar** *n.* Pole Star —**'lodestone** or **'loadstone** *n.* magnetic iron ore

lodge (lɒdʒ) *n.* 1. house, cabin used seasonally or occasionally, *eg* for hunting, skiing 2. gatekeeper's house 3. meeting place of branch of Freemasons *etc.* 4. the branch —*vt.* 5. house 6. deposit 7. bring (a charge *etc.*) against someone —*vi.* 8. live in another's house at fixed charge 9. come to rest —**'lodger** *n.* —**'lodgings** *pl.n.* rented room(s) in another person's house —**'lodgment** or **'lodgement** *n.* lodging, being lodged

loft (lɒft) *n.* 1. space between top storey and roof 2. gallery in church *etc.* —*vt.* 3. send (golf ball *etc.*) high —**'loftily** *adv.* haughtily —**'loftiness** *n.* —**'lofty** *a.* 1. of great height 2. elevated 3. haughty

log¹ (lɒg) *n.* 1. portion of felled tree stripped of branches 2. detailed record of voyages, time travelled *etc.* of ship, aircraft *etc.* 3. apparatus used formerly for measuring ship's speed —*vt.* 4. keep a record of 5. travel (specified distance, time) (**-gg-**) —**'logger** *n.* lumberjack —**'logging** *n.* US cutting and transporting logs to river —**'logbook** *n.*

log² (lɒg) *n.* logarithm

logan ('ləugən) *n.* C *see* BOGAN

loganberry ('ləugənbərɪ, -brɪ) *n.* 1. trailing prickly plant, cross between raspberry and blackberry 2. its purplish-red fruit

logarithm ('lɒgərɪðəm) *n.* one of series of arithmetical functions tabulated for use in calculation —**loga'rithmic** *a.*

loggerhead ('lɒgəhed) *n.* —**at loggerheads** quarrelling, disputing

loggia ('lɒdʒə, 'lɒdʒɪə) *n.* covered, arcaded gallery (*pl.* **-s, loggie** ('lɒdʒɛ))

logic ('lɒdʒɪk) *n.* 1. art or philosophy of reasoning 2. reasoned thought or argument 3. coherence of various facts, events *etc.* —**'logical** *a.* 1. of logic 2. according to reason 3. reasonable 4. apt to reason correctly —**'logically** *adv.* —**lo'gician** *n.*

logistics (lɒ'dʒɪstɪks) *pl.n.* (*with sing. or pl. v.*) 1. the transport, housing and feeding of troops 2. organization of any project, operation —**lo'gistical** *a.*

logo ('ləugəu, 'lɒg-) *n.* company emblem or similar device (*pl.* **-s**)

Logos ('lɒgɒs) *n.* the Divine Word incarnate, Christ

-logue or *U.S.* **-log** (*comb. form*) speech or discourse of particular kind, as in *travelogue, monologue*

-logy (*n. comb. form*) 1. science or study of, as in *musicology* 2. writing, discourse or body of writings, as in *trilogy, phraseology, martyrology* —**-logical** or **-logic** (*a. comb. form*) —**-logist** (*n. comb. form*)

loin (lɔɪn) *n.* 1. part of body between ribs and hip 2. cut of meat from this —*pl.* 3. hips and lower abdomen —**'loincloth** *n.* garment covering loins only

loiter ('lɔɪtə) *vi.* 1. dawdle, hang about 2. idle —**'loiterer** *n.*

loll (lɒl) *vi.* 1. sit, lie lazily 2. (*esp.* of the tongue) hang out —*vt.* 3. hang out (tongue)

lollipop ('lɒlɪpɒp) *n.* boiled sweet *etc.* on small wooden stick —**lollipop man** *UK inf.* person holding circular sign on pole who stops traffic so children may cross road (**lollipop lady** *fem.*)

lollop ('lɒləp) *vi. chiefly UK* 1. walk or run with clumsy or relaxed bouncing movement 2. lounge

lolly ('lɒlɪ) *n.* 1. *inf.* lollipop; ice lolly 2. *sl.* money

London pride ('lʌndən) saxifrage with pinkish-white flowers

lone (ləun) *a.* solitary —**'loneliness** *n.* —**'lonely** *a.* 1. sad because alone 2. unfrequented 3. solitary, alone —**'loner** *n. inf.* one who prefers to be alone —**'lonesome** *a. chiefly US* lonely

long¹ (lɒŋ) *a.* 1. having length, *esp.* great length, in space or time 2. extensive 3. protracted —*adv.* 4. for a long time —**'longways** or *U.S.* **'longwise** *adv. see* **lengthways** at LENGTH —**'longbow** *n. esp.* in medieval England, large powerful handdrawn bow —**long division** process of dividing one number by another and putting steps down in full —**long-drawn-out** *a.* overprolonged, extended —**long-hair** *a. inf.* of intellectuals or their tastes, *esp.* preferring classical music to jazz *etc.* (*also* **long-haired**) —**'longhand** *n.* writing of words, letters *etc.* in full —**long-headed** *a.* astute; shrewd; sagacious —**long johns** *inf.* underpants with long legs —**long jump** athletic contest in which competitors try to cover farthest distance possible with running jump from fixed board or mark —**long off** *Cricket* fielding position near boundary behind bowler on offside of pitch —**long on** *Cricket* fielding position near boundary behind bowler on leg side of pitch —**long-playing** *a.* (of record) lasting for 10 to 30 minutes because of its fine grooves —**long-range** *a.* 1. of the future 2. able to travel long distances without refuelling 3. (of weapons) designed to hit distant target —**long shot** competitor, undertaking, bet *etc.* with small chance of success —**long-standing** *a.* existing for a long time —**long-term** *a.* 1. lasting or extending over a long time 2. *Fin.* maturing after a long period —**long ton** the imperial ton (2240 lbs) —**long wave** radio wave with wavelength greater than

1000 metres —**long-winded** a. tediously loquacious

long² (lɒŋ) vi. have keen desire, yearn —'**longing** n. yearning

long. longitude

longeron ('lɒndʒərən) n. long spar running fore and aft in body of aircraft

longevity (lɒn'dʒɛvɪtɪ) n. long existence or life

longitude ('lɒndʒɪtjuːd) n. distance east or west from standard meridian —**longi'tudinal** a. 1. of length or longitude 2. lengthwise

longshoreman ('lɒŋʃɔːmən) n. US wharf labourer

loo (luː) n. inf. lavatory

loofah ('luːfə) n. 1. pod of plant used as sponge 2. the plant

look (luk) vi. 1. direct, use eyes 2. face 3. seem 4. (with for) search 5. (with for) hope 6. (with after) take care (of) —n. 7. looking 8. view 9. search 10. (oft. pl.) appearance —**looker-on** n. spectator —**looking glass** mirror —'**lookout** n. 1. guard 2. place for watching 3. prospect 4. watchman 5. inf. worry, concern —**good looks** beauty —**look after** tend —**look down on** despise

loom¹ (luːm) n. 1. machine for weaving 2. middle part of oar

loom² (luːm) vi. 1. appear dimly 2. seem ominously close 3. assume great importance

loon (luːn) n. inf. stupid, foolish person —'**loony** a./n. —**loony bin** inf. mental hospital

loop (luːp) n. 1. figure made by curved line crossing itself 2. similar rounded shape in cord, rope etc. crossed on itself 3. contraceptive coil 4. aerial manoeuvre in which aircraft describes complete circle 5. Figure skating curve crossing itself made on single edge —vt. 6. make loop in or of —**loop line** railway line which leaves, then rejoins, main line

loophole ('luːphəʊl) n. 1. means of escape, of evading rule without infringing it 2. vertical slit in wall, esp. for defence

loose (luːs) a. 1. not tight, fastened, fixed or tense 2. slack 3. vague 4. dissolute —vt. 5. free 6. unfasten 7. slacken —vi. 8. (with off) shoot, let fly (bullet etc.) —'**loosely** adv. —'**loosen** v. make or become loose —'**looseness** n. —**loose-jointed** a. 1. supple and easy in movement 2. loosely built; with ill-fitting joints —**loose-leaf** a. (of binder etc.) capable of being opened to allow removal and addition of pages —**on the loose** 1. free 2. inf. on a spree

loot (luːt) n./v. plunder

lop¹ (lɒp) vt. (usu. with off) 1. cut away (twigs and branches) from tree 2. chop (off) (**-pp-**)

lop² (lɒp) vi. hang limply (**-pp-**) —**lop-eared** a. having drooping ears —**lop'sided** a. with one side lower than the other, badly balanced

lope (ləʊp) vi. run with long, easy strides

loquacious (lɒ'kweɪʃəs) a. talkative —**loquacity** (lɒ'kwæsɪtɪ) n.

loquat ('ləʊkwɒt, -kwɒt) n. 1. Japanese plum tree 2. its fruit

lor (lɔː) interj. nonstandard exclamation of surprise or dismay

loran ('lɔːrən) n. radio navigation system operating over long distances

lord (lɔːd) n. 1. British nobleman, peer of the realm 2. feudal superior 3. one ruling others 4. owner 5. God —v. 6. be domineering (esp. in **lord it over someone**) —'**lordliness** n. —'**lordly** a. 1. imperious, proud 2. fit for a lord —'**lordship** n. 1. rule, ownership 2. domain 3. title of some noblemen —**Lord Chief Justice** judge second only to Lord Chancellor; president of one division of High Court of Justice —**Lord (High) Chancellor** Brit. government cabinet minister who is head of judiciary in England and Wales, and Speaker of the House of Lords —**Lord Lieutenant** 1. UK representative of Crown in county 2. formerly, British viceroy in Ireland —**Lord Mayor** mayor in City of London and certain other boroughs —**Lord President of the Council** UK cabinet minister who presides at meetings of Privy Council —**Lord Privy Seal** UK senior cabinet minister without official duties —**the Lord's Day** Christian Sabbath; Sunday —**the Lord's Prayer** prayer taught by Jesus Christ to his disciples (also **Our Father, Pater'noster**) —**the Lord's Supper** see Holy Communion at HOLY —**the Lords Temporal** peers other than bishops in their capacity as members of House of Lords

lore (lɔː) n. 1. learning 2. body of facts and traditions

lorgnette (lɔː'njɛt) n. pair of spectacles mounted on long handle

lorikeet ('lɒrɪkiːt, lɒrɪ'kiːt) n. small parrot

loris ('lɔːrɪs) n. tree-dwelling, nocturnal Asian animal (pl. **-ris**)

lorn (lɔːn) a. poet. 1. abandoned 2. desolate

lorry ('lɒrɪ) n. motor vehicle for transporting loads by road, truck

lory ('lɔːrɪ) n. **lowry** or **lowrie** ('laʊrɪ) n. small, brightly coloured parrot of Aust. and Indonesia

lose (luːz) vt. 1. be deprived of, fail to retain or use 2. let slip 3. fail to get 4. (of clock etc.) run slow by (specified amount) 5. be defeated in —vi. 6. suffer loss (**lost** pt./pp., '**losing** pr.p.) —'**loser** n. 1. person or thing that loses 2. inf. person or thing that seems destined to fail etc. —**loss** (lɒs) n. 1. a losing 2. what is lost 3. harm or damage resulting from losing —**lost** (lɒst) a. 1. unable to be found 2. unable to find one's way 3. bewildered 4. not won 5. not utilized

lot (lɒt) pron. 1. great number —n. 2. collection 3. large quantity 4. share 5. fate 6. destiny 7. item at auction 8. one of a set of objects used to decide something by chance (*esp. in* **to cast lots**) **9.** area of land —*pl.* **10.** *inf.* great numbers or quantity —*adv.* **11.** *inf.* a great deal

loth (ləʊθ) *a. see* LOATH

lotion ('ləʊʃən) *n.* liquid for washing wounds, improving skin *etc.*

lottery ('lɒtərɪ) *n.* **1.** method of raising funds by selling tickets and prizes by chance **2.** gamble

lotto ('lɒtəʊ) *n.* game of chance like bingo

lotus or **lotos** ('ləʊtəs) *n.* **1.** legendary plant whose fruits induce forgetfulness when eaten **2.** Egyptian water lily —**lotus-eater** *n. Gr. myth.* one of people encountered by Odysseus in N Afr. who lived in indolent forgetfulness, drugged by fruit of legendary lotus —**lotus position** seated cross-legged position used in yoga *etc.*

loud (laʊd) *a.* **1.** strongly audible **2.** noisy **3.** obtrusive —**'loudly** *adv.* —**'loudmouth** *n. inf.* person who brags or talks too loudly —**'loudmouthed** *a.* —**loud'speaker** *n.* instrument for converting electrical signals into sound audible at a distance

lough (lɒx) *n.* in Ireland, loch

lounge (laʊndʒ) *vi.* **1.** sit, lie, walk or stand in a relaxed manner —*n.* **2.** living room of house **3.** general waiting, relaxing area in airport, hotel *etc.* —**'lounger** *n.* loafer —**lounge suit** man's suit for daytime wear

lour (laʊə) *see* LOWER

lourie ('laʊrɪ) *n.* S Afr. bird with bright plumage

louse (laʊs) *n.* parasitic insect (*pl.* **lice**) —**lousy** ('laʊzɪ) *a.* **1.** *sl.* nasty, unpleasant **2.** (*with* with) *sl.* (too) generously provided, thickly populated (with) **3.** *sl.* bad, poor **4.** having lice

lout (laʊt) *n.* crude, oafish person —**'loutish** *a.*

louvre or *U.S.* **louver** ('luːvə) *n.* **1.** one of a set of boards or slats set parallel and slanted to admit air but not rain **2.** ventilating structure of these

lovage ('lʌvɪdʒ) *n.* European umbelliferous plant used for flavouring food

love (lʌv) *n.* **1.** warm affection **2.** benevolence **3.** charity **4.** sexual passion **5.** sweetheart **6.** *Tennis etc.* score of nothing —*vt.* **7.** admire passionately **8.** delight in —*vi.* **9.** be in love —**'lovable** or **'loveable** *a.* —**'loveless** *a.* —**'loveliness** *n.* —**'lovely** *a.* beautiful, delightful —**'lover** *n.* —**'loving** *a.* **1.** affectionate **2.** tender —**'lovingly** *adv.* —**'lovebird** *n.* **1.** small parrot **2.** *inf.* lover —**love child** euphemistic illegitimate child, bastard —**love-in-a-mist** *n.* plant with pale-blue flowers —**love letter** —**love-lies-bleeding** *n.* plant with long, drooping red flowers —**'lovelorn** *a.* forsaken by, pining for a lover —**'lovesick** *a.* pining or languishing because of love —**'lovesickness** *n.* —**lovey-dovey** *a.* making excessive or ostentatious display of affection —**loving cup** bowl formerly passed round at banquet —**make love (to)** have sexual intercourse (with)

low¹ (ləʊ) *a.* **1.** not tall, high or elevated **2.** humble **3.** coarse, vulgar **4.** dejected **5.** ill **6.** not loud **7.** moderate **8.** cheap —**'lower** *vt.* **1.** cause, allow to descend **2.** move down **3.** degrade —*vi.* **4.** diminish —*a.* **5.** below in position or rank **6.** at an early stage, period of development —**'lowliness** *n.* —**'lowly** *a.* modest, humble —**low'born** or **low'bred** *a.* rare of ignoble or common parentage —**'lowbrow** *n./a.* (one) having no intellectual or cultural interests —**Low Church** section of Anglican Church stressing evangelical beliefs and practices —**'lowdown** *n. inf.* inside information —**low-down** *a. inf.* mean, shabby, dishonourable —**lower case** bottom half of compositor's type case, in which small letters are kept —**lower-case** *a.* **1.** of small letters —*vt.* **2.** print with lower-case letters —**lower class** social stratum having lowest position in social hierarchy —**lower-class** *a.* **1.** of lower class **2.** inferior; vulgar —**lower house** one of houses of bicameral legislature, usu. the larger and more representative (*also* **lower chamber**) —**low frequency** **1.** in electricity, any frequency of alternating current from about 30 to 10,000 cycles **2.** frequency within audible range —**Low German** language of N Germany, spoken *esp.* in rural areas (*also* **'Plattdeutsch**) —**low-grade** *a.* of inferior quality —**low-key** *a.* subdued, restrained, not intense —**lowland** ('ləʊlənd) *n.* low-lying country —**Lowlander** ('ləʊləndə) *n.* —**Lowlands** ('ləʊləndz) *n.* less mountainous parts of Scotland —**Low Latin** any form of Latin other than classical, such as Medieval Latin —**Low Mass** Mass that has simplified ceremonial form and is spoken rather than sung —**low-minded** *a.* having vulgar or crude mind and character —**low profile** position or attitude characterized by deliberate avoidance of prominence or publicity —**low-tension** *a.* carrying, operating at low voltage —**low tide** **1.** tide at lowest level or time at which it reaches this **2.** lowest point —**low water** **1.** low tide **2.** state of any stretch of water at its lowest level

low² (ləʊ) *n.* **1.** cry of cattle, bellow —*vi.* **2.** (of cattle) utter their cry, bellow

lower ('laʊə) or **lour** *vi.* **1.** look gloomy or threatening, as sky **2.** scowl —*n.* **3.** scowl, frown

lox¹ (lɒks) *n.* kind of smoked salmon

lox² (lɒks) *n. short for* liquid oxygen, *esp.* when used as oxidizer for rocket fuels

loyal ('lɔɪəl) *a.* faithful, true to allegiance —**'loyalist** *n.* —**Loyalist** *n.* C United Empire Loyalist —**'loyally** *adv.* —**'loyalty** *n.* —**loyal toast** toast drunk in pledging allegiance to sovereign, usu. after meal

lozenge ('lɒzɪndʒ) *n.* **1.** small sweet or tablet of medicine **2.** rhombus, diamond figure

LP long-playing (record)

LPG or **LP gas** liquefied petroleum gas

L-plate *n.* sign on car driven by learner driver

Lr *Chem.* lawrencium

LSD 1. lysergic acid diethylamide (hallucinogenic drug) **2.** librae, solidi, denarii (*Lat.*, pounds, shillings, pence)

L.S.E. London School of Economics

Lt. Lieutenant

Ltd. or **ltd.** Limited (Liability)

Lu *Chem.* lutetium

lubber ('lʌbə) *n.* **1.** clumsy fellow **2.** unskilled seaman

lubricate ('lu:brɪkeɪt) *vt.* **1.** oil, grease **2.** make slippery —**'lubricant** *n.* substance used for this —**lubri'cation** *n.* —**lubricator** *n.* —**lu'bricity** *n.* **1.** slipperiness, smoothness **2.** lewdness

lucent ('lu:s²nt) *a.* bright, shining

lucerne (lu:'sɜːn) *n.* fodder plant like clover, alfalfa

lucid ('lu:sɪd) *a.* **1.** clear **2.** easily understood **3.** sane —**lu'cidity** or **'lucidness** *n.* —**'lucidly** *adv.*

luck (lʌk) *n.* **1.** fortune, good or bad **2.** good fortune **3.** chance —**'luckily** *adv.* fortunately —**'luckless** *a.* having bad luck —**'lucky** *a.* having good luck —**lucky dip** UK **1.** box containing small prizes for which children search **2.** *inf.* undertaking of uncertain outcome

lucre ('lu:kə) *n.* *usu. facetious* money, wealth —**'lucrative** *a.* very profitable —**filthy lucre** *inf.* money

ludicrous ('lu:dɪkrəs) *a.* absurd, laughable, ridiculous

ludo ('lu:dəʊ) *n.* game played with dice and counters on board

luff (lʌf) *n.* **1.** the part of fore-and-aft sail nearest mast —*v.* **2.** sail (ship) into wind so that sails flap —*vi.* **3.** (of sails) flap

lug¹ (lʌg) *v.* drag (something heavy) with effort (**-gg-**)

lug² (lʌg) *n.* **1.** projection, tag serving as handle or support **2.** *inf.* ear

luggage ('lʌgɪdʒ) *n.* traveller's trunks and other baggage

lugger ('lʌgə) *n.* working boat (*eg* fishing, prawning lugger) orig. fitted with lugsail

lugsail ('lʌgseɪl) *n.* oblong sail fixed on yard which hangs slanting on mast

lugubrious (lʊ'gu:brɪəs) *a.* mournful, doleful, gloomy —**lu'gubriously** *adv.*

lugworm ('lʌgwɜːm) *n.* large worm used as bait, lobworm

lukewarm (lu:k'wɔːm) *a.* **1.** moderately warm, tepid **2.** unenthusiastic

lull (lʌl) *vt.* **1.** soothe, sing (to sleep) **2.** make quiet —*vi.* **3.** become quiet, subside —*n.* **4.** brief time of quiet in storm *etc.* —**lullaby** ('lʌləbaɪ) *n.* lulling song, *esp.* for children

lumbar ('lʌmbə) *a.* relating to body between lower ribs and hips —**lumbago** (lʌm'beɪgəʊ) *n.* rheumatism in the lower part of the back

lumber ('lʌmbə) *n.* **1.** disused articles, useless rubbish **2.** sawn timber —*vi.* **3.**

move heavily —*vt.* **4.** *inf.* burden with something unpleasant —**'lumberjack** *n.* US, C man who fells trees and prepares logs for transport to mill

lumen ('lu:mɪn) *n.* SI unit of luminous flux (*pl.* **-s, -mina** (-mɪnə))

luminous ('lu:mɪnəs) *a.* **1.** bright **2.** shedding light **3.** glowing **4.** lucid —**'luminary** *n.* **1.** learned person **2.** heavenly body giving light —**lumi'nescence** *n.* emission of light at low temperatures by process (*eg* chemical) not involving burning —**lumi'nosity** *n.*

lump (lʌmp) *n.* **1.** shapeless piece or mass **2.** swelling **3.** large sum —*vt.* **4.** (*oft. with* together) throw (together) in one mass or sum —*vi.* **5.** move heavily —**'lumpish** *a.* **1.** clumsy **2.** stupid —**'lumpy** *a.* **1.** full of lumps **2.** uneven —**lump sum** relatively large sum of money, paid at one time —**lump it** *inf.* put up with something

lunar ('lu:nə) *a.* relating to the moon —**lunar module** module used to carry astronauts from spacecraft to surface of moon and back

lunatic ('lu:nətɪk) *a.* **1.** insane —*n.* **2.** insane person —**'lunacy** *n.* —**lunatic asylum** *old name for* institution for mentally ill —**lunatic fringe** extreme, radical section of group *etc.*

lunch (lʌntʃ) *n.* **1.** meal taken in the middle of the day —*v.* **2.** eat, entertain to lunch —**luncheon** ('lʌntʃən) *n.* a lunch —**luncheon voucher** voucher worth specified amount issued to employees and redeemable at restaurant for food

lung (lʌŋ) *n.* one of the two organs of respiration in vertebrates —**'lungfish** *n.* type of fish with air-breathing lung —**'lungworm** *n.* parasitic worm infesting lungs of some animals —**'lungwort** *n.* flowering plant

lunge (lʌndʒ) *vi.* **1.** thrust with sword *etc.* —*n.* **2.** such thrust **3.** sudden movement of body, plunge

lupin or US. **lupine** ('lu:pɪn) *n.* leguminous plant with tall spikes of flowers

lupine ('lu:paɪn) *a.* like a wolf

lupus ('lu:pəs) *n.* skin disease

lurch (lɜːtʃ) *n.* **1.** sudden roll to one side —*vi.* **2.** stagger —**leave in the lurch** leave in difficulties

lurcher ('lɜːtʃə) *n.* crossbred dog trained to hunt silently

lure (lʊə) *n.* **1.** something which entices **2.** bait **3.** power to attract —*vt.* **4.** entice **5.** attract

lurid ('lʊərɪd) *a.* **1.** vivid in shocking detail, sensational **2.** pale, wan **3.** lit with unnatural glare —**'luridly** *adv.*

lurk (lɜːk) *vi.* lie hidden —**'lurking** *a.* (of suspicion) not definite

luscious ('lʌʃəs) *a.* **1.** sweet, juicy **2.** extremely pleasurable or attractive

lush¹ (lʌʃ) *a.* (of grass *etc.*) luxuriant and juicy, fresh

lush² (lʌʃ) *n.* US *sl.* **1.** heavy drinker **2.** alcoholic —**'lushy** *a.*

lust (lʌst) *n.* **1.** strong desire for sexual gratification **2.** any strong desire —*vi.* **3.** have passionate desire —**'lustful** *a.* —**'lustily** *adv.* —**'lusty** *a.* vigorous, healthy

lustration (lʌs'treɪʃən) *n.* purification by sacrifice —**'lustral** *a.* used in lustration —**'lustrate** *vt.*

lustre or *U.S.* **luster** ('lʌstə) *n.* **1.** gloss, sheen **2.** splendour **3.** renown **4.** glory **5.** glossy material **6.** metallic pottery glaze —**'lustrous** *a.* shining, luminous

lute¹ (luːt) *n.* old stringed musical instrument played with the fingers —**'lutenist** or **'lutist** *n.*

lute² (luːt) *n.* **1.** composition to make joints airtight —*vt.* **2.** close with lute

lutetium or **lutecium** (luˈtiːʃɪəm) *n.* silvery-white metallic element of lanthanide series

Lutheran ('luːθərən) *n.* **1.** follower of Luther, German leader of Protestant Reformation, or member of Lutheran Church —*a.* **2.** of Luther or his doctrines **3.** of Lutheran Church —**'Lutheranism** *n.*

lutz (lʊts) *n. Ice-skating* jump from one skate with complete turn in air and return to other skate

lux (lʌks) *n.* SI unit of illumination (*pl.* **lux**)

luxe (lʌks, lʊks; *Fr.* lyks) *n.* see DE LUXE

luxury ('lʌkʃərɪ) *n.* **1.** possession and use of costly, choice things for enjoyment **2.** enjoyable but not necessary thing **3.** comfortable surroundings —**luxuriance** (lʌg'zjʊərɪəns) *n.* abundance, proliferation —**luxuriant** (lʌg'zjʊərɪənt) *a.* **1.** growing thickly **2.** abundant —**luxuriantly** (lʌg-'zjʊərɪəntlɪ) *adv.* —**luxuriate** (lʌg-'zjʊərɪeɪt) *vi.* **1.** indulge in luxury **2.** flourish profusely **3.** take delight —**luxurious** (lʌg-'zjʊərɪəs) *a.* **1.** fond of luxury **2.** self-indulgent **3.** sumptuous —**luxuriously** (lʌg-'zjʊərɪəslɪ) *adv.*

LV luncheon voucher

lyceum (laɪ'sɪəm) *n.* public building for concerts *etc.*

lychee (laɪ'tʃiː) *n.* see LITCHI

lych gate (lɪtʃ) see LICH GATE

lyddite ('lɪdaɪt) *n.* powerful explosive used in shells

lye (laɪ) *n.* water made alkaline with wood ashes *etc.* for use as cleansing agent

lying ('laɪɪŋ) *pr.p.* of LIE¹, LIE² —**lying-in** *n.* confinement in childbirth (*pl.* **lyings-in**)

lymph (lɪmf) *n.* colourless bodily fluid, mainly of white blood cells —**lym'phatic** *a.* **1.** of lymph **2.** flabby, sluggish —*n.* **3.** vessel in the body conveying lymph —**lymph node** any of numerous bean-shaped masses of tissue, situated along course of lymphatic vessels

lynch (lɪntʃ) *vt.* put to death without trial —**lynch law** procedure of self-appointed court trying and executing accused

lynx (lɪŋks) *n.* animal of cat family —**lynx-eyed** *a.* having keen sight

lyre (laɪə) *n* instrument like harp —**lyric** ('lɪrɪk) *n.* **1.** lyric poem —*pl.* **2.** words of popular song —**lyric(al)** ('lɪrɪk('l)) *a.* **1.** of short personal poems expressing emotion **2.** of lyre **3.** meant to be sung —**lyricist** ('lɪrɪsɪst) *n.* —**lyrist** ('lɪrɪst) *n.* **1.** lyric poet **2.** ('laɪərɪst) player on lyre —**'lyrebird** *n.* Aust. bird, the male of which displays tail shaped like a lyre —**wax lyrical** express great enthusiasm

-lyte (*n. comb. form*) substance that can be decomposed or broken down, as in *electrolyte* —**-lytic** (*a. comb. form*) loosening, dissolving, as in *paralytic*

M

m *or* **M** (εm) *n.* **1.** 13th letter of English alphabet **2.** speech sound represented by this letter (*pl.* **m's, M's** *or* **Ms**)

m metre(s)

M 1. Mach **2.** mega- **3.** *Currency* mark(s) **4.** million **5.** UK motorway **6.** Roman numeral, 1000

m. 1. male **2.** married **3.** masculine **4.** mile **5.** minute

M. 1. Medieval **2.** Monsieur

ma (mɑː) *n. inf.* mother

MA Massachusetts

M.A. Master of Arts

ma'am (mæm, mɑːm; *unstressed* məm) *n.* madam

mac *or* **mack** (mæk) *n.* UK *inf.* mackintosh

Mac-, Mc- *or* **M'-** (*comb. form*) in surnames of Gaelic origin, son of, as in *MacDonald*

macabre (məˈkɑːbə, -brə) *a.* gruesome, ghastly

macadam (məˈkædəm) *n.* road surface made of pressed layers of small broken stones —**maˈcadamize** *or* **-ise** *vt.* pave (road) with this

macaroni *or* **maccaroni** (mækəˈrəʊnɪ) *n.* pasta in long, thin tubes (*pl.* **-s, -es**)

macaroon (mækəˈruːn) *n.* small cake, biscuit containing almonds

macaw (məˈkɔː) *n.* kind of parrot

mace[1] (meɪs) *n.* **1.** staff with metal head **2.** staff of office

mace[2] (meɪs) *n.* spice made of the husk of the nutmeg

macerate (ˈmæsəreɪt) *v.* **1.** soften by soaking **2.** (cause to) waste away —**maceˈration** *n.*

machete (məˈʃɛtɪ, -ˈtʃeɪ-) *n.* broad, heavy knife used for cutting or as a weapon

Machiavellian (mækɪəˈvɛlɪən) *a.* politically unprincipled, crafty, perfidious, subtle, deep-laid

machination (mækɪˈneɪʃən) *n.* (*usu. pl.*) plotting, intrigue —**ˈmachinate** *v.* lay or devise (plots)

machine (məˈʃiːn) *n.* **1.** apparatus combining action of several parts to apply mechanical force **2.** controlling organization **3.** mechanical appliance **4.** vehicle —*vt.* **5.** sew, print, shape *etc.* with machine —**maˈchinery** *n.* **1.** parts of machine collectively **2.** machines —**maˈchinist** *n.* one who makes or works machines —**machine gun** gun firing repeatedly and continuously with an automatic loading and firing mechanism —**machine-readable** *a.* (of data) in a form that can be directly fed into a computer —**machine shop** workshop in which machine tools are operated —**machine tool** power-driven machine, such as lathe, for cutting or shaping metals *etc.*

machismo (mæˈkɪzməʊ, -ˈtʃɪz-) *n.* strong or exaggerated masculine pride or masculinity (*oft.* **macho** (ˈmætʃəʊ))

Mach (number) (mæx) *n.* the ratio of the air speed of an aircraft to the velocity of sound under given conditions

mack (mæk) *n.* UK *inf. see* MAC

mackerel (ˈmækrəl) *n.* edible sea fish with blue and silver stripes

mackintosh *or* **macintosh** (ˈmækɪntɒʃ) *n.* **1.** waterproof raincoat of rubberized cloth **2.** any raincoat

macramé (məˈkrɑːmɪ) *n.* ornamental work of knotted cord

macro- *or before vowel* **macr-** (*comb. form*) **1.** large, long, or great in size or duration, as in *macroscopic* **2.** *Pathol.* abnormal enlargement, as in *macrocephaly*

macrobiotics (mækrəʊbaɪˈɒtɪks) *pl.n.* (*with sing. v.*) dietary system advocating whole grain and vegetables grown without chemical additives

macrocosm (ˈmækrəkɒzəm) *n.* **1.** the universe **2.** any large, complete system

macron (ˈmækrɒn) *n.* diacritical mark (−) placed over letter to represent long vowel

macroscopic (mækrəʊˈskɒpɪk) *a.* **1.** visible to the naked eye **2.** concerned with large units —**macroˈscopically** *adv.*

mad (mæd) *a.* **1.** suffering from mental disease, insane **2.** wildly foolish **3.** very enthusiastic **4.** excited **5.** *inf.* furious, angry —**ˈmadden** *vt.* make mad —**ˈmadly** *adv.* —**ˈmadness** *n.* **1.** insanity **2.** folly —**ˈmadhouse** *n. inf.* **1.** mental hospital or asylum **2.** state of uproar or confusion —**ˈmadman** *n.*

madam (ˈmædəm) *n.* **1.** polite form of address to a woman **2.** *inf.* precocious or conceited girl

madame (ˈmædəm) *n.* married French-woman

madcap (ˈmædkæp) *n.* **1.** reckless person —*a.* **2.** reckless

madder (ˈmædə) *n.* **1.** climbing plant **2.** its root **3.** red dye made from this

made (meɪd) *pt./pp. of* MAKE —**made-up** *a.* **1.** invented **2.** wearing make-up **3.** put together

Madeira (məˈdɪərə) *n.* rich sherry wine —**Madeira cake** rich sponge cake

mademoiselle (mædmwɑːˈzɛl) *n.* **1.** young unmarried French girl or woman **2.** French teacher or governess

Madonna (məˈdɒnə) *n.* **1.** the Virgin Mary **2.** picture or statue of her

madrepore (mædrɪˈpɔː) *n.* kind of coral

madrigal (ˈmædrɪgəl) *n.* **1.** unaccompanied part song **2.** short love poem or song

maelstrom ('meɪlstrəʊm) *n.* **1.** great whirlpool **2.** turmoil

maenad ('miːnæd) *n. Class. lit.* frenzied female worshipper of Dionysus

maestoso (maɪ'stəʊsəʊ) *adv. Mus.* grandly, in majestic manner

maestro ('maɪstrəʊ) *n.* **1.** outstanding musician, conductor **2.** man regarded as master of any art (*pl.* **-tri** (trɪ), **-s**)

mae west (meɪ) *sl.* inflatable life jacket

Mafia ('mæfɪə) *n.* international secret criminal organization, *orig.* Italian

magazine (mægə'ziːn) *n.* **1.** periodical publication with stories and articles by different writers **2.** appliance for supplying cartridges automatically to gun **3.** storehouse for explosives or arms

magenta (mə'dʒɛntə) *a./n.* (of) deep purplish-red colour

maggot ('mægət) *n.* grub, larva —**'maggoty** *a.* infested with maggots

magi ('meɪdʒaɪ) *pl.n.* **1.** priests of ancient Persia **2.** the wise men from the East at the Nativity (*sing.* **-gus** (-gəs))

magic ('mædʒɪk) *n.* **1.** art of supposedly invoking supernatural powers to influence events *etc.* **2.** any mysterious agency or power **3.** witchcraft, conjuring —*a.* **4.** magical, enchanting —**'magical** *a.* —**'magically** *adv.* —**ma'gician** *n.* one skilled in magic, wizard, conjurer, enchanter —**magic lantern** early form of projector using slides

magistrate ('mædʒɪstreɪt, -strɪt) *n.* **1.** civil officer administering law **2.** justice of the peace —**magis'terial** *a.* **1.** of, referring to magistrate **2.** dictatorial —**'magistracy** *n.* **1.** office of magistrate **2.** magistrates collectively

magma ('mægmə) *n.* **1.** paste or suspension consisting of finely divided solid dispersed in liquid **2.** molten rock inside earth's crust

magnanimous (mæg'nænɪməs) *a.* noble, generous, not petty —**magna'nimity** *n.*

magnate ('mægneɪt, -nɪt) *n.* influential or wealthy person

magnesium (mæg'niːzɪəm) *n.* metallic element —**mag'nesia** *n.* white powder compound of this, used in medicine

magnet ('mægnɪt) *n.* **1.** piece of iron, steel having properties of attracting iron, steel and pointing north and south when suspended **2.** lodestone —**mag'netic** *a.* **1.** with properties of magnet **2.** exerting powerful attraction —**mag'netically** *adv.* —**'magnetism** *n.* **1.** magnetic phenomena **2.** science of magnetic phenomena **3.** personal charm or power of attracting others —**'magnetite** *n.* black magnetizable mineral that is important source of iron —**magneti'zation** *or* **-i'sation** *n.* —**'magnetize** *or* **-ise** *vt.* **1.** make into a magnet **2.** attract as if by magnet **3.** fascinate —**magneto** (mæg'niːtəʊ) *n.* apparatus for ignition in internal-combustion engine (*pl.* **-s**) —**magne'tometer** *n.* instrument used to measure

magnetic force —**'magnetron** *n.* two-electrode electronic valve used with applied magnetic field to generate high-power microwave oscillations —**magnetic field** field of force surrounding permanent magnet or moving charged particle —**magnetic mine** mine designed to activate when magnetic field is detected —**magnetic needle** magnetized rod used in certain instruments for indicating direction of magnetic field —**magnetic north** direction in which compass needle points, usu. at angle of true north —**magnetic pole 1.** either of two regions in magnet where magnetic induction is concentrated **2.** either of two variable points on earth's surface towards which magnetic needle points —**magnetic storm** sudden severe disturbance of earth's magnetic field —**magnetic tape** long coated plastic strip for recording sound or video signals

Magnificat (mæg'nɪfɪkæt) *n.* hymn of Virgin Mary in *Luke* 1. 46–55, used as canticle

magnificent (mæg'nɪfɪs²nt) *a.* **1.** splendid **2.** stately, imposing **3.** excellent —**mag'nificence** *n.* —**mag'nificently** *adv.*

magnify ('mægnɪfaɪ) *vt.* **1.** increase apparent size of, as with lens **2.** exaggerate **3.** make greater (**-fied, -fying**) —**magnifi'cation** *n.*

magniloquent (mæg'nɪləkwənt) *a.* **1.** speaking pompously **2.** grandiose —**mag'niloquence** *n.*

magnitude ('mægnɪtjuːd) *n.* **1.** importance **2.** greatness, size

magnolia (mæg'nəʊlɪə) *n.* shrub or tree with large white, sweet-scented flowers

magnox ('mægnɒks) *n.* alloy of mostly magnesium with small amounts of aluminium, used in fuel elements of nuclear reactor —**magnox reactor**

magnum ('mægnəm) *n.* large wine bottle (approx. 52 fluid ounces)

magnum opus great work of art or literature

magpie ('mægpaɪ) *n.* black-and-white bird

Magyar ('mægjɑː) *n.* **1.** member of prevailing race in Hungary **2.** native speech of Hungary —*a.* **3.** pert. to Magyars **4.** *Dressmaking* cut with sleeves and bodice of garment in one piece

maharajah *or* **maharaja** (mɑːhə'rɑːdʒə) *n.* former title of some Indian princes

maharani *or* **maharanee** (mɑːhə'rɑːniː) *n.* **1.** wife of maharajah **2.** woman holding rank of maharajah

maharishi (mɑːhɑː'riːʃɪ, məhɑːriːʃɪ) *n.* Hindu religious teacher or mystic

mahatma (mə'hɑːtmə) *n.* **1.** *Hinduism* man of saintly life with supernatural powers **2.** one endowed with great wisdom and power

mahjong *or* **mah-jongg** (mɑː'dʒɒŋ) *n.* Chinese table game for four, played with pieces called tiles

mahogany (mə'hɒgənɪ) n. tree yielding reddish-brown wood

mahout (mə'haʊt) n. in India and E Indies, elephant driver or keeper

maiden ('meɪdⁿ) n. 1. Lit. young unmarried woman —a. 2. unmarried 3. of, suited to maiden 4. first 5. having blank record —maid n. 1. Lit. young unmarried woman 2. woman servant —'maidenhood n. —'maidenly a. modest —'maidenhair n. fern with delicate stalks and fronds —'maidenhead n. 1. hymen 2. virginity —maiden name woman's surname before marriage —maid of honour 1. UK small tart with almond-flavoured filling 2. unmarried lady attending queen or princess 3. US principal unmarried attendant of bride —maiden over Cricket over in which no runs are scored

mail¹ (meɪl) n. 1. letters etc. transported and delivered by the post office 2. letters etc. conveyed at one time 3. the postal system 4. train, ship etc. carrying mail —vt. 5. send by post —mail order 1. order for merchandise sent by post 2. system of buying and selling merchandise through post

mail² (meɪl) n. armour of interlaced rings or overlapping plates —mailed a. covered with mail

maim (meɪm) vt. cripple, mutilate

main (meɪn) a. 1. chief, principal, leading —n. 2. principal pipe, line carrying water, electricity etc. 3. chief part 4. strength, power 5. obs. open sea —'mainly adv. for the most part, chiefly —main chance one's own interests (usu. in have an eye to the main chance) —main clause Gram. clause that can stand alone as sentence —main force physical strength —mainland ('meɪnlənd) n. stretch of land which forms main part of a country —main line 1. Railways trunk route between two points 2. sl. main vein into which narcotic drug can be injected —'mainline vi. sl. inject drug thus —'mainmast n. chief mast in ship —mainsail ('meɪnseɪl; Naut. 'meɪns'l) n. lowest sail of mainmast —'mainspring n. 1. chief spring of watch or clock 2. chief cause or motive —'mainstay n. 1. rope from mainmast 2. chief support —'mainstream n. 1. main current (of river, cultural trend etc.) —a. 2. of style of jazz that lies between traditional and modern

maintain (meɪn'teɪn) vt. 1. carry on 2. preserve 3. support 4. sustain 5. keep up 6. keep supplied 7. affirm 8. support by argument 9. defend —main'tainable a. —'maintenance n. 1. maintaining 2. means of support 3. upkeep of buildings etc. 4. provision of money for separated or divorced spouse

maisonette or **maisonnette** (meɪzə'nɛt) n. part of house, usu. on two floors, fitted as self-contained dwelling

maître d'hôtel (mɛtrə dəʊ'tɛl) Fr. restaurant manager

maize (meɪz) n. type of corn

Maj. Major

majesty ('mædʒɪstɪ) n. 1. stateliness 2. sovereignty 3. grandeur —ma'jestic a. 1. splendid 2. regal —ma'jestically adv.

majolica (mə'dʒɒlɪkə, mə'jɒl-) or maiolica (mə'jɒlɪkə) n. type of ornamented Italian pottery

major ('meɪdʒə) n. 1. army officer ranking next above captain 2. major scale in music 3. US, A, NZ principal field of study at university etc. 4. person of legal majority —a. 5. greater in number, quality, extent 6. significant, serious —vi. 7. (usu. with in) US, A, NZ do one's principal study (in particular subject) —ma'jority n. 1. greater number 2. larger party voting together 3. excess of the vote on one side 4. coming of age 5. rank of major —majordomo ('dəʊməʊ) n. house steward (pl. -s) —major general Mil. officer immediately junior to lieutenant general —major scale Mus. scale with semitones instead of whole tones after third and seventh notes

make (meɪk) vt. 1. construct 2. produce 3. create 4. establish 5. appoint 6. amount to 7. cause to (do something) 8. accomplish 9. reach 10. earn —vi. 11. tend (made, 'making) —n. 12. brand, type, style —'Maker n. title given to God (as Creator) —'making n. 1. creation —pl. 2. necessary requirements or qualities —make-believe n. fantasy or pretence —'makeshift n. temporary expedient —make-up n. 1. cosmetics 2. characteristics 3. layout —'makeweight n. trifle added to make something stronger or better —(go to) meet one's Maker die —make believe pretend; enact fantasy —make up 1. compose 2. compile 3. complete 4. compensate 5. apply cosmetics 6. invent —on the make sl. 1. intent on gain 2. in search of sexual partner

mako ('mɑːkəʊ) n. type of shark (pl. -s)

mal- (comb. form) ill, badly, as in malformation, malfunction

malacca or **malacca cane** (mə'lækə) n. brown cane used for walking stick

malachite ('mæləkaɪt) n. green mineral

maladjusted (mælə'dʒʌstɪd) a. 1. Psychol. unable to meet the demands of society 2. badly adjusted —malad'justment n.

maladministration (mælədmɪnɪ'streɪʃən) n. inefficient or dishonest administration

maladroit (mælə'drɔɪt) a. clumsy, awkward

malady ('mælədɪ) n. disease

malaise (mæ'leɪz) n. vague, unlocated feeling of discomfort

malapropism ('mæləprɒpɪzəm) or malaprop n. ludicrous misuse of word

malapropos (mælæprə'pəʊ) a./adv. inappropriate(ly)

malaria (mə'lɛərɪə) n. infectious disease caused by bite of some mosquitoes —ma'larial a.

Malathion (mælə'θaɪɒn) n. R insecticide consisting of organic phosphate

Malay (mə'leɪ) n. 1. native of Malaysia or Indonesia 2. language of this people —Ma'layan a./n.

malcontent ('mælkəntent) a. 1. actively discontented —n. 2. malcontent person

male (meɪl) a. 1. of sex producing gametes which fertilize female gametes 2. of men or male animals —n. 3. male person or animal

malediction (mælɪ'dɪkʃən) n. curse

malefactor ('mælɪfæktə) n. criminal

maleficent (mə'lɛfɪsənt) a. harmful, hurtful —ma'leficence n.

malevolent (mə'lɛvələnt) a. full of ill will —ma'levolence n.

malice ('mælɪs) n. 1. ill will 2. spite —ma'licious a. 1. intending evil or unkindness 2. spiteful 3. moved by hatred —ma'liciously adv.

malign (mə'laɪn) a. 1. evil in influence or effect —vt. 2. slander, misrepresent —malignancy (mə'lɪgnənsɪ) n. —malignant (mə'lɪgnənt) a. 1. feeling extreme ill will 2. (of disease) resistant to therapy —malignantly (mə'lɪgnəntlɪ) adv. —malignity (mə'lɪgnɪtɪ) n. malignant disposition

malinger (mə'lɪŋgə) vi. feign illness to escape duty —ma'lingerer n.

mall (mɔːl, mæl) n. 1. level, shaded walk 2. street, shopping area closed to vehicles

mallard ('mælɑːd) n. wild duck

malleable ('mælɪəbᵊl) a. 1. capable of being hammered into shape 2. adaptable —mallea'bility n.

mallet ('mælɪt) n. 1. (wooden) hammer 2. croquet or polo stick

mallow ('mæləʊ) n. wild plant with purple flowers

malmsey ('mɑːmzɪ) n. strong sweet wine

malnutrition (mælnjuː'trɪʃən) n. inadequate nutrition

malodorous (mæl'əʊdərəs) a. evil-smelling

malpractice (mæl'præktɪs) n. immoral, illegal or unethical conduct

malt (mɔːlt) n. 1. grain used for brewing —v. 2. make into or become malt —'maltster n. maker of malt

Maltese (mɔːl'tiːz) a. 1. of or relating to Malta, its inhabitants, or their language —n. 2. native or inhabitant of Malta (pl. -tese) 3. official language of Malta —Maltese cross cross with triangular arms that taper towards centre

maltreat (mæl'triːt) vt. treat badly, handle roughly —mal'treatment n.

mama or chiefly U.S. **mamma** (mə'mɑː) n. old-fashioned mother

mamba ('mæmbə) n. deadly S Afr. snake

mambo ('mæmbəʊ) n. Latin Amer. dance like rumba (pl. -s)

mamilla or U.S. **mammilla** (mæ'mɪlə) n. 1. nipple or teat 2. any nipple-shaped prominence (pl. -lae (-liː)) —'mamillary or U.S. 'mammillary a.

mamma ('mæmə) n. milk-secreting organ of female mammals: breast in women,

udder in cows etc. (pl. -mae (-miː)) —'mammary a.

mammal ('mæməl) n. animal of type that suckles its young —mammalian (mæ'meɪlɪən) a.

mammon ('mæmən) n. 1. wealth regarded as source of evil 2. (M-) false god of covetousness —'mammonism n. —'mammonist n.

mammoth ('mæməθ) n. 1. extinct animal like an elephant —a. 2. colossal

man (mæn) n. 1. human being 2. person 3. human race 4. adult male 5. SA sl. any person 6. manservant 7. piece used in chess etc. (pl. men) —vt. 8. supply (ship etc.) with necessary men 9. fortify (-nn-) —'manful a. brave, vigorous —'manfully adv. —'manhood n. —'manikin, 'manakin or 'mannikin 1. little man 2. model of human body 3. lay figure —'manlike a. —'manliness n. —'manly a. —'mannish a. like a man —man Friday 1. loyal male servant or assistant 2. any factotum, esp. in office (also Girl Friday, Person Friday) —'manhandle vt. treat roughly —'manhole n. opening through which man may pass to a drain, sewer etc. —man-hour n. unit of work in industry, equal to work done by one man in one hour —'manhunt n. organized search for fugitive —man-'kind n. human beings in general —man-of-war or man o' war n. 1. warship 2. see Portuguese man-of-war at PORTUGUESE —'manpower n. 1. power of human effort 2. available number of workers —'manslaughter n. culpable homicide without malice aforethought —man in the street typical person —man of letters 1. writer 2. scholar —man of the world man of wide experience

manacle ('mænəkᵊl) n. 1. fetter, handcuff —vt. 2. shackle

manage ('mænɪdʒ) v. 1. be in charge (of), administer 2. succeed in (doing) —vt. 3. control 4. handle, cope with 5. conduct, carry on —'manageable a. —'management n. 1. those who manage, as board of directors etc. 2. administration 3. skilful use of means 4. conduct —'manager n. 1. one in charge of business, institution, actor etc. (manage'ress fem.) 2. one who manages efficiently —mana'gerial a. —'managing a. having administrative control

mañana (mə'njɑːnə) Sp. 1. tomorrow 2. some other and later time

manatee (mænə'tiː) n. large, plant-eating aquatic mammal

Manchu (mæn'tʃuː) n. 1. member of Mongoloid people of Manchuria (pl. -s, -'chu) 2. language of this people

Mancunian (mæŋ'kjuːnɪən) n. 1. native or inhabitant of Manchester —a. 2. of Manchester

mandala ('mændələ, mæn'dɑːlə) n. any of various designs, usu. circular, symbolizing the universe

mandarin ('mændərɪn) n. 1. Hist. Chinese

high-ranking bureaucrat 2. *fig.* any high government official 3. Chinese variety of orange —**mandarin duck** Asian duck, the male of which has brightly coloured patterned plumage and crest

mandate ('mændeɪt, -dɪt) *n.* 1. command of, or commission to act for, another 2. commission from United Nations to govern a territory 3. instruction from electorate to representative or government —'**mandated** *a.* committed to a mandate —**mandatory** ('mændətərɪ, -trɪ) *n.* 1. holder of a mandate —*a., also* '**mandatary** 2. compulsory

mandible ('mændɪb'l) *n.* 1. lower jawbone 2. either part of bird's beak —**man'dibular** *a.* of, like mandible

mandolin *or* **mandoline** (mændə'lɪn) *n.* stringed musical instrument

mandrake ('mændreɪk) *or* **mandragora** (mæn'drægərə) *n.* narcotic plant

mandrel *or* **mandril** ('mændrəl) *n.* 1. axis on which material is supported in a lathe 2. rod round which metal is cast or forged

mandrill ('mændrɪl) *n.* large blue-faced baboon

mane (meɪn) *n.* long hair on neck of horse, lion *etc.* —**maned** *a.*

manganese (mæŋgə'niːz) *n.* 1. metallic element 2. black oxide of this

mange (meɪndʒ) *n.* skin disease of dogs *etc.* —'**mangy** *or* '**mangey** *a.* scruffy, shabby

mangelwurzel ('mæŋg'lwɜːz'l) *or* **mangoldwurzel** ('mæŋgəʊldwɜːz'l) *n.* variety of beet used as cattle food

manger ('meɪndʒə) *n.* eating trough in stable

mangle[1] ('mæŋg'l) *n.* 1. machine for rolling clothes *etc.* to remove water —*vt.* 2. press in mangle

mangle[2] ('mæŋg'l) *vt.* mutilate, spoil, hack

mango ('mæŋgəʊ) *n.* 1. tropical fruit 2. tree bearing it (*pl.* -**s**, -**es**)

mangrove ('mæŋgrəʊv, 'mæn-) *n.* tropical tree which grows on muddy banks of estuaries

mania ('meɪnɪə) *n.* 1. madness 2. prevailing craze —'**maniac**, **maniacal** (mə'naɪək'l) *or* **manic** ('mænɪk) *a.* affected by mania —'**maniac** *n. inf.* 1. mad person 2. crazy enthusiast —**manic-depressive** *a. Psych.* 1. pert. to mental disorder characterized by alternation between extreme confidence and deep depression —*n.* 2. person afflicted with this disorder

manicure ('mænɪkjʊə) *n.* 1. treatment and care of fingernails and hands —*vt.* 2. apply such treatment to —'**manicurist** *n.* one doing this professionally

manifest ('mænɪfest) *a.* 1. clearly revealed, visible, undoubted —*vt.* 2. make manifest —*n.* 3. list of cargo for customs —**manifes'tation** *n.* —'**manifestly** *adv.* clearly —**mani'festo** *n.* declaration of policy by political party, government, or movement (*pl.* -**s**, -**es**)

manifold ('mænɪfəʊld) *a.* 1. numerous and

varied —*n.* 2. in internal-combustion engine, pipe with several outlets —*vt.* 3. make copies of (document)

manikin, **manakin**, *or* **mannikin** ('mænɪkɪn) *n. see* MAN

Manila (mə'nɪlə) *n.* 1. fibre used for ropes 2. tough paper

manipulate (mə'nɪpjʊleɪt) *vt.* 1. handle 2. deal with skilfully 3. manage 4. falsify —**manipu'lation** *n.* 1. act of manipulating, working by hand 2. skilled use of hands —**ma'nipulative** *a.* —**ma'nipulator** *n.*

manna ('mænə) *n.* 1. food of Israelites in the wilderness 2. any spiritual or divine nourishment

mannequin ('mænɪkɪn) *n.* woman who models clothes, *esp.* at fashion shows

manner ('mænə) *n.* 1. way thing happens or is done 2. sort, kind 3. custom 4. style —*pl.* 5. social behaviour —'**mannered** *a.* having idiosyncrasies or mannerisms; affected —'**mannerism** *n.* person's distinctive habit, trait —'**mannerly** *a.* polite

manoeuvre *or U.S.* **maneuver** (mə-'nuːvə) *n.* 1. contrived, complicated, perhaps deceptive plan or action 2. skilful management —*vt.* 3. contrive or accomplish with skill or cunning —*vi.* 4. manipulate situations *etc.* in order to gain some end —*v.* 5. (cause to) perform manoeuvres

manor ('mænə) *n.* 1. *Hist.* land belonging to a lord 2. feudal unit of land —**ma'norial** *a.* —**manor house** residence of lord of manor

manqué ('mɒŋkeɪ) *Fr.* unfulfilled; would-be

mansard roof ('mænsɑːd, -səd) roof with break in its slope, lower part being steeper than upper

manse (mæns) *n.* house of minister in some religious denominations

mansion ('mænʃən) *n.* large house

mantel *or* **mantle** ('mænt'l) *n.* structure round fireplace —**mantel shelf** *or* '**mantelpiece** *n.* shelf at top of mantel

mantilla (mæn'tɪlə) *n.* in Spain, (lace) scarf worn as headdress

mantis ('mæntɪs) *n.* genus of insects including the stick insects and leaf insects (*pl.* **mantes** ('mæntiːz))

mantissa (mæn'tɪsə) *n.* fractional part of common logarithm

mantle ('mænt'l) *n.* 1. loose cloak 2. covering 3. incandescent gauze round gas jet —*vt.* 4. cover 5. conceal

mantra ('mæntrə, 'mʌn-) *n. Hinduism* any of those parts of the sacred literature which consist of metrical psalms of praise

manual ('mænjʊəl) *a.* 1. of, or done with, the hands 2. by human labour, not automatic —*n.* 3. handbook 4. textbook 5. organ keyboard

manufacture (mænjʊ'fæktʃə) *vt.* 1. process, make (materials) into finished articles 2. produce (articles) 3. invent, concoct —*n.* 4. making of articles, materials, *esp.* in large quantities 5.

anything produced from raw materials —**manu'facturer** *n.* owner of factory

manumit (mænju'mɪt) *vt.* free from slavery (**-tt-**) —**manu'mission** *n.*

manure (mə'njuə) *vt.* 1. enrich (land) —*n.* 2. dung or chemical fertilizer used to enrich land

manuscript ('mænjuskrɪpt) *n.* 1. book, document, written by hand 2. copy for printing —*a.* 3. handwritten

Manx (mæŋks) *a.* 1. of Isle of Man —*n.* 2. Manx language —**Manx cat** tailless breed of cat —'**Manxman** *n.*

many ('mɛnɪ) *a.* 1. numerous (**more** *comp.*, **most** *sup.*) —*n.* 2. large number

Maoism ('mauɪzəm) *n.* form of Marxism advanced by Mao Tse-Tung in China —'**Maoist** *n./a.*

Maori ('maurɪ, 'maːrɪ) *n.* 1. member of New Zealand native race (*pl.* **-s, -ri**) 2. their language

map (mæp) *n.* 1. flat representation of the earth or some part of it, or of the heavens —*vt.* 2. make a map of 3. (*with* out) plan (**-pp-**)

maple ('meɪp'l) *n.* tree of the sycamore family, a variety of which yields sugar —**maple leaf** leaf of maple tree, national emblem of Canada —**maple syrup** *chiefly US* sweet syrup made from sap of sugar maple

maquis (maː'kiː) *n.* 1. scrubby undergrowth of Mediterranean countries 2. (*oft.* M-) name adopted by French underground resistance movement in WWII

mar (maː) *vt.* spoil, impair (**-rr-**)

Mar. March

marabou ('mærəbuː) *n.* 1. kind of stork 2. its soft white lower tail feathers, used to trim hats *etc.* 3. kind of silk

maraca (mə'rækə) *n.* percussion instrument of gourd containing dried seeds *etc.*

maraschino (mærə'skiːnəu) *n.* liqueur made from cherries

marathon ('mærəθən) *n.* 1. long-distance race 2. endurance contest

maraud (mə'rɔːd) *vi.* 1. make raid for plunder —*v.* 2. pillage —**ma'rauder** *n.*

marble ('maːb'l) *n.* 1. kind of limestone capable of taking polish 2. slab of, sculpture in this 3. small ball used in children's game —'**marbled** *a.* having mottled appearance, like marble —'**marbly** *a.*

marc (maːk) *n.* 1. remains of grapes *etc.* that have been pressed for wine-making 2. brandy distilled from these

marcasite ('maːkəsaɪt) *n.* 1. pale yellow crystallized iron pyrites 2. polished form of steel or white metal used for making jewellery

march¹ (maːtʃ) *vi.* 1. walk with military step 2. go, progress —*vt.* 3. cause to march —*n.* 4. action of marching 5. distance marched in day 6. tune to accompany marching —**marching orders** 1. *Mil.* instructions about march, its destination *etc.* 2. *inf.* any notice of dismissal, *esp.*

from employment —**march-past** *n.* review of troops as they march past a saluting point

march² (maːtʃ) *n.* 1. border or frontier —*vi.* 2. (*oft. with* upon *or* with) share a common border (with)

March (maːtʃ) *n.* third month —**March hare** hare during its breeding season, noted for its excitable behaviour

marchioness ('maːʃənɪs, maːʃə'nɛs) *n.* wife, widow of marquis

Mardi Gras ('maːdɪ 'graː) 1. festival of Shrove Tuesday 2. revelry celebrating this

mare¹ (mɛə) *n.* female horse —**mare's nest** supposed discovery which proves worthless

mare² ('maːreɪ, -rɪ) *n.* (**M-** *when part of name*) huge dry plain on surface of moon (*pl.* **maria** ('maːrɪə))

margarine (maːdʒə'riːn, maːg-) *or* **margarin** ('maːdʒərɪn, 'maːg-, maːdʒə'riːn, maːg-) *n.* butter substitute made from vegetable fats

marge (maːdʒ) *n. inf.* margarine

margin ('maːdʒɪn) *n.* 1. border, edge 2. space round printed page 3. amount allowed beyond what is necessary —'**marginal** *a.* —**marginal seat** *Pol.* constituency in which political party cannot be certain of retaining majority

marguerite (maːgə'riːt) *n.* large daisy

marigold ('mærɪgəuld) *n.* plant with yellow flowers

marijuana (mærɪju'aːnə) *or* **marihuana** (mærɪ'hwaːnə) *n.* dried flowers and leaves of hemp plant, used as narcotic

marimba (mə'rɪmbə) *n.* Latin Amer. percussion instrument resembling a xylophone

marina (mə'riːnə) *n.* mooring facility for yachts and pleasure boats

marinade (mærɪ'neɪd) *n.* seasoned, flavoured liquid used to soak fish, meat *etc.* before cooking —'**marinate** *v.*

marine (mə'riːn) *a.* 1. of the sea or shipping 2. used at, found in sea —*n.* 3. shipping, fleet 4. soldier trained for land or sea combat —**mariner** ('mærɪnə) *n.* sailor

marionette (mærɪə'nɛt) *n.* puppet worked with strings

marital ('mærɪt'l) *a.* relating to a husband or to marriage

maritime ('mærɪtaɪm) *a.* 1. connected with seafaring, naval 2. bordering on the sea 3. (of climate) having small temperature differences between summer and winter —**Maritime Provinces** certain of the Canadian provinces with coasts facing the Gulf of St. Lawrence or Atlantic (*also* '**Maritimes**)

marjoram ('maːdʒərəm) *n.* aromatic herb

mark¹ (maːk) *n.* 1. line, dot, scar *etc.* 2. sign, token 3. inscription 4. letter, number showing evaluation of schoolwork *etc.* 5. indication 6. target —*vt.* 7. make a mark on 8. be distinguishing mark of 9. indicate 10. notice 11. watch 12. assess, *eg* examination paper 13. stay close to (sporting opponent) to hamper his play —**marked** *a.* **1.** obvious, evident, or noticeable **2.** singled out, *esp.* as target of attack **3.** *Linguis.* distinguished by specific feature, as in phonology —**markedly** ('ma:kɪdlɪ) *adv.* —'**marker** *n.* **1.** one who, that which keeps score at games **2.** counter used at card playing *etc.* —'**marksman** *n.* skilled shot

mark² (ma:k) *n.* German coin

market ('ma:kɪt) *n.* **1.** assembly, place for buying and selling **2.** demand for goods **3.** centre for trade —*vt.* **4.** offer or produce for sale —'**marketable** *a.* —'**marketing** *n.* business of selling goods, including advertising, packaging *etc.* —**market garden** *chiefly UK* establishment where fruit and vegetables are grown for sale —**market research** analysis of data relating to demand for product

marl (ma:l) *n.* **1.** clayey soil used as fertilizer —*vt.* **2.** fertilize with it

marline, marlin ('ma:lɪn), *or* **marling** ('ma:lɪŋ) *n.* two-strand cord —'**marline-spike, 'marlinspike** *or* '**marlingspike** *n.* pointed tool, *esp.* for unravelling rope to be spliced

marmalade ('ma:məleɪd) *n.* preserve usu. made of oranges, lemons *etc.*

marmoreal (ma:'mɔːrɪəl) *or* **marmorean** *a.* of or like marble

marmoset ('ma:məzɛt) *n.* small bushy-tailed monkey

marmot ('ma:mət) *n.* burrowing rodent

maroon¹ (mə'ru:n) *n.* **1.** brownish-crimson **2.** firework —*a.* **3.** of the colour

maroon² (mə'ru:n) *vt.* **1.** leave (person) on deserted island or coast **2.** isolate, cut off by any means

marquee (ma:'ki:) *n.* large tent

marquetry *or* **marqueterie** ('ma:kɪtrɪ) *n.* inlaid work, wood mosaic

marquis ('ma:kwɪs, ma:'ki:) *n.* nobleman of rank below duke —**marquisate** ('ma:kwɪzɪt) *n.*

marquise (ma:'ki:z) *n.* **1.** in various countries, marchioness **2.** gemstone cut in pointed oval shape

marrow ('mærəʊ) *n.* **1.** fatty substance inside bones **2.** vital part **3.** vegetable marrow —'**marrowy** *a.* —'**marrowfat** *n.* large pea

marry ('mærɪ) *v.* **1.** take (someone as husband or wife) in marriage **2.** unite closely —*vt.* **3.** join as husband and wife ('**married, 'marrying**) —**marriage** ('mærɪdʒ) *n.* **1.** state of being married **2.** wedding —**marriageable** ('mærɪdʒəb'l) *a.* —**marriage bureau** business concern set up to introduce people wishing to get married —**marriage guidance** advice given to couples who have problems in their married life —**marriage lines** certificate stating that marriage has taken place

Mars (ma:z) *n.* **1.** Roman god of war **2.** planet nearest but one to earth —**Martian**

('ma:ʃən) *n.* **1.** supposed inhabitant of Mars —*a.* **2.** of Mars

Marseillaise (ma:sə'leɪz) *n.* the French national anthem

marsh (ma:ʃ) *n.* low-lying wet land —'**marshy** *a.* —**marsh gas** gas composed of methane produced when vegetation decomposes under water —**marsh'mallow** *n.* spongy sweet orig. made from root of **marsh mallow,** shrubby plant growing near marshes

marshal ('ma:ʃəl) *n.* **1.** high officer of state **2.** US law enforcement officer —*vt.* **3.** arrange in due order **4.** conduct with ceremony (**-ll-**) —**field marshal** military officer of the highest rank —**marshalling yard** railway depot for goods trains —**Marshal of the Royal Air Force** rank in Royal Air Force comparable to that of field marshal in army

marsupial (ma:'sju:pɪəl, -'su:-) *n.* **1.** animal that carries its young in pouch, *eg* kangaroo —*a.* **2.** of marsupials —**mar'supium** *n.* external pouch in most female marsupials (*pl.* **-pia** (-pɪə))

mart (ma:t) *n.* **1.** place of trade **2.** market

Martello tower (ma:'tɛləʊ) round fort, for coast defence

marten ('ma:tɪn) *n.* **1.** weasel-like animal **2.** its fur

martial ('ma:ʃəl) *a.* **1.** relating to war **2.** warlike, brave —**court martial** *see* COURT —**martial law** law enforced by military authorities in times of danger or emergency

martin ('ma:tɪn) *n.* species of swallow

martinet (ma:tɪ'nɛt) *n.* strict disciplinarian

martingale ('ma:tɪŋgeɪl) *n.* strap to prevent horse from throwing up its head

martini (ma:'ti:nɪ) *n.* **1.** cocktail containing *esp.* vermouth, gin, bitters **2.** (**M-**) **R** Italian vermouth (*pl.* **-s**)

Martinmas ('ma:tɪnməs) *n.* feast of St. Martin, Nov. 11th

martlet ('ma:tlɪt) *n.* *Her.* bird without feet

martyr ('ma:tə) *n.* **1.** one put to death for his beliefs **2.** one who suffers in some cause **3.** one in constant suffering —*vt.* **4.** make martyr of —'**martyrdom** *n.* —**martyr'ology** *n.* list, history of Christian martyrs

marvel ('ma:v'l) *vi.* **1.** wonder (**-ll-**) —*n.* **2.** wonderful thing —'**marvellous** *or U.S.* '**marvelous** *a.* **1.** amazing **2.** wonderful

Marxism ('ma:ksɪzəm) *n.* state socialism as conceived by Karl Marx —'**Marxian** *a.* —'**Marxist** *n./a.*

marzipan ('ma:zɪpæn) *n.* paste of almonds, sugar *etc.* used in sweets, cakes *etc.*

Masai ('ma:saɪ, ma:'saɪ) *n.* **1.** member of Negroid pastoral people living chiefly in Kenya and Tanzania (*pl.* **-s, -sai**) **2.** language of this people

masc. masculine

mascara (mæ'ska:rə) *n.* cosmetic for darkening eyelashes

mascot ('mæskət) *n.* thing supposed to bring luck

masculine ('mæskjulin) *a.* 1. relating to males 2. manly 3. of the grammatical gender to which names of males belong

maser ('meizə) *n.* device for amplifying microwaves

mash (mæʃ) *n.* 1. meal mixed with warm water 2. warm food for horses *etc.* 3. *inf.* mashed potatoes —*vt.* 4. make into a mash 5. crush into soft mass or pulp

mashie *or* **mashy** ('mæʃı) *n. Golf* iron club with deep sloping blade for lob shots

mask (mɑːsk) *n.* 1. covering for face 2. *Surg.* covering for nose and mouth 3. disguise, pretence —*vt.* 4. cover with mask 5. hide, disguise —**masking tape** adhesive tape used to protect surfaces surrounding an area to be painted

masochism ('mæsəkızəm) *n.* abnormal condition where pleasure (*esp.* sexual) is derived from pain, humiliation *etc.* —'**masochist** *n.* —**maso'chistic** *a.*

mason ('meis'n) *n.* 1. worker in stone 2. (M-) Freemason —**Masonic** (mə'sɒnık) *a.* of Freemasonry —'**masonry** *n.* 1. stonework 2. (M-) Freemasonry

masque *or* **mask** (mɑːsk) *n. Hist.* form of theatrical performance —**masquerade** (mæskə'reıd) *n.* 1. masked ball —*vi.* 2. appear in disguise

mass (mæs) *n.* 1. quantity of matter 2. dense collection of this 3. large quantity or number —*v.* 4. form into a mass —'**massive** *a.* large and heavy —'**massy** *a.* solid, weighty —**mass market** market for mass-produced goods —**mass-market** *a.* of mass market —**mass media** means of communication to large numbers of people, such as television, newspapers *etc.* —**mass-produce** *vt.* produce (standardized articles) in large quantities —**mass production** —**mass spectrometer** instrument in which ions are separated by electric or magnetic fields according to their ratios of charge to mass (*also* '**spectroscope**) —**the masses** the populace

Mass (mæs, mɑːs) *n.* service of the Eucharist, *esp.* in R.C. Church

massacre ('mæsəkə) *n.* 1. indiscriminate, large-scale killing, *esp.* of unresisting people —*vt.* 2. kill indiscriminately

massage ('mæsɑːʒ, -sɑːdʒ) *n.* 1. rubbing and kneading of muscles *etc.* as curative treatment —*vt.* 2. apply this treatment to 3. manipulate (figures *etc.*) in order to deceive —**masseur** (mæ'sɜː) *n.* one who practises massage (**masseuse** (mæ'sɜːz) *fem.*)

massé *or* **massé shot** ('mæsı) *n. Billiards* stroke with cue upright

massif ('mæsiːf) *n.* compact group of mountains

mast¹ (mɑːst) *n.* 1. pole for supporting ship's sails 2. tall upright support for aerial *etc.* —'**masthead** *n.* 1. *Naut.* head of mast 2. name of newspaper, its proprietors, staff *etc.*, printed at top of front page —*vt.* 3. raise (sail) to masthead

mast² (mɑːst) *n.* fruit of beech, oak *etc.* used as pig fodder

mastectomy (mæ'stektəmı) *n.* surgical removal of a breast

master ('mɑːstə) *n.* 1. one in control 2. employer 3. head of household 4. owner 5. document *etc.* from which copies are made 6. captain of merchant ship 7. expert 8. great artist 9. teacher —*vt.* 10. overcome 11. acquire knowledge of or skill in —'**masterful** *a.* imperious, domineering —'**masterly** *a.* showing great competence —'**mastery** *n.* 1. full understanding 2. expertise 3. authority 4. victory —**master aircrew** warrant officer rank in Royal Air Force —**master key** key that opens many different locks —'**mastermind** *vt.* 1. plan, direct —*n.* 2. very intelligent person, *esp.* one who directs an undertaking —'**masterpiece** *n.* outstanding work —'**masterstroke** *n.* outstanding piece of strategy *etc.* —**Master of Arts** (*or* **Science** *etc.*) 1. degree given by university usu. to postgraduate 2. person who has this degree —**master of ceremonies** person who presides over public ceremony *etc.*, introducing events *etc.*

mastic ('mæstık) *n.* 1. gum got from certain trees 2. puttylike substance

masticate ('mæstıkeıt) *v.* chew —**masti'cation** *n.* —'**masticatory** *a.*

mastiff ('mæstıf) *n.* large dog

mastitis (mæ'staıtıs) *n.* inflammation of breast or udder

mastodon ('mæstədɒn) *n.* extinct elephantlike mammal

mastoid ('mæstɔıd) *a.* 1. nipple-shaped —*n.* 2. prominence on bone behind human ear —**mastoi'ditis** *n.* inflammation of this area

masturbate ('mæstəbeıt) *v.* stimulate (one's own or one's partner's) genital organs —**mastur'bation** *n.*

mat¹ (mæt) *n.* 1. small rug 2. piece of fabric to protect another surface or to wipe feet on *etc.* 3. thick tangled mass —*v.* 4. form into such mass (**-tt-**) —**on the mat** *inf.* called up for reprimand

mat² *or* **matt** (mæt) *a.* dull, lustreless, not shiny

matador ('mætədɔː) *n.* man who slays bull in bullfights

match¹ (mætʃ) *n.* 1. contest, game 2. equal 3. person, thing exactly corresponding to another 4. marriage 5. person regarded as eligible for marriage —*vt.* 6. get something corresponding to (colour, pattern *etc.*) 7. oppose, put in competition with 8. join (in marriage) —*vi.* 9. correspond —'**matchless** *a.* unequalled —'**matchboard** *n.* long, flimsy board tongued and grooved for lining work —'**matchmaker** *n.* one who schemes to bring about a marriage —**match play** *Golf* scoring according to number of holes won and lost

match² (mætʃ) *n.* 1. small stick with head

which ignites when rubbed **2.** fuse —'**matchbox** n. —'**matchlock** n. early musket fired by fuse —'**matchwood** n. small splinters

mate¹ (meɪt) n. **1.** comrade **2.** husband, wife **3.** one of pair **4.** officer in merchant ship **5.** inf. common Brit. and Aust. term of address, esp. between males —v. **6.** marry or join in marriage **7.** pair —'**matey** a. inf. friendly, sociable

mate² (meɪt) n./vt. Chess checkmate

mater ('meɪtə) n. sl. UK mother

material (mə'tɪərɪəl) n. **1.** substance from which thing is made **2.** cloth, fabric —a. **3.** of matter or body **4.** affecting physical wellbeing **5.** unspiritual **6.** important, essential —**ma'terialism** n. **1.** excessive interest in, desire for money and possessions **2.** doctrine that nothing but matter exists, denying independent existence of spirit —**ma'terialist** a./n. —**material'istic** a. —**ma'terialize** or -**ise** vi. **1.** come into existence or view —vt. **2.** make material —**ma'terially** adv. appreciably

materiel or **matériel** (mətɪərɪ'el) n. equipment of organization, esp. of military force

maternal (mə'tɜːnʲl) a. of, related through mother —**ma'ternity** n. motherhood

mathematics (mæθə'mætɪks) pl.n. (with sing. v.) science of number, quantity, shape and space —**mathe'matical** a. —**mathe'matically** adv. —**mathema'tician** n.

maths (mæθs) n. inf. mathematics

matinée ('mætɪneɪ) n. afternoon performance in theatre —**matinée coat** short coat for baby

matins or **mattins** ('mætɪnz) pl.n. morning prayers

matriarch ('meɪtrɪɑːk) n. mother as head and ruler of family —'**matriarchal** a. —'**matriarchy** n. society with matriarchal government and descent reckoned in female line

matricide ('mætrɪsaɪd, 'meɪ-) n. **1.** the crime of killing one's mother **2.** one who does this

matriculate (mə'trɪkjuleɪt) v. enrol, be enrolled in a college or university —**matricu'lation** n.

matrimony ('mætrɪmənɪ) n. marriage —**matri'monial** a.

matrix ('meɪtrɪks, 'mæ-) n. **1.** substance, situation in which something originates, takes form, or is enclosed **2.** mould for casting **3.** Maths. rectangular array of elements set out in rows and columns (pl. **matrices** ('meɪtrɪsiːz, 'mæ-))

matron ('meɪtrən) n. **1.** married woman **2.** former name for nursing officer **3.** woman who superintends domestic arrangements of public institution, boarding school etc. —'**matronly** a. sedate —**matron of honour** married woman serving as chief attendant to bride

matt (mæt) a. see MAT²

Matt. Bible Matthew

matter ('mætə) n. **1.** substance of which thing is made **2.** physical or bodily substance **3.** affair, business **4.** cause of trouble **5.** substance of book etc. **6.** pus —vi. **7.** be of importance, signify —**matter-of-fact** a. unimaginative or emotionless —**matter of fact** fact that is undeniably true —**as a matter of fact** actually; in fact

mattock ('mætək) n. tool like pick with ends of blades flattened for cutting, hoeing

mattress ('mætrɪs) n. **1.** stuffed flat case, often with springs, or foam rubber pad, used as part of bed **2.** underlay

mature (mə'tjʊə, -'tʃʊə) a. **1.** ripe, completely developed **2.** grown-up —v. **3.** bring, come to maturity —vi. **4.** (of bill) fall due —**matu'ration** n. process of maturing —**ma'turity** n. full development

matutinal (mætju'taɪnʲl) a. of, occurring in, or during morning

maudlin ('mɔːdlɪn) a. weakly or tearfully sentimental

maul (mɔːl) vt. **1.** handle roughly **2.** beat; bruise —n. **3.** heavy wooden hammer **4.** Rugby loose scrum

maulstick ('mɔːlstɪk) or **mahlstick** n. light stick with ball at one end, held in left hand to support right hand while painting

maunder ('mɔːndə) vi. talk, act aimlessly, dreamily

maundy ('mɔːndɪ) n. **1.** foot-washing ceremony on Thursday before Easter **2.** royal alms given on that day

mausoleum (mɔːsə'lɪəm) n. stately building as a tomb (pl. **-s, -lea** (-'lɪə))

mauve (məʊv) a./n. (of) pale purple colour

maverick ('mævərɪk) n. **1.** US unbranded steer, stray cow **2.** independent, unorthodox person

maw (mɔː) n. stomach, crop

mawkish ('mɔːkɪʃ) a. weakly sentimental, maudlin **2.** sickly

max. maximum

maxi ('mæksɪ) a. **1.** (of garment) reaching ankle **2.** large, considerable

maxilla (mæk'sɪlə) n. jawbone (pl. **-lae** (-liː)) —**max'illary** a. of the jaw

maxim ('mæksɪm) n. **1.** general truth, proverb **2.** rule of conduct, principle

maximum ('mæksɪməm) n. **1.** greatest size or number **2.** highest point (pl. **-s, -ma** (-mə)) —a. **3.** greatest —'**maximize** or -**ise** vt.

maxwell ('mækswəl) n. cgs unit of magnetic flux

may (meɪ) v. aux. expresses possibility, permission, opportunity etc. (**might** pt.) —**maybe** ('meɪbiː) adv. **1.** perhaps **2.** possibly

May (meɪ) n. **1.** fifth month **2.** (**m-**) hawthorn or its flowers —'**mayfly** n. short-lived flying insect, found near water —'**maypole** n. pole set up for dancing round on **May Day**, first day of May —**May queen** girl chosen to preside over May-Day celebrations

Maya ('maɪə) n. **1.** member of Amer.

Indian people of Yucatan, Belize and N Guatemala (*pl.* **-ya**, **-s**) 2. language of this people

Mayday ('meɪdeɪ) *n.* international radio-telephone distress signal

mayhap ('meɪhæp) *adv. obs.* perhaps

mayhem *or* **maihem** ('meɪhɛm) *n.* 1. depriving person by violence of limb, member or organ, or causing mutilation of body 2. any violent destruction 3. confusion

mayonnaise (meɪə'neɪz) *n.* creamy sauce of egg yolks, oil *etc.*, *esp.* for salads

mayor (mɛə) *n.* head of municipality —'**mayoral** *a.* —'**mayoralty** *n.* (time of) office of mayor —'**mayoress** *n.* 1. mayor's wife 2. lady mayor

maze (meɪz) *n.* 1. labyrinth 2. network of paths, lines 3. state of confusion

mazurka *or* **mazourka** (mə'zɜːkə) *n.* 1. lively Polish dance like polka 2. music for it

MB Manitoba

M.B. Bachelor of Medicine

M.B.E. Member of the Order of the British Empire

M.C. 1. Master of Ceremonies 2. Military Cross

M.C.C. Marylebone Cricket Club

M.Ch. Master of Surgery

Md *Chem.* mendelevium

MD Maryland

M.D. Doctor of Medicine

me[1] (miː; *unstressed* mɪ) *pron.* objective case of pronoun I

me[2] (miː) *n. Mus. see* MI

ME Maine

ME *or* **M.E.** Middle English

M.E. 1. Marine Engineer 2. Mechanical Engineer 3. Methodist Episcopal 4. Mining Engineer 5. in titles, Most Excellent

mea culpa ('meɪɑ: 'kʊlpɑ:) *Lat.* my fault

mead[1] (miːd) *n.* alcoholic drink made from honey

mead[2] (miːd) *n. obs., poet.* meadow

meadow ('mɛdəʊ) *n.* piece of grassland —'**meadowsweet** *n.* plant with dense heads of small fragrant flowers

meagre *or U.S.* **meager** ('miːgə) *a.* 1. lean, thin 2. scanty, insufficient

meal[1] (miːl) *n.* 1. occasion when food is served and eaten 2. the food —**meals-on-wheels** *n.* UK service taking hot meals to elderly, infirm *etc.* —**meal ticket** 1. US luncheon voucher 2. *sl.* person, situation *etc.* providing source of livelihood or income

meal[2] (miːl) *n.* grain ground to powder —'**mealy** *a.* —**mealy-mouthed** *a.* euphemistic, insincere in what one says

mealie ('miːlɪ) *n.* SA maize

mean[1] (miːn) *vt.* 1. intend 2. signify —*vi.* 3. have the intention of behaving (**meant** *pt./pp.*, '**meaning** *pr.p.*) —'**meaning** *n.* 1. sense, significance —*a.* 2. expressive —'**meaningful** *a.* of great meaning or significance —'**meaningless** *a.*

mean[2] (miːn) *a.* 1. ungenerous, petty 2. miserly, niggardly 3. unpleasant 4. callous 5. shabby 6. ashamed —'**meanly** *adv.* —'**meanness** *n.*

mean[3] (miːn) *n.* 1. thing which is intermediate 2. middle point —*pl.* 3. that by which thing is done 4. money 5. resources —*a.* 6. intermediate in time, quality *etc.* 7. average —**means test** enquiry into person's means to decide eligibility for pension, grant *etc.* —**meantime** *or* '**meanwhile** *adv./n.* (during) time between one happening and another —**by all means** certainly —**by no means** not at all

meander (mɪ'ændə) *vi.* 1. flow windingly 2. wander aimlessly

meant (mɛnt) *pt./pp. of* MEAN[1]

measles ('miːzəlz) *n.* infectious disease producing rash of red spots —'**measly** *a.* 1. *inf.* poor, wretched, stingy 2. of measles

measure ('mɛʒə) *n.* 1. size, quantity 2. vessel, rod, line *etc.* for ascertaining size or quantity 3. unit of size or quantity 4. course, plan of action 5. law 6. poetical rhythm 7. musical time 8. *Poet.* tune 9. *obs.* dance —*vt.* 10. ascertain size, quantity of 11. indicate measurement of 12. estimate 13. bring into competition against —*vi.* 14. make measurement(s) 15. be (so much) in size or quantity —'**measurable** *a.* —'**measured** *a.* 1. determined by measure 2. steady 3. rhythmical 4. carefully considered —'**measurement** *n.* 1. measuring 2. size —*pl.* 3. dimensions

meat (miːt) *n.* 1. animal flesh as food 2. food —'**meaty** *a.* 1. (tasting) of, like meat 2. brawny 3. full of import or interest

Mecca ('mɛkə) *n.* 1. holy city of Islam 2. place that attracts visitors

mech. 1. mechanical 2. mechanics 3. mechanism

mechanic (mɪ'kænɪk) *n.* 1. one employed in working with machinery 2. skilled workman —*pl.* 3. scientific theory of motion —me'**chanical** *a.* 1. concerned with machines or operation of them 2. worked, produced (as though) by machine 3. acting without thought —me'**chanically** *adv.* —mecha'**nician** *n.* —**mechanical drawing** *see* technical drawing *at* TECHNICAL

mechanism ('mɛkənɪzəm) *n.* 1. structure of machine 2. piece of machinery —mechani'**zation** *or* **-i'sation** *n.* —'**mechanize** *or* **-ise** *vt.* 1. equip with machinery 2. make mechanical, automatic 3. *Mil.* equip with armoured vehicles —'**mechanized** *or* **-ised** *a.*

med. 1. medical 2. medicine 3. medieval 4. medium

Med (mɛd) *n. inf.* Mediterranean region

M.Ed. Master of Education

medal ('mɛdʼl) *n.* piece of metal with inscription *etc.* used as reward or memento —me'**dallion** *n.* 1. large medal 2. any of various things like this in decorative work —'**medallist** *or U.S.*

'medalist n. **1.** winner of a medal **2.** maker of medals

meddle ('mɛd'l) vi. interfere, busy oneself unnecessarily —'**meddlesome** a.

media ('miːdɪə) n., pl. of MEDIUM, used esp. of the mass media, radio, television etc. —**media event** event staged for or exploited by the mass media

mediaeval (mɛdɪ'iːv'l) a. see MEDIEVAL

medial ('miːdɪəl) a. **1.** in the middle **2.** pert. to a mean or average —'**median** a./n. middle (point or line)

mediate ('miːdɪeɪt) vi. **1.** intervene to reconcile —vt. **2.** bring about by mediation —a. ('miːdɪɪt) **3.** depending on mediation —**medi'ation** n. **1.** intervention on behalf of another **2.** act of going between —'**mediator** n.

medicine ('mɛdɪsɪn, 'mɛdsɪn) n. **1.** drug or remedy for treating disease **2.** science of preventing, diagnosing, alleviating, or curing disease —'**medic** n. inf. **1.** doctor **2.** medical orderly **3.** medical student —'**medical** a. —'**medically** adv. —**me-'dicament** n. remedy —'**medicate** vt. impregnate with medicinal substances —**medi'cation** n. —'**medicative** a. healing —**me'dicinal** a. curative —'**medico** n. inf. **1.** doctor **2.** medical student (pl. -s) —**medical certificate** doctor's certificate giving evidence of person's fitness or unfitness for work etc. —**medicine ball** heavy ball for physical training —**medicine man** witch doctor

medieval or **mediaeval** (mɛdɪ'iːv'l) a. of Middle Ages —**medi'evalism** or **medi-'aevalism** n. **1.** spirit of Middle Ages **2.** cult of medieval ideals —**medi'evalist** or **medi'aevalist** n. student of the Middle Ages —**Medieval Greek** Greek language from 7th cent. A.D.–1204 —**Medieval Latin** Latin language as used throughout Europe in Middle Ages

mediocre (miːdɪ'əʊkə) a. **1.** neither bad nor good, ordinary, middling **2.** second-rate —**mediocrity** (miːdɪ'ɒkrɪtɪ, mɛd-) n.

meditate ('mɛdɪteɪt) vi. **1.** be occupied in thought **2.** reflect deeply on spiritual matters —**medi'tation** n. **1.** thought **2.** absorption in thought **3.** religious contemplation —'**meditative** a. **1.** thoughtful **2.** reflective —'**meditatively** adv.

Mediterranean (mɛdɪtə'reɪnɪən) n. **1.** short for **Mediterranean Sea**, sea between S Europe, N Afr., and SW Asia **2.** native or inhabitant of Mediterranean country —a. **3.** of Mediterranean Sea

medium ('miːdɪəm) a. **1.** between two qualities, degrees etc., average —n. **2.** middle quality, degree **3.** intermediate substance conveying force **4.** means, agency of communicating news etc. to public, as radio, newspapers etc. **5.** person through whom communication can supposedly be held with spirit world **6.** surroundings, environment (pl. -s, 'media) —**medium waves** Rad. waves between 100 and 1000 metres

medlar ('mɛdlə) n. **1.** tree with fruit like small apple **2.** the fruit, eaten when decayed

medley ('mɛdlɪ) n. miscellaneous mixture (pl. -s)

medulla (mɪ'dʌlə) n. **1.** marrow **2.** pith **3.** inner tissue —**me'dullary** a.

Medusa (mɪ'djuːzə) n. **1.** Myth. Gorgon whose head turned beholders into stone **2.** (m-) jellyfish (pl. -sae (-ziː))

meek (miːk) a. submissive, humble —'**meekly** adv. —'**meekness** n.

meerkat ('mɪəkæt) n. S Afr. mongoose

meerschaum ('mɪəʃəm) n. **1.** white substance like clay **2.** tobacco pipe bowl made of this

meet[1] (miːt) vt. **1.** come face to face with, encounter **2.** satisfy **3.** pay —vi. **4.** come face to face **5.** converge at specified point **6.** assemble **7.** come into contact (met pt./pp.) —n. **8.** meeting, esp. for sports —'**meeting** n. **1.** assembly **2.** encounter

meet[2] (miːt) a. obs. fit, suitable

mega- (comb. form) **1.** denoting 10⁶, as in megawatt **2.** in computer technology, denoting 2²⁰ (1 048 576), as in megabyte **3.** large, great, as in megalith

megadeath ('mɛgədɛθ) n. death of a million people, esp. in nuclear war

megahertz ('mɛgəhɜːts) n. one million hertz (pl. 'megahertz)

megalith ('mɛgəlɪθ) n. great stone —**mega'lithic** a.

megalomania (mɛgələʊ'meɪnɪə) n. desire for, delusions of grandeur, power etc. —**megalo'maniac** a./n.

megalopolis (mɛgə'lɒpəlɪs) n. urban complex, usu. comprising several towns —**megalopolitan** (mɛgələ'pɒlɪt'n) a./n.

megaphone ('mɛgəfəʊn) n. cone-shaped instrument to amplify voice

megaton ('mɛgətʌn) n. **1.** one million tons **2.** explosive power of 1 000 000 tons of TNT

megohm ('mɛgəʊm) n. Elec. one million ohms

meiosis (maɪ'əʊsɪs) n. type of cell division in which nucleus divides into four daughter nuclei, each containing half chromosome number of parent nucleus (pl. -ses (-siːz)) —**meiotic** (maɪ'ɒtɪk) a.

melamine ('mɛləmiːn) n. colourless crystalline compound used in making synthetic resins —**melamine resin** resilient kind of plastic

melancholy ('mɛlənkəlɪ) n. **1.** sadness, dejection, gloom —a. **2.** gloomy, dejected —**melancholia** (mɛlən'kəʊlɪə) n. mental disease accompanied by depression —**melancholic** ('mɛlənkɒlɪk) n./a.

Melanesian (mɛlə'niːzɪən) a. **1.** of Melanesia, its people, or their languages —n. **2.** native or inhabitant of Melanesia **3.** group or branch of languages spoken in Melanesia

mélange (me'lɑ̃ːʒ) Fr. mixture

melanin ('mɛlənɪn) n. dark pigment found in hair, skin etc. of man

Melba toast ('mɛlbə) very thin crisp toast

melee or **mêlée** ('mɛleɪ) n. confused, noisy fight or crowd

meliorate ('miːlɪəreɪt) v. improve —**melio'ration** n. —'**meliorism** n. doctrine that the world may be improved by human effort —'**meliorist** n.

mellifluous (mɪ'lɪfluəs) or **mellifluent** a. (of sound) smooth, sweet —**mel'lifluence** n.

mellow ('mɛləʊ) a. 1. ripe 2. softened by age, experience 3. soft, not harsh 4. genial, gay —v. 5. make, become mellow

melodeon or **melodion** (mɪ'ləʊdɪən) n. Mus. 1. small accordion 2. keyboard instrument similar to harmonium

melodrama ('mɛlədraːmə) n. 1. play full of sensational and startling situations, often highly emotional 2. overdramatic behaviour, emotion —**melodra'matic** a.

melody ('mɛlədɪ) n. 1. series of musical notes which make tune 2. sweet sound —**melodic** (mɪ'lɒdɪk) a. 1. of or relating to melody 2. of or relating to part in piece of music —**me'lodious** a. 1. pleasing to the ear 2. tuneful —'**melodist** n. 1. singer 2. composer

melon ('mɛlən) n. large, fleshy, juicy fruit

melt (mɛlt) v. 1. (cause to) become liquid by heat 2. dissolve 3. soften 4. (cause to) waste away 5. blend —vi. 6. disappear ('**melted** pt./pp., '**molten** pp.) —'**melting** a. 1. softening 2. languishing 3. tender —'**meltdown** n. (in nuclear reactor) melting of fuel rods as result of defect in cooling system, with possible escape of radiation —**melting point** temperature at which solid turns into liquid —'**meltwater** n. melted snow or ice

mem. 1. member 2. memoir 3. memorandum 4. memorial

member ('mɛmbə) n. 1. any of individuals making up body or society 2. limb 3. any part of complex whole —'**membership** n. —**Member of Parliament** member of House of Commons or similar legislative body

membrane ('mɛmbreɪn) n. thin flexible tissue in plant or animal body

memento (mɪ'mɛntəʊ) n. thing serving to remind, souvenir (pl. **-s, -es**) —**memento mori** ('mɔːriː) object intended to remind people of death

memo ('mɛməʊ, 'miːməʊ) memorandum

memoir ('mɛmwɑː) n. 1. autobiography, personal history or biography 2. record of events

memory ('mɛmərɪ) n. 1. faculty of recollecting, recalling to mind 2. recollection 3. thing remembered 4. length of time one can remember 5. commemoration 6. part or faculty of computer which stores information —**memorabilia** (mɛmərə-'bɪlɪə) pl.n. memorable events or things (sing. **-rabile** (-'ræbɪlɪ)) —'**memorable** a. worthy of remembrance, noteworthy —'**memorably** adv. —**memo'randum** n. 1. note to help the memory etc. 2. informal letter 3. note of contract (pl. **-s, -da** (-də))

—**me'morial** a. 1. of, preserving memory —n. 2. thing, esp. a monument, which serves to keep in memory —**me'morialist** n. —**me'morialize** or **-ise** vt. commemorate —'**memorize** or **-ise** vt. commit to memory

memsahib ('mɛmsɑːɪb, -hɪb) n. formerly in India, term of respect used of European married woman

men (mɛn) n., pl. of MAN

menace ('mɛnɪs) n. 1. threat —v. 2. threaten

ménage (meɪ'nɑːʒ) n. persons of a household —**ménage à trois** (mena:ʒ a 'trwa) Fr. sexual arrangement involving married couple and lover of one of them (pl. **ménages à trois** (mena:ʒ a 'trwa))

menagerie (mɪ'nædʒərɪ) n. exhibition, collection of wild animals

mend (mɛnd) vt. 1. repair, patch 2. reform, correct, put right —vi. 3. improve, esp. in health —n. 4. repaired breakage, hole —**on the mend** regaining health

mendacious (mɛn'deɪʃəs) a. untruthful —**mendacity** (mɛn'dæsɪtɪ) n. (tendency to) untruthfulness

mendelevium (mɛndɪ'liːvɪəm) n. transuranic element artificially produced by bombardment of einsteinium

mendicant ('mɛndɪkənt) a. 1. begging —n. 2. beggar —'**mendicancy** or **men'dicity** n. begging

menhir ('mɛnhɪə) n. single, upright monumental stone, monolith

menial ('miːnɪəl) a. 1. of work requiring little skill 2. of household duties or servants 3. servile —n. 4. servant 5. servile person

meninges (mɪ'nɪndʒiːz) pl.n. three membranes that envelop brain and spinal cord (sing. **meninx** ('miːnɪŋks)) —**me'ningeal** a. —**menin'gitis** n. inflammation of the membranes of the brain

meniscus (mɪ'nɪskəs) n. 1. curved surface of liquid 2. curved lens

menopause ('mɛnəʊpɔːz) n. final cessation of menstruation

menorah (mɪ'nɔːrə) n. Judaism seven-branched candelabrum used in ceremonies

menses ('mɛnsiːz) n. 1. menstruation 2. period of time during which one menstruation occurs 3. matter discharged during menstruation (pl. '**menses**)

menstruation (mɛnstru'eɪʃən) n. approximately monthly discharge of blood and cellular debris from womb of nonpregnant woman —'**menstrual** a. —'**menstruate** vi.

mensuration (mɛnʃə'reɪʃən) n. measuring, esp. of areas

-ment (comb. form) 1. state; condition; quality, as in enjoyment 2. result or product of action, as in embankment 3. process; action, as in management

mental ('mɛntl) a. 1. of, done by the mind 2. inf. feeble-minded, mad —**men'tality** n. state or quality of mind —'**mentally** adv.

menthol ('mɛnθɒl) n. organic compound found in peppermint, used medicinally

mention ('mɛnʃən) vt. 1. refer to briefly, speak of —n. 2. acknowledgment 3. reference to or remark about person or thing —**'mentionable** a. fit or suitable to be mentioned

mentor ('mɛntɔː) n. wise, trusted adviser, guide

menu ('mɛnjuː) n. list of dishes to be served, or from which to order

meow, miaou, miaow (mɪ'aʊ, mjaʊ), or **miaul** (mɪ'aʊl, mjaʊl) vi. 1. (of cat) make characteristic crying sound —interj. 2. imitation of this sound

M.E.P. Member of European Parliament

mercantile ('mɜːkəntaɪl) a. of, engaged in trade, commerce

mercenary ('mɜːsɪnərɪ, -sɪnrɪ) a. 1. influenced by greed 2. working merely for reward —n. 3. hired soldier

mercer ('mɜːsə) n. esp. formerly, dealer in fabrics —**'mercery** n. his trade, goods

mercerize or **-ise** ('mɜːsəraɪz) vt. give lustre to (cotton fabrics) by treating with chemicals —**'mercerized** or **-ised** a.

merchant ('mɜːtʃənt) n. 1. one engaged in trade 2. wholesale trader —**merchandise** ('mɜːtʃəndaɪs, -daɪz) n. his wares —**merchant bank UK** financial institution engaged in accepting foreign bills and underwriting new security issues —**'merchantman** n. trading ship —**merchant navy** ships engaged in a nation's commerce

mercury ('mɜːkjʊrɪ) n. 1. silvery metal, liquid at ordinary temperature, quicksilver 2. (M-) Roman myth. messenger of the gods 3. (M-) planet nearest to sun —**mer'curial** a. 1. relating to, containing mercury 2. lively, changeable

mercy ('mɜːsɪ) n. refraining from infliction of suffering by one who has right, power to inflict it, compassion —**'merciful** a. —**'merciless** a. —**mercy killing** see EUTHANASIA

mere[1] (mɪə) a. 1. only 2. not more than 3. nothing but —**'merely** adv.

mere[2] (mɪə) n. obs. lake

meretricious (mɛrɪ'trɪʃəs) a. 1. superficially or garishly attractive 2. insincere

merganser (mɜː'gænsə) n. large, crested diving duck

merge (mɜːdʒ) v. (cause to) lose identity or be absorbed —**'merger** n. 1. combination of business firms into one 2. absorption into something greater

meridian (mə'rɪdɪən) n. 1. circle of the earth passing through poles 2. imaginary circle in sky passing through celestial poles 3. highest point reached by star etc. 4. period of greatest splendour —a. 5. of meridian 6. at peak of something

meringue (mə'ræŋ) n. 1. baked mixture of white of eggs and sugar 2. cake of this

merino (mə'riːnəʊ) n. 1. breed of sheep originating in Spain (pl. -s) 2. long, fine wool of this sheep 3. yarn or cloth made from this wool

merit ('mɛrɪt) n. 1. excellence, worth 2. quality of deserving reward —pl. 3. excellence —vt. 4. deserve —**meri'tocracy** n. 1. rule by persons chosen for their superior talents or intellect 2. persons constituting such group —**meri'torious** a. deserving praise

merlin ('mɜːlɪn) n. small falcon

mermaid ('mɜːmeɪd) n. imaginary sea creature with upper part of woman and lower part of fish

merry ('mɛrɪ) a. joyous, cheerful —**'merrily** adv. —**'merriment** n. —**merry-go-round** n. roundabout

mésalliance (me'zælɪəns) n. marriage with person of lower social status

mescaline or **mescalin** ('mɛskəliːn, -lɪn) n. hallucinogenic drug derived from **mescal buttons**, button-like tubercles of the mescal cactus of Mexico

mesdames ('meɪdæm) n., pl. of MADAME

mesdemoiselles (meɪdmwɑ'zɛl) n., pl. of MADEMOISELLE

mesembryanthemum (mɪzɛmbrɪ'ænθɪməm) n. low-growing plant with daisy-like flowers of various colours

mesh (mɛʃ) n. 1. (one of the open spaces of, or wires etc. forming) network, net —v. 2. entangle, become entangled 3. (of gears) engage —vi. 4. coordinate

mesmerism ('mɛzmərɪzəm) n. former term for HYPNOTISM —**mes'meric** a. —**'mesmerist** n. —**'mesmerize** or **-ise** vt. 1. hypnotize 2. fascinate, hold spellbound

meso- or before vowel **mes-** (comb. form) middle or intermediate, as in mesomorph

Mesolithic (mɛsəʊ'lɪθɪk) n. 1. period between Palaeolithic and Neolithic —a. 2. of or relating to Mesolithic

meson ('miːzɒn) n. elementary atomic particle

Mesozoic (mɛsəʊ'zəʊɪk) a. of, denoting, or relating to era of geological time that began 225 000 000 years ago and lasted about 155 000 000 years

mess (mɛs) n. 1. untidy confusion 2. trouble, difficulty 3. group in armed services who regularly eat together 4. place where they eat —vi. 5. make mess 6. Mil. eat in a mess —vt. 7. muddle —**'messy** a. —**mess about** or **around** potter about

message ('mɛsɪdʒ) n. 1. communication sent 2. meaning, moral 3. errand —**'messenger** n. bearer of message

Messiah (mɪ'saɪə) n. 1. Jews' promised deliverer 2. Christ —**Messianic** (mɛsɪ'ænɪk) a.

messieurs ('mɛsəz) n., pl. of MONSIEUR

Messrs. ('mɛsəz) n., pl. of MR.

met (mɛt) pt./pp. of MEET[1]

Met (mɛt) a./n. inf. Meteorological (Office in London)

met. 1. meteorological 2. meteorology 3. metropolitan

meta- or sometimes before vowel **met-**

(comb. form) change, as in *metamorphose, metathesis*

metabolism (mɪ'tæbəlɪzəm) *n.* chemical process of living body —**meta'bolic** *a.* —**me'tabolize** *or* **-ise** *v.*

metacarpus (metə'kɑːpəs) *n.* **1.** skeleton of hand between wrist and fingers **2.** corresponding bones in other vertebrates *(pl.* **-pi** *(-*paɪ*))* —**meta'carpal** *a./n.*

metal ('metˀl) *n.* **1.** mineral substance, opaque, fusible and malleable, capable of conducting heat and electricity **2.** broken stone for macadamized roads —**me'tallic** *a.* —**'metalloid** *n.* **1.** nonmetallic element that has some of properties of metal —*a.* *(also* **metal'loidal)** **2.** of or being metalloid **3.** resembling metal —**metal'lurgic** *or* **metal'lurgical** *a.* —**me'tallurgist** *n.* —**me'tallurgy** *n.* scientific study of extracting, refining metals, and their structure and properties

metal. *or* **metall.** **1.** metallurgical **2.** metallurgy

metamorphosis (metə'mɔːfəsɪs) *n.* change of shape, character *etc.* *(pl.* **-phoses** *(-*fəsiːz*))* —**meta'morphic** *a.* *(esp.* of rocks) changed in texture, structure by heat, pressure *etc.* —**meta'morphose** *v.* transform

metaphor ('metəfə, -fɔː) *n.* **1.** figure of speech in which term is transferred to something it does not literally apply to **2.** instance of this —**meta'phorical** *a.* figurative —**meta'phorically** *adv.*

metaphysics (metə'fɪzɪks) *pl.n.* *(with sing. v.)* branch of philosophy concerned with being and knowing —**meta'physical** *a.* —**metaphy'sician** *n.*

metastasis (mɪ'tæstəsɪs) *n.* *Pathol.* spreading of disease, *esp.* cancer cells, from one part of body to another *(pl.* **-ses** *(-*siːz*))* —**metastatic** (metə'stætɪk) *a.*

metatarsus (metə'tɑːsəs) *n.* **1.** skeleton of foot between toes and ankle **2.** corresponding bones in other vertebrates *(pl.* **-si** *(-*saɪ*))* —**meta'tarsal** *a./n.*

metathesis (mɪ'tæθəsɪs) *n.* transposition, *esp.* of letters in word, *eg* Old English *bridd* gives modern *bird* *(pl.* **-eses** *(-*əsiːz*))*

metazoan (metə'zəʊən) *n.* **1.** any animal having a body composed of many cells —*a.* *(also* **meta'zoic)** **2.** of or relating to metazoans

mete (miːt) *vt.* measure —**mete out 1.** distribute **2.** allot as punishment

metempsychosis (metəmsaɪ'kəʊsɪs) *n.* migration of soul from one body to another *(pl.* **-ses** *(-*siːz*))* —**metempsy'chosist** *n.*

meteor ('miːtɪə) *n.* small, fast-moving celestial body, visible as streak of incandescence if it enters earth's atmosphere —**mete'oric** *a.* **1.** of, like meteor **2.** brilliant but short-lived —**'meteorite** *n.* fallen meteor —**'meteoroid** *n.* any of small celestial bodies that are thought to orbit sun —**meteor'oidal** *a.*

meteorology (miːtɪə'rɒlədʒɪ) *n.* study of earth's atmosphere, *esp.* for weather forecasting —**meteoro'logical** *a.* —**meteor'ologist** *n.*

meter ('miːtə) *n.* **1.** that which measures **2.** instrument for recording consumption of gas, electricity *etc.*

Meth. Methodist

methane ('miːθeɪn) *n.* inflammable gas, compound of carbon and hydrogen

methanol ('meθənɒl) *n.* colourless, poisonous liquid used as solvent and fuel *(also* **methyl alcohol)**

methinks (mɪ'θɪŋks) *v. impers. obs.* it seems to me (**me'thought** *pt.*)

method ('meθəd) *n.* **1.** way, manner **2.** technique **3.** orderliness, system —**me'thodical** *a.* orderly —**'methodize** *or* **-ise** *vt.* reduce to order —**metho'dology** *n.* particular method or procedure

Methodist ('meθədɪst) *n.* **1.** member of any of the churches originated by John Wesley and his followers —*a.* **2.** of or relating to Methodism or the Methodist Church —**'Methodism** *n.*

meths (meθs) *n. inf.* methylated spirits

methyl ('miːθaɪl, 'meθɪl) *n.* (compound containing) a saturated hydrocarbon group of atoms —**'methylate** *vt.* **1.** combine with methyl **2.** mix with methanol —**methylated spirits** alcoholic mixture denatured with methanol

meticulous (mɪ'tɪkjʊləs) *a.* (over)particular about details

métier ('metɪeɪ) *n.* **1.** profession, vocation **2.** forte

Métis (meˈtiːs) *n.* **C** person of mixed parentage

metonymy (mɪ'tɒnɪmɪ) *n.* figure of speech in which thing is replaced by another associated with it, *eg the Crown for the king* —**meto'nymical** *a.*

metre *or U.S.* **meter** ('miːtə) *n.* **1.** unit of length in decimal system **2.** SI unit of length **3.** rhythm of poem —**metric** ('metrɪk) *a.* of system of weights and measures in which metre is a unit —**metrical** ('metrɪkˀl) *a.* of measurement of poetic metre —**metricate** ('metrɪkeɪt) *v.* convert (measuring system *etc.*) from nonmetric to metric units —**metri'cation** *n.* —**metric ton** *see* TONNE

Metro ('metrəʊ) *n.* **C** metropolitan city administration

metronome ('metrənəʊm) *n.* instrument which marks musical time by means of ticking pendulum

metropolis (mɪ'trɒpəlɪs) *n.* chief city of a country, region —**metro'politan** *a.* **1.** of metropolis —*n.* **2.** bishop with authority over other bishops of a province

-metry *(n. comb. form)* process or science of measuring, as in *geometry* —**-metric** *(a. comb. form)*

mettle ('metˀl) *n.* courage, spirit —**'mettlesome** *a.* high-spirited

mew¹ (mjuː) *n.* **1.** cry of cat, gull —*vi.* **2.** utter this cry

mew² (mjuː) *n.* any sea gull, *esp.* common gull

mews (mjuːz) *pl.n.* (*sing. v.*) yard, street, orig. of stables, now oft. converted to houses

Mex. 1. Mexican 2. Mexico

mezzanine ('mɛzəniːn, 'mɛtsəniːn) *n.* intermediate storey, balcony between two main storeys, *esp.* between first and second floors

mezzo ('mɛtsəʊ) *adv. Mus.* moderately; quite —**mezzo-soprano** *n.* voice, singer between soprano and contralto (*pl.* -s)

mezzotint ('mɛtsəʊtɪnt) *n.* 1. method of engraving by scraping roughened surface 2. print so made

mf *Mus.* mezzo forte

MF 1. *Rad.* medium frequency. 2. Middle French

mfr. 1. manufacture 2. manufacturer

mg *or* **mg.** milligram(s)

Mg *Chem.* magnesium

M. Glam. Mid Glamorgan

Mgr. 1. manager 2. Monseigneur 3. Monsignor

MHG Middle High German

MHz megahertz

mi *or* **me** (miː) *n. Mus.* in tonic sol-fa, third degree of any major scale

MI 1. Military Intelligence 2. Michigan

MI5 Military Intelligence, section five

miaou *or* **miaow** ('miːaʊ, mjaʊ) *see* MEOW

miasma (mɪ'æzmə) *n.* unwholesome or foreboding atmosphere (*pl.* **-mata** (-mətə), **-s**) —**miasmatic** (miːəz'mætɪk) *a.*

mica ('maɪkə) *n.* mineral found as glittering scales, plates

mice (maɪs) *n., pl. of* MOUSE

Michaelmas ('mɪk'lməs) *n.* feast of Archangel St. Michael, 29th September —**Michaelmas daisy** common garden flower of aster family

mickey *or* **micky** ('mɪkɪ) *n. inf.* —**take the mickey** *or* **micky out of** tease

Mickey Finn (fɪn) *sl.* drink containing drug to make drinker unconscious

micro ('maɪkrəʊ) *n. inf.* 1. microcomputer 2. microprocessor (*pl.* -s)

micro- *or* before vowel **micr-** (*comb. form*) 1. small or minute, as in *microdot* 2. magnification or amplification, as in *microscope, microphone* 3. involving use of microscope, as in *microscopy*

microbe ('maɪkrəʊb) *n.* 1. minute organism 2. disease germ —**mi'crobial** *a.*

microbiology (maɪkrəʊbaɪ'ɒlədʒɪ) *n.* branch of biology involving study of microorganisms —**microbio'logic(al)** *a.*

microchemistry (maɪkrəʊ'kɛmɪstrɪ) *n.* chemical experimentation with minute quantities of material —**micro'chemical** *a.*

microchip ('maɪkrəʊtʃɪp) *n.* small wafer of silicon *etc.* containing electronic circuits (*also* **chip**)

microcircuit ('maɪkrəʊsɜːkɪt) *n.* minia-

ture electronic circuit, *esp.* integrated circuit —**micro'circuitry** *n.*

microcomputer (maɪkrəʊkəm'pjuːtə) *n.* computer in which central processing unit is contained in one or more silicon chips

microcopy ('maɪkrəʊkɒpɪ) *n.* minute photographic replica useful for storage because of its small size

microcosm ('maɪkrəʊkɒzəm) *or* **microcosmos** (maɪkrəʊ'kɒzmɒs) *n.* 1. miniature representation, model *etc.* of some larger system 2. man as epitome of universe —**micro'cosmic** *a.*

microdot ('maɪkrəʊdɒt) *n.* extremely small microcopy

microelectronics (maɪkrəʊɪlɛk'trɒnɪks) *pl.n.* (*with sing. v.*) branch of electronics concerned with microcircuits

microfiche ('maɪkrəʊfiːʃ) *n.* microfilm in sheet form

microfilm ('maɪkrəʊfɪlm) *n.* miniaturized recording of manuscript, book on roll of film

microgroove ('maɪkrəʊgruːv) *n.* 1. narrow groove of long-playing gramophone record —*a.* 2. (of a record) having such grooves

micrometer (maɪ'krɒmɪtə) *n.* instrument for measuring very small distances or angles

microminiaturization *or* **-isation** (maɪkrəʊmɪnɪtʃəraɪ'zeɪʃən) *n.* production of small components and circuits and equipment in which they are used

micron ('maɪkrɒn) *n.* unit of length, one millionth of a metre

microorganism (maɪkrəʊ'ɔːgənɪzəm) *n.* organism of microscopic size

microphone ('maɪkrəfəʊn) *n.* instrument for amplifying, transmitting sounds

microprint ('maɪkrəʊprɪnt) *n.* greatly reduced photographic copy of print, read by magnifying device

microprocessor (maɪkrəʊ'prəʊsɛsə) *n.* integrated circuit acting as central processing unit in small computer

microscope ('maɪkrəskəʊp) *n.* instrument by which very small body is magnified and made visible —**microscopic** (maɪkrə'skɒpɪk) *a.* 1. of microscope 2. very small —**microscopy** (maɪ'krɒskəpɪ) *n.* use of microscope

microstructure ('maɪkrəʊstrʌktʃə) *n.* structure on microscopic scale, *esp.* of alloy as observed by etching, polishing *etc.* under microscope

microsurgery (maɪkrəʊ'sɜːdʒərɪ) *n.* minute surgical dissection or manipulation of individual cells under a microscope

microwave ('maɪkrəʊweɪv) *n.* electromagnetic wave with wavelength of a few centimetres, used in radar, cooking *etc.*

micturate ('mɪktjʊreɪt) *vi.* urinate —**micturition** (mɪktjʊ'rɪʃən) *n.*

mid (mɪd) *a.* intermediate, in the middle of —**'mid'day** *n.* noon —**midland** ('mɪdlənd) *n.* 1. middle part of country —*pl.* 2. central England —**'midnight** *n.* twelve o'clock at night —**midnight sun** sun visible at midnight during summer inside Arctic and Antarctic circles —**mid-off** n. Cricket fielding position on off side closest to bowler —**mid-on** n. Cricket fielding position on on side closest to bowler —**'midshipman** n. naval officer of lowest commissioned rank —**'mid'summer** n. 1. summer solstice 2. middle of summer —**'midway** a./adv. halfway —**mid-wicket** n. Cricket fielding position on on side, midway between square leg and mid-on —**'mid'winter** n.

midden ('mɪdᵊn) n. 1. dunghill 2. rubbish heap

middle ('mɪdᵊl) a. 1. equidistant from two extremes 2. medium, intermediate —n. 3. middle point or part —**'middling** a. 1. mediocre 2. moderate —adv. 3. inf. moderately —**middle age** period of life between youth and old age, usu. considered to be between ages of 40 and 60 —**middle-aged** a. —**Middle Ages** period from end of Roman Empire to Renaissance, roughly A.D. 500–1500 —**middle C** Mus. note written on first ledger line below treble staff or first ledger line above bass staff —**middle class** social class of businessmen, professional people etc. —**middle-class** a. —**middle ear** sound-conducting part of ear —**Middle East** (loosely) area around E Mediterranean, esp. Israel and Arab countries from Turkey to N Afr. and eastwards to Iran —**Middle Eastern** —**Middle English** English language from about 1100 to about 1450 —**Middle High German** High German from about 1200 to about 1500 —**Middle Low German** Low German from about 1200 to about 1500 —**'middleman** n. trader between producer and consumer —**middle-of-the-road** a. not extreme; moderate —**middle school** UK school for children aged between 8 or 9 and 12 or 13 —**'middleweight** n. 1. professional boxer weighing 154-160 lbs. (70-72.5 kg); amateur boxer weighing 157-165 lbs. (71-75 kg) 2. wrestler weighing usu. 172-192 lbs. (78-87 kg)

midge (mɪdʒ) n. gnat or similar insect

midget ('mɪdʒɪt) n. very small person or thing

midi ('mɪdɪ) a. (of skirt etc.) reaching to below knee or midcalf

midriff ('mɪdrɪf) n. middle part of body

midst (mɪdst) prep. 1. in the middle of —n. 2. middle —**in the midst of** surrounded by, among

midwife ('mɪdwaɪf) n. trained person who assists at childbirth —**midwifery** ('mɪdwɪfərɪ) n. art, practice of this

mien (miːn) n. person's bearing, demeanour or appearance

might¹ (maɪt) pt. of MAY

might² (maɪt) n. power, strength —**'mightily** adv. 1. strongly 2. powerfully —**'mighty** a. 1. of great power 2. strong 3. valiant 4. important —adv. 5. inf. very

mignonette (mɪnjə'nɛt) n. grey-green plant with sweet-smelling flowers

migraine ('miːgreɪn, 'maɪ-) n. severe headache, often with nausea and other symptoms

migrate (maɪ'greɪt) vi. move from one place to another —**'migrant** n./a. —**mi'gration** n. 1. act of passing from one place, condition to another 2. number migrating together —**'migratory** a. 1. of, capable of migration 2. (of animals) changing from one place to another according to season

mikado (mɪ'kɑːdəʊ) n. (oft. M-) obs. Japanese emperor

mike (maɪk) n. inf. microphone

milady or **miladi** (mɪ'leɪdɪ) n. formerly, continental title used for English gentlewoman

milch (mɪltʃ) a. giving, kept for milk

mild (maɪld) a. 1. not strongly flavoured 2. gentle, merciful 3. calm or temperate —**'mildly** adv. —**'mildness** n. —**mild steel** any strong tough steel that contains low quantity of carbon

mildew ('mɪldjuː) n. 1. destructive fungus on plants or things exposed to damp —v. 2. become tainted, affect with mildew

mile (maɪl) n. measure of length, 1760 yards, 1.609 km —**'mileage** or **'milage** n. 1. distance in miles 2. travelling expenses per mile 3. miles travelled (per gallon of petrol) 4. inf. advantage, profit, use —**mile'ometer** or **mi'lometer** n. device that records number of miles vehicle has travelled —**'milestone** n. 1. stone marker showing distance 2. significant event, achievement

milfoil ('mɪlfɔɪl) n. yarrow

milieu ('miːljɜː) n. environment, condition in life

military ('mɪlɪtərɪ, -trɪ) a. 1. of, for, soldiers, armies or war —n. 2. armed services —**'militancy** n. —**'militant** a. 1. aggressive, vigorous in support of cause 2. prepared, willing to fight —**'militarism** n. enthusiasm for military force and methods —**'militarist** n. —**'militarize** or **-ise** vt. convert to military use —**militia** (mɪ'lɪʃə) n. military force of citizens for home service

militate ('mɪlɪteɪt) vi. (esp. with against) have strong influence, effect (on)

milk (mɪlk) n. 1. white fluid with which mammals feed their young 2. fluid in some plants —vt. 3. draw milk from —**'milky** a. 1. containing, like milk 2. (of liquids) opaque, clouded —**milk-and-water** a. weak, feeble, or insipid —**milk bar** snack bar specializing in milk drinks —**milk float** UK small motor vehicle used to deliver milk to houses —**'milkmaid** n. esp. formerly, woman working with cows or in dairy —**milk run** inf. Aeron. routine and uneventful flight —**milk shake** frothy drink made of milk, flavouring, and usu. ice cream —**'milksop** n. effeminate fellow —**milk teeth** first set of teeth in young mammals —**Milky Way** luminous band of stars *etc.* stretching across sky, the galaxy —**milk of magnesia** suspension of magnesium hydroxide in water, used as laxative

mill (mɪl) *n.* 1. factory 2. machine for grinding, pulverizing corn, paper *etc.* —*vt.* 3. put through mill 4. cut fine grooves across edges of (*eg* coins) —*vi.* 5. move in confused manner, as cattle or crowds of people —'**miller** *n.* —'**millpond** *n.* pool formed by damming stream to provide water to turn mill wheel —'**millrace** *n.* current of water driving mill wheel —'**millstone** *n.* flat circular stone for grinding

millennium (mɪ'lɛnɪəm) *n.* 1. period of a thousand years during which some claim Christ is to reign on earth 2. period of a thousand years 3. period of peace, happiness (*pl.* **-s, -ia** (-ɪə))

millepede ('mɪlɪpiːd) *or* **milleped** ('mɪlɪpɛd) *n.* small animal with jointed body and many pairs of legs

miller's thumb ('mɪləz) any of several small freshwater European fishes having flattened body

millet ('mɪlɪt) *n.* a cereal grass

milli- (*comb. form*) thousandth, as in *millilitre*

milliard ('mɪlɑːd, 'mɪljɑːd) *n.* UK thousand million

millibar ('mɪlɪbɑː) *n.* unit of atmospheric pressure

milligram *or* **milligramme** ('mɪlɪgræm) *n.* thousandth part of a gram

millimetre *or* *U.S.* **millimeter** ('mɪlɪmiːtə) *n.* thousandth part of a metre

milliner ('mɪlɪnə) *n.* maker of, dealer in women's hats, ribbons *etc.* —'**millinery** *n.* his goods or work

million ('mɪljən) *n.* 1000 thousands —**million'aire** *n.* 1. owner of a million pounds, dollars *etc.* 2. very rich man —'**millionth** *a./n.*

milometer (maɪ'lɒmɪtə) *n. see* **mileometer** *at* MILE

milt (mɪlt) *n.* spawn of male fish

mime (maɪm) *n.* 1. acting without the use of words —*v.* 2. act in mime

mimic ('mɪmɪk) *vt.* 1. imitate (person, manner *etc.*), *esp.* for satirical effect ('**mimicked**, '**mimicking**) —*n.* 2. one who, or animal which does this, or is adept at it —*a.* 3. imitative, simulated —**mi'metic** *a.* 1. of, resembling, or relating to imitation 2. *Biol.* of or exhibiting protective resemblance to another species —'**mimicry** *n.* mimicking

mimosa (mɪ'məʊsə, -zə) *n.* genus of plants with fluffy, yellow flowers and sensitive leaves

min. 1. minim 2. minimum 3. minute

Min. 1. Minister 2. Ministry

mina (maɪnə) *n. see* MYNA

minaret (mɪnə'rɛt, 'mɪnərɛt) *n.* tall slender tower of mosque

minatory ('mɪnətərɪ, -trɪ) *or* **minatorial** *a.* threatening or menacing

mince (mɪns) *vt.* 1. cut, chop small 2. soften or moderate (words *etc.*) —*vi.* 3. walk, speak in affected manner —*n.* 4. minced meat —'**mincer** *n.* —'**mincing** *a.* affected in manner —'**mincemeat** *n.* mixture of currants, spices, suet *etc.* —**mince pie** pie containing mincemeat or mince

mind (maɪnd) *n.* 1. thinking faculties as distinguished from the body, intellectual faculties 2. memory, attention 3. intention 4. opinion 5. sanity —*vt.* 6. take offence at 7. care for 8. attend to 9. be cautious, careful about —*vi.* 11. be careful —'**minder** *n.* 1. one who looks after someone or something 2. *see* child minder *at* CHILD 3. *sl.* aide to someone in public life, who keeps control of press and public relations 4. *sl.* bodyguard or assistant, *esp.* in criminal underworld —'**mindful** *a.* 1. heedful 2. keeping in memory —'**mindless** *a.* stupid, careless —**mind-reader** *n.* person seemingly able to discern thoughts of another —**mind's eye** visual memory or imagination

mine[1] (maɪn) *pron.* belonging to me

mine[2] (maɪn) *n.* 1. deep hole for digging out coal, metals *etc.* 2. in war, hidden deposit of explosive to blow up ship *etc.* 3. profitable source —*vt.* 4. dig from mine 5. make mine in or under 6. place explosive mines in, on —*vi.* 7. make, work in mine —'**miner** *n.* one who works in a mine —'**minefield** *n.* area of land or sea containing mines —'**minelayer** *n.* ship for laying mines —'**minesweeper** *n.* ship for clearing away mines

mineral ('mɪnərəl, 'mɪnrəl) *n.* 1. naturally occurring inorganic substance, *esp.* as obtained by mining —*a.* 2. of, containing minerals —'**mineralist** *n.* —**minera'logical** *a.* —**miner'alogy** *n.* science of minerals —**mineral water** water containing some mineral, *esp.* natural or artificial kinds for drinking

minestrone (mɪnɪ'strəʊnɪ) *n.* type of soup containing pasta

mingle ('mɪŋg'l) *v.* mix, blend, unite, merge

mingy ('mɪndʒɪ) *a.* UK *inf.* miserly, stingy, or niggardly

mini ('mɪnɪ) *n.* something small or miniature —'**miniskirt** *n.* very short skirt, one at least four inches above knee

mini- (*comb. form*) smaller or shorter than standard size

miniature ('mɪnɪtʃə) *n.* 1. small painted portrait 2. anything on small scale —*a.* 3. small-scale, minute —'**miniaturist** *n.* —'**miniaturize** *or* **-ise** *vt.* make or construct on a very small scale

minibus ('mɪnɪbʌs) *n.* small bus for about ten passengers

minim ('mɪnɪm) *n.* 1. unit of fluid measure, one sixtieth of a drachm 2. *Mus.* note half the length of semibreve

minimize *or* **-ise** ('mɪnɪmaɪz) *vt.* bring to,

estimate at smallest possible amount —'**minimal** a. —'**minimum** n. 1. lowest size or quantity (pl. -s, -ma (-mə)) —a. 2. least possible —**minimum lending rate** formerly, minimum rate of interest at which the Bank of England lent money —**minimum wage** lowest wage that employer is permitted to pay by law or union contract

minion ('mɪnjən) n. 1. favourite 2. servile dependant

minister ('mɪnɪstə) n. 1. person in charge of department of State 2. diplomatic representative 3. clergyman —vi. 4. (oft. with to) attend to needs (of), take care (of) —minis'**terial** a. —minis'**terialist** n. supporter of government —**ministrant** a./n. —minis'**tration** n. rendering help, esp. to sick —'**ministry** n. 1. office of clergyman 2. body of ministers forming government 3. act of ministering —**minister of state** UK minister, usu. below cabinet rank, appointed to assist senior minister —**Minister of the Crown** UK any Government minister of cabinet rank

miniver ('mɪnɪvə) n. a white fur used in ceremonial costumes

mink (mɪŋk) n. 1. variety of weasel 2. its (brown) fur

minnow ('mɪnəʊ) n. small freshwater fish

Minoan (mɪ'nəʊən) a. 1. of Bronze Age culture of Crete from about 3000 B.C. to about 1100 B.C. —n. 2. Cretan belonging to Minoan culture

minor ('maɪnə) a. 1. lesser 2. under age —n. 3. person below age of legal majority 4. minor scale in music —mi'**nority** n. 1. lesser number 2. smaller party voting together 3. ethical or religious group in a minority in any state 4. state of being a minor —**minor scale** Mus. scale with semitones instead of whole tones after second and seventh notes

Minotaur ('mɪnɔtɔː) n. fabled monster, half bull, half man

minster ('mɪnstə) n. 1. Hist. monastery church 2. cathedral, large church

minstrel ('mɪnstrəl) n. 1. medieval singer, musician, poet —pl. 2. performers of negro songs —'**minstrelsy** n. 1. art, body of minstrels 2. collection of songs

mint[1] (mɪnt) n. 1. place where money is coined —vt. 2. coin, invent

mint[2] (mɪnt) n. aromatic plant

minuet (mɪnjʊ'ɛt) n. 1. stately dance 2. music for it

minus ('maɪnəs) prep. 1. less, with the deduction of, deprived of —a. 2. lacking 3. negative —n. 4. the sign of subtraction (-)

minuscule ('mɪnəskjuːl) n. 1. lower-case letter 2. writing using such letters —a. 3. relating to, printed in, or written in small letters 4. very small —**minuscular** (mɪ-'nʌskjulə) a.

minute[1] (maɪ'njuːt) a. 1. very small 2. precise —mi'**nutely** adv. —**minutiae** (mɪ-'njuːʃiː) pl.n. trifles, precise details

minute[2] ('mɪnɪt) n. 1. 60th part of hour or degree 2. moment 3. memorandum —pl. 4. record of proceedings of meeting etc. —vt. 5. make minute of 6. record in minutes —**minute steak** small steak that can be cooked quickly

minx (mɪŋks) n. bold, flirtatious woman

Miocene ('maɪəsiːn) a. 1. of or denoting fourth epoch of Tertiary period —n. 2. this epoch or rock system

miracle ('mɪrək[l]) n. 1. supernatural event 2. marvel —mi'**raculous** a. —mi'**raculously** adv. —**miracle play** drama (esp. medieval) based on sacred subject

mirage ('mɪraːʒ) n. deceptive image in atmosphere, eg of lake in desert

mire (maɪə) n. 1. swampy ground, mud —vt. 2. stick in, dirty with mud

mirror ('mɪrə) n. 1. glass or polished surface reflecting images —vt. 2. reflect —**mirror image** 1. image as observed in mirror 2. object that corresponds to another in reverse as does image in mirror

mirth (mɜːθ) n. merriment, gaiety —'**mirthful** a. —'**mirthless** a.

mis- (comb. form) wrong(ly), bad(ly). See the list below

misadventure (mɪsəd'vɛntʃə) n. unlucky chance

misalliance (mɪsə'laɪəns) n. unsuitable alliance or marriage —misal'**ly** v.

misanthrope ('mɪzənθrəʊp) or **misanthropist** (mɪ'zænθrəpɪst) n. hater of mankind —**misanthropic** (mɪzən'θrɒpɪk) a. —mi'**santhropy** n.

misappropriate (mɪsə'prəʊprɪeɪt) vt. 1. put to dishonest use 2. embezzle —**misappropri'ation** n.

misbegotten (mɪsbɪ'gɒt[ə]n) a. 1. unlawfully obtained 2. badly conceived or designed 3. Lit., dial. illegitimate; bastard

miscarry (mɪs'kærɪ) vi. 1. bring forth young prematurely 2. go wrong, fail —**mis'carriage** n.

miscast (mɪs'kɑːst) v. 1. distribute (acting parts) wrongly —vt. 2. assign to unsuitable role

miscegenation (mɪsɪdʒɪ'neɪʃən) n. interbreeding of races

miscellaneous (mɪsə'leɪnɪəs) a. mixed, assorted —mis'**cellany** n. 1. collection of assorted writings in one book 2. medley

mischance (mɪs'tʃɑːns) n. unlucky event

mischief ('mɪstʃɪf) n. 1. annoying behaviour 2. inclination to tease, disturb 3. harm 4. source of harm or annoyance —'**mischievous** a. 1. (of a child) full of pranks 2.

---

misad'dress
misadminis'tration
misa'lignment

misap'ply
misbe'have
mis'calculate

disposed to mischief **3.** having harmful effect

miscible ('mısıb^əl) *a.* capable of mixing

misconception (mıskən'sɛpʃən) *n.* wrong idea, belief

miscreant ('mıskrıənt) *n.* wicked person, evildoer, villain

misdemeanour *or U.S.* **misdemeanor** (mısdı'mi:nə) *n.* **1.** formerly, offence less grave than a felony **2.** minor offence

misdoubt (mıs'daut) *v. obs.* doubt or suspect

mise en scène (miz ã 'sɛn) *Fr.* **1.** arrangement of scenery *etc.* in play; stage setting **2.** environment of event

miser ('maızə) *n.* **1.** hoarder of money **2.** stingy person —'**miserliness** *n.* —'**miserly** *a.* **1.** avaricious **2.** niggardly

miserable ('mızərəb^əl) *a.* **1.** very unhappy, wretched **2.** causing misery **3.** worthless **4.** squalid —'**misery** *n.* **1.** great unhappiness **2.** distress **3.** poverty **4. UK** *inf.* habitually depressed, discontented person

misericord *or* **misericorde** (mı'zɛrıkɔːd) *n.* ledge projecting from underside of hinged seat of choir stall in church, on which occupant can support himself while standing

misfire (mıs'faıə) *vi.* fail to fire, start, function successfully

misfit ('mısfıt) *n. esp.* person not suited to his environment or work

misgiving (mıs'gıvıŋ) *n.* (*oft. pl.*) feeling of fear, doubt *etc.*

misguided (mıs'gaıdıd) *a.* foolish, unreasonable

mishap ('mıshæp) *n.* minor accident

mishmash ('mıʃmæʃ) *n.* confused collection or mixture

mislay (mıs'leı) *vt.* put in place which cannot later be remembered

mislead (mıs'li:d) *vt.* **1.** give false information to **2.** lead astray (**mis'led** *pt./pp.*) —**mis'leading** *a.* deceptive

misnomer (mıs'nəumə) *n.* **1.** wrong name or term **2.** use of this

misogamy (mı'sɒgəmı, maı-) *n.* hatred of marriage —**mi'sogamist** *n.*

misogyny (mı'sɒdʒını, maı-) *n.* hatred of women —**mi'sogynist** *n.*

misrepresent (mısrɛprı'zɛnt) *vt.* portray in wrong or misleading light

misrule (mıs'ru:l) *vt.* **1.** govern inefficiently or without justice —*n.* **2.** inefficient or unjust government **3.** disorder

miss (mıs) *vt.* **1.** fail to hit, reach, find, catch, or notice **2.** not be in time for **3.**

omit **4.** notice or regret absence of **5.** avoid —*vi.* **6.** (of engine) misfire —*n.* **7.** fact, instance of missing —'**missing** *a.* **1.** lost **2.** absent —**missing link 1.** hypothetical extinct animal intermediate between anthropoid apes and man **2.** any missing section or part in series

Miss (mıs) *n.* **1.** title of unmarried woman **2.** (**m-**) girl

missal ('mıs^əl) *n.* book containing prayers *etc.* of the Mass

missile ('mısaıl) *n.* that which may be thrown, shot, homed to damage, destroy —**guided missile** *see* GUIDE

mission ('mıʃən) *n.* **1.** specific task or duty **2.** calling in life **3.** delegation **4.** sending or being sent on some service **5.** those sent —'**missionary** *n.* **1.** one sent to a place, society to spread religion —*a.* **2.** of, like missionary or religious mission

missis *or* **missus** ('mısıs, -ıs) *n.* (*usu. with* the) *inf.* one's wife or wife of person addressed or referred to

missive ('mısıv) *n.* letter

misspend (mıs'spɛnd) *v.* spend thoughtlessly or wastefully (-'**spending**, -'**spent**)

mist (mıst) *n.* water vapour in fine drops —'**mistily** *adv.* —'**misty** *a.* **1.** full of mist **2.** dim **3.** obscure

mistake (mı'steık) *n.* **1.** error, blunder —*vt.* **2.** fail to understand **3.** form wrong opinion about **4.** take (person or thing) for another —**mis'taken** *a.* **1.** wrong in opinion *etc.* **2.** arising from error in judgment *etc.*

mister ('mıstə) *n.* title of courtesy to man

mistle thrush *or* **missel thrush** ('mıs^əl) European thrush with brown back and spotted breast

mistletoe ('mıs^əltəu) *n.* evergreen parasitic plant with white berries, which grows on trees

mistook (mı'stuk) *pt. of* MISTAKE

mistral ('mıstrəl, mı'strɑːl) *n.* strong, dry, N wind in France

mistress ('mıstrıs) *n.* **1.** object of man's illicit love **2.** woman with mastery or control **3.** woman owner **4.** woman teacher **5.** *obs.* title given to married woman

mistrial (mıs'traıəl) *n. Law* trial made void because of some error

mistrust (mıs'trʌst) *vt.* **1.** have doubts or suspicions about —*n.* **2.** distrust —**mis-'trustful** *a.*

misunderstanding (mısʌndə'stændıŋ) *n.* **1.** failure to understand properly **2.**

---

miscon'ceive	mis'hear	misre'port
mis'conduct	mis'hit	mis'state
mis'count	mis'judge	mis'statement
mis'deed	mis'manage	mis'time
misem'ploy	mis'management	mis'treat
mis'fortune	mis'marriage	mis'type
mis'govern	misper'ception	misunder'stand
mis'government	mis'phrase	mis'use
mis'handle	mis'read	

disagreement —**misunder'stood** a. not properly or sympathetically understood

mite (mait) n. 1. very small insect 2. anything very small 3. small but well-meant contribution

mitigate ('mitigeit) vt. make less severe —**miti'gation** n. —**mitigating circumstances** circumstances which lessen the culpability of an offender

mitosis (mai'tǝusis, mi-) n. cell division in which nucleus divides into daughter nuclei, each containing same number of chromosomes as parent nucleus —**mitotic** (mai'tɒtik, mi-) a.

mitre or U.S. **miter** ('maitǝ) n. 1. bishop's headdress 2. joint between two pieces of wood etc. meeting at right angles —vt. 3. join with, shape for a mitre joint 4. put mitre on

mitt (mit) n. 1. glove leaving fingers bare 2. baseball catcher's glove 3. sl. hand

mitten ('mit²n) n. glove with two compartments, one for thumb and one for fingers

mix (miks) vt. 1. put together, combine, blend, mingle —vi. 2. be mixed 3. associate —**mixed** a. composed of different elements, races, sexes etc. —'**mixer** n. one who, that which mixes —'**mixture** n. —**mixed bag** inf. something composed of diverse elements, people etc. —**mixed blessing** situation etc. having advantages and disadvantages —**mixed doubles** Tennis game with man and woman as partners on each side —**mixed grill** dish of grilled chops, sausages, bacon etc. —**mixed marriage** marriage between persons of different races or religions —**mixed-up** a. inf. confused —**mix-up** n. confused situation

mizzen or **mizen** ('miz²n) n. lowest fore-and-aft sail on aftermost mast of ship —**mizzenmast** or **mizenmast** ('miz²n-mɑːst; Naut. 'miz²nmǝst) n. aftermost mast on full-rigged ship

mks units metric system of units based on the metre, kilogram and second

ml millilitre(s)

M.L. Medieval Latin

M.L.A. C Member of the Legislative Assembly

M.Litt. UK Master of Letters

Mlle or **Mlle.** Mademoiselle (pl. **Mlles**, **Mlles.**)

MLR minimum lending rate

mm millimetre(s)

M.M. Military Medal

Mme or **Mme.** Madame (pl. **Mmes**, **Mmes.**)

M.Mus. Master of Music

Mn Chem. manganese

MN Minnesota

MNA or **M.N.A.** C Member of the National Assembly

mnemonic (ni'mɒnik) a. 1. helping the memory —n. 2. something intended to help the memory

mo (mǝu) n. inf. moment

Mo Chem. molybdenum

MO Missouri

M.O. Medical Officer

-mo (comb. form) in bookbinding, indicating book size by specifying number of leaves formed by folding one sheet of paper, as in sixteenmo

moa ('mǝuǝ) n. any of various extinct flightless birds of New Zealand

moan (mǝun) n. 1. low murmur, usually of pain —v. 2. utter (words etc.) with moan —vi. 3. lament

moat (mǝut) n. 1. deep wide ditch, esp. round castle —vt. 2. surround with moat

mob (mɒb) n. 1. disorderly crowd of people 2. mixed assembly —vt. 3. attack in mob, hustle or ill-treat (-bb-) —'**mobster** n. US sl. gangster

mobcap ('mɒbkæp) n. formerly, woman's large cotton cap with pouched crown

mobile ('mǝubail) a. 1. capable of movement 2. easily moved or changed —n. 3. hanging structure of card, plastic etc., designed to move in air currents —**mobility** (mǝu'biliti) n.

mobilize or **-ise** ('mǝubilaiz) vi. 1. (of armed services) prepare for military service —vt. 2. organize for a purpose —**mobili'zation** or **-i'sation** n. in war time, calling up of men and women for active service

moccasin ('mɒkǝsin) n. Amer. Indian soft shoe, usu. of deerskin

mocha ('mɒkǝ) n. 1. type of strong, dark coffee 2. this flavour

mock (mɒk) vt. 1. make fun of, ridicule 2. mimic —vi. 3. scoff —n. 4. act of mocking 5. laughing stock —a. 6. sham, imitation —'**mocker** n. —'**mockery** n. 1. derision 2. travesty —**mocking bird** N Amer. bird which imitates songs of others —**mock orange** shrub with white fragrant flowers —**mock turtle soup** imitation turtle soup made from calf's head —**mock-up** n. scale model —**put the mockers on** inf. ruin chances of success of

mod[1] (mɒd) UK a. 1. of any fashion in dress regarded as stylish, esp. that of early 1960s —n. 2. member of group of teenagers, orig. in mid-1960s, noted for their clothes-consciousness

mod[2] (mɒd) n. annual Highland Gaelic meeting with musical and literary competitions

mod. 1. moderate 2. modern

mod cons (kɒnz) inf. modern conveniences

mode (mǝud) n. 1. method, manner 2. prevailing fashion 3. Mus. any of various scales of notes within one octave —'**modal** a. 1. of or relating to mode or manner 2. Gram. expressing distinction of mood 3. Metaphys. of or relating to form of thing as opposed to its substance etc. 4. Mus. of or relating to mode —**mo'dality** n. —'**modish** a. in the fashion —**modiste** (mǝu'diːst) n. fashionable dressmaker or milliner

model ('mɒdˀl) n. 1. miniature representation 2. pattern 3. person or thing worthy of imitation 4. person employed by artist to pose, or by dress designer to display clothing —vt. 5. make model of 6. mould —v. 7. display (clothing) for dress designer (-ll-)

moderate ('mɒdərɪt) a. 1. not going to extremes, temperate, medium —n. 2. person of moderate views —v. ('mɒdəreɪt) 3. make, become less violent or excessive 4. preside (over) —**mode'ration** n. —'**moderator** n. 1. mediator 2. president of Presbyterian body 3. arbitrator

moderato (mɒdə'rɑːtəʊ) adv. Mus. 1. at moderate tempo 2. direction indicating that tempo specified be used with restraint

modern ('mɒdən) a. 1. of present or recent times 2. in, of current fashion —n. 3. person living in modern times —'**modernism** n. (support of) modern tendencies, thoughts etc. —'**modernist** n. —mo'**dernity** n. —**moderni'zation** or -i'sation n. —'**modernize** or -ise vt. bring up to date —**Modern English** English language since about 1450 —**modern languages** current European languages as subject of study

modest ('mɒdɪst) a. 1. not overrating one's qualities or achievements 2. shy 3. moderate, not excessive 4. decorous, decent —'**modestly** adv. —'**modesty** n.

modicum ('mɒdɪkəm) n. small quantity

modify ('mɒdɪfaɪ) vt. 1. change slightly 2. tone down (-fied, -fying) —**modifi'cation** n. —'**modifier** n. esp. word qualifying another

modulate ('mɒdjʊleɪt) vt. 1. regulate 2. vary in tone —vi. 3. change key of music —**modu'lation** n. 1. modulating 2. Electron. superimposing signals on to high-frequency carrier —'**modulator** n.

module ('mɒdjuːl) n. (detachable) unit, section, component with specific function —'**modular** a. of, consisting of, or resembling module or modulus

modulus ('mɒdjʊləs) n. 1. Phys. coefficient expressing specified property of specified substance 2. Maths. number by which logarithm to one base is multiplied to give the corresponding logarithm to another base 3. Maths. integer that can be divided exactly into the difference between two other integers (pl. -li (-laɪ))

modus operandi ('məʊdəs ɒpə'rændiː) Lat. method of operating, tackling task (pl. **modi operandi** ('məʊdiː))

modus vivendi (vɪ'vɛndiː) Lat. working arrangement between conflicting interests (pl. **modi vivendi** ('məʊdiː))

mog (mɒg) or **moggy** n. UK sl. cat

mogul ('məʊgʌl, məʊ'gʌl) n. important or powerful person

M.O.H. Medical Officer of Health

mohair ('məʊhɛə) n. 1. fine cloth of goat's hair 2. hair of Angora goat

Mohammed (məʊ'hæmɪd) n. prophet and founder of Islam —**Mo'hammedan** a./n.

Muslim —**Mo'hammedanism** n. another word (not in Muslim use) for Islam

moiety ('mɔɪtɪ) n. a half

moire (mwɑː) n. fabric, usu. silk, having watered effect —**moiré** ('mwɑːreɪ) a. 1. having watered or wavelike pattern —n. 2. such pattern, impressed on fabrics by means of engraved rollers 3. any fabric having such pattern, moire

moist (mɔɪst) a. damp, slightly wet —**moisten** ('mɔɪsˀn) v. —'**moisture** n. liquid, esp. diffused or in drops —'**moisturize** or -ise vt. add, restore moisture to (skin etc.)

moke (məʊk) n. sl. donkey

mol Chem. mole

molar ('məʊlə) a. 1. (of teeth) for grinding —n. 2. molar tooth

molasses (mə'læsɪz) n. syrup, by-product of process of sugar refining

mole¹ (məʊl) n. small dark protuberant spot on the skin

mole² (məʊl) n. 1. small burrowing animal 2. spy, informer —'**molehill** n. small mound of earth thrown up by burrowing mole —**make a mountain out of a molehill** exaggerate unimportant matter out of all proportion

mole³ (məʊl) n. 1. pier or breakwater 2. causeway 3. harbour within this

mole⁴ (məʊl) n. SI unit of amount of substance

molecule ('mɒlɪkjuːl) n. 1. simplest freely existing chemical unit, composed of two or more atoms 2. very small particle —mo'**lecular** a. of, inherent in molecules —**molecular weight** sum of all atomic weights of atoms in a molecule

molest (mə'lɛst) vt. pester, interfere with so as to annoy or injure —**molestation** (məʊlɛ'steɪʃən) n.

moll (mɒl) n. sl. 1. gangster's female accomplice 2. prostitute

mollify ('mɒlɪfaɪ) vt. calm down, placate, soften (-fied, -fying) —**mollifi'cation** n.

mollusc or U.S. **mollusk** ('mɒləsk) n. soft-bodied, usu. hard-shelled animal, eg snail, oyster

mollycoddle ('mɒlɪkɒdˀl) vt. pamper

Molotov cocktail ('mɒlətɒf) incendiary petrol bomb

molten ('məʊltən) a. 1. liquefied; melted 2. made by having been melted —v. 3. pp. of MELT

molto ('mɒltəʊ) adv. Mus. very

molybdenum (mɒ'lɪbdɪnəm) n. silver-white metallic element

moment ('məʊmənt) n. 1. very short space of time 2. (present) point in time —'**momentarily** adv. —'**momentary** a. lasting only a moment —**moment of truth** moment when person or thing is put to test

momentous (məʊ'mɛntəs) a. of great importance

momentum (məʊ'mɛntəm) n. 1. force of a moving body 2. impetus gained from motion (pl. -ta (-tə), -s)

mon. monetary

Mon. Monday

monad ('mɒnæd, 'mɒ-) *n.* **1.** *Philos.* any fundamental singular metaphysical entity (*pl.* **-s, -ades** (-ədi:z)) **2.** single-celled organism **3.** atom, ion, or radical with valency of one —**monadic** (mɒ'nædɪk) *a.*

monandrous (mɒ'nændrəs) *a.* **1.** having only one male sexual partner over a period of time **2.** (of plants) having flowers with only one stamen —**mo'nandry** *n.*

monarch ('mɒnək) *n.* sovereign ruler of a state —**mon'archic** *a.* —**'monarchist** *n.* supporter of monarchy —**'monarchy** *n.* **1.** state ruled by sovereign **2.** his rule

monastery ('mɒnəstəri) *n.* house occupied by a religious order —**mo'nastic** *a.* **1.** relating to monks, nuns, or monasteries —*n.* **2.** monk, recluse —**mo'nasticism** *n.*

monaural (mɒ'nɔːrəl) *a.* relating to, having, or hearing with only one ear

Monday ('mʌndɪ) *n.* second day of the week, or first of working week

money ('mʌnɪ) *n.* banknotes, coin *etc.*, used as medium of exchange (*pl.* **-s, -ies**) —**'monetarism** *n.* theory that inflation is caused by increase in money supply —**'monetarist** *n./a.* —**'monetary** *a.* —**moneti'zation** *or* **-i'sation** *n.* —**'monetize** *or* **-ise** *vt.* make into, recognize as money —**'moneyed** *or* **'monied** *a.* rich —**'moneybags** *n. sl.* very rich person —**money-grubbing** *a. inf.* seeking greedily to obtain money —**'moneylender** *n.* person who lends money at interest as a living —**money-spinner** *n. inf.* enterprise, idea *etc.* that is source of wealth

monger ('mʌŋgə) *n.* trader or dealer: usu. in compounds, as in *ironmonger*

mongolism ('mɒŋgəlɪzəm) *n.* Down's syndrome —**'mongol** *n./a.* (one) afflicted with this —**'mongoloid** *a.* relating to or characterized by mongolism

Mongoloid ('mɒŋgəlɔɪd) *a.* of major racial group of mankind, including most of peoples of Asia, Eskimos, and N Amer. Indians

mongoose ('mɒŋguːs) *n.* small animal of Asia and Afr. noted for killing snakes (*pl.* **-s**)

mongrel ('mʌŋgrəl) *n.* **1.** animal, *esp.* dog, of mixed breed, hybrid —*a.* **2.** of mixed breed

monitor ('mɒnɪtə) *n.* **1.** person or device which checks, controls, warns or keeps record of something **2.** pupil assisting teacher with odd jobs in school **3.** television set used in a studio for checking programme being transmitted **4.** type of large lizard —*vt.* **5.** watch, check on —**mo'nition** *n.* warning —**'monitory** *a.*

monk (mʌŋk) *n.* one of a religious community of men bound by vows of poverty *etc.* —**'monkish** *a.* —**'monkshood** *n.* poisonous plant with hooded flowers

monkey ('mʌŋkɪ) *n.* **1.** long-tailed primate **2.** mischievous child —*vi.* **3.** meddle, fool —**monkey business** *inf.* mischievous or

dishonest behaviour or acts —**monkey nut** UK peanut —**monkey puzzle** coniferous tree with sharp stiff leaves —**monkey wrench** spanner with movable jaws

mono ('mɒnəʊ) *a.* **1.** monophonic —*n.* **2.** monophonic sound

mono- *or before vowel* **mon-** (*comb. form*) single, as in *monosyllabic*

monochrome ('mɒnəkrəʊm) *n.* **1.** representation in one colour —*a.* **2.** of one colour —**monochro'matic** *a.*

monocle ('mɒnək'l) *n.* single eyeglass

monocotyledon (mɒnəʊkɒtɪ'liːd'n) *n.* any of various flowering plants having single embryonic seed leaf and leaves with parallel veins —**monocoty'ledonous** *a.*

monocular (mɒ'nɒkjʊlə) *a.* one-eyed

monogamy (mɒ'nɒgəmɪ) *n.* custom of being married to one person at a time

monogram ('mɒnəgræm) *n.* design of letters interwoven

monograph ('mɒnəgrɑːf) *n.* short book on single subject

monogyny (mɒ'nɒdʒɪnɪ) *n.* having only one female sexual partner over a period of time —**mo'nogynous** *a.*

monolith ('mɒnəlɪθ) *n.* monument consisting of single standing stone

monologue ('mɒnəlɒg) *n.* **1.** dramatic composition with only one speaker **2.** long speech by one person

monomania (mɒnəʊ'meɪnɪə) *n.* excessive preoccupation with one thing

monomial (mɒ'nəʊmɪəl) *n.* **1.** *Maths.* expression consisting of single term —*a.* **2.** consisting of single algebraic term

mononucleosis (mɒnəʊnjuːklɪ'əʊsɪs) *n.* **1.** *Pathol.* presence of large number of monocytes in blood **2.** *see* **infectious mononucleosis** *at* INFECT

monophonic (mɒnəʊ'fɒnɪk) *a.* **1.** (of reproduction of sound) using only one channel between source and loudspeaker (*also* **mo'naural**) **2.** *Mus.* of style of musical composition consisting of single melodic line

monoplane ('mɒnəʊpleɪn) *n.* aeroplane with one pair of wings

monopoly (mə'nɒpəlɪ) *n.* **1.** exclusive possession of trade, privilege *etc.* **2.** (M-) R board game for two to six players —**mo'nopolist** *n.* —**mo'nopolize** *or* **-lise** *vt.* claim, take exclusive possession of

monorail ('mɒnəʊreɪl) *n.* railway with cars running on or suspended from single rail

monosodium glutamate (mɒnəʊ-'səʊdɪəm 'gluːtəmeɪt) white crystalline substance used as food additive

monosyllable ('mɒnəsɪləb'l) *n.* word of one syllable

monotheism ('mɒnəʊθɪɪzəm) *n.* belief in only one God —**'monotheist** *n.*

monotone ('mɒnətəʊn) *n.* continuing on one note —**mo'notonous** *a.* lacking in variety, dull, wearisome —**mo'notony** *n.*

monovalent (mɒnəʊ'veɪlənt) *a. Chem.* **1.** having valency of one **2.** having only one

valency (*also* uni'valent) —mono'valence
or mono'valency *n.*

monoxide (mɒ'nɒksaɪd) *n.* oxide that
contains one oxygen atom per molecule

Monseigneur (mɔ̃seˈnœːr) *Fr.* title given
to French bishops, prelates, and princes
(*pl. Messeigneurs* (meseˈnœːr))

monsieur (məsˈjɜː) *n.* French title of
address equivalent to *sir* when used alone
or *Mr.* before name

Monsignor (mɒnˈsiːnjə) *n. R.C.Ch.* ecclesiastical title attached to certain offices

monsoon (mɒnˈsuːn) *n.* 1. seasonal wind of
SE Asia 2. very heavy rainfall season

monster ('mɒnstə) *n.* 1. fantastic imaginary beast 2. misshapen animal or plant 3.
very wicked person 4. huge person, animal
or thing —*a.* 5. huge —**mon'strosity** *n.* 1.
monstrous being 2. deformity 3. distortion
—'**monstrous** *a.* 1. of, like monster 2.
unnatural 3. enormous 4. horrible —'**mon-
strously** *adv.*

monstrance ('mɒnstrəns) *n. R.C.Ch.*
vessel in which consecrated Host is
exposed for adoration

montage (mɒnˈtɑːʒ) *n.* 1. elements of two
or more pictures imposed upon a single
background to give a unified effect 2.
method of editing a film

montbretia (mɒnˈbriːʃə) *n.* plant with
orange flowers on long stems

month (mʌnθ) *n.* 1. one of twelve periods
into which the year is divided 2. period of
moon's revolution —'**monthly** *a.* 1.
happening or payable once a month
—*adv.* 2. once a month —*n.* 3. magazine
published every month

monument ('mɒnjumənt) *n.* anything that
commemorates, *esp.* a building or statue
—**monu'mental** *a.* 1. vast, lasting 2. of or
serving as monument —**monumental
mason** maker and engraver of tombstones

moo (muː) *n.* 1. cry of cow —*vi.* 2. make
this noise, low

mooch (muːtʃ) *vi. sl.* loaf, slouch

mood[1] (muːd) *n.* state of mind and feelings
—'**moody** *a.* 1. gloomy, pensive 2.
changeable in mood

mood[2] (muːd) *n. Gram.* form indicating
function of verb

Moog synthesizer (muːg, məʊg) **R**
electrophonic instrument operated by
keyboard and pedals

moon (muːn) *n.* 1. satellite which takes
lunar month to revolve round earth 2. any
secondary planet —*vi.* 3. (*oft. with* around)
go about dreamily —'**moony** *a. inf.*
dreamy or listless 2. of or like moon
—'**mooncalf** *n.* 1. born fool; dolt 2. person
who idles time away (*pl.* -**calves**)
—'**moonlight** *n.* 1. light of moon —*vi.* 2.
hold two paid occupations —**moonlight flit**
hurried departure by night to escape from
one's creditors —'**moonscape** *n.* general
surface of moon or representation of it
—'**moonshine** *n.* 1. whisky illicitly distilled
2. nonsense —'**moonshot** *n.* launching of
spacecraft *etc.* to moon —'**moonstone** *n.*

transparent semiprecious stone —'**moon-
struck** *a.* deranged

moor[1] (mʊə, mɔː) *n.* tract of open
uncultivated land, often hilly and heather-
clad —'**moorhen** *n.* water bird

moor[2] (mʊə, mɔː) *v.* secure (ship) with
chains or ropes —'**moorage** *n.* place,
charge for mooring —'**moorings** *pl.n.* 1.
ropes *etc.* for mooring 2. something
providing stability, security

Moor (mʊə, mɔː) *n.* member of race in
Morocco and adjoining parts of N Afr.

moose (muːs) *n.* N Amer. deer, like elk

moot (muːt) *a.* 1. that is open to argument,
debatable —*vt.* 2. bring for discussion —*n.*
3. meeting

mop (mɒp) *n.* 1. bundle of yarn, cloth *etc.*
on end of stick, used for cleaning 2. tangle
(of hair *etc.*) —*vt.* 3. clean, wipe with mop
or other absorbent stuff (-**pp-**)

mope (məʊp) *vi.* be gloomy, apathetic

moped ('məʊpɛd) *n.* light motorized
bicycle

moquette (mɒˈkɛt) *n.* thick fabric used for
upholstery *etc.*

moraine (mɒˈreɪn) *n.* accumulated mass
of debris, earth, stones *etc.*, deposited by
glacier

moral ('mɒrəl) *a.* 1. pert. to right and
wrong conduct 2. of good conduct —*n.* 3.
practical lesson, *eg* of fable —*pl.* 4. habits
with respect to right and wrong, *esp.* in
matters of sex —'**moralist** *n.* teacher of
morality —**mo'rality** *n.* 1. good moral
conduct 2. moral goodness or badness 3.
kind of medieval drama, containing moral
lesson —'**moralize** *or* -**lise** *vi.* 1. write, talk
about moral aspect of things —*vt.* 2.
interpret morally —'**morally** *adv.* —**moral
philosophy** branch of philosophy dealing
with ethics —**moral victory** triumph that
is psychological rather than practical

morale (mɒˈrɑːl) *n.* degree of confidence,
hope of person or group

morass (mɒˈræs) *n.* 1. marsh 2. mess

moratorium (mɒrəˈtɔːrɪəm) *n.* 1. act
authorizing postponement of payments
etc. 2. delay (*pl.* -**ria** (-**rɪə**))

moray (mɒˈreɪ) *n.* large, voracious eel

morbid ('mɔːbɪd) *a.* 1. unduly interested in
death 2. gruesome 3. diseased

mordant ('mɔːdənt) *a.* 1. biting 2. corrosive
3. scathing —*n.* 4. substance that fixes dyes

more (mɔː) *comp.* of MANY *and* MUCH *a.* 1.
greater in quantity or number —*adv.* 2. to
a greater extent 3. in addition —*pron.* 4.
greater or additional amount or number
—**more'over** *adv.* besides, further

morel (mɒˈrɛl) *n.* edible fungus in which
mushroom has pitted cap

morello (mɒˈrɛləʊ) *n.* variety of small
dark sour cherry (*pl.* -**s**)

mores ('mɔːreɪz) *pl.n.* customs and
conventions embodying fundamental
values of society *etc.*

morganatic marriage (mɔːgəˈnætɪk)
marriage of king or prince in which wife
does not share husband's rank or

possessions and children do not inherit from father

morgen ('mɔːgən) *n. SA* land unit, approx. two acres (0.8 hectare)

morgue (mɔːg) *n.* mortuary

moribund ('mɒrɪbʌnd) *a.* 1. dying 2. stagnant

Mormon ('mɔːmən) *n.* member of religious sect founded in U.S.A. —'**Mormonism** *n.*

mornay ('mɔːneɪ) *a.* denoting cheese sauce used in various dishes

morning ('mɔːnɪŋ) *n.* early part of day until noon —**morn** *n. Poet.* morning —**morning dress** formal day dress for men, comprising cutaway frock coat, usu. with grey trousers and top hat —**morning-glory** *n.* plant with trumpet-shaped flowers which close in late afternoon —**morning sickness** *inf.* nausea occurring shortly after rising during early months of pregnancy —**morning star** planet, usu. Venus, seen just before sunrise —**the morning after** *inf.* aftereffects of excess, *esp.* hangover

morocco (mə'rɒkəʊ) *n.* goatskin leather

moron ('mɔːrɒn) *n.* 1. mentally deficient person 2. *inf.* fool —**mo'ronic** *a.*

morose (mə'rəʊs) *a.* sullen, moody

morphine ('mɔːfiːn) *or* **morphia** ('mɔːfɪə) *n.* narcotic extract of opium, drug used to induce sleep and relieve pain

morphology (mɔː'fɒlədʒɪ) *n.* 1. science of structure of organisms 2. form and structure of words of a language —**mor-pho'logical** *a.*

morris dance ('mɒrɪs) English folk dance

morrow ('mɒrəʊ) *n. Poet.* next day

Morse (mɔːs) *n.* system of telegraphic signalling in which letters of alphabet are represented by combinations of dots and dashes, or short and long flashes

morsel ('mɔːs'l) *n.* fragment, small piece

mortal ('mɔːt'l) *a.* 1. subject to death 2. causing death —*n.* 3. mortal creature —**mor'tality** *n.* 1. state of being mortal 2. great loss of life 3. death rate —**mortally** *adv.* 1. fatally 2. deeply, intensely —**mortal sin** *R.C.Ch.* sin meriting damnation

mortar ('mɔːtə) *n.* 1. mixture of lime, sand and water for holding bricks and stones together 2. small cannon firing over short range 3. vessel in which substances are pounded —**'mortarboard** *n.* square academic cap

mortgage ('mɔːgɪdʒ) *n.* 1. conveyance of property as security for debt with provision that property be reconveyed on payment within agreed time —*vt.* 2. convey by mortgage 3. pledge as security —**mortga'gee** *n.* —**mortgagor** (mɔːgɪ'dʒɔː) *or* **mortga'ger** *n.*

mortify ('mɔːtɪfaɪ) *vt.* 1. humiliate 2. subdue by self-denial —*vi.* 3. (of flesh) be affected with gangrene (-**fied**, -**fying**) —**mortifi'cation** *n.*

mortise *or* **mortice** ('mɔːtɪs) *n.* 1. hole in piece of wood *etc.* to receive the tongue (tenon) and end of another piece —*vt.* 2. make mortise in 3. fasten by mortise and tenon —**mortise lock** lock embedded in door

mortuary ('mɔːtʃʊərɪ) *n.* 1. building where corpses are kept before burial —*a.* 2. of, for burial

mosaic (mə'zeɪɪk) *n.* 1. picture or pattern of small bits of coloured stone, glass *etc.* 2. this process of decoration

Mosaic (məʊ'zeɪɪk) *a.* of Moses

Moselle (məʊ'zel) *n.* light white wine

Moslem ('mɒzləm) *n. see* MUSLIM

mosque (mɒsk) *n.* Muslim temple

mosquito (mə'skiːtəʊ) *n.* various kinds of flying, biting insects (*pl.* -**es**)

moss (mɒs) *n.* 1. small plant growing in masses on moist surfaces 2. peat bog, swamp —**'mossy** *a.* covered with moss —**moss agate** agate with mosslike markings —**moss stitch** knitting stitch made up of alternate plain and purl stitches

mossie ('mɒsɪ) *n. SA* Cape sparrow

most (məʊst) *sup. of* MUCH *and* MANY *a.* 1. greatest in size, number, or degree —*n.* 2. greatest number, amount, or degree —*adv.* 3. in the greatest degree 4. *US* almost —**'mostly** *adv.* for the most part, generally, on the whole —**Most Reverend** courtesy title applied to archbishops

M.O.T. Ministry of Transport —**M.O.T.** (**test**) compulsory annual test of the roadworthiness of vehicles over a certain age

mote (məʊt) *n.* tiny speck

motel (məʊ'tel) *n.* roadside hotel with accommodation for motorists and vehicles

motet (məʊ'tet) *n.* short sacred vocal composition

moth (mɒθ) *n.* 1. usu. nocturnal insect like butterfly 2. its grub —**'mothy** *a.* infested with moths —**'mothball** *n.* 1. small ball of camphor or naphthalene to repel moths from stored clothing *etc.* —*vt.* 2. put in mothballs 3. store, postpone *etc.* —**'motheaten** *a.* 1. eaten, damaged by grub of moth 2. decayed, scruffy

mother ('mʌðə) *n.* 1. female parent 2. head of religious community of women —*a.* 3. natural, native, inborn —*vt.* 4. act as mother to —**'motherhood** *n.* —**'motherly** *a.* —**Mother Carey's chicken** ('kɛərɪz) *see* stormy petrel *at* STORM —**mother country** 1. original country of colonists or settlers 2. person's native country —**mother earth** 1. earth as a mother, particularly in its fertility 2. soil; ground —**mother-in-law** *n.* mother of one's husband or wife —**mother of pearl** iridescent lining of certain shells —**mother tongue** 1. language first learned by child 2. language from which another has evolved

motif (məʊ'tiːf) *n.* 1. dominating theme 2. recurring design

motion ('məʊʃən) *n.* 1. process or action or way of moving 2. proposal in meeting 3. application to judge 4. evacuation of

motive 315 MT

bowels —v. **5.** signal or direct by sign —'**motionless** a. still, immobile

motive ('məʊtɪv) n. **1.** that which makes person act in particular way **2.** inner impulse —a. **3.** causing motion —'**motivate** vt. **1.** instigate **2.** incite —moti'**vation** n. —'**motivative** a. —**motive power 1.** any source of energy used to produce motion **2.** means of supplying power to engine, vehicle etc.

mot juste (mo 'ʒyst) Fr. appropriate word or expression (pl. **mots justes** (mo 'ʒyst))

motley ('mɒtlɪ) a. **1.** miscellaneous, varied **2.** multicoloured —n. **3.** motley colour or mixture **4.** jester's particoloured dress

motocross ('məʊtəkrɒs) n. motorcycle race over rough course

motor ('məʊtə) n. **1.** that which imparts movement **2.** machine to supply motive power **3.** motorcar —vi. **4.** travel by car —'**motoring** n. —'**motorist** n. user of motorcar —'**motorize** or **-ise** vt. **1.** equip with motor **2.** provide with motor transport —'**motorbike**, '**motorboat**, '**motorcar**, '**motorcycle, motor scooter** n. vehicles driven by motor —**motorcade** ('məʊtəkeɪd) n. parade of cars —**motor nerve** nerve which controls muscular movement —'**motorway** n. main road for fast-moving traffic, with limited access

mottle ('mɒt³l) vt. **1.** mark with blotches, variegate —n. **2.** arrangement of blotches **3.** blotch on surface

motto ('mɒtəʊ) n. **1.** saying adopted as rule of conduct **2.** short inscribed sentence **3.** word or sentence on heraldic crest (pl. **-s**, **-es**)

moue (mu) Fr. pouting look

moufflon ('muːflɒn) n. wild mountain sheep

mould¹ or U.S. **mold** (məʊld) n. **1.** hollow object in which metal etc. is cast **2.** pattern for shaping **3.** character **4.** shape, form —vt. **5.** shape or pattern —'**moulding** or U.S. '**molding** n. **1.** moulded object **2.** ornamental edging **3.** decoration —'**mouldboard** or U.S. '**moldboard** n. curved blade of plough

mould² or U.S. **mold** (məʊld) n. fungoid growth caused by dampness —'**mouldy** or U.S. '**moldy** a. stale, musty

mould³ or U.S. **mold** (məʊld) n. loose or surface earth —'**moulder** or U.S. '**molder** vi. decay into dust

moult or U.S. **molt** (məʊlt) v. **1.** cast or shed (fur, feathers etc.) —n. **2.** moulting

mound (maʊnd) n. **1.** heap of earth or stones **2.** small hill

mount (maʊnt) vi. **1.** rise **2.** increase **3.** get on horseback —vt. **4.** get up on **5.** frame (picture) **6.** fix, set up **7.** provide with horse —n. **8.** that on which thing is supported or fitted **9.** horse **10.** hill

mountain ('maʊntɪn) n. **1.** hill of great size **2.** surplus —**mountain'eer** n. one who lives among or climbs mountains —**mountain**-'**eering** n. —'**mountainous** a. very high, rugged —**mountain lion** puma

mountebank ('maʊntɪbæŋk) n. charlatan, fake

Mountie or **Mounty** ('maʊntɪ) n. inf. member of Royal Canadian Mounted Police

mourn (mɔːn) v. feel, show sorrow (for) —'**mourner** n. —'**mournful** a. **1.** sad **2.** dismal —'**mournfully** adv. —'**mourning** n. **1.** grieving **2.** conventional signs of grief for death **3.** clothes of mourner —**mourning band** piece of black material, esp. armband, worn to indicate mourning

mouse (maʊs) n. **1.** small rodent (pl. **mice**) —vi. (maʊz) **2.** catch, hunt mice **3.** prowl —'**mouser** n. cat used for catching mice —'**mousy** or '**mousey** a. **1.** like mouse, esp. in colour **2.** meek, shy —'**mousetrap** n. **1.** any trap for catching mice **2.** UK inf. cheese of indifferent quality

mousse (muːs) n. sweet dish of flavoured cream whipped and chilled

moustache or U.S. **mustache** (məˈstɑːʃ) n. hair on the upper lip —**moustache cup** cup with partial cover to protect drinker's moustache

mouth (maʊθ) n. **1.** opening in head for eating, speaking etc. **2.** opening into anything hollow **3.** outfall of river **4.** entrance to harbour etc. —vt. (maʊð) **5.** declaim, esp. in public **6.** form (words) with lips without speaking **7.** take, move in mouth —'**mouthful** n. **1.** as much as is held in mouth at one time **2.** small quantity, as of food **3.** word etc. difficult to say —**mouth organ** harmonica —'**mouthpiece** n. **1.** end of anything placed between lips, eg pipe **2.** spokesman —'**mouthwash** n. medicated solution for cleansing mouth

move (muːv) vt. **1.** change position of **2.** stir emotions of **3.** incite **4.** propose for consideration —vi. **5.** change places **6.** change one's dwelling etc. **7.** take action —n. **8.** a moving **9.** motion towards some goal —'**movable** or '**moveable** a./n. —'**movement** n. **1.** process, action of moving **2.** moving parts of machine **3.** division of piece of music

movie ('muːvɪ) US inf. n. **1.** film —pl. **2.** cinema

mow (məʊ) v. cut (grass etc.) (**mown** pp.) —'**mower** n. man or machine that mows

mp or **m.p.** Mus. mezzo piano

M.P. 1. Member of Parliament **2.** Military Police **3.** Mounted Police

m.p.g. miles per gallon

m.p.h. miles per hour

M.Phil. or **M.Ph.** Master of Philosophy

Mr. ('mɪstə) mister

Mrs. ('mɪsɪz) title of married woman —**Mrs. Mopp** charwoman

MS Mississippi

Ms. (mɪz, məs) title used instead of Miss or Mrs.

MS. or **ms.** manuscript (pl. **MSS.** or **mss.**)

M.Sc. Master of Science

M.S.C. Manpower Services Commission

M.S.T. US, C Mountain Standard Time

MT Montana

Mt. *or* **mt.** Mount

M.Tech. Master of Technology

mu (mju:) *n.* 12th letter in Gr. alphabet (M, μ)

much (mʌtʃ) *a.* **1.** existing in quantity —*n.* **2.** large amount **3.** a great deal **4.** important matter —*adv.* **5.** in a great degree **6.** nearly (**more** *comp.,* **most** *sup.*)

mucilage ('mju:sɪlɪdʒ) *n.* gum, glue

muck (mʌk) *n.* **1.** cattle dung **2.** unclean refuse —'**mucky** *a.* **1.** dirty **2.** messy **3.** unpleasant —'**muckrake** *vi.* seek out and expose scandal, *esp.* concerning public figures —'**muckraking** *n.* —'**mucksweat** *n.* UK *inf.* profuse sweat or state of profuse sweating —**muck about** UK *sl.* **1.** waste time; misbehave **2.** annoy, interfere (with) —**muck up** UK *sl.* ruin, spoil

mucus ('mju:kəs) *n.* viscid fluid secreted by mucous membrane —**mu'cosity** *n.* —'**mucous** *a.* **1.** resembling mucus **2.** secreting mucus **3.** slimy —**mucous membrane** lining of canals and cavities of the body

mud (mʌd) *n.* **1.** wet and soft earth **2.** *inf.* slander —'**muddy** *a.* —'**mudguard** *n.* cover over wheel to prevent mud, water *etc.* being splashed —'**mudlark** *n.* **1.** formerly, one who made a living by picking up odds and ends in the mud of tidal rivers **2.** *sl., rare* street urchin —'**mudpack** *n.* cosmetic paste to improve complexion —'**mudslinger** *n.* —'**mudslinging** *n.* casting malicious slurs on an opponent, *esp.* in politics

muddle ('mʌd³l) *vt.* **1.** (*esp. with* up) confuse **2.** bewilder **3.** mismanage —*n.* **4.** confusion **5.** tangle

muesli ('mju:zlɪ) *n.* mixture of grain, dried fruit *etc.* eaten with milk

muezzin (mu:'ɛzɪn) *n.* crier who summons Muslims to prayer

muff[1] (mʌf) *n.* tube-shaped covering to keep the hands warm

muff[2] (mʌf) *vt.* miss, bungle, fail in

muffin ('mʌfɪn) *n.* round, spongy, flat scone

muffle ('mʌf³l) *vt.* wrap up, *esp.* to deaden sound —'**muffler** *n.* scarf

mufti ('mʌftɪ) *n.* plain clothes as distinguished from uniform, *eg* of soldier

mug[1] (mʌg) *n.* drinking cup

mug[2] (mʌg) *n.* *sl.* **1.** face **2.** fool, simpleton, one easily imposed upon —*vt.* **3.** *inf.* rob violently (**-gg-**) —'**mugger** *n.*

mug[3] (mʌg) *vi.* *inf.* (*esp. with* up) study hard (**-gg-**)

muggins ('mʌgɪnz) *n.* *inf.* fool, simpleton

muggy ('mʌgɪ) *a.* damp and stifling

mukluk ('mʌklʌk) *n.* C Eskimo's soft (sealskin) boot

mulatto (mju:'lætəʊ) *n.* child of one White and one Negro parent (*pl.* **-s, -es**)

mulberry ('mʌlbərɪ, -brɪ) *n.* **1.** tree whose leaves are used to feed silkworms **2.** its purplish fruit

mulch (mʌltʃ) *n.* **1.** straw, leaves *etc.,* spread as protection for roots of plants —*vt.* **2.** protect thus

mulct (mʌlkt) *vt.* **1.** defraud **2.** fine

mule[1] (mju:l) *n.* **1.** animal which is cross between horse and ass **2.** hybrid **3.** spinning machine —**muleteer** (mju:lɪ'tɪə) *n.* mule driver —'**mulish** *a.* obstinate

mule[2] (mju:l) *n.* backless shoe or slipper

mull[1] (mʌl) *vt.* heat (wine) with sugar and spices —**mull over** think over, ponder

mull[2] (mʌl) *n.* light muslin fabric of soft texture

mullah *or* **mulla** ('mʌlə, 'mʊlə) *n.* Muslim theologian

mullein ('mʌlɪn) *n.* plant with tall spikes of yellow flowers

mullet ('mʌlɪt) *n.* edible sea fish

mulligatawny (mʌlɪgə'tɔ:nɪ) *n.* soup made with curry powder

mullion ('mʌlɪən) *n.* upright dividing bar in window —'**mullioned** *a.*

multangular (mʌl'tæŋgjʊlə) *or* **multiangular** *a.* having many angles

multi- (*comb. form*) many, as in *multiracial, multistorey.* Such words are omitted where the meaning may easily be found from the simple word

multifarious (mʌltɪ'fɛərɪəs) *a.* of various kinds or parts —**multi'fariously** *adv.*

multilateral (mʌltɪ'lætərəl, -'lætrəl) *a.* **1.** of or involving more than two nations or parties **2.** having many sides

multinational (mʌltɪ'næʃən³l) *a.* (of large business company) operating in several countries

multiple ('mʌltɪp³l) *a.* **1.** having many parts —*n.* **2.** quantity which contains another an exact number of times —**multipli'cand** *n. Maths.* number to be multiplied —**multipli'cation** *n.* —**multi'plicity** *n.* variety, greatness in number —'**multiplier** *n.* **1.** person or thing that multiplies **2.** number by which multiplicand is multiplied **3.** *Phys.* any instrument, as photomultiplier, for increasing effect —'**multiply** *vt.* **1.** increase in number **2.** add (a number) to itself a given number of times —*vi.* **3.** increase in number or amount (**-plied, -plying**) —**multiple-choice** *a.* having a number of possible given answers out of which the correct one must be chosen —**multiple sclerosis** chronic disease of central nervous system, resulting in speech disorder, partial paralysis *etc.* —**multiplication table** one of group of tables giving results of multiplying two numbers together

multiplex ('mʌltɪplɛks) *a. Telecomm.* capable of transmitting numerous messages over same wire or channel

multitude ('mʌltɪtju:d) *n.* **1.** great number **2.** great crowd **3.** populace —**multi'tudinous** *a.* very numerous

mum (mʌm) *n. inf.* mother

mumble ('mʌmb³l) *vi.* **1.** speak indistinctly —*v.* **2.** mutter

mumbo jumbo ('mʌmbəʊ) **1.** foolish religious reverence or incantation **2.**

meaningless or unnecessarily complicated language

mummer ('mʌmə) n. actor in dumb show —**mum** a. 1. silent —v. 2. act in mime (-mm-) —'**mummery** n. dumb-show acting

mummy ('mʌmɪ) n. embalmed body —'**mummify** v. (-fied, -fying)

mumps (mʌmps) pl.n. infectious disease marked by swelling in the glands of the neck

mun. municipal

munch (mʌntʃ) v. 1. chew noisily and vigorously 2. crunch

mundane ('mʌndeɪn, mʌn'deɪn) a. 1. ordinary, everyday 2. belonging to this world, earthly

municipal (mjuː'nɪsɪpəl) a. belonging to affairs of city or town —**munici'pality** n. 1. city or town with local self-government 2. its governing body

munificent (mjuː'nɪfɪsənt) a. very generous —mu'**nificence** n. bounty

muniments ('mjuːnɪmənts) pl.n. title deeds, documents verifying ownership

munition (mjuː'nɪʃən) n. (usu. pl.) military stores

muon ('mjuːɒn) n. positive or negative elementary particle with mass 207 times that of electron

mural ('mjuərəl) n. 1. painting on a wall —a. 2. of or on a wall

murder ('mɜːdə) n. 1. unlawful premeditated killing of human being —vt. 2. kill thus —n. —'**murderer** n. ('**murderess** fem.) —'**murderous** a.

murk or **mirk** (mɜːk) n. thick darkness —'**murky** or '**mirky** a. gloomy

murmur ('mɜːmə) n. 1. low, indistinct sound —vi. 2. make such a sound 3. complain —vt. 4. utter in a low voice

murrain ('mʌrɪn) n. cattle plague

mus. 1. museum 2. music(al)

Mus.B. or **Mus.Bac.** Bachelor of Music

muscat ('mʌskət, -kæt) n. 1. muskflavoured grape 2. raisin —musca'tel n. 1. muscat 2. strong wine made from it

muscle ('mʌsəl) n. 1. part of body which produces movement by contracting 2. system of muscles —**muscular** ('mʌskjʊlə) a. 1. with well-developed muscles 2. strong 3. of, like muscle —**musculature** ('mʌskjʊlətʃə) n. 1. arrangement of muscles in organ or part 2. total muscular system of organism —**muscle-bound** a. with muscles stiff through overdevelopment —'**muscleman** n. 1. man with highly developed muscles 2. henchman employed by gangster etc. to intimidate or use violence upon victims —**muscular dystrophy** disease with wasting of muscles —**muscle in** inf. force one's way in

Muscovy duck ('mʌskəvɪ) or **musk duck** large crested widely domesticated S Amer. duck

Mus.D. or **Mus.Doc.** Doctor of Music

muse (mjuːz) vi. 1. ponder 2. consider meditatively 3. be lost in thought —n. 4. state of musing or abstraction 5. reverie

Muse (mjuːz) n. one of the nine goddesses inspiring learning and the arts

museum (mjuː'zɪəm) n. (place housing) collection of natural, artistic, historical or scientific objects —**museum piece** 1. object fit to be kept in museum 2. inf. person or thing regarded as antiquated

mush (mʌʃ) n. 1. soft pulpy mass 2. inf. cloying sentimentality —'**mushy** a.

mushroom ('mʌʃruːm, -rum) n. 1. fungoid growth, typically with stem and cap structure, some species edible —vi. 2. shoot up rapidly 3. expand —**mushroom cloud** mushroom-shaped cloud produced by nuclear explosion

music ('mjuːzɪk) n. 1. art form using melodious and harmonious combination of notes 2. laws of this 3. composition in this art —'**musical** a. 1. of, like music 2. interested in, or with instinct for, music 3. pleasant to ear —n. 4. show, film in which music plays essential part —'**musically** adv. —mu'**sician** n. —musi'**cologist** n. —musi'**cology** n. scientific study of music —**musical chairs** party game in which players walk around chairs to music, there being one fewer chairs than players: when music stops, player without a chair is eliminated —**musical comedy** light dramatic entertainment with songs, dances etc. —**music box** or **musical box** mechanical instrument that plays tunes by means of pins on revolving cylinder striking tuned teeth of comblike metal plate —**music centre** single hi-fi unit containing turntable, amplifier, radio and cassette player —**music hall** variety theatre

musk (mʌsk) n. 1. scent obtained from gland of **musk deer** 2. any of various plants with similar scent —'**musky** a. —'**muskmelon** n. any of several varieties of melon, such as cantaloupe, having ribbed or warty rind and musky aroma —**musk ox** ox of Arctic Amer. —'**muskrat** n. 1. N Amer. rodent found near water 2. its fur —**musk rose** rose cultivated for its white musk-scented flowers

muskeg ('mʌskɛg) n. C boggy hollow

muskellunge ('mʌskəlʌndʒ) or **maskinonge** ('mæskənɒndʒ) n. N Amer. freshwater game fish

musket ('mʌskɪt) n. Hist. infantryman's gun —muske'teer n. —'**musketry** n. (use of) small firearms

Muslim ('muzlɪm, 'mʌz-) or **Moslem** n. 1. follower of religion of Islam —a. 2. of religion, culture etc. of Islam

muslin ('mʌzlɪn) n. fine cotton fabric —'**muslined** a.

musquash ('mʌskwɒʃ) n. muskrat

mussel ('mʌsəl) n. bivalve shellfish

must¹ (mʌst; unstressed məst, məs) v. aux. 1. be obliged to, or certain to —n. 2. something one must do

must² (mʌst) n. 1. newly-pressed grape juice 2. unfermented wine

mustang ('mʌstæŋ) n. wild horse

mustard ('mʌstəd) n. 1. powder made from the seeds of a plant, used in paste as a condiment 2. the plant —**mustard gas** poisonous gas causing blistering

muster ('mʌstə) v. 1. assemble —n. 2. assembly, esp. for exercise, inspection

musty ('mʌsti) a. mouldy, stale —**must** or '**mustiness** n.

mutate (mju:'teit) v. (cause to) undergo mutation —'**mutable** a. liable to change —'**mutant** n. mutated animal, plant etc. —**mu'tation** n. change, esp. genetic change causing divergence from kind or racial type

mute (mju:t) a. 1. dumb 2. silent —n. 3. dumb person 4. Mus. contrivance to soften tone of instruments —'**muted** a. 1. (of sound) muffled 2. (of light) subdued —'**mutely** adv.

muti ('mu:ti) n. SA (herbal) medicine

mutilate ('mju:tileit) vt. 1. deprive of a limb or other part 2. damage, deface —**muti'lation** n. —'**mutilator** n.

mutiny ('mju:tini) n. 1. rebellion against authority, esp. against officers of disciplined body —vi. 2. commit mutiny ('**mutinied**, '**mutinying**) —**muti'neer** n. —'**mutinous** a. rebellious

mutt (mʌt) n. inf. 1. stupid person 2. dog

mutter ('mʌtə) vi. 1. speak with mouth nearly closed, indistinctly 2. grumble —vt. 3. utter in such tones —n. 4. act, sound of muttering

mutton ('mʌt⁸n) n. flesh of sheep used as food —**mutton bird** migratory seabird —'**muttonchops** pl.n. side whiskers trimmed in shape of chops —'**muttonhead** n. sl. fool

mutual ('mju:tʃʊəl) a. 1. done, possessed etc. by each of two with respect to the other 2. reciprocal 3. inf. common to both or all —'**mutually** adv.

Muzak ('mju:zæk) n. R recorded light music played in shops etc.

muzzle ('mʌz⁸l) n. 1. mouth and nose of animal 2. cover for these to prevent biting 3. open end of gun —vt. 4. put muzzle on 5. silence, gag

muzzy ('mʌzi) a. indistinct, confused, muddled

MV motor vessel

mW milliwatt(s)

MW megawatt(s)

Mx Phys. maxwell

my (mai) a. belonging to me —**my'self** pron. emphatic or reflexive form of I

myalgia (mai'ældʒiə) n. pain in a muscle

mycelium (mai'si:liəm) n. vegetative body of fungi (pl. -**lia** (-liə)) —**my'celial** a.

Mycenaean (maisi'ni:ən) a. 1. of ancient Mycenae or its inhabitants 2. of Aegean civilization of Mycenae (1400 to 1100 B.C.)

mycology (mai'kɒlədʒi) n. science of fungi

myna, mynah, or **mina** ('mainə) n. Indian bird related to starling

myopia (mai'əupiə) n. short-sightedness —**myopic** (mai'ɒpik) a.

myosotis (maiə'səutis) n. any of various kinds of small plant with blue, pink or white flowers, eg forget-me-not

myriad ('miriəd) a. 1. innumerable —n. 2. large indefinite number

myriapod ('miriəpɒd) n. 1. any of group of terrestrial arthropods having long segmented body, such as the centipede —a. 2. of or belonging to this group

myrmidon ('mɜ:midɒn, -d⁸n) n. follower or henchman

myrrh (mɜ:) n. aromatic gum, formerly used as incense

myrtle ('mɜ:t⁸l) n. flowering evergreen shrub

myself (mai'self) pron. see MY

mystery ('mistəri, -tri) n. 1. obscure or secret thing 2. anything strange or inexplicable 3. religious rite 4. in Middle Ages, biblical play —**mys'terious** a. —**mys'teriously** adv.

mystic ('mistik) n. 1. one who seeks divine, spiritual knowledge, esp. by prayer, contemplation etc. —a. 2. of hidden meaning, esp. in religious sense —'**mystical** a. —'**mysticism** n.

mystify ('mistifai) vt. bewilder, puzzle (-**fied**, -**fying**) —**mystifi'cation** n.

mystique (mi'sti:k) n. aura of mystery, power etc.

myth (miθ) n. 1. tale with supernatural characters or events 2. invented story 3. imaginary person or object —'**mythical** a. —**mytho'logical** a. —**my'thologist** n. —**my'thology** n. 1. myths collectively 2. study of them

myxomatosis (miksəmə'təusis) n. contagious, fatal disease of rabbits caused by a virus

N

n *or* **N** (ɛn) *n.* **1.** 14th letter of English alphabet **2.** speech sound represented by this letter (*pl.* **n's, N's** *or* **Ns**)

n (ɛn) *a.* indefinite number (of) —**nth** (ɛnθ) *a.* **1.** *Maths.* of unspecified ordinal number, usu. greatest in series **2.** *inf.* being last or most extreme of long series —**to the nth degree** *inf.* to the utmost extreme

N 1. *Chess* knight **2.** *Chem.* nitrogen **3.** *Phys.* newton **4.** north(ern)

n. 1. neuter **2.** noun **3.** number

Na *Chem.* sodium

NAAFI ('næfɪ) *n.* organization providing canteens *etc.* for the services (*N*avy, *A*rmy and *A*ir *F*orce *I*nstitutes)

naartjie ('nɑːtʃɪ) *n.* SA tangerine

nab (næb) *vt. inf.* **1.** arrest criminal **2.** catch suddenly (**-bb-**)

nacre ('neɪkə) *n.* **1.** mother-of-pearl **2.** shellfish

nadir ('neɪdɪə, 'næ-) *n.* **1.** point opposite the zenith **2.** lowest point

nae (neɪ) *Scots word for* no (sense 1)

naff (næf) *a.* UK *sl.* inferior, useless —**naff off** UK *sl.* forceful expression of dismissal or contempt

nag¹ (næg) *v.* **1.** scold or annoy constantly **2.** cause pain to constantly (**-gg-**) —*n.* **3.** nagging **4.** one who nags

nag² (næg) *n.* **1.** *inf.* horse **2.** small horse for riding

naiad ('naɪæd) *n.* water nymph (*pl.* **-s, -ades** (-ədiːz))

naïf (nɑːˈiːf) *a. see* NAIVE

nail (neɪl) *n.* **1.** horny shield at ends of fingers, toes **2.** claw **3.** small metal spike for fixing wood *etc.* —*vt.* **4.** fix, stud with nails **5.** *inf.* catch —**'nailfile** *n.* small file used to trim nails —**nail set** punch for driving head of nail below or flush with surrounding surface

naive, naïve (nɑːˈiːv, naɪˈiːv), *or* **naïf** *a.* simple, unaffected, ingenuous —**naiveté, naïveté** (nɑːiːvˈteɪ) *or* **naivety** (naɪˈiːvtɪ) *n.*

naked ('neɪkɪd) *a.* **1.** without clothes **2.** exposed, bare **3.** undisguised —**'nakedly** *adv.* —**'nakedness** *n.* —**naked eye** the eye unassisted by any optical instrument

NALGO ('nælgəʊ) *N*ational *a*nd *L*ocal *G*overnment *O*fficers' Association

namby-pamby (næmbɪˈpæmbɪ) *a.* **1.** weakly **2.** sentimental **3.** insipid —*n.* **4.** namby-pamby person

name (neɪm) *n.* **1.** word by which person, thing *etc.* is denoted **2.** reputation **3.** title **4.** credit **5.** family **6.** famous person —*vt.* **7.** give name to **8.** call by name **9.** entitle **10.** appoint **11.** mention **12.** specify —**'nameless** *a.* **1.** without a name **2.** indescribable **3.** too dreadful to be mentioned **4.** obscure —**'namely** *adv.* that is to say —**name day 1.** R.C.Ch. feast day of saint whose name one bears **2.** *St. Ex.* day before setting day, when stockbrokers are given names of purchasers (*also* **ticket day**) —**'name-dropper** *n.* —**name-dropping** *n. inf.* referring frequently to famous people, *esp.* as though they were intimate friends, in order to impress others —**'nameplate** *n.* small panel on door bearing occupant's name —**'namesake** *n.* person with same name as another

nancy *or* **nancy boy** ('nænsɪ) *n.* effeminate or homosexual boy or man

nankeen (næŋˈkiːn) *or* **nankin** ('nænkɪn) *n.* **1.** buff-coloured cotton fabric **2.** pale greyish-yellow colour

nanny ('nænɪ) *n.* child's nurse —**nanny goat** she-goat

nano- (*comb. form*) 10^{-9}, as in nanosecond

nap¹ (næp) *vi.* **1.** take short sleep, *esp.* in daytime (**-pp-**) —*n.* **2.** short sleep

nap² (næp) *n.* downy surface on cloth made by projecting fibres

nap³ (næp) *n.* card game similar to whist

napalm ('neɪpɑːm, 'næ-) *n.* jellied petrol, highly inflammable, used in bombs *etc.*

nape (neɪp) *n.* back of neck

naphtha ('næfθə, 'næp-) *n.* inflammable oil distilled from coal *etc.* —**'naphthalene** *n.* white crystalline product distilled from coal tar, used in disinfectants, mothballs *etc.*

napkin ('næpkɪn) *n.* **1.** cloth, paper for wiping fingers or lips at table, serviette **2.** small towel **3.** nappy

nappy ('næpɪ) *n.* towelling cloth or other material placed around waist, between legs, of baby to absorb its excrement

narcissus (nɑːˈsɪsəs) *n.* genus of bulbous plants including daffodil, jonquil, *esp.* one with white flowers (*pl.* **-cissi** (-ˈsɪsaɪ)) —**'narcissism** *n.* abnormal love and admiration of oneself —**'narcissist** *n.*

narcotic (nɑːˈkɒtɪk) *n.* **1.** any of a group of drugs, including morphine and opium, producing numbness and stupor, used medicinally but addictive —*a.* **2.** of narcotics or narcosis —**narcosis** (nɑːˈkəʊsɪs) *n.* effect of narcotic

nard (nɑːd) *n.* **1.** *see* **spikenard** *at* SPIKE. **2.** plant whose aromatic roots were formerly used in medicine

nark (nɑːk) *vt. sl.* annoy, irritate

narrate (nəˈreɪt) *vt.* relate, recount, tell (story) —**nar'ration** *n.* —**'narrative** *n.* **1.** account, story —*a.* **2.** relating —**nar'rator** *n.*

narrow ('nærəʊ) *a.* **1.** of little breadth, *esp.* in comparison to length **2.** limited **3.** barely adequate or successful —*v.* **4.** make, become narrow —**'narrowly** *adv.* —**'narrowness** *n.* —**'narrows** *pl.n.* narrow part of straits —**narrow boat** long narrow bargelike boat used on canals —**narrow gauge** smaller distance between lines of railway than standard gauge of 56½ inches —**narrow-gauge** a. of railway with narrow gauge —**narrow-minded** a. 1. illiberal 2. bigoted —**narrow-mindedness** n. prejudice, bigotry

narwhal, narwal ('nɑːwəl), or **narwhale** ('nɑːweil) n. arctic whale with tusk developed from teeth

NASA ('næsə) National Aeronautics and Space Administration

nasal ('neiz²l) a. 1. of nose —n. 2. sound partly produced in nose —'**nasalize** or -**lise** vt. make nasal in sound —'**nasally** adv.

nascent ('næs²nt, 'nei-) a. 1. just coming into existence 2. springing up

nasturtium (nə'stɜːʃəm) n. 1. genus of plants which includes the watercress 2. trailing garden plant with red or orange flowers

nasty ('nɑːstɪ) a. foul, disagreeable, unpleasant —'**nastily** adv. —'**nastiness** n.

NAS/UWT National Association of Schoolmasters/Union of Women Teachers

nat. 1. national 2. native 3. natural

natal ('neit²l) a. of birth

natatory (nə'teitərɪ) or **natatorial** (næ-tə'tɔːrɪəl) a. of swimming —**na'tation** n.

nation ('neiʃən) n. people or race organized as a state —**national** ('næʃən²l) a. 1. belonging or pert. to a nation 2. public, general —n. 3. member of a nation —**nationalism** ('næʃənəlɪzəm) n. 1. loyalty, devotion to one's country 2. movement for independence of state, people, ruled by another —**nationalist** ('næʃənəlɪst) n./a. —**nationality** (næʃə'nælɪtɪ) n. 1. national quality or feeling 2. fact of belonging to particular nation —**nationalization** or -**lisation** (næʃənəlaɪ'zeiʃən) n. acquisition and management of industries by the State —**nationalize** or -**lise** ('næʃənəlaɪz) vt. convert (private industry, resources etc.) to state control —**nationally** ('næʃənəlɪ) adv. —**national assistance** old name for supplementary benefit —**national debt** total financial obligations incurred by nation's central government —**National Front** political organization opposing immigration and advocating extreme nationalism —**national grid** UK 1. network of high-voltage electric power lines linking major electric power stations 2. metric coordinate system used in Ordnance Survey maps —**National Health Service** system of medical services financed mainly by taxation —**national insurance** state insurance scheme providing payments to the unemployed, sick etc. —**national park** area of land controlled by the state to preserve its natural beauty etc. —**National Trust** organization concerned with preservation of historic buildings and areas of countryside of great beauty

native ('neitiv) a. 1. inborn 2. born in particular place 3. found in pure state 4. that was place of one's birth —n. 5. one

born in a place 6. member of indigenous race of a country 7. species of plant, animal etc. originating in a place

nativity (nə'tivitɪ) n. 1. birth 2. time, circumstances of birth 3. (N-) birth of Christ

NATO ('neitəʊ) North Atlantic Treaty Organization

NATSOPA (næt'səʊpə) National Society of Operative Printers and Assistants

natter ('nætə) vi. inf. talk idly

natty ('nætɪ) a. neat and smart; spruce —'**nattily** adv.

nature ('neitʃə) n. 1. innate or essential qualities of person or thing 2. class, sort 3. life force 4. (oft. N-) power underlying all phenomena in material world 5. material world as a whole 6. natural unspoilt scenery or countryside, and plants and animals in it 7. disposition, temperament —**natural** ('nætʃrəl) a. 1. of, according to, occurring in, provided by, nature 2. inborn 3. normal 4. unaffected 5. illegitimate —n. 6. something, somebody well suited for something 7. Mus. character (♮) used to remove effect of sharp or flat preceding it —**naturalism** ('nætʃrəlɪzəm) n. 1. movement, esp. in art and literature, advocating realism 2. belief that all religious truth is based on study of natural causes and processes 3. Philos. rational account of world in terms of natural forces 4. action or thought caused by natural instincts —**naturalist** ('nætʃrəlɪst) n. student of natural history —**naturalistic** (nætʃrə-'lɪstɪk) a. of or imitating nature in effect or characteristics —**naturalization** or -**lisation** (nætʃrəlaɪ'zeiʃən) n. —**naturalize** or -**lise** ('nætʃrəlaɪz) vt. 1. admit to citizenship 2. accustom to new climate —**naturally** ('nætʃrəlɪ) adv. 1. of or according to nature 2. by nature 3. of course —'**naturism** n. 1. nature-worship 2. nudism —'**naturist** n. —**natural gas** gaseous mixture, consisting mainly of methane, trapped below ground; used extensively as fuel —**natural history** study of animals and plants —**natural number** any of positive integers 1, 2, 3, 4,... —**natural philosophy** physical science, esp. physics —**natural resources** naturally occurring materials such as coal etc. —**natural science** any of sciences that are involved in study of physical world, including biology, physics etc. —**natural selection** process resulting in survival of those individuals from population of animals etc. that are best adapted to prevailing environmental conditions —**nature trail** path through countryside of particular interest to naturalists

naught (nɔːt) n. 1. obs. nothing 2. cipher 0 —**set at naught** defy, disregard

naughty ('nɔːtɪ) a. 1. disobedient, not behaving well 2. inf. mildly indecent —'**naughtily** adv.

nausea ('nɔːzɪə, -sɪə) n. feeling that precedes vomiting —'**nauseate** vt. sicken

—'**nauseous** a. 1. disgusting 2. causing nausea

nautical ('nɔːtɪk²l) a. 1. of seamen or ships 2. marine —**nautical mile** 1852 metres

nautilus ('nɔːtɪləs) n. univalvular shellfish (pl. -es, -tili (-tɪlaɪ))

naval ('neɪv²l) a. see NAVY

nave¹ (neɪv) n. main part of church

nave² (neɪv) n. hub of wheel

navel ('neɪv²l) n. small scar, depression in middle of abdomen where umbilical cord was attached (also um'bilicus)

navigate ('nævɪgeɪt) v. 1. plan, direct, plot path or position of (ship etc.) 2. travel —'**navigable** a. —navi'**gation** n. 1. science of directing course of seagoing vessel, or of aircraft in flight 2. shipping —'**navigator** n. one who navigates

navvy ('nævɪ) n. labourer employed on roads, railways etc.

navy ('neɪvɪ) n. 1. fleet 2. warships of country with their crews and organization —a. 3. navy-blue —'**naval** a. of the navy —**navy-blue** a. very dark blue

Nazi ('nɑːtsɪ) n. 1. member of the National Socialist political party in Germany, 1919–45 2. one who thinks, acts like a Nazi (pl. -s) —a. 3. of Nazis —'**Nazism** or '**Naziism** n. Nazi doctrine

Nb Chem. niobium

NB New Brunswick

NB, N.B., or **n.b.** nota bene

NC North Carolina

N.C.B. National Coal Board

N.C.O. noncommissioned officer

Nd Chem. neodymium

ND North Dakota

N.D.P. C New Democratic Party

Ne Chem. neon

NE 1. northeast(ern) 2. Nebraska

Neanderthal (nɪ'ændətɑːl) a. of a type of primitive man

neap (niːp) a. low —**neap tide** the low tide at the first and third quarters of the moon

Neapolitan (nɪə'pɒlɪt²n) n. 1. native of Naples —a. 2. of Naples

near (nɪə) prep. 1. close to —adv. 2. at or to a short distance —a. 3. close at hand 4. closely related 5. narrow, so as barely to escape 6. stingy 7. (of vehicles, horses etc.) left —v. 8. approach —'**nearly** adv. 1. closely 2. almost —'**nearness** n. —'**nearby** a. adjacent —**Near East** 1. see Middle **East** at MIDDLE 2. formerly, Balkan States and area of Ottoman Empire —**nearsighted** a. relating to or suffering from myopia

neat (niːt) a. 1. tidy, orderly 2. efficient 3. precise, deft 4. cleverly worded 5. undiluted 6. simple and elegant 7. sl., chiefly US pleasing; admirable; excellent —'**neaten** vt. make neat; tidy —'**neatly** adv. —'**neatness** n.

neath or '**neath** (niːθ) prep. obs. beneath

N.E.B. 1. New English Bible 2. National Enterprise Board

nebula ('nɛbjʊlə) n. Astron. diffuse cloud of particles, gases (pl. -s, -ulae (-juliː))

—'**nebulous** a. 1. cloudy 2. vague, indistinct

necessary ('nɛsɪsərɪ) a. 1. needful, requisite, that must be done 2. unavoidable, inevitable —'**necessarily** adv. —ne'**cessitate** vt. make necessary —ne'**cessitous** a. poor, needy, destitute —ne'**cessity** n. 1. something needed, requisite 2. constraining power or state of affairs 3. compulsion 4. poverty

neck (nɛk) n. 1. part of body joining head to shoulders 2. narrower part of a bottle etc. 3. narrow piece of anything between wider parts —vi. 4. sl. embrace, cuddle —'**neckerchief** n. kerchief for the neck —'**necklet** n. neck ornament, piece of fur etc. —'**necklace** ('nɛklɪs) n. ornament round the neck —'**necktie** n. US see TIE (sense 6)

necro- or before vowel **necr-** (comb. form) death, dead body, dead tissue, as in necrosis

necromancy ('nɛkrəʊmænsɪ) n. magic, esp. by communication with dead —'**necromancer** n. wizard

necrophilia (nɛkrəʊ'fɪlɪə) n. sexual attraction for or intercourse with dead bodies (also necro'**mania**, ne'**crophilism**)

necropolis (nɛ'krɒpəlɪs) n. cemetery (pl. -es, -oleis (-əleɪs))

nectar ('nɛktə) n. 1. honey of flowers 2. drink of the gods —'**nectary** n. honey gland of flower

nectarine ('nɛktərɪn) n. variety of peach

N.E.D.C. National Economic Development Council

née or **nee** (neɪ) a. indicating maiden name of married woman

need (niːd) vt. 1. want, require —n. 2. (state, instance of) want 3. requirement 4. necessity 5. poverty —'**needful** a. necessary, requisite —'**needless** a. unnecessary —**needs** adv. of necessity (esp. in needs must or must needs) —'**needy** a. poor, in want

needle ('niːd²l) n. 1. pointed pin with an eye and no head, for sewing 2. long, pointed pin for knitting 3. pointer of gauge, dial 4. magnetized bar of compass 5. stylus for record player 6. leaf of fir or pine 7. obelisk 8. inf. hypodermic syringe —vt. 9. inf. goad, provoke —'**needlecord** n. corduroy fabric with narrow ribs —'**needlepoint** n. 1. embroidery done on canvas with various stitches so as to resemble tapestry 2. point lace —**needle time** chiefly UK time allocated by radio channel to broadcasting of recorded music —'**needlework** n. embroidery, sewing

ne'er (nɛə) adv. Lit. never —**ne'er-do-well** n. worthless person

nefarious (nɪ'fɛərɪəs) a. wicked

neg. negative(ly)

negate (nɪ'geɪt) vt. deny, nullify —ne'**gation** n. contradiction, denial

negative ('nɛgətɪv) a. 1. expressing denial or refusal 2. lacking enthusiasm, energy, interest 3. not positive 4. (of electrical charge) having the same polarity as the charge of an electron —n. 5. negative word or statement 6. *Photog.* picture made by action of light on chemicals in which lights and shades are reversed —*vt.* 7. disprove, reject —**negative feedback** *see* **feedback** *at* FEED

neglect (nɪ'glɛkt) *vt.* 1. disregard, take no care of 2. omit through carelessness —*vi.* 3. fail (to do) —*n.* 4. fact of neglecting or being neglected —**ne'glectful** *a.*

negligee, negligée, *or* **negligé** ('nɛglɪʒeɪ) *n.* woman's light, gauzy nightdress or dressing gown

negligence ('nɛglɪdʒəns) *n.* 1. neglect 2. carelessness —'**negligent** *a.* —'**negligible** *a.* 1. able to be disregarded 2. very small or unimportant

negotiate (nɪ'gəʊʃɪeɪt) *vi.* 1. discuss with view to mutual settlement —*vt.* 2. arrange by conference 3. transfer (bill, cheque *etc.*) 4. get over, past, around (obstacle) —**ne'gotiable** *a.* —**negoti'ation** *n.* 1. treating with another on business 2. discussion 3. transference (of bill, cheque *etc.*) —**ne'gotiator** *n.*

Negro ('niːgrəʊ) *n.* member of Black orig. Afr. race (*pl.* **-es**) ('Negress *fem.*) —'**negritude** *n.* 1. fact of being a Negro 2. awareness and cultivation of Negro culture *etc.* —'**Negroid** *a.* of or like a Negro

negus ('niːgəs) *n.* hot drink of port and lemon juice

neigh (neɪ) *n.* 1. cry of horse —*vi.* 2. utter this cry

neighbour *or U.S.* **neighbor** ('neɪbə) *n.* one who lives near another —'**neighbourhood** *or U.S.* '**neighborhood** *n.* 1. district 2. people of a district 3. region round about —'**neighbouring** *or U.S.* '**neighboring** *a.* situated nearby —'**neighbourly** *or U.S.* '**neighborly** *a.* 1. as or befitting a good or friendly neighbour 2. friendly 3. sociable 4. helpful

neither ('naɪðə, 'niːðə) *a./pron.* 1. not the one or the other —*adv.* 2. not on the one hand 3. not either —*conj.* 4. not

nelson ('nɛlsən) *n.* wrestling hold in which wrestler places his arm(s) under his opponent's arm(s) from behind and exerts pressure with his palms on back of opponent's neck

nematode ('nɛmətəʊd) *n.* any of class of unsegmented worms having tough outer cuticle, including hookworm and filaria (*also* **nematode worm, 'roundworm**)

nemesia (nɪ'miːʒə) *n.* garden plant with flowers of various colours

Nemesis ('nɛmɪsɪs) *n.* 1. retribution 2. the goddess of vengeance (*pl.* **-ses** (-siːz))

neo- *or sometimes before vowel* **ne-** (*comb. form*) new, later, revived in modified form, based upon

neodymium (niːəʊ'dɪmɪəm) *n.* silvery-white metallic element of lanthanide series

Neolithic (niːəʊ'lɪθɪk) *a.* of the later Stone Age

neologism (nɪ'ɒlədʒɪzəm) *or* **neology** *n.* new-coined word or phrase —**ne'ologize** *or* **-gise** *vi.*

neon ('niːɒn) *n.* one of the inert constituent gases of the atmosphere, used in illuminated signs and lights —**neon lamp** tube containing neon, that gives red glow when voltage is applied

neophyte ('niːəʊfaɪt) *n.* 1. new convert 2. beginner, novice

nephew ('nɛvjuː, 'nɛf-) *n.* brother's or sister's son

nephritis (nɪ'fraɪtɪs) *n.* inflammation of a kidney

nepotism ('nɛpətɪzəm) *n.* undue favouritism towards one's relations

Neptune ('nɛptjuːn) *n.* 1. god of the sea 2. planet second farthest from sun

neptunium (nɛp'tjuːnɪəm) *n.* synthetic metallic element

nerve (nɜːv) *n.* 1. sinew, tendon 2. fibre or bundle of fibres conveying feeling, impulses to motion *etc.* to and from brain and other parts of body 3. assurance 4. coolness in danger 5. audacity —*pl.* 6. irritability, unusual sensitiveness to fear, annoyance *etc.* —*vt.* 7. give courage or strength to —'**nerveless** *a.* 1. without nerves 2. useless 3. weak 4. paralysed —'**nervous** *a.* 1. excitable, timid 2. apprehensive, worried 3. of the nerves —'**nervously** *adv.* —'**nervousness** *n.* —'**nervy** *a.* 1. nervous 2. jumpy 3. irritable 4. on edge —**nerve cell** *see* NEURON —**nerve centre** 1. group of nerve cells associated with specific function 2. principal source of control over any complex activity —**nerve gas** poisonous gas that has paralysing effect on central nervous system that can be fatal —**nerve-racking** *or* **nerve-wracking** *a.* very distressing, exhausting or harrowing —**nervous breakdown** condition of mental, emotional disturbance, disability —**nervous system** sensory and control apparatus of animals, consisting of network of nerve cells (*see also* NEURON)

ness (nɛs) *n.* headland, cape

nest (nɛst) *n.* 1. place in which bird lays and hatches its eggs 2. animal's breeding place 3. snug retreat —*vi.* 4. make, have a nest —**nest egg** (fund of) money in reserve

nestle ('nɛsʲl) *vi.* settle comfortably, usu. pressing in or close to something

nestling ('nɛstlɪŋ, 'nɛslɪŋ) *n.* bird too young to leave nest

net¹ (nɛt) *n.* 1. openwork fabric of meshes of cord *etc.* 2. piece of it used to catch fish *etc.* —*vt.* 3. cover with, or catch in, net (-**tt**-) —'**netting** *n.* string or wire net —'**netball** *n.* game in which ball has to be thrown through elevated horizontal ring, from which hangs short piece of netting

net² *or* **nett** (nɛt) *a.* 1. left after all deductions 2. free from deduction —*vt.* 3.

gain, yield as clear profit —**net profit** gross profit minus all operating costs not included in calculation of gross profit

nether ('nɛðə) a. lower —'**nethermost** a. farthest down; lowest —**nether world** l. underworld 2. hell (also **nether regions**)

netsuke ('nɛtsʊkɪ) n. carved wooden or ivory toggle or button worn in Japan

nettle ('nɛt'l) n. 1. plant with stinging hairs on the leaves —vt. 2. irritate, provoke —**nettle rash** urticaria

network ('nɛtwɜːk) n. 1. system of intersecting lines, roads etc. 2. interconnecting group of people or things 3. in broadcasting, group of stations connected to transmit same programmes simultaneously

neural ('njʊərəl) a. of the nerves

neuralgia (njʊ'rældʒə) n. pain in, along nerves, esp. of face and head —**neu'ralgic** a.

neuritis (njʊ'raɪtɪs) n. inflammation of nerves

neuro- or before vowel **neur-** (comb. form) nerve; nervous system, as in neurology

neurology (njʊ'rɒlədʒɪ) n. science, study of nerves —**neu'rologist** n.

neuron ('njʊərɒn) or **neurone** ('njʊərəʊn) n. cell specialized to conduct nerve impulses (also **nerve cell**) —**neu'ronic** a.

neurosis (njʊ'rəʊsɪs) n. relatively mild mental disorder (pl. **-ses** (-siːz)) —**neurotic** (njʊ'rɒtɪk) a. 1. suffering from nervous disorder 2. abnormally sensitive —n. 3. neurotic person

neurosurgery (njʊərəʊ'sɜːdʒərɪ) n. branch of surgery concerned with nervous system —**neuro'surgical** a.

neuter ('njuːtə) a. 1. neither masculine nor feminine —n. 2. neuter word 3. neuter gender —vt. 4. castrate, spay (domestic animal)

neutral ('njuːtrəl) a. 1. taking neither side in war, dispute etc. 2. without marked qualities 3. belonging to neither of two classes —n. 4. neutral nation or a subject of one 5. neutral gear —**neu'trality** n. —'**neutralize** or **-ise** vt. 1. make ineffective 2. counterbalance —**neutral gear** in vehicle, position of gears that leaves transmission disengaged

neutrino (nju:'tri:nəʊ) n. Phys. stable elementary particle with zero rest mass (pl. **-s**)

neutron ('njuːtrɒn) n. electrically neutral particle of the nucleus of an atom —**neutron bomb** nuclear bomb designed to destroy people but not buildings

never ('nɛvə) adv. at no time —**never'more** adv. Lit. never again —**never-never** n. inf. hire-purchase system of buying —**neverthe'less** adv. for all that, notwithstanding

new (njuː) a. 1. not existing before, fresh 2. that has lately come into some state or existence 3. unfamiliar, strange —adv. 4. recently, fresh (usu. 'newly) —'**newly** adv. —'**newness** n. —'**newcomer** n. recent arrival —**new'fangled** a. of new fashion —**new maths** approach to mathematics in which basic principles of set theory are introduced at elementary level —**new moon** moon when it appears as narrow waxing crescent —'**newspeak** n. language of bureaucrats and politicians, regarded as deliberately ambiguous and misleading —**New Testament** collection of writings composed soon after Christ's death and added to Jewish writings of Old Testament to make up Christian Bible —**new town** UK town planned as complete unit and built with government sponsorship, esp. to accommodate overspill population —**New Year** first day or days of year —**the New World** the Americas; western hemisphere

newel ('njuːəl) n. 1. central pillar of winding staircase 2. post at top or bottom of staircase rail

news (njuːz) n. 1. report of recent happenings, tidings 2. interesting fact not previously known —'**newsy** a. full of news —**news agency** organization that collects news reports for newspapers etc. (also **press agency**) —'**newsagent** n. shopkeeper who sells and distributes newspapers —**news bulletin** the latest news, esp. as broadcast by radio and television —'**newscast** n. news broadcast —'**newscaster** n. —'**newsflash** n. brief item of important news, oft. interrupting radio or television programme —'**newsletter** n. 1. printed periodical bulletin circulated to members of group (also **news-sheet**) 2. Hist. written or printed account of news —'**newspaper** n. periodical publication containing news —'**newsprint** n. paper of the kind used for newspapers etc. —'**newsreel** n. cinema or television film giving news —'**newsstand** n. stand from which newspapers are sold —'**newsworthy** a. sufficiently interesting or important to be reported as news

newt (njuːt) n. small, tailed amphibious creature

newton ('njuːt²n) n. SI unit of force

next (nɛkst) a./adv. 1. nearest 2. immediately following —**next door** at or to adjacent house, flat etc. —**next-of-kin** n. nearest relative

nexus ('nɛksəs) n. tie, connection, link (pl. '**nexus**)

NF Newfoundland

N.F.U. National Farmers' Union

N.G.A. National Graphical Association

NH New Hampshire

N.H.S. National Health Service

Ni Chem. nickel

N.I. 1. UK National Insurance 2. Northern Ireland

nib (nɪb) n. 1. (split) pen point 2. bird's beak —pl. 3. crushed cocoa beans

nibble ('nɪb'l) v. 1. take little bites (of) —n. 2. little bite

nibs (nıbz) n. mock title of respect, as in *his nibs*

nice (naıs) a. 1. pleasant 2. friendly, kind 3. attractive 4. subtle, fine 5. careful, exact 6. difficult to decide —'**nicely** adv. —**nicety** ('naısıtı) n. 1. minute distinction or detail 2. subtlety 3. precision

niche (nıtʃ, niːʃ) n. 1. recess in wall 2. suitable place in life, public estimation *etc.*

nick (nık) vt. 1. make notch in, indent 2. sl. steal —n. 3. notch 4. exact point of time 5. sl. prison —**in good nick** inf. in good condition

nickel ('nık²l) n. 1. silver-white metal much used in alloys and plating 2. US, C five-cent piece —**nickel silver** white alloy containing copper, zinc and nickel (*also* **German silver**)

nicker[1] ('nıkə) vi. 1. (of horse) neigh softly 2. snigger

nicker[2] ('nıkə) n. UK sl. pound sterling (*pl.* '**nicker**)

nicknack ('nık‚næk) n. see KNICK-KNACK

nickname ('nıkneım) n. familiar name added to or replacing an ordinary name

nicotine ('nıkətiːn) n. poisonous oily liquid in tobacco —'**nicotinism** n. tobacco poisoning

nictitate ('nıktıteıt) *or* **nictate** ('nıkteıt) v. blink —**nicti'tation** *or* **nic'tation** n.

niece (niːs) n. brother's or sister's daughter

nifty ('nıftı) a. inf. 1. neat, smart 2. quick

niggard ('nıgəd) n. mean, stingy person —'**niggardly** a./adv.

nigger ('nıgə) n. offens. Negro

niggle ('nıg²l) vi. 1. find fault continually —vt. 2. annoy —'**niggling** a. 1. petty 2. irritating and persistent

nigh (naı) a./adv./prep. obs., poet. near

night (naıt) n. 1. time of darkness between sunset and sunrise 2. end of daylight 3. dark —'**nightie** *or* '**nighty** n. woman's nightdress —'**nightly** a. 1. happening, done every night 2. of the night —adv. 3. every night 4. by night —**nights** adv. inf. at night, esp. regularly —**night blindness** Pathol. inability to see normally in dim light (*also* **nycta'lopia**) —'**nightcap** n. 1. cap worn in bed 2. late-night (alcoholic) drink —'**nightclub** n. establishment for dancing, music *etc.* opening late at night —'**nightdress** n. woman's loose robe worn in bed —'**nightfall** n. approach of darkness; dusk —'**nightingale** n. small bird which sings usu. at night —'**nightjar** n. nocturnal bird with harsh cry —'**nightmare** n. 1. very bad dream 2. terrifying experience —**night safe** safe built into outside wall of bank, in which customers deposit money when bank is closed —**night school** educational institution that holds classes in evening —'**nightshade** n. any of various plants of potato family, some of them with very poisonous berries —'**nightspot** n. inf. nightclub —**night-time** n. —**night watch** 1. guard kept at night,

esp. for security 2. period of time watch is kept 3. night watchman

nihilism ('naıılızəm) n. 1. rejection of all religious and moral principles 2. opposition to all constituted authority or government —'**nihilist** n. —**nihil'istic** a.

nil (nıl) n. nothing, zero

nimble ('nımb²l) a. agile, active, quick, dexterous —'**nimbly** adv.

nimbus ('nımbəs) n. 1. rain or storm cloud 2. cloud of glory, halo (*pl.* **-bi** (-baı), **-es**)

nincompoop ('nınkəmpuːp, 'nıŋ-) n. fool, simpleton

nine (naın) a./n. cardinal number next above eight —'**nine'teen** a./n. nine more than ten —'**nine'teenth** a. —'**ninetieth** a. —'**ninety** a./n. nine tens —**ninth** (naınθ) a. —**ninthly** ('naınθlı) adv. —**nine-days wonder** something that arouses great interest but only for short period —'**ninepins** pl.n. (with sing. v.) game where wooden pins are set up to be knocked down by rolling ball, skittles —**nineteenth hole** Golf sl. bar in golf clubhouse

niobium (naı'əʊbıəm) n. white superconductive metallic element that occurs principally in black mineral columbite and tantalite

nip (nıp) vt. 1. pinch sharply 2. detach by pinching, bite 3. check growth of (plants) thus 4. sl. steal —vi. 5. inf. hurry (-pp-) —n. 6. pinch 7. check to growth 8. sharp coldness of weather 9. short drink —'**nipper** n. 1. thing (*eg* crab's claw) that nips 2. inf. small child —pl. 3. pincers —'**nippy** a. inf. 1. cold 2. quick

nipple ('nıp²l) n. 1. point of a breast, teat 2. anything like this

Nippon ('nıpɒn) n. Japan

nisi ('naısaı) a. see decree nisi at DECREE

Nissen hut ('nıs²n) temporary military building of corrugated sheet steel

nit (nıt) n. 1. egg of louse or other parasite 2. inf. nitwit —**nit-picking** a. inf. over concerned with detail, esp. to find fault —**nitty-gritty** n. inf. basic facts, details —'**nitwit** n. inf. fool

nitre *or* U.S. **niter** ('naıtə) n. 1. potassium nitrate 2. sodium nitrate

nitrogen ('naıtrədʒən) n. one of the gases making up the air —'**nitrate** n. compound of nitric acid and an alkali —'**nitric** *or* '**nitrous** a. —'**nitrify** vt. 1. treat or cause to react with nitrogen 2. treat (soil) with nitrates 3. (of nitrobacteria) convert (ammonium compounds) into nitrates by oxidation —**ni'trogenous** a. of, containing nitrogen —**nitric acid** colourless corrosive liquid —**nitrobac'teria** pl.n. soil bacteria involved in nitrification —**nitrogen cycle** natural circulation of nitrogen by living organisms —**nitroglycerin** (naıtrəʊ'glısərın) *or* **nitroglycerine** (naıtrəʊ'glısəriːn) n. explosive liquid —**nitrous oxide** colourless gas with sweet smell, used as anaesthetic in dentistry (*also* **laughing gas**)

nix (nɪks) *n. sl.* nothing

NJ New Jersey

NM New Mexico

NNE north-northeast

NNW north-northwest

no (nəʊ) *a.* 1. not any, not a 2. not at all —*adv.* 3. expresses negative reply to question or request —*n.* 4. refusal 5. denial 6. negative vote or voter (*pl.* **-es**) —**no-ball** *n.* 1. *Cricket* illegal ball for which batting side scores run 2. *Rounders* illegal ball, *esp.* one bowled too high or too low —*interj.* 3. *Cricket, rounders* call by umpire indicating no-ball —**no-claim bonus** reduction on insurance premium, *esp.* one covering motor vehicle, if no claims have been made within specified period (*also* **no-claims bonus**) —**no-go** *a. sl.* 1. not functioning properly 2. hopeless —**no-go area** district barricaded off, which police, army can only enter by force —**no-man's-land** *n.* 1. waste or unclaimed land 2. contested land between two opposing forces —**no-one** *or* **no one** nobody —**no-trump** *Cards n.* 1. bid or contract to play without trumps (*also* **no-trumps**) —*a.* 2. (of hand) of balanced distribution suitable for playing without trumps (*also* **no-trumper**) —**'noway** *adv. sl.* not at all

No *Chem.* nobelium

No. number (*pl.* **Nos.**)

n.o. *Cricket* not out

nob (nɒb) *n. sl.* 1. member of upper classes 2. head

nobble ('nɒb'l) *vt. sl.* 1. disable (*esp.* racehorse with drugs) 2. secure dishonestly 3. catch (criminal) 4. cheat, swindle

nobelium (nəʊ'biːlɪəm) *n.* synthetic element produced from curium

noble ('nəʊb'l) *a.* 1. of the nobility 2. showing, having high moral qualities 3. impressive, excellent —*n.* 4. member of the nobility —**no'bility** *n.* 1. class holding special rank, usu. hereditary, in state 2. quality of being noble —**'nobly** *adv.* —**'nobleman** *n.*

noblesse oblige (nəʊ'blɛs əʊ'bliːʒ) *oft. ironic* supposed obligation of nobility to be honourable and generous

nobody ('nəʊbədɪ) *n.* 1. no person 2. person of no importance

nocturnal (nɒk'tɜːn'l) *a.* 1. of, in, by, night 2. active by night

nocturne ('nɒktɜːn) *n.* 1. dreamy piece of music 2. night scene

nod (nɒd) *v.* 1. bow (head) slightly and quickly in assent, command *etc.* —*vi.* 2. let head droop with sleep (**-dd-**) —*n.* 3. act of nodding —**nodding acquaintance** slight knowledge of person or subject —**nod off** *inf.* fall asleep

noddle ('nɒd'l) *n. inf.* head

node (nəʊd) *n.* 1. knot or knob 2. point at which curve crosses itself —**'nodal** *a.* —**'nodical** *a.*

nodule ('nɒdjuːl) *n.* 1. little knot 2. rounded irregular mineral mass

Noel *or* **Noël** (nəʊ'ɛl) *n.* 1. Christmas 2. Christmas carol

noggin ('nɒgɪn) *n.* 1. small amount of liquor 2. small mug 3. *inf.* head

noise (nɔɪz) *n.* 1. any sound, *esp.* disturbing one 2. clamour, din 3. loud outcry 4. talk; interest —*vt.* 5. (*usu. with* abroad *or* about) spread (gossip *etc.*) —**'noiseless** *a.* without noise, quiet, silent —**'noisily** *adv.* —**'noisy** *a.* 1. making much noise 2. clamorous

noisome ('nɔɪsəm) *a.* 1. (*esp.* of smells) offensive 2. harmful, noxious

nom. nominative

nomad ('nəʊmæd) *n.* 1. member of tribe with no fixed dwelling place 2. wanderer —**no'madic** *a.*

nom de plume ('nɒm də 'pluːm) *Fr.* writer's assumed name, pen name, pseudonym (*pl.* **noms de plume**)

nomenclature (nəʊ'mɛnklətʃə; *U.S.* 'nəʊmənkleɪtʃər) *n.* terminology of particular science *etc.*

nominal ('nɒmɪn'l) *a.* 1. in name only 2. (of fee *etc.*) small, insignificant 3. of a name or names —**'nominalism** *n.* philosophical theory that general word, such as *dog*, is merely name and does not denote real object, the general idea 'dog' —**'nominalist** *n.* —**'nominally** *adv.* 1. in name only 2. not really

nominate ('nɒmɪneɪt) *vt.* 1. propose as candidate 2. appoint to office —**nomi'nation** *n.* —**'nominative** *a./n.* (of) case of nouns, pronouns when subject of verb —**'nominator** *n.* —**nomi'nee** *n.* candidate

non- (*comb. form*) negatives the idea of the simple word. See the list below

nonage ('nəʊnɪdʒ) *n.* 1. *Law* state of being under any of various ages at which person may legally enter into certain transactions 2. any period of immaturity

nonagenarian (nəʊnədʒɪ'nɛərɪən) *a.* 1. aged between ninety and ninety-nine —*n.* 2. person of such age

nonaligned (nɒnə'laɪnd) *a.* (of states *etc.*) not part of a major alliance or power bloc

nonce (nɒns) *n.* —**nonce word** word coined for single occasion —**for the nonce** 1. for the occasion only 2. for the present

nonchalant ('nɒnʃələnt) *a.* casually unconcerned, indifferent, cool —**'nonchalance** *n.*

noncombatant (nɒn'kɒmbətənt) *n.* 1. civilian during war 2. member of army who does not fight, *eg* doctor, chaplain

noncommissioned officer (nɒnkə'mɪʃənd) *Mil.* subordinate officer, risen from the ranks

nonac'ceptance	nonap'pearance	non'breakable
nonag'gression	nonbe'liever	non-Catholic
nonalco'holic	nonbel'ligerent	noncom'bustible

noncommittal (ˌnɒnkəˈmɪtˀl) a. avoiding definite preference or pledge

non compos mentis (ˈnɒn ˈkɒmpɒs ˈmentɪs) *Lat.* of unsound mind

nonconformist (ˌnɒnkənˈfɔːmɪst) n. dissenter, *esp.* from Established Church —**nonconformity** n.

nondescript (ˈnɒndɪskrɪpt) a. lacking distinctive characteristics, indeterminate

none (nʌn) *pron.* 1. no-one, not any —a. 2. no —adv. 3. in no way —**nonesuch** or **nonsuch** (ˈnʌnsʌtʃ) n. obs. matchless person or thing; nonpareil —**nonethe'less** adv. despite that, however

nonentity (nɒnˈentɪtɪ) n. 1. insignificant person, thing 2. nonexistent thing

nonevent (ˌnɒnɪˈvent) n. disappointing or insignificant occurrence, *esp.* one predicted to be important

nonferrous (nɒnˈferəs) a. 1. denoting metal other than iron 2. not containing iron

nonflammable (nɒnˈflæməbˀl) a. 1. incapable of burning 2. not easily set on fire

nonintervention (ˌnɒnɪntəˈvenʃən) n. refusal to intervene, *esp.* abstention by state from intervening in affairs of other states

noniron (nɒnˈaɪən) a. not requiring ironing

nonnuclear (nɒnˈnjuːklɪə) a. not operated by or using nuclear energy

nonpareil (ˌnɒnpərəl, nɒnpəˈreɪl) a. 1. unequalled, matchless —n. 2. person or thing unequalled or unrivalled

nonpartisan or **nonpartizan** (ˌnɒnpɑːtɪˈzæn) a. not supporting any single political party

nonplus (nɒnˈplʌs) vt. disconcert, confound or bewilder completely (-ss-)

nonproliferation (ˌnɒnprəlɪfərˈeɪʃən) n. limitation of production *esp.* of nuclear weapons

nonrepresentational (ˌnɒnreprɪzenˈteɪʃˀl) a. *Art* abstract

nonsectarian (ˌnɒnsekˈtɛərɪən) a. not sectarian; not confined to any specific religion

nonsense (ˈnɒnsəns) n. 1. lack of sense 2. absurd language 3. absurdity 4. silly conduct —**non'sensical** a. 1. ridiculous 2. meaningless 3. without sense

non sequitur (ˈnɒn ˈsekwɪtə) *Lat.* statement with little or no relation to what preceded it

nonstarter (nɒnˈstɑːtə) n. 1. horse that fails to run in race for which it has been entered 2. person or thing that has little chance of success

non-U a. UK *inf.* (*esp.* of language) not characteristic of upper class

noodle[1] (ˈnuːdˀl) n. strip of pasta served in soup *etc.*

noodle[2] (ˈnuːdˀl) n. simpleton, fool

nook (nʊk) n. sheltered corner, retreat —**'nooky** a.

noon (nuːn) n. midday, twelve o'clock —**'noonday** n. noon —**'noontide** n. the time about noon

noose (nuːs) n. 1. running loop 2. snare —vt. 3. catch, ensnare in noose, lasso

nor (nɔː; *unstressed* nə) *conj.* and not

nor' or **nor** (nɔː) north (*esp.* in compounds)

Nor. 1. Norman 2. north 3. Norway 4. Norwegian

Nordic (ˈnɔːdɪk) a. pert. to peoples of Germanic stock

norm (nɔːm) n. 1. average level of achievement 2. rule or authoritative standard 3. model 4. standard type or pattern —**'normal** a. 1. ordinary 2. usual 3. conforming to type —n. 4. *Geom.* perpendicular —**nor'mality** n. —**normali'zation** or **-i'sation** n. —**'normalize** or **-ise** vt. 1. bring or make into normal state 2. bring into conformity with standard 3. heat (steel) above critical temperature and allow it to cool in air to relieve internal stresses; anneal —**'normally** adv. —**'normative** a. creating or prescribing norm or standard

---

non'communist	non'member	nonse'lective
noncom'petitive	non'metal	non'shrink(able)
noncom'pliance	non'militant	non'slip
noncon'secutive	non-negotiable	non'smoker
noncon'tagious	nonob'servance	non'standard
noncon'tributory	nonoper'ational	non'stick
noncontro'versial	non'party	non'stop
noncooper'ation	non'payment	non'swimmer
nonde'livery	non-playing	non'taxable
nondenomi'national	non'poisonous	non'technical
non'drinker	non'porous	non'toxic
non'driver	non-profit-making	nontrans'ferable
nones'sential	non'racial	non'tropical
nonex'istent	non'reader	non'venomous
non'fiction	non'registered	non'verbal
nonin'fectious	nonrepre'sentative	non'violent
nonin'flammable	non'resident	non'voter
nonmag'netic	nonre'sistant	
nonma'lignant	nonre'turnable	

Norman ('nɔːmən) *n.* 1. in Middle Ages, member of people of Normandy in N France, descended from 10th-century Scandinavian conquerors of the country and native French 2. native of Normandy 3. medieval Norman and English dialect of Old French (*also* **Norman French**) —*a.* 4. of Normans or their dialect of French 5. of Normandy 6. denoting Romanesque architecture used in Britain from Norman Conquest until 12th century, characterized by massive masonry walls *etc.*

Norse (nɔːs) *a.* 1. of ancient and medieval Scandinavia 2. of Norway —*n.* 3. N group of Germanic languages, spoken in Scandinavia 4. any of these languages, *esp.* in ancient or medieval forms —'**Norseman** *n. see* VIKING —**the Norse** 1. Norwegians 2. Vikings

north (nɔːθ) *n.* 1. direction to the right of person facing the sunset 2. part of the world, of country *etc.* towards this point —*adv.* 3. towards or in the north —*a.* 4. to, from or in the north —**northerly** ('nɔːðəlɪ) *a.* 1. of or situated in north —*n.* 2. wind from the north —**northern** ('nɔːðən) *a.* —**northerner** ('nɔːðənə) *n.* person from the north —**northward** ('nɔːθwəd; *Naut.* 'nɔːðəd) *a./n./adv.* —**northwards** ('nɔːθwədz) *adv.* —**northeast** (nɔːθ'iːst; *Naut.* nɔːr'iːst) *n.* 1. direction midway between north and east 2. (*oft.* N-) area lying in or towards this direction —*a.* 3. (*sometimes* N-) of northeastern part of specified country *etc.* 4. in, towards or facing northeast 5. (*esp.* of wind) from northeast (*also* **north'eastern**) —*adv.* 6. in, to, towards or (*esp.* of wind) from northeast —**North'east** *n.* northeastern part of England, *esp.* Northumberland and Durham —**northeaster** (nɔːθ'iːstə; *Naut.* nɔːr'iːstə) *n.* strong wind or storm from northeast —**northern hemisphere** (*oft.* N-H-) half of globe lying north of equator —**northern lights** aurora borealis —**north-northeast** *n.* 1. direction midway between north and northeast —*a./adv.* 2. in, from or towards this direction —**north-northwest** *n.* 1. direction midway between northwest and north —*a./adv.* 2. in, from or towards this direction —**North Pole** 1. northernmost point on earth's axis 2. *Astron.* point of intersection of earth's extended axis and northern half of celestial sphere (*also* **north celestial pole**) —**North-Sea gas** UK natural gas obtained from deposits below North Sea —**northwest** (nɔːθ'wɛst; *Naut.* nɔː'wɛst) *n.* 1. direction midway between north and west 2. (*oft.* N-) area lying in or towards this direction —*a.* 3. (*sometimes* N-) of northwestern part of specified country *etc.* (*also* **north'western**) —*a./adv.* 4. in, to, towards or (*esp.* of wind) from northwest —**northwester** (nɔːθ'wɛstə; *Naut.* nɔː'wɛstə) *n.* strong wind or storm from northwest —**the North Star** *see the* **Pole Star** *at* POLE²

Northants. (nɔː'θænts) Northamptonshire

Northd. Northumberland
Northum. Northumbria
Norw. 1. Norway 2. Norwegian
Norwegian (nɔː'wiːdʒən) *a.* 1. of Norway —*n.* 2. any of various North Germanic languages of Norway 3. native of Norway
Nos. numbers
nose (nəʊz) *n.* 1. organ of smell, used also in breathing 2. any projection resembling a nose, as prow of ship, aircraft *etc.* —*v.* 3. (cause to) move forward slowly and carefully —*vt.* 4. touch with nose 5. smell, sniff —*vi.* 6. smell 7. (*with* into, around, about *etc.*) pry —'**nosy** *or* '**nosey** *a. inf.* inquisitive —'**nosebag** *n.* bag fastened around head of horse in which feed is placed —'**noseband** *n.* detachable part of horse's bridle that goes around nose —**nose dive** downward sweep of aircraft —'**nosegay** *n.* bunch of flowers —**nosy parker** *inf., chiefly* UK prying person
nosh (nɒʃ) *sl. n.* 1. food —*v.* 2. eat —**nosh-up** *n.* UK *sl.* large and satisfying meal
nostalgia (nɒ'stældʒə, -dʒɪə) *n.* 1. longing for return of past events 2. homesickness —**nos'talgic** *a.*
nostril ('nɒstrɪl) *n.* one of the two external openings of the nose
nostrum ('nɒstrəm) *n.* 1. quack medicine 2. secret remedy
not (nɒt) *adv.* expressing negation, refusal, denial —**not proven** ('prəʊv°n) a third verdict available to Scottish courts, returned when there is insufficient evidence to convict
nota bene ('nəʊtə 'biːnɪ) *Lat.* note well
notable ('nəʊtəb°l) *a.* 1. worthy of note, remarkable —*n.* 2. person of distinction —**nota'bility** *n.* an eminent person —'**notably** *adv.*
notary ('nəʊtərɪ) *n.* person authorized to draw up deeds, contracts
notation (nəʊ'teɪʃən) *n.* 1. representation of numbers, quantities, by symbols 2. set of such symbols 3. C footnote, memorandum
notch (nɒtʃ) *n.* 1. V-shaped cut or indentation 2. *inf.* step, grade —*vt.* 3. make notches in
note (nəʊt) *n.* 1. brief comment or record 2. short letter 3. banknote 4. symbol for musical sound 5. single tone 6. sign 7. indication, hint 8. fame 9. notice 10. regard —*pl.* 11. brief jottings written down for future reference —*vt.* 12. observe, record 13. heed —'**noted** *a.* well-known —'**notelet** *n.* folded card with printed design on front, for writing short letter —'**notebook** *n.* small book with blank pages for writing —'**notepaper** *n.* paper for writing letters; writing paper —'**noteworthy** *a.* 1. worth noting 2. remarkable
nothing ('nʌθɪŋ) *n.* 1. no thing 2. not anything, nought —*adv.* 3. not at all, in no way —'**nothingness** *n.*
notice ('nəʊtɪs) *n.* 1. observation 2. attention, consideration 3. warning, intimation, announcement 4. advance notification of intention to end a contract *etc.*,

as of employment **5.** review —*vt.* **6.** observe, mention **7.** give attention to —'**noticeable** *a.* **1.** conspicuous **2.** attracting attention **3.** appreciable

notify ('nəʊtɪfaɪ) *vt.* **1.** report **2.** give notice of or to (**-fied, -fying**) —'**notifiable** *a.* —notifi'**cation** *n.*

notion ('nəʊʃən) *n.* **1.** concept **2.** opinion **3.** whim —'**notional** *a.* speculative, imaginary, abstract

notorious (nəʊ'tɔːrɪəs) *a.* **1.** known for something bad **2.** well-known —**notoriety** (nəʊtə'raɪtɪ) *n.* discreditable publicity

Notts. (nɒts) Nottinghamshire

notwithstanding (nɒtwɪθ'stændɪŋ) *prep.* **1.** in spite of —*adv.* **2.** all the same —*conj.* **3.** although

nougat ('nuːgɑː) *n.* chewy sweet containing nuts, fruit *etc.*

nought (nɔːt) *n.* **1.** nothing **2.** cipher 0

noun (naʊn) *n.* word used as name of person, idea, or thing, substantive

nourish ('nʌrɪʃ) *vt.* **1.** feed **2.** nurture **3.** tend **4.** encourage —'**nourishment** *n.*

nous (naʊs) *n.* **1.** mind, intellect **2.** common sense

nouveau riche (nuvo 'riʃ) *Fr.* person who has acquired wealth recently and is regarded as vulgarly ostentatious (*pl.* *nouveaux riches* (nuvo 'riʃ))

nouvelle cuisine ('nuːvɛl kwiː'ziːn) style of preparing food, *oft.* raw or only lightly cooked, with unusual combinations of flavours

Nov. November

nova ('nəʊvə) *n.* star that suddenly becomes brighter then loses brightness through months or years (*pl.* **-vae** (-viː), **-s**)

novel[1] ('nɒv'l) *n.* fictitious tale in book form —**nove'lette** *n.* **1.** short novel **2.** trite, oversentimental novel —'**novelist** *n.* writer of novels

novel[2] ('nɒv'l) *a.* **1.** new, recent **2.** strange —'**novelty** *n.* **1.** newness **2.** something new or unusual **3.** small ornament, trinket

novella (nəʊ'vɛlə) *n.* **1.** short narrative tale, *esp.* one having satirical point **2.** short novel (*pl.* **-s, -le** (-leɪ))

November (nəʊ'vɛmbə) *n.* eleventh month

novena (nəʊ'viːnə) *n.* *R.C.Ch.* prayers, services, lasting nine consecutive days (*pl.* **-nae** (-niː))

novice ('nɒvɪs) *n.* **1.** one new to anything **2.** beginner **3.** candidate for admission to religious order —**novitiate** *or* **noviciate** (nəʊ'vɪʃɪt, -eɪt) *n.* **1.** probationary period **2.** part of religious house for novices **3.** novice

now (naʊ) *adv.* **1.** at the present time **2.** immediately **3.** recently (*oft. with* just) —*conj.* **4.** seeing that, since —'**nowadays** *adv.* in these times, at present

Nowel *or* **Nowell** (nəʊ'ɛl) *n. see* NOEL

nowhere ('nəʊwɛə) *adv.* not in any place or state

noxious ('nɒkʃəs) *a.* poisonous, harmful

nozzle ('nɒz'l) *n.* pointed spout, *esp.* at end of hose

Np *Chem.* neptunium

NS Nova Scotia

N.S.B. National Savings Bank

N.S.P.C.C. National Society for the Prevention of Cruelty to Children

N.S.T. Newfoundland Standard Time

N.S.W. New South Wales

N.T. 1. National Trust **2.** New Testament **3.** Northern Territory **4.** no trumps

nt. wt. *or* **wt wt** net weight

nu (njuː) *n.* 13th letter in Gr. alphabet (N, ν)

nuance (njuː'ɑːns, 'njuːɑːns) *n.* delicate shade of difference, in colour, tone of voice *etc.*

nub (nʌb) *n.* **1.** small lump **2.** main point (of story *etc.*)

nubile ('njuːbaɪl) *a.* marriageable

nucleus ('njuːklɪəs) *n.* **1.** centre, kernel **2.** beginning meant to receive additions **3.** core of the atom (*pl.* **-lei** (-lɪaɪ)) —'**nuclear** *a.* of, pert. to atomic nucleus —**nucle'onics** *pl.n.* (*with sing. v.*) branch of physics dealing with applications of nuclear energy —**nuclear bomb** bomb whose force is due to uncontrolled nuclear fusion or nuclear fission —**nuclear disarmament** elimination of nuclear weapons from country's armament —**nuclear energy** energy released by nuclear fission —**nuclear family** *Sociol., anthropol.* primary social unit consisting of parents and their offspring —**nuclear fission** disintegration of the atom —**nuclear fusion** reaction in which two nuclei combine to form nucleus with release of energy (*also* '**fusion**) —**nuclear physics** branch of physics concerned with structure of nucleus and particles of which it consists —**nuclear reaction** change in structure and energy content of atomic nucleus by interaction with another nucleus, particle —**nuclear reactor** *see* reactor *at* REACT —**nuclear winter** period of low temperatures and little light that has been suggested would occur after nuclear war —**nucleic acid** (njuː'kliːɪk, -'kleɪ-) *Biochem.* any of group of complex compounds with high molecular weight that are vital constituents of all living cells

nude (njuːd) *n.* **1.** state of being naked **2.** (picture, statue *etc.* of) naked person —*a.* **3.** naked —'**nudism** *n.* practice of nudity —'**nudist** *n.* —'**nudity** *n.*

nudge (nʌdʒ) *vt.* **1.** touch slightly with elbow —*n.* **2.** such touch

nugatory ('njuːgətərɪ, -trɪ) *a.* trifling, futile

nugget ('nʌgɪt) *n.* rough lump of native gold

nuisance ('njuːsəns) *n.* something or someone harmful, offensive, annoying or disagreeable

N.U.J. National Union of Journalists

null (nʌl) *a.* of no effect, void —'**nullify** *vt.* **1.** cancel **2.** make useless or ineffective (**-fied, -fying**) —'**nullity** *n.* state of being null and void —**null set** *Maths.* set having no members (*also* **empty set**)

num. 1. number **2.** numeral

Num. Numbers

N.U.M. National Union of Mineworkers

numb (nʌm) *a.* **1.** deprived of feeling, *esp.* by cold —*vt.* **2.** make numb **3.** deaden —'**numbskull** *n. see* NUMSKULL

number ('nʌmbə) *n.* **1.** sum, aggregate **2.** word or symbol saying how many **3.** single issue of a paper *etc.* issued in regular series **4.** classification as to singular or plural **5.** song, piece of music **6.** performance **7.** company, collection **8.** identifying number, as of particular house, telephone *etc.* **9.** *sl.* measure, correct estimation —*vt.* **10.** count **11.** class, reckon **12.** give a number to **13.** amount to —'**numberless** *a.* countless —**number crunching** the performing of complicated calculations involving large numbers, *esp.* at high speed by computer —**number one** *n.* **1.** *inf.* oneself —*a.* **2.** first in importance, urgency *etc.* —'**numberplate** *n.* plate mounted on front and back of motor vehicle bearing registration number —**Number Ten** 10 Downing Street, British prime minister's official London residence

numeral ('nju:mərəl) *n.* sign or word denoting a number —'**numerable** *a.* able to be numbered or counted —'**numeracy** *n.* —'**numerate** ('nju:mərɪt) *a.* **1.** able to use numbers in calculations —*vt.* ('nju:məreɪt) **2.** count —**nume'ration** *n.* —'**numerator** *n.* top part of fraction, figure showing how many of the fractional units are taken —**nu'merical** *a.* of, in respect of, number or numbers —**nume'rology** *n.* study of numbers, and of their supposed influence on human affairs —'**numerous** *a.* many

numismatic (nju:mɪz'mætɪk) *a.* of coins —**numis'matics** *pl.n.* (*with sing. v.*) the study of coins —**nu'mismatist** *n.*

numskull *or* **numbskull** ('nʌmskʌl) *n.* dolt, dunce

nun (nʌn) *n.* woman living (in convent) under religious vows —'**nunnery** *n.* convent of nuns

nuncio ('nʌnʃɪəʊ, -sɪ-) *n.* ambassador of the Pope (*pl.* **-s**)

nunny bag ('nʌnɪ) *C* small sealskin haversack

NUPE ('nju:pɪ) National Union of Public Employees

nuptial ('nʌpʃəl, -tʃəl) *a.* of, relating to marriage —'**nuptials** *pl.n.* (*sometimes with sing. v.*) **1.** marriage **2.** wedding ceremony

N.U.R. National Union of Railwaymen

nurse (nɜ:s) *n.* **1.** person trained for care of sick or injured **2.** woman tending another's child —*vt.* **3.** act as nurse to **4.** suckle **5.** pay special attention to **6.** harbour (grudge *etc.*) —'**nursery** *n.* **1.** room for children **2.** rearing place for plants —'**nursemaid** *or* '**nurserymaid** *n.* woman employed to look after children (*also* **nurse**) —'**nurseryman** *n.* one who raises plants for sale —**nursery rhyme** short traditional verse or song for children —**nursery school** school for young children —**nursery slope** gentle slope for beginners in skiing —**nursing home** private hospital or residence for aged or infirm persons —**nursing officer** administrative head of nursing staff of hospital

nurture ('nɜ:tʃə) *n.* **1.** bringing up **2.** education **3.** rearing **4.** nourishment —*vt.* **5.** bring up **6.** educate

N.U.S. 1. National Union of Seamen **2.** National Union of Students

nut (nʌt) *n.* **1.** fruit consisting of hard shell and kernel **2.** hollow metal collar into which a screw fits **3.** *inf.* head **4.** *inf.* eccentric or crazy person (*also* '**nutter**) —*vi.* **5.** gather nuts (**-tt-**) —'**nutty** *a.* **1.** of, like nut **2.** pleasant to taste and bite **3.** *sl.* insane, crazy (*also* **nuts**) —'**nutcase** *n. sl.* insane or foolish person —'**nutcracker** *n.* **1.** (*oft. pl.*) device for cracking shells of nuts **2.** Old World or North American bird having speckled plumage and feeding on nuts *etc.* —'**nuthatch** *n.* small songbird —'**nutmeg** *n.* aromatic seed of Indian tree —'**nutshell** *n.* shell around kernel of nut —**in a nutshell** in essence; briefly —**nuts and bolts** *inf.* essential or practical details

N.U.T. National Union of Teachers

nutria ('nju:trɪə) *n.* fur of coypu

nutrient ('nju:trɪənt) *a.* **1.** nourishing —*n.* **2.** something nutritious

nutriment ('nju:trɪmənt) *n.* nourishing food —**nu'trition** *n.* **1.** receiving foods **2.** act of nourishing —**nu'tritious** *or* '**nutritive** *a.* **1.** nourishing **2.** promoting growth

nux vomica ('nʌks 'vɒmɪkə) seed of tree which yields strychnine

nuzzle ('nʌz'l) *v.* **1.** burrow, press with nose —*vi.* **2.** nestle

NV Nevada

NW northwest(ern)

N.W.T. Northwest Territories (of Canada)

NY New York

nylon ('naɪlɒn) *n.* **1.** synthetic material used for fabrics, bristles, ropes *etc.* —*pl.* **2.** stockings made of this

nymph (nɪmf) *n.* **1.** legendary semidivine maiden of sea, woods, mountains *etc.*

nymphomania (nɪmfə'meɪnɪə) *n.* abnormally intense sexual desire in women —**nympho'maniac** *n.*

N.Z. *or* **N. Zeal.** New Zealand

O

o *or* **O** (əʊ) *n.* **1.** 15th letter of English alphabet **2.** any of several speech sounds represented by this letter, as in *code, pot, cow* or *form* **3.** *see* NOUGHT (*pl.* **o's, O's** *or* **Os**)

O[1] **1.** *Chem.* oxygen **2.** human blood type of ABO group **3.** Old

O[2] (əʊ) *interj.* **1.** *see* OH **2.** exclamation introducing invocation, entreaty, wish *etc.*

o' (ə) *prep. inf.* of

O'- (*comb. form*) in surnames of Irish Gaelic origin, descendant of, as in *O'Corrigan*

oaf (əʊf) *n.* **1.** lout **2.** dolt

oak (əʊk) *n.* **1.** common, deciduous forest tree —*pl.* **2.** (O-) horse race for fillies held annually at Epsom —'**oaken** *a.* of oak —**oak apple** *or* **gall** round gall on oak trees

oakum ('əʊkəm) *n.* loose fibre got by unravelling old rope

O. & M. organization and method (in studies of working methods)

O.A.P. old age pensioner

oar (ɔː) *n.* **1.** wooden lever with broad blade worked by the hands to propel boat **2.** oarsman —*v.* **3.** row —'**oarsman** *n.* —'**oarsmanship** *n.* skill in rowing

OAS 1. Organization of American States **2.** *Organisation de l'Armée Secrète*; organization which opposed Algerian independence by acts of terrorism

oasis (əʊ'eɪsɪs) *n.* fertile spot in desert (*pl.* **oases** (əʊ'eɪsiːz))

oast (əʊst) *n.* kiln for drying hops

oat (əʊt) *n.* **1.** (*usu. pl.*) grain of cereal plant **2.** the plant —'**oaten** *a.* —'**oatmeal** *n.*

oath (əʊθ) *n.* **1.** confirmation of truth of statement by naming something sacred **2.** curse (*pl.* **oaths** (əʊðz))

OAU Organization of African Unity

ob. 1. on tombstones *etc.*) obiit (*Lat.*, he or she died) **2.** obiter (*Lat.*, incidentally, in passing) **3.** oboe

ob- (*comb. form*) inverse; inversely, as in *obovate*

obbligato *or* **obligato** (ɒblɪ'ɡɑːtəʊ) *Mus. a.* **1.** not to be omitted —*n.* **2.** essential part in score (*pl.* **-s, -ti** (-tiː))

obdurate ('ɒbdjʊrɪt) *a.* stubborn, unyielding —'**obduracy** *or* '**obdurateness** *n.*

O.B.E. Officer of the Order of the British Empire

obedience (ə'biːdɪəns) *n.* submission to authority —o'**bedient** *a.* **1.** willing to obey **2.** compliant **3.** dutiful —o'**bediently** *adv.*

obeisance (əʊ'beɪsəns, əʊ'biː-) *n.* bow; curtsy

obelisk ('ɒbɪlɪsk) *n.* tapering rectangular stone column with pyramidal apex

obese (əʊ'biːs) *a.* very fat, corpulent —o'**besity** *n.*

obey (ə'beɪ) *vt.* **1.** do the bidding of **2.** act in accordance with —*vi.* **3.** do as ordered **4.** submit to authority

obfuscate ('ɒbfʌskeɪt) *vt.* **1.** perplex **2.** darken

obituary (ə'bɪtjʊərɪ) *n.* **1.** notice, record of death **2.** biographical sketch of deceased person, *esp.* in newspaper (*also* (*inf.*) '**obit**)

obj. 1. object **2.** objective

object[1] ('ɒbdʒɪkt) *n.* **1.** material thing **2.** that to which feeling or action is directed **3.** end, aim **4.** *Gram.* word dependent on verb or preposition —**object lesson** lesson with practical and concrete illustration —**no object** not an obstacle or hindrance

object[2] (əb'dʒɛkt) *vt.* **1.** state in opposition —*vi.* **2.** feel dislike or reluctance (to something) —**ob'jection** *n.* —**ob'jectionable** *a.* **1.** disagreeable **2.** justly liable to objection —**ob'jector** *n.*

objective (əb'dʒɛktɪv) *a.* **1.** external to the mind **2.** impartial —*n.* **3.** thing or place aimed at —**objec'tivity** *n.*

objet d'art (ɔbʒɛ 'daːr) *Fr.* small object considered to be of artistic worth (*pl.* **objets d'art** (ɔbʒɛ 'daːr))

oblate[1] ('ɒbleɪt) *a.* (of sphere) flattened at the poles

oblate[2] ('ɒbleɪt) *n.* person dedicated to religious work

oblation (ɒ'bleɪʃən) *n.* offering —**ob'lational** *a.*

obligato (ɒblɪ'ɡɑːtəʊ) *see* OBBLIGATO

oblige (ə'blaɪdʒ) *vt.* **1.** bind morally or legally to do service to **2.** compel —**obligate** ('ɒblɪɡeɪt) *vt.* bind, *esp.* by legal contract **2.** put under obligation —**obligation** (ɒblɪ'ɡeɪʃən) *n.* **1.** binding duty, promise **2.** debt of gratitude —**obligatory** (ɒ'blɪɡətərɪ, -trɪ) *a.* required **2.** binding —**o'bliging** *a.* ready to serve others, civil, helpful, courteous

oblique (ə'bliːk) *a.* **1.** slanting **2.** indirect —o'**bliquely** *adv.* —**obliquity** (ə'blɪkwɪtɪ) *n.* **1.** slant **2.** dishonesty —**oblique angle** angle not a right angle

obliterate (ə'blɪtəreɪt) *vt.* blot out, efface, destroy completely —**oblite'ration** *n.*

oblivion (ə'blɪvɪən) *n.* **1.** forgetting or being forgotten —**ob'livious** *a.* **1.** forgetful **2.** unaware

oblong ('ɒblɒŋ) *a.* **1.** rectangular, with adjacent sides unequal —*n.* **2.** oblong figure

obloquy ('ɒbləkwɪ) *n.* **1.** reproach, abuse **2.** disgrace **3.** detraction

obnoxious (əb'nɒkʃəs) *a.* offensive, disliked, odious

oboe ('əʊbəʊ) *n.* woodwind instrument, hautboy —'**oboist** *n.*

obs. 1. observation **2.** obsolete

obscene (əb'si:n) a. 1. indecent, lewd 2. repulsive —**obscenity** (əb'sɛnɪtɪ) n.

obscure (əb'skjuə) a. 1. unclear, indistinct 2. unexplained 3. dark, dim 4. humble —vt. 5. make unintelligible 6. dim 7. conceal —**ob'scurant** n. one who opposes enlightenment or reform —**obscu'rantism** n. —**ob'scurity** n. 1. indistinctness 2. lack of intelligibility 3. darkness 4. obscure, esp. unrecognized, place or position 5. retirement

obsequies ('ɒbsɪkwɪz) pl.n. funeral rites

obsequious (əb'si:kwɪəs) a. servile, fawning

observe (əb'zɜ:v) vt. 1. notice, remark 2. watch 3. note systematically 4. keep, follow —vi. 5. make a remark —**ob'servable** a. —**ob'servably** adv. —**ob'servance** n. 1. paying attention 2. keeping —**ob'servant** a. quick to notice —**obser'vation** n. 1. action, habit of observing 2. noticing 3. remark —**ob'servatory** n. place for watching stars etc. —**ob'server** n.

obsess (əb'sɛs) vt. haunt, fill the mind of —**ob'session** n. 1. fixed idea 2. domination of the mind by one idea —**ob'sessive** a.

obsidian (ɒb'sɪdɪən) n. fused volcanic rock, forming hard, dark, natural glass

obsolete ('ɒbsəli:t, ɒbsə'li:t) a. disused, out of date —**obso'lescent** a. going out of use

obstacle ('ɒbstək'l) n. 1. hindrance 2. impediment, barrier, obstruction

obstetrics (ɒb'stɛtrɪks) pl.n. (with sing. v.) branch of medicine concerned with childbirth and care of women before and after childbirth —**ob'stetric(al)** a. —**obste'trician** n.

obstinate ('ɒbstɪnɪt) a. 1. stubborn 2. self-willed 3. unyielding 4. hard to overcome or cure —**obstinacy** n. —**obstinately** adv.

obstreperous (əb'strɛpərəs) a. unruly, noisy, boisterous

obstruct (əb'strʌkt) vt. 1. block up 2. hinder, impede —**ob'struction** n. —**ob'structionist** n. one who deliberately opposes transaction of business —**ob'structive** a.

obtain (əb'teɪn) vt. 1. get 2. acquire 3. procure by effort —vi. 4. be customary —**ob'tainable** a. procurable

obtrude (əb'tru:d) v. thrust forward unduly —**ob'trusion** n. —**ob'trusive** a. forward, pushing —**ob'trusively** adv.

obtuse (əb'tju:s) a. 1. dull of perception 2. stupid 3. (of angle) greater than right angle 4. not pointed —**ob'tusely** adv.

obverse ('ɒbvɜ:s) n. 1. fact, idea etc. which is the complement of another 2. side of coin, medal etc. that has the principal design —a. 3. facing the observer 4. complementary, opposite

obviate ('ɒbvɪeɪt) vt. remove, make unnecessary

obvious ('ɒbvɪəs) a. 1. clear, evident 2. wanting in subtlety

O.C. Officer Commanding

occasion (ə'keɪʒən) n. 1. time when thing happens 2. reason, need 3. opportunity 4. special event —vt. 5. cause —**oc'casional** a. 1. happening, found now and then 2. produced for some special event, as occasional music —**oc'casionally** adv. sometimes, now and then

Occident ('ɒksɪdənt) n. the West —**Occi'dental** a.

occlude (ə'klu:d) vt. shut in or out —**oc'clusion** n. —**oc'clusive** a. serving to occlude —**occluded front** Met. line occurring where cold front of depression has overtaken warm front, raising warm sector from ground level (also **oc'clusion**)

occult (ɒ'kʌlt, 'ɒkʌlt) a. 1. secret, mysterious 2. supernatural —n. 3. esoteric knowledge —vt. (ɒ'kʌlt) 4. hide from view —**occul'tation** n. eclipse —**'occultism** n. study of supernatural —**oc'cultness** n. mystery

occupy ('ɒkjupaɪ) vt. 1. inhabit, fill 2. employ 3. take possession of (**-pied**, **-pying**) —**'occupancy** n. 1. fact of occupying 2. residing —**'occupant** n. —**occu'pation** n. 1. employment 2. pursuit 3. fact of occupying 4. seizure —**occu'pational** a. 1. pert. to occupation, esp. of diseases arising from a particular occupation 2. pert. to use of occupations, eg craft, hobbies etc. as means of rehabilitation —**'occupier** n. tenant —**occupational therapy** Med. therapeutic use of crafts, hobbies etc., esp. in rehabilitation of emotionally disturbed patients

occur (ə'kɜ:) vi. 1. happen 2. come to mind (**-rr-**) —**oc'currence** n. happening

ocean ('əʊʃən) n. 1. great body of water 2. large division of this 3. the sea —**oceanic** (əʊʃɪ'ænɪk) a. —**ocean'ographer** n. —**ocean'ography** n. study of physical and biological features of the sea —**ocean'ology** n. study of the sea, esp. of its economic geography —**ocean-going** a. (of ship, boat etc.) suited for travel on ocean

ocelot ('ɒsɪlɒt, 'əʊ-) n. Amer. leopard

oche ('ɒkɪ) n. Darts mark on floor behind which player must stand to throw

ochre or U.S. **ocher** ('əʊkə) n. various earths used as yellow or brown pigments —**ochreous** ('əʊkrɪəs, 'əʊkərəs), **ochrous** ('əʊkrəs), **ochry** ('əʊkərɪ, 'əʊkrɪ) or U.S. **'ocherous, 'ochery** a.

o'clock (ə'klɒk) adv. by the clock

OCR optical character reader or recognition

Oct. October

oct- (comb. form) eight

octagon ('ɒktəgən) n. plane figure with eight angles —**oc'tagonal** a.

octahedron (ɒktə'hi:drən) n. solid figure with eight sides (pl. **-s**, **-dra** (-drə))

octane ('ɒkteɪn) n. ingredient of motor fuel —**octane rating** measure of quality or type of petrol

octave ('ɒktɪv) n. 1. Mus. eighth note above or below given note 2. this space 3. eight lines of verse

octavo (ɒk'teɪvəʊ) n. book in which each

sheet is folded three times forming eight leaves (pl. **-s**)

octennial (ɒk'tɛnɪəl) a. lasting, happening every eight years

octet (ɒk'tɛt) n. **1.** group of eight **2.** music for eight instruments or singers

October (ɒk'təʊbə) n. tenth month

octogenarian (ɒktəʊdʒɪ'nɛərɪən) or **octogenary** (ɒk'tɒdʒɪnərɪ) n. **1.** person aged between eighty and ninety —a. **2.** of an octogenarian

octopus ('ɒktəpəs) n. mollusc with eight arms covered with suckers —'**octopod** n./a. (mollusc) with eight feet

octosyllable ('ɒktəsɪləb'l) n. word, line of verse of eight syllables

OCTU ('ɒktuː) UK Officer Cadets' Training Unit

ocular ('ɒkjʊlə) a. of eye or sight —'**ocularly** adv.

oculist ('ɒkjʊlɪst) n. Med. obs. ophthalmologist

O.D. Med. overdose

odd (ɒd) a. **1.** strange, queer **2.** incidental, random **3.** that is one in addition when the rest have been divided into equal groups **4.** not even **5.** not part of a set —'**oddity** n. **1.** odd person or thing **2.** quality of being odd —'**oddment** n. (oft. pl.) **1.** remnant **2.** trifle —**odds** pl.n. (with on or against) **1.** advantage conceded in betting **2.** likelihood —**odd-jobman** or **odd-jobber** n. person who does casual work, esp. domestic repairs —**odds-on** a. **1.** (of chance, horse etc.) rated at even money or less to win **2.** regarded as more or most likely to win, happen etc. —**odds and ends** odd fragments or scraps

ode (əʊd) n. lyric poem on particular subject

odium ('əʊdɪəm) n. hatred, widespread dislike —'**odious** a. hateful, repulsive, obnoxious

odometer (ɒ'dɒmɪtə, əʊ-) n. US mileometer

odour or U.S. **odor** ('əʊdə) n. smell —odo'**riferous** a. spreading an odour —'**odorous** a. **1.** fragrant **2.** scented —'**odourless** or U.S. '**odorless** a.

Odyssey ('ɒdɪsɪ) n. **1.** Homer's epic describing Odysseus' return from Troy **2.** any long adventurous journey

OE, O.E., or **OE** Old English (language)

O.E.C.D. Organization for Economic Co-operation and Development

oedema or **edema** (ɪ'diːmə) n. swelling in body tissues, due to accumulation of fluid (pl. **-mata** (-mətə))

Oedipus complex ('iːdɪpəs) Psychoanal. usu. unconscious desire of child to possess sexually parent of opposite sex —'**oedipal** or oedi'**pean** a.

o'er (ɔː, əʊə) prep./adv. Poet. over

oesophagus or U.S. **esophagus** (iː'sɒfəgəs) n. canal from mouth to stomach, gullet (pl. **-gi** (-gaɪ)) —**oesophageal** or U.S. **esophageal** (iːsɒfə'dʒiːəl) a.

oestrogen ('iːstrədʒən, 'ɛstrə-) or U.S.

estrogen n. hormone in females esp. controlling changes, cycles in reproductive organs

of (ɒv; unstressed əv) prep. denotes removal, separation, ownership, attribute, material, quality

off (ɒf) adv. **1.** away —prep. **2.** away from —a. **3.** not operative **4.** cancelled or postponed **5.** bad, sour etc. **6.** distant **7.** (of horses, vehicles etc.) right **8.** Cricket to bowler's left —'**offing** n. part of sea visible to observer on ship or shore —'**offbeat** n. **1.** Mus. any of normally unaccented beats in bar —a. **2.** unusual, unconventional or eccentric —**off chance** slight possibility —**off colour** slightly ill —**off cut** piece of paper, wood etc. remaining after main pieces have been cut; remnant —**off'hand** a. **1.** without previous thought **2.** curt (also **off'handed**) —**off key 1.** Mus. not in correct key; out of tune **2.** out of keeping; discordant —**off-licence** n. place where alcoholic drinks are sold for consumption elsewhere —**off line 1.** of or concerned with part of computer system not connected to central processing unit but controlled by computer storage device **2.** disconnected from computer —**off-load** vt. get rid of (something unpleasant or burdensome), as by delegation to another —**off-peak** a. of or relating to services as used outside periods of intensive use —**off-putting** a. UK inf. disconcerting or disturbing —**offset** ('ɒfsɛt) n. **1.** that which counterbalances, compensates **2.** method of printing —vt. (ɒf'sɛt) **3.** counterbalance, compensate for **4.** print (text etc.) using offset process —'**offshoot** n. **1.** shoot or branch growing from main stem of plant **2.** something that develops from principal source —'**off'side** a./adv. Sport illegally forward —'**offspring** n. children, issue —**off-the-peg** a. (of clothing) ready to wear; not produced especially for person buying —**in the offing** likely to happen soon —**on the off chance** with hope

off. **1.** office **2.** officer **3.** official

offal ('ɒf'l) n. **1.** edible entrails of animal **2.** refuse

offend (ə'fɛnd) vt. **1.** hurt feelings of, displease —vi. **2.** do wrong —of'**fence** or U.S. of'**fense** n. **1.** wrong **2.** crime **3.** insult —of'**fender** n. —of'**fensive** a. **1.** causing displeasure **2.** aggressive —n. **3.** position or movement of attack

offer ('ɒfə) vt. **1.** present for acceptance or refusal **2.** tender **3.** propose **4.** attempt —vi. **5.** present itself —n. **6.** offering, bid —'**offerer** or '**offeror** n. —'**offering** n. **1.** something that is offered **2.** contribution **3.** sacrifice, as of animal, to deity —'**offertory** n. **1.** offering of the bread and wine at the Eucharist **2.** collection in church service

office ('ɒfɪs) n. **1.** room(s), building, in which business, clerical work etc. is done **2.** commercial or professional organization **3.** official position **4.** service **5.** duty **6.** form of worship —pl. **7.** task **8.** service

—**'officer** n. 1. one in command in army, navy, ship etc. 2. official

official (ə'fɪʃəl) a. 1. with, by, authority —n. 2. one holding office, esp. in public body —**of'ficialdom** n. officials collectively, or their attitudes, work, usu. in contemptuous sense —**officia'lese** n. language characteristic of official documents, esp. when verbose —**Official Receiver** officer who manages estate of bankrupt

officiate (ə'fɪʃɪeɪt) vi. 1. perform duties of office 2. perform ceremony

officious (ə'fɪʃəs) a. 1. importunate in offering service 2. interfering

oft (ɒft) adv. often (obs., poet. except in combinations such as oft-repeated

often ('ɒf°n) adv. many times, frequently

ogee arch ('əʊdʒiː) pointed arch with S-shaped curve on both sides

ogle ('əʊg°l) v. 1. stare, look (at) amorously —n. 2. this look —**'ogler** n.

ogre ('əʊgə) n. 1. Folklore man-eating giant 2. monster (**'ogress** fem.)

oh (əʊ) interj. exclamation of surprise, pain etc.

OH Ohio

ohm (əʊm) n. unit of electrical resistance —**'ohmic** a. —**'ohmmeter** n.

O.H.M.S. On His (or Her) Majesty's Service

-**oid** (comb. form) likeness, resemblance, similarity, as in anthropoid

oil (ɔɪl) n. 1. any of a number of viscous liquids with smooth, sticky feel and wide variety of uses 2. petroleum 3. any of variety of petroleum derivatives, esp. as fuel or lubricant —vt. 4. lubricate with oil 5. apply oil to —**'oily** a. 1. soaked in or smeared with oil or grease 2. consisting of, containing or resembling oil 3. flatteringly servile or obsequious —**oil cake** stock feed consisting of compressed linseed —**'oilcloth** n. waterproof material made by treating cotton fabric with drying oil or synthetic resin —**'oilfield** n. area containing reserves of petroleum —**'oilfired** a. (of central heating etc.) using oil as fuel —**oil painting** 1. picture painted with oil paints 2. art of painting with oil paints 3. inf. person or thing regarded as good-looking (esp. in she's no oil painting) —**oil rig** see RIG (sense 6) —**'oilskin** n. cloth treated with oil to make it waterproof —**oil slick** mass of floating oil covering area of water —**oil well** boring into earth or sea bed for extraction of petroleum —**well oiled** sl. drunk

ointment ('ɔɪntmənt) n. greasy preparation for healing or beautifying the skin

OK Oklahoma

O.K. inf. a./adv. 1. all right —n. 2. approval —vt. 3. approve (**O.K.ing** (əʊ'keɪɪŋ), **O.K.ed** (əʊ'keɪd))

okapi (əʊ'kɑːpɪ) n. Afr. animal like short-necked giraffe (pl. **-s**, **-pi**)

okra ('əʊkrə) n. 1. annual plant with yellow-and-red flowers and edible pods 2. pod of this plant, eaten in soups, stews etc.

old (əʊld) a. 1. aged, having lived or existed long 2. belonging to earlier period (**'older**, **'elder** comp., **'oldest**, **'eldest** sup.) —**'olden** a. old —**'oldie** n. inf. old song, film, person etc. —**'oldish** a. —**old age pension** see PENSION¹ —**Old Bailey** Central Criminal Court of England —**old boy** 1. (sometimes **O- B-**) UK male ex-pupil of school 2. inf., chiefly UK familiar name used to refer to man; old man —**old country** country of origin of immigrant or immigrant's ancestors —**Old English** English language from time of earliest Saxon settlements in fifth century A.D. to about 1100 (also **Anglo-Saxon**) —**old-fashioned** a. 1. in style of earlier period, out of date 2. fond of old ways —n. 3. cocktail containing spirit, bitters, fruit etc. —**old guard** 1. group that works for long-established principles etc. 2. conservative element in political party or other groups —**old hat** old-fashioned; trite —**old maid** elderly spinster —**old man** 1. inf. father; husband 2. (sometimes **O- M-**) inf. man in command, such as employer, foreman etc. 3. jocular affectionate term used in addressing man —**old master** 1. one of great European painters before 19th cent. 2. painting by one of these —**Old Nick** inf., jocular Satan —**old school** 1. chiefly UK one's former school 2. group of people favouring traditional ideas etc. —**old school tie** 1. UK distinctive tie that indicates which school wearer attended 2. attitudes, values etc. associated with British public schools —**Old Testament** collection of books comprising sacred Scriptures of Hebrews; first part of Christian Bible —**old wives' tale** belief passed on as piece of traditional wisdom —**Old World** eastern hemisphere —**old-world** a. of former times, esp. quaint or traditional

oleaginous (əʊlɪ'ædʒɪnəs) a. 1. oily, producing oil 2. unctuous, fawning —**ole'aginousness** n.

oleander (əʊlɪ'ændə) n. poisonous evergreen flowering shrub

oleo- (comb. form) oil, as in oleomargarine

O level UK 1. basic level of General Certificate of Education 2. pass in subject at O level

olfactory (ɒl'fæktərɪ, -trɪ) a. of smelling

oligarchy ('ɒlɪgɑːkɪ) n. government by a few —**'oligarch** n. —**oli'garchic(al)** a.

Oligocene ('ɒlɪgəʊsiːn, ɒ'lɪg-) a. 1. of third epoch of Tertiary period —n. 2. Oligocene epoch or rock series

olive ('ɒlɪv) n. 1. evergreen tree 2. its oil-yielding fruit 3. its wood —a. 4. greyish-green —**olive branch** any offering of peace or conciliation —**olive oil** pale yellow oil extracted from olives, used in medicines etc.

Olympian (ə'lɪmpɪən) a. 1. of Mount Olympus or classical Greek gods 2. majestic in manner or bearing 3. of ancient Olympia or its inhabitants —n. 4.

god of Mount Olympus **5.** inhabitant of ancient Olympia

Olympic (ə'lɪmpɪk) a. **1.** of Olympic Games **2.** of ancient Olympia —**Olympic Games 1.** Panhellenic festival, held every fourth year in honour of Zeus at ancient Olympia **2.** modern revival of these games

O.M. Order of Merit

ombudsman ('ɒmbʊdzmən) n. official who investigates citizens' complaints against government etc.

omega ('əʊmɪgə) n. **1.** last letter in Gr. alphabet (Ω, ω) **2.** end

omelette or esp. U.S. **omelet** ('ɒmlɪt) n. dish of eggs beaten up and fried with seasoning

omen ('əʊmən) n. prophetic object or happening —**ominous** ('ɒmɪnəs) a. boding evil, threatening

omicron (əʊ'maɪkrɒn, 'ɒmɪkrɒn) n. 15th letter in Gr. alphabet (O, o)

omit (əʊ'mɪt) vt. **1.** leave out, neglect **2.** leave undone (**-tt-**) —**o'mission** n. —**o'missive** a.

omni- (comb. form) all

omnibus ('ɒmnɪbʌs, -bəs) n. **1.** large road vehicle travelling on set route and taking passengers at any stage (also **bus**) **2.** book containing several works —a. **3.** serving, containing several objects

omnidirectional (ɒmnɪdɪ'rekʃən³l, -daɪ-) a. in radio, denotes transmission, reception in all directions

omnipotent (ɒm'nɪpətənt) a. all-powerful —**om'nipotence** n.

omnipresent (ɒmnɪ'prez³nt) a. present everywhere —**omni'presence** n.

omniscient (ɒm'nɪsɪənt) a. knowing everything —**om'niscience** n.

omnivorous (ɒm'nɪvərəs) a. **1.** devouring all foods **2.** not fastidious

on (ɒn) prep. **1.** above and touching, at, near, towards etc. **2.** attached to **3.** concerning **4.** performed upon **5.** during **6.** taking regularly —a. **7.** operating **8.** taking place **9.** Cricket denoting part of field to left of right-handed batter, and to right of bowler —adv. **10.** so as to be on **11.** forwards **12.** continuously etc. **13.** in progress —'**oncoming** a. coming nearer in space or time; approaching —n. **2.** approach; onset —'**ongoing** a. actually in progress **2.** continually moving forward —**on line** of or concerned with peripheral device that is directly connected to and controlled by central processing unit of computer —'**onrush** n. forceful forward rush or flow —'**onset** n. **1.** violent attack **2.** assault **3.** beginning —'**onslaught** n. attack —**on stream** (of manufacturing process, equipment etc.) in or about to go into operation or production —'**onward** a. **1.** advanced or advancing —adv. **2.** in advance, ahead, forward —'**onwards** adv.

ON Ontario

on- (comb. form) on, as in onlooker

onager ('ɒnədʒə) n. wild ass (pl. **-gri** (-graɪ), **-s**)

onanism ('əʊnənɪzəm) n. masturbation

O.N.C. UK Ordinary National Certificate

once (wʌns) adv. **1.** one time **2.** formerly **3.** ever —**once-over** n. inf. quick examination —**at once** immediately; simultaneously

oncost ('ɒnkɒst) n. UK (sometimes pl.) see **overheads** at OVERHEAD

O.N.D. UK Ordinary National Diploma

one (wʌn) a. **1.** lowest cardinal number **2.** single **3.** united **4.** only, without others **5.** identical —n. **6.** number or figure 1 **7.** unity **8.** single specimen —pron. **9.** particular but not stated person **10.** any person —'**oneness** n. **1.** unity **2.** uniformity **3.** singleness —**one'self** pron. —**one-armed bandit** inf. fruit machine operated by pulling down lever at one side —**one-horse** a. inf. small; obscure —**one-night stand 1.** performance given only once at any one place **2.** inf. sexual encounter lasting only one night —**one-off** n. UK something that is carried out or made only once (also **one-shot**) —**one-sided** a. **1.** partial **2.** uneven —**one-track** a. **1.** inf. obsessed with one idea, subject etc. **2.** having or consisting of single track —**one-way** a. denotes system of traffic circulation in one direction only

onerous ('ɒnərəs, 'əʊ-) a. burdensome

onion ('ʌnjən) n. edible bulb of pungent flavour

only ('əʊnlɪ) a. **1.** being the one specimen —adv. **2.** solely, merely, exclusively —conj. **3.** but then, excepting that

o.n.o. or near(est) offer

onomatopoeia (ɒnəmætə'piːə) n. formation of a word by using sounds that resemble or suggest the object or action to be named —**onomato'poeic** or **onomato'poetic** (ɒnəmætəpəʊ'etɪk) a.

onto or **on to** ('ɒntʊ; unstressed 'ɒntə) prep. **1.** on top of **2.** aware of

ontology (ɒn'tɒlədʒɪ) n. science of being or reality —**onto'logical** a. —**on'tologist** n.

onus ('əʊnəs) n. responsibility, burden

onyx ('ɒnɪks) n. variety of chalcedony

oodles ('uːd³lz) pl.n. inf. abundance

oolite ('əʊəlaɪt) n. any sedimentary rock, esp. limestone, consisting of tiny spherical grains within fine matrix —**oolitic** (əʊə'lɪtɪk) a.

ooze (uːz) vi. **1.** pass slowly out —v. **2.** exude (moisture etc.) —n. **3.** sluggish flow **4.** wet mud, slime —'**oozy** a.

op. **1.** opera **2.** operation **3.** opus

o.p. or **O.P.** out of print

opal ('əʊp³l) n. glassy gemstone displaying variegated colours —**opa'lescent** a.

opaque (əʊ'peɪk) a. not allowing the passage of light, not transparent —**opacity** (əʊ'pæsɪtɪ) n.

op. cit. opere citato (Lat., in the work cited)

OPEC ('əʊpek) Organization of Petroleum Exporting Countries

open ('əʊp³n) a. **1.** not shut or blocked up **2.** without lid or door **3.** bare **4.** undisguised **5.**

not enclosed, covered or exclusive **6.** spread out, accessible **7.** frank, sincere —*vt.* **8.** set open, uncover, give access to **9.** disclose, lay bare **10.** begin **11.** make a hole in —*vi.* **12.** become open **13.** begin —*n.* **14.** clear space, unenclosed country **15.** *Sport* competition in which all may enter —'**opening** *n.* **1.** hole, gap **2.** beginning **3.** opportunity —*a.* **4.** first **5.** initial —'**openly** *adv.* without concealment —**open-and-shut** *a.* easily decided or solved —'**opencast** *a.* (of coal) mined from the surface, not underground —**open-ended** *a.* without definite limits, as of duration or amount —**open-handed** *a.* generous —**open-hearted** *a.* frank, magnanimous —**open-heart surgery** surgical repair of heart during which blood circulation is off. maintained mechanically —**open-minded** *a.* unprejudiced —**open-plan** *a.* having no or few dividing walls between areas —**open prison** prison without restraints to prevent absconding —**open secret** something that is supposed to be secret but is widely known —**Open University** UK university for mature students studying by television and radio lectures, correspondence courses *etc.* —**open verdict** coroner's verdict not stating cause (of death) —'**openwork** *n.* pattern with interstices

opera ('ɒpərə, 'ɒprə) *n.* musical drama —**oper'atic** *a.* of opera —**ope'retta** *n.* light, comic opera —**opera glasses** small binoculars used by audiences in theatres *etc.*

operation (ɒpə'reɪʃən) *n.* **1.** working, way things work **2.** scope **3.** act of surgery **4.** military action —**opera'bility** *n.* —'**operable** *a.* **1.** capable of being treated by surgical operation **2.** capable of being put into practice —'**operate** *vt.* **1.** cause to function **2.** control functioning of —*vi.* **3.** work **4.** produce an effect **5.** perform act of surgery **6.** exert power —**ope'rational** *a.* **1.** of operation(s) **2.** working —'**operative** *a.* **1.** working —*n.* **2.** worker, *esp.* with a special skill —'**operator** *n.* —**operating theatre** room in which surgical operations are performed —**operations research** analysis of problems in business involving quantitative techniques

operculum (ɒʊ'pɜːkjʊləm) *n.* lid; cover (*pl.* **-s, -la** (-lə))

ophidian (ɒʊ'fɪdɪən) *a.* **1.** snakelike **2.** of suborder of reptiles which comprises snakes —*n.* **3.** any reptile of this suborder

ophthalmic (ɒf'θælmɪk) *a.* of eyes —**oph'thalmia** *n.* inflammation of eye —**ophthal'mologist** *n.* —**ophthal'mology** *n.* study of eye and its diseases —**oph'thalmoscope** *n.* instrument for examining interior of eye —**ophthalmic optician** optician qualified to prescribe spectacles *etc.*

opiate ('əʊpɪɪt) *see* OPIUM

opinion (ə'pɪnjən) *n.* **1.** what one thinks about something **2.** belief, judgment —**opine** (əʊ'paɪn) *vt.* **1.** think —*vi.* **2.** utter opinion —**o'pinionated** *a.* **1.** stubborn in one's opinions **2.** dogmatic

opium ('əʊpɪəm) *n.* addictive narcotic drug made from poppy —'**opiate** *n.* **1.** drug containing opium **2.** narcotic —*a.* **3.** inducing sleep **4.** soothing

opossum (ə'pɒsəm) *or* **possum** *n.* small Amer. and Aust. marsupial animal

opp. 1. opposed **2.** opposite

opponent (ə'pəʊnənt) *n.* adversary, antagonist

opportune ('ɒpətjuːn) *a.* seasonable, well-timed —**oppor'tunism** *n.* policy of doing what is expedient at the time regardless of principle —**oppor'tunist** *n./a.* —**opportunity** *n.* **1.** favourable time or condition **2.** good chance

oppose (ə'pəʊz) *vt.* **1.** resist, withstand **2.** contrast **3.** set against —**op'poser** *n.* —'**opposite** *a.* **1.** contrary **2.** facing **3.** diametrically different **4.** adverse —*n.* **5.** the contrary —*prep./adv.* **6.** facing **7.** on the other side —**oppo'sition** *n.* **1.** antithesis **2.** resistance **3.** obstruction **4.** hostility **5.** group opposing another **6.** party opposing that in power —**opposite number** person holding corresponding position on another side or situation

oppress (ə'prɛs) *vt.* **1.** govern with tyranny **2.** weigh down —**op'pression** *n.* **1.** act of oppressing **2.** severity **3.** misery —**op'pressive** *a.* **1.** tyrannical **2.** hard to bear **3.** heavy **4.** (of weather) hot and tiring —**op'pressively** *adv.* —**op'pressor** *n.*

opprobrium (ə'prəʊbrɪəm) *n.* disgrace —**op'probrious** *a.* **1.** reproachful **2.** shameful **3.** abusive

oppugn (ə'pjuːn) *vt.* call into question, dispute

opt (ɒpt) *vi.* make a choice —'**optative** *a.* **1.** expressing wish or desire —*n.* **2.** mood of verb expressing wish

opt. 1. optical **2.** optional

optic ('ɒptɪk) *a.* **1.** of eye or sight —*n.* **2.** eye —*pl.* **3.** (*with sing. v.*) science of sight and light —'**optical** *a.* —**op'tician** *n.* maker of, dealer in spectacles, optical instruments —**optical character reader** computer device enabling characters, usu. printed on paper, to be optically scanned and input to storage device

optimism ('ɒptɪmɪzəm) *n.* **1.** disposition to look on the bright side **2.** doctrine that good must prevail in the end **3.** belief that the world is the best possible world —'**optimist** *n.* —**opti'mistic** *a.* —**opti'mistically** *adv.*

optimum ('ɒptɪməm) *a./n.* the best, the most favourable (*pl.* **-s, -ma** (-mə))

option ('ɒpʃən) *n.* **1.** choice **2.** preference **3.** thing chosen **4.** in business, purchased privilege of either buying or selling things at specified price within specified time —'**optional** *a.* leaving to choice

optometrist (ɒp'tɒmɪtrɪst) *n.* person *usu.* not medically qualified, testing eyesight, prescribing corrective lenses etc. —**op-ˈtometry** n.

opulent ('ɒpjulənt) a. 1. rich 2. copious —**ˈopulence** or **ˈopulency** n. riches, wealth

opus ('əupəs) n. 1. work 2. musical composition (pl. **opera** ('ɒpərə), **-es**)

or (ɔː; unstressed ə) conj. 1. introduces alternatives 2. if not

OR Oregon

-or¹ (comb. form) person or thing that does what is expressed by verb, as in actor, sailor

-or² (comb. form) 1. state, condition, activity, as in terror, error 2. US see -OUR

O.R. 1. Official Receiver 2. operational research

oracle ('ɒrək²l) n. 1. divine utterance, prophecy, oft. ambiguous, given at shrine of god 2. the shrine 3. wise or mysterious adviser 4. (O-) R ITV teletext service —**oˈracular** a. 1. of oracle 2. prophetic 3. authoritative 4. ambiguous

oral ('ɔːrəl, 'ɒrəl) a. 1. spoken 2. by mouth —n. 3. spoken examination —**ˈorally** adv.

orange ('ɒrɪndʒ) n. 1. bright reddish-yellow round fruit 2. tree bearing it 3. fruit's colour —**orangeˈade** n. effervescent orange-flavoured drink —**ˈorangery** n. building, such as greenhouse, in which orange trees are grown

Orangeman ('ɒrɪndʒmən) n. member of society founded as secret order in Ireland to uphold Protestantism

orang-utan (ɔːræŋuːˈtæn, ɔːræŋˈuːtæn) or **orang-outang** (ɔːræŋuːˈtæŋ, ɔːræŋ-ˈuːtæŋ) n. large Indonesian ape

orator ('ɒrətə) n. 1. maker of speech 2. skilful speaker —**oˈration** n. formal speech —**oraˈtorical** a. of orator or oration —**ˈoratory** n. 1. speeches 2. eloquence 3. small private chapel

oratorio (ɒrəˈtɔːrɪəʊ) n. semi-dramatic composition of sacred music (pl. **-s**)

orb (ɔːb) n. globe, sphere —**orˈbicular** a.

orbit ('ɔːbɪt) n. 1. track of planet, satellite, comet etc., around another heavenly body 2. field of influence, sphere 3. eye socket —v. 4. move in, or put into, an orbit

Orcadian (ɔːˈkeɪdɪən) n. 1. native or inhabitant of the Orkneys —a. 2. of or relating to the Orkneys

orchard ('ɔːtʃəd) n. 1. area for cultivation of fruit trees 2. the trees

orchestra ('ɔːkɪstrə) n. 1. band of musicians 2. place for such a band in theatre etc. (also **orchestra pit**) —**orˈchestral** a. —**ˈorchestrate** vt. 1. compose or arrange (music) for orchestra 2. organize, arrange

orchid ('ɔːkɪd) n. genus of various flowering plants

ordain (ɔːˈdeɪn) vt. 1. admit to Christian ministry 2. confer holy orders upon 3. decree, enact 4. destine —**ordiˈnation** n.

ordeal (ɔːˈdiːl) n. 1. severe, trying experience 2. Hist. form of trial by which accused underwent severe physical test

order ('ɔːdə) n. 1. regular or proper arrangement or condition 2. sequence 3. peaceful condition of society 4. rank, class 5. group 6. command 7. request for something to be supplied 8. mode of procedure 9. instruction 10. monastic society —vt. 11. command 12. request (something) to be supplied or made 13. arrange —**ˈorderliness** n. —**ˈorderly** a. 1. tidy 2. methodical 3. well-behaved —n. 4. hospital attendant 5. soldier following officer to carry orders —**ˈordinal** a. 1. showing position in a series —n. 2. ordinal number —**ordinal number** number denoting order, quality or degree in group, such as first, second, third —**Order of Merit** UK order conferred on civilians and service-men for eminence in any field

ordinance ('ɔːdɪnəns) n. 1. decree, rule 2. rite, ceremony

ordinary ('ɔːd²nrɪ) a. 1. usual, normal 2. common 3. plain 4. commonplace —n. 5. bishop in his province —**ˈordinarily** adv. —**Ordinary level** UK formal name for O LEVEL —**ordinary rating** rank in Royal Navy comparable to that of private in army

ordinate ('ɔːdɪnɪt) n. vertical or y-coordinate of point in two-dimensional system of Cartesian coordinates

ordnance ('ɔːdnəns) n. 1. big guns, artillery 2. military stores —**Ordnance Survey** official geographical survey of Britain

Ordovician (ɔːdəʊˈvɪʃɪən) a. 1. of, denoting or formed in second period of Palaeozoic era —n. 2 Ordovician period or rock system

ordure ('ɔːdjʊə) n. 1. dung 2. filth

ore (ɔː) n. naturally occurring mineral which yields metal

oregano (ɒrɪˈgɑːnəʊ) n. herb, variety of marjoram

organ ('ɔːgən) n. 1. musical wind instrument of pipes and stops, played by keys 2. member of animal or plant carrying out particular function 3. means of action 4. medium of information, esp. newspaper —**orˈganic** a. 1. of, derived from, living organisms 2. of bodily organs 3. affecting bodily organs 4. having vital organs 5. Chem. of compounds formed from carbon 6. grown with fertilizers derived from animal or vegetable matter 7. organized, systematic —**orˈganically** adv. —**ˈorganist** n. organ player —**organ loft** gallery in church etc. for an organ

organdie or esp. U.S. **organdy** ('ɔːgəndɪ) n. light, transparent muslin

organize or **-ise** ('ɔːgənaɪz) vt. 1. give definite structure to 2. get up, arrange 3. put into working order 4. unite in a society —**ˈorganism** n. 1. organized body or system 2. plant, animal —**organiˈzation** or **-iˈsation** n. 1. act of organizing 2. body of people 3. society —**ˈorganizer** or **-iser** n.

orgasm ('ɔːgæzəm) n. sexual climax

orgy ('ɔːdʒɪ) n. 1. drunken or licentious

revel, debauch **2.** act of immoderation, overindulgence

oriel ('ɔːrɪəl) *n.* **1.** projecting part of an upper room with a window **2.** the window

orient ('ɔːrɪənt) *n.* **1.** (**O-**) the East **2.** lustre of best pearls —*a.* **3.** rising **4.** (**O-**) Eastern —*vt.* ('ɔːrɪɛnt) **5.** place so as to face East **6.** adjust or align (oneself *etc.*) according to surroundings or circumstances **7.** position or set (map *etc.*) with reference to compass *etc.* —**ori'ental** *a./n.* —**ori'ental-ist** *n.* expert in Eastern languages and history —**'orientate** *vt.* orient —**orien'ta-tion** *n.* —**orien'teering** *n.* competitive sport involving compass and map-reading skills

orifice ('ɒrɪfɪs) *n.* opening, mouth of a cavity, eg pipe

orig. 1. origin **2.** original(ly)

origami (ɒrɪ'gɑːmɪ) *n.* Japanese art of paper folding

origin ('ɒrɪdʒɪn) *n.* **1.** beginning **2.** source **3.** parentage

original (ə'rɪdʒɪn°l) *a.* **1.** primitive, earliest **2.** new, not copied or derived **3.** thinking or acting for oneself **4.** eccentric —*n.* **5.** pattern, thing from which another is copied **6.** unconventional or strange person —**origi'nality** *n.* power of producing something individual to oneself —**o'riginally** *adv.* **1.** at first **2.** in the beginning —**original sin** *Theol.* state of sin held to be innate in mankind as descendants of Adam

originate (ə'rɪdʒɪneɪt) *v.* come or bring into existence, begin —**origi'nation** *n.* —**o'riginator** *n.*

oriole ('ɔːrɪəʊl) *n.* tropical thrushlike bird

orison ('ɒrɪz°n) *n.* prayer

Orlon ('ɔːlɒn) *n.* **R** crease-resistant acrylic fabric used for clothing *etc.*

ormolu ('ɔːməluː) *n.* **1.** gilded bronze **2.** gold-coloured alloy **3.** articles of these

ornament ('ɔːnəmənt) *n.* **1.** any object used to adorn or decorate **2.** decoration —*vt.* ('ɔːnəmɛnt) **3.** adorn —**orna'mental** *a.*

ornate (ɔː'neɪt) *a.* highly decorated or elaborate

ornery ('ɔːnərɪ) *a.* US *dial., inf.* **1.** stubborn; vile-tempered **2.** low; treacherous **3.** ordinary

ornithology (ɔːnɪ'θɒlədʒɪ) *n.* science of birds —**ornitho'logical** *a.* —**orni'tholo-gist** *n.*

orotund ('ɒrəʊtʌnd) *a.* **1.** full, clear and musical **2.** pompous

orphan ('ɔːfən) *n.* child bereaved of one or both parents —**'orphanage** *n.* institution for care of orphans —**'orphanhood** *n.*

orrery ('ɒrərɪ) *n.* mechanical model of solar system to show revolutions, planets *etc.*

orris *or* **orrice** ('ɒrɪs) *n.* any of various kinds of iris

ortho- *or before vowel* **orth-** (*comb. form*) right, correct

orthodontics (ɔːθəʊ'dɒntɪks) *or* **ortho-**

dontia (ɔːθəʊ'dɒntɪə) *n.* branch of dentis-try concerned with correcting irregu-larities of teeth —**ortho'dontic** *a.* —**ortho-'dontist** *n.*

orthodox ('ɔːθədɒks) *a.* **1.** holding accept-ed views **2.** conventional —**'orthodoxy** *n.* —**Orthodox Church 1.** collective body of Eastern Churches that were separated from western Church in 11th century and are in communion with Gr. patriarch of Constantinople **2.** any of these Churches

orthography (ɔː'θɒgrəfɪ) *n.* correct spell-ing

orthopaedics *or U.S.* **orthopedics** (ɔːθə-'piːdɪks) *pl.n.* (*with sing. v.*) branch of surgery concerned with disorders of spine and joints and repair of deformities of these parts —**ortho'paedic** *or U.S.* **ortho-'pedic** *a.*

orthopterous (ɔː'θɒptərəs) *a.* of large order of insects, including crickets, locusts and grasshoppers, having leathery fore-wings and membranous hind wings

ortolan ('ɔːtələn) *n.* a small bird, *esp.* as table delicacy

-ory[1] (*comb. form*) **1.** place for, as in *observatory* **2.** something having specified use, as in *directory*

-ory[2] (*comb. form*) of, relating to; characterized by; having effect of, as in *contributory*

oryx ('ɒrɪks) *n.* large Afr. antelope (*pl.* **-es**, **-yx**)

Os *Chem.* osmium

O.S. 1. Old Style **2.** Ordinary Seaman **3.** UK Ordnance Survey **4.** outsize **5.** (*also* **OS**) Old Saxon (language)

Oscar ('ɒskə) *n.* any of several small gold statuettes awarded annually in U.S.A. for outstanding achievements in films

oscillate ('ɒsɪleɪt) *vi.* **1.** swing to and fro **2.** waver **3.** fluctuate (regularly) —**oscil'la-tion** *n.* —**'oscillator** *n.* —**'oscillatory** *a.* —**os'cilloscope** *n.* electronic instrument producing visible representation of rapidly changing quantity

osculate ('ɒskjʊleɪt) *v. jocular* kiss —**'oscular** *a.* —**oscu'lation** *n.* —**'oscula-tory** *a.*

osier ('əʊzɪə) *n.* species of willow used for basketwork

-osis (*comb. form*) **1.** process; state, as in *metamorphosis* **2.** diseased condition, as in *tuberculosis* **3.** formation or development of something, as in *fibrosis*

osmium ('ɒzmɪəm) *n.* heaviest known of metallic elements

osmosis (ɒz'məʊsɪs, ɒs-) *n.* percolation of fluids through porous partitions —**osmotic** (ɒz'mɒtɪk, ɒs-) *a.*

osprey ('ɒsprɪ, -preɪ) *n.* **1.** fishing hawk **2.** plume

osseous ('ɒsɪəs) *a.* **1.** of, like bone **2.** bony —**ossifi'cation** *n.* —**'ossify** *v.* **1.** turn into bone —*vi.* **2.** grow rigid (**-fied**, **-fying**)

ostensible (ɒ'stɛnsɪb°l) *a.* **1.** apparent **2.** professed —**os'tensibly** *adv.*

ostentation (ɒstɛn'teɪʃən) *n.* show, pretentious display —**osten'tatious** a. 1. given to display 2. showing off —**osten'tatiously** adv.

osteo- or before vowel **oste-** (comb. form) bone(s)

osteomyelitis (ɒstɪəʊmaɪ'laɪtɪs) n. inflammation of bone marrow

osteopathy (ɒstɪ'ɒpəθɪ) n. art of treating disease by removing structural derangement by manipulation, esp. of spine —**'osteopath** n. one skilled in this art

ostler ('ɒslə) or **hostler** n. Hist. stableman at an inn

ostracize or **-ise** ('ɒstrəsaɪz) vt. exclude, banish from society, exile —**'ostracism** n. social boycotting

ostrich ('ɒstrɪtʃ) n. large swift-running flightless Afr. bird

O.T. 1. occupational therapy 2. Old Testament 3. overtime

O.T.C. UK Officers' Training Corps

other ('ʌðə) a. 1. not this 2. not the same 3. alternative, different —pron. 4. other person or thing —**'otherwise** adv. 1. differently 2. in another way —conj. 3. or else, if not —**other'worldly** a. 1. of or relating to spiritual or imaginative world 2. impractical, unworldly

otiose ('əʊtɪəʊs, -əʊz) a. 1. superfluous 2. useless

otitis (əʊ'taɪtɪs) n. inflammation of ear

otter ('ɒtə) n. furry aquatic fish-eating animal

Ottoman ('ɒtəmən) or **Othman** ('ɒθmən) a. 1. Turkish —n. 2. Turk 3. (o-) cushioned, backless seat, storage box (pl. **-s**)

ou (əʊ) n. SA sl. man —**oubaas** ('əʊbɑːs) n. man in authority

oubliette (uːblɪ'et) n. dungeon entered by trapdoor

ouch (aʊtʃ) interj. exclamation of sudden pain

ought (ɔːt) v. aux. 1. expressing duty, obligation or advisability 2. be bound

Ouija ('wiːdʒə) n. R board with letters and symbols used to obtain messages at seances

ouma ('əʊmɑː) n. SA 1. grandmother 2. elderly woman

ounce (aʊns) n. a weight, sixteenth of avoirdupois pound (28.4 grams), twelfth of troy pound (31.1 grams)

oupa ('əʊpɑː) n. SA 1. grandfather 2. elderly man

our (aʊə) a. belonging to us —**ours** pron. —**our'self** pron. myself, used in regal or formal style —**our'selves** pl. pron. emphatic or reflexive form of WE

-our (comb. form) state, condition, activity, as in behaviour, labour

-ous (comb. form) 1. having; full of, as in dangerous, spacious 2. Chem. indicating that element is chemically combined in

lower of two possible valency states, as in ferrous

ousel ('uːz'l) n. see OUZEL

oust (aʊst) vt. put out, expel

out (aʊt) adv. 1. from within, away 2. wrong 3. on strike —a. 4. not worth considering 5. not allowed 6. unfashionable 7. unconscious 8. not in use, operation etc. 9. at an end 10. not burning 11. Sport dismissed —**'outer** a. away from the inside —**'outermost** or **'outmost** a. on extreme outside —**'outing** n. pleasure excursion —**'outward** a./adv. —**'outwardly** adv. —**'outwards** adv. —**out-and-out** a. thoroughgoing; complete —**outer space** any region of space beyond atmosphere of earth —**out-of-the-way** a. 1. distant from more populous areas 2. uncommon or unusual —**out of date** no longer valid, current, or fashionable —**out of pocket** 1. having lost money, as in a commercial enterprise 2. without money to spend 3. (of expenses) unbudgeted and paid for in cash

out- (comb. form) 1. beyond, in excess, as in outclass, outdistance, outsize 2. so as to surpass or defeat, as in outfox, outmanoeuvre 3. outside, away from, as in outpatient, outgrowth. See the list below

outback ('aʊtbæk) n. A remote, sparsely populated country

outbalance (aʊt'bæləns) vt. 1. outweigh 2. exceed in weight

outboard ('aʊtbɔːd) a. (of boat's engine) mounted outside stern

outbreak ('aʊtbreɪk) n. sudden occurrence, esp. of disease or strife

outburst ('aʊtbɜːst) n. bursting out, esp. of violent emotion

outcast ('aʊtkɑːst) n. 1. someone rejected —a. 2. rejected, cast out

outclass (aʊt'klɑːs) vt. excel, surpass

outcome ('aʊtkʌm) n. result

outcrop ('aʊtkrɒp) n. Geol. 1. rock coming out of stratum to the surface —vi. (aʊt-'krɒp) 2. come out to the surface (**-pp-**)

outcry ('aʊtkraɪ) n. 1. widespread or vehement protest —vt. (aʊt'kraɪ) 2. cry louder or make more noise than

outdo (aʊt'duː) vt. surpass or exceed in performance (**-'doing, -'did, -'done**)

outdoors (aʊt'dɔːz) adv. in the open air —**'outdoor** a.

outfall ('aʊtfɔːl) n. mouth of river

outfit ('aʊtfɪt) n. 1. equipment 2. clothes and accessories 3. inf. group or association regarded as a unit —**'outfitter** n. one who deals in outfits

outflank (aʊt'flæŋk) vt. 1. get beyond the flank of (enemy army) 2. circumvent

outgoing ('aʊtgəʊɪŋ) a. 1. departing 2. friendly, sociable

outgrow (aʊt'grəʊ) vt. 1. become too large

out'bid	out'face	'outflow
out'box	'outfield	out'fox
out'distance	out'fight	

or too old for **2.** surpass in growth (-'**grew,** -'**grown,** -'**growing**)

outhouse ('авthaus) *n.* shed *etc.* near main building

outlandish (aut'lændɪʃ) *a.* queer, extravagantly strange

outlaw ('автlɔ:) *n.* **1.** one beyond protection of the law **2.** exile, bandit —*vt.* **3.** make (someone) an outlaw **4.** ban —'**outlawry** *n.*

outlay ('автleɪ) *n.* expenditure

outlet ('автlɛt, -lɪt) *n.* **1.** opening, vent **2.** means of release or escape **3.** market for product or service

outline ('автlaɪn) *n.* **1.** rough sketch **2.** general plan **3.** lines enclosing visible figure —*vt.* **4.** sketch **5.** summarize

outlook ('автluk) *n.* **1.** point of view **2.** probable outcome **3.** view

outlying ('автlaɪɪŋ) *a.* distant, remote

outmoded (aut'məudɪd) *a.* no longer fashionable or accepted

output ('автput) *n.* **1.** quantity produced **2.** *Comp.* information produced

outrage ('автreɪdʒ) *n.* **1.** violation of others' rights **2.** gross or violent offence or indignity **3.** anger arising from this —*vt.* **4.** offend grossly **5.** insult **6.** injure, violate —out'**rageous** *a.*

outré (u'tre) *a.* **1.** extravagantly odd **2.** bizarre

outrigger ('автrɪgə) *n.* **1.** frame, *esp.* with float attached, outside boat's gunwale **2.** frame on rowing boat's side with rowlock **3.** boat equipped with a framework

outright ('автraɪt) *a.* **1.** undisputed **2.** downright **3.** positive —*adv.* **4.** completely **5.** instantly **6.** openly

outset ('автsɛt) *n.* beginning

outside (aut'saɪd) *n.* **1.** exterior **2.** C settled parts of Canada —*adv.* (aut'saɪd) **3.** not inside **4.** in the open air —*a.* ('автsaɪd) **5.** on exterior **6.** remote, unlikely **7.** greatest possible, probable —out'**sider** *n.* **1.** person outside specific group **2.** contestant thought unlikely to win —**outside broadcast** *T.V., rad.* broadcast not made from studio

outskirts ('автskɜ:ts) *pl.n.* outer areas, districts, *esp.* of city

outspan ('автspæn) *n.* SA **1.** unyoking of oxen **2.** area for rest

outspoken (aut'spəukən) *a.* frank, candid

outstanding (aut'stændɪŋ) *a.* **1.** excellent **2.** remarkable **3.** unsettled, unpaid

outstrip (aut'strɪp) *vt.* outrun, surpass

outwit (aut'wɪt) *vt.* get the better of by cunning

outwork ('автwɜ:k) *n.* part of fortress outside main wall

ouzel *or* **ousel** ('u:z'l) *n.* **1.** type of thrush **2.** kind of diving bird

ouzo ('u:zəu) *n.* strong aniseed-flavoured spirit from Greece

ova ('əuvə) *n., pl. of* OVUM

oval ('əuv'l) *a.* **1.** egg-shaped, elliptical —*n.* **2.** something of this shape

ovary ('əuvərɪ) *n.* female egg-producing organ —o'**varian** *a.*

ovation (əu'veɪʃən) *n.* enthusiastic burst of applause

oven ('ʌv'n) *n.* heated chamber for baking in

over ('əuvə) *adv.* **1.** above, above and beyond, going beyond, in excess, too much, past, finished, in repetition, across, downwards *etc.* —*prep.* **2.** above **3.** on, upon **4.** more than, in excess of, along *etc.* —*a.* **5.** upper, outer —*n.* **6.** *Cricket* set of six balls bowled by bowler from same end of pitch

over- (*comb. form*) too, too much, in excess, above, to a prostrate position. See the list below

overall ('əuvərɔ:l) *n.* **1.** (*also pl.*) loose garment worn as protection against dirt *etc.* —*a.* **2.** total

overbalance (əuvə'bæləns) *v.* **1.** lose or cause to lose balance —*n.* ('əuvəbæləns) **2.** excess of weight, value *etc.*

overbearing (əuvə'bɛərɪŋ) *a.* domineering

overblown (əuvə'bləun) *a.* excessive, bombastic

overboard ('əuvəbɔ:d) *adv.* from a vessel into the water

overcast ('əuvəkɑ:st) *a.* covered over, *esp.* by clouds

overcoat ('əuvəkəut) *n.* warm coat worn over outer clothes

overcome (əuvə'kʌm) *vt.* **1.** conquer **2.** surmount **3.** make incapable or powerless —*vi.* **4.** be victorious

'outgrowth	'outsize	over'burden
out'last	out'smart	overca'pacity
out'live	'out'spread	over'cautious
outma'noeuvre	out'stare	over'charge
out'match	'outstation	'overcoat
out'number	out'stretch	over'compensate
'outpatient	out'value	over'confident
out'play	out'vote	overcon'sumption
'outpost	out'weigh	over'cook
out'rank	overa'bundance	over'crowd
out'reach	over'act	over'curious
'outrider	overam'bitious	overde'pendent
out'rival	over'anxious	overde'velop
out'run	over'awe	
out'shine	over'book	

overdraft ('əʊvədrɑːft) *n.* withdrawal of money in excess of credit balance on bank account

overdrive ('əʊvədraɪv) *n.* 1. very high gear in motor vehicle used at high speeds to reduce wear —*vt.* (əʊvə'draɪv) 2. drive too hard or too far; overwork (-'driving, -'drove, -'driven)

overhaul (əʊvə'hɔːl) *vt.* 1. examine and set in order, repair 2. overtake —*n.* ('əʊvəhɔːl) 3. thorough examination, *esp.* for repairs

overhead ('əʊvəhɛd) *a.* 1. over one's head, above —*adv.* (əʊvə'hɛd) 2. aloft, above —'**overheads** *pl.n.* expenses of running a business, over and above cost of manufacturing and of raw materials

overhear (əʊvə'hɪə) *vt.* hear (person, remark *etc.*) without knowledge of speaker (-'**hearing,** -'**heard**)

overkill ('əʊvəkɪl) *n.* capacity, advantage greater than required

overland ('əʊvəlænd) *a./adv.* by land

overlap (əʊvə'læp) *v.* 1. (of two things) extend or lie partly over (each other) 2. cover and extend beyond (something) —*vi.* 3. coincide partly in time, subject *etc.* (-pp-) —*n.* ('əʊvəlæp) 4. part that overlaps or is overlapped 5. amount, length *etc.* overlapping

overleaf ('əʊvəliːf) *adv.* on other side of page

overlook (əʊvə'lʊk) *vt.* 1. fail to notice 2. disregard 3. look over

overpower (əʊvə'paʊə) *vt.* 1. conquer by superior force 2. have such strong effect on as to make ineffective 3. supply with more power than necessary —over-'powering *a.*

override (əʊvə'raɪd) *vt.* 1. set aside, disregard 2. cancel 3. trample down

overrule (əʊvə'ruːl) *vt.* 1. disallow arguments of (person) by use of authority 2. rule or decide against (decision *etc.*) 3. prevail over; influence 4. exercise rule over

overseas ('əʊvə'siːz) *a.* 1. foreign 2. from or to a place over the sea (*also* over'**sea**) —*adv.* (əʊvə'siːz) 3. beyond the sea; abroad

overseer ('əʊvəsiːə) *n.* supervisor —over-'**see** *vt.* supervise

oversight ('əʊvəsaɪt) *n.* 1. failure to notice 2. mistake

overt ('əʊvɜːt) *a.* open, unconcealed

overtake (əʊvə'teɪk) *vt.* 1. move past (vehicle, person) travelling in same direction 2. come up with in pursuit 3. catch up

overthrow (əʊvə'θrəʊ) *vt.* 1. upset, overturn 2. defeat (-'**threw,** -'**thrown,** -'**throwing**) —*n.* ('əʊvəθrəʊ) 3. ruin 4. defeat 5. fall

overtime ('əʊvətaɪm) *n.* 1. time at work, outside normal working hours 2. payment for this time

overtone ('əʊvətəʊn) *n.* additional meaning, nuance

overture ('əʊvətjʊə) *n.* 1. *Mus.* orchestral introduction 2. opening of negotiations 3. formal offer

overweening (əʊvə'wiːnɪŋ) *a.* thinking too much of oneself

overwhelm (əʊvə'wɛlm) *vt.* 1. crush 2. submerge, engulf —over'**whelming** *a.* 1. decisive 2. irresistible —over'**whelmingly** *adv.*

overwrought (əʊvə'rɔːt) *a.* 1. overexcited 2. too elaborate

---

over'do
'overdose
over'due
over'eager
over'eat
over'emphasize
over'estimate
overex'cite
overex'ert
overex'pand
overex'penditure
over'fill
over'flow *v.*
'overflow *n.*
'overgarment
over'grow
over'hang
over'hasty
overin'dulge
overin'dulgence
overin'sistent
over'joy
'overlay
over'lie
over'load *v.*

'overload *n.*
'overlord
over'many
over'modest
over'much
over'night
'overpass
over'pay
over'play
overpopu'lation
over'praise
over'price
overpro'duce
overpro'duction
over'rate
over'reach
overre'act
over'ripe
over'run
over'sensitive
over'shadow
'overshoe
over'shoot
oversimplifi'cation
over'simplify

over'size
over'sleep
over'specialize
over'spend
over'spill *v.*
'overspill *n.*
over'stay
over'steer *v.*
'oversteer *n.*
over'step
over'stock *v.*
'overstock *n.*
over'stretch
over'tire
over'top
over'trump
over'turn
over'use
over'value
over'weight
over'work *v.*
'overwork *n.*
over'zealous

ovi- *or* **ovo-** (*comb. form*) egg; ovum, as in *oviform*

oviduct ('ɒvɪdʌkt, 'əʊ-) *n.* tube through which ova are conveyed from ovary (*also* (in mammals) **Fallopian tube**) —**oviducal** (ɒvɪ'djuːk*ə*l, əʊ-) *or* **ovi'ductal** *a.*

oviform ('əʊvɪfɔːm) *a.* egg-shaped

ovine ('əʊvaɪn) *a.* of, like, sheep

oviparous (əʊ'vɪpərəs) *a.* laying eggs

ovoid ('əʊvɔɪd) *a.* egg-shaped

ovoviviparous (əʊvəʊvaɪ'vɪpərəs) *a.* (of certain reptiles, fishes *etc.*) producing eggs that hatch within body of mother —**ovovivi'parity** *n.*

ovule ('ɒvjuːl) *n.* unfertilized seed —'**ovulate** *vi.* produce, discharge egg from ovary —**ovu'lation** *n.*

ovum ('əʊvəm) *n.* female egg cell, in which development of foetus takes place (*pl.* '**ova**)

owe (əʊ) *vt.* be bound to repay, be indebted for —'**owing** *a.* owed, due —**owing to** caused by, as a result of

owl (aʊl) *n.* night bird of prey —'**owlet** *n.* young owl —'**owlish** *a.* solemn and dull

own (əʊn) *a.* **1.** emphasizes possession —*vt.* **2.** possess **3.** acknowledge —*vi.* **4.** confess —'**owner** *n.* —'**ownership** *n.* possession

ox (ɒks) *n.* **1.** large cloven-footed and usu. horned farm animal **2.** bull or cow (*pl.* '**oxen**) —'**oxbow** *n.* **1.** U-shaped harness collar of ox **2.** lake formed from deep bend of river —'**oxeye** *n.* daisylike plant —'**oxtail** *n.* skinned tail of ox, used *esp.* in soups and stews —'**oxtongue** *n.* **1.** any of various plants having bristly tongue-shaped leaves **2.** tongue of ox, braised or boiled as food

oxalis ('ɒksəlɪs, ɒk'sælɪs) *n.* genus of plants —**oxalic acid** (ɒk'sælɪk) poisonous acid derived from oxalis

Oxbridge ('ɒksbrɪdʒ) *n.* Brit. universities of Oxford and Cambridge, *esp.* considered as prestigious academic institutions

oxen ('ɒksən) *n., pl. of* ox

Oxfam ('ɒksfæm) Oxford Committee for Famine Relief

oxide ('ɒksaɪd) *n.* compound of oxygen and one other element —**oxidate** ('ɒksɪdeɪt) *v.* —**oxidation** (ɒksɪ'deɪʃ*ə*n) *n.* act or process of oxidizing —**oxidization** *or* -**isation** (ɒksɪdaɪ'zeɪʃ*ə*n) *n.* —**oxidize** *or* -**ise** ('ɒksɪdaɪz) *v.* (cause to) combine with oxide, rust

Oxon. ('ɒksən) Oxfordshire

oxygen ('ɒksɪdʒ*ə*n) *n.* gas in atmosphere essential to life, combustion *etc.* —'**oxygenate,** '**oxygenize** *or* -**ise** *vt.* combine or treat with oxygen —**oxya'cetylene** *a.* denoting flame used for welding produced by mixture of oxygen and acetylene —**oxygen tent** *Med.* transparent enclosure covering patient, into which oxygen is released to help maintain respiration

oxymoron (ɒksɪ'mɔːrɒn) *n.* figure of speech in which two ideas of opposite meaning are combined to form an expressive phrase or epithet, as in *cruel kindness* (*pl.* -**mora** (-'mɔːrə))

oyez *or* **oyes** ('əʊjɛs, -jɛz) *n.* call, uttered three times by public crier or court official

oyster ('ɔɪstə) *n.* edible bivalve mollusc or shellfish —'**oystercatcher** *n.* shore bird

oz *or* **oz.** ounce

ozone ('əʊzəʊn, əʊ'zəʊn) *n.* form of oxygen with pungent odour —'**ozonize** *or* -**ise** *vt.*

P

p *or* **P** (piː) *n.* **1.** 16th letter of English alphabet **2.** speech sound represented by this letter (*pl.* **p's, P's** *or* **Ps**) —**mind one's p's and q's** be careful to use polite language

p 1. page **2.** pence **3.** penny **4.** *Mus.* piano (softly)

P 1. (car) park **2.** *Chess* pawn **3.** *Chem.* phosphorus **4.** pressure

Pa *Chem.* protactinium

PA Pennsylvania

P.A. 1. personal assistant **2.** *Mil.* Post Adjutant **3.** power of attorney **4.** press agent **5.** Press Association **6.** private account **7.** public-address system **8.** publicity agent **9.** Publishers Association **10.** purchasing agent

p.a. per annum

PABX *UK* private automatic branch exchange (*see also* PBX)

pace[1] (peɪs) *n.* **1.** step **2.** its length **3.** rate of movement **4.** walk, gait —*vi.* **5.** step —*vt.* **6.** set speed for **7.** cross, measure with steps —**'pacer** *n.* one who sets the pace for another —**'pacemaker** *n. esp.* electronic device surgically implanted in those with heart disease

pace[2] ('peɪsɪ; *Lat.* 'pɑːkɛ) *prep.* with due deference to: used to acknowledge politely someone who disagrees

pachyderm ('pækɪdɜːm) *n.* thick-skinned animal, *eg* elephant —**pachy'dermatous** *a.* thick-skinned, stolid

pacify ('pæsɪfaɪ) *vt.* **1.** calm **2.** restore to peace (**-ified, -ifying**) —**pa'cific** *a.* **1.** peaceable **2.** calm, tranquil —**pacifi'cation** *n.* —**pa'cificatory** *a.* tending to make peace —**'pacifier** *n.* **1.** person or thing that pacifies **2.** US baby's dummy or teething ring —**'pacifism** *n.* —**'pacifist** *n.* **1.** advocate of abolition of war **2.** one who refuses to participate in war

pack (pæk) *n.* **1.** bundle **2.** band of animals **3.** large set of people or things **4.** set of, container for, retail commodities **5.** set of playing cards **6.** mass of floating ice —*v.* **7.** put (articles) together in suitcase *etc.* **8.** press tightly together, cram —*vt.* **9.** make into a bundle **10.** fill with things **11.** fill (meeting *etc.*) with one's own supporters **12.** (*oft.* with *off* or *away*) order off —**'package** *n.* **1.** parcel **2.** set of items offered together —*vt.* **3.** wrap in or put into package —**'packet** *n.* **1.** small parcel **2.** small container (and contents) **3.** *sl.* large sum of money —**package holiday** holiday with fixed itinerary and at price inclusive of travel and lodging —**'packet (boat)** *n.* mail-boat —**'packhorse** *n.* horse for carrying goods —**pack ice** loose floating ice which has been compacted together —**pack saddle** saddle for carrying goods

pact (pækt) *n.* covenant, agreement, compact

pad[1] (pæd) *n.* **1.** piece of soft stuff used as a cushion, protection *etc.* **2.** block of sheets of paper **3.** foot or sole of various animals **4.** place for launching rockets **5.** *sl.* residence —*vt.* **6.** make soft, fill in, protect *etc.* with pad or padding (**-dd-**) —**'padding** *n.* **1.** material used for stuffing **2.** literary matter put in simply to increase quantity —**padded cell** room, *esp.* in mental hospital, with padded surfaces, in which violent inmates are placed

pad[2] (pæd) *vi.* **1.** walk with soft step **2.** travel slowly (**-dd-**) —*n.* **3.** sound of soft footstep

paddle[1] ('pæd'l) *n.* **1.** short oar with broad blade at one or each end —*v.* **2.** move by, as with, paddles **3.** row gently —**paddle wheel** wheel with crosswise blades striking water successively to propel ship

paddle[2] ('pæd'l) *vi.* **1.** walk with bare feet in shallow water —*n.* **2.** act of paddling

paddock ('pædək) *n.* small grass field or enclosure

paddy[1] ('pædɪ) *n.* rice growing or in the husk —**paddy field** field where rice is grown

paddy[2] ('pædɪ) *n. inf.* temper

padlock ('pædlɒk) *n.* **1.** detachable lock with hinged hoop to go through staple or ring —*vt.* **2.** fasten thus

padre ('pɑːdrɪ) *n.* chaplain with the armed forces

paean *or* U.S. (*sometimes*) **pean** ('piːən) *n.* song of triumph or thanksgiving

paederast ('pedəræst) *n. see* PEDERAST

paediatrics *or* U.S. **pediatrics** (piːdɪ-'ætrɪks) *n.* branch of medicine dealing with diseases and disorders of children —**paedia'trician** *or* U.S. **pedia'trician** *n.*

paedo-, pedo- *or before vowel* **paed-, ped-** (*comb. form*) child, children, as in **paedophilia**

paedophilia (piːdəʊ'fɪlɪə) *n.* condition of being sexually attracted to children —**paedophile** ('piːdəʊfaɪl) *or* **paedo'philiac** *n./a.*

paella (paɪ'elə) *n.* **1.** Sp. dish of rice, shellfish *etc.* **2.** pan in which paella is cooked

pagan ('peɪgən) *a./n.* heathen —**'paganism** *n.*

page[1] (peɪdʒ) *n.* one side of leaf of book *etc.*

page[2] (peɪdʒ) *n.* **1.** boy servant or attendant —*vt.* **2.** summon by loudspeaker announcement —**'pageboy** *n.* medium-length hairstyle with ends of hair curled under

pageant ('pædʒənt) *n.* **1.** show of persons in costume in procession, dramatic scenes *etc.*, usu. illustrating history **2.** brilliant show —**'pageantry** *n.*

paginate ('pædʒɪneɪt) *vt.* number pages of —**pagi'nation** *n.*

pagoda (pə'gəʊdə) *n.* pyramidal temple or tower of Chinese or Indian type

paid (peɪd) *pt./pp.* of PAY —**put paid to** *inf.* end, destroy

pail (peɪl) *n.* bucket —**'pailful** *n.*

paillasse ('pælɪæs, pælɪ'æs) *n.* see PALLIASSE

pain (peɪn) *n.* 1. bodily or mental suffering 2. penalty or punishment —*pl.* 3. trouble, exertion —*vt.* 4. inflict pain upon —**pained** *a.* having or expressing pain or distress, *esp.* mental or emotional —**'painful** *a.* —**'painfully** *adv.* —**'painless** *a.* —**'painlessly** *adv.* —**'painkiller** *n.* drug, as aspirin, that reduces pain —**'painstaking** *a.* diligent, careful

paint (peɪnt) *n.* 1. colouring matter spread on a surface with brushes, roller, spray gun *etc.* —*vt.* 2. portray, colour, coat, or make picture of, with paint 3. apply make-up to 4. describe —**'painter** *n.* —**'painting** *n.* picture in paint

painter ('peɪntə) *n.* line at bow of boat for tying it up

pair (peə) *n.* 1. set of two, *esp.* existing or generally used together —*v.* 2. (*oft.* with off) group or be grouped in twos

paisley ('peɪzlɪ) *n.* pattern of small curving shapes

pajamas (pə'dʒɑːməz) *pl.n.* US see PYJAMAS

Pakistani (pɑːkɪ'stɑːnɪ) *a.* 1. of Pakistan, country in Indian subcontinent —*n.* 2. native or inhabitant of Pakistan

pal (pæl) *n. inf.* friend —**'pally** *a. inf.* on friendly terms

palace ('pælɪs) *n.* 1. residence of king, bishop *etc.* 2. stately mansion —**pa'latial** *a.* 1. like a palace 2. magnificent —**'palatine** *a.* with royal privileges

paladin ('pælədɪn) *n. Hist.* knight errant

palaeo-, *before vowel* **palae-** *or esp. U.S.* **paleo-, pale-** (*comb. form*) old, ancient, prehistoric, as in *palaeography*

Palaeocene ('pælɪəʊsiːn) *a.* 1. of first epoch of Tertiary period —*n.* 2. Palaeocene epoch or rock series

Palaeolithic (pælɪəʊ'lɪθɪk) *a.* of the old Stone Age

palaeontology (pælɪɒn'tɒlədʒɪ) *n.* study of past geological periods and fossils —**palaeonto'logical** *a.*

Palaeozoic (pælɪəʊ'zəʊɪk) *a.* 1. of geological time that began with Cambrian period and lasted until end of Permian period —*n.* 2. Palaeozoic era

palanquin *or* **palankeen** (pælən'kiːn) *n.* covered litter, formerly used in Orient, carried on shoulders of four men

palate ('pælɪt) *n.* 1. roof of mouth 2. sense of taste —**'palatable** *a.* agreeable to eat —**'palatal** *or* **'palatine** *a.* 1. of the palate 2. made by placing tongue against palate —*n.* 3. palatal sound

palatial (pə'leɪʃəl) *a.* see PALACE

palaver (pə'lɑːvə) *n.* 1. fuss 2. conference, discussion

pale[1] (peɪl) *a.* 1. wan, dim, whitish —*vi.* 2. whiten 3. lose superiority or importance —**'paleface** *n.* derogatory term for White person, said to have been used by N Amer. Indians

pale[2] (peɪl) *n.* stake, boundary —**'paling** *n.* upright plank making up fence

paleo- *or before vowel* **pale-** (*comb. form*) *esp. US see* PALAEO-

Palestinian (pælɪ'stɪnɪən) *a.* 1. of Palestine, former country in Middle East —*n.* 2. native or inhabitant of this area 3. descendant of inhabitant of this area, displaced when Israel became state

palette *or* **pallet** ('pælɪt) *n.* artist's flat board for mixing colours on —**palette knife** spatula with thin flexible blade, used in painting *etc.*

palimony ('pælɪmənɪ) *n.* US alimony awarded to nonmarried partner after break-up of long relationship

palindrome ('pælɪndrəʊm) *n.* word, verse or sentence that is the same when read backwards or forwards

palisade (pælɪ'seɪd) *n.* 1. fence of stakes —*vt.* 2. enclose or protect with one

pall[1] (pɔːl) *n.* 1. cloth spread over a coffin 2. depressing, oppressive atmosphere —**'pallbearer** *n.* one carrying, attending coffin at funeral

pall[2] (pɔːl) *vi.* 1. become tasteless or tiresome 2. cloy

palladium (pə'leɪdɪəm) *n.* silvery-white element of platinum metal group, used in jewellery *etc.*

pallet[1] ('pælɪt) *n.* 1. straw mattress 2. small bed

pallet[2] ('pælɪt) *n.* portable platform for storing and moving goods

palliasse *or* **paillasse** ('pælɪæs, pælɪ'æs) *n.* straw mattress

palliate ('pælɪeɪt) *vt.* 1. relieve without curing 2. excuse —**palli'ation** *n.* —**palliative** ('pælɪətɪv) *a.* 1. giving temporary or partial relief —*n.* 2. that which excuses, mitigates or alleviates

pallid ('pælɪd) *a.* pale, wan, colourless —**'pallor** *n.* paleness

palm (pɑːm) *n.* 1. inner surface of hand 2. tropical tree 3. leaf of the tree as symbol of victory —*vt.* 4. conceal in palm of hand 5. pass off by trickery —**palmate** ('pælmeɪt, -mɪt) *or* **'palmated** *a.* 1. shaped like open hand 2. *Bot.* having five lobes that spread out from common point 3. (of water birds) having three toes connected by web —**'palmist** *n.* —**'palmistry** *n.* fortune-telling from lines on palm of hand —**'palmy** *a.* flourishing, successful —**palm oil** oil obtained from fruit of certain palms —**Palm Sunday** Sunday before Easter —**palm off** (*oft.* with on) 1. offer, sell or spend fraudulently 2. divert in order to be rid of

palomino (pælə'miːnəʊ) *n.* golden horse with white mane and tail (*pl.* -**s**)

palpable ('pælpəb'l) a. 1. obvious 2. certain 3. that may be touched or felt —'**palpably** adv.

palpate ('pælpeɪt) vt. Med. examine by touch

palpitate ('pælpɪteɪt) vi. 1. throb 2. pulsate violently —**palpi'tation** n. 1. throbbing 2. violent, irregular beating of heart

palsy ('pɔːlzɪ) n. paralysis

paltry ('pɔːltrɪ) a. worthless, contemptible, trifling

pampas ('pæmpəz) n. (oft. with pl. v.) vast grassy treeless plains in S Amer.

pamper ('pæmpə) vt. overindulge, spoil by coddling

pamphlet ('pæmflɪt) n. thin unbound book usu. on some topical subject

pan[1] (pæn) n. 1. broad, shallow vessel 2. bowl of lavatory 3. depression in ground, esp. where salt forms —vt. 4. wash (gold ore) in pan 5. inf. criticize harshly (**-nn-**) —'**pantile** n. curved roofing tile —**pan out** result

pan[2] (pæn) v. move (film camera) slowly while filming to cover scene, follow moving object etc. (**-nn-**)

pan- (comb. form) all, as in panacea, pantomime. Such words are not given here where the meaning may easily be inferred from simple word

panacea (pænə'sɪə) n. universal remedy, cure for all ills

panache (pə'næʃ, -'nɑːʃ) n. dashing style

Panama hat (pænə'mɑː) straw hat

Pan-American a. of North, South and Central Amer. collectively

pancake ('pænkeɪk) n. 1. thin cake of batter fried in pan 2. flat cake or stick of compressed make-up —vi. 3. Aviation make flat landing by dropping in a level position —**Pancake Day** see Shrove Tuesday at Shrovetide

panchromatic (pænkrəʊ'mætɪk) a. Photog. sensitive to light of all colours

pancreas ('pæŋkrɪəs) n. digestive gland behind stomach —**pancre'atic** a.

panda ('pændə) n. large black and white bearlike mammal of China —**panda car** police patrol car

pandemic (pæn'demɪk) a. (of disease) occurring over wide area

pandemonium (pændɪ'məʊnɪəm) n. scene of din and uproar

pander ('pændə) v. 1. (esp. with to) give gratification (to weakness or desires) —n. 2. pimp

pandit ('pʌndɪt; spelling pron. 'pændɪt) n. see PUNDIT (sense 2)

P. & L. profit and loss

p. & p. UK postage and packing

pane (peɪn) n. single piece of glass in window or door

panegyric (pænɪ'dʒɪrɪk) n. speech of praise —**pane'gyrical** a. laudatory —**pan-e'gyrist** n.

panel ('pæn'l) n. 1. compartment of surface, usu. raised or sunk, eg in door 2. any distinct section of something, eg of car body 3. strip of material inserted in garment 4. group of persons as team in quiz game etc. 5. list of jurors, doctors etc. 6. thin board with picture on it —vt. 7. adorn with panels (**-ll-**) —'**panelling** or U.S. '**paneling** n. panelled work —'**panellist** or U.S. '**panelist** n. member of panel —**panel beater** one who repairs damage to car body —**panel game** quiz etc. played by group of people, esp. on TV

pang (pæŋ) n. 1. sudden pain, sharp twinge 2. compunction

pangolin (pæŋ'gəʊlɪn) n. mammal with scaly body and long snout for feeding on ants etc. (also **scaly anteater**)

panic ('pænɪk) n. 1. sudden and infectious fear 2. extreme fright 3. unreasoning terror —a. 4. of fear etc. —v. 5. feel or cause to feel panic (**-icked, -icking**) —'**panicky** a. 1. inclined to panic 2. nervous —'**panicmonger** n. one who starts panic —**panic-stricken** or **panic-struck** a.

panicle ('pænɪk'l) n. compound raceme, as in oat

panjandrum (pæn'dʒændrəm) n. pompous self-important man

pannier ('pænɪə) n. basket carried by beast of burden, bicycle, or on person's shoulders

panoply ('pænəplɪ) n. complete, magnificent array —'**panoplied** a.

panorama (pænə'rɑːmə) n. 1. wide or complete view 2. picture arranged round spectator or unrolled before him —**pano'ramic** a.

panpipes ('pænpaɪps) pl.n. (oft. sing., oft. P-) number of reeds or whistles of graduated lengths bound together to form musical wind instrument (also **pipes of Pan, 'syrinx**)

pansy ('pænzɪ) n. 1. flower, species of violet 2. inf. effeminate man

pant (pænt) vi. 1. gasp for breath 2. yearn, long 3. throb —n. 4. gasp

pantaloon (pæntə'luːn) n. 1. in pantomime, foolish old man who is the butt of clown —pl. 2. inf. baggy trousers

pantechnicon (pæn'teknɪkən) n. large van, esp. for carrying furniture

pantheism ('pænθɪɪzəm) n. identification of God with the universe —'**pantheist** n. —**panthe'istic** a. —'**pantheon** n. temple of all gods

panther ('pænθə) n. variety of leopard

panties ('pæntɪz) pl.n. women's undergarment

pantihose ('pæntɪhəʊz) n. tights

panto ('pæntəʊ) n. UK inf. pantomime (pl. **-s**)

pantograph ('pæntəgrɑːf) n. instrument for copying maps etc. to any scale

pantomime ('pæntəmaɪm) n. 1. theatrical show, usu. produced at Christmastime, oft. founded on fairy tale 2. dramatic entertainment in dumbshow

pantry ('pæntrɪ) n. room for storing food or utensils

pants (pænts) *pl.n.* 1. undergarment for lower trunk 2. US trousers

panzer ('pænzə; *Ger.* 'pantsər) *a.* 1. of fast mechanized armoured units employed by German army in World War II —*n.* 2. vehicle belonging to panzer unit, *esp.* tank —*pl.* 3. armoured troops

pap¹ (pæp) *n.* 1. soft food for infants, invalids *etc.* 2. pulp, mash 3. SA maize porridge

pap² (pæp) *n.* 1. breast 2. nipple

papa (pə'pɑ:) *n. inf.* father

papacy ('peɪpəsɪ) *n.* 1. office of Pope 2. papal system —'**papal** *a.* of, relating to, the Pope

paparazzo (pæpə'rætsəʊ) *n.* freelance photographer who takes candid-camera shots of famous people (*pl.* **-razzi** (-'rætsi:))

papaw *or* **pawpaw** ('pɔːpɔː) *n.* 1. tree bearing melon-shaped fruit 2. its fruit (*also* **papaya** (pə'paɪə))

paper ('peɪpə) *n.* 1. material made by pressing pulp of rags, straw, wood *etc.* into thin, flat sheets 2. printed sheet of paper 3. newspaper 4. article, essay 5. set of examination questions —*pl.* 6. documents *etc.* —*vt.* 7. cover, decorate with paper —'**paperback** *n.* book with flexible covers —'**paperboy** *n.* boy employed to deliver newspapers ('**papergirl** *fem.*) —**paper chase** cross-country run in which runner lays trail of paper for others to follow —'**paperclip** *n.* clip for holding sheets of paper together, *esp.* one of bent wire —'**paperhanger** *n.* person who hangs wallpaper as occupation —'**paperknife** *n.* knife with comparatively blunt blade for opening sealed envelopes *etc.* —**paper money** paper currency issued by government or central bank as legal tender —'**paperweight** *n.* small heavy object to prevent loose papers from scattering —'**paperwork** *n.* clerical work, such as writing of reports or letters

papier-mâché (pæpɪeɪ'mæʃeɪ) *n.* pulp from rags or paper mixed with size, shaped by moulding and dried hard

papilla (pə'pɪlə) *n.* 1. small projection of tissue at base of hair *etc.* 2. any similar protuberance (*pl.* **-lae** (-liː)) —**pa'pillary**, '**papillate** *or* '**papillose** *a.*

papoose (pə'puːs) *n.* N Amer. Indian child

paprika ('pæprɪkə, pæ'priː-) *n.* (powdered seasoning prepared from) type of red pepper

Pap test *or* **smear** (pæp) *Med.* examination of stained cells in smear taken of bodily secretions, *esp.* from uterus, for detection of cancer

papyrus (pə'paɪrəs) *n.* 1. species of reed 2. (manuscript written on) kind of paper made from this plant (*pl.* **-ri** (-raɪ), **-es**)

par (pɑː) *n.* 1. equality of value or standing 2. face value (of stocks and shares) 3. *Golf* estimated standard score —'**parity** *n.* 1. equality 2. analogy —**par value** value

imprinted on face of share certificate or bond and used to assess dividend *etc.*

par. 1. paragraph 2. parallel 3. parenthesis

para- *or before vowel* **par-** (*comb. form*) beside, beyond, as in *paradigm, parallel, parody*

parable ('pærəb'l) *n.* allegory, story with a moral lesson —**para'bolic(al)** *a.* of parable

parabola (pə'ræbələ) *n.* section of cone cut by plane parallel to the cone's side —**para'bolic** *a.* of parabola

paracetamol (pærə'siːtəmɒl, -'sɛtə-) *n.* mild drug used as alternative to aspirin

parachute ('pærəʃuːt) *n.* 1. apparatus extending like umbrella used to retard the descent of a falling body —*v.* 2. land or cause to land by parachute —'**parachutist** *n.*

parade (pə'reɪd) *n.* 1. display 2. muster of troops 3. parade ground 4. public walk —*vi.* 5. march —*vt.* 6. display

paradigm ('pærədaɪm) *n.* example, model —**paradigmatic** (pærədɪg'mætɪk) *a.*

paradise ('pærədaɪs) *n.* 1. Heaven 2. state of bliss 3. Garden of Eden

paradox ('pærədɒks) *n.* statement that seems absurd or self-contradictory but may be true —**para'doxical** *a.*

paraffin ('pærəfɪn) *n.* waxlike or liquid hydrocarbon mixture used as fuel, solvent, in candles *etc.*

paragon ('pærəgən) *n.* pattern or model of excellence

paragraph ('pærəgrɑːf, -græf) *n.* 1. section of chapter or book 2. short notice, as in newspaper —*vt.* 3. arrange in paragraphs

parakeet *or* **parrakeet** ('pærəkiːt) *n.* small kind of parrot

parallax ('pærəlæks) *n.* apparent difference in object's position or direction as viewed from different points

parallel ('pærəlɛl) *a.* 1. continuously at equal distances 2. precisely corresponding —*n.* 3. line equidistant from another at all points 4. thing exactly like another 5. comparison 6. line of latitude —*vt.* 7. represent as similar, compare —'**parallelism** *n.* —**paral'lelogram** *n.* four-sided plane figure with opposite sides parallel —**parallel bars** *Gymnastics* pair of wooden bars on uprights used for exercises

paralysis (pə'rælɪsɪs) *n.* incapacity to move or feel, due to damage to nervous system (*pl.* **-yses** (-ɪsɪz)) —'**paralyse** *or U.S.* **-lyze** *vt.* 1. afflict with paralysis 2. cripple 3. make useless or ineffectual —**para'lytic** *a./n.* (person) afflicted with paralysis —**infantile paralysis** poliomyelitis

paramedical (pærə'mɛdɪk'l) *a.* of persons working in various capacities in support of medical profession

parameter (pə'ræmɪtə) *n.* any constant limiting factor

paramilitary (pærə'mɪlɪtərɪ, -trɪ) *a.* of

civilian group organized on military lines or in support of the military

paramount ('pærəmaunt) *a.* supreme, eminent, pre-eminent, chief

paramour ('pærəmuə) *n. esp.* formerly, illicit lover, mistress

parang ('pɑːræŋ) *n.* heavy Malay knife

paranoia (pærə'nɔɪə) *n.* mental disease with delusions of fame, grandeur, persecution —**paranoiac** (pærə'nɔɪɪk) *a./n.* —'**paranoid** *a.* 1. of paranoia 2. *inf.* exhibiting fear of persecution *etc.* —*n.* 3. person afflicted with paranoia

parapet ('pærəpɪt, -pɛt) *n.* low wall, railing along edge of balcony, bridge *etc.*

paraphernalia (pærəfə'neɪlɪə) *pl.n.* (*sometimes with sing. v.*) 1. personal belongings 2. odds and ends of equipment

paraphrase ('pærəfreɪz) *n.* 1. expression of meaning of passage in other words 2. free translation —*vt.* 3. put into other words

paraplegia (pærə'pliːdʒə) *n.* paralysis of lower half of body —**para'plegic** *n./a.*

parapsychology (pærəsaɪ'kɒlədʒɪ) *n.* study of subjects pert. to extrasensory perception, *eg* telepathy

Paraquat ('pærəkwɒt) *n.* **R** very poisonous weedkiller

parasite ('pærəsaɪt) *n.* 1. animal or plant living in or on another 2. self-interested hanger-on —**parasitic** (pærə'sɪtɪk) *a.* of the nature of, living as, parasite —'**parasitism** *n.*

parasol ('pærəsɒl) *n.* sunshade

parataxis (pærə'tæksɪs) *n.* arrangement of sentences which omits connecting words

parathion (pærə'θaɪɒn) *n.* toxic oil used as insecticide

paratroops ('pærətruːps) *pl.n.* troops trained to descend by parachute

paratyphoid fever (pærə'taɪfɔɪd) infectious disease similar to but distinct from typhoid fever

parboil ('pɑːbɔɪl) *vt.* boil until partly cooked

parcel ('pɑːs°l) *n.* 1. packet of goods, *esp.* one enclosed in paper 2. quantity dealt with at one time 3. piece of land —*vt.* 4. wrap up 5. divide into parts (**-ll-**)

parch (pɑːtʃ) *v.* 1. dry by heating 2. make, become hot and dry 3. scorch 4. roast slightly

parchment ('pɑːtʃmənt) *n.* 1. sheep, goat, calf skin prepared for writing 2. manuscript of this

pardon ('pɑːd°n) *vt.* 1. forgive, excuse —*n.* 2. forgiveness 3. release from punishment —'**pardonable** *a.* —'**pardonably** *adv.*

pare (pɛə) *vt.* 1. trim, cut edge or surface of 2. decrease bit by bit —'**paring** *n.* piece pared off, rind

parent ('pɛərənt) *n.* father or mother —'**parentage** *n.* descent, extraction —**pa'rental** *a.* —'**parenthood** *n.* —**parent teacher association** group of parents of children at school and their teachers

formed in order to foster better understanding between them *etc.*

parenthesis (pə'rɛnθɪsɪs) *n.* word or sentence inserted in passage independently of grammatical sequence and usu. marked off by brackets, dashes, or commas —**pa'rentheses** *pl.n.* round brackets, ( ), used for this —**pa'renthesize** *or* -**sise** *vt.* 1. place in parentheses 2. insert as parenthesis 3. intersperse with parentheses —**paren'thetical** *a.*

par excellence (par ɛksɛ'lɑːs; *English* pɑːr 'ɛksələns) *Fr.* to degree of excellence; beyond comparison

pariah (pə'raɪə, 'pærɪə) *n.* social outcast

parietal (pə'raɪɪt°l) *a.* of the walls of bodily cavities, *eg* skull

pari-mutuel (pæri'mjuːtjʊəl) *n.* system of betting in which those who have bet on winners of race share in total amount wagered less percentage for management (*pl.* **pari-mutuels, paris-mutuels** (pæri'mjuːtjʊəlz))

parish ('pærɪʃ) *n.* 1. district under one clergyman 2. subdivision of county —**pa'rishioner** *n.* inhabitant of parish —**parish clerk** person designated to assist in various church duties —**parish register** book in which births, baptisms, marriages, and deaths in parish are recorded

parity ('pærɪtɪ) *n. see* PAR

park (pɑːk) *n.* 1. large area of land in natural state preserved for recreational use 2. large enclosed piece of ground, usu. with grass or woodland, attached to country house or for public use 3. area designed to accommodate a number of related enterprises 4. space in camp for military supplies —*vt.* 5. leave for a short time 6. manoeuvre (car) into a suitable space 7. arrange or leave in a park —**parking meter** timing device, usu. coin-operated, that indicates how long vehicle may be left parked —**parking ticket** summons served for parking offence —'**parkland** *n.* grassland with scattered trees

parka ('pɑːkə) *n.* warm waterproof coat, oft. with hood

parkin ('pɑːkɪn) *n.* **UK** moist spicy ginger cake

Parkinson's disease ('pɑːkɪnsənz) progressive chronic disorder of central nervous system characterized by impaired muscular coordination and tremor (*also* '**parkinsonism**)

Parkinson's law notion, expressed facetiously as law of economics, that work expands to fill time available

Parl. 1. Parliament 2. parliamentary (*also* **parl.**)

parlance ('pɑːləns) *n.* 1. way of speaking, conversation 2. idiom

parley ('pɑːlɪ) *n.* 1. meeting between leaders or representatives of opposing forces to discuss terms —*vi.* 2. hold discussion about terms

parliament ('pɑːləmənt) *n.* 1. the legislature of the United Kingdom 2. any similar legislative assembly —**parliamen'tarian** *n.* member of parliament —**parlia'mentary** *a.* —**parliamentary private secretary** UK backbencher in Parliament who assists minister

parlour *or U.S.* **parlor** ('pɑ:lə) *n.* 1. sitting room, room for receiving company in small house 2. place for milking cows 3. US room or shop as business premises, *esp.* hairdresser *etc.*

Parmesan cheese (pɑ:mɪ'zæn) hard dry cheese used grated, *esp.* on pasta dishes *etc.*

parochial (pə'rəʊkɪəl) *a.* 1. narrow, provincial 2. of a parish —**pa'rochialism** *n.*

parody ('pærədɪ) *n.* 1. composition in which author's style is made fun of by imitation 2. travesty —*vt.* 3. write parody of (-**odied, -odying**) —**'parodist** *n.*

parole (pə'rəʊl) *n.* 1. early freeing of prisoner on condition he is of good behaviour 2. word of honour —*vt.* 3. place on parole

parotid (pə'rɒtɪd) *a.* 1. relating to or situated near parotid gland —*n.* 2. parotid gland —**parotid gland** large salivary gland in front of and below each ear

-**parous** (*comb. form*) giving birth to, as in *oviparous*

paroxysm ('pærəksɪzəm) *n.* sudden violent attack of pain, rage, laughter

parquet ('pɑ:keɪ, -kɪ) *n.* 1. flooring of wooden blocks arranged in pattern —*vt.* 2. cover (floor) with parquet —**parquetry** ('pɑ:kɪtrɪ) *n.*

parr (pɑ:) *n.* salmon up to two years of age (*pl.* -**s, parr**)

parrakeet ('pærəki:t) *n. see* PARAKEET

parricide ('pærɪsaɪd) *n.* murder or murderer of a parent

parrot ('pærət) *n.* 1. any of several related birds with short hooked beak, some varieties of which can imitate speaking 2. unintelligent imitator —**parrot fever** *or* **disease** *see* psittacosis *at* PSITTACINE

parry ('pærɪ) *vt.* 1. ward off, turn aside ('**parried, 'parrying**) —*n.* 2. act of parrying, *esp.* in fencing

parse (pɑ:z) *vt.* 1. describe (word) 2. analyse (sentence) in terms of grammar —'**parser** *n. Comp.* program that interprets ordinary language typed into computer by recognizing key words or analysing sentence structure and translating into machine language

parsec ('pɑ:sɛk) *n.* unit of length used in expressing distance of stars

parsimony ('pɑ:sɪmənɪ) *n.* 1. stinginess 2. undue economy —**parsi'monious** *a.* sparing

parsley ('pɑ:slɪ) *n.* herb used for seasoning, garnish *etc.*

parsnip ('pɑ:snɪp) *n.* edible yellow root vegetable

parson ('pɑ:sᵊn) *n.* 1. clergyman of parish or church 2. clergyman —**'parsonage** *n.*

parson's house —**parson's nose** fatty extreme end portion of tail of fowl when cooked

part (pɑ:t) *n.* 1. portion, section, share 2. division 3. actor's role 4. duty 5. (*oft. pl.*) region 6. interest —*v.* 7. divide 8. separate —'**parting** *n.* 1. division between sections of hair on head 2. separation 3. leavetaking —'**partly** *adv.* in part —**part exchange** transaction in which used goods are taken as partial payment —**part of speech** class of words sharing important syntactic or semantic features; group of words in language that may occur in similar positions or fulfil similar functions in sentence —**part song** song for several voices singing in harmony —**part-time** *a.* 1. for less than entire time appropriate to activity —*adv.* 2. on part-time basis —**part-timer** *n.*

part. 1. participle 2. particular

partake (pɑ:'teɪk) *vi.* 1. (*with* of) take or have share (in) 2. take food or drink (-'**took**, -'**taken**, -'**taking**)

parterre (pɑ:'tɛə) *n.* 1. ornamental arrangement of beds in a flower garden 2. the pit of a theatre

parthenogenesis (pɑ:θɪnəʊ'dʒɛnɪsɪs) *n.* type of reproduction, occurring in some insects and flowers, in which unfertilized ovum develops directly into new individual —**parthenoge'netic** *a.*

Parthian shot ('pɑ:θɪən) hostile remark or gesture delivered while departing

partial ('pɑ:ʃəl) *a.* 1. not general or complete 2. prejudiced 3. (*with* to) fond (of) —**parti'ality** *n.* 1. favouritism 2. fondness —**'partially** *adv.* partly

participate (pɑ:'tɪsɪpeɪt) *v.* (*with* in) 1. share (in) 2. take part (in) —**par'ticipant** *n.* —**partici'pation** *n.* —**par'ticipator** *n.*

participle ('pɑ:tɪsɪpᵊl) *n.* adjective made by inflection from verb and keeping verb's relation to dependent words —**parti'cipial** *a.*

particle ('pɑ:tɪkᵊl) *n.* 1. minute portion of matter 2. least possible amount 3. minor part of speech in grammar, prefix, suffix

parti-coloured ('pɑ:tɪkʌləd) *a.* differently coloured in different parts, variegated

particular (pə'tɪkjʊlə) *a.* 1. relating to one, not general 2. distinct 3. minute 4. very exact 5. fastidious —*n.* 6. detail, item —*pl.* 7. detailed account 8. items of information —**particu'larity** *n.* —**par'ticularize** *or* -**ise** *vt.* mention in detail —**par'ticularly** *adv.*

partisan *or* **partizan** (pɑ:tɪ'zæn, 'pɑ:tɪzæn) *n.* 1. adherent of a party 2. guerrilla, member of resistance movement —*a.* 3. adhering to faction 4. prejudiced

partition (pɑ:'tɪʃən) *n.* 1. division 2. interior dividing wall —*vt.* 3. divide, cut into sections

partitive ('pɑ:tɪtɪv) *a.* 1. *Gram.* indicating that noun involved in construction refers only to part of what it otherwise refers to

2. serving to separate or divide into parts —*n.* **3.** *Gram.* partitive linguistic element or feature

partner ('pɑːtnə) *n.* **1.** ally or companion **2.** a member of a partnership **3.** one that dances with another **4.** a husband or wife **5.** *Golf, Tennis etc.* one who plays with another against opponents —*vt.* **6.** (cause to) be a partner (of) —'**partnership** *n.* association of persons for business *etc.*

partridge ('pɑːtrɪdʒ) *n.* any of various game birds of the grouse family

parturition (pɑːtjʊ'rɪʃən) *n.* **1.** act of bringing forth young **2.** childbirth —**par-'turient** *a.* **1.** of childbirth **2.** giving birth **3.** producing new idea *etc.*

party ('pɑːtɪ) *n.* **1.** social assembly **2.** group of persons travelling or working together **3.** group of persons united in opinion **4.** side **5.** person —*a.* **6.** of, belonging to, a party or faction —**party line 1.** telephone line serving two or more subscribers **2.** policies of political party —**party wall** common wall separating adjoining premises

parvenu *or* (*fem.*) **parvenue** ('pɑːvənjuː) *n.* **1.** one newly risen into position of notice, power, wealth **2.** upstart

pas (pɑː) *n.* dance step or movement, *esp.* in ballet (*pl.* **pas**)

pascal ('pæsk'l) *n.* SI unit of pressure

Paschal ('pɑːsk'l, 'pæsk'l) *a.* of the Passover or Easter

pasha *or* **pacha** ('pɑːʃə, 'pæʃə) *n.* formerly, high official of Ottoman Empire or modern Egyptian kingdom: placed after name when used as title

pasqueflower ('pɑːskflaʊə) *n.* **1.** small purple-flowered plant of N and Central Europe and W Asia **2.** any of several related N Amer. plants

pass (pɑːs) *vt.* **1.** go by, beyond, through *etc.* **2.** exceed **3.** be accepted by **4.** undergo successfully **5.** spend **6.** transfer **7.** exchange **8.** disregard **9.** undergo (examination) successfully **10.** bring into force, sanction (a parliamentary bill *etc.*) —*vi.* **11.** go **12.** be transferred from one state or person to another **13.** elapse —*n.* **14.** way, *esp.* a narrow and difficult way **15.** permit, licence, authorization **16.** successful result from test **17.** condition **18.** *Sport* transfer of ball —'**passable** *a.* (just) acceptable —'**passing** *a.* **1.** transitory **2.** cursory, casual —'**passbook** *n.* **1.** book for keeping record of withdrawals from and payments into building society **2.** bankbook **3. SA** official document to identify bearer, his race, residence and employment —**passer-by** *n.* person that is passing by, *esp.* on foot (*pl.* **passers-by**) —'**passkey** *n.* **1.** any of various keys, *esp.* latchkey **2.** master key **3.** skeleton key —**pass up** ignore, neglect; reject

passage ('pæsɪdʒ) *n.* **1.** channel, opening **2.** way through, corridor **3.** part of book *etc.* **4.** journey, voyage, fare **5.** enactment of law by parliament *etc.* **6.** *rare* conversa-

tion; dispute —'**passageway** *n.* way, *esp.* one in or between buildings; passage

passé ('pɑːseɪ, 'pæseɪ) *a.* **1.** out of date **2.** past the prime

passenger ('pæsɪndʒə) *n.* **1.** traveller, *esp.* by public conveyance **2.** one of a team who does not pull his weight

passerine ('pæsəraɪn, -riːn) *a.* of the order of perching birds

passim ('pæsɪm) *Lat.* everywhere, throughout

passion ('pæʃən) *n.* **1.** ardent desire, *esp.* sexual **2.** any strongly felt emotion **3.** suffering (*esp.* that of Christ) —'**passion-ate** *a.* (easily) moved by strong emotions —'**passionflower** *n.* tropical Amer. plant —**passion fruit** edible fruit of passion-flower —**Passion play** play depicting Passion of Christ

passive ('pæsɪv) *a.* **1.** unresisting **2.** submissive **3.** inactive **4.** denoting grammatical mood of verb in which the action is suffered by the subject —**pas'sivity** *n.* —**passive resistance** resistance to government *etc.* without violence, as by fasting, demonstrating or refusing to cooperate —**passive smoking** inhalation of smoke from other people's cigarettes by non-smoker

Passover ('pɑːsəʊvə) *n.* Jewish spring festival

passport ('pɑːspɔːt) *n.* official document granting permission to pass, travel abroad *etc.*

password ('pɑːswɜːd) *n.* **1.** word, phrase, to distinguish friend from enemy **2.** countersign

past (pɑːst) *a.* **1.** ended **2.** gone by **3.** elapsed —*n.* **4.** bygone times —*adv.* **5.** by **6.** along —*prep.* **7.** beyond **8.** after —**past master 1.** person with talent for, or experience in a particular activity **2.** person who has held office of master in guild *etc.* —**past participle** participial form of verbs used to modify noun that is logically object of verb, also used in certain compound tenses and passive forms of verb —**past perfect** *Gram. a.* **1.** denoting tense of verbs used in relating past events where action had already occurred at time of action of main verb that is itself in past tense —*n.* **2.** past perfect tense **3.** verb in this tense

pasta ('pæstə) *n.* any of several variously shaped edible preparations of dough, *eg* spaghetti

paste (peɪst) *n.* **1.** soft composition, as toothpaste **2.** soft plastic mixture or adhesive **3.** fine glass to imitate gems —*vt.* **4.** fasten with paste —'**pasty** *a.* **1.** like paste **2.** white **3.** sickly —'**pasteboard** *n.* stiff thick paper

pastel ('pæst'l, pæ'stɛl) *n.* **1.** coloured crayon **2.** art of drawing with crayons **3.** pale, delicate colour —*a.* **4.** delicately tinted

pastern ('pæstən) *n.* part of horse's foot between fetlock and hoof

pasteurize or **-ise** ('pæstəraɪz, -stjə-, 'pɑ:-) vt. sterilize by heat —**pasteuri'zation** or **-i'sation** n.

pastiche (pæ'sti:ʃ) or **pasticcio** (pæ-'stɪtʃəʊ) n. 1. literary, musical, artistic work composed of parts borrowed from other works and loosely connected together 2. work imitating another's style

pastille or **pastil** ('pæstɪl) n. 1. lozenge 2. aromatic substance burnt as fumigator

pastime ('pɑ:staɪm) n. 1. that which makes time pass agreeably 2. recreation

pastor ('pɑ:stə) n. clergyman in charge of a congregation —**'pastoral** a. 1. of, or like, shepherd's or rural life 2. of office of pastor —n. 3. poem describing rural life —**pastorale** (pæstə'rɑ:l) n. Mus. 1. composition evocative of rural life 2. musical play based on rustic story (pl. **-s, -rali** (It. -'rɑ:li)) —**'pastorate** n. office, jurisdiction of pastor

pastry ('peɪstrɪ) n. article of food made chiefly of flour, fat and water

pasture ('pɑ:stʃə) n. 1. grass for food of cattle 2. ground on which cattle graze —v. 3. (cause to) graze —**'pasturage** n. (right to) pasture

pasty ('pæstɪ) n. small pie of meat and crust, baked without a dish

pat[1] (pæt) vt. 1. tap (**-tt-**) —n. 2. light, quick blow 3. small mass, as of butter, beaten into shape

pat[2] (pæt) adv. 1. exactly 2. fluently 3. opportunely —a. 4. glib 5. exactly right

pat. patent(ed)

patch (pætʃ) n. 1. piece of cloth sewed on garment 2. spot 3. plot of ground 4. protecting pad for the eye 5. small contrasting area 6. short period —vt. 7. mend 8. repair clumsily —**'patchy** a. 1. of uneven quality 2. full of patches —**'patchwork** n. 1. work composed of pieces sewn together 2. jumble

patchouli or **patchouly** ('pætʃʊlɪ, pə'tʃuːlɪ) n. 1. Indian herb 2. perfume made from it

pate (peɪt) n. 1. head 2. top of head

pâté ('pæteɪ) n. spread of finely minced liver etc. —**pâté de foie gras** (Fr. pate də fwa 'grɑ) smooth rich paste made from liver of specially fattened goose (pl. **pâtés de foie gras** (Fr. pate))

patella (pə'tɛlə) n. kneecap (pl. **patellae** (pə'tɛli:)) —**pa'tellar** a.

paten ('pæt²n) n. plate for bread in the Eucharist

patent ('peɪt²nt, 'pæt²nt) n. 1. deed securing to person exclusive right to invention —a. 2. open 3. ('peɪt²nt) evident; manifest 4. open to public perusal, as in letters patent —vt. 5. secure a patent for —**paten'tee** n. one that has a patent —**patently** ('peɪt²ntlɪ) adv. obviously —**patent leather** ('peɪt²nt) (imitation) leather processed to give hard, glossy surface —**patent medicine** ('peɪt²nt) medicine with patent, available without prescription

—**Patent Office** government department that issues patents

pater ('peɪtə) n. UK sl. father

paterfamilias (peɪtəfə'mɪlɪæs) n. father of a family (pl. **patresfamilias** (pɑ:treɪzfə'mɪlɪæs))

paternal (pə'tɜ:n²l) a. 1. fatherly 2. of a father —**pa'ternalism** n. authority exercised in a way that limits individual responsibility —**paternal'istic** a. —**pa'ternity** n. 1. relation of a father to his offspring 2. fatherhood

paternoster (pætə'nɒstə) n. 1. Lord's Prayer 2. beads of rosary 3. type of lift

path (pɑ:θ) n. 1. way or track 2. course of action —**'pathway** n. 1. path 2. Biochem. chain of reactions associated with particular metabolic process

-path (comb. form) 1. person suffering from specified disease or disorder, as in neuropath 2. practitioner of particular method of treatment, as in osteopath

pathetic (pə'θɛtɪk) a. 1. affecting or moving tender emotions 2. distressingly inadequate —**pa'thetically** adv. —**pathetic fallacy** Lit. presentation of nature etc. as possessing human feelings

pathogenic (pæθə'dʒɛnɪk) a. producing disease —**pa'thogeny** n. mode of development of disease

pathology (pə'θɒlədʒɪ) n. science of diseases —**patho'logical** a. 1. of the science of disease 2. due to disease 3. inf. compulsively motivated

pathos ('peɪθɒs) n. power of exciting tender emotions

-pathy (n. comb. form) 1. feeling, perception, as in telepathy 2. disease, as in psychopathy 3. method of treating disease, as in osteopathy —**-pathic** (a. comb. form)

patient ('peɪʃənt) a. 1. bearing trials calmly —n. 2. person under medical treatment —**'patience** n. 1. quality of enduring 2. card game for one

patina ('pætɪnə) n. 1. fine layer on a surface 2. sheen of age on woodwork

patio ('pætɪəʊ) n. paved area adjoining house (pl. **-s**)

patois ('pætwɑ:; Fr. pa'twa) n. regional dialect (pl. **patois** ('pætwɑ:z; Fr. pa'twa)

pat. pend. patent pending

patriarch ('peɪtrɪɑ:k) n. father and ruler of family, esp. Biblical —**patri'archal** a. venerable —**'patriarchy** n. 1. form of social organization in which male is head of family and descent, kinship and title are traced through male line 2. society governed by such system

patrician (pə'trɪʃən) n. 1. noble of ancient Rome 2. one of noble birth —a. 3. of noble birth

patricide ('pætrɪsaɪd) n. murder or murderer of father

patriot ('peɪtrɪət, 'pæt-) n. one that loves his country and maintains its interests —**patriotic** (pætrɪ'ɒtɪk) a. inspired by love of one's country —**patriotism** ('pætrɪətɪzəm) n.

patrol (pə'trəʊl) *n.* 1. regular circuit by guard 2. person, small group patrolling 3. unit of Scouts or Guides —*v.* 4. go round on guard or reconnoitring (-**ll-**)

patron ('peɪtrən) *n.* 1. one who sponsors or aids artists, charities *etc.* 2. protector 3. regular customer 4. guardian saint 5. one that has disposition of church living *etc.* —**patronage** ('pætrənɪdʒ) *n.* support given by, or position of, a patron —**patronize** *or* **-ise** ('pætrənaɪz) *vt.* 1. assume air of superiority towards 2. frequent as customer 3. encourage —**'patronizing** *or* **-ising** *a.* condescending

patronymic (pætrə'nɪmɪk) *n.* name derived from that of parent or an ancestor

patter ('pætə) *vi.* 1. make noise, as sound of quick, short steps 2. tap in quick succession 3. pray, talk rapidly —*n.* 4. quick succession of taps 5. *inf.* glib, rapid speech

pattern ('pæt'n) *n.* 1. arrangement of repeated parts 2. design 3. shape to direct cutting of cloth *etc.* 4. model 5. specimen —*vt.* 6. (*with* on, after) model 7. decorate with pattern

paucity ('pɔːsɪtɪ) *n.* 1. scarcity 2. smallness of quantity 3. fewness

paunch (pɔːntʃ) *n.* belly

pauper ('pɔːpə) *n.* poor person, *esp.,* formerly, one supported by the public —**'pauperism** *n.* 1. destitution 2. extreme poverty

pause (pɔːz) *vi.* 1. cease for a time —*n.* 2. stop or rest

pavane *or* **pavan** (pə'vɑːn, 'pæv'n) *n.* 1. slow, stately dance of 16th and 17th centuries 2. music for this dance

pave (peɪv) *vt.* 1. form surface on with stone or brick 2. prepare, make easier (*esp. in* pave the way) —**'pavement** *n.* 1. paved floor, footpath 2. material for paving

pavilion (pə'vɪljən) *n.* 1. clubhouse on playing field *etc.* 2. building for housing exhibition *etc.* 3. large ornate tent

pavlova (pæv'ləʊvə) *n.* meringue cake with whipped cream and fruit

paw (pɔː) *n.* 1. foot of animal —*v.* 2. scrape with forefoot —*vt.* 3. handle roughly 4. stroke with the hands

pawl (pɔːl) *n.* pivoted lever shaped to engage with ratchet wheel to prevent motion in particular direction

pawn¹ (pɔːn) *vt.* 1. deposit (article) as security for money borrowed —*n.* 2. article deposited —**'pawnbroker** *n.* lender of money on goods pledged

pawn² (pɔːn) *n.* 1. piece in chess 2. *fig.* person used as mere tool

pawpaw ('pɔːpɔː) *n. see* PAPAW

pax (pæks) *n. chiefly R.C.Ch.* 1. kiss of peace 2. small plate formerly used to convey kiss of peace from celebrant at Mass to those attending it —*interj.* 3. UK *school sl.* call signalling end to hostilities or claiming immunity from rules of game

P.A.X. UK private automatic exchange

pay (peɪ) *vt.* 1. give (money *etc.*) for goods or services rendered 2. compensate 3. give, bestow 4. be profitable to 5. (*with* out) release bit by bit, as rope 6. (*with* out) spend —*vi.* 7. be remunerative or profitable (paid, 'paying) —*n.* 8. wages 9. paid employment —**'payable** *a.* 1. justly due 2. profitable —**pay'ee** *n.* person to whom money is paid or due —**'payment** *n.* discharge of debt —**pay'ola** *n. inf.* 1. bribe given to secure special treatment, *esp.* to disc jockey to promote commercial product 2. practice of paying or receiving such bribes —**pay bed** bed in hospital for which user has paid as private patient —**paying guest** boarder, lodger, *esp.* in private house —**'payload** *n.* 1. part of cargo earning revenue 2. explosive power of missile *etc.* —**'paymaster** *n.* official of government *etc.,* responsible for payment of wages and salaries —**'payoff** *n.* 1. final settlement, *esp.* in retribution 2. *inf.* climax, consequence or outcome of events *etc.* 3. final payment of debt *etc.* 4. time of such payment 5. *inf.* bribe —**pay packet** 1. envelope containing employee's wages 2. the wages —**'payroll** *n.* 1. list of employees, specifying salary or wage of each 2. total of these amounts or actual money equivalent —**pay as you earn** UK, NZ system by which income tax is paid by employers directly to government —**pay off** 1. pay all that is due in wages *etc.* and discharge from employment 2. pay complete amount of (debt *etc.*) 3. turn out to be profitable 4. take revenge on (person) or for (wrong done) 5. *inf.* give bribe to

P.A.Y.E. pay as you earn

Pb *Chem.* lead

PBX UK private branch exchange; telephone system that handles internal and external calls of building *etc.*

P.C. 1. Police Constable 2. Privy Councillor 3. C Progressive Conservative

p.c. 1. per cent 2. personal computer 3. postcard

Pd *Chem.* palladium

pd. paid

P.D.S.A. UK People's Dispensary for Sick Animals

PE Prince Edward Island

P.E. physical education

pea (piː) *n.* 1. fruit, growing in pods, of climbing plant 2. the plant —**pea-green** *a.* of shade of green like colour of green peas —**pea jacket** *or* **'peacoat** *n.* sailor's short heavy woollen overcoat —**pea'souper** *n. inf.* thick fog

peace (piːs) *n.* 1. freedom from war 2. harmony 3. quietness of mind 4. calm 5. repose —**'peaceable** *a.* disposed to peace —**'peaceably** *adv.* —**'peaceful** *a.* 1. free from war, tumult 2. mild 3. undisturbed —**'peacefully** *adv.* —**'peacemaker** *n.* person who establishes peace, *esp.* between others —**peace offering** 1. something given to adversary in hope of procuring or maintaining peace 2. *Judaism* sacrificial meal shared between offerer and Jehovah —**peace pipe** pipe smoked by N Amer. Indians, *esp.* as token of peace (*also* '**calumet**)

peach[1] (piːtʃ) *n.* 1. stone fruit of delicate flavour 2. *inf.* anything very pleasant 3. pinkish-yellow colour —'**peachy** *a.* 1. like peach 2. *inf.* fine, excellent

peach[2] (piːtʃ) *vi. sl.* become informer

peacock ('piːkɒk) *n.* 1. male of bird ('**peafowl**) with fanlike tail, brilliantly coloured ('**peahen** *fem.*) —*vi.* 2. strut about or pose, like a peacock

peak (piːk) *n.* 1. pointed end of anything, *esp.* hill's sharp top 2. point of greatest development *etc.* 3. sharp increase 4. projecting piece on front of cap —*v.* 5. (cause to) form, reach peaks —**peaked** *or* '**peaky** *a.* 1. like, having a peak 2. sickly, wan, drawn —**peak hour** time at which maximum occurs, either in amount of traffic or demand for gas *etc.* —**peak load** maximum load on electrical power-supply system

peal (piːl) *n.* 1. loud sound or succession of loud sounds 2. changes rung on set of bells 3. chime —*v.* 4. sound loudly

peanut ('piːnʌt) *n.* 1. pea-shaped nut that ripens underground —*pl.* 2. *inf.* trifling amount of money

pear (pɛə) *n.* 1. tree yielding sweet, juicy fruit 2. the fruit —**pear-shaped** *a.* shaped like a pear, heavier at the bottom than the top

pearl (pɜːl) *n.* hard, lustrous structure found in several molluscs, *esp.* pearl oyster and used as jewel —'**pearly** *a.* like pearls —**pearl barley** barley with skin ground off —**pearl diver** *or* **fisher** person who dives for pearl-bearing molluscs

peasant ('pɛz'nt) *n.* member of low social class, *esp.* in rural district —'**peasantry** *n.* peasants collectively

pease (piːz) *n. obs., dial.* pea (*pl.* **pease**) —**pease pudding** *chiefly* UK dish of boiled split peas

peat (piːt) *n.* 1. decomposed vegetable substance found in bogs 2. turf of it used for fuel —**peat moss** any of various mosses, *esp.* sphagnum, that grow in wet places and decay to form peat (*see also* SPHAGNUM)

pebble ('pɛb'l) *n.* 1. small roundish stone 2. pale, transparent rock crystal 3. grainy, irregular surface —*vt.* 4. pave, cover with pebbles —**pebble dash** finish for exterior walls with small stones in plaster

pecan (pɪ'kæn, 'piːkən) *n.* 1. N Amer. tree, species of hickory, allied to walnut 2. its edible nut

peccadillo (pɛkə'dɪləʊ) *n.* 1. slight offence 2. petty crime (*pl.* **-es, -s**)

peccary ('pɛkərɪ) *n.* vicious Amer. animal allied to pig

peck[1] (pɛk) *n.* 1. fourth part of bushel, 2 gallons 2. great deal

peck[2] (pɛk) *v.* 1. pick, strike with or with

beak 2. nibble —*vt.* 3. *inf.* kiss quickly —*n.* 4. act, instance of pecking —'**peckish** *a. inf.* hungry

pecker ('pɛkə) *n.* UK *sl.* good spirits (*esp. in* **keep one's pecker up**)

pectin ('pɛktɪn) *n.* gelatinizing substance obtained from ripe fruits —'**pectic** *a.* 1. congealing 2. denoting pectin

pectoral ('pɛktərəl) *a.* 1. of the breast —*n.* 2. chest medicine 3. breastplate —**pectoral fin** either of pair of fins, situated just behind head in fishes

peculate ('pɛkjʊleɪt) *v.* 1. embezzle 2. steal —**pecu'lation** *n.* —'**peculator** *n.*

peculiar (pɪ'kjuːlɪə) *a.* 1. strange 2. particular 3. (*with* to) belonging (to) —**pecu'liarity** *n.* 1. oddity 2. characteristic 3. distinguishing feature

pecuniary (pɪ'kjuːnɪərɪ) *a.* relating to, or consisting of, money

-**ped** *or* -**pede** (*comb. form*) foot or feet, as in *quadruped, centipede*

pedagogue *or* U.S. (*sometimes*) **pedagog** ('pɛdəɡɒɡ) *n.* 1. schoolmaster 2. pedant —**peda'gogic** *a.* —**pedagogy** ('pɛdəɡɒɡɪ, -ɡɒdʒɪ, -ɡəʊdʒɪ) *n.* principles, practice or profession of teaching

pedal ('pɛd'l) *n.* 1. something to transmit motion from foot 2. foot lever to modify tone or swell of musical instrument 3. *Mus.* note, *usu.* bass, held through successive harmonies —*a.* ('piːd'l) 4. of a foot —*v.* 5. propel (bicycle) by using pedals —*vi.* 6. use pedals (**-ll-**)

pedalo ('pɛdələʊ) *n.* small watercraft with paddle wheel propelled by foot pedals

pedant ('pɛd'nt) *n.* one who overvalues, or insists on, petty details of book-learning, grammatical rules *etc.* —**pe'dantic** *a.*

peddle ('pɛd'l) *v.* go round selling (goods) —'**peddler** *n.* one who sells narcotic drugs

pederast *or* **paederast** ('pɛdəræst) *n.* man who has homosexual relations with boy —'**pederasty** *or* '**paederasty** *n.*

pedestal ('pɛdɪst'l) *n.* base of column, pillar

pedestrian (pɪ'dɛstrɪən) *n.* 1. one who walks on foot —*a.* 2. going on foot 3. commonplace; dull, uninspiring —**pe'destrianism** *n.* the practice of walking —**pe'destrianize** *or* **-ise** *vt.* convert into area for use of pedestrians only —**pedestrian crossing** place marked where pedestrians may cross road —**pedestrian precinct** area for pedestrians only to shop *etc.*

pedi- (*comb. form*) foot, as in *pedicure*

pediatrics (piːdɪ'ætrɪks) *n. see* PAEDIATRICS

pedicure ('pɛdɪkjʊə) *n.* medical or cosmetic treatment of feet

pedigree ('pɛdɪɡriː) *n.* 1. register of ancestors 2. genealogy

pediment ('pɛdɪmənt) *n.* triangular part over Greek portico *etc.* —**pedi'mental** *a.*

pedlar *or esp.* U.S. **peddler** ('pɛdlə) *n.* 1. one who sells 2. hawker

pedo- *or before vowel* **ped-** (*comb. form*) US *see* PAEDO-

peduncle (pɪ'dʌŋk'l) n. 1. flower stalk 2. stalklike structure

peek (piːk) vi./n. peep, glance

peel¹ (piːl) vt. 1. strip off skin, rind or any form of covering from —vi. 2. come off, as skin, rind —n. 3. rind, skin —peeled a. inf. (of eyes) watchful

peel² (piːl) n. UK fortified tower of 16th cent. on borders of Scotland

peen (piːn) n. 1. end of hammer head opposite striking face, oft. rounded or wedge-shaped —vt. 2. strike with peen of hammer or stream of metal shot

peep¹ (piːp) vi. 1. look slyly or quickly —n. 2. such a look —'**peeper** n. 1. person who peeps 2. (oft. pl.) sl. eye —**Peeping Tom** man who furtively observes women undressing; voyeur —'**peepshow** n. box with peephole through which series of pictures can be seen

peep² (piːp) vi. 1. cry, as chick 2. chirp —n. 3. such a cry

peer¹ (pɪə) n. 1. nobleman 2. one of the same rank ('**peeress** fem.) —'**peerage** n. 1. body of peers 2. rank of peer —'**peerless** a. without match or equal —**peer group** social group composed of individuals of approximately same age

peer² (pɪə) vi. look closely and intently

peevish ('piːvɪʃ) a. 1. fretful 2. irritable —**peeved** a. inf. sulky, irritated —'**peevishly** adv. —'**peevishness** n. annoyance

peewit or **pewit** ('piːwɪt) n. see LAPWING

peg (pɛg) n. 1. nail or pin for joining, fastening, marking etc. 2. (mark of) level, standard etc. —vt. 3. fasten with pegs 4. stabilize (prices) 5. inf. throw —vi. 6. (with away) persevere (-**gg**-) —'**pegboard** n. 1. board having pattern of holes into which small pegs can be fitted, used for playing certain games or keeping score 2. see solitaire (sense 1) at SOLITARY 3. hardboard perforated by pattern of holes in which articles may be hung, as for display —**peg leg** inf. 1. artificial leg, esp. one made of wood 2. person with artificial leg —**peg out** sl. die

peignoir ('peɪnwɑː) n. lady's dressing gown, jacket, wrapper

pejorative (pɪ'dʒɒrətɪv, 'piːdʒər-) a. (of words etc.) with unpleasant, disparaging connotation

Pekingese (piːkɪŋ'iːz) or **Pekinese** (piːkə'niːz) n. small Chinese dog (also **peke**) —**Peking man** (piː'kɪŋ) early type of man, remains of which were found in cave near Peking

pelargonium (pɛlə'gəʊnɪəm) n. plant with red, white or pink flowers

pelf (pɛlf) n. contemptuous money; wealth

pelican ('pɛlɪkən) n. large, fish-eating waterfowl with large pouch beneath its bill —**pelican crossing** road crossing with pedestrian-operated traffic-light system

pelisse (pɛ'liːs) n. 1. fur-trimmed cloak 2. loose coat, usu. fur-trimmed, worn esp. by women in early 19th cent.

pellagra (pə'leɪɡrə, -'læ-) n. Pathol. disease caused by dietary deficiency of niacin, characterized by scaling of skin etc.

pellet ('pɛlɪt) n. little ball, pill

pellicle ('pɛlɪk'l) n. thin skin, film

pell-mell ('pɛl'mɛl) adv. in utter confusion, headlong

pellucid (pɛ'luːsɪd) a. 1. translucent 2. clear —**pellu'cidity** n.

pelmet ('pɛlmɪt) n. ornamental drapery or board, concealing curtain rail

pelt¹ (pɛlt) vt. 1. strike with missiles —vi. 2. throw missiles 3. rush 4. fall persistently, as rain

pelt² (pɛlt) n. raw hide or skin

pelvis ('pɛlvɪs) n. bony cavity at base of human trunk (pl. -es, -ves (-viːz)) —'**pelvic** a. pert. to pelvis

Pemb. Pembrokeshire

pen¹ (pɛn) n. 1. instrument for writing —vt. 2. compose 3. write (-**nn**-) —**pen friend** pen pal —'**penknife** n. small knife with one or more blades that fold into handle; pocketknife —'**penmanship** n. style or technique of writing by hand —**pen name** author's pseudonym —**pen pal** person with whom one exchanges letters, oft. person in another country whom one has not met (also **pen friend**) —'**penpusher** n. clerk involved with boring paperwork

pen² (pɛn) n. 1. small enclosure, as for sheep —vt. 2. put, keep in enclosure (-**nn**-)

pen³ (pɛn) n. female swan

Pen. Peninsula

penal ('piːn'l) a. of, incurring, inflicting, punishment —'**penalize** or -**ise** vt. 1. impose penalty on 2. handicap —**penalty** ('pɛn'ltɪ) n. 1. punishment for crime or offence 2. forfeit 3. Sport handicap or disadvantage imposed for infringement of rule etc. —**penal code** codified body of laws that relate to crime and punishment

penance ('pɛnəns) n. 1. suffering submitted to as expression of penitence 2. repentance

pence (pɛns) n., pl. of PENNY

penchant ('pɛntʃənt; Fr. pɑ̃'ʃɑ̃) n. inclination, decided taste

pencil ('pɛns'l) n. 1. instrument as of graphite, for writing etc. 2. Optics narrow beam of light —vt. 3. paint or draw 4. mark with pencil (-**ll**-)

pendant ('pɛndənt) n. hanging ornament —'**pendent** a. 1. suspended, hanging 2. projecting

pending ('pɛndɪŋ) prep. 1. during, until —a. 2. awaiting settlement 3. undecided 4. imminent

pendulous ('pɛndjʊləs) a. hanging, swinging —'**pendulum** n. suspended weight swinging to and fro, esp. as regulator for clock

penetrate ('pɛnɪtreɪt) vt. 1. enter into 2. pierce 3. arrive at the meaning of —penetra'bility n. quality of being penetrable —'**penetrable** a. capable of being entered or pierced —'**penetrating** a. 1. sharp 2. easily heard 3. subtle 4. quick to understand —**pene'tration** n. insight, acuteness —**'penetrative** a. 1. piercing 2. discerning —**'penetrator** n.

penguin ('pengwin) n. flightless, short-legged swimming bird

penicillin (penɪ'sɪlɪn) n. antibiotic drug effective against a wide range of diseases, infections

peninsula (pɪ'nɪnsjulə) n. portion of land nearly surrounded by water —**pe'ninsular** a.

penis ('piːnɪs) n. male organ of copulation (and of urination) in man and many mammals (pl. -es, penes ('piːniːz))

penitent ('penɪtənt) a. 1. affected by sense of guilt —n. 2. one that repents of sin —**'penitence** n. 1. sorrow for sin 2. repentance —**peni'tential** a. of, or expressing, penitence —**peni'tentiary** a. 1. relating to penance, or to the rules of penance —n. 2. US prison

pennant ('penənt) n. long narrow flag

pennon ('penən) n. small pointed or swallow-tailed flag

penny ('penɪ) n. 1. Brit. bronze coin, now 100th part of pound (pl. pence, 'pennies) —**'penniless** a. 1. having no money 2. poor —**Penny Black** first postage stamp, issued in Brit. in 1840 —**penny-dreadful** n. UK inf. cheap, oft. lurid book or magazine (pl. -s) —**penny-farthing** n. UK early type of bicycle with large front wheel and small rear wheel —**penny-pincher** n. inf. person who is excessively careful with money —**penny-pinching** n./a. —**penny-wise** a. greatly concerned with saving small sums of money —**'pennyworth** n. 1. amount that can be bought for a penny 2. small amount —**penny-wise and pound-foolish** careful about trifles but wasteful in large ventures

penology (piː'nɒlədʒɪ) n. study of punishment and prevention of crime

pension[1] ('penʃən) n. 1. regular payment to old people, retired public officials, soldiers etc. —vt. 2. grant pension to —**'pensioner** n.

pension[2] (pã'sjɔ̃) Fr. 1. continental boarding house 2. (full) board

pensive ('pensɪv) a. 1. thoughtful with sadness 2. wistful

penstemon (pen'stiːmən) n. see PENTSTE-MON

pent (pent) a. shut up, kept in —**pent-up** a. not released, repressed

penta- (comb. form) five, as in pentagon, pentameter

pentacle ('pentək'l) n. 1. star-shaped figure with five points 2. such figure used by Pythagoreans, black magicians etc. (also **'pentagram, 'pentangle**)

pentagon ('pentəgon) n. plane figure having five angles —**pen'tagonal** a.

Pentagon ('pentəgon) n. military headquarters in U.S.A.

pentameter (pen'tæmɪtə) n. verse of five metrical feet

Pentateuch ('pentətjuːx) n. first five books of Old Testament

pentathlon (pen'tæθlən) n. athletic contest of five events

pentatonic scale (pentə'tɒnɪk) Mus. scale consisting of five notes

Pentecost ('pentɪkɒst) n. 1. Whitsuntide 2. Jewish harvest festival on 50th day after Passover —**Pente'costal** a. 1. of any of various Christian groups that emphasize charismatic aspects of Christianity 2. of Pentecost or influence of Holy Ghost —n. 3. member of a Pentecostal Church —**Pente'costalist** n./a.

penthouse ('penthaus) n. apartment, flat or other structure on top, or top floor, of building

pentode ('pentəud) n. Electron. five-electrode thermionic valve, having anode, cathode and three grids

pentstemon (pent'stiːmən) or **penstemon** n. bright-flowered garden plant

penult ('penʌlt, pɪ'nʌlt) n. last syllable but one of word —**pe'nultimate** a. next before the last

penumbra (pɪ'nʌmbrə) n. 1. imperfect shadow 2. in an eclipse, the partially shadowed region which surrounds the full shadow

penury ('penjurɪ) n. 1. extreme poverty 2. extreme scarcity —**pe'nurious** a. 1. niggardly, stingy 2. poor, scanty

peony ('piːənɪ) n. any of genus of N Amer. plants with showy red, pink or white flowers

people ('piːp'l) pl.n. 1. persons generally 2. community, nation 3. family —n. 4. race —vt. 5. stock with inhabitants, populate

pep (pep) n. 1. vigour 2. energy 3. enthusiasm —vt. (usu. with up) 4. impart energy to 5. speed up (-pp-) —**pep pill** inf. tablet containing stimulant —**pep talk** inf. enthusiastic talk designed to increase confidence, production etc.

pepper ('pepə) n. 1. fruit of climbing plant, which yields pungent aromatic spice 2. various slightly pungent vegetables, eg capsicum —vt. 3. season with pepper 4. sprinkle, dot 5. pelt with missiles —**'peppery** a. 1. having the qualities of pepper 2. irritable —**pepper-and-salt** a. 1. (of cloth etc.) marked with fine mixture of black and white 2. (of hair) streaked with grey —**'peppercorn** n. 1. dried pepper berry 2. something trifling —**pepper mill** hand mill used to grind peppercorns —**'peppermint** n. 1. plant noted for aromatic pungent liquor distilled from it 2. a sweet flavoured with this

pepsin ('pepsɪn) n. enzyme produced in stomach, which, when activated by acid, breaks down proteins

peptic ('peptɪk) a. relating to digestion or digestive juices

per (pɜː; unstressed pə) prep. 1. for each 2. by 3. in manner of

per- (comb. form) through, thoroughly, as in perfect, perspicacious

peradventure (pərəd'ventʃə, pɜːr-) obs.

adv. **1.** by chance; perhaps —*n.* **2.** chance; doubt

perambulate (pə'ræmbjʊleɪt) *vt.* **1.** walk through or over **2.** traverse —*vi.* **3.** walk about —**per'ambulator** *n.* pram

per annum ('ænəm) *Lat.* by the year

per capita ('kæpɪtə) of or for each person

perceive (pə'siːv) *vt.* **1.** obtain knowledge of through senses **2.** observe **3.** understand —**per'ceivable** *a.* —**percepti'bility** *n.* —**per'ceptible** *a.* discernible, recognizable —**per'ception** *n.* **1.** faculty of perceiving **2.** intuitive judgment —**per'ceptive** *a.*

percentage (pə'sɛntɪdʒ) *n.* proportion or rate per hundred —**per cent** in each hundred —**per'centile** *n.* one of 99 actual or notional values of a variable dividing its distribution into 100 groups with equal frequencies (*also* (US) **'centile**)

perception (pə'sɛpʃən) *n. see* PERCEIVE

perch[1] (pɜːtʃ) *n.* any of a family of freshwater fishes

perch[2] (pɜːtʃ) *n.* **1.** resting place, as for bird **2.** formerly, measure of 5½ yards —*vt.* **3.** place, as on perch —*vi.* **4.** alight, settle on fixed body **5.** roost **6.** balance

perchance (pə'tʃɑːns) *adv. Poet.* perhaps

percipient (pə'sɪpɪənt) *a.* **1.** having faculty of perception **2.** perceiving —*n.* **3.** one who perceives

percolate ('pɜːkəleɪt) *v.* **1.** pass through fine mesh as liquor **2.** permeate **3.** filter —**perco'lation** *n.* —**'percolator** *n.* coffeepot with filter

percussion (pə'kʌʃən) *n.* **1.** collision, impact **2.** vibratory shock —**per'cussionist** *n. Mus.* person who plays percussion instrument —**per'cussive** *a.* —**percussion cap** detonator consisting of paper or thin metal cap containing material that explodes when struck —**percussion instrument** one played by being struck, *eg* drum, cymbals *etc.*

perdition (pə'dɪʃən) *n.* spiritual ruin

peregrinate ('pɛrɪɡrɪneɪt) *vi.* travel about, roam —**peregri'nation** *n.*

peregrine ('pɛrɪɡrɪn) *n.* type of falcon

peremptory (pə'rɛmptərɪ) *a.* **1.** authoritative, imperious **2.** forbidding debate **3.** decisive

perennial (pə'rɛnɪəl) *a.* **1.** lasting through the years **2.** perpetual, unfailing —*n.* **3.** plant lasting more than two years —**pe'rennially** *adv.*

perfect ('pɜːfɪkt) *a.* **1.** complete **2.** finished **3.** whole **4.** unspoilt **5.** faultless **6.** correct, precise **7.** excellent **8.** of highest quality —*n.* **9.** tense denoting a complete act —*vt.* (pə'fɛkt) **10.** improve **11.** finish **12.** make skilful —**per'fectable** *a.* capable of becoming perfect —**per'fection** *n.* **1.** state of being perfect **2.** faultlessness —**per'fectionism** *n.* **1.** *Philos.* doctrine that man can attain perfection in this life **2.** demand for highest standard of excellence —**per'fectionist** *n.* —**'perfectly** *adv.* —**perfect participle** past participle

perfidy ('pɜːfɪdɪ) *n.* treachery, disloyalty —**per'fidious** *a.*

perforate ('pɜːfəreɪt) *vt.* make holes in, penetrate —**perfo'ration** *n.*

perforce (pə'fɔːs) *adv.* of necessity

perform (pə'fɔːm) *vt.* **1.** bring to completion **2.** accomplish; fulfil **3.** represent on stage —*vi.* **4.** function **5.** act part **6.** play, as on musical instrument —**per'formance** *n.* —**per'former** *n.*

perfume ('pɜːfjuːm) *n.* **1.** agreeable scent **2.** fragrance —*vt.* (pə'fjuːm) **3.** imbue with an agreeable odour, scent —**per'fumer** *n.* —**per'fumery** *n.* perfumes in general

perfunctory (pə'fʌŋktərɪ) *a.* **1.** superficial **2.** hasty **3.** done indifferently

pergola ('pɜːɡələ) *n.* **1.** area covered by plants growing on trellis **2.** the trellis

perhaps (pə'hæps; *inf.* præps) *adv.* possibly

peri- (*comb. form*) round, as in *perimeter, period, periphrasis*

perianth ('pɛrɪænθ) *n.* outer part of flower, consisting of calyx and corolla

pericardium (pɛrɪ'kɑːdɪəm) *n.* membrane enclosing the heart (*pl.* **-dia** (-dɪə)) —**peri'cardiac** *or* **peri'cardial** *a.* —**peri-car'ditis** *n.* inflammation of this

perigee ('pɛrɪdʒiː) *n.* point in its orbit around earth when moon or satellite is nearest earth

perihelion (pɛrɪ'hiːlɪən) *n.* point in orbit of planet or comet when nearest to sun (*pl.* **-lia** (-lɪə))

peril ('pɛrɪl) *n.* **1.** danger **2.** exposure to injury —**'perilous** *a.* full of peril, hazardous

perimeter (pə'rɪmɪtə) *n.* **1.** *Maths.* outer boundary of an area; length of this **2.** medical instrument for measuring the field of vision

perineum (pɛrɪ'niːəm) *n.* **1.** region of body between anus and genital organs **2.** surface of human trunk between thighs (*pl.* **-nea** (-'niːə))

period ('pɪərɪəd) *n.* **1.** particular portion of time **2.** a series of years **3.** single occurrence of menstruation **4.** cycle **5.** conclusion **6.** full stop (.) at end of sentence **7.** complete sentence —*a.* **8.** (of furniture, dress, play *etc.*) belonging to particular time in history —**peri'odic** *a.* recurring at regular intervals —**peri'odical** *a./n.* **1.** (of) publication issued at regular intervals —*a.* **2.** of a period **3.** periodic —**perio'dicity** *n.* —**periodic law** principle that chemical properties of elements are periodic functions of their atomic weights or, more accurately, of their atomic numbers —**periodic table** table of elements, arranged in order of increasing atomic number, based on periodic law

peripatetic (pɛrɪpə'tɛtɪk) *a.* itinerant, walking, travelling about

periphery (pə'rɪfərɪ) *n.* **1.** circumference **2.** surface, outside —**pe'ripheral** *a.* **1.** minor, unimportant **2.** of periphery

periphrasis (pə'rıfrəsıs) n. 1. roundabout speech or phrase 2. circumlocution (pl. -rases (-rəsi:z)) —peri'phrastic a.

periscope ('periskəup) n. instrument, used esp. in submarines, for giving view of objects on different level —periscopic (peri'skopik) a.

perish ('peri∫) vi. 1. die, waste away 2. decay, rot —perisha'bility n. —'perishable a. 1. that will not last long —pl.n. 2. perishable food —'perishing a. 1. inf. (of weather etc.) extremely cold 2. sl. confounded

peristalsis (peri'stælsıs) n. Physiol. succession of waves of involuntary muscular contraction of various bodily tubes, esp. of alimentary tract (pl. -ses (-si:z))

peristyle ('peristail) n. 1. range of pillars surrounding building, square etc. 2. court within this

peritoneum (peritə'ni:əm) n. membrane lining internal surface of abdomen (pl. -s, -nea (-'ni:ə)) —perito'nitis n. inflammation of peritoneum

periwig ('periwig) n. Hist. wig

periwinkle ('periwıŋk'l) n. 1. flowering plant 2. small edible shellfish (also 'winkle)

perjure ('pɜ:dʒə) vt. render (oneself) guilty of perjury —'perjury n. 1. crime of false testimony on oath 2. false swearing

perk¹ (pɜ:k) n. inf. perquisite

perk² (pɜ:k) vi. inf. (of coffee) percolate

perky ('pɜ:kı) a. lively, cheerful, jaunty, gay —perk up make, become cheerful

perm (pɜ:m) n. inf. see permutation (sense 3) at PERMUTE

permafrost ('pɜ:məfrost) n. permanently frozen ground

permanent ('pɜ:mənənt) a. 1. continuing in same state 2. lasting —'permanence or 'permanency n. fixedness —permanent wave (treatment of hair producing) long-lasting style (also perm) —permanent way chiefly UK track of railway, including sleepers, rails etc.

permanganate (pə'mæŋgəneit, -nıt) n. salt of an acid of manganese

permeate ('pɜ:mıeit) vt. 1. pervade, saturate 2. pass through pores of —'permeable a. admitting of passage of fluids

Permian ('pɜ:mıən) a. 1. of last period of Palaeozoic era, between Carboniferous and Triassic periods —n. 2. Permian period or rock system

permit (pə'mıt) vt. 1. allow 2. give leave to (-tt-) —n. ('pɜ:mıt) 3. warrant or licence to do something 4. written permission —per'missible a. allowable —per'mission n. authorization, leave, liberty —per'missive a. (too) tolerant, lenient, esp. sexually

permute (pə'mju:t) vt. change sequence of —permu'tation n. 1. mutual transference 2. Maths. arrangement of a number of quantities in every possible order 3. fixed combinations for selections of results on football pools

pernicious (pə'nı∫əs) a. 1. wicked or mischievous 2. extremely hurtful 3. having quality of destroying or injuring —pernicious anaemia form of anaemia characterized by lesions of spinal cord, weakness, diarrhoea etc.

pernickety (pə'nıkıtı) a. inf. fussy, fastidious about trifles

peroration (perə'rei∫ən) n. concluding part of oration —'perorate vi.

peroxide (pə'roksaid) n. 1. oxide of a given base containing greatest quantity of oxygen 2. see hydrogen peroxide at HYDROGEN

perpendicular (pɜ:pən'dıkjulə) a. 1. at right angles to the plane of the horizon 2. at right angles to given line or surface 3. exactly upright —n. 4. line falling at right angles on another line or plane

perpetrate ('pɜ:pıtreit) vt. perform or be responsible for (deception, crime etc.) —perpe'tration n. —'perpetrator n.

perpetual (pə'petjuəl) a. 1. continuous 2. lasting for ever —per'petually adv. —per'petuate vt. 1. make perpetual 2. not to allow to be forgotten —perpetu'ation n. —perpe'tuity n. —perpetual motion motion of hypothetical mechanism that continues indefinitely without any external source of energy

perplex (pə'pleks) vt. 1. puzzle, bewilder 2. make difficult to understand —per'plexity n. puzzled or tangled state

perquisite ('pɜ:kwızıt) n. 1. any incidental benefit from a certain type of employment 2. casual payment in addition to salary

perry ('perı) n. fermented drink made from pears

per se (sei) Lat. by or in itself

persecute ('pɜ:sıkju:t) vt. 1. oppress because of race, religion etc. 2. subject to persistent ill-treatment —perse'cution n. —'persecutor n.

persevere (pɜ:sı'vıə) vi. (oft. with in) persist, maintain effort —perse'verance n. persistence

Persian ('pɜ:∫ən) a. 1. of ancient Persia or modern Iran —n. 2. native or inhabitant of modern Iran; Iranian 3. language of Iran or Persia in any of ancient or modern forms —Persian cat long-haired domestic cat —Persian lamb 1. black loosely curled fur from karakul lamb 2. karakul lamb

persimmon (pɜ:'sımən) n. 1. any of several tropical trees typically having hard wood 2. its fruit

persist (pə'sıst) vi. (oft. with in) continue in spite of obstacles or objections —per'sistence or per'sistency n. —per'sistent a. 1. persisting 2. steady 3. persevering 4. lasting

person ('pɜ:s'n) n. 1. individual (human) being 2. body of human being 3. Gram. classification, or one of the classes, of pronouns and verb forms according to the person speaking, spoken to, or spoken of —per'sona n. assumed character (pl. -nae (-ni:)) —'personable a. good-looking

—'**personage** n. notable person —'**personal** a. 1. individual, private, or one's own 2. of, relating to grammatical person —**perso'nality** n. 1. distinctive character 2. a celebrity —'**personalize** or -**ise** vt. 1. endow with personal or individual qualities 2. mark with person's initials, name etc. 3. take personally 4. personify —'**personally** adv. in person —'**personalty** n. personal property —'**personate** vt. pass oneself off as —**perso'nation** n. —**personal column** newspaper column containing personal messages etc. —**personal computer** small inexpensive computer used in word processing etc. —**personal property** Law all property except land and interests in land that pass to heir —**in person** actually present

persona non grata (pɜː'səʊnə nɒn 'grɑːtə) Lat. 1. unacceptable or unwelcome person 2. diplomat who is not acceptable to government to whom he is accredited (pl. **personae non gratae** (pɜː'səʊniː nɒn 'grɑːtiː))

personify (pɜː'sɒnɪfaɪ) vt. 1. represent as person 2. typify (-**ified**, -**ifying**) —**personifi'cation** n.

personnel (pɜːsə'nɛl) n. 1. staff employed in a service or institution 2. department that interviews or keeps records of employees

perspective (pə'spɛktɪv) n. 1. mental view 2. art of drawing on flat surface to give effect of solidity and relative distances and sizes 3. drawing in perspective

Perspex ('pɜːspɛks) n. R transparent acrylic substitute for glass

perspicacious (pɜːspɪ'keɪʃəs) a. having quick mental insight —**perspicacity** (pɜːspɪ'kæsɪtɪ) n.

perspicuous (pə'spɪkjʊəs) a. 1. clearly expressed 2. lucid 3. plain 4. obvious —**perspi'cuity** n.

perspire (pə'spaɪə) vi. sweat —**perspiration** (pɜːspə'reɪʃən) n. sweating

persuade (pə'sweɪd) vt. 1. bring (one to do something) by argument, charm etc. 2. convince —**per'suasion** n. 1. art, act of persuading 2. way of thinking or belief —**per'suasive** a.

pert (pɜːt) a. forward, saucy

pertain (pə'teɪn) vi. (oft. with to) 1. belong, relate, have reference (to) 2. concern

pertinacious (pɜːtɪ'neɪʃəs) a. obstinate, persistent —**pertinacity** (pɜːtɪ'næsɪtɪ) or **perti'naciousness** n. doggedness, resolution

pertinent ('pɜːtɪnənt) a. relating to the matter at hand —'**pertinence** or '**pertinency** n. relevance

perturb (pə'tɜːb) vt. 1. disturb greatly 2. alarm —**per'turbable** a. —**pertur'bation** n. agitation of mind

peruke (pə'ruːk) n. Hist. wig

peruse (pə'ruːz) vt. read, esp. in slow and careful, or leisurely, manner —**pe'rusal** n.

pervade (pɜː'veɪd) vt. 1. spread through 2.

be rife among —**per'vasion** n. —**per'vasive** a.

pervert (pə'vɜːt) vt. 1. turn to wrong use 2. lead astray —n. ('pɜːvɜːt) 3. one who shows unhealthy abnormality, esp. in sexual matters —**per'verse** a. 1. obstinately or unreasonably wrong 2. self-willed 3. headstrong 4. wayward —**per'versely** adv. —**per'version** n.

pervious ('pɜːvɪəs) a. 1. permeable 2. penetrable, giving passage

peseta (pə'seɪtə; Sp. pe'seta) n. Sp. monetary unit

peso ('peɪsəʊ; Sp. 'peso) n. standard monetary unit of Argentina, Mexico etc. (pl. **pesos** ('peɪsəʊz; Sp. 'pesos))

pessary ('pɛsərɪ) n. 1. instrument used to support mouth and neck of uterus 2. appliance to prevent conception 3. medicated suppository

pessimism ('pɛsɪmɪzəm) n. 1. tendency to see the worst side of things 2. theory that everything turns to evil —'**pessimist** n. —**pessi'mistic** a.

pest (pɛst) n. 1. troublesome or harmful thing, person or insect 2. rare plague —'**pesticide** n. chemical for killing pests, esp. insects —**pes'tiferous** a. 1. troublesome 2. bringing plague

pester ('pɛstə) vt. trouble or vex persistently, harass

pestilence ('pɛstɪləns) n. epidemic disease, esp. bubonic plague —'**pestilent** a. 1. troublesome 2. deadly —**pesti'lential** a.

pestle ('pɛsl) n. 1. instrument with which things are pounded in a mortar —v. 2. pound with pestle

pet (pɛt) n. 1. animal kept for companionship etc. 2. person regarded with affection —vt. 3. make pet of —v. 4. inf. hug, embrace, fondle (-tt-)

pet (pɛt) n. fit of sulkiness, esp. at what is felt to be a slight; pique —'**pettish** a. peevish, petulant

Pet. Bible Peter

petal ('pɛtˀl) n. white or coloured leaflike part of flower —'**petalled** a.

petard (pɪ'tɑːd) n. formerly, an explosive device

peter ('piːtə) vi. —**peter out** inf. disappear, lose power gradually

Peter Pan youthful or immature man

petersham ('piːtəʃəm) n. thick corded ribbon used to stiffen belts etc.

pethidine ('pɛθɪdiːn) n. water-soluble drug used as analgesic (also me'peridine)

petiole ('pɛtɪəʊl) n. 1. stalk by which leaf is attached to plant 2. Zool. slender stalk or stem, as between thorax and abdomen of ants —'**petiolate** a.

petit ('pɛtɪ) a. Law small, petty —**petit bourgeois** n. 1. section of middle class with lowest social status, as shopkeepers etc. 2. member of this stratum (pl. **petits bourgeois** ('pɛtɪ 'bʊəʒwɑːz)) (also **petite bourgeoisie, petty bourgeoisie**) —a. 3. of petit bourgeois, esp. indicating sense of self-righteousness etc. —**petit four** any of various small fancy cakes and biscuits (*pl.* **petits fours** ('peti 'fo:z)) —**petit jury** jury of 12 persons empanelled to determine facts of case and decide issue pursuant to direction of court on points of law (*also* **petty jury**) —**petit mal** (mæl) mild form of epilepsy characterized by periods of impairment or loss of consciousness for up to 30 seconds —**petit point** (point, pwo:) 1. small diagonal needlepoint stitch used for fine detail 2. work done with such stitches

petite (pə'ti:t) *a.* (of women) small, dainty

petition (pɪ'tɪʃən) *n.* 1. entreaty, request, *esp.* one presented to sovereign or parliament —*vt.* 2. present petition to —**pe'titionary** *a.*

petrel ('petrəl) *n.* any of a family of sea birds

petrify ('petrɪfaɪ) *vt.* 1. turn to stone 2. *fig.* make motionless with fear 3. make dumb with amazement (**-ified, -ifying**) —**petri'faction** *or* **petrifi'cation** *n.*

petrochemical (petrəu'kemɪkəl) *n.* 1. any substance, such as acetone or ethanol, obtained from petroleum —*a.* 2. of petrochemicals; related to petrochemistry —**petro'chemistry** *n.*

petrocurrency ('petrəu'kʌrənsɪ) *n.* currency oil-producing countries acquire as profit from oil sales to other countries

petrodollar ('petrəudɒlə) *n.* money earned by country by exporting of petroleum

petrolatum (petrə'leɪtəm) *n.* translucent gelatinous substance obtained from petroleum

petroleum (pə'trəulɪəm) *n.* mineral oil —**'petrol** *n.* refined petroleum used in motorcars *etc.* —**petroleum jelly** *see* PETROLATUM —**petrol station** UK filling station

petrology (pe'trɒlədʒɪ) *n.* study of rocks and their structure

petticoat ('petɪkəut) *n.* women's undergarment worn under skirts, dresses *etc.*

pettifogger ('petɪfɒgə) *n.* 1. low-class lawyer 2. one given to mean dealing in small matters

petty ('petɪ) *a.* 1. unimportant, trivial 2. small-minded, mean 3. on a small scale —**petty cash** cash kept by firm to pay minor incidental expenses —**petty jury** *see* petit jury *at* PETIT —**petty officer** noncommissioned officer in Navy

petulant ('petjulənt) *a.* given to small fits of temper, peevish —**'petulance** *or* **'petulancy** *n.*

petunia (pɪ'tju:nɪə) *n.* any plant of tropical Amer. genus with funnel-shaped purple or white flowers

pew (pju:) *n.* 1. fixed seat in church 2. *inf.* chair, seat

pewit *or* **peewit** ('pi:wɪt) *n. see* LAPWING

pewter ('pju:tə) *n.* 1. alloy of tin and lead 2. ware made of this

pH potential of hydrogen; measure of acidity or alkalinity of solution

phalanx ('fælæŋks) *n.* body of men formed in close array (*pl.* **-es, phalanges** (fæ-'lændʒi:z))

phalarope ('fælərəup) *n.* any of a family of small wading birds

phallus ('fæləs) *n.* 1. penis 2. symbol of it used in primitive rites (*pl.* **-es, -li** (-laɪ)) —**'phallic** *a.* —**'phallicism** *n.*

phantasm ('fæntæzəm) *n.* 1. vision of absent person 2. illusion —**phantasma'goria** *or* **phan'tasmagory** *n.* 1. crowd of dim or unreal figures 2. exhibition of illusions —**phan'tasmal** *a.* —**'phantasy** *n. see* FANTASY

phantom ('fæntəm) *n.* 1. apparition, spectre, ghost 2. fancied vision

Pharaoh ('fɛərəu) *n.* title of ancient Egyptian kings

Pharisee ('færɪsi:) *n.* 1. sanctimonious person 2. hypocrite —**phari'saic(al)** *a.*

pharmaceutical (fɑ:mə'sju:tɪk'l) *or* **pharmaceutic** *a.* of pharmacy —**pharma'ceutics** *pl.n.* (*with sing. v.*) science of pharmacy —**'pharmacist** *n.* person qualified to dispense drugs —**pharma'cology** *n.* study of drugs —**pharmacopoeia** *or U.S.* (*sometimes*) **pharmacopeia** (fɑ:məkə-'pi:ə) *n.* official book with list and directions for use of drugs —**'pharmacy** *n.* 1. preparation and dispensing of drugs 2. dispensary

pharos ('fɛərɒs) *n.* marine lighthouse or beacon

pharynx ('færɪŋks) *n.* cavity forming back part of mouth and terminating in gullet (*pl.* **pharynges** (fæ'rɪndʒi:z)) —**pharyn'geal** *or* **pha'ryngal** *a.* —**pharyn'gitis** *n.* inflammation of pharynx

phase (feɪz) *n.* 1. any distinct or characteristic period or stage in a development or chain of events —*vt.* 2. arrange, execute in stages or to coincide with something else

Ph.D. Doctor of Philosophy (*also* **D.Phil.**)

pheasant ('fez'nt) *n.* any of various game birds with bright plumage

pheno- *or before vowel* **phen-** (*comb. form*) 1. showing, manifesting, as in *phenotype* 2. indicating that molecule contains benzene rings, as in *phenobarbitone*

phenobarbitone (fi:nəu'bɑ:bɪtəun) *or* **phenobarbital** (fi:nəu'bɑ:bɪt'l) *n.* drug inducing sleep

phenol ('fi:nɒl) *n.* carbolic acid

phenomenon (fɪ'nɒmɪnən) *n.* 1. anything appearing or observed 2. remarkable person or thing (*pl.* **phenomena** (fɪ'nɒmɪnə)) —**phe'nomenal** *a.* 1. relating to phenomena 2. remarkable 3. recognizable or evidenced by senses —**phe'nomenalism** *n.* 1. theory that only phenomena are real and can be known 2. tendency to think about things as phenomena only —**phe'nomenalist** *n./a.*

phenyl ('fi:naɪl, 'fenɪl) *a.* of, containing or consisting of monovalent group C_6H_5, derived from benzene

phew (fju:) *interj.* exclamation of relief, surprise *etc.*

phi (faɪ) *n.* 21st letter in Gr. alphabet (Φ, φ) (*pl.* **-s**)

phial ('faɪəl) *n.* small bottle for medicine *etc.*

Phil. 1. *Bible* Philippians **2.** Philippines **3.** Philadelphia

philander (fɪ'lændə) *vi.* (of man) flirt with women

philanthropy (fɪ'lænθrəpɪ) *n.* **1.** practice of doing good to one's fellow men **2.** love of mankind —**philan'thropic** *a.* loving mankind, benevolent —**phi'lanthropist** *or* **'philanthrope** *n.*

philately (fɪ'lætəlɪ) *n.* stamp collecting —**phila'telic** *a.* —**phi'latelist** *n.*

-phile *or* **-phil** (*comb. form*) person or thing having fondness for something specified, as in *bibliophile*

philharmonic (fɪlhɑ:'mɒnɪk, fɪlə-) *a.* **1.** fond of music **2.** (**P-** *when part of name*) denoting orchestra, choir *etc.* devoted to music

philhellene (fɪl'heliːn) *n.* **1.** lover of Greece and Greek culture **2.** *European hist.* supporter of cause of Greek national independence —**philhel'lenic** *a.*

philippic (fɪ'lɪpɪk) *n.* bitter or impassioned speech of denunciation; invective

Philistine ('fɪlɪstaɪn) *n.* **1.** ignorant, smug person **2.** member of non-Semitic people who inhabited ancient Philistia —*a.* **3.** (*sometimes* **p-**) boorishly uncultured **4.** of the ancient Philistines —**philistinism** ('fɪlɪstɪnɪzəm) *n.*

Phillips ('fɪlɪps) *n.* screwdriver that can be used on screw (**Phillips screw**) that has two slots crossing at centre of head

philo- *or before vowel* **phil-** (*comb. form*) love of, as in *philology, philanthropic*

philology (fɪ'lɒlədʒɪ) *n.* science of structure and development of languages —**philo'logical** *a.* —**phi'lologist** *or* **phi'lologer** *n.*

philos. 1. philosopher **2.** philosophical

philosophy (fɪ'lɒsəfɪ) *n.* **1.** pursuit of wisdom **2.** study of realities and general principles **3.** system of theories on nature of things or on conduct **4.** calmness of mind —**phi'losopher** *n.* one who studies, possesses or originates philosophy —**philo'sophic(al)** *a.* **1.** of, like philosophy **2.** wise, learned **3.** calm, stoical —**phi'losophize** *or* **-phise** *vi.* **1.** reason like philosopher **2.** theorize **3.** moralize

philtre *or U.S.* **philter** ('fɪltə) *n.* love potion

phlebitis (flɪ'baɪtɪs) *n.* inflammation of a vein

phlegm (flɛm) *n.* **1.** viscid substance formed by mucous membrane and ejected by coughing *etc.* **2.** calmness, sluggishness —**phlegmatic(al)** (flɛg'mætɪk(ə)l) *a.* **1.** not easily agitated **2.** composed

phloem ('fləʊɛm) *n.* tissue in higher plants that conducts synthesized food substances to all parts of plant

phlogiston (flɒ'dʒɪstɒn, -tən) *n. Chem.* hypothetical substance formerly thought to be present in all combustible materials

phlox (flɒks) *n.* any of chiefly N Amer. genus of flowering plants (*pl.* **phlox, -es**)

phobia ('fəʊbɪə) *n.* **1.** fear, aversion **2.** unreasoning dislike

-phobia (*n. comb. form*) extreme abnormal fear of or aversion to, as in *acrophobia, claustrophobia* —**phobe** (*n. comb. form*) one that fears or hates, as in *xenophobe* —**-phobic** (*a. comb. form*)

Phoenician (fə'nɪʃɪən, -'niːʃən) *n.* **1.** member of ancient Semitic people of NW Syria **2.** extinct language of this people —*a.* **3.** of Phoenicia, Phoenicians or their language

phoenix *or U.S.* **phenix** ('fiːnɪks) *n.* **1.** legendary bird **2.** unique thing

phone (fəʊn) *n./v. inf.* telephone —**'phonecard** *n.* **1.** public telephone operated by special card instead of coins **2.** the card used —**phone-in** *n. Rad., T.V.* programme in which listeners' or viewers' questions, comments *etc.* are telephoned to studio and broadcast live as part of discussion

-phone (*n. comb. form*) **1.** device giving off sound, as in *telephone* —(*a. comb. form*) **2.** speaking a particular language, as in *Francophone* —**-phonic** (*a. comb. form*)

phoneme ('fəʊniːm) *n. Linguis.* one of set of speech sounds in a language, that serve to distinguish one word from another —**pho'nemic** *a.* —**pho'nemics** *pl. n.* (*with sing. v.*) aspect of linguistics concerned with classification and analysis of phonemes of a language

phonetic (fə'nɛtɪk) *a.* of vocal sounds —**phone'tician** *or* **'phonetist** *n.* —**pho'netics** *pl.n.* (*with sing. v.*) science of vocal sounds

phoney *or* **phony** ('fəʊnɪ) *a. inf.* **1.** counterfeit, sham, fraudulent **2.** suspect

phono- *or before vowel* **phon-** (*comb. form*) sounds, as in *phonology*

phonograph ('fəʊnəɡrɑːf, -ɡræf) *n.* instrument recording and reproducing sounds —**phono'graphic** *a.*

phonology (fə'nɒlədʒɪ) *n.* **1.** study of speech sounds and their development **2.** system of sounds in a language —**phono'logic(al)** *a.* —**pho'nologist** *n.*

phosphorus ('fɒsfərəs) *n.* toxic, flammable, nonmetallic element which appears luminous in the dark —**'phosphate, 'phosphide, 'phosphite** *n.* compounds of phosphorus —**'phosphor** *n.* substance capable of emitting light when irradiated with particles of electromagnetic radiation —**phospho'resce** *vi.* exhibit phosphorescence —**phospho'rescence** *n.* faint glow in the dark —**phos'phoric** *a.* of or containing phosphorus with valence of five —**'phosphorous** *a.* of or containing phosphorus in trivalent state

photo ('fəʊtəʊ) *n. inf.* photograph (*pl.* **-s**)

photo- 359 **physiography**

—photo finish photo taken at end of race to show placing of contestants

photo- (*comb. form*) light, as in *photometer, photosynthesis*

photocell ('fəutəusel) *n.* device in which photoelectric or photovoltaic effect or photoconductivity is used to produce current or voltage when exposed to light or other electromagnetic radiation (*also* **photoelectric cell, electric eye**)

photochemistry (fəutəu'kemistri) *n.* study of chemical action of light

photoconductivity (fəutəukɒndʌk'tiviti) *n.* change in electrical conductivity of certain substances as a result of absorption of electromagnetic radiation

photocopy ('fəutəukɒpi) *n.* **1.** photographic reproduction —*vt.* **2.** make photocopy of —'**photocopier** *n.* instrument using light-sensitive photographic materials to reproduce written, printed or graphic work

photoelectricity (fəutəuilek'trisiti) *n.* electricity produced or affected by action of light —**photoe'lectric** *a.* of electric or electronic effects caused by light or other electromagnetic radiation —**photoelectric cell** *see* PHOTOCELL

photoelectron (fəutəui'lektrɒn) *n.* electron liberated from metallic surface by action of beam of light

Photofit ('fəutəufit) *n.* **R** method of combining photographs of facial features, hair *etc.* into composite picture of face: used by police to trace suspects, criminals *etc.*

photoflood ('fəutəuflʌd) *n.* highly incandescent tungsten lamp used for indoor photography, television *etc.*

photogenic (fəutə'dʒenik) *a.* (*esp.* of person) capable of being photographed attractively

photograph ('fəutəgrɑ:f, -græf) *n.* **1.** picture made by chemical action of light on sensitive film —*vt.* **2.** take photograph of —**pho'tographer** *n.* —**photo'graphic** *a.* —**pho'tography** *n.*

photogravure (fəutəugrə'vjuə) *n.* **1.** process of etching, product of photography **2.** picture so reproduced

photolithography (fəutəuli'θɒgrəfi) *n.* art of printing from photographs transferred to stone or metal plate —**photolitho-'graphic** *a.*

photometer (fəu'tɒmitə) *n.* instrument for measuring intensity of light —**pho'tometry** *n.*

photomontage (fəutəumɒn'tɑ:ʒ) *n.* **1.** technique of producing composite picture by combining several photographs **2.** composite picture so produced

photon ('fəutɒn) *n.* quantum of electromagnetic radiation energy, as of light *etc.* having both particle and wave behaviour

photosensitive (fəutəu'sensitiv) *a.* sensitive to electromagnetic radiation, *esp.* light —**photosensi'tivity** *n.* —**photo'sensi-tize** *or* -**tise** *vt.*

Photostat ('fəutəustæt) *n.* **1.** R apparatus for obtaining direct, facsimile, photographic reproductions of documents, manuscripts, drawings *etc.*, without printing from negatives —*vt.* **2.** take Photostat copy of

photosynthesis (fəutəu'sinθisis) *n.* process by which green plant uses sun's energy to build up carbohydrate reserves

phototropism (fəutəu'trəupizəm) *n.* growth response of plant parts to stimulus of light

photovoltaic effect (fəutəuvɒl'teiik) effect when electromagnetic radiation falls on thin film of one solid deposited on surface of dissimilar solid producing a difference in potential between the two materials

phrase (freiz) *n.* **1.** group of words **2.** pithy expression **3.** mode of expression —*vt.* **4.** express in words —**phraseology** (freizi-'ɒlədʒi) *n.* manner of expression, choice of words —**phrasal verb** phrase consisting of verb and preposition, oft. with meaning different to the parts (*eg* take in)

phrenology (fri'nɒlədʒi) *n.* **1.** formerly, study of skull's shape **2.** theory that character and mental powers are indicated by shape of skull —**phreno'logical** *a.* —**phre'nologist** *n.*

phut (fʌt) *n. inf.* dull, heavy sound —**go phut** collapse

phylactery (fi'læktəri) *n.* leather case containing religious texts worn by Jewish men

phylum ('failəm) *n.* **1.** major taxonomic division of animals and plants that contain one or more classes **2.** group of related language families or linguistic stocks (*pl.* -**la** (-lə))

phys. 1. physical **2.** physician **3.** physics **4.** physiological **5.** physiology

physic ('fizik) *n.* **1.** *rare* medicine, *esp.* cathartic —*pl.* **2.** (*with sing. v.*) science of properties of matter and energy —'**physical** *a.* **1.** bodily, as opposed to mental or moral **2.** material **3.** of physics of body —'**physically** *adv.* —**phy'sician** *n.* qualified medical practitioner —'**physicist** *n.* one skilled in, or student of physics —**physical chemistry** chemistry concerned with way in which physical properties of substances depend on their chemical structure, properties and reactions —**physical education** training and practice in sports, gymnastics *etc.* —**physical geography** branch of geography that deals with natural features of earth's surface —**physical jerks** *sl.* physical exercises —**physical science** any science concerned with nonliving matter, such as physics, chemistry *etc.* —**physical training** method of keeping fit by following course of bodily exercises

physiognomy (fizi'ɒnəmi) *n.* **1.** judging character by face **2.** face **3.** outward appearance of something

physiography (fizi'ɒgrəfi) *n.* science of the earth's surface —**physi'ographer** *n.*

physiology (fɪzɪ'ɒlədʒɪ) n. science of normal function of living things —**physi-'ologist** n.

physiotherapy (fɪzɪəʊ'θerəpɪ) n. therapeutic use of physical means, as massage etc. —**physio'therapist** n.

physique (fɪ'ziːk) n. bodily structure, constitution and development

pi¹ (paɪ) n. 1. 16th letter in Gr. alphabet (Π, π) 2. Maths. ratio of circumference of circle to its diameter (pl. -s)

pi² or **pie** (paɪ) n. 1. jumbled pile of printer's type 2. jumbled mixture (pl. **pies**) —vt. 3. spill and mix (set type) indiscriminately 4. mix up (**pied** pt./pp., '**piing**, '**pieing** pr.p.)

pia mater ('paɪə 'meɪtə) innermost of three membranes that cover brain and spinal cord

piano (pɪ'ænəʊ) n. 1. (orig. **pianoforte** (pɪænəʊ'fɔːtɪ)) musical instrument with strings which are struck by hammers worked by keyboard (pl. -s) —a./adv. ('pjɑːnəʊ) 2. Mus. to be performed softly —**pia'nissimo** a./adv. Mus. to be performed very quietly —'**pianist** n. performer on piano —**Pia'nola** n. R mechanically played piano —**piano accordion** accordion in which right hand plays pianolike keyboard (also **ac'cordion**) —**piano accordionist**

piazza (pɪ'ætsə; It. 'pjattsa) n. square, marketplace

pibroch ('piːbrɒx) n. form of bagpipe music

pica ('paɪkə) n. 1. printing type of 6 lines to the inch (also **em, pica em**) 2. formerly, size of type equal to 12 point 3. typewriter type size (10 letters to inch)

picador ('pɪkədɔː) n. mounted bullfighter with lance

picaresque (pɪkə'resk) a. (of fiction) episodic and dealing with adventures of rogues

piccalilli ('pɪkəlɪlɪ) n. pickle of mixed vegetables in mustard sauce

piccaninny or **pickaninny** (pɪkə'nɪnɪ) n. offens. small Negro child —'**piccanin** n. SA male Afr. child

piccolo ('pɪkələʊ) n. small flute (pl. -s)

pick¹ (pɪk) vt. 1. choose, select carefully 2. pluck, gather 3. peck at 4. pierce with something pointed 5. find occasion for —n. 6. act of picking 7. choicest part —**picked** a. selected with care —'**pickings** pl.n. 1. gleanings 2. odds and ends of profit —'**picky** a. inf. fussy; finicky —'**picklock** n. instrument for opening locks —**pick-me-up** n. inf. 1. tonic 2. stimulating drink —'**pickpocket** n. one who steals from another's pocket —**pick-up** n. 1. device for conversion of mechanical energy into electric signals, as in record player etc. 2. small truck —**pick on** find fault with —**pick up 1.** raise, lift 2. collect 3. improve, get better 4. accelerate

pick² (pɪk) n. tool with curved iron crossbar and wooden shaft, used for

breaking up hard ground or masonry —'**pickaxe** n. pick

pickaback ('pɪkəbæk) n. see PIGGYBACK

picket ('pɪkɪt) n. 1. prong, pointed stake 2. party of trade unionists posted to deter would-be workers during strike 3. post as picket 4. beset with pickets 5. tether to peg —**picket fence** fence of pickets —**picket line** line of people acting as pickets

pickle ('pɪk²l) n. 1. food preserved in brine, vinegar etc. 2. liquid used for preserving 3. awkward situation 4. mischievous child —pl. 5. pickled vegetables —vt. 6. preserve in pickle —'**pickled** a. inf. drunk

picnic ('pɪknɪk) n. 1. pleasure excursion during which food is consumed outdoors —vi. 2. take part in picnic ('**picnicked**, '**picnicking**)

picot ('piːkəʊ) n. any of pattern of small loops, as on lace

picric acid ('pɪkrɪk) powerful acid used in dyeing, medicine and as ingredient in certain explosives

Pict (pɪkt) n. member of ancient race of NE Scotland —'**Pictish** a.

pictograph ('pɪktəgrɑːf) n. 1. picture or symbol standing for word or group of words, as in written Chinese 2. chart on which symbols are used to represent values (also '**pictogram**)

picture ('pɪktʃə) n. 1. drawing or painting 2. mental image 3. beautiful or picturesque object —pl. 4. cinema —vt. 5. represent in, or as in, a picture —**pic'torial** a. 1. of, in, with, painting or pictures 2. graphic —n. 3. newspaper with pictures —**pic'torially** adv. —**picturesque** (pɪktʃə'resk) a. 1. such as would be effective in picture 2. striking, vivid —**picture card** see **court card** at COURT —**picture moulding 1.** edge around framed picture 2. moulding or rail near top of wall from which pictures are hung (also **picture rail**) —**picture postcard** postcard with picture on one side —**picture window** large window having single pane of glass, usu. facing view

piddling ('pɪdlɪŋ) a. inf. petty; trifling

pidgin ('pɪdʒɪn) n. language made up of elements of two or more other languages

pie (paɪ) n. 1. baked dish of meat or fruit etc., usu. with pastry crust 2. obs. magpie —**pie chart** circular graph divided into sectors proportional to magnitudes of quantities represented —**pie in the sky** inf. illusory hope of some future good

piebald ('paɪbɔːld) a. 1. irregularly marked with black and white 2. motley —n. 3. piebald horse or other animal —**pied** a. 1. piebald 2. variegated

piece (piːs) n. 1. bit, part, fragment 2. single object 3. literary or musical composition etc. 4. sl. young woman 5. small object used in draughts, chess etc. —vt. 6. (with together) mend, put together —**piece goods** goods, esp. fabrics, made in standard widths and lengths —'**piecemeal** adv. by, in, or into pieces, a bit at a time

—**'piecework** *n.* work paid for according to quantity produced

pièce de résistance (pjɛs də rezisˈtɑːs) *Fr.* principal item

pied-à-terre (pjetaˈtɛːr) *Fr.* flat or other lodging for occasional use (*pl.* **pieds-à-terre** (pjetaˈtɛːr))

pier (pɪə) *n.* **1.** structure running into sea as landing stage **2.** piece of solid upright masonry, *esp.* supporting bridge —**pier glass** tall narrow mirror designed to hang on wall between windows

pierce (pɪəs) *vt.* **1.** make hole in **2.** make a way through —**'piercing** *a.* keen, penetrating

Pierrot (ˈpɪərəʊ; *Fr.* pjɛˈro) *n.* pantomime character, clown

piety (ˈpaɪtɪ) *n.* **1.** godliness **2.** devoutness, goodness **3.** dutifulness —**'pietism** *n.* exaggerated or affected piety

piezoelectric effect (paɪːzəʊɪˈlɛktrɪk) or **piezoelectricity** (paɪːzəʊɪlɛkˈtrɪsɪtɪ) *n. Phys.* **1.** production of electricity or electric polarity by applying mechanical stress to certain crystals **2.** converse effect in which stress is produced in crystal as result of applied potential difference

piffle (ˈpɪfˈl) *n. inf.* rubbish, twaddle, nonsense

pig (pɪg) *n.* **1.** wild or domesticated mammal killed for pork, ham, bacon **2.** *inf.* greedy, dirty person **3.** *sl.* policeman **4.** oblong mass of smelted metal —*vi.* **5.** (of sow) produce litter (**-gg-**) —**'piggery** *n.* **1.** place for keeping, breeding pigs **2.** greediness —**'piggish** *a.* **1.** dirty **2.** greedy **3.** stubborn —**'piggy** *n.* child's word for a pig —**'piglet** *n.* young pig —**piggy bank** child's bank shaped like pig with slot for coins —**pig-headed** *a.* obstinate —**pig iron** crude iron produced in blast furnace and poured into moulds —**'pigskin** *n.* **1.** skin of domestic pig **2.** leather made of this skin **3.** US *inf.* football —*a.* **4.** made of pigskin —**'pigsty** or U.S. **'pigpen** *n.* pen for pigs; sty **2.** UK untidy place —**'pigswill** *n.* waste food *etc.* fed to pigs (*also* **pig's wash**) —**'pigtail** *n.* plait of hair hanging from back or either side of head

pigeon (ˈpɪdʒɪn) *n.* **1.** bird of many wild and domesticated varieties, oft. trained to carry messages **2.** *inf.* concern, responsibility (*oft. in* **it's his, her** *etc.*, **pigeon**) —**'pigeonhole** *n.* **1.** compartment for papers in desk *etc.* —*vt.* **2.** defer **3.** classify —**pigeon-toed** *a.* with feet, toes turned inwards

piggyback (ˈpɪgɪbæk) *or* **pickaback** *n.* ride on back of man or animal, given to child

pigment (ˈpɪgmənt) *n.* colouring matter, paint or dye —**pigmenˈtation** *n.* **1.** coloration in plants, animals or man caused by presence of pigments **2.** deposition of pigment in animals, plants or man

pigmy (ˈpɪgmɪ) *see* PYGMY

pike[1] (paɪk) *n.* any of various types of large, predatory freshwater fishes

pike[2] (paɪk) *n.* spear formerly used by infantry

pilaster (pɪˈlæstə) *n.* square column, usu. set in wall

pilau (pɪˈlaʊ), **pilaf, pilaff** (ˈpɪlæf), or **pilaw** (pɪˈlɔː) *n.* Oriental dish of meat or fowl boiled with rice, spices *etc.*

pilchard (ˈpɪltʃəd) *n.* small sea fish like the herring

pile[1] (paɪl) *n.* **1.** heap **2.** great mass of building —*vt.* **3.** heap (up), stack (load) —*vi.* **4.** (*with* in, out, off *etc.*) move in a group —**pile-up** *n. inf.* multiple collision of vehicles —**atomic pile** nuclear reactor —**pile up 1.** gather or be gathered in pile **2.** *inf.* (cause to) crash

pile[2] (paɪl) *n.* beam driven into the ground, *esp.* as foundation for building in water or wet ground —**'piledriver** *n.* machine for driving down piles

pile[3] (paɪl) *n.* **1.** nap of cloth, *esp.* of velvet, carpet *etc.* **2.** down

piles (paɪlz) *pl.n.* tumours of veins of rectum, haemorrhoids

pilfer (ˈpɪlfə) *v.* steal in small quantities

pilgrim (ˈpɪlgrɪm) *n.* **1.** one who journeys to sacred place **2.** wanderer, wayfarer —**'pilgrimage** *n.* —**the Pilgrim Fathers** *or* **Pilgrims** English Puritans who founded Plymouth Colony in Massachusetts

pill (pɪl) *n.* **1.** small ball of medicine swallowed whole **2.** anything disagreeable which has to be endured —**'pillbox** *n.* **1.** small box for pills **2.** small round hat —**the pill** oral contraceptive

pillage (ˈpɪlɪdʒ) *v.* **1.** plunder, ravage, sack —*n.* **2.** seizure of goods, *esp.* in war **3.** plunder

pillar (ˈpɪlə) *n.* **1.** slender, upright structure, column **2.** prominent supporter —**pillar box** UK red pillar-shaped public letter box situated on pavement

pillion (ˈpɪljən) *n.* seat, cushion, for passenger behind rider of motorcycle or horse

pillory (ˈpɪlərɪ) *n.* **1.** frame with holes for head and hands in which offender was formerly confined and exposed to public abuse and ridicule —*vt.* **2.** expose to ridicule and abuse **3.** set in pillory (**'pilloried, 'pillorying**)

pillow (ˈpɪləʊ) *n.* **1.** cushion for the head, *esp.* in bed —*vt.* **2.** lay on, or as on, pillow —**'pillowcase** *or* **'pillowslip** *n.* removable washable cover of cotton *etc.* for pillow

pilot (ˈpaɪlət) *n.* **1.** person qualified to fly an aircraft or spacecraft **2.** one qualified to take charge of ship entering or leaving harbour **3.** steersman **4.** guide —*a.* **5.** experimental and preliminary —*vt.* **6.** act as pilot to **7.** steer —**'pilotage** *n.* **1.** act of piloting ship or aircraft **2.** pilot's fee —**pilot fish** small fish of tropical and subtropical seas which oft. accompanies sharks —**pilot house** *Naut.* enclosed structure on bridge of vessel from which it can be navigated; wheelhouse —**pilot lamp** small light in electric circuit that lights when current is on —**pilot light 1.** small auxiliary flame lighting main burner in gas appliance *etc.* **2.** small electric light as indicator —**pilot officer** most junior commissioned rank in British Royal Air Force and in certain other air forces

pilule ('pɪljuːl) *n.* small pill

pimento (pɪ'mɛntəʊ) *n.* **1.** allspice **2.** sweet red pepper (*pl.* **-s**) (*also* **pimiento** (pɪ'mjɛntəʊ, -'mɛn-))

pimp (pɪmp) *n.* **1.** one who solicits for prostitute —*vi.* **2.** act as pimp

pimpernel ('pɪmpənɛl, -n'l) *n.* any of several plants with small scarlet, blue or white flowers closing in dull weather

pimple ('pɪmp'l) *n.* small pus-filled spot on skin

pin (pɪn) *n.* **1.** short thin piece of stiff wire with point and head, for fastening **2.** wooden or metal peg or rivet —*vt.* **3.** fasten with pin **4.** seize and hold fast (-**nn**-) —'**pinball** *n.* electrically operated table game, where small ball is shot through various hazards —'**pincushion** *n.* small cushion in which pins are stuck ready for use —'**pinhead** *n.* **1.** head of pin **2.** something very small **3.** *sl.* stupid person —**pin money** trivial sum —'**pinpoint** *vt.* mark exactly —'**pinprick** *n.* **1.** slight puncture made (as if) by pin **2.** small irritation —*vt.* **3.** puncture (as if) with pin —'**pinstripe** *n.* in textiles, very narrow stripe in fabric or fabric itself —**pin tuck** narrow, ornamental fold, *esp.* on shirt fronts *etc.* —'**pinwheel** *n. see* CATHERINE WHEEL (sense 1) —**on pins and needles** in a state of anxious suspense —**pins and needles** *inf.* tingling sensation in fingers *etc.* caused by return of normal blood circulation after its temporary impairment

pinafore ('pɪnəfɔː) *n.* **1.** apron **2.** dress with a bib top (*also* **pinafore dress**)

pince-nez ('pænsneɪ, 'pɪns-; *Fr.* pɛ̃s'ne) *n.* eyeglasses kept on nose by spring (*pl.* **pince-nez**)

pincers ('pɪnsəz) *pl.n.* **1.** tool for gripping, composed of two limbs crossed and pivoted **2.** claws of lobster *etc.*

pinch (pɪntʃ) *vt.* **1.** nip, squeeze **2.** stint **3.** *inf.* steal **4.** *inf.* arrest —*n.* **5.** nip **6.** as much as can be taken up between finger and thumb **7.** stress **8.** emergency —'**pinchbar** *n.* jemmy

pinchbeck ('pɪntʃbɛk) *n.* **1.** zinc and copper alloy —*a.* **2.** counterfeit, flashy

pine[1] (paɪn) *n.* **1.** any of a genus of evergreen coniferous trees **2.** its wood —**pine cone** seed-producing structure of pine tree

pine[2] (paɪn) *vi.* **1.** yearn **2.** waste away with grief

pineal ('pɪnɪəl) *a.* shaped like pine cone —**pineal gland** small cone-shaped gland situated at base of brain

pineapple ('paɪnæp'l) *n.* **1.** tropical plant with spiny leaves bearing large edible fruit **2.** the fruit

ping (pɪŋ) *n.* **1.** short high-pitched resonant sound, as of bullet striking metal or sonar echo —*vi.* **2.** make such noise

Ping-Pong ('pɪŋpɒŋ) *n.* **R** table tennis

pinion[1] ('pɪnjən) *n.* **1.** bird's wing —*vt.* **2.** disable or confine by binding wings, arms *etc.*

pinion[2] ('pɪnjən) *n.* small cogwheel

pink (pɪŋk) *n.* **1.** pale reddish colour **2.** garden plant **3.** best condition, fitness —*a.* **4.** of colour pink —*vt.* **5.** pierce **6.** ornament with perforations or scalloped, indented edge —*vi.* **7.** (of engine) knock

pinkie *or* **pinky** ('pɪŋkɪ) *n.* US, *Scot.* little finger

pinnace ('pɪnɪs) *n.* ship's tender

pinnacle ('pɪnək'l) *n.* **1.** highest pitch or point **2.** mountain peak **3.** pointed turret on buttress or roof

pinnate ('pɪneɪt, 'pɪnɪt) *a.* **1.** like feather **2.** (of compound leaves) having leaflets growing opposite each other in pairs on either side of stem

pinny ('pɪnɪ) *n. inf.* pinafore

pint (paɪnt) *n.* liquid measure, half a quart, 1/8 gallon (.568 litre) —**pint-size** *or* **pint-sized** *a. inf.* very small

pintle ('pɪnt'l) *n.* pivot pin

pinto ('pɪntəʊ) US *a.* **1.** marked with patches of white; piebald —*n.* **2.** pinto horse (*pl.* **-s**)

pin-up *n. inf.* picture of sexually attractive person, *esp.* (partly) naked

pion ('paɪɒn) *or* **pi meson** *n. Phys.* meson having positive or negative charge and rest mass 273 times that of electron, or no charge and rest mass 264 times that of electron

pioneer (paɪə'nɪə) *n.* **1.** explorer **2.** early settler **3.** originator **4.** one of advance party preparing road for troops —*vi.* **5.** act as pioneer or leader

pious ('paɪəs) *a.* **1.** devout **2.** righteous

pip[1] (pɪp) *n.* seed in fruit

pip[2] (pɪp) *n.* **1.** high-pitched sound used as time signal on radio **2.** spot on playing cards, dice or dominoes **3.** *inf.* star on junior officer's shoulder showing rank

pip[3] (pɪp) *n.* disease of fowl —**give someone the pip** *sl.* annoy someone

pip[4] (pɪp) *vt.* UK *sl.* **1.** wound, *esp.* with gun **2.** defeat (person), *esp.* when his success seems certain (*oft. in* **pip at the post**) **3.** blackball, ostracize (-**pp**-)

pipe (paɪp) *n.* **1.** tube of metal or other material **2.** tube with small bowl at end for smoking tobacco **3.** musical instrument, whistle **4.** wine cask —*pl.* **5.** bagpipes —*v.* **6.** play on pipe **7.** utter (something) shrilly —*vt.* **8.** convey by pipe **9.** ornament with a piping or fancy edging —'**piper** *n.* player of pipe or bagpipes —'**piping** *n.* **1.** system of pipes **2.** decoration of icing on cake **3.** fancy edging or trimming on clothes **4.** act or art of playing pipe, *esp.* bagpipes —'**pipeclay** *n.* **1.** white clay used in manufacture of tobacco pipes *etc.* and for whitening leather *etc.* —*vt.* **2.** whiten with pipeclay —**pipe cleaner** short length of thin wires twisted so as to hold tiny tufts of yarn: used to clean stem of tobacco pipe —**pipe dream** fanciful, impossible plan *etc.* —'**pipeline** *n.* **1.** long pipe for transporting oil, water *etc.* **2.** means of communication —**pipe down** *sl.* stop talking, making noise *etc.* —**pipe up 1.** commence singing or playing musical instrument **2.** speak up, *esp.* in shrill voice —**in the pipeline 1.** yet to come **2.** in process of completion *etc.*

pipette (pɪ'pɛt) *n.* slender glass tube to transfer fluids from one vessel to another

pipit ('pɪpɪt) *n.* any of various songbirds, *esp.* meadow pipit

pippin ('pɪpɪn) *n.* any of several kinds of apple

pipsqueak ('pɪpskwiːk) *n. inf.* insignificant or contemptible person or thing

piquant ('piːkənt, -kɑːnt) *a.* **1.** pungent **2.** stimulating —'**piquancy** *or* '**piquant- ness** *n.*

pique (piːk) *n.* **1.** feeling of injury, baffled curiosity or resentment —*vt.* **2.** hurt pride of **3.** irritate **4.** stimulate

piranha *or* **piraña** (pɪ'rɑːnjə) *n.* any of various small voracious freshwater fishes of tropical Amer.

pirate ('paɪrɪt) *n.* **1.** sea robber **2.** publisher *etc.* who infringes copyright —*n./a.* **3.** (person) broadcasting illegally —*vt.* **4.** use or reproduce (artistic work *etc.*) illicitly —'**piracy** *n.* —**pi'ratic(al)** *a.* —**pi'ratical- ly** *adv.*

pirouette (pɪrʊ'ɛt) *n.* **1.** spinning round on the toe —*vi.* **2.** perform pirouette

Pisces ('paɪsiːz, 'pɪ-) *pl.n.* (fishes) 12th sign of zodiac, operative *c.* Feb. 19th-Mar. 20th —**piscatorial** (pɪskə'tɔːrɪəl) *or* **piscatory** ('pɪskətərɪ) *a.* of fishing or fishes —**piscine** ('pɪsaɪn) *a.* of fish

pistachio (pɪ'stɑːʃɪəʊ) *n.* **1.** small hard- shelled, sweet-tasting nut **2.** tree producing it (*pl.* **-s**)

pistil ('pɪstɪl) *n.* seed-bearing organ of flower —'**pistillate** *a.* (of plants) **1.** having pistils but no anthers **2.** producing pistils

pistol ('pɪstʳl) *n.* **1.** small firearm for one hand —*vt.* **2.** shoot with pistol (**-ll-**)

piston ('pɪstən) *n.* in internal-combustion engine, steam engine *etc.*, cylindrical part propelled to and fro in hollow cylinder by pressure of gas *etc.* to convert reciprocat- ing motion to rotation

pit¹ (pɪt) *n.* **1.** deep hole in ground **2.** mine or its shaft **3.** depression **4.** part of theatre occupied by orchestra (*also* **orchestra pit**) **5.** enclosure where animals were set to fight **6.** servicing, refuelling area on motor-racing track —*vt.* **7.** set to fight, match **8.** mark with small dents or scars (**-tt-**) —'**pitfall** *n.* **1.** any hidden danger **2.** covered pit for catching animals or men —'**pithead** *n.* top of mine shaft and buildings *etc.* around it

pit² (pɪt) *chiefly US n.* **1.** stone of cherry *etc.* —*vt.* **2.** extract stone from (fruit) (**-tt-**)

pitapat ('pɪtəpæt) *adv.* **1.** with quick light taps —*vi.* **2.** make quick light taps (**-tt-**) —*n.* **3.** such taps

pitch¹ (pɪtʃ) *vt.* **1.** cast or throw **2.** set up **3.** set the key of (a tune) —*vi.* **4.** fall headlong **5.** (of ship) plunge lengthwise —*n.* **6.** act of pitching **7.** degree, height, intensity **8.** slope **9.** distance airscrew advances during one revolution **10.** distance between threads of screw, teeth of saw *etc.* **11.** acuteness of tone **12.** part of ground where wickets are set up **13.** *Sport* field of play **14.** station of street vendor *etc.* **15.** *inf.* persuasive sales talk —'**pitcher** *n.* US *Baseball* player who delivers ball to batter —**pitched battle 1.** battle ensuing from deliberate choice of time and place **2.** any fierce encounter, *esp.* one with large numbers —'**pitchfork** *n.* **1.** fork for lifting hay *etc.* —*vt.* **2.** throw with, as with, pitchfork —**pitch pipe** small pipe that sounds note or notes of standard frequen- cy, used for establishing correct starting note for unaccompanied singing —**pitch in 1.** cooperate; contribute **2.** begin energeti- cally —**pitch into 1.** assail physically or verbally **2.** get on with doing (something)

pitch² (pɪtʃ) *n.* **1.** dark sticky substance obtained from tar or turpentine —*vt.* **2.** coat with this —'**pitchy** *a.* **1.** covered with pitch **2.** black as pitch —**pitch-black** *or* **pitch-dark** *a.* very dark —**pitch pine** any of various kinds of resinous pine

pitchblende ('pɪtʃblɛnd) *n.* mineral com- posed largely of uranium oxide, yielding radium

pitcher ('pɪtʃə) *n.* large jug —**pitcher plant** insectivorous plant with leaves modified to form pitcherlike organs that attract and trap insects

pith (pɪθ) *n.* **1.** tissue in stems and branches of certain plants **2.** essential substance, most important part —'**pithily** *adv.* —'**pithless** *a.* —'**pithy** *a.* **1.** terse, cogent, concise **2.** consisting of pith —**pith helmet** lightweight hat made of pith that protects wearer from sun (*also* '**topee,** '**topi**)

piton ('piːtɒn) *n. Mountaineering* metal spike that may be driven into crevice and used to secure rope *etc.*

pittance ('pɪtⁿs) *n.* **1.** small allowance **2.** inadequate wages

pitter-patter ('pɪtəpætə) *n.* **1.** sound of light rapid taps or pats, as of raindrops —*vi.* **2.** make such sound —*adv.* **3.** with such sound

pituitary (pɪ'tjuːɪtərɪ) *a.* of, pert. to, endocrine gland at base of brain

pity ('pɪtɪ) *n.* **1.** sympathy, sorrow for others' suffering **2.** regrettable fact —*vt.* **3.** feel pity for ('**pitied,** '**pitying**) —'**piteous** *a.* **1.** deserving pity **2.** sad, wretched —'**pitiable** *a.* —'**pitiably** *adv.* —'**pitiful** *a.* **1.** woeful **2.** contemptible —'**pitiless** *a.* feeling no pity, hard, merciless

più (pjuː) *adv. Mus.* more (quickly *etc.*)

pivot ('pɪvət) n. 1. shaft or pin on which thing turns —vt. 2. furnish with pivot —vi. 3. hinge on pivot —'**pivotal** a. 1. of, acting as, pivot 2. of crucial importance

pixie or **pixy** ('pɪksɪ) n. fairy

pizza ('piːtsə) n. dish, orig. It., of baked disc of dough covered with wide variety of savoury toppings —**pizzeria** (piːtsə'riːə) n. place selling pizzas

pizzicato (pɪtsɪ'kɑːtəu) a./n. Mus. (note, passage) played by plucking string of violin etc. with finger

pl. 1. place 2. plate 3. plural

plaas (plɑːs) n. SA farm

placard ('plækɑːd) n. 1. paper or card with notice on one side for posting up or carrying; poster —vt. 2. post placards on 3. advertise, display on placards

placate (plə'keɪt) vt. conciliate, pacify, appease —**pla'catory** a.

place (pleɪs) n. 1. locality, spot 2. position 3. stead 4. duty 5. town, village, residence, buildings 6. office, employment 7. seat, space —vt. 8. put in particular place 9. set 10. identify 11. make (order, bet etc.) —'**placement** n. 1. act of placing or state of being placed 2. arrangement, position 3. process of finding employment —**place kick** Football kick in which ball is placed in position before it is kicked —**place-kick** v. kick (ball) in this way —**place mat** small mat serving as individual table cover for person at meal —**place setting** cutlery, crockery and glassware laid for one person at dining table

placebo (plə'siːbəu) n. sugar pill etc. given to unsuspecting patient as active drug (pl. **-s, -es**)

placenta (plə'sɛntə) n. 1. organ formed in uterus during pregnancy, providing nutrients for foetus 2. afterbirth (pl. **-s, -tae** (-tiː)) —**pla'cental** a.

placer ('plæsə) n. surface sediment containing particles of gold or some other valuable mineral

placid ('plæsɪd) a. 1. calm 2. equable —**pla'cidity** n. mildness, quiet

placket ('plækɪt) n. opening at top of skirt etc. fastened with buttons, zip etc.

plagiarism ('pleɪdʒərɪzəm) n. act of taking ideas, passages etc. from an author and presenting them as one's own —'**plagiarize** or **-ise** v.

plague (pleɪg) n. 1. highly contagious disease, esp. bubonic plague 2. inf. nuisance 3. affliction —vt. 4. trouble, annoy

plaice (pleɪs) n. European flatfish

plaid (plæd) n. 1. long Highland cloak or shawl 2. checked or tartan pattern

Plaid Cymru (plaɪd 'kʌmrɪ) Welsh nationalist party

plain (pleɪn) a. 1. flat, level 2. unobstructed, not intricate 3. clear, obvious 4. easily understood 5. simple 6. ordinary 7. without decoration 8. not beautiful —n. 9. tract of level country —adv. 10. clearly —'**plainly** adv. —'**plainness** n. —**plain chocolate**

chocolate with slightly bitter flavour and dark colour —**plain clothes** civilian dress, as opposed to uniform —**plain flour** flour to which no raising agent has been added —**plain sailing** unobstructed course of action —**plain speaking** frankness, candour

plainsong ('pleɪnsɒŋ) n. style of unison unaccompanied vocal music used in medieval Church

plaint (pleɪnt) n. 1. Law statement of complaint 2. obs. lament —'**plaintiff** n. Law one who sues in court —'**plaintive** a. sad, mournful

plait (plæt) n. 1. braid of hair, straw etc. —vt. 2. form or weave into plaits

plan (plæn) n. 1. scheme 2. way of proceeding 3. project, design 4. drawing of horizontal section 5. diagram, map —vt. 6. make plan of 7. arrange beforehand (**-nn-**)

planchette (plɑːn'ʃɛt) n. small board used in spiritualism

plane¹ (pleɪn) n. 1. smooth surface 2. a level 3. carpenter's tool for smoothing wood —vt. 4. make smooth with plane —a. 5. perfectly flat or level —'**planar** a. 1. of plane 2. lying in one plane; flat —'**planer** n. planing machine

plane² (pleɪn) vi. 1. (of aeroplane) glide 2. (of boat) rise and partly skim over water —n. 3. wing of aeroplane 4. aeroplane

plane³ (pleɪn) n. tree with broad leaves

planet ('plænɪt) n. heavenly body revolving round the sun —'**planetary** a. of planets

planetarium (plænɪ'tɛərɪəm) n. 1. an apparatus that shows the movement of sun, moon, stars and planets by projecting lights on the inside of a dome 2. building in which the apparatus is housed (pl. **-s, -ia** (-ɪə))

plangent ('plændʒənt) a. resounding

plank (plæŋk) n. 1. long flat piece of sawn timber —vt. 2. cover with planks

plankton ('plæŋktən) n. minute animal and vegetable organisms floating in ocean

plant (plɑːnt) n. 1. any living organism feeding on inorganic substances and without power of locomotion 2. such an organism that is smaller than tree or shrub 3. equipment or machinery needed for manufacture 4. building and equipment for manufacturing purposes 5. heavy vehicles used for road building etc. —vt. 6. set in ground to grow 7. support, establish 8. stock with plants 9. sl. hide, esp. to deceive or observe —'**planter** n. 1. one who plants 2. ornamental pot or stand for house plants

plantain¹ ('plæntɪn) n. any of various low-growing herbs with broad leaves

plantain² ('plæntɪn) n. 1. tropical plant like banana 2. its fruit

plantation (plæn'teɪʃən) n. 1. estate for cultivation of tea, tobacco etc. 2. wood of planted trees 3. formerly, colony

plaque (plæk, plɑːk) n. 1. ornamental plate, tablet 2. plate of clasp or brooch 3.

filmy deposit on surfaces of teeth, conducive to decay

-plasm (*n. comb. form*) *Biol.* material forming cells, as in *protoplasm* —**-plasmic** (*a. comb. form*)

plasma ('plæzmə) *or* **plasm** ('plæzəm) *n.* clear yellowish fluid portion of blood —**'plasmic** *a.*

plaster ('plɑːstə) *n.* 1. mixture of lime, sand *etc.* for coating walls *etc.* 2. piece of fabric spread with medicinal or adhesive substance —*vt.* 3. apply plaster to 4. apply like plaster —**'plastered** *a. sl.* intoxicated; drunk —**'plasterer** *n.* —**'plasterboard** *n.* thin board in form of layer of plaster compressed between two layers of fibreboard, used to form or cover walls *etc.* —**plaster of Paris** ('pæris) 1. white powder that sets to hard solid when mixed with water, used for sculptures and casts *etc.* 2. hard plaster produced when this powder is mixed with water

plastic ('plæstik) *n.* 1. any of a group of synthetic products derived from casein, cellulose *etc.*, which can be readily moulded into any form and are extremely durable —*a.* 2. made of plastic 3. easily moulded, pliant 4. capable of being moulded 5. produced by moulding 6. *sl.* superficially attractive yet unoriginal or artificial —**plasticity** (plæ'stisiti) *n.* ability to be moulded —**'plasticizer** *or* **-ciser** *n.* any of number of substances added to materials to soften and improve flexibility *etc.* —**plastic bomb** bomb consisting of adhesive jellylike explosive fitted around detonator —**plastic bullet** bullet consisting of cylinder of plastic about four inches long, usu. causing less severe injuries than ordinary bullet, and used *esp.* for riot control (*also* **baton round**) —**plastic surgery** repair or reconstruction of missing or malformed parts of the body for medical or cosmetic reasons

Plasticine ('plæstisiːn) *n.* **R** modelling material like clay

plate (pleit) *n.* 1. shallow round dish 2. flat thin sheet of metal, glass *etc.* 3. utensils of gold or silver 4. device for printing 5. illustration in book 6. device used by dentists to straighten children's teeth 7. *inf.* set of false teeth —*vt.* 8. cover with thin coating of gold, silver or other metal —**'plateful** *n.* —**'plater** *n.* —**plate glass** kind of thick glass used for mirrors, windows *etc.*

plateau ('plætəʊ) *n.* 1. tract of level high land, tableland 2. period of stability (*pl.* **-s**, **-eaux** (-əʊz))

platelet ('pleitlit) *n.* minute particle occurring in blood of vertebrates and involved in clotting of blood

platen ('plæt'n) *n.* 1. *Printing* plate by which paper is pressed against type 2. roller in typewriter

platform ('plætfɔːm) *n.* 1. raised level surface or floor, stage 2. raised area in station from which passengers board

trains 3. political programme —**platform ticket** ticket for admission to railway platforms but not for travel

platinum ('plætinəm) *n.* white heavy malleable metal —**platinum-blond** *or* **platinum-blonde** *a.* 1. (of hair) of pale silver-blond colour 2. having hair of this colour

platitude ('plætitjuːd) *n.* commonplace remark —**plati'tudinous** *a.*

Platonic (plə'tɒnik) *a.* 1. of Plato or his philosophy 2. (*oft.* **p-**) (of love) purely spiritual, friendly —**Platonism** ('pleitə-nizəm) *n.* 1. teachings of Plato, Gr. philosopher, and his followers 2. philosophical theory that meanings of general words are real entities (forms) and describe particular objects *etc.* by virtue of some relationship of these to form —**Platonist** ('pleitənist) *n.*

platoon (plə'tuːn) *n.* body of soldiers employed as unit

platteland ('platəlant) *n.* **SA** rural district

platter ('plætə) *n.* flat dish

platypus ('plætipəs) *n.* small Aust. egg-laying amphibious mammal, with dense fur, webbed feet and ducklike bill (*also* **duck-billed platypus**)

plaudit ('plɔːdit) *n.* act of applause, hand-clapping

plausible ('plɔːzəb'l) *a.* 1. apparently fair or reasonable 2. fair-spoken —**plausi'bility** *n.*

play (plei) *vi.* 1. amuse oneself 2. take part in game 3. behave carelessly; trifle 4. act a part on the stage 5. perform on musical instrument 6. move with light or irregular motion, flicker *etc.* —*vt.* 7. contend with in game 8. take part in (game) 9. act the part of 10. perform (music) 11. perform on (instrument) 12. use, work (instrument) —*n.* 13. dramatic piece or performance 14. sport 15. amusement 16. manner of action or conduct 17. activity 18. brisk or free movement 19. gambling —**'player** *n.* —**'playful** *a.* lively —**'playback** *n.* 1. act or process of reproducing recording, *esp.* on magnetic tape 2. part of tape recorder serving to or used for reproducing recorded material —**'playbill** *n.* 1. poster or bill advertising play 2. programme of play —**'playboy** *n.* man, *esp.* of private means, who devotes himself to the pleasures of nightclubs, female company *etc.* —**'playground** *n.* 1. outdoor area for children's play, *esp.* one having swings *etc.* or adjoining school 2. place popular as sports or holiday resort —**'playgroup** *n.* group of young children playing regularly under adult supervision —**'playhouse** *n.* theatre —**playing card** one of set of 52 cards used in card games —**playing fields** extensive piece of ground for open-air games —**'playmate** *or* **'playfellow** *n.* friend or partner in play or recreation —**play-off** *n.* 1. *Sport* extra contest to decide winner when competitors are tied 2. *chiefly US* contest or series of games to determine championship —**'playpen** n. small enclosure, usu. portable, in which young child can be left to play in safety —**'plaything** n. toy —**'playtime** n. time for play or recreation, esp. school break —**'playwright** n. author of plays —**play back** reproduce (recorded material) on (magnetic tape) by means of tape recorder —**play off** 1. (usu. with against) manipulate as if playing game 2. take part in play-off —**play on words** pun

plaza ('plɑːzə) n. 1. open space or square 2. complex of shops etc.

PLC Public Limited Company

plea (pliː) n. 1. entreaty 2. statement of prisoner or defendant 3. excuse —**plead** vi. 1. make earnest appeal 2. address court of law —vt. 3. bring forward as excuse or plea (**'pleaded** or (US, Scot.) **pled** (pled), **'pleading**) —**'pleadings** pl.n. Law formal written statements presented alternately by plaintiff and defendant in lawsuit

please (pliːz) vt. 1. be agreeable to 2. gratify 3. delight —vi. 4. like, be willing —adv. 5. word of request —**pleasance** ('plɛzəns) n. secluded part of garden —**pleasant** ('plɛz'nt) a. pleasing, agreeable —**pleasantly** ('plɛz'ntlı) adv. —**pleasantry** ('plɛz'ntrı) n. joke, humour —**pleasurable** ('plɛʒərəb'l) a. giving pleasure —**pleasure** ('plɛʒə) n. 1. enjoyment, satisfaction 2. will, choice

pleat (pliːt) n. 1. any of various types of fold made by doubling material back on itself —vt. 2. make, gather into pleats

plebeian (plə'biːən) a. 1. belonging to the common people 2. low or rough —n. 3. one of the common people (also (offens. sl.) **pleb** (plɛb))

plebiscite ('plɛbɪsaɪt, -sɪt) n. decision by direct voting of the electorate

plectrum ('plɛktrəm) or **plectron** ('plɛktrən) n. small implement for plucking strings of guitar etc. (pl. **-tra** (-trə), **-trums** or **-tra, -trons**)

pledge (plɛdʒ) n. 1. promise 2. thing given over as security 3. toast —vt. 4. promise formally 5. bind or secure by pledge 6. give over as security

Pleiocene ('plaɪəʊsiːn) n. see PLIOCENE

Pleistocene ('plaɪstəsiːn) a. 1. of glacial period of formation —n. 2. Pleistocene epoch or rock series

plenary ('pliːnərı, 'plɛn-) a. 1. complete, without limitations, absolute 2. (of meeting etc.) with all members present

plenipotentiary (plɛnɪpə'tɛnʃərı) a./n. (envoy) having full powers

plenitude ('plɛnɪtjuːd) n. 1. completeness, entirety 2. abundance

plenty ('plɛntı) n. 1. abundance 2. quite enough —**plenteous** a. 1. ample 2. rich 3. copious —**'plentiful** a. abundant

plenum ('pliːnəm) n. 1. space as considered to be full of matter (opposed to vacuum) 2. condition of fullness (pl. **-s, -na** (-nə))

plethora ('plɛθərə) n. oversupply

pleura ('plʊərə) n. membrane lining the chest and covering the lungs (pl. **pleurae** ('plʊəriː)) —**'pleurisy** n. inflammation of the pleura

pliable ('plaɪəb'l) a. easily bent or influenced —**plia'bility** n. —**'pliancy** n. —**'pliant** a. pliable

pliers ('plaɪəz) pl.n. tool with hinged arms and jaws for gripping

plight¹ (plaɪt) n. 1. distressing state 2. predicament

plight² (plaɪt) vt. promise —**plight one's troth** make a promise, esp. of marriage

Plimsoll line ('plɪmsəl) mark on ships indicating maximum draught permitted when loaded

plimsolls or **plimsoles** ('plɪmsəlz) pl.n. rubber-soled canvas shoes

plinth (plɪnθ) n. slab as base of column etc.

Pliocene or **Pleiocene** ('plaɪəʊsiːn) a. 1. of the most recent tertiary deposits —n. 2. Pliocene epoch or rock series

plissé ('pliːseɪ, 'plɪs-) n. 1. fabric with wrinkled finish, achieved by treatment involving caustic soda 2. such finish on fabric

P.L.O. Palestine Liberation Organization

plod (plɒd) vi. walk or work doggedly (**-dd-**)

plonk¹ (plɒŋk) v. 1. drop, fall suddenly and heavily —n. 2. act or sound of this

plonk² (plɒŋk) n. inf. alcoholic drink, esp. (cheap) wine

plop (plɒp) n. 1. sound of object falling into water without splash —v. 2. (cause to) fall with such sound (**-pp-**)

plosion ('pləʊʒən) n. Phonet. sound of abrupt break or closure, esp. audible release of stop (also **ex'plosion**) —**'plosive** Phonet. a. 1. accompanied by plosion —n. 2. plosive consonant; stop

plot¹ (plɒt) n. 1. secret plan, conspiracy 2. essence of story, play etc. —vt. 3. devise secretly 4. mark position of 5. make map of —vi. 6. conspire (**-tt-**)

plot² (plɒt) n. small piece of land

plough or esp. U.S. **plow** (plaʊ) n. 1. implement for turning up soil 2. similar implement for clearing snow etc. —vt. 3. turn up with plough, furrow —vi. 4. (with through) work (at) slowly —**'ploughman** or esp. U.S. **'plowman** n. —**ploughman's lunch** meal of cheese, bread and oft. beer —**'ploughshare** or esp. U.S. **'plowshare** n. blade of plough —**the Plough** group of seven brightest stars in constellation Ursa Major (also **Charles's Wain**)

plover ('plʌvə) n. any of various shore birds, typically with round head, straight bill and long pointed wings

plow (plaʊ) US see PLOUGH

ploy (plɔɪ) n. 1. stratagem 2. occupation 3. prank

P.L.R. Public Lending Right

pluck (plʌk) vt. 1. pull, pick off 2. strip 3. sound strings of (guitar etc.) with fingers, plectrum —n. 4. courage 5. sudden pull or tug —'**pluckily** *adv.* —'**plucky** *a.* courageous

plug (plʌg) *n.* 1. thing fitting into and filling a hole 2. *Elec.* device connecting appliance to electricity supply 3. tobacco pressed hard 4. *inf.* recommendation, advertisement —*vt.* 5. stop with plug 6. *inf.* advertise (product, show *etc.*) by constant repetition, as on television 7. *sl.* punch 8. *sl.* shoot —*vi.* 9. *inf.* (*with* away) work hard (**-gg-**) —**plug in** connect (electrical appliance) with power source by means of plug

plum (plʌm) *n.* 1. stone fruit 2. tree bearing it 3. choicest part, piece, position *etc.* —*a.* 4. choice 5. dark reddish-purple colour —'**plummy** *a.* 1. of plums 2. *UK inf.* (of speech) deep, refined and somewhat drawling 3. *UK inf.* choice; desirable

plumage ('plu:mɪdʒ) *n. see* PLUME

plumb (plʌm) *n.* 1. ball of lead (**plumb bob**) attached to string used for sounding, finding the perpendicular *etc.* —*a.* 2. perpendicular —*adv.* 3. perpendicularly 4. exactly 5. *US inf.* downright 6. honestly 7. exactly —*vt.* 8. set exactly upright 9. find depth of 10. reach, undergo 11. equip with, connect to plumbing system —'**plumber** *n.* worker who attends to water and sewage systems —'**plumbing** *n.* 1. trade of plumber 2. system of water and sewage pipes —'**plumbline** *n.* cord with plumb attached

plume (plu:m) *n.* 1. feather 2. ornament of feathers or horsehair —*vt.* 3. furnish with plumes 4. pride (oneself) —'**plumage** *n.* bird's feathers collectively

plummet ('plʌmɪt) *vi.* 1. plunge headlong —*n.* 2. plumbline

plump[1] (plʌmp) *a.* 1. of rounded form, moderately fat, chubby —*v.* 2. (*oft. with* up *or* out) make, become plump

plump[2] (plʌmp) *vi.* 1. sit, fall abruptly —*vt.* 2. drop, throw abruptly —*adv.* 3. suddenly 4. heavily 5. directly —**plump for** choose, vote only for

plunder ('plʌndə) *vt.* 1. take by force 2. rob systematically —*vi.* 3. rob —*n.* 4. pillage 5. booty, spoils

plunge (plʌndʒ) *vt.* 1. put forcibly —*vi.* 2. throw oneself 3. enter, rush with violence 4. descend very suddenly —*n.* 5. dive —'**plunger** *n.* 1. rubber suction cap to unblock drains 2. pump piston —**take the plunge** *inf.* 1. embark on risky enterprise 2. get married

plunk (plʌŋk) *v.* 1. pluck (string of banjo *etc.*) 2. drop suddenly

pluperfect (plu:'pɜːfɪkt) *a./n.* (tense) expressing action completed before past point of time

plural ('plʊərəl) *a.* 1. of, denoting more than one person or thing —*n.* 2. word in its plural form —'**pluralism** *n.* 1. holding of more than one appointment, vote *etc.* 2. coexistence of different social groups *etc.* in one society —'**pluralist** *n./a.* —plu'**rality** *n.* majority of votes *etc.*

plus (plʌs) *prep.* 1. with addition of (*usu.* indicated by the sign +) —*a.* 2. to be added 3. positive —**plus fours** men's baggy knickerbockers reaching below knee, now only worn for golf *etc.*

plush (plʌʃ) *n.* 1. fabric with long nap, long-piled velvet —*a.* 2. luxurious

Pluto[1] ('plu:təʊ) *n. Gr. myth.* god of underworld; Hades —**Plu'tonian** *a.* pert. to Pluto or the infernal regions, dark —**plutonic** (plu:'tɒnɪk) *a.* (of igneous rocks) derived from magma that has cooled and solidified below surface of earth

Pluto[2] ('plu:təʊ) *n.* second smallest planet and farthest known from sun

plutocracy (plu:'tɒkrəsɪ) *n.* 1. government by the rich 2. state ruled thus 3. wealthy class —'**plutocrat** *n.* wealthy man —**pluto-'cratic** *a.*

plutonium (plu:'təʊnɪəm) *n.* radioactive metallic element used *esp.* in nuclear reactors and weapons

pluvial ('plu:vɪəl) *a.* of, caused by the action of rain

ply[1] (plaɪ) *vt.* 1. wield 2. work at 3. supply pressingly 4. urge 5. keep busy —*vi.* 6. go to and fro, run regularly (**plied, 'plying**)

ply[2] (plaɪ) *n.* 1. fold or thickness 2. strand of yarn —'**plywood** *n.* board of thin layers of wood glued together with grains at right angles

Plymouth Brethren ('plɪməθ) strongly Puritanical religious sect having no organized ministry

Pm *Chem.* promethium

p.m. *or* **P.M.** 1. post meridiem (*Lat.,* after noon) 2. post-mortem

P.M. 1. Paymaster 2. Postmaster 3. Prime Minister

P.M.G. 1. Paymaster General 2. Postmaster General

PMS premenstrual syndrome

PMT premenstrual tension

pneumatic (njuː'mætɪk) *a.* of, worked by, inflated with wind or air —**pneu'matics** *pl.n.* (*with sing. v.*) branch of physics concerned with mechanical properties of gases, *esp.* air

pneumonia (njuː'məʊnɪə) *n.* inflammation of the lungs

po (pəʊ) *n. UK inf.* chamber pot (*pl.* **-s**)

Po *Chem.* polonium

P.O. 1. Petty Officer 2. postal order (*also* **p.o.**) 3. Post Office

poach[1] (pəʊtʃ) *vt.* 1. catch (game) illegally 2. trample, make swampy or soft —*vi.* 3. trespass for purpose of poaching 4. encroach

poach[2] (pəʊtʃ) *vt.* simmer (eggs, fish *etc.*) gently in water *etc.* —'**poacher** *n.*

pock (pɒk) *n.* pustule, as in smallpox *etc.*

pocket ('pɒkɪt) *n.* 1. small bag inserted in garment 2. cavity filled with ore *etc.* 3. socket, cavity, pouch or hollow 4. mass of water or air differing from that surrounding it 5. isolated group or area 6. *SA* bag of vegetables or fruit —*vt.* 7. put into one's pocket **8.** appropriate, steal —*a.* **9.** small —'**pocketbook** *n. chiefly* US small bag or case for money, papers *etc.* —'**pocketknife** *n.* small knife with one or more blades that fold into handle; penknife —**pocket money 1.** small, regular allowance given to children by parents **2.** allowance for small, occasional expenses

poco ('pəʊkəʊ; *It.* 'pɔːko) *or* **un poco** *a./adv. Mus.* little; to a small degree

pod (pɒd) *n.* **1.** long seed vessel, as of peas, beans *etc.* —*vi.* **2.** form pods —*vt.* **3.** shell (**-dd-**)

-pod *or* **-pode** (*comb. form*) indicating certain type or number of feet, as in *arthropod, tripod*

podgy ('pɒdʒɪ) *a.* short and fat

podium ('pəʊdɪəm) *n.* small raised platform (*pl.* **-s, -dia** (-dɪə))

poem ('pəʊɪm) *n.* imaginative composition in rhythmic lines —**poesy** ('pəʊɪzɪ) *n.* poetry —**poet** *n.* writer of poems ('**poetess** *fem.*) —**poetaster** (pəʊ'tæstə, -'teɪ-) *n.* would-be or inferior poet —**po'etic(al)** *a.* —**po'etically** *adv.* —'**poetry** *n.* art or work of poet, verse —**poetic justice** fitting retribution —**poetic licence** justifiable departure from conventional rules of form, fact *etc.*, as in poetry

po-faced *a.* wearing disapproving stern expression

pogey *or* **pogy** ('pəʊgɪ) *n.* C *sl.* **1.** unemployment insurance **2.** dole

pogo stick ('pəʊgəʊ) stout pole with handle at top, steps for feet and spring at bottom, so that user can spring up, down and along on it

pogrom ('pɒgrəm) *n.* organized persecution and massacre, *esp.* of Jews in Russia

poignant ('pɔɪnjənt, -nənt) *a.* **1.** moving **2.** biting, stinging **3.** vivid **4.** pungent —'**poignancy** *or* '**poignance** *n.*

poinciana (pɔɪnsɪ'ɑːnə) *n.* tropical tree with scarlet flowers

poinsettia (pɔɪn'sɛtɪə) *n. orig.* Amer. shrub, widely cultivated for its clusters of scarlet leaves, resembling petals

point (pɔɪnt) *n.* **1.** dot, mark **2.** punctuation mark **3.** item, detail **4.** unit of value **5.** position, degree, stage **6.** moment **7.** gist of an argument **8.** purpose **9.** striking or effective part or quality **10.** essential object or thing **11.** sharp end **12.** single unit in scoring **13.** headland **14.** one of direction marks of compass **15.** movable rail changing train to other rails **16.** fine kind of lace **17.** act of pointing **18.** power point **19.** printing unit, one twelfth of a pica —*pl.* **20.** electrical contacts in distributor of engine —*vi.* **21.** show direction or position by extending finger **22.** direct attention **23.** (of dog) indicate position of game by standing facing it —*vt.* **24.** aim, direct **25.** sharpen **26.** fill up joints of (brickwork *etc.*) with mortar *etc.* **27.** give value to (words *etc.*) —'**pointed** *a.* **1.** sharp **2.** direct, telling —'**pointedly** *adv.* —'**pointer** *n.* **1.** index **2.** indicating rod *etc.* used for pointing **3.**

indication **4.** dog trained to point —'**pointless** *a.* **1.** blunt **2.** futile, irrelevant —**point-blank** *a.* **1.** aimed horizontally **2.** plain, blunt —*adv.* **3.** with level aim (there being no necessity to elevate for distance) **4.** at short range —**point duty** police regulation of traffic —**point-to-point** *n.* steeplechase usu. for amateur riders only —**point of no return 1.** point at which irreversible commitment must be made to action *etc.* **2.** point in journey at which, if one continues, supplies will be insufficient for return to starting place —**point of order** question raised in meeting as to whether rules governing procedures are being breached (*pl.* **points of order**) —**point of sale** (in retail distribution) place and time when sale is made —**point of view 1.** position from which someone or something is observed **2.** mental viewpoint or attitude (*pl.* **points of view**)

pointillism ('pwæntɪlɪzəm) *n.* technique of painting elaborated from impressionism, in which dots of unmixed colour are juxtaposed on white ground so that from distance they fuse in viewer's eye into appropriate intermediate tones —'**pointillist** *n./a.*

poise (pɔɪz) *n.* **1.** composure **2.** self-possession **3.** balance, equilibrium, carriage (of body *etc.*) —*v.* **4.** (cause to) be balanced or suspended —*vt.* **5.** hold in readiness

poison ('pɔɪzⁿn) *n.* **1.** substance which kills or injures when introduced into living organism —*vt.* **2.** give poison to **3.** infect **4.** pervert, spoil —'**poisoner** *n.* —'**poisonous** *a.* —**poison ivy** N Amer. shrub or climbing plant that causes itching rash on contact —**poison-pen letter** malicious anonymous letter

poke[1] (pəʊk) *vt.* **1.** push, thrust with finger, stick *etc.* **2.** thrust —*vi.* **3.** make thrusts **4.** pry —*n.* **5.** act of poking —'**poker** *n.* metal rod for poking fire —'**poky** *or* '**pokey** *a.* small, confined, cramped

poke[2] (pəʊk) —**pig in a poke** something bought *etc.* without previous inspection

poker ('pəʊkə) *n.* card game —**poker face** *inf.* face without expression, as of poker player concealing value of his cards —**poker-faced** *a.*

pol. 1. political **2.** politics

Pol. 1. Poland **2.** Polish

polar ('pəʊlə) *a. see* POLE[2]

Polaris (pə'lɑːrɪs) *n.* **1.** brightest star in constellation Ursa Minor, situated slightly less than 1° from north celestial pole (*also* **Pole Star, North Star**) **2.** type of Amer. ballistic missile, usu. fired by submarine

Polaroid ('pəʊlərɔɪd) *n.* R **1.** type of plastic which polarizes light **2.** camera that develops print very quickly inside itself

polder ('pəʊldə, 'pɒl-) *n.* land reclaimed from the sea

pole[1] (pəʊl) *n.* **1.** long rounded piece of wood *etc.* —*vt.* **2.** propel with pole —**pole-vault** *vi.* perform or compete in the pole vault —**pole-vaulter** n. —**the pole vault** field event in which competitors attempt to clear high bar with aid of long flexible pole —**up the pole** inf. 1. slightly mad 2. in error, confused

pole² (pəul) n. 1. either of the ends of axis of earth or celestial sphere 2. either of opposite ends of magnet, electric cell etc. —**'polar** a. 1. pert. to the N and S pole, or to magnetic poles 2. directly opposite in tendency, character etc. —**po'larity** n. —**polari'zation** or **-i'sation** n. —**'polarize** or **-ise** vt. give polarity to —**polar bear** white Arctic bear —**polar circle** either Arctic Circle or Antarctic Circle —**the Pole Star** star closest to N celestial pole at any particular time, at present Polaris

poleaxe or U.S. **poleax** ('pəulæks) n. 1. battle-axe —vt. 2. hit, fell as with poleaxe

polecat ('pəulkæt) n. small animal of weasel family

polemic (pə'lɛmɪk) a. 1. controversial (also **po'lemical**) —n. 2. war of words, argument —**po'lemics** pl.n. (with sing. v.) art or practice of dispute or argument

police (pə'liːs) n. 1. the civil force which maintains public order —vt. 2. keep in order —**police dog** dog trained to help police —**po'liceman** n. member of police force (**po'licewoman** fem.) —**police state** state or country in which repressive government maintains control through police —**police station** office or head-quarters of police force of district

policy¹ ('pɒlɪsɪ) n. 1. course of action adopted, esp. in state affairs 2. prudence

policy² ('pɒlɪsɪ) n. insurance contract

poliomyelitis (pəulɪəumaɪə'laɪtɪs) n. disease of spinal cord characterized by fever and sometimes paralysis (also **infantile paralysis**)

polish ('pɒlɪʃ) vt. 1. make smooth and glossy 2. refine —n. 3. shine 4. polishing 5. substance for polishing 6. refinement

Polish ('pəulɪʃ) a. 1. of Poland —n. 2. official language of Poland

Politburo ('pɒlɪtbjuərəu) n. 1. executive committee of a Communist Party 2. supreme policy-making authority in most Communist countries

polite (pə'laɪt) a. 1. showing regard for others in manners, speech etc. 2. refined, cultured —**po'litely** adv. —**po'liteness** n. courtesy

politic ('pɒlɪtɪk) a. 1. wise 2. shrewd 3. expedient 4. cunning —**po'litical** a. of the state or its affairs —**poli'tician** n. one engaged in politics —**'politics** pl.n. 1. (with sing. v.) art of government 2. political affairs or life —**'polity** n. 1. form of government 2. organized state 3. civil government —**political asylum** refuge given to someone for political reasons —**political economy** former name for economics —**political prisoner** someone imprisoned for holding or expressing particular political beliefs —**political**

science study of state, government and politics —**political scientist**

polka ('pɒlkə) n. 1. lively dance in 2/4 time 2. music for it —**polka dot** one of pattern of bold spots on fabric etc.

poll (pəul) n. 1. voting 2. counting of votes 3. number of votes recorded 4. canvassing of sample of population to determine general opinion 5. (top of) head —vt. 6. receive (votes) 7. take votes of 8. lop, shear 9. cut horns from (animals) —vi. 10. vote —**'pollster** n. one who conducts polls —**polling booth** voting place at election —**polling station** place to which voters go during election to cast votes —**poll tax** tax levied per head of adult population (also **community charge**)

pollard ('pɒləd) n. 1. hornless animal of normally horned variety 2. tree on which a close head of young branches has been made by polling —vt. 3. make a pollard of

pollen ('pɒlən) n. fertilizing dust of flower —**'pollinate** vt. —**pollen count** measure of pollen present in air over 24-hour period

pollute (pə'luːt) vt. 1. make foul 2. corrupt 3. desecrate —**pol'lutant** n. —**pol'lution** n.

polo ('pəuləu) n. game like hockey played by teams of 4 players on horseback —**polo neck** 1. collar on garment, worn rolled over to fit closely round neck 2. sweater with such collar

polonaise (pɒlə'neɪz) n. 1. Polish dance 2. music for it

polonium (pə'ləunɪəm) n. radioactive element that occurs in trace amounts in uranium ores

poltergeist ('pɒltəgaɪst) n. noisy mischievous spirit

poltroon (pɒl'truːn) n. abject coward

poly ('pɒlɪ) n. inf. polytechnic

poly- (comb. form) many, as in polysyllabic

polyamide (pɒlɪ'æmaɪd) n. any of a class of synthetic polymeric materials

polyandry ('pɒlɪændrɪ) n. polygamy in which woman has more than one husband

polyanthus (pɒlɪ'ænθəs) n. cultivated primrose

polychrome ('pɒlɪkrəum) a. 1. having various colours —n. 2. work of art in many colours —**polychro'matic** a.

polyester (pɒlɪ'ɛstə) n. any of large class of synthetic materials used as plastics, textile fibres etc.

polygamy (pə'lɪgəmɪ) n. custom of being married to several persons at same time —**po'lygamist** n.

polyglot ('pɒlɪglɒt) a. speaking, writing in several languages

polygon ('pɒlɪgən) n. figure with many angles or sides —**po'lygonal** a.

polygraph ('pɒlɪgrɑːf, -græf) n. 1. instrument for recording pulse rate and perspiration, used esp. as lie detector 2. device for producing copies of written matter

polygyny (pə'lɪdʒənɪ) n. polygamy in which man has more than one wife

polyhedron (pɒlɪ'hiːdrən) n. solid figure contained by many faces (pl. **-s, -dra** (-drə))

polymath ('pɒlɪmæθ) n. person of great and varied learning

polymer ('pɒlɪmə) n. compound, as polystyrene, that has large molecules formed from repeated units —**poly'meric** a. of polymer —**polymeri'zation** or **-i'sation** n. —**'polymerize** or **-ise** v.

polymorphous (pɒlɪ'mɔːfəs) or **polymorphic** a. 1. having, taking or passing through many different forms or stages 2. exhibiting or undergoing polymorphism

Polynesian (pɒlɪ'niːʒən, -ʒɪən) a. 1. of Polynesia, group of Pacific islands, its people or any of their languages —n. 2. member of people of Polynesia, generally of Caucasoid features with light skin and wavy hair 3. branch of Malayo-Polynesian family of languages, including Maori and Hawaiian

polynomial (pɒlɪ'nəʊmɪəl) a. 1. of two or more names or terms —n. 2. mathematical expression consisting of sum of terms each of which is product of constant and one or more variables raised to positive or zero integral power 3. mathematical expression consisting of sum of a number of terms (also **multi'nomial**)

polyp ('pɒlɪp) n. 1. sea anemone or allied animal 2. tumour with branched roots (also **'polypus**)

polyphase ('pɒlɪfeɪz) a. (of alternating current of electricity) possessing number of regular sets of alternations

polyphony (pə'lɪfənɪ) n. polyphonic style of composition or piece of music utilizing it —**poly'phonic** a. 1. Mus. composed of relatively independent parts; contrapuntal 2. many-voiced

polystyrene (pɒlɪ'staɪriːn) n. synthetic material used esp. as white rigid foam for packing etc.

polytechnic (pɒlɪ'tɛknɪk) n. 1. college dealing mainly with various arts and crafts —a. 2. of or relating to technical instruction

polytheism ('pɒlɪθiːɪzəm, pɒlɪ'θiːɪzəm) n. belief in many gods —**'polytheist** n.

polythene ('pɒlɪθiːn) n. tough thermoplastic material

polyunsaturated (pɒlɪʌn'sætʃʊreɪtɪd) a. of group of fats that do not form cholesterol in blood

polyurethane (pɒlɪ'jʊərəθeɪn) n. class of synthetic materials, oft. in foam or flexible form

polyvalent (pɒlɪ'veɪlənt, pə'lɪvələnt) a. having more than one valency

pomace ('pʌmɪs) n. 1. pulpy residue of apples or similar fruit after crushing and pressing, as in cider-making 2. any pulpy substance left after crushing etc.

pomade (pə'mɑːd) n. 1. perfumed oil or ointment applied to hair, to make it smooth and shiny —vt. 2. put pomade on

pomander (pəʊ'mændə) n. (container for) mixture of sweet-smelling herbs etc.

pomegranate ('pɒmɪgrænɪt, 'pɒmgrænɪt) n. 1. tree cultivated for its edible fruit 2. its fruit with thick rind containing many seeds in red pulp

Pomeranian (pɒmə'reɪnɪən) n. breed of small dog

pomfret or **pomfret-cake** ('pʌmfrɪt, 'pɒm-) n. small black rounded confection of liquorice (also **Pontefract cake**)

pommel ('pʌməl, 'pɒm-) n. 1. front of saddle 2. knob of sword hilt —vt. 3. see PUMMEL

pommy ('pɒmɪ) n. (sometimes P-) A, NZ sl. British person (also **pom**)

pomp (pɒmp) n. splendid display or ceremony

pompon ('pɒmpɒn) or **pompom** ('pɒmpɒm) n. tuft of ribbon, wool, feathers etc. decorating hat, shoe etc.

pompous ('pɒmpəs) a. 1. self-important 2. ostentatious 3. (of language) inflated, stilted —**pom'posity** n.

ponce (pɒns) n. sl. 1. effeminate man 2. pimp

poncho ('pɒntʃəʊ) n. loose circular cloak with hole for head (pl. **-s**)

pond (pɒnd) n. small body, pool or lake of still water

ponder ('pɒndə) v. 1. muse, meditate, think over 2. consider, deliberate (on)

ponderous ('pɒndərəs) a. 1. heavy, unwieldy 2. boring

pong (pɒŋ) inf. n. 1. strong (unpleasant) smell —vi. 2. stink

pontiff ('pɒntɪf) n. 1. Pope 2. high priest 3. bishop —**pon'tifical** a. —**pontificate** (pɒn'tɪfɪkɪt) n. 1. dignity or office of pontiff —vi. (pɒn'tɪfɪkeɪt) 2. speak bombastically (also **'pontify**) 3. act as pontiff

pontoon[1] (pɒn'tuːn) n. flat-bottomed boat or metal drum for use in supporting temporary bridge

pontoon[2] (pɒn'tuːn) n. gambling card game (also **twenty-one**)

pony ('pəʊnɪ) n. 1. horse of small breed 2. very small glass, esp. for liqueurs —**'ponytail** n. long hair tied in one bunch at back of head —**pony trekking** act of riding ponies cross-country, esp. as pastime

poodle ('puːd'l) n. pet dog with long curly hair oft. clipped fancifully

poof (puf, puːf) or **poove** (puːv) n. sl. homosexual man

pooh (puː) interj. exclamation of disdain, contempt or disgust —**pooh-pooh** vt. express disdain or scorn for; dismiss, belittle

Pooh-Bah ('puː'bɑː) n. pompous official

pool[1] (puːl) n. 1. small body of still water 2. deep place in river or stream 3. puddle 4. swimming pool

pool[2] (puːl) n. 1. common fund or resources 2. group of people, eg typists, any of whom can work for any of several employers 3. collective stakes in various games 4.

cartel 5. variety of billiards —pl. 6. see football pools at FOOT —vt. 7. put in common fund

poop (puːp) n. ship's stern

poor (puə, pɔː) a. 1. having little money 2. unproductive 3. inadequate, insignificant 4. needy 5. miserable, pitiable 6. feeble 7. not fertile —'**poorly** adv. 1. badly —a. 2. inf. not in good health —'**poorness** n. —**poor box** box, esp. in church, used for collection of alms or money for poor —'**poorhouse** n. formerly, publicly maintained institution offering accommodation to the poor

poort (puət) n. SA narrow mountain pass

pop[1] (pɒp) vi. 1. make small explosive sound 2. inf. go or come unexpectedly or suddenly —vt. 3. cause to make small explosive sound 4. put or place suddenly (-pp-) —n. 5. small explosive sound 6. inf. nonalcoholic fizzy drink —'**popper** n. 1. person or thing that pops 2. UK inf. press stud 3. chiefly US container for cooking popcorn in —'**popcorn** n. 1. any kind of maize that puffs up when roasted 2. the roasted product —'**popgun** n. toy gun that fires pellet or cork by means of compressed air

pop[2] (pɒp) n. inf. 1. father 2. old man

pop[3] (pɒp) n. 1. music of general appeal, esp. to young people —a. inf. 2. popular

pop. 1. popular 2. population

P.O.P. Post Office Preferred (size of envelopes etc.)

pope (pəup) n. (oft. P-) bishop of Rome and head of R.C. Church —'**popery** n. offens. papal system, doctrines —'**popish** a. derogatory belonging to or characteristic of Roman Catholicism

popeyed ('pɒpaɪd) a. 1. having bulging, prominent eyes 2. staring in astonishment

popinjay ('pɒpɪndʒeɪ) n. 1. conceited or talkative person 2. obs. parrot

poplar ('pɒplə) n. tree noted for its slender tallness

poplin ('pɒplɪn) n. corded fabric usu. of cotton

poppadom or **poppadum** ('pɒpədəm) n. thin, round, crisp Indian bread

poppet ('pɒpɪt) n. 1. term of affection for small child or sweetheart 2. mushroom-shaped valve lifted from seating by applying axial force to stem (also **poppet valve**) 3. Naut. temporary supporting brace for vessel hauled on land

poppy ('pɒpɪ) n. bright-flowered plant yielding opium —**Poppy Day** inf. Remembrance Sunday

poppycock ('pɒpɪkɒk) n. inf. nonsense

popsy ('pɒpsɪ) n. old-fashioned UK sl. attractive young woman

populace ('pɒpjuləs) n. (sometimes with pl. v.) the common people, the masses

popular ('pɒpjulə) a. 1. finding general favour 2. of, by the people —**popu'larity** n. state or quality of being generally liked —populari'zation or -i'sation n. —'**popularize** or -**ise** vt. make popular —'**popularly** adv. —**popular front** (oft. P- F-) left-

wing group or party that opposes spread of fascism

populate ('pɒpjuleɪt) vt. fill with inhabitants —popu'lation n. 1. inhabitants 2. the number of such inhabitants —'**populous** a. thickly populated or inhabited

porbeagle ('pɔːbiːgəl) n. any of several sharks of northern seas (also **mackerel shark**)

porcelain ('pɔːslɪn) n. fine earthenware, china —**porcelain clay** kaolin

porch (pɔːtʃ) n. covered approach to entrance of building

porcine ('pɔːsaɪn) a. of, like pigs

porcupine ('pɔːkjupaɪn) n. any of various rodents covered with long, pointed quills

pore[1] (pɔː) vi. 1. fix eye or mind 2. (with over) study closely

pore[2] (pɔː) n. minute opening, esp. in skin —po'rosity n. —'**porous** a. 1. allowing liquid to soak through 2. full of pores

pork (pɔːk) n. pig's flesh used as food —'**porker** n. pig raised for food —'**porky** a. fleshy, fat —**porkpie hat** hat with round flat crown and brim that can be turned up or down

porn (pɔːn) or **porno** n. inf. pornography

pornography (pɔːˈnɒɡrəfɪ) n. indecent literature, films etc. —**por'nographer** n. —**porno'graphic** a. —**porno'graphically** adv.

porphyry ('pɔːfɪrɪ) n. reddish stone with embedded crystals

porpoise ('pɔːpəs) n. blunt-nosed sea mammal like dolphin (pl. **-poise, -s**)

porridge ('pɒrɪdʒ) n. 1. soft food of oatmeal etc. boiled in water 2. sl. imprisonment

porringer ('pɒrɪndʒə) n. small dish, oft. with handle, for soup, porridge etc.

port[1] (pɔːt) n. 1. harbour, haven 2. town with harbour

port[2] (pɔːt) n. 1. left side of ship or aircraft (also (formerly) '**larboard**) —v. 2. turn to left side of ship

port[3] (pɔːt) n. strong red wine

port[4] (pɔːt) n. opening in side of ship —'**porthole** n. small opening or window in side of ship

port[5] (pɔːt) Mil. vt. 1. carry (rifle etc.) diagonally across body —n. 2. this position

Port. 1. Portugal 2. Portuguese

portable ('pɔːtəbəl) n./a. (something) easily carried

portage ('pɔːtɪdʒ) n. (cost of) transport

portal ('pɔːtəl) n. large doorway or imposing gate

portcullis (pɔːtˈkʌlɪs) n. defence grating to raise or lower in front of castle gateway

portend (pɔːˈtend) vt. foretell, be an omen of —'**portent** n. 1. omen, warning 2. marvel —por'tentous a. 1. ominous, threatening 2. pompous

porter[1] ('pɔːtə) n. 1. person employed to carry burden, eg on railway 2. doorkeeper —'**porterage** n. (charge for) carrying of supplies

porter[2] ('pɔːtə) n. UK dark sweet ale

brewed from black malt —**'porterhouse** *n.* thick choice steak of beef cut from middle ribs or sirloin (*also* **porterhouse steak**)

portfolio (pɔːt'fəʊlɪəʊ) *n.* **1.** flat portable case for loose papers **2.** office of minister of state (*pl.* **-s**)

portico ('pɔːtɪkəʊ) *n.* **1.** colonnade **2.** covered walk (*pl.* **-es, -s**)

portière (pɔːtɪ'ɛə; *Fr.* pɔr'tjɛːr) *n.* curtain hung in doorway

portion ('pɔːʃən) *n.* **1.** part **2.** share **3.** helping **4.** destiny, lot —*vt.* **5.** divide into shares —**'portionless** *a.*

portly ('pɔːtlɪ) *a.* bulky, stout

portmanteau (pɔːt'mæntəʊ) *n.* leather suitcase, *esp.* one opening into two compartments (*pl.* **-s, -teaux** (-təʊz)) —**portmanteau word** word formed by joining together beginning and end of two other words (*also* **blend**)

portray (pɔː'treɪ) *vt.* make pictures of, describe —**portrait** ('pɔːtrɪt, -treɪt) *n.* likeness of (face of) individual —**portraiture** ('pɔːtrɪtʃə) *n.* —**por'trayal** *n.* act of portraying

Portuguese (pɔːtjʊ'giːz) *a.* pert. to Portugal or its inhabitants —**Portuguese man-of-war** kind of jellyfish

pose (pəʊz) *vt.* **1.** place in attitude **2.** put forward —*vi.* **3.** assume attitude, affect or pretend to be a certain character —*n.* **4.** attitude, *esp.* one assumed for effect —**'poser** *n.* one who poses —**poseur** (pəʊ'zɜː) *n.* one who assumes affected attitude to create impression

poser ('pəʊzə) *n.* puzzling question

posh (pɒʃ) *a. inf.* **1.** smart, elegant, stylish **2.** upper-class or genteel

posit ('pɒzɪt) *vt.* lay down as principle

position (pə'zɪʃən) *n.* **1.** place **2.** situation **3.** location, attitude **4.** status **5.** state of affairs **6.** employment **7.** strategic point **8.** *Mus.* vertical spacing or layout of written notes in chord —*vt.* **9.** place in position

positive ('pɒzɪtɪv) *a.* **1.** certain, sure **2.** definite, absolute, unquestionable **3.** utter, downright **4.** confident **5.** not negative **6.** greater than zero **7.** *Elec.* having deficiency of electrons —*n.* **8.** something positive **9.** *Photog.* print in which lights and shadows are not reversed —**'positively** *adv.* —**'positivism** *n.* philosophy recognizing only matters of fact and experience —**'positivist** *a./n.* (one) believing in this —**positive discrimination** provision of special opportunities for disadvantaged group —**positive feedback** *see* **feedback** (sense 1) *at* FEED

positron ('pɒzɪtrɒn) *n.* positive electron

poss. 1. possession **2.** possessive **3.** possible **4.** possibly

posse ('pɒsɪ) *n.* **1.** US body of men, *esp.* for maintaining law and order **2.** C group of trained horsemen who perform at rodeos

possess (pə'zɛs) *vt.* **1.** own **2.** (of evil spirit *etc.*) have mastery of —**pos'session** *n.* **1.** act of possessing **2.** thing possessed **3.** ownership —**pos'sessive** *a.* **1.** of, indicating possession **2.** with excessive desire to possess, control —*n.* **3.** possessive case in grammar

possible ('pɒsɪb'l) *a.* **1.** that can, or may, be, exist, happen or be done **2.** worthy of consideration —*n.* **3.** possible candidate —**possi'bility** *n.* —**'possibly** *adv.* perhaps

possum ('pɒsəm) *n. see* OPOSSUM —**play possum** pretend to be dead, asleep *etc.* to deceive opponent

post[1] (pəʊst) *n.* **1.** upright pole of timber or metal fixed firmly, usu. to support or mark something —*vt.* **2.** display **3.** put up (notice *etc.*) on wall *etc.* —**'poster** *n.* **1.** large advertising bill **2.** one who posts bills —**poster paints** *or* **colours** lustreless paints used for writing posters *etc.*

post[2] (pəʊst) *n.* **1.** official carrying of letters or parcels **2.** collection or delivery of these **3.** office **4.** situation **5.** point, station, place of duty **6.** place where soldier is stationed **7.** place held by body of troops **8.** fort —*vt.* **9.** put into official box for carriage by post **10.** supply with latest information **11.** station (soldiers *etc.*) in particular spot **12.** transfer (entries) to ledger —*adv.* **13.** in haste —**'postage** *n.* charge for delivering letters or parcels —**'postal** *a.* —**postage stamp 1.** printed paper label with gummed back for attaching to mail as official indication that required postage has been paid **2.** mark printed on envelope *etc.* serving same function —**postal order** written order, available at post office, for payment of sum of money —**'postbag** *n.* **1.** *chiefly UK* mailbag **2.** mail received by magazine, radio programme *etc.* —**'postbox** *n. chiefly UK* box into which mail is put for collection —**'postcard** *n.* stamped card sent by post —**'postcode** *or* **postal code** *n.* system of letters and numbers used to aid sorting of mail —**post-free** *adv./a.* **1.** UK with postage prepaid; postpaid **2.** free of postal charge —**'postman** *n.* man who collects or delivers post —**postman's knock** parlour game involving exchange of kisses —**'postmark** *n.* official mark with name of office *etc.* stamped on letters —**'postmaster** *or* **'postmistress** *n.* official in charge of post office —**postmaster general** executive head of postal service in certain countries (*pl.* **postmasters general**) —**post office** place where postal business is conducted —**'post'paid** *adv./a.* with postage prepaid

post- (*comb. form*) after, behind, later than, as in *postwar*. Such compounds are not given here where the meaning can easily be found from the simple word

postdate (pəʊst'deɪt) *vt.* assign date to (event *etc.*) that is later than actual date

poste restante ('pəʊst rɪ'stænt) *Fr.* department of post office where travellers' letters are kept till called for

posterior (pɒ'stɪərɪə) *a.* **1.** later **2.** hinder —*n.* **3.** the buttocks

posterity (pɒ'stɛrɪtɪ) *n.* **1.** later generations **2.** descendants

postern ('pɒstən) n. 1. private entrance 2. small door, gate

postgraduate (pəust'grædjuıt) a. 1. carried on after graduation —n. 2. student taking course of study after graduation

posthaste ('pəust'heɪst) adv. 1. with great haste —n. 2. obs. great haste

posthumous ('pɒstjuməs) a. 1. occurring after death 2. born after father's death 3. (of book etc.) published after author's death —'**posthumously** adv.

posthypnotic suggestion (pəusthɪp-'nɒtɪk) suggestion made to subject while in hypnotic trance, to be acted upon some time after emerging from trance

postilion or **postillion** (pɒ'stɪljən) n. Hist. man riding one of pair of horses drawing a carriage

postimpressionism (pəustɪm'preʃənɪzəm) n. movement in painting at end of 19th cent. which rejected naturalism and momentary effects of impressionism but adapted its use of pure colour to paint subjects with greater subjective emotion —postim'pressionist n./a.

post meridiem (mə'rɪdɪəm) see P.M.

postmortem (pəust'mɔːtəm) n. 1. analysis of recent event —a. 2. taking place after death —**postmortem examination** medical examination of dead body

postnatal (pəust'neɪt'l) a. after birth

post-obit (pəust'əubɪt, -'ɒbɪt) a. taking effect after death

postoperative (pəust'ɒpərətɪv) a. of period following surgical operation

postpone (pəust'pəun, pə'spəun) vt. put off to later time, defer —**post'ponement** n.

postprandial (pəust'prændɪəl) a. after-dinner

postscript ('pəusskrɪpt) n. 1. note added at end of letter, after signature 2. supplement added to book, document etc.

postulant ('pɒstjulənt) n. candidate for admission to religious order

postulate ('pɒstjuleɪt) vt. 1. take for granted 2. lay down as self-evident 3. stipulate —n. ('pɒstjulɪt) 4. proposition assumed without proof 5. prerequisite —postu'lation n.

posture ('pɒstʃə) n. 1. attitude, position of body —vi. 2. pose

posy ('pəuzɪ) n. bunch of flowers

pot (pɒt) n. 1. round vessel 2. cooking vessel 3. trap, esp. for crabs, lobsters 4. sl. cannabis —pl. 5. inf. a lot —vt. 6. put into, preserve in pot (-tt-) —'**potted** a. 1. preserved in a pot 2. inf. abridged —'**potbellied** a. —'**potbelly** n. 1. protruding belly 2. one having such a belly —'**potboiler** n. inf. artistic work of little merit produced quickly to make money —**pot-bound** a. (of pot plant) having grown to fill all available root space and lacking room for continued growth —'**potherb** n. any plant having leaves, stems etc. that are used in cooking —'**pothole** n. 1. pitlike cavity in rocks, usu. limestone, produced by faulting and water action 2. hole worn

in road —'**potholer** n. —'**potholing** n. UK sport in which participants explore underground caves —'**pothook** n. 1. S-shaped hook for suspending pot over fire 2. long hook for lifting hot pots etc. 3. S-shaped mark, oft. made by children when learning to write —'**pothunter** n. 1. person who hunts for profit without regard to rules of sport 2. inf. person who enters competitions for sole purpose of winning prizes —'**pot'luck** n. 1. whatever food is available without special preparation 2. choice dictated by lack of alternative (esp. in **take potluck**) —**pot plant** plant grown in flowerpot —**pot roast** meat cooked slowly in covered pot with little water —'**potsherd** n. broken fragment of pottery —**pot shot** easy or random shot —**potter's wheel** device with horizontal rotating disc, on which clay is moulded by hand —**potting shed** building in which plants are grown in flowerpots before being planted outside —**the Potteries** region of W central England in which china industries are concentrated

potable ('pəutəb'l) a. drinkable

potage (pɒ'tɑːʒ; English pəu'tɑːʒ) Fr. thick soup

potash ('pɒtæʃ) n. 1. alkali used in soap etc. 2. crude potassium carbonate

potassium (pə'tæsɪəm) n. white metallic element —**potassium nitrate** crystalline compound used in gunpowders, fertilizers and as preservative (also **salt'petre, 'nitre**)

potato (pə'teɪtəu) n. plant with tubers grown for food (pl. **-es**) —**potato crisp** see CRISP (sense 6) —**sweet potato** 1. trailing plant 2. its edible sweetish tubers

poteen (pɒ'tiːn) n. in Ireland, illicitly distilled alcoholic liquor

potent ('pəut'nt) a. 1. powerful, influential 2. (of male) capable of sexual intercourse —'**potency** n. 1. physical or moral power 2. efficacy

potentate ('pəut'nteɪt) n. ruler

potential (pə'tenʃəl) a. 1. latent, that may or might but does not now exist or act —n. 2. possibility 3. amount of potential energy 4. Elec. level of electric pressure —potenti'ality n. —**potential difference** difference in electric potential between two points in electric field

pother ('pɒðə) n. 1. commotion, fuss 2. choking cloud of smoke etc.

potion ('pəuʃən) n. dose of medicine or poison

potpourri (pəu'puərɪ) n. 1. mixture of rose petals, spices etc. 2. musical, literary medley (pl. **-s**)

pottage ('pɒtɪdʒ) n. thick soup containing vegetables and meat

potter[1] ('pɒtə) n. maker of earthenware vessels —'**pottery** n. 1. earthenware 2. place where it is made 3. art of making it

potter[2] ('pɒtə) or esp. U.S. **putter** ('pʌtə) vi. work, act in feeble, unsystematic way

potty ('pɒtɪ) a. inf. 1. (of person) mad 2. (of thing) silly, trivial

pouch (pautʃ) n. 1. small bag 2. Anat. any sac, pocket or pouchlike cavity —vt. 3. put into pouch

pouf or **pouffe** (pu:f) n. large solid cushion

poultice ('pəʊltɪs) n. soft composition of mustard, kaolin etc., applied hot to sore or inflamed parts of body

poultry ('pəʊltrɪ) n. domestic fowls collectively —'**poulterer** n. dealer in poultry

pounce (pauns) vi. 1. spring suddenly, swoop —n. 2. swoop or sudden descent

pound[1] (paund) vt. 1. beat, thump 2. crush to pieces or powder —vi. 3. walk, run heavily

pound[2] (paund) n. 1. unit of troy weight 2. unit of avoirdupois weight equal to 0.454 kg 3. monetary unit in U.K. —'**poundage** n. 1. charge of so much per pound of weight 2. charge of so much per pound sterling 3. weight expressed in pounds —**pound note** banknote valued at one pound sterling

pound[3] (paund) n. 1. enclosure for stray animals or officially removed vehicles 2. confined space

poundal ('paund'l) n. unit of force in the foot-pound-second system

pour (pɔː) vi. 1. come out in a stream, crowd etc. 2. flow freely 3. rain heavily —vt. 4. give out thus 5. cause to run out

pourboire (pur'bwa:r) Fr. tip; gratuity

pout[1] (paut) v. 1. thrust out (lips) —vi. 2. look sulky —n. 3. act of pouting —'**pouter** n. pigeon with power of inflating its crop

pout[2] (paut) n. type of food fish (pl. pout, -s)

poverty ('pɒvətɪ) n. 1. state of being poor 2. poorness 3. lack of means 4. scarcity —**poverty-stricken** a. suffering from extreme poverty —**poverty trap** situation of being unable to raise one's living standard because one is dependent on state benefits which are reduced if one gains any extra income

P.O.W. prisoner of war

powder ('paudə) n. 1. solid matter in fine dry particles 2. medicine in this form 3. gunpowder 4. face powder etc. —vt. 5. apply powder to 6. reduce to powder; pulverize —'**powdery** a. —**powder keg** 1. small barrel to hold gunpowder 2. potential source of violence etc. —**powder puff** soft pad for applying cosmetic powder —**powder room** ladies' cloakroom

power ('pauə) n. 1. ability to do or act 2. strength 3. authority 4. control 5. person or thing having authority 6. mechanical energy 7. electricity supply 8. rate of doing work 9. product from continuous multiplication of number by itself —'**powered** a. having or operated by mechanical or electrical power —'**powerful** a. —'**powerless** a. —'**powerhouse** or **power station** n. installation for generating and distributing electric power —**power point** socket on wall for plugging in electrical appliance —**power of attorney** 1. legal authority to act for another person in certain specified matters 2. document conferring such authority

powwow ('pauwau) n. 1. conference —vi. 2. confer

pox (pɒks) n. 1. one of several diseases marked by pustular eruptions of skin 2. inf. syphilis

pp or **pp.** 1. per procurationem (Lat., by proxy; for and on behalf of) 2. pianissimo

pp. pages

p.p. 1. parcel post 2. past participle 3. prepaid 4. post paid 5. by delegation to 6. on prescriptions, after meal

ppd. 1. postpaid 2. prepaid

P.P.S. 1. parliamentary private secretary 2. post postscriptum (also **p.p.s.**)

PQ Quebec

Pr Chem. praseodymium

pr. 1. pair (pl. **prs.**) 2. present 3. price 4. pronoun

P.R. 1. proportional representation 2. public relations

practical ('præktɪk'l) a. 1. given to action rather than theory 2. relating to action or real existence 3. useful 4. in effect though not in name 5. virtual —practica'**bility** n. —'**practicable** a. that can be done, used etc. —'**practically** adv. —**prac**'**titioner** n. one engaged in a profession —**practical joke** trick usu. intended to make victim appear foolish

practice ('præktɪs) n. 1. habit 2. mastery, skill 3. exercise of art or profession 4. action, not theory —v. 5. US see PRACTISE

practise or U.S. **practice** ('præktɪs) vt. 1. do repeatedly, work at to gain skill 2. do habitually 3. put into action —vi. 4. exercise oneself 5. exercise profession

praetor or **pretor** ('pri:tə, -tɔː) n. in ancient Rome, senior magistrate ranking just below consul

pragmatic (præg'mætɪk) a. 1. concerned with practical consequence 2. of the affairs of state —prag'**matical** a. —'**pragmatism** n.

prairie ('preərɪ) n. large treeless tract of grassland of Central U.S.A. and Canad. —**prairie dog** small Amer. rodent allied to marmot —**prairie oyster** drink consisting of raw egg, vinegar, salt and pepper: supposed cure for hangover

praise (preɪz) n. 1. commendation 2. fact, state of being praised —vt. 3. express approval, admiration of 4. speak well of 5. glorify —'**praiseworthy** a.

praline ('prɑːliːn) n. sweet composed of nuts and sugar

pram (præm) n. carriage for baby

prance (prɑːns) vi. 1. swagger 2. caper 3. walk with bounds —n. 4. prancing

prandial ('prændɪəl) a. of dinner

prang (præŋ) inf. v. 1. crash or damage (car, aircraft etc.) 2. damage (town etc.) by bombing —n. 3. crash in a car, aircraft etc.

prank (præŋk) n. mischievous trick or escapade, frolic

prase (preiz) n. light green translucent chalcedony

praseodymium (preɪzɪəʊ'dɪmɪəm) n. malleable element of lanthanide series of metals

prate (preɪt) vi. 1. talk idly, chatter —n. 2. idle or trivial talk

prattle ('præt'l) vi. 1. talk like child —n. 2. trifling, childish talk —'**prattler** n. babbler

prawn (prɔːn) n. edible sea crustacean like shrimp but larger

praxis ('præksɪs) n. practice, esp. as opposed to theory (pl. -es, praxes ('præksiːz))

pray (preɪ) vt. 1. ask earnestly, entreat —vi. 2. offer prayers, esp. to God —**prayer** (preə) n. 1. action, practice of praying to God 2. earnest entreaty —**prayer rug** small carpet on which Muslim kneels while saying prayers (also **prayer mat**) —**prayer wheel** Buddhism esp. in Tibet, wheel or cylinder inscribed with prayers, each revolution of which is counted as uttered prayer —**praying mantis** or **mantid** see MANTIS

pre- (comb. form) before, beforehand, as in prenatal, prerecord, preshrunk. Such compounds are not given here where the meaning can easily be found from the simple word

preach (priːtʃ) vi. 1. deliver sermon 2. give moral, religious advice —vt. 3. set forth in religious discourse 4. advocate —'**preacher** n.

preamble (priː'æmb'l) n. introductory part of story etc.

prebend ('prɛbənd) n. stipend of canon or member of cathedral chapter —'**prebendary** n. holder of this

Precambrian or **Pre-Cambrian** (priː-'kæmbrɪən) a. 1. of earliest geological era, which lasted for about 4000 000 000 years before Cambrian period —n. 2. Precambrian era

precarious (prɪ'kɛərɪəs) a. insecure, unstable, perilous

precaution (prɪ'kɔːʃən) n. 1. previous care to prevent evil or secure good 2. preventative measure —**pre'cautionary** a.

precede (prɪ'siːd) vt. go, come before in rank, order, time etc. —**precedence** ('prɛsɪdəns) n. priority in position, rank, time etc. —**precedent** ('prɛsɪdənt) n. previous example or occurrence taken as rule

precentor (prɪ'sɛntə) n. leader of singing choir or congregation

precept ('priːsɛpt) n. rule for conduct, maxim —**pre'ceptor** n. instructor —**precep'torial** a.

precinct ('priːsɪŋkt) n. 1. enclosed, limited area 2. area in town, oft. closed to traffic, reserved for particular activity 3. US administrative area of city —pl. 4. environs

precious ('prɛʃəs) a. 1. beloved, cherished 2. of great value, highly valued 3. rare —**preci'osity** n. overrefinement in art or literature —'**preciously** adv. —'**preciousness** n. —**precious metal** gold, silver or platinum —**precious stone** rare mineral, such as diamond, ruby etc., highly valued as gemstone

precipice ('prɛsɪpɪs) n. very steep cliff or rockface —**precipitous** (prɪ'sɪpɪtəs) a. sheer

precipitant (prɪ'sɪpɪtənt) a. 1. hasty, rash 2. abrupt —**pre'cipitance** or **pre'cipitancy** n.

precipitate (prɪ'sɪpɪteɪt) vt. 1. hasten happening of 2. throw headlong 3. Chem. cause to be deposited in solid form from solution —a. (prɪ'sɪpɪtɪt) 4. too sudden 5. rash, impetuous —n. (prɪ'sɪpɪtɪt) 6. substance chemically precipitated —**pre'cipitately** adv. —**precipi'tation** n. rain, snow, sleet etc.

precis or **précis** ('preɪsiː) n. abstract, summary (pl. **precis** or **précis** ('preɪsiːz))

precise (prɪ'saɪs) a. 1. definite 2. particular 3. exact, strictly worded 4. careful in observance 5. punctilious, formal —**pre'cisely** adv. —**precision** (prɪ'sɪʒən) n. accuracy

preclude (prɪ'kluːd) vt. 1. prevent from happening 2. shut out

precocious (prɪ'kəʊʃəs) a. developed, matured early or too soon —**precocity** (prɪ'kɒsɪtɪ) or **pre'cociousness** n.

precognition (priːkɒg'nɪʃən) n. Psychol. alleged ability to foresee future events —**pre'cognitive** a.

preconceive (priːkən'siːv) vt. form an idea of beforehand —**precon'ception** n.

precondition (priːkən'dɪʃən) n. necessary or required condition

precursor (prɪ'kɜːsə) n. forerunner —**pre'cursive** or **pre'cursory** a.

pred. predicate

predate (priː'deɪt) vt. 1. affix date to (document etc.) that is earlier than actual date 2. assign date to (event etc.) that is earlier than actual or previously assigned date of occurrence 3. be or occur at earlier date than; precede in time

predatory ('prɛdətərɪ) a. 1. hunting, killing other animals etc. for food 2. plundering —'**predator** n. predatory animal

predecease (priːdɪ'siːs) vt. die before (some other person)

predecessor ('priːdɪsɛsə) n. 1. one who precedes another in an office or position 2. ancestor

predestine (priː'dɛstɪn) or **predestinate** (priː'dɛstɪneɪt) vt. decree beforehand, foreordain —**predesti'nation** n.

predetermine (priːdɪ'tɜːmɪn) vt. 1. determine beforehand 2. influence, bias —**predetermi'nation** n.

predicament (prɪ'dɪkəmənt) n. perplexing, embarrassing or difficult situation

predicant ('prɛdɪkənt) a. 1. of preaching

—n. 2. member of religious order founded for preaching, *esp.* Dominican

predicate ('predıkeıt) *vt.* 1. affirm, assert 2. (*with* on *or* upon) *chiefly US* base (argument *etc.*) —n. ('predıkıt) 3. that which is predicated 4. *Gram.* statement made about a subject —'**predicable** *a.* 1. capable of being predicated —n. 2. quality that can be predicated 3. *Logic* any of five general forms of attribution, namely genus, species, differentia, property and accident —**predi'cation** *n.* —**pre'dicative** *a.*

predict (prɪ'dɪkt) *vt.* foretell, prophesy —**pre'dictable** *a.* —**pre'diction** *n.*

predikant (predɪ'kænt) *n.* in S Afr., minister in Dutch Reformed Church

predilection (priːdɪ'lekʃən) *n.* preference, liking, partiality

predispose (priːdɪ'spəʊz) *vt.* 1. incline, influence 2. make susceptible

predominate (prɪ'dɒmɪneɪt) *vi.* be main or controlling element —**pre'dominance** *n.* —**pre'dominant** *a.* chief

pre-eminent (prɪ'emɪnənt) *a.* excelling all others, outstanding —**pre-eminence** *n.* —**pre-eminently** *adv.*

pre-empt (prɪ'empt) *vt.* acquire in advance of or to exclusion of others —**pre-emption** *n.* —**pre-emptive** *a.*

preen (priːn) *vt.* 1. (of birds) trim (feathers) with beak, plume 2. smarten (oneself)

pref. 1. preface 2. preference 3. prefix

prefabricate (priː'fæbrɪkeɪt) *vt.* manufacture (buildings *etc.*) in shaped sections, for rapid assembly on site —'**prefab** *n.* prefabricated building, *esp.* house

preface ('prefıs) *n.* 1. introduction to book *etc.* —*vt.* 2. introduce —'**prefatory** *a.*

prefect ('priːfekt) *n.* 1. person put in authority 2. schoolchild in position of limited power over others —'**prefecture** *n.* office, residence, district of a prefect

prefer (prɪ'fɜː) *vt.* 1. like better 2. promote (**-rr-**) —**preferable** ('prefərəb'l) *a.* more desirable —**preferably** ('prefərəblɪ) *adv.* —**preference** ('prefərəns, 'prefrəns) *n.* —**preferential** (prefə'renʃəl) *a.* giving, receiving preference —**pre'ferment** *n.* promotion, advancement

prefigure (priː'fɪgə) *vt.* exhibit, suggest by previous types, foreshadow —**pre'figurative** *a.*

prefix ('priːfɪks) *n.* 1. preposition or particle put at beginning of word or title —*vt.* (priː'fɪks, 'priːfɪks) 2. put as introduction 3. put before word to make compound

pregnant ('pregnənt) *a.* 1. carrying foetus in womb 2. full of meaning, significance 3. inventive —'**pregnancy** *n.*

prehensile (prɪ'hensaɪl) *a.* capable of grasping —**prehensility** (priːhen'sɪlɪtɪ) *n.*

prehistoric (priːhɪ'stɒrɪk) *or* **prehistorical** *a.* before period in which written history begins —**pre'history** *n.*

prejudge (priː'dʒʌdʒ) *vt.* judge beforehand, *esp.* without sufficient evidence

prejudice ('predʒʊdɪs) *n.* 1. preconceived opinion 2. bias, partiality 3. injury likely to happen to person or his rights as result of others' action or judgment —*vt.* 4. influence 5. bias 6. injure —**preju'dicial** *a.* 1. injurious 2. disadvantageous

prelate ('prelɪt) *n.* bishop or other church dignitary of equal or higher rank —'**prelacy** *n.* his office —**prelatical** (prɪ'lætɪk'l) *a.*

preliminary (prɪ'lɪmɪnərɪ) *a.* 1. preparatory, introductory —n. 2. introductory, preparatory statement, action 3. eliminating contest held before main competition

prelims ('priːlɪmz, prə'lɪmz) *pl.n.* 1. pages of book, such as title page *etc.* before main text (*also* **front matter**) 2. first public examinations taken for bachelor's degree in some universities 3. in Scotland, school examinations taken before public examinations

prelude ('preljuːd) *n.* 1. *Mus.* introductory movement 2. performance, event *etc.* serving as introduction —*vt.* 3. serve as prelude to (something) —*vt.* 4. introduce

premarital (priː'mærɪt'l) *a.* occurring before marriage

premature (premə'tjʊə, 'premətjʊə) *a.* 1. happening, done before proper time 2. impulsive, hasty 3. (of infant) born before end of full period of gestation

premeditate (prɪ'medɪteɪt) *vt.* consider, plan beforehand —**premedi'tation** *n.*

premenstrual (priː'menstrʊəl) *a.* of period in menstrual cycle just before menstruation

premier ('premjə) *n.* 1. prime minister 2. head of government of Aust. state —*a.* 3. chief, foremost 4. first —'**premiership** *n.*

premiere ('premɪeə, 'premɪə) *n.* first public performance of a play, film *etc.*

premise ('premıs) *n.* 1. *Logic* proposition from which inference is drawn (*also* '**premiss**) —*pl.* 2. house, building with its belongings 3. *Law* beginning of deed —*vt.* (prɪ'maɪz, 'premɪs) 4. state by way of introduction

premium ('priːmɪəm) *n.* 1. bonus 2. sum paid for insurance 3. excess over nominal value 4. great value or regard —**Premium Savings Bond** issued by government on which no interest is paid but cash prizes can be won

premonition (premə'nɪʃən) *n.* presentiment, foreboding

preoccupy (priː'ɒkjʊpaɪ) *vt.* occupy to the exclusion of other things (**-pying, -pied**) —**preoccu'pation** *n.* mental concentration or absorption

preordain (priːɔː'deɪn) *vt.* ordain or decree beforehand

prep (prep) *n. inf.* 1. preparation for schoolwork 2. *chiefly US* preparatory school

prep. 1. preparation 2. preparatory 3. preposition

prepare (prɪ'pɛə) vt. 1. make ready 2. make —vi. 3. get ready —**preparation** (prɛpə'reɪʃən) n. 1. making ready beforehand 2. something that is prepared, as a medicine 3. at school, (time spent) preparing work for lesson —**preparatory** (prɪ'pærətərɪ) a. 1. serving to prepare 2. introductory —**preparedness** (prɪ'pɛərɪdnɪs) n. state of being prepared —**preparatory school** 1. UK private school for children between ages of 6 and 13, generally preparing pupils for public school 2. in Amer., private secondary school preparing pupils for college (also **prep school**)

prepay (priː'peɪ) vt. pay in advance

prepense (prɪ'pɛns) a. usu. in legal contexts, premeditated (esp. in **malice prepense**)

preponderate (prɪ'pɒndəreɪt) vi. be of greater weight or power —**pre'ponderance** n. superiority of power, numbers etc.

preposition (prɛpə'zɪʃən) n. word marking relation between noun or pronoun and other words —**prepo'sitional** a.

prepossess (priːpə'zɛs) vt. 1. preoccupy or engross mentally 2. impress, esp. favourably, beforehand —**prepos'sessing** a. inviting favourable opinion, attractive, winning —**prepos'session** n.

preposterous (prɪ'pɒstərəs) a. utterly absurd, foolish

prepuce ('priːpjuːs) n. 1. retractable fold of skin covering tip of penis; foreskin 2. similar fold of skin covering tip of clitoris

Pre-Raphaelite (priː'ræfəlaɪt) n. 1. member of **Pre-Raphaelite Brotherhood**, association of painters and writers founded in 1848 to revive qualities of It. painting before Raphael —a. 2. of Pre-Raphaelite painting and painters

prerequisite (priː'rɛkwɪzɪt) n./a. (something) required as prior condition

prerogative (prɪ'rɒgətɪv) n. 1. peculiar power or right, esp. as vested in sovereign —a. 2. privileged

pres. 1. present (time) 2. presidential

Pres. President

presage ('prɛsɪdʒ) n. 1. omen, indication of something to come —vt. ('prɛsɪdʒ, prɪ'seɪdʒ) 2. foretell

presbyopia (prɛzbɪ'əʊpɪə) n. progressively diminishing ability of the eye to focus, esp. on near objects; long-sightedness

presbyter ('prɛzbɪtə) n. 1. elder in early Christian church 2. priest 3. member of a presbytery —**Presby'terian** a./n. (member) of Protestant church governed by lay elders —**Presby'terianism** n. —**presbytery** n. 1. church court composed of all ministers within a certain district and one ruling elder from each church 2. R.C.Ch. priest's house

prescience ('prɛsɪəns) n. foreknowledge —**'prescient** a.

prescribe (prɪ'skraɪb) v. 1. set out rules (for) 2. order 3. ordain 4. order use of (medicine) —**prescription** (prɪ'skrɪpʃən)

n. 1. prescribing 2. thing prescribed 3. written statement of it —**prescriptive** (prɪ'skrɪptɪv) a.

present' ('prɛznt) a. 1. that is here 2. now existing or happening —n. 3. present time or tense —'**presence** n. 1. being present 2. appearance, bearing —'**presently** adv. 1. soon 2. US at present —**presence of mind** ability to remain calm and act constructively during crises —**present-day** a. of modern day; current —**present participle** participial form of verbs used adjectivally when action it describes is contemporaneous with that of main verb of sentence and also used in formation of certain compound tenses —**present perfect** Gram. see PERFECT (sense 9)

present' (prɪ'zɛnt) vt. 1. introduce formally 2. show 3. give 4. offer 5. point, aim —n. ('prɛz'nt) 6. gift —**pre'sentable** a. fit to be seen —**presentation** (prɛzən'teɪʃən) n.

presentiment (prɪ'zɛntɪmənt) n. sense of something (esp. evil) about to happen

preserve (prɪ'zɜːv) vt. 1. keep from harm, injury or decay 2. maintain 3. pickle —n. 4. special area 5. that which is preserved, as fruit etc. 6. place where game is kept for private fishing, shooting —**preservation** (prɛzə'veɪʃən) n. —**pre'servative** n. 1. chemical added to perishable foods, drinks etc. to prevent them from rotting —a. 2. tending to preserve 3. having quality of preserving

preside (prɪ'zaɪd) vi. 1. be chairman 2. (with over) superintend —**presidency** ('prɛzɪdənsɪ) n. —**president** ('prɛzɪdənt) n. head of society, company, republic etc. —**presidential** (prɛzɪ'dɛnʃəl) a.

presidium (prɪ'sɪdɪəm) n. 1. (oft. P-) in Communist countries, permanent committee of larger body, such as legislature, that acts for it when it is in recess 2. collective presidency

press' (prɛs) vt. 1. subject to push or squeeze 2. smooth by pressure or heat 3. urge steadily, earnestly —vi. 4. bring weight to bear 5. throng 6. hasten —n. 7. a pressing 8. machine for pressing, esp. printing machine 9. printing house 10. art or process of printing 11. newspapers collectively 12. crowd 13. stress 14. large cupboard —'**pressing** a. 1. urgent 2. persistent —**press agent** person employed to advertise and secure press publicity for any person, enterprise etc. —**press conference** interview for press reporters given by politician etc. —**press gallery** area for newspaper reporters, esp. in legislative assembly —'**pressman** n. 1. printer who attends to the press 2. journalist —**press stud** fastening device, one part with projecting knob that snaps into hole on another part —**press-up** n. exercise in which body is alternately raised and lowered by arms only, trunk being kept straight (also (US) **push-up**)

press' (prɛs) vt. force to serve in navy or army —**press gang** formerly, body of men employed to press men into naval service

—**press-gang** vt. force (someone) to do something

pressure ('preʃə) n. 1. act of pressing 2. influence 3. authority 4. difficulties 5. Phys. thrust per unit area —**pressuri'zation** or **-i'sation** n. in aircraft, maintenance of normal atmospheric pressure at high altitudes —**'pressurize** or **-ise** vt. —**pressure cooker** vessel like saucepan which cooks food rapidly by steam under pressure —**pressure group** organized group which exerts influence on policies, public opinion etc.

Prestel ('prestel) n. R Post Office viewdata service

prestidigitation (prestidiʒɪ'teiʃən) n. see **sleight of hand** at SLEIGHT —**presti'digitator** n.

prestige (pre'sti:ʒ) n. 1. reputation based on high achievement, character, wealth etc. 2. power to impress or influence —**prestigious** (pre'stidʒəs) a.

presto ('prestəu) adv. 1. Mus. quickly 2. immediately (esp. in **hey presto**)

prestressed (pri:'strest) a. (of concrete) containing stretched steel cables for strengthening

presume (prɪ'zju:m) vt. 1. take for granted —vi. 2. take liberties —**pre'sumably** adv. 1. probably 2. doubtlessly —**presumption** (prɪ'zʌmpʃən) n. 1. forward, arrogant opinion or conduct 2. strong probability —**presumptive** (prɪ'zʌmptɪv) a. that may be assumed as true or valid until contrary is proved —**presumptuous** (prɪ'zʌmptjuəs) a. forward, impudent, taking liberties —**presumptuously** (prɪ'zʌmptjuəslɪ) adv. —**heir presumptive** heir whose right may be defeated by birth of nearer relative

presuppose (pri:sə'pəuz) vt. assume or take for granted beforehand —**presuppo'sition** n.

pretend (prɪ'tend) vt. 1. claim or allege (something untrue) 2. make believe, as in play —vi. 3. lay claim (to) —**pre'tence** or U.S. **pre'tense** n. 1. simulation 2. pretext —**pre'tender** n. claimant (to throne) —**pre'tension** n. —**pre'tentious** a. 1. making claim to special merit or importance 2. given to outward show

preter- (comb. form) beyond, more than

preterite or esp. U.S. **preterit** ('pretərɪt) a. 1. past 2. expressing past state or action —n. 3. past tense

preternatural (pri:tə'nætʃrəl) n. 1. out of ordinary way of nature 2. abnormal, supernatural

pretext ('pri:tekst) n. 1. excuse 2. pretence

pretty ('prɪtɪ) a. 1. having beauty that is attractive rather than imposing 2. charming —adv. 3. fairly, moderately —**'prettify** vt. make pretty, esp. in trivial way; embellish —**'prettily** adv. —**'prettiness** n. —**pretty-pretty** a. inf. excessively or ostentatiously pretty

pretzel ('pretsəl) n. small, brittle, savoury biscuit

prevail (prɪ'veɪl) vi. 1. gain mastery 2.

triumph 3. be in fashion, generally established —**pre'vailing** a. 1. widespread 2. predominant —**prevalence** ('prevələns) n. —**prevalent** ('prevələnt) a. extensively existing, rife

prevaricate (prɪ'værɪkeɪt) vi. 1. make evasive or misleading statements 2. quibble —**prevari'cation** n. —**pre'varicator** n.

prevent (prɪ'vent) vt. stop, hinder —**pre'ventable** a. —**pre'ventative** a. preventing, or serving to prevent, esp. disease (also **pre'ventive**) —**pre'vention** n. —**pre'ventive** a./n.

preview ('pri:vju:) n. 1. advance showing 2. showing of scenes from forthcoming film

previous ('pri:vɪəs) a. 1. earlier 2. preceding 3. inf. hasty —**'previously** adv. before

prey (preɪ) n. 1. animal hunted and killed by another carnivorous animal 2. victim —vi. (oft. with (up)on) 3. seize for food 4. treat as prey 5. afflict, obsess

price (praɪs) n. 1. that for which thing is bought or sold 2. cost 3. value 4. reward 5. odds in betting —vt. 6. fix, ask price for —**'priceless** a. 1. invaluable 2. inf. very funny —**'pricey** or **'pricy** a. inf. expensive —**price control** establishment of maximum price levels for basic goods and services by government —**at any price** whatever the price or cost

prick (prɪk) vt. 1. pierce slightly with sharp point 2. cause to feel mental pain 3. mark by prick —v. 4. (usu. with up) erect (ears) —n. 5. slight hole made by pricking 6. pricking or being pricked 7. sting 8. remorse 9. that which pricks 10. sharp point —**'prickle** n. 1. thorn, spike —vi. 2. feel tingling or pricking sensation —**'prickly** a. —**prickly heat** inflammation of skin with stinging pains —**prickly pear** 1. tropical cactus having flattened or cylindrical spiny joints and oval fruit 2. fruit of prickly pear

pride (praɪd) n. 1. too high an opinion of oneself, inordinate self-esteem 2. worthy self-esteem 3. feeling of elation or great satisfaction 4. something causing this 5. group (of lions) —v.refl. 6. take pride

prie-dieu (pri:'djɜ:) n. piece of furniture consisting of low surface for kneeling upon and narrow front surmounted by rest, for use when praying

priest (pri:st) or (fem.) **priestess** n. official minister of religion, clergyman —**'priesthood** n. —**'priestly** a.

prig (prɪg) n. self-righteous person who professes superior culture, morality etc. —**'priggery** n. —**'priggish** a.

prim (prɪm) a. very restrained, formally prudish

prima ('pri:mə) a. first —**prima ballerina** leading female ballet dancer —**prima donna** ('dɒnə) 1. principal female singer in opera 2. inf. temperamental person (pl. -s)

primacy ('praiməsi) *n.* 1. state of being first in rank, grade *etc.* 2. office of archbishop

prima facie ('praimə 'feiʃi) *Lat.* at first sight

primal ('praiməl) *a.* 1. of earliest age 2. first, original —'**primarily** *adv.* —'**primary** *a.* 1. chief 2. of the first stage, decision *etc.* 3. elementary —**primary accent** *or* **stress** *Linguis.* strongest accent in word or breath group —**primary school** 1. in England and Wales, school for children below age of 11 2. in Scotland, school for children below age of 12 3. in U.S., school equivalent to first three or four grades of elementary school

primate[1] ('praimeit) *n.* one of order of mammals including monkeys and man

primate[2] ('praimeit) *n.* archbishop

prime[1] (praim) *a.* 1. fundamental 2. original 3. chief 4. best —*n.* 5. first, best part of anything 6. youth 7. full health and vigour —*vt.* 8. prepare (gun, engine, pump *etc.*) for use 9. fill up, *eg* with information, liquor —'**priming** *n.* powder mixture used for priming gun —**prime meridian** the 0° meridian from which other meridians are calculated, usu. taken to pass through Greenwich —**Prime Minister** leader of government —**prime number** integer that cannot be divided into other integers but is only divisible by itself or 1

prime[2] (praim) *vt.* prepare for paint with preliminary coating of oil, size *etc.* —'**primer** *n.* paint *etc.* for priming

primer ('praimə) *n.* elementary school book or manual

primeval *or* **primaeval** (prai'miːvᵊl) *a.* of the earliest age of the world

primitive ('primitiv) *a.* 1. of an early undeveloped kind, ancient 2. crude, rough

primogeniture (praiməu'dʒɛnitʃə) *n.* rule by which real estate passes to the first-born son —**primo'genital** *a.* —**primo'genitor** *n.* 1. forefather; ancestor 2. earliest parent or ancestor, as of race

primordial (prai'mɔːdiəl) *a.* existing at or from the beginning

primp (primp) *v.* dress (oneself), *esp.* in fine clothes; prink

primrose ('primrəuz) *n.* 1. any of various pale-yellow spring flowers of the genus *Primula* 2. this colour —*a.* 3. of this colour —**primrose path** pleasurable way of life

primula ('primjulə) *n.* any of a genus of plants including primrose, oxlip *etc.*

Primus ('praiməs) *n.* **R** portable cooking stove, used *esp.* by campers

prince (prins) *n.* 1. son or in Brit. grandson of king or queen 2. ruler, chief (**prin'cess** *fem.*) —'**princely** *a.* generous, lavish 2. stately 3. magnificent —**princess royal** eldest daughter of Brit. or, formerly, Prussian sovereign —**Prince of Wales** eldest son and heir apparent of Brit. sovereign

principal ('prinsipᵊl) *a.* 1. chief in importance —*n.* 2. person for whom

another is agent 3. head of institution, *esp.* school or college 4. sum of money lent and yielding interest 5. chief actor —**princi'pality** *n.* territory, dignity of prince —**principal boy** leading male role in pantomime, played by woman —**principal parts** *Gram.* main inflected forms of verb, from which all other inflections may be deduced

principle ('prinsipᵊl) *n.* 1. moral rule 2. settled reason of action 3. uprightness 4. fundamental truth or element —'**principled** *a.* having high moral principles

prink (priŋk) *v.* 1. dress (oneself *etc.*) finely; deck out —*vi.* 2. preen oneself

print (print) *vt.* 1. reproduce (words, pictures *etc.*) by pressing inked types on blocks to paper *etc.* 2. produce thus 3. write in imitation of this 4. impress 5. *Photog.* produce (pictures) from negatives 6. stamp (fabric) with coloured design —*n.* 7. printed matter 8. printed lettering 9. written imitation of printed type 10. photograph 11. impression, mark left on surface by thing that has pressed against it 12. printed cotton fabric —'**printer** *n.* one engaged in printing —'**printing** *n.* 1. business or art of producing printed matter 2. printed text 3. copies of book *etc.* printed at one time (*also* **im'pression**) 4. form of writing in which letters resemble printed letters —**printed circuit** electronic circuit with wiring printed on an insulating base —**printer's devil** apprentice or errand boy in printing establishment —**printing press** machine for printing —**print-out** *n.* printed information from computer, teleprinter *etc.* —**out of print** no longer available from publisher

prior ('praiə) *a.* 1. earlier —*n.* 2. chief of religious house or order (**-ess** *fem.*) —**pri'ority** *n.* 1. precedence 2. something given special attention —'**priory** *n.* monastery, nunnery under prior, prioress

prise *or* **prize** (praiz) *vt.* 1. force open by levering 2. obtain (information *etc.*) with difficulty

prism ('prizəm) *n.* transparent solid usu. with triangular ends and rectangular sides, used to disperse light into spectrum or refract it in optical instruments *etc.* —**pris'matic** *a.* 1. of prism shape 2. (of colour) such as is produced by refraction through prism, rainbowlike, brilliant

prison ('prizᵊn) *n.* jail —'**prisoner** *n.* 1. one kept in prison 2. captive —**prisoner of war** person, *esp.* serviceman, captured by enemy in time of war

prissy ('prisi) *a.* *inf.* fussy, prim

pristine ('pristain, -tiːn) *a.* 1. original 2. primitive 3. unspoiled, good

private ('praivit) *a.* 1. secret, not public 2. reserved for, or belonging to, or concerning, an individual only 3. personal 4. secluded 5. denoting soldier of lowest rank 6. not part of National Health Service 7. not controlled by State —*n.* 8. private soldier —**privacy** ('praivəsi, 'privəsi) *n.*

—**'privately** adv. —**privati'zation** or **-i'sation** n. —**'privatize** or **-ise** vt. take into or return to private ownership (a company or concern previously owned by the State) —**private bill** bill presented to Parliament or Congress on behalf of individual, corporation etc. —**private company** limited company that does not issue shares for public subscription —**private eye** inf. private detective —**private member's bill** parliamentary bill sponsored by Member of Parliament who is not government minister —**private parts** or **'privates** pl.n. genitals —**private school** school accepting mostly fee-paying pupils

privateer (praivə'tiə) n. Hist. 1. privately owned armed vessel authorized by government to take part in war 2. captain of such ship

privation (prai'veiʃən) n. 1. loss or lack of comforts or necessities 2. hardship 3. act of depriving —**privative** ('privətiv) a.

privet ('privit) n. bushy evergreen shrub used for hedges

privilege ('privilidʒ) n. 1. advantage or favour that only a few obtain 2. right, advantage belonging to person or class —**'privileged** a. enjoying special right or immunity

privy ('privi) a. 1. admitted to knowledge of secret —n. 2. lavatory, esp. outhouse 3. Law person having interest in an action —**'privily** adv. —**privy council** council of state of monarch —**privy purse** (oft. P- P-) 1. allowance voted by Parliament for private expenses of monarch 2. official responsible for dealing with monarch's private expenses (also **Keeper of the Privy Purse**) —**privy seal** (oft. P- S-) UK seal affixed to documents issued by royal authority: of less importance than great seal

prize¹ (praiz) n. 1. reward given for success in competition 2. thing striven for 3. thing won, eg in lottery etc. —a. 4. winning or likely to win a prize —vt. 5. value highly —**'prizefight** n. boxing match for money —**'prizefighter** n.

prize² (praiz) n. ship, property captured in (naval) warfare

pro¹ (prəu) adv./prep. in favour (of)

pro² (prəu) n. 1. professional 2. prostitute (pl. -s) —a. 3. professional

P.R.O. 1. Public Records Office 2. public relations officer

pro- (comb. form) for, instead of, before, in front, as in proconsul, pronoun, project. Such compounds are not given here where the meaning may easily be found from the simple word

probable ('probəb'l) a. likely —**proba'bility** n. 1. likelihood 2. anything that has appearance of truth —**'probably** adv.

probate ('prəubit, -beit) n. 1. proving of authenticity of will 2. certificate of this

probation (prə'beiʃən) n. 1. system of dealing with lawbreakers, esp. juvenile

ones, by placing them under supervision of probation officer for stated period 2. testing of candidate before admission to full membership —**pro'bationer** n. person on probation —**probation officer** officer of court who supervises offenders placed on probation

probe (prəub) vt. 1. search into, examine, question closely —n. 2. that which probes, or is used to probe 3. thorough inquiry

probity ('prəubiti) n. honesty, uprightness, integrity

problem ('probləm) n. 1. matter etc. difficult to deal with or solve 2. question set for solution 3. puzzle —**proble'matic(al)** a. 1. questionable; uncertain 2. disputable

proboscis (prə'bosis) n. trunk or long snout, eg of elephant (pl. -es, **proboscides** (prəu'bosidiːz))

proceed (prə'siːd) vi. 1. go forward, continue 2. be carried on 3. go to law —**pro'cedural** a. —**pro'cedure** n. 1. act, manner of proceeding 2. conduct —**pro-'ceeding** n. 1. act or course of action 2. transaction —pl. 3. minutes of meeting 4. methods of prosecuting charge, claim etc. —**'proceeds** pl.n. price or profit

process ('prəuses) n. 1. series of actions or changes 2. method of operation 3. state of going on 4. action of law 5. outgrowth —vt. 6. handle, treat, prepare by special method of manufacture etc. —**pro'cession** n. 1. regular, orderly progress 2. train of persons in formal order

proclaim (prə'kleim) vt. announce publicly, declare —**proclamation** (proklə-'meiʃən) n.

proclivity (prə'kliviti) n. inclination, tendency

proconsul (prəu'kons'l) n. Hist. governor of province

procrastinate (prəu'kræstineit, prə-) vi. put off (an action) until later, delay —**procrasti'nation** n. —**pro'crastinator** n.

procreate ('prəukrieit) v. produce (offspring) —**procre'ation** n.

Procrustean (prəu'krʌstiən) a. compelling uniformity by violence

proctor ('proktə) n. university official with disciplinary powers

procure (prə'kjuə) vt. 1. obtain, acquire 2. provide 3. bring about —vi. 4. act as pimp —**pro'curable** a. —**procuration** (prokju-'reiʃən) n. —**procurator** ('prokjureitə) n. one who manages another's affairs —**pro'curement** n. —**pro'curer** n. 1. one who procures 2. pimp —**procurator fiscal** in Scotland, legal officer who performs functions of public prosecutor and coroner

prod (prod) vt. 1. poke with something pointed (-dd-) —n. 2. prodding 3. goad 4. pointed instrument

prodigal ('prodig'l) a. 1. wasteful 2. extravagant —n. 3. spendthrift —**prodi'gality** n. reckless extravagance

prodigy ('prodidʒi) n. 1. person with some marvellous gift 2. thing causing wonder

—**pro'digious** *a.* 1. very great, immense 2. extraordinary —**pro'digiously** *adv.*

produce (prə'djuːs) *vt.* 1. bring into existence 2. yield 3. make 4. bring forward 5. manufacture 6. exhibit 7. present on stage, film, television 8. *Geom.* extend in length —*n.* ('prɒdjuːs) 9. that which is yielded or made —**pro'ducer** *n.* person who produces, *esp.* play, film *etc.* —**product** ('prɒdʌkt) *n.* 1. result of process of manufacture 2. number resulting from multiplication —**pro'duction** *n.* 1. producing 2. things produced —**pro'ductive** *a.* 1. fertile 2. creative 3. efficient —**productivity** (prɒdʌk'tɪvɪtɪ) *n.*

proem ('prəʊɛm) *n.* introduction or preface, such as to work of literature

Prof. Professor

profane (prə'feɪn) *a.* 1. irreverent, blasphemous 2. not sacred —*vt.* 3. pollute, desecrate —**profanation** (prɒfə'neɪʃən) *n.* —**profanity** (prə'fænɪtɪ) *n.* profane talk or behaviour, blasphemy

profess (prə'fɛs) *vt.* 1. affirm, acknowledge 2. confess publicly 3. assert 4. claim, pretend —**professedly** (prə'fɛsɪdlɪ) *adv.* avowedly —**pro'fession** *n.* 1. calling or occupation, *esp.* learned, scientific or artistic 2. a professing 3. vow of religious faith on entering religious order —**pro'fessional** *a.* 1. engaged in a profession 2. engaged in a game or sport for money —*n.* 3. paid player —**pro'fessor** *n.* teacher of highest rank in university —**professorial** (prɒfɪ'sɔːrɪəl) *a.* —**professoriate** (prɒfɪ'sɔːrɪɪt) *n.* body of university professors —**pro'fessorship** *n.*

proffer ('prɒfə) *vt./n.* offer

proficient (prə'fɪʃənt) *a.* skilled; expert —**pro'ficiency** *n.*

profile ('prəʊfaɪl) *n.* 1. outline, *esp.* of face, as seen from side 2. brief biographical sketch

profit ('prɒfɪt) *n.* 1. (*oft. pl.*) money gained 2. benefit obtained —*v.* 3. benefit —**'profitable** *a.* yielding profit —**profi'teer** *n.* 1. one who makes excessive profits at the expense of the public —*vi.* 2. make excessive profits —**'profitless** *a.* —**profit-sharing** *n.* system in which portion of net profit of business is distributed to employees, usu. in proportion to wages or length of service

profligate ('prɒflɪgɪt) *a.* 1. dissolute 2. reckless, wasteful —*n.* 3. dissolute person —**'profligacy** *n.*

pro forma ('prəʊ 'fɔːmə) *Lat.* prescribing a set form

profound (prə'faʊnd) *a.* 1. very learned 2. deep —**profundity** (prə'fʌndɪtɪ) *n.*

profuse (prə'fjuːs) *a.* abundant, prodigal —**pro'fusion** *n.*

progeny ('prɒdʒɪnɪ) *n.* children —**progenitor** (prəʊ'dʒɛnɪtə) *n.* ancestor

progesterone (prəʊ'dʒɛstərəʊn) *n.* hormone which prepares uterus for pregnancy and prevents further ovulation

prognathous (prɒg'neɪθəs) *or* **prognath-** **ic** (prɒg'næθɪk) *a.* with projecting lower jaw

prognosis (prɒg'nəʊsɪs) *n.* 1. art of foretelling course of disease by symptoms 2. forecast (*pl.* **-noses** (-'nəʊsiːz)) —**prognostic** (prɒg'nɒstɪk) *a./n.* 1. serving as prognosis —*n.* 2. *Med.* any symptom used in making prognosis 3. sign of some future occurrence —**prognosticate** (prɒg'nɒstɪkeɪt) *vt.* foretell —**prognostication** (prɒgnɒstɪ'keɪʃən) *n.*

programme *or U.S.* **program** ('prəʊgræm) *n.* 1. plan, detailed notes of intended proceedings 2. broadcast on radio or television 3. syllabus or curriculum —**'program** *n.* 1. detailed instructions for computer —*vt.* 2. feed program into (computer) 3. arrange detailed instructions for (computer) (**-mm-**) —**'programmer** *n.* person who writes program

progress ('prəʊgrɛs) *n.* 1. onward movement 2. development —*vi.* (prə'grɛs) 3. go forward 4. improve —**pro'gression** *n.* 1. moving forward 2. advance, improvement 3. increase or decrease of numbers or magnitudes according to fixed law 4. *Mus.* regular succession of chords —**pro'gressive** *a.* 1. progressing by degrees 2. favouring political or social reform

prohibit (prə'hɪbɪt) *vt.* forbid —**prohibition** (prəʊɪ'bɪʃən) *n.* 1. act of forbidding 2. interdict 3. interdiction of supply and consumption of alcoholic drinks —**pro'hibitive** *a.* 1. tending to forbid or exclude 2. (of prices) very high —**pro'hibitory** *a.*

project ('prɒdʒɛkt) *n.* 1. plan, scheme 2. design —*vt.* (prə'dʒɛkt) 3. plan 4. throw 5. cause to appear on distant background —*vi.* (prə'dʒɛkt) 6. stick out, protrude —**projectile** (prə'dʒɛktaɪl) *n.* 1. heavy missile, *esp.* shell or ball —*a.* 2. designed for throwing —**projection** (prə'dʒɛkʃən) *n.* —**projectionist** (prə'dʒɛkʃənɪst) *n.* operator of film projector —**projector** (prə'dʒɛktə) *n.* 1. apparatus for projecting photographic images, films, slides on screen 2. one that forms scheme or design

prolapse ('prəʊlæps, prəʊ'læps) *n.* falling, slipping down of part of body from normal position (*also* **pro'lapsus**)

prolate ('prəʊleɪt) *a.* having polar diameter greater than the equatorial diameter

prole (prəʊl) *n. derogatory sl., chiefly UK* proletarian

prolegomena (prəʊlɛ'gɒmɪnə) *pl.n.* introductory remarks prefixed to book; preface

proletariat (prəʊlɪ'tɛərɪət) *n.* 1. all wage earners collectively 2. lowest class of community, working class —**prole'tarian** *a./n.*

proliferate (prə'lɪfəreɪt) *v.* grow or reproduce rapidly —**prolifer'ation** *n.*

prolific (prə'lɪfɪk) *a.* 1. producing fruit, offspring *etc.* in abundance 2. producing constant or successful results 3. fruitful

prolix ('prəʊlɪks, prəʊ'lɪks) *a.* (of speech *etc.*) wordy, long-winded —**pro'lixity** *n.*

prologue or U.S. (oft.) **prolog** ('prəʊlɒg) n. preface, esp. speech before play

prolong (prə'lɒŋ) vt. lengthen, protract —**prolongation** (prəʊlɒŋ'geɪʃən) n.

prom (prɒm) n. promenade (concert)

promenade (prɒmə'nɑːd) n. 1. leisurely walk 2. place made or used for this —vi. 3. take leisurely walk 4. go up and down —**promenade concert** concert at which audience stands

promethium (prə'miːθɪəm) n. radioactive element of lanthanide series artificially produced by fission of uranium

prominent ('prɒmɪnənt) a. 1. sticking out 2. conspicuous 3. distinguished —**prominence** n.

promiscuous (prə'mɪskjʊəs) a. 1. indiscriminate, esp. in sexual relations 2. mixed without distinction —**promiscuity** (prɒmɪ'skjuːɪtɪ) n.

promise ('prɒmɪs) v. 1. give undertaking or assurance (of) —vi. 2. be likely —n. 3. undertaking to do or not to do something 4. potential —**promising** a. showing good signs, hopeful —**promissory** a. containing promise —**Promised Land** 1. O.T. land of Canaan, promised by God to Abraham and his descendants as their heritage 2. Christianity heaven 3. place where one expects to find greater happiness —**promissory note** written promise to pay sum to person named, at specified time

promontory ('prɒməntərɪ, -trɪ) n. point of high land jutting out into the sea, headland

promote (prə'məʊt) vt. 1. help forward 2. move up to higher rank or position 3. work for 4. encourage sale of —**pro'moter** n. —**pro'motion** n. 1. advancement 2. preferment

prompt (prɒmpt) a. 1. done at once 2. acting with alacrity 3. punctual 4. ready —vt. 5. urge, suggest —v. 6. help out (actor or speaker) by reading or suggesting next words —**prompter** n. —**promptitude** or **promptness** n. —**promptly** adv.

promulgate ('prɒməlgeɪt) vt. proclaim, publish —**promul'gation** n. —**'promulgator** n.

pron. 1. pronoun 2. pronunciation

prone (prəʊn) a. 1. lying face or front downwards 2. inclined —**proneness** n.

prong (prɒŋ) n. single spike of fork or similar instrument

pronghorn ('prɒŋhɔːn) n. Amer. antelope

pronoun ('prəʊnaʊn) n. word used to replace noun —**pro'nominal** a. pert. to, like pronoun

pronounce (prə'naʊns) vt. 1. utter formally 2. form with organs of speech 3. say distinctly 4. declare —vi. 5. give opinion or decision —**pro'nounceable** a. —**pro'nounced** a. strongly marked, decided —**pro'nouncement** n. declaration —**pronunci'ation** n. 1. manner in which word etc. is pronounced 2. articulation 3. phonetic transcription of a word

pronto ('prɒntəʊ) adv. inf. at once, immediately, quickly

proof (pruːf) n. 1. evidence 2. thing which proves 3. test, demonstration 4. trial impression from type or engraved plate 5. Photog. print from a negative 6. standard of strength of alcoholic drink —a. 7. giving impenetrable defence 8. of proved strength —**proofread** v. read and correct (proofs) —**proofreader** n. —**proofreading** n. —**proof spirit** UK mixture of alcohol and water or alcoholic beverage that contains 49.28 per cent of alcohol by weight, 57.1 per cent by volume at 60°F (15.6°C): used as standard of alcoholic liquids

-proof (comb. form) impervious to; resisting effects of, as in waterproof

prop¹ (prɒp) vt. 1. support, sustain, hold up (-**pp**-) —n. 2. pole, beam etc. used as support

prop² (prɒp) n. propeller —**'propjet** n. see TURBOPROP

prop³ (prɒp) n. (theatrical) property

prop. 1. proper(ly) 2. property 3. proposition 4. proprietor

propaganda (prɒpə'gændə) n. organized dissemination of information to assist or damage political cause etc. —**propa'gandist** a./n.

propagate ('prɒpəgeɪt) vt. 1. reproduce, breed, spread by sowing, breeding etc. 2. transmit —vi. 3. breed, multiply —**propa'gation** n. —**'propagative** a.

propane ('prəʊpeɪn) n. colourless, flammable gas from petroleum

propel (prə'pɛl) vt. cause to move forward (-**ll**-) —**pro'pellant** or **pro'pellent** n. something causing propulsion, eg rocket fuel —**pro'peller** n. revolving shaft with blades for driving ship or aircraft —**pro'pulsion** n. act of driving forward —**pro'pulsive** or **pro'pulsory** a. 1. tending, having power to propel 2. urging on

propene ('prəʊpiːn) n. colourless gaseous alkene obtained by cracking petroleum (also **'propylene**)

propensity (prə'pɛnsɪtɪ) n. 1. inclination or bent 2. tendency 3. disposition

proper ('prɒpə) a. 1. appropriate 2. correct 3. conforming to etiquette, decorous 4. strict 5. (of noun) denoting individual person or place —**'properly** adv. —**proper fraction** fraction in which numerator has lower absolute value than denominator

property ('prɒpətɪ) n. 1. that which is owned 2. estate whether in lands, goods or money 3. quality, attribute of something 4. article used on stage in play etc.

prophet ('prɒfɪt) n. 1. inspired teacher or revealer of Divine Will 2. foreteller of future (-**ess** fem.) —**prophecy** ('prɒfɪsɪ) n. prediction, prophetic utterance —**prophesy** ('prɒfɪsaɪ) v. foretell —**prophetic** (prə'fɛtɪk) a.

prophylactic (prɒfɪ'læktɪk) n./a. 1. (something) done or used to ward off disease —n. 2. US condom —**prophy'laxis** n.

propinquity (prə'pɪŋkwɪtɪ) *n.* nearness, proximity, close kinship

propitiate (prə'pɪʃɪeɪt) *vt.* appease, gain favour of —**propiti'ation** *n.* —**pro'pitiatory** *a.* —**pro'pitious** *a.* favourable, auspicious

proponent (prə'pəʊnənt) *n.* one who advocates something

proportion (prə'pɔːʃən) *n.* 1. relative size or number 2. comparison 3. due relation between connected things or parts 4. share 5. relation —*pl.* 6. dimensions —*vt.* 7. arrange proportions of —**pro'portionable** *a.* —**pro'portional** or **pro'portionate** *a.* 1. having a due proportion 2. corresponding in size, number *etc.* —**pro'portionally** *adv.* —**proportional representation** representation of parties in elective body in proportion to votes they win

propose (prə'pəʊz) *vt.* 1. put forward for consideration 2. nominate 3. intend —*vi.* 4. offer marriage —**pro'posal** *n.* —**pro'poser** *n.* —**proposition** (prɒpə'zɪʃən) *n.* 1. offer 2. statement, assertion 3. theorem 4. suggestion of terms 5. *inf.* thing to be dealt with

propound (prə'paʊnd) *vt.* put forward for consideration or solution

proprietor (prə'praɪətə) *n.* owner (**-tress**, **-trix** *fem.*) —**pro'prietary** *a.* 1. belonging to owner 2. made by firm with exclusive rights of manufacture

propriety (prə'praɪətɪ) *n.* properness, correct conduct, fitness

propulsion (prə'pʌlʃən) *n.* *see* PROPEL

propylene (ˈprəʊpɪliːn) *n.* *see* PROPENE

pro rata (ˈrɑːtə) *Lat.* in proportion

prorogue (prə'rəʊg) *vt.* dismiss (parliament) at end of session without dissolution

prosaic (prəʊ'zeɪɪk) *a.* commonplace, unromantic

pros and cons various arguments in favour of and against motion, course of action *etc.*

proscenium (prə'siːnɪəm) *n.* arch or opening framing stage (*pl.* **-nia** (-nɪə))

proscribe (prəʊ'skraɪb) *vt.* outlaw, condemn —**proscription** (prəʊ'skrɪpʃən) *n.*

prose (prəʊz) *n.* speech or writing without rhyme or metre —**'prosily** *adv.* —**'prosiness** *n.* —**'prosy** *a.* tedious, dull

prosecute (ˈprɒsɪkjuːt) *vt.* carry on, bring legal proceedings against —**prose'cution** *n.* —**'prosecutor** *n.* (**-trix** *fem.*)

proselyte (ˈprɒsɪlaɪt) *n.* convert —**proselytism** (ˈprɒsɪlɪtɪzəm) *n.* —**proselytize** or **-ise** (ˈprɒsɪlɪtaɪz) *v.*

prosody (ˈprɒsədɪ) *n.* system, study of versification —**'prosodist** *n.*

prospect (ˈprɒspɛkt) *n.* 1. (*sometimes pl.*) expectation, chance for success 2. view, outlook 3. likely customer or subscriber 4. mental view —*v.* (prə'spɛkt) 5. explore, *esp.* for gold —**pro'spective** *a.* 1. anticipated 2. future —**pro'spectively** *adv.* —**pro'spector** *n.* —**pro'spectus** *n.* circular describing company, school *etc.*

prosper (ˈprɒspə) *v.* (cause to) do well —**pros'perity** *n.* good fortune, wellbeing

—**'prosperous** *a.* 1. doing well, successful 2. flourishing, rich, well-off —**'prosperously** *adv.*

prostate (ˈprɒsteɪt) *n.* gland accessory to male generative organs

prosthesis (ˈprɒsθɪsɪs) *n.* (replacement of part of body with) artificial substitute (*pl.* **-ses** (-siːz))

prostitute (ˈprɒstɪtjuːt) *n.* 1. one who offers sexual intercourse in return for payment —*vt.* 2. make a prostitute of 3. put to unworthy use —**prosti'tution** *n.*

prostrate (ˈprɒstreɪt) *a.* 1. lying flat 2. crushed, submissive, overcome —*vt.* (prɒ-'streɪt) 3. throw flat on ground 4. reduce to exhaustion —**pros'tration** *n.*

Prot. 1. Protestant 2. Protectorate

protactinium (prəʊtæk'tɪnɪəm) *n.* toxic radioactive element that occurs in uranium ores and is produced by neutron irradiation of thorium

protagonist (prəʊ'tægənɪst) *n.* 1. leading character 2. principal actor 3. champion of a cause

protasis (ˈprɒtəsɪs) *n.* introductory clause of conditional sentence (*pl.* **-ses** (-siːz))

protean (prəʊ'tiːən, 'prəʊtɪən) *a.* 1. variable 2. versatile

protect (prə'tɛkt) *vt.* defend, guard, keep from harm —**pro'tection** *n.* —**pro'tectionist** *n.* one who advocates protecting industries by taxing competing imports —**pro'tective** *a.* —**pro'tector** *n.* 1. one who protects 2. regent —**pro'tectorate** *n.* 1. relation of state to territory it protects and controls 2. such territory 3. office, period of protector of a state

protégé or (*fem.*) **protégée** (ˈprəʊtɪʒeɪ) *n.* one under another's care, protection or patronage

protein (ˈprəʊtiːn) *n.* any of various kinds of organic compound which form most essential part of food of living creatures

pro tempore (ˈprəʊ 'tɛmpərɪ) *Lat.* for the time being (*also* **pro tem**)

protest (ˈprəʊtɛst) *n.* 1. declaration or demonstration of objection —*vi.* (prə'tɛst) 2. object —*v.* 3. make declaration (against) 4. assert formally —**protes'tation** *n.* strong declaration

Protestant (ˈprɒtɪstənt) *a.* 1. belonging to any branch of the Western Church outside the Roman Catholic Church —*n.* 2. member of such a church —**'Protestantism** *n.*

protium (ˈprəʊtɪəm) *n.* most common isotope of hydrogen

proto- or *sometimes before vowel* **prot-** (*comb. form*) first, as in *prototype*

protocol (ˈprəʊtəkɒl) *n.* 1. diplomatic etiquette 2. draft of terms signed by parties as basis of formal treaty

proton (ˈprəʊtɒn) *n.* positively charged particle in nucleus of atom

protoplasm (ˈprəʊtəplæzəm) *n.* substance that is living matter of all animal and plant cells —**proto'plasmic** *a.*

prototype (ˈprəʊtətaɪp) *n.* 1. original or

model after which thing is copied **2.** pattern

protozoan (prəʊtə'zəʊən) *n.* minute animal of lowest and simplest class (*pl.* **-zoa** (-'zəʊə))

protract (prə'trækt) *vt.* **1.** lengthen **2.** prolong **3.** delay **4.** draw to scale —**pro'tracted** *a.* **1.** long-drawn-out **2.** tedious —**pro'traction** *n.* —**pro'tractor** *n.* instrument for measuring angles on paper

protrude (prə'truːd) *v.* stick out, (cause to) project —**pro'trusile** *a. Zool.* capable of being thrust forward —**pro'trusion** *n.* —**pro'trusive** *a.* thrusting forward —**pro'trusively** *adv.*

protuberant (prə'tjuːbərənt) *a.* bulging out —**pro'tuberance** *or* **pro'tuberancy** *n.* bulge, swelling

proud (praʊd) *a.* **1.** feeling or displaying pride **2.** arrogant **3.** gratified **4.** noble **5.** self-respecting **6.** stately —**'proudly** *adv.* —**proud flesh** flesh growing around healing wound

Prov. 1. Provençal **2.** *Bible* Proverbs **3.** Province **4.** Provost

prove (pruːv) *vt.* **1.** establish validity of **2.** demonstrate, test —*vi.* **3.** turn out (to be *etc.*) **4.** (of dough) rise in warm place before baking (**proved, 'proven** *pp.*) —**proven** ('pruːvªn, 'prəʊ-) *a.* proved —**proving ground** place for testing new equipment *etc.*

provenance ('prɒvɪnəns) *n.* place of origin, source

Provençal (prɒvɒn'sɑːl; *Fr.* prɔvãˈsal) *a.* **1.** of Provence, former province of SE France, its dialect of French or its Romance language —*n.* **2.** language of Provence, closely related to French and Italian, belonging to Romance group of Indo-European family **3.** native or inhabitant of Provence

provender ('prɒvɪndə) *n.* fodder

proverb ('prɒvɜːb) *n.* short, pithy, traditional saying in common use —**pro'verbial** *a.*

provide (prə'vaɪd) *vi.* **1.** make preparation —*vt.* **2.** supply, equip, prepare, furnish, give —**pro'vider** *n.* —**pro'viding** *or* **pro'vided** *conj.* (*sometimes with* that) on condition or understanding (that)

provident ('prɒvɪdənt) *a.* **1.** thrifty **2.** showing foresight —**'providence** *n.* **1.** kindly care of God or nature **2.** foresight **3.** economy —**provi'dential** *a.* strikingly fortunate, lucky —**provi'dentially** *adv.*

province ('prɒvɪns) *n.* **1.** division of a country, district **2.** sphere of action —*pl.* **3.** any part of country outside capital —**pro'vincial** *a.* **1.** of a province **2.** unsophisticated **3.** narrow in outlook —*n.* **4.** unsophisticated person **5.** inhabitant of province —**pro'vincialism** *n.* **1.** narrowness of outlook **2.** lack of refinement **3.** idiom peculiar to province

provision (prə'vɪʒn) *n.* **1.** a providing, *esp.* for the future **2.** thing provided —*pl.* **3.** food **4.** *Law* articles of instrument or statute —*vt.* **5.** supply with food —**pro'visional** *a.* **1.** temporary **2.** conditional

proviso (prə'vaɪzəʊ) *n.* condition (*pl.* **-s, -es**)

provoke (prə'vəʊk) *vt.* **1.** irritate **2.** incense **3.** arouse **4.** excite **5.** cause —**provocation** (prɒvə'keɪʃən) *n.* —**provocative** (prə'vɒkətɪv) *a.*

provost ('prɒvəst) *n.* **1.** one who superintends or presides **2.** head of certain colleges **3.** administrative head of Scottish burgh

prow (praʊ) *n.* bow of vessel

prowess ('praʊɪs) *n.* **1.** bravery, fighting capacity **2.** skill

prowl (praʊl) *vi.* **1.** roam stealthily, *esp.* in search of prey or booty —*n.* **2.** act of prowling —**'prowler** *n.* —**on the prowl 1.** moving about stealthily **2.** pursuing members of opposite sex

prox. proximo

proximate ('prɒksɪmɪt) *a.* nearest, next, immediate —**prox'imity** *n.* —**'proximo** *adv.* in the next month

proxy ('prɒksɪ) *n.* **1.** authorized agent or substitute **2.** writing authorizing one to act as this

prude (pruːd) *n.* one who affects excessive modesty or propriety —**'prudery** *n.* —**'prudish** *a.*

prudent ('pruːdªnt) *a.* **1.** careful, discreet **2.** sensible —**'prudence** *n.* **1.** habit of acting with careful deliberation **2.** wisdom applied to practice —**pru'dential** *a.*

prune[1] (pruːn) *n.* dried plum

prune[2] (pruːn) *vt.* **1.** cut out (dead parts, excessive branches *etc.*) from **2.** shorten, reduce —**pruning hook** tool with curved blade terminating in hook, used for pruning

prurient ('prʊərɪənt) *a.* **1.** given to, springing from lewd thoughts **2.** having unhealthy curiosity or desire —**'prurience** *or* **'pruriency** *n.*

pruritus (prʊə'raɪtəs) *n. Pathol.* intense itching —**pruritic** (prʊə'rɪtɪk) *a.*

prussic acid ('prʌsɪk) extremely poisonous aqueous solution of hydrogen cyanide

pry (praɪ) *vi.* **1.** make furtive or impertinent inquiries **2.** look curiously —*vt.* **3.** US force open (**pried, 'prying**)

P.S. postscript (*also* **p.s.**)

Ps. *or* **Psa.** *Bible* Psalm(s)

psalm (sɑːm) *n.* **1.** sacred song **2.** (**P-**) any of the sacred songs making up the Book of Psalms in the Bible —**'psalmist** *n.* writer of psalms —**psalmody** ('sɑːmədɪ, 'sæl-) *n.* art, act of singing sacred music —**Psalter** ('sɔːltə) *n.* **1.** book of psalms **2.** copy of the Psalms as separate book —**psaltery** ('sɔːltərɪ) *n.* obsolete stringed instrument like lyre

PSBR public sector borrowing requirement

psephology (sɛ'fɒlədʒɪ) *n.* statistical study of elections

pseud (sjuːd) *inf. n.* **1.** false or pretentious person —*a.* **2.** sham, fake (*also* **'pseudo**)

pseudo- *or sometimes before vowel* **pseud-** *(comb. form)* sham, as in *pseudo-Gothic, pseudomodern*. Such compounds are not given here where the meaning may easily be inferred from the simple word

pseudonym ('sjuːdənɪm) *n.* **1.** false, fictitious name **2.** pen name —**pseudonymous** (sjuː'dɒnɪməs) *a.*

pshaw (pʃɔː) *interj. rare* exclamation of disgust, impatience, disbelief *etc.*

psi (psaɪ) *n.* 23rd letter in Gr. alphabet (Ψ, ψ), transliterated as *ps*

psittacine ('sɪtəsaɪn, -sɪn) *a.* pert. to, like parrots —**psitta'cosis** *n.* dangerous infectious disease, germ of which is carried by parrots

psoriasis (sə'raɪəsɪs) *n.* skin disease characterized by formation of reddish spots and patches covered with silvery scales

psst (pst) *interj.* exclamation of beckoning, *esp.* made surreptitiously

P.S.T. US, C Pacific Standard Time

P.S.V. public service vehicle

psyche ('saɪkɪ) *n.* human mind or soul

psychedelic (saɪkɪ'dɛlɪk) *a.* **1.** of or causing hallucinations **2.** like intense colours *etc.* experienced during hallucinations

psychic ('saɪkɪk) *a.* **1.** sensitive to phenomena lying outside range of normal experience **2.** of soul or mind **3.** that appears to be outside region of physical law —**psy'chiatry** *n.* medical treatment of mental diseases —**psychical** *a.* psychic —**psycho'analyse** *or esp. U.S.* **psycho'analyze** *vt.* treat by psychoanalysis —**psychoa'nalysis** *n.* method of studying and treating mental disorders —**psycho'analyst** *n.* —**psychogenic** (saɪkəʊ'dʒɛnɪk) *a. Psychol.* (esp. of disorders or symptoms) of mental, rather than organic origin —**psychoki'nesis** *n.* (in parapsychology) alteration of state of object supposedly by mental influence alone —**psycho'logical** *a.* of psychology **2.** of the mind —**psy'chologist** *n.* —**psy'chology** *n.* **1.** study of mind **2.** *inf.* person's mental make-up —**psy'chometry** *n.* **1.** measurement, testing of psychological processes **2.** supposed ability to divine unknown person's qualities by handling object used or worn by him —**'psychopath** *n.* person afflicted with severe mental disorder causing him to commit antisocial, oft. violent acts —**psycho'pathic** *a.* —**psy'chosis** *n.* severe mental disorder in which person's contact with reality becomes distorted (*pl.* **-choses** (-'kəʊsiːz)) —**psychoso'matic** *a.* of physical disorders thought to have psychological causes —**psycho'therapy** *n.* treatment of disease by psychological, rather than by physical, means —**psychological moment** most appropriate time for producing desired effect —**psychological warfare** military

application of psychology, *esp.* to manipulation of morale in time of war

psycho ('saɪkəʊ) *sl. n.* **1.** psychopath (*pl.* **-s**) —*a.* **2.** psychopathic

psycho- *or sometimes before vowel* **psych-** *(comb. form)* mind, psychological or mental processes, as in *psychology, psychosomatic*

Pt *Chem.* platinum

pt. 1. part **2.** pint **3.** point

Pt. 1. Point **2.** Port

p.t. 1. past tense **2.** pro tempore

P.T. 1. physical therapy **2.** physical training

P.T.A. parent teacher association

ptarmigan ('tɑːmɪgən) *n.* bird of grouse family which turns white in winter (*pl.* **-s**, **-gan**)

Pte. Private (soldier)

ptero- *(comb. form)* wing, as in *pterodactyl*

pterodactyl (tɛrə'dæktɪl) *n.* extinct flying reptile with batlike wings

P.T.O. *or* **p.t.o.** please turn over

ptomaine *or* **ptomain** ('təʊmeɪn) *n.* any of group of poisonous alkaloids found in decaying matter

Pu *Chem.* plutonium

pub (pʌb) *n.* public house, building with bar(s) and licence to sell alcoholic drinks —**pub-crawl** *sl., chiefly* UK *n.* **1.** drinking tour of number of pubs or bars —*vi.* **2.** make such tour

pub. 1. public **2.** publication **3.** published **4.** publisher **5.** publishing

puberty ('pjuːbətɪ) *n.* sexual maturity —**'pubertal** *a.*

pubes ('pjuːbiːz) *n.* **1.** region above external genital organs, covered with hair from time of puberty **2.** pubic hair (*pl.* **'pubes**) **3.** *pl. of* PUBIS

pubescent (pjuː'bɛsʔnt) *a.* **1.** arriving or arrived at puberty **2.** (of certain plants and animals or their parts) covered with fine short hairs or down —**pu'bescence** *n.*

pubic ('pjuːbɪk) *a.* of the lower abdomen

pubis ('pjuːbɪs) *n.* one of three sections of hipbone that forms part of pelvis (*pl.* **-bes** (-biːz))

public ('pʌblɪk) *a.* **1.** of or concerning the public as a whole **2.** not private **3.** open to general observation or knowledge **4.** accessible to all **5.** serving the people —*n.* **6.** the community or its members —**'publican** *n.* keeper of public house —**'publicly** *adv.* —**public-address system** system of microphones, amplifiers and loudspeakers for increasing sound level, used in auditoriums *etc.* (*also* **P.A. system**) —**public company** limited company whose shares may be purchased by the public —**public convenience** public lavatory —**public enemy** notorious person, such as criminal, regarded as menace to public —**public house** pub —**public lending right** right of authors to receive payment when books are borrowed from public libraries —**public relations** promotion of good relations of an organization or authority with the general public —**public school 1.** in England and Wales, private independent fee-paying school **2.** in some Canad. provinces, a local elementary school —**public servant 1.** elected or appointed holder of public office **2.** A, NZ civil servant —**public service** government employment —**public spirit** interest in and devotion to welfare of community —**public-spirited** a. having or showing active interest in good of community —**public transport** trains, buses etc. that have fixed routes and are available to general public —**public utility** enterprise concerned with provision to public of essentials, such as electricity etc.

publicist ('pʌblɪsɪst) n. **1.** writer on public concerns **2.** journalist —**pub'licity** n. **1.** process of attracting public attention **2.** attention thus gained —a. **3.** pert. to advertisement —**'publicize** or **-ise** vt. advertise

publish ('pʌblɪʃ) vt. **1.** prepare and issue for sale (books, music etc.) **2.** make generally known **3.** proclaim —**publi'cation** n. —**'publisher** n.

puce (pju:s) a./n. purplish-brown (colour)

puck[1] (pʌk) n. rubber disc used instead of ball in ice hockey

puck[2] (pʌk) n. mischievous sprite —**'puckish** a.

pucker ('pʌkə) v. **1.** gather into wrinkles —n. **2.** crease, fold

pudding ('pudɪŋ) n. **1.** sweet, usu. cooked dessert, oft. made from suet, flour etc. **2.** sweet course of meal **3.** soft savoury dish with pastry or batter **4.** kind of sausage

puddle ('pʌd'l) n. **1.** small muddy pool **2.** rough cement for lining ponds etc. —vt. **3.** line with puddle **4.** make muddy

pudendum (pju:'dɛndəm) n. (oft. pl.) human external genital organs, esp. of female (pl. **-da** (-də)) —**pu'dendal** or **'pudic** a.

pudgy ('pʌdʒɪ) a. esp. US see PODGY

puerile ('pjʊəraɪl) a. **1.** childish **2.** foolish **3.** trivial

puerperium (pjuə'pɪərɪəm) n. period of about six weeks after childbirth —**puerperal** (pju:'ɜːpərəl) a. —**puerperal fever** formerly, blood poisoning caused by infection during childbirth

puff (pʌf) n. **1.** short blast of breath, wind etc. **2.** its sound **3.** type of pastry **4.** laudatory notice or advertisement —vi. **5.** blow abruptly **6.** breathe hard —vt. **7.** send out in a puff **8.** blow out, inflate **9.** advertise **10.** smoke hard —**puffed** a. **1.** breathless; winded **2.** swollen; puffy —**'puffy** a. **1.** short-winded **2.** swollen —**puff adder 1.** large venomous Afr. viper that inflates its body when alarmed **2.** N Amer. nonvenomous snake that inflates its body when alarmed (also **hognose snake**) —**'puffball** n. **1.** ball-shaped fungus **2.** skirt that puffs out wide and is nipped into narrow hem —**puff pastry** or U.S. **puff paste** dough for making a rich flaky pastry

puffin ('pʌfɪn) n. any of various sea birds with large brightly-coloured beaks

pug (pʌg) n. **1.** small snub-nosed dog **2.** sl. boxer —**pug nose** snub nose

pugilism ('pju:dʒɪlɪzəm) n. art, practice or profession of fighting with fists; boxing —**'pugilist** n. —**pugi'listic** a.

pugnacious (pʌg'neɪʃəs) a. given to fighting —**pugnacity** (pʌg'næsɪtɪ) n.

puissant ('pju:ɪs²nt) a. Poet. powerful, mighty —**puissance** ('pju:ɪs²ns, 'pwi:sɑ:ns) n. showjumping competition over very high fences

puke (pju:k) sl. vi. **1.** vomit —n. **2.** act of vomiting

pukka or **pucka** ('pʌkə) a. Anglo-Indian properly or perfectly done, constructed etc.; good; genuine

pulchritude ('pʌlkrɪtju:d) n. Lit. beauty

pule (pju:l) vi. whine; whimper

pull (pul) vt. **1.** exert force on (object) to move it towards source of force **2.** strain, stretch **3.** tear **4.** propel by rowing —n. **5.** act of pulling **6.** force exerted by it **7.** draught of liquor **8.** inf. power, influence —**pull in 1.** (of train) arrive **2.** (of car etc.) draw in to side of road, stop **3.** attract **4.** sl. arrest —**pull off** inf. carry through to successful issue —**pull out 1.** withdraw **2.** extract **3.** (of train) depart **4.** (of car etc.) move away from side of road; move out to overtake —**pull (someone's) leg** inf. make fun of (someone) —**pull up 1.** tear up **2.** recover lost ground **3.** improve **4.** come to a stop **5.** halt **6.** reprimand

pullet ('pulɪt) n. young hen

pulley ('pulɪ) n. wheel with groove in rim for cord, used to raise weights by downward pull

Pullman ('pulmən) n. railway saloon car (pl. **-s**) (also **Pullman car**)

pullover ('puləʊvə) n. jersey, sweater without fastening, to be pulled over head

pulmonary ('pʌlmənərɪ, 'pul-) a. **1.** of lungs **2.** having lungs or lunglike organs

pulp (pʌlp) n. **1.** soft, moist, vegetable or animal matter **2.** flesh of fruit **3.** any soft soggy mass —vt. **4.** reduce to pulp

pulpit ('pulpɪt) n. raised (enclosed) platform for preacher

pulsar ('pʌlsɑ:) n. small dense star emitting radio waves

pulse[1] (pʌls) n. **1.** movement of blood in arteries corresponding to heartbeat, discernible to touch, eg in wrist **2.** any regular beat or vibration —**pul'sate** vi. throb, quiver —**pul'sation** n.

pulse[2] (pʌls) n. edible seeds of pod-bearing plants, eg beans

pulverize or **-ise** ('pʌlvəraɪz) vt. **.1.** reduce to powder **2.** smash, demolish —**pulveri'zation** or **-i'sation** n.

puma ('pju:mə) n. large Amer. feline carnivore, cougar

pumice ('pʌmɪs) n. light porous variety of volcanic rock used to scour, smooth and polish (also **pumice stone**)

pummel ('pʌməl) vt. strike repeatedly (-ll-)

pump¹ (pʌmp) n. 1. appliance in which piston and handle are used for raising water, or putting in or taking out air, liquid etc. —vt. 2. raise, put in, take out etc. with pump 3. empty by means of pump 4. extract information from —vi. 5. work pump 6. work like pump —**pump iron** sl. lift weights

pump² (pʌmp) n. light shoe

pumpernickel ('pʌmpənık³l) n. sour black bread made of coarse rye flour

pumpkin ('pʌmpkın) n. any of several varieties of gourd, eaten esp. as vegetable

pun (pʌn) n. 1. humorous use of words that have the same sound, but have different meanings —vi. 2. make pun (-nn-) —'**punster** n.

punch¹ (pʌntʃ) n. 1. tool for perforating or stamping 2. blow with fist 3. inf. vigour —vt. 4. stamp, perforate with punch 5. strike with fist —'**punchball** n. 1. stuffed or inflated ball or bag, either suspended or supported by flexible rod, that is punched for exercise, esp. boxing training 2. US game resembling baseball —**punch-drunk** or (inf.) '**punchy** a. dazed, as by repeated blows —**punched card** or esp. U.S. **punch card** card on which data can be coded in form of punched holes —**punched tape** or U.S. **perforated tape** strip of paper used in computers etc. for recording information in form of punched holes (also **paper tape**) —**punch line** culminating part of joke etc., that gives it its point —**punch-up** n. UK sl. fight, brawl

punch² (pʌntʃ) n. drink of spirits or wine with fruit juice, spice etc.

punctilious (pʌŋk'tılıəs) a. 1. making much of details of etiquette 2. very exact, particular

punctual ('pʌŋktjuəl) a. in good time, not late, prompt —**punctu'ality** n. —'**punctually** adv.

punctuate ('pʌŋktjueıt) vt. 1. insert punctuation marks into 2. interrupt at intervals —**punctu'ation** n. marks, eg commas, colons etc., put in writing to assist in making sense clear

puncture ('pʌŋktʃə) n. 1. small hole made by sharp object, esp. in tyre 2. act of puncturing —vt. 3. prick hole in, perforate

pundit or **pandit** ('pʌndıt) n. 1. self-appointed expert 2. Brahman learned in Sanskrit and, esp. in Hindu religion, philosophy or law

pungent ('pʌndʒənt) a. 1. biting 2. irritant 3. piercing 4. tart 5. caustic —'**pungency** n.

punish ('pʌnıʃ) vt. 1. cause (someone) to suffer for offence 2. inflict penalty on 3. use or treat roughly —'**punishable** a. —'**punishment** n. —**punitive** ('pju:nıtıv) a. inflicting or intending to inflict punishment

punk¹ (pʌŋk) a./n. 1. inferior, rotten,

worthless (person or thing) 2. petty (hoodlum) 3. (of) style of rock music

punk² (pʌŋk) n. dried decayed wood or other substance that smoulders when ignited: used as tinder

punka or **punkah** ('pʌŋkə) n. 1. fan made of palm leaf or leaves 2. large fan made of palm leaves etc. worked mechanically to cool room

punnet ('pʌnıt) n. small basket for fruit

punt¹ (pʌnt) n. 1. flat-bottomed, square-ended boat, propelled by pushing with pole —vt. 2. propel thus

punt² (pʌnt) Sport vt. 1. kick (ball) before it touches ground, when let fall from hands —n. 2. such a kick

punt³ (pʌnt) vi. gamble, bet —'**punter** n. 1. one who punts 2. professional gambler 3. inf. customer or client, esp. prostitute's client

puny ('pju:nı) a. small and feeble

pup (pʌp) n. young of certain animals, eg dog

pupa ('pju:pə) n. stage between larva and adult in metamorphosis of insect, chrysalis (pl. **pupae** ('pju:pi:)) —'**pupal** a.

pupil ('pju:p³l) n. 1. person being taught 2. opening in iris of eye

puppet ('pʌpıt) n. small doll or figure of person etc. controlled by operator's hand —**puppe'teer** n. —'**puppetry** n. —**puppet show** show with puppets worked by hidden showman —**puppet state** state that appears independent but is controlled by another

puppy ('pʌpı) n. young dog —**puppy fat** fatty tissue in child or adolescent, usu. disappearing with age

purblind ('pɜːblaınd) a. 1. partly or nearly blind 2. lacking in insight or understanding

purchase ('pɜːtʃıs) vt. 1. buy —n. 2. act of buying 3. what is bought 4. leverage, grip

purdah ('pɜːdə) n. 1. Muslim, Hindu custom of keeping women in seclusion 2. screen, veil to achieve this

pure (pjuə) a. 1. unmixed, untainted 2. simple 3. spotless 4. faultless 5. innocent 6. concerned with theory only —'**purely** adv. —**purifi'cation** n. —'**purificatory** a. —'**purify** v. make, become pure, clear or clean (-ified, -ifying) —'**purism** n. excessive insistence on correctness of language —'**purist** n. —'**purity** n. state of being pure —**purebred** ('pjuə'brɛd) a. 1. denoting pure strain obtained through many generations of controlled breeding —n. ('pjuəbrɛd) 2. purebred animal

purée ('pjuəreı) n. 1. pulp of cooked fruit or vegetables —vt. 2. make (cooked foods) into purée

purgatory ('pɜːgətərı) n. place or state of torment, pain or distress, esp. temporary —purga'torial a.

purge (pɜːdʒ) vt. 1. make clean, purify 2. remove, get rid of 3. clear out —n. 4. act, process of purging 5. removal of undesirable members from political party, army *etc.* —**purgation** (pɜ:ˈgeɪʃən) *n.* —**purgative** (ˈpɜ:gətɪv) *a./n.*

Puritan (ˈpjʊərɪtˀn) *n.* 1. *Hist.* member of extreme Protestant party 2. (**p-**) person of extreme strictness in morals or religion —**puriˈtanic(al)** *a.* 1. strict in the observance of religious and moral duties 2. overscrupulous —ˈ**puritanism** *n.*

purl¹ (pɜ:l) *n.* 1. stitch that forms ridge in knitting —*v.* 2. knit in purl stitch

purl² (pɜ:l) *vi.* flow with burbling sound, swirl, babble

purlieus (ˈpɜ:lju:z) *pl.n.* outlying parts, outskirts

purlin *or* **purline** (ˈpɜ:lɪn) *n.* horizontal beam that provides support for rafters of roof

purloin (pɜ:ˈlɔɪn) *vt.* 1. steal 2. pilfer

purple (ˈpɜ:pˀl) *n./a.* (of) colour between crimson and violet —**Purple Heart** decoration awarded to members of U.S. Armed Forces for wound received in action

purport (pɜ:ˈpɔ:t) *vt.* 1. claim to be (true *etc.*) 2. signify, imply —*n.* (ˈpɜ:pɔ:t) 3. meaning 4. apparent meaning 5. significance

purpose (ˈpɜ:pəs) *n.* 1. reason, object 2. design 3. aim, intention —*vt.* 4. intend —ˈ**purposely** *adv.* —**purpose-built** *a.* made to serve specific purpose —**on purpose** intentionally

purr (pɜ:) *n.* 1. (*esp.* of cats) make low vibrant sound, usu. considered as expressing pleasure *etc.* —*vi.* 2. utter this sound

purse (pɜ:s) *n.* 1. small bag for money 2. resources 3. money as prize —*vt.* 4. pucker (mouth, lips *etc.*) in wrinkles —*vi.* 5. become wrinkled and drawn in —ˈ**purser** *n.* ship's officer who keeps accounts —**purse strings** control of expenditure (*esp.* **in hold** *or* **control the purse strings**)

purslane (ˈpɜ:slɪn) *n.* plant used (*esp.* formerly) in salads and as potherb

pursue (pəˈsju:) *vt.* 1. run after 2. chase 3. aim at 4. engage in 5. continue 6. follow —*vi.* 7. go in pursuit 8. continue —**purˈsuance** *n.* carrying out —**purˈsuant** *adj. chiefly law* in agreement or conformity —**purˈsuer** *n.* —**purˈsuit** *n.* 1. running after, attempt to catch 2. occupation

pursuivant (ˈpɜ:sɪvənt) *n.* officer of College of Arms below herald

purulent (ˈpjʊərʊlənt) *a. see* PUS

purvey (pəˈveɪ) *vt.* supply (provisions) —**purˈveyance** *n.* —**purˈveyor** *n.*

purview (ˈpɜ:vju:) *n.* scope, range

pus (pʌs) *n.* yellowish matter produced by suppuration —**purulence** (ˈpjʊərʊləns) *n.* —ˈ**purulent** *a.* 1. forming, discharging pus 2. septic

push (pʊʃ) *vt.* 1. move, try to move away by pressure 2. drive, impel 3. *inf.* sell (*esp.* narcotic drugs) illegally —*vi.* 4. make thrust 5. advance with steady effort —*n.* 6. thrust 7. persevering self-assertion 8. big military advance 9. *sl.* dismissal —ˈ**pusher** *n.* —ˈ**pushing** *or inf.* ˈ**pushy** *a.* given to

pushing oneself —**push-bike** *n.* UK *inf.* bicycle —**push button** electrical switch operated by pressing button, which closes or opens circuit —**push-button** *a.* 1. operated by push button 2. initiated as simply as by pressing button —ˈ**pushchair** *n.* (collapsible) chair-shaped carriage for baby —ˈ**pushover** *n. sl.* 1. something easily achieved 2. person *etc.* easily taken advantage of or defeated —**push-start** *vt.* 1. start (motor vehicle) by pushing while in gear, thus turning engine —*n.* 2. this process

pusillanimous (pju:sɪˈlænɪməs) *a.* cowardly —**pusillaˈnimity** *n.*

puss (pʊs) *n.* cat (*also* ˈ**pussy**) —**pussy willow** willow tree with silvery silky catkins

pussyfoot (ˈpʊsɪfʊt) *vi. inf.* 1. move stealthily 2. act indecisively, procrastinate

pustule (ˈpʌstju:l) *n.* pimple containing pus —ˈ**pustular** *a.* —**pustulate** (ˈpʌstjʊleɪt) *v.* 1. (cause to) form into pustules —*a.* (ˈpʌstjʊlɪt) 2. covered with pustules

put (pʊt) *vt.* 1. place 2. set 3. express 4. throw (*esp.* shot) (**put**, ˈ**putting**) —*n.* 5. throw —**put across** express successfully —**put-down** *n.* cruelly critical remark —**put-up** *a.* dishonestly or craftily prearranged (*esp.* **in put-up job**) —**put down** 1. make written record of 2. repress 3. consider 4. attribute 5. put (animal) to death because of old age or illness 6. table on agenda 7. *sl.* reject, humiliate —**put off** 1. postpone 2. disconcert 3. repel —**put up** 1. erect 2. accommodate 3. nominate

putative (ˈpju:tətɪv) *a.* reputed, supposed —ˈ**putatively** *adv.*

putrid (ˈpju:trɪd) *a.* 1. decomposed 2. rotten —ˈ**putrefy** *v.* make or become rotten (**-efied**, **-efying**) —**putreˈfaction** *n.* —puˈ**trescence** *n.* —puˈ**trescent** *a.* becoming rotten —puˈ**tridity** *n.*

Putsch (pʊtʃ) *n.* surprise attempt to overthrow the existing power, political revolt

putt (pʌt) *vt.* strike (golf ball) along ground in direction of hole —ˈ**putter** *n.* golf club for putting —**putting green** 1. on golf course, area of closely mown grass at end of fairway where hole is 2. area of smooth grass with several holes for putting games

puttee *or* **putty** (ˈpʌtɪ) *n.* strip of cloth wound round leg like bandage, serving as gaiter

putty (ˈpʌtɪ) *n.* 1. paste of whiting and oil as used by glaziers 2. jeweller's polishing powder —*vt.* 3. fix, fill with putty (**-ied**, **-ying**)

puzzle (ˈpʌzˀl) *v.* 1. perplex or be perplexed —*n.* 2. bewildering, perplexing question, problem or toy —ˈ**puzzlement** *n.*

PVC polyvinyl chloride (synthetic thermoplastic material used in insulation, shoes *etc.*)

pyaemia *or* **pyemia** (paɪˈi:mɪə) *n.* form of blood poisoning —pyˈ**aemic** *or* pyˈ**emic** *a.*

pye-dog *or* **pie-dog** ('paidɒg) *n.* ownerless half-wild Asian dog

pygmy *or* **pigmy** ('pigmi) *n.* **1.** abnormally undersized person **2.** (**P-**) member of one of dwarf peoples of Equatorial Afr. —*a.* **3.** undersized

pyjamas *or U.S.* **pajamas** (pə'dʒɑːməz) *pl.n.* sleeping suit of trousers and jacket

pylon ('pailən) *n.* towerlike erection, *esp.* to carry electric cables

pyo- *or before vowel* **py-** (*comb. form*) pus, as in *pyosis*

pyorrhoea *or esp. U.S.* **pyorrhea** (paiə-'riə) *n.* inflammation of the gums with discharge of pus and loosening of teeth

pyramid ('pirəmid) *n.* **1.** solid figure with sloping sides meeting at apex **2.** structure of this shape, *esp.* ancient Egyptian **3.** group of persons or things highest in the middle —**py'ramidal** *a.* —**pyramid selling** practice adopted by some manufacturers of advertising for distributors and selling them batches of goods. The first distributors then advertise for more distributors who are sold subdivisions of original batches at increased price. This process continues until final distributors are left with stock that is unsaleable except at loss

pyre (paiə) *n.* pile of wood for burning a dead body

pyrethrum (pai'riːθrəm) *n.* **1.** any of several types of cultivated chrysanthemums **2.** insecticide made from it

pyretic (pai'retik) *a. Pathol.* of fever

Pyrex ('paireks) *n.* **R** glassware resistant to heat

pyrite ('pairait) *n.* yellow mineral consisting of iron sulphide in cubic crystalline form

pyrites (pai'raitiːz) *n.* **1.** *see* PYRITE **2.** any of a number of other disulphides of metals, *esp.* of copper and tin (*pl.* **py'rites**)

pyro- *or before vowel* **pyr-** (*comb. form*) **1.** fire or heat, as in *pyromania, pyrometer* **2.** *Chem.* new substance obtained by heating another, as in *pyroboric acid* **3.** *Min.* having property that changes upon application of heat; having flame-coloured appearance, as in *pyroxylin*

pyrogenic (pairəʊ'dʒenik) *or* **pyrogenous** (pai'rɒdʒinəs) *a.* **1.** produced by or producing heat **2.** causing or resulting from fever

pyrography (pai'rɒgrəfi) *n.* **1.** art of burning designs on wood or leather with heated tools **2.** design made by this process

pyromania (pairəʊ'meiniə) *n. Psych.* uncontrollable impulse and practice of setting things on fire —**pyro'maniac** *n.*

pyrometer (pai'rɒmitə) *n.* instrument for measuring very high temperature —**py'rometry** *n.*

pyrotechnics (pairəʊ'tekniks) *pl.n.* **1.** (*with sing. v.*) manufacture of fireworks **2.** (*with sing. or pl. v.*) firework display —**pyro'technist** *n.*

Pyrrhic victory ('pirik) victory won at high cost

Pythagoras' theorem (pai'θægərəs) theorem that in right-angled triangle square of length of hypotenuse equals sum of squares of other two sides

python ('paiθən) *n.* large nonpoisonous snake that crushes its prey —**'pythoness** *n.* woman, such as Apollo's priestess at Delphi, believed to be possessed by oracular spirit —**pythonic** (pai'θɒnik) *a.*

pyx *or* **pix** (piks) *n.* **1.** box in Brit. Royal Mint holding specimen coins kept to be tested for weight (*also* **pyx chest**) **2.** vessel in which consecrated Host is preserved

Q

q *or* **Q** (kju:) *n.* **1.** 17th letter of English alphabet **2.** speech sound represented by this letter (*pl.* **q's, Q's** *or* **Qs**)

Q 1. *Chess* Queen **2.** Question

q. 1. quart **2.** quarter **3.** quarto (*pl.* **qq., Qq.**) (*also* **Q.**) **4.** question

Q.C. Queen's Counsel

Q.E.D. quod erat demonstrandum (*Lat.*, which was to be proved)

Qld. Queensland

Q.M. Quartermaster

qr. 1. quarter **2.** quire (*pl.* **qrs.**)

qt. 1. quart (*pl.* **qt., qts.**) **2.** quantity

q.t. *inf.* quiet —**on the q.t.** secretly

qua (kwei, kwɑː) *prep.* in the capacity of

quack (kwæk) *n.* **1.** harsh cry of duck **2.** pretender to medical or other skill —*vi.* **3.** (of duck) utter cry

quad (kwɒd) *n.* **1.** quadrangle **2.** quadrant **3.** quadraphonic **4.** quadruplet

quadrangle ('kwɒdræŋg'l) *n.* **1.** four-sided figure **2.** four-sided courtyard in a building —**quad'rangular** *a.*

quadrant ('kwɒdrənt) *n.* **1.** quarter of circle **2.** instrument for taking angular measurements —**quad'rate** *vt.* make square —**quadratic** (kwɒ'drætɪk) *a.* (of equation) involving square of unknown quantity

quadraphonic *or* **quadrophonic** (kwɒdrə'fɒnɪk) *a.* (of a sound system) using four independent speakers

quadrennial (kwɒ'drɛnɪəl) *a.* **1.** occurring every four years **2.** lasting four years —*n.* **3.** period of four years

quadri- *or before vowel* **quadr-** (*comb. form*) four

quadrilateral (kwɒdrɪ'lætərəl) *a.* **1.** four-sided —*n.* **2.** four-sided figure

quadrille (kwə'drɪl, kwɒ-) *n.* **1.** square dance **2.** music played for it **3.** old card game

quadrillion (kwɒ'drɪljən) *n.* **1.** in Brit. and Germany, number represented as one followed by 24 zeros (10^{24}) **2.** in Amer. and France, number represented as one followed by 15 zeros (10^{15}) (*pl.* **-s, quad'rillion** *a.*

quadriplegia (kwɒdrɪ'pliːdʒɪə) *n.* paralysis of all four limbs (*also* **tetra'plegia**) —**quadri'plegic** *a.*

quadrivalent (kwɒdrɪ'veɪlənt) *a. Chem.* having four valencies (*also* **tetra'valent**) —**quadri'valency** *or* **quadri'valence** *n.*

quadruped ('kwɒdrupɛd) *n.* four-footed animal —**quad'rupedal** *a.*

quadruple ('kwɒdrup'l, kwɒ'druːp'l) *a.* **1.** fourfold —*v.* **2.** make, become four times as much —**quad'ruplicate** *a.* fourfold

quadruplet ('kwɒdruplɪt, kwɒ'druːplɪt) *n.* one of four offspring born at one birth

quaff (kwɒf) *v.* drink heartily or in one draught

quag (kwæg) *n.* bog, swamp

quagga ('kwægə) *n.* recently extinct member of horse family

quail[1] (kweɪl) *n.* small bird of partridge family

quail[2] (kweɪl) *vi.* flinch; cower

quaint (kweɪnt) *a.* **1.** interestingly old-fashioned or odd **2.** curious **3.** whimsical —'**quaintly** *adv.* —'**quaintness** *n.*

quake (kweɪk) *vi.* shake, tremble

Quaker ('kweɪkə) *n.* member of Christian sect, the **Society of Friends** ('**Quakeress** *fem.*)

qualify ('kwɒlɪfaɪ) *vi.* **1.** make oneself competent —*vt.* **2.** moderate **3.** limit **4.** make competent **5.** ascribe quality to **6.** describe (**-fied, -fying**) —**qualifi'cation** *n.* **1.** thing that qualifies, attribute **2.** restriction **3.** qualifying

quality ('kwɒlɪtɪ) *n.* **1.** attribute, characteristic, property **2.** degree of excellence **3.** rank —'**qualitative** *a.* depending on quality —**qualitative analysis** *Chem.* decomposition of substance to determine kinds of constituents present; result obtained by such determination —**quality control** control of relative quality of manufactured product, usu. by statistical sampling techniques

qualm (kwɑːm) *n.* **1.** misgiving **2.** sudden feeling of sickness —'**qualmish** *a.*

quandary ('kwɒndrɪ) *n.* state of perplexity; puzzling situation; dilemma

quango ('kwæŋgəʊ) *n.* quasi-autonomous national government (*or* nongovernmental) organization (*pl.* **-s**)

quantity ('kwɒntɪtɪ) *n.* **1.** size, number, amount **2.** specified or considerable amount —'**quantify** *vt.* discover, express quantity of —'**quantitative** *a.* **1.** involving considerations of amount or size **2.** capable of being measured **3.** *Prosody* of metrical system based on length of syllables —'**quantum** *n.* desired or required amount (*pl.* **-ta**) —**quantitative analysis** *Chem.* decomposition of substance to determine amount of each constituent; result obtained by such determination —**quantity surveyor** one who estimates cost of materials, labour for building job —**quantum theory** theory that in radiation, energy of electrons is discharged not continuously but in discrete units or quanta

quarantine ('kwɒrəntiːn) *n.* **1.** isolation to prevent spreading of infection —*vt.* **2.** put, keep in quarantine

quark (kwɑːk) *n. Phys.* any of several hypothetical particles thought to be fundamental units of matter

quarrel[1] ('kwɒrəl) *n.* **1.** angry dispute **2.**

argument —*vi.* **3.** argue **4.** find fault (**-ll-**) —**'quarrelsome** *a.*

quarrel[2] ('kwɒrəl) *n.* **1.** crossbow arrow **2.** diamond-shaped pane

quarry[1] ('kwɒrɪ) *n.* **1.** object of hunt or pursuit **2.** prey

quarry[2] ('kwɒrɪ) *n.* **1.** excavation where stone *etc.* is got from ground for building *etc.* —*v.* **2.** get (stone *etc.*) from quarry (**'quarried, 'quarrying**)

quart (kwɔːt) *n.* liquid measure equal to quarter of gallon or 2 pints (1.1 litres)

quarter ('kwɔːtə) *n.* **1.** fourth part **2.** US, C 25 cents **3.** unit of weight, 28 lbs. **4.** region, district **5.** mercy —*pl.* **6.** lodgings —*vt.* **7.** divide into quarters —*v.* **8.** billet or be billeted in lodgings —**'quarterly** *a.* **1.** happening, due *etc.* each quarter of year —*n.* **2.** quarterly periodical —**quar'tet** *or* **quar'tette** *n.* **1.** group of four musicians **2.** music for four performers —**'quarto** *n.* **1.** size of book in which sheets are folded into four leaves (*pl.* **-s**) —*a.* **2.** of this size —**quarter day** any of four days in the year when certain payments become due —**'quarterdeck** *n.* after part of upper deck used *esp.* for official, ceremonial purposes —**quarter'final** *n.* round before semifinal in competition —**quarter horse** small, powerful breed of horse —**'quarterlight** *n.* UK small pivoted window in door of car —**'quartermaster** *n.* **1.** officer responsible for stores **2.** rating in navy, usu. petty officer, with particular responsibility for navigational duties —**'quarterstaff** *n.* long staff for fighting (*pl.* **-staves**)

quartz (kwɔːts) *n.* stone of pure crystalline silica —**'quartzite** *n.* quartz rock

quasar ('kweɪzɑː, -sɑː) *n.* extremely distant starlike object emitting powerful radio waves

quash (kwɒʃ) *vt.* **1.** annul **2.** reject **3.** subdue forcibly

quasi- (*comb. form*) seemingly, resembling but not actually being, as in *quasiscientific*

quassia ('kwɒʃə) *n.* tropical Amer. tree

quaternary (kwə'tɜːnərɪ) *a.* **1.** of the number four **2.** having four parts **3.** (Q-) *Geol.* of most recent period, after Tertiary —*n.* **4.** (Q-) Quaternary period or rock system

quatrain ('kwɒtreɪn) *n.* four-line stanza, *esp.* rhymed alternately

quatrefoil ('kætrəfɔɪl) *n.* **1.** leaf composed of four leaflets **2.** *Archit.* carved ornament having four arcs arranged about common centre

quaver ('kweɪvə) *vt.* **1.** say or sing in quavering tones —*vi.* **2.** tremble, shake, vibrate —*n.* **3.** musical note half length of crotchet **4.** quavering trill

quay (kiː) *n.* **1.** solid, fixed landing stage **2.** wharf

queasy ('kwiːzɪ) *a.* inclined to, or causing, sickness

queen (kwiːn) *n.* **1.** king's wife **2.** female sovereign **3.** piece in chess **4.** fertile female bee, wasp *etc.* **5.** court card with picture of a queen, ranking between king and jack **6.** *inf.* male homosexual —**'queenly** *a./adv.* —**Queen-Anne** (æn) *n.* **1.** style of furniture popular in early 18th century, characterized by use of curves, cabriole leg *etc.* —*a.* **2.** in or of this style **3.** of style of architecture popular in early 18th-century England, characterized by red-brick construction with classical ornamentation —**queen consort** wife of reigning king —**queen dowager** widow of king —**queen mother** widow of former king who is also mother of reigning sovereign —**Queen's Bench** one of the divisions of the High Court in England —**Queen's Counsel 1.** in England when sovereign is female, barrister appointed Counsel to Crown on recommendation of Lord Chancellor **2.** in Canad., honorary title which may be bestowed by government on lawyers with long experience —**Queen's English** when Brit. sovereign is female, standard S Brit. English —**queen's evidence** evidence given by criminal against his accomplice(s) —**queen's highway 1.** in Brit. when sovereign is female, any public road or right of way **2.** in Canad., main road maintained by provincial government

Queensberry rules ('kwiːnzbərɪ) **1.** code of rules followed in modern boxing **2.** *inf.* gentlemanly conduct, *esp.* in dispute

queer (kwɪə) *a.* **1.** odd, strange **2.** *inf.* homosexual —*n.* **3.** *inf.* homosexual —*vt.* *inf.* **4.** spoil **5.** interfere with

quell (kwel) *vt.* **1.** crush, put down **2.** allay **3.** pacify

quench (kwentʃ) *vt.* **1.** slake **2.** extinguish, put out **3.** suppress

quern (kwɜːn) *n.* stone hand mill

querulous ('kwerʊləs, 'kwerjʊ-) *a.* **1.** fretful **2.** peevish, whining

query ('kwɪərɪ) *n.* **1.** question **2.** mark of interrogation —*vt.* **3.** question (**'queried, 'querying**)

quest (kwest) *n./vi.* search

question ('kwestʃən) *n.* **1.** sentence seeking for answer **2.** that which is asked **3.** interrogation **4.** inquiry **5.** problem **6.** point for debate **7.** debate, strife —*vt.* **8.** ask questions of, interrogate **9.** dispute **10.** doubt —**'questionable** *a.* doubtful, *esp.* not clearly true or honest —**questionnaire** (kwestʃə'neə, kes-) *n.* list of questions drawn up for formal answer —**question mark 1.** punctuation mark **?**, used at end of questions *etc.* where doubt or ignorance is implied **2.** this mark used for any other purpose, as to draw attention to possible mistake (*also* **interrogation mark**) —**question time** in parliamentary bodies of British type, time set aside each day for questions to government ministers

queue (kjuː) *n.* **1.** line of waiting persons, vehicles —*vi.* **2.** (*with* up) wait in queue

quibble ('kwɪb[ə]l) *n.* **1.** trivial objection —*vi.* **2.** make this

quiche (kiːʃ) *n.* open savoury tart

quick (kwɪk) *a.* 1. rapid, swift 2. keen 3. brisk 4. hasty —*n.* 5. sensitive flesh 6. innermost feelings (*esp. in* cut to the quick) —*adv.* 7. *inf.* rapidly —'**quicken** *v.* make, become faster or more lively —'**quickie** *n. inf.* a quick one —'**quickly** *adv.* —'**quicklime** *n.* calcium oxide —'**quicksand** *n.* loose wet sand easily yielding to pressure and engulfing persons, animals *etc.* —'**quickset** *chiefly* UK *n.* 1. plant or cutting, *esp.* of hawthorn, set so as to form hedge; such plants or cuttings collectively 2. hedge composed of such plants —*a.* 3. composed of such plants —'**quicksilver** *n.* mercury —'**quickstep** *n.* 1. ballroom dance —*vi.* 2. perform this dance —**quick-tempered** *a.* irascible —**quick-witted** *a.* having keenly alert mind —**quick-wittedness** *n.* —**the quick** *obs.* living people

quid¹ (kwɪd) *n.* piece of tobacco suitable for chewing

quid² (kwɪd) *n. inf.* pound (sterling) (*pl.* quid)

quiddity ('kwɪdɪtɪ) *n.* 1. essential nature 2. petty or trifling distinction; quibble

quid pro quo ('kwɪd prəʊ 'kwəʊ) *Lat.* something given in exchange

quiescent (kwɪ'ɛsˀnt) *a.* 1. at rest, inactive, inert 2. silent —**qui'escence** *or* **qui'escency** *n.*

quiet ('kwaɪət) *a.* 1. with little or no motion or noise 2. undisturbed 3. not showy or obtrusive —*n.* 4. state of peacefulness, absence of noise or disturbance —*v.* 5. make, become quiet —'**quieten** *v.* make, become quiet —'**quietly** *adv.* —'**quietness** *or* '**quietude** *n.*

quietism ('kwaɪətɪzəm) *n.* passive attitude to life, *esp.* as form of religion —'**quietist** *n.*

quietus (kwaɪ'iːtəs, -'eɪtəs) *n.* 1. anything that serves to quash, eliminate or kill 2. release from life; death 3. discharge or settlement of debts, duties *etc.*

quiff (kwɪf) UK tuft of hair brushed up above forehead

quill (kwɪl) *n.* 1. large feather 2. hollow stem of this 3. pen, plectrum made from feather 4. spine of porcupine

quilt (kwɪlt) *n.* 1. padded coverlet —*vt.* 2. stitch (two pieces of cloth) with pad between

quin (kwɪn) quintuplet

quince (kwɪns) *n.* 1. acid pear-shaped fruit 2. tree bearing it

quincunx ('kwɪŋkʌŋks) *n.* group of five objects arranged in shape of rectangle with one at each corner and fifth in centre

quinine (kwɪ'niːn; *U.S.* 'kwaɪnaɪn) *n.* bitter drug made from bark of tree, used to treat fever, and as tonic

Quinquagesima (kwɪŋkwə'dʒɛsɪmə) *n.* Sunday 50 days before Easter

quinquennial (kwɪn'kwɛnɪəl) *a.* occurring once in, or lasting, five years

quinquereme ('kwɪŋkwɪriːm) *n.* ancient Roman galley with five banks of oars

quinsy ('kwɪnzɪ) *n.* inflammation of throat or tonsils

quintessence (kwɪn'tɛsəns) *n.* 1. purest form, essential feature 2. embodiment —**quintes'sential** *a.*

quintet *or* **quintette** (kwɪn'tɛt) *n.* 1. set of five singers or players 2. composition for five voices or instruments

quintillion (kwɪn'tɪljən) *n.* 1. in Brit. and Germany, number represented as one followed by 30 zeros (10^{30}) 2. in Amer. and France, number represented as one followed by 18 zeros (10^{18}) (*pl.* -s, **quin'tillion**) —**quin'tillionth** *a.*

quintuple ('kwɪntjʊpˀl, kwɪn'tjuːpˀl) *vt.* 1. multiply by five —*a.* 2. five times as much or as many; fivefold 3. consisting of five parts —*n.* 4. quantity or number five times as great as another

quintuplet ('kwɪntjʊplɪt, kwɪn'tjuːplɪt) *n.* one of five offspring born at one birth

quip (kwɪp) *n.* 1. witty saying —*vi.* 2. make quip (**-pp-**)

quire (kwaɪə) *n.* 24 sheets of writing paper

quirk (kwɜːk) *n.* 1. individual peculiarity of character 2. unexpected twist or turn

quisling ('kwɪzlɪŋ) *n.* traitor who aids occupying enemy force

quit (kwɪt) *vi.* 1. stop doing a thing 2. depart —*vt.* 3. leave, go away from 4. cease from (**quit** *or* '**quitted** *pt./pp.*) —*a.* 5. free, rid —**quits** *a.* on equal or even terms by repayment *etc.* —'**quittance** *n.* 1. discharge 2. receipt —'**quitter** *n.* one lacking perseverance

quitch grass (kwɪtʃ) *see* COUCH GRASS

quite (kwaɪt) *adv.* 1. wholly, completely 2. very considerably 3. somewhat, rather —*interj.* 4. exactly, just so

quiver¹ ('kwɪvə) *vi.* 1. shake, tremble —*n.* 2. quivering 3. vibration

quiver² ('kwɪvə) *n.* carrying case for arrows

quixotic (kwɪk'sɒtɪk) *a.* unrealistically and impractically optimistic, idealistic, chivalrous

quiz (kwɪz) *n.* 1. entertainment in which general or specific knowledge of players is tested by questions 2. examination, interrogation —*vt.* 3. question, interrogate (**-zz-**) —'**quizzical** *a.* 1. questioning 2. mocking

quod (kwɒd) *n. sl.* prison

quoin (kɔɪn, kwɔɪn) *n.* 1. external corner of building 2. small wedge for locking printing type into forme

quoit (kɔɪt) *n.* 1. ring for throwing at peg as a game —*pl.* 2. (*with sing. v.*) the game

quondam ('kwɒndæm) *a.* of an earlier time; former

quorum ('kwɔːrəm) *n.* least number that must be present in meeting to make its transactions valid

quota ('kwəʊtə) *n.* 1. share to be contributed or received 2. specified number, quantity, which may be imported or admitted

quote (kwəʊt) *vt.* **1.** copy or repeat passages from **2.** refer to, *esp.* to confirm view **3.** state price for —**'quotable** *a.* —**quo'tation** *n.* —**quotation mark** either of punctuation marks used to begin or end quotation, respectively " and " or ' and '

quoth (kwəʊθ) *v. obs.* said

quotidian (kwəʊ'tɪdɪən) *a.* **1.** daily **2.** everyday, commonplace

quotient ('kwəʊʃənt) *n.* number resulting from dividing one number by another

q.v. quod vide (*Lat.*, which see)

qwerty *or* **QWERTY** ('kwɜːtɪ) *n. inf.* standard typewriter keyboard

R

r *or* **R** (ɑː) *n.* **1.** 18th letter of English alphabet **2.** speech sound represented by this letter (*pl.* **r's, R's** *or* **Rs**) —**the three Rs** three skills regarded as fundamentals of education: reading, writing and arithmetic

R 1. *Chem.* radical **2.** rand **3.** rupee **4.** Réaumur (scale) **5.** *Phys., electron.* resistance **6.** roentgen *or* röntgen **7.** *Chess* rook **8.** Royal **9.** *Chem.* gas constant **10.** radius

R. 1. Regina (*Lat.,* Queen) **2.** Rex (*Lat.,* King) **3.** River

Ra *Chem.* radium

R.A. 1. Rear Admiral **2.** Royal Academy **3.** Royal Artillery

R.A.A.F. Royal Australian Air Force

rabbet ('ræbɪt) *see* REBATE²

rabbi ('ræbaɪ) *n.* Jewish learned man, spiritual leader (*pl.* **-s**) —**rabbinical** (rə'bɪnɪk°l) *or* **rab'binic** *a.*

rabbit ('ræbɪt) *n.* **1.** small burrowing rodent like hare —*vi.* **2.** hunt rabbits —**rabbit punch** sharp blow to back of neck

rabble ('ræb°l) *n.* **1.** crowd of vulgar, noisy people **2.** mob —**rabble-rouser** *n.* person who manipulates passions of mob; demagogue

Rabelaisian (ræbə'leɪzɪən, -ʒən) *a.* **1.** of or resembling work of François Rabelais, Fr. writer, characterized by broad, oft. bawdy humour and sharp satire —*n.* **2.** student or admirer of Rabelais

rabid ('ræbɪd, 'reɪ-) *a.* **1.** relating to or having rabies **2.** furious **3.** mad **4.** fanatical —**'rabidly** *adv.* —**'rabidness** *n.*

rabies ('reɪbiːz) *n. Pathol.* acute infectious viral disease transmitted by dogs *etc.*

R.A.C. 1. Royal Automobile Club **2.** Royal Armoured Corps

raccoon *or* **racoon** (rə'kuːn) *n.* small N Amer. mammal

race¹ (reɪs) *n.* **1.** contest of speed, as in running, swimming *etc.* **2.** contest, rivalry **3.** strong current of water, *esp.* leading to water wheel —*pl.* **4.** meeting for horse racing —*vt.* **5.** cause to run rapidly —*vi.* **6.** run swiftly **7.** (of engine, pedal *etc.*) move rapidly and erratically, *esp.* on removal of resistance —**'racer** *n.* person, vehicle, animal that races —**'racecourse** *n.* long broad track, over which horses are raced (*also* (*esp.* US) **'racetrack**) —**race meeting** prearranged fixture for racing horses *etc.* over set course —**'racetrack** *n.* **1.** circuit for motor racing *etc.* **2.** *esp.* US racecourse

race² (reɪs) *n.* **1.** group of people of common ancestry with distinguishing physical features, skin colour *etc.* **2.** species **3.** type —**'racial** *a.* —**'racialism** *or* **'racism** *n.* **1.** belief in innate superiority of particular race **2.** antagonism towards members of different race based on this belief —**'racialist** *or* **'racist** *a./n.* —**race relations 1.** (*with pl. v.*) relations between members of two or more human races, *esp.* within single community **2.** (*with sing. v.*) branch of sociology concerned with such relations —**race riot** riot among members of different races in same community

raceme (rə'siːm) *n.* cluster of flowers along a central stem, as in foxglove

rack¹ (ræk) *n.* **1.** framework for displaying or holding baggage, books, hats, bottles *etc.* **2.** *Mech.* straight bar with teeth on its edge, to work with pinion **3.** instrument of torture by stretching —*vt.* **4.** stretch on rack or wheel **5.** torture **6.** stretch, strain —**'racking** *a.* agonizing —**rack-and-pinion** *n.* **1.** device for converting rotary into linear motion and vice versa, in which gearwheel (pinion) engages with flat toothed bar (rack) —*a.* **2.** (of type of steering gear in motor vehicles) having track rod with rack along part of its length that engages with pinion attached to steering column —**rack railway** mountain railway having middle rail fitted with rack that engages pinion on locomotive (*also* **cog railway**) —**rack-rent** *n.* **1.** high rent that annually equals value of property upon which it is charged **2.** any extortionate rent —*vt.* **3.** charge extortionate rent for

rack² (ræk) *n.* destruction (*esp. in* **rack and ruin**)

rack³ *or* **wrack** (ræk) *n.* broken mass of clouds blown by wind

rack⁴ (ræk) *vt.* clear (wine, beer *etc.*) by drawing it off from dregs

rack⁵ (ræk) *n.* neck or rib section of mutton, lamb or pork

racket¹ ('rækɪt) *n.* **1.** loud noise, uproar **2.** occupation by which money is made illegally —**racket'eer** *n.* one making illegal profits —**racket'eering** *n.* —**'rackety** *a.* noisy

racket² *or* **racquet** ('rækɪt) *n.* **1.** bat used in tennis *etc.* —*pl.n.* **2.** (*with sing. v.*) ball game played in paved, walled court

raconteur (rækɒn'tɜː) *n.* skilled storyteller

racy ('reɪsɪ) *a.* **1.** spirited **2.** lively **3.** having strong flavour **4.** spicy **5.** piquant —**'racily** *adv.* —**'raciness** *n.*

RADA ('rɑːdə) UK Royal Academy of Dramatic Art

radar ('reɪdɑː) *n.* device for finding range and direction by ultrahigh-frequency point-to-point radio waves, which reflect back to their source and reveal position and nature of objects sought —**radar trap**

device using radar to detect motorists exceeding speed limit

raddled ('ræd'ld) *a.* (*esp.* of person) unkempt or run-down in appearance

radial ('reidiəl) *a. see* RADIUS

radiate ('reidieit) *v.* 1. emit, be emitted in rays —*vi.* 2. spread out from centre —'**radiance** *n.* 1. brightness 2. splendour —'**radiant** *a.* 1. beaming 2. shining 3. emitting rays —*n.* 4. point or object that emits radiation, *esp.* part of heater that gives out heat 5. *Astron.* the point in space from which a meteor shower appears to emanate —**radi'ation** *n.* 1. transmission of heat, light *etc.* from one body to another 2. particles, rays, emitted in nuclear decay 3. act of radiating —'**radiator** *n.* 1. that which radiates, *esp.* heating apparatus for rooms 2. cooling apparatus of car engine —**radiant energy** energy emitted or propagated in form of particles or electromagnetic radiation —**radiation sickness** *Pathol.* illness caused by overexposure of body to ionizing radiations from radioactive material *etc.*

radical ('rædik'l) *a.* 1. fundamental, thorough 2. extreme 3. *Maths.* of roots of numbers or quantities —*n.* 4. person of extreme (political) views 5. radicle 6. *Maths.* number expressed as root of another 7. group of atoms of several elements which remain unchanged in a series of chemical compounds —'**radicalism** *n.* —**radical sign** symbol √ placed before number or quantity to indicate extraction of root, *esp.* square root

radicle ('rædik'l) *n. Bot.* root

radio ('reidiəʊ) *n.* 1. use of electromagnetic waves for broadcasting, communication *etc.* 2. device for receiving, amplifying radio signals 3. broadcasting, content of radio programmes —*vt.* 4. transmit (message *etc.*) by radio —**radio'active** *a.* emitting invisible rays that penetrate matter —**radioac'tivity** *n.* —**radio astronomy** astronomy in which radio telescope is used to detect and analyse radio signals received on earth from radio sources in space —**radiocarbon dating** technique for determining age of organic materials based on their content of radioisotope ¹⁴C acquired from atmosphere when they formed part of living plant (*see also* **carbon dating** *at* CARBON) —**radio'chemical** *a.* —**radio'chemist** *n.* —**radio'chemistry** *n.* chemistry of radioactive elements and their compounds —**radio frequency** 1. any frequency that lies in range 10 kilohertz to 300 000 megahertz and can be used for broadcasting 2. frequency transmitted by particular radio station —'**radiogram** *n.* 1. UK unit comprising radio and gramophone 2. message transmitted by radiotelegraphy 3. radiograph —'**radiograph** *n.* image produced on sensitized film or plate by radiation —**radi'ographer** *n.* —**radi'ography** *n.* production of image on film or plate by radiation —**radio'isotope** *n.*

radioactive isotope —**radi'ologist** *n.* —**radi'ology** *n.* science of use of rays in medicine —**radioscopic** (reidiəʊ'skɒpik) *a.* —**radi'oscopy** *n. see* **fluoroscopy** *at* FLUORESCENCE —**radiosonde** ('reidiəʊsɒnd) *n.* airborne instrument to send meteorological information back to earth by radio —**radio'telegraph** *v./n.* —**radiote'legraphy** *n.* telegraphy in which messages (usu. in Morse code) are transmitted by radio waves —**radio'telephone** *n.* 1. device for communications by means of radio waves —*v.* 2. telephone (person) by radiotelephone —**radiote'lephony** *n.* —**radio telescope** instrument used in radio astronomy to pick up and analyse radio waves from space and to transmit radio waves —**radio'therapy** *n.* diagnosis and treatment of disease by x-rays

radio- (*comb. form*) 1. denoting radio, broadcasting or radio frequency, as in *radiogram* 2. indicating radioactivity or radiation, as in *radiochemistry*

radish ('rædiʃ) *n.* pungent root vegetable

radium ('reidiəm) *n.* radioactive metallic element

radius ('reidiəs) *n.* 1. straight line from centre to circumference of circle 2. outer of two bones in forearm (*pl.* **radii** ('reidiai), **-es**) —'**radial** *a.* 1. arranged like radii of circle 2. of ray or rays 3. of radius —'**radian** *n.* SI unit of plane angle; angle between two radii of circle that cut off on circumference arc equal in length to radius —**radial-ply** *a.* (of motor tyre) having fabric cords in outer casing running radially, enabling sidewalls to be flexible

radon ('reidɒn) *n.* radioactive gaseous element

RAF (*nonstandard* ræf) *or* **R.A.F.** Royal Air Force

raffia *or* **raphia** ('ræfiə) *n.* prepared palm fibre for making mats *etc.*

raffish ('ræfiʃ) *a.* disreputable

raffle ('ræf'l) *n.* 1. lottery in which an article is assigned by lot to one of those buying tickets —*vt.* 2. dispose of by raffle

raft (rɑːft) *n.* floating structure of logs, planks *etc.*

rafter ('rɑːftə) *n.* one of main beams of roof

rag¹ (ræg) *n.* 1. fragment of cloth 2. torn piece 3. *inf.* newspaper *etc.*, *esp.* one considered worthless 4. piece of ragtime music —*pl.* 5. tattered clothing —**ragged** ('rægid) *a.* 1. shaggy 2. torn 3. clothed in torn clothes 4. lacking smoothness —**rag-and-bone man** UK man who buys and sells discarded clothing *etc.* —'**ragbag** *n.* confused assortment —'**ragtag** *n. derogatory* common people; rabble (*esp.* in **ragtag and bobtail**) —'**ragtime** *n.* style of jazz piano music —**rag trade** *inf.* clothing industry, trade —'**ragwort** *n.* European plant with yellow daisylike flowers (*see also* GROUNDSEL)

rag² (ræg) *vt.* 1. tease 2. torment 3. play

practical jokes on (**-gg-**) —*n*. **4. a.** period of carnival with procession *etc*. organized by students to raise money for charities **b.** (*as modifier*): rag day

ragamuffin (ˈrægəmʌfɪn) *n*. ragged, dirty person

rage (reɪdʒ) *n*. **1.** violent anger or passion **2.** fury —*vi*. **3.** speak, act with fury **4.** proceed violently and without check (as storm, battle *etc*.) **5.** be widely and violently prevalent —**all the rage** very popular

raglan (ˈræglən) *a*. of sleeves that continue to the neck so that there are no shoulder seams

ragout (ræˈguː) *n*. highly seasoned stew of meat and vegetables

raid (reɪd) *n*. **1.** rush, attack **2.** foray —*vt*. **3.** make raid on —**ˈraider** *n*.

rail¹ (reɪl) *n*. horizontal bar, *esp*. as part of fence, track *etc*. —**ˈrailing** *n*. fence, barrier made of rails supported by posts —**ˈrailhead** *n*. farthest point to which railway line extends —**ˈrailway** *or U.S.* **ˈrailroad** *n*. **1.** track of iron rails on which trains run **2.** company operating railway —**off the rails** *inf*. **1.** astray **2.** on wrong track **3.** in error **4.** leading reckless, dissipated life

rail² (reɪl) *vi*. (*with* at *or* against) **1.** utter abuse **2.** scoff **3.** scold **4.** reproach —**ˈraillery** *n*. banter

rail³ (reɪl) *n*. any of various kinds of marsh bird

raiment (ˈreɪmənt) *n*. *obs*. clothing

rain (reɪn) *n*. **1.** moisture falling in drops from clouds **2.** fall of such drops —*vi*. **3.** fall as rain —*vt*. **4.** pour down like rain —**ˈrainy** *a*. —**ˈrainbow** *n*. arch of prismatic colours in sky —**ˈraincoat** *n*. light water-resistant overcoat —**ˈrainfall** *n*. precipitation in form of raindrops **2.** *Met*. amount of precipitation in specified place and time —**ˈrainforest** *n*. dense forest found in tropical areas of heavy rainfall —**rain gauge** instrument for measuring rainfall —**rain shadow** relatively dry area on leeward side of high ground in path of rain-bearing winds —**rainy day** future time of need, *esp*. financial —**take a rain check** *Inf*. accept postponement of offer

raise (reɪz) *vt*. **1.** lift up **2.** set up **3.** build **4.** increase **5.** elevate **6.** promote **7.** heighten, as pitch of voice **8.** breed into existence **9.** levy, collect **10.** end (siege)

raisin (ˈreɪzᵊn) *n*. dried grape

raison d'être (rɛzɔ̃ ˈdɛtr) *Fr*. reason or justification for existence (*pl*. **raisons d'être** (rɛzɔ̃ ˈdɛtr))

raj (rɑːdʒ) *n*. rule, sway, *esp*. in India —**ˈrajah** *or* **ˈraja** *n*. (formerly) Indian prince or ruler

rake¹ (reɪk) *n*. **1.** tool with long handle and crosspiece with teeth for gathering hay, leaves *etc*. —*vt*. **2.** gather, smooth with rake **3.** sweep, search over **4.** sweep with shot —**rake-off** *n*. *inf*. monetary commission, *esp*. illegal

rake² (reɪk) *n*. dissolute or dissipated man —**ˈrakish** *a*. dissolute; profligate

rake³ (reɪk) *n*. **1.** slope, *esp*. backwards, of ship's funnel *etc*. —*v*. **2.** incline from perpendicular —**ˈrakish** *a*. appearing dashing or speedy

rally¹ (ˈrælɪ) *vt*. **1.** bring together, *esp*. what has been scattered, as routed army or dispersed troops —*vi*. **2.** come together **3.** regain health or strength, revive (**ˈrallied**, **ˈrallying**) —*n*. **4.** act of rallying **5.** assembly, *esp*. outdoor, of any organization **6.** *Tennis* lively exchange of strokes

rally² (ˈrælɪ) *v*. mock or ridicule (someone) in good-natured way; chaff; tease

ram (ræm) *n*. **1.** male sheep **2.** hydraulic machine **3.** battering engine —*vt*. **4.** force, drive **5.** strike against with force **6.** stuff **7.** strike with ram (**-mm-**) —**ˈramrod** *n*. **1.** rod for cleaning barrel of rifle *etc*. **2.** rod for ramming in charge of muzzle-loading firearm

RAM (ræm) *Comp*. random access memory

R.A.M. Royal Academy of Music

Ramadan, Rhamadhan (ræməˈdɑːn) *or* **Ramazan** (ræməˈzɑːn) *n*. **1.** 9th Mohammedan month **2.** strict fasting observed during this time

ramble (ˈræmbᵊl) *vi*. **1.** walk without definite route **2.** wander **3.** talk incoherently **4.** spread in random fashion —*n*. **5.** rambling walk —**ˈrambler** *n*. **1.** climbing rose **2.** one who rambles

rambutan (ræmˈbuːtᵊn) *n*. **1.** SE Asian tree **2.** its bright red edible fruit

R.A.M.C. Royal Army Medical Corps

ramekin *or* **ramequin** (ˈræmɪkɪn) *n*. **1.** small fireproof dish **2.** savoury food baked in it

ramify (ˈræmɪfaɪ) *v*. **1.** spread in branches, subdivide —*vi*. **2.** become complex (**-ified**, **-ifying**) —**ramifiˈcation** *n*. **1.** branch, subdivision **2.** process of branching out **3.** consequence

ramp (ræmp) *n*. gradual slope joining two level surfaces

rampage (ræmˈpeɪdʒ) *vi*. **1.** dash about violently —*n*. (ˈræmpeɪdʒ, ræmˈpeɪdʒ) **2.** angry or destructive behaviour —**ramˈpageous** *a*. —**on the rampage** behaving violently or destructively

rampant (ˈræmpənt) *a*. **1.** violent **2.** rife **3.** rearing

rampart (ˈræmpɑːt) *n*. **1.** mound, wall for defence —*vt*. **2.** defend with rampart

rampike (ˈræmpaɪk) *n*. *C* tall tree, burnt or bare of branches

ramshackle (ˈræmʃækᵊl) *a*. tumbledown, rickety, makeshift

ran (ræn) *pt. of* RUN

ranch (rɑːntʃ) *n*. **1.** Amer. cattle farm —*vi*. **2.** manage a ranch —**ˈrancher** *n*.

rancherie (ˈrɑːntʃərɪ) *n*. *C* Indian reservation

rancid ('rænsɪd) a. (of food) having unpleasant smell or taste —**ran'cidity** n.

rancour or U.S. **rancor** ('ræŋkə) n. bitter, inveterate hate —**rancorous** a. 1. malignant 2. virulent

rand (rænd, rɒnt) n. monetary unit of S Afr.

R & B rhythm-and-blues

R & D research and development

random ('rændəm) a. made or done by chance, without plan —**at random** haphazard(ly)

randy ('rændɪ) a. sl. sexually aroused

rang (ræŋ) pt. of RING²

range (reɪndʒ) n. 1. limits 2. row 3. scope, sphere 4. distance missile can travel 5. distance of mark shot at 6. place for shooting practice or rocket testing 7. rank 8. kitchen stove —vt. 9. set in row 10. classify 11. roam —vi. 12. extend 13. roam 14. pass from one point to another 15. fluctuate (as prices) —**'ranger** n. 1. official in charge of or patrolling park etc. 2. (R-) member of senior branch of Guides —**'rangy** a. 1. with long, slender limbs 2. spacious —**'rangefinder** n. instrument for finding distance away of given object

rani or **ranee** ('rɑːnɪ) n. queen or princess; wife of rajah

rank¹ (ræŋk) n. 1. row, line 2. place where taxis wait 3. order 4. social class 5. status 6. relative place or position —pl. 7. common soldiers 8. great mass or majority of people (also **rank and file**) —vt. 9. draw up in rank, classify —vi. 10. have rank, place 11. have certain distinctions

rank² (ræŋk) a. 1. growing too thickly, coarse 2. offensively strong 3. rancid 4. vile 5. flagrant —**'rankly** adv.

rankle ('ræŋk³l) vi. fester, continue to cause anger, resentment or bitterness

ransack ('rænsæk) vt. 1. search thoroughly 2. pillage, plunder

ransom ('rænsəm) n. 1. release from captivity by payment 2. amount paid —vt. 3. pay ransom for —**'ransomer** n.

rant (rænt) vi. 1. rave in violent, high-sounding language —n. 2. noisy, boisterous speech 3. wild gaiety —**'ranter** n.

ranunculus (rə'nʌŋkjʊləs) n. any of a genus of plants that includes buttercup, crowfoot and spearwort

rap¹ (ræp) n. 1. smart slight blow 2. fast, rhythmic monologue over musical backing —vt. 3. give rap to (-**pp**-) —**rap music** —**take the rap** sl. suffer punishment, whether guilty or not

rap² (ræp) n. the least amount (esp. in **not to care a rap**)

rapacious (rə'peɪʃəs) a. 1. greedy 2. grasping —**rapacity** (rə'pæsɪtɪ) n.

rape¹ (reɪp) vt. 1. force (woman) to submit unwillingly to sexual intercourse —n. 2. act of raping 3. any violation or abuse

rape² (reɪp) n. plant with oil-yielding seeds, also used as fodder (also **'colza, cole**)

rapid ('ræpɪd) a. 1. quick, swift —pl.n. 2. part of river with fast, turbulent current —**ra'pidity** or **'rapidness** n. —**'rapidly** adv. —**rapid eye movement** movement of eyeballs during sleep, while sleeper is dreaming

rapier ('reɪpɪə) n. fine-bladed sword used as thrusting weapon

rapine ('ræpaɪn) n. plunder

rapport (ræ'pɔː) n. harmony, agreement

rapprochement (raprɔʃ'mɑ̃) Fr. reestablishment of friendly relations between nations

rapscallion (ræp'skæljən) n. rascal, rogue

rapt (ræpt) a. engrossed, spellbound —**'rapture** n. ecstasy —**'rapturous** a.

raptorial (ræp'tɔːrɪəl) a. 1. predatory 2. of the order of birds of prey

rare¹ (reə) a. 1. uncommon 2. infrequent 3. of uncommon quality 4. (of atmosphere) having low density, thin —**'rarely** adv. seldom —**'rarity** n. 1. anything rare 2. rareness —**rare earth** 1. any oxide of lanthanide 2. any element of lanthanide series (also **rare-earth element**)

rare² (reə) a. (of meat) lightly cooked

rarebit ('reəbɪt) n. savoury cheese dish (also **Welsh rabbit**)

rarefy ('reərɪfaɪ) v. 1. make, become thin, rare or less dense (-**fied**, -**fying**) —**rare'faction** or **rarefi'cation** n.

raring ('reərɪŋ) a. enthusiastically willing, ready

rascal ('rɑːsk³l) n. 1. rogue 2. naughty (young) person —**ras'cality** n. roguery, baseness —**'rascally** a./adv.

rase (reɪz) vt. see RAZE

rash¹ (ræʃ) a. hasty, reckless, incautious —**'rashly** adv.

rash² (ræʃ) n. 1. skin eruption 2. outbreak, series of (unpleasant) occurrences

rasher ('ræʃə) n. thin slice of bacon or ham

rasp (rɑːsp) n. 1. harsh, grating noise 2. coarse file —vt. 3. scrape with rasp —vi. 4. grate upon 5. irritate 6. make scraping noise 7. speak in grating voice

raspberry ('rɑːzbərɪ, -brɪ) n. 1. red, juicy, edible berry 2. plant which bears it 3. inf. spluttering noise with tongue and lips to show contempt

Rastafarian (ræstə'feərɪən) n. 1. member of Jamaican cult that regards Ras Tafari, former emperor of Ethiopia, Haile Selassie, as God —a. 2. of Rastafarians —**'Rasta** a./n.

rat (ræt) n. 1. small rodent 2. inf. contemptible person, esp. deserter, informer etc. —vi. 3. inform 4. (with on) betray 5. (with on) desert, abandon 6. hunt rats (-**tt**-) —**'ratter** n. 1. dog or cat that catches and kills rats 2. inf. worker who works during strike; blackleg; scab (also **rat**) —**'ratty** a. sl. 1. mean, ill-tempered, irritable 2. (of hair) straggly, unkempt, greasy —**rat-catcher** n. one whose job is to drive away or destroy vermin, esp. rats —**rat race** continual hectic competitive activity —**'ratsbane** n. rat poison, esp.

arsenic oxide —**smell a rat** have suspicions of some treacherous practice

ratchet ('rætʃɪt) *n.* set of teeth on bar or wheel allowing motion in one direction only

rate[1] (reɪt) *n.* **1.** proportion between two things **2.** charge **3.** degree of speed *etc.* —*pl.* **4.** local tax on property —*vt.* **5.** value **6.** estimate value of **7.** assess for local taxation —'**ratable** *or* '**rateable** *a.* **1.** that can be rated **2.** liable to pay rates —**ratable value** *or* **rateable value** UK fixed value assigned to property by local authority, on basis of which variable annual rates are charged —**rate-cap** *vt.* UK impose on (local authority) upper limit on rates it may levy —**rate-capping** *n.* —'**ratepayer** *n.*

rate[2] (reɪt) *vt.* scold, chide

rather ('rɑːðə) *adv.* **1.** to some extent **2.** preferably **3.** more willingly

ratify ('rætɪfaɪ) *vt.* confirm (-**ified**, -**ifying**) —**ratifi'cation** *n.*

rating ('reɪtɪŋ) *n.* **1.** valuing or assessing **2.** fixing a rate **3.** classification, *esp.* of ship **4.** rank or grade as of naval personnel **5.** angry rebuke

ratio ('reɪʃɪəʊ) *n.* **1.** proportion **2.** quantitative relation

ratiocinate (rætɪ'ɒsɪneɪt) *vi.* reason —**ratioci'nation** *n.*

ration ('ræʃən) *n.* **1.** fixed allowance of food *etc.* —*vt.* **2.** supply with, limit to certain amount

rational ('ræʃənəl) *a.* **1.** reasonable, sensible **2.** capable of thinking, reasoning —**rationale** (ræʃə'nɑːl) *n.* reasons given for actions *etc.* —'**rationalism** *n.* philosophy which regards reason as only guide or authority —'**rationalist** *n.* —**ratio'nality** *n.* —**rationali'zation** *or* **-i'sation** *n.* —'**rationalize** *or* **-ise** *vt.* **1.** justify by plausible reasoning **2.** reorganize to improve efficiency *etc.* —'**rationally** *adv.*

ratline *or* **ratlin** ('rætlɪn) *n.* Naut. any of light lines tied across shrouds of sailing vessel for climbing aloft

rattan *or* **ratan** (ræ'tæn) *n.* **1.** climbing palm with jointed stems **2.** cane made of this

rattle ('ræt°l) *vi.* **1.** give out succession of short sharp sounds **2.** clatter —*vt.* **3.** shake briskly causing a sharp clatter of sounds **4.** *inf.* confuse, fluster —*n.* **5.** succession of short sharp sounds **6.** baby's toy filled with small pellets for making this sound **7.** set of horny rings in rattlesnake's tail —'**rattling** *adv. inf.* very —'**rattlesnake** *n.* poisonous snake —'**rattletrap** *n. inf.* broken-down old vehicle, *esp.* car

raucous ('rɔːkəs) *a.* **1.** hoarse **2.** harsh

raunchy ('rɔːntʃɪ) *a.* US *sl.* **1.** lecherous, smutty **2.** slovenly; dirty

ravage ('rævɪdʒ) *vt.* **1.** lay waste, plunder —*n.* **2.** destruction

rave (reɪv) *vi.* **1.** talk wildly, as in delirium **2.** write or speak (about) enthusiastically —*n.* **3.** enthusiastic or extravagant praise

—'**raving** *a.* **1.** delirious; frenzied **2.** *inf.* exciting admiration —*adv.* **3.** so as to cause raving —**rave-up** *n. sl.* party

ravel ('ræv°l) *vt.* **1.** entangle **2.** fray out **3.** disentangle (**-ll-**)

raven[1] ('reɪv°n) *n.* **1.** black bird like crow —*a.* **2.** jet-black

raven[2] ('ræv°n) *v.* seek (prey, plunder) —'**ravening** *a.* (of animals) voracious; predatory —'**ravenous** *a.* very hungry

ravine (rə'viːn) *n.* narrow steep-sided valley worn by stream, gorge

ravioli (rævɪ'əʊlɪ) *n.* small, thin pieces of dough filled with highly seasoned, chopped meat and cooked

ravish ('rævɪʃ) *vt.* **1.** enrapture **2.** commit rape upon —'**ravishing** *a.* lovely, entrancing

raw (rɔː) *a.* **1.** uncooked **2.** not manufactured or refined **3.** skinned **4.** inexperienced, unpractised, as recruits **5.** sensitive **6.** chilly —'**raw'boned** *a.* having lean bony physique —**raw deal** unfair or dishonest treatment —'**rawhide** *n.* **1.** untanned hide **2.** whip made of this —**in the raw 1.** *inf.* without clothes; naked **2.** in natural or unmodified state

ray[1] (reɪ) *n.* **1.** single line or narrow beam of light, heat *etc.* **2.** any of set of radiating lines —*vi.* **3.** come out in rays **4.** radiate

ray[2] (reɪ) *n.* marine fish, oft. very large, with winglike pectoral fins and whiplike tail

ray[3] (reɪ) *n. Mus.* in tonic solfa, second degree of any major scale; supertonic

rayon ('reɪɒn) *n.* (fabric made of) synthetic fibre

raze *or* **rase** (reɪz) *vt.* **1.** destroy completely **2.** wipe out, delete **3.** level

razor ('reɪzə) *n.* sharp instrument for shaving or for cutting hair —'**razorbill** *n.* N Atlantic auk

razzle-dazzle ('ræz°l'dæz°l) *or* **razzmatazz** ('ræzmə'tæz) *n. sl.* **1.** noisy or showy fuss or activity **2.** spree; frolic

Rb *Chem.* rubidium

R.C. 1. Red Cross **2.** Roman Catholic

R.C.A. 1. Radio Corporation of America **2.** Royal College of Art

R.C.A.F. Royal Canadian Air Force

R.C.M. Royal College of Music

R.C.M.P. Royal Canadian Mounted Police

R.C.N. 1. Royal Canadian Navy **2.** Royal College of Nursing

Rd. Road

re[1] (reɪ, riː) *n. Mus. see* RAY[3]

re[2] (riː) *prep.* with reference to, concerning

Re *Chem.* rhenium

R.E. 1. Royal Engineers **2.** religious education

re- (*comb. form*) again. See the list below, where the meaning may be inferred from the word to which *re-* is prefixed

reach (riːtʃ) *vt.* **1.** arrive at **2.** extend as far as **3.** succeed in touching **4.** attain to —*vi.* **5.** stretch out hand **6.** extend —*n.* **7.** act of reaching **8.** power of touching **9.** grasp, scope **10.** range **11.** stretch of river

between two bends —'**reachable** a.
—**reach-me-down** n. 1. see **hand-me-down**
at HAND 2. ready-made garment

react (rɪ'ækt) vi. act in return, opposition
or towards former state —re'**actance** n.
Elec. resistance in coil, apart from ohmic
resistance, due to current reacting on
itself —re'**action** n. 1. any action resisting
another 2. counter or backward tendency
3. mental depression following
overexertion 4. *inf.* response 5. chemical
or nuclear change, combination or
decomposition —re'**actionary** n./a. (person) opposed to change, *esp.* in politics
etc. —re'**active** a. chemically active
—**nuclear reactor** apparatus in which
nuclear reaction is maintained and
controlled to produce nuclear energy

read (ri:d) vt. 1. look at and understand
(written or printed matter) 2. learn by
reading 3. interpret mentally 4. read and
utter 5. interpret 6. study 7. understand
(any indicating instrument) 8. (of instrument) register —vi. 9. be occupied in
reading 10. find mentioned in reading
(**read** (rɛd) *pt./pp.*) —**reada**'**bility** n.
—'**readable** a. that can be read, or read
with pleasure —'**reader** n. 1. one who
reads 2. university lecturer 3. school
textbook 4. one who reads manuscripts
submitted to publisher 5. one who reads
printer's proofs —'**readership** n. all
readers of particular publication or author
—'**reading** n. —**read-out** n. 1. retrieving of
information from computer memory or
storage device 2. information retrieved
—**read between the lines** *inf.* deduce a
meaning that is implied —**read out** 1. read
aloud 2. US expel from political party *etc.*
3. retrieve information from computer
memory or storage device

ready ('rɛdɪ) a. 1. prepared for use or
action 2. willing, prompt —'**readily** adv. 1.
promptly 2. willingly —'**readiness** n.
—**ready-made** a. 1. made for purchase and
immediate use by customer 2. extremely
convenient; ideally suited 3. unoriginal,
conventional —n. 4. ready-made article,
esp. garment —**ready reckoner** table of
numbers used to facilitate simple calculations, *esp.* for working out interest *etc.*

reagent (ri:'eidʒənt) n. chemical substance that reacts with another and is
used to detect presence of the other
—re'**agency** n.

real (rɪəl) a. 1. existing in fact 2. happening
3. actual 4. genuine 5. (of property)
consisting of land and houses —'**realism**

n. 1. regarding things as they are 2. artistic
treatment with this outlook —'**realist** n.
—**rea**'**listic** a. —**reality** (rɪ'ælɪtɪ) n. real
existence —'**really** adv. —'**realty** n. real
estate —**real estate** landed property
—**real tennis** ancient form of tennis
played in four-walled indoor court

realize or -**ise** ('rɪəlaɪz) vt. 1. apprehend,
grasp significance of 2. make real 3.
convert into money —**reali**'**zation** or
-**i**'**sation** n.

realm (rɛlm) n. 1. kingdom, domain 2.
province, sphere

ream¹ (ri:m) n. 1. twenty quires of paper,
generally 480 sheets —pl. 2. *inf.* large
quantity of written matter

ream² (ri:m) vt. enlarge, bevel out, as hole
in metal —'**reamer** n. tool for this

reap (ri:p) v. 1. cut and gather (harvest)
—vt. 2. receive as fruit of previous activity
—'**reaper** n.

rear¹ (rɪə) n. 1. back part 2. part of army,
procession *etc.* behind others —'**rearmost**
a. —**rear admiral** lowest flag rank in
certain navies —'**rearguard** n. troops
protecting rear of army —**rear light** or
lamp red light attached to rear of motor
vehicle —**rear-view mirror** mirror on
motor vehicle enabling driver to see
traffic behind —'**rearward** a. 1. towards
or in rear —adv. 2. towards or in rear (also
'**rearwards**) —n. 3. position in rear, *esp.*
rear division of military formation

rear² (rɪə) vt. 1. care for and educate
(children) 2. breed 3. erect —vi. 4. rise,
esp. on hind feet

reason ('ri:z³n) n. 1. ground, motive 2.
faculty of thinking 3. sanity 4. sensible or
logical thought or view —vi. 5. think
logically in forming conclusions 6. (*usu.*
with with) persuade by logical argument
into doing *etc.* —'**reasonable** a. 1. sensible,
not excessive 2. suitable 3. logical
—'**reasoning** n. 1. drawing of conclusions
from facts *etc.* 2. arguments, proofs *etc.* so
adduced

reassure (ri:ə'ʃʊə) vt. restore confidence
to

rebate¹ ('ri:beɪt) n. 1. discount, refund —vt.
(rɪ'beɪt) 2. deduct

rebate² ('ri:beɪt, 'ræbɪt) or **rabbet** n. 1.
recess, groove cut into piece of timber to
join with matching piece —vt. 2. cut
rebate in

rebel (rɪ'bɛl) vi. 1. revolt, resist lawful
authority, take arms against ruling power
(-**ll**-) —n. ('rɛb³l) 2. one who rebels 3.
insurgent —a. ('rɛb³l) 4. in rebellion

—**re'bellion** n. organized open resistance to authority, revolt —**re'bellious** a. —**re'belliously** adv.

rebirth (riːˈbɜːθ) n. 1. revival, renaissance 2. second or new birth

rebore (ˈriːbɔː) n. boring of cylinder to regain true shape

rebound (rɪˈbaʊnd) vi. 1. spring back 2. misfire, esp. so as to hurt perpetrator (of plan, deed etc.) —n. (ˈriːbaʊnd) 3. act of springing back or recoiling 4. return —**re'bounder** n. small trampoline, used esp. at home, for aerobic exercising

rebuff (rɪˈbʌf) n. 1. blunt refusal 2. check —vt. 3. repulse, snub

rebuke (rɪˈbjuːk) vt. 1. reprove, reprimand, find fault with —n. 2. reprimand, scolding

rebus (ˈriːbəs) n. riddle in which names of things etc. are represented by pictures standing for syllables etc. (pl. **-es**)

rebut (rɪˈbʌt) vt. refute, disprove (**-tt-**) —**re'buttal** n.

rec. 1. receipt 2. recipe 3. record

recalcitrant (rɪˈkælsɪtrənt) a./n. wilfully disobedient (person) —**re'calcitrance** n.

recall (rɪˈkɔːl) vt. 1. recollect, remember 2. call, summon, order back 3. annul, cancel 4. revive, restore —n. 5. summons to return 6. ability to remember

recant (rɪˈkænt) v. withdraw (statement, opinion etc.) —**recan'tation** n.

recap (ˈriːkæp, riːˈkæp) v. 1. recapitulate (**-pp-**) —n. (ˈriːkæp) 2. recapitulation

recapitulate (riːkəˈpɪtjʊleɪt) vt. 1. state again briefly 2. repeat —**recapitu'lation** n.

recce (ˈrɛkɪ) sl. n. 1. reconnaissance —v. 2. reconnoitre

recd. or **rec'd.** received

recede (rɪˈsiːd) vi. 1. go back 2. become distant 3. slope backwards 4. start balding

receipt (rɪˈsiːt) n. 1. written acknowledgment of money received 2. receiving or being received —vt. 3. acknowledge payment of in writing

receive (rɪˈsiːv) vt. 1. take, accept, get 2. experience 3. greet (guests) —**re'ceivable** a. —**re'ceiver** n. 1. officer appointed to take public money 2. one who takes stolen goods knowing them to have been stolen 3. equipment in telephone, radio or television that converts electrical signals into sound and light

recent (ˈriːsənt) a. 1. that has lately happened 2. new 3. (**R-**) of second and most recent epoch of Quaternary period, which began 10 000 years ago (also **'Holocene**) —n. 4. (**R-**) the Recent epoch or rock series (also **'Holocene**) —**'recently** adv.

receptacle (rɪˈsɛptəkˀl) n. vessel, place or space to contain anything

reception (rɪˈsɛpʃən) n. 1. receiving 2.

manner of receiving 3. welcome 4. formal party 5. area for receiving guests, clients etc. 6. in broadcasting, quality of signals received —**re'ceptionist** n. person who receives guests, clients etc. —**reception room** 1. room in house suitable for entertaining guests 2. room in hotel suitable for receptions etc.

receptive (rɪˈsɛptɪv) a. able, quick, willing to receive new ideas, suggestions etc. —**receptivity** (riːsɛpˈtɪvɪtɪ) or **re'ceptiveness** n.

recess (rɪˈsɛs, ˈriːsɛs) n. 1. niche, alcove 2. hollow 3. secret, hidden place 4. remission or suspension of business 5. vacation, holiday

recession (rɪˈsɛʃən) n. 1. period of reduction in trade 2. act of receding —**re'cessive** a. receding

recessional (rɪˈsɛʃənˀl) n. hymn sung while clergy retire

recherché (rəˈʃɛəʃeɪ) a. 1. of studied elegance 2. exquisite 3. choice

recidivism (rɪˈsɪdɪvɪzəm) n. habitual relapse into crime —**re'cidivist** n./a.

recipe (ˈrɛsɪpɪ) n. 1. directions for cooking a dish 2. prescription 3. expedient

recipient (rɪˈsɪpɪənt) a. 1. that can or does receive —n. 2. one who, that which receives —**re'cipience** or **re'cipiency** n.

reciprocal (rɪˈsɪprəkˀl) a. 1. complementary 2. mutual 3. moving backwards and forwards 4. alternating —**re'ciprocally** adv. —**re'ciprocate** vt. 1. give and receive mutually 2. return —vi. 3. move backwards and forwards —**recipro'cation** n. —**reciprocity** (rɛsɪˈprɒsɪtɪ) n.

recite (rɪˈsaɪt) vt. repeat aloud, esp. to audience —**re'cital** n. 1. musical performance, usu. by one person 2. act of reciting 3. narration of facts etc. 4. story 5. public entertainment of recitations etc. —**recitation** (rɛsɪˈteɪʃən) n. 1. recital, usu. from memory, of poetry or prose 2. recountal —**recitative** (rɛsɪtəˈtiːv) n. musical declamation —**re'citer** n.

reckless (ˈrɛklɪs) a. heedless, incautious —**'recklessness** n.

reckon (ˈrɛkən) v. 1. count —vt. 2. include 3. consider 4. think, deem —vi. 5. make calculations —**'reckoner** n. —**'reckoning** n. 1. counting, calculating 2. settlement of account etc. 3. bill, account 4. retribution for one's actions (esp. in **day of reckoning**) 5. Navigation see **dead reckoning** at DEAD

reclaim (rɪˈkleɪm) vt. 1. make fit for cultivation 2. bring back 3. reform 4. demand the return of —**re'claimable** a.

recline (rɪˈklaɪn) vi. sit, lie back or on one's side

recluse (rɪˈkluːs) n. 1. hermit —a. 2. living

---

re'bid v.	**re'build**	**re'cast**
'rebid n.	**re'calculate**	**re'charge**
re'born	**re'capture**	

in complete retirement —re'clusion n.
—re'clusive a.

recognize or -ise ('rɛkəgnaɪz) vt. 1. know
again 2. treat as valid 3. notice, show
appreciation of —recognition (rɛkəg-
'nɪʃən) n. —'recognizable or -isable a.
—recognizance or recognisance (rɪ'kɒgnɪzəns) n. 1. avowal 2. bond by which
person undertakes before court to observe
some condition 3. obs. recognition

recoil (rɪ'kɔɪl) vi. 1. draw back in horror
etc. 2. go wrong so as to hurt the
perpetrator 3. (esp. of gun when fired)
rebound —n. (rɪ'kɔɪl, 'riː.kɔɪl) 4. backward
spring 5. retreat 6. recoiling

recollect (rɛkə'lɛkt) vt. call back to mind,
remember —recol'lection n.

recommend (rɛkə'mɛnd) vt. 1. advise,
counsel 2. praise, commend 3. make
acceptable —recommen'dation n.

recompense ('rɛkəmpɛns) vt. 1. reward 2.
compensate, make up for —n. 3. compensation 4. reward 5. requital

reconcile ('rɛkənsaɪl) vt. 1. bring back
into friendship 2. adjust, settle, harmonize
—'reconcilable a. —'reconcilement n.
—reconciliation (rɛkənsɪlɪ'eɪʃən) n.

recondite (rɪ'kɒndaɪt, 'rɛkəndaɪt) a. obscure, abstruse, little known

recondition (riːkən'dɪʃən) vt. restore to
good condition or working order

reconnoitre or U.S. reconnoiter (rɛkə-
'nɔɪtə) vt. 1. make preliminary survey of 2.
survey position of (enemy) —vi. 3. make
reconnaissance —reconnaissance (rɪ-
'kɒnɪsəns) n. 1. an examination or survey
for military or engineering purposes 2.
scouting

reconstitute (riː'kɒnstɪtjuːt) vt. restore
(food) to former state, esp. by addition of
water to a concentrate

record ('rɛkɔːd) n. 1. being recorded 2.
document or other thing that records 3.
disc with indentations which gramophone
transforms into sound 4. best recorded
achievement 5. known facts about person's past —vt. (rɪ'kɔːd) 6. put in writing 7.
register —v. (rɪ'kɔːd) 8. preserve (sound,
TV programmes etc.) on plastic disc,
magnetic tape etc. for reproduction on
playback device —re'corder n. 1. one
who, that which records 2. type of flute 3.
judge in certain courts —re'cording n. 1.
process of making records from sound 2.
something recorded, eg radio or TV
programme —recorded delivery Post
Office service by which official record of
posting and delivery is obtained for letter
or package —Record Office institution in
which official records are stored and kept
(also Public Record Office) —record-
player n. machine for playing gramophone records —for the record for the

sake of strict factual accuracy —off the
record confidential or confidentially

recount (rɪ'kaʊnt) vt. tell in detail

re-count (riː'kaʊnt) v. 1. count (votes etc.)
again —n. ('riː.kaʊnt) 2. second or further
count, esp. of votes

recoup (rɪ'kuːp) vt. 1. recompense,
compensate 2. recover (what has been
expended or lost)

recourse (rɪ'kɔːs) n. 1. (resorting to)
source of help 2. Law right of action or
appeal

recover (rɪ'kʌvə) vt. 1. regain, get back
—vi. 2. get back health —re'coverable a.
—re'covery n.

recreant ('rɛkrɪənt) a. 1. cowardly,
disloyal —n. 2. recreant person 3.
renegade —'recreance or 'recreancy n.

recreation (rɛkrɪ'eɪʃən) n. agreeable or
refreshing occupation, relaxation, amusement —'recreative a.

recriminate (rɪ'krɪmɪneɪt) vi. make
countercharge or mutual accusation —re-
crimi'nation n. mutual abuse and blame
—re'criminative or re'criminatory a.

recrudesce (riːkruː'dɛs) vi. break out
again —recru'descence n. —recru'descent a.

recruit (rɪ'kruːt) n. 1. newly-enlisted
soldier 2. one newly joining society etc.
—vt. 3. enlist (fresh soldiers etc.)
—re'cruitment n.

rectangle ('rɛktæŋgl) n. oblong four-
sided figure with four right angles
—rec'tangular a. shaped thus

rectify ('rɛktɪfaɪ) vt. 1. put right, correct,
remedy 2. purify (-fied, -fying) —rectifi-
'cation n. 1. act of setting right 2. refining
by repeated distillation 3. Elec. conversion
of alternating current into direct current
—'rectifier n. thing that rectifies

rectilinear (rɛktɪ'lɪnɪə) or rectilineal a.
1. in straight line 2. characterized by
straight lines

rectitude ('rɛktɪtjuːd) n. 1. moral uprightness 2. honesty of purpose

recto ('rɛktəʊ) n. right-hand page of book,
front of leaf (pl. -s)

rector ('rɛktə) n. 1. clergyman with care
of parish 2. head of certain institutions,
chiefly academic —'rectorship n. —'rectory n. rector's house

rectum ('rɛktəm) n. final section of large
intestine (pl. -s, -ta (-tə)) —'rectal a.

recumbent (rɪ'kʌmbənt) a. lying down
—re'cumbence or re'cumbency n.

recuperate (rɪ'kuːpəreɪt, -'kjuː-) vi. 1.
recover from illness, convalesce —v. 2.
restore, be restored from losses etc.
—recuper'ation n.

recur (rɪ'kɜː) vi. 1. happen again 2. return
again and again 3. go or come back in

mind (-**rr**-) —re**'currence** n. repetition —re**'current** a.

recusant ('rɛkjuzənt) n. 1. one who refused to conform to rites of Established Anglican Church —a. 2. obstinate in refusal

recycle (riː'saɪkˀl) vt. 1. reprocess (manufactured substance) for use again 2. reuse

red (rɛd) a. 1. of colour varying from crimson to orange and seen in blood, rubies, glowing fire etc. —n. 2. the colour 3. inf. communist —**'redden** vt. 1. make red —vi. 2. become red 3. flush —**'reddish** a. —**red blood cell** see ERYTHROCYTE —**red-blooded** a. 1. vigorous 2. virile —**'red-breast** n. robin —**'redbrick** a. of provincial and relatively new university —**red carpet** 1. strip of red carpeting laid for important dignitaries to walk on 2. deferential treatment accorded to person of importance —**'redcoat** n. 1. obs. soldier 2. C inf. Mountie —**Red Crescent** emblem of Red Cross Society in Muslim country —**Red Cross** international humanitarian organization providing medical care for war casualties, famine relief etc. —**red deer** large deer formerly widely distributed in woodlands of Europe and Asia —**Red Ensign** ensign of British Merchant Navy, having Union Jack on red background at upper corner; also national flag of Canad. until 1965 —**'redfish** n. any of various types of fish —**red flag** 1. emblem of communist party 2. (**R- F-**) their song 3. danger signal —**red-handed** a. inf. (caught) in the act —**red hat** broad-brimmed crimson hat given to cardinals as symbol of rank —**'redhead** n. person with red hair —**'redheaded** a. —**red herring** topic introduced to divert attention from main issue —**red-hot** a. 1. (esp. of metal) heated to temperature at which it glows red 2. extremely hot 3. keen, excited, eager 4. furious; violent 5. very recent or topical —**red-hot poker** garden plant with tall spikes of red or orange flowers —**Red Indian** N Amer. Indian —**red lead** red poisonous insoluble oxide of lead —**red-letter day** memorably important or happy occasion —**red light** 1. signal to stop, esp. traffic signal 2. danger signal 3. red lamp hanging outside house indicating it is a brothel —**red-light district** containing many brothels —**red pepper** 1. pepper plant cultivated for its hot pungent red podlike fruits 2. this fruit 3. ripe red fruit of sweet pepper 4. see CAYENNE PEPPER —**red rag** provocation; something that infuriates —**'redshank** n. large European sandpiper —**red shift** shift in spectral lines of stellar spectrum towards red end of visible region relative to wavelength of these lines in terrestrial spectrum —**'redskin** n. inf. Amer. Indian —**'redstart** n. 1. European songbird of thrush family 2. N Amer. warbler —**red tape** excessive adherence to official rules —**'redwing** n. small European thrush having speckled breast and reddish flanks —**'redwood** n. giant coniferous tree of California —**in the red** inf. in debt —**see red** inf. be angry

redeem (rɪ'diːm) vt. 1. buy back 2. set free 3. free from sin 4. make up for —re**'deemable** a. —**redemption** (rɪ'dɛmpʃən) n. —**The Redeemer** Jesus Christ

redeploy (riːdɪ'plɔɪ) v. assign new positions or tasks to (labour etc.) —rede**'ployment** n.

redolent ('rɛdəʊlənt) a. 1. smelling strongly, fragrant 2. reminiscent —**'redolence** n.

redouble (rɪ'dʌbˀl) v. 1. increase, multiply, intensify 2. Bridge double a second time

redoubt (rɪ'daʊt) n. detached outwork in fortifications

redoubtable (rɪ'daʊtəbˀl) a. dreaded, formidable

redound (rɪ'daʊnd) vi. 1. contribute 2. recoil

redress (rɪ'drɛs) vt. 1. set right 2. make amends for —n. 3. compensation, amends

reduce (rɪ'djuːs) vt. 1. bring down, lower 2. lessen, weaken 3. bring by force or necessity to some state or action 4. slim 5. simplify 6. dilute —vi. 7. Chem. separate substance from others with which it is combined —re**'ducible** a. —**reduction** (rɪ'dʌkʃən) n. —**reducing agent** substance used to deoxidize or lessen density of another substance

redundant (rɪ'dʌndənt) a. 1. superfluous 2. (of worker) deprived of job because it is no longer needed —re**'dundancy** n. —**redundancy payment** sum of money given to worker made redundant by employer

reduplicate (rɪ'djuːplɪkeɪt) v. 1. make or become double; repeat 2. repeat (sound or syllable) in word or (of sound or syllable) be repeated —a. (rɪ'djuːplɪkɪt) 3. doubled; repeated 4. (of petals or sepals) having margins curving outwards —**redupli'cation** n.

reed (riːd) n. 1. any of various marsh or water plants 2. tall straight stem of one 3. Mus. vibrating cane or metal strip of certain wind instruments —**'reedy** a. 1. full of reeds 2. like reed instrument 3. harsh and thin in tone —**'reedbuck** n. S Afr. antelope with buff coat —**reed bunting** common European bunting that has brown streaked plumage

reef (riːf) *n.* 1. ridge of rock or coral near surface of sea 2. vein of ore 3. part of sail which can be rolled up to reduce area —*vt.* 4. take in a reef of —**'reefer** *n.* 1. sailor's jacket 2. *sl.* hand-rolled cigarette, *esp.* containing cannabis —**reef knot** knot consisting of two overhand knots turned opposite ways (*also* **square knot**)

reek (riːk) *n.* 1. strong (unpleasant) smell —*vi.* 2. emit fumes 3. smell

reel (riːl, rɪəl) *n.* 1. spool on which film is wound 2. *Cine.* portion of film 3. winding apparatus 4. bobbin 5. thread wound on this 6. lively dance 7. music for it 8. act of staggering —*vt.* 9. wind on to reel 10. draw (in) by means of reel —*vi.* 11. stagger, sway, rock —**reel off** recite, write fluently, quickly

re-entry (riːˈɛntrɪ) *n.* 1. retaking possession of land *etc.* 2. return of spacecraft into earth's atmosphere

reeve[1] (riːv) *n.* 1. *Hist.* manorial steward or official 2. **C** president of local (rural) council

reeve[2] (riːv) *vt.* pass (rope) through hole, in block *etc.*

reeve[3] (riːv) *n.* female of ruff (bird)

ref. 1. referee 2. reference 3. reformed

refectory (rɪˈfɛktərɪ, -trɪ) *n.* room for meals in college *etc.* —**reˈfection** *n.* meal —**refectory table** long narrow dining table supported by two trestles

refer (rɪˈfɜː) *vi.* 1. relate, allude —*vt.* 2. send for information 3. trace, ascribe 4. submit for decision (**-rr-**) —**referable** (ˈrɛfərəbˈl) *or* **reˈferrable** *a.* —**referee** (rɛfəˈriː) *n.* 1. arbitrator 2. person willing to testify to someone's character *etc.* 3. umpire —*v.* 4. act as referee (in) —**reference** (ˈrɛfərəns, ˈrɛfrəns) *n.* 1. act of referring 2. citation or direction in book 3. appeal to judgment of another 4. testimonial 5. one to whom inquiries as to character *etc.* may be made —**referendum** (rɛfəˈrɛndəm) *n.* submitting of question to electorate (*pl.* **-s, -da** (-də)) —**reˈferral** *n.* act, instance of referring —**reference library** library where books may be consulted but not taken away by readers

refine (rɪˈfaɪn) *vt.* purify —**reˈfined** *a.* 1. not coarse or vulgar; genteel, elegant, polite 2. freed from impurities; purified —**reˈfinement** *n.* 1. subtlety 2. improvement, elaboration 3. fineness of feeling, taste or manners —**reˈfiner** *n.* —**reˈfinery** *n.* place where sugar, oil *etc.* is refined

refit (riːˈfɪt) *v.* 1. make or be made ready for use again by repairing *etc.* (**-tt-**) —*n.*

(ˈriːfɪt) 2. repair or re-equipping, as of ship, for further use

reflation (riːˈfleɪʃən) *n.* (steps taken to produce) increase in economic activity of country *etc.*

reflect (rɪˈflɛkt) *vt.* 1. throw back, *esp.* rays of light 2. cast (discredit *etc.*) upon —*vi.* 3. meditate —**reˈflection** *or* **reˈflexion** *n.* 1. act of reflecting 2. return of rays of heat, light or waves of sound from surface 3. image of object given back by mirror *etc.* 4. conscious thought 5. meditation 6. expression of thought —**reˈflective** *a.* 1. meditative, quiet, contemplative 2. throwing back images —**reˈflector** *n.* polished surface for reflecting light *etc.*

reflex (ˈriːflɛks) *n.* 1. reflex action 2. reflected image 3. reflected light, colour *etc.* —*a.* 4. (of muscular action) involuntary 5. reflected 6. bent back —**reˈflexive** *a.* *Gram.* denoting agent's action on himself —**reflex action** involuntary response to (nerve) stimulation

reflux (ˈriːflʌks) *n.* flowing back, ebb —**refluence** (ˈrɛfluəns) *n.* —**refluent** (ˈrɛfluənt) *a.* returning, ebbing

reform (rɪˈfɔːm) *vt.* 1. improve 2. reconstruct —*vi.* 3. abandon evil practices —*n.* 4. improvement —**reformation** (rɛfəˈmeɪʃən) *n.* —**reˈformatory** *n.* 1. institution for reforming juvenile offenders —*a.* 2. reforming —**reˈformer** *n.*

refract (rɪˈfrækt) *vt.* change course of (light *etc.*) passing from one medium to another —**reˈfraction** *n.* —**reˈfractive** *a.*

refractory (rɪˈfræktərɪ) *a.* 1. unmanageable 2. difficult to treat or work 3. *Med.* resistant to treatment 4. resistant to heat

refrain[1] (rɪˈfreɪn) *vi.* abstain

refrain[2] (rɪˈfreɪn) *n.* chorus

refresh (rɪˈfrɛʃ) *vt.* 1. give freshness to 2. revive 3. renew 4. brighten 5. provide with refreshment —**reˈfresher** *n.* that which refreshes —**reˈfreshment** *n.* 1. that which refreshes, *esp.* food, drink 2. restorative

refrigerate (rɪˈfrɪdʒəreɪt) *vt.* 1. freeze 2. cool —**reˈfrigerant** *n.* 1. refrigerating substance —*a.* 2. causing cooling or freezing —**refrigerˈation** *n.* —**reˈfrigerator** *n.* apparatus in which foods, drinks are kept cool

refuge (ˈrɛfjuːdʒ) *n.* shelter, protection, retreat, sanctuary —**refuˈgee** *n.* one who seeks refuge, *esp.* in foreign country

refulgent (rɪˈfʌldʒənt) *a.* shining, radiant —**reˈfulgence** *n.* —**reˈfulgency** *n.* splendour

refund (rɪˈfʌnd) *vt.* 1. pay back —*n.*

re-elect	re-enactment	**'refill** *n.*
re-election	re-enforce	re'float
re-emerge	re-enforcement	re'forest
re-emergence	re-enter	re-form
re-emphasize	re-equip	re'fuel
re-employ	re-examine	
re-enact	re'fill *v.*	

('riːfʌnd) 2. return of money to purchaser or amount so returned

refurbish (riːˈfɜːbɪʃ) vt. furbish, furnish or polish anew

refuse[1] (rɪˈfjuːz) v. decline, deny, reject —**re'fusal** n. 1. denial of anything demanded or offered 2. option

refuse[2] ('refjuːs) n. rubbish, useless matter

refute (rɪˈfjuːt) vt. disprove —**refutable** ('refjutəb'l, rɪˈfjuː-) a. —**refutation** (refjuˈteɪʃən) n.

regal ('riːg'l) a. of, like a king —**regalia** (rɪˈɡeɪlɪə) pl.n. (sometimes with sing. v.) 1. insignia of royalty, as used at coronation etc. 2. emblems of high office, an order etc. —**re'gality** n. —**'regally** adv.

regale (rɪˈɡeɪl) vt. 1. give pleasure to 2. feast —**re'galement** n.

regard (rɪˈɡɑːd) vt. 1. look at 2. consider 3. relate to 4. heed —n. 5. look 6. attention 7. particular respect 8. esteem —pl. 9. expression of good will —**re'gardful** a. heedful, careful —**re'garding** prep. in respect of; on the subject of —**re'gardless** a. 1. heedless —adv. 2. in spite of everything

regatta (rɪˈɡætə) n. meeting for yacht or boat races

regenerate (rɪˈdʒɛnəreɪt) v. 1. (cause to) undergo spiritual rebirth 2. reform morally 3. reproduce, re-create 4. reorganize —a. (rɪˈdʒɛnərɪt) 5. born anew —**regener'ation** n. —**re'generative** a. —**re'generator** n.

regent ('riːdʒənt) n. 1. ruler of kingdom during absence, minority etc., of its monarch —a. 2. ruling —**'regency** n. status of, (period of) office of regent

reggae ('rɛɡeɪ) n. style of popular West Indian music with strong beat

regicide ('rɛdʒɪsaɪd) n. 1. one who kills a king 2. this crime

regime or **régime** (reɪˈʒiːm) n. 1. system of government, administration 2. see REGIMEN (sense 1)

regimen ('rɛdʒɪmɛn) n. 1. prescribed system of diet etc. (also re'gime) 2. rule

regiment ('rɛdʒɪmənt) n. 1. organized body of troops as unit of army —vt. ('rɛdʒɪmɛnt) 2. discipline, organize rigidly or too strictly —**regi'mental** a. of regiment —**regi'mentals** pl.n. uniform

region ('riːdʒən) n. 1. area, district 2. stretch of country 3. part of the body 4. sphere, realm 5. (oft. R-) administrative division of a country —**'regional** a.

register ('rɛdʒɪstə) n. 1. list 2. catalogue 3. roll 4. device for registering 5. written record 6. range of voice or instrument —v. 7. show, be shown on meter, face etc. —vt. 8. enter in register 9. record 10. show 11. set down in writing 12. Print., photog. cause to correspond precisely —**regis-**

'trar n. 1. keeper of a register 2. senior hospital doctor, junior to consultant —**regis'tration** n. —**'registry** n. 1. registering 2. place where registers are kept, esp. of births, marriages, deaths —**registered post** 1. Post Office service by which compensation is paid for loss of or damage to mail for which registration fee has been paid 2. mail sent by this service —**registration number** sequence of numbers and letters displayed on motor vehicle to identify it

regorge (rɪˈɡɔːdʒ) vt. vomit up

regress (rɪˈɡrɛs) vi. 1. return, revert to former place, condition etc. —n. ('riːɡrɛs) 2. movement in backward direction —**re'gression** n. 1. act of returning 2. retrogression —**re'gressive** a. falling back —**re'gressively** adv.

regret (rɪˈɡrɛt) vt. 1. feel sorry, distressed for loss of or on account of (-tt-) —n. 2. sorrow, distress for thing done or left undone or lost —**re'gretful** a. —**re'grettable** a.

regular ('rɛɡjʊlə) a. 1. normal 2. habitual 3. done, occurring, according to rule 4. periodical 5. straight, level 6. living under rule 7. belonging to standing army —n. 8. regular soldier 9. inf. regular customer —**regu'larity** n. —**'regularize** or **-ise** v.

regulate ('rɛɡjʊleɪt) vt. 1. adjust 2. arrange 3. direct 4. govern 5. put under rule —**regu'lation** n. —**'regulator** n. contrivance to produce uniformity of motion, as fly wheel, governor valve etc.

regurgitate (rɪˈɡɜːdʒɪteɪt) v. 1. vomit 2. bring back (swallowed food) into mouth —**regurgi'tation** n.

rehabilitate (riːəˈbɪlɪteɪt) vt. 1. help (person) to readjust to society after period of illness, imprisonment etc. 2. restore to reputation or former position 3. make fit again 4. reinstate —**rehabili'tation** n.

rehash (riːˈhæʃ) vt. 1. rework, reuse —n. 2. old materials presented in new form

rehearse (rɪˈhɜːs) vt. 1. practise (play etc.) 2. repeat aloud 3. say over again 4. train, drill —**re'hearsal** n.

Reich (raɪx) n. 1. Holy Roman Empire (962-1806) (**First Reich**) 2. Hohenzollern empire in Germany from 1871 to 1918 (**Second Reich**) 3. Nazi dictatorship in Germany from 1933-45 (**Third Reich**)

reign (reɪn) n. 1. period of sovereign's rule —vi. 2. be sovereign 3. be supreme

reimburse (riːɪmˈbɜːs) vt. 1. refund 2. pay back —**reim'bursement** n.

rein (reɪn) n. 1. (oft. pl.) narrow strap attached to bit to guide horse 2. instrument for governing —vt. 3. check, manage with reins 4. control —**give (a) free rein** remove restraints

reincarnation (riːɪnkɑːˈneɪʃən) n. 1. re-

re'furnish	re'grow	re'house
re'gain	re'harden	reim'pose
re'gather	re'heat	

birth of soul in successive bodies **2.** one of series of such transmigrations —**re'incarnate** *vt.*

reindeer ('reɪndɪə) *n.* deer of cold regions, eg Lapland (*pl.* **-deer, -s**)

reinforce (riːɪn'fɔːs) *vt.* **1.** strengthen with new support, material, force **2.** strengthen with additional troops, ships *etc.* —**rein'forcement** *n.* —**reinforced concrete 1.** concrete strengthened internally by steel bars **2.** ferroconcrete

reinstate (riːɪn'steɪt) *vt.* replace, restore, re-establish —**rein'statement** *n.*

reiterate (riː'ɪtəreɪt) *vt.* repeat again and again —**reiter'ation** *n.* repetition

reject (rɪ'dʒɛkt) *vt.* **1.** refuse to accept **2.** put aside **3.** discard **4.** renounce —*n.* ('riːdʒɛkt) **5.** person or thing rejected as not up to standard —**re'jection** *n.* refusal

rejig (riː'dʒɪg) *vt.* **1.** re-equip (factory, plant) **2.** *inf.* rearrange (**-gg-**)

rejoice (rɪ'dʒɔɪs) *v.* **1.** make or be joyful, merry —*vt.* **2.** exult **3.** gladden

rejoin (rɪ'dʒɔɪn) *vt.* **1.** reply **2.** (riː'dʒɔɪn) join again —**re'joinder** *n.* answer, retort

rejuvenate (rɪ'dʒuːvɪneɪt) *vt.* restore to youth —**rejuve'nation** *n.* —**rejuve'nescence** *n.* process of growing young again

relapse (rɪ'læps) *vi.* **1.** fall back (into evil, illness *etc.*) —*n.* **2.** act or instance of relapsing

relate (rɪ'leɪt) *vt.* **1.** narrate, recount **2.** establish relation between —*vi.* (**with** to) **3.** have reference or relation **4.** form sympathetic relationship —**re'lated** *a.* **1.** connected; associated **2.** connected by kinship or marriage

relation (rɪ'leɪʃən) *n.* **1.** relative quality or condition **2.** connection by blood or marriage **3.** connection (between things) **4.** act of relating **5.** narrative —**re'lationship** *n.* —**relative** ('rɛlətɪv) *a.* **1.** dependent on relation to something else, not absolute **2.** having reference or relation —*n.* **3.** one connected by blood or marriage **4.** relative word or thing —**relatively** ('rɛlətɪvlɪ) *adv.* —**relativity** (rɛlə'tɪvɪtɪ) *n.* **1.** state of being relative **2.** subject of two theories of Albert Einstein, dealing with relationships of space, time and motion and acceleration and gravity

relax (rɪ'læks) *vt.* **1.** make loose or slack —*vi.* **2.** become loosened or slack **3.** ease up from effort or attention **4.** become more friendly, less strict —**relax'ation** *n.* **1.** relaxing recreation **2.** alleviation **3.** abatement

relay ('riːleɪ) *n.* **1.** fresh set of people or animals relieving others **2.** *Elec.* device for making or breaking local circuit **3.** *Rad., T.V.* broadcasting station receiving programmes from another station —*vt.*

(rɪ'leɪ) **4.** pass on, as message (**re'layed, re'laying**) —**relay race** race between teams of which each runner races part of distance

release (rɪ'liːs) *vt.* **1.** give up, surrender, set free **2.** permit public showing of (film *etc.*) —*n.* **3.** setting free **4.** releasing **5.** written discharge **6.** permission to show publicly **7.** film, record *etc.* newly issued

relegate ('rɛlɪgeɪt) *vt.* **1.** banish, consign **2.** demote —**rele'gation** *n.*

relent (rɪ'lɛnt) *vi.* give up harsh intention, become less severe —**re'lentless** *a.* **1.** pitiless **2.** merciless

relevant ('rɛlɪvənt) *a.* having to do with the matter in hand, to the point —**'relevance** *n.*

reliable (rɪ'laɪəb'l) *a. see* RELY

relic ('rɛlɪk) *n.* **1.** thing remaining, *esp.* as memorial of saint **2.** memento —*pl.* **3.** remains, traces **4.** *obs.* dead body —**'relict** *n. obs.* widow

relief (rɪ'liːf) *n.* **1.** alleviation, end of pain, distress *etc.* **2.** money, food given to victims of disaster, poverty *etc.* **3.** release from duty **4.** one who relieves another from work or duty **5.** bus, plane *etc.* that carries passengers when a scheduled service is full **6.** freeing of besieged city *etc.* **7.** projection of carved design from surface **8.** distinctness, prominence —**re'lieve** *vt.* bring or give relief to —**relief map** map showing elevations and depressions of country in relief

religion (rɪ'lɪdʒən) *n.* system of belief in, worship of a supernatural power or god —**religiose** (rɪ'lɪdʒɪəʊs) *a.* affectedly or extremely pious; sanctimoniously religious —**religiosity** (rɪlɪdʒɪ'ɒsɪtɪ) *n.* —**re'ligious** *a.* **1.** pert. to religion **2.** pious **3.** conscientious —**re'ligiously** *adv.* **1.** in religious manner **2.** scrupulously **3.** conscientiously

relinquish (rɪ'lɪŋkwɪʃ) *vt.* **1.** give up, abandon **2.** surrender or renounce (claim, right *etc.*) —**re'linquishment** *n.*

reliquary ('rɛlɪkwərɪ) *n.* case or shrine for holy relics

relish ('rɛlɪʃ) *vt.* **1.** enjoy, like —*n.* **2.** liking, gusto **3.** savoury taste **4.** taste, flavour

relive (riː'lɪv) *vt.* experience (sensation *etc.*) again, *esp.* in imagination —**re'livable** *a.*

reluctant (rɪ'lʌktənt) *a.* unwilling, loath, disinclined —**re'luctance** *n.*

rely (rɪ'laɪ) *vi.* **1.** depend **2.** (**with** on) trust (**re'lied, re'lying**) —**relia'bility** *n.* —**re'liable** *a.* trustworthy, dependable —**re'liance** *n.* **1.** trust **2.** confidence **3.** dependence —**re'liant** *a.* confident

REM rapid eye movement

remain (rɪ'meɪn) *vi.* **1.** stay, be left behind

2. continue 3. abide 4. last —**re'mainder** n. 1. rest, what is left after subtraction —vt. 2. offer (end of consignment of goods, material etc.) at reduced prices —**re'mains** pl.n. 1. relics, esp. of ancient buildings 2. dead body

remand (rı'mɑːnd) vt. send back, esp. into custody —**remand home** or **centre** place of detention for young delinquents

remark (rı'mɑːk) vi. 1. make casual comment —vt. 2. comment, observe 3. say 4. take notice of —n. 5. observation, comment —**re'markable** a. noteworthy, unusual —**re'markably** adv. 1. exceedingly 2. unusually

REME ('riːmiː) Royal Electrical and Mechanical Engineers

remedy ('rɛmıdı) n. 1. means of curing, counteracting or relieving disease, trouble etc. —vt. 2. put right (**-edied, -edying**) —**remediable** (rı'miːdıəb'l) a. —**remedial** (rı'miːdıəl) a. designed, intended to correct specific disability, handicap etc.

remember (rı'mɛmbə) vt. 1. retain in, recall to memory 2. have in mind —**re'membrance** n. 1. memory 2. token 3. souvenir 4. reminiscence —**Remembrance Day** 1. UK Sunday closest to Nov. 11th, on which the dead of both World Wars are commemorated (also **Remembrance Sunday**) 2. C statutory holiday observed on Nov. 11th in memory of the dead of both World Wars

remind (rı'maınd) vt. 1. cause to remember 2. put in mind —**re'minder** n.

reminisce (rɛmı'nıs) vi. talk, write of past times, experiences etc. —**remi'niscence** n. 1. remembering 2. thing recollected —pl. 3. memoirs —**remi'niscent** a. reminding, suggestive

remiss (rı'mıs) a. negligent, careless —**re'missly** adv.

remit (rı'mıt) v. 1. send (money) for goods, services etc., esp. by post 2. refrain from exacting (penalty) —vt. 3. give up 4. restore, return 5. slacken 6. obs. forgive (**-tt-**) —n. ('riːmıt, rı'mıt) 7. area of competence, authority —**re'missible** a. —**re'mission** n. 1. abatement 2. reduction in length of prison term 3. pardon, forgiveness —**re'mittance** n. 1. sending of money 2. money sent —**re'mittence** n. —**re'mittent** a. (of symptoms of disease) characterized by periods of diminished severity —**re'mittently** adv.

remix (riː'mıks) v. 1. change balance and separation of (a recording) —n. ('riːmıks) 2. remixed version of a recording

remnant ('rɛmnənt) n. 1. (oft. pl.) fragment or small piece remaining 2. oddment

remonstrate ('rɛmənstreıt) vi. protest, reason, argue —**re'monstrance** n.

remorse (rı'mɔːs) n. regret and repent-

ance —**re'morseful** a. —**re'morsefully** adv. —**re'morseless** a. pitiless

remote (rı'məut) a. 1. far away, distant 2. aloof 3. slight —**re'motely** adv. —**remote control** control of apparatus from a distance by electrical device

remould (riː'məuld) see RETREAD

remove (rı'muːv) vt. 1. take away or off 2. transfer 3. withdraw —vi. 4. go away, change residence —n. 5. degree of difference —**re'movable** a. —**re'moval** n.

remunerate (rı'mjuːnəreıt) vt. reward, pay —**remuner'ation** n. —**re'munerative** a.

renaissance (rə'neısəns; U.S. also 'rɛnəsɒns) or **renascence** (rı'næsəns, -'neı-) n. revival, rebirth, esp. (**R-**) revival of learning in 14th-16th centuries

renal ('riːn'l) a. of the kidneys

renascent (rı'næs'nt, -'neı-) a. springing up again into being

rend (rɛnd) v. 1. tear, wrench apart 2. burst, break, split (**rent, 'rending**)

render ('rɛndə) vt. 1. submit, present 2. give in return, deliver up 3. cause to become 4. portray, represent 5. melt down 6. cover with plaster

rendezvous ('rɒndıvuː) n. 1. meeting place 2. appointment 3. haunt 4. assignation (pl. **-vous** (-vuːz)) —vi. 5. meet, come together

rendition (rɛn'dıʃən) n. 1. performance 2. translation

renegade ('rɛnıgeıd) n. 1. deserter 2. outlaw 3. rebel

renege or **renegue** (rı'niːg, -'neıg) vi. go back (on promise etc.)

renew (rı'njuː) vt. 1. begin again 2. reaffirm 3. make valid again 4. make new 5. revive 6. restore to former state 7. replenish —vi. 8. be made new 9. grow again —**renewa'bility** n. quality of being renewable —**re'newable** a. —**re'newal** n. 1. revival, restoration 2. regeneration

rennet ('rɛnıt) n. preparation for curdling milk

renounce (rı'nauns) vt. 1. give up, cast off, disown 2. abjure 3. resign, as title or claim —**renunci'ation** n. 1. act or instance of renouncing 2. formal declaration renouncing something

renovate ('rɛnəveıt) vt. restore, repair, renew, do up —**reno'vation** n.

renown (rı'naun) n. fame

rent[1] (rɛnt) n. 1. payment for use of land, buildings, machines etc. —vt. 2. hold by lease 3. hire 4. let —**'rental** n. sum payable as rent —**rent boy** young male prostitute

rent[2] (rɛnt) n. 1. tear 2. fissure —v. 3. pt./pp. of REND

renunciation (rınʌnsı'eıʃən) n. see RENOUNCE

re'marriage	'rematch n.	re'occupy
re'marry	re'model	re'open
re'match v.	re'number	re'order

rep¹ or **repp** (rɛp) n. fabric with corded surface for upholstery etc.

rep² (rɛp) a./n. repertory (company, theatre, group)

rep³ (rɛp) n. representative, travelling salesman

repaid (rɪ'peɪd) pt./pp. of REPAY

repair¹ (rɪ'pɛə) vt. 1. make whole, sound again 2. mend 3. patch 4. restore —n. 5. act or process of repairing —re'pairable a. —**reparation** (rɛpə'reɪʃən) n. 1. repairing 2. amends, compensation

repair² (rɪ'pɛə) vi. (usu. with to) resort, go

repartee (rɛpɑː'tiː) n. 1. witty retort 2. interchange of witty retorts

repast (rɪ'pɑːst) n. meal

repatriate (riː'pætrɪeɪt) vt. send (someone) back to his own country —**repatri'ation** n.

repay (rɪ'peɪ) vt. 1. pay back, refund 2. make return for (**re'paid, re'paying**) —**re'payable** a. —**re'payment** n.

repeal (rɪ'piːl) vt. 1. revoke, annul, cancel —n. 2. act of repealing

repeat (rɪ'piːt) vt. 1. say, do again 2. reproduce —vi. 3. recur —n. 4. act, instance of repeating, esp. TV show broadcast again —re'peatedly adv. 1. again and again 2. frequently —re'peater n. 1. firearm that may be discharged many times without reloading 2. timepiece that strikes hours —repe'tition n. 1. act of repeating 2. thing repeated 3. piece learnt by heart and repeated —**repetitious** (rɛpɪ'tɪʃəs) a. repeated unnecessarily —**repetitive** (rɪ'pɛtɪtɪv) a. repeated

repel (rɪ'pɛl) vt. 1. drive back, ward off, refuse 2. be repulsive to (-ll-) —re'pellent a. 1. distasteful 2. resisting (water etc.) —n. 3. that which repels, esp. chemical to repel insects

repent (rɪ'pɛnt) vi. 1. wish one had not done something 2. feel regret for deed or omission —vt. 3. feel regret for —re'pentance n. contrition —re'pentant a.

repercussion (riːpə'kʌʃən) n. 1. (oft. pl.) indirect effect, oft. unpleasant 2. recoil 3. echo

repertory ('rɛpətərɪ, -trɪ) n. 1. repertoire 2. store —**repertoire** ('rɛpətwɑː) n. stock of plays, songs etc. that player or company can give —**repertory company, theatre** or **group** (theatre etc. with) permanent company producing succession of plays

repetition (rɛpɪ'tɪʃən) n. see REPEAT

repine (rɪ'paɪn) vi. fret, complain

replace (rɪ'pleɪs) vt. 1. substitute for 2. put back —re'placement n.

replay ('riːpleɪ) n. 1. immediate reshowing on TV of incident in sport, esp. in slow motion (also **action replay**) 2. replaying of a match —vt. (riː'pleɪ) 3. play again

replenish (rɪ'plɛnɪʃ) vt. fill up again —re'plenishment n.

replete (rɪ'pliːt) a. filled, gorged —re'pletion n. complete fullness

replica ('rɛplɪkə) n. 1. exact copy 2. facsimile, duplicate —'replicate vt. make, be a copy of

reply (rɪ'plaɪ) v. 1. answer (re'plied, re'plying) —n. 2. an answer; response

report (rɪ'pɔːt) n. 1. account, statement 2. written statement of child's progress at school 3. rumour 4. repute 5. bang —vt. 6. announce, relate 7. make, give account of 8. take down in writing 9. complain about —vi. 10. make report 11. act as reporter 12. present oneself (to) —re'porter n. one who reports, esp. for newspaper —reported speech see indirect speech at INDIRECT

repose (rɪ'pəʊz) n. 1. peace 2. composure 3. sleep —vi. 4. rest —vt. 5. lay at rest 6. place 7. rely, lean (on) —re'pository (rɪ'pɒzɪtərɪ, -trɪ) n. 1. place where valuables are deposited for safekeeping 2. store

repossess (riːpə'zɛs) vt. take back possession of (property), esp. for nonpayment of money due under hire-purchase agreement —repos'session n.

repoussé (rə'puːseɪ) a. 1. embossed 2. hammered into relief from reverse side —n. 3. metal work so produced

reprehend (rɛprɪ'hɛnd) vt. find fault with —repre'hensible a. deserving censure 2. unworthy —repre'hension n. censure

represent (rɛprɪ'zɛnt) vt. 1. stand for 2. deputize for 3. act, play 4. symbolize 5. make out to be 6. call up by description or portrait —represen'tation n. —repre'sentative n. 1. one chosen to stand for group 2. travelling salesman —a. 3. typical

repress (rɪ'prɛs) vt. keep down or under, quell, check —re'pression n. restraint —re'pressive a.

reprieve (rɪ'priːv) vt. 1. suspend execution of (condemned person) 2. give temporary relief to —n. 3. postponement or cancellation of punishment 4. respite 5. last-minute intervention

reprimand ('rɛprɪmɑːnd) n. 1. sharp rebuke —vt. 2. rebuke sharply

reprisal (rɪ'praɪzˡl) n. retaliation

reproach (rɪ'prəʊtʃ) vt. 1. blame, rebuke —n. 2. scolding, upbraiding 3. expression of this 4. thing bringing discredit —re'proachful a.

reprobate ('rɛprəʊbeɪt) a. 1. depraved 2. cast off by God —n. 3. depraved or disreputable person —vt. 4. disapprove of, reject —repro'bation n.

reproduce (riːprə'djuːs) vt. 1. produce copy of 2. bring (new individuals) into existence 3. re-create, produce anew —vi. 4. propagate 5. generate —repro'ducible

reorgani'zation	re'paint	re'plant
re'organize	re'paper	re'print v.
re'pack	re'phrase	'reprint n.

a. —**repro'duction** n. 1. process of reproducing 2. that which is reproduced 3. facsimile, as of painting etc. —**repro'ductive** a.

reprove (rɪ'pruːv) vt. censure, rebuke —**re'proof** n.

reptile ('rɛptaɪl) n. cold-blooded, air-breathing vertebrate with horny scales or plates, as snake, tortoise etc. —**reptilian** (rɛp'tɪlɪən) a.

republic (rɪ'pʌblɪk) n. state without monarch in which supremacy of people or their elected representatives is formally acknowledged —**re'publican** a./n. —**re'publicanism** n.

repudiate (rɪ'pjuːdɪeɪt) vt. 1. reject authority or validity of 2. cast off, disown

repugnant (rɪ'pʌgnənt) a. 1. offensive 2. distasteful 3. contrary —**re'pugnance** n. 1. dislike, aversion 2. incompatibility

repulse (rɪ'pʌls) vt. 1. drive back 2. rebuff 3. repel —n. 4. driving back, rejection, rebuff —**re'pulsion** n. 1. distaste, aversion 2. Phys. force separating two objects —**re'pulsive** a. loathsome, disgusting

repute (rɪ'pjuːt) vt. 1. reckon, consider —n. 2. reputation, credit —**reputable** ('rɛpjutəb'l) a. 1. of good repute 2. respectable —**reputation** (rɛpju'teɪʃən) n. 1. estimation in which person is held 2. character 3. good name —**re'puted** a. generally reckoned or considered; supposed —**re'putedly** adv.

request (rɪ'kwɛst) n. 1. asking 2. thing asked for —vt. 3. ask

Requiem ('rɛkwɪɛm) n. 1. Mass for the dead 2. music for this

requiescat in pace (rɛkwɪ'ɛskæt ɪn 'paːkɛ) Lat. may he (or she) rest in peace

require (rɪ'kwaɪə) vt. 1. want, need 2. demand —**re'quirement** n. 1. essential condition 2. specific need 3. want

requisite ('rɛkwɪzɪt) a. 1. necessary 2. essential —n. 3. something indispensable; necessity

requisition (rɛkwɪ'zɪʃən) n. 1. formal demand, eg for materials or supplies —vt 2. demand (supplies) 3. press into service

requite (rɪ'kwaɪt) vt. repay —**re'quital** n.

reredos ('rɪədɒs) n. ornamental screen behind altar

rerun (riː'rʌn) vt. 1. broadcast or put on (film etc.) again 2. run (race etc.) again —n. ('riːrʌn) 3. film etc. that is broadcast again; repeat 4. race that is run again

resale price maintenance ('riːseɪl) practice by which manufacturer establishes fixed or minimum price for resale of brand product by retailers or other distributors

rescind (rɪ'sɪnd) vt. cancel, annul —**re'scindment** or **rescission** (rɪ'sɪʒən) n.

rescue ('rɛskjuː) vt. 1. save, deliver, extricate (-cuing, -cued) —n. 2. act or instance of rescuing —**'rescuer** n. —**'rescuing** n.

research (rɪ'sɜːtʃ) n. 1. investigation, esp. scientific study to discover facts —v. 2. carry out investigations (on, into) —**re'searcher** n.

resemble (rɪ'zɛmb'l) vt. 1. be like 2. look like —**re'semblance** n.

resent (rɪ'zɛnt) vt. 1. show, feel indignation at 2. retain bitterness about —**re'sentful** a. —**re'sentment** n.

reserve (rɪ'zɜːv) vt. 1. hold back, set aside, keep for future use —n. 2. (also pl.) something, esp. money, troops etc., kept for emergencies 3. area of land reserved for particular purpose or for use by particular group of people etc. (also reser'vation) 4. reticence, concealment of feelings or friendliness —**reservation** (rɛzə'veɪʃən) n. 1. reserving 2. thing reserved 3. doubt 4. exception; limitation —**re'served** a. not showing feelings, lacking cordiality —**re'servist** n. one serving in reserve —**reserve price** UK minimum price acceptable to owner of property being auctioned

reservoir ('rɛzəvwɑː) n. 1. enclosed area for storage of water, esp. for community supplies 2. receptacle for liquid, gas etc. 3. place where anything is kept in store

reside (rɪ'zaɪd) vi. dwell permanently —**residence** ('rɛzɪdəns) n. 1. home 2. house —**residency** ('rɛzɪdənsɪ) n. official dwelling, esp., formerly, of Brit. government agent —**resident** ('rɛzɪdənt) a./n. —**residential** (rɛzɪ'dɛnʃəl) a. 1. (of part of town) consisting mainly of residences 2. of, connected with residence 3. providing living accommodation

residue ('rɛzɪdjuː) n. what is left, remainder —**residual** (rɪ'zɪdjʊəl) a. —**residuary** (rɪ'zɪdjʊərɪ) a. —**re'siduum** n. formal residue (pl. -ua (-juə))

resign (rɪ'zaɪn) vt. 1. give up 2. reconcile (oneself) —vi. 3. give up office, employment etc. —**resignation** (rɛzɪg'neɪʃən) n. 1. resigning 2. being resigned, submission —**re'signed** a. content to endure

resilient (rɪ'zɪlɪənt) a. 1. (of an object) capable of returning to normal after stretching etc.; elastic 2. (of a person) recovering quickly from shock etc. —**re'silience** or **re'siliency** n.

resin ('rɛzɪn) n. sticky substance formed in and oozing from plants, esp. firs and pines (also **'rosin**) —**'resinous** a. of, like resin

resist (rɪ'zɪst) v. 1. withstand 2. oppose —**re'sistance** n. 1. act of resisting 2. opposition 3. hindrance 4. Elec. opposition offered by circuit to passage of current through it —**re'sistant** a. —**re'sistible** a. —**resis'tivity** n. measure of electrical resistance —re'**sistor** n. component of electrical circuit producing resistance

resit (riː'sɪt) vt. 1. sit (examination) again —n. ('riːsɪt) 2. examination one must sit again

resolute ('rɛzəluːt) a. determined —'**resolutely** adv. —**reso'lution** n. 1. resolving 2. firmness 3. purpose or thing resolved upon 4. decision of court or vote of assembly

resolve (rɪ'zɒlv) vi. 1. make up one's mind 2. decide with effort of will —vt. 3. form by resolution of vote 4. separate component parts of 5. make clear —n. 6. resolution 7. fixed purpose —**resolu'bility, resolva'bility** or re'**solubleness, re'solvableness** n. —**resoluble** (rɪ'zɒljubˀl, 'rɛzəl-) or re'**solvable** a. able to be resolved or analysed —re'**solved** a. fixed in purpose or intention; determined —**resolvedly** (rɪ'zɒlvɪdlɪ) adv. —re'**solvent** a./n. —re'**solver** n.

resonance ('rɛzənəns) n. 1. echoing, esp. in deep tone 2. sound produced by body vibrating in sympathy with neighbouring source of sound —'**resonant** a. —'**resonate** v. —'**resonator** n.

resort (rɪ'zɔːt) vi. 1. have recourse 2. (with to) frequent —n. 3. place of recreation, eg beach 4. recourse 5. frequented place 6. haunt

resound (rɪ'zaund) vi. echo, ring, go on sounding —re'**sounding** a. 1. echoing 2. thorough

resource (rɪ'zɔːs, -'sɔːs) n. 1. capability, ingenuity 2. that to which one resorts for support 3. expedient —pl. 4. source of economic wealth 5. stock that can be drawn on 6. means of support, funds —re'**sourceful** a. —re'**sourcefully** adv. —re'**sourcefulness** n.

respect (rɪ'spɛkt) n. 1. deference, esteem 2. point, aspect 3. reference, relation —vt. 4. treat with esteem 5. show consideration for —respecta'**bility** n. —re'**spectable** a. 1. worthy of respect, decent 2. fairly good —re'**specter** n. —re'**spectful** a. —re'**specting** prep. concerning —re'**spective** a. 1. relating separately to each of those in question 2. several, separate —re'**spectively** adv.

respire (rɪ'spaɪə) v. breathe —**respirable** ('rɛspɪrəbˀl) a. —**respiration** (rɛspə'reɪʃən) n. —**respirator** ('rɛspəreɪtə) n. apparatus worn over mouth and breathed through as protection against dust, poison gas etc. or to provide artificial respiration —**respiratory** ('rɛspərətərɪ, -trɪ) a.

respite ('rɛspɪt, -paɪt) n. 1. pause 2. interval 3. suspension of labour 4. delay 5. reprieve

resplendent (rɪ'splɛndənt) a. 1. brilliant, splendid 2. shining —re'**splendence** or re'**splendency** n.

respond (rɪ'spɒnd) vi. 1. answer 2. act in answer to any stimulus 3. react —re'**spondent** a. 1. replying —n. 2. one who answers 3. defendant —re'**sponse** n. answer —re'**sponsive** a. readily reacting to some influence —re'**sponsiveness** n.

responsible (rɪ'spɒnsəbˀl) a. 1. liable to answer (for) 2. accountable 3. dependable 4. involving responsibility 5. of good credit or position —**responsi'bility** n. 1. state of being answerable 2. duty 3. charge 4. obligation

rest[1] (rɛst) n. 1. repose 2. freedom from exertion etc. 3. that on which anything rests or leans 4. pause, esp. in music 5. support —vi. 6. take rest 7. be supported —vt. 8. give rest to 9. place on support —'**restful** a. —'**restless** a.

rest[2] (rɛst) n. 1. remainder 2. others —vi. 3. remain 4. continue to be

restaurant ('rɛstərɒn, 'rɛstrɒn) n. commercial establishment serving food —**restaurateur** (rɛstərə'tɜː) n. keeper of restaurant —**restaurant car** UK railway coach in which meals are served (also **dining car**)

restitution (rɛstɪ'tjuːʃən) n. 1. giving back or making up 2. reparation, compensation

restive ('rɛstɪv) a. 1. restless 2. resisting control, impatient

restore (rɪ'stɔː) vt. 1. build up again, repair, renew 2. re-establish 3. give back —**restoration** (rɛstə'reɪʃən) n. —**restorative** (rɪ'stɒrətɪv) a. 1. restoring —n. 2. medicine to strengthen etc. —re'**storer** n.

restrain (rɪ'streɪn) vt. 1. check, hold back 2. prevent 3. confine —re'**straint** n. restraining, control, esp. self-control

restrict (rɪ'strɪkt) vt. limit, bound —re'**striction** n. 1. limitation 2. restraint 3. rule —re'**strictive** a. —**restricted area** area in which speed limit for vehicles applies —**restrictive practice** UK a trading agreement against the public interest

result (rɪ'zʌlt) vi. 1. follow as consequence 2. happen 3. end —n. 4. effect, outcome —re'**sultant** a. arising as result

resume (rɪ'zjuːm) v. begin again —**résumé** ('rɛzjumeɪ) n. summary, abstract —**resumption** (rɪ'zʌmpʃən) n. 1. resuming 2. fresh start —**resumptive** (rɪ'zʌmptɪv) a.

resurgence (rɪ'sɜːdʒəns) n. rising again —re'**surgent** a.

resurrect (rɛzə'rɛkt) vt. 1. restore to life, resuscitate 2. use once more (something discarded etc.) —**resur'rection** n. 1. rising again (esp. from dead) 2. revival

resuscitate (rɪ'sʌsɪteɪt) vt. revive to life, consciousness —**resusci'tation** n.

retail ('riːteɪl) n. 1. sale of goods in small quantities —adv. 2. by retail —v. 3. sell, be sold, retail 4. (rɪ'teɪl) recount —'**retailer** n.

retain (rɪ'teɪn) vt. 1. keep 2. engage

---

re'**spray** v.
'**respray** n.

re'**start**
re'**stock**

re'**surface**

services of —**re'tainer** n. 1. fee to retain professional adviser, esp. barrister 2. Hist. follower of nobleman etc. —**retention** (rɪ'tɛnʃən) n. —**retentive** (rɪ'tɛntɪv) a. capable of retaining, remembering —**retaining wall** wall constructed to hold back earth etc. (also **re'vetment**)

retake (ri:'teɪk) vt. 1. take back, capture again 2. Cine. shoot (scene) again 3. tape (recording) again —n. ('ri:teɪk) 4. Cine. rephotographed scene 5. retaped recording

retaliate (rɪ'tælɪeɪt) vi. 1. repay someone in kind 2. revenge oneself —**retali'ation** n. —**re'taliative** or **re'taliatory** a.

retard (rɪ'tɑ:d) vt. 1. make slow or late 2. keep back 3. impede development of —**retar'dation** n. —**re'tarded** a. underdeveloped, esp. mentally

retch (rɛtʃ, ri:tʃ) vi. try to vomit

reticent ('rɛtɪsənt) a. 1. reserved in speech 2. uncommunicative —'**reticence** n.

reticulate (rɪ'tɪkjʊlɪt) a. 1. made or arranged like a net (also **re'ticular**) —v. (rɪ'tɪkjʊleɪt) 2. make, be like net —**reticu'lation** n.

retina ('rɛtɪnə) n. light-sensitive membrane at back of eye (pl. -s, -nae (-ni:))

retinue ('rɛtɪnju:) n. band of followers or attendants

retire (rɪ'taɪə) vi. 1. give up office or work 2. go away 3. withdraw 4. go to bed —vt. 5. cause to retire —**re'tired** a. that has retired from office etc. —**re'tirement** n. —**re'tiring** a. unobtrusive, shy —**retirement pension** UK weekly payment made by government to retired man over 65 or woman over 60

retort (rɪ'tɔ:t) vt. 1. reply 2. repay in kind, retaliate 3. hurl back (charge etc.) —vi. 4. reply with countercharge —n. 5. vigorous reply or repartee 6. vessel with bent neck used for distilling

retouch (ri:'tʌtʃ) vt. touch up, improve by new touches, esp. of paint etc.

retrace (rɪ'treɪs) vt. go back over (a route etc.) again

retract (rɪ'trækt) v. draw back, recant —**re'tractable** or **re'tractible** a. —**re'tractile** a. capable of being drawn in —**re'traction** n. drawing or taking back, esp. of statement etc. —**re'tractor** n. 1. muscle 2. surgical instrument

retread (ri:'trɛd) vt. 1. renovate (worn rubber tyre) (-'**treaded**, -'**treading**) —n. ('ri:trɛd) 2. renovated tyre (also '**remould**)

retreat (rɪ'tri:t) vi. 1. move back from any position 2. retire —n. 3. act of, or military signal for, retiring, withdrawal 4. place to which anyone retires 5. refuge 6. sunset call on bugle

retrench (rɪ'trɛntʃ) v. 1. reduce (expenditure), esp. by dismissing staff —vt. 2. cut down —**re'trenchment** n.

retribution (rɛtrɪ'bju:ʃən) n. 1. recompense, esp. for evil deeds 2. vengeance —**retributive** (rɪ'trɪbjutɪv) a.

retrieve (rɪ'tri:v) vt. 1. fetch back again 2. restore 3. rescue from ruin 4. recover, esp. information from computer 5. regain —**re'trievable** a. —**re'trieval** n. —**re'triever** n. dog trained to retrieve game

retro- (comb. form) 1. back; backwards, as in retroactive 2. located behind, as in retrochoir

retroact ('rɛtrəʊækt) vi. 1. react 2. act in opposite direction —**retro'active** a. applying or referring to the past —**retro'actively** adv.

retrochoir ('rɛtrəʊkwaɪə) n. space in large church or cathedral behind high altar

retrograde ('rɛtrəʊgreɪd) a. 1. going backwards, reverting 2. reactionary —**retro'gress** vi. 1. go back to earlier, esp. worse, condition; degenerate, deteriorate 2. move backwards; recede —**retro'gression** n. —**retro'gressive** a.

retrorocket ('rɛtrəʊrɒkɪt) n. rocket engine to slow or reverse spacecraft etc.

retrospect ('rɛtrəʊspɛkt) n. looking back, survey of past —**retro'spection** n. —**retro'spective** a.

retroussé (rə'tru:seɪ) a. (of nose) turned upwards, pug

retsina (rɛt'si:nə) n. Gr. wine

return (rɪ'tɜ:n) vi. 1. go, come back —vt. 2. give, send back 3. report officially 4. elect —n. 5. returning, being returned 6. profit 7. official report 8. return ticket —**returning officer** officer conducting election —**return ticket** ticket allowing passenger to travel to and from a place

reunion (ri:'ju:njən) n. gathering of people who have been apart

rev (rɛv) inf. n. 1. revolution (of engine) —v. 2. (oft. with up) increase speed of revolution (of) —**rev counter** UK inf. tachometer

Rev. 1. Bible Revelation 2. Reverend

revalue (ri:'vælju:) or U.S. **revaluate** v. adjust exchange value of (currency) upwards —**revalu'ation** n.

revamp (ri:'væmp) vt. renovate, restore

reveal (rɪ'vi:l) vt. 1. make known 2. show —**revelation** (rɛvə'leɪʃən) n.

reveille (rɪ'vælɪ) n. morning bugle call etc. to waken soldiers

revel ('rɛv'l) vi. 1. take pleasure (in) 2. make merry (-ll-) —n. 3. (usu. pl.) merrymaking —'**reveller** n. —'**revelry** n. festivity

revenge (rɪ'vɛndʒ) n. 1. retaliation for wrong done 2. act that satisfies this 3.

re'think v.   **re'try**   **re'use**
'**rethink** n.   **re'type**
re'trial   **reu'nite**

desire for this —*vt.* 4. avenge 5. make retaliation for —*v.refl.* 6. avenge oneself —**re'vengeful** *a.* 1. vindictive 2. resentful

revenue ('rɛvɪnjuː) *n.* income, *esp.* of state, as taxes *etc.* —**Inland Revenue** government department that administers and collects direct taxes, *eg* income tax

reverberate (rɪ'vɜːbəreɪt) *v.* echo, resound, throw back (sound *etc.*) —**rever-ber'ation** *n.*

revere (rɪ'vɪə) *vt.* hold in great regard or religious respect —**reverence** ('rɛvərəns) *n.* 1. revering 2. awe mingled with respect and esteem 3. veneration —**reverend** ('rɛvərənd) *a.* (*esp.* as prefix to clergyman's name) worthy of reverence —**rev-erent** ('rɛvərənt, 'rɛvrənt) *a.* showing reverence —**reverential** (rɛvə'rɛnʃəl) *a.* marked by reverence

reverie ('rɛvərɪ) *n.* daydream, absent-minded state

revers (rɪ'vɪə) *n.* part of garment which is turned back, *eg* lapel (*pl.* **-vers** (-'vɪəz))

reverse (rɪ'vɜːs) *v.* 1. (of vehicle) (cause to) move backwards —*vt.* 2. turn upside down or other way round 3. change completely —*n.* 4. opposite, contrary 5. side opposite, obverse 6. defeat 7. reverse gear —*a.* 8. opposite, contrary —**re'versal** *n.* —**re'versible** *a.* —**reverse charge** telephone call made at recipient's expense —**reverse gear** mechanism enabling vehicle to move backwards —**reversing light** light on rear of motor vehicle to provide illumination when reversing

revert (rɪ'vɜːt) *vi.* 1. return to former state 2. come back to subject 3. refer (to) a second time 4. turn backwards —**re'ver-sion** *n.* (of property) rightful passing to owner or designated heir *etc.* —**re'verted** *a.* —**re'vertible** *a.*

review (rɪ'vjuː) *vt.* 1. examine 2. look back on 3. reconsider 4. hold, make, write review of —*n.* 5. general survey 6. critical notice of book *etc.* 7. periodical with critical articles 8. inspection of troops —**re'viewer** *n.* writer of reviews

revile (rɪ'vaɪl) *vt.* be viciously scornful of, abuse —**re'viler** *n.*

revise (rɪ'vaɪz) *vt.* 1. look over and correct 2. restudy (work done previously) in preparation for examination 3. change, alter —**re'viser** *n.* —**revision** (rɪ'vɪʒən) *n.* 1. re-examination for purpose of correcting 2. revising of notes, subject for examination 3. revised copy —**revision-ism** (rɪ'vɪʒənɪzəm) *n.* 1. (*sometimes* R-) moderate, nonrevolutionary version of Marxism developed in Germany around 1900 2. (*sometimes* R-) in Marxist-Leninist ideology, dangerous departure from true interpretation of Marx's teachings 3. advocacy of revision of some political theory *etc.* —**revisionist** (rɪ'vɪʒənɪst) *n./a.* —**re'visory** *a.* of revision

revive (rɪ'vaɪv) *v.* bring, come back to life, vigour, use *etc.* —**re'vival** *n.* reviving, *esp.* of religious fervour —**re'vivalist** *n./a.*

revoke (rɪ'vəʊk) *vt.* 1. take back, withdraw 2. cancel —**revocable** ('rɛvəkəb'l) *a.* —**revocation** (rɛvə'keɪʃən) *n.* repeal

revolt (rɪ'vəʊlt) *n.* 1. rebellion —*vi.* 2. rise in rebellion 3. feel disgust —*vt.* 4. affect with disgust —**re'volting** *a.* disgusting, horrible

revolve (rɪ'vɒlv) *vi.* 1. turn round, rotate 2. be centred (on) —*vt.* 3. rotate —**revolu-tion** (rɛvə'luːʃən) *n.* 1. violent overthrow of government 2. great change 3. complete rotation, turning or spinning round —**revolutionary** (rɛvə'luːʃənərɪ) *a./n.* —**revolutionize** *or* **-ise** (rɛvə'luːʃənaɪz) *vt.* 1. change considerably 2. bring about revolution in —**revolving door** door that rotates about vertical axis, *esp.* with four leaves at right angles to each other

revolver (rɪ'vɒlvə) *n.* repeating pistol with revolving magazine

revue *or* **review** (rɪ'vjuː) *n.* theatrical entertainment with topical sketches and songs

revulsion (rɪ'vʌlʃən) *n.* 1. sudden violent change of feeling 2. marked repugnance or abhorrence

reward (rɪ'wɔːd) *vt.* 1. pay, make return to (someone) for service, conduct *etc.* —*n.* 2. something given in return for a deed or service rendered —**re'warding** *a.* giving personal satisfaction, worthwhile

rewire (riː'waɪə) *vt.* provide (house *etc.*) with new wiring

RF radio frequency

R.F.C. Rugby Football Club

R.G.S. Royal Geographical Society

Rh 1. *Chem.* rhodium 2. rhesus (*esp. in* **Rh factor** (*see also* **rhesus factor** *at* RHESUS))

rhapsody ('ræpsədɪ) *n.* enthusiastic or high-flown (musical) composition or utter-ance —**rhapsodic** (ræp'sɒdɪk) *a.* —**'rhap-sodist** *n.* —**rhapsodize** *or* **-ise** ('ræpsədaɪz) *v.*

rhea ('rɪə) *n.* S Amer. three-toed ostrich

rhebuck *or* **rhebok** ('riːbʌk) *n.* brownish-grey S Afr. antelope

rhenium ('riːnɪəm) *n.* dense silvery-white metallic element that has high melting point

rheostat ('rɪəstæt) *n.* instrument for regulating the value of the resistance in an electric circuit

rhesus ('riːsəs) *n.* small, long-tailed monkey of S Asia —**rhesus factor** feature distinguishing different types of human blood (*also* **Rh factor**)

rhetoric ('rɛtərɪk) *n.* 1. art of effective speaking or writing 2. artificial or exaggerated language —**rhe'torical** *a.* (of question) not requiring an answer —**rhe-to'rician** *n.*

rheum (ruːm) *n.* 1. watery discharge, mucus 2. catarrh —'**rheumy** *a.*

rheumatism ('ruːmətɪzəm) *n.* painful inflammation of joints or muscles —**rheu-'matic** *a./n.* —'**rheumatoid** *a.* of, like rheumatism —**rheumatic fever** disease characterized by inflammation and pain in joints —**rheumatoid arthritis** chronic disease characterized by inflammation and swelling of joints

Rh factor *see* **rhesus factor** *at* RHESUS

rhinestone ('raɪnstəʊn) *n.* imitation gem made of paste

rhino ('raɪnəʊ) *n.* rhinoceros (*pl.* -s, 'rhino)

rhino- *or before vowel* **rhin-** (*comb. form*) nose, as in *rhinology*

rhinoceros (raɪ'nɒsərəs, -'nɒsrəs) *n.* large thick-skinned animal with one or two horns on nose (-es, -ros)

rhizome ('raɪzəʊm) *n.* thick horizontal underground stem whose buds develop into new plants (*also* 'rootstock, 'rootstalk)

rho (rəʊ) *n.* 17th letter in Gr. alphabet (P, ρ) (*pl.* -s)

rhodium ('rəʊdɪəm) *n.* hard metal like platinum —'**rhodic** *a.*

rhododendron (rəʊdə'dendrən) *n.* any of various evergreen flowering shrubs

rhombus ('rɒmbəs) *n.* equilateral but not right-angled parallelogram, diamond-shaped figure (*pl.* -es, -bi (-baɪ)) —**rhombohedron** (rɒmbəʊ'hiːdrən) *n.* six-sided prism whose sides are parallelograms —'**rhomboid** *n./a.* —**rhom'boidal** *a.*

rhubarb ('ruːbɑːb) *n.* 1. garden plant of which the fleshy stalks are cooked and used as fruit 2. laxative from root of allied Chinese plant

rhumba ('rʌmbə, 'rum-) *n. see* RUMBA

rhumb line (rʌm) 1. imaginary line on surface of sphere that intersects all meridians at same angle 2. course navigated by vessel or aircraft that maintains uniform compass heading (*also* rhumb)

rhyme *or* **rime** (raɪm) *n.* 1. identity of sounds at ends of lines of verse, or in words 2. word or syllable identical in sound to another 3. verse marked by rhyme —*vt.* 4. use (word) to make rhymes —**rhymester, rimester** ('raɪmstə), 'rhymer *or* 'rimer *n.* poet, *esp.* one considered mediocre; poetaster; versifier —**rhyme scheme** pattern of rhymes used in piece of verse, usu. indicated by letters —**rhyming slang** slang in which word is replaced by word or phrase that rhymes with it

rhythm ('rɪðəm) *n.* measured beat or flow, *esp.* of words, music *etc.* —'**rhythmic(al)** *a.* —'**rhythmically** *adv.* —**rhythm-and-blues** *n.* kind of popular music derived from or influenced by blues —**rhythm method** method of contraception by restricting sexual intercourse to days in woman's menstrual cycle when conception is considered least likely to occur

RI Rhode Island

R.I. 1. Regina et Imperatrix (*Lat.*, Queen and Empress) 2. Rex et Imperator (*Lat.*, King and Emperor) 3 Royal Institution 4. religious instruction

ria ('rɪə) *n.* long narrow inlet of sea coast, being former valley submerged by sea

rib[1] (rɪb) *n.* 1. one of curved bones springing from spine and forming framework of upper part of body 2. cut of meat including rib(s) 3. curved timber of framework of boat 4. raised series of rows in knitting *etc.* —*vt.* 5. furnish, mark with ribs 6. knit to form rib pattern (-bb-) —'**ribbing** *n.*

rib[2] (rɪb) *vt. inf.* tease, ridicule (-bb-)

R.I.B.A. Royal Institute of British Architects

ribald ('rɪb'ld) *a.* 1. irreverent, scurrilous 2. indecent —*n.* 3. ribald person —'**ribaldry** *n.* vulgar, indecent talk

ribbon ('rɪb'n) *n.* 1. narrow band of fabric used for trimming, tying *etc.* 2. long strip or line of anything —**ribbon development** building of houses along main road leading out of town *etc.*

riboflavin *or* **riboflavine** (raɪbəʊ'fleɪvɪn) *n.* form of vitamin B

ribonucleic acid (raɪbəʊnjuː'kliːɪk, -'kleɪ-) *see* RNA

rice (raɪs) *n.* 1. Eastern cereal plant 2. its seeds as food —**rice paper** fine, edible Chinese paper

rich (rɪtʃ) *a.* 1. wealthy 2. fertile 3. abounding 4. valuable 5. (of food) containing much fat or sugar 6. mellow 7. amusing —*n.* 8. the wealthy classes —'**riches** *pl.n.* wealth —'**richly** *adv.*

Richter scale ('rɪxtə) scale for expressing intensity of earthquake

rick[1] (rɪk) *n.* stack of hay *etc.*

rick[2] (rɪk) *vt./n.* sprain, wrench

rickets ('rɪkɪts) *n.* disease of children marked by softening of bones, bow legs *etc.*, caused by vitamin D deficiency —'**rickety** *a.* 1. shaky, insecure, unstable 2. suffering from rickets

rickshaw ('rɪkʃɔː) *or* **ricksha** ('rɪkʃə) *n.* light two-wheeled man-drawn Asian vehicle

ricochet ('rɪkəʃeɪ, 'rɪkəʃet) *vi.* 1. (of bullet) rebound or be deflected by solid surface or water —*n.* 2. bullet or shot to which this happens

rid (rɪd) *vt.* 1. clear, relieve 2. free 3. deliver (rid, 'ridding) —'**riddance** *n.* 1. clearance 2. act of ridding 3. deliverance 4. relief

ridden ('rɪd'n) *pp. of* RIDE

-ridden (*comb. form*) afflicted by, affected by, as in *disease-ridden*

riddle[1] ('rɪd'l) *n.* 1. question made puzzling to test one's ingenuity 2. enigma 3. puzzling thing, person —*vi.* 4. speak in, make riddles

riddle[2] ('rɪd'l) *vt.* 1. pierce with many holes —*n.* 2. coarse sieve for gravel *etc.* —**riddled with** full of, *esp.* holes

ride (raɪd) v. 1. sit on and control or propel (horse, bicycle *etc.*) —*vi.* 2. go on horseback or in vehicle 3. lie at anchor 4. be carried on or across —*vt.* 5. travel over (**rode, 'ridden, 'riding**) —*n.* 6. journey on horse *etc.*, or in any vehicle 7. riding track —'**rider** *n.* 1. one who rides 2. supplementary clause 3. addition to a document 4. mathematical problem on given proposition —'**riderless** *a.* —**riding crop** short whip with handle at one end for opening gates —**riding lamp** *or* **light** light on vessel showing it is at anchor

ridge (rɪdʒ) *n.* 1. long, narrow hill 2. long, narrow elevation on surface 3. line of meeting of two sloping surfaces —*v.* 4. form into ridges —'**ridgepole** *n.* 1. timber along ridge of roof, to which rafters are attached 2. horizontal pole at apex of tent

ridiculous (rɪ'dɪkjʊləs) *a.* deserving to be laughed at; absurd, foolish —'**ridicule** *n.* 1. language or behaviour intended to humiliate or mock —*vt.* 2. laugh at, deride

riding ('raɪdɪŋ) *n.* 1. (**R-** *when part of name*) former administrative district of Yorkshire 2. C parliamentary constituency

riesling ('riːzlɪŋ, 'raɪz-) *n.* 1. dry white wine 2. type of grape used to make this wine

rife (raɪf) *a.* prevalent, common

riffle ('rɪf'l) *v.* flick through (pages *etc.*) quickly

riffraff ('rɪfræf) *n.* disreputable people, *esp.* collectively; rabble

rifle ('raɪf'l) *vt.* 1. search and rob 2. ransack 3. make spiral grooves in (gun barrel *etc.*) —*n.* 4. firearm with long barrel —'**rifling** *n.* 1. arrangement of grooves in gun barrel 2. pillaging

rift (rɪft) *n.* crack, split, cleft —**rift valley** long narrow valley resulting from subsidence of land between two faults

rig (rɪg) *vt.* 1. provide (ship) with spars, ropes *etc.* 2. equip 3. set up, *esp.* as makeshift 4. arrange in dishonest way (**-gg-**) —*n.* 5. way ship's masts and sails are arranged 6. apparatus for drilling for oil and gas 7. US articulated lorry —'**rigger** *n.* —'**rigging** *n.* ship's spars and ropes —'**rigout** *n. inf.* person's clothing or costume, *esp.* bizarre outfit —**rig out** 1. (*oft. with* **with**) equip or fit out (with) 2. dress or be dressed

right (raɪt) *a.* 1. just 2. in accordance with truth and duty 3. true 4. correct 5. proper 6. of side that faces east when front is turned to north 7. *Pol.* conservative or reactionary (*also* **right-wing**) 8. straight 9. upright 10. of outer or more finished side of fabric —*vt.* 11. bring back to vertical position 12. do justice to —*vi.* 13. come back to vertical position —*n.* 14. claim, title *etc.* allowed or due 15. what is right, just or due 16. conservative political party 17. *Boxing* punch, blow with right hand —*adv.* 18. straight 19. properly 20. very 21. on or to right side —'**rightful** *a.* —'**rightly** *adv.* —**right angle** angle of 90 degrees

—**right-angled triangle** triangle one angle of which is right angle —**right-hand** *a.* 1. of, located on or moving towards the right 2. for use by right hand —**right-handed** *a.* 1. using right hand with greater skill than left 2. performed with right hand 3. for use by right hand 4. turning from left to right —**right-minded** *a.* holding opinions or principles that accord with what is right or with opinions of speaker —**Right Reverend** title of respect for bishop —**right whale** large, grey or black whalebone whale with large head and no dorsal fin —**right-hand man** most valuable assistant —**right of way** *Law* 1. right to pass over someone's land 2. path used (*pl.* **rights of way**)

righteous ('raɪtʃəs) *a.* 1. just, upright 2. godly 3. virtuous 4. good 5. honest —'**righteousness** *n.*

rigid ('rɪdʒɪd) *a.* 1. inflexible 2. harsh, stiff —ri'**gidity** *n.*

rigmarole ('rɪgmərəʊl) *or* **rigamarole** ('rɪgəmərəʊl) *n.* 1. meaningless string of words 2. long, complicated procedure

rigor ('raɪgɔː, 'rɪgə) *n.* sudden coldness attended by shivering —**rigor mortis** ('rɪgə 'mɔːtɪs) stiffening of body after death

rigour *or U.S.* **rigor** ('rɪgə) *n.* 1. harshness, severity, strictness 2. hardship —'**rigorous** *a.* stern, harsh, severe

rile (raɪl) *vt. inf.* anger, annoy

rill (rɪl) *n.* small stream

rim (rɪm) *n.* 1. edge, border, margin 2. outer ring of wheel —**rimmed** *a.* bordered, edged

rime[1] (raɪm) *n.* hoarfrost —'**rimy** *a.*

rime[2] (raɪm) *n. see* RHYME

rind (raɪnd) *n.* outer coating of fruits *etc.*

rinderpest ('rɪndəpɛst) *n.* malignant infectious disease of cattle

ring[1] (rɪŋ) *n.* 1. circle of gold *etc.*, *esp.* for finger 2. any circular band, coil, rim *etc.* 3. people or things arranged so as to form circle 4. group of people working together to advance their own interests 5. enclosed area, *esp.* roped-in square for boxing —*vt.* 6. put ring round 7. mark (bird *etc.*) with ring —'**ringer** *n.* 1. one who rings bells 2. *sl.* person, thing apparently identical to another (*esp. in* **dead ringer**) —'**ringlet** *n.* curly lock of hair —'**ringbark** *v.* kill (tree) by cutting bark round trunk —**ring finger** third finger, *esp.* of left hand, on which wedding ring is worn —'**ringleader** *n.* instigator of mutiny, riot *etc.* —**ring main** domestic electrical supply in which outlet sockets are connected to mains supply through continuous closed circuit (**ring circuit**) —'**ringmaster** *n.* master of ceremonies in circus —**ring road** main road that bypasses a town (centre) —'**ringside** *n.* 1. row of seats nearest boxing or wrestling ring 2. any place affording close uninterrupted view —'**ringworm** *n.* fungal skin disease in circular patches

ring² (rɪŋ) vi. 1. give out clear resonant sound, as bell 2. resound —vt. 3. cause (bell) to sound 4. call (person) by telephone (**rang** pt., **rung** pp.) —n. 5. a ringing 6. telephone call

rink (rɪŋk) n. 1. sheet of ice for skating or curling 2. floor for roller skating

rinkhals ('rɪŋkhaus) n. S Afr. ring-necked cobra

rinse (rɪns) vt. 1. remove soap from (washed clothes, hair etc.) by applying clean water 2. wash lightly —n. 3. a rinsing 4. liquid to tint hair

riot ('raɪət) n. 1. tumult, disorder 2. loud revelry 3. disorderly, unrestrained disturbance 4. profusion —vi. 5. make, engage in riot —'**riotous** a. unruly, rebellious, wanton

rip¹ (rɪp) vt. 1. cut, tear away, slash, rend (**-pp-**) —n. 2. rent, tear —'**ripcord** n. cord pulled to open parachute —**rip-roaring** a. inf. characterized by excitement, intensity or boisterous behaviour —'**ripsaw** n. handsaw with coarse teeth (used for cutting wood along grain) —**rip-off** n. sl. act of stealing, overcharging etc. —**rip off** sl. 1. steal 2. overcharge

rip² (rɪp) n. strong current, esp. one moving away from the shore

R.I.P. requiescat in pace

riparian (raɪ'pɛərɪən) a. of, on banks of river

ripe (raɪp) a. 1. ready to be reaped, eaten etc. 2. matured 3. (of judgment etc.) sound —'**ripen** v. 1. make or grow ripe —vi. 2. mature

riposte (rɪ'pɒst, rɪ'pəʊst) n. 1. verbal retort 2. counterstroke 3. Fencing quick lunge after parry

ripple ('rɪp²l) n. 1. slight wave, ruffling of surface 2. sound like ripples of water —vi. 3. flow, form into little waves 4. (of sounds) rise and fall gently —vt. 5. form ripples on

rise (raɪz) vi. 1. get up 2. move upwards 3. appear above horizon 4. reach higher level 5. increase in value or price 6. rebel 7. adjourn 8. originate; begin (**rose**, **risen** ('rɪz²n), '**rising**) —n. 9. rising 10. slope upwards 11. increase, esp. of wages —'**riser** n. 1. one who rises, esp. from bed 2. vertical part of step —'**rising** n. 1. revolt —a. 2. increasing in rank, maturity

risible ('rɪzɪb²l) a. 1. inclined to laugh 2. laughable —**risi'bility** n.

risk (rɪsk) n. 1. chance of disaster or loss —vt. 2. venture 3. put in jeopardy 4. take chance of —'**riskily** adv. —'**risky** a. 1. dangerous 2. hazardous —**take or run a risk** proceed in an action regardless of danger involved

risotto (rɪ'zɒtəʊ) n. dish of rice cooked in stock and served with various other ingredients

risqué ('rɪskeɪ) a. suggestive of indecency

rissole ('rɪsəʊl) n. dish of fish or meat minced, coated with egg and breadcrumbs and fried

rite (raɪt) n. formal practice or custom,

esp. religious —**ritual** ('rɪtjʊəl) n. 1. prescribed order or book of rites 2. regular, stereotyped action or behaviour —a. 3. concerning rites —**ritualism** ('rɪtjʊəlɪzəm) n. practice of ritual —**ritualist** ('rɪtjʊəlɪst) n.

ritzy ('rɪtsɪ) a. sl. luxurious; elegant

rival ('raɪv²l) n. 1. one that competes with another for favour, success etc. —vt. 2. vie with (**-ll-**) —a. 3. in position of rival —'**rivalry** n. keen competition

rive (raɪv) v. (usu. as pp./a. **riven**) 1. split asunder 2. tear apart (**rived** pt., **rived**, '**riven** pp., '**riving** pr.p.) —**riven** ('rɪv²n) a. split

river ('rɪvə) n. 1. large natural stream of water 2. copious flow —**river basin** area drained by river and its tributaries —'**riverbed** n. channel in which river flows or has flowed

rivet ('rɪvɪt) n. 1. bolt for fastening metal plates, the end being put through holes and then beaten flat —vt. 2. fasten with rivets 3. cause to be fixed or held firmly, esp. (fig.) in surprise, horror etc. —'**riveter** n.

rivulet ('rɪvjʊlɪt) n. small stream

R.L. Rugby League

rly. railway

R.M. 1. Royal Mail 2. Royal Marines 3. C Rural Municipality

R.M.A. Royal Military Academy (Sandhurst)

rms or **r.m.s.** root mean square

Rn Chem. radon

R.N. Royal Navy

RNA Biochem. ribonucleic acid; any of group of nucleic acids, present in all living cells, that play essential role in synthesis of proteins

R.N.(V.)R. Royal Naval (Volunteer) Reserve

roach (rəʊtʃ) n. European freshwater fish (pl. **roach**, **-es**)

road (rəʊd) n. 1. track, way prepared for passengers, vehicles etc. 2. direction, way 3. street —'**roadster** n. 1. obs. touring car 2. kind of bicycle —'**roadblock** n. barricade across road to stop traffic for inspection etc. —**road-fund licence** UK licence showing that tax payable in respect of motor vehicle has been paid —**road hog** selfish, aggressive driver —'**roadholding** n. extent to which motor vehicle is stable and does not skid, esp. on sharp bends etc. —'**roadhouse** n. public house, restaurant on country route —**road metal** broken stones used in macadamizing roads —**road sense** sound judgment in driving road vehicles —**road show** 1. Rad. live programme, usu. with audience participation, transmitted from radio van taking particular show on the road 2. group of entertainers on tour —'**roadside** n./a. —'**roadstead** n. Naut. partly sheltered anchorage (also **roads**) —**road test** test to ensure that vehicle is roadworthy, esp. after repair etc., by driving it on roads

—**road-test** *vt.* test (vehicle) in this way —**'roadway** *n.* **1.** surface of road **2.** part of road used by vehicles —**'roadworks** *pl.n.* repairs to road, *esp.* blocking part of road —**'roadworthy** *a.* (of vehicle) mechanically sound —**hit the road** *sl.* start or resume travelling —**one for the road** a last alcoholic drink before leaving

roam (rəʊm) *v.* wander about, rove —**'roamer** *n.*

roan (rəʊn) *a.* **1.** (of horses) having coat in which main colour is thickly interspersed with another, *esp.* bay, sorrel or chestnut mixed with white or grey —*n.* **2.** horse having such a coat

roar (rɔː) *vi.* **1.** make or utter loud, deep, hoarse sound, as of lion —*v.* **2.** (of people) utter (something) with loud deep cry, as in anger or triumph —*n.* **3.** such a sound —**'roaring** *a.* **1.** *inf.* brisk and profitable —*adv.* **2.** noisily

roast (rəʊst) *v.* **1.** bake, cook in closed oven **2.** cook by exposure to open fire **3.** make, be very hot —*n.* **4.** roasted joint —*a.* **5.** roasted —**'roaster** *n.* **1.** oven *etc.* for roasting meat **2.** chicken *etc.* suitable for roasting —**'roasting** *n.* *inf.* severe criticism, scolding

rob (rɒb) *vt.* **1.** plunder, steal from **2.** pillage, defraud (**-bb-**) —**'robber** *n.* —**'robbery** *n.*

robe (rəʊb) *n.* **1.** any long outer garment, oft. denoting rank or office —*vt.* **2.** dress —*vi.* **3.** put on robes, vestments

robin ('rɒbɪn) *n.* small brown bird with red breast (*also* **robin redbreast**)

robot ('rəʊbɒt) *n.* **1.** automated machine, *esp.* performing functions in human manner **2.** person of machinelike efficiency **3.** SA traffic lights —**ro'botic** *a.* of or like robot —**ro'botics** *pl.n.* (*with sing. v.*) study of use of robots

robust (rəʊ'bʌst, 'rəʊbʌst) *a.* sturdy, strong —**ro'bustious** *a.* *obs.* **1.** rough; boisterous **2.** strong, robust, stout —**ro-'bustness** *n.*

roc (rɒk) *n.* monstrous bird of Arabian mythology

R.O.C. Royal Observer Corps

rock[1] (rɒk) *n.* **1.** stone **2.** large rugged mass of stone **3.** hard sweet in sticks —**'rockery** *n.* mound or grotto of stones or rocks for plants in garden —**'rocky** *a.* **1.** having many rocks **2.** rugged —**rock bottom** lowest possible level —**rock-bound** *a.* hemmed in or encircled by rocks (*also* (*poet.*) **rock-girt**) —**rock cake** small cake containing dried fruit, with rough surface supposed to resemble rock —**rock crystal** transparent colourless quartz —**rock garden** garden featuring rocks or rockeries —**rock plant** plant that grows on rocks or in rocky ground —**rock rabbit** SA dassie, hyrax —**rock salmon** various food fishes, *esp.* dogfish —**rock salt** mineral consisting of sodium chloride in crystalline form, occurring in sedimentary beds

etc.: important source of table salt (*also* **'halite**)

rock[2] (rɒk) *v.* **1.** (cause to) sway to and fro **2.** reel or sway or cause (someone) to reel or sway, as with shock or emotion —*vi.* **3.** dance in rock-and-roll style —*n.* **4.** rocking motion **5.** rock-and-roll —**'rocker** *n.* **1.** curved piece of wood *etc.* on which thing may rock **2.** rocking chair —**'rocky** *a.* **1.** weak, unstable **2.** *inf.* (of person) dizzy; nauseated —**rock-and-roll** *or* **rock-'n'-roll** *n.* **1.** type of pop music of 1950s as blend of rhythm-and-blues and country-and-western **2.** dancing performed to such music —**rocking horse** toy horse mounted on rockers, on which child can rock to and fro in seesaw movement —**off one's rocker** *inf.* insane

rocket[1] ('rɒkɪt) *n.* **1.** self-propelling device powered by burning of explosive contents, used as firework, for display, signalling, line carrying, weapon *etc.* **2.** vehicle propelled by rocket engine, as weapon or carrying spacecraft —*vi.* **3.** move fast, *esp.* upwards, as rocket —**'rocketry** *n.*

rocket[2] ('rɒkɪt) *n.* any of several kinds of flowering plant

rococo (rə'kəʊkəʊ) *a.* (*oft.* R-) **1.** of furniture, architecture *etc.* having much conventional decoration in style of early 18th-cent. work in France **2.** tastelessly florid

rod (rɒd) *n.* **1.** slender cylinder of metal, wood *etc.* **2.** cane **3.** unit of length equal to 5½ yards

rode (rəʊd) *pt. of* RIDE

rodent ('rəʊdˀnt) *n.* any gnawing animal, eg rat

rodeo ('rəʊdɪəʊ) *n.* US, A display of skills of cowboys, with bareback riding, cattle-handling techniques *etc.* (*pl.* **-s**)

rodomontade (rɒdəmɒn'teɪd, -'tɑːd) *Lit.* *n.* **1.** boastful words or behaviour —*vi.* **2.** boast; rant

roe[1] (rəʊ) *n.* small species of deer

roe[2] (rəʊ) *n.* mass of eggs in fish

roentgen *or* **röntgen** ('rɒntgən, -tjən, 'rɛnt-) *n.* measuring unit of radiation dose

rogation (rəʊ'geɪʃən) *n.* (*usu. pl.*) *Christianity* solemn supplication, *esp.* in form of ceremony prescribed by Church —**Rogation Days** three days preceding Ascension Day

roger ('rɒdʒə) *interj.* **1.** *Telecomm. etc.* message received and understood **2.** expression of agreement

rogue (rəʊg) *n.* **1.** rascal, knave, scoundrel **2.** mischief-loving person, *oft.* child **3.** wild beast of savage temper, living apart from herd —**'roguery** *n.* —**'roguish** *a.* —**rogues' gallery** collection of portraits of known criminals kept by police for identification purposes

roister ('rɔɪstə) *vi.* **1.** be noisy or boisterous **2.** brag, bluster or swagger —**'roisterer** *n.* reveller

role *or* **rôle** (rəʊl) *n.* **1.** actor's part **2.** specific task or function

roll (rəʊl) v. **1.** move by turning over and over —vt. **2.** wind round **3.** smooth out with roller —vi. **4.** move, sweep along **5.** undulate **6.** (of ship) swing from side to side **7.** (of aircraft) turn about a line from nose to tail in flight —n. **8.** act of lying down and turning over and over or from side to side **9.** piece of paper etc. rolled up **10.** any object thus shaped, as meat roll, swiss roll, etc. **11.** official list or register, esp. of names **12.** bread baked into small oval or round **13.** continuous sound, as of drums, thunder etc. —'**roller** n. **1.** cylinder of wood, stone, metal etc. used for pressing, crushing, smoothing, supporting thing to be moved, winding thing on etc. **2.** long wave of sea **3.** any of various Old World birds that have blue, green and brown plumage and erratic flight —'**rolling** a. **1.** having gentle rising and falling slopes **2.** reverberating **3.** that may be turned up or down **4.** sl. extremely rich —adv. **5.** sl. swaying, staggering (esp. in **rolling drunk**) —**roll call** act, time of calling over list of names, as in schools or army —**rolled gold** metal coated with thin layer of gold —**roller bearings** bearings of hardened steel rollers —**roller coaster** see **big dipper** at BIG —**roller skate** skate with wheels instead of runner —**roller skating** —**roller towel** loop of towel on roller —**rolling mill 1.** mill or factory where ingots of heated metal are passed between rollers to produce sheets or bars of a required cross section and form **2.** machine used for this purpose —**rolling pin** cylindrical roller for pastry or dough —**rolling stock** locomotives, carriages etc. of railway —**rolling stone** restless or wandering person —'**rollmop** n. herring fillet rolled, usu. around onion slices, and pickled in spiced vinegar —**roll-on** a. **1.** (of deodorant etc.) dispensed by means of revolving ball fitted into neck of container —n. **2.** woman's foundation garment —**roll-top** a. (of desk) with flexible lid sliding in grooves —**roll on** UK used to express wish that eagerly anticipated event or date will come quickly —**roll up** inf. appear, turn up

rollick ('rɒlɪk) vi. **1.** behave in carefree or boisterous manner —n. **2.** boisterous or carefree escapade —'**rollicking** a.

roly-poly ('rəʊlɪ'pəʊlɪ) n. **1.** pudding of suet pastry covered with jam and rolled up —a. **2.** round, plump

ROM (rɒm) Comp. read only memory

rom. Print. roman (type)

Rom. Bible Romans

Roman ('rəʊmən) a. of Rome or Church of Rome —**Roman alphabet** alphabet evolved by ancient Romans for writing of Latin and still used for writing most of languages of Western Europe —**Roman candle** firework that produces continuous shower of sparks punctuated by coloured balls of fire —**Roman Catholic** member of that section of Christian Church which acknowledges supremacy of the Pope

—**Roman nose** nose having high prominent bridge —**Roman numerals** letters I, V, X, L, C, D, M used to represent numbers in manner of Romans —**roman type** plain upright letters, ordinary style of printing

romance (rə'mæns, 'rəʊmæns) n. **1.** love affair, esp. intense and happy one **2.** mysterious or exciting quality **3.** tale of chivalry **4.** tale with scenes remote from ordinary life **5.** literature like this **6.** picturesque falsehood —vi. (rə'mæns) **7.** exaggerate, fantasize —ro'**mancer** n. —ro'**mantic** a. **1.** characterized by romance **2.** of or dealing with love **3.** (of literature etc.) preferring passion and imagination to proportion and finish —n. **4.** romantic person **5.** person whose tastes in art, literature etc. lie mainly in romanticism —ro'**manticism** n. —ro-'**manticist** n. —ro'**manticize** or -**cise** v.

Romance (rə'mæns, 'rəʊmæns) a. **1.** of vernacular language of certain countries, developed from Latin, as French, Spanish etc. —n. **2.** this group of languages

Romanesque (rəʊmə'nɛsk) a./n. (in) style of round-arched vaulted architecture of period between Classical and Gothic

Romany or **Rommany** ('rɒmənɪ, 'rəʊ-) n. **1.** Gypsy **2.** Gypsy language —a. **3.** of the Gypsies or their language

romp (rɒmp) vi. **1.** run, play wildly, joyfully —n. **2.** spell of romping —'**rompers** pl.n. child's one-piece garment consisting of trousers and bib with straps —**romp home** win easily

rondavel (rɒn'dɑːvəl) n. SA circular building, oft. thatched

rondo ('rɒndəʊ) n. piece of music with leading theme to which return is continually made (pl. -s)

röntgen ('rɒntgən, -tjən, 'rɛnt-) n. see ROENTGEN

roo (ruː) n. A inf. kangaroo

rood (ruːd) n. **1.** the Cross **2.** crucifix **3.** quarter of acre —**rood screen** screen separating nave from choir

roof (ruːf) n. **1.** outside upper covering of building **2.** top, covering part of anything —vt. **3.** put roof on, over —'**roofing** n. **1.** material used to construct roof **2.** act of constructing roof —**roof rack** rack attached to roof of motor vehicle for carrying luggage etc. —'**rooftree** n. see ridgepole at RIDGE —**hit** (or **raise** or **go through**) **the roof** inf. become extremely angry

rooibos ('rʊɪbɒs) n. S Afr. red-leafed tree

rooikat ('rʊɪkæt) n. S Afr. lynx

rook¹ (rʊk) n. **1.** bird of crow family —vt. **2.** sl. swindle, cheat —'**rookery** n. colony of rooks

rook² (rʊk) n. chess piece (also '**castle**)

rookie ('rʊkɪ) n. inf. recruit, esp. in army

room (ruːm, rʊm) n. **1.** space **2.** space enough **3.** division of house **4.** scope, opportunity —pl. **5.** lodgings —'**roomy** a. spacious —'**roommate** n. person with whom one shares room or lodging —**room**

service service in hotel providing meals *etc.* in guests' rooms

roost (ruːst) *n.* **1.** perch for fowls —*vi.* **2.** perch —**'rooster** *n.* US domestic cock —**come home to roost** have unfavourable repercussions

root (ruːt) *n.* **1.** part of plant that grows down into earth and conveys nourishment to plant **2.** plant with edible root, *eg* carrot **3.** vital part **4.** source, origin, original cause of anything **5.** *Anat.* embedded portion of tooth, nail, hair *etc.* **6.** primitive word from which other words are derived **7.** *Maths.* factor of a quantity which, when multiplied by itself the number of times indicated, gives the quantity —*v.* **8.** (cause to) take root —*vt.* **9.** pull by roots —*vi.* **10.** dig, burrow —**'rootless** *a.* having no roots or ties —**root mean square** square root of average of squares of set of numbers —**'rootstock** *n.* **1.** *see* RHIZOME **2.** *see* STOCK (sense 6) **3.** *Biol.* basic structure from which offshoots have developed —**root out** remove or eliminate completely

root for *inf.* cheer, applaud, encourage —**'rooter** *n.*

rope (rəʊp) *n.* **1.** thick cord —*vt.* **2.** secure, mark off with rope —**'ropiness** *n.* —**'ropy** *a.* **1.** *inf.* inferior, inadequate **2.** *inf.* not well **3.** (of liquid) sticky and stringy —**'rope- walk** *n.* long narrow shed where ropes are made —**know the ropes** know details or procedures, as of job

ro-ro (ˈrəʊrəʊ) *a.* roll-on/roll-off: of cargo ship or ferry designed so that vehicles can be driven straight on and straight off

rorqual (ˈrɔːkwəl) *n.* whalebone whale with dorsal fin and series of grooves along throat and chest (*also* **'finback**)

rosaceous (rəʊˈzeɪʃəs) *a.* **1.** of *Rosaceae*, family of plants typically having five- petalled flowers, including rose, strawberry *etc.* **2.** like rose, esp. rose-coloured

rosary (ˈrəʊzərɪ) *n.* **1.** *R.C.Ch.* series of prayers **2.** string of beads for counting these prayers as they are recited **3.** rose garden

rose[1] (rəʊz) *n.* **1.** shrub, climbing plant *usu.* with prickly stems and fragrant flowers **2.** the flower **3.** perforated flat nozzle for hose *etc.* **4.** pink colour —*a.* **5.** of this colour —**roseate** (ˈrəʊzɪeɪt) *a.* rose- coloured, rosy —**ro'sette** *n.* **1.** rose-shaped bunch of ribbon **2.** rose-shaped architec- tural ornament —**'rosy** *a.* **1.** flushed **2.** hopeful, promising —**rose-coloured** *a.* **1.** having colour of rose **2.** unwarrantably optimistic —**rose-water** *n.* **1.** scented water made by distillation of rose petals or by impregnation with oil of roses —*a.* **2.** elegant or delicate, *esp.* excessively so —**rose window** circular window with series of mullions branching from centre —**'rosewood** *n.* fragrant wood —**rose of Sharon** (ˈʃærən) low, spreading shrub with yellow flowers

rose[2] (rəʊz) *pt. of* RISE

rosé (ˈrəʊzeɪ) *n.* pink wine

rosemary (ˈrəʊzmərɪ) *n.* evergreen fra- grant flowering shrub

Rosh Hashanah *or* **Rosh Hashana** (ˈrɒʃ həˈʃɑːnə; *Hebrew* ˈrɔʃ haʃaˈna) Jewish New Year

Rosicrucian (rəʊzɪˈkruːʃən) *n.* **1.** member of secret order devoted to occult beliefs —*a.* **2.** of the Rosicrucians or Rosicrucian- ism —**Rosi'crucianism** *n.*

rosin (ˈrɒzɪn) *n.* resin

ROSPA (ˈrɒspə) UK Royal Society for Prevention of Accidents

roster (ˈrɒstə) *n.* **1.** list or plan showing turns of duty —*vt.* **2.** place on roster

rostrum (ˈrɒstrəm) *n.* **1.** platform, stage, pulpit **2.** beak or bill of bird (*pl.* **-s, -tra** (-trə))

rot (rɒt) *v.* **1.** (cause to) decompose naturally —*vt.* **2.** corrupt (**-tt-**) —*n.* **3.** decay, putrefaction **4.** any disease produc- ing decomposition of tissue **5.** *inf.* nonsense —**'rotten** *a.* **1.** decomposed, putrid **2.** corrupt —**'rotter** *n. sl.*, *chiefly* UK worthless, unpleasant or despicable person

rota (ˈrəʊtə) *n.* roster, list

rotary (ˈrəʊtərɪ) *a.* **1.** (of movement) circular **2.** operated by rotary movement —**Ro'tarian** *n.* member of Rotary Club —**ro'tate** *v.* (cause to) move round centre or on pivot —**ro'tation** *n.* **1.** rotating **2.** regular succession —**'rotatory** *a.* —**'rotovate** *vt.* —**'rotovator** *n.* R mechani- cal cultivator with rotary blades —**Rotary Club** one of international association of businessmen's clubs

rote (rəʊt) *n.* mechanical repetition —**by rote** by memory

rotisserie (rəʊˈtɪsərɪ) *n.* (electrically- driven) rotating spit for cooking meat

rotor (ˈrəʊtə) *n.* **1.** revolving portion of a dynamo motor or turbine

rotten (ˈrɒt'n) *a. see* ROT

rotund (rəʊˈtʌnd) *a.* **1.** round **2.** plump **3.** sonorous —**ro'tundity** *n.*

rotunda (rəʊˈtʌndə) *n.* circular building or room, *esp.* with dome

rouble *or* **ruble** (ˈruːb'l) *n.* monetary unit of Soviet Union

roué (ˈruːeɪ) *n.* debauched or lecherous man; rake

rouge (ruːʒ) *n.* **1.** red powder, cream used to colour cheeks —*vt.* **2.** colour with rouge

rough (rʌf) *a.* **1.** not smooth, of irregular surface **2.** violent, stormy, boisterous **3.** rude **4.** uncivil **5.** lacking refinement **6.** approximate **7.** in preliminary form —*vt.* **8.** make rough **9.** plan out approximately **10.** (*with* it) live without usual comforts *etc.* —*n.* **11.** rough state or area **12.** sketch —**'roughage** *n.* unassimilated portion of food promoting proper intestinal action —**'roughen** *v.* —**'roughly** *adv.* —**rough- and-ready** *a.* **1.** crude, unpolished or hastily prepared, but sufficient for purpose **2.** (of person) without formality or refinement —**rough-and-tumble** *n.* **1.** fight or scuffle without rules —*a.* **2.** characterized by disorderliness and disregard for rules —'**roughcast** a. 1. coated with mixture of lime and gravel —n. 2. such mixture —vt. 3. coat (wall etc.) with roughcast —**rough diamond** trustworthy but unsophisticated person —**rough-dry** a. 1. (of clothes or linen) dried ready for pressing —vt. 2. dry (clothes etc.) without ironing —**rough-hew** vt. shape roughly —'**roughhouse** n. sl. fight, row —'**rough-shod** a. (of horse) shod with rough-bottomed shoes to prevent sliding —**ride roughshod over** treat harshly and without consideration

roulette (ruː'lɛt) n. game of chance played with revolving wheel and ball

round (raund) a. 1. spherical 2. cylindrical 3. circular 4. curved 5. full, complete 6. roughly correct 7. large, considerable 8. plump 9. positive —adv. 10. with circular or circuitous course —n. 11. thing round in shape 12. recurrent duties 13. stage in competition 14. customary course, as of milkman 15. game (of golf) 16. one of several periods in boxing match etc. 17. cartridge for firearm 18. rung 19. movement in circle —prep. 20. about 21. on all sides of —v. 22. make, become round —vt. 23. move round —'**rounders** n. ball game —'**roundly** adv. 1. plainly 2. thoroughly —'**roundabout** n. 1. revolving circular platform on which people ride for amusement 2. road junction at which traffic passes round a central island —a. 3. indirect; devious —**round dance** 1. dance in which dancers form circle 2. ballroom dance in which couples revolve —'**Round-head** n. English hist. supporter of Parliament against Charles I during Civil War —**round robin** petition signed with names in circle to conceal order —**round-shouldered** a. denoting faulty posture characterized by drooping shoulders and slight forward bending of back —**round table** meeting of parties or people on equal terms for discussion —**round-the-clock** a. throughout day and night —**round trip** trip to place and back again —'**roundup** n. 1. act of gathering together cattle etc. for branding, counting or selling 2. inf. any similar act of bringing together —'**roundworm** n. nematode worm that is common intestinal parasite of man and pigs —**round up** 1. drive (cattle) together 2. collect and arrest criminals

roundel ('raundʲl) n. 1. rondeau 2. small disc —'**roundelay** n. simple song with refrain

rouse (rauz) vt. 1. wake up, stir up, excite to action 2. cause to rise —vi. 3. waken

rout¹ (raut) n. 1. overwhelming defeat, disorderly retreat 2. noisy rabble —vt. 3. scatter and put to flight

rout² (raut) v. 1. dig over or turn up (something), esp. (of animal) with snout; root —vt. 2. (usu. with out or up) find by searching 3. (usu. with out) drive out 4. (oft. with out) hollow or gouge out —vi. 5. search, poke, rummage

route (ruːt) n. road, chosen way —'**route-march** n. 1. Mil. long march undertaken for training purposes 2. inf. any long exhausting walk

routine (ruː'tiːn) n. 1. regularity of procedure, unvarying round 2. regular course —a. 3. ordinary, regular

rove (rəuv) v. wander, roam —'**rover** n. 1. one who roves 2. pirate

row¹ (rəu) n. 1. number of things in a straight line 2. rank 3. file 4. line

row² (rəu) v. 1. propel (boat) by oars —n. 2. spell of rowing —**rowing boat**

row³ (rau) inf. n. 1. dispute 2. disturbance —vi. 3. quarrel noisily

rowan ('rəuən, 'rau-) n. native Brit. tree producing bright red berries (also (European) **mountain ash**)

rowdy ('raudɪ) a. 1. disorderly, noisy and rough —n. 2. person like this

rowel ('rauəl) n. small wheel with points on spur

rowlock ('rɒlək) n. appliance on gunwale of boat serving as point of leverage for oar

royal ('rɔɪəl) a. 1. of, worthy of, befitting, patronized by, king or queen 2. splendid —'**royalist** n. supporter of monarchy —'**royalty** n. 1. royal dignity or power 2. royal persons 3. payment to owner of land for right to work minerals, or to inventor for use of his invention 4. payment to author depending on sales —**Royal Air Force** air force of Great Brit. —**royal blue** (of) deep blue colour —**royal jelly** substance secreted by pharyngeal glands of worker bees and fed to all larvae when very young and to larvae destined to become queens throughout their development —**Royal Marines** UK corps of soldiers trained in amphibious warfare —**Royal Navy** navy of Great Brit. —**royal palm** palm tree of tropical Amer. having tall trunk with tuft of feathery pinnate leaves —**royal warrant** authorization to tradesman to supply goods to royal household

r.p.m. revolutions per minute

R.R. 1. Right Reverend 2. C Rural Route

R.S. UK Royal Society

R.S.A. 1. Republic of South Africa 2. Royal Scottish Academy 3. Royal Scottish Academician 4. Royal Society of Arts 5. NZ Returned Services Association

RSFSR Russian Soviet Federated Socialist Republic

R.S.P.C.A. UK Royal Society for the Prevention of Cruelty to Animals

R.S.V. Revised Standard Version (of the Bible)

R.S.V.P. répondez s'il vous plaît (Fr., please reply)

Rt. Hon. Right Honourable

Rt. Rev. Right Reverend

Ru Chem. ruthenium

R.U. Rugby Union

rub (rʌb) vt. 1. apply pressure to with circular or backwards and forwards movement 2. clean, polish, dry, thus 3.

pass hand over 4. abrade, chafe 5. remove by friction —*vi.* 6. come into contact accompanied by friction 7. become frayed or worn by friction (-bb-) —*n.* 8. rubbing 9. impediment —'**rubbing** *n.* impression taken of incised or raised surface by laying paper over it and rubbing with wax *etc.*

rubato (ru:'bɑːtəu) *Mus. n.* 1. flexibility of tempo in performance (*pl.* -s) —*a./adv.* 2. to be played with flexible tempo

rubber[1] ('rʌbə) *n.* 1. coagulated sap of rough, elastic consistency, of certain tropical trees (*also* **India rubber, gum elastic, 'caoutchouc**) 2. piece of rubber *etc.* used for erasing 3. thing for rubbing 4. person who rubs —*a.* 5. made of rubber —'**rubberize** *or* -**ise** *vt.* coat, impregnate, treat with rubber —'**rubbery** *a.* —**rubber band** continuous loop of thin rubber, used to hold papers *etc.* together (*also* **elastic band**) —'**rubberneck** *sl. n.* 1. person who gapes inquisitively 2. sightseer, tourist —*vi.* 3. stare in naive or foolish manner —**rubber plant** 1. plant with glossy leathery leaves, cultivated as house plant in Europe and N Amer. 2. any of several tropical trees, sap of which yields crude rubber —**rubber stamp** 1. device for imprinting dates *etc.* 2. automatic authorization

rubber[2] ('rʌbə) *n.* 1. series of odd number of games or contests at various games 2. two out of three games won

rubbish ('rʌbɪʃ) *n.* 1. refuse, waste material 2. anything worthless 3. trash, nonsense —'**rubbishy** *a.* valueless

rubble ('rʌbʰl) *n.* 1. fragments of stone *etc.* 2. builders' rubbish

rubella (ru:'belə) *n.* mild contagious viral disease (*also* **German measles**)

rubicund ('ru:bɪkənd) *a.* of reddish colour; ruddy

rubidium (ru:'bɪdɪəm) *n.* soft highly reactive radioactive element of alkali metal group

rubric ('ru:brɪk) *n.* 1. title, heading 2. direction in liturgy 3. instruction

ruby ('ru:bɪ) *n.* 1. precious red gem 2. its colour —*a.* 3. of this colour —**ruby wedding** fortieth wedding anniversary

ruche (ru:ʃ) *n.* strip of pleated or frilled lace *etc.* used to decorate blouses *etc.*

ruck[1] (rʌk) *n.* 1. crowd 2. common herd 3. rank and file 4. *Rugby* loose scrummage or maul

ruck[2] (rʌk) *n.* 1. crease —*v.* 2. make, become wrinkled

rucksack ('rʌksæk) *n.* pack carried on back, knapsack (*also* **back pack**)

ruction ('rʌkʃən) *n. inf.* noisy disturbance

rudder ('rʌdə) *n.* flat piece hinged to boat's stern or rear of aircraft used to steer

ruddy ('rʌdɪ) *a.* 1. of fresh or healthy red colour 2. rosy 3. florid

rude (ru:d) *a.* 1. impolite 2. coarse 3. vulgar

4. primitive 5. roughly made 6. uneducated 7. sudden, violent —'**rudely** *adv.*

rudiments ('ru:dɪmənts) *pl.n.* elements, first principles —**rudi'mentary** *a.*

rue[1] (ru:) *v.* 1. grieve (for) —*vt.* 2. regret 3. deplore —*vi.* 4. repent —*n.* 5. *obs.* repentance —'**rueful** *a.* 1. sorry 2. regretful 3. dejected 4. deplorable —'**ruefully** *adv.*

rue[2] (ru:) *n.* plant with evergreen bitter leaves

ruff[1] (rʌf) *n.* 1. starched and frilled collar 2. natural collar of feathers, fur *etc.* on some birds and animals 3. type of shore bird —'**ruffle** *vt.* 1. rumple, disorder 2. annoy, put out 3. frill, pleat —*n.* 4. frilled trimming

ruff[2] (rʌf) *n./v. Cards* trump

ruffian ('rʌfɪən) *n.* violent, lawless person —'**ruffianism** *n.* —'**ruffianly** *a.*

rufous ('ru:fəs) *a.* reddish-brown

rug (rʌg) *n.* 1. small, oft. shaggy or thick-piled floor mat 2. thick woollen wrap, coverlet

rugby *or* **rugby football** ('rʌgbɪ) *n.* form of football in which the ball may be carried in the hands (*inf.* '**rugger**)

rugged ('rʌgɪd) *a.* 1. rough 2. broken 3. unpolished 4. harsh, austere

ruin ('ru:ɪn) *n.* 1. decay, destruction 2. downfall 3. fallen or broken state 4. loss of wealth, position *etc.* —*pl.* 5. ruined buildings *etc.* —*vt.* 6. reduce to ruins 7. bring to decay or destruction 8. spoil 9. impoverish —**rui'nation** *n.* —'**ruinous** *a.* causing or characterized by ruin or destruction —'**ruinously** *adv.*

rule (ru:l) *n.* 1. principle 2. precept 3. authority 4. government 5. what is usual 6. control 7. measuring stick —*vt.* 8. govern 9. decide 10. mark with straight lines 11. draw (line) —'**ruler** *n.* 1. one who governs 2. stick for measuring or ruling lines —'**ruling** *n.* 1. decision of someone in authority, such as judge 2. one or more parallel ruled lines —*a.* 3. controlling or exercising authority 4. predominant —**rule of thumb** rough and practical approach, based on experience, rather than theory

rum (rʌm) *n.* spirit distilled from sugar cane

rumba *or* **rhumba** ('rʌmbə, 'rum-) *n.* 1. rhythmic dance, *orig.* Cuban 2. music for it

rumble ('rʌmbʰl) *vi.* 1. make noise as of distant thunder, heavy vehicle *etc.* —*n.* 2. such noise

rumbustious (rʌm'bʌstjəs) *a.* boisterous, unruly

ruminate ('ru:mɪneɪt) *vi.* 1. chew cud 2. ponder, meditate —'**ruminant** *a./n.* cud-chewing (animal) —**rumi'nation** *n.* quiet meditation and reflection —'**ruminative** *a.*

rummage ('rʌmɪdʒ) *v.* 1. search thoroughly —*n.* 2. act of rummaging

rummy ('rʌmɪ) *or* **rum** *n.* card game

rumour *or U.S.* **rumor** ('ru:mə) *n.* 1.

hearsay, common talk, unproved statement —vt. 2. put round as, by way of, rumour

rump ('rʌmp) n. 1. hindquarters of mammal, not including legs 2. person's buttocks

rumple ('rʌmp'l) v./n. crease, wrinkle

rumpus ('rʌmpəs) n. 1. disturbance 2. noise and confusion

run (rʌn) vi. 1. move with more rapid gait than walking 2. go quickly 3. flow 4. flee 5. compete in race, contest, election 6. revolve 7. continue 8. function 9. travel according to schedule 10. fuse 11. melt 12. spread 13. have certain meaning —vt. 14. cross by running 15. expose oneself to (risk etc.) 16. cause to run 17. (of newspaper) print, publish 18. land and dispose of (smuggled goods) 19. manage 20. operate (ran pt., run pp., 'running pr.p.) —n. 21. act, spell of running 22. rush 23. tendency, course 24. period 25. sequence 26. heavy demand 27. enclosure for domestic fowls, animals 28. ride in car 29. series of unravelled stitches, ladder 30. score of one at cricket 31. steep snow-covered course for skiing —'runner n. 1. racer 2. messenger 3. curved piece of wood on which sledge slides 4. any similar appliance 5. slender stem of plant running along ground forming new roots at intervals 6. strip of lace etc. placed on table for decoration 7. strip of carpet —'running a. 1. continuous 2. consecutive 3. flowing 4. discharging 5. effortless 6. entered for race 7. used for running —n. 8. act of moving or flowing quickly 9. management —'runny a. tending to flow or exude moisture —'runabout n. small light vehicle or aeroplane —'runaway n. 1. person or animal that runs away 2. act or instance of running away —a. 3. rising rapidly, as prices 4. (of race etc.) easily won —'rundown n. summary —run-down a. exhausted —runner-up n. contestant finishing race or competition in second place (pl. runners-up) —running board ledge beneath doors of old cars —running commentary commentary maintained continuously —running head or title Print. heading printed at top of every page of book —running knot knot that moves or slips easily —running repairs repairs that do not (greatly) interrupt operations —run-of-the-mill a. ordinary —run-up n. 1. approach run by athlete for long jump, pole vault etc. 2. preliminary or preparatory period —'runway n. level stretch where aircraft take off and land —run about move busily from place to place —run away 1. take flight; escape 2. go away; depart 3. (of horse) gallop away uncontrollably —run away with 1. abscond or elope with 2. make off with; steal 3. escape from control of 4. win easily or be assured of victory in (competition) —run down 1. stop working 2. reduce 3. exhaust 4. denigrate —run up 1. amass; incur 2. make by sewing together quickly

3. hoist —in the running having a fair chance in a competition

rune (ru:n) n. 1. character of earliest Germanic alphabet 2. magic sign —'runic a.

rung[1] (rʌŋ) n. crossbar or spoke, esp. in ladder

rung[2] (rʌŋ) pp. of RING[2]

runnel ('rʌn'l) n. 1. gutter 2. small brook or rivulet

running ('rʌnɪŋ) see RUN

runt (rʌnt) n. 1. smallest young animal in litter 2. offens. undersized person

rupee (ru:'pi:) n. monetary unit of India, Pakistan, Sri Lanka etc.

rupture ('rʌptʃə) n. 1. breaking, breach 2. hernia —v. 3. break 4. burst, sever

rural ('ruərəl) a. 1. of the country 2. rustic —'ruralize or -ise v. —rural route C mail service in rural area

rusbank ('rʌsbæŋk) n. SA wooden bench, settle

ruse (ru:z) n. stratagem, trick

rush[1] (rʌʃ) vt. 1. impel, carry along violently and rapidly 2. take by sudden assault —vi. 3. cause to hurry 4. move violently or rapidly —n. 5. rushing, charge 6. hurry 7. eager demand 8. heavy current (of air, water etc.) —a. 9. done with speed 10. characterized by speed —rush hour period at beginning and end of day when many people are travelling to and from work

rush[2] (rʌʃ) n. 1. marsh plant with slender pithy stem 2. the stems used as material for baskets —'rushy a. full of rushes

rusk (rʌsk) n. kind of light biscuit

Russ. Russia(n)

russet ('rʌsɪt) a. 1. reddish-brown —n. 2. the colour

Russian ('rʌʃən) n. 1. official language of Soviet Union: Indo-European language belonging to East Slavonic branch 2. native or inhabitant of Russia or Soviet Union —a. 3. of Russia or Soviet Union —Russian roulette 1. act of bravado in which each person in turn spins cylinder of revolver loaded with only one cartridge and presses trigger with barrel against his own head 2. any foolish or potentially suicidal undertaking

rust (rʌst) n. 1. reddish-brown coating formed on iron by oxidation 2. disease of plants —v. 3. contract, affect with rust —'rusty a. 1. coated with, affected by, or consisting of rust 2. of rust colour 3. out of practice —'rustproof a.

rustic ('rʌstɪk) a. 1. of or as of country people 2. rural 3. of rude manufacture 4. made of untrimmed branches —n. 5. countryman, peasant —'rusticate vt. 1. banish from university —vi. 2. live a country life —rusti'cation n. —rus'ticity n.

rustle[1] ('rʌs'l) vi. 1. make sound as of blown dead leaves etc. —n. 2. this sound

rustle[2] ('rʌs'l) vt. US steal (cattle) —'rustler n. US cattle thief

rut[1] (rʌt) *n.* **1.** furrow made by wheel **2.** settled habit or way of living **3.** groove —**'rutty** *a.*

rut[2] (rʌt) *n.* **1.** periodic sexual excitement among animals —*vi.* **2.** be under influence of this (**-tt-**)

ruthenium (ruːˈθiːnɪəm) *n.* hard brittle white element of platinum metal group

ruthless (ˈruːθlɪs) *a.* pitiless, merciless —**'ruthlessly** *adv.*

R.V. Revised Version (of the Bible)

-ry (*comb. form*) *see* -ERY

rye (raɪ) *n.* **1.** grain used for fodder and bread **2.** plant bearing it **3.** whisky made from rye —**rye bread** bread made entirely or partly from rye flour

rye-grass *n.* any of various kinds of grasses cultivated for fodder

S

s *or* **S** (ɛs) *n.* **1.** 19th letter of English alphabet **2.** speech sound represented by this letter, either voiceless, as in *sit*, or voiced, as in *dogs* **3.** something shaped like S (*pl.* **s's, S's** *or* **Ss**)

S 1. Society **2.** South(ern) **3.** *Chem.* sulphur **4.** *Phys.* entropy **5.** *Phys.* siemens **6.** *Phys.* strangeness

s. 1. second (of time) **2.** shilling **3.** singular **4.** son **5.** succeeded

-'s (*comb. form*) **1.** forming possessive singular of nouns and some pronouns, as in *man's* **2.** forming possessive plural of nouns whose plurals do not end in *-s*, as in *children's* **3.** forming plural of numbers, letters, or symbols, as in *20's*

-s' (*comb. form*) forming possessive of plural nouns, and some singular nouns, ending in sounded *s*, as in *girls'; for goodness' sake*

S.A. 1. Salvation Army **2.** South Africa **3.** South Australia **4.** *Sturmabteilung*: Nazi terrorist militia

Sabbath ('sæbəθ) *n.* **1.** Jewish and Christian day of worship and rest **2.** Sunday —**sab'batical** *a./n.* (denoting) leave granted to university staff *etc.* for study

sable ('seib'l) *n.* **1.** small weasellike Arctic animal **2.** its fur **3.** black (*pl.* **-s, 'sable**) —*a.* **4.** black

sabot ('sæbəʊ) *n.* shoe made of wood, or with wooden sole

sabotage ('sæbətɑːʒ) *n.* **1.** intentional damage done to roads, machines *etc.*, *esp.* secretly in war —*vt.* **2.** carry out sabotage on **3.** destroy, disrupt —**saboteur** (sæbə-'tɜː) *n.*

sabre *or U.S.* **saber** ('seibə) *n.* curved cavalry sword —**sabre rattling** menacing display of armed force

sac (sæk) *n.* pouchlike structure in an animal or vegetable body

saccharin ('sækərɪn) *n.* artificial sweetener —**saccharine** ('sækəriːn) *a. lit., fig.* excessively sweet

sacerdotal (sæsə'dəʊt'l) *a.* of priests

sachet ('sæʃeɪ) *n.* small envelope or bag, *esp.* one holding liquid, as shampoo

sack¹ (sæk) *n.* **1.** large bag, *orig.* of coarse material **2.** pillaging **3.** *inf.* dismissal **4.** *sl.* bed —*vt.* **5.** pillage (captured town) **6.** *inf.* dismiss —**'sacking** *n.* material for sacks —**'sackcloth** *n.* coarse fabric used for sacks —**sackcloth and ashes** public display of extreme grief

sack² (sæk) *n. obs.* dry white wine from SW Europe

sacrament ('sækrəmənt) *n.* one of certain ceremonies of Christian Church, *esp.* Eucharist —**sacra'mental** *a.*

sacred ('seikrɪd) *a.* **1.** dedicated, regarded as holy **2.** set apart, reserved **3.** inviolable

4. connected with, intended for religious use —**'sacredly** *adv.* —**sacred cow** *inf.* person *etc.* held to be beyond criticism

sacrifice ('sækrɪfaɪs) *n.* **1.** giving something up for sake of something else **2.** act of giving up **3.** thing so given up **4.** making of offering to a god **5.** thing offered —*vt.* **6.** offer as sacrifice **7.** give up **8.** sell at very cheap price —**sacrificial** (sækrɪ'fɪʃəl) *a.*

sacrilege ('sækrɪlɪdʒ) *n.* misuse, desecration of something sacred —**sacrilegious** (sækrɪ'lɪdʒəs) *a.* **1.** profane **2.** desecrating

sacristan ('sækrɪstən) *or* **sacrist** ('sækrɪst, 'seɪ-) *n.* official in charge of vestments and sacred vessels of church —**'sacristy** *n.* room where sacred vessels *etc.* are kept

sacrosanct ('sækrəʊsæŋkt) *a.* **1.** preserved by religious fear against desecration or violence **2.** inviolable —**sacro'sanctity** *n.*

sacrum ('seikrəm) *n.* five vertebrae forming compound bone at base of spinal column (*pl.* **-cra** (-krə))

sad (sæd) *a.* **1.** sorrowful **2.** unsatisfactory, deplorable —**'sadden** *vt.* make sad

saddle ('sæd'l) *n.* **1.** rider's seat to fasten on horse, bicycle *etc.* **2.** anything resembling a saddle **3.** joint of mutton or venison **4.** ridge of hill —*vt.* **5.** put saddle on **6.** lay burden, responsibility on —*a.* **7.** resembling a saddle, as in *saddleback* —**'saddler** *n.* maker of saddles *etc.* —**'saddlery** *n.* —**'saddlebag** *n.* small bag attached to saddle of bicycle *etc.* —**saddle soap** soft soap for preserving and cleaning leather —**'saddletree** *n.* frame of saddle

Sadducee ('sædjʊsiː) *n. Judaism* member of ancient Jewish sect, denying resurrection of dead and validity of oral tradition

sadism ('seɪdɪzəm) *n.* form of (sexual) perversion marked by love of inflicting pain —**'sadist** *n.* —**sadistic** (sə'dɪstɪk) *a.* —**sado'masochism** *n.* sadistic and masochistic elements in one person —**sadomaso'chistic** *a.*

s.a.e. stamped addressed envelope

safari (sə'fɑːrɪ) *n.* (party making) overland (hunting) journey, *esp.* in Afr. (*pl.* **-s**) —**safari park** park where lions *etc.* may be viewed by public from cars

safe (seɪf) *a.* **1.** secure, protected **2.** uninjured, out of danger **3.** not involving risk **4.** trustworthy **5.** sure, reliable **6.** cautious —*n.* **7.** strong lockable container **8.** ventilated cupboard for meat *etc.* —**'safely** *adv.* —**'safety** *n.* —**safe-conduct** *n.* passport, permit to pass somewhere —**safe-deposit** *or* **safety-deposit** *n.* place with facilities for safe storage of money *etc.* —**'safeguard** *n.* **1.** protection —*vt.* **2.** protect —**safety belt 1.** *see* seat belt *at* SEAT **2.** belt worn by person working at great height —**safety curtain** fireproof curtain that can be lowered to separate auditorium and stage —**safety glass** unsplinterable glass —**safety lamp** miner's oil lamp in which flame is surrounded by metal gauze to prevent it igniting combustible gas —**safety match** match that will light only when struck against prepared surface —**safety pin** spring clasp with covering catch, designed to shield point when closed —**safety razor** razor with guard over blade —**safety valve 1.** valve in pressure vessel that allows fluid to escape at excess pressure **2.** harmless outlet for emotion *etc.*

safflower ('sæflaυə) *n.* thistlelike plant with flowers used for dye, oil

saffron ('sæfrən) *n.* **1.** crocus **2.** orange-coloured flavouring obtained from it **3.** the colour —*a.* **4.** orange

S.Afr. South Africa(n)

sag (sæg) *vi.* **1.** sink in middle **2.** hang sideways **3.** curve downwards under pressure **4.** give way **5.** tire **6.** (of clothes) hang loosely (**-gg-**) —*n.* **7.** droop

saga ('sɑːgə) *n.* **1.** legend of Norse heroes **2.** any long (heroic) story

sagacious (sə'geɪʃəs) *a.* wise —**sa'gaciously** *adv.* —**sagacity** (sə'gæsɪtɪ) *n.*

sage[1] (seɪdʒ) *n.* **1.** very wise man —*a.* **2.** wise —**'sagely** *adv.*

sage[2] (seɪdʒ) *n.* aromatic herb

sagebrush ('seɪdʒbrʌʃ) *n.* aromatic plant of West N Amer.

Sagittarius (sædʒɪ'tɛərɪəs) *n.* (archer) 9th sign of zodiac, operative *c.* Nov. 22nd-Dec. 20th

sago ('seɪgəʊ) *n.* starchy cereal from powdered pith of sago palm

sahib ('sɑːhɪb) *n.* in India, form of address placed after man's name

said (sɛd) *pt./pp. of* SAY

sail (seɪl) *n.* **1.** piece of fabric stretched to catch wind for propelling ship *etc.* **2.** act of sailing **3.** journey upon the water **4.** ships collectively **5.** arm of windmill —*vi.* **6.** travel by water **7.** move smoothly **8.** begin voyage —*vt.* **9.** navigate —**'sailor** *n.* **1.** seaman **2.** one who sails —**'sailboard** *n.* floatable board, comprising sail, rudder and centreboard, used in windsurfing —**'sailcloth** *n.* **1.** fabric from which sails are made **2.** canvas-like cloth used for clothing *etc.*

saint (seɪnt; *unstressed* sənt) *n.* **1.** (title of) person formally recognized (*esp.* by R.C. Church) after death as having gained by holy deeds a special place in heaven **2.** exceptionally good person —**'sainted** *a.* **1.** canonized **2.** sacred —**'saintliness** *n.* holiness —**'saintly** *a.* —**Saint Bernard** large breed of dog with dense red-and-white coat —**Saint Leger** annual horse race run at Doncaster, England —**saintpaulia** (sənt'pɔːlɪə) *n.* Afr. violet —**Saint Swithin's Day** July 15th; if it rains on this day it is traditionally believed it will rain for the next forty days —**Saint Valentine's**

Day Feb. 14th; observed as day for sending valentines —**Saint Vitus's dance** *Pathol. see* CHOREA

saithe (seɪθ) *n.* coalfish

sake[1] (seɪk) *n.* **1.** cause, account **2.** end, purpose —**for the sake of 1.** on behalf of **2.** to please or benefit

sake[2], **saké** *or* **saki** ('sɑːkɪ) *n.* Japanese alcoholic drink made of fermented rice

salaam (sə'lɑːm) *n.* **1.** bow of salutation, mark of respect in East —*vt.* **2.** salute

salacious (sə'leɪʃəs) *a.* excessively concerned with sex, lewd —**salacity** (sə'læsɪtɪ) *n.*

salad ('sæləd) *n.* mixed vegetables, or fruit, used as food without cooking —**salad days** period of youth and inexperience —**salad dressing** oil, vinegar, herbs *etc.* mixed together as sauce for salad

salamander ('sæləmændə) *n.* **1.** variety of lizard **2.** mythical lizardlike fire spirit

salami (sə'lɑːmɪ) *n.* variety of highly-spiced sausage

salary ('sælərɪ) *n.* fixed regular payment to persons employed usu. in nonmanual work —**'salaried** *a.*

salchow ('sɔːlkəʊ) *n. Figure skating* jump from inner backward edge of one foot with full turn in air, returning to outer backward edge of opposite foot

sale (seɪl) *n.* **1.** selling **2.** selling of goods at unusually low prices **3.** auction —**'saleable** *or U.S.* **'salable** *a.* capable of being sold —**sale of work** sale of articles, proceeds of which benefit charities —**'saleroom** *n. chiefly UK* room where objects are displayed for sale, *esp.* by auction —**'salesman** *n.* **1.** shop assistant **2.** one travelling to sell goods, *esp.* as representative of firm —**'salesmanship** *n.* art of selling or presenting goods in most effective way —**sales talk** *or* **pitch** argument or other persuasion used in selling

salicin ('sælɪsɪn) *n.* substance obtained from poplars and used in medicine —**sali'cylic** *a.* —**salicylic acid** white crystalline substance used in manufacture of aspirin, and as fungicide

salient ('seɪlɪənt) *a.* **1.** prominent, noticeable **2.** jutting out —*n.* **3.** salient angle, *esp.* in fortification —**'salience** *or* **'saliency** *n.*

saline ('seɪlaɪn) *a.* **1.** containing, consisting of a chemical salt, *esp.* common salt **2.** salty —**salinity** (sə'lɪnɪtɪ) *n.*

saliva (sə'laɪvə) *n.* liquid which forms in mouth, spittle —**sa'livary** *a.* —**salivate** ('sælɪveɪt) *v.* —**saliva test** test for use of drugs in athletes, racehorses *etc.*

Salk vaccine (sɔːlk) vaccine against poliomyelitis

sallow[1] ('sæləʊ) *a.* of unhealthy pale or yellowish colour

sallow[2] ('sæləʊ) *n.* tree or low shrub allied to the willow

sally ('sælɪ) *n.* **1.** rushing out, *esp.* by troops **2.** outburst **3.** witty remark —*vi.* **4.** rush **5.** set out (**'sallied, 'sallying**)

Sally Lunn (lʌn) flat cake made from sweet yeast dough

salmagundi (sælmə'gʌndɪ) n. 1. mixed salad dish of cooked meats, eggs, beetroot etc. 2. miscellany

salmon ('sæmən) n. 1. large silvery fish with orange-pink flesh valued as food 2. colour of its flesh —a. 3. of this colour —**salmon ladder** series of steps designed to enable salmon to move upstream to their breeding grounds

salmonella (sælmə'nɛlə) n. any of genus of bacteria causing disease, esp. food poisoning (pl. -**lae** (-liː))

salon ('sælɒn) n. 1. (reception room for) guests in fashionable household 2. commercial premises of hairdressers, beauticians etc.

saloon (sə'luːn) n. 1. principal cabin or public room in passenger ship 2. public room for specified use, eg billiards 3. closed car with 2 or 4 doors and 4-6 seats —**saloon bar** first-class bar in hotel etc.

salpiglossis (sælpɪ'glɒsɪs) n. plant with bright funnel-shaped flowers

salsify ('sælsɪfɪ) n. purple-flowered plant with edible root

SALT (sɔːlt) Strategic Arms Limitation Talks or Treaty

salt (sɔːlt) n. 1. white powdery or granular crystalline substance consisting mainly of sodium chloride, used to season or preserve food 2. chemical compound of acid and metal 3. wit —vt. 4. season, sprinkle with, preserve with salt —**saltless** a. —**saltness** n. —**salty** a. of, like salt —**saltbush** n. shrub that grows in alkaline desert regions —**saltcellar** n. small vessel for salt at table —**salt lick** deposit, block of salt licked by game, cattle etc. —**saltpan** n. depression encrusted with salt after draining away of water —**saltpetre** or U.S. **saltpeter** (sɔːlt'piːtə) n. potassium nitrate used in gunpowder —**saltwater** a. —**old salt** sailor —**salt away** or **down** hoard or save (money, valuables etc.) —**with a pinch, grain, of salt** allowing for exaggeration —**worth one's salt** efficient

saltant ('sæltənt) a. 1. leaping 2. dancing —**sal'tation** n. —**'saltatory** a.

salubrious (sə'luːbrɪəs) a. favourable to health, beneficial —**sa'lubrity** n.

Saluki (sə'luːkɪ) n. tall hound with silky coat

salutary ('sæljutərɪ) a. wholesome, resulting in good —**'salutarily** adv.

salute (sə'luːt) vt. 1. greet with words or sign 2. acknowledge with praise —vi. 3. perform military salute —n. 4. word, sign by which one person greets another 5. motion of arm as mark of respect to superior etc. in military usage 6. firing of guns as military greeting of honour —**salutation** (sælju'teɪʃən) n.

salvage ('sælvɪdʒ) n. 1. act of saving ship or other property from danger of loss 2. property so saved —vt. 3. rescue, save from wreck or ruin

salvation (sæl'veɪʃən) n. (esp. of soul) fact or state of being saved —**Salvation Army** Christian body organized for evangelism and social work among poor

salve (sælv, sɑːv) n. 1. healing ointment —vt. 2. anoint with salve 3. soothe

salver ('sælvə) n. (silver) tray for presentation of food, letters etc.

salvia ('sælvɪə) n. plant with blue or red flowers

salvo ('sælvəu) n. simultaneous discharge of guns etc. (pl. -**s**, -**es**)

sal volatile (sæl vɒ'lætɪlɪ) preparation of ammonia used to revive persons who faint etc.

SAM (sæm) surface-to-air missile

Sam. Bible Samuel

Samaritan (sə'mærɪt'n) n. 1. native of ancient Samaria 2. benevolent person

samarium (sə'mɛərɪəm) n. silvery metallic element of lanthanide series

samba ('sæmbə) n. 1. dance of S Amer. origin 2. music for it

same (seɪm) a. (usu. with the) 1. identical, not different, unchanged 2. uniform 3. just mentioned previously —**'sameness** n. 1. similarity 2. monotony

samite ('sæmaɪt) n. rich silk cloth

samovar ('sæməvɑː) n. Russian tea urn

Samoyed (sə'mɔɪɛd) n. dog with thick white coat and tightly curled tail

samp (sæmp) n. SA crushed maize used for porridge

sampan ('sæmpæn) n. small oriental boat

samphire ('sæmfaɪə) n. herb found on rocks by seashore

sample ('sɑːmp'l) n. 1. specimen —vt. 2. take, give sample of 3. try 4. test 5. select —**'sampler** n. beginner's exercise in embroidery —**'sampling** n. 1. the taking of samples 2. sample

Samson ('sæmsən) n. 1. O.T. judge of Israel, who performed herculean feats of strength until he was betrayed by his mistress Delilah 2. any man of outstanding physical strength

samurai ('sæmuraɪ) n. member of ancient Japanese warrior caste (pl. -**rai**)

sanatorium (sænə'tɔːrɪəm) or U.S. **sanitarium** n. 1. hospital, esp. for chronically ill 2. health resort (pl. -**s**, -**ria** (-rɪə)) —**'sanatory** or **'sanative** a. curative

sanctify ('sæŋktɪfaɪ) vt. 1. set apart as holy 2. free from sin (-**fied**, -**fying**) —**sanctifi'cation** n. —**'sanctity** n. 1. saintliness 2. sacredness 3. inviolability —**'sanctuary** n. 1. holy place 2. part of church nearest altar 3. formerly, place where fugitive was safe from arrest or violence 4. place protected by law where animals etc. can live without interference —**'sanctum** n. 1. sacred place or shrine 2. person's private room (pl. -**s**, -**ta**)

sanctimonious (sæŋktɪ'məunɪəs) a. making a show of piety. holiness —**'sanctimony** or **sancti'moniousness** n.

sanction ('sæŋkʃən) n. 1. permission, authorization 2. penalty for breaking law —pl. 3. boycott or other coercive measure, esp. by one state against another regarded as having violated a law, right etc. —vt. 4. allow, authorize, permit

sand (sænd) n. 1. substance consisting of small grains of rock or mineral, esp. on beach or in desert —pl. 2. stretches or banks of this, usu. forming seashore —vt. 3. polish, smooth with sandpaper 4. cover, mix with sand —'**sander** n. power tool for smoothing surfaces —'**sandy** a. 1. like sand 2. sand-coloured 3. consisting of, covered with sand —'**sandbag** n. bag filled with sand or earth, used as protection against gunfire, floodwater etc., and as weapon —**sand bar** ridge of sand in river or sea, built up by action of tides etc. —'**sandblast** n. 1. jet of sand blown from a nozzle under pressure for cleaning, grinding etc. —vt. 2. clean or decorate (surface) with sandblast —**sand castle** sand moulded into castle-like shape, esp. on seashore —'**sandman** n. in folklore, magical person supposed to put children to sleep by sprinkling sand in their eyes —**sand martin** small brown European songbird with white underparts —'**sandpaper** n. paper with sand stuck on it for scraping or polishing wood etc. —'**sandpiper** n. shore bird —'**sandpit** n. quantity of sand for children to play in —'**sandshoes** pl.n. canvas shoes for beach wear etc. —'**sandstone** n. rock composed of sand —'**sandstorm** n. strong wind that whips up clouds of sand —**sand yacht** wheeled boat with sails, built to be propelled over sand

sandal ('sænd'l) n. shoe consisting of sole attached by straps

sandalwood ('sænd'lwʊd) or **sandal** n. sweet-scented wood

sanderling ('sændəliŋ) n. small sandpiper that frequents sandy shores

sandwich ('sænwidʒ, -witʃ) n. 1. two slices of bread with meat or other substance between —vt. 2. insert between two other things —**sandwich board** one of two connected boards hung over shoulders in front of and behind person to display advertisements —**sandwich course** course consisting of alternate periods of study and industrial work —**sandwich man** man who carries sandwich board

sane (sein) a. 1. of sound mind 2. sensible, rational —**sanity** ('sæniti) n.

Sanforize or **-rise** ('sænfəraiz) vt. R preshrink (fabric) using a patented process

sang (sæŋ) pt. of SING

sang-froid (Fr. sã'frwa) n. composure; self-possession

Sangraal (sæŋ'greil), **Sangrail** or **Sangreal** ('sæŋgriəl) n. see Holy Grail at HOLY

sangria (sæŋ'griːə) n. Sp. drink of red wine and fruit juice, sometimes laced with brandy

sanguine ('sæŋgwin) a. 1. cheerful, confident 2. ruddy in complexion —'**sanguinary** a. 1. accompanied by bloodshed 2. bloodthirsty

Sanhedrin ('sænidrin) n. Judaism supreme judicial, ecclesiastical, and administrative council of Jews in New Testament times

sanitary ('sænitəri) a. helping protection of health against dirt etc. —**sani'tation** n. measures, apparatus for preservation of public health —**sanitary towel** or esp. U.S. **napkin** absorbent pad worn externally by women during menstruation

sank (sæŋk) pt. of SINK

sans (sænz) prep. without —**sans-culotte** (-kju'lɒt) n. 1. revolutionary of poorer class during French Revolution 2. any revolutionary extremist

Sanskrit ('sænskrit) n. ancient language of India

Santa Claus ('sæntə klɔːz) legendary patron saint of children, who brings presents at Christmas (also **Father Christmas**)

sap[1] (sæp) n. 1. moisture which circulates in plants 2. energy —vt. 3. drain of sap (-pp-) —'**sapless** a. —'**sapling** n. young tree

sap[2] (sæp) vt. 1. undermine 2. destroy insidiously 3. weaken (-pp-) —n. 4. trench dug in order to approach or undermine enemy position —'**sapper** n. soldier in engineering unit

sap[3] (sæp) n. inf. gullible person —'**sappy** a.

sapid ('sæpid) a. 1. having pleasant taste 2. agreeable or engaging —sa'**pidity** n.

sapient ('seipiənt) a. (usu. ironical) wise, discerning, shrewd, knowing —'**sapience** n.

saponify (sə'pɒnifai) Chem. v. 1. convert (fat) into soap by treatment with alkali —vi. 2. undergo reaction in which ester is hydrolysed to acid and alcohol as result of treatment with alkali —saponifi'**cation** n.

Sapphic ('sæfik) a. 1. of Sappho, 6th-cent. B.C. Grecian poetess 2. of metre associated with Sappho —n. 3. Sapphic verse —'**sapphism** n. lesbianism

sapphire ('sæfaiə) n. 1. (usu. blue) precious stone 2. deep blue —a. 3. of sapphire (blue) 4. denoting 45th anniversary

saprophyte ('sæprəufait) n. plant that lives on dead organic matter

saraband or **sarabande** ('særəbænd) n. 1. slow, stately Sp. dance 2. music for it

Saracen ('særəs'n) n. 1. Arabian 2. adherent of Mohammedanism in Syria and Palestine 3. infidel —**Saracenic** (særə'senik) a.

sarcasm ('sɑːkæzəm) n. 1. bitter or wounding ironic remark 2. such remarks 3. taunt; sneer 4. irony 5. use of such expressions —**sar'castic** a. —**sar'castically** adv.

sarcoma (saː'kəʊmə) n. Pathol. usu. malignant tumour arising from connective tissue (pl. -**s**, -**mata** (-mətə)) —**sar'comatous** a.

sarcophagus (saː'kɒfəgəs) n. stone coffin (pl. -**gi** (-gaɪ), -**es**)

sard (saːd) or **sardius** ('saːdɪəs) n. precious stone, variety of chalcedony

sardine (saː'diːn) n. small fish of herring family, usu. preserved in oil

sardonic (saː'dɒnɪk) a. characterized by irony, mockery or derision

sardonyx ('saːdɒnɪks) n. gemstone, variety of chalcedony

sargassum (saː'gæsəm) n. gulfweed, type of floating seaweed

sari ('saːrɪ) n. Hindu woman's robe (pl. -**s**)

sarong (sə'rɒŋ) n. skirtlike garment worn in Asian and Pacific countries

sarsaparilla (saːsəpə'rɪlə) n. (flavour of) drink, orig. made from root of plant

sartorial (saː'tɔːrɪəl) a. of tailor, tailoring or men's clothes

sash¹ (sæʃ) n. decorative belt or ribbon, wound around the body

sash² (sæʃ) n. wooden window frame opened by moving up and down in grooves

saskatoon (sæskə'tuːn) n. Canad. shrub with purplish berries

sassafras ('sæsəfræs) n. laurel-like tree with aromatic bark used medicinally

Sassenach ('sæsənæx) n. Scot. English person

sat (sæt) pt./pp. of SIT

Sat. 1. Saturday 2. Saturn

Satan ('seɪt³n) n. the devil —**satanic(al)** (sə'tænɪk(³l)) a. devilish, fiendish —**satanically** (sə'tænɪkəlɪ) adv. —**'Satanism** n. 1. worship of Satan 2. satanic disposition —**'Satanist** n./a.

satchel ('sætʃəl) n. small bag, esp. for school books

sate (seɪt) vt. satisfy (a desire or appetite) fully or excessively

sateen (sæ'tiːn) n. glossy linen or cotton fabric that resembles satin

satellite ('sætəlaɪt) n. 1. celestial body or man-made projectile orbiting planet 2. person, country etc. dependent on another

satiate ('seɪʃɪeɪt) vt. 1. satisfy to the full 2. surfeit —**'satiable** a. —**sati'ation** n. —**satiety** (sə'taɪɪtɪ) n. feeling of having had too much

satin ('sætɪn) n. fabric (of silk, rayon etc.) with glossy surface on one side —**'satiny** a. of, like satin —**'satinwood** n. any of various tropical trees that yield hard satiny wood

satire ('sætaɪə) n. 1. composition in which vice, folly or foolish person is held up to ridicule 2. use of ridicule or sarcasm to expose vice and folly —**satiric(al)** (sə'tɪrɪk(³l)) a. 1. of nature of satire 2. sarcastic 3. bitter —**satirist** ('sætərɪst) n. —**satirize** or -**rise** ('sætəraɪz) vt. 1. make object of satire 2. censure thus

satisfy ('sætɪsfaɪ) vt. 1. content, meet wishes of 2. pay 3. fulfil, supply adequately 4. convince (-**fied**, -**fying**) —**satis'faction** n. —**satis'factory** a.

satsuma (sæt'suːmə) n. kind of small orange

saturate ('sætʃəreɪt) vt. 1. soak thoroughly 2. cause to absorb maximum amount 3. Chem. cause (substance) to combine to its full capacity with another 4. shell or bomb heavily —**satu'ration** n. act, result of saturating

Saturday ('sætədɪ) n. seventh day of week

Saturn ('sætɜːn) n. 1. Roman god 2. one of planets —**Saturnalia** (sætə'neɪlɪə) n. 1. ancient festival of Saturn 2. (also **s-**) noisy revelry, orgy —**'saturnine** a. 1. gloomy 2. sluggish in temperament, dull, morose

satyr ('sætə) n. 1. woodland deity, part man, part goat 2. lustful man —**satyric** (sə'tɪrɪk) a.

sauce (sɔːs) n. 1. liquid added to food to enhance flavour 2. inf. impudence —vt. 3. add sauce to 4. inf. be cheeky, impudent to —**'saucily** adv. —**'saucy** a. impudent —**saucepan** ('sɔːspən) n. cooking pot with long handle

saucer ('sɔːsə) n. 1. curved plate put under cup 2. shallow depression

sauerkraut ('saʊəkraʊt) n. Ger. dish of finely shredded and pickled cabbage

sauna ('sɔːnə) n. steam bath, orig. Finnish

saunter ('sɔːntə) vi. 1. walk in leisurely manner, stroll —n. 2. leisurely walk or stroll

-**saur** or -**saurus** (comb. form) lizard, as in dinosaur

saurian ('sɔːrɪən) n. one of the order of reptiles including the alligator, lizard etc.

sausage ('sɒsɪdʒ) n. minced meat enclosed in thin tube of animal intestine or synthetic material —**sausage roll** pastry cylinder filled with sausage

sauté ('səʊteɪ) a. fried quickly with little fat

Sauternes (səʊ'tɜːn) n. sweet white Fr. wine

savage ('sævɪdʒ) a. 1. wild 2. ferocious 3. brutal 4. uncivilized, primitive —n. 5. member of savage tribe, barbarian —vt. 6. attack ferociously —**'savagely** adv. —**'savagery** n.

savanna or **savannah** (sə'vænə) n. extensive open grassy plain

savant ('sævənt) n. man of learning

save (seɪv) vt. 1. rescue, preserve 2. protect 3. secure 4. keep for future, lay by 5. prevent need of 6. spare 7. except —vi. 8. lay by money —prep. 9. obs. except —conj. 10. obs. but —**'saving** a. 1. frugal 2. thrifty 3. delivering from sin 4. excepting 5. compensating —prep. 6. excepting —n. 7. economy —pl. 8. money, earnings put by for future use —**savings bank** bank that accepts savings of depositors and pays interest on them —**save as you earn** UK savings scheme in which monthly contributions earn tax-free interest

saveloy ('sævɪlɔɪ) n. type of smoked red sausage

saviour or U.S. **savior** ('seɪvjə) n. 1. person who rescues another 2. (S-) Christ

savoir-faire ('sævwɑː'fɛə; Fr. savwar-'fɛːr) ability to do, say, the right thing in any situation

savory ('seɪvərɪ) n. aromatic herb used in cooking

savour or U.S. **savor** ('seɪvə) n. 1. characteristic taste 2. flavour 3. odour 4. distinctive quality —vi. 5. have particular smell or taste 6. (with of) have suggestion (of) —vt. 7. give flavour to 8. have flavour of 9. enjoy, appreciate —'**savoury** or U.S. '**savory** a. 1. attractive to taste or smell 2. not sweet —n. 3. savoury snack (before meal)

savoy (sə'vɔɪ) n. variety of cabbage

savvy ('sævɪ) sl. v. 1. understand —n. 2. wits, intelligence

saw[1] (sɔː) n. 1. tool for cutting wood etc. by tearing it with toothed edge —vt. 2. cut with saw —vi. 3. make movements of sawing (sawed, sawn, 'sawing) —'**sawyer** n. one who saws timber —'**sawbones** n. sl. surgeon or doctor —'**sawdust** n. fine wood fragments made in sawing —'**sawfish** n. fish armed with toothed snout —'**sawhorse** n. stand for supporting timber during sawing —'**sawmill** n. mill where timber is sawn into planks etc.

saw[2] (sɔː) pt. of SEE[1]

saw[3] (sɔː) n. wise saying, proverb

sawn (sɔːn) pp. of SAW[1]

sax (sæks) inf. saxophone

saxe (sæks) n. shade of blue

saxhorn ('sækshɔːn) n. instrument of trumpet class

saxifrage ('sæksɪfreɪdʒ) n. Alpine or rock plant

Saxon ('sæksən) n. 1. member of West Germanic people who settled widely in Europe in the early Middle Ages —a. 2. of this people or their language

saxophone ('sæksəfəʊn) n. keyed wind instrument

say (seɪ) vt. 1. speak 2. pronounce 3. state 4. express 5. take as example or as near enough 6. make a case for (said pt./pp., 'saying pr.p., says (sɛz) 3rd pers. sing. pres. ind.) —n. 7. what one has to say 8. chance of saying it 9. share in decision —'**saying** n. maxim, proverb

S.A.Y.E. save as you earn

Sb Chem. antimony

Sc Chem. scandium

SC South Carolina

sc. 1. scale 2. scene 3. science 4. screw 5. scruple (unit of weight)

s.c. Print. small capitals

S.C. 1. A, NZ School Certificate 2. Signal Corps 3. C Social Credit

scab (skæb) n. 1. crust formed over wound 2. skin disease 3. disease of plants 4. offens. blackleg —'**scabby** a.

scabbard ('skæbəd) n. sheath for sword or dagger

scabies ('skeɪbiːz) n. contagious skin disease —'**scabious** a. having scabies, scabby

scabrous ('skeɪbrəs) a. 1. having rough surface 2. thorny 3. indecent 4. risky

scaffold ('skæfəld) n. 1. temporary platform for workmen 2. gallows —'**scaffolding** n. (material for building) scaffold

scalar ('skeɪlə) n./a. (variable quantity, eg time) having magnitude but no direction

scalawag ('skæləwæg) n. see SCALLYWAG

scald (skɔːld) vt. 1. burn with hot liquid or steam 2. clean, sterilize with boiling water 3. heat (liquid) almost to boiling point —n. 4. injury by scalding

scale[1] (skeɪl) n. 1. one of the thin, overlapping plates covering fishes and reptiles 2. thin flake 3. incrustation which forms in boilers etc. —vt. 4. remove scales from —vi. 5. come off in scales —'**scaly** a. resembling or covered in scales

scale[2] (skeɪl) n. (chiefly in pl.) 1. weighing instrument —vt. 2. weigh in scales 3. have weight of

scale[3] (skeɪl) n. 1. graduated table or sequence of marks at regular intervals used as reference or for fixing standards, as in making measurements, in music etc. 2. ratio of size between a thing and a model or map of it 3. (relative) degree, extent —vt. 4. climb —a. 5. proportionate —**scale up** or **down** increase or decrease proportionately in size

scalene ('skeɪliːn) a. (of triangle) with three unequal sides

scallion ('skæljən) n. onion with small bulb and long leaves

scallop ('skɒləp, 'skæl-) n. 1. edible shellfish 2. edging in small curves like edge of scallop shell —vt. 3. shape like scallop shell 4. cook in scallop shell or dish like one

scallywag ('skælɪwæg) n. inf. scamp, rascal (also 'scalawag, 'scallawag)

scalp (skælp) n. 1. skin and hair of top of head —vt. 2. cut off scalp of

scalpel ('skælp'l) n. small surgical knife

scamp (skæmp) n. 1. mischievous person or child —vt. 2. skimp

scamper ('skæmpə) vi. 1. run about 2. run hastily from place to place —n. 3. act of scampering

scampi ('skæmpɪ) n. (with sing. or pl. v.) large prawns usu. eaten fried in batter

scan (skæn) vt. 1. look at carefully, scrutinize 2. measure or read (verse) by metrical feet 3. examine, search by systematically varying the direction of a radar or sonar beam 4. glance over quickly —vi. 5. (of verse) conform to metrical rules (-nn-) —n. 6. scanning —'**scanner** n. device, esp. electronic, which scans —'**scansion** n. analysis of metrical structure of verse

Scand. or **Scan.** Scandinavia(n)

scandal ('skænd'l) n. 1. action, event generally considered disgraceful 2. malicious gossip —'**scandalize** or **-ise** vt.

shock —**'scandalous** a. outrageous, disgraceful —**'scandalmonger** n. person who spreads gossip etc.

Scandinavian (skændɪ'neɪvɪən) a. 1. of Scandinavia, its inhabitants or their languages —n. 2. native or inhabitant of Scandinavia

scandium ('skændɪəm) n. rare silvery-white metallic element occurring in numerous minerals

scant (skænt) a. barely sufficient or not sufficient —**'scantily** adv. —**'scanty** a.

scapegoat ('skeɪpgəʊt) n. person bearing blame due to others

scapegrace ('skeɪpgreɪs) n. mischievous person

scapula ('skæpjʊlə) n. shoulder blade (pl. -lae (-liː), -s) —**'scapular** a. 1. of scapula —n. 2. part of habit of certain religious orders in R.C. Church

scar¹ (skɑː) n. 1. mark left by healed wound, burn or sore 2. change resulting from emotional distress —v. 3. mark, heal with scar (-rr-)

scar² (skɑː) n. bare craggy rock formation

scarab ('skærəb) n. 1. sacred beetle of ancient Egypt 2. gem cut in shape of this

scarce (skɛəs) a. 1. hard to find 2. existing or available in insufficient quantity 3. uncommon —**'scarcely** adv. 1. only just 2. not quite 3. definitely or probably not —**'scarceness** or **'scarcity** n.

scare (skɛə) vt. 1. frighten —n. 2. fright, sudden panic —**'scary** a. —**'scarecrow** n. 1. thing set up to frighten birds from crops 2. badly dressed or miserable-looking person —**'scaremonger** n. one who spreads alarming rumours

scarf¹ (skɑːf) n. long narrow strip, large piece of material to put round neck, head etc. (pl. **-s, scarves**)

scarf² (skɑːf) n. 1. part cut away from each of two pieces of timber to be jointed longitudinally 2. joint so made (pl. **-s**) —vt. 3. cut or join in this way —**'scarfing** n.

scarify ('skɛərɪfaɪ, 'skær-) vt. 1. scratch, cut slightly all over 2. lacerate 3. stir surface soil of 4. criticize mercilessly (-**fied, -fying**) —scarifi'cation n.

scarlatina (skɑːlə'tiːnə) n. scarlet fever

scarlet ('skɑːlɪt) n. 1. brilliant red colour 2. cloth or clothing of this colour, esp. military uniform —a. 3. of this colour 4. immoral, esp. unchaste —**scarlet fever** infectious fever with scarlet rash

scarp (skɑːp) n. 1. steep slope 2. inside slope of ditch in fortifications

scarper ('skɑːpə) vi. sl. depart in haste

scarves (skɑːvz) n., pl. of SCARF¹

scat¹ (skæt) vi. inf. (usu. imp.) go away

scat² (skæt) n. Jazz singing characterized by improvised vocal sounds instead of words

scathe (skeɪð) (usu. now as pp./a. **scathed** & **un'scathed**) n. 1. injury, harm, damage —vt. 2. injure, damage —**'scathing** a. 1. harshly critical 2. cutting 3. damaging

scatology (skæ'tɒlədʒɪ) n. 1. scientific study of excrement, esp. in medicine and palaeontology 2. preoccupation with obscenity, esp. in form of references to excrement —scato'logical a.

scatter ('skætə) vt. 1. throw in various directions 2. put here and there 3. sprinkle —vi. 4. disperse —n. 5. sprinkling —**'scatterbrain** n. silly, careless person —**'scatty** a. inf. silly, useless

scavenge ('skævɪndʒ) v. search for (anything usable), usu. among discarded material —**'scavenger** n. 1. person who scavenges 2. animal, bird which feeds on refuse

Sc.D. Doctor of Science

S.C.E. Scottish Certificate of Education

scene (siːn) n. 1. place of action of novel, play etc. 2. place of any action 3. subdivision of play 4. view 5. episode 6. display of strong emotion —**scenario** (sɪ'nɑːrɪəʊ) n. summary of plot (of play etc.) or plan (pl. **-s**) —**'scenery** n. 1. natural features of district 2. constructions of wood, canvas etc. used on stage to represent a place where action is happening —**'scenic** a. 1. picturesque 2. of or on the stage

scent (sɛnt) n. 1. distinctive smell, esp. pleasant one 2. trail, clue 3. perfume —vt. 4. detect or track by or as if by smell 5. suspect, sense 6. fill with fragrance

sceptic or U.S. **skeptic** ('skɛptɪk) n. 1. one who maintains doubt or disbelief 2. agnostic 3. unbeliever —**'sceptical** or U.S. **'skeptical** a. —**'scepticism** or U.S. **'skepticism** n.

sceptre or U.S. **scepter** ('sɛptə) n. 1. ornamental staff as symbol of royal power 2. royal dignity

schedule ('ʃɛdjuːl; also, esp. U.S. 'skɛdʒʊəl) n. 1. plan of procedure for a project 2. list 3. timetable —vt. 4. enter in schedule 5. plan to occur at certain time —**on schedule** on time

schema ('skiːmə) n. overall plan or diagram (pl. **-mata (-mətə)**) —**sche'matic** a. presented as plan or diagram —**'schematize** or **-ise** vt.

scheme (skiːm) n. 1. plan, design 2. project 3. outline —v. 4. devise, plan, esp. in underhand manner —**'schemer** n.

scherzo ('skɛətsəʊ) n. Mus. light playful composition (pl. **-s, -zi (-tsiː)**)

schism ('sɪzəm, 'skɪz-) n. (group resulting from) division in political party, church etc. —**schis'matic** n./a.

schist (ʃɪst) n. crystalline rock which splits into layers —**'schistose** a.

schizanthus (skɪz'ænθəs) n. plant with divided leaves

schizo ('skɪtsəʊ) inf. a. 1. schizophrenic —n. 2. schizophrenic person (pl. **-s**)

schizo- or before vowel **schiz-** (comb. form) indicating cleavage, split, or division, as in schizophrenia

schizophrenia (skɪtsəʊ'friːnɪə) n. mental disorder involving deterioration of, confusion about personality —'**schizoid** a. of schizophrenia —**schizo'phrenic** a./n.

schmaltz or **schmalz** (ʃmælts, ʃmɔːlts) n. excessive sentimentality —'**schmaltzy** a.

schnapps or **schnaps** (ʃnæps) n. 1. spirit distilled from potatoes 2. inf. any strong spirit

schnitzel ('ʃnɪtsəl) n. thin slice of meat, esp. veal

scholar ('skɒlə) n. see SCHOOL¹

scholium ('skəʊlɪəm) n. 1. marginal annotation 2. note 3. comment (pl. -lia (-lɪə)) —'**scholiast** n. 1. commentator 2. annotator

school¹ (skuːl) n. 1. institution for teaching children or for giving instruction in any subject 2. buildings of such institution 3. group of thinkers, writers, artists etc. with principles or methods in common —vt. 4. educate 5. bring under control, train —'**scholar** n. 1. learned person 2. one taught in school 3. one quick to learn —**scholarly** ('skɒləlɪ) a. learned, erudite —**scholarship** ('skɒləʃɪp) n. 1. learning 2. prize, grant to student for payment of school or college fees —**scholastic** (skə-'læstɪk) a. 1. of schools or scholars, or education 2. pedantic —'**schooling** n. 1. education, esp. when received at school 2. training of animal, esp. of horse for dressage —'**schoolhouse** n. 1. building used as school 2. house attached to school —'**schoolman** n. medieval philosopher —'**schoolmarm** n. inf. woman school-teacher 2. woman considered old-fashioned or prim —'**schoolmaster** or '**schoolmistress** n. person who teaches in or runs a school

school² (skuːl) n. shoal (of fish, whales etc.)

schooner ('skuːnə) n. 1. fore-and-aft rigged vessel with two or more masts 2. tall glass

schottische (ʃɒ'tiːʃ) n. 1. 19th-century German dance 2. music for this

schwa or **shwa** (ʃwɑː) n. 1. central vowel represented in International Phonetic Alphabet by (ə), eg 'a' in around 2. symbol (ə) used to represent this sound

sciatica (saɪ'ætɪkə) n. 1. neuralgia of hip and thigh 2. pain in sciatic nerve —**sci'atic** a. 1. of the hip 2. of sciatica

science ('saɪəns) n. 1. systematic study and knowledge of natural or physical phenomena 2. any branch of study concerned with observed material facts —**scien'tific** a. 1. of the principles of science 2. systematic —**scien'tifically** adv. —'**scientist** n. one versed in natural sciences —**science fiction** stories set in the future making imaginative use of scientific knowledge

Scientology (saɪən'tɒlədʒɪ) n. religious cult based on belief that self-awareness is paramount

sci-fi ('saɪ'faɪ) n. inf. science fiction

scimitar ('sɪmɪtə) n. oriental curved sword

scintilla (sɪn'tɪlə) n. rare minute amount

scintillate ('sɪntɪleɪt) vi. 1. sparkle 2. be animated, witty, clever —**scintil'lation** n. —**scintillation counter** instrument for detecting and measuring intensity of high-energy radiation

scion ('saɪən) n. 1. descendant, heir 2. slip for grafting

scission ('sɪʒən) n. act of cutting, dividing, splitting —'**scissile** a.

scissors ('sɪzəz) pl.n. 1. cutting instrument of two blades pivoted together (also **pair of scissors**) —n./a. 2. (with) scissorlike action of limbs in swimming, athletics etc.

sclerosis (sklɪə'rəʊsɪs) n. a hardening of bodily organs, tissues etc. (pl. -ses (-siːz)) —'**sclera** n. firm white fibrous membrane that forms outer covering of eyeball —**sclerotic** (sklɪə'rɒtɪk) a. 1. of sclera 2. of or having sclerosis —n. 3. sclera

scoff¹ (skɒf) vi. 1. (oft. with at) express derision (for) —n. 2. derision 3. mocking words —'**scoffer** n.

scoff² (skɒf) v. sl. eat rapidly

scold (skəʊld) v. 1. find fault (with) —vt. 2. reprimand, be angry with —n. 3. one who does this

scollop ('skɒləp) see SCALLOP

sconce¹ (skɒns) n. bracket candlestick on wall

sconce² (skɒns) n. small protective fortification

scone (skəʊn, skɒn) n. small plain cake baked on griddle or in oven

scoop (skuːp) n. 1. small shovel-like tool for ladling, hollowing out etc. 2. sl. profitable deal 3. Journalism exclusive news item —vt. 4. ladle out 5. hollow out, rake in with scoop 6. make sudden profit 7. beat (rival newspaper etc.)

scoot (skuːt) vi. sl. move off quickly —'**scooter** n. 1. child's vehicle propelled by pushing on ground with one foot 2. light motorcycle (also **motor scooter**)

scope (skəʊp) n. 1. range of activity or application 2. opportunity

-scope (n. comb. form) indicating instrument for observing or detecting, as in microscope —**-scopic** (a. comb. form)

scopolamine (skə'pɒləmiːn) n. colourless viscous liquid alkaloid used in preventing travel sickness and as sedative and truth serum (also '**hyoscine**)

scorbutic (skɔː'bjuːtɪk) or **scorbutical** a. of or having scurvy —**scor'butically** adv.

scorch (skɔːtʃ) v. 1. burn, be burnt, on surface 2. parch 3. shrivel 4. wither —n. 5. slight burn —'**scorcher** n. inf. very hot day

score (skɔː) n. 1. points gained in game, competition 2. group of 20 3. (esp. pl.) a lot 4. musical notation 5. mark or notch, esp. to keep tally 6. reason, account 7. grievance —v. 8. gain (points) in game —vt. 9. mark 10. (with out) cross out 11. arrange music for —vi. 12. keep tally of points 13. succeed —'**scorecard** n. 1. card on which scores are recorded 2. card identifying players in sports match

scoria ('skɔːrɪə) n. 1. solidified lava

scorn (skɔːn) *n*. 1. contempt, derision —*vt*. 2. despise —'**scorner** *n*. —'**scornful** *a*. derisive —'**scornfully** *adv*.

Scorpio ('skɔːpɪəʊ) *n*. (scorpion) 8th sign of zodiac, operative *c*. Oct. 23rd - Nov. 21st

scorpion ('skɔːpɪən) *n*. small lobster-shaped animal with sting at end of jointed tail

Scot (skɒt) *n*. native of Scotland —**Scotch** *n*. whisky made in Scotland —'**Scottish** *or* **Scots** *a*. —**Scotch broth** UK soup made from beef stock, vegetables, and pearl barley —**Scotch egg** UK hard-boiled egg enclosed in layer of sausage meat and covered in breadcrumbs —**Scotch mist** 1. heavy wet mist 2. drizzle —'**Scotsman** *n*. —**Scots pine** *or* **Scotch pine** 1. coniferous tree of Europe and W and N Asia 2. its wood —**Scottish Certificate of Education** Scottish examination equivalent to General Certificate of Education in England —**Scottish terrier** small long-haired breed of terrier

Scot. 1. Scotch (whisky) 2. Scotland 3. Scottish

scotch (skɒtʃ) *vt*. 1. put an end to 2. *obs.* wound

scoter ('skəʊtə) *n*. sea duck of northern regions

scot-free *a*. without harm or loss

Scotland Yard ('skɒtlənd) headquarters of police force of metropolitan London

Scottie *or* **Scotty** ('skɒtɪ) *n*. 1. Scottish terrier 2. *inf.* Scotsman

scoundrel ('skaʊndrəl) *n*. villain, blackguard —'**scoundrelly** *a*.

scour[1] (skaʊə) *vt*. 1. clean, polish by rubbing 2. clear or flush out

scour[2] (skaʊə) *v*. move rapidly along or over (territory) in search of something

scourge (skɜːdʒ) *n*. 1. whip, lash 2. severe affliction 3. pest 4. calamity —*vt*. 5. flog 6. punish severely

Scouse (skaʊs) UK *inf. n*. 1. person from Liverpool 2. dialect of such person —*a*. 3. of or from Liverpool

scout (skaʊt) *n*. 1. one sent out to reconnoitre 2. (S-) member of **Scout Association**, organization to develop character and responsibility —*vi*. 3. go out, act as scout 4. reconnoitre —'**scouter** *n*. leader of troop of scouts

scow (skaʊ) *n*. unpowered barge

scowl (skaʊl) *vi*. 1. frown gloomily or sullenly —*n*. 2. angry or gloomy expression

scrabble ('skræbʰl) *vi*. 1. scrape with hands, claws in disorderly manner —*n*. 2. (S-) R word game

scrag (skræg) *n*. 1. lean person or animal 2. lean end of a neck of mutton —'**scraggy** *a*. thin, bony

scraggly ('skræglɪ) *a*. untidy

scram (skræm) *vi. inf.* (*oft. imp.*) go away hastily, get out (-**mm**-)

scramble ('skræmbʰl) *vi*. 1. move along or up by crawling, climbing *etc*. 2. struggle with others 3. (of aircraft, aircrew) take off hurriedly —*vt*. 4. mix up 5. cook (eggs) beaten up with milk 6. render (speech) unintelligible by electronic device —*n*. 7. scrambling 8. rough climb 9. disorderly proceeding 10. motorcycle race over rough ground —'**scrambler** *n*. electronic device that renders speech unintelligible during transmission

scrap (skræp) *n*. 1. small piece or fragment 2. leftover material 3. *inf.* fight —*vt*. 4. break up, discard as useless —*vi*. 5. *inf.* fight (-**pp**-) —'**scrappy** *a*. 1. unequal in quality 2. badly finished —'**scrapbook** *n*. book in which newspaper cuttings *etc*. are kept —**scrap merchant** person dealing in scrap, *esp*. scrap metal

scrape (skreɪp) *vt*. 1. rub with something sharp 2. clean, smooth thus 3. grate 4. scratch 5. rub with harsh noise —*n*. 6. act, sound of scraping 7. *inf.* awkward situation, *esp*. as result of escapade —'**scraper** *n*. 1. instrument for scraping 2. contrivance on which mud is scraped from shoes *etc*.

scratch (skrætʃ) *vt*. 1. score, make narrow surface wound on with claws, nails, or anything pointed 2. make marks on with pointed instruments 3. scrape (skin) with nails to relieve itching 4. remove, withdraw from list, race *etc*. —*vi*. 5. use claws or nails, *esp*. to relieve itching —*n*. 6. wound, mark or sound made by scratching 7. line or starting point —*a*. 8. got together at short notice 9. impromptu —'**scratching** *n*. percussive effect obtained by rotating gramophone record manually: a disc-jockey technique —'**scratchy** *a*.

scrawl (skrɔːl) *vt*. 1. write, draw untidily —*n*. 2. thing scrawled 3. careless writing

scrawny ('skrɔːnɪ) *a*. thin, bony

scream (skriːm) *vi*. 1. utter piercing cry, *esp*. of fear, pain *etc*. 2. be very obvious —*vt*. 3. utter in a scream —*n*. 4. shrill, piercing cry 5. *inf.* very funny person or thing

scree (skriː) *n*. 1. loose shifting stones 2. slope covered with these

screech (skriːtʃ) *vi./n*. scream —**screech owl** 1. small N Amer. owl having reddish-brown or grey plumage 2. UK any owl that utters screeching cry

screed (skriːd) *n*. 1. long (tedious) letter, passage or speech 2. thin layer of cement

screen (skriːn) *n*. 1. device to shelter from heat, light, draught, observation *etc*. 2. anything used for such purpose 3. mesh over doors, windows to keep out insects 4. white or silvered surface on which photographic images are projected 5. windscreen 6. wooden or stone partition in church —*vt*. 7. shelter, hide 8. protect from detection 9. show (film) 10. scrutinize 11. examine (group of people) for presence of disease, weapons *etc*. 12. examine for political motives 13. *Elec.*

protect from stray electric or magnetic fields —**'screenplay** n. script for film, including instructions for sets and camera work —**screen process** see **silk-screen** at SILK —**the screen** cinema generally

screw (skru:) n. **1.** (nail-like device or cylinder with) spiral thread cut to engage similar thread or to bore into material (wood etc.) to pin or fasten **2.** anything resembling a screw in shape, esp. in spiral form **3.** propeller **4.** twist —vt. **5.** fasten with screw **6.** twist around **7.** inf. extort —**'screwy** a. inf. crazy, eccentric —**'screwball** US sl. n. **1.** eccentric person —a. **2.** odd; eccentric —**'screwdriver** n. tool for turning screws —**screw top** bottle top that screws on to bottle, allowing bottle to be resealed after use —**screw-top** a. —**screw up 1.** distort **2.** inf. bungle

scribble ('skrɪbʰl) v. **1.** write, draw carelessly —vi. **2.** make meaningless marks with pen or pencil —n. **3.** something scribbled —**'scribbly** a.

scribe (skraɪb) n. **1.** writer **2.** copyist —v. **3.** scratch a line on (a surface) with pointed instrument

scrimmage ('skrɪmɪdʒ) n. scuffle

scrimp (skrɪmp) vt. **1.** make too small or short **2.** treat meanly —**'scrimpy** a.

script (skrɪpt) n. **1.** (system or style of) handwriting **2.** written characters **3.** written text of film, play, radio or television programme **4.** answer paper in examination

scripture ('skrɪptʃə) n. **1.** sacred writings **2.** the Bible —**'scriptural** a.

scrofula ('skrɒfjʊlə) n. tuberculosis of lymphatic glands, esp. of neck —**'scrofulous** a.

scroll (skrəʊl) n. **1.** roll of parchment or paper **2.** list **3.** ornament shaped thus

Scrooge (skru:dʒ) n. miserly person

scrotum ('skrəʊtəm) n. pouch containing testicles (pl. **-ta** (-tə)) —**'scrotal** a.

scrounge (skraʊndʒ) v. inf. get (something) without cost, by begging —**'scrounger** n.

scrub[1] (skrʌb) vt. **1.** clean with hard brush and water **2.** scour **3.** inf. cancel, get rid of (**-bb-**) —n. **4.** scrubbing —**'scrubber** n. **1.** person or thing that scrubs **2.** apparatus for purifying gas **3.** derogatory sl. promiscuous girl

scrub[2] (skrʌb) n. **1.** stunted trees **2.** brushwood —**'scrubby** a. **1.** covered with scrub **2.** stunted **3.** inf. messy

scruff (skrʌf) n. nape (of neck)

scruffy ('skrʌfɪ) a. unkempt or shabby

scrum (skrʌm) n. **1.** Rugby restarting of play in which opposing packs of forwards push against each other to try to gain possession of the ball (also **'scrummage**) **2.** crush, crowd

scrump (skrʌmp) v. UK dial. steal (apples) from orchard or garden

scrumptious ('skrʌmpʃəs) a. inf. very pleasing; delicious —**'scrumptiously** adv.

scrumpy ('skrʌmpɪ) n. rough dry cider

scrunch (skrʌntʃ) v. **1.** crumple or crunch or be crumpled or crunched —n. **2.** act or sound of scrunching

scruple ('skru:pʰl) n. **1.** doubt or hesitation about what is morally right **2.** weight of 20 grains —vi. **3.** hesitate —**'scrupulous** a. **1.** extremely conscientious **2.** thorough, attentive to small points

scrutiny ('skru:tɪnɪ) n. **1.** close examination **2.** critical investigation **3.** official examination of votes etc. **4.** searching look —**scruti'neer** n. examiner of votes —**'scrutinize** or **-nise** vt. examine closely

scuba ('skju:bə) n./a. (relating to) self-contained underwater breathing apparatus

scud (skʌd) vi. **1.** run fast **2.** run before the wind (**-dd-**)

scuff (skʌf) vi. **1.** drag, scrape with feet in walking —vt. **2.** scrape with feet **3.** graze —n. **4.** act, sound of scuffing —pl. **5.** thong sandals —**scuffed** a. (of shoes) scraped or slightly grazed

scuffle ('skʌfʰl) vi. **1.** fight in disorderly manner **2.** shuffle —n. **3.** disorderly struggle

scull (skʌl) n. **1.** oar used in stern of boat **2.** short oar used in pairs —v. **3.** propel, move by means of scull(s)

scullery ('skʌlərɪ) n. place for washing dishes etc. —**'scullion** n. **1.** despicable person **2.** obs. kitchen underservant

sculpture ('skʌlptʃə) n. **1.** art of forming figures in relief or solid **2.** product of this art —vt. **3.** represent by sculpture —**sculpt** v. —**'sculptor** n. ('sculptress fem.) —**'sculptural** a. with qualities proper to sculpture

scum (skʌm) n. **1.** froth or other floating matter on liquid **2.** waste part of anything **3.** vile person(s) or thing(s) —**'scummy** a.

scunner ('skʌnə) dial., chiefly Scot. vt. **1.** produce feeling of aversion in —n. **2.** strong aversion (oft. in **take a scunner**) **3.** object of aversion

scupper ('skʌpə) n. **1.** hole in ship's side level with deck to carry off water —vt. **2.** inf. ruin, destroy, kill

scurf (sk3:f) n. flaky matter on scalp, dandruff

scurrilous ('skʌrɪləs) a. coarse, indecently abusive —**scur'rility** n.

scurry ('skʌrɪ) vi. **1.** run hastily ('scurried, 'scurrying) —n. **2.** bustling haste **3.** flurry

scurvy ('sk3:vɪ) n. **1.** disease caused by lack of vitamin C —a. **2.** mean, contemptible

scut (skʌt) n. short tail of hare or other animal

scuttle[1] ('skʌtʰl) n. fireside container for coal

scuttle[2] ('skʌtʰl) vi. **1.** rush away —n. **2.** hurried pace, run

scuttle[3] ('skʌtʰl) vt. cause (ship) to sink by making holes in bottom

scythe (saɪð) n. **1.** manual implement with

long curved blade for cutting grass —*vt.* 2. cut with scythe

SD South Dakota

Se *Chem.* selenium

SE southeast(ern)

sea (siː) *n.* 1. mass of salt water covering greater part of earth 2. broad tract of this 3. waves 4. swell 5. large quantity 6. vast expanse —**sea anchor** *Naut.* device dragged in water to slow vessel —**sea anemone** sea animal with suckers like petals —**'seaboard** *n.* chiefly US coast —**sea cow** 1. dugong or manatee 2. *obs.* walrus —**sea dog** experienced or old sailor —**'seafaring** *a.* occupied in sea voyages —**'seafood** *n.* edible saltwater fish or shellfish —**sea-girt** *a. Lit.* surrounded by sea —**sea gull** gull —**sea horse** fish with bony plated body and horselike head —**sea kale** European coastal plant with edible asparagus-like shoots —**sea legs** *inf.* 1. ability to maintain one's balance on board ship 2. ability to resist seasickness —**sea level** level of surface of sea, taken to be mean level between high and low tide —**sea lion** kind of large seal —**'seaman** *n.* sailor —**'seamanship** *n.* skill in navigating, maintaining and operating vessel —**'seaplane** *n.* aircraft that lands on and takes off from water —**Sea Scout** Scout belonging to any of number of Scout troops whose main activities are sailing *etc.* —**'seashell** *n.* empty shell of marine mollusc —**'seasick** *a.* —**'seasickness** *n.* nausea caused by motion of ship —**'seaside** *n.* place, *esp.* holiday resort, on coast —**sea urchin** marine animal with globular body enclosed in rigid, spiny test —**'seaweed** *n.* plant growing in sea —**'seaworthy** *a.* in fit condition to put to sea

seal¹ (siːl) *n.* 1. device impressed on piece of wax *etc.*, fixed to letter *etc.* as mark of authentication 2. impression thus made 3. device, material preventing passage of water, air, oil *etc.* (*also* **'sealer**) —*vt.* 4. affix seal to 5. ratify, authorize 6. mark with stamp as evidence of some quality 7. keep close or secret 8. settle 9. make watertight, airtight *etc.* —**sealing wax** hard material made of shellac and turpentine that softens when heated

seal² (siːl) *n.* 1. amphibious furred carnivorous mammal with flippers as limbs —*vi.* 2. hunt seals —**'sealer** *n.* man or ship engaged in sealing —**'sealskin** *n.* skin, fur of seals

seam (siːm) *n.* 1. line of junction of two edges, *eg* of two pieces of cloth, or two planks 2. thin layer, stratum —*vt.* 3. mark with furrows or wrinkles —**'seamless** *a.* —**seamstress** (**'sɛmstrɪs**) *or* **sempstress** (**'sɛmpstrɪs**) *n.* woman who sews and makes clothes, *esp.* professionally —**'seamy** *a.* 1. sordid 2. marked with seams

seance (**'seɪɒns**) *n.* meeting of spiritualists

sear (sɪə) *vt.* 1. scorch, brand with hot iron 2. deaden

search (sɜːtʃ) *v.* 1. look over or through (a place *etc.*) to find something —*vt.* 2. probe into, examine —*n.* 3. act of searching 4. quest —**'searcher** *n.* —**'searching** *a.* 1. keen 2. thorough 3. severe —**'searchlight** *n.* powerful electric light with concentrated beam —**search warrant** legal document authorizing search of premises for stolen goods *etc.*

season (**'siːzⁿn**) *n.* 1. one of four divisions of year (spring, summer, autumn and winter), which have characteristic weather conditions 2. period during which thing takes place, grows, is active *etc.* 3. proper time —*vt.* 4. flavour with salt, herbs *etc.* 5. make reliable or ready for use 6. make experienced —**'seasonable** *a.* 1. appropriate for the season 2. opportune 3. fit —**'seasonal** *a.* depending on, varying with seasons —**'seasoning** *n.* flavouring —**season ticket** ticket for series of journeys, events *etc.* within a certain time

seat (siːt) *n.* 1. thing for sitting on 2. buttocks 3. base 4. right to sit (eg in council *etc.*) 5. place where something is located, centred 6. locality of disease, trouble *etc.* 7. country house —*vt.* 8. bring to or place on seat 9. provide sitting accommodation for 10. install firmly —**seat belt** belt worn in car, aircraft *etc.* to secure seated passenger (*also* **safety belt**)

SEATO (**'siːtəʊ**) South East Asia Treaty Organization

sebaceous (sɪ'beɪʃəs) *a.* 1. of, pert. to fat 2. secreting fat, oil

sec¹ (sɛk) *a.* 1. (of wines) dry 2. (of champagne) of medium sweetness

sec² (sɛk) *inf.* second (of time)

sec³ (sɛk) secant

sec. 1. second (of time) 2. secondary 3. secretary 4. section 5. sector

secant (**'siːkənt**) *n. Maths.* 1. (of angle) the reciprocal of its cosine 2. line that intersects a curve

secateurs (**'sɛkətəz**) *pl.n.* small pruning shears

secede (sɪ'siːd) *vi.* withdraw formally from federation, Church *etc.* —**secession** (sɪ'sɛʃən) *n.* —**secessionist** (sɪ'sɛʃənɪst) *n.*

seclude (sɪ'kluːd) *vt.* guard from, remove from sight, view, contact with others —**se'cluded** *a.* 1. remote 2. private —**se'clusion** *n.*

second¹ (**'sɛkənd**) *a.* 1. next after first 2. alternate 3. additional 4. of lower quality —*n.* 5. person or thing coming second 6. attendant 7. sixtieth part of minute 8. SI unit of time 9. moment 10. (*esp. pl.*) inferior goods —*vt.* 11. support 12. support (motion in meeting) so that discussion may be in order —**'seconder** *n.* —**'secondly** *adv.* —**second-best** *a.* next to best —**second chamber** upper house of bicameral legislative assembly —**second class** class next in value *etc.* to first —**second-**

class *a.* **1.** of grade next to best in quality *etc.* **2.** shoddy or inferior **3.** (of accommodation in hotel, on aircraft *etc.*) next in quality to first class **4.** UK (of letters) handled more slowly than first-class letters —*adv.* **5.** by second-class mail *etc.* —**Second Coming** or **Advent** *Christian theol.* prophesied return of Christ to earth at Last Judgment —**second cousin** child of first cousin of either of one's parents —**second fiddle** *inf.* **1.** second violin in string quartet **2.** person who has secondary status —**second generation** offspring of parents born in a given country —**second-generation** *a.* of refined stage of development in manufacture —**second hand** pointer on face of timepiece that indicates seconds —**second-hand** *a.* **1.** bought after use by another **2.** not original **3.** dealing in goods that are not new —*adv.* **4.** not directly —**second lieutenant** officer holding lowest commissioned rank in armed forces of certain nations —**second nature** habit *etc.* long practised so as to seem innate —**second person** grammatical category of pronouns and verbs used when referring to individual(s) being addressed —**second-rate** *a.* **1.** mediocre **2.** second in importance *etc.* —**second sight** faculty of seeing events before they occur —**second thought** revised opinion on matter already considered —**second wind 1.** return of breath at normal rate, *esp.* following exertion **2.** renewed ability to continue in effort —**come off second best** *inf.* be defeated in competition

second² (sə'kɒnd) *vt.* transfer (employee, officer) temporarily

secondary ('sɛkəndərı) *a.* **1.** subsidiary, of less importance **2.** developed from, or dependent on, something else —**'secondarily** *adv.* —**secondary education** education of young people between ages of 11 and 18 —**secondary picketing** picketing by striking workers of distribution outlet *etc.* that supplies goods to or distributes goods from their employer

secret ('si:krɪt) *a.* **1.** kept, meant to be kept from knowledge of others **2.** hidden **3.** private —*n.* **4.** thing kept secret —**'secrecy** *n.* keeping or being kept secret —**'secretive** *a.* given to having secrets; uncommunicative, reticent —**'secretiveness** *n.* —**'secretly** *adv.* —**secret agent** person employed in espionage —**secret police** police force that operates secretly to check subversion —**secret service** government department that conducts intelligence or counterintelligence operations

secretary ('sɛkrətrı) *n.* **1.** one employed by individual or organization to deal with papers and correspondence, keep records, prepare business *etc.* **2.** head of a state department —**secre'tarial** *a.* —**secre'tariat** *n.* **1.** body of secretaries **2.** building occupied by secretarial staff —**'secretaryship** *n.* —**secretary bird** large Afr. bird of prey

secrete (sɪ'kri:t) *vt.* **1.** hide, conceal **2.** (of gland *etc.*) collect and supply (particular substance in body) —**se'cretion** *n.* —**se'cretory** *a.*

sect (sɛkt) *n.* **1.** group of people (within religious body *etc.*) with common interest **2.** faction —**sec'tarian** *a.* **1.** of a sect **2.** narrow-minded

section ('sɛkʃən) *n.* **1.** part cut off **2.** division **3.** portion **4.** distinct part of city, country, people *etc.* **5.** cutting **6.** drawing of anything as if cut through **7.** smallest military unit —**'sectional** *a.*

sector ('sɛktə) *n.* **1.** part, subdivision **2.** part of circle enclosed by two radii and the arc which they cut off

secular ('sɛkjulə) *a.* **1.** worldly **2.** lay, not religious **3.** not monastic **4.** lasting for, or occurring once in, an age **5.** centuries old —**'secularism** *n.* —**'secularist** *n.* one who believes that religion should have no place in civil affairs —**seculari'zation** or **-ri'sation** *n.* —**'secularize** or **-rise** *vt.* transfer from religious to lay possession or use

secure (sɪ'kjuə) *a.* **1.** safe **2.** free from fear, anxiety **3.** firmly fixed **4.** certain **5.** sure, confident —*vt.* **6.** gain possession of **7.** make safe **8.** free (creditor) from risk of loss **9.** make firm —**se'curely** *adv.* —**se'curity** *n.* **1.** state of safety **2.** protection **3.** that which secures **4.** assurance **5.** anything given as bond, caution or pledge **6.** one that becomes surety for another —**security risk** person deemed to be threat to state security

sedan (sɪ'dæn) *n.* US saloon car —**sedan chair** *Hist.* closed chair for one person, carried on poles by bearers

sedate¹ (sɪ'deɪt) *a.* **1.** calm, collected **2.** serious

sedate² (sɪ'deɪt) *vt.* make calm by sedative —**se'dation** *n.* —**sedative** ('sɛdətɪv) *a.* **1.** having soothing or calming effect —*n.* **2.** sedative drug

sedentary ('sɛd³ntərı) *a.* **1.** done sitting down **2.** sitting much **3.** (of birds) not migratory

sedge (sɛdʒ) *n.* plant like coarse grass growing in swampy ground —**sedge warbler** European songbird having streaked brownish plumage with white eye stripes

sedilia (sɛ'daɪlɪə) *n.* (*with sing. v.*) stone seats on south side of altar for priests

sediment ('sɛdɪmənt) *n.* **1.** matter which settles to the bottom of liquid **2.** matter deposited from water, ice or wind —**sedi'mentary** *a.*

sedition (sɪ'dɪʃən) *n.* speech or action threatening authority of a state —**se'ditious** *a.*

seduce (sɪ'dju:s) *vt.* **1.** persuade to commit some (wrong) deed, *esp.* sexual intercourse **2.** tempt **3.** attract —**se'ducer** *n.* (**seductress** (sɪ'dʌktrıs) *fem.*) —**seduction** (sɪ'dʌkʃən) *n.* —**seductive** (sɪ'dʌktɪv) *a.* **1.** alluring **2.** winning

sedulous ('sɛdjuləs) a. 1. diligent 2. industrious 3. persevering, persistent —se'dulity n.

sedum ('si:dəm) n. rock plant

see¹ (si:) vt. 1. perceive with eyes or mentally 2. observe 3. watch 4. find out 5. consider 6. have experience of 7. interview 8. make sure 9. accompany —vi. 10. have power of sight 11. consider 12. understand (**saw, seen, 'seeing**) —'**seeing** conj. since, in view of the fact that

see² (si:) n. diocese, office or jurisdiction of bishop

seed (si:d) n. 1. reproductive germs of plants 2. one grain of this 3. such grains saved or used for sowing 4. origin 5. sperm 6. obs. offspring —vt. 7. sow with seed 8. arrange (draw for lawn tennis or other tournament) so that best players do not meet in early rounds —vi. 9. produce seed —'**seedling** n. young plant raised from seed —'**seedy** a. 1. shabby 2. (of plant) at seed-producing stage 3. inf. unwell, ill —**seed pearl** tiny pearl weighing less than a quarter of a grain

seek (si:k) vt. 1. make search or enquiry for —vi. 2. search (**sought, 'seeking**)

seem (si:m) vi. 1. appear (to be or to do) 2. look 3. appear to one's judgment —'**seeming** a. apparent but not real —'**seemingly** adv.

seemly ('si:mlɪ) a. becoming and proper —'**seemliness** n.

seen (si:n) pp. of SEE¹

seep (si:p) vi. trickle through slowly, as water, ooze

seer (sɪə) n. prophet

seersucker ('sɪəsʌkə) n. light cotton fabric with slightly crinkled surface

seesaw ('si:sɔ:) n. 1. game in which children sit at opposite ends of plank supported in middle and swing up and down 2. plank used for this —vi. 3. move up and down

seethe (si:ð) vi. 1. boil, foam 2. be very agitated 3. be in constant movement (as large crowd etc.) (**seethed, 'seething**)

segment ('sɛgmənt) n. 1. piece cut off 2. section —v. (sɛg'mɛnt) 3. divide into segments —seg'mental a. —segmen'tation n.

segregate ('sɛgrɪgeɪt) vt. set apart from the rest —segre'gation n.

seigneur (sɛ'njɜ:; Fr. sɛ'nœ:r) n. feudal lord, esp. in France —sei'gneurial a. —'seigneury n. estate of seigneur

seignior ('seɪnjə) n. 1. less common name for seigneur 2. in England, lord of

seigniory —sei'gniorial a. —'seigniory or 'signory n. 1. less common names for seigneury 2. in England, fee or manor of seignior 3. authority of seignior

seine (seɪn) n. type of large fishing net

seismic ('saɪzmɪk) a. pert. to earthquakes —'seismograph n. instrument that records earthquakes (also seis'mometer) —seismo'logic(al) a. pert. to seismology —seis'mologist n. one versed in seismology —seis'mology n. science of earthquakes

seismo- or before vowel **seism-** (comb. form) earthquake, as in seismology

seize (si:z) vt. 1. grasp 2. lay hold of 3. capture —vi. 4. (of mechanical parts) stick tightly through overheating —'seizable a. —'seizure n. 1. act of taking, esp. by warrant, as goods 2. sudden onset of disease

seldom ('sɛldəm) adv. not often, rarely

select (sɪ'lɛkt) vt. 1. pick out, choose —a. 2. choice, picked 3. exclusive —se'lection n. —se'lective a. —selec'tivity n. —se'lector n.

selenium (sɪ'li:nɪəm) n. nonmetallic element with photoelectric properties —se'lenic a.

self (sɛlf) pron. 1. used reflexively or to express emphasis (pl. selves) —a. 2. (of colour) same throughout, uniform —n. 3. one's own person or individuality (pl. selves) —'selfish a. 1. concerned unduly over personal profit or pleasure 2. lacking consideration for others 3. greedy —'selfishly adv. —'selfless a. 1. having no regard to self 2. unselfish

self- (comb. form) of oneself or itself. See the list below

self-abnegation n. denial of one's own interests

self-abuse n. 1. misuse of one's own abilities etc. 2. euphemistic masturbation

self-aggrandizement n. act of increasing one's own power etc. —self-aggrandizing a.

self-assertion n. act of putting forward one's own opinions etc., esp. in aggressive manner —self-asserting a. —self-assertive a.

self-assurance n. confidence in validity etc. of one's own opinions etc. —self-assured a.

self-conscious a. 1. unduly aware of oneself 2. conscious of one's acts or states

self-determination n. the right of person or nation to decide for himself or itself

self-abasement	self-catering	self-deception
self-absorbed	self-centred	self-defeating
self-absorption	self-complacent	self-defence
self-addressed	self-confessed	self-delusion
self-adhesive	self-confidence	self-denial
self-appointed	self-confident	
self-assurance	self-contained	
self-assured	self-control	

self-discipline *n.* disciplining of one's own feelings, desires *etc.* —**self-disciplined** *a.*

self-educated *a.* educated through one's own efforts without formal instruction

self-effacement *n.* act of making oneself, one's actions *etc.* inconspicuous —**self-effacing** *a.*

self-employed *a.* earning one's living in one's own business —**self-employment** *n.*

self-expression *n.* expression of one's own personality *etc.* as in painting *etc.* —**self-expressive** *a.*

self-government *n.* government of country *etc.* by its own people —**self-governed** *a.* —**self-governing** *a.*

selfheal ('sɛlfhiːl) *n.* European herbaceous plant reputedly having healing powers

self-important *a.* having unduly high opinion of one's own importance *etc.* —**self-importance** *n.*

self-improvement *n.* improvement of one's status, education *etc.* by one's own efforts

self-induced *a.* induced by oneself or itself

self-interest *n.* **1.** one's personal interest or advantage **2.** act of pursuing one's own interest

self-made *a.* having achieved wealth, status *etc.* by one's own efforts

self-opinionated *a.* **1.** having unduly high regard for oneself or one's own opinions **2.** clinging stubbornly to one's own opinions

self-possessed *a.* calm, composed —**self-possession** *n.*

self-propelled *a.* (of vehicle) provided with its own source of tractive power

self-raising *a.* (of flour) having raising agent already added

self-respect *n.* proper sense of one's own dignity and integrity

self-righteous *a.* smugly sure of one's own virtue

self-sacrifice *n.* sacrifice of one's own desires *etc.* for sake of well-being of others —**self-sacrificing** *a.*

selfsame ('sɛlfseɪm) *a.* very same

self-satisfied *a.* having or showing complacent satisfaction with oneself, one's own actions *etc.* —**self-satisfaction** *n.*

self-sealing *a.* (*esp.* of envelope) designed to become sealed by pressure only

self-seeking *n.* **1.** act of seeking one's own profit or interest —*a.* **2.** having exclusive preoccupation with one's own profit or interest —**self-seeker** *n.*

self-service *a./n.* (of) shop or restaurant where customers serve themselves

self-starter *n.* **1.** electric motor used to start internal-combustion engine **2.** switch that operates this motor

self-styled *a.* claiming to be of specified nature, profession *etc.*

self-sufficient *or* **self-sufficing** *a.* **1.** sufficient in itself **2.** relying on one's own powers

self-will *n.* **1.** obstinacy **2.** wilfulness —**self-willed** *a.* headstrong

self-winding *a.* (of wrist watch) winding automatically

sell (sɛl) *vt.* **1.** hand over for a price **2.** stock, have for sale **3.** make (someone) accept **4.** *inf.* betray, cheat —*vi.* **5.** find purchasers (**sold**, '**selling**) —*n. inf.* **6.** hoax —'**seller** *n.* —**selling race** *or* **plate** horse race in which winner must be offered for sale at auction —'**sellout** *n.* **1.** disposing of completely by selling **2.** betrayal

Sellotape ('sɛləteɪp) *n.* **1. R** type of adhesive tape —*vt.* **2.** seal using adhesive tape

Seltzer ('sɛltsə) *n.* aerated mineral water

selvage *or* **selvedge** ('sɛlvɪdʒ) *n.* finished, nonfraying edge of cloth

selves (sɛlvz) *n., pl. of* SELF

Sem. 1. Seminary **2.** Semitic

semantic (sɪ'mæntɪk) *a.* relating to meaning of words or symbols —**se'mantics** *pl.n.* (*with sing. v.*) study of linguistic meaning

semaphore ('sɛməfɔː) *n.* **1.** post with movable arms for signalling **2.** system of signalling by human or mechanical arms

semblance ('sɛmbləns) *n.* **1.** (false) appearance **2.** image, likeness

semen ('siːmɛn) *n.* **1.** fluid carrying sperm of male animals **2.** sperm

semester (sɪ'mɛstə) *n.* **US** half-year session in many universities, colleges

semi ('sɛmɪ) *inf.* semidetached house

semi- (*comb. form*) half, partly, not completely, as in *semicircle*

semiannual (sɛmɪ'ænjʊəl) *a.* **1.** occurring every half-year **2.** lasting for half a year —**semi'annually** *adv.*

semibreve ('sɛmɪbriːv) *n.* musical note half length of breve

semicircle ('sɛmɪsɜːk³l) *n.* half of circle —**semi'circular** *a.* —**semicircular canal** *Anat.* any of three looped fluid-filled membranous tubes that comprise labyrinth of ear

self-employed	self-justification	self-reliant
self-esteem	self-knowledge	self-reproach
self-evident	self-pity	self-restraint
self-explanatory	self-portrait	self-righting
self-help	self-preservation	self-sacrifice
self-indulgence	self-raising	self-satisfied
self-indulgent	self-realization	self-supporting
self-inflicted	self-regard	self-taught
self-interest	self-reliance	

semicolon (sɛmɪˈkəʊlən) *n.* punctuation mark (;)

semiconductor (sɛmɪkənˈdʌktə) *n.* **1.** substance, as silicon, having electrical conductivity that increases with temperature **2.** device, as transistor, dependent on properties of such substance

semidetached (sɛmɪdɪˈtætʃt) *a./n.* (of) house joined to another on one side only

semifinal (sɛmɪˈfaɪnˀl) *n.* match, round *etc.* before final

seminal (ˈsɛmɪnəl) *a.* **1.** capable of developing **2.** influential, important **3.** rudimentary **4.** of semen or seed

seminar (ˈsɛmɪnɑː) *n.* meeting of group (of students) for discussion

seminary (ˈsɛmɪnərɪ) *n.* college for priests

semiprecious (sɛmɪˈprɛʃəs) *a.* (of gemstones) having less value than precious stones

semiprofessional (sɛmɪprəˈfɛʃənˀl) *a.* **1.** (of person) engaged in activity or sport part-time but for pay **2.** (of activity or sport) engaged in by semiprofessionals **3.** of person whose activities are professional in some respects —*n.* **4.** semiprofessional person

semiquaver (ˈsɛmɪkweɪvə) *n. Mus.* note having time value of one-sixteenth of semibreve

semiskilled (sɛmɪˈskɪld) *a.* partly skilled, trained but not for specialized work

Semite (ˈsiːmaɪt) *n.* member of race including Jews and Arabs —**Semitic** (sɪˈmɪtɪk) *a.* **1.** denoting a Semite **2.** Jewish

semitone (ˈsɛmɪtəʊn) *n.* musical halftone

semitrailer (sɛmɪˈtreɪlə) *n.* type of trailer that has wheels only at rear, front end being supported by towing vehicle

semivowel (ˈsɛmɪvaʊəl) *n. Phonet.* vowel-like sound that acts like consonant, as (w) in *well* and (j), represented as *y*, in *yell* (*also* **glide**)

semolina (sɛməˈliːnə) *n.* hard grains left after sifting of flour, used for puddings *etc.*

sempervivum (sɛmpəˈvaɪvəm) *n.* plant with ornamental rosettes of leaves

sempre (ˈsɛmprɪ) *adv. Mus.* always; consistently

S.E.N. State Enrolled Nurse

Sen. *or* **sen. 1.** senate **2.** senator **3.** senior

senate (ˈsɛnɪt) *n.* upper council of state, university *etc.* —**senator** *n.* —**sena'torial** *a.*

send (sɛnd) *vt.* **1.** cause to go or be conveyed **2.** dispatch **3.** transmit (by radio) (**sent**, **'sending**) —**'sendoff** *n. inf.* demonstration of good wishes to person about to set off on journey *etc.* —**send-up** *n.* UK parody or imitation —**send off 1.** cause to depart **2.** *Soccer, rugby etc.* (of referee) dismiss (player) from field of play for some offence —**send up** *sl.* **1.** send to prison **2.** UK make fun of, *esp.* by doing parody of

senescent (sɪˈnɛsˀnt) *a.* **1.** growing old **2.** characteristic of old age —**se'nescence** *n.*

senile (ˈsiːnaɪl) *a.* showing weakness of old age —**senility** (sɪˈnɪlɪtɪ) *n.*

senior (ˈsiːnjə) *a.* **1.** superior in rank or standing **2.** older —*n.* **3.** superior **4.** elder person —**seni'ority** *n.* —**senior aircraftman** rank in Royal Air Force comparable to that of private in army, though with lowest rank in Royal Air Force —**senior citizen UK, A, NZ,** *euphemistic* elderly person —**senior service UK** Royal Navy

senna (ˈsɛnə) *n.* **1.** tropical plant **2.** its dried leaves or pods, used as laxative

señor (sɛˈnjɔː; *Sp.* seˈɲor) *n.* Sp. title of respect, like Mr. (*pl.* **-s, -ñores** (*Sp.* -ˈɲores)) —**se'ñora** *n.* Mrs. —**seño'rita** *n.* Miss

sensation (sɛnˈseɪʃən) *n.* **1.** operation of sense, feeling, awareness **2.** excited feeling, state of excitement **3.** exciting event **4.** strong impression **5.** commotion —**sen'sational** *a.* **1.** producing great excitement **2.** melodramatic **3.** of perception by senses —**sen'sationalism** *n.* **1.** use of sensational language *etc.* to arouse intense emotional excitement **2.** doctrine that sensations are basis of all knowledge

sense (sɛns) *n.* **1.** any of bodily faculties of perception or feeling **2.** sensitiveness of any or all of these faculties **3.** ability to perceive, mental alertness **4.** consciousness **5.** meaning **6.** coherence, intelligible meaning **7.** sound practical judgment —*vt.* **8.** perceive **9.** understand —**'senseless** *a.* —**'senselessly** *adv.* —**sense organ** structure in animals that is specialized for receiving external stimuli and transmitting them to brain

sensible (ˈsɛnsɪbˀl) *a.* **1.** reasonable, wise **2.** perceptible by senses **3.** aware, mindful **4.** considerable, appreciable —**sensi'bility** *n.* ability to feel, *esp.* emotional or moral feelings —**'sensibly** *adv.*

sensitive (ˈsɛnsɪtɪv) *a.* **1.** open to, acutely affected by, external impressions **2.** easily affected or altered **3.** easily upset by criticism **4.** responsive to slight changes —**'sensitively** *adv.* —**sensi'tivity** *or* **'sensitiveness** *n.* —**'sensitize** *or* **-tise** *vt.* make sensitive, *esp.* make (photographic film *etc.*) sensitive to light

sensor (ˈsɛnsə) *n.* device that responds to stimulus

sensory (ˈsɛnsərɪ) *or* **sensorial** (sɛnˈsɔːrɪəl) *a.* relating to organs, operation, of senses

sensual (ˈsɛnsjʊəl) *a.* **1.** of senses only and not of mind **2.** given to pursuit of pleasures of sense **3.** self-indulgent **4.** licentious —**'sensualism** *n.* —**'sensualist** *n.* —**sen-su'ality** *n.*

sensuous (ˈsɛnsjʊəs) *a.* stimulating, or apprehended by senses, *esp.* in aesthetic manner

sent (sɛnt) *pt./pp. of* SEND

sentence (ˈsɛntəns) *n.* **1.** combination of words, which is complete as expressing a thought **2.** judgment passed on criminal by court or judge —*vt.* **3.** pass sentence on, condemn —**sen'tential** a. of sentence —**sen'tentious** a. 1. full of axioms and maxims 2. pithy 3. pompously moralizing —**sen'tentiously** adv. —**sen'tentiousness** n.

sentient ('sɛntɪənt) a. 1. capable of feeling 2. feeling 3. thinking —**'sentience** or **'sentiency** n.

sentiment ('sɛntɪmənt) n. 1. tendency to be moved by feeling rather than reason 2. verbal expression of feeling 3. mental feeling, emotion 4. opinion —**senti'mental** a. 1. given to indulgence in sentiment and in its expression 2. weak 3. sloppy —**senti'mentalist** n. —**sentimen'tality** n. —**senti'mentalize** or **-lise** v.

sentinel ('sɛntɪnˀl) n. sentry

sentry ('sɛntrɪ) n. soldier on watch —**sentry box** small shelter in which sentry may stand to be sheltered from weather

sepal ('sɛpˀl) n. leaf or division of the calyx of a flower

separate ('sɛpəreɪt) vt. 1. part 2. divide 3. sever 4. put apart 5. occupy place between —vi. 6. withdraw, become parted —a. ('sɛprɪt, 'sɛpərɪt) 7. disconnected, apart 8. distinct, individual —**'separable** a. —**separately** ('sɛprɪtlɪ, 'sɛpərɪtlɪ) adv. —**sepa'ration** n. 1. disconnection 2. Law living apart of married people without divorce —**'separatism** n. —**'separatist** n. person who advocates secession from organization, union etc. —**'separator** n. 1. that which separates 2. apparatus for separating cream from milk —**separate school** C school for a large religious minority

sepia ('siːpɪə) n. 1. reddish-brown pigment made from a fluid secreted by the cuttlefish —a. 2. of this colour

sepoy ('siːpɔɪ) n. formerly, Indian soldier in service of Brit.

sepsis ('sɛpsɪs) n. presence of pus-forming bacteria in body

Sept. September

September (sɛp'tɛmbə) n. 9th month

septennial (sɛp'tɛnɪəl) a. lasting, occurring every seven years

septet (sɛp'tɛt) n. 1. music for seven instruments or voices 2. group of seven performers

septic ('sɛptɪk) a. 1. of, caused by, sepsis 2. (of wound) infected —**septicaemia** or **septicemia** (sɛptɪ'siːmɪə) n. blood poisoning —**septic tank** tank for containing sewage to be decomposed by anaerobic bacteria

septuagenarian (sɛptjuədʒɪ'nɛərɪən) a. 1. aged between seventy and eighty —n. 2. person of this age

Septuagesima (sɛptjuə'dʒɛsɪmə) n. third Sunday before Lent

septum ('sɛptəm) n. Biol., anat. dividing partition between two tissues or cavities (pl. **-ta** (-tə))

septuple ('sɛptjupˀl) a. 1. seven times as much or many 2. consisting of seven parts or members —vt. 3. multiply by seven —**septuplicate** (sɛp'tjuːplɪkət) n./a.

sepulchre or U.S. **sepulcher** ('sɛpəlkə) n. tomb, burial vault —**se'pulchral** a. 1. of burial, or the grave 2. mournful 3. gloomy —**'sepulture** n. burial

sequel ('siːkwəl) n. 1. consequence 2. continuation, eg of story

sequence ('siːkwəns) n. 1. arrangement of things in successive order 2. section, episode of film —**'sequent** or **se'quential** a.

sequester (sɪ'kwɛstə) vt. 1. separate 2. seclude 3. put aside —**se'questrate** vt. 1. confiscate 2. divert or appropriate income of (property) to satisfy claims against its owner —**sequestration** (siːkwɛ'streɪʃən) n.

sequin ('siːkwɪn) n. 1. small ornamental metal disc on dresses etc. 2. formerly, Venetian gold coin

sequoia (sɪ'kwɔɪə) n. giant Californian coniferous tree

seraglio (sɛ'rɑːlɪəʊ) or **serail** (sə'raɪ) n. harem, palace, of Turkish sultan (pl. **-s**)

seraph ('sɛrəf) n. member of highest order of angels (pl. **-s**, **-aphim** (-əfɪm)) —**se'raphic** a.

Serbian ('sɜːbɪən) a. 1. of Serbia, its people or their dialect of Serbo-Croatian —n. 2. dialect of Serbo-Croatian spoken in Serbia 3. native or inhabitant of Serbia (also **Serb**) —**Serbo-Croatian** or **Serbo-Croat** n. 1. chief official language of Yugoslavia —a. 2. of this language

serenade (sɛrɪ'neɪd) n. 1. sentimental piece of music or song of type addressed to woman by lover, esp. at evening —v. 2. sing serenade (to)

serendipity (sɛrən'dɪpɪtɪ) n. faculty of making fortunate discoveries by accident

serene (sɪ'riːn) a. 1. calm, tranquil 2. unclouded 3. quiet, placid —**se'renely** adv. —**serenity** (sɪ'rɛnɪtɪ) n.

serf (sɜːf) n. one of class of medieval labourers bound to, and transferred with, land —**'serfdom** or **'serfhood** n.

serge (sɜːdʒ) n. strong hard-wearing twilled worsted fabric

sergeant ('sɑːdʒənt) n. 1. noncommissioned officer in army 2. police officer above constable —**sergeant major** highest noncommissioned officer in regiment —**sergeant at arms** parliamentary, court officer with ceremonial duties

series ('sɪəriːz) n. 1. sequence 2. succession, set (eg of radio, TV programmes with same characters, setting, but different stories) (pl. **-ries**) —**'serial** n. 1. story or play produced in successive episodes or instalments 2. periodical publication —a. 3. of, in or forming a series —**'serialize** or **-lise** vt. publish, present as serial —**seriatim** (sɪərɪ'ætɪm) adv. one after another

serif or **seriph** ('sɛrɪf) n. Print. small line finishing off stroke of letter

seriocomic (sɪərɪəʊ'kɒmɪk) a. mixing serious and comic elements —**serio'comically** adv.

serious ('sɪərɪəs) a. 1. thoughtful, solemn 2.

earnest, sincere **3.** of importance **4.** giving cause for concern —'**seriously** adv.

sermon ('sɜːmən) n. **1.** discourse of religious instruction or exhortation spoken or read from pulpit **2.** any similar discourse —'**sermonize** or **-ise** vi. **1.** talk like preacher **2.** compose sermons

serpent ('sɜːpənt) n. Lit. snake —'**serpentine** a. **1.** like, shaped like, serpent —n. **2.** any of several kinds of green to black rock

serrate ('sɛrɪt, -eɪt) a. having notched, sawlike edge —**ser'rated** a. —**ser'ration** n.

serried ('sɛrɪd) a. in close order, shoulder to shoulder

serum ('sɪərəm) n. watery animal fluid, esp. thin part of blood as used for inoculation or vaccination (pl. **-s, -ra** (-rə)) —**se'rosity** n. —'**serous** a. of or producing serum

serval ('sɜːvᵊl) n. feline Afr. mammal

serve (sɜːv) vt. **1.** work for, under **2.** attend to (customers) in shop etc. **3.** provide **4.** provide (guests) with (food etc.) **5.** present (food etc.) in particular way **6.** provide with regular supply of **7.** pay homage to **8.** go through (period of service etc.) **9.** suit **10.** Tennis etc. put (ball) into play —vi. **11.** be member of military unit —n. **12.** Tennis etc. act of serving ball —'**servant** n. personal or domestic attendant —'**service** n. **1.** the act of serving, helping, assisting **2.** system organized to provide for needs of public **3.** maintenance of vehicle **4.** use **5.** readiness, availability for use **6.** department of State employ **7.** employment of persons engaged in this **8.** set of dishes etc. **9.** form, session, of public worship —pl. **10.** armed forces —vt. **11.** overhaul —'**serviceable** a. **1.** in working order, usable **2.** durable —'**serving** n. portion of food or drink —**service area** place on motorway providing facilities as garage, restaurant etc. —**service charge** percentage of bill added to total to pay for service —**service flat** rented flat where landlord provides services such as cleaning etc. —'**serviceman** n. member of the armed forces —**service road** narrow road giving access to houses, shops etc. —**service station** place supplying fuel, oil, maintenance for motor vehicles —**service tree** Eurasian rosaceous tree with white flowers and brown edible apple-like fruits

serviette (sɜːvɪ'ɛt) n. table napkin

servile ('sɜːvaɪl) a. **1.** slavish, without independence **2.** cringing, fawning **3.** menial —**servility** (sɜː'vɪlɪtɪ) n.

servitude ('sɜːvɪtjuːd) n. bondage, slavery

servomechanism ('sɜːvəʊmɛkənɪzəm) n. device for converting small mechanical force into larger force, esp. in steering mechanisms

servomotor ('sɜːvəʊməʊtə) n. motor that supplies power to servomechanism

sesame ('sɛsəmɪ) n. plant with seeds used as herbs and for making oil

sesqui- (comb. form) one and a half, as in sesquicentennial

sessile ('sɛsaɪl) a. **1.** (of flowers or leaves) having no stalk **2.** (of animals such as barnacle) permanently attached —**sessility** (sɛ'sɪlɪtɪ) n.

session ('sɛʃən) n. **1.** meeting of court etc. **2.** assembly **3.** continuous series of such meetings **4.** any period devoted to an activity **5.** school or university term or year

sestet (sɛ'stɛt) n. **1.** Prosody last six lines of sonnet **2.** see SEXTET (sense 1)

set (sɛt) vt. **1.** put or place in specified position or condition **2.** cause to sit **3.** fix **4.** point **5.** put up **6.** make ready **7.** establish **8.** prescribe, allot **9.** put to music **10.** (of hair) arrange while wet, so that it dries in position —vi. **11.** become firm or fixed **12.** (of sun) go down **13.** have direction (**set, 'setting**) —a. **14.** fixed, established **15.** deliberate **16.** formal **17.** arranged beforehand **18.** unvarying —n. **19.** act or state of being set **20.** bearing, posture **21.** Rad., T.V. complete apparatus for reception or transmission **22.** Theat., cine. organized settings and equipment to form ensemble of scene **23.** number of things, persons associated as being similar, complementary or used together **24.** Maths. group of numbers, objects etc. with at least one common property —'**setback** n. anything that hinders or impedes —**set piece 1.** work of literature etc. intended to create impressive effect **2.** display of fireworks —'**setscrew** n. screw that fits into coupling, cam etc. and prevents motion of part relative to shaft on which it is mounted —**set square** thin flat piece of plastic etc. in shape of right-angled triangle, used in technical drawing —**set-to** n. inf. brief disagreement or fight —'**setup** n. **1.** position **2.** organization —**set to 1.** begin working **2.** start fighting —**set up** establish

sett or **set** (sɛt) n. badger's burrow

settee (sɛ'tiː) n. couch

setter ('sɛtə) n. any of various breeds of gun dog

setting ('sɛtɪŋ) n. **1.** background **2.** surroundings **3.** scenery and other stage accessories **4.** act of fixing **5.** decorative metalwork holding precious stone etc. in position **6.** tableware and cutlery for (single place at) table **7.** descending below horizon of sun **8.** music for song

settle¹ ('sɛtᵊl) vt. **1.** arrange, put in order **2.** establish, make firm or secure **3.** make quiet or calm **4.** decide upon **5.** end (dispute etc.) **6.** pay **7.** bestow (property) by legal deed —vi. **8.** come to rest **9.** subside **10.** become clear **11.** take up residence **12.** sink to bottom **13.** come to agreement —'**settlement** n. **1.** act of settling **2.** place newly inhabited **3.** money bestowed legally **4.** subsidence (of building) —'**settler** n. colonist

settle² ('sɛtªl) *n.* seat, usu. made of wood with high back and arms

seven ('sɛvªn) *a./n.* cardinal number, next after six —'**seven'teen** *a./n.* ten and seven —'**seventh** *a.* ordinal number of seven —'**seventy** *a./n.* ten times seven —**seven seas** all the oceans of the world —**seventh heaven 1.** final state of eternal bliss **2.** state of supreme happiness

sever ('sɛvə) *v.* **1.** separate, divide —*vt.* **2.** cut off —'**severance** *n.* —**severance pay** compensation paid by a firm to employee for loss of employment

several ('sɛvrəl) *a.* **1.** some, a few **2.** separate; individual **3.** various **4.** different —*pron.* **5.** indefinite small number —'**severally** *adv.* apart from others

severe (sɪ'vɪə) *a.* **1.** strict; rigorous **2.** hard to do **3.** harsh **4.** austere **5.** extreme —se'**verely** *adv.* —**severity** (sɪ'vɛrɪtɪ) *n.*

Seville orange (sə'vɪl) **1.** orange tree grown for its bitter fruit, used *esp.* to make marmalade **2.** its fruit

sew (səʊ) *v.* **1.** join (pieces of fabric *etc.*) with needle and thread —*vt.* **2.** make by sewing (**sewed** *pt.,* **sewed, sewn** *pp.,* '**sewing** *pr.p.*) —'**sewing** *n.*

sewage ('suːɪdʒ) *n.* refuse, waste matter, excrement conveyed in sewer —'**sewer** *n.* underground drain to remove waste water and refuse —'**sewerage** *n.* **1.** arrangement of sewers **2.** sewage —**sewage farm** place where sewage is treated, *esp.* for use as manure

sex (sɛks) *n.* **1.** state of being male or female **2.** males or females collectively **3.** sexual intercourse —*a.* **4.** concerning sex —*vt.* **5.** ascertain sex of —'**sexism** *n.* discrimination on basis of sex —'**sexist** *n./a.* —'**sexless** *a.* **1.** having no sexual differentiation **2.** having no sexual appeal or desires —'**sexual** *a.* —'**sexually** *adv.* —'**sexy** *a. inf.* provoking or intended to provoke sexual interest —**sex appeal** quality of attracting opposite sex —**sex change** change of sex, *esp.* involving medical or surgical treatment to alter sexual characteristics to those of opposite sex —**sex chromosome** either of chromosomes determining sex of animals —**sexual intercourse** act of procreation in which male's penis is inserted into female's vagina

sex- (*comb. form*) six, as in *sexcentenary*

sexagenarian (sɛksədʒɪ'nɛərɪən) *a./n.* (person) sixty years old

Sexagesima (sɛksə'dʒɛsɪmə) *n.* the second Sunday before Lent

sexennial (sɛk'sɛnɪəl) *a.* lasting, occurring every six years

sextant ('sɛkstənt) *n.* navigator's instrument for measuring elevations of heavenly body *etc.*

sextet *or* **sextette** (sɛks'tɛt) *n.* **1.** (composition for) six singers or players **2.** group of six

sexton ('sɛkstən) *n.* official in charge of a church, oft. acting as gravedigger

sextuple ('sɛkstjʊpªl) *n.* **1.** quantity or number six times as great as another —*a.* **2.** six times as much or as many **3.** consisting of six parts or members —'**sextuplet** *n.* **1.** one of six offspring born at one birth **2.** *Mus.* group of six notes played in time value of four

SF *or* **sf** science fiction

SFA Scottish Football Association

Sgt. Sergeant

sh (*spelling pron.* ʃʃʃ) *interj.* exclamation to request silence or quiet

shabby ('ʃæbɪ) *a.* **1.** faded, worn, ragged **2.** poorly dressed **3.** mean, dishonourable **4.** stingy —'**shabbily** *adv.* —'**shabbiness** *n.*

shack (ʃæk) *n.* rough hut —**shack up** (*usu.* with *with*) *sl.* live (*esp.* with lover)

shackle ('ʃækªl) *n.* (*oft. pl.*) **1.** metal ring or fastening for prisoner's wrist or ankle **2.** anything that confines —*vt.* **3.** fasten with shackles **4.** hamper

shad (ʃæd) *n.* herringlike fish

shade (ʃeɪd) *n.* **1.** partial darkness **2.** shelter, place sheltered from light, heat *etc.* **3.** darker part of anything **4.** depth of colour **5.** tinge **6.** ghost **7.** screen **8.** anything used to screen **9.** US windowblind —*pl.* **10.** US *sl.* sunglasses —*vt.* **11.** screen from light, darken **12.** represent (shades) in (drawing) —'**shady** *a.* **1.** shielded from sun **2.** dim **3.** dubious **4.** dishonest **5.** dishonourable

shadow ('ʃædəʊ) *n.* **1.** dark figure projected by anything that intercepts rays of light **2.** patch of shade **3.** slight trace **4.** indistinct image **5.** gloom **6.** inseparable companion —*vt.* **7.** cast shadow over **8.** follow and watch closely —'**shadowy** *a.* —**shadow cabinet** (in Brit. Parliament) members of opposition party, who would hold ministerial office if their party were in power

shaft (ʃɑːft) *n.* **1.** straight rod, stem **2.** handle **3.** arrow **4.** ray, beam (of light) **5.** revolving rod for transmitting power **6.** one of the bars between which horse is harnessed **7.** entrance boring of mine

shag¹ (ʃæg) *n.* **1.** matted wool or hair **2.** long-napped cloth **3.** coarse shredded tobacco —'**shaggy** *a.* **1.** covered with rough hair or wool **2.** tousled, unkempt

shag² (ʃæg) *n.* any of various varieties of cormorant

shagreen (ʃæ'griːn) *n.* **1.** rough skin of certain sharks and rays **2.** rough grainy leather made from certain animal hides

shah (ʃɑː) *n.* formerly, ruler of Iran

shake (ʃeɪk) *v.* **1.** (cause to) move with quick vibrations **2.** grasp the hand (of another) in greeting —*vi.* **3.** tremble —*vt.* **4.** upset **5.** wave, brandish (**shook, 'shaken**) —*n.* **6.** act of shaking **7.** vibration **8.** jolt **9.** *inf.* short period of time, jiffy

—'**shaker** n. 1. person or thing that shakes 2. container from which condiment is shaken 3. container in which ingredients of alcoholic drinks are shaken together —'**shakily** adv. —'**shaky** a. unsteady, insecure

shale (ʃeɪl) n. flaky, sedimentary rock

shall (ʃæl; unstressed ʃəl) v. aux. makes compound tenses or moods to express obligation, command, condition or intention (**should** pt.)

shallot (ʃəˈlɒt) n. kind of small onion

shallow ('ʃæləʊ) a. 1. not deep 2. having little depth of water 3. superficial 4. not sincere —n. 5. shallow place —'**shallowness** n.

shalom aleichem (ʃəˈlɒm əˈlexɛm) Hebrew peace be to you: used by Jews as greeting or farewell (oft. also **shaˈlom**)

sham (ʃæm) a./n. 1. imitation, counterfeit —vi. 2. pretend —v. 3. feign (**-mm-**)

shaman ('ʃæmən) n. 1. priest of shamanism 2. medicine man of similar religion —'**shamanism** n. religion of certain peoples of northern Asia, based on belief in good and evil spirits who can be controlled only by shamans

shamble ('ʃæmbˀl) vi. walk in shuffling, awkward way

shambles ('ʃæmbˀlz) pl.n. (with sing. v.) messy, disorderly thing or place

shame (ʃeɪm) n. 1. emotion caused by consciousness of guilt or dishonour in one's conduct or state 2. cause of disgrace 3. ignominy 4. pity, hard luck —vt. 5. cause to feel shame 6. disgrace 7. force by shame —'**shameful** a. disgraceful —'**shamefully** adv. —'**shameless** a. 1. with no sense of shame 2. indecent —'**shamefaced** a. ashamed

shammy ('ʃæmɪ) inf. chamois leather

shampoo (ʃæmˈpuː) n. 1. any of various preparations of liquid soap for washing hair, carpets etc. 2. this process —vt. 3. use shampoo to wash

shamrock ('ʃæmrɒk) n. clover leaf, esp. as Irish emblem

shandy ('ʃændɪ) or U.S. **shandygaff** ('ʃændɪgæf) n. mixed drink, esp. beer diluted with soft drink

shanghai ('ʃæŋhaɪ, ʃæŋˈhaɪ) vt. force, trick (someone) to do something

shank (ʃæŋk) n. 1. lower leg 2. shinbone 3. stem of thing

shantung (ʃænˈtʌŋ) n. soft, natural Chinese silk

shanty[1] ('ʃæntɪ) n. 1. temporary wooden building 2. crude dwelling

shanty[2] ('ʃæntɪ) n. sailor's song with chorus

shape (ʃeɪp) n. 1. external form or appearance 2. mould, pattern 3. inf. condition, esp. of physical fitness —vt. 4. form, mould, fashion, make —v. 5. develop (**shaped**, '**shaping**) —'**shapeless** a. —'**shapely** a. well-proportioned

SHAPE (ʃeɪp) Supreme Headquarters Allied Powers Europe

shard (ʃɑːd) or **sherd** n. broken fragment, esp. of earthenware

share[1] (ʃɛə) n. 1. portion, quota, lot 2. unit of ownership in public company —v. 3. give, take a share (of) 4. join with others in doing, using (something) —'**shareholder** n.

share[2] (ʃɛə) n. blade of plough

shark (ʃɑːk) n. 1. large usu. predatory sea fish 2. person who cheats others

sharkskin ('ʃɑːkskɪn) n. stiff rayon fabric

sharp (ʃɑːp) a. 1. having keen cutting edge or fine point 2. keen 3. not gradual or gentle 4. brisk 5. clever 6. harsh 7. dealing cleverly but unfairly 8. shrill 9. strongly marked, esp. in outline —adv. 10. promptly —n. 11. Mus. note half a tone above natural pitch 12. sl. cheat, swindler —'**sharpen** vt. make sharp —'**sharper** n. person who cheats or swindles —'**sharply** adv. —'**sharpness** n. —**sharp practice** dishonest dealings —**sharp-set** a. 1. set to give acute cutting angle 2. keenly hungry —'**sharpshooter** n. marksman —**sharp-witted** a. having or showing keen intelligence

shatter ('ʃætə) v. 1. break in pieces —vt. 2. ruin (plans etc.) 3. disturb (person) greatly

shave (ʃeɪv) v. 1. cut close (esp. hair of face or head) —vt. 2. pare away 3. graze 4. reduce (**shaved**, '**shaven**, '**shaving**) —n. 5. shaving —'**shaver** n. 1. person or thing that shaves 2. electrical implement for shaving —'**shavings** pl.n. parings —**close** or **near shave** narrow escape

Shavian ('ʃeɪvɪən) a. 1. of or like George Bernard Shaw, his works, ideas etc. —n. 2. admirer of Shaw or his works

shawl (ʃɔːl) n. piece of fabric to cover woman's shoulders or wrap baby

she (ʃiː) pron. 3rd person singular feminine pronoun

sheaf (ʃiːf) n. 1. bundle, esp. corn 2. loose leaves of paper (pl. **sheaves**)

shear (ʃɪə) vt. 1. clip hair, wool from 2. cut (through) 3. fracture (**sheared** pt., **shorn**, **sheared** pp., '**shearing** pr.p.) —'**shearer** n. —**shears** pl.n. 1. large pair of scissors 2. any of various analogous cutting instruments

shearwater ('ʃɪəwɔːtə) n. any of various sea birds

sheath (ʃiːθ) n. 1. close-fitting cover, esp. for knife or sword 2. scabbard 3. condom (pl. **sheaths** (ʃiːðz)) —**sheathe** vt. put into sheath

sheave (ʃiːv) n. wheel with grooved rim, esp. one used as pulley

sheaves (ʃiːvz) n., pl. of SHEAF

shebang (ʃɪˈbæŋ) n. sl. situation, matter (esp. in **the whole shebang**)

shebeen or **shebean** (ʃəˈbiːn) n. 1. Irish, Scot., SA place where alcohol is sold illegally 2. in S Afr., place where Black Afr. men engage in social drinking

shed[1] (ʃɛd) n. roofed shelter used as store or workshop

shed[2] (ʃɛd) v. 1. (cause to) pour forth (eg

tears, blood) —vt. **2.** cast off (**shed, 'shedding**)

sheen (ʃiːn) n. gloss —'**sheeny** a.

sheep (ʃiːp) n. ruminant animal bred for wool and meat (pl. **sheep**) —'**sheepish** a. embarrassed, shy —**sheep-dip** n. (deep trough containing) solution in which sheep are immersed to kill vermin and germs in fleece —'**sheepdog** n. any of various breeds of dog, orig. for herding sheep —'**sheepfold** n. pen or enclosure for sheep —'**sheepshank** n. knot etc. made in rope to shorten it temporarily

sheer[1] (ʃɪə) a. **1.** perpendicular **2.** (of material) very fine, transparent **3.** absolute, unmitigated

sheer[2] (ʃɪə) vi. deviate from course, swerve, turn aside

sheet[1] (ʃiːt) n. **1.** large piece of cotton etc. to cover bed **2.** broad piece of any thin material **3.** large expanse —vt. **4.** cover with sheet —**sheet music** printed copy of short composition or piece

sheet[2] (ʃiːt) n. rope fastened in corner of sail —**sheet anchor** large anchor for emergency

sheik or **sheikh** (ʃeɪk) n. Arab chief

shekel ('ʃek'l) n. **1.** Jewish weight and silver coin **2.** (oft. pl.) inf. money, cash

shelf (ʃelf) n. **1.** board fixed horizontally (on wall etc.) for holding things **2.** ledge (pl. **shelves**) —**shelf life** length of time packaged food etc. will last without deteriorating

shell (ʃel) n. **1.** hard outer case (esp. of egg, nut etc.) **2.** husk **3.** explosive projectile **4.** outer part of structure left when interior is removed —vt. **5.** take shell from **6.** take out of shell **7.** fire at with shells —'**shellfish** n. **1.** mollusc **2.** crustacean —**shell shock** nervous disorder caused by bursting of shells or bombs —**shell out** inf. pay up

shellac (ʃə'læk, 'ʃelæk) n. **1.** resin usu. produced in thin plates for use as varnish —vt. **2.** coat with shellac (-'**lacked**, -'**lacking**)

shelter ('ʃeltə) n. **1.** place, structure giving protection **2.** protection **3.** refuge; haven —vt. **4.** give protection to **5.** screen —vi. **6.** take shelter

shelve (ʃelv) vt. **1.** put on a shelf **2.** put off, defer indefinitely **3.** cease to employ —vi. **4.** slope gradually —'**shelving** n. **1.** material for making shelves **2.** set of shelves

shelves (ʃelvz) n., pl. of SHELF

shenanigan (ʃɪ'nænɪgən) n. sl. **1.** frolicking **2.** act of playing tricks etc.

shepherd ('ʃepəd) n. **1.** man who tends sheep ('**shepherdess** fem.) —vt. **2.** guide, watch over —**shepherd's pie** chiefly UK dish of minced meat covered with mashed potato —**shepherd's-purse** n. plant with white flowers

sherbet ('ʃɜːbət) n. fruit-flavoured effervescent powder, eaten as sweet or used in drinks

sherd (ʃɜːd) n. see SHARD

sheriff ('ʃerɪf) n. **1.** US law enforcement officer **2.** in England and Wales, chief executive representative of the crown in a county **3.** in Scotland, chief judge of a district **4.** C municipal officer who enforces court orders etc. —'**sheriffdom** n.

Sherpa ('ʃɜːpə) n. member of a Tibetan people (pl. **-s**, '**Sherpa**)

sherry ('ʃerɪ) n. fortified wine

Shetland pony ('ʃetlənd) very small sturdy breed of pony

shewbread or **showbread** ('ʃəʊbred) n. unleavened bread used in Jewish ritual

shield (ʃiːld) n. **1.** piece of armour carried on arm **2.** any protection used to stop blows, missiles etc. **3.** any protective device **4.** sports trophy —vt. **5.** cover, protect

shieling ('ʃiːlɪŋ) n. chiefly Scot. **1.** temporary shelter used by people tending cattle on high ground **2.** grazing ground

shift (ʃɪft) v. **1.** (cause to) move, change position —n. **2.** relay of workers **3.** time of their working **4.** evasion **5.** expedient **6.** removal **7.** woman's underskirt or dress —'**shiftiness** n. —'**shiftless** a. lacking in resource or character —'**shifty** a. **1.** evasive **2.** of dubious character

shillelagh or **shillala** (ʃə'leɪlə, -lɪ) n. in Ireland, cudgel

shilling ('ʃɪlɪŋ) n. **1.** former Brit. coin, now 5p **2.** monetary unit in various countries

shillyshally ('ʃɪlɪʃælɪ) vi. **1.** waver —n. **2.** wavering, indecision

shim (ʃɪm) n. **1.** thin washer used to adjust clearance for gears etc. —vt. **2.** modify clearance on (gear etc.) by use of shims (-**mm-**)

shimmer ('ʃɪmə) vi. **1.** shine with quivering light —n. **2.** such light **3.** glimmer

shimmy ('ʃɪmɪ) n. **1.** Amer. ragtime dance with much shaking of hips and shoulders **2.** abnormal wobbling motion in motor vehicle

shin (ʃɪn) n. **1.** front of lower leg —v. **2.** climb with arms and legs —vt. **3.** kick on shin (-**nn-**) —'**shinbone** n. see TIBIA

shindig ('ʃɪndɪg) or **shindy** ('ʃɪndɪ) n. inf. row; noisy disturbance

shine (ʃaɪn) vi. **1.** give out, reflect light **2.** perform very well, excel —vt. **3.** cause to shine by polishing (**shone**, '**shining**) —n. **4.** brightness, lustre **5.** polishing —'**shiner** n. **1.** something that shines, such as polishing device **2.** small N Amer. freshwater cyprinid fish **3.** inf. black eye —'**shiny** a.

shingle[1] ('ʃɪŋg'l) n. **1.** wooden roof tile —vt. **2.** cover with shingles

shingle[2] ('ʃɪŋg'l) n. mass of pebbles

shingles ('ʃɪŋg'lz) n. disease causing inflammation along a nerve

Shinto ('ʃɪntəʊ) n. native Japanese religion —'**Shintoism** n.

shinty ('ʃɪntɪ) n. **1.** simple form of hockey

played with ball and sticks curved at lower end 2. stick used in this game

ship (ʃip) *n.* 1. large seagoing vessel —*vt.* 2. put on or send by ship —*vi.* 3. embark 4. take service in ship (-**pp**-) —'**shipment** *n.* 1. act of shipping 2. goods shipped —'**shipper** *n.* company *etc.* in business of shipping freight —'**shipping** *n.* 1. freight transport business 2. ships collectively —'**shipboard** *a.* taking place, used, or intended for use aboard ship —'**shipmate** *n.* sailor who serves on same ship as another —'**shipshape** *a.* orderly, trim —'**shipwreck** *n.* 1. destruction of ship through storm, collision *etc.* —*vt.* 2. cause to undergo shipwreck —'**shipwright** *n.* artisan skilled in tasks required to build vessels —'**shipyard** *n.* place for building and repair of ships

-**ship** (*comb. form*) 1. state, condition, as in *fellowship* 2. rank, office, position, as in *lordship* 3. craft, skill, as in *scholarship*

shire (ʃaɪə) *n.* county —**shire horse** large heavy breed of carthorse

shirk (ʃɜːk) *vt.* evade, try to avoid (duty *etc.*)

shirr (ʃɜː) *vt.* 1. gather (fabric) into parallel rows —*n.* 2. series of gathered rows decorating dress *etc.*

shirt (ʃɜːt) *n.* garment for upper part of body —'**shirty** *a. sl.* annoyed —**shirt-tail** *n.* part of shirt that extends below waist —'**shirtwaister** *or U.S.* '**shirtwaist** *n.* woman's dress with bodice resembling shirt

shish kebab ('ʃiːʃ kə'bæb) *see* KEBAB

shiver¹ ('ʃɪvə) *vi.* 1. tremble, usu. with cold or fear; shudder; vibrate —*n.* 2. act, state of shivering

shiver² ('ʃɪvə) *v.* 1. splinter, break in pieces —*n.* 2. splinter

shoal¹ (ʃəʊl) *n.* 1. stretch of shallow water 2. sandbank, sandbar —*v.* 3. make, become shallow

shoal² (ʃəʊl) *n.* 1. large number of fish swimming together —*vi.* 2. form shoal

shock¹ (ʃɒk) *vt.* 1. horrify, scandalize —*n.* 2. violent or damaging blow 3. emotional disturbance 4. state of weakness, illness, caused by physical or mental shock 5. paralytic stroke 6. collision 7. effect on sensory nerves of electric discharge —'**shocker** *n.* person or thing which shocks or distresses —'**shocking** *a.* 1. causing shock, disgust *etc.* 2. *inf.* very bad or terrible —**shock absorber** device, *esp.* in cars, to absorb shocks —**shock therapy** *or* **treatment** treatment of certain psychotic conditions by injecting drugs or by passing electric current through brain

shock² (ʃɒk) *n.* group of corn sheaves placed together

shock³ (ʃɒk) *n.* 1. mass of hair —*a.* 2. shaggy —'**shockheaded** *a.*

shod (ʃɒd) *pt./pp. of* SHOE

shoddy ('ʃɒdɪ) *a.* 1. worthless, trashy 2. second-rate 3. made of poor material

shoe (ʃuː) *n.* 1. covering for foot, not

enclosing ankle 2. metal rim or curved bar put on horse's hoof 3. any of various protective plates or undercoverings —*vt.* 4. protect, furnish with shoe or shoes (**shod** *pt./pp.*, '**shoeing** *pr.p.*) —'**shoehorn** *n.* curved plastic or metal implement, inserted at back of shoe, used to ease in heel —'**shoestring** *a./n.* very small (amount of money *etc.*) —'**shoetree** *n.* wooden or metal block inserted into shoe to preserve shape

shone (ʃɒn; *U.S.* ʃəʊn) *pt./pp. of* SHINE

shoo (ʃuː) *interj.* 1. go away —*vt.* 2. drive away

shook (ʃʊk) *pt. of* SHAKE

shoot (ʃuːt) *vt.* 1. hit, wound, kill with missile fired from weapon 2. send, slide, push rapidly —*v.* 3. discharge (weapon) 4. photograph, film —*vi.* 5. hunt 6. sprout (**shot**, '**shooting**) —*n.* 7. young branch, sprout 8. shooting competition 9. hunting expedition —'**shooter** *n.* —**shooting brake** *UK* estate car —**shooting star** *inf.* meteor —**shooting stick** device resembling walking stick, having spike at one end and folding seat at other

shop (ʃɒp) *n.* 1. place for retail sale of goods and services 2. workshop, works building —*vi.* 3. visit shops to buy —*vt.* 4. *sl.* inform against (-**pp**-) —**shop floor** 1. part of factory housing machines 2. workers in factory —'**shopkeeper** *n.* person who owns or manages shop —'**shoplifter** *n.* one who steals from shop —**shopping centre** 1. area of town where most of shops are situated 2. complex of stores, restaurants *etc.* with adjoining car park —'**shopsoiled** *a.* faded *etc.* from being displayed in shop —**shop steward** trade union representative of workers in factory *etc.* —'**shoptalk** *n.* conversation concerning one's work, *esp.* outside business hours —'**shopwalker** *n.* overseer who directs customers *etc.* —**talk shop** talk of one's business *etc.* at unsuitable moments

shore¹ (ʃɔː) *n.* edge of sea or lake

shore² (ʃɔː) *vt.* (*oft. with* up) prop (up)

shorn (ʃɔːn) *pp. of* SHEAR

short (ʃɔːt) *a.* 1. not long 2. not tall 3. brief, hasty 4. not reaching quantity or standard required 5. wanting, lacking 6. abrupt, rude 7. friable —*adv.* 8. suddenly, abruptly 9. without reaching end —*n.* 10. drink of spirits, as opposed to beer *etc.* 11. short film —*pl.* 12. short trousers —'**shortage** *n.* deficiency —'**shorten** *v.* —'**shortening** *n.* butter, lard or other fat, used in cake mixture *etc.* to make pastry light —'**shortly** *adv.* 1. soon 2. briefly —'**shortcake** *or* '**shortbread** *n.* sweet, brittle cake made of butter, flour and sugar —**shortchange** *vt.* 1. give less than correct change to 2. *sl.* cheat, swindle —**short circuit** faulty connection between two points in electric circuit, establishing path of low resistance through which excessive current can flow —**short-circuit** *v.* 1. develop or cause to develop short circuit —vt. **2.** bypass (procedure etc.) —'**shortcoming** n. failing, defect —**short cut 1.** shorter route than usual one **2.** means of saving time or effort —**short-cut** vi. use short cut —'**shortfall** n. failure to meet requirement —'**shorthand** n. method of rapid writing by signs or contractions —**short-handed** a. lacking the usual or necessary number of workers, helpers —'**shorthorn** n. short-horned breed of cattle with several regional varieties —**short list** selected list of candidates (esp. for job) from which final selection will be made —**short-lived** a. living or lasting only for a short time —**short-range** a. of limited extent in time or distance —**short shrift** summary treatment —**short-sighted** a. **1.** relating to or suffering from myopia **2.** lacking foresight —**short-tempered** a. easily moved to anger —**short-term** a. **1.** extending over limited period **2.** Fin. extending over or maturing within short period of time —**short ton** US ton (2000 lbs.) —**short wave** radio wave between 10 and 50 metres —**short-winded** a. **1.** tending to run out of breath, esp. after exertion **2.** (of speech or writing) abrupt

shot (ʃɒt) n. **1.** act of shooting **2.** missile **3.** lead in small pellets **4.** marksman, shooter **5.** try, attempt **6.** photograph **7.** short film sequence **8.** dose **9.** inf. injection —a. **10.** woven so that colour is different, according to angle of light —v. **11.** pt./pp. of SHOOT —'**shotgun** n. **1.** firearm with unrifled bore used mainly for hunting small game —a. **2.** chiefly US involving coercion or duress —**shot put** athletic event in which contestants hurl heavy metal ball as far as possible

should (ʃʊd) pt. of SHALL

shoulder ('ʃəʊldə) n. **1.** part of body to which arm or foreleg is attached **2.** anything resembling shoulder **3.** side of road —vt. **4.** undertake **5.** bear (burden) **6.** accept (responsibility) **7.** put on one's shoulder —vi. **8.** make way by pushing —**shoulder blade** shoulder bone

shout (ʃaʊt) n. **1.** loud cry —v. **2.** utter (cry etc.) with loud voice

shove (ʃʌv) vt. **1.** push **2.** inf. put —n. **3.** push —**shove off** inf. go away

shovel ('ʃʌvəl) n. **1.** instrument for scooping, lifting earth etc. —vt. **2.** lift, move (as) with shovel (-ll-) —'**shoveler** n. duck with spoon-shaped bill

show (ʃəʊ) vt. **1.** expose to view **2.** point out **3.** display, exhibit **4.** explain; prove **5.** guide **6.** accord (favour etc.) —vi. **7.** appear **8.** be noticeable (showed, shown, 'showing) —n. **9.** display, exhibition **10.** spectacle **11.** theatrical or other entertainment **12.** indication **13.** competitive event **14.** ostentation **15.** semblance **16.** pretence —'**showily** adv. —'**showy** a. gaudy **2.** ostentatious —**show business** entertainment industry (also (inf.) **show biz**) —'**showcase** n. **1.** glass case used for displaying and protecting objects in

museum etc. **2.** setting in which anything may be displayed to best advantage —'**showdown** n. **1.** confrontation **2.** final test —'**showjumping** n. horse-riding competition to demonstrate skill in jumping obstacles —'**showman** n. **1.** one employed in, or owning, show at fair etc. **2.** one skilled at presenting anything in effective way —**show-off** n. —'**showpiece** n. **1.** anything exhibited **2.** anything prized as fine example of its type —**show off 1.** exhibit to invite admiration **2.** behave in such a way as to make an impression —**show up 1.** reveal **2.** expose **3.** inf. embarrass **4.** inf. arrive

shower ('ʃaʊə) n. **1.** short fall of rain **2.** anything coming down like rain **3.** kind of bath in which person stands while being sprayed with water **4.** US party to present gifts to a person, such as a prospective bride —vt. **5.** bestow liberally —vi. **6.** take bath in shower —'**showery** a.

shrank (ʃræŋk) pt. of SHRINK

shrapnel ('ʃræpnʲl) n. **1.** shell filled with pellets which scatter on bursting **2.** shell splinters

shred (ʃred) n. **1.** fragment, torn strip **2.** small amount —vt. **3.** cut, tear to shreds (shred or 'shredded, 'shredding)

shrew (ʃruː) n. **1.** animal like mouse **2.** bad-tempered woman **3.** scold —'**shrewish** a. nagging

shrewd (ʃruːd) a. **1.** astute, intelligent **2.** crafty

shriek (ʃriːk) n. **1.** shrill cry **2.** piercing scream —v. **3.** screech

shrift (ʃrɪft) n. **1.** confession **2.** absolution

shrike (ʃraɪk) n. bird of prey

shrill (ʃrɪl) a. **1.** piercing, sharp in tone —v. **2.** utter (words etc.) in such tone —'**shrilly** adv.

shrimp (ʃrɪmp) n. **1.** small edible crustacean **2.** inf. undersized person —vi. **3.** fish for shrimps

shrine (ʃraɪn) n. place (building, tomb, alcove) of worship, usu. associated with saint

shrink (ʃrɪŋk) vi. **1.** become smaller **2.** retire, flinch, recoil —vt. **3.** make smaller (shrank pt., 'shrunken, shrunk pp., 'shrinking pr.p.) —n. **4.** sl. psychiatrist —'**shrinkage** n. —**shrink-wrap** vt. package (product) in flexible plastic wrapping designed to shrink about its contours

shrivel ('ʃrɪvʲl) vi. shrink and wither (-ll-)

shroud (ʃraʊd) n. **1.** sheet, wrapping, for corpse **2.** anything which covers, envelops like shroud —pl. **3.** set of ropes to masthead —vt. **4.** put shroud on **5.** screen, veil **6.** wrap up

Shrovetide ('ʃrəʊvtaɪd) n. the three days preceding Lent —**Shrove Tuesday** day before Ash Wednesday

shrub (ʃrʌb) n. bushy plant —'**shrubbery** n. plantation, part of garden, filled with shrubs

shrug (ʃrʌg) vi. **1.** raise shoulders, as sign of indifference, ignorance etc. —vt. **2.**

move (shoulders) thus **3.** (*with* off) dismiss as unimportant (**-gg-**) —*n.* **4.** shrugging

shrunk (ʃrʌŋk) *pp. of* SHRINK

shuck (ʃʌk) *n.* shell, husk, pod

shudder ('ʃʌdə) *vi.* **1.** shake, tremble violently, *esp.* with horror —*n.* **2.** shuddering, tremor

shuffle ('ʃʌfˀl) *vi.* **1.** move feet without lifting them **2.** act evasively —*vt.* **3.** mix (cards) **4.** (*with* off) evade, pass to another —*n.* **5.** shuffling **6.** rearrangement —'**shuffler** *n.*

shun (ʃʌn) *vt.* **1.** avoid **2.** keep away from (**-nn-**)

shunt (ʃʌnt) *vt.* **1.** push aside **2.** divert **3.** move (train) from one line to another

shush (ʃuʃ) *interj.* **1.** be quiet, hush —*vt.* **2.** silence or calm by saying 'shush'

shut (ʃʌt) *v.* **1.** close —*vt.* **2.** bar **3.** forbid entrance to (**shut, 'shutting**) —'**shutter** *n.* **1.** movable window screen, usu. hinged to frame **2.** device in camera admitting light as required to film or plate —'**shuteye** *n. sl.* sleep —**shut down** close or stop (factory, machine *etc.*)

shuttle ('ʃʌtˀl) *n.* **1.** instrument which threads weft between threads of warp in weaving **2.** similar appliance in sewing machine **3.** plane, bus *etc.* travelling to and fro over short distance —'**shuttlecock** *n.* small, light cone with cork stub and fan of feathers used as a ball in badminton

shy¹ (ʃaɪ) *a.* **1.** awkward in company **2.** timid, bashful **3.** reluctant **4.** scarce, lacking (*esp.* in card games, not having enough money for bet *etc.*) —*vi.* **5.** start back in fear **6.** show sudden reluctance (**shied, 'shying**) —*n.* **7.** start of fear by horse —'**shyly** *adv.* —'**shyness** *n.*

shy² (ʃaɪ) *vt./n.* throw (**shied, 'shying**)

Shylock ('ʃaɪlɒk) *n.* heartless or demanding creditor

shyster ('ʃaɪstə) *n. sl.* dishonest, deceitful person

si (siː) *n. Mus. see* TE

Si *Chem.* silicon

SI *Fr.* Système International (d'Unités), international system of units of measurement based on units of ten

Siamese (saɪə'miːz) *a.* of Siam, former name of Thailand —**Siamese cat** breed of cat with blue eyes —**Siamese twins** twins born joined to each other by some part of body

sibilant ('sɪbɪlənt) *a.* **1.** hissing —*n.* **2.** speech sound with hissing effect

sibling ('sɪblɪŋ) *n.* person's brother or sister

sibyl ('sɪbɪl) *n.* woman endowed with spirit of prophecy —**sibylline** ('sɪbɪlaɪn) *a.* occult

sic (sɪk) *Lat.* thus: oft. used to call attention to a quoted mistake

sick (sɪk) *a.* **1.** inclined to vomit, vomiting **2.** not well or healthy, physically or mentally **3.** *inf.* macabre, sadistic, morbid **4.** *inf.* bored, tired **5.** *inf.* disgusted —'**sicken** *v.* **1.** make, become sick —*vt.* **2.** disgust; nauseate —'**sickening** *a.* **1.**

causing sickness or revulsion **2.** *inf.* extremely annoying —'**sickly** *a.* **1.** unhealthy, weakly **2.** inducing nausea —'**sickness** *n.* —'**sickbay** *n.* place set aside for treating sick people, *esp.* in ships

sickle ('sɪkˀl) *n.* reaping hook —**sickle cell anaemia** inherited form of anaemia in which large number of red blood cells become sickle-shaped

side (saɪd) *n.* **1.** one of the surfaces of object, *esp.* upright inner or outer surface **2.** either surface of thing having only two **3.** part of body that is to right or left **4.** region nearer or farther than, or right or left of, dividing line *etc.* **5.** region **6.** aspect or part **7.** one of two parties or sets of opponents **8.** sect, faction **9.** line of descent traced through one parent **10.** *sl.* swank, conceit —*a.* **11.** at, in the side **12.** subordinate, incidental —*vi.* **13.** (*usu. with* with) take up cause (of) —'**siding** *n.* short line of rails on which trains or wagons are shunted from main line —**side arms** weapons carried on person, by belt or holster, such as sword, pistol *etc.* —'**sideboard** *n.* piece of furniture for holding dishes *etc.* in dining room —'**sideboards** *pl.n.* UK man's whiskers grown down either side of face in front of ears (*also* US '**sideburns**) —'**sidecar** *n.* small car attached to side of motorcycle —'**sidekick** *n. sl., chiefly* US close friend or follower —'**sidelight** *n.* either of two small lights on front of motor vehicle —'**sideline** *n.* **1.** *Sport* boundary of playing area **2.** subsidiary interest or activity —'**sidelong** *a.* **1.** lateral, not directly forward —*adv.* **2.** obliquely —**side-saddle** *n.* riding saddle orig. designed for women riders in skirts, who sit with both legs on near side of horse —'**sideshow** *n.* **1.** small show offered in conjunction with larger attraction, as at circus **2.** subordinate event —'**sideslip** *n.* skid —'**sidesman** *n.* *Anglican Ch.* man elected to help parish churchwarden —**side-splitting** *a.* **1.** producing great mirth **2.** (of laughter) very hearty —'**sidestep** *v.* **1.** step aside from or out of way of (something) —*vt.* **2.** dodge —**side step** movement to one side, as in boxing *etc.* —'**sidetrack** *v.* **1.** distract or be distracted from main topic —*n.* **2.** digression —'**sidewalk** *n.* US footpath beside road —'**sideways** *adv.* **1.** to or from the side **2.** laterally

sidereal (saɪ'dɪərɪəl) *a.* relating to, fixed by, stars

sidle ('saɪdˀl) *vi.* **1.** move in furtive or stealthy manner **2.** move sideways

SIDS sudden infant death syndrome

siege (siːdʒ) *n.* besieging of town or fortified place

siemens ('siːmənz) *n.* derived SI unit of electrical conductance

sienna (sɪ'ɛnə) *n.* (pigment of) brownish-yellow colour

sierra (sɪ'ɛərə) *n.* range of mountains with jagged peaks

siesta (sɪˈɛstə) n. rest, sleep in afternoon

sieve (sɪv) n. 1. device with network or perforated bottom for sifting —vt. 2. sift 3. strain

sift (sɪft) vt. 1. separate (eg with sieve) coarser portion from finer 2. examine closely

sigh (saɪ) vi./n. (utter) long audible breath —**sigh for** yearn for, grieve for

sight (saɪt) n. 1. faculty of seeing 2. seeing 3. thing seen 4. view 5. glimpse 6. device for guiding eye 7. spectacle 8. inf. pitiful or ridiculous object 9. inf. large number, great deal —vt. 10. catch sight of 11. adjust sights of (gun etc.) —ˈsightless a. —ˈsight-read v. play, sing (music) without previous preparation —ˈsightscreen n. Cricket white screen placed near boundary behind bowler to help batsman see ball —ˈsightsee v. visit (place) to look at interesting sights —ˈsightseeing n.

sigma (ˈsɪgmə) n. 1. 18th letter in Gr. alphabet (Σ, σ or, when final, ς), consonant, transliterated as S 2. Maths. symbol Σ, indicating summation

sign (saɪn) n. 1. mark, gesture etc. to convey some meaning 2. (board, placard bearing) notice, warning etc. 3. symbol 4. omen 5. evidence —vt. 6. put one's signature to 7. ratify —vi. 8. make sign or gesture 9. affix signature —**sign language** any system of communication by signs, esp. used by deaf —ˈsignpost n. 1. post bearing sign that shows way, as at roadside 2. something that serves as indication —vt. 3. mark with signposts

signal (ˈsɪgnˀl) n. 1. sign to convey order or information, esp. on railway 2. that which in first place impels any action 3. Rad. etc. sequence of electrical impulses transmitted or received —a. 4. remarkable, striking —vt. 5. make signals to —vi. 6. give orders etc. by signals (-ll-) —ˈsignalize or -lise vt. make notable —ˈsignally adv. —**signal box** 1. building containing signal levers for railway lines 2. control point for large area of railway system —ˈsignalman n. railway employee in charge of signals

signatory (ˈsɪgnətərɪ) n. one of those who sign agreements, treaties

signature (ˈsɪgnɪtʃə) n. 1. person's name written by himself 2. act of writing it —**signature tune** tune associated with particular programme, person etc.

signet (ˈsɪgnɪt) n. small seal —**signet ring** finger ring bearing signet

significant (sɪgˈnɪfɪkənt) a. 1. revealing 2. designed to make something known 3. important —sigˈnificance n. 1. import, weight 2. meaning —sigˈnificantly adv. —signifiˈcation n. meaning —**significant figures** 1. figures of number that express magnitude to specified degree of accuracy 2. number of such figures

signify (ˈsɪgnɪfaɪ) vt. 1. mean 2. indicate 3. denote 4. imply —vi. 5. be of importance (ˈsignified, ˈsignifying)

signor or **signior** (ˈsiːnjɔː; It. siɲˈɲoːr) n. It. title of respect, like Mr. (pl. -s, -gnori (It. -ˈɲoːri)) —**signora** (siːnˈjɔːrə; It. siɲˈɲoːra) n. Mrs. (pl. -s, -re (It. -re)) —**signorina** (siːnjɔːˈriːnə; It. siɲɲoˈriːna) n. Miss (pl. -s, -ne (It. -ne))

Sikh (siːk) n. member of Indian religious sect

silage (ˈsaɪlɪdʒ) n. fodder crop harvested while green and stored in state of partial fermentation

silence (ˈsaɪləns) n. 1. absence of noise 2. refraining from speech —vt. 3. make silent 4. put a stop to —ˈsilencer n. device to reduce noise of engine exhaust, firearm —ˈsilent a.

silhouette (sɪluːˈɛt) n. 1. outline of object seen against light 2. profile portrait in black

silica (ˈsɪlɪkə) n. naturally occurring dioxide of silicon —siliceous or silicious (sɪˈlɪʃəs) a. —siliˈcosis n. lung disease caused by inhaling silica dust over a long period

silicon (ˈsɪlɪkən) n. brittle metalloid element found in sand, clay, stone, widely used in chemistry, industry —ˈsilicone n. large class of synthetic substances, related to silicon and used in chemistry, industry and medicine —**silicon chip** see CHIP (sense 4)

silk (sɪlk) n. 1. fibre made by larvae (**silkworm**) of certain moth 2. thread, fabric made from this —ˈsilken a. 1. made of, like silk 2. soft 3. smooth 4. dressed in silk —ˈsilkily adv. —ˈsilkiness n. —ˈsilky a. —**silk hat** man's top hat covered with silk —**silk-screen** n. stencil process of printing a design through screen of fine mesh cloth

sill (sɪl) n. 1. ledge beneath window 2. bottom part of door or window frame

sillabub (ˈsɪləbʌb) n. see SYLLABUB

silly (ˈsɪlɪ) a. 1. foolish 2. trivial 3. feeble-minded —ˈsilliness n.

silo (ˈsaɪləʊ) n. 1. pit, tower for storing fodder or grain 2. underground missile launching site (pl. -s)

silt (sɪlt) n. 1. mud deposited by water —v. 2. fill, be choked with silt —silˈtation n. —ˈsilty a.

Silurian (saɪˈlʊərɪən) a. 1. of or formed in third period of Palaeozoic era, during which fishes first appeared —n. 2. Silurian period or rock system

silvan (ˈsɪlvən) a. see SYLVAN

silver (ˈsɪlvə) n. 1. white precious metal 2. things made of it 3. silver coins 4. cutlery —a. 5. made of silver 6. resembling silver or its colour 7. having pale lustre, as moon 8. soft, melodious, as sound 9. bright —vt. 10. coat with silver —ˈsilvery a. —**silver birch** tree having silvery-white peeling bark —**silver jubilee** 25th anniversary —**silver lining** hopeful aspect of otherwise desperate situation —**silver plate** 1. thin layer of silver deposited on base metal 2. articles, esp. tableware, made of silver plate —**silver-plate** *vt.* coat (metal *etc.*) with silver —**silver screen** *inf.* 1. films collectively 2. screen on to which films are projected —**'silverside** *n.* UK cut of beef below aitchbone and above leg —**'silversmith** *n.* craftsman who makes articles of silver —**silver wedding** 25th wedding anniversary

silviculture ('sɪlvɪkʌltʃə) *n.* branch of forestry concerned with cultivation of trees

simian ('sɪmɪən) *a.* of, like apes

similar ('sɪmɪlə) *a.* resembling, like —**simi'larity** *n.* likeness, close resemblance

simile ('sɪmɪlɪ) *n.* comparison of one thing with another, using *as* or *like*, *esp.* in poetry

similitude (sɪ'mɪlɪtjuːd) *n.* 1. outward appearance, likeness 2. guise

simmer ('sɪmə) *v.* 1. keep or be just bubbling or just below boiling point —*vi.* 2. be in state of suppressed anger or laughter

simnel cake ('sɪmn'l) UK fruit cake covered with layer of marzipan

simper ('sɪmpə) *v.* 1. smile, utter in silly or affected way —*n.* 2. simpering smile

simple ('sɪmp'l) *a.* 1. not complicated 2. plain 3. not combined or complex 4. ordinary, mere 5. guileless 6. stupid —**'simpleton** *n.* foolish person —**sim'plicity** *n.* 1. simpleness 2. clearness 3. artlessness —**simplifi'cation** *n.* —**'simplify** *vt.* make simple, plain or easy (**-plified, -plifying**) —**sim'plistic** *a.* very simple, naive —**'simply** *adv.* —**simple fraction** fraction in which both the numerator and the denominator are integers —**simple fracture** fracture in which broken bone does not pierce skin —**simple interest** interest paid on principal alone —**simple-minded** *a.* 1. stupid; feeble-minded 2. mentally defective 3. unsophisticated —**simple-mindedness** *n.* —**simple sentence** sentence consisting of single main clause

simulate ('sɪmjʊleɪt) *vt.* 1. make pretence of 2. reproduce, copy (*esp.* conditions of particular situation) —**simu'lation** *n.* —**'simulator** *n.*

simultaneous (sɪməl'teɪnɪəs) *a.* occurring at the same time —**simultaneity** (sɪməltə'niːɪtɪ) *or* **simul'taneousness** *n.* —**simul'taneously** *adv.*

sin[1] (sɪn) *n.* 1. transgression of divine or moral law, *esp.* committed consciously 2. offence against principle or standard —*vi.* 3. commit sin (**-nn-**) —**'sinful** *a.* 1. of nature of sin 2. guilty of sin —**'sinfully** *adv.* —**'sinner** *n.* —**sin bin** C *sl.* penalty box used in ice hockey

sin[2] *Maths.* sine

SIN C Social Insurance Number

since (sɪns) *prep.* 1. during or throughout period of time after —*conj.* 2. from time when 3. because —*adv.* 4. from that time

sincere (sɪn'sɪə) *a.* 1. not hypocritical, actually moved by or feeling apparent emotions 2. true, genuine 3. unaffected —**sin'cerely** *adv.* —**sincerity** (sɪn'sɛrɪtɪ) *n.*

sine (saɪn) *n.* mathematical function, *esp.* ratio of length of hypotenuse to opposite side in right-angled triangle

sinecure ('saɪnɪkjʊə) *n.* office with pay but minimal duties

sine die ('saɪnɪ 'daɪɪ) *Lat.* with no date, indefinitely postponed

sine qua non ('saɪnɪ kweɪ 'nɒn) *Lat.* essential condition or requirement

sinew ('sɪnjuː) *n.* 1. tough, fibrous cord joining muscle to bone —*pl.* 2. muscles, strength —**'sinewy** *a.* 1. stringy 2. muscular

sing (sɪŋ) *vi.* 1. utter musical sounds 2. hum, whistle, ring —*vt.* 3. utter (words) with musical modulation 4. celebrate in song or poetry (**sang, sung, 'singing**) —**'singer** *n.* —**'singsong** *n.* 1. informal singing session —*a.* 2. monotonously regular in tone, rhythm

singe (sɪndʒ) *vt.* 1. burn surface of (**singed, 'singeing**) —*n.* 2. act or effect of singeing

Singh (sɪŋ) *n.* title assumed by Sikh on becoming full member of community

single ('sɪŋg'l) *a.* 1. one only 2. alone, separate 3. unmarried 4. for one 5. formed of only one part, fold *etc.* 6. denoting ticket for train *etc.* valid for outward journey only 7. whole-hearted, straightforward —*n.* 8. single thing 9. gramophone record with one short item on each side 10. single ticket —*vt.* 11. (*with* out) pick (out) —**'singleton** *n.* 1. *Bridge etc.* original holding of one card only in suit 2. single object as distinguished from pair or group 3. *Maths.* set containing only one member —**'singly** *adv.* —**single-breasted** *a.* (of garment) overlapping only slightly and with one row of fastenings —**single entry** *Book-keeping* entered in one account only —**single file** persons, things arranged in one line —**single-handed** *a./adv.* without assistance —**single-minded** *a.* having but one aim or purpose —**single-mindedness** *n.*

singlet ('sɪŋglɪt) *n.* sleeveless undervest

singular ('sɪŋgjʊlə) *a.* 1. remarkable 2. unusual 3. unique 4. denoting one person or thing —**singu'larity** *n.* something unusual —**'singularly** *adv.* 1. particularly 2. peculiarly

Sinhalese (sɪnhə'liːz) *or* **Singhalese** (sɪŋə'liːz) *n.* 1. member of people living chiefly in Sri Lanka 2. language of this people —*a.* 3. of this people or their language

sinister ('sɪnɪstə) *a.* 1. threatening 2. evil-looking 3. wicked 4. unlucky 5. *Her.* on left-hand side

sink (sɪŋk) *vi.* 1. become submerged (in water) 2. drop, give way 3. decline in value, health *etc.* 4. penetrate —*vt.* 5. cause to sink 6. make by digging out 7. invest (**sank** *pt.*, **sunk**, **'sunken** *pp.*, **'sinking** *pr.p.*) —*n.* 8. receptacle with pipe for carrying away waste water 9. cesspool 10. place of corruption, vice —**'sinker** *n.*

weight for fishing line —**sinking fund** money set aside at intervals for payment of particular liability at fixed date

Sinn Fein ('ʃɪn 'feɪn) Irish republican political movement

Sino- (*comb. form*) Chinese, of China, as in *Sino-Tibetan*

Sinology (saɪ'nɒlədʒɪ) *n.* study of Chinese history, language, culture *etc.* —**Sinological** (saɪnə'lɒdʒɪk'l) *a.* —**Si'nologist** *n.*

sinuous ('sɪnjʊəs) *a.* 1. curving 2. devious 3. lithe —**'sinuate** *a.* —**sinu'osity** *n.*

sinus ('saɪnəs) *n.* cavity, *esp.* any of air passages in bones of skull —**sinu'sitis** *n.* inflammation of sinus

Sion ('saɪən) *n. see* ZION

sip (sɪp) *v.* 1. drink in very small portions (**-pp-**) —*n.* 2. small drink

siphon *or* **syphon** ('saɪf'n) *n.* 1. device, *esp.* bent tube, which uses atmospheric or gaseous pressure to draw liquid from container —*vt.* 2. draw off thus 3. draw off in small amounts

sir (sɜː) *n.* 1. polite term of address for a man 2. (**S-**) title of knight or baronet

sire (saɪə) *n.* 1. male parent, *esp.* of horse or domestic animal 2. term of address to king —*vt.* 3. beget

siren ('saɪərən) *n.* 1. device making loud wailing noise, *esp.* giving warning of danger 2. legendary sea nymph who lured sailors to destruction 3. alluring woman

Sirius ('sɪrɪəs) *n.* brightest star in sky, lying in constellation Canis Major (*also* **Dog Star**)

sirloin ('sɜːlɔɪn) *n.* prime cut of loin of beef

sirocco (sɪ'rɒkəʊ) *n.* hot oppressive wind beginning in N Afr. and reaching S Europe (*pl.* **-s**)

sisal ('saɪs'l) *n.* (fibre of) plant used in making ropes

siskin ('sɪskɪn) *n.* small olive-green bird of finch family

sissy ('sɪsɪ) *a./n.* weak, cowardly (person)

sister ('sɪstə) *n.* 1. daughter of same parents 2. woman fellow-member, *esp.* of religious body 3. senior nurse —*a.* 4. closely related, similar —**'sisterhood** *n.* relation of sister 2. order, band of women —**'sisterly** *a.* —**sister-in-law** *n.* 1. sister of husband or wife 2. brother's wife

sit (sɪt) *vi.* 1. adopt posture or rest on buttocks, thighs 2. perch 3. (of bird) cover eggs to hatch them 4. pose for portrait 5. occupy official position 6. hold session 7. remain 8. keep watch over baby *etc.* —*vt.* 9. take (examination) (**sat**, **'sitting**) —**'sitter** *n.* 1. person or animal that sits 2. person who is posing for portrait 3. *see* **baby-sitter** at BABY —**'sitting** *n.* 1. continuous period of being seated 2. in canteen *etc.*, such period during which one of two or more meals is served 3. meeting, *esp.* of official body 4. incubation period of bird's eggs during which mother sits on them —**sit-down** *a.* (of meal *etc.*) eaten while sitting down at table —**sit-**

down strike strike in which employees refuse to leave their place of employment —**sit-in** *n.* protest involving refusal to move from place —**sitting duck** *inf.* person or thing in defenceless position —**sitting tenant** tenant already occupying flat *etc.* —**sit down** 1. adopt sitting posture 2. (*with* under) suffer (insults *etc.*) without protest —**sit in** protest by sit-in

sitar (sɪ'tɑː) *n.* stringed musical instrument, *esp.* of India

site (saɪt) *n.* 1. place, location 2. space for, with, a building —*vt.* 3. locate in specific place

situate ('sɪtjʊeɪt) *vt.* place, locate —**situ'a-tion** *n.* 1. place, position 2. state of affairs 3. employment, post —**situation comedy** comedy based on humorous situations that could arise in day-to-day life

six (sɪks) *a./n.* cardinal number one more than five —**'six'teen** *n./a.* six and ten —**sixth** *a.* 1. ordinal number of six —*n.* 2. sixth part —**'sixty** *n./a.* six times ten —**six-shooter** *n.* US *inf.* revolver with six chambers —**sixth sense** any supposed means of perception, such as intuition

size[1] (saɪz) *n.* 1. bigness, dimensions 2. one of series of standard measurements of clothes *etc.* 3. *inf.* state of affairs —*vt.* 4. arrange according to size —**'sizable** *or* **'sizeable** *a.* quite large —**size up** *inf.* assess (person, situation *etc.*)

size[2] (saɪz) *n.* 1. gluelike sealer, filler —*vt.* 2. coat, treat with size

sizzle ('sɪz'l) *vi./n.* (make) hissing, spluttering sound, as of frying —**'sizzler** *n. inf.* hot day

SJA Saint John's Ambulance (Brigade *or* Association)

SK Saskatchewan

skate[1] (skeɪt) *n.* 1. steel blade attached to boot, for gliding over ice —*vi.* 2. glide as on skates —**'skateboard** *n.* small board mounted on roller-skate wheels

skate[2] (skeɪt) *n.* large marine ray

skean-dhu (skiːən'duː) *n.* dagger worn in stocking as part of Highland dress

skedaddle (skɪ'dæd'l) *vi. inf.* scamper off

skein (skeɪn) *n.* 1. quantity of yarn, wool *etc.* in loose knot 2. flight of wildfowl

skeleton ('skɛlɪtən) *n.* 1. bones of animal 2. bones separated from flesh and preserved in their natural position 3. very thin person 4. outline, draft, framework 5. nucleus —*a.* 6. reduced to a minimum 7. drawn in outline 8. not in detail —**'skeletal** *a.* —**skeleton key** key filed down so as to open many different locks

skeptic ('skɛptɪk) *n.* US *see* SCEPTIC

skerry ('skɛrɪ) *n.* rocky island or reef

sketch (skɛtʃ) *n.* 1. rough drawing 2. brief account 3. essay 4. short humorous play —*v.* 5. make sketch (of) —**'sketchy** *a.* 1. omitting detail 2. incomplete 3. inadequate

skew (skjuː) *vi.* 1. move obliquely —*a.* 2. slanting 3. crooked —**'skew'whiff** *a. inf.* aslant 2. crooked

skewbald ('skjuːbɔːld) *a.* (*esp.* of horse)

white and any other colour (except black) in patches

skewer ('skjuə) n. 1. pin to fasten meat together —vt. 2. pierce or fasten with skewer

ski (skiː) n. 1. long runner fastened to foot for sliding over snow or water (pl. -s, ski) —vi. 2. slide on skis (**skied**, '**skiing**) —**ski jump** ramp overhanging slope from which skiers compete to make longest jump —**ski-jump** vi.

skid (skɪd) v. 1. (cause (esp. vehicle) to) slide (sideways) out of control with wheels not revolving (**-dd-**) —n. 2. instance of this 3. device to facilitate sliding, eg in moving heavy objects —'**skidpan** n. area made slippery so that drivers can practise controlling skids —**skid row** or **road** sl., chiefly US dilapidated section of city inhabited by vagrants etc.

skidoo ('skiduː) n. C snowmobile

skiff (skɪf) n. small boat

skill (skɪl) n. practical ability, cleverness, dexterity —'**skilful** or U.S. '**skillful** a. expert, masterly, adroit —'**skilfully** or U.S. '**skillfully** adv. —**skilled** a. having, requiring knowledge, united with readiness and dexterity

skillet ('skɪlɪt) n. small frying pan

skim (skɪm) vt. 1. remove floating matter from surface of (liquid) 2. glide over lightly and rapidly 3. read thus —vi. 4. move thus (**-mm-**) —**skim** or **skimmed milk** milk from which cream has been removed

skimp (skɪmp) v. 1. give short measure (on) 2. do (thing) imperfectly —'**skimpy** a. 1. meagre 2. scanty

skin (skɪn) n. 1. outer covering of vertebrate body, lower animal or fruit 2. animal skin used as material or container 3. film on surface of cooling liquid etc. 4. complexion —vt. 5. remove skin of (**-nn-**) —'**skinless** a. —'**skinned** a. 1. stripped of skin 2. having skin of specified kind —'**skinner** n. 1. dealer in hides 2. furrier —'**skinny** a. thin —**skin-deep** a. 1. superficial 2. slight —**skin diving** underwater swimming using breathing apparatus —**skin flick** film containing much nudity and explicit sex scenes —'**skinflint** n. miser, niggard —**skin graft** transplant of piece of healthy skin to wound to form new skin —'**skintight** a. fitting close to skin —**keep one's eyes skinned** watch carefully

skint (skɪnt) a. sl. without money

skip[1] (skɪp) vi. 1. leap lightly 2. jump a rope as it is swung under one —vt. 3. pass over, omit (**-pp-**) —n. 4. act of skipping —**skipping-rope** n. UK cord that is held in hands and swung round so that holder or others can jump over it

skip[2] (skɪp) n. 1. large open container for builders' rubbish etc. 2. large bucket, container for transporting men, materials in mines etc.

skipper ('skɪpə) n. 1. captain of ship, plane or team —vt. 2. captain

skirl (skɜːl) n. sound of bagpipes

skirmish ('skɜːmɪʃ) n. 1. fight between small parties, small battle —vi. 2. fight briefly or irregularly

skirt (skɜːt) n. 1. woman's garment hanging from waist 2. lower part of woman's dress, coat etc. 3. outlying part 4. sl. woman —vt. 5. border 6. go round —'**skirting** n. 1. vertical board round margin of floor (also **skirting board**) 2. material for women's skirts

skit (skɪt) n. satire, esp. theatrical burlesque

skittish ('skɪtɪʃ) a. frisky, frivolous

skittles ('skɪt'lz) pl.n. ninepins

skive (skaɪv) v. evade (work or responsibility)

skivvy ('skɪvɪ) n. female servant who does menial work

skokiaan ('skɔːkɪɑːn) n. SA potent alcoholic beverage

skua ('skjuːə) n. large predatory gull

skulduggery or U.S. **skullduggery** (skʌl-'dʌgərɪ) n. inf. trickery

skulk (skʌlk) vi. 1. sneak out of the way 2. lurk

skull (skʌl) n. bony case that encloses brain —**skull and crossbones** picture of human skull above two crossed thighbones, used as warning of danger or death —'**skullcap** n. close-fitting cap

skunk (skʌŋk) n. 1. small N Amer. animal which emits evil-smelling fluid 2. sl. mean person

sky (skaɪ) n. 1. apparently dome-shaped expanse extending upwards from the horizon 2. outer space 3. heavenly regions (pl. **skies**) —vt. 4. hit (cricket ball) high —'**skydiving** n. parachute jumping with delayed opening of parachute —**sky-high** a./adv. 1. at or to unprecedented level —adv. 2. high into air —'**skyjack** vt. hijack (an aircraft) —'**skylark** n. 1. lark, noted for singing while hovering at great height —vi. 2. inf. romp or play jokes —'**skylight** n. window in roof or ceiling —'**skyline** n. 1. line at which earth and sky appear to meet 2. outline of trees etc. seen against sky —'**skyscraper** n. very tall building —**blow sky-high** destroy

Skye terrier (skaɪ) short-legged breed of terrier with long wiry hair

slab (slæb) n. thick, broad piece

slack[1] (slæk) a. 1. loose 2. sluggish 3. careless, negligent 4. not busy —n. 5. loose part, as of rope —vi. 6. be idle or lazy —'**slacken** v. 1. make or become looser 2. make or become slower —'**slacker** n. person who evades work —'**slackly** adv. —**slack water** period of still water around turn of tide

slack[2] (slæk) n. coal dust, small pieces of coal

slacks (slæks) pl.n. informal trousers worn by men or women

slag (slæg) n. 1. refuse of smelted metal 2.

sl. coarse woman —**slag heap** hillock of waste matter from coal-mining *etc.*

slain (sleɪn) *pp. of* SLAY

slake (sleɪk) *vt.* 1. satisfy (thirst, desire *etc.*) 2. combine (lime) with water to produce calcium hydroxide

slalom ('slɑːləm) *n.* race over winding course in skiing *etc.*

slam (slæm) *v.* 1. shut noisily 2. bang —*vt.* 3. hit 4. dash down 5. *inf.* criticize harshly (-**mm-**) —*n.* 6. (noise of) this action —**grand slam** *Cards* winning of all tricks

slander ('slɑːndə) *n.* 1. false or malicious statement about person —*vt.* 2. utter such statement (about) —'**slanderer** *n.* —'**slanderous** *a.*

slang (slæŋ) *n.* 1. colloquial language —*vt.* 2. *sl.* scold, abuse violently

slant (slɑːnt) *v.* 1. slope —*vt.* 2. put at angle 3. write, present (news *etc.*) with bias —*n.* 4. slope 5. point of view 6. idea —*a.* 7. sloping, oblique —'**slantwise** *or* '**slantways** *adv.*

slap (slæp) *n.* 1. blow with open hand or flat instrument —*vt.* 2. strike thus 3. *inf.* put (on, down) carelessly or messily (-**pp-**) —'**slapdash** *a.* careless and abrupt —'**slaphappy** *a. inf.* cheerfully irresponsible 2. dazed as if from repeated blows —'**slapstick** *n.* boisterous knockabout comedy —**slap-up** *a.* UK *inf.* (*esp.* of meals) lavish

slash (slæʃ) *vt.* 1. gash 2. lash 3. cut, slit 4. criticize unmercifully —*n.* 5. gash 6. cutting stroke

slat (slæt) *n.* narrow strip of wood or metal as in blinds *etc.*

slate (sleɪt) *n.* 1. kind of stone which splits easily in flat sheets 2. piece of this for covering roof or, formerly, for writing on —*vt.* 3. cover with slates 4. abuse —'**slating** *n.* severe reprimand

slater ('sleɪtə) *n.* woodlouse

slattern ('slætən) *n.* slut —'**slatternly** *a.* slovenly, untidy

slaughter ('slɔːtə) *n.* 1. killing —*vt.* 2. kill —'**slaughterous** *a.* —'**slaughterhouse** *n.* place for killing animals for food

Slav (slɑːv) *n.* member of any of peoples of E Europe or Soviet Asia who speak Slavonic language —**Sla'vonic** *or* '**Slavic** *n.* 1. branch of Indo-European family of languages, including Bulgarian, Russian, Polish, Czech *etc.* —*a.* 2. of this group of languages

slave (sleɪv) *n.* 1. captive, person without freedom or personal rights 2. one dominated by another or by a habit *etc.* —*vi.* 3. work like slave —'**slaver** *n.* person, ship engaged in slave traffic —'**slavery** *n.* —'**slavish** *a.* servile —**slave-driver** *n.* 1. *esp.* formerly, person forcing slaves to work 2. employer demanding excessively hard work from employees

slaver ('slævə) *vi.* 1. dribble saliva from mouth 2. fawn —*n.* 3. saliva running from mouth

slaw (slɔː) *n. chiefly US short for* COLESLAW

slay (sleɪ) *vt.* 1. kill 2. *inf.* impress, *esp.* by being very funny (**slew, slain,** '**slaying**)

sleazy ('sliːzɪ) *a.* sordid

sledge¹ (slɛdʒ) *or* (*esp. U.S.*) **sled** (slɛd) *n.* 1. carriage on runners for sliding on snow 2. toboggan —*v.* 3. convey, travel by sledge

sledge² (slɛdʒ) *n.* heavy hammer with long handle (*also* '**sledgehammer**)

sleek (sliːk) *a.* glossy, smooth, shiny

sleep (sliːp) *n.* 1. unconscious state regularly occurring in man and animals 2. slumber, repose 3. *inf.* dried particles *oft.* found in corners of eyes after sleeping —*vi.* 4. take rest in sleep, slumber (**slept,** '**sleeping**) —'**sleeper** *n.* 1. one who sleeps 2. beam supporting rails of railway 3. railway sleeping car —'**sleepily** *adv.* —'**sleepiness** *n.* —'**sleepless** *a.* —'**sleepy** *a.* —**sleeping bag** large well-padded bag for sleeping in, *esp.* outdoors —**sleeping car** railway car fitted with compartments containing bunks for sleeping in —**sleeping partner** partner in business who does not play active role (*also* **silent partner**) —**sleeping policeman** protuberance built across roads to deter motorists from speeding —**sleeping sickness** Afr. disease spread by tsetse fly —'**sleepwalk** *vi.* walk while asleep

sleet (sliːt) *n.* rain and snow or hail falling together

sleeve (sliːv) *n.* 1. part of garment which covers arm 2. case surrounding shaft 3. gramophone record cover —*vt.* 4. furnish with sleeves —**sleeved** *a.* —'**sleeveless** *a.* —**have (something) up one's sleeve** have (something) prepared secretly for emergency

sleigh (sleɪ) *n.* sledge

sleight (slaɪt) *n.* 1. dexterity 2. trickery 3. deviousness —**sleight of hand** 1. (manual dexterity in) conjuring, juggling 2. legerdemain

slender ('slɛndə) *a.* 1. slim, slight 2. feeble

slept (slɛpt) *pt./pp. of* SLEEP

sleuth (sluːθ) *n.* 1. detective 2. tracking dog (*also* '**sleuthhound**) —*vt.* 3. track

slew¹ (sluː) *pt. of* SLAY

slew² *or esp. U.S.* **slue** (sluː) *v.* swing round

slice (slaɪs) *n.* 1. thin flat piece cut off 2. share 3. flat culinary tool —*vt.* 4. cut into slices 5. cut cleanly 6. hit (ball) with bat *etc.* at angle

slick (slɪk) *a.* 1. smooth 2. smooth-tongued 3. flattering 4. superficially attractive 5. sly —*vt.* 6. make glossy, smooth —*n.* 7. slippery area 8. patch of oil on water

slide (slaɪd) *vi.* 1. slip smoothly along 2. glide, as over ice 3. deteriorate morally —*v.* 4. pass imperceptibly (**slid** (slɪd) *pt.,* **slid, slidden** ('slɪdᵊn) *pp.,* '**sliding** *pr.p.*) —*n.* 5. sliding 6. surface, track for sliding 7. sliding part of mechanism 8. piece of glass holding object to be viewed under microscope 9. photographic transparency 10. ornamental clip to hold hair in place, hair slide —**slide rule** mathematical instrument of two parts, one of which slides upon the other, for rapid calculations —**sliding scale** schedule for automatically varying one thing (*eg* wages) according to fluctuations of another (*eg* cost of living)

slight (slaɪt) *a.* 1. small, trifling 2. not substantial, fragile 3. slim, slender —*vt.* 4. disregard 5. neglect —*n.* 6. indifference 7. act of discourtesy —**'slightly** *adv.*

slim (slɪm) *a.* 1. thin 2. slight —*v.* 3. make or become slim by diet and exercise (-**mm**-)

slime (slaɪm) *n.* greasy, thick, liquid mud or similar substance —**'slimy** *a.* 1. like slime 2. fawning

sling[1] (slɪŋ) *n.* 1. strap, loop with string attached at each end for hurling stone 2. bandage for supporting wounded limb 3. rope, belt *etc.* for hoisting, carrying weights —*vt.* 4. throw 5. hoist, swing by rope (**slung, 'slinging**) —**'slingback** *n.* shoe with strap instead of full covering for heel

slink (slɪŋk) *vi.* move stealthily, sneak (**slunk, 'slinking**) —**'slinky** *a.* 1. sinuously graceful 2. (of clothes *etc.*) figure-hugging

slip[1] (slɪp) *v.* 1. (cause to) move smoothly, easily, quietly 2. pass out of (mind *etc.*) 3. (of motor vehicle clutch) engage partially, fail —*vi.* 4. lose balance by sliding 5. fall from person's grasp 6. (*usu. with* up) make mistake 7. decline in health, morals —*vt.* 8. put on or take off easily, quickly 9. let go (anchor *etc.*) 10. dislocate (bone) (-**pp**-) —*n.* 11. act or occasion of slipping 12. mistake 13. petticoat 14. small piece of paper 15. plant cutting 16. launching slope on which ships are built 17. *Cricket* (fieldsman in) position offside and a little behind wicket 18. covering for pillow —**'slippy** *a. see* SLIPPERY (sense 1) 2. UK *inf.* alert —**'slipknot** *n.* knot tied so that it will slip along rope round which it is made (*also* **running knot**) —**slip-on** *a.* 1. (of garment or shoe) easily put on or removed —*n.* 2. slip-on garment or shoe —**slipped disc** *Pathol.* herniated intervertebral disc, oft. resulting in pain due to pressure on spinal nerves —**slip road** narrow road giving access to motorway *etc.* —**'slipshod** *a.* slovenly, careless —**'slipstream** *n. Aviation* stream of air driven astern by engine —**slip-up** *n. inf.* mistake or mishap —**'slipway** *n.* incline for launching ships —**slip up** *inf.* blunder

slip[2] (slɪp) *n.* clay mixed with water to creamy consistency, used for decorating ceramic ware

slipper ('slɪpə) *n.* light shoe for indoor use

slippery ('slɪpərɪ, -prɪ) *a.* 1. so smooth as to cause slipping or to be difficult to hold or catch 2. changeable 3. unreliable 4. crafty, wily

slit (slɪt) *vt.* 1. make long straight cut in 2. cut in strips (**slit, 'slitting**) —*n.* 3. long narrow cut or opening

slither ('slɪðə) *vi.* slide unsteadily (down slope *etc.*)

sliver ('slɪvə) *n.* 1. thin small piece torn off something 2. splinter

slob (slɒb) *n. inf.* stupid, coarse person

slobber ('slɒbə) *or* **slabber** ('slæbə) *vi.* 1. slaver 2. be weakly and excessively demonstrative —*n.* 3. running saliva 4. maudlin speech —**'slobbery** *or* **'slabbery** *a.*

slob ice C sludgy masses of floating ice

sloe (sləʊ) *n.* blue-black, sour fruit of blackthorn —**sloe-eyed** *a.* having dark slanted or almond-shaped eyes

slog (slɒg) *vt.* 1. hit vigorously, *esp.* at cricket —*vi.* 2. work or study with dogged determination 3. move, work with difficulty (-**gg**-) —*n.* 4. tiring walk 5. long exhausting work 6. heavy blow

slogan ('sləʊgən) *n.* distinctive phrase (in advertising *etc.*)

sloop (sluːp) *n.* 1. small one-masted vessel 2. *Hist.* small warship

sloot (sluːt) *n.* SA ditch for irrigation or drainage

slop (slɒp) *vi.* 1. spill —*vt.* 2. spill, splash (-**pp**-) —*n.* 3. liquid spilt 4. liquid food 5. dirty liquid —*pl.* 6. liquid refuse —**'sloppy** *a.* 1. careless, untidy 2. sentimental 3. wet, muddy

slope (sləʊp) *vt.* 1. place slanting —*vi.* 2. lie in, follow an inclined course 3. go furtively —*n.* 4. slant 5. upward, downward inclination

slosh (slɒʃ) *n.* 1. watery mud, snow *etc.* 2. *sl.* heavy blow —*v.* 3. splash —*vt.* 4. hit —**sloshed** *a. sl.* drunk

slot (slɒt) *n.* 1. narrow hole or depression 2. slit for coins —*vt.* 3. put in slot 4. sort 5. *inf.* place in series, organization (-**tt**-) —**slot machine** automatic machine worked by insertion of coin

sloth (sləʊθ) *n.* 1. sluggish S Amer. animal 2. sluggishness —**'slothful** *a.* lazy, idle

slouch (slaʊtʃ) *vi.* 1. walk, sit *etc.* in lazy or ungainly, drooping manner —*n.* 2. drooping bearing 3. incompetent or slovenly person —*a.* 4. (of hat) with wide, flexible brim

slough[1] (slaʊ) *n.* 1. bog 2. (sluː) C hole where water collects

slough[2] (slʌf) *n.* 1. skin shed by snake —*v.* 2. shed (skin) —**slough off** cast off (cares *etc.*)

sloven ('slʌv³n) *n.* dirty, untidy person —**'slovenly** *a.* 1. untidy 2. careless 3. disorderly —*adv.* 4. in slovenly manner

slow (sləʊ) *a.* 1. lasting a long time 2. moving at low speed 3. behind the true time 4. dull —*v.* 5. (cause to) decrease in speed —**'slowly** *adv.* —**'slowness** *n.* —**'slowcoach** *n.* person slow in moving, acting, deciding *etc.* —**slow-motion** *a.* (of film) showing movement greatly slowed down

slowworm ('sləʊwɜːm) *n.* small legless lizard, blindworm

sludge (slʌdʒ) *n.* 1. slush, ooze 2. sewage

slue[1] (sluː) *v. esp. US see* SLEW[2]

slue[2] (sluː) *n. see* SLOUGH[1] (sense 2)

slug¹ (slʌg) *n.* **1.** land snail with no shell **2.** bullet —**'sluggard** *n.* lazy, idle person —**'sluggish** *a.* **1.** slow **2.** lazy, inert **3.** not functioning well

slug² (slʌg) *vt.* **1.** hit, slog (**-gg-**) —*n.* **2.** heavy blow **3.** portion of spirits —**'slugger** *n.* hard-hitting boxer, slogger

sluice (sluːs) *n.* **1.** gate, door to control flow of water —*vt.* **2.** pour water over, through

slum (slʌm) *n.* **1.** squalid street or neighbourhood —*vi.* **2.** visit slums (**-mm-**)

slumber (ˈslʌmbə) *vi./n.* sleep —**'slumberer** *n.*

slump (slʌmp) *vi.* **1.** fall heavily **2.** relax ungracefully **3.** decline suddenly in value, volume or esteem —*n.* **4.** sudden decline **5.** (of prices *etc.*) sharp fall **6.** depression

slung (slʌŋ) *pt./pp.* of SLING

slunk (slʌŋk) *pt./pp.* of SLINK

slur (slɜː) *vt.* **1.** pass over lightly **2.** run together (words, musical notes) **3.** disparage (**-rr-**) —*n.* **4.** slight, stigma **5.** *Mus.* curved line above or below notes to be slurred

slurp (slɜːp) *v. inf.* eat, drink noisily

slurry (ˈslʌrɪ) *n.* muddy liquid mixture, such as cement, mud *etc.*

slush (slʌʃ) *n.* **1.** watery, muddy substance **2.** excess sentimentality —**slush fund** US fund for financing bribery, corruption

slut (slʌt) *n.* dirty (immoral) woman —**'sluttish** *a.* —**'sluttishness** *n.*

sly (slaɪ) *a.* **1.** cunning, wily, knowing **2.** secret, deceitful —**'slyly** *or* **'slily** *adv.* —**'slyness** *n.*

Sm *Chem.* samarium

smack¹ (smæk) *n.* **1.** taste, flavour **2.** *sl.* heroin —*vi.* (**with** of) **3.** have taste (of) **4.** be suggestive (of)

smack² (smæk) *vt.* **1.** slap **2.** open and close (lips) with loud sound —*n.* **3.** smacking slap **4.** crack **5.** such sound **6.** loud kiss —*adv.* **7.** *inf.* squarely; directly —**'smacker** *n. sl.* **1.** loud kiss **2.** pound note or dollar bill

smack³ (smæk) *n.* small sailing vessel, usu. for fishing

small (smɔːl) *a.* **1.** little **2.** unimportant, petty **3.** short **4.** weak **5.** mean —*n.* **6.** small slender part, *esp.* of the back —*pl.* **7.** *inf.* personal laundry, underwear —**'smallness** *n.* —**small beer** *inf.*, *chiefly* UK people or things of no importance —**small change 1.** coins, *esp.* those of low value **2.** *rare* person or thing of little importance —**'smallholding** *n.* small area of farming land —**small hours** hours just after midnight —**small-minded** *a.* having narrow views; petty —**'smallpox** *n.* contagious disease —**small-scale** *a.* **1.** of limited size **2.** (of map *etc.*) giving small representation of something —**small talk** light, polite conversation —**small-time** *a. inf.* insignificant —**small-timer** *n.*

smarm (smɑːm) *vi. inf.* fawn —**'smarmy** *a. inf.* unpleasantly suave; fawning

smart (smɑːt) *a.* **1.** astute **2.** brisk **3.** clever, witty **4.** impertinent **5.** trim, well dressed **6.** fashionable **7.** causing stinging pain —*v.* **8.** feel, cause pain —*n.* **9.** sharp pain —**'smarten** *v.* —**'smartly** *adv.* —**'smartness** *n.* —**smart aleck** (ˈælɪk) *or* **'smarty** *inf.* conceited person, know-all

smash (smæʃ) *vt.* **1.** break violently **2.** strike hard **3.** ruin **4.** destroy —*vi.* **5.** break **6.** dash violently —*n.* **7.** heavy blow **8.** collision (of vehicles *etc.*) **9.** total financial failure **10.** *inf.* popular success —**smashed** *a. sl.* very drunk or affected by drugs —**'smasher** *n. inf.* attractive person, thing —**'smashing** *a. inf.*, *chiefly* UK excellent —**smash-and-grab** *a. inf.* of robbery in which shop window is broken and contents removed

smattering (ˈsmætərɪŋ) *n.* slight superficial knowledge

smear (smɪə) *vt.* **1.** rub with grease *etc.* **2.** smudge, spread with dirt, grease *etc.* —*n.* **3.** mark made thus **4.** sample of secretion for medical examination **5.** slander

smell (smel) *vt.* **1.** perceive by nose **2.** *fig.* suspect —*vi.* **3.** give out odour **4.** use nose (**smelt** *or* **smelled, 'smelling**) —*n.* **5.** faculty of perceiving odours by nose **6.** anything detected by sense of smell —**'smelly** *a.* with strong (unpleasant) smell —**smelling salts** preparation of ammonium carbonate that has stimulant action when sniffed in cases of faintness *etc.*

smelt¹ (smelt) *vt.* extract (metal) from (ore) —**'smeltery** *n.*

smelt² (smelt) *n.* fish of salmon family

smew (smjuː) *n.* type of duck

smilax (ˈsmaɪlæks) *n.* **1.** climbing shrub having slightly lobed leaves and berry-like fruits **2.** much branched vine of S Afr. with glossy green foliage

smile (smaɪl) *n.* **1.** curving or parting of lips in pleased or amused expression —*vi.* **2.** wear, assume a smile **3.** (**with** on) approve, favour

smirch (smɜːtʃ) *vt.* **1.** dirty, sully **2.** disgrace, discredit **3.** stain **4.** disgrace

smirk (smɜːk) *n.* **1.** smile expressing scorn, smugness —*vi.* **2.** give such smile

smite (smaɪt) *vt.* **1.** strike **2.** attack **3.** afflict **4.** affect, *esp.* with love or fear (**smote, 'smitten, 'smiting**)

smith (smɪθ) *n.* worker in iron, gold *etc.* —**smithy** (ˈsmɪðɪ) *n.* blacksmith's workshop

smithereens (smɪðəˈriːnz) *pl.n.* small bits

smitten (ˈsmɪtən) *pp.* of SMITE

smock (smɒk) *n.* **1.** loose outer garment —*vt.* **2.** gather by sewing in honeycomb pattern

smog (smɒg) *n.* mixture of smoke and fog

smoke (sməʊk) *n.* **1.** cloudy mass of suspended particles that rises from fire or anything burning **2.** spell of tobacco smoking —*vi.* **3.** give off smoke **4.** inhale and expel tobacco smoke —*vt.* **5.** use (tobacco) by smoking **6.** expose to smoke (*esp.* in curing fish *etc.*) —**'smoker** *n.* —**'smokily** *adv.* —**'smoky** *a.* —**smoke**

screen 1. *Mil.* cloud of smoke produced to obscure movements **2.** something said or done to conceal truth —**'smokestack** *n.* chimney that conveys smoke into air

smolt (sməʊlt) *n.* young salmon at stage when it migrates from fresh water to sea

smooch (smuːtʃ) *vi./n. inf.* kiss, cuddle

smooth (smuːð) *a.* **1.** not rough, even of surface or texture **2.** sinuous **3.** flowing **4.** calm, soft, soothing **5.** suave, plausible **6.** free from jolts —*vt.* **7.** make smooth **8.** quieten —**'smoothly** *adv.* —**smooth-spoken** *a.* speaking in gently persuasive manner —**smooth-tongued** *a.* suave or persuasive in speech

smorgasbord ('smɔːgəsbɔːd) *n.* buffet meal of assorted dishes

smote (sməʊt) *pt. of* SMITE

smother ('smʌðə) *vt.* **1.** suffocate **2.** envelop **3.** suppress —*vi.* **4.** be suffocated

smoulder *or U.S.* **smolder** ('sməʊldə) *vi.* **1.** burn slowly without flame **2.** (of feelings) exist in suppressed state

smudge (smʌdʒ) *vt.* **1.** make smear, stain, dirty mark on —*n.* **2.** smear or dirty mark

smug (smʌg) *a.* self-satisfied, complacent

smuggle ('smʌgl) *vt.* **1.** import, export without paying customs duties **2.** conceal, take secretly

smut (smʌt) *n.* **1.** piece of soot, particle of dirt **2.** lewd or obscene talk *etc.* **3.** disease of grain —*vt.* **4.** blacken, smudge (-tt-) —**'smutty** *a.* **1.** soiled with smut, soot **2.** obscene, lewd

Sn *Chem.* tin

snack (snæk) *n.* light, hasty meal —**snack bar** bar at which snacks are served

snaffle ('snæf'l) *n.* **1.** light bit for horse —*vt.* **2.** *sl.* appropriate, scrounge **3.** put snaffle on

snag (snæg) *n.* **1.** difficulty **2.** sharp protuberance **3.** hole, loop in fabric caused by sharp object **4.** obstacle (*eg* tree branch *etc.* in river bed) —*vt.* **5.** catch, damage on snag (-gg-)

snail (sneɪl) *n.* **1.** slow-moving mollusc with shell **2.** slow, sluggish person —**snail-like** *a.* —**snail's pace** very slow rate

snake (sneɪk) *n.* **1.** long scaly limbless reptile, serpent —*vi.* **2.** move like snake —**'snaky** *a.* of, like snakes —**snake charmer** entertainer who appears to charm snakes by playing music —**snakes and ladders** board game in which tossed dice determine how far counters move either to climb up ladders or slide down snakes

snap (snæp) *v.* **1.** break suddenly **2.** (cause to) make cracking sound **3.** bite (at) suddenly **4.** speak (words) suddenly, angrily (-pp-) —*n.* **5.** act of snapping **6.** fastener **7.** *inf.* snapshot **8.** *inf.* easy task **9.** brief period, *esp.* of cold weather —*a.* **10.** sudden, unplanned, arranged quickly —**'snapper** *n.* perchlike fish —**'snappy** *a.* **1.** irritable **2.** *sl.* quick **3.** *sl.* well-dressed, fashionable —**'snapdragon** *n.* plant with flowers that can be opened like a mouth

—**snap fastener** press stud —**'snapshot** *n.* photograph

snare[1] (snɛə) *n.* **1.** (noose used as) trap —*vt.* **2.** catch with one

snare[2] (snɛə) *n. Mus.* set of gut strings wound with wire fitted across bottom of drum to increase vibration —**snare drum** *Mus.* cylindrical double-headed drum with snares

snarl (snɑːl) *n.* **1.** growl of angry dog **2.** tangle, knot —*vi.* **3.** utter snarl **4.** grumble —**snarl-up** *n. inf.* confusion, obstruction, *esp.* traffic jam

snatch (snætʃ) *vt.* **1.** make quick grab or bite at **2.** seize, catch —*n.* **3.** grab **4.** fragment **5.** short spell

snazzy ('snæzɪ) *a. inf.* stylish, flashy

sneak (sniːk) *vi.* **1.** slink **2.** move about furtively **3.** act in mean, underhand manner —*n.* **4.** mean, treacherous person **5.** petty informer —**'sneaking** *a.* secret but persistent —**sneak thief** person who steals articles from premises which he enters through open windows *etc.*

sneakers ('sniːkəz) *pl.n. chiefly* US flexible, informal sports shoes

sneer (snɪə) *n.* **1.** scornful, contemptuous expression or remark —*vi.* **2.** assume scornful expression —*v.* **3.** speak or utter contemptuously

sneeze (sniːz) *vi.* **1.** emit breath through nose with sudden involuntary spasm and noise —*n.* **2.** sound or act of sneezing

snick (snɪk) *n.* **1.** small cut or notch, nick —*vt.* **2.** cut; clip; nick

snicker ('snɪkə) *see* SNIGGER

snide (snaɪd) *a.* malicious, supercilious

sniff (snɪf) *vi.* **1.** inhale through nose with sharp hiss **2.** (*with* at) express disapproval *etc.* by sniffing —*vt.* **3.** take up through nose **4.** smell —*n.* **5.** act or sound of sniffing —**'sniffle** *vi.* sniff noisily through nose, *esp.* when suffering from a cold in the head, snuffle

snifter ('snɪftə) *n.* **1.** pear-shaped glass with bowl that narrows towards the top so that aroma of brandy *etc.* is retained **2.** *inf.* small alcoholic drink

snigger ('snɪgə) *n.* **1.** sly, disrespectful laugh, *esp.* partly stifled —*vi.* **2.** utter such laugh

snip (snɪp) *v.* **1.** cut (bits off) (-pp-) —*n.* **2.** act, sound of snipping **3.** bit cut off **4.** *inf.* bargain **5.** *inf.* certainty —**'snippet** *n.* shred, fragment, clipping —**snips** *pl.n.* tool for cutting

snipe (snaɪp) *n.* **1.** wading bird —*v.* **2.** shoot at (enemy) from cover **3.** (*with* at) criticize, attack (person) slyly —**'sniper** *n.*

snitch (snɪtʃ) *inf. vt.* **1.** steal —*vi.* **2.** inform on someone —*n.* **3.** telltale

snivel ('snɪv'l) *vi.* **1.** sniffle to show distress **2.** whine (-ll-)

snob (snɒb) *n.* one who pretentiously judges others by social rank *etc.* —**'snobbery** *n.* —**'snobbish** *a.* of, like snob —**'snobbishly** *adv.*

snoek (snʊk) *n. SA* barracouta

snood (snu:d) *n.* **1.** pouchlike hat, worn at back of head to hold woman's hair **2.** *Scot.* headband, *esp.* formerly worn by young unmarried women

snook (snu:k) *n.* UK rude gesture, made by putting one thumb to nose with fingers outstretched (*esp. in* **cock a snook at**)

snooker ('snu:kə) *n.* **1.** game played on billiard table —*vt.* **2.** leave (opponent) in unfavourable position **3.** place (someone) in difficult situation

snoop (snu:p) *vi.* **1.** pry, meddle **2.** peer —*n.* **3.** one who acts thus **4.** act or instance of snooping

snooty ('snu:tɪ) *a. sl.* haughty

snooze (snu:z) *vi.* **1.** take short sleep, be half asleep —*n.* **2.** nap

snore (snɔ:) *vi.* **1.** breathe noisily when asleep —*n.* **2.** noise of snoring

snorkel ('snɔ:k⁰l) *n.* **1.** tube for breathing underwater —*vi.* **2.** swim, fish using this (**-ll-**)

snort (snɔ:t) *vi.* **1.** make (contemptuous) noise by driving breath through nostrils —*n.* **2.** such noise

snot (snɒt) *n. vulg.* mucus from nose

snout (snaut) *n.* animal's nose

snow (snəu) *n.* **1.** frozen vapour which falls in flakes **2.** *sl.* cocaine —*v.* **3.** fall, sprinkle as snow —*vt.* **4.** let fall, throw down like snow **5.** cover with snow —'**snowy** *a.* **1.** of, like snow **2.** covered with snow **3.** very white —'**snowball** *n.* **1.** snow pressed into hard ball for throwing —*vi.* **2.** increase rapidly in importance *etc.* **3.** play, fight with snowballs —'**snowberry** *n.* shrub with small pink flowers and white berries —**snow blindness** temporary blindness due to brightness of snow —'**snowdrift** *n.* bank of deep snow —'**snowdrop** *n.* small, white, bell-shaped spring flower —'**snowfall** *n.* **1.** fall of snow **2.** *Met.* amount of snow received in specified place and time —**snow fence** C fence erected in winter beside exposed road —'**snowflake** *n.* **1.** one of mass of ice crystals that fall as snow **2.** any of various European plants that have white bell-shaped flowers —**snow goose** white N Amer. goose —**snow-in-summer** *n.* rock plant with white flowers —**snow line** elevation above which snow does not melt —'**snowman** *n.* figure shaped out of snow —'**snowmobile** *n.* C motor vehicle with caterpillar tracks and front skis —'**snowplough** *n.* implement or vehicle for clearing away snow —'**snowshoes** *pl.n.* shoes like rackets for travelling on snow —**snow under 1.** cover and block with snow **2.** *fig.* overwhelm

SNP Scottish National Party

snub (snʌb) *vt.* **1.** insult (*esp.* by ignoring) intentionally (**-bb-**) —*n.* **2.** snubbing, rebuff —*a.* **3.** short and blunt

snuff¹ (snʌf) *n.* powdered tobacco for inhaling through nose —**snuff-dipping** *n.* absorbing nicotine by holding in mouth, between cheek and gum, a small amount of tobacco

snuff² (snʌf) *vt.* extinguish (*esp.* light from candle) —'**snuffer** *n.* **1.** cone-shaped implement for extinguishing candles —*pl.* **2.** instrument resembling scissors for trimming wick of candle —**snuff it** *sl.* die

snuffle ('snʌf⁰l) *vi.* breathe noisily or with difficulty

snug (snʌg) *a.* warm, comfortable —'**snuggle** *v.* lie close to, for warmth or affection —'**snugly** *adv.*

snye (snaɪ) *n.* C side channel of river

so¹ (səu) *adv.* **1.** to such an extent **2.** in such a manner **3.** very **4.** the case being such **5.** accordingly —*conj.* **6.** therefore **7.** in order that **8.** with the result that —*interj.* **9.** well —**so-and-so** *n. inf.* **1.** person whose name is forgotten or ignored **2.** *euphemistic* person or thing regarded as unpleasant —**so-called** *a.* called by but doubtfully deserving the name —**so long** *interj.* **1.** *inf.* farewell; goodbye —*adv.* **2.** SA *sl.* in the meantime, for the time being

so² (səu) *n. Mus. see* SOH

So. south(ern)

soak (səuk) *v.* **1.** steep —*vt.* **2.** absorb **3.** drench —*vi.* **4.** lie in liquid —*n.* **5.** soaking **6.** *sl.* habitual drunkard

soap (səup) *n.* **1.** compound of alkali and oil used in washing —*vt.* **2.** apply soap to —'**soapy** *a.* —'**soapbox** *n.* crate used as platform for speech-making —**soap opera** radio or television serial of domestic life —'**soapstone** *n.* massive compact variety of talc, used for making hearths *etc.* (*also* '**steatite**)

soar (sɔ:) *vi.* **1.** fly high **2.** increase, rise (in price *etc.*)

sob (sɒb) *vi.* **1.** catch breath, *esp.* in weeping (**-bb-**) —*n.* **2.** sobbing —**sob story** tale of personal distress told to arouse sympathy

sober ('səubə) *a.* **1.** not drunk **2.** temperate **3.** subdued **4.** dull, plain **5.** solemn —*v.* **6.** make, become sober —'**soberly** *adv.* —so'**briety** *n.* state of being sober

sobriquet *or* **soubriquet** ('səubrɪkeɪ) *n.* **1.** nickname **2.** assumed name

Soc. *or* **soc.** Society

soccer ('sɒkə) *n.* game of football played with spherical ball

sociable ('səuʃəb⁰l) *a.* **1.** friendly **2.** convivial —**socia'bility** *n.* —'**sociably** *adv.*

social ('səuʃəl) *a.* **1.** living in communities **2.** relating to society **3.** sociable —*n.* **4.** informal gathering —'**socialite** *n.* member of fashionable society —**sociali'zation** *or* **-li'sation** *n.* —'**socialize** *or* **-lise** *v.* —'**socially** *adv.* —**social contract** *or* **compact** agreement entered into by individuals, that results in formation of state and entails surrender of some personal liberties —**social science** study of society and of relationship of individual members within society, including economics, history, psychology *etc.* —**social security** state provision for the unemployed, aged *etc.* —**social services** welfare activities organized by state

—**social studies** (*with sing. v.*) study of how people live and organize themselves in society, embracing geography, economics *etc.* —**social work** work to improve welfare of others

socialism ('səuʃəlızəm) *n.* political system which advocates public ownership of means of production, distribution and exchange —**'socialist** *n./a.* —**socia'listic** *a.*

society (sə'saıətı) *n.* 1. living associated with others 2. those so living 3. companionship 4. company 5. association 6. club 7. fashionable people collectively

socio- (*comb. form*) denoting social or society, as in *socioeconomic*

socioeconomic (səusıəui:kə'nɒmık) *a.* of or involving both economic and social factors

sociology (səusı'ɒlədʒı) *n.* study of societies

sociopolitical (səusıəupə'lıtık²l) *a.* of or involving both political and social factors

sock¹ (sɒk) *n.* cloth covering for foot

sock² (sɒk) *sl. vt.* 1. hit —*n.* 2. blow

socket ('sɒkıt) *n.* hole or recess for something to fit into

Socratic (sɒ'krætık) *a.* of, like Gr. philosopher Socrates

sod (sɒd) *n.* 1. lump of earth with grass 2. *sl.* person considered obnoxious 3. *sl.* person, as specified

soda ('səudə) *n.* 1. compound of sodium 2. soda water —**soda fountain** US 1. counter that serves drinks, snacks *etc.* 2. apparatus dispensing soda water —**soda water** water charged with carbon dioxide

sodden ('sɒd²n) *a.* 1. soaked 2. drunk 3. heavy and doughy

sodium ('səudıəm) *n.* metallic alkaline element —**sodium bicarbonate** white crystalline soluble compound used in baking powder *etc.* (*also* **bicarbonate of soda**) —**sodium carbonate** soluble crystalline compound used in manufacture of glass, ceramics, soap and paper, and as cleansing agent —**sodium chloride** common table salt

Sodom ('sɒdəm) *n.* 1. *O.T.* city that, with Gomorrah, traditionally typifies depravity 2. this city as representing homosexuality 3. any place notorious for depravity

sodomy ('sɒdəmı) *n.* anal intercourse —'**sodomite** *n.*

sofa ('səufə) *n.* upholstered seat with back and arms, for two or more people

soft (sɒft) *a.* 1. yielding easily to pressure 2. mild 3. easy 4. subdued 5. quiet, gentle 6. (too) lenient 7. oversentimental 8. feeble-minded 9. (of water) containing few mineral salts 10. (of drugs) not liable to cause addiction —**soften** ('sɒf²n) *v.* 1. make, become soft or softer —*vt.* 2. mollify 3. lighten 4. mitigate 5. make less loud —'**softly** *adv.* gently, quietly —'**softy** *or* '**softie** *n. inf.* person who is sentimental, weakly foolish or lacking in physical endurance —**soft-boiled** *a.* (of egg) boiled

for a short time so that yolk remains soft —**soft drink** drink that is nonalcoholic —**soft furnishings** curtains, rugs *etc.* —**soft'hearted** *a.* easily moved to pity —**soft palate** posterior fleshy portion of roof of mouth —**soft-pedal** *vt.* 1. mute tone of (piano) 2. *inf.* make (something) less obvious by deliberately failing to emphasize it —**soft pedal** foot-operated lever on piano that causes fewer of strings to sound —**soft sell** *chiefly* US method of selling based on indirect suggestion or inducement —**soft shoe** (of tap dancing) done without metal taps on shoes —**soft soap** flattery —**soft spot** sentimental fondness —'**software** *n.* computer programs, tapes *etc.* for a particular computer system —'**softwood** *n.* wood of coniferous tree

SOGAT ('səugæt) UK Society of Graphical and Allied Trades

soggy ('sɒgı) *a.* 1. soaked with liquid 2. damp and heavy

soh *or* **so** (səu) *n. Mus.* in tonic sol-fa, name used for fifth note or dominant of any scale

soigné *or* (*fem.*) **soignée** ('swɑːnjeı) *a.* well-groomed

soil¹ (sɔıl) *n.* 1. earth, ground 2. country, territory

soil² (sɔıl) *v.* 1. make, become dirty —*vt.* 2. tarnish, defile —*n.* 3. dirt 4. sewage 5. stain

soiree ('swɑːreı) *n.* private evening party, *esp.* with music

sojourn ('sɒdʒɜːn, 'sʌdʒ-) *vi.* 1. stay for a time —*n.* 2. short stay —'**sojourner** *n.*

sol (sɒl) *n. Mus. see* SOH

solace ('sɒlıs) *n./vt.* comfort in distress

solar ('səulə) *a.* of the sun —**solari'zation** *or* **-i'sation** *n.* —'**solarize** *or* **-ise** *vt.* affect by sunlight —**solar cell** that produces electricity from sun's rays —**solar plexus** ('plɛksəs) network of nerves at pit of stomach —**solar system** system containing sun and heavenly bodies held in its gravitational field

solarium (səu'lɛərıəm) *n.* 1. room built mainly of glass to give exposure to sun 2. (place with) bed for acquiring suntan by artificial means

sold (səuld) *pt./pp. of* SELL

solder ('sɒldə; *U.S.* 'sɒdər) *n.* 1. easily-melted alloy used for joining metal —*vt.* 2. join with solder —**soldering iron**

soldier ('səuldʒə) *n.* 1. one serving in army —*vi.* 2. serve in army 3. (*with* on) persist doggedly —'**soldierly** *a.* —'**soldiery** *n.* troops —**soldier of fortune** man who seeks money or adventure as soldier

sole¹ (səul) *a.* 1. one and only, unique 2. solitary —'**solely** *adv.* 1. alone 2. only 3. entirely

sole² (səul) *n.* 1. underside of foot 2. underpart of boot *etc.* —*vt.* 3. fit with sole

sole³ (səul) *n.* small edible flatfish

solecism ('sɒlısızəm) *n.* breach of grammar or etiquette

solemn ('sɒləm) *a.* 1. serious 2. formal 3. impressive —**solemnity** (sə'lɛmnıtı) *n.*

—**solemnization** or **-isation** (sɒləmnaɪ-
ˈzeɪʃən) n. —**solemnize** or **-ise**
(ˈsɒləmnaɪz) vt. 1. celebrate, perform 2.
make solemn —**solemnly** adv.

solenoid (ˈsəʊlɪnɔɪd) n. coil of wire as part
of electrical apparatus

sol-fa (ˈsɒlˈfɑː) n. Mus. system of syllables
sol, fa etc. sung in scale

solicit (səˈlɪsɪt) vt. 1. request 2. accost 3.
urge 4. entice —**solici'tation** n. —**so'lici-
tor** n. lawyer who prepares documents,
advises clients, but represents them in
lower courts only —**so'licitous** a. 1.
anxious 2. eager 3. earnest —**so'licitude** n.
—Solicitor General UK law officer of
Crown ranking next to Attorney General

solid (ˈsɒlɪd) a. 1. not hollow 2. compact 3.
composed of one substance 4. firm 5.
massive 6. reliable, sound —n. 7. body of
three dimensions 8. substance not liquid or
gas —**soli'darity** n. 1. unity of interests 2.
united state —**solidifi'cation** n. —**so'lidify**
v. 1. make, become solid or firm 2. harden
(**-ified**, **-ifying**) —**so'lidity** n. —**'solidly**
adv. —**solid geometry** branch of geometry
concerned with solid geometric figures
—**solid-state** a. (of electronic device)
consisting chiefly of semiconductor materials and controlled by means of their
electrical properties

solidus (ˈsɒlɪdəs) n. short stroke (/) used
in text to separate items (pl. **-di** (-daɪ))

soliloquy (səˈlɪləkwɪ) n. esp. in drama,
thoughts spoken by person while alone
—**so'liloquize** or **-ise** v.

solipsism (ˈsɒlɪpsɪzəm) n. doctrine that
self is the only thing known to exist
—**'solipsist** n.

solitary (ˈsɒlɪtərɪ, -trɪ) a. 1. alone, single
—n. 2. hermit —**soli'taire** n. 1. game for
one person played with pegs set in board
2. single precious stone, esp. diamond, set
by itself —**'solitude** n. 1. state of being
alone 2. loneliness —**solitary confinement**
isolation imposed on prisoner

solo (ˈsəʊləʊ) n. 1. music for one
performer (pl. **-s**, **-li** (-liː)) 2. card game
like whist (pl. **-s**) —a. 3. not concerted 4.
unaccompanied, alone 5. piloting aeroplane alone —**'soloist** n.

solstice (ˈsɒlstɪs) n. either shortest
(winter) or longest (summer) day of year
—**solstitial** (sɒlˈstɪʃəl) a.

solve (sɒlv) vt. 1. work out, explain 2. find
answer to —**solubility** (sɒljʊˈbɪlɪtɪ) n.
—**soluble** (ˈsɒljʊbᵊl) a. 1. capable of being
dissolved in liquid 2. able to be solved or
explained —**so'lute** n. 1. substance
dissolved in solution —a. 2. Bot. unattached —**solution** (səˈluːʃən) n. 1. answer
to problem 2. dissolving 3. liquid with
something dissolved in it —**'solvable** a.
—**'solvency** n. —**'solvent** a. 1. able to
meet financial obligations —n. 2. liquid
with power of dissolving

Som. Somerset

somatic (səʊˈmætɪk) a. 1. of the body, as
distinct from the mind 2. of animal body or

body wall as distinct from viscera, limbs
and head

sombre or U.S. **somber** (ˈsɒmbə) a. dark,
gloomy

sombrero (sɒmˈbreərəʊ) n. wide-brimmed
hat (pl. **-s**)

some (sʌm; unstressed səm) a. 1. denoting
an indefinite number, amount or extent 2.
one or other 3. amount of 4. certain 5.
approximately —pron. 6. portion, quantity
—**'somebody** pron. 1. some person —n. 2.
important person —**'somehow** adv. by
some means unknown —**'someone** pron.
some person —**'something** pron. 1. thing
not clearly defined 2. indefinite amount,
quantity or degree —**'sometime** adv. 1.
formerly 2. at some (past or future) time
—a. 3. former —**'sometimes** adv. 1.
occasionally 2. now and then —**'somewhat**
adv. to some extent, rather —**'somewhere**
adv.

somersault or **summersault** (ˈsʌmə-
sɔːlt) n. tumbling head over heels

somnambulist (sɒmˈnæmbjʊlɪst) n. sleep-
walker —**som'nambulism** n. —**somnam-
bu'listic** a.

somnolent (ˈsɒmnələnt) a. 1. drowsy 2.
causing sleep —**'somnolence** or **'somno-
lency** n.

son (sʌn) n. 1. male child —**'sonny** n.
familiar term of address to boy or man
—son-in-law n. daughter's husband

sonar (ˈsəʊnɑː) n. device like echo
sounder

sonata (səˈnɑːtə) n. piece of music in
several movements —**sonatina** (sɒnə-
ˈtiːnə) n. short sonata

son et lumière (ˈsɒn eɪ ˈluːmɪɛə) Fr.
entertainment staged at night at famous
place, building, giving dramatic history of
it with lighting and sound effects

song (sɒŋ) n. 1. singing 2. poem etc. for
singing —**'songster** n. 1. singer 2. songbird
(**'songstress** fem.)

sonic (ˈsɒnɪk) a. pert. to sound waves
—**sonic barrier** see **sound barrier** at
SOUND —**sonic boom** explosive sound
caused by aircraft travelling at supersonic
speed

sonnet (ˈsɒnɪt) n. fourteen-line poem with
definite rhyme scheme —**sonne'teer** n.
writer of this

sonorous (səˈnɔːrəs, ˈsɒnərəs) a. giving
out (deep) sound, resonant —**sonority**
(səˈnɒrɪtɪ) n. —**so'norously** adv.

soon (suːn) adv. 1. in a short time 2. before
long 3. early, quickly

soot (sʊt) n. black powdery substance
formed by burning of coal etc. —**'sooty** a.
of, like soot

sooth (suːθ) n. truth —**'soothsayer** n. one
who foretells future, diviner

soothe (suːð) vt. 1. make calm, tranquil 2.
relieve (pain etc.)

sop (sɒp) n. 1. piece of bread etc. soaked in
liquid 2. concession, bribe —vt. 3. steep in
water etc. 4. soak (up) (**-pp-**) —**'sopping** a.

completely soaked —'**soppy** a. inf. over-sentimental

sophist ('sofist) n. fallacious reasoner, quibbler —'**sophism** n. specious argument —so'**phistical** a. —'**sophistry** n.

sophisticate (sə'fistikeit) vt. 1. make artificial, spoil, falsify, corrupt —n. (sə'fistikeit, -kit) 2. sophisticated person —so'**phisticated** a. 1. having refined or cultured tastes, habits 2. worldly-wise 3. superficially clever 4. complex —sophisti-'**cation** n.

sophomore ('sofəmɔ:) n. US student in second year at college

-**sophy** (n. comb. form) indicating knowledge or intellectual system, as in philosophy —**sophic** or -**sophical** (a. comb. form)

soporific (sopə'rifik) a. 1. causing sleep (esp. by drugs) —n. 2. drug or other agent that induces sleep

soprano (sə'prɑ:nəʊ) n. 1. highest voice in women and boys 2. singer with this voice 3. musical part for it (pl. -s)

sorbet ('sɔ:bit, -bei) n. (fruit-flavoured) water ice

sorcerer ('sɔ:sərə) or (fem.) **sorceress** ('sɔ:sərɪs) n. magician —'**sorcery** n. witchcraft, magic

sordid ('sɔ:dɪd) a. 1. mean, squalid 2. ignoble, base —'**sordidly** adv. —'**sordidness** n.

sore (sɔ:) a. 1. painful 2. causing annoyance 3. severe 4. distressed 5. annoyed —adv. 6. obs. grievously, intensely —n. 7. sore place, ulcer, boil etc. —'**sorely** adv. 1. grievously 2. greatly

sorghum ('sɔ:gəm) n. kind of grass cultivated for grain

sorority (sə'rorɪtɪ) n. chiefly US social club or society for university women

sorrel ('sorəl) n. 1. plant 2. reddish-brown colour 3. horse of this colour —a. 4. of this colour

sorrow ('sorəʊ) n. 1. pain of mind, grief, sadness —vi. 2. grieve —'**sorrowful** a.

sorry ('sorɪ) a. 1. feeling pity or regret 2. distressed 3. miserable, wretched 4. mean, poor —'**sorrily** adv. —'**sorriness** n.

sort (sɔ:t) n. 1. kind or class —vt. 2. classify

sortie ('sɔ:tɪ) n. sally by besieged forces

SOS 1. international code signal of distress 2. call for help

so-so a. inf. mediocre

sostenuto (sostə'nu:təʊ) a./adv. Mus. in smooth sustained manner

sot (sot) n. habitual drunkard

sotto voce ('sotəʊ 'vəʊtʃɪ) It. in an undertone

sou (su:) n. 1. former French coin 2. small amount of money

soubrette (su:'brɛt) n. 1. minor female role in comedy 2. any flirtatious girl

soufflé (su:'fleɪ) n. dish of eggs beaten to froth, flavoured and baked

sough (saʊ) n. low murmuring sound as of wind in trees

sought (sɔ:t) pt./pp. of SEEK

souk (su:k) n. open-air marketplace, esp. in N Afr. and Middle East

soul (səʊl) n. 1. spiritual and immortal part of human being 2. example, pattern 3. person —'**soulful** a. full of emotion or sentiment —'**soulless** a. 1. mechanical 2. lacking sensitivity or nobility 3. heartless, cruel —**soul-destroying** a. (of occupation etc.) monotonous —**soul food** inf. food, as yams etc., traditionally eaten by U.S. Negroes —**soul mate** person for whom one has deep affinity —**soul music** type of Black music resulting from addition of jazz and gospel to urban blues style —**soul-searching** n. deep or critical examination of one's motives, actions etc.

sound[1] (saʊnd) n. 1. what is heard 2. noise —vi. 3. make sound 4. seem 5. resonate with a certain quality —vt. 6. cause to sound 7. utter —**sound barrier** large increase in resistance encountered by aircraft approaching speed of sound —**sound effect** sound artificially produced to create theatrical effect, as in plays, films etc. —**sounding board** 1. thin wooden board in violin etc. designed to reflect sound 2. person etc. used to test new idea etc. —**sound track** recorded sound accompaniment of film etc. —**sound wave** wave that propagates sound

sound[2] (saʊnd) a. 1. in good condition 2. solid 3. of good judgment 4. legal 5. solvent 6. thorough 7. effective 8. watertight 9. deep —'**soundly** adv. thoroughly

sound[3] (saʊnd) vt. 1. measure depth of (well, sea etc.) 2. probe —'**soundings** pl.n. measurements taken by sounding —**sound out** ascertain views of

sound[4] (saʊnd) n. channel, strait

soup (su:p) n. liquid food made by boiling meat, vegetables etc. —'**soupy** a. 1. like soup 2. murky 3. sentimental —**soup kitchen** 1. place where food, esp. soup, is served to destitute people 2. Mil. mobile kitchen

soupçon (sup'sɔ̃) Fr. small amount

sour (saʊə) a. 1. acid 2. gone bad 3. rancid 4. peevish 5. disagreeable —v. 6. make, become sour —'**sourly** adv. —'**sourness** n. —**sour grapes** attitude of despising something because one cannot have it oneself —'**sourpuss** n. sullen, sour-faced person

source (sɔ:s) n. 1. origin, starting point 2. spring

souse (saʊs) v. 1. plunge, drench or be drenched 2. pickle —n. 3. sousing 4. brine for pickling

soutane (su:'tæn) n. priest's cassock

south (saʊθ) n. 1. cardinal point opposite north 2. region, part of country etc. lying to that side —a./adv. 3. (that is) towards south —'**southerly** ('sʌðəlɪ) a. 1. towards south —n. 2. wind from the south —'**southern** ('sʌðən) a. in south —'**Southerner** n. (sometimes s-) native or inhabitant of south of any specified region —'**southwards** adv. —'**Southdown** n.

breed of sheep —**south'east** n. 1. point of compass midway between south and east —a. 2. (sometimes S-) denoting southeastern part of specified country etc. 3. in, towards or facing southeast —adv. 4. in, to, towards or (esp. of wind) from southeast —**South'east** n. (usu. with the) southeastern part of Britain —**Southern Cross** small constellation in S hemisphere whose four brightest stars form cross —**southern hemisphere** (oft. S- H-) that half of earth lying south of equator —**southern lights** aurora australis —**'southpaw** inf. n. 1. any left-handed person, esp. a boxer —a. 2. of or relating to southpaw —**South Pole** southernmost point on earth's axis —**South Seas** seas south of equator —**south-southeast** n. 1. point on compass midway between southeast and south —a./adv. 2. in, from or towards this direction —**south-southwest** n. 1. point on compass midway between south and southwest —a./adv. 2. in, from or towards this direction —**south'west** n. 1. point on compass midway between west and south —a. 2. (sometimes S-) of or denoting southwestern part of specified country etc. 3. in or towards southwest —adv. 4. in, to, towards or (esp. of wind) from southwest —**South'west** n. (usu. with the) southwestern part of Britain

souvenir (suːvəˈnɪə, ˈsuːvənɪə) n. keepsake, memento

sou'wester (sauˈwɛstə) n. waterproof hat

sovereign (ˈsɒvrɪn) n. 1. king, queen 2. former Brit. gold coin worth 20 shillings —a. 3. supreme 4. efficacious —**'sovereignty** n. 1. supreme power and right to exercise it 2. dominion 3. independent state

soviet (ˈsəʊvɪət, ˈsɒv-) n. 1. elected council at various levels of government in U.S.S.R. 2. (S-) citizen of U.S.S.R. —a. 3. (S-) of U.S.S.R., its people or its government —**'sovietism** n.

sow[1] (səʊ) vi. 1. scatter, plant seed —vt. 2. scatter, deposit (seed) 3. spread abroad (**sowed** pt., **sown** or **sowed** pp., **'sowing** pr.p.)

sow[2] (saʊ) n. female adult pig

soya bean (ˈsɔɪə) or U.S. **soybean** (ˈsɔɪbiːn) n. edible bean used as meat substitute, in making soy sauce etc. —**soy sauce** (sɔɪ) salty, dark brown sauce made from fermented soya beans, used esp. in Chinese cookery (also **soya sauce**)

sozzled (ˈsɒzəld) a. sl. drunk

sp. 1. special 2. species (pl. **spp.**) 3. specific 4. specimen 5. spelling

spa (spɑː) n. 1. medicinal spring 2. place or resort with such a spring

space (speɪs) n. 1. extent 2. room 3. period 4. empty place 5. area 6. expanse 7. region beyond earth's atmosphere —vt. 8. place at intervals —**spacious** (ˈspeɪʃəs) a. roomy, extensive —**space age** period in which exploration of space has become possible —**space-age** a. ultramodern

—**'spacecraft** or **'spaceship** n. vehicle for travel beyond earth's atmosphere —**'spaceman** n. —**space shuttle** vehicle designed to carry men and materials to space stations etc. —**space station** any manned artificial satellite designed to orbit earth and provide base for scientific research in space —**'spacesuit** n. sealed, pressurized suit worn by astronaut —**space-time** n. Phys. continuum having three spatial coordinates and one time coordinate that together specify location of particle or event (also **space-time continuum**)

spade[1] (speɪd) n. tool for digging —**'spadework** n. arduous preparatory work

spade[2] (speɪd) n. leaf-shaped black symbol on playing card

spadix (ˈspeɪdɪks) n. spike of small flowers on fleshy stem, whole being enclosed in spathe (pl. **spadices** (speɪˈdaɪsiːz))

spaghetti (spəˈgɛtɪ) n. pasta in form of long strings

Spam (spæm) n. R kind of tinned luncheon meat

span (spæn) n. 1. space from thumb to little finger as measure 2. extent, space 3. stretch of arch etc. 4. distance from wingtip to wingtip (also **'wingspan**) —vt. 5. stretch over 6. measure with hand (**-nn-**)

spangle (ˈspæŋg'l) n. 1. small shiny metallic ornament —vt. 2. decorate with spangles

spaniel (ˈspænjəl) n. breed of dog with long ears and silky hair

Spanish (ˈspænɪʃ) n. 1. official language of Spain, Mexico and most countries of S and Central Amer., except Brazil —a. 2. of Spanish language or its speakers 3. of Spain or Spaniards —**'Spaniard** n. native or inhabitant of Spain —**Spanish America** parts of America colonized by Spaniards and now chiefly Spanish-speaking —**Spanish fly** 1. European blister beetle, the dried bodies of which yield cantharides 2. cantharides —**Spanish Main** 1. mainland of Spanish America 2. Caribbean Sea

spank (spæŋk) vt. 1. slap with flat of hand, esp. on buttocks —n. 2. one or series of these slaps —**'spanking** n. 1. series of spanks —a. 2. quick, lively 3. large, fine

spanner (ˈspænə) n. tool for gripping nut or bolt head

spanspek (ˈspænspɛk) n. SA sweet melon

spar[1] (spɑː) n. pole, beam, esp. as part of ship's rigging

spar[2] (spɑː) vi. 1. box 2. dispute, esp. in fun (**-rr-**) —n. 3. sparring —**sparring partner** person who practises with boxer during training

spar[3] (spɑː) n. any of various kinds of crystalline mineral

spare (speə) vt. 1. leave unhurt 2. show mercy 3. abstain from using 4. do without 5. give away —a. 6. additional 7. in reserve 8. thin, lean 9. scanty —n. 10. spare part (for machine) —**'sparing** a. economical, careful —**'sparerib** n. cut of pork ribs with most of meat trimmed off —**spare tyre** UK *sl.* roll of fat just above waist

spark (spɑːk) *n.* **1.** small glowing or burning particle **2.** flash of light produced by electrical discharge **3.** vivacity, humour **4.** trace **5.** in internal-combustion engines, electric spark (in sparking plug) which ignites explosive mixture in cylinder —*vi.* **6.** emit sparks —*vt.* **7.** (*oft. with* off) kindle, excite —**sparking plug** device screwed into cylinder head of internal-combustion engine to ignite explosive mixture by means of electric spark (*also* **spark plug**)

sparkle ('spɑːkˀl) *vi.* **1.** glitter **2.** effervesce **3.** scintillate —*n.* **4.** small spark **5.** glitter **6.** flash **7.** lustre —**'sparkler** *n.* **1.** type of firework that throws out sparks **2.** *inf.* sparkling gem

sparrow ('spærəʊ) *n.* small brownish bird —**sparrow hawk** hawk that hunts small birds

sparse (spɑːs) *a.* thinly scattered

Spartan ('spɑːtˀn) *a.* **1.** of ancient Gk. city of Sparta, its inhabitants or their culture **2.** (*sometimes* s-) very strict or austere **3.** (*sometimes* s-) possessing courage and resolve

spasm ('spæzəm) *n.* **1.** sudden convulsive (muscular) contraction **2.** sudden burst of activity *etc.* —**spas'modic** *a.* occurring in spasms

spastic ('spæstɪk) *a.* **1.** affected by spasms, suffering cerebral palsy —*n.* **2.** person who has cerebral palsy

spat[1] (spæt) *pt./pp. of* SPIT[1]

spat[2] (spæt) *n.* short gaiter

spat[3] (spæt) *n.* slight quarrel

spate (speɪt) *n.* **1.** rush, outpouring **2.** flood

spathe (speɪð) *n.* large sheathlike leaf enclosing flower cluster

spatial *or* **spacial** ('speɪʃəl) *a.* of, in space

spatter ('spætə) *vt.* **1.** splash, cast drops over —*vi.* **2.** be scattered in drops —*n.* **3.** slight splash **4.** sprinkling

spatula ('spætjʊlə) *n.* utensil with broad, flat blade used for various purposes

spawn (spɔːn) *n.* **1.** eggs of fish or frog **2.** *oft. offens.* offspring —*vi.* **3.** (of fish or frog) cast eggs —*vt.* **4.** produce, engender

spay (speɪ) *vt.* remove ovaries from (animal)

speak (spiːk) *vi.* **1.** utter words **2.** converse **3.** deliver discourse —*vt.* **4.** utter **5.** pronounce **6.** express **7.** communicate in (**spoke, 'spoken, 'speaking**) —**'speakable** *a.* —**'speaker** *n.* **1.** one who speaks **2.** one who specializes in speech-making **3.** (*oft.* S-) official chairman of many legislative bodies **4.** loudspeaker —**'speakeasy** *n.* US place where alcoholic drink was sold illicitly during Prohibition —**speaking clock** UK telephone service giving verbal statement of time

spear (spɪə) *n.* **1.** long pointed weapon **2.** slender shoot, as of asparagus —*vt.* **3.** transfix, pierce, wound with spear —**'spearhead** *n.* **1.** leading force in attack,

campaign —*vt.* **2.** lead, initiate (attack, campaign *etc.*)

spearmint ('spɪəmɪnt) *n.* type of mint

spec (spɛk) *n. inf.* speculation, gamble (*esp.* **in on spec**)

spec. 1. special **2.** specification **3.** speculation

special ('spɛʃəl) *a.* **1.** beyond the usual **2.** particular, individual **3.** distinct **4.** limited —**'specialism** *n.* —**'specialist** *n.* one who devotes himself to special subject or branch of subject —**speci'ality** *n.* special product, skill, characteristic *etc.* —**speciali'zation** *or* **-i'sation** *n.* —**'specialize** *or* **-ise** *vi.* **1.** be specialist —*vt.* **2.** make special —**'specially** *adv.* —**Special Branch** UK department of police force concerned with political security —**special constable** person recruited for temporary police duties, *esp.* in time of emergency —**special delivery** delivery of mail outside time of scheduled delivery —**special licence** UK licence permitting marriage to take place without usual legal conditions

specie ('spiːʃiː) *n.* coined, as distinct from paper, money

species ('spiːʃiːz; *Lat.* 'spiːʃiːz) *n.* **1.** sort, kind, *esp.* of animals *etc.* **2.** class **3.** subdivision (*pl.* **-cies**)

specific (spɪ'sɪfɪk) *a.* **1.** definite **2.** exact in detail **3.** characteristic of a thing or kind —**spe'cifically** *adv.* —**specifi'cation** *n.* detailed description of something to be made, done —**'specify** *vt.* state definitely or in detail (**-ified, -ifying**) —**specific gravity** ratio of density of substance to that of water

specimen ('spɛsɪmɪn) *n.* **1.** part typifying whole **2.** individual example **3.** *Med.* sample of tissue, urine *etc.* taken for diagnostic examination

specious ('spiːʃəs) *a.* deceptively plausible, but false —**'speciously** *adv.* —**'speciousness** *n.*

speck (spɛk) *n.* **1.** small spot, particle —*vt.* **2.** spot —**'speckle** *n./vt.* speck

specs (spɛks) *pl.n.* spectacles

spectacle ('spɛktəkˀl) *n.* **1.** show **2.** thing exhibited **3.** ridiculous sight —*pl.* **4.** pair of lenses for correcting defective sight —**spec'tacular** *a.* **1.** impressive **2.** showy **3.** grand **4.** magnificent —*n.* **5.** lavishly produced performance —**spec'tator** *n.* one who looks on

spectra ('spɛktrə) *n., pl. of* SPECTRUM

spectre *or* U.S. **specter** ('spɛktə) *n.* **1.** ghost **2.** image of something unpleasant —**'spectral** *a.* ghostly

spectrum ('spɛktrəm) *n.* band of colours into which beam of light can be decomposed, *eg* by prism (*pl.* **-tra**) —**'spectroscope** *n.* instrument for producing, examining spectra —**spec'troscopist** *n.* —**spec'troscopy** *n.* study of spectra by use of spectroscopes *etc.*

speculate ('spɛkjʊleɪt) *vi.* **1.** guess, conjecture **2.** engage in (risky) commercial transactions **—specu'lation** n. **—'speculative** a. given to, characterized by speculation **—'speculator** n.

speculum ('spɛkjuləm) n. 1. mirror 2. reflector of polished metal, esp. in reflecting telescopes (pl. **-la** (-lə), **-s**) **—'specular** a.

sped (spɛd) pt./pp. of SPEED

speech (spi:tʃ) n. 1. act, faculty of speaking 2. words, language 3. conversation 4. discourse 5. (formal) talk given before audience **—'speechify** vi. make speech, esp. long and tedious one (**-ified, -ifying**) **—'speechless** a. 1. dumb 2. at a loss for words **—speech day** UK in schools, annual prize-giving day at which speeches are made

speed (spi:d) n. 1. swiftness 2. rate of progress 3. degree of sensitivity of photographic film 4. sl. amphetamine —vi. 5. move quickly 6. drive vehicle at high speed 7. obs. succeed —vt. 8. further 9. expedite (**sped** or **'speeded** pt./pp.) **—'speedily** adv. **—'speeding** n. driving (vehicle) at high speed, esp. over legal limit **—'speedo** n. inf. speedometer (pl. **-s**) **—'speedy** a. 1. quick 2. rapid 3. nimble 4. prompt **—'speedboat** n. light, fast motor-boat **—speed limit** maximum permitted speed at which vehicle may travel on certain roads **—speed'ometer** n. instrument to show speed of vehicle **—'speed-way** n. track for motorcycle racing **—'speedwell** n. plant with small, usu. blue flowers

spek (spɛk) n. SA bacon

speleology or **spelaeology** (spi:lɪ'ɒlədʒɪ) n. study, exploring of caves **—speleo'logi-cal** or **spelaeo'logical** a.

spell' (spɛl) vt. 1. give letters of in order 2. read letter by letter 3. indicate, result in (**spelled** or **spelt** pt./pp., **'spelling** pr.p.) **—'spelling** n. **—spell out** make explicit

spell² (spɛl) n. 1. magic formula 2. enchantment **—'spellbound** a. enchanted, entranced

spell³ (spɛl) n. (short) period of time, work

spelt (spɛlt) pt./pp. of SPELL'

spend (spɛnd) vt. 1. pay out 2. pass (time) on activity etc. 3. use up completely (**spent** pt./pp., **'spending** pr.p.) **—'spender** n. **—spent** a. used up, exhausted **—'spend-thrift** n. wasteful person

sperm (spɜːm) n. 1. male reproductive cell 2. semen **—spermaceti** (spɜːmə'sɛtɪ, -'si:tɪ) n. white, waxy substance obtained from oil from head of sperm whale **—sper'matic** a. of sperm **—spermatozoon** (spɜːmətəʊ'zəʊɒn) n. any of male reproductive cells released in semen during ejaculation (pl. **-zoa** (-'zəʊə)) (also **sperm**, **'zoosperm**) **—'spermicide** n. drug etc. that kills sperm **—sperm whale** large, toothed whale hunted for sperm oil, spermaceti and ambergris (also **'cacha-lot**)

spew (spju:) v. vomit

sphagnum ('sfægnəm) n. moss that grows in bogs

sphere (sfɪə) n. 1. ball, globe 2. range 3. field of action 4. status 5. position 6. province **—spherical** ('sfɛrɪk°l) a. **—'spheroid** n. 1. geometric surface produced by rotating ellipse about one of its two axes —a. 2. shaped like but not exactly a sphere

sphincter ('sfɪŋktə) n. ring of muscle surrounding opening of hollow bodily organ

sphinx (sfɪŋks) n. 1. statue in Egypt with lion's body and human head 2. (**S-**) monster with woman's head and lion's body 3. enigmatic person (pl. **-es, sphinges** ('sfɪndʒi:z))

spice (spaɪs) n. 1. aromatic or pungent vegetable substance 2. spices collectively 3. anything that adds flavour, relish, piquancy, interest etc. —vt. 4. season with spices, flavour **—'spicily** adv. **—'spicy** a. 1. flavoured with spices 2. inf. slightly indecent, risqué

spick-and-span or **spic-and-span** ('spɪk-ən'spæn) a. 1. neat, smart 2. new-looking

spider ('spaɪdə) n. small eight-legged creature which spins web to catch prey **—'spidery** a. **—spider plant** hardy house plant with long thin leaves

spiel (ʃpi:l) inf. n. 1. glib (sales) talk —vi. 2. deliver spiel, recite **—'spieler** n.

spigot ('spɪgət) n. peg, plug

spike (spaɪk) n. 1. sharp point 2. sharp pointed object 3. long flower cluster with flowers attached directly to the stalk —vt. 4. pierce, fasten with spike 5. render ineffective 6. add alcohol to (drink) **—'spiky** a. **—'spikenard** n. 1. aromatic Indian plant with rose-purple flowers 2. aromatic ointment obtained from this plant

spill' (spɪl) v. 1. (cause to) pour, flow over, fall out, esp. unintentionally 2. upset —vi. 3. be lost or wasted (**spilt** (spɪlt) or **spilled** pt./pp.) —n. 4. fall 5. amount spilt **—'spillage** n.

spill² (spɪl) n. thin strip of wood, twisted paper etc. for lighting fires etc.

spin (spɪn) v. 1. (cause to) revolve rapidly 2. whirl —vt. 3. twist into thread 4. (with out) prolong 5. inf. tell (a story) —vi. 6. fish with lure (**spun, obs. span** (spæn) pt., **spun** pp., **'spinning** pr.p.) —n. 7. spinning 8. (of aircraft) descent in dive with continued rotation 9. rapid run or drive 10. in skating, rapid turning on the spot 11. angular momentum of elementary particle **—'spinner** n. 1. person or thing that spins 2. Cricket ball that is bowled with spinning motion; spin bowler 3. fishing lure with fin or wing that revolves **—'spinneret** n. any of several organs in spiders etc. through which silk threads are exuded **—'spinning** n. act, process of drawing out and twisting into threads, as wool, cotton, flax etc. **—spin bowler** Cricket bowler who specializes in bowling balls with spinning motion

—**spin-dry** vt. spin (clothes) in spin-dryer —**spin-dryer** n. device that extracts water from clothes etc. by spinning them in perforated drum —**spinning jenny** early type of spinning frame with several spindles —**spinning wheel** household machine with large wheel turned by treadle for spinning wool etc. into thread —**spin-off** n. any product or development derived incidentally from application of existing knowledge or enterprise

spina bifida ('spaɪnə 'bɪfɪdə) congenital condition in which meninges of spinal cord protrude through gap in backbone

spinach ('spɪnɪdʒ, -ɪtʃ) n. 1. annual plant with edible leaves 2. the leaves, eaten boiled as vegetable

spindle ('spɪnd'l) n. rod, axis for spinning —'**spindly** a. long and slender 2. attenuated —'**spindlelegs** or '**spindle-shanks** pl.n. 1. long thin legs 2. person who has such legs

spindrift ('spɪndrɪft) or **spoondrift** ('spuːndrɪft) n. spray blown along surface of sea

spine (spaɪn) n. 1. backbone 2. thin spike, esp. on fish etc. 3. ridge 4. back of book —'**spinal** a. —'**spineless** a. 1. lacking spine 2. cowardly —'**spiny** a. 1. (of animals) having or covered with quills or spines 2. (of plants) covered with spines 3. troublesome —**spinal column** series of contiguous bony segments that surround spinal cord (also **spine, vertebral column**) —**spinal cord** cord of nerve tissue within spinal canal, which together with brain forms central nervous system —**spine-chiller** n. film etc. that arouses terror

spinet (spɪ'nɛt, 'spɪnɪt) n. keyboard instrument like harpsichord

spinnaker ('spɪnəkə; Naut. 'spæŋkə) n. large yacht sail

spinney ('spɪnɪ) n. small wood

spinster ('spɪnstə) n. unmarried woman

spiracle ('spaɪərək'l, 'spaɪrə-) n. Zool. opening for breathing

spiraea or esp. U.S. **spirea** (spaɪ'rɪə) n. any of various plants with small white or pink flower sprays

spiral ('spaɪərəl) n. 1. continuous curve drawn at ever-increasing distance from fixed point 2. anything resembling this —a. 3. having shape of spiral —'**spirally** adv.

spirant ('spaɪərənt) a. 1. Phonet. see FRICATIVE —n. 2. fricative consonant

spire (spaɪə) n. 1. pointed part of steeple 2. pointed stem

spirit ('spɪrɪt) n. 1. life principle animating body 2. disposition 3. liveliness 4. courage 5. frame of mind 6. essential character or meaning 7. soul 8. ghost 9. liquid got by distillation, alcohol —pl. 10. emotional state 11. strong alcoholic drink, eg whisky —vt. 12. (usu. with away or off) carry away mysteriously —'**spirited** a. lively —'**spiritless** a. listless, apathetic —'**spiritual** a. 1. given to, interested in things of the spirit —n. 2. Negro sacred song, hymn

—'**spiritualism** n. belief that spirits of the dead communicate with the living —'**spiritualist** n. —**spiritu'ality** n. —'**spiritually** adv. —'**spirituous** a. alcoholic —**spirit gum** glue made from gum dissolved in ether —**spirit lamp** lamp that burns methylated or other spirits —**spirit level** glass tube containing bubble in liquid, used to check horizontal, vertical surfaces —**spirits of salts** hydrochloric acid

spirt (spɜːt) see SPURT

spit[1] (spɪt) vi. 1. eject saliva —vt. 2. eject from mouth (**spat, spit** pt./pp., '**spitting** pr.p.) —n. 3. spitting, saliva —'**spittle** n. saliva —**spit'toon** n. vessel to spit into —'**spitfire** n. person with fiery temper —**spitting image** inf. person who bears physical resemblance to another —**spit and polish** inf. punctilious attention to neatness, discipline etc., esp. in armed forces

spit[2] (spɪt) n. 1. sharp rod to put through meat for roasting 2. sandy point projecting into the sea —vt. 3. thrust through (-**tt**-)

spite (spaɪt) n. 1. malice —vt. 2. thwart spitefully —'**spiteful** a. —'**spitefully** adv. —**in spite of** regardless of; notwithstanding

spiv (spɪv) n. smartly dressed man, esp. one who makes living by shady dealings

splake (spleɪk) n. type of hybrid Canad. trout

splash (splæʃ) v. 1. scatter (liquid) about, on or over (something) —vt. 2. print, display prominently —n. 3. sound of water being scattered 4. patch, esp. of colour 5. (effect of) extravagant display 6. small amount —'**splashdown** n. 1. controlled landing of spacecraft on water 2. time scheduled for this event —**splash down**

splat (splæt) n. wet, slapping sound

splatter ('splætə) v./n. spatter

splay (spleɪ) a. 1. spread out 2. slanting 3. turned outwards —v. 4. spread out 5. twist outwards —n. 6. slant surface 7. spread —'**splayfooted** a. flat and broad (of foot)

spleen (spliːn) n. 1. organ in abdomen 2. anger 3. irritable or morose temper —**splenetic** (splɪ'nɛtɪk) a. —'**spleenwort** n. any of various ferns

splendid ('splɛndɪd) a. 1. magnificent 2. brilliant 3. excellent —'**splendidly** adv. —'**splendour** or U.S. '**splendor** n.

splice (splaɪs) vt. 1. join by interweaving strands 2. join (wood) by overlapping 3. sl. join in marriage —n. 4. spliced joint

spline (splaɪn) n. narrow groove, ridge, strip, esp. joining wood etc.

splint (splɪnt) n. rigid support for broken limb etc.

splinter ('splɪntə) n. 1. thin fragment of glass, wood etc. —v. 2. break into fragments, shiver —**splinter group** group that separates from main party, organization, oft. after disagreement

split (splɪt) v. 1. break asunder 2. separate 3. divide —vi. 4. sl. depart; leave (**split,** '**splitting**) —n. 5. crack, fissure 6. dessert of fruit and ice cream —**'splitting** a. 1. (of headache) acute 2. (of head) assailed by overpowering unbearable pain —**split infinitive** in English grammar, infinitive used with another word between *to* and verb —**split-level** a. (of house *etc.*) having floor level of one part about half storey above floor level of adjoining part —**split pea** pea dried and split and used in soups *etc.* —**split personality** 1. tendency to change rapidly in mood or temperament 2. schizophrenia —**split second** infinitely small period of time —**split-second** a. made or arrived at in infinitely short time

splotch (splɒtʃ) *or* **splodge** (splɒdʒ) n./vt. splash, daub —**'splotchy** *or* **'splodgy** a.

splurge (splɜːdʒ) v. 1. spend (money) extravagantly —n. 2. ostentatious display, *esp.* of wealth 3. bout of unrestrained extravagance

splutter ('splʌtə) vi. 1. make hissing, spitting sounds —vt. 2. utter incoherently with spitting sounds —n. 3. process or noise of spluttering 4. spluttering incoherent speech

spode (spəʊd) n. (*sometimes* S-) china or porcelain manufactured by Josiah Spode, English potter, or his company

spoil (spɔɪl) vt. 1. damage, injure 2. damage manners or behaviour of (*esp.* child) by indulgence 3. pillage —vi. 4. go bad (**spoiled** *or* **spoilt** pt./pp., **'spoiling** pr.p.) —n. 5. booty 6. waste material, *esp.* in mining (*also* **'spoilage**) —**'spoiler** n. slowing device on aircraft wing *etc.* —**'spoilsport** n. *inf.* one who spoils pleasure of other people —**spoiling for** eager for

spoke[1] (spəʊk) pt. of SPEAK —**'spoken** pp. of SPEAK —**'spokesman** n. one deputed to speak for others

spoke[2] (spəʊk) n. radial bar of wheel

spoliation (spəʊlɪ'eɪʃən) n. 1. act of spoiling 2. robbery 3. destruction

spondee ('spɒndiː) n. metrical foot consisting of two long syllables (‾ ‾)

sponge (spʌndʒ) n. 1. marine animal 2. its skeleton, or a synthetic substance like it, used to absorb liquids 3. type of light cake —vt. 4. wipe with sponge —vi. 5. live meanly at expense of others —v. 6. cadge —**'sponger** n. *sl.* one who cadges or lives at expense of others —**'spongy** a. 1. spongelike 2. wet and soft —**sponge bag** small bag usu. made of plastic that holds toilet articles

sponsor ('spɒnsə) n. 1. one promoting, advertising something 2. one who agrees to give money to a charity on completion of specified activity by another 3. one taking responsibility (*esp.* for welfare of child at baptism, *ie* godparent) 4. guarantor —vt. 5. act as sponsor for —**'sponsorship** n.

spontaneous (spɒn'teɪnɪəs) a. 1. voluntary 2. natural 3. not forced 4. produced without external force —**spontaneity** (spɒntə-'niːɪtɪ, -'neɪ-) n. —**spon'taneously** adv.

—**spon'taneousness** n. —**spontaneous combustion** ignition of substance as result of internal oxidation processes

spoof (spuːf) n. 1. mild satirical mockery 2. trick, hoax

spook (spuːk) n. ghost —**'spooky** a.

spool (spuːl) n. reel, bobbin

spoon (spuːn) n. 1. implement with shallow bowl at end of handle for eating or serving food *etc.* —vt. 2. lift with spoon —**'spoonful** n. —**'spoonbill** n. any of several wading birds having long horizontally flattened bill —**spoon-feed** vt. 1. feed with spoon 2. spoil 3. provide (person) with ready-made opinions *etc.*

spoonerism ('spuːnərɪzəm) n. amusing transposition of initial consonants, *eg* 'half-warmed fish' for 'half-formed wish'

spoor (spʊə, spɔː) n. 1. trail of wild animals —v. 2. follow spoor (of)

sporadic (spə'rædɪk) *or* **sporadical** a. 1. intermittent 2. scattered —**spo'radically** adv.

spore (spɔː) n. minute reproductive organism of some plants and protozoans

sporran ('spɒrən) n. pouch worn in front of kilt

sport (spɔːt) n. 1. game, activity for pleasure, competition, exercise 2. enjoyment 3. mockery 4. cheerful person, good loser —vt. 5. wear, *esp.* ostentatiously —vi. 6. frolic 7. play (sport) —**'sportiness** n. —**'sporting** a. 1. of sport 2. behaving with fairness, generosity —**'sportive** a. playful —**'sporty** a. 1. stylish, loud or gay 2. relating to or appropriate to sportsman —**sporting chance** sufficient prospect of success to justify the attempt —**sports car** fast (open) car —**sports jacket** man's casual jacket —**'sportsman** n. 1. one who engages in sport 2. good loser

spot (spɒt) n. 1. small mark, stain 2. blemish 3. pimple 4. place 5. (difficult) situation 6. *inf.* small quantity —vt. 7. mark with spots 8. detect 9. observe (**-tt-**) —**'spotless** a. 1. unblemished 2. pure —**'spotlessly** adv. —**'spotty** a. 1. with spots 2. uneven —**spot check** random examination —**'spotlight** n. 1. powerful light illuminating small area 2. centre of attention —**spot-on** a. UK *inf.* absolutely correct —**spotted dick** *or* **dog** UK steamed or boiled suet pudding containing dried fruit —**spot-weld** vt. 1. join (two pieces of metal) by electrically generated heat —n. 2. weld so formed

spouse (spaʊs, spaʊz) n. husband or wife —**spousal** ('spaʊz'l) n. marriage

spout (spaʊt) v. 1. pour out —vi. 2. *sl.* speechify —n. 3. projecting tube or lip for pouring liquids 4. copious discharge —**up the spout** *sl.* 1. ruined; lost 2. pregnant

SPQR Senatus Populusque Romanus (*Lat.*, the Senate and people of Rome)

sprain (spreɪn) n./vt. wrench or twist (of muscle *etc.*)

sprang (spræŋ) pt. of SPRING

sprat (spræt) n. small sea fish

sprawl (sprɔːl) *vi.* 1. lie or sit about awkwardly —*v.* 2. spread in rambling, unplanned way —*n.* 3. sprawling

spray[1] (spreɪ) *n.* 1. (device for producing) fine drops of liquid —*vt.* 2. sprinkle with shower of fine drops —**spray gun** device that sprays fluid in finely divided form by atomizing it in air jet

spray[2] (spreɪ) *n.* 1. branch, twig with buds, flowers *etc.* 2. floral ornament, brooch *etc.* like this

spread (sprɛd) *v.* 1. extend 2. stretch out 3. open out 4. scatter 5. distribute or be distributed 6. unfold —*vt.* 7. cover (**spread, 'spreading**) —*n.* 8. extent 9. increase 10. ample meal 11. food which can be spread on bread *etc.* —**spread-eagle** *a.* with arms and legs outstretched (*also* **spread-eagled**)

spree (spriː) *n.* 1. session of overindulgence 2. romp

sprig (sprɪg) *n.* 1. small twig 2. ornamental design like this 3. small nail

sprightly ('spraɪtlɪ) *a.* lively, brisk —'**sprightliness** *n.*

spring (sprɪŋ) *vi.* 1. leap 2. shoot up or forth 3. come into being 4. appear 5. grow 6. become bent or split —*vt.* 7. produce unexpectedly 8. set off (trap) (**sprang, sprung, 'springing**) —*n.* 9. leap 10. recoil 11. piece of coiled or bent metal with much resilience 12. flow of water from earth 13. first season of year —'**springy** *a.* elastic —**spring balance** device in which object to be weighed is attached to end of helical spring, extension of which indicates weight on calibrated scale —'**springboard** *n.* flexible board for diving —**spring-clean** *v.* clean (house) thoroughly —**spring-cleaning** *n.* —**springer spaniel** breed of spaniel with silky coat, used for flushing or springing game —**spring onion** immature onion cultivated for its tiny bulb and long green leaves which are eaten in salads *etc.* —**spring tide** high tide at new or full moon

springbok *or* **springbuck** ('sprɪŋbʌk) *n.* 1. S Afr. antelope 2. (S-) South African national sportsman

sprinkle ('sprɪŋk'l) *vt.* scatter small drops on, strew —'**sprinkler** *n.* —'**sprinkling** *n.* small quantity or number

sprint (sprɪnt) *vi.* 1. run short distance at great speed —*n.* 2. such run, race

sprit (sprɪt) *n.* small spar set diagonally across fore-and-aft sail in order to extend it —**spritsail** ('sprɪtseɪl; *Naut.* 'sprɪtsəl) *n.* sail extended by sprit

sprite (spraɪt) *n.* fairy, elf

sprocket ('sprɒkɪt) *n.* 1. projection on wheel or capstan for engaging chain 2. wheel with sprockets (*also* **sprocket wheel**)

sprout (spraʊt) *v.* 1. put forth (shoots) —*vi.* 2. spring up —*n.* 3. shoot

spruce[1] (spruːs) *n.* variety of fir

spruce[2] (spruːs) *a.* neat in dress

sprung (sprʌŋ) *pp.* of SPRING

spry (spraɪ) *a.* nimble, vigorous

spud (spʌd) *n. inf.* potato

spume (spjuːm) *n./vi.* foam, froth

spun (spʌn) *pt./pp.* of SPIN

spunk (spʌŋk) *n.* courage, spirit

spur (spɜː) *n.* 1. pricking instrument attached to horseman's heel 2. incitement 3. stimulus 4. projection on cock's leg 5. projecting mountain range 6. railway branch line or siding —*vt.* 7. ride hard (**-rr-**)

spurious ('spjʊərɪəs) *a.* not genuine

spurn (spɜːn) *vt.* reject with scorn, thrust aside

spurt *or* **spirt** (spɜːt) *v.* 1. send, come out in jet —*vi.* 2. rush suddenly —*n.* 3. jet 4. short sudden effort, *esp.* in race

sputnik ('sputnɪk, 'spʌt-) *n.* any of series of Russian satellites

sputter ('spʌtə) *v.* splutter

sputum ('spjuːtəm) *n.* spittle (*pl.* **-ta** (-tə))

spy (spaɪ) *n.* 1. one who watches (*esp.* in rival countries, companies *etc.*) and reports secretly —*vi.* 2. act as spy —*vt.* 3. catch sight of (**spied, 'spying**) —'**spyglass** *n.* small telescope

Sq. 1. Square 2. Squadron

squab (skwɒb) *n.* 1. young unfledged bird, *esp.* pigeon 2. short fat person 3. well-stuffed cushion —*a.* 4. (of birds) unfledged 5. short and fat

squabble ('skwɒb'l) *vi.* 1. engage in petty, noisy quarrel, bicker —*n.* 2. petty quarrel

squad (skwɒd) *n.* small party, *esp.* of soldiers —'**squadron** *n.* division of cavalry regiment, fleet or air force —**squadron leader** officer holding commissioned rank, between flight lieutenant and wing commander in air forces of Brit. and certain other countries

squalid ('skwɒlɪd) *a.* mean and dirty —'**squalor** *n.*

squall (skwɔːl) *n.* 1. harsh cry 2. sudden gust of wind 3. short storm —*vi.* 4. yell

squander ('skwɒndə) *vt.* spend wastefully, dissipate

square (skwɛə) *n.* 1. equilateral rectangle 2. area of this shape 3. in town, open space (of this shape) 4. product of a number multiplied by itself 5. instrument for drawing right angles —*a.* 6. square in form 7. honest 8. straight, even 9. level, equal 10. denoting a measure of area 11. *inf.* old-fashioned, conservative —*vt.* 12. make square 13. find square of 14. pay 15. bribe —*vi.* 16. fit, suit —'**squarely** *adv.* —**square-bashing** *n.* UK *Mil. sl.* drill on barrack square —**square dance** any of various formation dances in which couples form squares —**square-dance** *vi.* perform such dance —**square deal** any transaction *etc.* that is honest and fair —**square leg** *Cricket* 1. fielding position on on side approximately at right angles to batsman 2. person who fields in this position —**square measure** unit or system of units for measuring areas —**square metre** *etc.* area equal to that of square with sides one metre *etc.* long —**square root** number that, multiplied by itself, gives number of which it is factor

squash (skwɒʃ) *vt.* **1.** crush flat **2.** pulp **3.** suppress **4.** humiliate —*n.* **5.** juice of crushed fruit **6.** crowd **7.** game played with rackets and soft balls in walled court **8.** marrowlike plant

squat (skwɒt) *vi.* **1.** sit on heels **2.** act as squatter (-**tt**-) —*a.* **3.** short and thick —'**squatter** *n.* one who settles on land or occupies house without permission

squaw (skwɔː) *n.* N Amer. Indian woman

squawk (skwɔːk) *n.* **1.** short harsh cry, *esp.* of bird —*vi.* **2.** utter this cry

squeak (skwiːk) *vi./n.* (make) short shrill sound

squeal (skwiːl) *n.* **1.** long piercing squeak —*vi.* **2.** make one **3.** *sl.* confess information (about another)

squeamish ('skwiːmɪʃ) *a.* **1.** easily made sick **2.** easily shocked **3.** overscrupulous

squeegee ('skwiːdʒiː) *or* **squilgee** ('skwɪldʒiː) *n.* **1.** tool with rubber blade for clearing water (from glass *etc.*), spreading wet paper *etc.* —*vt.* **2.** press, smooth with squeegee

squeeze (skwiːz) *vt.* **1.** press **2.** wring **3.** force **4.** hug **5.** subject to extortion —*n.* **6.** act of squeezing **7.** period of hardship, difficulty caused by financial weakness

squelch (skwɛltʃ) *vi.* **1.** make, walk with wet sucking sound, as in walking through mud —*n.* **2.** squelching sound

squib (skwɪb) *n.* **1.** small firework that hisses before exploding **2.** insignificant person

squid (skwɪd) *n.* type of cuttlefish

squiffy ('skwɪfɪ) *a.* UK *inf.* slightly drunk

squiggle ('skwɪgʰl) *n.* **1.** wavy, wriggling mark —*vi.* **2.** wriggle **3.** draw squiggle

squill (skwɪl) *n.* **1.** Mediterranean plant of lily family **2.** its bulb, used medicinally as expectorant

squint (skwɪnt) *vi.* **1.** have the eyes turned in different directions **2.** glance sideways —*n.* **3.** this eye disorder **4.** glance —*a.* **5.** having a squint

squire (skwaɪə) *n.* country gentleman

squirm (skwɜːm) *vi.* **1.** wriggle **2.** be embarrassed —*n.* **3.** squirming movement

squirrel ('skwɪrəl) *n.* small graceful bushy-tailed tree animal

squirt (skwɜːt) *v.* **1.** force (liquid) or (of liquid) be forced through narrow opening —*n.* **2.** jet **3.** *inf.* short or insignificant person

Sr *Chem.* strontium

Sr. *or* **Sr 1.** Senior **2.** Sister

S.R.C. UK Science Research Council

S.R.N. State Registered Nurse

SS 1. Saints **2.** paramilitary organization within Nazi party that provided Hitler's bodyguard, security forces, concentration camp guards *etc.* **3.** (*also* **S.S.**) steamship

SSE south-southeast

SSR Soviet Socialist Republic

S.S.R.C. UK Social Science Research Council

SSW south-southwest

st. stone (weight)

St. *or* **St 1.** Saint **2.** Strait **3.** Street

stab (stæb) *v.* **1.** pierce, strike (at) with pointed weapon (-**bb**-) —*n.* **2.** blow, wound so inflicted **3.** sudden sensation, *eg* of fear **4.** attempt

stabilize *or* -**ise** ('steɪbɪlaɪz) *vt.* make steady, restore to equilibrium, *esp.* of money values, prices and wages —**stabili-** '**zation** *or* -**i**'**sation** *n.* —'**stabilizer** *or* -**iser** *n.* device to maintain equilibrium of ship, aircraft *etc.*

stable[1] ('steɪbʰl) *n.* **1.** building for horses **2.** racehorses of particular owner, establishment **3.** such establishment —*vt.* **4.** put into stable

stable[2] ('steɪbʰl) *a.* **1.** firmly fixed **2.** steadfast, resolute —**stability** (stə'bɪlɪtɪ) *n.* **1.** steadiness **2.** ability to resist change of any kind —'**stably** *adv.*

staccato (stə'kɑːtəʊ) *a.* **1.** *Mus.* with notes sharply separated **2.** abrupt

stack (stæk) *n.* **1.** ordered pile, heap **2.** chimney —*vt.* **3.** pile in stack **4.** control (aircraft waiting to land) so that they fly at different altitudes

stadium ('steɪdɪəm) *n.* open-air arena for athletics *etc.* (*pl.* -**s, -dia** (-dɪə))

staff (stɑːf) *n.* **1.** body of officers or workers employed by a company *etc.*; personnel (*pl.* -**s**) **2.** pole (*pl.* -**s, staves**) **3.** set of five lines on which music is written (*pl.* -**s, staves**) —*vt.* **4.** supply with personnel —**staff nurse** qualified nurse ranking immediately below sister —**staff sergeant** *Mil.* **1.** UK noncommissioned officer holding sergeant's rank and carrying out certain special duties **2.** US noncommissioned officer who ranks: in Army, above sergeant and below sergeant first class; in Air Force, above airman first class and below technical sergeant; in Marine Corps, above sergeant and below gunnery sergeant

Staffs. (stæfs) Staffordshire

stag (stæg) *n.* **1.** male deer —*a.* **2.** for men only

stage (steɪdʒ) *n.* **1.** period, division of development **2.** raised floor or platform **3.** (platform of) theatre **4.** scene of action **5.** stopping-place on road, distance between two of them **6.** separate unit of space rocket that can be jettisoned —*vt.* **7.** put (play) on stage **8.** arrange, bring about —'**staging** *n.* any temporary structure used in building, *esp.* platforms supported by scaffolding —'**stagy** *a.* theatrical —'**stagecoach** *n.* formerly, four-wheeled horse-drawn vehicle used to carry passengers *etc.* on regular route —**stage fright** panic that may beset person about to appear in front of audience —'**stagehand** *n.* person who sets stage, moves props *etc.* in theatrical production —**stage-manage** *v.* **1.** work as stage manager for (play *etc.*)

—*vt.* **2.** arrange or supervise from behind the scenes —**stage manager** person who supervises stage arrangements of theatrical production —**stage-struck** *a.* infatuated with glamour of theatrical life —**stage whisper** loud whisper intended to be heard by audience

stagflation (stæg'fleɪʃən) *n.* inflationary economic situation characterized by decline in industrial output

stagger ('stægə) *vi.* **1.** walk unsteadily —*vt.* **2.** astound **3.** arrange in overlapping or alternating positions, times **4.** distribute over a period —*n.* **5.** act of staggering —*pl.* **6.** form of vertigo **7.** disease of horses —'**staggering** *a.* astounding

stagnate (stæg'neɪt) *vi.* cease to flow or develop —'**stagnant** *a.* **1.** sluggish **2.** not flowing **3.** foul, impure —**stag'nation** *n.*

staid (steɪd) *a.* of sober and quiet character, sedate —'**staidly** *adv.* —'**staidness** *n.*

stain (steɪn) *vt.* **1.** spot, mark **2.** apply liquid colouring to (wood *etc.*) **3.** bring disgrace upon —*n.* **4.** spot, mark, discoloration **5.** moral taint —'**stainless** *a.* —**stainless steel** rustless steel alloy

stairs (stɛəz) *pl.n.* set of steps, *esp.* as part of house —'**staircase** *or* '**stairway** *n.* **1.** structure enclosing stairs **2.** stairs —'**stairwell** *n.* vertical shaft that contains staircase

stake (steɪk) *n.* **1.** sharpened stick or post **2.** money wagered or contended for —*vt.* **3.** secure, mark out with stakes **4.** wager, risk —**stake out** US *sl.* keep under surveillance

stalactite ('stæləktaɪt) *n.* lime deposit like icicle on roof of cave

stalagmite ('stæləgmaɪt) *n.* lime deposit like pillar on floor of cave

stale (steɪl) *a.* **1.** old, lacking freshness **2.** hackneyed **3.** lacking energy, interest through monotony —'**stalemate** *n.* **1.** Chess draw through one player being unable to move **2.** deadlock, impasse

stalk[1] (stɔːk) *n.* **1.** plant's stem **2.** anything like this

stalk[2] (stɔːk) *v.* **1.** follow, approach (game *etc.*) stealthily —*vi.* **2.** walk in stiff and stately manner —*n.* **3.** stalking —**stalking-horse** *n.* pretext

stall[1] (stɔːl) *n.* **1.** compartment in stable *etc.* **2.** erection for display and sale of goods **3.** seat in chancel of church **4.** finger sheath —*pl.* **5.** area of seats on ground floor of theatre or cinema, nearest to orchestra pit or screen —*vt.* **6.** put in stall **7.** hinder **8.** stick fast —*v.* **9.** delay **10.** stop unintentionally (motor engine) **11.** lose flying speed (of aircraft) —*vi.* **12.** prevaricate

stallion ('stæljən) *n.* uncastrated male horse, *esp.* one used for breeding

stalwart ('stɔːlwət) *a.* **1.** strong **2.** brave **3.** staunch —*n.* **4.** stalwart person

stamen ('steɪmen) *n.* male organ of flowering plant (*pl.* **-s,** **stamina** ('stæmɪnə))

stamina ('stæmɪnə) *n.* power of endurance, vitality

stammer ('stæmə) *v.* **1.** speak, say with repetition of syllables, stutter —*n.* **2.** habit of so speaking —'**stammerer** *n.*

stamp (stæmp) *vi.* **1.** put down foot with force —*vt.* **2.** impress mark on **3.** affix postage stamp to **4.** fix (in memory) **5.** reveal, characterize —*n.* **6.** stamping with foot **7.** imprinted mark **8.** appliance for marking **9.** piece of gummed paper printed with device as evidence of postage *etc.* **10.** character —**stamping ground** habitual meeting or gathering place

stampede (stæm'piːd) *n.* **1.** sudden frightened rush, *esp.* of herd of cattle **2.** headlong rush of a crowd **3.** C rodeo —*vi.* **4.** cause, take part in stampede

stance (stæns, stɑːns) *n.* **1.** manner, position of standing **2.** attitude **3.** point of view

stanch (stɑːntʃ) *vt. see* STAUNCH

stanchion ('stɑːnʃən) *n.* **1.** upright bar, support —*vt.* **2.** support

stand (stænd) *v.* **1.** have, take, set in upright position —*vi.* **2.** remain **3.** be situated **4.** remain firm or stationary **5.** cease to move **6.** adhere to principles **7.** offer oneself as a candidate **8.** (*with* for) be symbol *etc.* (of) —*vt.* **9.** endure **10.** *inf.* provide free, treat to (**stood,** '**standing**) —*n.* **11.** holding firm **12.** position **13.** halt **14.** something on which thing may be placed **15.** structure from which spectators watch sport *etc.* **16.** stop made by pop group *etc.* —'**standing** *n.* **1.** reputation, status **2.** duration —*a.* **3.** erect **4.** permanent, lasting **5.** stagnant **6.** performed from stationary position, as in *standing jump* —**stand-by** *n.* person or thing that is ready for use or can be relied on in emergency —**stand-in** *n.* person, thing that acts as substitute —**standing order 1.** instruction to bank by depositor to pay stated amount at regular intervals **2.** rule governing procedure *etc.* of legislative body **3.** *Mil.* one of number of orders which have long-term validity —**stand'offish** *a.* reserved or aloof —'**standstill** *n.* complete cessation of movement —**stand by 1.** be available and ready to act if needed **2.** be present as onlooker **3.** be faithful to —**stand in** deputize —**stand over 1.** watch closely **2.** postpone

standard ('stændəd) *n.* **1.** accepted example of something against which others are judged **2.** degree, quality **3.** flag **4.** weight or measure to which others must conform **5.** post **6.** SA school form or grade —*a.* **7.** usual, regular **8.** average **9.** of recognized authority, competence **10.** accepted as correct —**standardi'zation** *or* **-i'sation** *n.* —'**standardize** *or* **-ise** *vt.* regulate by a standard —**standard-bearer** *n.* **1.** man who carries a standard **2.** leader of party *etc.* —**standard gauge** railway track with distance of 56½ inches between lines —**standard-gauge** *or* **standard-**

gauged a. of or denoting railway with standard gauge —**standard lamp** electric light fixed to tall support standing on floor —**standard time** official local time of region or country determined by distance from Greenwich of line of longitude passing through area —**standard of living** level of subsistence or material welfare of community, person etc.

standpoint ('stændpɔɪnt) n. 1. point of view, opinion 2. mental attitude

stank (stæŋk) pt. of STINK

stannary ('stænərɪ) n. place or region where tin is mined or worked

stannous ('stænəs) a. of, containing tin

stanza ('stænzə) n. group of lines of verse

staple ('steɪp'l) n. 1. U-shaped piece of wire used to fasten papers, cloth etc. 2. short length of stiff wire formed into U-shape with pointed ends, used for holding hasp to post, securing electrical cables etc. 3. main product 4. fibre 5. pile of wool etc. —a. 6. principal 7. regularly produced or made for market —vt. 8. fasten with staple 9. sort, classify (wool etc.) according to length of fibre —**stapler** n. small device for fastening papers together

star (stɑː) n. 1. celestial body, seen as twinkling point of light 2. asterisk (*) 3. celebrated player, actor etc. 4. medal, jewel etc. of apparent shape of star —vt. 5. adorn with stars 6. mark (with asterisk) 7. feature as star performer —vi. 8. play leading role (in film etc.) (-rr-) —a. 9. leading, most important, famous —**stardom** n. —**starlet** n. young actress who is projected as potential star —**starry** a. covered with stars —**star-crossed** a. dogged by ill luck —**starfish** n. small star-shaped sea creature —**stargaze** vi. 1. observe stars 2. daydream —**stargazing** n./a. —**starry-eyed** a. given to naive wishes, judgments etc. —**Star-Spangled Banner** 1. national anthem of the United States 2. Stars and Stripes —**star-studded** a. featuring large proportion of well-known performers —**Star of David** emblem symbolizing Judaism, consisting of six-pointed star formed by superimposing one equilateral triangle upon another —**Stars and Stripes** national flag of the United States, consisting of 50 white stars and seven red and six white horizontal stripes

starboard ('stɑːbəd, -bɔːd) n. 1. right-hand side of ship, looking forward —a. 2. of, on this side

starch (stɑːtʃ) n. 1. substance forming the main food element in bread, potatoes etc., and used mixed with water, for stiffening linen etc. —vt. 2. stiffen thus —**starchy** a. 1. containing starch 2. stiff 3. formal 4. prim

stare (stɛə) vi. 1. look fixedly 2. gaze with wide-open eyes —n. 3. staring, fixed gaze —**stare one in the face** be obvious or visible to one —**stare out** abash by staring at

stark (stɑːk) a. 1. blunt, bare 2. desolate 3. absolute —adv. 4. completely

starling ('stɑːlɪŋ) n. glossy black speckled songbird

start (stɑːt) vt. 1. begin 2. set going —vi. 3. begin, esp. journey 4. make sudden movement —n. 5. beginning 6. abrupt movement 7. advantage of a lead in a race —**starter** n. 1. electric motor starting car engine 2. competitor in, supervisor of, start of race

startle ('stɑːt'l) vt. surprise, frighten or alarm suddenly

starve (stɑːv) v. (cause to) suffer or die from hunger —**star'vation** n.

stash (stæʃ) vt. inf. put away, hide

-stat (comb. form) device that causes something to remain stationary or constant, as in thermostat

state (steɪt) n. 1. condition 2. place, situation 3. politically organized people 4. government 5. rank 6. pomp —vt. 7. express in words —**stated** a. 1. fixed 2. regular 3. settled —**stateless** a. 1. without nationality 2. without state or states —**stately** a. dignified, lofty —**statement** n. 1. expression in words 2. account —**State Enrolled Nurse** nurse who has passed examinations enabling him or her to perform many nursing services —**stately home** UK large mansion, esp. one open to public —**state-of-the-art** a. (of hi-fi equipment etc.) up-to-the-minute —**State Registered Nurse** nurse who has passed examinations enabling him or her to perform all nursing services —**stateroom** n. 1. private cabin on ship 2. large room in palace, mansion, used for ceremonial occasions —**state school** any school maintained by the state —**statesman** n. respected political leader

static ('stætɪk) a. 1. motionless, inactive 2. pert. to bodies at rest or in equilibrium 3. Comp. (of a memory) not needing its contents refreshed periodically —n. 4. electrical interference in radio reception —pl. 5. (with sing. v.) branch of physics —**statically** adv.

station ('steɪʃən) n. 1. place where thing stops or is placed 2. stopping place for railway trains 3. local office for police force, fire brigade etc. 4. place equipped for radio or television transmission 5. bus garage 6. post, employment 7. status 8. position in life —vt. 9. put in position —**stationary** a. 1. not moving, fixed 2. not changing —**station wagon** estate car

stationer ('steɪʃənə) n. dealer in writing materials etc. —**stationery** n.

statistics (stə'tɪstɪks) pl.n. 1. numerical facts collected systematically and arranged 2. (with sing. v.) the study of them —**sta'tistical** a. —**sta'tistically** adv. —**statis'tician** n. one who compiles and studies statistics

statue ('stætjuː) n. solid carved or cast image of person, animal etc. —**statuary** n. statues collectively —**statuesque**

(stætju'ɛsk) a. 1. like statue 2. dignified —**statu'ette** n. small statue

stature ('stætʃə) n. 1. bodily height 2. greatness

status ('steɪtəs) n. 1. position, rank 2. prestige 3. relation to others —**status quo** (kwəʊ) existing state of affairs —**status symbol** possession regarded as proof of owner's wealth etc.

statute ('stætjuːt) n. written law —'**statutory** a. enacted, defined or authorized by statute

staunch (stɔːntʃ) vt. 1. stop flow of (blood) (also **stanch**) —a. 2. trustworthy, loyal

stave (steɪv) n. 1. one of the pieces forming barrel 2. verse, stanza 3. Mus. staff —vt. 4. (usu. with in) burst or force (hole in something) 5. (with off) ward (off) (**stove**, **staved** pt./pp., '**staving** pr.p.)

staves (steɪvz) n., pl. of STAFF, STAVE

stay[1] (steɪ) vi. 1. remain 2. sojourn 3. pause 4. wait 5. endure —vt. 6. stop 7. hinder 8. postpone (**stayed**, '**staying**) —n. 9. remaining, sojourning 10. check 11. restraint 12. deterrent 13. postponement —**stay-at-home** a./n. (person) enjoying quiet and unadventurous use of leisure —**staying power** endurance

stay[2] (steɪ) n. 1. support, prop 2. rope supporting mast etc. —pl. 3. formerly, laced corsets

S.T.D. subscriber trunk dialling

stead (stɛd) n. rare place —**stand (someone) in good stead** be useful or of good service to (someone)

steady ('stɛdɪ) a. 1. firm 2. regular 3. temperate 4. industrious 5. reliable —vt. 6. make steady —'**steadily** adv. —'**steadiness** n. —'**steadfast** a. firm, fixed, unyielding —'**steadfastly** adv. —**steady state** Phys. condition of system when some or all of quantities describing it are independent of time —**steady (on)** be careful

steak (steɪk) n. 1. thick slice of meat, esp. beef 2. slice of fish

steal (stiːl) v. 1. take (something) without right or leave —vi. 2. move silently (**stole**, '**stolen**, '**stealing**)

stealth (stɛlθ) n. secret or underhand procedure, behaviour —'**stealthily** adv. —'**stealthy** a.

steam (stiːm) n. 1. vapour of boiling water 2. inf. power, energy —vi. 3. give off steam 4. rise in vapour 5. move by steam power —vt. 6. cook or treat with steam —'**steamer** n. 1. steam-propelled ship 2. vessel for cooking or treating with steam —'**steamy** a. 1. of, full of, or covered with steam 2. inf. lustful —**steam-engine** n. engine worked or propelled by steam —**steam iron** electric iron that emits steam to facilitate pressing and ironing —'**steamroller** n. 1. large roller, orig. moved by steam, for levelling road surfaces etc. 2. any great power used to crush opposition —vt. 3. crush

stearin or **stearine** ('stɪərɪn) n. 1. colourless crystalline ester, present in fats and used in soap and candles (also **tri'stearin**) 2. fat in its solid form

steatite ('stɪətaɪt) n. soapstone

steed (stiːd) n. Poet. horse

steel (stiːl) n. 1. hard and malleable metal made by mixing carbon in iron 2. tool, weapon of steel 3. C railway track, line —vt. 4. harden —'**steely** a. —**steel band** type of band consisting mainly of percussion instruments made from oildrums —**steel wool** woven mass of fine steel fibres, used for cleaning or polishing

steelyard ('stiːljɑːd) n. kind of balance with unequal arms

steep[1] (stiːp) a. 1. rising, sloping abruptly 2. precipitous 3. inf. difficult 4. (of prices) very high or exorbitant 5. inf. unreasonable —'**steepen** v. —'**steeply** adv.

steep[2] (stiːp) vt. 1. soak, saturate —vi. 2. be soaked —n. 3. act or process of steeping 4. the liquid used for this purpose

steeple ('stiːpʳl) n. church tower with spire —'**steeplechase** n. 1. horse race with ditches and fences to jump 2. foot race with hurdles etc. to jump —'**steeplejack** n. one who builds, repairs chimneys, steeples etc.

steer[1] (stɪə) vt. 1. guide, direct course of (vessel, motor vehicle etc.) —vi. 2. direct one's course —'**steerage** n. 1. effect of a helm 2. formerly, cheapest accommodation on ship —**steering committee** committee set up to prepare topics to be discussed, order of business etc. for legislative assembly etc. —**steering gear, wheel** etc. mechanism for steering —'**steersman** n. helmsman of vessel

steer[2] (stɪə) n. castrated male ox

stein (staɪn) n. earthenware beer mug

stele ('stiːlɪ, stiːl) n. ancient carved stone pillar or slab (pl. **stelae** ('stiːliː), **steles** ('stiːlɪz, stiːlz))

stellar ('stɛlə) a. of stars

stem[1] (stɛm) n. 1. stalk, trunk 2. long slender part, as in tobacco pipe 3. part of word to which inflections are added 4. foremost part of ship

stem[2] (stɛm) vt. check, stop, dam up (-**mm**-)

stench (stɛntʃ) n. offensive smell

stencil ('stɛnsʳl) n. 1. thin sheet of plastic or metal pierced with pattern, which is brushed over with paint or ink, leaving pattern on surface under it 2. pattern produced by this process —vt. 3. mark (surface) with stencil (-**ll**-)

Sten gun (stɛn) light sub-machine-gun

stenography (stə'nɒgrəfɪ) n. shorthand writing —**ste'nographer** n. —**steno'graphic** a.

stentorian (stɛn'tɔːrɪən) a. (of voice) very loud

step (stɛp) vi. 1. move and set down foot 2. proceed (in this way) —vt. 3. measure in paces (-**pp**-) —n. 4. act of stepping 5. sound made by stepping 6. mark made by foot 7. manner of walking 8. series of foot movements forming part of dance **9.** gait **10.** pace **11.** measure, act, stage in proceeding **12.** board, rung *etc.* to put foot on **13.** degree in scale **14.** mast socket **15.** promotion —*pl.* **16.** stepladder (*also* **pair of steps**) —'**stepladder** *n.* four-legged ladder having broad flat steps —**stepping stone 1.** one of series of stones acting as footrests for crossing streams *etc.* **2.** circumstance that assists progress towards some goal

stepchild ('stɛptʃaɪld) *n.* child of husband or wife by former marriage —'**stepbrother** *n.* —'**stepfather** *n.* —'**stepmother** *n.* —'**stepsister** *n.*

stephanotis (stɛfə'nəʊtɪs) *n.* climbing shrub with fragrant waxy flowers

steppe (stɛp) *n.* (*oft. pl.*) extensive treeless plain in European and Asiatic Russia

-ster (*comb. form*) **1.** indicating person who is engaged in certain activity, as in *prankster* **2.** indicating person associated with or being something specified, as in *mobster, youngster*

stere (stɪə) *n.* cubic metre

stereo- *or sometimes before vowel* **stere-** (*comb. form*) three-dimensional quality or solidity, as in *stereoscope*

stereophonic (stɛrɪə'fɒnɪk, stɪər-) *a.* (of sound reproduction) using two or more separate microphones to feed two or more loudspeakers through separate channels in order to give spatial effect to sound —'**stereo** *a./n.* (of, for) stereophonic gramophone *etc.*

stereoscope ('stɛrɪəskəʊp, 'stɪər-) *n.* optical instrument for viewing two-dimensional pictures, giving illusion of depth and relief —**stereoscopic** (stɛrɪə'skɒpɪk, stɪər-) *a.*

stereotype ('stɛrɪətaɪp, 'stɪər-) *n.* **1.** metal plate for printing cast from set-up type **2.** something (monotonously) familiar, conventional, predictable —*vt.* **3.** make stereotype of —'**stereotyped** *a.* **1.** lacking originality or individuality **2.** reproduced from or on stereotype printing plate

sterile ('stɛraɪl) *a.* **1.** unable to produce fruit, crops, young *etc.* **2.** free from (harmful) germs —**sterility** (stɛ'rɪlɪtɪ) *n.* —**sterilization** *or* **-isation** (stɛrɪlaɪ'zeɪʃən) *n.* process or act of making sterile —**sterilize** *or* **-ise** ('stɛrɪlaɪz) *vt.* render sterile

sterling ('stɜːlɪŋ) *a.* **1.** genuine, true **2.** of solid worth, dependable **3.** in British money —*n.* **4.** British money

stern¹ (stɜːn) *a.* severe, strict

stern² (stɜːn) *n.* rear part of ship

sternum ('stɜːnəm) *n.* breastbone (*pl.* **-na** (-nə), **-s**)

sterols ('stɛrɒlz) *pl.n.* class of complex organic alcohols, including ergosterol, cholesterol —'**steroid** *n.* *Biochem.* any of group of organic compounds including sterols, bile acids, many hormones, and D vitamins

stertorous ('stɜːtərəs) *a.* **1.** with sound of heavy snoring **2.** breathing in this way

stet (stɛt) *Lat.*, let it stand (proofreader's direction to cancel alteration previously made)

stethoscope ('stɛθəskəʊp) *n.* instrument for listening to action of heart, lungs *etc.*

stetson ('stɛts⁾n) *n.* type of broad-brimmed felt hat

stevedore ('stiːvɪdɔː) *n.* one who loads or unloads ships

stew (stjuː) *n.* **1.** food cooked slowly in closed vessel **2.** state of excitement, agitation or worry —*v.* **3.** cook by stewing —**stewed** *a.* **1.** (of fish *etc.*) cooked by stewing **2.** UK (of tea) bitter through having been left to infuse for too long **3.** *sl.* drunk

steward ('stjʊəd) *n.* **1.** one who manages another's property **2.** official managing race meeting, assembly *etc.* **3.** attendant on ship's or aircraft's passengers (**'stewardess** *fem.*)

stick (stɪk) *n.* **1.** long, thin piece of wood **2.** anything shaped like a stick **3.** *inf.* person, as in *good stick* —*vt.* **4.** pierce, stab **5.** place, fasten, as by pins, glue **6.** (*with* out) protrude **7.** *inf.* tolerate, abide —*vi.* **8.** adhere **9.** come to stop, jam **10.** remain **11.** be fastened **12.** (*with* out) protrude (**stuck** *pt./pp.*) —'**sticker** *n.* adhesive label, poster —'**sticky** *a.* **1.** covered with, adhesive substance **2.** (of weather) warm, humid **3.** *inf.* difficult, unpleasant —**sticking plaster** thin cloth with adhesive substance on one side, used for covering slight wounds —**stick insect** insect that resembles a twig —**stick-in-the-mud** *n. inf.* person who lacks initiative or imagination —**stick-up** *n. sl.*, *chiefly US* robbery at gunpoint —**sticky wicket 1.** cricket pitch rapidly dried by sun after rain and particularly conducive to spin **2.** *inf.* difficult situation —**stick up** *sl.*, *chiefly US* rob, *esp.* at gunpoint —**stick up for** *inf.* support or defend

stickleback ('stɪk⁾lbæk) *n.* small fish with sharp spines on back

stickler ('stɪklə) *n.* (*usu. with* for) person who insists on something

stiff (stɪf) *a.* **1.** not easily bent or moved **2.** rigid **3.** awkward **4.** difficult **5.** thick, not fluid **6.** formal **7.** stubborn **8.** unnatural **9.** strong or fresh, as breeze **10.** *inf.* excessive —*n.* **11.** *sl.* corpse —'**stiffen** *v.* —'**stiffly** *adv.* —'**stiffness** *n.* —**stiff-necked** *a.* obstinate, stubborn

stifle ('staɪf⁾l) *vt.* smother, suppress

stigma ('stɪgmə) *n.* distinguishing mark, *esp.* of disgrace (*pl.* **-s**, **stigmata** ('stɪgmətə, stɪg'mɑːtə)) —'**stigmatism** *n.* —'**stigmatize** *or* **-ise** *vt.* mark with stigma

stile (staɪl) *n.* arrangement of steps for climbing a fence

stiletto (stɪ'lɛtəʊ) *n.* **1.** small dagger **2.** small boring tool **3.** very high heel on woman's shoe, tapering to very narrow tip (*pl.* **-s**) —*a.* **4.** thin, pointed like stiletto

still¹ (stɪl) *a.* **1.** motionless **2.** noiseless **3.** at rest —*vt.* **4.** quiet —*adv.* **5.** to this time **6.**

yet 7. even —n. 8. photograph, *esp.* of film scene —'**stillness** n. —'**stillborn** a. born dead —**still life** painting of inanimate objects

still² (stɪl) n. apparatus for distilling —**still room** pantry, storeroom in large house

stilt (stɪlt) n. 1. pole with footrests for walking raised from ground 2. long post supporting building *etc.* 3. shore bird similar to avocet but having straight bill —'**stilted** a. stiff in manner, pompous —'**stiltedly** adv.

Stilton ('stɪltən) n. either of two rich cheeses, blue-veined or white

stimulus ('stɪmjʊləs) n. 1. something that rouses to activity 2. incentive (*pl.* -**uli** (-jʊlaɪ, -jʊliː)) —'**stimulant** n. drug *etc.* acting as a stimulus —'**stimulate** vt. rouse up, spur —'**stimulating** a. acting as stimulus —**stimu'lation** n. —'**stimulative** a./n.

sting (stɪŋ) vt. 1. thrust sting into 2. cause sharp pain to 3. *sl.* impose upon by asking for money 4. overcharge —vi. 5. feel sharp pain (**stung**, '**stinging**) —n. 6. (wound, pain, caused by) sharp pointed organ, oft. poisonous, of certain insects and animals —'**stingray** n. ray having whiplike tail bearing serrated venomous spine capable of inflicting painful weals

stingy ('stɪndʒɪ) a. 1. mean 2. avaricious 3. niggardly —'**stingily** adv. —'**stinginess** n.

stink (stɪŋk) vi. 1. give out strongly offensive smell 2. *sl.* be abhorrent (**stank, stunk, 'stinking**) —n. 3. such smell, stench 4. *inf.* fuss, bother —'**stinker** n. *sl.* 1. difficult or unpleasant person or thing 2. something of very poor quality —**stink bomb** small bomb containing liquid with offensive smell

stint (stɪnt) v. 1. be frugal, miserly to (someone) with (something) —n. 2. allotted amount of work or time 3. limitation, restriction

stipend ('staɪpɛnd) n. salary, *esp.* of clergyman —**sti'pendiary** a. receiving stipend

stipple ('stɪpᵊl) vt. engrave, paint in dots —n. 2. this process

stipulate ('stɪpjʊleɪt) vt. specify in making a bargain —**stipu'lation** n. proviso, condition —'**stipulator** n.

stipule ('stɪpjuːl) n. small paired outgrowth occurring at base of leaf or its stalk —'**stipular** a.

stir¹ (stɜː) v. 1. (begin to) move —vt. 2. set, keep in motion 3. excite; rouse 4. (*with* up) cause (trouble) (-**rr**-) —n. 5. commotion, disturbance —'**stirring** a. 1. exciting emotions; stimulating 2. active or busy

stir² (stɜː) n. 1. *sl.* prison 2. NZ *sl.* noisy party —**stir-crazy** a. US *sl.* mentally disturbed as result of being in prison

stirk (stɜːk) n. 1. heifer of 6 to 12 months old 2. yearling heifer or bullock

stirrup ('stɪrəp) n. metal loop hung from strap for supporting foot of rider on horse (*also* **stirrup iron**) —**stirrup cup** cup

containing alcoholic drink offered to horseman ready to depart —**stirrup pump** hand-operated pump, base of cylinder of which is placed in bucket of water: used in fighting fires

stitch (stɪtʃ) n. 1. movement of needle in sewing *etc.* 2. its result in the work 3. sharp pain in side 4. least fragment (of clothing) —vt. 5. sew, fasten *etc.* with stitches

stoat (stəʊt) n. small mammal with brown coat and black-tipped tail

stock (stɒk) n. 1. goods, material stored, *esp.* for sale or later use 2. reserve, fund 3. financial shares in, or capital of, company *etc.* 4. standing, reputation 5. farm animals, livestock 6. plant, stem from which cuttings are taken 7. handle of gun, tool *etc.* 8. liquid broth produced by boiling meat *etc.* 9. flowering plant 10. lineage —*pl.* 11. *Hist.* frame to secure feet, hands (of offender) 12. frame to support ship during construction —a. 13. kept in stock 14. standard, hackneyed —vt. 15. keep, store 16. supply with livestock, fish *etc.* —'**stockist** n. dealer who maintains stocks of specified product —'**stocky** a. thickset —'**stockbreeder** n. person who breeds livestock as occupation —'**stockbroker** n. agent for buying, selling shares in companies —**stock car** ordinary car strengthened and modified for a form of racing in which cars often collide —**stock exchange** institution for buying and selling shares —'**stockjobber** n. dealer on a stock exchange —'**stockman** n. man experienced in driving, handling cattle, sheep —**stock market** stock exchange —'**stockpile** v. acquire and store large quantity of (something) —**stock-still** a. motionless —'**stocktaking** n. examination, counting and valuing of goods in shop *etc.* —'**stockyard** n. yard with pens or covered buildings where farm animals are assembled, sold *etc.* —**stock in trade** 1. goods necessary for carrying on business 2. anything constantly used by someone as part of his occupation, trade *etc.*

stockade (stɒ'keɪd) n. enclosure of stakes, barrier

stockinet (stɒkɪ'nɛt) n. machine-knitted elastic fabric

stocking ('stɒkɪŋ) n. one of pair of close-fitting coverings for legs and feet —'**stockinged** a.

stodgy ('stɒdʒɪ) a. (*esp.* of food) heavy, dull —**stodge** n. heavy, solid food

stoep (stuːp) n. SA veranda

stoic ('stəʊɪk) n. 1. capable of much self-control, great endurance without complaint —n. 2. stoical person —'**stoical** a. —**stoicism** ('stəʊɪsɪzəm) n.

stoke (stəʊk) v. feed, tend (fire or furnace) —'**stoker** n. —'**stokehold** n. *Naut.* 1. coal bunker for ship's furnace 2. hold for ship's boilers; fire room —'**stokehole** n. 1. stokehold 2. hole in furnace through which it is stoked

stole[1] (stəul) *pt.* of STEAL —**'stolen** *pp.* of STEAL

stole[2] (stəul) *n.* long scarf or shawl

stolid ('stɒlɪd) *a.* 1. hard to excite 2. heavy, slow, apathetic —**sto'lidity** *n.* —**'stolidly** *adv.*

stoma ('stəumə) *n.* 1. *Bot.* epidermal pore in plant leaves, that controls passage of gases through plant 2. *Zool., anat.* mouth or mouthlike part (*pl.* **stomata** ('stəumətə, 'stɒm-, stəu'mɑːtə))

stomach ('stʌmək) *n.* 1. sac forming chief digestive organ in any animal 2. appetite 3. desire, inclination —*vt.* 4. put up with —**stomach pump** *Med.* suction device for removing stomach contents —**stomach upset** slight digestive disorder

stomp (stɒmp) *vi. inf.* stamp

stone (stəun) *n.* 1. (piece of) rock 2. gem 3. hard seed of fruit 4. hard deposit formed in kidneys, bladder 5. weight, 14 lbs. —*vt.* 6. throw stones at 7. free (fruit) from stones —**stoned** *a. sl.* stupefied by alcohol or drugs —**'stonily** *adv.* —**'stony** *or* **'stoney** *a.* 1. of, like stone 2. hard 3. cold —**Stone Age** period in human culture identified by use of stone implements —**stone-blind** *a.* completely blind —**'stonechat** *n.* black songbird with reddish-brown breast —**stone-cold** *a.* completely cold —**stonecold sober** completely sober —**'stonecrop** *n.* N temperate plant having fleshy leaves and typically red, yellow or white flowers —**stone deaf** completely deaf —**'stonemason** *n.* person skilled in preparing stone for building —**stone's throw** short distance —**stone'wall** *vi.* 1. obstruct business 2. play slow game, *esp.* in cricket —**'stoneware** *n.* heavy common pottery —**'stonewashed** *a.* (of clothes or fabric) given a faded look by being subjected to abrasive action of many small pieces of pumice —**stony-broke** *a. sl.* with no money left

stood (stud) *pt./pp.* of STAND

stooge (stuːdʒ) *n.* 1. *Theat. etc.* performer who is always the butt of another's jokes 2. *sl.* one taken advantage of by another

stook (stuːk) *n.* group of sheaves set upright in field to dry

stool (stuːl) *n.* 1. backless chair 2. excrement —**stool ball** game resembling cricket —**stool pigeon** 1. living or dummy pigeon used as decoy 2. police informer

stoop (stuːp) *vi.* 1. lean forward or down, bend 2. swoop 3. abase, degrade oneself —*n.* 4. stooping carriage of the body

stop (stɒp) *vt.* 1. check, bring to halt 2. prevent 3. interrupt 4. suspend 5. desist from 6. fill up (an opening) —*vi.* 7. cease, come to a halt 8. stay (-pp-) —*n.* 9. stopping or becoming stopped 10. punctuation mark, *esp.* full stop 11. any device for altering or regulating pitch 12. set of pipes in organ having tones of a distinct quality —**'stoppage** *n.* —**'stopper** *n.* plug for closing bottle *etc.* —**'stopcock** *n.* valve to control or stop flow of fluid in pipe

—**'stopgap** *n.* temporary substitute —**'stopoff** *or* **'stopover** *n.* short break in journey —**stop press** news put into a newspaper at the last minute —**'stopwatch** *n.* watch which can be stopped for exact timing of race

store (stɔː) *vt.* 1. stock, furnish, keep —*n.* 2. shop 3. abundance 4. stock 5. department store 6. place for keeping goods 7. warehouse —*pl.* 8. stocks of goods, provisions —**'storage** *n.* —**storage battery** *esp.* US accumulator —**storage heater** electric device which accumulates and radiates heat generated by off-peak electricity —**store cattle** cattle bought lean to be fattened for market

storey *or U.S.* **story** ('stɔːrɪ) *n.* horizontal division of a building

stork (stɔːk) *n.* large wading bird

storm (stɔːm) *n.* 1. violent weather with wind, rain, hail, sand, snow *etc.* 2. assault on fortress 3. violent outbreak, discharge —*vt.* 4. assault 5. take by storm —*vi.* 6. rage —**'stormy** *a.* 1. like storm 2. (emotionally) violent —**storm centre** 1. centre of cyclonic storm *etc.* where pressure is lowest 2. centre of disturbance or trouble —**storm door** additional door outside ordinary door, providing extra insulation against wind *etc.* —**stormtrooper** *n.* 1. member of Nazi S.A. 2. member of force of shock troops —**stormy petrel** 1. any of various small petrels typically having dark plumage and paler underparts 2. person who brings trouble

story ('stɔːrɪ) *n.* 1. (book, piece of prose *etc.*) telling about events, happenings 2. *inf.* lie 3. US *see* STOREY —**'storybook** *n.* book containing stories, *esp.* for children

stoup *or* **stoop** (stuːp) *n.* small basin for holy water

stout (staut) *a.* 1. fat 2. sturdy 3. resolute —*n.* 4. kind of beer —**'stoutly** *adv.* —**'stoutness** *n.* —**stout'hearted** *a.* brave

stove[1] (stəuv) *n.* apparatus for cooking, heating *etc.* —**'stovepipe** *n.* 1. pipe that serves as flue to stove 2. man's tall silk hat

stove[2] (stəuv) *pt./pp.* of STAVE

stow (stəu) *vt.* pack away —**'stowage** *n.* —**'stowaway** *n.* one who hides in ship to obtain free passage

strabismus (strə'bɪzməs) *n.* abnormal parallel alignment of one or both eyes, characterized by turning inwards or outwards from nose (*also* **squint**)

straddle ('strædʲl) *vt.* 1. bestride —*vi.* 2. spread legs wide —*n.* 3. act or position of straddling

Stradivarius (strædɪ'vɑːrɪəs) *n.* violin manufactured in Italy by Antonio Stradivari or his family

strafe (streɪf, strɑːf) *vt.* attack (*esp.* with bullets, rockets) from air

straggle ('strægʲl) *vi.* stray, get dispersed, linger —**'straggler** *n.*

straight (streɪt) *a.* 1. without bend 2. honest 3. level 4. in order 5. (of spirits) undiluted, neat 6. expressionless 7. (of drama, actor *etc.*) serious **8.** *sl.* heterosexual —*n.* **9.** straight state or part —*adv.* **10.** direct —'**straighten** *v.* —**straighta'way** *adv.* immediately (*also* **straight away**) —**straight face** serious facial expression, *esp.* one that conceals impulse to laugh —**straight-faced** *a.* —**straight'forward** *a.* **1.** open, frank **2.** simple **3.** honest —**straight'forwardly** *adv.* —**straight man** subsidiary actor who acts as stooge to comedian

strain¹ (strein) *vt.* **1.** stretch tightly **2.** stretch to full or to excess **3.** filter —*vi.* **4.** make great effort —*n.* **5.** stretching force **6.** violent effort **7.** injury from being strained **8.** burst of music or poetry **9.** great demand **10.** (condition caused by) overwork, worry *etc.* **11.** tone of speaking or writing —**strained** *a.* —'**strainer** *n.* filter, sieve

strain² (strein) *n.* **1.** breed or race **2.** *esp. Biol.* type **3.** trace, streak

strait (streit) *n.* **1.** channel of water connecting two larger areas of water —*pl.* **2.** position of difficulty or distress —*a.* **3.** narrow **4.** strict —'**straiten** *vt.* **1.** make strait, narrow **2.** press with poverty —'**straitjacket** *or* '**straightjacket** *n.* jacket to confine arms of violent person —**strait-laced** *a.* **1.** austere, strict **2.** puritanical

strand¹ (strænd) *v.* **1.** run aground **2.** leave, be left helpless or in difficulties —*n.* **3.** *Poet.* shore

strand² (strænd) *n.* one of individual fibres or threads of string, wire *etc.*

strange (streindʒ) *a.* **1.** odd, queer **2.** unaccustomed **3.** foreign **4.** uncommon **5.** wonderful **6.** singular —'**strangely** *adv.* —'**strangeness** *n.* —'**stranger** *n.* **1.** unknown person **2.** foreigner **3.** (*with* to) one unaccustomed (to)

strangle ('stræŋg'l) *vt.* **1.** kill by squeezing windpipe **2.** suppress —**strangu'lation** *n.* strangling —'**stranglehold** *n.* **1.** wrestling hold in which wrestler's arms are pressed against opponent's windpipe **2.** complete control over person or situation

strap (stræp) *n.* **1.** strip, *esp.* of leather —*vt.* **2.** fasten, beat with strap (-**pp-**) —'**strapping** *a.* tall and well-made —'**straphanger** *n.* in bus, train, one who has to stand, steadying himself with strap provided for this

strata ('strɑːtə) *n.*, *pl. of* STRATUM

stratagem ('strætidʒəm) *n.* plan, trick —**strategic(al)** (strə'tiːdʒik('l)) *a.* —**stra'tegically** *adv.* —'**strategist** *n.* —'**strategy** *n.* **1.** art of war **2.** overall plan

strathspey (stræθ'spei) *n.* type of Scottish dance with gliding steps

stratosphere ('strætəsfiə) *n.* upper part of the atmosphere, approx. 11 kms above earth's surface

stratum ('strɑːtəm) *n.* **1.** layer, *esp.* of rock **2.** class in society (*pl.* **-s, -ta**) —**stratifi'cation** *n.* —'**stratify** *v.* form, deposit in layers (-**ified, -ifying**)

stratus ('streitəs) *n.* grey layer cloud (*pl.* **-ti** (-tai))

straw (strɔː) *n.* **1.** stalks of grain **2.** single stalk **3.** long, narrow tube used to suck up liquid —'**strawberry** ('strɔːbəri, -bri) *n.* **1.** creeping plant producing red, juicy fruit **2.** the fruit —**strawberry blonde** (of hair) reddish blonde —**strawberry mark** soft vascular red birthmark

stray (strei) *vi.* **1.** wander **2.** digress **3.** get lost —*a.* **4.** strayed **5.** occasional, scattered —*n.* **6.** stray animal

streak (striːk) *n.* **1.** long line or band **2.** element, trace —*vt.* **3.** mark with streaks —*vi.* **4.** move fast **5.** *inf.* run naked in public —'**streaky** *a.* **1.** having streaks **2.** striped —**streaky bacon** bacon having alternating strips of fat and lean meat

stream (striːm) *n.* **1.** flowing body of water or other liquid **2.** steady flow **3.** class, division of schoolchildren grouped together because of similar ability —*vi.* **4.** flow **5.** run with liquid **6.** float, wave in the air —*vt.* **7.** group (schoolchildren) in streams —'**streamer** *n.* **1.** (paper) ribbon **2.** narrow flag —**stream of consciousness 1.** *Psychol.* continuous flow of ideas, feelings *etc.* forming content of individual's consciousness **2.** literary technique that reveals flow of thoughts and feelings of characters through long passages of soliloquy

streamlined ('striːmlaind) *a.* (of car, plane *etc.*) built so as to offer least resistance to air

street (striːt) *n.* road in town or village, usu. lined with houses —**street credibility** a command of style, knowledge *etc.* associated with urban counterculture (*also* **street cred**) —**street-credible** *a.* —'**streetwalker** *n.* prostitute —'**streetwise** *a.* adept at surviving in urban, poor and oft. criminal environment

strength (streŋθ) *n.* **1.** quality of being strong **2.** power **3.** capacity for exertion or endurance **4.** vehemence **5.** force **6.** full or necessary number of people —'**strengthen** *v.* make or become stronger —**on the strength of 1.** relying on **2.** because of

strenuous ('strenjuəs) *a.* **1.** energetic **2.** earnest —'**strenuously** *adv.*

streptomycin (streptəʊ'maisin) *n.* antibiotic drug

stress (stres) *n.* **1.** emphasis **2.** strain **3.** impelling force **4.** effort **5.** tension —*vt.* **6.** emphasize **7.** accent **8.** put mechanical stress on

stretch (stretʃ) *vt.* **1.** extend **2.** exert to utmost **3.** tighten, pull out **4.** reach out —*vi.* **5.** reach **6.** have elasticity —*n.* **7.** stretching, being stretched, expanse **8.** spell —'**stretcher** *n.* **1.** person, thing that stretches **2.** appliance on which ill, wounded or dead person is carried

strew (struː) *vt.* scatter over surface, spread (**strewed** *pt.*, **strewn** *or* **strewed** *pp.*, '**strewing** *pr.p.*)

strewth (struːθ) *interj.* expression of surprise or dismay

stria ('straɪə) *n.* small channel or threadlike line in surface of shell or other object (*pl.* **striae** ('straiːː)) —**striate** ('straɪɪt) *a.* 1. streaked, furrowed, grooved (*also* **stri'ated**) —*vt.* ('straɪeɪt) 2. mark with streaks 3. score —**stri'ation** *n.*

stricken ('strɪkən) *a.* 1. seriously affected by disease, grief, famine 2. afflicted —*v.* 3. *pp. of* STRIKE

strict (strɪkt) *a.* 1. stern, not lax or indulgent 2. defined 3. without exception

stricture ('strɪktʃə) *n.* 1. critical remark 2. constriction

stride (straɪd) *vi.* 1. walk with long steps (**strode, stridden** ('strɪdᵊn), **'striding**) —*n.* 2. single step 3. its length 4. regular pace

strident ('straɪdᵊnt) *a.* 1. harsh in tone 2. loud 3. urgent

strife (straɪf) *n.* 1. conflict 2. quarrelling

strike (straɪk) *v.* 1. hit (against) 2. ignite 3. (of snake) bite 4. (of plants) (cause to) take root 5. attack 6. hook (fish) 7. sound (time) as bell in clock *etc.* —*vt.* 8. affect 9. arrive at, come upon 10. enter mind of 11. discover (gold, oil *etc.*) 12. dismantle, remove 13. make (coin) —*vi.* 14. cease work as protest or to make demands (**struck** *pt.*, **'stricken, struck** *pp.*, **'striking** *pr.p.*) —*n.* 15. act of striking —**'striker** *n.* —**'striking** *a.* noteworthy, impressive —**'strikebreaker** *n.* person who tries to make strike ineffectual by working —**'strikebreaking** *n./a.* —**strike pay** allowance paid by trade union to members on strike —**strike off** remove

Strine (straɪn) *n.* humorous transliteration of Australian pronunciation

string (strɪŋ) *n.* 1. (length of) thin cord or other material 2. strand, row 3. series 4. fibre in plants —*pl.* 5. conditions —*vt.* 6. provide with, thread on string 7. form in line, series (**strung, 'stringing**) —**stringed** *a.* (of musical instruments) furnished with strings —**'stringer** *n.* 1. *Archit.* horizontal timber beam used for structural purposes 2. *Naut.* longitudinal structural brace for strengthening hull of vessel 3. part-time journalist retained by newspaper to cover particular area —**'stringy** *a.* 1. like string 2. fibrous —**string course** *Archit.* ornamental projecting band or continuous moulding along wall (*also* **'cordon**) —**string vest** undergarment made from large-meshed material

stringent ('strɪndʒənt) *a.* strict, rigid, binding —**'stringency** *n.* severity —**'stringently** *adv.*

strip (strɪp) *vt.* 1. lay bare, take covering off 2. dismantle 3. deprive —*vi.* 4. undress (**-pp-**) —*n.* 5. long, narrow piece 6. act of undressing or performing striptease —**'stripper** *n.* —**strip cartoon** *see* comic **strip** *at* COMIC —**strip lighting** electric lighting by means of long glass tubes that are fluorescent lamps —**'striptease** *n.*

cabaret or theatre act in which person undresses

stripe (straɪp) *n.* 1. narrow mark, band 2. chevron as symbol of military rank —**'stripy** *a.*

stripling ('strɪplɪŋ) *n.* youth

strive (straɪv) *vi.* try hard, struggle, contend (**strove, striven** ('strɪvᵊn), **'striving**)

strobe (strəʊb) *n.* apparatus which produces high-intensity flashing light

stroboscope ('strəʊbəskəʊp) *n.* 1. instrument producing intense flashing light 2. similar device synchronized with shutter of camera so that series of still photographs can be taken of moving object —**strobo'scopic(al)** *a.*

strode (strəʊd) *pt. of* STRIDE

stroke (strəʊk) *n.* 1. blow 2. sudden action, occurrence 3. apoplexy 4. mark of pen, pencil, brush *etc.* 5. chime of clock 6. completed movement in series 7. act, manner of striking (ball *etc.*) 8. style, method of swimming 9. rower sitting nearest stern setting the rate of rowing 10. act of stroking —*vt.* 11. set stroke for (rowing crew) 12. pass hand lightly over

stroll (strəʊl) *vi.* 1. walk in leisurely or idle manner —*n.* 2. leisurely walk

strong (strɒŋ) *a.* 1. powerful 2. robust 3. healthy 4. difficult to break 5. noticeable 6. intense 7. emphatic 8. not diluted 9. having a certain number —**'strongly** *adv.* —**strong-arm** *inf. a.* 1. of or involving physical force or violence —*vt.* 2. show violence towards —**'strongbox** *n.* box or safe in which valuables are locked for safety —**strong drink** alcoholic drink —**'stronghold** *n.* fortress —**strong language** swearing —**'strongroom** *n.* specially designed room for storing valuables

strontium ('strɒntɪəm) *n.* silvery-white chemical element —**strontium 90** radioactive isotope of strontium present in fallout of nuclear explosions

strop (strɒp) *n.* 1. leather for sharpening razors —*vt.* 2. sharpen on strop (**-pp-**) —**'stroppy** *a. sl.* angry, awkward

strophe ('strəʊfɪ) *n.* division of ode —**strophic** ('strɒfɪk, 'strəʊ-) *a.*

strove (strəʊv) *pt. of* STRIVE

struck (strʌk) *pt./pp. of* STRIKE

structure ('strʌktʃə) *n.* 1. (arrangement of parts in) construction, building *etc.* 2. form 3. organization —*vt.* 4. give structure to —**'structural** *a.*

strudel ('struːdᵊl) *n.* thin sheet of dough usu. filled with apple and baked

struggle ('strʌgᵊl) *vi.* 1. contend 2. fight 3. proceed, work, move with difficulty and effort —*n.* 4. act of struggling

strum (strʌm) *v.* strike strings of (guitar *etc.*) (**-mm-**)

strumpet ('strʌmpɪt) *n. obs.* promiscuous woman

strung (strʌŋ) *pt./pp. of* STRING

strut (strʌt) *vi.* 1. walk affectedly or

pompously (-tt-) —n. 2. brace 3. rigid support, usu. set obliquely 4. strutting gait

strychnine ('strɪkniːn) n. poison obtained from nux vomica seeds —'**strychnic** a.

stub (stʌb) n. 1. remnant of anything, eg pencil, cigarette etc. 2. counterfoil of cheque etc. —vt. 3. strike (toes) against fixed object 4. extinguish by pressing against surface (-bb-) —'**stubby** a. short, broad

stubble ('stʌbʔl) n. 1. stumps of cut grain after reaping 2. short growth of beard

stubborn ('stʌbʔn) a. unyielding, obstinate

stucco ('stʌkəʊ) n. plaster (pl. -s, -es) —'**stuccoed** a.

stuck (stʌk) pt./pp. of STICK —**stuck-up** a. inf. conceited; snobbish

stud[1] (stʌd) n. 1. nail with large head 2. removable double-headed button 3. vertical wall support —vt. 4. set with studs (-dd-)

stud[2] (stʌd) n. set of animals, esp. horses, kept for breeding —'**studbook** n. book giving pedigree of noted or thoroughbred animals, esp. horses —**stud farm**

studio ('stjuːdɪəʊ) n. 1. workroom of artist, photographer etc. 2. building, room where film, television or radio shows are made, broadcast (pl. -s) —**studio couch** upholstered couch that can be converted into double bed

study ('stʌdɪ) vi. 1. be engaged in learning —vt. 2. make study of 3. try constantly to do 4. consider 5. scrutinize ('**studied**, '**studying**) —n. 6. effort to acquire knowledge 7. subject of this 8. room to study in 9. book, report etc. produced as .result of study 10. sketch —**student** ('stjuːdʔnt) n. one who studies, esp. at university etc. —'**studied** a. carefully designed, premeditated —**studious** ('stjuːdɪəs) a. 1. fond of study 2. thoughtful 3. painstaking 4. deliberate

stuff (stʌf) vi. 1. eat (large amount) —vt. 2. pack, cram, fill (completely) 3. fill with seasoned mixture 4. fill (animal's skin) with material to preserve lifelike form —n. 5. material, fabric 6. any substance —'**stuffing** n. material for stuffing, esp. seasoned mixture for inserting in poultry etc. before cooking —'**stuffy** a. lacking fresh air 2. inf. dull, conventional —**do your stuff** inf. do what is required or expected of you

stultify ('stʌltɪfaɪ) vt. make ineffectual (-ified, -ifying) —stultifi'cation n.

stumble ('stʌmbʔl) vi. 1. trip and nearly fall 2. falter —n. 3. act of stumbling —**stumbling block** obstacle

stump (stʌmp) n. 1. remnant of tree, tooth etc. when main part has been cut away 2. one of uprights of wicket in cricket —vt. 3. confuse, puzzle 4. break wicket of (batsman out of his ground in playing ball) —vi. 5. walk heavily, noisily —'**stumpy** a. short and thickset

stun (stʌn) vt. 1. knock senseless 2. amaze

(-nn-) —'**stunner** n. inf. person or thing of great beauty, quality etc. —'**stunning** a.

stung (stʌŋ) pt./pp. of STING

stunk (stʌŋk) pp. of STINK

stunt[1] (stʌnt) vt. check growth of, dwarf —'**stunted** a. 1. underdeveloped 2. undersized

stunt[2] (stʌnt) n. 1. feat of dexterity or daring 2. anything spectacular, unusual, done to gain publicity —**stunt man** professional acrobat substituted for actor when dangerous scenes are filmed

stupefy ('stjuːpɪfaɪ) vt. 1. make insensitive, lethargic 2. astound (-efied, -efying) —stupe'faction n.

stupendous (stjuːˈpɛndəs) a. 1. astonishing, amazing 2. huge

stupid ('stjuːpɪd) a. 1. slow-witted 2. silly 3. dazed or stupefied

stupor ('stjuːpə) n. 1. dazed state 2. insensibility

sturdy ('stɜːdɪ) a. 1. robust 2. strongly built 3. vigorous —'**sturdily** adv. —'**sturdiness** n.

sturgeon ('stɜːdʒən) n. fish yielding caviar and isinglass

stutter ('stʌtə) v. 1. speak (word etc.) with difficulty 2. stammer —n. 3. act or habit of stuttering

sty[1] (staɪ) n. 1. place in which pigs are kept 2. hovel, dirty place

sty[2] or **stye** (staɪ) n. inflammation on edge of eyelid

Stygian ('stɪdʒɪən) a. 1. of river Styx in Hades 2. gloomy 3. infernal

style (staɪl) n. 1. manner of writing, doing etc. 2. designation 3. sort 4. elegance, refinement 5. superior manner, quality 6. design —vt. 7. shape, design 8. adapt 9. designate —'**stylish** a. fashionable —'**stylishly** adv. —'**stylist** n. 1. one cultivating style in literary or other execution 2. designer 3. hairdresser —sty'**listic** a. —'**stylize** or -**ise** vt. give conventional stylistic form to

stylus ('staɪləs) n. 1. writing instrument 2. in record-player, tiny point running in groove of record (pl. -li (-laɪ), -es)

stymie or **stymy** ('staɪmɪ) vt. hinder, thwart

styptic ('stɪptɪk) a./n. (designating) a substance that stops bleeding

styrene ('staɪriːn) n. colourless liquid used in making synthetic rubber, plastics

suave (swɑːv) a. smoothly polite, affable, bland —'**suavity** n.

sub (sʌb) n. 1. subeditor 2. submarine 3. subscription 4. substitute 5. inf. advance payment of wages, salary —vi. 6. inf. serve as substitute —v. 7. inf. grant or receive (advance payment) —vt. 8. subedit (-bb-)

sub- (comb. form) under, less than, in lower position, subordinate, forming subdivision, as in subaqua, subeditor, subheading, subnormal, subsoil. Such words are not given here where the meaning may be easily inferred from the simple word

subaltern ('sʌb³ltən) n. army officer below rank of captain

subcommittee (sʌbkə'mɪtɪ) n. section of committee functioning separately from main body

subconscious (sʌb'kɒnʃəs) a. 1. acting, existing without one's awareness —n. 2. Psychol. that part of human mind unknown, or only partly known, to possessor

subcontinent (sʌb'kɒntɪnənt) n. large land mass that is distinct part of continent —subconti'nental a.

subcontract (sʌb'kɒntrækt) n. 1. subordinate contract under which supply of materials or labour is let out to someone other than party to main contract —vi. (sʌbkən'trækt) 2. (oft. with for) enter into subcontract —vt. (sʌbkən'trækt) 3. let out (work) on subcontract —subcon'tractor n.

subculture ('sʌbkʌltʃə) n. subdivision of national culture with distinct integrated network of behaviour, beliefs and attitudes

subcutaneous (sʌbkju:'teɪnɪəs) a. under the skin

subdivide (sʌbdɪ'vaɪd, 'sʌbdɪvaɪd) vt. divide again —subdivision ('sʌbdɪvɪʒən) n.

subdominant (sʌb'dɒmɪnənt) Mus. n. 1. fourth degree of major or minor scale 2. key or chord based on this —a. 3. of the subdominant

subdue (səb'dju:) vt. 1. win control over; conquer 2. overcome 3. render less intense or less conspicuous (-'dued, -'duing)

subfusc ('sʌbfʌsk) a. devoid of brightness; drab, dull or dark

subject ('sʌbdʒɪkt) n. 1. theme, topic 2. that about which something is predicated 3. conscious self 4. one under power of another —a. 5. owing allegiance 6. subordinate 7. dependent 8. liable —vt. (səb'dʒɛkt) 9. cause to undergo 10. make liable 11. subdue —sub'jection n. act of bringing, or state of being, under control —sub'jective a. 1. based on personal feelings, not impartial 2. of the self 3. existing in the mind 4. displaying artist's individuality —subjec'tivity n.

subjoin (sʌb'dʒɔɪn) vt. add to end of something written etc.

sub judice ('dʒu:dɪsɪ) Lat. under judicial consideration

subjugate ('sʌbdʒʊgeɪt) vt. 1. force to submit 2. conquer —subju'gation n. —'subjugator n.

subjunctive (səb'dʒʌŋktɪv) Gram. n. 1. mood used mainly in subordinate clauses expressing wish, possibility —a. 2. in, of that mood

sublease ('sʌbli:s) n. 1. lease of property made by lessee of that property —v. (sʌb-'li:s) 2. grant sublease of (property); sublet

sublet (sʌb'lɛt) vt. (of tenant) let whole or part of what he has rented to another

sublieutenant (sʌblə'tɛnənt) n. most junior commissioned officer in Royal Navy and certain other navies —sublieu-'tenancy n.

sublimate ('sʌblɪmeɪt) vt. 1. Psychol. direct energy (esp. sexual) into activities considered more socially acceptable 2. refine —n. 3. Chem. material obtained when substance is sublimed —subli'mation n.

sublime (sə'blaɪm) a. 1. elevated 2. eminent 3. majestic 4. inspiring awe 5. exalted —v. 6. Chem. (cause to) change from solid to vapour —sub'limely adv. —sublimity (sə'blɪmɪtɪ) or su'blimeness n.

subliminal (sʌb'lɪmɪn³l) a. resulting from processes of which the individual is not aware

sub-machine-gun n. portable automatic gun with short barrel

submarine ('sʌbməri:n, sʌbmə'ri:n) n. 1. (war)ship which can travel (and attack from) below surface of sea and remain submerged for long periods —a. 2. below surface of sea

submerge (səb'mɜːdʒ) or **submerse** (səb'mɜːs) v. place, go under water —sub'mergence or sub'mersion n. —sub'mersible or sub'mergible a. 1. able to be submerged 2. capable of operating under water etc. —n. 3. warship designed to operate under water

submit (səb'mɪt) vt. 1. surrender 2. put forward for consideration —vi. 3. surrender 4. defer (-tt-) —sub'mission n. —sub'missive a. meek, obedient

subordinate (sə'bɔːdɪnɪt) a. 1. of lower rank or less importance —n. 2. inferior 3. one under order of another —vt. (sə'bɔːdɪneɪt) 4. make, treat as subordinate —sub'ordinately adv. —subordi'nation n. —subordinate clause Gram. clause with adjectival, adverbial or nominal function, rather than one that functions as separate sentence in its own right

suborn (sə'bɔːn) vt. bribe to do evil —subornation (sʌbɔː'neɪʃən) n. —sub'orner n.

subplot ('sʌbplɒt) n. subordinate plot in novel, film etc.

subpoena (səb'pi:nə) n. 1. writ requiring attendance at court of law —vt. 2. summon by such order (-naed, -naing)

sub rosa ('rəʊzə) in secret

subscribe (səb'skraɪb) vt. 1. pay, promise to pay (contribution) —v. 2. write (one's name) at end of document —sub'scriber n. —subscription (səb'skrɪpʃən) n. 1. subscribing 2. money paid —subscriber trunk dialling UK service by which telephone subscribers can obtain trunk calls by dialling direct without aid of operator

subscript ('sʌbskrɪpt) a. 1. Print. (of character) printed below base line —n. 2. subscript character (also sub'index)

subsection (sʌb'sɛkʃən) n. division of a section

subsequent ('sʌbsɪkwənt) a. later, following or coming after in time —**'subse-quence** n.

subservient (səb'sɜːvɪənt) a. submissive, servile —**sub'servience** n.

subset ('sʌbsɛt) n. mathematical set contained within larger set

subside (səb'saɪd) vi. 1. abate, come to an end 2. sink 3. settle 4. collapse —**subsidence** (səb'saɪd°ns, 'sʌbsɪd°ns) n.

subsidiary (səb'sɪdɪərɪ) a. 1. supplementing 2. secondary 3. auxiliary —n. 4. subsidiary person or thing

subsidize or **-ise** ('sʌbsɪdaɪz) vt. 1. help financially 2. pay grant to —**'subsidy** n. money granted

subsist (səb'sɪst) vi. exist, sustain life —**sub'sistence** n. 1. the means by which one supports life 2. livelihood

subsonic (sʌb'sɒnɪk) a. concerning speeds less than that of sound

substance ('sʌbstəns) n. 1. matter 2. particular kind of matter 3. chief part, essence 4. wealth —**sub'stantial** a. 1. considerable 2. of real value 3. solid, big 4. important 5. really existing —**substanti'ality** n. —**sub'stantially** adv. —**sub'stantiate** vt. bring evidence for, confirm, prove —**substanti'ation** n. —**'substantive** a. 1. having independent existence 2. real, fixed —n. 3. noun

substitute ('sʌbstɪtjuːt) v. 1. put, serve in exchange (for) —n. 2. thing, person put in place of another 3. deputy —**substi'tution** n.

substratum (sʌb'strɑːtəm, -'streɪ-) n. 1. that which is laid or spread under 2. layer of earth lying under another 3. basis (pl. **-ta** (-tə), **-s**)

subsume (səb'sjuːm) vt. incorporate (idea, case etc.) under comprehensive heading, classification

subtenant (sʌb'tɛnənt) n. person who rents property from tenant —**sub'tenancy** n.

subtend (səb'tɛnd) vt. Geom. be opposite to and delimit

subterfuge ('sʌbtəfjuːdʒ) n. trick, lying excuse used to evade something

subterranean (sʌbtə'reɪnɪən) a. underground (also **subter'restrial**)

subtitle ('sʌbtaɪt°l) n. 1. secondary title of book 2. (oft. pl.) written translation of film dialogue superimposed on film

subtle ('sʌt°l) a. 1. not immediately obvious 2. ingenious, acute 3. crafty 4. intricate 5. delicate 6. making fine distinctions —**'subtlety** n. —**'subtly** adv.

subtonic (sʌb'tɒnɪk) n. Mus. seventh degree of major or minor scale

subtract (səb'trækt) vt. take away, deduct —**sub'traction** n.

subtrahend ('sʌbtrəhɛnd) n. number to be subtracted from another number (**minuend**)

subtropical (sʌb'trɒpɪk°l) a. of regions bordering on the tropics

suburb ('sʌbɜːb) n. residential area on outskirts of city —**sub'urban** a./n. —**sub-**

'urbia n. 1. suburbs or people living in them considered as an identifiable community or class in society 2. life, customs etc. of suburban people

subvention (səb'vɛnʃən) n. subsidy

subvert (səb'vɜːt) vt. 1. overthrow 2. corrupt —**sub'version** n. —**sub'versive** a.

subway ('sʌbweɪ) n. 1. underground passage 2. underground railway

succeed (sək'siːd) vi. 1. accomplish purpose 2. turn out satisfactorily 3. follow —vt. 4. follow, take place of —**success** (sək'sɛs) n. 1. favourable accomplishment, attainment, issue or outcome 2. successful person or thing —**successful** (sək'sɛsfʊl) a. —**successfully** (sək'sɛsfʊlɪ) adv. —**succession** (sək'sɛʃən) n. 1. following 2. series 3. succeeding —**successive** (sək'sɛsɪv) a. following in order, consecutive —**successively** (sək'sɛsɪvlɪ) adv. —**successor** (sək'sɛsə) n.

succinct (sək'sɪŋkt) a. terse, concise

succour or U.S. **succor** ('sʌkə) vt./n. help in distress

succubus ('sʌkjʊbəs) n. female demon fabled to have sexual intercourse with sleeping men (pl. **-bi** (-baɪ))

succulent ('sʌkjʊlənt) a. 1. juicy, full of juice 2. (of plant) having thick, fleshy leaves —n. 3. such plant —**'succulence** or **'succulency** n.

succumb (sə'kʌm) vi. 1. yield, give way to 2. die

such (sʌtʃ) a. 1. of the kind or degree mentioned 2. so great, so much 3. so made etc. 4. of the same kind —**such and such** particular thing that is unspecified —**'suchlike** inf. a. 1. such —pron. 2. other such things

suck (sʌk) vt. 1. draw into mouth 2. hold, dissolve in mouth 3. draw in —n. 4. sucking —**'sucker** n. 1. person, thing that sucks 2. organ, appliance which adheres by suction 3. shoot coming from root or base of stem of plant 4. inf. person easily deceived or taken in

suckle ('sʌk°l) v. feed from the breast —**'suckling** n. unweaned infant

sucrose ('sjuːkrəʊz, -krəʊs) n. sugar

suction ('sʌkʃən) n. 1. drawing or sucking of air or fluid 2. force produced by difference in pressure

Sudanese (suːdᵊ'niːz) a. 1. of Sudan, in NE Afr. —n. 2. native or inhabitant of Sudan

sudden ('sʌd°n) a. 1. done, occurring unexpectedly 2. abrupt, hurried —**'suddenly** adv. —**'suddenness** n. —**sudden infant death syndrome** unexplained death of infant during sleep

sudorific (sjuːdə'rɪfɪk) a. 1. causing perspiration —n. 2. medicine that produces sweat

suds (sʌdz) pl.n. froth of soap and water, lather

sue (sjuː, suː) vt. 1. prosecute 2. seek justice from 3. beseech —vi. 4. make application or entreaty (**sued**, **'suing**)

suede (sweɪd) n. leather with soft, velvety finish

suet ('suːɪt, 'sjuːɪt) n. hard animal fat from sheep, ox etc.

suffer ('sʌfə) v. 1. undergo, endure, experience (pain etc.) —vt. 2. obs. allow —'**sufferable** a. —'**sufferance** n. toleration —'**sufferer** n.

suffice (sə'faɪs) v. be adequate, satisfactory (for) —**sufficiency** (sə'fɪʃənsɪ) n. adequate amount —**sufficient** (sə'fɪʃənt) a. enough, adequate

suffix ('sʌfɪks) n. 1. letter or word added to end of word —vt. ('sʌfɪks, sə'fɪks) 2. add, annex to the end

suffocate ('sʌfəkeɪt) v. 1. kill, be killed by deprivation of oxygen 2. smother —'**suffo-cation** n.

suffrage ('sʌfrɪdʒ) n. vote or right of voting —'**suffragist** n. one claiming a right of voting (**suffra'gette** fem.)

suffuse (sə'fjuːz) vt. well up and spread over —suf'**fusion** n.

sugar ('ʃʊgə) n. 1. sweet crystalline vegetable substance —vt. 2. sweeten, make pleasant (with sugar) —'**sugary** a. —**sugar beet** variety of common beet grown for sugar —**sugar cane** plant from whose juice sugar is obtained —**sugar daddy** sl. wealthy (elderly) man who pays for (esp. sexual) favours of younger person —**sugar loaf** conical mass of hard refined sugar

suggest (sə'dʒɛst) vt. 1. propose 2. call up the idea of —suggesti'**bility** n. —sug-'**gestible** a. easily influenced —sug'**gestion** n. 1. hint 2. proposal 3. insinuation of impression, belief etc. into mind —sug-'**gestive** a. containing, open to suggestion, esp. of something indecent

suicide ('suːɪsaɪd, 'sjuː-) n. 1. act or instance of killing oneself intentionally 2. person who does this —sui'**cidal** a.

suit (suːt) n. 1. set of clothing 2. garment worn for particular event, purpose 3. one of four sets in pack of cards 4. action at law —v. 5. make, be fit or appropriate (for) 6. be acceptable (to) —suita'**bility** n. —'**suitable** a. 1. fitting, proper 2. convenient 3. becoming —'**suit-ably** adv. —'**suitcase** n. flat rectangular travelling case

suite (swiːt) n. 1. matched set, esp. of furniture 2. set of rooms 3. retinue

suitor ('suːtə, 'sjuːt-) n. 1. wooer 2. one who sues 3. petitioner

sulk (sʌlk) vi. 1. be silent, resentful, esp. to draw attention to oneself —n. 2. sulky mood —'**sulkily** adv. —'**sulky** a.

sullen ('sʌlən) a. 1. unwilling to talk or be sociable; morose 2. dismal, dull —'**sullenly** adv.

sully ('sʌlɪ) vt. stain, tarnish, disgrace ('**sullied, 'sullying**)

sulpha drug ('sʌlfə) sulphonamide used to treat bacterial infections

sulphate ('sʌlfeɪt) n. salt formed by sulphuric acid in combination with any base

sulphonamide (sʌl'fɒnəmaɪd) n. any of group of drugs used as internal germicides in treatment of many bacterial diseases

sulphur or U.S. **sulfur** ('sʌlfə) n. pale yellow nonmetallic element —'**sulphide** n. compound of sulphur with more electropositive element —'**sulphite** n. salt or ester of acid —**sulphitic** (sʌl'fɪtɪk) a. —**sulphu-ric** or U.S. **sulfuric** (sʌl'fjʊərɪk) a. —'**sulphurous** a. —**sulphur dioxide** colourless soluble pungent gas used in manufacture of sulphuric acid, preservation of foodstuffs, bleaching and disinfecting —**sulphuric acid** colourless oily corrosive liquid used in manufacture of fertilizers, dyes and explosives

sultan ('sʌltən) n. ruler of Muslim country —sul'**tana** n. 1. sultan's wife 2. kind of raisin —'**sultanate** n. 1. territory or country ruled by sultan 2. office, rank or jurisdiction of sultan

sultry ('sʌltrɪ) a. 1. (of weather) hot, humid 2. (of person) looking sensual

sum (sʌm) n. 1. amount, total 2. problem in arithmetic —v. 3. add up 4. (with up) make summary of (main parts) (-mm-) —'**summing-up** n. summary of main points of speech etc. —**sum total** 1. total obtained by adding up sum or sums 2. everything included

sumach or U.S. **sumac** ('suːmæk, 'ʃuː-) n. shrub with clusters of green flowers and red hairy fruits

summary ('sʌmərɪ) n. 1. abridgment or statement of chief points of longer document, speech etc. 2. abstract —a. 3. done quickly —'**summarily** adv. 1. speedily 2. abruptly —'**summarize** or -ise vt. 1. make summary of 2. present briefly and concisely —sum'**mation** n. adding up

summer ('sʌmə) n. 1. second, warmest season —vi. 2. pass the summer —'**sum-mery** a. —'**summerhouse** n. small building in garden or park, used for shade in summer —**summer school** academic course etc. held during summer —**sum-mer solstice** 1. time at which sun is at its northernmost point in sky; June 21st 2. Astron. point on celestial sphere at which ecliptic is furthest north from celestial equator —'**summertime** n. daylight-saving time, ie time shown by clocks etc. put forward one hour during certain period of year

summit ('sʌmɪt) n. top, peak —**summit conference** meeting of heads of governments

summon ('sʌmən) vt. 1. demand attendance of 2. call on 3. bid (witness) appear in court 4. gather up (energies etc.) —'**summons** n. 1. call 2. authoritative demand

sump (sʌmp) n. place or receptacle (esp. as oil reservoir in engine) where fluid collects

sumptuous ('sʌmptjʊəs) a. 1. lavish,

magnificent **2.** costly —**'sumptuary** a. pert. to or regulating expenditure —**'sumptuously** adv. —**'sumptuousness** n.

sun (sʌn) n. **1.** luminous body round which earth and other planets revolve **2.** its rays —vt. **3.** expose to sun's rays (-nn-) —**'sunless** a. —**'sunny** a. **1.** like the sun **2.** warm **3.** cheerful —**'sunbathing** n. exposure of whole or part of body to sun's rays —**'sunbeam** n. ray of sun —**'sunburn** n. inflammation of skin due to excessive exposure to sun —**'sundial** n. device indicating time during hours of sunlight by means of pointer that casts shadow on to surface marked in hours —**'sundown** n. sunset —**'sunfish** n. sea fish with large rounded body —**'sunflower** n. plant with large golden flowers —**'sunglasses** pl.n. glasses with darkened or polarizing lenses that protect eyes from sun's glare —**sun-god** n. sun considered as personal deity —**sun lamp** lamp that generates ultraviolet rays —**'sunrise** n. **1.** daily appearance of sun above horizon **2.** atmospheric phenomena accompanying this appearance **3.** time at which sun rises at particular locality —**sunrise industry** any of the high-technology industries, such as electronics, that hold promise of future development —**'sunset** n. **1.** daily disappearance of sun below horizon **2.** atmospheric phenomena accompanying this disappearance **3.** time at which sun sets at particular locality —**'sunshade** n. device, esp. parasol or awning, serving to shade from sun —**'sunshine** n. **1.** light or warmth received directly from sun **2.** light-hearted term of affection —**'sunshiny** a. —**'sunspot** n. dark patch appearing temporarily on sun's surface —**'sunstroke** n. illness caused by prolonged exposure to intensely hot sun —**'suntan** n. colouring of skin by exposure to sun

Sun. Sunday

sundae (**'sʌndi:**, **-deɪ**) n. ice cream topped with fruit etc.

Sunday (**'sʌndɪ**) n. **1.** first day of week **2.** Christian Sabbath —**Sunday best** one's best clothes —**Sunday school** school for religious instruction of children

sunder (**'sʌndə**) vt. separate, sever

sundry (**'sʌndrɪ**) a. several, various —**'sundries** pl.n. odd items not mentioned in detail

sung (sʌŋ) pp. of SING

sunk (sʌŋk) pp. of SINK

sup (sʌp) vt. **1.** take by sips —vi. **2.** take supper (-pp-) —n. **3.** mouthful of liquid

sup. 1. above **2.** superior **3.** Gram. superlative **4.** supplement **5.** supplementary **6.** supply

super (**'su:pə**, **'sju:pə**) a. inf. very good

super- (comb. form) above, greater, exceeding(ly), as in superhuman, superman, superstore, supertanker. Such compounds are not given here where the

meaning may be inferred from the simple word

superable (**'su:pərəbᵊl**, **'sju:-**) a. **1.** capable of being overcome **2.** surmountable

superannuate (su:pər'ænjʊeɪt, sju:-) vt. **1.** pension off **2.** discharge or dismiss as too old —**super'annuated** a. —**superannu'ation** n. **1.** pension given on retirement **2.** contribution by employee to pension

superb (sʊ'pɜːb, sju:-) a. **1.** splendid **2.** grand **3.** impressive —**su'perbly** adv.

supercargo (su:pə'kɑːɡəʊ, sju:-) n. officer on merchant ship in charge of cargo

supercharge (**'su:pətʃɑːdʒ**, **'sju:-**) vt. charge, fill to excess —**'supercharged** a. —**'supercharger** n. in internal-combustion engine, device to ensure complete filling of cylinder with explosive mixture when running at high speed

supercilious (su:pə'sɪlɪəs, sju:-) a. displaying arrogant pride, scorn, indifference

superconductivity (su:pəkɒndʌk'tɪvɪtɪ, sju:-) n. Phys. property of certain substances that have almost no electrical resistance at temperatures close to absolute zero —**supercon'ductive** or **supercon'ducting** a. —**supercon'ductor** n.

supercool (su:pə'ku:l, sju:-) v. Chem. cool without freezing or crystallization to temperature below that at which freezing or crystallization should occur

superego (su:pər'i:ɡəʊ, -'eɡəʊ, sju:-) n. Psychoanal. that part of the unconscious mind that acts as conscience for the ego

supererogation (su:pərerə'ɡeɪʃən, sju:-) n. **1.** performance of work in excess of that required **2.** R.C.Ch. prayers, devotions etc. beyond those prescribed as obligatory

superficial (su:pə'fɪʃəl, sju:-) a. **1.** of or on surface **2.** not careful or thorough **3.** without depth, shallow —**superfici'ality** n.

superfluous (su:'pɜːflʊəs, sju:-) a. **1.** extra, unnecessary **2.** excessive **3.** left over —**super'fluity** n. **1.** superabundance **2.** unnecessary amount —**su'perfluously** adv.

supergrass (**'su:pəɡrɑːs**) n. person who acts as police informer on a large scale

superheat (su:pə'hi:t, sju:-) vt. **1.** heat (vapour, esp. steam) to temperature above its saturation point for given pressure **2.** heat (liquid) to temperature above its boiling point without boiling occurring **3.** overheat —**super'heater** n.

superheterodyne receiver (su:pə'hetərədaɪn, sju:-) radio receiver that combines two radio-frequency signals by heterodyne action to produce signal above audible frequency limit

superimpose (su:pərɪm'pəʊz, sju:-) vt. **1.** set or place on or over something else **2.** (usu. with on or upon) add (to) —**superim-po'sition** n.

superintend (su:pərɪn'tend, sju:-) vt. **1.** have charge of **2.** overlook **3.** supervise —**superin'tendence** n. —**superin'tendent** n. senior police officer

superior (su:'pɪərɪə, sju:-) a. **1.** greater in

quality or quantity **2.** upper, higher in position, rank or quality **3.** showing consciousness of being so —**superi'ority** *n.* quality of being higher, greater or more excellent

superlative (su:'pɜːlətɪv, sju:-) *a.* **1.** of, in highest degree or quality **2.** surpassing **3.** *Gram.* denoting form of adjective, adverb meaning 'most' —*n.* **4.** *Gram.* superlative degree of adjective or adverb

supermarket ('su:pəmɑːkɪt, 'sju:-) *n.* large self-service store selling chiefly food and household goods

supernatural (su:pə'nætʃərəl, sju:-) *a.* **1.** being beyond the powers or laws of nature **2.** miraculous —**super'naturally** *adv.*

supernova (su:pə'nəuvə, sju:-) *n.* star that explodes and is for a few days up to one hundred million times brighter than sun (*pl.* **-vae** (-viː), **-s**)

supernumerary (su:pə'njuːmərərɪ, sju:-) *a.* **1.** in excess of normal number, extra —*n.* **2.** extra person or thing

superphosphate (su:pə'fosfeɪt, sju:-) *n.* chemical fertilizer

superpose (su:pə'pəuz, sju:-) *vt. Geom.* place (one figure) upon another so that their perimeters coincide

superpower ('su:pəpauə, 'sju:-) *n.* **1.** an extremely powerful state, such as U.S.A. **2.** extremely high power, *esp.* electrical —'**superpowered** *a.*

superscribe (su:pə'skraɪb, sju:-) *vt.* write (inscription *etc.*) above, on top of or outside —**superscription** (su:pə'skrɪpʃən, sju:-) *n.*

superscript ('su:pəskrɪpt, 'sju:-) *n./a.* (character) printed, written above the line

supersede (su:pə'siːd, sju:-) *vt.* **1.** take the place of **2.** set aside, discard, supplant —**supersession** (su:pə'seʃən, sju:-) *n.*

supersonic (su:pə'sonɪk, sju:-) *a.* denoting speed greater than that of sound

superstition (su:pə'stɪʃən, sju:-) *n.* religion, opinion or practice based on belief in luck or magic —**super'stitious** *a.* —**super-'stitiously** *adv.*

superstructure ('su:pəstrʌktʃə, 'sju:-) *n.* **1.** structure above foundations **2.** part of ship above deck

supertax ('su:pətæks, 'sju:-) *n.* tax on large incomes in addition to usual income tax

supervene (su:pə'viːn, sju:-) *vi.* happen, as an interruption or change —**supervention** (su:pə'venʃən, sju:-) *n.*

supervise ('su:pəvaɪz, 'sju:-) *vt.* **1.** oversee **2.** direct **3.** inspect and control **4.** superintend —**supervision** (su:pə'vɪʒən, sju:-) *n.* —'**supervisor** *n.* —'**supervisory** *a.*

supine (su:'paɪn, sju:-; 'su:paɪn, 'sju:-) *a.* **1.** lying on back with face upwards **2.** indolent —*n.* ('su:paɪn, 'sju:-) **3.** Latin verbal noun

supper ('sʌpə) *n.* (light) evening meal

supplant (sə'plɑːnt) *vt.* take the place of, *esp.* unfairly **2.** oust —**sup'planter** *n.*

supple ('sʌpˀl) *a.* **1.** pliable **2.** flexible **3.** compliant —'**supply** *or* '**supplely** *adv.*

supplement ('sʌplɪmənt) *n.* **1.** thing added to fill up, supply deficiency, *esp.* extra part added to book *etc.* **2.** additional number of periodical, usu. on special subject **3.** separate, oft. illustrated section published periodically with newspaper —*vt.* ('sʌplɪment) **4.** add to **5.** remedy deficiency of —**supple'mentary** *a.* additional —**supplementary angle** either of two angles whose sum is 180° —**supplementary benefit** UK allowance paid to various groups of people by state to bring their incomes up to minimum levels established by law

suppliant ('sʌplɪənt) *a.* **1.** petitioning —*n.* **2.** petitioner

supplicate ('sʌplɪkeɪt) *v.* **1.** beg humbly —*vt.* **2.** entreat —**suppli'cation** *n.* —'**supplicatory** *a.*

supply (sə'plaɪ) *vt.* **1.** furnish **2.** make available **3.** provide (**sup'plied, sup'plying**) —*n.* **4.** supplying, substitute **5.** stock, store

support (sə'pɔːt) *vt.* **1.** hold up **2.** sustain **3.** assist —*n.* **4.** supporting, being supported **5.** means of support —**sup'portable** *a.* —**sup'porter** *n.* adherent —**sup'porting** *a.* (of film *etc.* role) less important —**sup'portive** *a.*

suppose (sə'pəuz) *vt.* **1.** assume as theory **2.** take for granted **3.** accept as likely **4.** (in passive) be expected, obliged **5.** (in passive) ought —**supposed** (sə'pəuzd, -'pəuzɪd) *a.* —**supposedly** (sə'pəuzɪdlɪ) *adv.* —**suppo'sition** *n.* **1.** assumption **2.** belief without proof **3.** conjecture —**suppo'sitious** *or* **supposititious** (səpɒzɪ'tɪʃəs) *a.* sham, spurious, counterfeit

suppository (sə'pɒzɪtərɪ, -trɪ) *n.* medication (in capsule) for insertion in orifice of body

suppress (sə'pres) *vt.* **1.** put down, restrain **2.** crush, stifle **3.** keep or withdraw from publication —**sup'pression** *n.*

suppurate ('sʌpjureɪt) *vi.* fester, form pus —**suppu'ration** *n.*

supra- (*comb. form*) above, over, as in supranational. Such words are not given here where the meaning may easily be inferred from the simple word

supreme (su'priːm, sju-) *a.* **1.** highest in authority or rank **2.** utmost —**supremacy** (su'preməsɪ, sju-) *n.* position of being supreme —**su'premely** *adv.* —**su'premo** *n.* person with overall authority (*pl.* **-s**) —**Supreme Being** God

Supt. *or* **supt.** superintendent

sur-[1] (*comb. form*) over, above; beyond, as in surcharge

sur-[2] (*comb. form*) see SUB-

surcease (sɜː'siːs) *v.* **1.** (cause to) cease —*n.* **2.** cessation

surcharge ('sɜːtʃɑːdʒ) *n.* **1.** additional charge —*vt.* (sɜː'tʃɑːdʒ, 'sɜːtʃɑːdʒ) **2.** subject to additional charge

surd (sɜːd) *n.* **1.** *Maths.* sum containing one

or more irrational roots of numbers **2.** *Phonet.* voiceless consonant —*a.* **3.** of or relating to surd

sure (ʃʊə, ʃɔː) *a.* **1.** certain **2.** trustworthy **3.** without doubt —*adv.* **4.** *inf.* certainly —**'surely** *adv.* —**surety** (ˈʃʊətɪ, ˈʃʊərɪtɪ) *n.* one who makes himself responsible for another's obligations —**sure-fire** *a. inf.* certain to succeed or meet expectations —**sure-footed** *a.* **1.** unlikely to fall, slip or stumble **2.** not likely to err or fall

surf (sɜːf) *n.* **1.** waves breaking on shore —*vi.* **2.** swim in, ride surf —**'surfer** *n.* —**'surfboard** *n.* board used in sport of riding over surf

surface (ˈsɜːfɪs) *n.* **1.** outside face of body **2.** exterior **3.** plane **4.** top, visible side **5.** superficial appearance, outward impression —*a.* **6.** involving the surface only **7.** going no deeper than the surface only —*v.* **8.** (cause to) come to surface —*vt.* **9.** put a surface on —**surface tension** property of liquids caused by intermolecular forces near surface leading to apparent presence of surface film

surfeit (ˈsɜːfɪt) *n.* **1.** excess **2.** disgust caused by excess —*vt.* **3.** feed to excess

surge (sɜːdʒ) *n.* **1.** wave **2.** sudden increase **3.** *Elec.* sudden rush of current in circuit —*vi.* **4.** move in large waves **5.** swell, billow

surgeon (ˈsɜːdʒən) *n.* medical expert who performs operations —**'surgery** *n.* **1.** medical treatment by operation **2.** doctor's, dentist's consulting room —**'surgical** *a.* —**'surgically** *adv.* —**surgical spirit** methylated spirit

surly (ˈsɜːlɪ) *a.* **1.** gloomily morose **2.** ill-natured **3.** cross and rude —**'surlily** *adv.* —**'surliness** *n.*

surmise (sɜːˈmaɪz) *v./n.* guess, conjecture

surmount (sɜːˈmaʊnt) *vt.* get over, overcome —**sur'mountable** *a.*

surname (ˈsɜːneɪm) *n.* family name

surpass (sɜːˈpɑːs) *vt.* **1.** go beyond **2.** excel **3.** outstrip —**sur'passable** *a.* —**sur'passing** *a.* **1.** excellent **2.** exceeding others

surplice (ˈsɜːplɪs) *n.* loose white vestment worn by clergy and choristers

surplus (ˈsɜːpləs) *n.* what remains over in excess

surprise (səˈpraɪz) *vt.* **1.** cause surprise to **2.** astonish **3.** take, come upon unexpectedly **4.** startle (someone) into action thus —*n.* **5.** what takes unawares **6.** something unexpected **7.** emotion aroused by being taken unawares

surrealism (səˈrɪəlɪzəm) *n.* movement in art and literature emphasizing expression of the unconscious —**sur'real** *a.* —**sur'realist** *n./a.*

surrender (səˈrɛndə) *vt.* **1.** hand over, give up —*vi.* **2.** yield **3.** cease resistance **4.** capitulate —*n.* **5.** act of surrendering

surreptitious (sʌrəpˈtɪʃəs) *a.* **1.** done secretly or stealthily **2.** furtive —**surrep'titiously** *adv.*

surrogate (ˈsʌrəgɪt) *n.* **1.** deputy, *esp.* of bishop **2.** substitute

surround (səˈraʊnd) *vt.* **1.** be, come all round, encompass **2.** encircle **3.** hem in —*n.* **4.** border, edging —**sur'roundings** *pl.n.* conditions, scenery *etc.* around a person, place, environment

surtax (ˈsɜːtæks) *n.* additional tax

surveillance (sɜːˈveɪləns) *n.* close watch, supervision —**sur'veillant** *a./n.*

survey (sɜːˈveɪ, ˈsɜːveɪ) *vt.* **1.** view, scrutinize **2.** inspect, examine **3.** measure, map (land) —*n.* (ˈsɜːveɪ) **4.** a surveying **5.** inspection **6.** report incorporating results of survey —**sur'veyor** *n.*

survive (səˈvaɪv) *vt.* **1.** outlive **2.** come through alive —*vi.* **3.** continue to live or exist —**sur'vival** *n.* continuation of existence of persons, things *etc.* —**sur'vivor** *n.* one left alive when others have died —**survival of the fittest** natural selection

sus (sʌs) *n. sl.* **1.** suspect **2.** suspicion

susceptible (səˈsɛptəbˈl) *a.* **1.** yielding readily **2.** capable **3.** impressionable —**suscepti'bility** *n.*

suspect (səˈspɛkt) *vt.* **1.** doubt innocence of **2.** have impression of existence or presence of **3.** be inclined to believe **4.** mistrust —*a.* (ˈsʌspɛkt) **5.** of suspected character —*n.* (ˈsʌspɛkt) **6.** suspected person

suspend (səˈspɛnd) *vt.* **1.** hang up **2.** cause to cease for a time **3.** debar from an office or privilege **4.** keep inoperative **5.** sustain in fluid —**sus'penders** *pl.n.* straps for supporting stockings —**suspended animation** temporary cessation of vital functions —**suspended sentence** prison sentence that is not served by offender unless he commits further offence during its currency —**suspender belt** belt with suspenders hanging from it to hold up women's stockings

suspense (səˈspɛns) *n.* **1.** state of uncertainty, *esp.* while awaiting news, an event *etc.* **2.** anxiety, worry —**sus'pension** *n.* **1.** state of being suspended **2.** springs on axle of body of vehicle —**sus'pensory** *a.* —**suspension bridge** bridge suspended from cables that hang between two towers and are anchored at both ends

suspicion (səˈspɪʃən) *n.* **1.** suspecting, being suspected **2.** slight trace —**sus'picious** *a.*

suss (sʌs) *vt. sl.* **1.** suspect **2.** (*oft. with* out) investigate, find (out)

sustain (səˈsteɪn) *vt.* **1.** keep, hold up **2.** endure **3.** keep alive **4.** confirm —**sus'tainable** *a.* —**sustenance** (ˈsʌstənəns) *n.* food

suture (ˈsuːtʃə) *n.* **1.** act of sewing **2.** sewing up of a wound **3.** material used for this **4.** a joining of the bones of the skull —**'sutural** *a.*

suzerain (ˈsuːzəreɪn) *n.* **1.** sovereign with rights over autonomous state **2.** feudal lord —**suzerainty** (ˈsuːzərəntɪ) *n.*

svelte (svɛlt, sfɛlt) *a.* **1.** lightly built, slender **2.** sophisticated

SW or **S.W.** southwest(ern)

Sw. 1. Sweden **2.** Swedish

swab (swɒb) n. **1.** mop **2.** pad of surgical wool etc. for cleaning, taking specimen etc. **3.** sl. low or unmannerly fellow —vt. **4.** clean with swab (-bb-) —'**swabber** n.

swaddle ('swɒd³l) vt. swathe —**swaddling clothes** Hist. long strips of cloth for wrapping newborn baby

swag (swæg) n. **1.** sl. stolen property **2.** A inf. bag carried by swagman —'**swagman** n. A itinerant tramp

swagger ('swægə) vi. **1.** strut **2.** boast —n. **3.** strutting gait **4.** boastful, overconfident manner —**swagger stick** or esp. U.K. **swagger cane** short cane or stick carried on occasion by army officers

Swahili (swɑː'hiːlɪ) n. **1.** Bantu language widely used as lingua franca throughout E and central Afr. **2.** member of people speaking this language (pl. **-s**, **-li**) —**Swa'hilian** a.

swain (sweɪn) n. rustic lover

swallow[1] ('swɒləʊ) vt. **1.** cause, allow to pass down gullet **2.** engulf **3.** suppress, keep back **4.** inf. believe gullibly —n. **5.** act of swallowing

swallow[2] ('swɒləʊ) n. migratory bird with forked tail and skimming manner of flight —**swallow dive** dive in which diver arches back, keeping his legs straight and his arms outstretched —'**swallowtail** n. **1.** butterfly having tail-like extension of each hind wing **2.** forked tail of swallow or similar bird

swam (swæm) pt. of SWIM

swami ('swɑːmɪ) n. in India, title of respect for Hindu saint or religious teacher (pl. **-es**, **-s**)

swamp (swɒmp) n. **1.** bog —vt. **2.** entangle in swamp **3.** overwhelm **4.** flood —'**swampy** a.

swan (swɒn) n. **1.** large, webfooted water bird with graceful curved neck —vi. **2.** inf. stroll idly (-nn-) —'**swannery** n. —**swan's-down** n. **1.** fine soft down feathers of swan, used to trim clothes etc. **2.** thick soft fabric of wool with silk, cotton or rayon **3.** cotton fabric with heavy nap —**swan song 1.** fabled song of a swan before death **2.** last act etc. before death —**swan-upping** n. UK practice of marking nicks in swans' beaks as sign of ownership

swank (swæŋk) vi. sl. **1.** swagger **2.** show off —'**swanky** a. sl. **1.** smart **2.** showy

swap or **swop** (swɒp) n./v. inf. **1.** exchange **2.** barter (-pp-)

sward (swɔːd) or **swarth** (swɔːθ) n. green turf

swarm[1] (swɔːm) n. **1.** large cluster of insects **2.** vast crowd —vi. **3.** (of bees) to be on the move in swarm **4.** gather in large numbers

swarm[2] (swɔːm) v. climb (rope etc.) by grasping with hands and knees

swarthy ('swɔːðɪ) a. dark-complexioned

swashbuckler ('swɒʃˌbʌklə) n. swaggering daredevil person —'**swashbuckling** a.

swastika ('swɒstɪkə) n. form of cross with arms bent at right angles, used as badge by Nazis

swat (swɒt) vt. **1.** hit smartly **2.** kill, esp. insects (-tt-)

swatch (swɒtʃ) n. **1.** sample of cloth or other material **2.** a number of such samples, usu. fastened together in book form

swathe (sweɪð) vt. cover with wraps or bandages

sway (sweɪ) v. **1.** swing unsteadily **2.** (cause to) vacillate in opinion etc. —vt. **3.** influence opinion etc. of —n. **4.** control **5.** power **6.** swaying motion

swear (sweə) vt. **1.** promise on oath **2.** cause to take an oath —vi. **3.** declare **4.** curse (**swore**, **sworn**, '**swearing**) —'**swearword** n. socially taboo word of a profane, obscene or insulting character

sweat (swɛt) n. **1.** moisture oozing from, forming on skin, esp. in humans —v. **2.** (cause to) exude sweat —vi. **3.** toil **4.** inf. worry —vt. **5.** employ at wrongfully low wages (**sweat** or '**sweated** pt./pp., '**sweating** pr.p.) —'**sweaty** a. —'**sweatband** n. **1.** band of material set in hat to protect it from sweat **2.** piece of cloth tied around forehead to keep sweat out of eyes or around wrist to keep hands dry, as in sports —**sweat shirt** long-sleeved knitted cotton sweater —'**sweatshop** n. workshop where employees work long hours for low wages

sweater ('swɛtə) n. woollen jersey

Swede (swiːd) n. **1.** native of Sweden **2.** (s-) variety of turnip —'**Swedish** a. **1.** of Sweden, its people or their language —n. **2.** official language of Sweden

sweep (swiːp) vi. **1.** effect cleaning with broom **2.** pass quickly or magnificently **3.** extend in continuous curve —vt. **4.** clean with broom **5.** carry impetuously (**swept**, '**sweeping**) —n. **6.** act of cleaning with broom **7.** sweeping motion **8.** wide curve **9.** range **10.** long oar **11.** one who cleans chimneys —'**sweeping** a. **1.** wide-ranging **2.** without limitations, reservations —**sweep** or '**sweepstake** n. gamble in which winner takes stakes contributed by all

sweet (swiːt) a. **1.** tasting like sugar **2.** agreeable **3.** kind, charming **4.** fresh, fragrant **5.** in good condition **6.** tuneful **7.** gentle, dear, beloved —n. **8.** small piece of sweet food **9.** sweet course served at end of meal —'**sweeten** v. —'**sweetener** n. **1.** sweetening agent, esp. one that is sugar-free **2.** sl. bribe —'**sweetish** a. —'**sweetly** adv. —'**sweetbread** n. animal's pancreas used as food —'**sweetbrier** n. wild rose —**sweet corn** variety of maize whose kernels are rich in sugar and eaten as vegetable when young —'**sweetheart** n. lover —'**sweetmeat** n. sweetened delicacy, eg small cake, sweet —**sweet pea** plant of pea family with bright flowers —**sweet potato 1.** trailing plant **2.** its edible, sweetish, starchy tubers —**sweet-talk** vt. inf. coax, flatter —**sweet tooth** strong liking for sweet foods —**sweet william** ('wɪljəm) garden plant with flat flower clusters

swell (swɛl) v. 1. expand —vi. 2. be greatly filled with pride, emotion (**swelled**, **'swollen, 'swelling**) —n. 3. act of swelling or being swollen 4. wave of sea 5. mechanism in organ to vary volume of sound 6. sl. person of high social standing —a. 7. sl. smart, fine —**swelled head** or **swollen head** inf. inflated view of one's own worth

swelter ('swɛltə) vi. be oppressed with heat

swept (swɛpt) pt./pp. of SWEEP —**'swept-wing** a. (of aircraft etc.) having wings swept backwards

swerve (swɜːv) vi. 1. swing round, change direction during motion 2. turn aside (from duty etc.) —n. 3. swerving

swift (swɪft) a. 1. rapid, quick, ready —n. 2. bird like a swallow —**'swiftly** adv.

swig (swɪg) n. 1. large swallow of drink —v. 2. drink thus (**-gg-**)

swill (swɪl) v. 1. drink greedily —vt. 2. pour water over or through —n. 3. liquid pig food 4. greedy drinking 5. rinsing

swim (swɪm) vi. 1. support and move oneself in water 2. float 3. be flooded 4. have feeling of dizziness —vt. 5. cross by swimming 6. compete in by swimming (**swam, swum, 'swimming**) —n. 7. spell of swimming —**'swimmer** n. —**'swimmingly** adv. successfully, effortlessly —**'swimming pool** artificial pool for swimming —**'swimsuit** n. woman's one-piece swimming garment

swindle ('swɪnd'l) n./v. cheat —**'swindler** n.

swine (swaɪn) n. 1. pig 2. contemptible person (pl. **swine**) —**'swinish** a. —**swine fever** infectious viral disease of pigs —**'swineherd** n.

swing (swɪŋ) v. 1. (cause to) move to and fro 2. (cause to) pivot, turn 3. hang 4. arrange, play (music) with (jazz) rhythm —vi. 5. be hanged 6. hit out (at) (**swung** pt./pp.) —n. 7. act, instance of swinging 8. seat hung to swing on 9. fluctuation (esp. in voting pattern) 10. C train of freight sleighs, canoes —**'swinger** n. inf. person regarded as modern, lively —**'swingboat** n. piece of fairground equipment consisting of boat-shaped carriage for swinging in

swingeing ('swɪndʒɪŋ) a. 1. severe 2. huge

swipe (swaɪp) v. 1. (sometimes with at) strike with wide, sweeping or glancing blow —vt. 2. sl. steal

swirl (swɜːl) v. 1. (cause to) move with eddying motion —n. 2. such motion

swish (swɪʃ) v. 1. (cause to) move with audible hissing sound —n. 2. the sound —a. 3. inf. fashionable, smart

Swiss (swɪs) n. 1. native of Switzerland —a. 2. of Switzerland —**swiss roll** type of rolled-up sponge cake

switch (swɪtʃ) n. 1. mechanism to complete or interrupt electric circuit etc. 2. abrupt change 3. flexible stick or twig 4. tufted end of animal's tail 5. tress of false hair —vi. 6. shift, change 7. swing —vt. 8. affect (current etc.) with switch 9. change abruptly 10. strike with switch —**'switchback** n. road, railway with steep rises and descents —**'switchboard** n. installation for establishing or varying connections in telephone and electric circuits

swither ('swɪðə) Scot. dial. vi. 1. hesitate; be perplexed —n. 2. hesitation; perplexity; agitation

swivel ('swɪv'l) n. 1. mechanism of two parts which can revolve the one on the other —v. 2. turn (on swivel) (**-ll-**)

swizzle ('swɪz'l) n. 1. an alcoholic drink containing gin or rum 2. inf. UK swindle or disappointment (also **swizz**) —**swizzle stick** small rod used to agitate effervescent drink to facilitate escape of carbon dioxide

swob (swɒb) see SWAB

swollen ('swəʊlən) pp. of SWELL

swoon (swuːn) vi./n. faint

swoop (swuːp) vi. 1. dive, as hawk —n. 2. act of swooping 3. sudden attack

swoosh (swuːʃ) vi. 1. make rustling, swirling sound, esp. when moving, pouring out —n. 2. swirling, rustling sound or movement

swop (swɒp) see SWAP

sword (sɔːd) n. weapon with long blade for cutting or thrusting —**sword dance** dance in which performers dance nimbly over swords on ground or brandish them in the air —**'swordfish** n. fish with elongated sharp upper jaw, like sword —**'swordplay** n. 1. action or art of fighting with sword 2. verbal sparring —**sword swallower** person who swallows or appears to swallow swords, in a circus etc.

swore (swɔː) pt. of SWEAR —**sworn** pp. of SWEAR

swot (swɒt) inf. v. 1. study hard (**-tt-**) —n. 2. one who works hard at lessons or studies

swum (swʌm) pp. of SWIM

swung (swʌŋ) pt./pp. of SWING

sybarite ('sɪbəraɪt) n. person who loves luxury —**sybaritic** (sɪbə'rɪtɪk) a.

sycamore ('sɪkəmɔː) n. tree allied to plane tree and maple

sycophant ('sɪkəfənt) n. one using flattery to gain favours —**'sycophancy** n. —**syco-'phantic** a.

syllable ('sɪləb'l) n. division of word as unit for pronunciation —**syl'labic** a. —**syl'labify** vt.

syllabub or **sillabub** ('sɪləbʌb) n. 1. sweet frothy dish of cream, sugar and wine 2. something insubstantial

syllabus ('sɪləbəs) n. 1. outline of a course of study 2. programme, list of subjects studied on course (pl. **-es**, **-bi** (**-baɪ**))

syllogism ('sɪlədʒɪzəm) n. form of logical

reasoning consisting of two premisses and conclusion —syllo'gistic a.

sylph (sɪlf) n. 1. slender, graceful woman 2. sprite —'sylphlike a.

sylvan or **silvan** ('sɪlvən) a. of forests, trees

sym- see SYN-

symbiosis (sɪmbɪ'əʊsɪs) n. living together of two organisms of different kinds, esp. to their mutual benefit —symbiotic (sɪmbɪ-'ɒtɪk) a.

symbol ('sɪmb'l) n. 1. sign 2. thing representing or typifying something —sym'bolic a. —sym'bolically adv. —'symbolism n. 1. use of, representation by symbols 2. movement in art holding that work of art should express idea in symbolic form —'symbolist n./a. —'symbolize or -ise v.

symmetry ('sɪmɪtrɪ) n. 1. proportion between parts 2. balance of arrangement between two sides 3. order —sym'metrical a. 1. having due proportion in parts 2. harmonious 3. regular

sympathy ('sɪmpəθɪ) n. 1. feeling for another in pain etc. 2. compassion, pity 3. sharing of emotion, interest, desire etc. 4. fellow feeling —sympa'thetic a. —sympa'thetically adv. —'sympathize or -ise vi. —sympathetic magic type of magic in which it is sought to produce large-scale effect by performing some small-scale ceremony resembling it, as pouring of water on altar to induce rainfall

symphony ('sɪmfənɪ) n. 1. composition for full orchestra 2. harmony of sounds —symphonic (sɪm'fɒnɪk) a. —sym'phonious a. harmonious —symphonic poem extended orchestral composition, based on nonmusical material, such as work of literature or folk tale —symphony orchestra large orchestra comprising strings, brass, woodwind, harp and percussion

symposium (sɪm'pəʊzɪəm) n. 1. conference, meeting 2. discussion, writings on a given topic (pl. -s, -sia (-zɪə))

symptom ('sɪmptəm) n. 1. change in body indicating its state of health or disease 2. sign, token —sympto'matic a.

syn- or **sym-** (comb form) with, together, alike

synagogue ('sɪnəgɒg) n. (place of worship of) Jewish congregation

synchromesh ('sɪŋkrəʊmɛʃ) a. (of gearbox) having device that synchronizes speeds of gears before they engage

synchronize or **-ise** ('sɪŋkrənaɪz) vt. 1. make agree in time —vi. 2. happen at same time —'synchronism n. —synchroni'zation or -i'sation n. —'synchronous a. simultaneous

synchrotron ('sɪŋkrətrɒn) n. device for acceleration of stream of electrons

syncopate ('sɪŋkəpeɪt) vt. accentuate (weak beat in bar of music) —synco'pation n.

syndicate ('sɪndɪkɪt) n. 1. body of people, delegates associated for some enterprise —vt. ('sɪndɪkeɪt) 2. form into syndicate 3. publish in many newspapers at the same time —'syndicalism n. economic movement aiming at combination of workers in all trades to enforce demands of labour

syndrome ('sɪndrəʊm) n. 1. combination of several symptoms in disease 2. symptom, set of symptoms or characteristics

synod ('sɪnɒd, 'sɪnəd) n. 1. church council 2. convention

synonym ('sɪnənɪm) n. word with same meaning as another —syno'nymity n. —synonymous (sɪ'nɒnɪməs) a.

synopsis (sɪ'nɒpsɪs) n. summary, outline (pl. -ses (-siːz)) —syn'optic a. 1. of, like synopsis 2. having same viewpoint

syntax ('sɪntæks) n. part of grammar treating of arrangement of words in sentence —syn'tactic a. —syn'tactically adv.

synthesis ('sɪnθɪsɪs) n. putting together, combination (pl. -theses (-θɪsiːz)) —'synthesize or -ise v. (cause to) combine into a whole —'synthesizer n. 1. see MOOG SYNTHESIZER 2. person or thing that synthesizes —synthetic (sɪn'θɛtɪk) a. 1. artificial 2. of synthesis

syphilis ('sɪfɪlɪs) n. contagious venereal disease —syphi'litic a.

Syrian ('sɪrɪən) a. 1. of Syria, republic in W. Asia, its people or their dialect of Arabic —n. 2. native or inhabitant of Syria

syringe ('sɪrɪndʒ, sɪ'rɪndʒ) n. 1. instrument for drawing in liquid by piston and forcing it out in fine stream or spray 2. squirt —vt. 3. spray, cleanse with syringe

syrup ('sɪrəp) n. 1. thick solution obtained in process of refining sugar 2. any liquid like this, esp. in consistency —'syrupy a.

system ('sɪstəm) n. 1. complex whole, organization 2. method 3. classification —syste'matic a. methodical —syste'matically adv. —'systematize or -ise vt. 1. reduce to system 2. arrange methodically —systemic (sɪ'stɛmɪk, -'stiː-) a. affecting entire body or organism —systems analysis analysis of methods involved in scientific and industrial operations, usu. with computer so that improved system can be designed

systole ('sɪstəlɪ) n. contraction of heart and arteries for expelling blood and carrying on circulation —systolic (sɪ'stɒlɪk) a. 1. contracting 2. of systole

T

t or **T** (tiː) *n.* **1.** 20th letter of English alphabet **2.** speech sound represented by this letter **3.** something shaped like T (*pl.* **t's, T's** or **Ts**) —**to a T** in every detail; perfectly

t 1. tense **2.** ton

T 1. absolute temperature **2.** *Chem.* tritium **3.** surface tension **4.** tablespoon

ta (tɑː) *interj.* UK *inf.* thank you

Ta *Chem.* tantalum

TA Territorial Army

Taal (tɑːl) *n.* SA language, *esp.* Afrikaans

tab¹ (tæb) *n.* tag, label, short strap —**keep tabs on** *inf.* keep watchful eye on

tab² (tæb) **1.** tabulator **2.** tablet

tabard ('tæbəd) *n.* (herald's) short tunic open at sides

tabby ('tæbɪ) *n./a.* (cat) with markings of stripes *etc.* on lighter background

tabernacle ('tæbənæk'l) *n.* **1.** portable shrine of Israelites **2.** *R.C.Ch.* receptacle containing consecrated Host **3.** place of worship not called a church

table ('teɪb'l) *n.* **1.** piece of furniture consisting of flat board supported by legs **2.** food **3.** set of facts, figures arranged in lines or columns —*vt.* **4.** lay on table **5.** submit (motion *etc.*) for consideration by meeting **6.** suspend discussion of (bill *etc.*) indefinitely —**'tablecloth** *n.* cloth for covering table —**'tableland** *n.* plateau, high flat area —**table licence** licence authorizing sale of alcoholic drinks with meals only —**'tablespoon** *n.* spoon used for serving food *etc.* —**table tennis** ball game played on table with small bats and light hollow ball

tableau ('tæbləʊ) *n.* **1.** group of persons, silent and motionless, arranged to represent some scene **2.** dramatic scene (*pl.* **-leaux** (-ləʊ, -ləʊz))

table d'hôte ('tɑːb'l 'dəʊt) *Fr.* (meal) with limited choice of dishes, at a fixed price

tablet ('tæblɪt) *n.* **1.** pill of compressed powdered medicinal substance **2.** flattish cake of soap *etc.* **3.** slab of stone, wood *etc.*, *esp.* used formerly for writing on

tabloid ('tæblɔɪd) *n.* illustrated popular small-sized newspaper with terse, sensational headlines

taboo or **tabu** (tə'buː) *a.* **1.** forbidden; disapproved of —*n.* **2.** prohibition resulting from social conventions *etc.* **3.** thing prohibited —*vt.* **4.** place under taboo

tabor or **tabour** ('teɪbə) *n.* small drum, used *esp.* in Middle Ages, struck with one hand while other held pipe

tabular ('tæbjʊlə) *a.* shaped, arranged like a table —**'tabulate** *vt.* arrange (figures, facts *etc.*) in tables —**tabu'lation** *n.* —**'tabulator** *n.* **1.** device for setting stops that locate column margins on typewriter **2.** *Comp.* machine that reads data from

punched cards *etc.*, producing lists, tabulations or totals

tacho- (*comb. form*) speed, as in *tachometer*

tachograph ('tækəɡrɑːf) *n.* device for recording speed and distance travelled by lorries

tachometer (tæ'kɒmɪtə) *n.* device for measuring speed, *esp.* of revolving shaft (in car) and hence revolutions per minute

tacit ('tæsɪt) *a.* **1.** implied but not spoken **2.** silent —**'tacitly** *adv.* —**'taciturn** *a.* **1.** talking little **2.** habitually silent —**taci'turnity** *n.*

tack¹ (tæk) *n.* **1.** small nail **2.** long, loose, temporary stitch **3.** *Naut.* course of ship obliquely to windward **4.** course, direction **5.** *inf.* food —*vt.* **6.** nail with tacks **7.** stitch (garment) with long, loose temporary stitches **8.** append, attach —*v.* **9.** sail to windward —**on the wrong tack** under false impression

tack² (tæk) *n.* riding harness for horses

tackies ('tækɪz) *pl.n.* SA plimsolls

tackle ('tæk'l) *n.* **1.** equipment, apparatus, *esp.* lifting appliances with ropes **2.** *Sport* physical challenge of opponent —*vt.* **3.** take in hand **4.** grapple with **5.** challenge

tacky¹ ('tækɪ) *a.* sticky, not quite dry —**'tackiness** *n.*

tacky² ('tækɪ) *a.* US *inf.* **1.** shabby, shoddy **2.** ostentatious and vulgar **3.** (of person) eccentric; crazy

tact (tækt) *n.* **1.** skill in dealing with people or situations **2.** delicate perception of the feelings of others —**'tactful** *a.* —**'tactfully** *adv.* —**'tactless** *a.* —**'tactlessly** *adv.*

tactics ('tæktɪks) *pl.n.* **1.** (*with sing. v.*) art of handling troops, ships in battle **2.** adroit management of a situation **3.** plans for this —**'tactical** *a.* —**tac'tician** *n.* —**tactical voting** (in election) casting vote not for party of one's choice but for second strongest contender in consitituency, in order to defeat likeliest winner

tactile ('tæktaɪl) *a.* of the sense of touch

tadpole ('tædpəʊl) *n.* immature frog, in its first state before gills and tail are absorbed

taffeta ('tæfɪtə) *n.* smooth, stiff fabric of silk, rayon *etc.*

taffrail ('tæfreɪl) *n.* **1.** rail at stern of ship **2.** flat ornamental part of stern

Taffy ('tæfɪ) *n. sl.* Welshman

tag¹ (tæɡ) *n.* **1.** label identifying or showing price of something **2.** ragged, hanging end **3.** pointed end of shoelace *etc.* **4.** trite quotation **5.** any appendage —*vt.* **6.** append, add (on) —*vi.* **7.** (*usu.* with on or along) trail behind (**-gg-**)

tag² (tæɡ) *n.* **1.** children's game where one being chased becomes the chaser upon being touched by chaser —*vt.* **2.** touch

(-gg-) —**tag wrestling** wrestling match for teams of two, where one partner may replace the other upon being touched on hand

tagetes (tæ'dʒːitiːz) *n.* plant with yellow or orange flowers

tail (teɪl) *n.* **1.** flexible prolongation of animal's spine **2.** lower or inferior part of anything **3.** appendage **4.** rear part of aircraft **5.** *inf.* person employed to follow and spy on another —*pl.* **6.** reverse side of coin **7.** *inf.* tail coat —*vt.* **8.** remove tail of **9.** *inf.* follow closely, trail —**tailed** *a.* —'**tailings** *pl.n.* waste left over from some (*eg* industrial) process —'**tailless** *a.* —'**tailback** *n.* queue of traffic stretching back from an obstruction —'**tailboard** *n.* removable or hinged rear board on lorry *etc.* —**tail coat** man's evening dress jacket —**tail end** last part —**tail gate** gate used to control flow of water at lower end of lock —'**tailgate** *n.* **1.** *esp.* US tailboard —*v.* **2.** US drive very close behind (vehicle) —'**taillight** *or* '**taillamp** *n.* light at rear of vehicle —'**tailpiece** *n.* **1.** extension or appendage that lengthens or completes something **2.** decorative design at foot of page *etc.* **3.** piece of wood to which strings of violin *etc.* are attached at lower end **4.** short beam or rafter with one end embedded in wall —'**tailpipe** *n.* pipe from which exhaust gases are discharged, *esp.* at rear of motor vehicle —'**tailplane** *n.* stabilizing surface at rear of aircraft —'**tailspin** *n.* spinning dive of aircraft —'**tailwind** *n.* wind blowing in same direction as course of aircraft or ship —**tail off** diminish gradually, dwindle —**turn tail** run away

tailor ('teɪlə) *n.* maker of outer clothing, *esp.* for men —'**tailored** *a.* **1.** having simple lines, as some women's garments **2.** specially fitted —'**tailorbird** *n.* tropical Asian warbler that builds nest by sewing together large leaves using plant fibres —**tailor-made** *a.* **1.** made by tailor **2.** well-fitting **3.** appropriate —*n.* **4.** *inf.* factory-made cigarettes

taint (teɪnt) *v.* **1.** affect or be affected by pollution *etc.* —*n.* **2.** defect, flaw **3.** infection, contamination

take (teɪk) *vt.* **1.** grasp, get hold of **2.** get, receive **3.** assume **4.** adopt **5.** accept **6.** understand **7.** consider **8.** carry, conduct **9.** use **10.** capture **11.** consume **12.** require —*vi.* **13.** be effective **14.** please **15.** go (**took**, **taken**, **taking**) —*n.* **16.** *esp.* Cine. (recording of) scene, sequence photographed without interruption —'**taking** *a.* charming —'**takings** *pl.n.* earnings, receipts —'**takeaway** UK, A, NZ *a.* **1.** sold for consumption away from premises **2.** selling food for consumption away from premises —*n.* **3.** shop or restaurant that sells such food —**take-home pay** remainder of one's pay after all income tax and other compulsory deductions have been made —**take-off** *n.* **1.** instant at which aircraft becomes airborne **2.** commence-

ment of flight **3.** *inf.* act of mimicry —'**takeover** *n.* act of assuming power, control *etc.* —**take after** resemble in appearance or character —**take down 1.** write down **2.** dismantle **3.** humiliate —**take in 1.** understand **2.** make (garment *etc.*) smaller **3.** deceive —**take in vain 1.** blaspheme **2.** mention (person's name) —**take off 1.** (of aircraft) leave ground **2.** *inf.* go away **3.** *inf.* mimic —**take over 1.** assume control or management (of) **2.** *Print.* move (copy) to next line —**take to** become fond of

talc (tælk) *n.* **1.** soft mineral of magnesium silicate **2.** talcum powder —**talcum powder** powder, *usu.* scented, to absorb body moisture, deodorize *etc.*

tale (teɪl) *n.* **1.** story, narrative, report **2.** fictitious story —**tell tales 1.** tell fanciful lies **2.** report malicious stories *etc.*, *esp.* to someone in authority

talent ('tælənt) *n.* **1.** natural ability or power **2.** ancient weight or money **3.** *inf.* (*esp.* attractive) members of opposite sex —'**talented** *a.* gifted —**talent scout** person whose occupation is searching for talented sportsmen, performers *etc.* for engagement as professionals

talisman ('tælɪzmən) *n.* **1.** object supposed to have magic power **2.** amulet (*pl.* -s) —talis'**manic** *a.*

talk (tɔːk) *vi.* **1.** express, exchange ideas *etc.* in words **2.** spread rumours or gossip —*vt.* **3.** express in speech, utter **4.** discuss —*n.* **5.** speech, lecture **6.** conversation **7.** rumour —'**talkative** *a.* fond of talking —'**talker** *n.* —**talking book** recording of book, designed to be used by blind —**talking head** (on television) person, shown only from shoulders up, who speaks without illustrative material —**talking-to** *n.* *inf.* reproof —**talk back** answer boldly or impudently —**talk into** persuade to by talking —**talk out of** dissuade from by talking

tall (tɔːl) *a.* **1.** high, of great stature **2.** incredible, untrue (*esp.* in **tall story**) —'**tallboy** *n.* high chest of drawers —**tall order** demand which is difficult to accomplish

tallow ('tæləʊ) *n.* **1.** melted and clarified animal fat —*vt.* **2.** smear with this

tally ('tælɪ) *vi.* **1.** correspond one with the other **2.** keep score (-**lied**, -**lying**) —*n.* **3.** record, account, total number —'**tallier** *n.*

tally-ho (tælɪ'həʊ) *interj.* huntsman's cry to urge on hounds

Talmud ('tælmʊd) *n.* body of Jewish law —Tal'**mudic** *a.*

talon ('tælən) *n.* claw

tamarind ('tæmərɪnd) *n.* **1.** tropical tree **2.** its pods containing sour brownish pulp

tamarisk ('tæmərɪsk) *n.* ornamental, evergreen tree or shrub with slender branches, very small leaves and spiky flowers

tambour ('tæmbʊə) *n.* **1.** *Real tennis* sloping buttress on one side of receiver's end of court **2.** embroidery frame consisting of two hoops over which fabric is stretched while being worked **3.** embroidered work done on such frame **4.** sliding door on desks etc., made of thin strips of wood glued on to canvas backing **5.** Archit. wall that is circular in plan, esp. supporting dome or surrounded by colonnade **6.** drum —v. **7.** embroider on tambour

tambourine (tæmbə'ri:n) n. flat half-drum with jingling discs of metal attached

tame (teim) a. **1.** not wild, domesticated **2.** subdued **3.** uninteresting —vt. **4.** make tame —'**tamely** adv. **1.** in a tame manner **2.** without resisting —'**tamer** n.

Tamil ('tæmɪl) n. **1.** member of a people of S India and Sri Lanka **2.** language of this people (pl. -s, 'Tamil) —a. **3.** of this people

tam-o'-shanter (tæmə'ʃæntə) n. Scottish brimless wool cap with bobble in centre

tamp (tæmp) vt. pack, force down by repeated blows

tamper ('tæmpə) vi. (usu. with with) interfere improperly, meddle

tampon ('tæmpɒn) n. plug of lint, cotton etc. inserted in wound, body cavity, to stop flow of blood, absorb secretions etc.

tan¹ (tæn) a./n. **1.** (of) brown colour of skin after long exposure to rays of sun etc. —v. **2.** (cause to) go brown —vt. **3.** (of animal hide) convert to leather by chemical treatment **4.** inf. beat, flog (-nn-) —'**tanner** n. —'**tannery** n. place where hides are tanned —'**tannic** a. of tan, tannin or tannic acid —'**tannin** n. vegetable substance used as tanning agent —'**tanbark** n. bark of certain trees, yielding tannin —**tannic acid** astringent derived from oak bark etc., used in tanning etc.

tan² (tæn) Trig. tangent

tanager ('tænədʒə) n. any of family of Amer. songbirds having short thick bill and, in male, brilliantly coloured plumage

tandem ('tændəm) n. bicycle for two riders, one behind the other

tandoori (tæn'duərɪ) n. Indian method of cooking meat or vegetables on a spit in clay oven

tang (tæŋ) n. **1.** strong pungent taste or smell **2.** trace, hint **3.** spike, barb —'**tangy** a.

tangent ('tændʒənt) n. **1.** line that touches a curve without cutting **2.** divergent course **3.** Trig. ratio of side opposite given acute angle in right-angled triangle to adjacent side —a. **4.** touching, meeting without cutting —**tan'gential** a. —**tan'gentially** adv.

tangerine (tændʒə'ri:n) n. **1.** Asian citrus tree **2.** its fruit, a variety of orange **3.** reddish-orange colour

tangible ('tændʒəbʰl) a. **1.** that can be touched **2.** definite **3.** palpable; concrete —**tangi'bility** n.

tangle ('tæŋgʰl) n. **1.** confused mass or situation —vt. **2.** twist together in muddle —vi. **3.** contend

tango ('tæŋgəʊ) n. dance of S Amer. origin (pl. -s)

tank (tæŋk) n. **1.** storage vessel for liquids or gas **2.** armoured motor vehicle moving on tracks **3.** cistern **4.** UK, US dial. reservoir —'**tanker** n. ship, lorry etc. for carrying liquid in bulk —**tank farming** see HYDROPONICS —**tank up** chiefly UK sl. imbibe large quantity of alcoholic drink

tankard ('tæŋkəd) n. **1.** large drinking cup of metal or glass **2.** its contents, esp. beer

tanner ('tænə) n. UK inf. sixpence

tannin ('tænɪn) n. see TAN¹

Tannoy ('tænɔɪ) n. **R** type of public-address system

tansy ('tænzɪ) n. yellow-flowered aromatic herb

tantalize or -**ise** ('tæntəlaɪz) vt. torment by appearing to offer something desired, tease —'**tantalus** n. UK case in which bottles may be locked with their contents visible

tantalum ('tæntələm) n. hard greyish-white metallic element

tantamount ('tæntəmaʊnt) a. **1.** equivalent in value or signification **2.** equal, amounting

tantrum ('tæntrəm) n. childish outburst of temper

Taoism ('taːəʊɪzəm) n. system of religion and philosophy based on teachings of Laotse, Chinese philosopher, and advocating simple, honest life and noninterference with course of natural events —'**Taoist** n./a. —**Tao'istic** a.

tap¹ (tæp) v. **1.** strike lightly but with some noise (-pp-) —n. **2.** slight blow, rap —**tap dance** step dance in which performer makes makes sharp, loud taps of the foot, toe or heal on stage as he dances —**tap-dance** vi. perform tap dance —**tap-dancer** n. —**tap-dancing** n.

tap² (tæp) n. **1.** valve with handle to regulate or stop flow of fluid in pipe etc. **2.** stopper, plug permitting liquid to be drawn from cask etc. **3.** steel tool for forming internal screw threads —vt. **4.** put tap in **5.** draw off (as) with tap **6.** make secret connection to (telephone wire) to overhear conversation on it **7.** make connection to (pipe, drain etc.) **8.** form internal threads in **9.** UK sl. ask (someone) for money; obtain (money) from someone (-pp-) —'**taproom** n. bar, as in hotel or pub

tape (teɪp) n. **1.** narrow long strip of fabric, paper etc. **2.** magnetic recording of music etc. —vt. **3.** record (speech, music etc.) —**tape deck** platform supporting spools etc. of tape recorder, incorporating motor and playback, recording and erasing heads —**tape machine** telegraphic device that records current stock quotations electronically or on ticker tape —**tape measure** tape of fabric or metal, marked off in centimetres, inches etc. —**tape recorder** apparatus for recording sound on magnetized tape and playing it back —**tape recording 1.** act of recording on magnetic tape **2.** magnetized tape used for this **3.** music *etc.* so recorded —'**tapeworm** *n.* long flat worm parasitic in animals and man —**have (someone) taped** *inf.* have (someone) sized up, have measure of (someone)

taper ('teɪpə) *vi.* **1.** become gradually thinner towards one end —*n.* **2.** thin candle **3.** long wick covered with wax; spill **4.** a narrowing

tapestry ('tæpɪstrɪ) *n.* fabric decorated with designs in colours woven by needles, not in shuttles —'**tapestried** *a.*

tapioca (tæpɪ'əʊkə) *n.* beadlike starch made from cassava root, used *esp.* in puddings

tapir ('teɪpə) *n.* Amer. animal with elongated snout, allied to pig

tappet ('tæpɪt) *n.* in internal-combustion engine, short steel rod conveying movement imparted by the lift of a cam to the valve stem

taproot ('tæpruːt) *n.* large single root growing straight down

tar¹ (tɑː) *n.* **1.** thick black liquid distilled from coal *etc.* —*vt.* **2.** coat, treat with tar (**-rr-**)

tar² (tɑː) *n. inf.* sailor

tarantella (tærən'tɛlə) *n.* **1.** lively It. dance **2.** music for it

tarantula (tə'ræntjʊlə) *n.* any of various large (poisonous) hairy spiders (*pl.* **-s, -lae** (-liː))

tarboosh (tɑː'buːʃ) *n.* felt brimless cap, usu. red and oft. with silk tassel, worn by Muslim men

tardy ('tɑːdɪ) *a.* **1.** slow **2.** late —'**tardily** *adv.*

tare¹ (tɛə) *n.* **1.** weight of wrapping or container for goods **2.** unladen weight of vehicle

tare² (tɛə) *n.* **1.** vetch **2.** weed

target ('tɑːgɪt) *n.* **1.** mark to aim at in shooting *etc.* **2.** thing aimed at **3.** object of criticism **4.** *esp.* **target language** language into which text *etc.* is translated

tariff ('tærɪf) *n.* **1.** tax levied on imports *etc.* **2.** list of charges **3.** method of charging for supply of services, *eg* electricity

Tarmac ('tɑːmæk) *n.* **R** mixture of tar, bitumen and crushed stones rolled to give hard, smooth surface *esp.* as used for road, airport runway *etc.* (*also* **Tarma'cadam**)

tarn (tɑːn) *n.* small mountain lake

tarnish ('tɑːnɪʃ) *v.* **1.** (cause to) become stained, lose shine or become dimmed or sullied —*n.* **2.** discoloration, blemish

taro ('tɑːrəʊ) *n.* **1.** plant of Pacific islands **2.** its edible roots

tarot ('tærəʊ) *n.* one of special pack of cards now used mainly in fortune-telling

tarpaulin (tɑː'pɔːlɪn) *n.* (sheet of) heavy hard-wearing waterproof fabric

tarragon ('tærəgən) *n.* aromatic herb

tarry ('tærɪ) *vi.* **1.** linger, delay **2.** stay behind (**-ried, -rying**)

tarsier ('tɑːsɪə) *n.* nocturnal tree-dwelling mammal of Indonesia *etc.*

tarsus ('tɑːsəs) *n.* **1.** bones of ankle and heel collectively **2.** corresponding part in other mammals *etc.* **3.** connective tissue supporting free edge of each eyelid (*pl.* **-si** (-saɪ)) —'**tarsal** *a.* **1.** of tarsus or tarsi —*n.* **2.** tarsal bone

tart¹ (tɑːt) *n.* **1.** pie or flan filled with fruit, jam *etc.* **2.** *inf., offens.* promiscuous woman, *esp.* prostitute —**tart up** *UK sl.* **1.** dress and make (oneself) up in provocative or promiscuous way **2.** reissue or decorate in cheap and flashy way

tart² (tɑːt) *a.* **1.** sour, bitter **2.** sharp

tartan ('tɑːt²n) *n.* **1.** woollen cloth woven in pattern of coloured checks, *esp.* in colours, patterns associated with Scottish clans **2.** such pattern

tartar¹ ('tɑːtə) *n.* **1.** crust deposited on teeth **2.** deposit formed during fermentation of wine —**tar'taric** *a.* —**tartaric acid** colourless crystalline acid found in many fruits

tartar² ('tɑːtə) *n.* vicious-tempered person, difficult to deal with

Tartar ('tɑːtə) *see* TATAR

tartar sauce mayonnaise sauce mixed with chopped herbs, capers *etc.*

tartrazine ('tɑːtrəziːn, -zɪn) *n.* artificial dye that produces yellow colour: used as food additive, in drugs *etc.*

Tas. Tasmania

task (tɑːsk) *n.* **1.** piece of work (*esp.* unpleasant or difficult) set or undertaken —*vt.* **2.** assign task to **3.** exact —**task force** naval or military unit dispatched to carry out specific undertaking —'**taskmaster** *n.* overseer —**take to task** reprove

Tasmanian devil (tæz'meɪnɪən) small, ferocious, carnivorous marsupial of Tasmania

Tass (tæs) *n.* principal news agency of Soviet Union

tassel ('tæs²l) *n.* **1.** ornament of fringed knot of threads *etc.* **2.** tuft

taste (teɪst) *n.* **1.** sense by which flavour, quality of substance is detected by the tongue **2.** this act or sensation **3.** (brief) experience of something **4.** small amount **5.** preference, liking **6.** power of discerning, judging **7.** discretion, delicacy —*v.* **8.** observe or distinguish the taste of (a substance) **9.** take small amount of (food *etc.*) into mouth —*vt.* **10.** experience —*vi.* **11.** have specific flavour —'**tasteful** *a.* **1.** in good style **2.** with, showing good taste —'**tastefully** *adv.* —'**tasteless** *a.* —'**taster** *n.* **1.** person who samples food or drink for quality **2.** device used in tasting or sampling **3.** *esp.* formerly, person employed to taste food and drink prepared for king *etc.* to test for poison —'**tasty** *a.* pleasantly or highly flavoured —**taste bud** small organ of taste on tongue

tat¹ (tæt) *v.* make (something) by tatting (**-tt-**) —'**tatter** *n.* —'**tatting** *n.* type of handmade lace

tat² (tæt) *n.* **1.** ragged, shoddy article **2.** tattiness

ta-ta (tæˈtɑː) *interj.* UK *inf.* goodbye; farewell

Tatar *or* **Tartar** (ˈtɑːtə) *n.* 1. member of Mongoloid people who established powerful state in central Asia in 13th century 2. descendant of this people, now scattered throughout Soviet Union 3. Turkic language or dialect spoken by this people —*a.* 4. of Tatars

tater (ˈteɪtə) *n. dial.* potato

tatter (ˈtætə) *v.* 1. make or become ragged, worn to shreds —*n.* 2. ragged piece

tattle (ˈtætʳl) *vi./n.* gossip, chatter —ˈ**tattletale** *chiefly* US *n.* 1. scandalmonger, gossip —*a.* 2. telltale

tattoo[1] (tæˈtuː) *n.* 1. formerly, beat of drum and bugle call 2. military spectacle or pageant

tattoo[2] (tæˈtuː) *vt.* 1. mark (skin) in patterns *etc.* by pricking and filling punctures with indelible coloured inks (-ˈtooed, -ˈtooing) —*n.* 2. mark so made

tatty (ˈtætɪ) *a.* shabby, worn-out —ˈ**tattiness** *n.*

tau (tɔː, taʊ) *n.* 19th letter in Gr. alphabet (T, τ)

taught (tɔːt) *pt./pp. of* TEACH

taunt (tɔːnt) *vt.* 1. provoke, deride with insulting words *etc.* 2. tease; tantalize —*n.* 3. instance of this

taupe (təʊp) *n.* brownish-grey colour

Taurus (ˈtɔːrəs) *n.* (bull) 2nd sign of zodiac, operative *c.* Apr. 21st-May 20th

taut (tɔːt) *a.* 1. drawn tight 2. under strain —ˈ**tauten** *vt.* make tight or tense

tauto- *or before vowel* **taut-** (*comb. form*) identical, same, as in *tautology*

tautology (tɔːˈtɒlədʒɪ) *n.* repetition of same thing in other words in same sentence —**tauto**ˈ**logical** *a.*

tavern (ˈtævən) *n.* inn, public house

tawdry (ˈtɔːdrɪ) *a.* showy, but cheap and without taste, flashy —ˈ**tawdrily** *adv.* —ˈ**tawdriness** *n.*

tawny (ˈtɔːnɪ) *a./n.* (of) light (yellowish) brown —**tawny owl** European owl having reddish-brown plumage and round head

tawse *or* **taws** (tɔːz) *n.* in Scotland, leather strap used *esp.* formerly by schoolteacher to punish pupils

tax (tæks) *n.* 1. compulsory payments by wage earners, companies *etc.* imposed by government to raise revenue 2. heavy demand (on something) —*vt.* 3. impose tax on 4. strain 5. accuse, blame —ˈ**taxable** *a.* —**tax**ˈ**ation** *n.* levying of taxes —**tax-deductible** *a.* legally deductible from income before tax assessment —**tax exile** person who lives abroad to avoid paying high taxes —**tax-free** *a.* exempt from taxation —ˈ**taxpayer** *n.* —**tax return** statement of personal income for tax purposes

taxi (ˈtæksɪ) *n.* 1. motor vehicle for hire with driver (*pl.* -s) (*also* **cab**, ˈ**taxicab**) —*vi.* 2. (of aircraft) run along ground under its own power 3. go in taxi (ˈ**taxied**

pt./pp., ˈ**taxying**, ˈ**taxiing** *pr.p.*) —ˈ**taximeter** *n.* meter fitted to taxi to register fare, based on length of journey —**taxi rank** place where taxis wait to be hired

taxidermy (ˈtæksɪdɜːmɪ) *n.* art of stuffing, mounting animal skins to give them lifelike appearance —**taxi**ˈ**dermal** *or* **taxi**ˈ**dermic** *a.* —ˈ**taxidermist** *n.*

taxonomy (tækˈsɒnəmɪ) *n.* science, practice of classification, *esp.* of biological organisms

Tb *Chem.* terbium

T.B. *or* **t.b.** tuberculosis

T-bone steak steak cut from sirloin of beef, containing T-shaped bone

tbs. *or* **tbsp.** tablespoon(ful)

Tc *Chem.* technetium

tch *interj./n.* 1. clicking sound made with tongue, to express disapproval *etc.* —*vi.* 2. utter tch's

te *or* **ti** (tiː) *n. Mus.* in tonic sol-fa, syllable used for seventh note or subtonic of any scale

Te *Chem.* tellurium

tea (tiː) *n.* 1. dried leaves of plant cultivated *esp.* in (sub)tropical Asia 2. infusion of it as beverage 3. any of various herbal infusions 4. tea, cakes *etc.* as light afternoon meal 5. main evening meal —**tea bag** small porous bag of paper containing tea leaves —**tea ball** *chiefly* US perforated metal ball filled with tea leaves and used to make tea —ˈ**teacake** *n.* UK flat bun, usu. eaten toasted and buttered —**tea-chest** *n.* square wooden box lined with foil for exporting tea *etc.* —**tea cosy** covering for teapot to keep contents hot —ˈ**teacup** *n.* 1. cup out of which tea may be drunk 2. amount teacup will hold, about four fluid ounces (*also* ˈ**teacupful**) —ˈ**teahouse** *n.* restaurant, *esp.* in Japan or China, where tea and light refreshments are served —**tea leaf** 1. dried leaf of tea shrub, used to make tea 2. (*usu. pl.*) shredded parts of these leaves, *esp.* after infusion —**tea party** social gathering at which tea is served —ˈ**teapot** *n.* container with lid, spout and handle, in which tea is made —ˈ**tearoom** *n.* UK restaurant where tea and light refreshments are served (*also* ˈ**teashop**) —ˈ**teaspoon** *n.* small spoon for stirring tea *etc.* —**tea tree** Aust., N.Z. tree

teach (tiːtʃ) *vt.* 1. instruct 2. educate 3. train 4. impart knowledge of —*vi.* 5. act as teacher (**taught**, ˈ**teaching**) —ˈ**teacher** *n.* —ˈ**teaching** *n.* —**teaching machine** machine that presents information and questions to user, registers answers, and indicates whether these are correct or acceptable

teak (tiːk) *n.* 1. E Indian tree 2. very hard wood obtained from it

teal (tiːl) *n.* 1. type of small duck 2. greenish-blue colour

team (tiːm) *n.* 1. set of animals, players of game *etc.* associated in activity —*v.* 2. (*usu. with* up) (cause to) make a team

—'**teamster** *n.* driver of team of draught animals —'**team-mate** *n.* fellow member of team —**team spirit** subordination of individual desire for good of team —'**teamwork** *n.* cooperative work by team acting as unit

tear[1] (tɪə) *n.* drop of fluid appearing in and falling from eye —'**tearful** *a.* 1. inclined to weep 2. involving tears —'**tearless** *a.* —'**teardrop** *n.* —**tear gas** irritant gas causing abnormal watering of eyes and temporary blindness —**tear-jerker** *n. inf.* excessively sentimental film *etc.*

tear[2] (tɛə) *vt.* 1. pull apart, rend —*vi.* 2. become torn 3. rush (**tore, torn, 'tearing**) —*n.* 4. hole, cut; split —'**tearaway** *n.* UK reckless impetuous person —**tear away** persuade (oneself or someone else) to leave

tease (tiːz) *vt.* 1. tantalize, torment, irritate, bait 2. pull apart fibres of —*n.* 3. one who teases —'**teaser** *n.* annoying or puzzling problem —'**teasing** *a.*

teasel, teazel, *or* **teazle** ('tiːzəl) *n.* plant with prickly leaves and head

teat (tiːt) *n.* 1. nipple of female breast 2. rubber nipple of baby's feeding bottle

tech (tɛk) *a./n. inf.* technical (college)

tech. 1. technical 2. technology

technetium (tɛk'niːʃɪəm) *n.* silvery-grey metallic element, artificially produced by bombardment of molybdenum by deuterons

technical ('tɛknɪkəl) *a.* 1. of, specializing in industrial, practical or mechanical arts and applied sciences 2. skilled in practical and mechanical arts 3. belonging to particular art or science 4. according to letter of the law —**techni'cality** *n.* 1. point of procedure 2. state of being technical —'**technically** *adv.* —**tech'nician** *n.* one skilled in technique of an art —**technique** (tɛk'niːk) *n.* 1. method of performance in an art 2. skill required for mastery of subject —**technical college** higher educational institution, with courses in art, technology *etc.* —**technical drawing** drawing done with T-squares, scales *etc.* —**technical knockout** *Boxing* judgment of knockout given when boxer is in referee's opinion too badly beaten to continue

Technicolor ('tɛknɪkʌlə) *n.* R colour photography, *esp.* in cinema

techno- (*comb. form*) 1. craft; art, as in *technology, technography* 2. technological; technical, as in *technocracy*

technocracy (tɛk'nɒkrəsɪ) *n.* 1. government by technical experts 2. group of these experts

technology (tɛk'nɒlədʒɪ) *n.* 1. application of practical, mechanical sciences to industry, commerce 2. technical methods, skills, knowledge —**techno'logical** *a.* —**tech'nologist** *n.*

tectonic (tɛk'tɒnɪk) *a.* of construction or building —**tec'tonics** *pl.n.* (*with sing. v.*) art, science of building

ted (tɛd) *inf.* teddy boy

teddy bear ('tɛdɪ) child's soft toy bear (*also* '**teddy**)

teddy boy 1. UK *esp.* in mid-1950s, one of cult of youths who wore mock Edwardian fashions 2. any tough or delinquent youth

Te Deum (tiː 'diːəm) 1. ancient Latin hymn in rhythmic prose 2. musical setting of this hymn 3. service of thanksgiving in which recital of this hymn forms central part

tedious ('tiːdɪəs) *a.* causing fatigue or boredom, monotonous —'**tedium** *n.* monotony

tee (tiː) *n.* 1. *Golf* slightly raised ground from which first stroke of hole is made 2. small peg supporting ball for this stroke 3. target in some games (*eg* quoits) —**tee off** make first stroke of hole in golf

teem (tiːm) *vi.* 1. abound, swarm, be prolific 2. pour, rain heavily

teens (tiːnz) *pl.n.* years of life from 13 to 19 —'**teenage** *a.* —'**teenager** *n.* young person between 13 and 19 —'**teenybopper** *n. sl.* young teenager, usu. girl, who avidly follows fashions

teeny ('tiːnɪ) *a.* extremely small; tiny (*also* **teeny-weeny** ('tiːnɪ'wiːnɪ), **teensy-weensy** ('tiːnzɪ'wiːnzɪ))

teepee ('tiːpiː) *n. see* TEPEE

tee shirt *see* T-SHIRT

teeter ('tiːtə) *vi.* 1. seesaw or make similar movements 2. vacillate

teeth (tiːθ) *n., pl. of* TOOTH —**teethe** (tiːð) *vi.* (of baby) grow first teeth —**teething ring** hard ring on which babies may bite while teething —**teething troubles** problems, difficulties at first stage of something

teetotal (tiː'təʊt°l) *a.* pledged to abstain from alcohol —**tee'totalism** *n.* —**tee'totaller** *n.*

Teflon ('tɛflɒn) *n.* R polymer used to make nonstick coatings on cooking utensils

tel. 1. telegram 2. telegraph(ic) 3. telephone

tel- (*comb. form*) *see* TELE-

tele- (*comb. form*) at a distance, from far off, as in *telescope*

telecast ('tɛlɪkɑːst) *vi./n.* (broadcast) television programme

telecommunications (tɛlɪkəmjuːnɪ'keɪʃənz) *pl.n.* (*with sing. v.*) science and technology of communications by telephony, radio, television *etc.*

telegram ('tɛlɪɡræm) *n.* message sent by telegraph

telegraph ('tɛlɪɡrɑːf) *n.* 1. electrical apparatus for transmitting messages to a distance 2. any signalling device for transmitting messages —*v.* 3. communicate by telegraph —*vt.* 4. C cast (votes) illegally by impersonating registered voters —**tele'graphic** *a.* —**tele'graphically** *adv.* —**te'legraphist** *n.* one who works telegraph —**te'legraphy** *n.* 1. science of telegraph 2. use of telegraph

telekinesis (tɛlɪkaɪ'niːsɪs) *n.* 1. movement of a body caused by thought or willpower

2. ability to cause such movement —**telekinetic** (tɛlɪkɪˈnɛtɪk) a.

teleology (tɛliˈɒlədʒi, tiːlɪ-) n. **1.** doctrine of final causes **2.** belief that things happen because of the purpose or design that will be fulfilled by them —**teleoˈlogic(al)** a.

telepathy (tɪˈlɛpəθɪ) n. action of one mind on another at a distance —**teleˈpathic** a. —**teleˈpathically** adv.

telephone (ˈtɛlɪfəʊn) n. **1.** apparatus for communicating sound to hearer at a distance —v. **2.** communicate, speak by telephone —**telephonic** (tɛlɪˈfɒnɪk) a. —**teˈlephonist** n. person operating telephone switchboard —**teˈlephony** n. —**telephone box** soundproof enclosure from which paid telephone call can be made (also **telephone kiosk, telephone booth**) —**telephone directory** book listing names, addresses and telephone numbers of subscribers in particular area

telephoto (ˈtɛlɪfəʊtəʊ) a. (of lens) producing magnified image of distant object —**telephoˈtography** n. process or technique of photographing distant objects using telephoto lens

teleprinter (ˈtɛlɪprɪntə) n. apparatus like typewriter, by which typed messages are sent and received by wire

Teleprompter (ˈtɛlɪprɒmptə) n. **R** T.V. device to enable speaker to refer to his script out of sight of the cameras

telesales (ˈtɛlɪseɪlz) pl.n. selling of commodity or service by salesperson who makes initial approach by telephone

telescope (ˈtɛlɪskəʊp) n. **1.** optical instrument for magnifying distant objects —v. **2.** slide or drive together, esp. parts designed to fit one inside the other **3.** make smaller, shorter —**telescopic** (tɛlɪˈskɒpɪk) a.

teletext (ˈtɛlɪtɛkst) n. electronic system which shows information, news on subscribers' television screens

television (ˈtɛlɪvɪʒən) n. **1.** system of producing on screen images of distant objects, events etc. by electromagnetic radiation **2.** device for receiving this transmission and converting it to optical images **3.** programmes etc. viewed on television set —**televise** vt. **1.** transmit by television **2.** make, produce as television programme

telex (ˈtɛlɛks) n. **1.** international telegraph service using teleprinters —v. **2.** transmit (message) to (person etc.) by telex

tell (tɛl) vt. **1.** let know **2.** order, direct **3.** narrate, make known **4.** discern **5.** distinguish **6.** count —vi. **7.** give account **8.** be of weight, importance **9.** inf. reveal secrets (**told, 'telling**) —**'teller** n. **1.** narrator **2.** bank cashier —**'telling** a. effective, striking —**'telltale** n. **1.** sneak **2.** automatic indicator —a. **3.** revealing

tellurian (tɛˈlʊərɪən) a. of the earth —**telˈluric** a. —**telˈlurium** n. nonmetallic bluish-white element —**tellurous** (ˈtɛljʊrəs, tɛˈlʊərəs) a.

telly (ˈtɛlɪ) inf. television (set)

temerity (tɪˈmɛrɪtɪ) n. boldness, audacity

temp (tɛmp) inf. n. **1.** one employed on temporary basis —vi. **2.** work as temp

temp. **1.** temperature **2.** temporary

temper (ˈtɛmpə) n. **1.** frame of mind **2.** anger, oft. noisy **3.** mental constitution **4.** degree of hardness of steel etc. —vt. **5.** restrain, qualify, moderate **6.** harden **7.** bring to proper condition —**'tempered** a. having temper or temperament as specified, as in ill-tempered

tempera (ˈtɛmpərə) n. emulsion used as painting medium

temperament (ˈtɛmpərəmənt) n. **1.** natural disposition **2.** excitability; moodiness; anger —**temperaˈmental** a. **1.** given to extremes of temperament, moody **2.** of, occasioned by temperament **3.** inf. working erratically and inconsistently; unreliable —**temperaˈmentally** adv.

temperate (ˈtɛmpərɪt) a. **1.** not extreme **2.** showing, practising moderation —**'temperance** n. **1.** moderation **2.** abstinence, esp. from alcohol —**'temperately** adv. —**Temperate Zone** parts of earth's surface lying between Arctic Circle and tropic of Cancer and between Antarctic Circle and tropic of Capricorn

temperature (ˈtɛmprɪtʃə) n. **1.** degree of heat or coldness **2.** inf. (abnormally) high body temperature

tempest (ˈtɛmpɪst) n. violent storm —**temˈpestuous** a. **1.** turbulent **2.** violent, stormy —**temˈpestuously** adv.

template or **templet** (ˈtɛmplɪt) n. mould, pattern to help shape something accurately

temple [1] (ˈtɛmp[2]l) n. **1.** building for worship **2.** shrine

temple [2] (ˈtɛmp[2]l) n. flat part on either side of forehead

tempo (ˈtɛmpəʊ) n. rate, rhythm, esp. in music (pl. **-s, -pi** (-piː))

temporal [1] (ˈtɛmpərəl) a. **1.** of time **2.** of this life or world, secular **3.** Gram. of tense or linguistic expression of time —**tempoˈrality** n.

temporal [2] (ˈtɛmpərəl) a. Anat. of temple or temples —**temporal bone** either of two compound bones forming sides of skull

temporary (ˈtɛmpərərɪ) a. lasting, used only for a time —**'temporarily** adv.

temporize or **-ise** (ˈtɛmpəraɪz) vi. **1.** use evasive action; hedge; gain time by negotiation etc. **2.** conform to circumstances —**'temporizer** or **-iser** n.

tempt (tɛmpt) vt. **1.** try to persuade, entice, esp. to something wrong or unwise **2.** dispose, cause to be inclined —**tempˈtation** n. **1.** act of tempting **2.** thing that tempts —**'tempter** n. (**'temptress** fem.) —**'tempting** a. attractive, inviting

tempus fugit (ˈtɛmpəs ˈfjuːdʒɪt) Lat. time flies

ten (tɛn) n./a. cardinal number next after nine —**tenth** a./n. ordinal number —**tengallon hat** US cowboy's broad-brimmed felt hat with high crown —**tenpin bowling**

('tɛnpɪn) bowling game in which bowls are rolled down lane to knock over ten target pins (also (esp. US) **'tenpins**) —the **Ten Commandments** O.T. commandments summarizing basic obligations of man towards God and his fellow men

ten. Mus. 1. tenor 2. tenuto

tenable ('tɛnəb°l) a. able to be held, defended, maintained

tenacious (tɪ'neɪʃəs) a. 1. holding fast 2. retentive 3. stubborn —**tenacity** (tɪ'næsɪtɪ) n.

tenant ('tɛnənt) n. one who holds lands, house etc. on rent or lease —**'tenancy** n. —**'tenantry** n. body of tenants —**tenant farmer** person who farms land rented from another, rent usu. taking form of crops etc.

tench (tɛntʃ) n. freshwater game fish

tend[1] (tɛnd) vi. 1. be inclined 2. be conducive 3. go or move (in particular direction) —**'tendency** n. inclination, bent —**ten'dentious** or **ten'dencious** a. having, showing tendency or bias, controversial

tend[2] (tɛnd) vt. take care of, watch over —**'tender** n. 1. small boat carried by yacht or ship 2. carriage for fuel and water attached to steam locomotive 3. one who tends, eg bar tender

tender[1] ('tɛndə) a. 1. not tough or hard 2. easily injured 3. gentle, loving, affectionate 4. delicate, soft —**'tenderize** or **-ise** vt. soften (meat) by pounding or by treating with substance made for this purpose —**'tenderly** adv. —**'tenderness** n. —**'tenderfoot** n. newcomer, esp. to ranch etc. —**'tenderloin** n. tender cut of pork etc. from between sirloin and ribs

tender[2] ('tɛndə) vt. 1. offer —vi. 2. make offer or estimate —n. 3. offer 4. offer or estimate for contract to undertake specific work 5. what may legally be offered in payment

tendon ('tɛndən) n. sinew attaching muscle to bone etc.

tendril ('tɛndrɪl) n. 1. slender curling stem by which climbing plant clings to anything 2. curl, as of hair

tenement ('tɛnəmənt) n. building divided into separate flats (also **tenement building**)

tenet ('tɛnɪt, 'tiːnɪt) n. doctrine, belief

tenner ('tɛnə) inf. ten-pound note

tennis ('tɛnɪs) n. game in which ball is struck with racket by players on opposite sides of net, lawn tennis —**tennis elbow** strained muscle as a result of playing tennis —**tennis shoe** rubber-soled canvas shoe tied with laces

tenon ('tɛnən) n. tongue put on end of piece of wood etc. to fit into a mortise —**tenon saw**

tenor ('tɛnə) n. 1. male voice between alto and bass 2. music for, singer with this 3. saxophone etc. intermediate between alto and baritone or bass 4. general course, meaning

tense[1] (tɛns) n. modification of verb to show time of action

tense[2] (tɛns) a. 1. stretched tight, strained; taut 2. emotionally strained —v. 3. make, become tense —**'tensile** a. 1. of tension 2. capable of being stretched —**'tension** n. 1. stretching 2. strain when stretched 3. emotional strain or excitement 4. hostility 5. suspense 6. Elec. voltage —**tensile strength** measure of ability of material to withstand longitudinal stress

tent (tɛnt) n. portable shelter of canvas —**tent stitch** see petit point at PETIT

tentacle ('tɛntək°l) n. elongated, flexible organ of some animals (eg octopus) used for grasping, feeding etc.

tentative ('tɛntətɪv) a. 1. done as a trial 2. experimental, cautious —**'tentatively** adv.

tenterhooks ('tɛntəhʊks) pl.n. —**on tenterhooks** in anxious suspense

tenuous ('tɛnjʊəs) a. 1. flimsy, uncertain 2. thin, fine, slender —**te'nuity** n.

tenure ('tɛnjʊə, 'tɛnjə) n. (length of time of) possession, holding of office, position etc.

tenuto (tɪ'njuːtəʊ) a./adv. Mus. (of note) to be held for or beyond its full time value

tepee or **teepee** ('tiːpiː) n. N Amer. Indian cone-shaped tent of animal skins

tepid ('tɛpɪd) a. 1. moderately warm, lukewarm 2. half-hearted

tequila (tɪ'kiːlə) n. Mexican alcoholic spirit

ter. 1. terrace 2. territory

terbium ('tɜːbɪəm) n. rare metallic element

tercel ('tɜːs°l) or **tiercel** n. male falcon or hawk, esp. as used in falconry

tercentenary (tɜːsɛn'tiːnərɪ) or **tercentennial** a./n. (of) three hundredth anniversary

tergiversate ('tɜːdʒɪvəseɪt) vi. 1. change sides or loyalties 2. be evasive or ambiguous —**tergiver'sation** n.

term (tɜːm) n. 1. word; expression 2. limited period of time 3. period during which courts sit, schools are open etc. 4. limit, end —pl. 5. conditions 6. mutual relationship —vt. 7. name, designate —**terms of reference** specific limits of responsibility that determine activities of investigating body etc. —**terms of trade** UK Econ. ratio of export prices to import prices

termagant ('tɜːməgənt) n. rare shrewish woman; scold

terminal ('tɜːmɪn°l) a. 1. at, forming an end 2. pert. to, forming a terminus 3. (of disease) ending in death —n. 4. terminal part or structure 5. extremity 6. point where current enters, leaves electrical device (eg battery) 7. device permitting operation of computer at some distance from it —**terminal velocity** 1. constant maximum velocity reached by body falling under gravity through fluid, esp. atmosphere 2. velocity of missile or projectile when it reaches target 3.

maximum velocity attained by rocket *etc.* flying in parabolic flight path **4.** maximum velocity that aircraft can attain

terminate ('tɜːmɪneɪt) *v.* bring, come to an end —'**terminable** *a.* —**termi'nation** *n.*

terminology (tɜːmɪ'nɒlədʒɪ) *n.* **1.** set of technical terms or vocabulary **2.** study of terms —**termino'logical** *a.*

terminus ('tɜːmɪnəs) *n.* **1.** finishing point **2.** farthest limit **3.** railway station, bus station *etc.* at end of long-distance line (*pl.* **-ni** (-naɪ), **-es**)

termite ('tɜːmaɪt) *n.* insect, some species of which feed on and damage wood (*also* **white ant**)

tern (tɜːn) *n.* sea bird like gull

ternary ('tɜːnərɪ) *a.* **1.** consisting of three **2.** proceeding in threes

Terpsichore (tɜːp'sɪkərɪ) *n.* Muse of dance and choral song —**Terpsichorean** (tɜːpsɪkə'riːən, -'kɔːrɪən) *oft. jocular a.* **1.** of dancing (*also* **Terpsicho'real**) —*n.* **2.** dancer

Terr. 1. Terrace **2.** Territory

terrace ('tɛrəs) *n.* **1.** raised level place **2.** level cut out of hill **3.** row, street of houses built as one block **4.** (*oft. pl.*) unroofed tier for spectators at football stadium —*vt.* **5.** form into, furnish with terrace

terra cotta ('tɛrə 'kɒtə) **1.** hard unglazed pottery **2.** its colour, brownish red

terra firma ('fɜːmə) *Lat.* firm ground; dry land

terrain (tə'reɪn) *n.* area of ground, *esp.* with reference to its physical character

terra incognita (ɪn'kɒgnɪtə) *Lat.* unexplored or unknown area

terrapin ('tɛrəpɪn) *n.* type of aquatic tortoise

terrazzo (tɛ'rætsəʊ) *n.* floor, wall finish of chips of stone set in mortar and polished

terrene (tɛ'riːn) *a.* **1.** of earth; worldly; mundane **2.** *rare* of earth; earthy —*n.* **3.** land **4.** *rare* earth

terrestrial (tə'rɛstrɪəl) *a.* **1.** of the earth **2.** of, living on land

terrible ('tɛrəbʲl) *a.* **1.** serious **2.** dreadful, frightful **3.** excessive **4.** causing fear —'**terribly** *adv.*

terrier ('tɛrɪə) *n.* small dog of various breeds, *orig.* for following quarry into burrow

terrific (tə'rɪfɪk) *a.* **1.** very great **2.** *inf.* good, excellent **3.** terrible, awe-inspiring

terrify ('tɛrɪfaɪ) *vt.* fill with fear, dread

terrine (tɛ'riːn) *n.* **1.** oval earthenware cooking dish **2.** food cooked or served in such dish, *esp.* paté

territory ('tɛrɪtərɪ) *n.* **1.** region **2.** geographical area under control of a political unit, *esp.* a sovereign state **3.** area of knowledge —**terri'torial** *a.* of territory —**Territorial Army** locally recruited volunteer force —**territorial waters** waters over which nation exercises jurisdiction

terror ('tɛrə) *n.* **1.** great fear **2.** *inf.* troublesome person or thing —'**terrorism**

n. **1.** use of violence, intimidation to achieve ends **2.** state of terror —'**terrorist** *n./a.* —'**terrorize** *or* **-ise** *vt.* force, oppress by fear, violence

terry ('tɛrɪ) *n./a.* (pile fabric) with the loops uncut

terse (tɜːs) *a.* **1.** expressed in few words, concise **2.** abrupt

tertiary ('tɜːʃərɪ) *a.* **1.** third in degree, order *etc.* **2.** (**T-**) of Tertiary period or rock system —*n.* **3.** (**T-**) geological period before Quaternary

Terylene ('tɛrəliːn) *n.* **R 1.** synthetic yarn **2.** fabric made of it

tessellate ('tɛsɪleɪt) *vt.* **1.** make, pave, inlay with mosaic of small tiles **2.** (of identical shapes) fit together exactly —'**tessellated** *a.* —**tessel'lation** *n.* —**tessera** ('tɛsərə) *n.* stone used in mosaic (*pl.* **-ae** (-iː))

test (tɛst) *vt.* **1.** try, put to the proof **2.** carry out test(s) on —*n.* **3.** critical examination **4.** means of trial —'**testing** *a.* difficult —**test case** lawsuit viewed as means of establishing precedent —**test match** one of series of international sports contests, *esp.* cricket —**test paper 1.** *Chem.* paper impregnated with indicator for chemical tests **2.** question sheet of test **3.** paper completed by test candidate —**test pilot** pilot who flies aircraft of new design to test performance in air —**test tube** narrow cylindrical glass vessel used in scientific experiments —**test-tube baby** baby conceived in artificial womb

testament ('tɛstəmənt) *n.* **1.** *Law* will **2.** declaration **3.** (**T-**) one of the two main divisions of the Bible —**testa'mentary** *a.*

testate ('tɛsteɪt, 'tɛstɪt) *a.* having left a valid will —'**testacy** *n.* state of being testate —**tes'tator** *n.* maker of will (**tes'tatrix** *fem.*)

testicle ('tɛstɪkʲl) *n.* either of two male reproductive glands

testify ('tɛstɪfaɪ) *v.* **1.** declare **2.** bear witness (to) (**-fied, -fying**)

testimony ('tɛstɪmənɪ) *n.* **1.** affirmation **2.** evidence —**testi'monial** *n.* **1.** certificate of character, ability *etc.* **2.** tribute given by person expressing regard for recipient —*a.* **3.** of testimony or testimonial

testis ('tɛstɪs) *n.* testicle (*pl.* **testes** ('tɛstiːz)) —**tes'tosterone** *n.* hormone secreted mainly by testes

testy ('tɛstɪ) *a.* irritable, short-tempered —'**testily** *adv.*

tetanus ('tɛtənəs) *n.* acute infectious disease producing muscular spasms, contractions (*also* '**lockjaw**)

tetchy ('tɛtʃɪ) *a.* cross, irritable, touchy —'**tetchiness** *n.*

tête-à-tête (teɪtə'teɪt) *n.* **1.** private conversation between two people **2.** small sofa for two people, *esp.* S-shaped (*pl.* **-s, -tête**) —*adv.* **3.** intimately; in private

tether ('tɛðə) *n.* **1.** rope or chain for fastening (grazing) animal —*vt.* **2.** tie up with rope —**be at the end of one's tether** have reached limit of one's endurance

tetra- *or before vowel* **tetr-** (*comb. form*) four, as in *tetrameter*

tetrad ('tɛtræd) *n.* group or series of four

tetraethyl lead (tɛtrə'iːθail lɛd) colourless oily insoluble liquid used in petrol to prevent knocking

tetragon ('tɛtrəgɒn) *n.* figure with four angles and four sides —**te'tragonal** *a.* —**tetra'hedron** *n.* solid contained by four plane faces

tetralogy (tɛ'trælədʒı) *n.* series of four related works, as in drama or opera

tetrameter (tɛ'træmıtə) *n. Prosody* 1. line of verse consisting of four metrical feet 2. verse composed of such lines

Teuton ('tjuːtɒn) *n.* 1. member of ancient Germanic people from Jutland who migrated to S Gaul in 2nd century B.C. 2. member of any Germanic-speaking people, *esp.* German —*a.* 3. Teutonic —**Teu'tonic** *a.* 1. German 2. of ancient Teutons

text (tɛkst) *n.* 1. (actual words of) book, passage *etc.* 2. passage of Scriptures *etc.*, *esp.* as subject of discourse —**'textual** *a.* of, in a text —**'textbook** *n.* book of instruction on particular subject —**textual criticism** 1. scholarly study of manuscripts, *esp.* of Bible, to establish original text 2. literary criticism emphasizing close analysis of text

textile ('tɛkstail) *n.* 1. any fabric or cloth, *esp.* woven —*a.* 2. of (the making of) fabrics

texture ('tɛkstʃə) *n.* 1. surface of material, *esp.* as perceived by sense of touch 2. character, structure 3. consistency —*vt.* 4. give distinctive texture to

T.G.W.U. Transport and General Workers' Union

Th *Chem.* thorium

-th¹ (*comb. form*) 1. action or its consequence, as in *growth* 2. quality, as in *width*

-th² *or* **-eth** (*comb. form*) forming ordinal numbers, as in *fourth, thousandth*

Thai (tai) *a.* 1. of Thailand —*n.* 2. native of Thailand (*pl.* **-s, Thai**) 3. language of Thailand

thalidomide (θə'lıdəmaıd) *n.* drug formerly used as sedative, but found to cause abnormalities in developing foetus

thallium ('θælıəm) *n.* highly toxic metallic element —**'thallic** *a.*

than (ðæn; *unstressed* ðən) *conj.* introduces second part of comparison

thane *or* **thegn** (θeın) *n. Hist.* nobleman holding lands in return for certain services

thank (θæŋk) *vt.* 1. express gratitude to 2. say thanks to 3. hold responsible —**'thankful** *a.* grateful, appreciative —**'thankless** *a.* 1. having, bringing no thanks 2. unprofitable —**thanks** *pl.n.* words of gratitude —**Thanksgiving Day** public holiday in Canad. and U.S.A.

that (ðæt; *unstressed* ðət) *a.* 1. demonstrates or particularizes (*pl.* **those**) —*demonstrative pron.* 2. particular thing meant (*pl.* **those**) —*adv.* 3. as —*relative pron.* 4. which, who —*conj.* 5. introduces noun or adverbial clauses

thatch (θætʃ) *n.* 1. reeds, straw *etc.* used as roofing material —*vt.* 2. roof (a house) with reeds, straw *etc.* —**'thatcher** *n.*

thaw (θɔː) *v.* 1. melt 2. (cause to) unfreeze 3. defrost —*vi.* 4. become warmer or more genial —*n.* 5. a melting (of frost *etc.*)

Th.D. Doctor of Theology

the (*stressed or emphatic* ðiː; *unstressed before consonant* ðə; *unstressed before vowel* ðı) the definite article

theatre *or U.S.* **theater** ('θıətə) *n.* 1. place where plays *etc.* are performed 2. drama, dramatic works generally 3. large room with (tiered) seats, used for lectures *etc.* 4. surgical operating room —**theatrical** (θı'ætrık²l) *a.* 1. of, for the theatre 2. exaggerated, affected —**theatrically** (θı'ætrıkəlı) *adv.* 4. —**theatricals** (θı'ætrık²lz) *pl.n.* amateur dramatic performances

thee (ðiː) *pron. obs.* objective and dative of THOU¹

theft (θɛft) *n.* stealing

their (ðɛə) *a.* belonging to them —**theirs** *pron.* something or someone belonging to them

theism ('θiːızəm) *n.* belief in creation of universe by one god —**'theist** *n.* —**the'istic(al)** *a.*

them (ðɛm; *unstressed* ðəm) *pron.* 1. objective case of THEY 2. those persons or things —**them'selves** *pron.* emphatic and reflexive form of THEY

theme (θiːm) *n.* 1. main idea or topic of conversation, book *etc.* 2. subject of composition 3. recurring melody in music —**the'matic** *a.*

then (ðɛn) *adv.* 1. at that time 2. next 3. that being so

thence (ðɛns) *adv.* from that place, point of reasoning *etc.*

theo- *or before vowel* **the-** (*comb. form*) God; gods, as in *theology*

theocracy (θı'ɒkrəsı) *n.* government by a deity or a priesthood —**theo'cratic** *a.*

theodolite (θı'ɒdəlait) *n.* surveying instrument for measuring angles

theology (θı'ɒlədʒı) *n.* systematic study of religion(s) and religious belief(s) —**theologian** (θıə'ləudʒıən) *n.* —**theo'logical** *a.* —**theo'logically** *adv.*

theorem ('θıərəm) *n.* proposition which can be demonstrated by argument —**theore'matic** *or* **theo'remic** *a.*

theory ('θıərı) *n.* 1. supposition to account for something 2. system of rules and principles 3. rules and reasoning *etc.* as distinguished from practice —**theo'retic(al)** *a.* 1. based on theory 2. speculative, as opposed to practical —**theo'retically** *adv.* —**theore'tician** *n.* student or user of theory rather than practical aspects of subject —'**theorist** n. —'**theorize** or -ise vi. form theories, speculate

theosophy (θɪ'ɒsəfɪ) n. any of various religious, philosophical systems claiming possibility of intuitive insight into divine nature

therapy ('θerəpɪ) n. healing treatment (usu. in comb. forms as radiotherapy) —**therapeutic** (θerə'pjuːtɪk) a. 1. of healing 2. serving to improve or maintain health —**therapeutics** (θerə'pjuːtɪks) pl.n. (with sing. v.) art of healing —'**therapist** n.

there (ðeə) adv. 1. in that place 2. to that point —'**thereabouts** or '**thereabout** adv. near that place, time etc. —**there'after** adv. from that time on; after that time —**there'by** adv. by that means —'**therefore** adv. in consequence, that being so —**there'in** adv. Formal, law in or into that place etc. —**there'of** adv. Formal, law 1. of or concerning that or it 2. from or because of that —**there'to** adv. 1. Formal, law to that or it 2. obs. in addition to that —**there'under** adv. Formal, law 1. in documents etc., below that or it; subsequently in that; thereafter 2. under terms or authority of that —**thereu'pon** adv. at that point, immediately afterwards —**there'with** or **therewith'al** adv. 1. Formal, law with or in addition to that 2. rare thereupon 3. obs. by means of or on account of that

therm (θɜːm) n. unit of measurement of heat —'**thermal** or '**thermic** a. 1. of, pert. to heat 2. hot, warm (esp. of spring etc.) 3. (of garments) specially made so as to have exceptional heat-retaining qualities

thermion ('θɜːmɪən) n. Phys. ion emitted by incandescent body —**thermi'onic** a. pert. to thermion —**thermionic valve** electronic valve in which electrons are emitted from a heated rather than a cold cathode

thermo- or before vowel **therm-** (comb. form) related to, caused by or producing heat, as in thermopile

thermocouple ('θɜːməʊkʌp²l) n. 1. device for measuring temperature consisting of pair of wires of different metals joined at both ends 2. similar device with only one junction between two dissimilar metals

thermodynamics (θɜːməʊdaɪ'næmɪks) pl.n. (with sing. v.) the science that deals with the interrelationship and interconversion of different forms of energy

thermoelectricity (θɜːməʊɪlek'trɪsɪtɪ) n. electricity developed by the action of heat —**thermoe'lectric(al)** a. 1. of conversion of heat energy to electrical energy 2. of conversion of electrical energy

thermometer (θə'mɒmɪtə) n. instrument to measure temperature —**thermo'metric** a.

thermonuclear (θɜːməʊ'njuːklɪə) a. involving nuclear fusion

thermoplastic (θɜːməʊ'plæstɪk) n. 1. plastic that retains its properties after

being melted and solidified —a. 2. (of plastic etc.) becoming soft when heated and rehardening on cooling without appreciable change of properties

Thermos or **Thermos flask** ('θɜːmɒs) n. R vacuum flask

thermosetting (θɜːməʊ'setɪŋ) a. (of material, esp. synthetic plastic) hardening permanently after one application of heat and pressure

thermostat ('θɜːməstæt) n. apparatus for automatically regulating temperature —**thermo'static** a.

thesaurus (θɪ'sɔːrəs) n. 1. book containing lists of synonyms and sometimes antonyms 2. dictionary of selected words, topics (pl. -es, -ri (-raɪ))

these (ðiːz) pron., pl. of THIS

thesis ('θiːsɪs) n. 1. written work submitted for degree, diploma 2. theory maintained in argument (pl. **theses** ('θiːsiːz))

Thespian ('θespɪən) a. 1. theatrical —n. 2. actor, actress

Thess. Bible Thessalonians

theta ('θiːtə) n. eighth letter in Gr. alphabet (Θ, θ)

they (ðeɪ) pron. the third person plural pronoun

thick (θɪk) a. 1. having great thickness, not thin 2. dense, crowded 3. viscous 4. (of voice) throaty 5. inf. stupid, insensitive 6. inf. friendly (esp. in **thick as thieves**) —n. 7. busiest, most intense part —'**thicken** v. 1. make, become thick —vi. 2. become more involved, complicated —'**thickening** n. 1. something added to liquid to thicken it 2. thickened part or piece —'**thicket** n. thick growth of small trees —'**thickly** adv. —'**thickness** n. 1. dimensions of anything measured through it, at right angles to length and breadth 2. state of being thick 3. layer —'**thickhead** n. 1. stupid or ignorant person; fool 2. Aust. or SE Asian songbird —**thick'headed** a. —**thick-'headedness** n. —**thick'set** a. 1. sturdy and solid of body 2. set closely together —**thick-skinned** a. insensitive to criticism or hints; not easily upset or affected

thief (θiːf) n. one who steals (pl. **thieves** (θiːvz)) —**thieve** v. steal —'**thievish** a.

thigh (θaɪ) n. upper part of leg

thimble ('θɪmb²l) n. cap protecting end of finger when sewing

thin (θɪn) a. 1. of little thickness 2. slim, lean 3. of little density 4. sparse; fine 5. loose, not close-packed 6. inf. unlikely —v. 7. make, become thin (-nn-) —'**thinner** n. —'**thinness** n. —**thin-skinned** a. sensitive to criticism or hints; easily upset or affected

thine (ðaɪn) pron./a. (thing) belonging to thee

thing (θɪŋ) n. 1. material object 2. any possible object of thought 3. preoccupation, obsession (esp. in **have a thing about**) —**thingumabob** or **thingamabob** ('θɪŋəməbɒb) n. inf. a person or thing the name of which is unknown, temporarily forgotten or deliberately overlooked (*also* **'thingumajig, 'thingamajig** *or* **'thingummy**)

think (θɪŋk) *vi.* 1. have one's mind at work 2. reflect, meditate 3. reason 4. deliberate 5. imagine 6. hold opinion — *vt.* 7. conceive, consider in the mind 8. believe 9. esteem (**thought, 'thinking**) — **'thinkable** *a.* able to be conceived, considered, possible, feasible — **'thinker** *n.* — **'thinking** *a.* reflecting — **think-tank** *n.* group of experts studying specific problems

thio- *or before vowel* **thi-** (*comb. form*) sulphur, *esp.* denoting replacement of oxygen atom with sulphur atom, as in *thiol, thiosulphate*

thiopentone sodium (θaɪəʊ'pentəʊn) *or* **thiopental sodium** (θaɪəʊ'pentæl) barbiturate drug used as intravenous general anaesthetic (*also* **sodium pentothal**)

third (θɜːd) *a.* 1. ordinal number corresponding to *three* — *n.* 2. third part — **third degree** *see* DEGREE — **third dimension** dimension of depth by which solid object may be distinguished from two-dimensional drawing or picture of it — **third man** *Cricket* fielding position on off side near boundary behind batsman's wicket — **third party** *Law, insurance etc.* person involved by chance or only incidentally in legal proceedings *etc.* — **third person** grammatical category of pronouns and verbs used when referring to objects or individuals other than speaker or his addressee(s) — **third-rate** *a.* mediocre, inferior — **Third World** developing countries of Afr., Asia, Latin Amer.

thirst (θɜːst) *n.* 1. desire to drink 2. feeling caused by lack of drink 3. craving, yearning — *vi.* 4. feel lack of drink — **'thirstily** *adv.* — **'thirsty** *a.*

thirteen ('θɜː'tiːn) *n./a.* three plus ten — **'thirty** *n./a.* three times ten

this (ðɪs) *demonstrative a./pron.* denotes thing, person near, or just mentioned (*pl.* **these**)

thistle ('θɪs'l) *n.* prickly plant with dense flower heads — **'thistledown** *n.* mass of feathery plumed seeds produced by thistle

thither ('ðɪðə) *or* **thitherward** *adv. obs.* to or towards that place

thixotropic (θɪksə'trɒpɪk) *a.* (of certain liquids, as paints) having property of thickening if left undisturbed but becoming less viscous when stirred

tho *or* **tho'** (ðəʊ) *US, poet. see* THOUGH

thole[1] (θəʊl) *or* **tholepin** ('θəʊlpɪn) *n.* wooden pin set upright in gunwale of rowing boat to serve as fulcrum in rowing

thole[2] (θəʊl) *vt.* 1. *dial.* put up with; bear 2. suffer

thong (θɒŋ) *n.* 1. narrow strip of leather, strap 2. *chiefly US, A, NZ* flip-flop (sandal)

thorax ('θɔːræks) *n.* part of body between neck and belly — **thoracic** (θɔː'ræsɪk) *a.*

thorium ('θɔːrɪəm) *n.* radioactive metallic element

thorn (θɔːn) *n.* 1. prickle on plant 2. spine 3. bush noted for its thorns 4. *fig.* anything which causes trouble or annoyance (*esp.* in **thorn in one's side** *or* **flesh**) — **'thorny** *a.*

thorough ('θʌrə) *a.* 1. careful, methodical 2. complete, entire — **'thoroughly** *adv.* — **'thoroughbred** *a.* 1. of pure breed — *n.* 2. purebred animal, *esp.* horse — **'thoroughfare** *n.* 1. road or passage open at both ends 2. right of way — **'thoroughgoing** *a.* 1. extremely thorough 2. absolute; complete

those (ðəʊz) *pron., pl. of* THAT

thou[1] (ðaʊ) *pron. obs.* the second person singular pronoun (*pl.* **ye, you**)

thou[2] (θaʊ) *n.* 1. thousandth of inch 2. *inf.* thousand (*pl.* **-s, thou**)

though (ðəʊ) *conj.* 1. in spite of the fact that, even if — *adv.* 2. nevertheless

thought (θɔːt) *n.* 1. process of thinking 2. what one thinks 3. product of thinking 4. meditation — *v.* 5. *pt./pp. of* THINK — **'thoughtful** *a.* 1. considerate 2. showing careful thought 3. engaged in meditation 4. attentive — **'thoughtless** *a.* inconsiderate, careless, heedless — **thought transference** *Psychol. see* TELEPATHY

thousand ('θaʊzənd) *n./a.* cardinal number, ten hundred

thrall (θrɔːl) *n.* 1. slavery 2. slave, bondsman — *vt.* 3. enslave — **'thralldom** *or* **'thraldom** *n.* bondage

thrash (θræʃ) *vt.* 1. beat, whip soundly 2. defeat soundly 3. thresh — *vi.* 4. move, plunge, *esp.* arms, legs in wild manner — **thrash out** 1. argue about from every angle 2. solve by exhaustive discussion

thread (θrɛd) *n.* 1. fine cord 2. yarn 3. ridge cut spirally on screw 4. theme, meaning — *vt.* 5. put thread into 6. fit film, magnetic tape *etc.* into (machine) 7. put on thread 8. pick (one's way *etc.*) — **'threadbare** *a.* 1. worn, with nap rubbed off 2. meagre 3. shabby

threat (θrɛt) *n.* 1. declaration of intention to harm, injure *etc.* 2. person or thing regarded as dangerous — **'threaten** *vt.* 1. utter threats against 2. menace

three (θriː) *n./a.* cardinal number, one more than two — **'threesome** *n.* group of three — **three-D** *or* **3-D** *n.* three-dimensional effect — **three-dimensional** *a.* 1. having three dimensions 2. simulating the effect of depth — **three-legged race** race in which pairs of competitors run with adjacent legs tied together — **three-penny bit** *or* **thrupenny bit** ('θrʌpnɪ, -ənɪ, 'θrɛp-) former twelve-sided Brit. coin valued at three old pence — **three-ply** *a.* having three layers (as wood) or strands (as wool) — **three-point turn** complete turn of motor vehicle using forward and reverse gears — **three-quarter** *a.* 1. being three quarters of something 2. being of three quarters the normal length — *n.* 3. *Rugby* any of players between full back and forwards — **'three'score** *n./a. obs.* sixty

threnody ('θrɛnədɪ, 'θriː-) *or* **threnode**

('θriːnəʊd, 'θrɛn-) n. ode, song or speech of lamentation, esp. for dead —'threnodist n.

thresh (θrɛʃ) v. 1. beat, rub (wheat, etc.) to separate grain from husks and straw 2. thrash

threshold ('θrɛʃəʊld, 'θrɛʃhəʊld) n. 1. bar of stone or wood forming bottom of doorway 2. entrance 3. starting point 4. point at which a stimulus is perceived, or produces a response

threw (θruː) pt. of THROW

thrice (θraɪs) adv. three times

thrift (θrɪft) n. 1. saving, economy 2. genus of plant, sea pink —'thrifty a. economical, frugal, sparing

thrill (θrɪl) n. 1. sudden sensation of excitement and pleasure —v. 2. (cause to) feel a thrill —vi. 3. vibrate, tremble —'thriller n. book, film etc. with story of mystery, suspense —'thrilling a. exciting

thrips (θrɪps) n. small slender-bodied insect that feeds on plant sap (pl. thrips)

thrive (θraɪv) vi. 1. grow well 2. flourish, prosper (throve, thrived pt., thriven ('θrɪv'n), thrived pp., 'thriving pr.p.)

thro' or thro (θruː) Poet. see THROUGH

throat (θrəʊt) n. 1. front of neck 2. either or both of passages through it —'throaty a. (of voice) hoarse

throb (θrɒb) vi. 1. beat, quiver strongly, pulsate (-bb-) —n. 2. pulsation, beat; vibration

throes (θrəʊz) pl.n. condition of violent pangs, pain etc. —in the throes of inf. in the process of

thrombosis (θrɒm'bəʊsɪs) n. formation of clot of coagulated blood in blood vessel or heart

throne (θrəʊn) n. 1. ceremonial seat, powers and duties of king or queen —vt. 2. place on throne, declare king etc.

throng (θrɒŋ) n./v. crowd

throstle ('θrɒs'l) n. thrush

throttle ('θrɒt'l) n. 1. device controlling amount of fuel entering engine and thereby its speed —vt. 2. strangle 3. suppress 4. restrict (flow of liquid etc.)

through (θruː) prep. 1. from end to end, from side to side of 2. between the sides of 3. in consequence of 4. by means or fault of —adv. 5. from end to end 6. to the end —a. 7. completed 8. inf. finished 9. continuous 10. (of transport, traffic) not stopping —through'out adv./prep. in every part (of) —'throughput n. quantity of material processed, esp. by computer —through ticket ticket for whole of journey —through train, bus etc. train, bus etc. which travels whole (unbroken) length of long journey —carry through accomplish

throve (θrəʊv) pt. of THRIVE

throw (θrəʊ) vt. 1. fling, cast 2. move, put abruptly, carelessly 3. give, hold (party etc.) 4. cause to fall 5. shape on potter's wheel 6. move (switch, lever etc.) 7. inf. baffle, disconcert (threw, thrown, 'throwing) —n. 8. act or distance of throwing

—'throwaway a. 1. chiefly UK said incidentally, esp. for rhetorical effect; casual —n. 2. anything that can be thrown away or discarded 3. chiefly US handbill —throw away 1. get rid of; discard 2. fail to make good use of; waste —'throwback n. 1. one who, that which reverts to character of an ancestor 2. this process

thrum (θrʌm) v. 1. strum rhythmically but without expression on (musical instrument) —vi. 2. drum incessantly (-mm-) —n. 3. repetitive strumming

thrush¹ (θrʌʃ) n. songbird

thrush² (θrʌʃ) n. 1. fungal disease of mouth, esp. in infants 2. vaginal infection caused by same fungus 3. foot disease of horses

thrust (θrʌst) vt. 1. push, drive —v. 2. (make a) stab —vi. 3. push one's way (thrust, 'thrusting) —n. 4. lunge, stab with pointed weapon etc. 5. cutting remark 6. propulsive force or power

thud (θʌd) n. 1. dull heavy sound —vi. 2. make thud (-dd-)

thug (θʌg) n. brutal, violent person —'thuggery n. —'thuggish a.

thuja or thuya ('θuːjə) n. any of various coniferous trees of N Amer. and E Asia

thulium ('θjuːlɪəm) n. malleable ductile silvery-grey element

thumb (θʌm) n. 1. first, shortest, thickest finger of hand —vt. 2. handle, dirty with thumb 3. signal for (lift in vehicle) 4. flick through (pages of book etc.) —thumb index series of indentations cut into fore-edge of book to facilitate quick reference —thumb-index vt. furnish with thumb index —'thumbnail n. 1. nail of thumb —a. 2. concise and brief —'thumbscrew n. 1. instrument of torture that pinches or crushes thumbs 2. screw with projections on head enabling it to be turned by thumb and forefinger

thump (θʌmp) n. 1. dull heavy blow 2. sound of one —vt. 3. strike heavily —vi. 4. throb, beat or pound violently —'thumping a. sl. huge; excessive

thunder ('θʌndə) n. 1. loud noise accompanying lightning —vi. 2. rumble with thunder 3. make noise like thunder —vt. 4. utter loudly —'thundering a. sl. very great; excessive —'thunderous a. —'thundery a. sultry —'thunderbolt or 'thunderclap n. 1. lightning flash followed by peal of thunder 2. anything totally unexpected and unpleasant —'thundercloud n. electrically charged cumulonimbus cloud associated with thunderstorms —'thunderstorm n. storm with thunder and lightning and usu. heavy rain or hail —'thunderstruck a. amazed

thurible ('θjʊərɪb'l) n. see CENSER

Thurs. Thursday

Thursday ('θɜːzdɪ) n. fifth day of week

thus (ðʌs) adv. 1. in this way 2. therefore

thwack (θwæk) vt./n. whack

thwart (θwɔːt) vt. 1. foil, frustrate —adv. 2. obs. across —n. 3. seat across a boat

thy (ðaɪ) *a.* belonging to thee —**thy'self** *pron.* emphatic form of THOU[1]

thyme (taɪm) *n.* aromatic herb

thymol ('θaɪmɒl) *n.* white crystalline substance obtained from thyme and used as antiseptic *etc.*

thymus ('θaɪməs) *n.* small ductless gland in upper part of chest (*pl.* **-es, -mi** (-maɪ))

thyroid ('θaɪrɔɪd) *a.* 1. of thyroid gland 2. of largest cartilage of larynx —*n.* 3. thyroid gland 4. p eparation of thyroid gland of certain animals, used to treat hypothyroidism —**thyroid gland** endocrine gland controlling body growth, situated (in man) at base of neck

ti (tiː) *n. Mus. see* TE

Ti *Chem.* titanium

tiara (tɪ'ɑːrə) *n.* jewelled head ornament, coronet

tibia ('tɪbɪə) *n.* inner and thicker of two bones of the leg below the knee (*pl.* **-biae** (-biːi), **-s**) —**'tibial** *a.*

tic (tɪk) *n.* spasmodic twitch in muscles, *esp.* of face

tick[1] (tɪk) *n.* 1. slight tapping sound, as of watch movement 2. small mark (✓) 3. *inf.* moment —*vt.* 4. mark with tick —*vi.* 5. make ticking sound —'**ticker** *n.* 1. *sl.* heart 2. *sl.* watch 3. person or thing that ticks 4. US tape machine —**ticker tape** continuous paper ribbon —'**ticktack** *n.* 1. UK system of sign language, mainly using hands, by which bookmakers transmit their odds to each other at racecourses 2. US ticking sound —'**ticktock** *n.* 1. ticking sound as made by clock —*vi.* 2. make ticking sound —**tick off** 1. mark off 2. reprimand —**tick over** 1. (of engine) idle 2. continue to function smoothly

tick[2] (tɪk) *n.* small insectlike parasite living on and sucking blood of warm-blooded animals

tick[3] (tɪk) *n.* mattress case —'**ticking** *n.* strong material for mattress covers

tick[4] (tɪk) *n. inf.* credit, account

ticket ('tɪkɪt) *n.* 1. card, paper entitling holder to admission, travel *etc.* 2. label 3. summons served for parking or traffic offence 4. US list of candidates of one party for election —*vt.* 5. attach label to 6. issue tickets to

tickle ('tɪk²l) *vt.* 1. touch, stroke, poke (person, part of body *etc.*) to produce laughter *etc.* 2. please, amuse (*oft. in* **tickle one's fancy**) —*vi.* 3. be irritated, itch —*n.* 4. act, instance of this 5. C narrow strait —'**ticklish** *a.* 1. sensitive to tickling 2. requiring care or tact

tiddler ('tɪdlə) *n. inf.* very small fish *etc.* —'**tiddly** *a.* tiny

tiddly ('tɪdlɪ) *a. inf.* slightly drunk

tiddlywinks ('tɪdlɪwɪŋks) *pl.n.* game of trying to flip small plastic discs into cup

tide (taɪd) *n.* 1. rise and fall of sea happening twice each lunar day 2. stream 3. season, time —'**tidal** *a.* of, like tide —**tidal wave** great wave, *esp.* produced by earthquake —'**tidemark** *n.* 1. mark left by

highest or lowest point of tide 2. *chiefly UK* mark showing level reached by liquid 3. *inf., chiefly UK* dirty mark on skin, indicating extent to which someone has washed —**tide someone over** help someone for a while, *esp.* by loan *etc.*

tidings ('taɪdɪŋz) *pl.n.* news

tidy ('taɪdɪ) *a.* 1. orderly, neat 2. *inf.* of fair size —*vt.* 3. put in order

tie (taɪ) *vi.* 1. make an equal score —*vt.* 2. fasten, bind, secure 3. restrict (**tied**, '**tying**) —*n.* 4. that with which anything is bound 5. restriction, restraint 6. long, narrow piece of material worn knotted round neck 7. bond, link 8. drawn game, contest 9. match, game in eliminating competition —**tied** *a.* 1. (of public house) obliged to sell beer *etc.* of only one brewer 2. (of cottage *etc.*) rented to tenant only as long as he is employed by owner —**tie-dyeing** *n.* way of dyeing cloth in patterns by tying sections tightly so they will not absorb dye —'**tiepin** *n.* ornamental pin used to pin ends of tie to shirt —**tie-up** *n.* 1. link, connection 2. *chiefly US* standstill 3. *chiefly US inf.* traffic jam —**tie up** 1. bind securely (as if) with string *etc.* 2. moor (vessel) 3. engage attentions of 4. conclude (organization of something) 5. come or bring to complete standstill 6. commit (funds *etc.*) and so make unavailable for other uses 7. subject (property) to conditions that prevent sale *etc.*

tier (tɪə) *n.* row, rank, layer

tiercel ('tɪəs²l) *n. see* TERCEL

tiff (tɪf) *n.* petty quarrel

tiffin ('tɪfɪn) *n.* in India, light meal, *esp.* at midday

tiger ('taɪgə) *n.* large carnivorous feline animal —'**tigress** *n.* 1. female tiger 2. fierce, cruel or wildly passionate woman —**tiger lily** lily plant cultivated for its flowers, which have black-spotted orange petals —**tiger moth** moth with wings conspicuously marked with stripes and spots —**tiger's-eye** *or* '**tigereye** *n.* semi-precious golden-brown stone

tight (taɪt) *a.* 1. taut, tense 2. closely fitting 3. secure, firm 4. not allowing passage of water *etc.* 5. cramped 6. *inf.* mean 7. *inf.* drunk —'**tighten** *v.* —'**tightly** *adv.* —**tights** *pl.n.* one-piece clinging garment covering body from waist to feet —**tight'fisted** *a.* mean; miserly —**tight-'knit** *a.* 1. closely integrated 2. organized carefully —**tight-lipped** *a.* 1. secretive; taciturn 2. with lips pressed tightly together, as through anger —'**tightrope** *n.* rope stretched taut above the ground, on which acrobats perform

tigon ('taɪgɒn) *or* **tiglon** ('tɪglɒn) *n.* offspring of tiger and lioness

tike (taɪk) *n. see* TYKE

tiki ('tiːkiː) *n.* amulet, figurine of Maori cultures

tilde ('tɪldə) *n.* diacritical mark (˜) placed over letter to indicate nasal sound, as in Sp. *señor*

tile ('tatl) n. 1. flat piece of ceramic, plastic etc. material used for roofs, walls, floors, fireplaces etc. —vt. 2. cover with tiles —tiled a. —'tiling n. —on the tiles inf. on a spree, esp. of drinking or debauchery

till' ('til) prep. 1. up to the time of —conj. 2. to the time that

till² ('til) vt. cultivate —'tillage n. —'tiller n.

till³ ('til) n. 1. drawer for money in shop counter 2. cash register

tiller ('tilə) n. lever to move rudder of boat

tilt (tilt) v. 1. incline, slope, slant 2. tip up —vi. 3. take part in medieval combat with lances 4. thrust, aim —n. 5. slope, incline 6. Hist. combat for mounted men with lances, joust

tilth (tilθ) n. 1. tilled land 2. condition of soil

Tim. Bible Timothy

timber ('timbə) n. 1. wood for building etc. 2. trees suitable for the sawmill —'timbered a. 1. made of wood 2. covered with trees —timber limit 1. C area to which rights of cutting trees are limited 2. timber line —timber line geographical limit beyond which trees will not grow

timbre ('timbə, 'tæmbə) n. 1. Mus. quality of sound 2. Phonet. tone differentiating one vowel etc. from another

time (taim) n. 1. existence as a succession of states 2. hour 3. duration 4. period 5. point in duration 6. opportunity 7. occasion 8. leisure 9. tempo —vt. 10. choose time for 11. note time taken by —'timeless a. 1. unaffected or unchanged by time; ageless 2. eternal —'timely a. at opportune or appropriate time —'timer n. person, device for recording or indicating time —'timing n. regulation of actions or remarks in relation to others to produce best effect, as in theatre etc. —time and motion study analysis of industrial or work procedures to determine most efficient methods of operation (also time and motion, time study, motion study) —time bomb bomb designed to explode at prearranged time —time clock clock which records, by punching or stamping timecards inserted into it, time of arrival or departure of employees —time exposure 1. exposure of photographic film for a relatively long period, usu. a few seconds 2. photograph produced by such exposure —time-honoured a. respectable because old —time-lag n. period of time between cause and effect —time off period when one is absent from work for holiday, through sickness etc. —time-out n. chiefly US 1. Sport interruption in play during which players rest, discuss tactics etc. 2. period of rest; break —'timepiece n. watch or clock —'timeserver n. person who compromises and changes his opinions etc. to suit current fashions —time sharing 1. system by which users at different terminals of computer can apparently communicate with it at same time 2. system of part-ownership of holiday home, whereby each participant owns property for particular period every year for specified number of years —time signature Mus. sign, usu. consisting of two figures, one above other, after key signature, indicating tempo —'timetable n. plan showing hours of work, times of arrival and departure etc. —'timeworn a. 1. showing adverse effects of overlong use or of old age 2. hackneyed; trite —time zone region throughout which same standard time is used —Greenwich Mean Time world standard time, time as settled by passage of sun over the meridian at Greenwich —time and a half rate of pay equalling one and a half times normal rate, oft. for overtime

timid ('timid) a. 1. easily frightened 2. lacking self-confidence —ti'midity or 'timidness n. —'timidly adv. —'timorous a. 1. timid 2. indicating fear

timpani or **tympani** ('timpəni) pl.n. set of kettledrums —'timpanist or 'tympanist n.

tin (tin) n. 1. malleable metal 2. container made of tin or tinned iron —vt. 3. put in tin, esp. for preserving (food) 4. coat with tin (-nn-) —'tinny a. 1. (of sound) thin, metallic 2. cheap, shoddy —'tin'foil n. 1. thin foil made of tin or alloy of tin and lead 2. thin foil made of aluminium; used for wrapping foodstuffs —tin god 1. self-important person 2. person erroneously regarded as holy or venerable —tin lizzie ('lizi) inf. old or decrepit car —tin plate thin steel sheet coated with layer of tin that protects steel from corrosion —tin-plate vt. coat with layer of tin —'tinpot a. inf. inferior, worthless —'tinsmith n. person who works with tin or tin plate

tincture ('tiŋktʃə) n. 1. solution of medicinal substance in alcohol 2. colour, stain —vt. 3. colour, tint

tinder ('tində) n. dry, easily-burning material used to start fire —'tinderbox n. 1. formerly, box for holding tinder, esp. one fitted with flint and steel 2. touchy or explosive person or thing

tine (tain) n. tooth, spike of fork, antler, harrow etc.

tinea ('tiniə) n. fungal skin disease

ting (tiŋ) n. 1. sharp sound, as of bell 2. tinkling —vi. 3. tinkle —ting-a-ling n. sound of small bell

tinge (tindʒ) n. 1. slight trace, flavour —vt. 2. colour, flavour slightly

tingle ('tiŋg'l) vi. 1. feel thrill or pricking sensation —n. 2. sensation of tingling

tinker ('tiŋkə) n. 1. formerly, travelling mender of pots and pans —vi. 2. fiddle, meddle (eg with machinery), oft. inexpertly —tinker's damn or cuss sl. slightest heed (esp. in not give a tinker's damn or cuss)

tinkle ('tiŋk'l) v. 1. (cause to) give out series of light sounds like small bell —n. 2. this sound or action

tinsel ('tinsəl) n. 1. glittering, metallic

substance for decoration **2.** anything sham and showy

tint (tɪnt) *n.* **1.** colour **2.** shade of colour **3.** tinge —*vt.* **4.** dye, give tint to

tintinnabulation (tɪntɪnæbjuˈleɪʃən) *n.* act or instance of ringing or pealing of bells

tiny (ˈtaɪnɪ) *a.* very small, minute

-tion (*comb. form*) state, condition, action, process, result, as in *election, prohibition*

tip¹ (tɪp) *n.* **1.** slender or pointed end of anything **2.** piece of metal, leather *etc.* protecting an extremity —*vt.* **3.** put a tip on (**-pp-**) —**ˈtipstaff** *n.* **1.** court official **2.** metal-tipped staff formerly used as symbol of office

tip² (tɪp) *n.* **1.** small present of money given for service rendered **2.** helpful piece of information **3.** warning, hint —*vt.* **4.** give tip to (**-pp-**) —**ˈtipster** *n.* one who sells tips about races —**tip-off** *n.* warning or hint, *esp.* given confidentially and based on inside information —**tip off**

tip³ (tɪp) *vt.* **1.** tilt, upset **2.** touch lightly —*vi.* **3.** topple over (**-pp-**) —*n.* **4.** place where rubbish is dumped

tippet (ˈtɪpɪt) *n.* covering for the neck and shoulders

tipple (ˈtɪpˀl) *v.* **1.** drink (alcohol) habitually, *esp.* in small quantities —*n.* **2.** alcoholic drink —**ˈtippler** *n.*

tipsy (ˈtɪpsɪ) *a.* (slightly) drunk

tiptoe (ˈtɪptəʊ) *vi.* **1.** walk on ball of foot and toes **2.** walk softly

tiptop (tɪpˈtɒp) *a.* of the best quality or highest degree

TIR Transports Internationaux Routiers (*Fr.,* International Road Transport)

tirade (taɪˈreɪd) *n.* long speech, generally vigorous and hostile, denunciation

tire¹ (taɪə) *vt.* **1.** reduce energy of, *esp.* by exertion **2.** bore **3.** irritate —*vi.* **4.** become tired, wearied, bored —**tired** *a.* **1.** weary; fatigued **2.** no longer fresh; hackneyed —**ˈtireless** *a.* unable to be tired —**ˈtirelessly** *adv.* —**ˈtiresome** *a.* wearisome, irritating, tedious —**ˈtiring** *a.*

tire² (taɪə) *n.* US tyre

tiro (ˈtaɪrəʊ) *n. see* TYRO

tissue (ˈtɪsjuː, ˈtɪʃuː) *n.* **1.** substance of animal body, plant *etc.* **2.** fine, soft paper, *esp.* used as handkerchief *etc.* **3.** fine woven fabric

tit¹ (tɪt) *n.* any of numerous small, active Old World songbirds *esp.* bluetit, tomtit *etc.*

tit² (tɪt) *n.* **1.** *vulg. sl.* female breast **2.** *sl.* despicable, stupid person

Tit. *Bible* Titus

titan (ˈtaɪtˀn) *n.* person of great strength or size —**tiˈtanic** *a.* huge, epic

titanium (taɪˈteɪnɪəm) *n.* rare metal of great strength and rust-resisting qualities

titbit (ˈtɪtbɪt) *or esp. U.S.* **tidbit** (ˈtɪdbɪt) *n.* **1.** tasty morsel of food **2.** pleasing scrap (of scandal *etc.*)

tit for tat blow for blow, retaliation

tithe (taɪð) *n.* **1.** *esp. Hist.* tenth part of agricultural produce paid for the upkeep of the clergy or as tax —*vt.* **2.** exact tithes from —**tithe barn** formerly, large barn where agricultural tithe of parish was stored

Titian red (ˈtɪʃən) *a.* (of hair) reddish-gold, auburn

titillate (ˈtɪtɪleɪt) *vt.* tickle, stimulate agreeably —**titilˈlation** *n.* —**ˈtitillator** *n.*

titivate *or* **tittivate** (ˈtɪtɪveɪt) *v.* dress or smarten up —**titiˈvation** *or* **tittiˈvation** *n.*

title (ˈtaɪtˀl) *n.* **1.** name of book **2.** heading **3.** name **4.** appellation denoting rank **5.** legal right or document proving it **6.** *Sport* championship —**ˈtitled** *a.* of the aristocracy —**title deed** legal document as proof of ownership —**ˈtitleholder** *n.* person who holds title, *esp.* sporting championship —**title page** page in book that gives title, author, publisher *etc.* —**title role** role of character after whom play *etc.* is named

titration (taɪˈtreɪʃən) *n.* operation in which measured amount of one solution is added to known quantity of another solution until reaction between the two is complete —**ˈtitrate** *vt.* measure volume or concentration of (solution) by titration

titter (ˈtɪtə) *vi.* **1.** laugh in suppressed way —*n.* **2.** such laugh

tittle (ˈtɪtˀl) *n.* whit, detail

tittle-tattle *n./vi.* gossip

titular (ˈtɪtjʊlə) *a.* **1.** pert. to title **2.** nominal **3.** held by virtue of a title

tizzy (ˈtɪzɪ) *n. inf.* state of confusion, anxiety

Tl *Chem.* thallium

Tm *Chem.* thulium

TN Tennessee

tn. ton(s)

TNT trinitrotoluene

to (tuː; *unstressed* tʊ, tə) *prep.* **1.** towards, in the direction of **2.** as far as **3.** used to introduce a comparison, ratio, indirect object, infinitive mood *etc.* —*adv.* **4.** to the required or normal state or position —**to and fro** *a./adv.* **1.** back and forth **2.** here and there —**toing and froing**

toad (təʊd) *n.* animal like large frog —**toad-in-the-hole** *n.* sausages baked in batter

toadflax (ˈtəʊdflæks) *n.* perennial plant having yellow-orange flowers (*also* **butter-and-eggs**)

toadstool (ˈtəʊdstuːl) *n.* fungus like mushroom, but usu. poisonous

toady (ˈtəʊdɪ) *n.* **1.** one who flatters, ingratiates himself —*vi.* **2.** do this (**ˈtoadied, ˈtoadying**)

toast (təʊst) *n.* **1.** slice of bread crisped and browned on both sides by heat **2.** tribute, proposal of health, success *etc.* made by company of people and marked by drinking together **3.** person toasted —*vt.* **4.** crisp and brown (as bread) **5.** drink toast to **6.** dry or warm at fire —**ˈtoaster** *n.* electrical device for toasting bread —**ˈtoastmaster** *n.* person who introduces speakers, proposes toasts *etc.* at public dinners (**ˈtoastmistress** *fem.*) —**toast-**

rack n. small, partitioned stand of metal etc. for serving toasted bread

tobacco (təˈbækəʊ) n. **1.** plant with leaves used for smoking **2.** the prepared leaves (pl. **-s**, **-es**) —**toˈbacconist** n. one who sells tobacco products

toboggan (təˈbɒgən) n. **1.** sledge for sliding down slope of snow —vi. **2.** slide on toboggan

toby jug (ˈtəʊbɪ) mug in form of stout, seated man

toccata (təˈkɑːtə) n. rapid piece of music for keyboard instrument

tocsin (ˈtɒksɪn) n. alarm signal, bell

today (təˈdeɪ) n. **1.** this day —adv. **2.** on this day **3.** nowadays

toddle (ˈtɒdˀl) vi. **1.** walk with unsteady, short steps **2.** inf. stroll —n. **3.** toddling —ˈ**toddler** n. child beginning to walk

toddy (ˈtɒdɪ) n. sweetened mixture of alcoholic spirit, hot water etc.

to-do n. inf. fuss, commotion (pl. **-s**)

toe (təʊ) n. **1.** digit of foot **2.** anything resembling toe in shape or position —vt. **3.** reach, touch or kick with toe —ˈ**toecap** n. reinforced covering for toe of shoe —ˈ**toehold** n. **1.** small foothold to facilitate climbing **2.** any means of gaining access, support etc. **3.** wrestling hold in which opponent's toe is held and leg twisted —**toe the line** conform

toff (tɒf) n. sl. well-dressed or upper-class person

toffee or **toffy** (ˈtɒfɪ) n. chewy sweet made of boiled sugar etc. —**toffee-apple** n. apple fixed on stick and coated with toffee —**toffee-nosed** a. sl., chiefly UK pretentious; supercilious; snobbish

tofu (ˈtəʊfuː) n. unfermented soya bean curd

tog (tɒg) n. unit of measurement of warmth of continental quilts etc. —**tog rating** or **value**

toga (ˈtəʊgə) n. loose outer garment worn by ancient Romans

together (təˈgeðə) adv. **1.** in company **2.** simultaneously —a./adv. **3.** inf. (well) organized —toˈ**getherness** n. feeling of closeness or affection from being united with other people

toggle (ˈtɒgˀl) n. **1.** small wooden, metal peg fixed crosswise on cord, wire etc. and used for fastening as button **2.** any similar device —**toggle joint** device consisting of two arms pivoted at common joint and at outer ends, and used to apply pressure by straightening angle between two arms —**toggle switch** electric switch having projecting lever that is manipulated in particular way to open or close circuit

togs (tɒgz) pl.n. inf. clothes

toil (tɔɪl) n. **1.** heavy work or task —vi. **2.** labour —ˈ**toilsome** or ˈ**toilful** a. laborious —ˈ**toilworn** a. **1.** weary with toil **2.** hard and lined

toilet (ˈtɔɪlɪt) n. **1.** lavatory **2.** process of washing, dressing **3.** articles used for this —ˈ**toiletry** n. object or cosmetic used in making up etc. —**toilet paper** or **tissue** thin absorbent paper, oft. wound in roll round cardboard cylinder (**toilet roll**), used for cleaning oneself after defecation or urination —**toilet training** training of young child to use toilet when he needs to discharge bodily waste —**toilet water** form of liquid perfume lighter than cologne

token (ˈtəʊkən) n. **1.** sign or object used as evidence **2.** symbol **3.** disc used as money **4.** gift card, voucher exchangeable for goods of a certain value —a. **5.** nominal, slight —ˈ**tokenism** n. practice of making only token effort or doing no more than minimum, esp. to comply with law

tokoloshe (tɒkɒˈlɒʃ, -ˈlɒʃɪ) n. SA malevolent imp in Bantu folklore

told (təʊld) pt./pp. of TELL

tolerate (ˈtɒləreɪt) vt. **1.** put up with **2.** permit —ˈ**tolerable** a. **1.** bearable **2.** moderate —ˈ**tolerably** adv. —ˈ**tolerance** n. (degree of) ability to endure stress, pain, radiation etc. —ˈ**tolerant** a. **1.** disinclined to interfere with others' ways or opinions **2.** forbearing **3.** broad-minded —ˈ**tolerantly** adv. —toleˈ**ration** n.

toll[1] (təʊl) vt. **1.** make (bell) ring slowly at regular intervals **2.** announce death thus —vi. **3.** ring thus —n. **4.** tolling sound

toll[2] (təʊl, tɒl) n. **1.** tax, esp. for the use of bridge or road **2.** loss, damage incurred through accident, disaster etc.

tollie (ˈtɒlɪ) n. SA steer calf

toluene (ˈtɒljuːiːn) n. colourless volatile flammable liquid obtained from petroleum and coal tar

tom (tɒm) n. male of some animals, esp. cat

tomahawk (ˈtɒməhɔːk) n. **1.** fighting axe of N Amer. Indians —vt. **2.** strike, kill with tomahawk

tomato (təˈmɑːtəʊ) n. **1.** plant with red fruit **2.** the fruit, used in salads etc. (pl. **-es**)

tomb (tuːm) n. **1.** grave **2.** monument over grave —ˈ**tombstone** n. gravestone

tombola (tɒmˈbəʊlə) n. lottery with tickets drawn to win prizes

tomboy (ˈtɒmbɔɪ) n. girl who acts, dresses in boyish way

Tom, Dick, and (or) Harry ordinary, undistinguished or common person (esp. **in every Tom, Dick, and Harry; any Tom, Dick, or Harry**)

tome (təʊm) n. large book or volume

tomfoolery (tɒmˈfuːlərɪ) n. nonsense, silly behaviour

tommy (ˈtɒmɪ) n. sl. private soldier in Brit. army —**Tommy gun** type of sub-machine-gun —ˈ**tommyrot** n. utter nonsense

tomorrow (təˈmɒrəʊ) adv./n. (on) the day after today

tom-tom or **tam-tam** n. drum associated with N Amer. Indians or with Asia

ton (tʌn) n. **1.** measure of weight, 1016 kg (2240 lbs) (**also long ton**) **2.** US measure of weight, 907 kg (2000 lbs) (**also short ton**) —ˈ**tonnage** n. **1.** carrying capacity **2.**

charge per ton 3. ships collectively —**ton-up** UK inf. a. 1. (esp. of motorcycle) capable of speeds of a hundred miles per hour or more 2. liking to travel at such speeds —n. 3. person who habitually rides at such speeds

tone (təʊn) n. 1. quality of musical sound 2. quality of voice, colour etc. 3. general character, style 4. healthy condition —vt. 5. give tone to —v. 6. blend, harmonize —'**tonal** a. —to'**nality** n. —**tone-deaf** a. unable to distinguish subtle differences in musical pitch —**tone deafness** —**tone poem** orchestral work based on story, legend etc.

tong (tɒŋ) n. formerly, secret society of Chinese Americans

tongs (tɒŋz) pl.n. large pincers, esp. for handling coal, sugar

tongue (tʌŋ) n. 1. muscular organ inside mouth, used for speech, taste etc. 2. various things shaped like this 3. language; speech; voice —**tongue-and-groove joint** joint made by means of tongue along edge of one board that fits into groove along edge of another board —**tongue-lash** vt. reprimand severely; scold —**tongue-lashing** n./a. —**tongue-tie** n. congenital condition in which tongue has restricted mobility as result of abnormally short fold of skin under tongue —**tongue-tied** a. 1. speechless, esp. with embarrassment or shyness 2. having condition of tongue-tie —**tongue twister** sentence or phrase difficult to articulate clearly and quickly

tonic ('tɒnɪk) n. 1. medicine to improve bodily tone or condition 2. Mus. first keynote of scale —a. 3. invigorating, restorative 4. of tone —**tonic sol-fa** method of teaching music, by which syllables are used as names for notes of major scale in any key —**tonic water** or **tonic** n. mineral water oft. containing quinine

tonight (tə'naɪt) n. 1. this night 2. the coming night —adv. 3. on this night

tonne (tʌn) n. metric ton, 1000 kg

tonsil ('tɒnsəl) n. gland in throat —'**tonsillar** a. —**tonsil'lectomy** n. surgical removal of tonsils —**tonsil'litis** n. inflammation of tonsils

tonsorial (tɒn'sɔːrɪəl) a. oft. jocular of barbering or hairdressing

tonsure ('tɒnʃə) n. 1. shaving of part of head as religious or monastic practice 2. part shaved —vt. 3. shave thus

too (tuː) adv. 1. also, in addition 2. in excess, overmuch

took (tʊk) pt. of TAKE

tool (tuːl) n. 1. implement or appliance for mechanical operations 2. servile helper 3. means to an end —vt. 4. work on with tool 5. indent design on (leather book cover etc.) —'**tooling** n. 1. decorative work 2. setting up etc. of tools, esp. for machine operation

toot (tuːt) v. 1. (cause to) give short blast, hoot or whistle —n. 2. short sound of horn, trumpet etc.

tooth (tuːθ) n. 1. bonelike projection in gums of upper and lower jaws of vertebrates 2. various pointed things like this 3. prong, cog (pl. teeth) —'**toothsome** a. of delicious or appetizing appearance, flavour or smell —'**toothy** a. having or showing numerous, large or projecting teeth —'**toothache** n. pain in or about tooth —'**toothbrush** n. small brush, usu. with long handle, for cleaning teeth —**tooth-comb** n. small comb with teeth close together —'**toothpaste** n. paste for cleaning teeth, applied with toothbrush —'**toothpick** n. small sharp sliver of wood etc. for extracting pieces of food from between teeth

tootle ('tuːt'l) inf. v. 1. toot —n. 2. soft hoot or series of hoots

top¹ (tɒp) n. 1. highest part, summit 2. highest rank 3. first in merit 4. garment for upper part of body 5. lid, stopper of bottle etc. 6. platform on ship's mast —vt. 7. cut off, pass, reach, surpass top of 8. provide top for (-pp-) —'**topless** a. (of costume, woman) with no covering for breasts —'**topmost** a. 1. supreme 2. highest —'**topper** n. 1. inf. top hat 2. person or thing that tops or excels —'**topping** n. 1. something that tops something else, esp. sauce or garnish for food —a. 2. high or superior in rank, degree etc. 3. UK sl. excellent; splendid —**top brass** inf. 1. high-ranking army officers 2. important officials —'**topcoat** n. outdoor coat worn over suit etc. —**top dog** inf. leader or chief of group —**top-drawer** a. of highest standing, esp. socially —**top-dress** vt. spread soil, fertilizer etc. on surface of (land) —**top dressing** —**top-flight** a. of superior or excellent quality —**topgallant** (tɒp'gælənt; Naut. tə'gælənt) n. 1. mast on square-rigger above topmast or extension of topmast 2. sail set on yard of topgallant mast —a. 3. of topgallant —**top gear** 1. highest forward ratio of gearbox in motor vehicle 2. highest speed, greatest energy etc. (also **top**) —**top hat** man's hat with tall cylindrical crown —**top-heavy** a. 1. unbalanced 2. with top too heavy for base —**top-hole** interj./a. UK inf. excellent; splendid —'**topknot** n. 1. crest, tuft, chignon etc. on top of head 2. European flatfish —**top-level** a. of those on highest level of influence or authority —**topmast** ('tɒpmɑːst; Naut. 'tɒpməst) n. mast next above lower mast on sailing vessel —(also **top**) —**top notch** a. excellent, first-class —**topsail** ('tɒpseɪl; Naut. 'tɒpsəl) n. square sail carried on yard set on topmast —**top-secret** a. needing highest level of secrecy, security —'**topside** n. 1. uppermost side 2. UK lean cut of beef from thigh, containing no bone 3. (oft. pl.) part of ship's sides above waterline 4. (oft. pl.) part of ship above decks —'**topsoil** n. surface layer of soil

top² (top) *n.* toy which spins on tapering point

topaz ('təupæz) *n.* precious stone of various colours

tope¹ (təup) *v.* consume (alcoholic drink) as regular habit, usu. in large quantities —'**toper** *n.*

tope² (təup) *n.* small grey shark of European coastal waters

topee *or* **topi** ('təupi:, -pɪ) *n.* lightweight hat made of pith (*pl.* **-s**)

topiary ('təupɪərɪ) *a.* **1.** (of shrubs) shaped by cutting or pruning, made ornamental by trimming or training —*n.* **2.** topiary work **3.** topiary garden —'**topiarist** *n.*

topic ('topɪk) *n.* subject of discourse, conversation *etc.* —'**topical** *a.* **1.** up-to-date, having news value **2.** of topic

topography (tə'pogrəfɪ) *n.* (description of) surface features of a place —to'**pographer** *n.* —topo'**graphic** *a.* —topo'**graphically** *adv.*

topology (tə'polədʒɪ) *n.* **1.** branch of mathematics concerned with generalization of concepts of continuity, limit *etc.* **2.** branch of geometry describing properties of figure that are unaffected by continuous distortion **3.** *Maths.* family of subsets of given set *S*, such that *S* is topological space **4.** study of topography of given place **5.** anatomy of any specific bodily area, structure or part —topo'**logic(al)** *a.* —to'**pologist** *n.*

topple ('top²l) *v.* (cause to) fall over, collapse

topsy-turvy ('topsɪ'tɜ:vɪ) *a.* **1.** upside down **2.** in confusion

toque (təuk) *n.* **1.** small round hat **2.** C knitted cap

tor (tɔ:) *n.* high, rocky hill

Torah ('tɔːrə) *n.* **1.** the Pentateuch **2.** scroll on which this is written **3.** whole body of Jewish sacred writings and tradition, including oral expositions of the Law

torch (tɔːtʃ) *n.* **1.** portable hand light containing electric battery and bulb **2.** burning brand *etc.* **3.** any apparatus burning with hot flame (*eg* for welding) —'**torchbearer** *n.* —**torch singer** —**torch song** sentimental song, usu. sung by woman —**carry a torch for** be in love with, *esp.* unrequitedly

tore (tɔ:) *pt.* of TEAR² —**torn** *pp.* of TEAR²

toreador ('torɪədɔ:) *n.* bullfighter

torment (tɔː'mɛnt) *vt.* **1.** torture in body or mind **2.** afflict **3.** tease —*n.* ('tɔːmɛnt) **4.** suffering, torture, agony of body or mind —tor'**mentor** *n.*

tornado (tɔː'neɪdəu) *n.* **1.** whirlwind **2.** violent storm (*pl.* **-es, -s**)

torpedo (tɔː'piːdəu) *n.* **1.** cylindrical, self-propelled underwater missile with explosive warhead, fired *esp.* from submarine (*pl.* **-es**) —*vt.* **2.** strike, sink with, as with, torpedo

torpid ('tɔːpɪd) *a.* sluggish, apathetic

—**tor'pidity** *or* '**torpidness** *n.* —'**torpor** *n.* torpid state

torque (tɔːk) *n.* **1.** collar, similar ornament of twisted gold or other metal **2.** *Mech.* rotating or twisting force

torr (tɔː) *n.* unit of pressure equal to one millimetre of mercury (133.322 newtons per square metre)

torrent ('torənt) *n.* **1.** rushing stream **2.** downpour —tor'**rential** *a.* **1.** resembling a torrent **2.** overwhelming

torrid ('torɪd) *a.* **1.** parched, dried with heat **2.** highly emotional —tor'**ridity** *or* '**torridness** *n.* —**Torrid Zone** land between tropics

torsion ('tɔːʃən) *n.* twist, twisting

torso ('tɔːsəu) *n.* **1.** (statue of) body without head or limbs **2.** trunk (*pl.* **-s, -si** (-sɪ))

tort (tɔːt) *n.* *Law* private or civil wrong

tortilla (tɔː'tiːə) *n.* thin Mexican pancake

tortoise ('tɔːtəs) *n.* four-footed reptile covered with shell of horny plates —'**tortoiseshell** *n.* **1.** mottled brown shell of hawksbill turtle used commercially —*a.* **2.** of yellowish-brown mottled colour **3.** made of tortoiseshell

tortuous ('tɔːtjuəs) *a.* **1.** winding, twisting **2.** involved, not straightforward —tortu-'**osity** *n.*

torture ('tɔːtʃə) *n.* **1.** infliction of severe pain —*vt.* **2.** subject to torture —'**torturer** *n.* —**torture chamber**

Tory ('tɔːrɪ) *n.* **1.** member of Brit., Canad. conservative party **2.** politically reactionary person

toss (tos) *vt.* **1.** throw up, about —*vi.* **2.** be thrown, fling oneself about —*n.* **3.** act of tossing —**toss-up** *n.* **1.** instance of tossing up coin **2.** *inf.* even chance or risk —**toss up** spin (coin) in air to decide between alternatives by guessing which side will fall uppermost

tot¹ (tot) *n.* **1.** very small child **2.** small quantity, *esp.* of drink

tot² (tot) *v.* (*with* up) total; add (**-tt-**)

total ('təut²l) *n.* **1.** whole amount **2.** sum, aggregate —*a.* **3.** complete, entire, full, absolute —*v.* **4.** (*sometimes with* to) amount —*vt.* **5.** add up (**-ll-**) —to'**tality** *n.* —'**totalizator**, '**totalizer** *or* '**totalisator**, '**totaliser** *n.* machine to operate system of betting on racecourse in which money is paid out to winners in proportion to their stakes —**total allergy syndrome** combination of symptoms produced by allergic reaction to various elements of modern everyday life

totalitarian (təutælɪ'tɛərɪən) *a.* of dictatorial, one-party government

totalizator ('təutəlaɪzeɪtə) *n.* totalizator

tote² (təut) *vt.* haul, carry —**tote bag** large handbag or shopping bag

totem ('təutəm) *n.* tribal badge or emblem —to'**temic** *a.* —**totem pole** post carved, painted with totems, *esp.* by Amer. Indians

totter ('totə) *vi.* **1.** walk unsteadily **2.** begin to fall

toucan ('tu:kən) *n.* tropical Amer. bird with large bill

touch (tʌtʃ) *n.* **1.** sense by which qualities of object *etc.* are perceived by touching **2.** characteristic manner or ability **3.** touching **4.** slight blow, stroke, contact, amount *etc.* —*vt.* **5.** come into contact with **6.** put hand on **7.** reach **8.** affect emotions of **9.** deal with, handle **10.** eat, drink **11.** *inf.* (try to) borrow from —*vi.* **12.** be in contact **13.** (*with* on) refer (to) —**touched** *a.* **1.** moved to sympathy or emotion **2.** showing slight insanity —**'touching** *a.* **1.** emotionally moving —*prep.* **2.** concerning —**'touchy** *a.* easily offended, sensitive —**'touchdown** *n.* **1.** moment at which landing aircraft or spacecraft comes into contact with landing surface **2.** *Rugby* act of placing or touching ball on ground behind goal line, as in scoring try **3.** *American football* scoring play for six points achieved by being in possession of ball in opponents' end zone —**touch judge** one of two linesmen in rugby —**'touchline** *n.* side line of pitch in some games —**'touchpaper** *n.* paper soaked in saltpetre for firing gunpowder —**'touchstone** *n.* criterion —**touch-type** *vi.* type without looking at keyboard —**touch-typist** *n.* —**'touchwood** *n.* tinder —**touch and go** precarious (situation) —**touch down 1.** (of aircraft *etc.*) land **2.** *Rugby* place ball behind goal line, as when scoring try

touché (tu:'ʃeɪ) *interj.* *orig.* in fencing, acknowledgment that blow, witty remark *etc.* has been successful

tough (tʌf) *a.* **1.** strong, resilient, not brittle **2.** sturdy **3.** able to bear hardship, strain **4.** difficult **5.** needing effort to chew **6.** *sl.* rough, uncivilized, violent **7.** *inf.* unlucky, unfair —*n.* **8.** *inf.* rough, violent person —**'toughen** *v.* —**'toughness** *n.*

toupee ('tu:peɪ) *n.* hairpiece

tour (tuə) *n.* **1.** travelling round **2.** journey to one place after another **3.** excursion —*v.* **4.** make tour (of) —**'tourism** *n.* **1.** tourist travel **2.** this as an industry —**'tourist** *n.* one who travels for pleasure —**'touristy** *a.* *inf.*, *oft.* derogatory abounding in or designed for tourists

tour de force (tur də 'fɔrs) *Fr.* brilliant stroke, achievement

tourmaline ('tuəməli:n) *n.* crystalline mineral used for optical instruments and as gem

tournament ('tuənəmənt) *n.* **1.** competition, contest usu. with several stages to decide overall winner **2.** *Hist.* contest between knights on horseback —**'tourney** *n.* *Hist.* knightly tournament

tourniquet ('tuənɪkeɪ) *n.* *Med.* bandage, surgical instrument to constrict artery and stop bleeding

tousle ('tauz²l) *vt.* **1.** tangle, ruffle **2.** treat roughly —*n.* **3.** disorderly, tangled or rumpled state **4.** dishevelled or disordered mass, *esp.* of hair

tout (taut) *vi.* **1.** solicit custom (usu. in undesirable fashion) **2.** obtain and sell information about racehorses —*n.* **3.** one who touts

tow¹ (təu) *vt.* **1.** drag along behind, *esp.* at end of rope —*n.* **2.** towing or being towed **3.** vessel, vehicle in tow —**'towage** *n.* —**'towbar** *n.* metal bar attached to car for towing caravan *etc.* —**'towpath** *n.* path beside canal, river, *orig.* for towing —**'towrope** *n.* rope or cable used for towing vehicle or vessel (*also* **'towline**)

tow² (təu) *n.* fibre of hemp, flax —**tow-headed** *a.* with pale-coloured or rumpled hair

towards (tə'wɔːdz, tɔːdz) *prep.* **1.** in direction of **2.** with regard to **3.** as contribution to (*also* **to'ward**)

towel ('tauəl) *n.* **1.** cloth for wiping off moisture after washing —*vt.* **2.** dry or wipe with towel (**-ll-**) —**'towelling** *n.* material used for making towels —**throw in the towel** give up completely

tower ('tauə) *n.* **1.** tall strong structure oft. forming part of church or other large building **2.** fortress —*vi.* **3.** stand very high **4.** loom —**'towering** *a.* **1.** very tall; lofty **2.** outstanding, as in importance or stature **3.** very intense —**tower block** a building of many storeys, as for offices or flats

town (taun) *n.* collection of dwellings *etc.*, larger than village and smaller than city —**'township** *n.* **1.** small town **2.** C land-survey area —**town clerk** chief administrative officer of town —**town crier** formerly, person employed to make public announcements in streets —**town hall** chief building in which municipal business is transacted, oft. with hall for public meetings —**town planning** comprehensive planning of physical and social development of town —**'townspeople** *pl.n.*

toxic ('tɒksɪk) *a.* **1.** poisonous **2.** due to poison —**toxaemia** *or U.S.* **toxemia** (tɒk-'si:mɪə) *n.* blood poisoning —**tox'icity** *n.* strength of a poison —**toxi'cology** *n.* study of poisons —**'toxin** *n.* poison of bacterial origin

toy (tɔɪ) *n.* **1.** something designed to be played with **2.** (miniature) replica —*a.* **3.** very small —*vi.* **4.** act idly, trifle —**toy boy** very young male lover of older woman

trace¹ (treɪs) *n.* **1.** track left by anything **2.** indication **3.** minute quantity —*vt.* **4.** follow course, track of **5.** find out **6.** make plan of **7.** draw or copy exactly, *esp.* using tracing paper —**'tracer** *n.* **1.** person or thing that traces **2.** ammunition that can be observed when in flight by burning of chemical substances in base of projectile **3.** *Med.* radioactive isotope introduced into body to study metabolic processes *etc.* by following its progress with Geiger counter or other detector **4.** investigation to trace missing cargo *etc.* —**'tracery** *n.* interlaced ornament, *esp.* stonework of Gothic window —**'tracing** *n.* traced copy of drawing —**trace element** chemical element occurring in very small quantity in soil *etc.* —**tracer bullet** bullet which leaves visible trail so that aim can be checked —**tracing paper** transparent paper placed over drawing, map *etc.* to enable exact copy to be taken

trace² (treɪs) *n.* 1. chain, strap by which horse pulls vehicle 2. *Angling* short piece of gut, nylon attaching hook or fly to line

trachea (trə'kiːə) *n.* windpipe (*pl.* **tracheae** (trə'kiːiː)) —**tra'cheal** *or* **tra'cheate** *a.* —**trache'otomy** *n.* surgical incision into trachea

track (træk) *n.* 1. mark, line of marks, left by passage of anything 2. path, rough road 3. course 4. railway line 5. distance between two road wheels on one axle 6. circular jointed metal band driven by wheels as on tank, bulldozer *etc.* 7. course for running or racing 8. separate section on gramophone record —*vt.* 9. follow trail or path of 10. (*with* down) find thus —**track events** athletic sports held on a track —**track record** past accomplishments of person, company *etc.* —**track shoe** light running shoe fitted with steel spikes for better grip —'**tracksuit** *n.* warm, two-piece garment worn *esp.* by athletes

tract¹ (trækt) *n.* 1. wide expanse, area 2. *Anat.* system of organs *etc.* with particular function

tract² (trækt) *n.* treatise or pamphlet, *esp.* religious one —'**tractate** *n.* short tract

tractable ('træktəbºl) *a.* easy to manage, docile, amenable

traction ('trækʃən) *n.* action of drawing, pulling —**traction engine** steam-powered locomotive used, *esp.* formerly, for drawing heavy loads along roads or over rough ground

tractor ('træktə) *n.* motor vehicle for hauling, pulling *etc.*

trad (træd) *n.* 1. *chiefly* UK traditional jazz —*a.* 2. traditional

trade (treɪd) *n.* 1. commerce, business 2. buying and selling 3. any profitable pursuit 4. those engaged in trade —*vi.* 5. engage in trade —*vt.* 6. buy and sell 7. barter 8. exchange (one thing) for another —'**trader** *n.* —**trade-in** *n.* used article given in part payment for new —'**trademark** *or* **trade name** *n.* distinctive mark (secured by legal registration) on maker's goods —**trade price** price of commodities as sold by wholesalers to retailers —**trade secret** secret formula, process *etc.* known and used to advantage by only one manufacturer —'**tradesman** *n.* 1. shopkeeper 2. skilled worker —**Trades Union Congress** major association of British trade unions —**trade union** *or* **trades union** society of workers for protection of their interests —**trade wind** wind blowing constantly towards equator in certain parts of globe —**trading estate** *chiefly* UK large area in which a number of commercial or industrial firms are situated —**trading stamp** stamp given by some retail

organizations to customers, redeemable for merchandise or cash

tradescantia (trædes'kænʃɪə) *n.* widely cultivated plant with striped variegated leaves

tradition (trə'dɪʃən) *n.* 1. unwritten body of beliefs, facts *etc.* handed down from generation to generation 2. custom, practice of long standing 3. process of handing down —**tra'ditional** *a.* —**tra'ditionally** *adv.*

traduce (trə'djuːs) *vt.* slander

traffic ('træfɪk) *n.* 1. vehicles passing to and fro in street, town *etc.* 2. (illicit) trade —*vi.* 3. trade, *esp.* in illicit goods (*eg* drugs) ('**trafficked,** '**trafficking**) —'**trafficker** *n.* trader —**traffic island** *see* ISLAND (sense 2) —**traffic lights** set of coloured lights at road junctions *etc.* to control flow of traffic —**traffic warden** one employed to supervise road traffic, parking *etc.*

tragedy ('trædʒɪdɪ) *n.* 1. sad or calamitous event 2. dramatic, literary work dealing with serious, sad topic and with ending marked by (inevitable) disaster —**tra'gedian** *n.* actor in, writer of tragedies (**tragedi'enne** *fem.*) —'**tragic** *a.* 1. of, in manner of tragedy 2. disastrous 3. appalling —'**tragically** *adv.* —**tragi'comedy** *n.* play with both tragic and comic elements

trail (treɪl) *vt.* 1. drag behind one —*vi.* 2. be drawn behind 3. hang, grow loosely —*n.* 4. track, trace 5. thing that trails 6. rough, ill-defined track in wild country —'**trailer** *n.* 1. vehicle towed by another vehicle 2. *Cine.* advertisement of forthcoming film 3. trailing plant —'**trailblazer** *n.* 1. pioneer in particular field 2. person who blazes trail

train (treɪn) *vt.* 1. educate, instruct, exercise 2. cause to grow in particular way 3. aim (gun *etc.*) —*vi.* 4. follow course of training, *esp.* to achieve physical fitness for athletics —*n.* 5. line of railway vehicles joined to locomotive 6. succession, *esp.* of thoughts, events *etc.* 7. procession of animals, vehicles *etc.* travelling together 8. trailing part of dress 9. body of attendants —**trai'nee** *n.* one training to be skilled worker, *esp.* in industry —'**trainer** *n.* 1. person who trains athletes 2. piece of equipment employed in training, such as simulated aircraft cockpit 3. person who schools racehorses —'**training** *n.* —'**trainbearer** *n.* attendant who holds up train of dignitary's robe —**train spotter** person who collects numbers of railway locomotives

traipse *or* **trapes** (treɪps) *vi. inf.* walk wearily

trait (treɪt, treɪ) *n.* characteristic feature

traitor ('treɪtə) *n.* one who betrays or is guilty of treason —'**traitorous** *a.* 1. disloyal 2. guilty of treachery —'**traitorously** *adv.*

trajectory (trə'dʒektərɪ) *n.* line of flight, (curved) path of projectile

tram (træm) *n.* vehicle (*esp.* electrically driven and for public transport) running on rails laid on roadway (*also* **'tramcar**) —**'tramway** *n.* rails for trams in street

trammel ('træməl) *n.* **1.** anything that restrains or holds captive **2.** type of compasses —*vt.* **3.** restrain, hinder (-**ll**-)

tramp (træmp) *vi.* **1.** travel on foot, *esp.* as vagabond or for pleasure **2.** walk heavily —*n.* **3.** (homeless) person who travels about on foot **4.** walk **5.** tramping **6.** vessel that takes cargo wherever shippers desire **7.** *sl., chiefly* US prostitute; promiscuous woman

trample ('træmp'l) *v.* tread (on) and crush under foot

trampoline ('træmpəlin, -li:n) *n.* tough canvas sheet stretched horizontally with elastic cords *etc.* to frame, for gymnastic, acrobatic use

trance (trɑːns) *n.* **1.** unconscious or dazed state **2.** state of ecstasy or total absorption

trannie *or* **tranny** ('træni) *inf.* transistor radio

tranquil ('træŋkwil) *a.* calm, quiet, serene —**tran'quillity** *or* U.S. (*sometimes*) **tran'quility** *n.* —**'tranquillize, -ise** *or* U.S. **'tranquilize** *vt.* make calm —**'tranquilliz er** *or* **-iser** *n.* drug which induces calm, tranquil state —**'tranquilly** *adv.*

trans. **1.** transaction **2.** transferred **3.** transitive **4.** translated **5.** translator **6.** transport(ation) **7.** transverse

trans- (*comb. form*) across, through, beyond, on the other side, as in *transatlantic*

transact (træn'zækt) *vt.* **1.** carry through **2.** negotiate **3.** conduct (affair *etc.*) —**trans'action** *n.* **1.** performing of any business **2.** that which is performed **3.** single sale or purchase —*pl.* **4.** proceedings **5.** reports of a society

transatlantic (trænzət'læntik) *a.* **1.** on or from the other side of the Atlantic **2.** crossing the Atlantic

transceiver (træn'si:və) *n.* combined radio transmitter and receiver

transcend (træn'send) *vt.* **1.** rise above **2.** exceed, surpass —**tran'scendence** *n.* —**tran'scendent** *a.* —**transcen'dental** *a.* **1.** surpassing experience **2.** supernatural **3.** abstruse —**transcen'dentalism** *n.* —**transcendental meditation** technique, based on Hindu traditions, for relaxing and refreshing mind and body through silent repetition of mantra

transcribe (træn'skraib) *vt.* **1.** copy out **2.** transliterate, translate **3.** record for later broadcast **4.** arrange (music) for different instrument —**'transcript** *n.* copy —**tran'scription** *n.* **1.** act or instance of transcribing or state of being transcribed **2.** something transcribed **3.** representation in writing of actual pronunciation of word *etc.* using phonetic symbols

transducer (trænz'dju:sə) *n.* any device that converts one form of energy into another

transept ('trænsept) *n.* **1.** transverse part of cruciform church **2.** either of its arms

transfer (træns'fɜː) *v.* **1.** move, send from one person, place *etc.* to another (-**rr**-) —*n.* ('trænsfɜː) **2.** removal of person or thing from one place to another **3.** design which can be transferred from one surface to another by pressure, heat *etc.* —**trans'ferable** *or* **trans'ferrable** *a.* —**transference** ('trænsfərəns) *n.* transfer

transfigure (træns'figə) *vt.* alter appearance of —**transfiguration** (trænsfigju'reiʃən) *n.*

transfix (træns'fiks) *vt.* **1.** astound, stun **2.** pierce

transform (træns'fɔːm) *vt.* change shape, character of —**transfor'mation** *n.* —**trans'former** *n.* Elec. apparatus for changing voltage of alternating current

transfuse (træns'fjuːz) *vt.* convey from one vessel to another, *esp.* blood from healthy person to one injured or ill —**trans'fusion** *n.*

transgress (trænz'gres) *vt.* **1.** break (law) —*vi.* **2.** sin —**trans'gression** *n.* —**trans'gressor** *n.*

tranship (træn'ʃip) *v. see* TRANSSHIP

transient ('trænziənt) *a.* fleeting, not permanent —**'transience** *n.*

transistor (træn'zistə) *n.* **1.** Electron. small, semiconducting device used to amplify electric currents **2.** portable radio using transistors —**tran'sistorize** *or* **-ise** *v.* **1.** convert to use or manufacture of transistors and other solid-state components —*vt.* **2.** equip with transistors and other solid-state components

transit ('trænsit, 'trænz-) *n.* passage, crossing —**transition** (træn'ziʃən) *n.* change from one state to another —**transitional** (træn'ziʃən'l) *a.* —**'transitive** *a.* (of verb) requiring direct object —**'transitory** *a.* not lasting long, transient —**transit camp** camp in which refugees *etc.* live temporarily

translate (træns'leit, trænz-) *vt.* **1.** turn from one language into another **2.** interpret —**trans'lation** *n.* —**trans'lator** *n.*

transliterate (trænz'litəreit) *vt.* write in the letters of another alphabet —**translit er'ation** *n.*

translucent (trænz'luːs'nt) *a.* letting light pass through, semitransparent —**trans'lu cence** *n.*

transmigrate (trænzmai'greit) *vi.* (of soul) pass into another body —**transmi 'gration** *n.*

transmit (trænz'mit) *vt.* **1.** send, cause to pass to another place, person *etc.* **2.** communicate **3.** send out (signals) by means of radio waves **4.** broadcast (radio, television programme) (-**tt**-) —**trans'mission** *n.* **1.** transference **2.** gear by which power is communicated from engine to road wheels —**trans'mitter** *n.* **1.** person or thing that transmits **2.** equipment used for generating and amplifying radio-frequency carrier, modulating carrier with information and feeding it to aerial for transmission **3.** microphone in telephone that converts sound waves into audio-frequency electrical signals **4.** device that converts mechanical movements into coded electrical signals transmitted along telegraph circuit

transmogrify (trænz'mɒgrɪfaɪ) *vt. inf.* change completely *esp.* into bizarre form

transmute (trænz'mjuːt) *vt.* change in form, properties or nature —**transmu'ta-tion** *n.*

transom ('trænzəm) *n.* **1.** crosspiece **2.** lintel

transparent (træns'pærənt) *a.* **1.** letting light pass without distortion **2.** that can be seen through distinctly **3.** obvious —**trans'parence** *n.* —**trans'parency** *n.* **1.** quality of being transparent **2.** photographic slide **3.** picture made visible by light behind it —**trans'parently** *adv.*

transpire (træn'spaɪə) *vi.* **1.** become known **2.** *inf.* happen **3.** (of plants) give off water vapour through leaves —**transpira-tion** (trænspə'reɪʃən) *n.*

transplant (træns'plɑːnt) *vt.* **1.** move and plant again in another place **2.** transfer (organ) surgically from one body to another —*n.* ('trænsplɑːnt) **3.** surgical transplanting of organ **4.** anything transplanted —**transplan'tation** *n.*

transponder (træn'spɒndə) *n.* radio or radar transmitter-receiver that transmits signals automatically when it receives predetermined signals

transport (træns'pɔːt) *vt.* **1.** convey from one place to another **2.** *Hist.* banish, as criminal, to penal colony **3.** enrapture —*n.* ('trænspɔːt) **4.** means of conveyance **5.** ships, aircraft *etc.* used in transporting stores, troops *etc.* **6.** a ship *etc.* so used **7.** ecstasy, rapture or any powerful emotion —**transpor'tation** *n.* **1.** transporting **2.** *Hist.* deportation to penal colony —**transport café** *UK* inexpensive eating place on main route, used mainly by long-distance lorry drivers

transpose (træns'pəʊz) *vt.* **1.** change order of, interchange **2.** put (music) into different key —**trans'posal** *n.* —**transpo-'sition** *n.*

transsexual (trænz'sɛksjuəl) *n.* **1.** person who is completely identified with opposite sex **2.** person who has undergone medical procedures to alter sexual characteristics to those of opposite sex

transship (træns'ʃɪp) *or* **tranship** *v.* move from one ship, train *etc.* to another

transubstantiation (trænsəbstænʃɪ'eɪʃən) *n.* doctrine that substance of bread and wine changes into substance of Christ's body when consecrated in Eucharist

transuranic (trænzju'rænɪk), **transura-nian** (trænzju'reɪnɪən), *or* **transuranium** *a.* **1.** (of element) having atomic number greater than that of uranium **2.** of behaviour of transuranic elements

transverse (trænz'vɜːs) *a.* **1.** lying across **2.** at right angles

transvestite (trænz'vɛstaɪt) *n.* person seeking sexual pleasure by wearing clothes normally worn by opposite sex

trap[1] (træp) *n.* **1.** snare, device for catching game *etc.* **2.** anything planned to deceive, betray *etc.* **3.** arrangement of pipes to prevent escape of gas **4.** movable opening, *esp.* through ceiling *etc.* **5.** *Hist.* two-wheeled carriage **6.** *sl.* mouth —*vt.* **7.** catch, ensnare (**-pp-**) —**'trapper** *n.* one who traps animals for their fur —**trap door** door in floor or roof

trap[2] (træp) *vt.* (*oft. with* out) dress, adorn (**-pp-**)

trapeze (trə'piːz) *n.* horizontal bar suspended from two ropes for use in gymnastics, acrobatic exhibitions *etc.*

trapezium (trə'piːzɪəm) *n.* quadrilateral figure with only two sides parallel (*pl.* **-s, -zia** (-zɪə)) —**'trapezoid** *n.* quadrilateral with no parallel sides

trappings ('træpɪŋz) *pl.n.* equipment, ornaments

Trappist ('træpɪst) *n.* member of Cistercian order of monks who observe strict silence

trash (træʃ) *n.* **1.** *chiefly US* rubbish **2.** nonsense —**'trashy** *a.* worthless, cheap

trauma ('trɔːmə) *n.* **1.** nervous shock **2.** injury (*pl.* **-ta** (-tə), **-s**) —**trau'matic** *a.* of, causing, caused by trauma

travail ('træveɪl) *vi./n.* labour, toil

travel ('træv'l) *vi.* **1.** go, move from one place to another (**-ll-**) —*n.* **2.** act of travelling, *esp.* as tourist **3.** *Machinery* distance component is permitted to move —*pl.* **4.** (account of) travelling —**'traveller** *n.* —**'travelogue** *or* **U.S.** (*sometimes*) **'travelog** *n.* film *etc.* about travels —**travel agency** *or* **bureau** agency that arranges and negotiates holidays *etc.* for travellers —**travel agent** —**traveller's cheque** cheque sold by bank *etc.* to bearer, who signs it on purchase and can cash it abroad by signing it again —**travelling salesman** salesman who travels within assigned territory to sell merchandise or solicit orders for commercial enterprise he represents by direct personal contact with (potential) customers

traverse ('trævɜːs) *vt.* **1.** cross, go through or over —*vi.* **2.** (of gun) move laterally —*n.* **3.** anything set across **4.** partition **5.** *Mountaineering* face, steep slope to be crossed from side to side —*a.* **6.** being, lying across

travesty ('trævɪstɪ) *n.* **1.** farcical, grotesque imitation **2.** mockery —*vt.* **3.** make, be a travesty of (**-estied, -estying**)

trawl (trɔːl) *n.* **1.** net dragged at deep levels behind special boat, to catch fish —*vi.* **2.** fish with one —**'trawler** *n.* trawling vessel

tray (treɪ) *n.* **1.** flat board, usu. with rim, for carrying things **2.** any similar utensil

treachery ('trɛtʃərɪ) *n.* deceit, betrayal —'**treacherous** *a.* **1.** disloyal **2.** unreliable, dangerous —'**treacherously** *adv.*

treacle ('triːk'l) *n.* thick syrup produced when sugar is refined —'**treacly** *a.*

tread (trɛd) *vt.* **1.** set foot on **2.** trample —*vi.* **3.** walk **4.** (*sometimes with* on) repress (**trod** *pt.*, '**trodden** *or* **trod** *pp.*, '**treading** *pr.p.*) —*n.* **5.** treading **6.** fashion of walking **7.** upper surface of step **8.** part of rubber tyre in contact with ground —'**treadmill** *n.* **1.** *Hist.* cylinder turned by treading on steps projecting from it **2.** dreary routine *etc.*

treadle ('trɛd'l) *n.* lever worked by foot to turn wheel

treason ('triːz'n) *n.* **1.** violation by subject of allegiance to sovereign or state **2.** treachery; disloyalty —'**treasonable** *or* '**treasonous** *a.* constituting treason —'**treasonably** *adv.*

treasure ('trɛʒə) *n.* **1.** riches **2.** stored wealth or valuables —*vt.* **3.** prize, cherish **4.** store up —'**treasurer** *n.* official in charge of funds —'**treasury** *n.* **1.** place for treasure **2.** (**T-**) government department in charge of finance —**treasure-trove** *n.* treasure found hidden with no evidence of ownership

treat (triːt) *n.* **1.** pleasure, entertainment given —*vt.* **2.** deal with, act towards **3.** give medical treatment to **4.** give (someone) gift, food *etc.* at one's own expense —*vi.* **5.** negotiate **6.** (*with* of) discourse (on) —'**treatment** *n.* **1.** method of counteracting a disease **2.** act or mode of treating **3.** manner of handling an artistic medium

treatise ('triːtɪz) *n.* book discussing a subject, formal essay

treaty ('triːtɪ) *n.* signed contract between states *etc.*

treble ('trɛb'l) *a.* **1.** threefold, triple **2.** *Mus.* high-pitched —*n.* **3.** soprano voice **4.** part of music for it **5.** singer with such voice —*v.* **6.** increase threefold —'**trebly** *adv.* —**treble chance** method of betting in football pools in which chances of winning are related to number of draws and number of home and away wins forecast by competitor —**treble clef** *Mus.* clef that establishes G fifth above middle C as being on second line of staff

tree (triː) *n.* **1.** large perennial plant with woody trunk **2.** beam **3.** anything (*eg* genealogical chart) resembling tree or tree's structure —*vt.* **4.** force, drive up tree —**tree creeper** small songbird

trefoil ('trɛfɔɪl) *n.* **1.** plant with three-lobed leaf, clover **2.** carved ornament like this

trek (trɛk) *n.* **1.** long difficult journey, esp. on foot **2.** SA journey or stage of journey, esp. migration by ox wagon —*vi.* **3.** make a trek (**-kk-**) —'**trekker** *n.*

trellis ('trɛlɪs) *n.* **1.** lattice or grating of light bars fixed crosswise —*vt.* **2.** screen, supply with one

tremble ('trɛmb'l) *vi.* **1.** quiver, shake **2.** feel fear, anxiety —*n.* **3.** involuntary shaking, quiver, tremor —'**trembler** *n.* trembling spring that makes electrical contact when shaken

tremendous (trɪ'mɛndəs) *a.* **1.** vast, immense **2.** *inf.* exciting, unusual **3.** *inf.* excellent

tremolo ('trɛmələʊ) *n.* quivering or vibrating effect in singing or playing (*pl.* **-s**)

tremor ('trɛmə) *n.* **1.** quiver **2.** shaking **3.** minor earthquake

tremulous ('trɛmjʊləs) *a.* **1.** quivering slightly **2.** timorous, agitated

trench (trɛntʃ) *n.* **1.** long narrow ditch, esp. as shelter in war —*vt.* **2.** cut grooves or ditches in —**trench coat** double-breasted waterproof coat

trenchant ('trɛntʃənt) *a.* cutting, incisive, biting

trencher ('trɛntʃə) *n.* *Hist.* wooden plate on which food was served —'**trencherman** *n.* person who enjoys food; hearty eater

trend (trɛnd) *n.* **1.** direction, tendency, inclination, drift **2.** fashion; mode —'**trendiness** *n.* —'**trendy** *a./n. inf.* consciously fashionable (person) —'**trendsetter** *n.* person or thing that creates or may create new fashion —'**trendsetting** *a.*

trephine (trɪ'fiːn) *or* **trepan** (trɪ'pæn) *n.* **1.** instrument for cutting circular pieces, esp. from skull —*vt.* **2.** remove circular section of bone, esp. from skull, of (someone)

trepidation (trɛpɪ'deɪʃən) *n.* fear, anxiety

trespass ('trɛspəs) *vi.* **1.** intrude (on property *etc.* of another) **2.** transgress, sin —*n.* **3.** wrongful entering on another's land **4.** wrongdoing —'**trespasser** *n.*

tress (trɛs) *n.* long lock of hair

trestle ('trɛs'l) *n.* board fixed on pairs of spreading legs and used as support

trews (truːz) *pl.n.* close-fitting trousers, orig. of tartan

tri- (*comb. form*) three, as in *trisect*

triad ('traɪæd) *n.* **1.** group of three **2.** *Chem.* element, radical with valency of three

trial ('traɪəl, traɪl) *n.* **1.** act of trying, testing **2.** experimental examination **3.** *Law* investigation of case before judge **4.** thing, person that strains endurance or patience —**trial and error** method of discovery *etc.* based on practical experiment and experience rather than theory —**trial balance** *Book-keeping* statement of all debit and credit balances in ledger of double-entry system

triangle ('traɪæŋg'l) *n.* **1.** figure with three angles **2.** percussion musical instrument —**tri'angular** *a.* —**triangulate** (traɪ-'æŋgjʊleɪt) *vt.* **1.** survey by method of triangulation **2.** calculate trigonometrically **3.** divide into triangles **4.** make triangular —*a.* (traɪ'æŋgjʊlɪt, -leɪt) **5.** marked with or composed of triangles —**triangu'lation** *n.* method of surveying in which area is divided into triangles, one side and all angles of which are measured and lengths of other lines calculated trigonometrically

Triassic (traɪˈæsɪk) *a.* **1.** of first period of Mesozoic era —*n.* **2.** Triassic period or rock system (*also* **'Trias**)

tribe (traɪb) *n.* **1.** race **2.** subdivision of race of people —**'tribal** *a.*

tribulation (trɪbjʊˈleɪʃən) *n.* **1.** misery, trouble, affliction, distress **2.** cause of this

tribune (ˈtrɪbjuːn) *n.* person or institution upholding public rights —**tribunal** (traɪ-ˈbjuːnˀl, trɪ-) *n.* **1.** lawcourt **2.** body appointed to inquire into and decide specific matter **3.** seat of judge

tributary (ˈtrɪbjʊtərɪ) *n.* **1.** stream flowing into another —*a.* **2.** auxiliary **3.** contributory **4.** paying tribute

tribute (ˈtrɪbjuːt) *n.* **1.** sign of honour or recognition **2.** tax paid by one state to another

trice (traɪs) *n.* moment —**in a trice** instantly

triceps (ˈtraɪsɛps) *n.* muscle having three heads, *esp.* one that extends forearm (*pl.* **-es, -ceps**)

trichina (trɪˈkaɪnə) *n.* minute parasitic worm (*pl.* **-nae** (-niː)) —**trichinosis** (trɪkɪ-ˈnəʊsɪs) *n.* disease caused by this

trichromatic (traɪkrəʊˈmætɪk) *or* **trichromic** (traɪˈkrəʊmɪk) *a.* **1.** involving combination of three primary colours **2.** of normal colour vision **3.** having three colours —**tri'chromatism** *n.*

trick (trɪk) *n.* **1.** deception **2.** prank **3.** mannerism **4.** illusion **5.** feat of skill or cunning **6.** knack **7.** cards played in one round **8.** spell of duty —*vt.* **9.** cheat, hoax, deceive —**'trickery** *n.* —**'trickster** *n.* —**'tricky** *a.* **1.** difficult, needing careful handling **2.** crafty

trickle (ˈtrɪkˀl) *v.* (cause to) run, flow, move in thin stream or drops

tricolour *or U.S.* **tricolor** (ˈtrɪkələ, ˈtraɪkʌlə) *a.* **1.** three-coloured —*n.* **2.** tricolour flag (*eg* of France)

tricot (ˈtrɪkəʊ, ˈtriː-) *n.* **1.** thin rayon or nylon fabric knitted or resembling knitting **2.** ribbed dress fabric

tricycle (ˈtraɪsɪkˀl) *n.* three-wheeled cycle

trident (ˈtraɪdˀnt) *n.* three-pronged fork or spear

triennial (traɪˈɛnɪəl) *a.* happening every, or lasting, three years

trifle (ˈtraɪfˀl) *n.* **1.** insignificant thing or matter **2.** small amount **3.** pudding of sponge cake, whipped cream *etc.* —*v.* **4.** toy **5.** act, speak idly —**'trifler** *n.* —**'trifling** *a.* **1.** insignificant, petty **2.** frivolous; idle

trig. **1.** trigonometry **2.** trigonometrical —**trig station** *or* **point** landmark which surveyor uses

trigger (ˈtrɪgə) *n.* **1.** catch which releases spring, *esp.* to fire gun —*vt.* **2.** (oft. with off) start, set in action *etc.* —**trigger-happy** *a.* tending to irresponsible, ill-considered behaviour, *esp.* in use of firearms

trigonometry (trɪgəˈnɒmɪtrɪ) *n.* branch of mathematics dealing with relations of sides and angles of triangles —**trigono'metrical** *a.*

trike (traɪk) tricycle

trilateral (traɪˈlætərəl) *a.* having three sides —**tri'laterally** *adv.*

trilby (ˈtrɪlbɪ) *n.* man's soft felt hat

trill (trɪl) *vi.* **1.** sing with quavering voice **2.** sing lightly **3.** warble —*n.* **4.** such singing or sound

trillion (ˈtrɪljən) *n.* **1.** one million million million, 10^{18} **2.** US one million million, 10^{12}

trilobite (ˈtraɪləbaɪt) *n.* extinct marine arthropod abundant in Palaeozoic times, having segmented exoskeleton divided into three parts —**trilobitic** (traɪləˈbɪtɪk) *a.*

trilogy (ˈtrɪlədʒɪ) *n.* series of three related (literary) works

trim (trɪm) *a.* **1.** neat, smart **2.** slender **3.** in good order —*vt.* **4.** shorten slightly by cutting, prune **5.** decorate **6.** adjust **7.** put in good order **8.** adjust balance of (ship, aircraft) (**-mm-**) —*n.* **9.** decoration **10.** order, state of being trim **11.** haircut that neatens existing style **12.** upholstery, accessories in car **13.** edging material, as inside woodwork round doors, windows *etc.* —**'trimming** *n.* (*oft. pl.*) decoration, addition

trimaran (ˈtraɪməræn) *n.* three-hulled vessel

trinitrotoluene (traɪnaɪtrəʊˈtɒljuːiːn) *or* **trinitrotoluol** (traɪnaɪtrəʊˈtɒljʊɒl) *n.* a high explosive derived from toluene

trinity (ˈtrɪnɪtɪ) *n.* **1.** the state of being threefold **2.** (T-) the three persons of the Godhead —**trini'tarian** *n./a.* —**Trinity Sunday** Sunday after Whit Sunday

trinket (ˈtrɪŋkɪt) *n.* small ornament, trifle —**'trinketry** *n.*

trio (ˈtriːəʊ) *n.* **1.** group of three **2.** music for three parts (*pl.* **-s**)

triode (ˈtraɪəʊd) *n. Electron.* three-electrode valve

trip (trɪp) *n.* **1.** (short) journey for pleasure **2.** stumble **3.** switch **4.** *inf.* hallucinatory experience caused by drug —*v.* **5.** (*oft. with* up) (cause to) stumble **6.** (cause to) make false step, mistake —*vi.* **7.** run lightly; skip; dance **8.** *inf.* take hallucinatory drugs —*vt.* **9.** operate (switch) (**-pp-**) —**'tripper** *n.* tourist

tripartite (traɪˈpɑːtaɪt) *a.* having, divided into three parts

tripe (traɪp) *n.* **1.** stomach of cow *etc.* prepared for food **2.** *inf.* nonsense

triplane (ˈtraɪpleɪn) *n.* aeroplane with three wings one above another

triple (ˈtrɪpˀl) *a.* **1.** threefold —*v.* **2.** treble —**'triplet** *n.* **1.** three of a kind **2.** one of three offspring born at one birth —**'triply** *adv.* —**triple jump** athletic event in which competitor has to perform hop, step and jump in continuous movement —**triple point** *Chem.* temperature and pressure at which three phases of substance are in equilibrium

triplicate ('trɪplɪkɪt) a. 1. threefold —vt. ('trɪplɪkeɪt) 2. make threefold —n. 3. state of being triplicate 4. one of set of three copies —tripli'cation n.

tripod ('traɪpɒd) n. stool, stand etc. with three feet

tripos ('traɪpɒs) n. degree examination at Cambridge University

triptych ('trɪptɪk) n. carving, set of pictures, esp. altarpiece, on three panels hinged side by side

trireme ('traɪriːm) n. ancient Gr. galley with three banks of oars on each side

trisect (traɪ'sɛkt) vt. divide into three (equal) parts —tri'section n.

trite (traɪt) a. hackneyed, banal

tritium ('trɪtɪəm) n. radioactive isotope of hydrogen

triumph ('traɪəmf) n. 1. great success 2. victory 3. exultation —vi. 4. achieve great success or victory 5. exult —tri'umphal a. —tri'umphant a. victorious

triumvirate (traɪ'ʌmvɪrɪt) n. joint rule by three persons

trivalent (traɪ'veɪlənt, 'trɪvələnt) a. Chem. 1. having valency of three 2. having three valencies (also ter'valent) —tri'valency n.

trivet ('trɪvɪt) n. metal bracket or stand for pot or kettle

trivia ('trɪvɪə) pl.n. petty, unimportant things, details —'trivial a. 1. of little consequence 2. commonplace —trivi'ality n.

trochee ('trəʊkiː) n. in verse, foot of two syllables, first long and second short —tro'chaic a.

trod (trɒd) pt. of TREAD —'trodden or trod pp. of TREAD

troglodyte ('trɒɡlədaɪt) n. cave dweller

troika ('trɔɪkə) n. 1. Russian vehicle drawn by three horses abreast 2. three horses harnessed abreast 3. triumvirate

Trojan ('trəʊdʒən) n./a. 1. (inhabitant) of ancient Troy 2. steadfast or persevering (person) —Trojan Horse 1. Gr. myth. hollow wooden figure of horse left outside Troy by Greeks and dragged inside by Trojans. Men concealed inside opened city to final Greek assault 2. trap intended to undermine enemy

troll[1] ('trəʊl) vt. fish for by dragging baited hook or lure through water

troll[2] ('trəʊl) n. supernatural being in Scandinavian mythology and folklore

trolley ('trɒlɪ) n. 1. small wheeled table for food and drink 2. wheeled cart for moving goods etc. 3. US tram —trolley bus bus deriving power from overhead electric wire but not running on rails

trollop ('trɒləp) n. promiscuous or slovenly woman

trombone (trɒm'bəʊn) n. deep-toned brass wind instrument with sliding tube —trom'bonist n.

troop (truːp) n. 1. group or crowd of persons or animals 2. unit of cavalry —pl. 3. soldiers —vi. 4. move in a troop, flock —'trooper n. cavalry soldier

trope (trəʊp) n. figure of speech

trophy ('trəʊfɪ) n. 1. prize, award, as shield, cup 2. memorial of victory, hunt etc.

-trophy (n. comb. form) certain type of nourishment or growth, as in dystrophy —-trophic (a. comb. form)

tropic ('trɒpɪk) n. 1. either of two lines of latitude at 23½° N (tropic of Cancer) or 23½° S (tropic of Capricorn) —pl. 2. area of earth's surface between these lines —'tropical a. 1. pert. to, within tropics 2. (of climate) very hot —'tropicbird n. tropical aquatic bird having long tail feathers and white plumage with black markings

tropism ('trəʊpɪzəm) n. response of organism, esp. plant, to external stimulus by growth in direction determined by stimulus

troposphere ('trɒpəsfɪə) n. lowest atmospheric layer, in which air temperature decreases normally with height at about 6.5° C per km

trot (trɒt) vi. 1. (of horse) move at medium pace, lifting feet in diagonal pairs 2. (of person) run easily with short strides (-tt-) —n. 2. trotting, jog —'trotter n. 1. horse trained to trot in race 2. foot of certain animals, esp. pig

Trot (trɒt) n. inf. follower of Trotsky; Trotskyite

troth (trəʊθ) n. obs. fidelity, truth

Trotskyism ('trɒtskɪɪzəm) n. theory of communism of Leon Trotsky, Russian revolutionary and writer, in which he called for immediate worldwide revolution by proletariat —'Trotskyite or 'Trotskyist n./a.

troubadour ('truːbədʊə) n. one of school of early poets and singers

trouble ('trʌb'l) n. 1. state or cause of mental distress, pain, inconvenience etc. 2. care, effort —vt. 3. be trouble to —vi. 4. be inconvenienced, concerned 5. be agitated 6. take pains; exert oneself —'troublesome a. —'troubleshooter n. person who locates cause of trouble and removes or treats it, as in running of machine —'troubleshooting n./a.

trough (trɒf) n. 1. long open vessel, esp. for animals' food or water 2. hollow between two waves 3. Met. area of low pressure

trounce (traʊns) vt. beat thoroughly, thrash

troupe (truːp) n. company of performers —'trouper n. 1. member of troupe 2. dependable worker or associate

trousers ('traʊzəz) pl.n. two-legged outer garment with legs reaching to the ankles

trousseau ('truːsəʊ) n. bride's outfit of clothing (pl. -seaux (-səʊz), -s)

trout (traʊt) n. freshwater sport and food fish

trowel ('traʊəl) n. small tool like spade for spreading mortar, lifting plants etc.

troy weight or **troy** (troɪ) n. system of weights used for gold, silver and gems

truant ('truːənt) n. 1. one absent without leave, esp. child so absenting himself or herself from school —a. 2. being or relating to truant —'**truancy** n.

truce (truːs) n. 1. temporary cessation of fighting 2. respite, lull

truck¹ (trʌk) n. wheeled (motor) vehicle for moving goods

truck² (trʌk) n. 1. barter 2. dealing (esp. in **have no truck with**) 3. payment of workmen in goods 4. inf. rubbish

truckle ('trʌk'l) vi. yield weakly

truckle bed low bed on wheels, stored under larger bed

truculent ('trʌkjʊlənt) a. aggressive, defiant

trudge (trʌdʒ) vi. 1. walk laboriously —n. 2. laborious or wearisome walk

true (truː) a. 1. in accordance with facts 2. faithful 3. exact, correct 4. genuine —'**truism** n. self-evident truth —'**truly** adv. 1. exactly 2. really 3. sincerely —**truth** n. 1. state of being true 2. something that is true —'**truthful** a. 1. accustomed to speak the truth 2. accurate, exact —'**truthfully** adv. —**true-blue** a. unwaveringly or staunchly loyal —**true blue** chiefly UK staunch royalist or conservative

truffle ('trʌf'l) n. 1. edible fungus growing underground 2. sweet resembling this

trug (trʌg) n. long shallow basket used by gardeners

truism ('truːɪzəm) n. see TRUE

trump¹ (trʌmp) n. 1. card of suit temporarily ranking above others —v. 2. play trump card on (plain suit) —**trump up** invent, concoct —**turn up** or **out trumps** turn out (unexpectedly) well, successfully

trump² (trʌmp) n. 1. trumpet 2. blast on trumpet —**the last trump** final trumpet call on Day of Judgment

trumpery ('trʌmpərɪ) a. 1. showy but worthless —n. 2. worthless finery 3. trash, rubbish

trumpet ('trʌmpɪt) n. 1. metal wind instrument like horn —vi. 2. blow trumpet 3. make sound like one, as elephant —vt. 4. proclaim, make widely known

truncate (trʌŋ'keɪt, 'trʌŋkeɪt) vt. cut short —'**truncated** a. 1. (of cone etc.) having apex or end removed by plane intersection 2. shortened (as if) by cutting off (also '**truncate**)

truncheon ('trʌntʃən) n. 1. short thick club or baton 2. staff of office or authority —vt. 3. cudgel

trundle ('trʌnd'l) vt. roll, as a thing on little wheels

trunk (trʌŋk) n. 1. main stem of tree 2. person's body without or excluding head and limbs 3. box for clothes etc. 4. elephant's proboscis —pl. 5. man's swimming costume —**trunk call** long-distance telephone call —**trunk line** main line of railway, canal, telephone etc. —**trunk road** main road

truss (trʌs) vt. 1. (oft. with up) fasten, tie —n. 2. support 3. medical device of belt etc. to hold hernia in place 4. package, bundle (of hay etc.) 5. cluster of flowers at end of single stalk

trust (trʌst) n. 1. confidence 2. firm belief 3. reliance 4. combination of producers to reduce competition and keep up prices 5. care, responsibility 6. property held for another —vt. 7. rely on 8. believe in 9. consign for care —v. 10. expect, hope —**trus'tee** n. one legally holding property on another's behalf —**trus'teeship** n. —'**trustful** a. 1. inclined to trust 2. credulous —'**trustworthy** a. 1. reliable, dependable, honest 2. safe —'**trusty** a. 1. faithful 2. reliable —**trust fund** money, securities etc. held in trust

truth (truːθ) n. see TRUE

try (traɪ) vi. 1. attempt, endeavour —vt. 2. attempt 3. test 4. make demands upon 5. investigate (case) 6. examine (person) in court of law 7. purify; refine (as metals) (**tried**, '**trying**) —n. 8. attempt, effort 9. Rugby score gained by touching ball down over opponent's goal line —**tried** a. 1. proved 2. afflicted —'**trying** a. 1. upsetting, annoying 2. difficult —**try-on** n. UK inf. something done to test out person's tolerance etc. —'**tryout** n. —**trysail** ('traɪseɪl; Naut. 'traɪs'l) n. small fore-and-aft sail set on sailing vessel in foul weather to help keep her head to wind —**try on** 1. put on (garment) to find out whether it fits etc. 2. inf. attempt to deceive or fool (esp. in **try it on**) —**try out** 1. test; put to experimental use 2. (usu. with for) US (of actor etc.) undergo test; submit (actor etc.) to test to determine suitability for role etc.

tryst (trɪst, traɪst) n. 1. appointment to meet 2. place appointed

tsar (zɑː) n. see CZAR

tsetse fly or **tzetze fly** ('tsɛtsɪ) Afr. bloodsucking fly whose bite transmits various diseases to man and animals

T-shirt or **tee-shirt** n. informal (short-sleeved) sweater, usu. of cotton

tsp. teaspoon

T-square n. T-shaped ruler for drawing parallel lines, right angles etc.

TT or **T.T.** 1. teetotal 2. Tourist Trophy 3. tuberculin tested

tub (tʌb) n. 1. open wooden vessel like bottom half of barrel 2. small round container 3. bath 4. inf. old, slow ship etc. —'**tubby** a. 1. plump 2. shaped like tub

tuba ('tjuːbə) n. valved brass wind instrument of low pitch

tube (tjuːb) n. 1. long, narrow, hollow cylinder 2. flexible cylinder with cap to hold liquids, pastes 3. (sometimes T-) underground electric railway, esp. in London 4. sl., chiefly US television set —'**tubing** n. 1. tubes collectively 2. length of tube **3.** system of tubes **4.** fabric in form of tube —**'tubular** a. like tube

tuber ('tjuːbə) n. fleshy underground stem of some plants, eg potato —**'tuberous** a.

tubercle ('tjuːbəkʰl) n. **1.** any small rounded nodule on skin etc. **2.** small lesion of tissue, esp. produced by tuberculosis —**tu'bercular** a. —**tu'berculin** n. extraction from bacillus used to test for and treat tuberculosis —**tubercu'losis** n. communicable disease, esp. of lungs —**tuberculin tested** (of milk) produced by cows certified as free of tuberculosis

T.U.C. Trades Union Congress

tuck (tʌk) vt. **1.** push, fold into small space **2.** gather, stitch in folds **3.** draw, roll together —n. **4.** stitched fold **5.** inf. food —**'tucker** n. strip of linen or lace formerly worn across bosom by women —**tuck-in** n. UK inf. meal, esp. large —**tuck shop** chiefly UK shop, esp. near school, where cakes and sweets are sold —**tuck in 1.** put to bed and make snug **2.** thrust loose ends or sides of (something) into confining space **3.** inf. eat, esp. heartily

Tudor ('tjuːdə) a. **1.** of the English royal house ruling 1485-1603 **2.** in, resembling style of this period, esp. of architecture

Tues. Tuesday

Tuesday ('tjuːzdɪ) n. third day of week

tufa ('tjuːfə) n. porous rock formed as deposit from springs etc.

tuff (tʌf) n. hard volcanic rock consisting of consolidated fragments of lava

tuffet ('tʌfɪt) n. small mound or seat

tuft (tʌft) n. bunch of feathers, threads etc.

tug (tʌg) vt. **1.** pull hard or violently **2.** haul **3.** jerk forward (-gg-) —n. **4.** violent pull **5.** ship used to tow other vessels —**tug of war** contest in which two teams pull against one another on a rope

tuition (tjuːˈɪʃən) n. **1.** teaching, instruction **2.** private coaching —**tu'itional** a.

tulip ('tjuːlɪp) n. plant with bright cup-shaped flowers

tulle (tjuːl) n. kind of fine thin silk or lace

tullibee ('tʌlɪbiː) n. Canad. whitefish

tumble ('tʌmbʰl) v. **1.** (cause to) fall, roll, twist etc., esp. in play —vt. **2.** rumple, disturb —n. **3.** fall **4.** somersault —**'tumbler** n. **1.** stemless drinking glass **2.** acrobat **3.** spring catch in lock —**tumble-down** a. dilapidated —**tumble drier** or **tumbler drier** machine that dries clothes etc. by tumbling in warm air —**tumble to** inf. realize, understand

tumbrel or **tumbril** ('tʌmbrəl) n. open cart for taking victims of French Revolution to guillotine

tumefy ('tjuːmɪfaɪ) v. (cause to) swell —**tu'mescence** n. —**tu'mescent** a. (becoming) swollen

tummy ('tʌmɪ) n. inf. childish word for stomach

tumour or U.S. **tumor** ('tjuːmə) n. abnormal growth in or on body

tumult ('tjuːmʌlt) n. violent uproar, commotion —**tu'multuous** a.

tumulus ('tjuːmjʊləs) n. burial mound, barrow (pl. **-li** (-laɪ))

tun (tʌn) n. **1.** large cask **2.** measure of liquid

tuna ('tjuːnə) n. see TUNNY

tundra ('tʌndrə) n. vast treeless zone between icecap and timber line of N Amer. and Eurasia

tune (tjuːn) n. **1.** melody **2.** quality of being in pitch **3.** adjustment of musical instrument **4.** concord **5.** frame of mind —vt. **6.** put in tune **7.** adjust (machine) to obtain most efficient running **8.** adjust (radio circuit) —**'tuneful** a. —**'tunefully** adv. —**'tuner** n. —**tune-up** n. adjustments to engine to improve performance —**tuning fork** two-pronged metal fork that when struck produces pure note of constant specified pitch —**tune in** adjust (radio, television) to receive (a station, programme) —**tune up 1.** adjust (musical instrument) to particular pitch **2.** tune (instruments) to common pitch **3.** adjust (engine) in (car etc.) to improve performance

tungsten ('tʌŋstən) n. greyish-white metal, used in lamp filaments, some steels etc.

tunic ('tjuːnɪk) n. **1.** close-fitting jacket forming part of uniform **2.** loose hiplength or kneelength garment

tunnel ('tʌnʰl) n. **1.** underground passage, esp. as track for railway line **2.** burrow of a mole etc. —vt. **3.** make tunnel through —vi. **4.** (with through, under etc.) make or force a way (through or under something) (-ll-) —**'tunneller** n.

tunny ('tʌnɪ) n. large marine food and game fish

tup (tʌp) n. male sheep, ram

tupik ('tuːpək) n. C tent used as summer shelter by Eskimos

tuppence ('tʌpəns) n. see twopence at TWO

tuque (tuːk) n. C knitted cap with tapering end

turban ('tɜːbʰn) n. **1.** in certain countries, man's headdress, made by coiling length of cloth round head or a cap **2.** woman's hat like this

turbid ('tɜːbɪd) a. **1.** muddy, not clear **2.** disturbed —**tur'bidity** or **'turbidness** n.

turbine ('tɜːbɪn, -baɪn) n. rotary engine driven by steam, gas, water or air playing on blades

turbo- (comb. form) of, relating to, or driven by a turbine, as in turbofan

turbofan (tɜːbəʊˈfæn) n. **1.** bypass engine in which large fan driven by turbine forces air rearwards around exhaust gases to increase propulsive thrust **2.** aircraft driven by turbofans **3.** fan in such engine

turbojet (tɜːbəʊˈdʒɛt) n. **1.** turbojet engine **2.** aircraft powered by turbojet engines, in which exhaust gasses provide propulsion

turboprop (tɜːbəʊˈprɒp) n. **1.** gas turbine for driving aircraft propeller **2.** aircraft powered by turboprops

turbot ('tɜːbət) n. large European flatfish

turbulent ('tɜːbjʊlənt) a. **1.** in commotion

2. swirling 3. riotous —'**turbulence** n. Met. instability of atmosphere causing gusty air currents etc.

tureen (tə'riːn) n. serving dish for soup

turf (tɜːf) n. 1. short grass with earth bound to it by matted roots 2. grass, esp. as lawn (pl. -s, **turves**) —vt. 3. lay with turf —**turf accountant** bookmaker —**the turf** 1. horse racing 2. racecourse —**turf out** inf. dismiss, throw out

turgid ('tɜːdʒɪd) a. 1. swollen, inflated 2. bombastic —**tur'gescent** a. —**tur'gidity** n.

turkey ('tɜːkɪ) n. large bird reared for its flesh

Turkish ('tɜːkɪʃ) a. of, pert. to Turkey, the Turks —**Turk** n. 1. native of Turkey 2. native speaker of any Turkic language 3. brutal or domineering person —'**Turkic** n. branch of Altaic family of languages, including Turkish —**Turkish bath** steam bath —**Turkish coffee** very strong black coffee —**Turkish delight** gelatin flavoured and coated with powdered sugar —**Turkish towel** rough, loose-piled towel

turmeric ('tɜːmərɪk) n. 1. Asian plant 2. powdered root of this used as dye, medicine and condiment

turmoil ('tɜːmɔɪl) n. confusion and bustle, commotion

turn (tɜːn) v. 1. move around, rotate 2. change, reverse, alter position or direction (of) —vi. 3. (oft. with into) change in nature, character etc. 4. (of milk) become rancid or sour —vt. 5. make, shape on lathe —n. 6. act of turning 7. inclination 8. period, spell 9. turning 10. short walk 11. (part of) rotation 12. performance —'**turner** n. —'**turning** n. road, path leading off main route —'**turnabout** n. 1. act of turning so as to face different direction 2. reversal of opinion etc. —'**turncoat** n. one who forsakes his party or principles —**turning circle** smallest circle in which vehicle can turn —**turning point** 1. moment when course of events is changed 2. point at which there is change in direction or motion —'**turnkey** n. obs. keeper of keys, esp. in prison; warder, jailer —**turn-off** n. 1. road etc. branching off from main thoroughfare 2. something or someone that turns one off —**turn-on** n. something or someone that turns one on —'**turnout** n. 1. number of people appearing for some purpose, occasion 2. way in which person is dressed, equipped —'**turnover** n. 1. total sales made by business over certain period 2. rate at which staff leave and are replaced 3. small pasty —'**turnpike** n. Hist. (gate across) road where toll was paid —'**turnstile** n. revolving gate for controlling admission of people —'**turnstone** n. shore bird that lifts up stones in search of food —'**turntable** n. revolving platform, esp. on record-player —**turn-up** n. 1. turned-up fold at bottom of trouser leg 2. unexpected or chance occurrence —**turn down** refuse —**turn off** 1. leave (road etc.) 2. (of road etc.) deviate from (another road etc.) 3. cause

(something) to cease operating by turning knob etc. 4. inf. cause (person etc.) to feel dislike or distaste for (something) —**turn on** 1. cause (something) to operate by turning knob etc. 2. depend or hinge on 3. become hostile; retaliate 4. inf. produce (charm etc.) suddenly or automatically 5. sl. arouse emotionally or sexually 6. sl. take or become intoxicated by drugs 7. sl. introduce to drugs —**turn up** 1. appear 2. be found 3. increase (flow, volume)

turnip ('tɜːnɪp) n. plant with globular root used as food

turpentine ('tɜːpˌntaɪn) n. 1. resin got from certain trees 2. oil, spirits made from this

turpitude ('tɜːpɪtjuːd) n. depravity

turps (tɜːps) turpentine

turquoise ('tɜːkwɔːz, -kwɑːz) n. 1. bluish-green precious stone 2. this colour —a. 3. bluish-green

turret ('tʌrɪt) n. 1. small tower 2. revolving armoured tower for guns on warship, tank etc.

turtle ('tɜːt'l) n. sea tortoise —'**turtleneck** n. 1. round high close-fitting neck on sweater 2. sweater itself

turtledove ('tɜːt'lˌdʌv) n. 1. Old World dove having brown plumage with speckled wings and long dark tail 2. gentle or loving person

tusk (tʌsk) n. long pointed side tooth of certain animals (eg elephant, wild boar etc.) —'**tusker** n. animal with tusks fully developed

tussle ('tʌs'l) n./vi. fight, wrestle, struggle

tussock ('tʌsək) n. 1. clump of grass 2. tuft —'**tussocky** a.

tutelage ('tjuːtɪlɪdʒ) n. act, office of tutor or guardian —'**tutelary** or '**tutelar** a.

tutor ('tjuːtə) n. 1. one teaching individuals or small groups —v. 2. teach thus —tu'**torial** n. period of instruction with tutor

tutti ('tutɪ) a./adv. Mus. to be performed by whole orchestra, choir etc.

tutti-frutti ('tuːtɪ'fruːtɪ) n. 1. ice cream or confection containing small pieces of candied or fresh fruits 2. preserve of chopped mixed fruits 3. flavour like that of many fruits combined

tutu ('tuːtuː) n. short, stiff skirt worn by ballerinas

tu-whit tu-whoo (tə'wɪt tə'wuː) imitation of sound made by owl

tuxedo (tʌk'siːdəʊ) n. US dinner jacket (pl. -s)

TV television

twaddle ('twɒd'l) n. silly talk

twain (tweɪn) n. obs. two —**in twain** asunder

twang (twæŋ) n. 1. vibrating metallic sound 2. nasal speech —v. 3. (cause to) make such sounds

tweak (twiːk) vt. 1. pinch and twist or pull —n. 2. a tweaking

twee (twiː) a. inf. excessively sentimental, sweet, pretty

tweed (twiːd) n. 1. rough-surfaced cloth used for clothing —pl. 2. suit of tweed —'**tweedy** a. 1. of tweed 2. showing fondness for hearty outdoor life, usu. associated with wearers of tweeds

tweet (twiːt) n./vi. chirp —'**tweeter** n. loudspeaker reproducing high-frequency sounds

tweezers ('twiːzəz) pl.n. small forceps or tongs

twelve (twelv) n./a. cardinal number two more than ten —**twelfth** a./n. ordinal number —**Twelfth Day** Jan. 6th, twelfth day after Christmas; feast of Epiphany —**twelve-tone** a. of type of serial music which uses as musical material tone row formed by 12 semitones of chromatic scale

twenty ('twenti) n./a. cardinal number, twice ten —'**twentieth** a./n. ordinal number

twerp or **twirp** (twɜːp) n. inf. silly person

twice (twais) adv. two times

twiddle ('twidᵊl) v. 1. fiddle —vt. 2. twist

twig¹ (twig) n. small branch, shoot

twig² (twig) v. inf. notice; understand (-**gg**-)

twilight ('twailait) n. soft light after sunset —'**twilit** a. —**twilight zone** 1. inner-city area where houses have become dilapidated 2. any indefinite or transitional condition or area

twill (twil) n. fabric woven so as to have surface of parallel ridges

twin (twin) n. 1. one of pair, esp. of two children born together —a. 2. being a twin —v. 3. pair, be paired —**twin-set** n. UK matching jumper and cardigan —**twin town** UK town that has civic associations with foreign town

twine (twain) v. 1. twist, coil round —n. 2. string, cord

twinge (twindʒ) n. 1. momentary sharp, shooting pain 2. qualm

twinkle ('twiŋkᵊl) vi. 1. shine with dancing or quivering light, sparkle —n. 2. twinkling 3. flash 4. gleam of amusement in eyes —'**twinkling** n. very brief time

twirl (twɜːl) v. 1. turn or twist round quickly 2. whirl —vt. 3. twiddle —n. 4. rotating; being rotated; whirl, twist 5. something wound around or twisted; coil 6. written flourish

twist (twist) v. 1. make, become spiral, by turning with one end fast 2. distort, change 3. wind —n. 4. thing twisted 5. dance popular in 1960s, in which dancers vigorously twist the hips —'**twister** n. inf. swindler —'**twisty** a.

twit (twit) n. 1. inf. foolish person —vt. 2. taunt (-**tt**-)

twitch (twitʃ) v. 1. give momentary sharp pull or jerk (to) —n. 2. such pull or jerk 3. spasmodic jerk, spasm

twitter ('twitə) vi. 1. (of birds) utter succession of tremulous sounds —n. 2. such succession of notes

two (tuː) n./a. cardinal number, one more than one —'**twofold** a./adv. —'**twosome** n.

1. two together, esp. two people 2. match between two people —**two-edged** a. 1. having two cutting edges 2. (esp. of remark) having two interpretations —**two-faced** a. 1. double-dealing, deceitful 2. with two faces —**twopence** or **tuppence** ('tʌpəns) n. UK 1. sum of two pennies 2. something of little value (esp. in **not care** or **give twopence**) 3. formerly, Brit. silver coin —**twopenny** or **tuppenny** ('tʌpəni) a. chiefly UK 1. cheap, tawdry (also **twopenny-halfpenny**) 2. worth two pence —**two-ply** a. 1. made of two layers, strands etc. —n. 2. two-ply knitting yarn etc. —**two-step** n. 1. ballroom dance in duple time 2. music for such dance —**two-stroke** a. (of internal-combustion engine) making one explosion to every two strokes of piston —**two-time** v. inf. deceive (someone, esp. lover) by carrying on relationship with another —**two-timer** n.

TX Texas

-ty¹ (comb. form) multiple of ten, as in sixty, seventy

-ty² (comb. form) state, condition, quality, as in cruelty

tycoon (tai'kuːn) n. powerful, influential businessman

tyke or **tike** (taik) n. 1. inf. small, cheeky child 2. small (mongrel) dog

tympani ('timpəni) pl.n. see TIMPANI

tympanum ('timpənəm) n. 1. cavity of middle ear 2. tympanic membrane 3. any diaphragm resembling that in middle ear in function 4. Archit. recessed space, esp. triangular, bounded by cornices of pediment 5. recessed space bounded by arch and lintel of doorway or window below it 6. Mus. drum 7. scoop wheel for raising water (pl. -s, -na (-nə)) —**tym'panic** a. —**tympanic membrane** thin membrane separating external ear from middle ear

Tynwald ('tinwəld, 'tain-) n. Parliament of Isle of Man

type (taip) n. 1. class, sort 2. model; pattern 3. characteristic build 4. specimen 5. block bearing letter used for printing 6. such pieces collectively —vt. 7. print with typewriter 8. typify 9. classify —'**typist** n. one who operates typewriter —'**typo** n. inf. error in typing —'**typecast** vt. cast (actor) in same kind of role continually —'**typeface** n. 1. printing surface of any type character 2. style or design of character on type (also **face**) —'**type-script** n. typewritten document or copy —'**typesetter** n. 1. person who sets type; compositor 2. typesetting machine —'**typewrite** v. —'**typewriter** n. keyed writing machine

-type (comb. form) 1. type, form, as in archetype 2. printing type; photographic process, as in collotype

typhoid ('taifoid) n. 1. acute infectious disease, affecting esp. intestines —a., also **ty'phoidal** 2. resembling typhus —'**typhus** n. infectious disease

typhoon (taɪˈfuːn) n. violent tropical storm or cyclone —**typhonic** (taɪˈfonɪk) a.

typical (ˈtɪpɪkˀl) or **typic** a. 1. true to type 2. characteristic —**ˈtypically** adv.

typify (ˈtɪpɪfaɪ) vt. serve as type or model of (-**ified**, -**ifying**)

typography (taɪˈpɒgrəfɪ) n. 1. art of printing 2. style of printing —**tyˈpographer** n. —**typoˈgraphical** a.

tyrannosaur (tɪˈrænəsɔː) or **tyrannosaurus** (tɪrænəˈsɔːrəs) n. large carnivorous two-footed dinosaur common in N Amer. in Upper Jurassic and Cretaceous times

tyrant (ˈtaɪrənt) n. 1. oppressive or cruel ruler 2. one who forces his will on others cruelly and arbitrarily —**tyrannical** (tɪˈrænɪkˀl) a. 1. despotic 2. ruthless —**tyrannically** (tɪˈrænɪkəlɪ) adv. —**tyrannicide** (tɪˈrænɪsaɪd) n. 1. slayer of tyrant 2. his deed —**tyrannize** or -**ise** (ˈtɪrənaɪz) v. exert ruthless or tyrannical authority (over) —**tyrannous** (ˈtɪrənəs) a. —**tyranny** (ˈtɪrənɪ) n. despotism

tyre or U.S. **tire** (taɪə) n. 1. (inflated) rubber ring over rim of road vehicle 2. metal band on rim of cart wheel

Tyrian (ˈtɪrɪən) n. 1. native of ancient Tyre, port in S Lebanon and centre of ancient Phoenician culture —a. 2. of ancient Tyre

tyro or **tiro** (ˈtaɪrəʊ) n. novice, beginner (pl. -**s**)

tzar (zɑː) n. see CZAR

tzetze fly (ˈtsɛtsɪ) see TSETSE FLY

U

u or **U** (juː) *n.* **1.** 21st letter of English alphabet **2.** any of several speech sounds represented by this letter, as in *mute, cut* or *minus* **3.** something shaped like U (*pl.* **u's, U's** or **Us**)

U 1. united **2.** unionist **3.** university **4.** UK universal (used to describe category of film certified as suitable for viewing by anyone) **5.** *Chem.* uranium

U.A.E. United Arab Emirates

UB40 *n.* UK **1.** registration card issued by Department of Employment to person registering as unemployed **2.** *inf.* person registered as unemployed

ubiquitous (juːˈbɪkwɪtəs) *a.* **1.** everywhere at once **2.** omnipresent —**uˈbiquity** *n.*

U-boat *n.* German submarine

u.c. *Print.* upper case

udder (ˈʌdə) *n.* milk-secreting organ of cow *etc.*

UDI Unilateral Declaration of Independence

UEFA (juːˈeɪfə, ˈjuːfə) Union of European Football Associations

UFO (*sometimes* ˈjuːfəʊ) unidentified flying object

ugh (ux, ʊh, ʌh) *interj.* exclamation of disgust, annoyance *etc.*

ugly (ˈʌglɪ) *a.* **1.** unpleasant or repulsive to the sight, hideous **2.** ill-omened **3.** threatening —**ˈuglify** *v.* —**ˈugliness** *n.* —**ugly duckling** person or thing, initially ugly or unprepossessing, that changes into something beautiful or admirable

UHF ultrahigh frequency

UHT ultra heat treated

U.K. United Kingdom

ukase (juːˈkeɪz) *n.* in imperial Russia, edict of Czar

Ukrainian (juːˈkreɪnɪən) *a.* **1.** of Ukraine —*n.* **2.** East Slavonic language of Ukrainians **3.** native or inhabitant of Ukraine

ukulele or **ukelele** (juːkəˈleɪlɪ) *n.* small four-stringed guitar, *esp.* of Hawaii

ulcer (ˈʌlsə) *n.* open sore on skin, mucous membrane that is slow to heal —**ˈulcerate** *v.* make, form ulcer(s) —**ˈulcerated** *a.* —**ulceˈration** *n.* —**ˈulcerous** *a.*

ulna (ˈʌlnə) *n.* longer of two bones of forearm (*pl.* **ulnae** (ˈʌlniː), **-s**)

ulster (ˈʌlstə) *n.* man's heavy double-breasted overcoat

ult. 1. ultimate **2.** ultimo

ulterior (ʌlˈtɪərɪə) *a.* **1.** lying beneath, beyond what is revealed or evident (*eg* motives) **2.** situated beyond

ultimate (ˈʌltɪmɪt) *a.* **1.** last **2.** highest **3.** most significant **4.** fundamental —**ˈultimately** *adv.* —**ultimatum** (ʌltɪˈmeɪtəm) *n.* **1.** final proposition **2.** final terms offered (*pl.* **-s, -ta** (-tə)) —**ˈultimo** *adv.* in last month

ultra (ˈʌltrə) *a.* **1.** extreme, *esp.* in beliefs or opinions —*n.* **2.** extremist

ultra- (*comb. form*) beyond, excessive(ly), extreme(ly) as in *ultramodern*

ultrahigh frequency (ˈʌltrəhaɪ) (band of) radio waves of very short wavelength

ultramarine (ʌltrəməˈriːn) *n.* blue pigment

ultrasonic (ʌltrəˈsɒnɪk) *a.* of sound waves beyond the range of human ear —**ultraˈsonics** *pl.n.* (*with sing. v.*) branch of physics concerned with ultrasonic waves (*also* **superˈsonics**)

ultrasound (ʌltrəˈsaʊnd) *n.* ultrasonic waves, used in cleaning metallic parts, echo sounding, medical diagnosis *etc.*

ultraviolet (ʌltrəˈvaɪəlɪt) *a.* of electromagnetic radiation, *eg* of sun *etc.*, beyond limit of visibility at violet end of spectrum

ululate (ˈjuːljʊleɪt) *vi.* howl, wail —**ˈululant** *a.* —**uluˈlation** *n.*

umbel (ˈʌmbəl) *n.* umbrellalike flower cluster with stalks springing from central point —**umbelˈliferous** *a.*

umber (ˈʌmbə) *n.* dark brown pigment

umbilical (ʌmˈbɪlɪkəl, ʌmbɪˈlaɪkəl) *a.* of (region of) navel —**umˈbilicus** *n.* **1.** *Biol.* hollow structure, such as cavity at base of gastropod shell **2.** *Anat.* navel (*pl.* **-bilici** (-ˈbɪlɪsaɪ, -bəˈlaɪsaɪ)) —**umbilical cord 1.** cordlike structure connecting foetus with placenta of mother **2.** cord joining astronaut to spacecraft *etc.*

umbra (ˈʌmbrə) *n.* **1.** region of complete shadow due to obstruction of light by opaque object, *esp.* shadow cast by moon onto earth during solar eclipse **2.** darker inner region of sunspot (*pl.* **-brae** (-briː), **-s**) —**ˈumbral** *a.*

umbrage (ˈʌmbrɪdʒ) *n.* offence, resentment (*esp. in* give *or* take umbrage)

umbrella (ʌmˈbrelə) *n.* **1.** folding circular cover of nylon *etc.* on stick, carried in hand to protect against rain, heat of sun **2.** anything shaped or functioning like an umbrella

umiak or **oomiak** (ˈuːmɪæk) *n.* Eskimo boat made of skins

umlaut (ˈʊmlaʊt) *n.* **1.** mark (¨) placed over vowel in some languages, such as German **2.** *esp.* in Germanic languages, change of vowel within word caused by assimilating influence of vowel or semivowel in preceding or following syllable

umpire (ˈʌmpaɪə) *n.* **1.** person chosen to decide question, or to decide disputes and enforce rules in a game —*v.* **2.** act as umpire in or for (game *etc.*)

umpteen (ʌmpˈtiːn) *a.* *inf.* many —**ˈumpteenth** *n./a.*

UN or **U.N.** United Nations

un- (*comb. form*) not, contrary to, opposite

of, reversal of an action, removal from, release, deprivation. See the list below

unaccountable (ʌnəˈkaʊntəbʲl) *a.* that cannot be explained

unaffected[1] (ʌnəˈfɛktɪd) *a.* unpretentious, natural, sincere —**unaf'fectedly** *adv.*

unaffected[2] (ʌnəˈfɛktɪd) *a.* not affected

unanimous (juːˈnænɪməs) *a.* 1. in complete agreement 2. agreed by all —**una'nimity** *n.* —**u'nanimously** *adv.*

unassailable (ʌnəˈseɪləbʲl) *a.* 1. able to withstand attack 2. irrefutable —**unas'sailably** *adv.*

unassuming (ʌnəˈsjuːmɪŋ) *a.* not pretentious, modest

unattached (ʌnəˈtætʃt) *a.* 1. not connected with any specific thing, group *etc.* 2. not engaged or married

unavailing (ʌnəˈveɪlɪŋ) *a.* useless, futile

unaware (ʌnəˈwɛə) *a.* not aware, uninformed —**una'wares** *adv.* 1. without previous warning 2. unexpectedly

unbend (ʌnˈbɛnd) *v.* 1. release or be released from restraints of formality 2. *inf.* relax (mind) or (of mind) become relaxed 3. make or become straight from original bent shape (-'bent, -'bending) —**un'bending** *a.* 1. rigid, inflexible 2. characterized by sternness or severity

unbidden (ʌnˈbɪdʲn) *a.* 1. not commanded; voluntary, spontaneous 2. not invited

unbosom (ʌnˈbuzəm) *vt.* tell or reveal (one's secrets *etc.*)

unbounded (ʌnˈbaʊndɪd) *a.* having no boundaries or limits —**un'boundedly** *adv.*

unbridled (ʌnˈbraɪdʲld) *a.* 1. with all restraints removed 2. (of horse *etc.*) wearing no bridle

unburden (ʌnˈbɜːdʲn) *vt.* 1. remove load or burden from 2. relieve, make free (one's mind, oneself *etc.*) of worry *etc.* by revelation or confession

uncalled-for *a.* unnecessary; unwarranted

uncanny (ʌnˈkænɪ) *a.* weird, mysterious

uncial (ˈʌnsɪəl) *a.* 1. of majuscule letters, as used in Greek and Latin manuscripts of third to ninth centuries, that resemble modern capitals but are more rounded —*n.* 2. uncial letter or manuscript —'**uncially** *adv.*

uncle (ˈʌŋkʲl) *n.* 1. brother of father or mother 2. husband of aunt

uncompromising (ʌnˈkɒmprəmaɪzɪŋ) *a.* not prepared to compromise —**un'compromisingly** *adv.*

unconscionable (ʌnˈkɒnʃənəbʲl) *a.* 1. unscrupulous, unprincipled 2. excessive

unconscious (ʌnˈkɒnʃəs) *a.* 1. insensible 2. not aware 3. not knowing 4. of thoughts, memories *etc.* of which one is not normally aware —*n.* 5. these thoughts —**un'consciously** *adv.* —**un'consciousness** *n.*

uncounted (ʌnˈkaʊntɪd) *a.* 1. innumerable 2. not counted

uncouth (ʌnˈkuːθ) *a.* 1. clumsy, boorish 2. without ease or polish

uncover (ʌnˈkʌvə) *vt.* 1. remove cover, top *etc.* from 2. reveal, disclose —*v.* 3. take off (one's head covering), *esp.* as mark of respect

unction (ˈʌŋkʃən) *n.* 1. anointing 2.

una'bated	un'bearable	un'clear
una'bridged	un'beaten	un'clothe
unac'ceptable	unbe'coming	un'cluttered
unac'companied	unbe'lievable	un'coil
unac'customed	unbe'liever	un'combed
unac'knowledged	unbe'lieving	un'comfortable
unac'quainted	un'bias(s)ed	uncom'mitted
una'dorned	un'bind	un'common
una'dulterated	un'blemished	uncom'municative
unad'venturous	un'blinking	uncom'plaining
una'fraid	un'block	un'complicated
un'aided	un'bolt	uncompli'mentary
unal'loyed	un'born	uncon'cerned
un'alterable	un'breakable	uncon'ditional
unam'biguous	un'broken	uncon'firmed
un'answerable	un'buckle	uncon'nected
unap'pealing	uncared-for	uncon'quered
un'appetizing	un'ceasing	uncon'trollable
unap'preciated	un'censored	uncon'trolled
unap'proachable	un'censured	uncontro'versial
un'armed	un'certain	uncon'ventional
una'shamed	un'challenged	uncon'vincing
un'asked	uncharacte'ristic	unco'operative
unat'tainable	un'charitable	unco'ordinated
unat'tended	un'checked	un'cork
unat'tractive	un'christian	uncor'roborated
un'authorized	un'circumcised	un'couple
una'vailable	un'civil	un'critical
un'balanced	un'claimed	un'crowned

excessive politeness **3.** soothing words or thoughts —**'unctuous** a. **1.** slippery, greasy **2.** oily in manner, ingratiating

undeceive (ʌndɪ'siːv) vt. reveal truth to (someone mistaken, misled)

under ('ʌndə) prep. **1.** below, beneath **2.** bound by, included in **3.** less than **4.** subjected to **5.** known by **6.** in the time of —adv. **7.** in lower place or condition —a. **8.** lower —**under way 1.** in progress **2.** Naut. in motion in direction headed

under- (comb. form) beneath, below, lower, too little, as in underground, underbid. Such words are not given where the meaning can be deduced from the meaning(s) of the simple word

underage (ʌndər'eɪdʒ) a. below required age, esp. below legal age for voting or drinking

undercarriage ('ʌndəkærɪdʒ) n. landing gear of aircraft

undercoat ('ʌndəkəʊt) n. coat of paint applied before top coat

undercover (ʌndə'kʌvə) a. done or acting in secret

undercurrent ('ʌndəkʌrənt) n. **1.** current that lies beneath another current **2.** opinion, emotion etc. lying beneath apparent feeling or meaning (also **'underflow**)

undercut (ʌndə'kʌt) v. **1.** charge less than (competitor) in order to obtain trade **2.** cut away under part of (something) **3.** Sport hit (ball) in such a way as to impart backspin —n. ('ʌndəkʌt) **4.** act of cutting underneath **5.** tenderloin of beef **6.** Sport stroke that imparts backspin to ball

underdeveloped (ʌndədɪ'vɛləpt) a. **1.** immature; undersized **2.** relating to societies lacking economical and industrial development necessary to advance **3.** Photog. (of film etc.) processed in developer for less than required time

underdog ('ʌndədɒg) n. **1.** losing competitor in contest etc. **2.** person in position of inferiority

underestimate (ʌndər'ɛstɪmeɪt) vt. **1.** make too low an estimate of **2.** think insufficiently highly of —n. (ʌndər'ɛstɪmɪt) **3.** too low an estimate —**underestima'tion** n.

underexpose (ʌndərɪk'spəʊz) vt. **1.** Photog. expose (film etc.) for too short a period or with insufficient light **2.** fail to

subject to appropriate publicity —**underex'posure** n.

undergo (ʌndə'gəʊ) vt. experience, endure, sustain (-'went, -'gone, -'going)

undergraduate (ʌndə'grædjʊt) n. student member of university or college who has not taken degree

underground ('ʌndəgraʊnd) a. **1.** under the ground **2.** secret —adv. (ʌndə'graʊnd) **3.** under earth's surface **4.** secretly —n. **5.** secret but organized resistance to government in power **6.** railway system under the ground

undergrowth ('ʌndəgrəʊθ) n. small trees, bushes etc. growing beneath taller trees in wood or forest

underhand ('ʌndəhænd) a. **1.** secret, sly **2.** Sport underarm

underlay (ʌndə'leɪ) vt. **1.** place (something) under or beneath **2.** support by something laid beneath (-'laid, -'laying) —n. ('ʌndəleɪ) **3.** lining, support etc. laid underneath something else **4.** felt, rubber etc. laid beneath carpet to increase insulation

underline (ʌndə'laɪn) vt. **1.** put line under **2.** emphasize

underling ('ʌndəlɪŋ) n. subordinate

underlying (ʌndə'laɪɪŋ) a. **1.** concealed but detectable **2.** fundamental; basic **3.** lying under

undermine (ʌndə'maɪn) vt. **1.** wear away base, support of **2.** weaken insidiously

underneath (ʌndə'niːθ) adv. **1.** below —prep. **2.** under —a. **3.** lower —n. **4.** lower part, surface etc.

underpass ('ʌndəpɑːs) n. section of road passing under another road, railway line etc.

underpin (ʌndə'pɪn) vt. **1.** support from beneath, esp. by prop **2.** give corroboration or support to (-nn-)

underprivileged (ʌndə'prɪvɪlɪdʒd) a. lacking rights and advantages of other members of society

underseal ('ʌndəsiːl) n. UK coating of tar etc., applied to underside of motor vehicle to retard corrosion

underside ('ʌndəsaɪd) n. bottom or lower surface

understand (ʌndə'stænd) v. **1.** know and comprehend **2.** realize —vt. **3.** infer **4.** take for granted (-'stood, -'standing) —**under'standable** a. —**under'standably** adv.

---

un'cultivated	unde'niable	under'nourish
un'cultured	undera'chieve	under'paid
un'curbed	under'bid v.	'underpants
un'curl	'underbid n.	'underpart
un'damaged	'underclothes	under'priced
un'daunted	under'do	under'sea
unde'cided	under'done	under'sexed
unde'feated	underem'ployed	'undershirt
unde'fended	under'foot	under'sized
unde'manding	'undergarment	'underskirt
undemo'cratic	under'lie	under'staffed
unde'monstrative	under'manned	

—**under'standing** n. 1. intelligence 2. opinion 3. agreement —a. 4. sympathetic

understudy ('ʌndəstʌdɪ) n. 1. one prepared to take over theatrical part from performer if necessary —vt. 2. act as understudy (to) or learn (part) thus

undertake (ʌndə'teɪk) vt. 1. make oneself responsible for 2. enter upon 3. promise (-'took, -'taken, -'taking) —'**undertaker** n. one who arranges funerals —'**undertaking** n. 1. that which is undertaken 2. project 3. guarantee

undertone ('ʌndətəʊn) n. 1. quiet, dropped tone of voice 2. underlying tone or suggestion

undertow ('ʌndətəʊ) n. 1. backwash of wave 2. current beneath surface moving in different direction from surface current

underwear ('ʌndəwɛə) n. garments worn next to skin (also '**underclothes**)

underworld ('ʌndəwɜːld) n. 1. criminals and their associates 2. Myth. abode of the dead

underwrite ('ʌndəraɪt, ʌndə'raɪt) vt. 1. agree to pay 2. accept liability in (insurance policy) (-'wrote, -'written, -'writing) —'**underwriter** n. 1. one that underwrites 2. agent for insurance company who assesses risks

undies ('ʌndɪz) pl.n. inf. women's underwear

undo (ʌn'duː) vt. 1. untie, unfasten 2. reverse 3. cause downfall of (-'did, -'done, -'doing) —un'**doing** n. —un'**done** a. 1. ruined 2. not performed

undoubted (ʌn'daʊtɪd) a. certain; indisputable —un'**doubtedly** adv.

undue (ʌn'djuː) a. 1. excessive 2. improper; illegal —un'**duly** adv. immoderately

undulate ('ʌndjʊleɪt) v. move up and down like waves —undu'**lation** n. —'**undulatory** a.

unearth (ʌn'ɜːθ) vt. 1. dig up 2. discover

unearthly (ʌn'ɜːθlɪ) a. 1. ghostly; eerie 2. heavenly; sublime 3. ridiculous or unreasonable (esp. in unearthly hour) —un'**earthliness** n.

uneasy (ʌn'iːzɪ) a. 1. anxious 2. uncomfortable

unemployed (ʌnɪm'plɔɪd) a. having no paid employment, out of work —unem'**ployment** n.

unerring (ʌn'ɜːrɪŋ) a. 1. not missing the mark 2. consistently accurate

UNESCO (juː'nɛskəʊ) United Nations Educational, Scientific and Cultural Organization

unexceptionable (ʌnɪk'sɛpʃənəbʰl) a. beyond criticism or objection —unex'**ceptionably** adv.

unexceptional (ʌnɪk'sɛpʃənʰl) a. 1. ordinary or normal 2. subject to or allowing no exceptions —unex'**ceptionally** adv.

unfortunate (ʌn'fɔːtʃənɪt) a. 1. causing or attended by misfortune 2. unlucky or unhappy 3. regrettable; unsuitable —n. 4. unlucky person —un'**fortunately** adv.

unfounded (ʌn'faʊndɪd) a. 1. (of ideas, allegations etc.) baseless 2. not yet established —un'**foundedly** adv.

unfrock (ʌn'frɒk) vt. deprive (person in holy orders) of ecclesiastical status

ungainly (ʌn'geɪnlɪ) a. awkward, clumsy

unguarded (ʌn'gɑːdɪd) a. 1. unprotected; vulnerable 2. open; frank 3. incautious

unguent ('ʌŋgwənt) n. ointment

ungulate ('ʌŋgjʊlɪt, -leɪt) n. any of large group of mammals all of which have hooves

unhinge (ʌn'hɪndʒ) vt. 1. remove (door etc.) from its hinges 2. unbalance (person, his mind etc.)

unholy (ʌn'həʊlɪ) a. 1. not holy or sacred 2.

under'state	un'equal	un'fortunate
under'value	un'equalled	un'founded
under'water	une'quivocal	un'freeze
under'weight	un'ethical	un'furl
unde'served	un'even	un'godly
unde'serving	une'ventful	un'governable
unde'sirable	unex'pected	un'gracious
unde'tected	unex'plained	ungram'matical
unde'terred	un'failing	un'grateful
unde'veloped	un'fair	un'hallowed
undi'minished	un'faithful	un'happy
un'disciplined	unfa'miliar	un'harmed
undis'covered	un'fashionable	un'healthy
undis'puted	un'favourable	un'heard
undis'turbed	un'feeling	unheard-of
un'drinkable	un'feigned	un'heated
un'dying	un'finished	un'heeded
un'earned	un'fit	un'helpful
un'eatable	un'flinching	un'hurried
uneco'nomic	un'fold	un'hurt
un'educated	unfore'seen	unhy'gienic
une'motional	unfor'gettable	
un'ending	unfor'givable	

immoral or depraved **3.** *inf.* outrageous; unnatural

uni- (*comb. form*) one, as in *unicorn, uniform.* Such words are not given here where the meanings may easily be inferred from the simple word

UNICEF (' juːnɪsɛf) United Nations International Children's Emergency Fund

unicellular (juːnɪ'sɛljʊlə) *a.* (of organisms and certain algae) consisting of single cell —**unicellu'larity** *n.*

unicorn ('juːnɪkɔːn) *n.* mythical horselike animal with single long horn

uniform ('juːnɪfɔːm) *n.* **1.** identifying clothes worn by members of same group, *eg* soldiers, nurses *etc.* —*a.* **2.** not changing, unvarying **3.** regular, consistent **4.** conforming to same standard or rule —**uni'formity** *n.* sameness —**'uniformly** *adv.*

unify ('juːnɪfaɪ) *v.* make or become one (-**ified, -ifying**) —**unifi'cation** *n.* —**Unification Church** religious sect founded by Rev. Sun Myung Moon, S Korean industrialist and religious leader

unilateral (juːnɪ'lætərəl) *a.* **1.** one-sided **2.** (of contract) binding one party only —**uni'laterally** *adv.*

unimpeachable (ʌnɪm'piːtʃəbªl) *a.* unquestionable as to honesty, truth *etc.*

union ('juːnjən) *n.* **1.** joining into one **2.** state of being joined **3.** result of being joined **4.** federation, combination of societies *etc.* **5.** trade union —**'unionism** *n.* —**'unionist** *n.* supporter of union —**'unionize** *or* **-nise** *v.* organize (workers) into trade union —**Union Jack** national flag of United Kingdom

unique (juː'niːk) *a.* **1.** being only one of its kind **2.** unparalleled

unisex ('juːnɪsɛks) *a.* of clothing, hair style, hairdressers *etc.* that can be worn or used by either sex

unison ('juːnɪsªn) *n.* **1.** *Mus.* singing *etc.* of same note as others **2.** agreement, harmony, concord

unit ('juːnɪt) *n.* **1.** single thing or person **2.** standard quantity **3.** group of people or things with one purpose —**Uni'tarian** *n.* member of Christian body that denies doctrine of the Trinity —**Uni'tarianism** *n.* —**'unitary** *a.* —**unit trust** UK investment

trust that issues units for public sale, holders of which are creditors with their interests represented by independent trust company

unite (juː'naɪt) *vt.* **1.** join into one, connect **2.** associate **3.** cause to adhere —*vi.* **4.** become one **5.** combine —**unity** *n.* **1.** state of being one **2.** harmony **3.** agreement, uniformity **4.** combination of separate parts into connected whole **5.** *Maths.* the number one —**United Empire Loyalist** American colonist who settled in Canada in War of Amer. Independence from loyalty to Britain —**United Kingdom** island of Great Britain together with Northern Ireland —**United Nations Organization** organization formed in 1945 to promote peace and international cooperation

Univ. University

univalent (juːnɪ'veɪlənt; juː'nɪvələnt) *a.* **1.** (of chromosome during meiosis) not paired with its homologue **2.** *Chem. see* MONOVALENT —**uni'valency** *n.*

universe ('juːnɪvɜːs) *n.* **1.** all existing things considered as constituting systematic whole **2.** the world —**uni'versal** *a.* **1.** relating to all things or all people **2.** applying to all members of a community —**univer'sality** *n.* —**uni'versally** *adv.* —**universal joint** *or* **coupling** form of coupling between two rotating shafts allowing freedom of movement in all directions

university (juːnɪ'vɜːsɪtɪ) *n.* educational institution for study, examination and conferment of degrees in various branches of learning

unjust (ʌn'dʒʌst) *a.* not in accordance with accepted standards of justice; unfair —**un'justly** *adv.*

unkempt (ʌn'kɛmpt) *a.* of rough or uncared-for appearance

unless (ʌn'lɛs) *conj.* except under the circumstances that

unloose (ʌn'luːs) *or* **unloosen** *vt.* **1.** release **2.** loosen (hold, grip *etc.*) **3.** unfasten, untie

unman (ʌn'mæn) *vt.* **1.** cause to lose nerve *etc.* **2.** make effeminate **3.** remove men from (-**nn-**)

uni'dentified	unin'tentional	un'likely
uni'maginable	un'interesting	un'limited
uni'maginative	uninter'rupted	un'lined
unim'paired	unin'vited	un'load
unim'portant	unin'viting	un'lock
unim'pressed	un'justified	unlooked-for
unin'formed	un'kind	un'lucky
unin'habited	un'known	un'made
unin'hibited	un'labelled	un'make
un'injured	un'ladylike	un'manageable
unin'spired	un'lawful	un'manned
unin'sured	un'learned	un'mannerly
unin'telligent	un'leash	un'marked
unin'telligible	un'lettered	un'married
unin'tended	un'like	

unmitigated (ʌnˈmɪtɪɡeɪtɪd) *a.* not diminished in intensity, severity *etc.*

unnatural (ʌnˈnætʃərəl) *a.* 1. abnormal 2. not in accordance with accepted standards of behaviour 3. uncanny; supernatural 4. affected, forced 5. inhuman, monstrous —**un'naturally** *adv.*

unnerve (ʌnˈnɜːv) *vt.* cause to lose courage, confidence *etc.*

U.N.O. United Nations Organization

unparalleled (ʌnˈpærəleld) *a.* unmatched; unequalled

unprincipled (ʌnˈprɪnsɪpˈld) *a.* lacking moral principles

unquote (ʌnˈkwəʊt) *interj.* expression used parenthetically to indicate that preceding quotation is finished

unravel (ʌnˈrævˈl) *vt.* undo, untangle (-ll-)

unread (ʌnˈred) *a.* 1. (of book *etc.*) not yet read 2. (of person) having read little

unregenerate (ʌnrɪˈdʒɛnərɪt) *a.* 1. unrepentant; unreformed 2. obstinately adhering to one's own views —**unre'generacy** *n.* —**unre'generately** *adv.*

unremitting (ʌnrɪˈmɪtɪŋ) *a.* never slackening or stopping

unrest (ʌnˈrest) *n.* troubled or rebellious state of discontent

unroll (ʌnˈrəʊl) *v.* 1. open out (something rolled or folded) or (of something rolled *etc.*) become unwound —*vi.* 2. become visible or apparent, *esp.* gradually

unruly (ʌnˈruːlɪ) *a.* badly behaved, ungovernable, disorderly

unsaturated (ʌnˈsætʃəreɪtɪd) *a.* 1. not saturated 2. (of chemical compound, *esp.* organic compound) containing one or more double or triple bonds and thus capable of undergoing addition reactions —**unsatu'ration** *n.*

unsavoury or *U.S.* **unsavory** (ʌnˈseɪvərɪ) *a.* distasteful, disagreeable

unsightly (ʌnˈsaɪtlɪ) *a.* ugly

unspeakable (ʌnˈspiːkəbˈl) *a.* incapable of expression in words 2. indescribably bad or evil 3. not to be uttered —**un'speakably** *adv.*

unstructured (ʌnˈstrʌktʃəd) *a.* without formal or systematic organization

unstrung (ʌnˈstrʌŋ) *a.* 1. emotionally distressed 2. (of stringed instrument) with strings detached

unstudied (ʌnˈstʌdɪd) *a.* 1. natural 2. (*with* in) without knowledge or training

unsung (ʌnˈsʌŋ) *a.* 1. not acclaimed or honoured 2. not yet sung

---

un'mask
un'mentionable
un'merciful
un'merited
unmis'tak(e)able
un'moved
un'musical
un'named
un'natural
un'necessary
un'noticed
unob'servant
unob'served
unob'tainable
unob'trusive
un'occupied
unof'ficial
un'opened
unop'posed
un'organized
un'orthodox
un'pack
un'paid
un'pardonable
un'pick
un'pin
un'playable
un'pleasant
un'pleasing
un'plumbed
un'popular
un'practised
unpre'cedented
unpre'dictable
unpre'pared
unprepos'sessing
unpre'tentious
un'printable

unpro'ductive
unpro'fessional
un'profitable
un'promising
unpro'pitious
unpro'tected
unpro'voked
un'qualified
un'questionable
un'real
unrea'listic
un'reasonable
un're'registered
unre'lenting
unre'liable
unre'pentant
unrepre'sentative
unre'quited
unre'served
unre'solved
unre'strained
un'righteous
un'ripe
un'rivalled
un'ruffled
un'saddle
un'safe
un'said
un'saleable
unsatis'factory
un'scathed
un'scheduled
unscien'tific
un'scramble
un'screw
un'scrupulous
un'seasonable
un'seat

un'seemly
unself'conscious
un'selfish
un'settle
un'shak(e)able
un'sheathe
un'skilful
un'skilled
un'sociable
un'social
unso'licited
un'solved
unso'phisticated
un'sound
un'sparing
un'specified
un'spoken
un'sporting
un'stable
un'steady
un'stinted
un'string
un'strung
unsub'stantiated
unsuc'cessful
un'suitable
un'sure
unsur'passed
unsus'pected
unsus'pecting
un'sweetened
unsympa'thetic
unsyste'matic
un'tainted
un'tamed
un'tangle

untenable (ʌnˈtɛnəb'l) *a.* (of theories *etc.*) incapable of being maintained, defended

unthinkable (ʌnˈθɪŋkəb'l) *a.* **1.** out of the question **2.** inconceivable **3.** unreasonable

untie (ʌnˈtaɪ) *v.* **1.** unfasten or free (knot or something that is tied) or (of knot *etc.*) become unfastened —*vt.* **2.** free from restriction (-ˈtied, -ˈtying)

until (ʌnˈtɪl) *conj.* **1.** to the time that **2.** (with a negative) before —*prep.* **3.** up to the time of

unto (ˈʌntuː) *prep. obs.* to

untold (ʌnˈtəʊld) *a.* **1.** incapable of description **2.** incalculably great in number or quantity **3.** not told

untouched (ʌnˈtʌtʃt) *a.* **1.** not touched **2.** not harmed —**unˈtouchable** *a.* **1.** not able to be touched —*n.* **2.** *esp.* formerly, non-caste Hindu, forbidden to be touched by one of caste

untoward (ʌntəˈwɔːd) *a.* awkward, inconvenient

unutterable (ʌnˈʌtərəb'l) *a.* incapable of being expressed in words —**unˈutterably** *adv.*

unwell (ʌnˈwɛl) *a.* not well, ill

unwieldy (ʌnˈwiːldɪ) *a.* **1.** awkward, big, heavy to handle **2.** clumsy

unwitting (ʌnˈwɪtɪŋ) *a.* **1.** not knowing **2.** not intentional

up (ʌp) *prep.* **1.** from lower to higher position **2.** along —*adv.* **3.** in or to higher position, source, activity *etc.* **4.** indicating completion (ˈupper *comp.*, ˈuppermost *sup.*) —ˈupward *a./adv.* —ˈupwards or ˈupward *adv.* —up-and-coming *a.* promising continued or future success; enterprising —ˈupˈhill *a.* **1.** inclining; sloping **2.** requiring protracted effort —*adv.* **3.** up incline or slope **4.** against difficulties —*n.* **5.** rising incline —**up time** time during which computer *etc.* actually operates —up-to-date *a.* modern; fashionable —**upwardly mobile** (of person or social group) moving or aspiring to move to higher class or status —**upward mobility** —**up against** confronted with

up- (*comb. form*) up, upper, upwards as in *uproot, upgrade.* Such words are not given here where the meaning may easily be inferred from the simple word

upbeat (ˈʌpbiːt) *n.* **1.** *Mus.* unaccented beat; upward gesture of conductor's baton indicating this —*a.* **2.** *inf.* cheerful; optimistic

upbraid (ʌpˈbreɪd) *vt.* scold, reproach

upbringing (ˈʌpbrɪŋɪŋ) *n.* rearing and education of children

update (ʌpˈdeɪt) *vt.* bring up to date

upfront (ˈʌpˈfrʌnt) *a.* **1.** open and frank —*adv./a.* **2.** (of money) paid out at beginning of business arrangement

upgrade (ʌpˈgreɪd) *vt.* **1.** promote to higher position **2.** improve

upheaval (ʌpˈhiːv'l) *n.* sudden or violent disturbance

uphold (ʌpˈhəʊld) *vt.* **1.** maintain **2.** support (upˈheld, upˈholding)

upholster (ʌpˈhəʊlstə) *vt.* fit springs, padding and coverings on (chairs *etc.*) —upˈholsterer *n.* —upˈholstery *n.*

upkeep (ˈʌpkiːp) *n.* act, process or cost of keeping something in good repair

upland (ˈʌplənd) *n.* high land

uplift (ʌpˈlɪft) *vt.* **1.** raise aloft **2.** *Scot.*, NZ collect; pick up (documents *etc.*) —*n.* (ˈʌplɪft) **3.** a lifting up **4.** mental, social or emotional improvement —*a.* (ˈʌplɪft) **5.** designating brassiere for lifting and supporting breasts

upon (əˈpɒn) *prep.* on

upper (ˈʌpə) *a. comp. of* UP **1.** higher, situated above —*n.* **2.** upper part of boot or shoe —ˈuppermost *a. sup. of* UP —**upper-case** *a.* of or relating to capital letters used in setting or production of printed or typed matter —ˈuppercut *n.* short-arm upward blow —**the upper hand** position of control

uppish (ˈʌpɪʃ) *a. inf.* **1.** self-assertive **2.** arrogant **3.** affectedly superior

upright (ˈʌpraɪt) *a.* **1.** erect **2.** honest, just —*adv.* **3.** vertically —*n.* **4.** thing standing upright, eg post in framework **5.** upright piano —**upright piano** piano with rectangular vertical case

uprising (ˈʌpraɪzɪŋ, ʌpˈraɪzɪŋ) *n.* rebellion, revolt

uproar (ˈʌprɔː) *n.* tumult, disturbance —upˈroarious *a.* rowdy —upˈroariously *adv.*

uproot (ʌpˈruːt) *vt.* **1.** pull up by or as if by the roots **2.** displace (person or persons) from native or habitual surroundings

unˈtapped	unˈtypical	unˈwept
unˈtaught	unˈusable	unˈwholesome
unˈtaxed	unˈused	unˈwilling
unˈthinking	unˈusual	unˈwind
unˈthrone	unˈutterable	unˈwise
unˈtidy	unˈvell	unˈworkable
unˈtimely	unˈverified	unˈworldly
unˈtrained	unˈvoiced	unˈworn
unˈtroubled	unˈwanted	unˈworthy
unˈtrue	unˈwarranted	unˈwrap
unˈtrustworthy	unˈwary	unˈwritten
unˈtruthful	unˈwashed	unˈyielding
unˈtutored	unˈwavering	unˈzip
unˈtwist	unˈwelcome	

upset (ʌp'sɛt) vt. **1.** overturn **2.** distress **3.** disrupt **4.** make ill (**up'set, up'setting**) —n. ('ʌpsɛt) **5.** unexpected defeat **6.** confusion **7.** trouble **8.** overturning

upshot ('ʌpʃɒt) n. outcome, end

upside down ('ʌpsaid) **1.** turned over completely; inverted **2.** in disorder or chaos

upsilon ('ʌpsilon) n. 20th letter in Gr. alphabet (Υ, υ), vowel transliterated as y or u

upstage ('ʌp'steidʒ) a. **1.** of back of stage —vt. **2.** inf. draw attention away from (another) to oneself

upstanding (ʌp'stændɪŋ) a. **1.** of good character **2.** upright and vigorous in build

upstart ('ʌpstɑ:t) n. one suddenly raised to wealth, power etc.

uptake ('ʌpteik) n. **1.** shaft etc. used to convey smoke or gases, esp. one that connects furnace to chimney **2.** lifting up —**quick** (or **slow**) **on the uptake** inf. quick (or slow) to understand or learn

uptight (ʌp'tait) a. inf. **1.** displaying tense nervousness, irritability **2.** repressed

upturn (ʌp'tɜ:n) v. **1.** turn or cause to turn over or upside down —vt. **2.** create disorder in **3.** direct upwards —n. ('ʌptɜ:n) **4.** upward trend or improvement

uranium (ju'reiniəm) n. white radioactive metallic element, used as chief source of nuclear energy

urban ('ɜ:b'n) a. relating to town or city —**'urbanize** or **-nise** vt. change (countryside) to residential or industrial area

urbane (ɜ:'bein) a. elegant, sophisticated —**urbanity** (ɜ:'bæniti) n.

urchin ('ɜ:tʃin) n. mischievous, unkempt child

Urdu ('uədu:, 'ɜ:-) n. official language of Pakistan, belonging to Indic branch of Indo-European family of languages, closely related to Hindi

urea ('juəriə) n. substance occurring in urine

ureter (ju'ri:tə) n. tube that conveys urine from kidney to urinary bladder or cloaca —**u'reteral** or **ureteric** (juəri'tɛrik) a.

urethra (ju'ri:θrə) n. canal conveying urine from bladder out of body (pl. -**thrae** (-θri:), -s)

urge (ɜ:dʒ) vt. **1.** exhort earnestly **2.** entreat **3.** drive on —n. **4.** strong desire —**'urgency** n. —**'urgent** a. **1.** pressing **2.** needing attention at once —**'urgently** adv.

urine ('juərin) n. fluid excreted by kidneys to bladder and passed as waste from body —**'uric** a. —**urinal** (ju'rain'l, 'juəri-) n. (place with) sanitary fitting(s) used by men for urination —**'urinary** a. —**'urinate** vi. discharge urine —**uri'nation** n.

urn (ɜ:n) n. **1.** vessel like vase, esp. for ashes of the dead **2.** large container with tap for making and dispensing tea, coffee etc.

urogenital (juərəu'dʒɛnit'l) or **urinogenital** a. of urinary and genital organs and their functions (also **genito'urinary**)

Ursa Major ('ɜ:sə 'meidʒə) extensive conspicuous constellation in N hemisphere. The seven brightest stars form Plough (also **the Great Bear, the Bear**)

Ursa Minor ('ɜ:sə 'mainə) small faint constellation, brightest star of which is Pole Star (also **the Little Bear, the Bear**)

ursine ('ɜ:sain) a. of, like a bear

us (ʌs) pron. pl. the objective case of WE

U.S. United States (of America)

use (ju:z) vt. **1.** employ, avail oneself of **2.** exercise **3.** exploit **4.** consume —n. (ju:s) **5.** employment, application to a purpose **6.** need to employ **7.** serviceableness **8.** profit **9.** habit —**'usable** or **'useable** a. fit for use —**usage** ('ju:sidʒ, -zidʒ) n. **1.** act of using **2.** custom **3.** customary way of using —**used** a. second-hand, not new —**useful** ('ju:sful) a. **1.** of use **2.** helpful **3.** serviceable —**usefully** ('ju:sfəli) adv. —**usefulness** ('ju:sfulnis) n. —**useless** ('ju:slis) a. —**uselessly** ('ju:slisli) adv. —**uselessness** ('ju:slisnis) n. —**user-friendly** a. (esp. of computer system) easily operated and understood —**used to** (ju:st) a. **1.** accustomed to —vt. **2.** did so formerly

usher ('ʌʃə) n. **1.** doorkeeper, one showing people to seats etc. (**ushe'rette** fem.) —vt. **2.** introduce, announce **3.** inaugurate

U.S.S.R. Union of Soviet Socialist Republics

usual ('ju:ʒuəl) a. habitual, ordinary —**'usually** adv. **1.** as a rule **2.** generally, commonly

usurp (ju:'zɜ:p) vt. seize wrongfully —**usur'pation** n. violent or unlawful seizing of power —**u'surper** n.

usury ('ju:ʒəri) n. **1.** lending of money at excessive interest **2.** such interest —**'usurer** n. money lender —**u'surious** a.

UT Utah

utensil (ju:'tɛnsəl) n. vessel, implement, esp. in domestic use

uterus ('ju:tərəs) n. womb (pl. **uteri** ('ju:tərai)) —**uterine** ('ju:tərain) a. of the uterus

utilidor (ju:'tilədə; Canad. -dɒr) n. C aboveground insulated casing for pipes

utility (ju:'tiliti) n. **1.** usefulness **2.** benefit **3.** useful thing —a. **4.** made for practical purposes —**utili'tarian** a. **1.** useful rather than beautiful **2.** of utilitarianism —n. **3.** believer in utilitarianism —**utili'tarianism** n. doctrine that morality of actions is to be tested by their utility, esp. that the greatest good of the greatest number should be the sole end of public action —**utili'zation** or **-li'sation** n. —**'utilize** or **-lise** vt. make use of —**utility room** room used for storage, laundry etc. —**utility truck A, NZ** small truck with open body and low sides

utmost ('ʌtməust) or **uttermost** a. **1.** to the highest degree **2.** extreme, furthest —n. **3.** greatest possible amount

Utopia (ju:'təupiə) n. (sometimes **u-**) imaginary state with perfect political and social conditions or constitution —**U'to-**

pian *a.* (*sometimes* **u-**) ideally perfect but impracticable

utter[1] ('ʌtə) *vt.* 1. express, emit audibly, say 2. put in circulation (forged banknotes, counterfeit coin) —'**utterance** *n.* 1. act of speaking 2. expression in words 3. spoken words

utter[2] ('ʌtə) *a.* complete, total, absolute —'**utterly** *adv.*

uttermost ('ʌtəməʊst) *see* UTMOST

U-turn *n.* 1. U-shaped turn by vehicle in order to go in opposite direction 2. reversal of political policy

U.V. ultraviolet

uvula ('juːvjʊlə) *n.* pendent fleshy part of soft palate (*pl.* **-lae** (-liː), **-s**) —'**uvular** *a.*

uxorious (ʌk'sɔːrɪəs) *a.* excessively fond of one's wife

V

v *or* **V** (viː) *n.* **1.** 22nd letter of English alphabet **2.** speech sound represented by this letter, as in *vote* **3.** something shaped like V (*pl.* **v's, V's** *or* **Vs**)

v volt

V *Chem.* vanadium

v. 1. verb **2.** verso **3.** versus **4.** very **5.** vide

V-1 *n.* flying robot bomb invented by Germans in World War II (*also* **'doodle-bug, 'buzzbomb'**)

VA Virginia

V.A. 1. Vicar Apostolic **2.** (Order of) Victoria and Albert

vacant ('veɪkənt) *a.* **1.** without thought, empty **2.** unoccupied —**'vacancy** *n.* **1.** state of being unoccupied **2.** unfilled post, accommodation *etc.* —**'vacantly** *adv.*

vacate (və'keɪt) *vt.* quit, leave empty —**va'cation** *n.* **1.** time when universities and law courts are closed **2.** US holidays **3.** act of vacating

vaccinate ('væksɪneɪt) *vt.* inoculate with vaccine as protection against a specific disease —**vacci'nation** *n.* —**'vaccinator** *n.* —**vaccine** ('væksiːn) *n.* any substance used for inoculation against disease

vacillate ('væsɪleɪt) *vi.* **1.** fluctuate in opinion **2.** waver **3.** move to and fro —**vacil'lation** *n.* **1.** indecision **2.** wavering **3.** unsteadiness

vacuum ('vækjʊəm) *n.* **1.** place, region containing no matter and from which all or most air, gas has been removed (*pl.* **-s, -ua** (-jʊə)) —*v.* **2.** clean with vacuum cleaner —**va'cuity** *n.* —**'vacuous** *a.* **1.** vacant **2.** expressionless **3.** unintelligent —**vacuum cleaner** apparatus for removing dust by suction —**vacuum flask** double-walled flask with vacuum between walls, for keeping contents of inner flask at temperature at which they were inserted —**vacuum-packed** *a.* packed in airtight container to maintain freshness *etc.* —**vacuum pump** pump for producing low gas pressure —**vacuum tube** *or* **valve** *see* **VALVE** (sense 3)

vade mecum ('vɑːdɪ 'meɪkʊm) handbook *etc.* carried on person for immediate use when needed

vagabond ('vægəbɒnd) *n.* **1.** person with no fixed home **2.** wandering beggar or thief —*a.* **3.** like a vagabond

vagary ('veɪgərɪ, və'gɛərɪ) *n.* **1.** something unusual, erratic **2.** whim

vagina (və'dʒaɪnə) *n.* passage from womb to exterior —**va'ginal** *a.*

vagrant ('veɪgrənt) *n.* **1.** vagabond, tramp —*a.* **2.** wandering, *esp.* without purpose —**'vagrancy** *n.*

vague (veɪg) *a.* **1.** indefinite, uncertain **2.** indistinct **3.** not clearly expressed **4.** absent-minded

vain (veɪn) *a.* **1.** conceited **2.** worthless,

useless **3.** unavailing **4.** foolish —**'vainly** *adv.*

vainglory (veɪn'glɔːrɪ) *n.* boastfulness, vanity —**vain'glorious** *a.*

valance ('væləns) *n.* short curtain round base of bed *etc.*

vale (veɪl) *n. Poet.* valley

valediction (vælɪ'dɪkʃən) *n.* farewell —**vale'dictory** *n.* **1.** farewell address —*a.* **2.** parting, farewell

valency ('veɪlənsɪ) *or esp. U.S.* **valence** ('veɪləns) *n. Chem.* combining power of element or atom

valentine ('væləntaɪn) *n.* (one receiving) card, gift, expressing affection on Saint Valentine's Day, Feb. 14th

valet ('vælɪt, 'væleɪ) *n.* gentleman's personal servant

valetudinarian (vælɪtjuːdɪ'nɛərɪən) *or* **valetudinary** (vælɪ'tjuːdɪnərɪ) *a.* **1.** sickly **2.** infirm —*n.* **3.** person obliged or disposed to live the life of an invalid

valiant ('væljənt) *a.* brave, courageous

valid ('vælɪd) *a.* **1.** sound **2.** capable of being justified **3.** of binding force in law —**va'lidity** *n.* **1.** soundness **2.** power to convince **3.** legal force —**'validate** *vt.* make valid

valise (və'liːz) *n.* travelling bag

valley ('vælɪ) *n.* **1.** low area between hills **2.** river basin

valour *or U.S.* **valor** ('vælə) *n.* bravery —**'valorous** *a.*

value ('væljuː) *n.* **1.** worth **2.** utility **3.** equivalent **4.** importance —*pl.* **5.** principles, standards —*vt.* **6.** estimate value of **7.** hold in respect **8.** prize —**'valuable** *a.* **1.** precious **2.** worthy **3.** capable of being valued —*n.* **4.** (*usu. pl.*) valuable thing —**valu'ation** *n.* estimated worth —**'valued** *a.* **1.** estimated; appraised **2.** highly thought of —**'valueless** *a.* worthless —**'valuer** *n.* —**value added tax** tax on difference between cost of basic materials and cost of article made from them —**value judgment** subjective assessment based on one's own values or those of one's class

valve (vælv) *n.* **1.** device to control passage of fluid *etc.* through pipe **2.** *Anat.* part of body allowing one-way passage of fluids **3.** part of radio or television which controls flow of current **4.** any of separable parts of shell of mollusc **5.** *Mus.* device on brass instrument for lengthening tube —**'valvular** *a.* of, like valves

vamoose (və'muːs) *vi. sl.* depart quickly

vamp¹ (væmp) *inf. n.* **1.** woman who deliberately allures men —*v.* **2.** exploit (man) as vamp

vamp² (væmp) *n.* **1.** something patched up (*also* **re'vamp**) **2.** front part of shoe upper —*vt.* **3.** patch up, rework

vampire ('væmpaɪə) *n.* in folklore, corpse

that rises from dead to drink blood of the living —**vampire bat** bat that sucks blood of animals

van[1] (væn) *n.* 1. covered vehicle, *esp.* for goods 2. railway carriage for goods and use of guard

van[2] (væn) *n.* vanguard

vanadium (və'neɪdɪəm) *n.* metallic element used in manufacture of hard steel

vandal ('vændˀl) *n.* one who wantonly and deliberately damages or destroys —**'vandalism** *n.* —**'vandalize** *or* **-lise** *vt.*

Vandyke beard ('vændaɪk) short pointed beard (*also* **'Vandyke**)

vane (veɪn) *n.* 1. weathercock 2. blade of propeller 3. fin on bomb *etc.* 4. sight on quadrant

vanguard ('vænɡɑːd) *n.* leading, foremost group, position *etc.*

vanilla (və'nɪlə) *n.* 1. tropical climbing orchid 2. its seed(pod) 3. essence of this for flavouring

vanish ('vænɪʃ) *vi.* 1. disappear 2. fade away —**vanishing cream** cosmetic cream that is colourless once applied, used as foundation or cleansing cream —**vanishing point** 1. point to which parallel lines appear to converge 2. point at which something disappears

vanity ('vænɪtɪ) *n.* 1. excessive pride or conceit 2. ostentation —**vanity case** *or* **box** woman's small hand case for carrying cosmetics *etc.*

vanquish ('væŋkwɪʃ) *vt.* 1. subdue in battle 2. conquer, overcome —**'vanquishable** *a.* —**'vanquisher** *n.*

vantage ('vɑːntɪdʒ) *n.* advantage

vapid ('væpɪd) *a.* flat, dull, insipid —**va'pidity** *n.*

vapour *or U.S.* **vapor** ('veɪpə) *n.* 1. gaseous form of a substance more familiar as liquid or solid 2. steam, mist 3. invisible moisture in air —**'vaporize** *or* **-rise** *v.* convert into, pass off in, vapour —**'vaporizer** *or* **-riser** *n.* —**'vaporous** *a.*

variable ('vɛərɪəbˀl) *see* VARY

varicose ('værɪkəʊs) *a.* (of vein) swollen, twisted

variegate ('vɛərɪɡeɪt) *vt.* diversify by patches of different colours —**'variegated** *a.* streaked, spotted, dappled —**varie'gation** *n.*

variety (və'raɪɪtɪ) *n.* 1. state of being varied or various 2. diversity 3. varied assortment 4. sort, kind

various ('vɛərɪəs) *a.* manifold, diverse, of several kinds

varlet ('vɑːlɪt) *n.* formerly, menial servant; rascal

varmint ('vɑːmɪnt) *n. inf.* obnoxious person or animal

varnish ('vɑːnɪʃ) *n.* 1. resinous solution put on a surface to make it hard and shiny —*vt.* 2. apply varnish to

varsity ('vɑːsɪtɪ) *n. UK inf.* university

vary ('vɛərɪ) *v.* (cause to) change, diversify, differ, deviate (**'varied**, **'varying**) —**varia'bility** *n.* —**'variable** *a.* 1.

changeable 2. unsteady; fickle —*n.* 3. something subject to variation —**'variance** *n.* state of discord, discrepancy —**'variant** *a.* 1. different —*n.* 2. difference in form 3. alternative form or reading —**vari'ation** *n.* 1. alteration 2. extent to which thing varies 3. modification —**vari-'ational** *a.* —**'varied** *a.* 1. diverse 2. modified 3. variegated

vas (væs) *n. Anat.* vessel, tube carrying bodily fluid (*pl.* **vasa** ('veɪsə)) —**vas deferens** ('dɛfərɛnz) duct within each testis that conveys spermatozoa to ejaculatory duct (*pl.* **vasa deferentia** (dɛfə-'rɛnʃɪə))

vascular ('væskjʊlə) *a.* of, with vessels for conveying sap, blood *etc.*

vase (vɑːz) *n.* vessel, jar as ornament or for holding flowers

vasectomy (væ'sɛktəmɪ) *n.* contraceptive measure of surgical removal of part of vas bearing sperm from testicle

Vaseline ('væsɪliːn) *n.* **R** jellylike petroleum product

vassal ('væsˀl) *n.* 1. holder of land by feudal tenure 2. dependant —**'vassalage** *n.*

vast (vɑːst) *a.* very large —**'vastly** *adv.* —**'vastness** *n.*

vat (væt) *n.* large tub, tank

VAT (*sometimes* væt) value added tax

Vatican ('vætɪkən) *n.* 1. Pope's palace 2. papal authority

vaudeville ('vəʊdəvɪl, 'vɔː-) *n.* theatrical entertainment with songs, juggling acts, dance *etc.*

vault[1] (vɔːlt) *n.* 1. arched roof 2. arched apartment 3. cellar 4. burial chamber 5. place for storing valuables —*vt.* 6. build with arched roof —**'vaulting** *n.* one or more vaults in building or such structures collectively

vault[2] (vɔːlt) *v.* 1. spring, jump over (object) with the hands resting on something —*n.* 2. such jump —**'vaulting** *a.* 1. excessively confident 2. used to vault

vaunt (vɔːnt) *v./n.* boast

vb. verb

V.C. 1. Vice Chairman 2. Vice Chancellor 3. Victoria Cross 4. Viet Cong

VCR 1. video cassette recorder 2. visual control room (at airfield)

VD venereal disease

VDU visual display unit

veal (viːl) *n.* calf flesh as food

vector ('vɛktə) *n.* 1. quantity (*eg* force) having both magnitude and direction 2. disease-carrying organism, *esp.* insect 3. compass direction, course

V-E Day day marking Allied victory in Europe in World War II (May 8th, 1945)

veer (vɪə) *vi.* 1. change direction 2. change one's mind

vegan ('viːɡən) *n.* strict vegetarian, who does not eat animal products

vegetable ('vɛdʒtəbˀl) *n.* 1. plant, *esp.* edible one 2. *inf.* person who has lost use of his mental faculties, limbs *etc.* 3. *inf.* dull person —*a.* 4. of, from, concerned with plants —**vegetable marrow** plant with long, green-striped fruit, eaten as vegetable —**vegetable oil** any of group of oils obtained from plants

vegetarian (vɛdʒɪ'tɛərɪən) n. 1. one who does not eat meat —a. 2. not eating meat; without meat —**vege'tarianism** n.

vegetate ('vɛdʒɪteɪt) vi. 1. (of plants) grow, develop 2. (of person) live dull, unproductive life —**vege'tation** n. 1. plants collectively 2. plants growing in a place 3. process of plant growth —**vegetative** ('vɛdʒɪtətɪv) a.

vehement ('viːmənt) a. 1. marked by intensity of feeling 2. vigorous 3. forcible —'**vehemence** n. —'**vehemently** adv.

vehicle ('viːɪk²l) n. 1. means of conveying 2. means of expression 3. medium —**vehicular** (vɪ'hɪkjʊlə) a.

veil (veɪl) n. 1. light material to cover face or head 2. mask, cover —vt. 3. cover with, as with, veil —**veiled** a. disguised —**take the veil** become a nun

vein (veɪn) n. 1. tube in body taking blood to heart 2. rib of leaf or insect's wing 3. fissure in rock filled with ore 4. streak 5. distinctive trait, strain etc. 6. mood —vt. 7. mark with streaks —'**veiny** a. —**venation** (viː'neɪʃən) n. 1. arrangement of veins in leaf etc. 2. such veins collectively —'**venous** a. of veins

Velcro ('vɛlkrəʊ) n. **R** fastening consisting of two strips of nylon fabric, one having tiny hooked threads and the other a coarse surface, that form strong bond when pressed together

veld or **veldt** (fɛlt, vɛlt) n. elevated grassland in S Afr. —**veldskoen** ('fɛltskʊn, 'vɛlt-) n. SA ankle-length boot orig. of raw hide

veleta or **valeta** (və'liːtə) n. ballroom dance in triple time

vellum ('vɛləm) n. 1. parchment of calfskin used for manuscripts or bindings 2. paper resembling this

velocipede (vɪ'lɒsɪpiːd) n. early form of bicycle

velocity (vɪ'lɒsɪtɪ) n. 1. rate of motion in given direction, esp. of inanimate things 2. speed

velodrome ('viːlədrəʊm, 'vɛl-) n. area with banked track for cycle racing

velours or **velour** (vɛ'lʊə) n. fabric with velvety finish

velum ('viːləm) n. 1. Zool. membranous covering or organ 2. soft palate (pl. **vela** ('viːlə))

velvet ('vɛlvɪt) n. silk or cotton fabric with thick, short pile —**velve'teen** n. cotton fabric resembling velvet —'**velvety** a. 1. of, like velvet 2. soft and smooth

vena cava ('viːnə 'keɪvə) either of two large veins that convey oxygen-depleted blood to heart (pl. **venae cavae** ('viːniː 'keɪviː))

venal ('viːn²l) a. 1. guilty of taking, prepared to take, bribes 2. corrupt —**ve'nality** n.

vend (vɛnd) vt. sell —'**vendible** a. 1. saleable, marketable —n. 2. (usu. pl.) rare saleable object —'**vendor** n. —**vending machine** machine that automatically dispenses goods when money is inserted

vendetta (vɛn'dɛtə) n. bitter, prolonged feud

veneer (vɪ'nɪə) n. 1. thin layer of fine wood 2. superficial appearance —vt. 3. cover with veneer

venerable ('vɛnərəb²l) a. worthy of reverence —'**venerate** vt. look up to, respect, revere —**vener'ation** n.

venereal (vɪ'nɪərɪəl) a. 1. (of disease) transmitted by sexual intercourse 2. infected with venereal disease 3. of genitals or sexual intercourse

venery[1] ('vɛnərɪ, 'viː-) n. obs. pursuit of sexual gratification

venery[2] ('vɛnərɪ, 'viː-) n. Hist. art, practice of hunting

Venetian (vɪ'niːʃən) a. 1. of Venice, port in NE Italy —n. 2. native or inhabitant of Venice —**Venetian blind** window blind made of thin horizontal slats arranged to turn so as to admit or exclude light

vengeance ('vɛndʒəns) n. 1. revenge 2. retribution for wrong done —'**vengeful** a.

venial ('viːnɪəl) a. pardonable

venison ('vɛnɪz²n, -s²n) n. flesh of deer as food

venom ('vɛnəm) n. 1. poison 2. spite —'**venomous** a. poisonous

venous ('viːnəs) a. see VEIN

vent[1] (vɛnt) n. 1. small hole or outlet —vt. 2. give outlet to 3. utter 4. pour forth

vent[2] (vɛnt) n. vertical slit in garment, esp. at back of jacket

ventilate ('vɛntɪleɪt) vt. 1. supply with fresh air 2. bring into discussion —**venti'lation** n. —'**ventilator** n.

ventral ('vɛntrəl) a. abdominal

ventricle ('vɛntrɪk²l) n. cavity, hollow in body, esp. in heart or brain —**ven'tricular** a.

ventriloquist (vɛn'trɪləkwɪst) n. one who can so speak that the sounds seem to come from some other person or place —**ven'triloquism** n.

venture ('vɛntʃə) vt. 1. expose to hazard 2. risk —vi. 3. dare 4. have courage (to do something or go somewhere) —n. 5. risky undertaking 6. speculative commercial undertaking —'**venturesome** or '**venturous** a.

venue ('vɛnjuː) n. 1. Law district in which case is tried 2. meeting place 3. location

Venus ('viːnəs) n. 1. Roman goddess of love 2. planet between earth and Mercury —**Venus's flytrap** insect-eating plant

veracious (vɛ'reɪʃəs) a. 1. truthful 2. true —**veracity** (vɛ'ræsɪtɪ) n.

veranda or **verandah** (və'rændə) n. open or partly enclosed porch on outside of house

verb (vɜːb) n. part of speech used to express action or being —'**verbal** a. 1. of, by, or relating to words spoken rather than written **2.** of, like a verb —'**verbalism** n. **1.** verbal expression; phrase; word **2.** exaggerated emphasis on importance of words **3.** statement lacking real content —'**verbalize** or **-lise** vt. **1.** put into words —vi. **2.** speak —'**verbally** adv. —**verbatim** (vɜː'beɪtɪm) adv./a. word for word, literal(ly) —**verbal noun** noun derived from verb

verbascum (vɜː'bæskəm) n. perennial garden plant

verbena (vɜː'biːnə) n. **1.** genus of fragrant, beautiful plants **2.** their characteristic scent

verbiage ('vɜːbɪɪdʒ) n. excess of words —**verbose** (vɜː'bəʊs) a. wordy, longwinded —**verbosity** (vɜː'bɒsɪtɪ) n.

verdant ('vɜːdˀnt) a. green and fresh —'**verdure** n. **1.** greenery **2.** freshness —'**verdurous** a.

verdict ('vɜːdɪkt) n. **1.** decision of a jury **2.** opinion reached after examination of facts

verdigris ('vɜːdɪɡrɪs) n. green film on copper

verdure ('vɜːdʒə) n. see VERDANT

verge (vɜːdʒ) n. **1.** edge **2.** brink **3.** grass border along a road —vi. **4.** (with on) come close (to) **5.** (sometimes with on) be on the border (of)

verger ('vɜːdʒə) n. **1.** caretaker and attendant in church **2.** bearer of wand of office

verify ('vɛrɪfaɪ) vt. **1.** prove, confirm truth of **2.** test accuracy of (**-ified, -ifying**) —'**verifiable** a. —**verifi'cation** n.

verily ('vɛrɪlɪ) adv. obs. **1.** truly **2.** in truth

verisimilitude (vɛrɪsɪ'mɪlɪtjuːd) n. **1.** appearance of truth **2.** likelihood —**veri'similar** a. probable; likely

veritable ('vɛrɪtəbˀl) a. actual, true, genuine —'**veritably** adv.

verity ('vɛrɪtɪ) n. **1.** truth **2.** reality **3.** true assertion

verkrampte (fə'kramtə) n. SA Afrikaner Nationalist opposed to liberal trends in government policy, particularly those related to race

verligte (fə'lɒxtə) n. SA member of any white political party who supports more liberal trends in government policy

vermi- (comb. form) worm, as in vermicide, vermiform, vermifuge

vermicelli (vɜːmɪ'sɛlɪ, -'tʃɛlɪ) n. **1.** pasta in fine strands, used in soups **2.** tiny chocolate strands used to coat cakes etc.

vermicide ('vɜːmɪsaɪd) n. substance to destroy worms —**ver'micular** a. **1.** resembling form, motion or tracks of worms **2.** of worms —'**vermiform** a. shaped like a worm (eg **vermiform appendix**)

vermilion (və'mɪljən) a./n. (of) bright red colour or pigment

vermin ('vɜːmɪn) n. (with pl. v.) injurious animals, parasites etc. —'**verminous** a.

vermouth ('vɜːməθ) n. wine flavoured with aromatic herbs etc.

vernacular (və'nækjʊlə) n. **1.** commonly spoken language or dialect of particular country or place —a. **2.** of vernacular **3.** native

vernal ('vɜːnˀl) a. of spring

vernier ('vɜːnɪə) n. sliding scale for obtaining fractional parts of subdivision of graduated scale

veronica (və'rɒnɪkə) n. genus of plants including speedwell

verruca (vɛ'ruːkə) n. wart, esp. on foot

versatile ('vɜːsətaɪl) a. **1.** capable of or adapted to many different uses, skills etc. **2.** liable to change —**versatility** (vɜːsə'tɪlɪtɪ) n.

verse (vɜːs) n. **1.** stanza or short subdivision of poem or the Bible **2.** poetry **3.** line of poetry —**versifi'cation** n. —'**versify** v. turn (something) into verse (**-ified, -ifying**) —**versed** in skilled in

version ('vɜːʃən) n. **1.** description from certain point of view **2.** translation **3.** adaptation

verso ('vɜːsəʊ) n. back of sheet of printed paper, left-hand page (pl. **-s**)

versus ('vɜːsəs) prep. against

vertebra ('vɜːtɪbrə) n. single section of backbone (pl. **-brae** (-briː), **-s**) —'**vertebral** a. of the spine —'**vertebrate** n. **1.** animal with backbone —a. **2.** having a backbone

vertex ('vɜːtɛks) n. summit (pl. **-es**, **vertices** ('vɜːtɪsiːz))

vertical ('vɜːtɪkˀl) a. **1.** at right angles to the horizon **2.** upright **3.** overhead

vertigo ('vɜːtɪɡəʊ) n. giddiness (pl. **-es**, **vertigines** (vɜː'tɪdʒɪniːz)) —**vertiginous** (vɜː'tɪdʒɪnəs) a. dizzy

vertu (vɜː'tuː) n. see VIRTU

verve (vɜːv) n. **1.** enthusiasm **2.** spirit **3.** energy, vigour

very ('vɛrɪ) a. **1.** exact, ideal **2.** same **3.** complete **4.** actual —adv. **5.** extremely, to great extent —**very high frequency** radio frequency or band lying between 300 and 30 megahertz —**very low frequency** radio frequency band or radio frequency lying between 30 and 3 kilohertz

vesicle ('vɛsɪkˀl) n. small blister, bubble or cavity —**ve'sicular** a.

vespers ('vɛspəz) n. **1.** evening church service **2.** evensong

vessel ('vɛsˀl) n. **1.** any object used as container, esp. for liquids **2.** ship, large boat **3.** tubular structure conveying liquids (eg blood) in body

vest (vɛst) n. **1.** undergarment for the trunk —vt. **2.** place **3.** bestow **4.** confer **5.** clothe —'**vestment** n. robe or official garment —**vested interest** strong personal interest in particular state of affairs

vestal ('vɛstˀl) a. pure, chaste —**vestal virgin** in ancient Rome, one of virgin priestesses whose lives were dedicated to Vesta and to maintaining sacred fire in her temple

vestibule ('vɛstɪbjuːl) n. entrance hall, lobby

vestige ('vɛstɪdʒ) *n.* small trace, amount —**ves'tigial** *a.*

vestry ('vɛstrɪ) *n.* room in church for keeping vestments, holding meetings *etc.*

vet (vɛt) *n.* **1.** veterinary surgeon —*vt.* **2.** examine **3.** check (**-tt-**)

vet. 1. veteran **2.** veterinary

vetch (vɛtʃ) *n.* plant of bean family

veteran ('vɛtərən) *n.* **1.** one who has served a long time, *esp.* in fighting services —*a.* **2.** long-serving —**veteran car** UK car constructed before 1919, *esp.* before 1905

veterinary ('vɛtərɪnərɪ) *a.* of, concerning the health of animals —**veterinary surgeon** surgeon qualified to treat animal ailments

veto ('viːtəʊ) *n.* **1.** power of rejecting piece of legislation or preventing it from coming into effect **2.** any prohibition (*pl.* -es) —*vt.* **3.** enforce veto against **4.** forbid with authority

vex (vɛks) *vt.* **1.** annoy **2.** distress —**vex'ation** *n.* **1.** cause of irritation **2.** state of distress —**vex'atious** *a.* —**vexed** *a.* **1.** cross, annoyed **2.** much discussed

VHF *or* **vhf** very high frequency

V.I. Vancouver Island

via ('vaɪə) *prep.* by way of

viable ('vaɪəb'l) *a.* **1.** practicable **2.** able to live and grow independently —**via'bility** *n.*

viaduct ('vaɪədʌkt) *n.* bridge over valley for a road or railway

vial ('vaɪəl) *n. see* PHIAL

viands ('viːəndz) *pl.n.* food

viaticum (vaɪ'ætɪkəm) *n.* **1.** Holy Communion as administered to person dying or in danger of death **2.** *rare* provisions or travel allowance for journey (*pl.* **-ca** (-kə), -s)

vibes (vaɪbz) *pl.n. inf.* **1.** vibrations **2.** vibraphone

vibraphone ('vaɪbrəfəʊn) *n.* musical instrument like xylophone, but with electronic resonators, that produces a gentle vibrato

vibrate (vaɪ'breɪt) *v.* **1.** (cause to) move to and fro rapidly and continuously **2.** give off (light or sound) by vibration —*vi.* **3.** oscillate **4.** quiver —**'vibrant** *a.* **1.** throbbing **2.** vibrating **3.** appearing vigorous, lively —**vi'bration** *n.* **1.** a vibrating —*pl.* **2.** *inf.* instinctive feelings about a place, person *etc.* —**vibrato** (vɪ'brɑːtəʊ) *n.* vibrating effect in music (*pl.* -s) —**vi'brator** *n.* —**'vibratory** *a.*

viburnum (vaɪ'bɜːnəm) *n.* subtropical shrub with white flowers and berrylike fruits

Vic. A Victoria (state)

vicar ('vɪkə) *n.* clergyman in charge of parish —**'vicarage** *n.* vicar's house —**vicarial** (vɪ'kɛərɪəl) *a.* of vicar —**vicar apostolic** *R.C. Ch.* titular bishop having jurisdiction in missionary countries —**vicar general** official appointed to assist bishop of diocese in administrative or judicial duties (*pl.* **vicars general**) —**Vicar of Christ** *R.C.Ch.* the Pope

vicarious (vɪ'kɛərɪəs, vaɪ-) *a.* **1.** obtained, enjoyed or undergone at second hand through sympathetic participation in another's experiences **2.** suffered, done *etc.* as substitute for another —**vi'cariously** *adv.*

vice¹ (vaɪs) *n.* **1.** evil or immoral habit or practice **2.** criminal immorality, *esp.* prostitution **3.** fault, imperfection —**vice squad** police division which deals with enforcement of gaming and prostitution laws

vice² *or U.S.* (*oft.*) **vise** (vaɪs) *n.* appliance with screw jaw for holding things while working on them

vice³ (vaɪs) *n. inf.* person who serves as deputy to another

vice- (*comb. form*) in place of, second to, as in *vice-chairman*, *viceroy*. Such compounds are not given here where meaning may be inferred from simple word

vice admiral commissioned officer of flag rank in certain navies, junior to admiral and senior to rear admiral

vicegerent (vaɪs'dʒɛrənt) *n.* **1.** person appointed to exercise all or some of authority of another **2.** *R.C.Ch.* representative of God or Christ on earth, such as pope —*a.* **3.** invested with or characterized by delegated authority —**vice'gerency** *n.*

vice president officer ranking immediately below president and serving as his deputy —**vice-presidency** *n.*

viceroy ('vaɪsrɔɪ) *n.* ruler acting for king in province or dependency (**vicereine** (vaɪs'reɪn) *fem.*) —**vice'regal** *a.* of viceroy —**vice'royalty** *n.*

vice versa ('vaɪsɪ 'vɜːsə) *Lat.* conversely, the other way round

vichy water ('viʃɪ) **1.** (*sometimes* V-) mineral water from Vichy in France, reputed to be beneficial to health **2.** any sparkling mineral water resembling this

vicinage ('vɪsɪnɪdʒ) *n. rare* **1.** residents of particular neighbourhood **2.** vicinity

vicinity (vɪ'sɪnɪtɪ) *n.* neighbourhood

vicious ('vɪʃəs) *a.* **1.** wicked, cruel **2.** ferocious, dangerous **3.** leading to vice —**'viciously** *adv.* —**vicious circle 1.** situation in which attempt to resolve one problem creates new problems that lead back to original situation **2.** *Logic* invalid form of reasoning in which conclusion is derived from premiss orig. deduced from same conclusion **3.** *Logic* circular definition

vicissitude (vɪ'sɪsɪtjuːd) *n.* **1.** change of fortune —*pl.* **2.** ups and downs of fortune —**vicissi'tudinous** *a.*

victim ('vɪktɪm) *n.* **1.** person or thing killed, injured *etc.* as result of another's deed, or accident, circumstances *etc.* **2.** person cheated **3.** sacrifice —**victimi'zation** *or* **-mi'sation** *n.* —**'victimize** *or* **-mise** *vt.* **1.** punish unfairly **2.** make victim of

victor ('vɪktə) *n.* **1.** conqueror **2.** winner

—**vic'torious** a. 1. winning 2. triumphant —**'victory** n. winning of battle etc.

victoria (vɪk'tɔːrɪə) n. 1. four-wheeled horse-drawn carriage with folding hood 2. UK large sweet plum, red and yellow in colour (also **victoria plum**)

Victorian (vɪk'tɔːrɪən) a. 1. of Victoria, queen of Great Brit. and Ireland, or period of her reign 2. exhibiting characteristics popularly attributed to Victorians, esp. prudery etc. 3. of Victoria (state in Aust. or any of the cities) —n. 4. person who lived during reign of Queen Victoria 5. inhabitant of Victoria (state or any of the cities) —**Victoria Cross** highest decoration for gallantry in face of enemy awarded to Brit. and Commonwealth armed forces —**Victoria Day** Monday preceding May 24th: national holiday in Canad. in commemoration of Queen Victoria's birthday

victual (ˈvɪtʰl) n. 1. (usu. pl.) food —v. 2. supply with or obtain food (**-ll-**) —**'victualler** n.

vicuña (vɪ'kjuːnə, -'kuːnjə) n. 1. S Amer. animal like llama 2. fine, light cloth made from its wool

vide (ˈvaɪdɪ) Lat. see —**vide infra** see below —**vide supra** see above

videlicet (vɪ'diːlɪsɛt) Lat. namely

video (ˈvɪdɪəʊ) a. 1. relating to or used in transmission or production of television image —n. 2. film recorded on video cassette 3. video cassette (recorder) (pl. **videos**) —v. 4. record (television programme etc.) on video cassette recorder (**'videoed, 'videoing**) —**video cassette** cassette containing video tape —**video cassette recorder** tape recorder for vision and sound signals using magnetic tape in closed plastic cassettes: used for recording and playing back television programmes and films —**video disc** or **'videodisc** n. disc stored with information, which one plays like a gramophone record, the result being translated, in sound and vision, on to TV set —**video nasty** film, usu. specially made for video, that is explicitly horrific and pornographic —**'videophone** n. telephonic device in which there is both verbal and visual communication between parties —**video tape** magnetic tape on which to record television programme

vie (vaɪ) vi. (with with or for) contend, compete (against or for someone, something) (**vied, 'vying**)

Vietnamese (vjɛtnəˈmiːz) a. 1. of Vietnam, in SE Asia —n. 2. native of Vietnam (pl. **-ese**) 3. language of Vietnam

view (vjuː) n. 1. survey by eyes or mind 2. range of vision 3. picture 4. scene 5. opinion 6. purpose —vt. 7. look at 8. survey 9. consider —**'viewer** n. 1. one who views 2. one who watches television 3. optical device to assist viewing of photographic slides —**'viewfinder** n. device on camera enabling user to see what will be included in photograph —**'viewpoint** n. 1. way of

regarding a subject 2. position commanding view of landscape

viewdata (ˈvjuːdeɪtə) n. see TELETEXT

vigil (ˈvɪdʒɪl) n. 1. a keeping awake, watch 2. eve of feast day —**'vigilance** n. —**'vigilant** a. watchful, alert —**vigilance committee** US self-appointed body of citizens organized to maintain order etc.

vigilante (vɪdʒɪˈlæntɪ) n. one, esp. as member of group, who unofficially takes it upon himself to enforce law

vignette (vɪ'njɛt) n. 1. short literary essay, sketch 2. photograph or portrait with the background shaded off

vigour or U.S. **vigor** (ˈvɪgə) n. 1. force, strength 2. energy, activity —**'vigorous** a. 1. strong 2. energetic 3. flourishing —**'vigorously** adv.

Viking (ˈvaɪkɪŋ) n. medieval Scandinavian seafarer, raider, settler

vile (vaɪl) a. 1. very wicked, shameful 2. disgusting 3. despicable —**'vilely** adv. —**'vileness** n. —**vilification** (vɪlɪfɪ'keɪʃən) n. —**vilify** (ˈvɪlɪfaɪ) vt. 1. speak ill of 2. slander (**-ified, -ifying**)

villa (ˈvɪlə) n. 1. large, luxurious, country house 2. detached or semidetached suburban house

village (ˈvɪlɪdʒ) n. small group of houses in country area —**'villager** n.

villain (ˈvɪlən) n. 1. wicked person 2. inf. mischievous person —**'villainous** a. 1. wicked 2. vile —**'villainy** n.

villein (ˈvɪlən) n. in medieval Europe, peasant personally bound to his lord, to whom he paid dues and services in return for land —**'villeinage** n.

vim (vɪm) n. inf. force, energy

vinaigrette (vɪneɪ'grɛt) n. 1. small bottle of smelling salts 2. type of salad dressing

vinculum (ˈvɪŋkjʊləm) n. 1. line drawn above group of mathematical terms, used as sign of aggregation in mathematical expressions, as in $x + y$ 2. Anat. bandlike structure, esp. uniting two or more parts (pl. **-la** (-lə))

vindicate (ˈvɪndɪkeɪt) vt. 1. clear of charges 2. justify 3. establish the truth or merit of —**'vindicable** a. capable of being vindicated; justifiable —**vindi'cation** n. —**'vindicator** n. —**vindicatory** a.

vindictive (vɪn'dɪktɪv) a. 1. revengeful 2. inspired by resentment

vine (vaɪn) n. climbing plant bearing grapes —**'vinery** n. 1. hothouse for growing grapes 2. vineyard 3. vines collectively —**vinosity** (vɪ'nɒsɪtɪ) n. distinctive and essential quality and flavour of wine —**vintage** (ˈvɪntɪdʒ) n. 1. gathering of the grapes 2. the yield 3. wine of particular year 4. time of origin —a. 5. best and most typical —**vintner** (ˈvɪntnə) n. dealer in wine —**vintage car** chiefly UK old car, esp. constructed between 1919 and 1930 —**vineyard** (ˈvɪnjəd) n. plantation of vines

vinegar (ˈvɪnɪgə) n. acid liquid obtained from wine and other alcoholic liquors

—'**vinegary** *a.* 1. like vinegar 2. sour 3. bad-tempered

vingt-et-un (vĕte' œ̃) *Fr. see* PONTOON²

vini- *or before vowel* **vin-** (*comb. form*) wine, as in viniculture

viniculture ('vɪnɪkʌltʃə) *n.* process or business of growing grapes and making wine

vinyl ('vaɪnɪl) *n.* plastic material with variety of domestic and industrial uses

viol ('vaɪəl) *n.* early stringed instrument preceding violin —'**violist** *n.* person who plays viol

viola¹ (vɪ'əʊlə) *n. see* VIOLIN

viola² ('vaɪələ, vaɪ'əʊ-) *n.* single-coloured variety of pansy

violate ('vaɪəleɪt) *vt.* 1. break (law, agreement *etc.*), infringe 2. rape 3. outrage, desecrate —'**violable** *a.* —**vio'lation** *n.* —'**violator** *n.*

violent ('vaɪələnt) *a.* 1. marked by, due to, extreme force, passion or fierceness 2. of great force 3. intense —'**violence** *n.* —'**violently** *adv.*

violet ('vaɪəlɪt) *n.* 1. plant with small bluish-purple or white flowers 2. the flower 3. bluish-purple colour —*a.* 4. of this colour

violin (vaɪə'lɪn) *n.* small four-stringed musical instrument —**vi'ola** *n.* large violin with lower range —**vio'linist** *n.* —**violon-cello** (vaɪələn'tʃeləʊ) *n. see* CELLO —**viola da gamba** (vɪ'əʊlə də 'gæmbə) second largest and lowest member of viol family

V.I.P. very important person

viper ('vaɪpə) *n.* venomous snake

virago (vɪ'rɑːgəʊ) *n.* abusive woman (*pl.* -**es, -s**)

virgin ('vɜːdʒɪn) *n.* 1. one who has not had sexual intercourse —*a.* 2. without experience of sexual intercourse 3. unsullied, fresh 4. (of land) untilled —'**virginal** *a.* 1. of, like virgin —*n.* 2. (*oft. pl.*) type of spinet —**vir'ginity** *n.* —**Virgin Birth** doctrine that Jesus Christ was conceived solely by direct intervention of Holy Spirit so that Mary remained a virgin after his birth —**Virgin Mary** Mary, mother of Christ (*also* **the Virgin**)

Virginia creeper (və'dʒɪnɪə) climbing plant that turns red in autumn

Virgo ('vɜːgəʊ) *n.* (virgin) 6th sign of the zodiac operative c. Aug. 22nd-Sept. 21st

virgule ('vɜːgjuːl) *n. Print. see* SOLIDUS

virile. ('vɪraɪl) *a.* 1. (of male) capable of copulation or procreation 2. strong, forceful —**virility** (vɪ'rɪlɪtɪ) *n.*

virology (vaɪ'rɒlədʒɪ) *n. see* VIRUS

virtu *or* **vertu** (vɜː'tuː) *n.* 1. taste or love for curios or works of fine art 2. such objects collectively 3. quality or being appealing to connoisseur (*esp. in* **articles of virtu, objects of virtu**)

virtual ('vɜːtʃʊəl) *a.* so in effect, though not in appearance or name —'**virtually** *adv.* practically, almost

virtue ('vɜːtjuː) *n.* 1. moral goodness 2. good quality 3. merit 4. inherent power

—'**virtuous** *a.* 1. morally good 2. chaste —'**virtuously** *adv.*

virtuoso (vɜːtjʊ'əʊzəʊ) *n.* one with special skill, *esp.* in a fine art (*pl.* -**s, -si** (-ziː)) —**virtuosity** (vɜːtjʊ'ɒsɪtɪ) *n.* great technical skill, *esp.* in a fine art, as music

virulent ('vɪrʊlənt) *a.* 1. very infectious, poisonous *etc.* 2. malicious

virus ('vaɪrəs) *n.* any of various submicroscopic organisms, some causing disease —'**viral** *a.* of virus —**vi'rology** *n.* study of viruses

visa ('viːzə) *n.* endorsement on passport permitting the bearer to travel into country of issuing government —'**visaed** *a.*

visage ('vɪzɪdʒ) *n.* face

vis-à-vis (viːzɑː'viː) *Fr.* 1. in relation to, regarding 2. opposite to

Visc. Viscount

viscera ('vɪsərə) *pl.n.* large internal organs of body, *esp.* of abdomen (*sing.* **viscus** ('vɪskəs)) —'**visceral** *a.*

viscid ('vɪsɪd) *a.* sticky, of a consistency like treacle —**vis'cidity** *n.*

viscose ('vɪskəʊs) *n.* (substance used to produce) synthetic fabric

viscount ('vaɪkaʊnt) *n.* Brit. nobleman ranking below earl and above baron ('**viscountess** *fem.*)

viscous ('vɪskəs) *a.* thick and sticky —**vis'cosity** *n.*

visible ('vɪzɪbⁱl) *a.* that can be seen —**visi'bility** *n.* degree of clarity of atmosphere, *esp.* for navigation —'**visibly** *adv.*

vision ('vɪʒən) *n.* 1. sight 2. insight 3. dream 4. phantom 5. imagination —'**visionary** *a.* 1. marked by vision 2. impractical —*n.* 3. mystic 4. impractical person

visit ('vɪzɪt) *v.* 1. go, come and see, stay temporarily with (someone) —*n.* 2. stay 3. call at person's home *etc.* 4. official call —'**visitant** *n.* 1. ghost; apparition 2. visitor or guest, usu. from far away 3. migratory bird that is present in particular region only at certain times (*also* '**visitor**) —**visi'tation** *n.* 1. formal visit or inspection 2. affliction or plague —'**visitor** *n.*

visor *or* **vizor** ('vaɪzə) *n.* 1. front part of helmet made to move up and down before face 2. eyeshade, *esp.* on car 3. peak or cap

vista ('vɪstə) *n.* view, *esp.* distant view

visual ('vɪʒʊəl, -zjʊ-) *a.* 1. of sight 2. visible —**visuali'zation** *or* -**li'sation** *n.* —'**visualize** *or* -**lise** *vt.* form mental image of —**visual aids** devices, such as films, slides *etc.*, that display in visual form material to be understood or remembered

vital ('vaɪtⁱl) *a.* 1. necessary to, affecting life 2. lively, animated 3. essential 4. highly important —**vi'tality** *n.* life, vigour —'**vitalize** *or* -**lise** *vt.* 1. give life to 2. lend vigour to —'**vitally** *adv.* —'**vitals** *pl.n.* vital organs of body —**vital statistics** 1. data concerning human life or conditions affecting it, such as death rate **2.** *inf.* measurements of woman's bust, waist and hips

vitamin ('vɪtəmɪn, 'vaɪ-) *n.* any of group of substances occurring in foodstuffs and essential to health

vitiate ('vɪʃɪeɪt) *vt.* **1.** spoil **2.** deprive of efficacy **3.** invalidate —**viti'ation** *n.*

viticulture ('vɪtɪkʌltʃə) *n.* **1.** science, art or process of cultivating grapevines **2.** study of (growing of) grapes —**viti'culturist** *n.*

vitreous ('vɪtrɪəs) *a.* **1.** of glass **2.** glassy —**vitrifi'cation** *n.* —**'vitrify** *v.* convert or be converted into glass, or glassy substance (**-ified, -ifying**) —**vitreous humour** *or* **body** transparent gelatinous substance that fills eyeball between lens and retina

vitriol ('vɪtrɪɒl) *n.* **1.** sulphuric acid **2.** caustic speech —**vitri'olic** *a.*

vituperate (vɪ'tjuːpəreɪt) *vt.* abuse in words, revile —**vituper'ation** *n.* —**vi'tuperative** *a.*

viva ('viːvə) *interj.* long live; up with (specified person or thing)

vivace (vɪ'vɑːtʃɪ) *a./adv.* Mus. to be performed in brisk lively manner

vivacious (vɪ'veɪʃəs) *a.* lively, gay, sprightly —**vivacity** (vɪ'væsɪtɪ) *n.*

vivarium (vaɪ'vɛərɪəm) *n.* place where animals are kept under natural conditions for study *etc.* (*pl.* **-s, -ia** (-ɪə))

viva voce ('vaɪvə 'vəʊtʃɪ) *Lat. adv.* **1.** by word of mouth —*n.* **2.** oral examination (*oft.* **'viva**)

vivid ('vɪvɪd) *a.* **1.** bright, intense **2.** clear **3.** lively, animated **4.** graphic —**'vividly** *adv.*

vivify ('vɪvɪfaɪ) *vt.* animate, inspire (**-ified, -ifying**)

viviparous (vɪ'vɪpərəs) *a.* bringing forth young alive

vivisection (vɪvɪ'sɛkʃən) *n.* dissection of, or operating on, living animals —**'vivisect** *v.* subject (animal) to vivisection —**vivi'sectionist** *n.* —**'vivisector** *n.*

vixen ('vɪksən) *n.* **1.** female fox **2.** spiteful woman —**'vixenish** *a.*

viz. videlicet

vizier (vɪ'zɪə) *n.* high official in some Muslim countries

V-J Day day marking Allied victory over Japan in World War II (Aug. 15th, 1945)

V.L. Vulgar Latin

VLF *or* **vlf** *Rad.* very low frequency

V neck neck on garment resembling shape of letter 'V' —**V-neck** *or* **V-necked** *a.*

voc. *or* **vocat.** vocative

vocable ('vəʊkəb'l) *n.* word regarded as sequence of letters or spoken sounds

vocabulary (və'kæbjʊlərɪ) *n.* **1.** list of words, usu. in alphabetical order **2.** stock of words used in particular language *etc.*

vocal ('vəʊk'l) *a.* **1.** of, with, or giving out voice **2.** outspoken, articulate —*n.* **3.** piece of popular music that is sung —**'vocalist** *n.* singer —**'vocalize** *or* **-ise** *vt.* utter with voice —**'vocally** *adv.* —**vocal cords** either

of two pairs of membranous folds in larynx

vocalic (vəʊ'kælɪk) *a.* of vowel(s)

vocation (vəʊ'keɪʃən) *n.* (urge, inclination, predisposition to) particular career, profession *etc.* —**vo'cational** *a.* —**vocational guidance** guidance service based on psychological tests and interviews to find out what career may best suit person

vocative ('vɒkətɪv) *n.* in some languages, case of nouns used in addressing a person

vociferate (vəʊ'sɪfəreɪt) *v.* exclaim, cry out —**vocifer'ation** *n.* —**vo'ciferous** *a.* shouting, noisy

vodka ('vɒdkə) *n.* Russian spirit distilled from grain, potatoes *etc.*

vogue (vəʊg) *n.* **1.** fashion, style **2.** popularity

voice (vɔɪs) *n.* **1.** sound given out by person in speaking, singing *etc.* **2.** quality of the sound **3.** expressed opinion **4.** (right to) share in discussion **5.** verbal form proper to relation of subject and action —*vt.* **6.** give utterance to, express —**'voiceless** *a.* —**voice-over** *n.* voice of unseen commentator heard during film *etc.* —**'voiceprint** *n.* graphic representation of person's voice recorded electronically

void (vɔɪd) *a.* **1.** empty **2.** destitute **3.** not legally binding —*n.* **4.** empty space —*vt.* **5.** make ineffectual or invalid **6.** empty out

voile (vɔɪl) *n.* light semitransparent fabric

vol. volume

volatile ('vɒlətaɪl) *a.* **1.** evaporating quickly **2.** lively **3.** fickle, changeable —**volatility** (vɒlə'tɪlɪtɪ) *n.* —**volatilization** *or* **-lisation** (vɒlætɪlaɪ'zeɪʃən) *n.* —**volatilize** *or* **-lise** (vɒ'lætɪlaɪz) *v.* (cause to) evaporate

vol-au-vent (*Fr.* vɒlɒ'vɑ̃) *n.* small, light pastry case with savoury filling

volcano (vɒl'keɪnəʊ) *n.* **1.** hole in earth's crust through which lava, ashes, smoke *etc.* are discharged **2.** mountain so formed (*pl.* **-es, -s**) —**volcanic** (vɒl'kænɪk) *a.* —**volcanology** (vɒlkə'nɒlədʒɪ) *or* **vulca'nology** *n.* study of volcanoes and volcanic phenomena

vole (vəʊl) *n.* small rodent

volition (və'lɪʃən) *n.* **1.** act, power of willing **2.** exercise of the will —**vo'litional** *a.*

volley ('vɒlɪ) *n.* **1.** simultaneous discharge of weapons or missiles **2.** rush of oaths, questions *etc.* **3.** *Sport* kick, stroke *etc.* at moving ball before it touches ground —*v.* **4.** discharge or be discharged —*vt.* **5.** utter **6.** fly, strike *etc.* in volley —**'volleyball** *n.* team game where large ball is hit by hand over high net

volt (vəʊlt) *n.* unit of electric potential —**'voltage** *n.* electric potential difference expressed in volts —**'voltmeter** *n.*

voltaic (vɒl'teɪɪk) *a. see* GALVANIC (sense 1)

volte-face ('vɒlt'fɑːs) *Fr. n.* complete reversal of opinion or direction (*pl.* **volte-face**)

voluble ('vɒljʊb'l) *a.* talking easily, readily

and at length —**volu'bility** n. —**'volubly** adv.

volume ('vɒljuːm) n. 1. space occupied 2. bulk, mass 3. amount 4. power, fullness of voice or sound 5. control on radio etc. for adjusting this 6. book 7. part of book bound in one cover —**volu'metric** a. pert. to measurement by volume —**voluminous** (vɒ'luːmɪnəs) a. bulky, copious

voluntary ('vɒləntərɪ) a. 1. having, done by free will 2. done without payment 3. supported by freewill contributions 4. spontaneous —n. 5. organ solo in church service —**'voluntarily** adv. —**volun'teer** n. 1. one who offers service, joins force etc. of his own free will —v. 2. offer oneself or one's services

voluptuous (vɒ'lʌptjʊəs) a. of, contributing to pleasures of the senses —**vo'luptuary** n. one given to luxury and sensual pleasures

vomit ('vɒmɪt) v. 1. eject (contents of stomach) through mouth —n. 2. matter vomited

voodoo ('vuːduː) n. 1. practice of black magic, esp. in W Indies, witchcraft —vt. 2. affect by voodoo

voracious (vɒ'reɪʃəs) a. greedy, ravenous —**vo'raciously** adv. —**voracity** (vɒ-'ræsɪtɪ) n.

-vorous (a. comb. form) feeding on; devouring, as in carnivorous —**-vore** (n. comb. form)

vortex ('vɔːtɛks) n. 1. whirlpool 2. whirling motion (pl. **-es**, **vortices** ('vɔːtɪsiːz))

votary ('vəʊtərɪ) n. one vowed to service or pursuit (**'votaress** fem.) —**'votive** a. given, consecrated by vow

vote (vəʊt) n. 1. formal expression of choice 2. individual pronouncement 3. right to give it, in question or election 4. result of voting 5. that which is given or allowed by vote —v. 6. express, declare opinion, choice, preference etc. by vote 7. authorize, enact etc. by vote —**'voter** n.

vouch (vaʊtʃ) vi. (usu. with for) guarantee, make oneself responsible (for) —**'voucher** n. 1. document proving correctness of item in accounts, or to establish facts 2. ticket as substitute for cash —**vouch'safe** vt. condescend to grant or do

vow (vaʊ) n. 1. solemn promise, esp. religious one —vt. 2. promise, threaten by vow

vowel ('vaʊəl) n. 1. any speech sound pronounced without stoppage or friction of

the breath 2. letter standing for such sound, as a, e, i, o, u

vox (vɒks) n. voice; sound (pl. **voces** ('vəʊsiːz)) —**vox populi** ('pɒpjʊlaɪ) voice of the people; popular or public opinion

voyage ('vɔɪɪdʒ) n. 1. journey, esp. long one, by sea or air —vi. 2. make voyage —**'voyager** n. —**voyageur** (vwɑː jɑːˈʒɜː; Fr. vwaja'ʒœːr) n. C guide, trapper in N regions

voyeur (vwaɪ'ɜː) n. one obtaining sexual pleasure by watching sexual activities of others

vs. versus

V-sign n. 1. UK offensive gesture made by sticking up index and middle fingers with palm of hand inwards 2. similar gesture with palm outwards meaning victory or peace

V.S.O. Voluntary Service Overseas

V.S.O.P. very superior old pale

VT Vermont

VTOL ('viːtɒl) vertical takeoff and landing

VTR video tape recorder

vulcanize or **-nise** ('vʌlkənaɪz) vt. treat (rubber) with sulphur at high temperature to increase its durability —**'vulcanite** n. rubber so hardened —**vulcani'zation** or **-ni'sation** n. —**vulca'nology** n. see volcanology at VOLCANO

vulgar ('vʌlgə) a. 1. offending against good taste 2. coarse 3. common —**vulgarian** (vʌl'gɛərɪən) n. vulgar (rich) person —**'vulgarism** n. coarse, obscene word, phrase —**vulgarity** (vʌl'gærɪtɪ) n. —**vulgari'zation** or **-ri'sation** n. —**'vulgarize** or **-rise** vt. make vulgar or too common —**'vulgarly** adv. —**vulgar fraction** simple fraction —**Vulgar Latin** any of dialects of Latin spoken in Roman Empire other than classical Latin

Vulgate ('vʌlgeɪt, -gɪt) n. fourth-century Latin version of the Bible

vulnerable ('vʌlnərəb'l) a. 1. capable of being physically or emotionally wounded or hurt 2. exposed, open to attack, persuasion etc. —**vulnera'bility** n.

vulpine ('vʌlpaɪn) a. 1. of foxes 2. foxy

vulture ('vʌltʃə) n. large bird which feeds on carrion —**'vulturine** or **'vulturous** a. 1. of vulture 2. rapacious

vulva ('vʌlvə) n. external genitals of human female

v.v. vice versa

vying ('vaɪɪŋ) pr.p. of VIE

W

w *or* **W** ('dʌb°ljuː) *n.* **1.** 23rd letter of English alphabet **2.** speech sound represented by this letter, usu. bilabial semivowel, as in *web* (*pl.* **w's, W's** *or* **Ws**)

W 1. *Chem.* tungsten **2.** watt **3.** Wednesday **4.** west(ern)

w. 1. week **2.** weight **3.** width

W. 1. Wales **2.** Welsh

WA Washington

W.A. 1. West Africa **2.** Western Australia

WAAC (wæk) *n.* **1.** Women's Army Auxiliary Corps **2.** member of this corps (*also* **waac**)

WAAF (wæf) *n.* **1.** Women's Auxiliary Air Force **2.** member of this force (*also* **Waaf**)

wacky ('wækɪ) *a. sl.* eccentric or unpredictable

wad (wɒd) *n.* **1.** small pad of fibrous material **2.** thick roll of banknotes **3.** sum of money —*vt.* **4.** line, pad, stuff *etc.* with wad (**-dd-**) —'**wadding** *n.* stuffing

waddle ('wɒd°l) *vi.* **1.** walk like duck —*n.* **2.** this gait

wade (weɪd) *vi.* **1.** walk through something that hampers movement, *esp.* water **2.** proceed with difficulty —'**wader** *n.* **1.** person or bird that wades —*pl.* **2.** angler's high waterproof boots

wafer ('weɪfə) *n.* **1.** thin, crisp biscuit **2.** thin slice of anything

waffle[1] ('wɒf°l) *n.* kind of pancake with deep indentations on both sides —**waffle iron** utensil for cooking waffles, having two flat, studded plates hinged together

waffle[2] ('wɒf°l) *inf. vi.* **1.** speak, write in vague wordy manner —*n.* **2.** vague speech *etc.* **3.** nonsense

waft (wɑːft, wɒft) *vt.* **1.** convey smoothly through air or water —*n.* **2.** breath of wind **3.** odour, whiff

wag (wæg) *v.* **1.** (cause to) move rapidly from side to side (**-gg-**) —*n.* **2.** instance of wagging **3.** *inf.* humorous, witty person —'**waggish** *a.* —'**wagtail** *n.* small bird with wagging tail

wage (weɪdʒ) *n.* (*oft. pl.*) payment for work done —*vt.* **2.** engage in

wager ('weɪdʒə) *n./v.* bet

waggle ('wæg°l) *v.* wag —'**waggly** *a.*

Wagnerian (vɑːɡ'nɪərɪən) *a.* pert. to German composer Richard Wagner, his music or his theories

wagon *or* **waggon** ('wægən) *n.* **1.** four-wheeled vehicle for heavy loads **2.** railway freight truck —'**wagoner** *or* '**waggoner** *n.* —**wago'nette** *or* **waggo'nette** *n.* four-wheeled horse-drawn vehicle with two lengthwise seats facing each other behind driver's seat

waif (weɪf) *n.* homeless person, *esp.* child

wail (weɪl) *v.* **1.** cry out —*vt.* **2.** lament —*n.* **3.** mournful cry

wainscot ('weɪnskət) *n.* **1.** wooden lining of walls of room —*vt.* **2.** line thus

waist (weɪst) *n.* **1.** part of body between hips and ribs **2.** various narrow central parts —'**waistband** *n.* encircling band of material to finish and strengthen skirt *etc.* at waist —**waistcoat** ('weɪskəʊt) *n.* sleeveless garment worn under jacket or coat —'**waistline** *n.* line, size of waist (of person, garment)

wait (weɪt) *v.* **1.** stay in one place, remain inactive in expectation (of something) **2.** be prepared (for something) **3.** delay —*vi.* **4.** serve in restaurant *etc.* —*n.* **5.** act or period of waiting —*pl.* **6.** street musicians, carol singers —'**waiter** *n.* **1.** attendant on guests at hotel, restaurant *etc.* ('**waitress** *fem.*) **2.** one who waits —**waiting game** postponement of action in order to gain advantage —**waiting list** list of people waiting to obtain some object, treatment *etc.*

waive (weɪv) *vt.* **1.** forgo **2.** not insist on —'**waiver** *n.* (written statement of) this act

wake[1] (weɪk) *v.* **1.** rouse from sleep **2.** stir (up) (**woke, 'woken, 'waking**) —*n.* **3.** vigil **4.** watch beside corpse **5.** (*oft. pl.*) annual holiday in parts of N England —'**wakeful** *a.* —'**waken** *v.* wake

wake[2] (weɪk) *n.* track or path left by anything that has passed, as track of turbulent water behind ship

wale (weɪl) *n.* **1.** raised mark left on skin after stroke of whip **2.** weave of fabric, such as ribs in corduroy **3.** *Naut.* ridge of planking along rail of ship —*v.* **4.** raise wales (on) by striking **5.** weave with wale

walk (wɔːk) *v.* **1.** (cause, assist to) move, travel on foot at ordinary pace —*vt.* **2.** cross, pass through by walking **3.** escort, conduct by walking —*n.* **4.** act, instance of walking **5.** path or other place or route for walking **6.** manner of walking **7.** occupation, career —'**walker** *n.* —'**walkabout** *n.* informal walk among crowd by royalty *etc.* —**walkie-talkie** *or* **walky-talky** *n.* portable radio set containing both transmission and receiver units —**walking stick** stick, cane carried to assist walking —**walk-on** *n.* small part in play *etc.*, *esp.* one without lines —'**walkout** *n.* **1.** strike **2.** act of leaving as a protest —'**walkover** *n.* unopposed or easy victory

wall (wɔːl) *n.* **1.** structure of brick, stone *etc.* serving as fence, side of building *etc.* **2.** surface of one **3.** anything resembling this —*vt.* **4.** enclose with wall **5.** block up with wall —'**wallboard** *n.* thin board made of materials, such as compressed wood fibres or gypsum plaster, used to cover walls *etc.* —'**wallflower** *n.* **1.** garden flower, oft. growing on walls **2.** woman who remains seated at dance *etc.* for lack of partner —'**wallpaper** *n.* paper, usu. patterned, to cover interior walls

wallaby ('wɒləbɪ) *n.* Aust. marsupial similar to and smaller than kangaroo

wallet ('wɒlɪt) *n.* small folding case, *esp.* for paper money, documents *etc.*

walleyed ('wɔːlaɪd) *a.* 1. squinting 2. having eyes with pale irises

Walloon (wɒ'luːn) *n.* 1. member of French-speaking people living chiefly in S and SE Belgium 2. French dialect of Belgium —*a.* 3. of Walloons or their dialect

wallop ('wɒləp) *inf. vt.* 1. beat soundly 2. strike hard —*n.* 3. stroke or blow —'**walloper** *n. inf.* one who wallops —'**walloping** *inf. n.* 1. thrashing —*adv.* 2. very, greatly —*a.* 3. great

wallow ('wɒləʊ) *vi.* 1. roll (in liquid or mud) 2. revel —*n.* 3. act or instance of wallowing 4. muddy place where animals wallow

Wall Street street in New York, where Stock Exchange and major banks are situated

wally ('wɒlɪ) *n. sl.* stupid person

walnut ('wɔːlnʌt) *n.* large nut with crinkled shell splitting easily into two halves 2. the tree 3. its wood

walrus ('wɔːlrəs, 'wɒl-) *n.* large sea mammal with long tusks (*pl.* **-es, -rus**)

waltz (wɔːls) *n.* 1. ballroom dance 2. music for it —*v.* 3. dance or lead (someone) in or as in a waltz

wampum ('wɒmpəm) *n.* beads made of shells, formerly used by N Amer. Indians as money and for ornament

wan (wɒn) *a.* pale, sickly complexioned, pallid

wand (wɒnd) *n.* stick, usu. straight and slender, *esp.* as carried by magician *etc.*

wander ('wɒndə) *v.* 1. roam, ramble —*vi.* 2. go astray, deviate —*n.* 3. stroll —'**wanderer** *n.* —'**wanderlust** *n.* irrepressible urge to wander or travel

wane (weɪn) *vi./n.* 1. decline 2. (of moon) decrease in size

wangle ('wæŋg'l) *inf. vt.* 1. manipulate, manage in skilful way —*n.* 2. intrigue, trickery, something obtained by craft

Wankel engine ('wæŋk'l) type of rotary four-stroke internal-combustion engine without reciprocating parts

want (wɒnt) *v.* 1. desire —*vt.* 2. lack —*n.* 3. desire 4. need 5. deficiency —'**wanted** *a.* being sought, *esp.* by the police —'**wanting** *a.* 1. lacking 2. below standard

wanton ('wɒntən) *a.* 1. dissolute 2. without motive, thoughtless 3. unrestrained —*n.* 4. wanton person *esp.* woman

war (wɔː) *n.* 1. fighting between nations 2. state of hostility 3. conflict, contest —*vi.* 4. make war (**-rr-**) —'**warlike** *a.* 1. of, for war 2. fond of war —'**warrior** *n.* fighter —**war crime** crime committed in wartime in violation of accepted customs of war —**war cry** 1. cry used by attacking troops in war 2. distinctive word, phrase used by

political party *etc.* —'**warfare** *n.* hostilities —**war game** 1. notional tactical exercise for training military commanders, in which no military units are actually deployed 2. game in which model soldiers are used to create battles in order to study tactics —'**warhead** *n.* part of missile *etc.* containing explosives —'**warhorse** *n.* 1. horse used in battle 2. *inf.* veteran soldier or politician —**war memorial** monument to those who die in war —'**warmonger** *n.* one fostering, encouraging war —**war paint** 1. painted decoration of face and body applied by certain N Amer. Indians before battle 2. *inf.* cosmetics —'**warpath** *n.* route taken by N Amer. Indians on warlike expedition —'**warship** *n.* vessel armed, armoured for naval warfare —**on the warpath** *inf.* in a state of anger

War. Warwickshire

warble ('wɔːb'l) *v.* sing with trills —'**warbler** *n.* 1. person or bird that warbles 2. kind of small songbird

ward (wɔːd) *n.* 1. division of city, hospital *etc.* 2. minor under care of guardian 3. guardianship 4. bar in lock, groove in key that prevents incorrectly cut key opening lock —'**warder** *n.* jailer ('**wardress** *fem.*) —'**wardship** *n.* 1. office of guardian 2. state of being under guardian —'**wardroom** *n.* senior officers' mess on warship —**ward off** avert, repel

-ward (*comb. form*) 1. indicating direction towards, as in *backward step* 2. *esp.* US *see* **-WARDS**

warden ('wɔːd'n) *n.* person, officer in charge of building, institution, college *etc.*

wardrobe ('wɔːdrəʊb) *n.* 1. piece of furniture for hanging clothes in 2. person's supply of clothes 3. costumes of theatrical company

-wards *or* **-ward** (*comb. form*) indicating direction towards, as in *step backwards*

ware (weə) *n.* 1. goods 2. articles collectively —*pl.* 3. goods for sale 4. commodities 5. merchandise —'**warehouse** *n.* storehouse for goods prior to distribution and sale

warlock ('wɔːlɒk) *n.* wizard, sorcerer

warm (wɔːm) *a.* 1. moderately hot 2. serving to maintain heat 3. affectionate 4. ardent 5. earnest 6. hearty 7. (of colour) having yellow or red base —*v.* 8. make, become warm —'**warmly** *adv.* —**warmth** *n.* 1. mild heat 2. cordiality 3. vehemence, anger —**warm-blooded** *a.* ardent —**warm-bloodedness** *n.* —**warm front** *Met.* boundary between warm air mass and cold air above

warn (wɔːn) *vt.* 1. put on guard 2. caution, admonish 3. give advance information to 4. notify authoritatively —'**warning** *n.* 1. hint of harm *etc.* 2. admonition 3. advance notice

warp (wɔːp) *v.* 1. (cause to) twist (out of shape) 2. pervert or be perverted —*n.* 3. state, condition of being warped 4. lengthwise threads on loom

warrant ('wɒrənt) n. 1. authority 2. document giving authority —vt. 3. guarantee 4. authorize, justify —**warran'tee** n. person given warranty —**'warrantor** n. person, company giving warranty —**'warranty** n. 1. guarantee of quality of goods 2. security —**warrant officer** officer in certain armed services who holds a rank between those of commissioned and noncommissioned officers.

warren ('wɒrən) n. (burrows inhabited by) colony of rabbits

wart (wɔ:t) n. small hard growth on skin —**wart hog** kind of Afr. wild pig

wary ('weərɪ) a. watchful, cautious, alert

was (wɒz; unstressed wəz) pt. first and third person sing. of BE

wash (wɒʃ) v. 1. clean (oneself, clothes etc.), esp. with water, soap etc. 2. move, be moved by water —vi. 3. be washable 4. inf. be able to be proved true —vt. 5. flow, sweep over, against —n. 6. act of washing 7. clothes washed at one time 8. sweep of water, esp. set up by moving ship 9. thin coat of colour —**'washable** a. capable of being washed without damage etc. —**'washer** n. 1. one who, that which, washes 2. ring put under a nut —**'washing** n. clothes to be washed —**'washy** a. 1. dilute 2. watery 3. insipid —**'washboard** n. 1. board having surface, usu. of corrugated metal, on which, esp. formerly, clothes are scrubbed 2. Naut. planklike shield fastened to gunwales of boat to prevent water from splashing over side —**wash drawing** pen-and-ink drawing that has been lightly brushed over with water —**washing-up** n. UK 1. washing of dishes, cutlery etc. after meal 2. dishes, cutlery etc. waiting to be washed up —**wash leather** piece of leather, usu. chamois, used for washing windows etc. —**'washout** n. inf. complete failure —**washed out** 1. faded or colourless 2. exhausted, pale

wasp (wɒsp) n. striped stinging insect resembling bee —**'waspish** a. irritable, snappish —**wasp waist** very small waist

Wasp or **WASP** (wɒsp) n. US usu. derogatory person descended from N European Protestant stock

wassail ('wɒseɪl) n. 1. formerly, toast made to person at festivities 2. festivity when much drinking takes place 3. alcoholic drink drunk at such festivity, esp. spiced beer —v. 4. drink health of (person) at wassail —vi. 5. go from house to house singing carols at Christmas

waste (weɪst) vt. 1. expend uselessly, use extravagantly 2. fail to take advantage of 3. lay desolate —vi. 4. dwindle 5. pine away —n. 6. act of wasting 7. what is wasted 8. desert —a. 9. worthless, useless 10. desert 11. wasted —**'wastage** n. 1. loss by use or decay 2. reduction in numbers, esp. of workforce —**'wasteful** a. extravagant —**'wastefully** adv. —**'wasting** a. reducing vitality, strength, or robustness of body —**'wastrel** n. wasteful person, idler

—**'wasteland** n. barren or desolate area of land

watch (wɒtʃ) vt. 1. observe closely 2. guard —vi. 3. wait expectantly 4. be on watch —n. 5. portable timepiece for wrist, pocket etc. 6. state of being on the lookout 7. guard 8. spell of duty —**'watchful** a. —**'watchfully** adv. —**'watchdog** n. 1. dog trained to guard property 2. person or group that acts as protector against inefficiency etc. —**'watchmaker** n. one skilled in making and repairing watches —**'watchman** n. man guarding building etc., esp. at night —**watch night** in Protestant churches, service held on night of Dec. 31st, to mark passing of old year —**'watchword** n. 1. password 2. rallying cry

water ('wɔ:tə) n. 1. transparent, colourless, odourless, tasteless liquid, substance of rain, river etc. 2. body of water 3. river 4. lake 5. sea 6. tear 7. urine —vt. 8. put water on or into 9. irrigate, provide with water —vi. 10. salivate 11. (of eyes) fill with tears 12. take in or obtain water —**'watery** a. —**water bed** waterproof mattress filled with water —**water biscuit** thin crisp plain biscuit —**'waterbuck** n. Afr. antelope —**water buffalo** oxlike Asian animal —**water butt** barrel with one end open, used for collecting and storing rainwater —**water chestnut** floating aquatic plant of Asia, having edible nutlike fruits —**water closet** sanitary convenience flushed by water —**'watercolour** or U.S. **'watercolor** n. 1. pigment mixed with water 2. painting in this —**'watercourse** n. stream —**'watercress** n. plant growing in clear ponds and streams —**'waterfall** n. perpendicular descent of waters of river —**'waterfront** n. area of town alongside body of water, such as harbour —**water gauge** instrument that indicates presence or quantity of water in tank etc. (also **water glass**) —**water glass** 1. syrupy solution of sodium silicate dissolved in water, used as preservative, esp. for eggs 2. water gauge —**water hole** depression, such as pool, containing water, esp. one used by animals as drinking place —**water ice** ice cream made from frozen sugar syrup flavoured with fruit juice etc. —**watering place** 1. place where drinking water may be obtained 2. UK spa 3. UK seaside resort —**water jump** ditch over which athletes or horses must jump, as in steeplechase —**water lily** plant that floats on surface of fresh water —**water line** 1. line marked at level around vessel's hull to which vessel will be immersed when afloat 2. line marking level reached by body of water —**'waterlogged** a. saturated, filled with water —**water main** principal supply pipe in arrangement of water pipes —**'watermark** n. faint translucent design stamped on substance of sheet of paper —**water meadow** meadow that remains fertile due to periodic flooding by stream —**'watermelon** n. large edible fruit which has hard green rind and sweet watery reddish flesh —**water pistol** toy pistol that squirts stream of water —**water power** 1. power latent in dynamic or static head of water as used to drive machinery 2. source of such power, such as drop in level of river etc. —'**waterproof** a. 1. not letting water through —vt. 2. make waterproof —n. 3. waterproof garment —**water rate** charge levied for use of public water supply —**water-repellent** a. (of garments etc.) having water-resistant finish —'**watershed** n. 1. line separating two river systems 2. divide —**water-ski** n. 1. type of ski used for gliding over water —vi. 2. ride over water on water-skis, while holding rope towed by speedboat —'**waterspout** n. 1. Met. tornado occurring over water, that forms column of water and mist; sudden heavy rainfall 2. pipe or channel through which water is discharged —**water table** level below which ground is saturated with water —'**watertight** a. 1. so fitted as to prevent water entering or escaping 2. with no loopholes or weak points —**water tower** storage tank mounted on towerlike structure so that water can be distributed at uniform pressure —**water vapour** water in gaseous state, esp. when due to evaporation at temperature below boiling point —**water wheel** 1. water-driven turbine consisting of wheel having vanes set axially across its rim, used to drive machinery 2. wheel with buckets attached to its rim for raising water from pond etc. —**water wings** inflatable rubber device, placed under arms of person learning to swim —'**waterworks** pl.n. 1. (with sing. v.) establishment for storing, purifying, and distributing water for community supply 2. (with pl. v.) display of water in movement, as in fountains 3. (with pl. v.) sl. crying; tears

Watergate ('wɔːtəgeɪt) n. political scandal when agents employed by U.S. President Richard Nixon's re-election organization were caught breaking into Democratic Party headquarters in Watergate building, Washington, D.C.; exacerbated by attempts to conceal the fact that White House officials had approved the burglary

Waterloo (wɔːtə'luː) n. 1. town in Belgium, site of battle where Napoleon met his final defeat 2. total or crushing defeat (esp. in **meet one's Waterloo**)

watt (wɒt) n. unit of electric power —'**wattage** n. electric power expressed in watts

wattle ('wɒtʳl) n. 1. frame of woven branches etc. as fence 2. fleshy pendent lobe of neck of certain birds, eg turkey —**wattle and daub** form of wall construction consisting of interwoven twigs plastered with mixture of clay and water

waul or **wawl** (wɔːl) vi. cry or wail plaintively like cat

wave (weɪv) v. 1. move to and fro, as hand in greeting or farewell 2. signal by waving 3. give, take shape of waves (as hair etc.) —n. 4. ridge and trough on water etc. 5. act, gesture of waving 6. vibration, as in radio waves, of electric and magnetic forces alternating in direction 7. prolonged spell of something 8. upsurge 9. wavelike shape in the hair etc. —'**wavy** a. —'**waveband** n. range of wavelengths or frequencies used for particular type of radio transmission —'**wavelength** n. distance between same points of two successive sound waves

waver ('weɪvə) vi. 1. hesitate, be irresolute 2. be, become unsteady —'**waverer** n.

wax[1] (wæks) n. 1. yellow, soft, pliable material made by bees 2. this or similar substance used for sealing, making candles etc. 3. waxy secretion of ear —vt. 4. put wax on —'**waxen** a. 1. made of, treated with, or covered with wax 2. resembling wax in colour or texture —'**waxy** a. like wax —'**waxbill** n. Afr. finchlike weaverbird —**wax paper** paper coated with wax or paraffin to make it waterproof —'**waxwing** n. small songbird —'**waxwork** n. lifelike figure, esp. of famous person, reproduced in wax

wax[2] (wæks) vi. grow, increase

way (weɪ) n. 1. manner 2. method, means 3. track 4. direction 5. path 6. passage 7. course 8. route 9. progress 10. state or condition —'**waybill** n. document attached to goods in transit specifying their nature, point of origin, destination and rate to be charged —'**wayfarer** n. traveller, esp. on foot —**way'lay** vt. lie in wait for and accost, attack (-'**laid**, -'**laying**) —**way-out** a. inf. 1. extremely unconventional or experimental 2. excellent or amazing —'**wayside** n. 1. side or edge of a road —a. 2. situated by the wayside —'**wayward** a. capricious, perverse, wilful —'**waywardly** adv. —'**waywardness** n. —**ways and means** 1. revenues and methods of raising revenues needed for functioning of state etc. 2. methods and resources for accomplishing some purpose

-ways (comb. form) indicating direction or manner, as in sideways

Wb Phys. weber

w.b. 1. water ballast 2. waybill (also **W/B, W.B.**) 3. westbound

W.C. or **WC** water closet

we (wiː) pron. first person plural pronoun

weak (wiːk) a. 1. lacking strength 2. feeble 3. fragile 4. defenceless 5. easily influenced 6. faint —'**weaken** v. —'**weakling** n. feeble creature —'**weakly** a. 1. weak 2. sickly —adv. 3. in a weak or feeble manner —'**weakness** n. —**weak-kneed** a. inf. yielding readily to force, intimidation etc.

weal[1] (wiːl) n. streak left on flesh by blow of stick or whip

weal[2] (wiːl) n. obs. prosperity or wellbeing (esp. in **the public weal, common weal**)

weald (wiːld) n. obs. forested country

wealth (wɛlθ) n. 1. riches 2. abundance —'**wealthiness** n. —'**wealthy** a.

wean (wiːn) *vt.* 1. accustom to food other than mother's milk 2. win over, coax away

weapon ('wɛpən) *n.* 1. implement to fight with 2. anything used to get the better of an opponent

wear (wɛə) *vt.* 1. have on the body 2. show 3. produce (hole *etc.*) by rubbing *etc.* 4. harass; weaken 5. *inf.* allow, tolerate —*vi.* 6. last 7. become impaired by use 8. (*with* on) (of time) pass slowly (**wore, worn, 'wearing**) —*n.* 9. act of wearing 10. things to wear 11. damage caused by use 12. ability to resist effects of constant use —'**wearer** *n.* —**wear and tear** depreciation or loss resulting from ordinary use

weary ('wɪərɪ) *a.* 1. tired, exhausted, jaded 2. tiring 3. tedious —*v.* 4. make, become weary (**'wearied, 'wearying**) —'**wearily** *adv.* —'**weariness** *n.* —'**wearisome** *a.* causing weariness

weasel ('wiːzˀl) *n.* small carnivorous mammal with long body and short legs

weather ('wɛðə) *n.* 1. day-to-day meteorological conditions, *esp.* temperature, cloudiness *etc.* of a place —*a.* 2. towards the wind —*v.* 3. affect or be affected by weather —*vt.* 4. endure 5. resist 6. come safely through 7. sail to windward of —'**weathering** *n.* mechanical and chemical breakdown of rocks by action of rain, cold *etc.* —**weather-beaten** *a.* showing signs of exposure to weather —'**weatherboard** *n.* timber boards used as external cladding of house —**weather-bound** *a.* (of vessel, aircraft *etc.*) delayed by bad weather —'**weathercock** *n.* revolving vane to show which way wind blows —**weather eye** 1. vision of person trained to observe changes in weather 2. *inf.* alert or observant gaze —**weather house** model house, usu. with two human figures, one that enters to foretell bad weather and one that enters to foretell good weather —**weather strip** thin strip of metal, felt *etc.* fitted between frame of door or window and opening part to exclude draughts and rain —**weather vane** vane designed to indicate direction in which wind is blowing

weave (wiːv) *vt.* 1. form into texture or fabric by interlacing, *esp.* on loom 2. fashion, construct —*vi.* 3. practise weaving 4. make one's way, *esp.* with side to side motion (**wove** *or* **weaved, 'woven** *or* **weaved, 'weaving**) —'**weaver** *n.*

web (wɛb) *n.* 1. woven fabric 2. net spun by spider 3. membrane between toes of waterfowl, frogs *etc.* —'**webbing** *n.* strong fabric woven in strips

weber ('veɪbə) *n.* SI unit of magnetic flux

wed (wɛd) *v.* 1. marry —*vt.* 2. unite closely (**'wedded, wed** *pt./pp.*, '**wedding**) —'**wedding** *n.* act of marrying, nuptial ceremony —'**wedlock** *n.* marriage

Wed. Wednesday

wedge (wɛdʒ) *n.* 1. piece of wood, metal *etc.*, thick at one end, tapering to a thin edge —*vt.* 2. fasten, split with wedge 3. stick by compression or crowding

Wedgwood ('wɛdʒwʊd) *n.* **R** kind of pottery with ornamental reliefs

Wednesday ('wɛnzdɪ) *n.* fourth day of week

wee (wiː) *a.* small, little

weed (wiːd) *n.* 1. plant growing where undesired 2. *inf.* tobacco 3. *inf.* marijuana 4. *inf.* thin, sickly person, animal —*vt.* 5. clear of weeds —'**weedy** *a.* 1. full of weeds 2. *inf.* thin, weakly —**weed out** remove, eliminate what is unwanted

weeds (wiːdz) *pl.n.* (widow's) mourning clothes

week (wiːk) *n.* 1. period of seven days, *esp.* one beginning on Sunday and ending on Saturday 2. hours, days of work in seven-day period —'**weekly** *a./adv.* 1. (happening, done, published *etc.*) once a week —*n.* 2. newspaper or magazine issued every week —'**weekday** *n.* any day of week except Sunday and *usu.* Saturday —**weekend** *n.* Saturday and Sunday, *esp.* considered as rest period

weep (wiːp) *v.* 1. shed (tears) 2. grieve (**wept, 'weeping**) —'**weepy** *a.* —**weeping willow** willow with drooping branches

weevil ('wiːvɪl) *n.* small beetle harmful to grain *etc.*

weft (wɛft) *n.* cross threads in weaving, woof

weigh (weɪ) *vt.* 1. find weight of 2. consider 3. raise (anchor) —*vi.* 4. have weight 5. be burdensome —**weight** *n.* 1. measure of the heaviness of an object 2. quality of heaviness 3. heavy mass 4. object of known mass for weighing 5. unit of measurement of weight 6. importance, influence —*vt.* 7. add weight to —'**weightily** *adv.* —'**weighting** *n.* additional allowance payable in particular circumstances —'**weightlessness** *n.* having little or no weight, experienced *esp.* at great distances from earth because of reduced gravitational attraction (*also* **zero gravity**) —'**weighty** *a.* 1. heavy 2. onerous 3. important 4. momentous —'**weighbridge** *n.* machine for weighing vehicles *etc.* by means of metal plate set into road —'**weightlifting** *n.* sport of lifting barbells of specified weights in prescribed manner —**weight training** physical exercise using heavy or light weights, to improve muscle performance

weir (wɪə) *n.* river dam

weird (wɪəd) *a.* 1. unearthly, uncanny 2. strange, bizarre

welch (wɛlʃ) *vi. see* WELSH

welcome ('wɛlkəm) *a.* 1. received gladly 2. freely permitted —*n.* 3. kindly greeting —*vt.* 4. greet with pleasure 5. receive gladly (**-comed, -coming**)

weld (wɛld) *vt.* 1. unite (metal) by softening with heat 2. unite closely —*n.* 3. welded joint —'**welder** *n.* 1. tradesman who welds 2. machine used in welding

welfare ('wɛlfɛə) *n.* wellbeing —**welfare**

state system in which the government takes responsibility for the social, economic *etc.* security of its citizens

well¹ (wɛl) *adv.* **1.** in good manner or degree **2.** suitably **3.** intimately **4.** fully **5.** favourably, kindly **6.** to a considerable degree —*a.* **7.** in good health **8.** suitable ('**better** *comp.*, **best** *sup.*) —*interj.* **9.** exclamation of surprise, interrogation *etc.* —**well-appointed** *a.* well equipped or furnished —**well-balanced** *a.* **1.** having good balance or proportions **2.** sane or sensible —'**well'being** *n.* state of being well, happy, or prosperous —**well-connected** *a.* having influential or important relatives or friends —**well-disposed** *a.* inclined to be friendly, kindly (towards) —**well-done** *a.* **1.** (of food, *esp.* meat) cooked thoroughly **2.** accomplished satisfactorily —**well-grounded** *a.* **1.** well instructed in basic elements of subject **2.** based on good reasons —**well-heeled** *a. sl.* rich; wealthy —**well-intentioned** *a.* having benevolent intentions, usu. with unfortunate results —**well-mannered** *a.* having good manners —**well-nigh** *adv. poet.* nearly; almost —**well-off** *a.* fairly rich —**well-read** *a.* having read much —**well-spoken** *a.* speaking fluently, graciously, aptly —**well-to-do** *a.* moderately wealthy —**well tried** proved to be satisfactory by long experience —**well-wisher** *n.* person who shows benevolence towards person, cause *etc.* —**well-wishing** *a./n.* —**well-worn** *a.* **1.** so much used as to be affected by wear **2.** hackneyed

well² (wɛl) *n.* **1.** hole sunk into the earth to reach water, gas, oil *etc.* **2.** spring **3.** any shaft like a well **4.** space in a lawcourt where solicitors sit —*vi.* **5.** spring, gush —'**wellhead** *n.* **1.** source of well or stream **2.** source, fountainhead or origin —'**well-spring** *n.* **1.** source of spring or stream **2.** source of abundant supply

Wellington boots ('wɛlɪŋtən) high waterproof boots (*also* '**Wellingtons**, '**wellies**)

welsh *or* **welch** (wɛlʃ) *vi.* fail to pay debt or fulfil obligation —'**welsher** *or* '**welcher** *n.*

Welsh (wɛlʃ) *a.* **1.** of Wales —*n.* **2.** language, natives or inhabitants of Wales —**Welsh rabbit** *or* **rarebit** savoury dish of melted cheese on toast —**Welsh terrier** wire-haired breed of terrier with black-and-tan coat

welt (wɛlt) *n.* **1.** raised, strengthened seam **2.** weal —*vt.* **3.** provide with welt **4.** thrash

welter ('wɛltə) *vi.* **1.** roll or tumble —*n.* **2.** turmoil, disorder

welterweight ('wɛltəweɪt) *n.* **1.** professional boxer weighing 140-147 lbs (63.5-66.5 kg); amateur boxer weighing 63.5-67 kg (140-148 lbs) **2.** wrestler weighing usu. 154-172 lbs (70-78 kg)

wen (wɛn) *n.* cyst, *esp.* on scalp

wench (wɛntʃ) *n.* now *oft.* facetious young woman

wend (wɛnd) *v.* go, travel

wendigo ('wɛndɪɡʊ) *n.* C *see* SPLAKE

wensleydale ('wɛnzlɪdeɪl) *n.* **1.** type of white cheese with flaky texture **2.** breed of sheep with long woolly fleece

went (wɛnt) *pt. of* GO

wept (wɛpt) *pt./pp. of* WEEP

were (wɜː; *unstressed* wə) imperfect indicative plural and subjunctive sing. and pl. of BE

werewolf ('wɪəwʊlf, 'wɛə-) *n.* in folklore, human being turned into wolf

Wesleyan ('wɛzlɪən) *a.* **1.** pert. to English preacher, John Wesley (1703-91), who founded Methodism **2.** of Methodism, *esp.* in its original form —*n.* **3.** follower of John Wesley **4.** member of Methodist Church —'**Wesleyanism** *n.*

west (wɛst) *n.* **1.** part of sky where sun sets **2.** part of country *etc.* lying to this side **3.** occident —*a.* **4.** that is toward or in this region —*adv.* **5.** to the west —'**westerly** *a.* —'**western** *a.* **1.** of, in the west —*n.* **2.** film, story *etc.* about cowboys or frontiersmen in western U.S. —'**westernize** *or* **-ise** *vt.* influence with customs, practices *etc.* of West —'**westward** *a./adv.* —'**westwards** *adv.* towards the west —**western hemisphere** (*oft.* W- H-) that half of the globe containing N and S Amer. —**go west** *inf.* **1.** disappear **2.** die **3.** be lost —**the West Country** southwest of England, *esp.* Cornwall, Devon and Somerset —**the West End** part of W central London containing main shopping and entertainment areas

Westminster ('wɛstmɪnstə) *n.* British Houses of Parliament

wet (wɛt) *a.* **1.** having water or other liquid on a surface or being soaked in it **2.** rainy **3.** not yet dry (paint, ink *etc.*) **4.** *inf.* (of person) feeble, dull *etc.* ('**wetter** *comp.*, '**wettest** *sup.*) —*vt.* **5.** make wet (**wet**, '**wetted** *pt./pp.*, '**wetting** *pr.p.*) —*n.* **6.** moisture, rain **7.** (*oft.* W-) UK *inf.* Conservative politician who is not a hardliner —**wet blanket** *inf.* one depressing spirits of others —**wet dream** erotic dream accompanied by emission of semen —**wetland** ('wɛtlənd) *n.* (*sometimes pl.*) area of marshy land, *esp.* considered as part of ecological system —**wet nurse** woman suckling another's child —**wet suit** close-fitting rubber suit worn by divers *etc.*

wether ('wɛðə) *n.* castrated ram

W. Glam. West Glamorgan

whack (wæk) *vt.* **1.** strike with sharp resounding blow —*n.* **2.** such blow **3.** *inf.* share **4.** *inf.* attempt —**whacked** *a.* exhausted —'**whacking** *a. inf.* big, enormous

whale (weɪl) *n.* large fish-shaped sea mammal —'**whaler** *n.* man, ship employed in hunting whales —'**whaling** *n.* work or industry of hunting and processing whales for food, oil *etc.* —'**whalebone** *n.* horny elastic substance from projections of upper jaw of certain whales

wham (wæm) *n.* **1.** forceful blow or sound

produced by it —*v.* **2.** strike or cause to strike with great force (-**mm**-)

wharf (wɔːf) *n.* platform at harbour, on river *etc.* for loading and unloading ships (*pl.* **wharves** (wɔːvz), -**s**)

what (wɒt; *unstressed* wət) *pron.* **1.** which thing **2.** that which **3.** request for statement to be repeated —*a.* **4.** which **5.** as much as **6.** how great, surprising *etc.* —*interj.* **7.** exclamation of surprise, anger *etc.* —**what'ever** *pron.* **1.** anything which **2.** of what kind it may be —**whatso'ever** *a.* **1.** at all: used as intensifier with indefinite pronouns and determiners such as *none, anybody etc.* —*pron.* **2.** *rare* whatever —'**whatnot** *n.* **1.** *inf.* person, thing whose name is unknown, forgotten *etc.* **2.** small stand with shelves

wheat (wiːt) *n.* cereal plant with thick four-sided seed spikes of which bread is chiefly made —'**wheaten** *a.* —'**wheatear** *n.* small songbird —**wheat germ** embryo of wheat kernel —'**wheatmeal** *n.* wholemeal flour made from wheat

wheedle ('wiːdᵊl) *v.* coax, cajole

wheel (wiːl) *n.* **1.** circular frame or disc (with spokes) revolving on axle **2.** anything like a wheel in shape or function **3.** act of turning **4.** steering wheel —*v.* **5.** (cause to) turn as if on axle **6.** (cause to) move on or as if on wheels **7.** (cause to) change course, *esp.* in opposite direction —'**wheelbarrow** *n.* barrow with one wheel —'**wheelbase** *n.* distance between front and rear hubs of vehicle —'**wheelchair** *n.* chair mounted on large wheels, used by people who cannot walk —'**wheelhouse** *n.* enclosed structure on vessel's bridge for steersman —'**wheelspin** *n.* revolution of wheels without full grip of road —'**wheelwright** *n.* person who makes or mends wheels as trade

wheeze (wiːz) *vi.* **1.** breathe with difficulty and whistling noise —*n.* **2.** this sound **3.** *inf.* trick, idea, plan —'**wheezy** *a.*

whelk (wɛlk) *n.* sea snail, *esp.* edible variety

whelp (wɛlp) *n.* **1.** young of certain animals, *esp.* of wolf or dog **2.** *disparaging* youth **3.** *jocular* child —*v.* **4.** give birth to (whelps)

when (wɛn) *adv.* **1.** at what time —*conj.* **2.** at the time that **3.** although **4.** since —*pron.* **5.** at which (time) —**when'ever** *adv./conj.* at whatever time —**whenso'ever** *conj./adv.* rare whenever

whence (wɛns) *adv./conj. formal* **1.** from what place or source **2.** how

where (wɛə) *adv./conj.* **1.** at what place **2.** at or to the place in which —'**whereabouts** *adv./conj.* **1.** in what, which place —*n.* **2.** present position —**where'as** *conj.* **1.** considering that **2.** while, on the contrary —**where'by** *conj.* by which —'**wherefore** *adv. obs.* **1.** why **2.** consequently —**where-'of** *obs., formal adv.* **1.** of what or which person or thing? —*pron.* **2.** of which (person or thing) —**whereu'pon** *conj.* at

which point —**wher'ever** *adv.* at whatever place —'**wherewithal** *n.* necessary funds, resources *etc.*

whet (wɛt) *vt.* **1.** sharpen **2.** stimulate (-**tt**-) —'**whetstone** *n.* stone for sharpening tools

whether ('wɛðə) *conj.* introduces the first of two alternatives, of which the second may be expressed or implied

whew (hwjuː) *interj.* exclamation expressing relief, delight *etc.*

whey (weɪ) *n.* watery part of milk left after separation of curd in cheese making

which (wɪtʃ) *a.* **1.** used in requests for a selection from alternatives —*pron.* **2.** which person or thing **3.** the thing 'who' —**which'ever** *pron.*

whiff (wɪf) *n.* **1.** brief smell or suggestion of **2.** puff of air —*vt.* **3.** smell

Whig (wɪg) *n.* member of British political party that preceded the Liberal Party

while (waɪl) *conj.* **1.** in the time that **2.** in spite of the fact that, although **3.** whereas —*vt.* **4.** pass (time, usu. idly) —*n.* **5.** period of time —**whilst** *conj.* while

whim (wɪm) *n.* sudden, passing fancy —'**whimsical** *a.* **1.** fanciful **2.** full of whims —**whimsi'cality** *n.* —'**whimsy** *or* 'whim**sey** *n.* **1.** whim **2.** caprice —*a.* **3.** quaint, comical or unusual, oft. in tasteless way

whimper ('wɪmpə) *vi.* **1.** cry or whine softly **2.** complain in this way —*n.* **3.** such cry or complaint

whin (wɪn) *n.* gorse

whine (waɪn) *n.* **1.** high-pitched plaintive cry **2.** peevish complaint —*vi.* **3.** utter this

whinge (wɪndʒ) *inf. vi.* **1.** whine, complain —*n.* **2.** complaint

whinny ('wɪnɪ) *vi.* **1.** neigh softly ('whinnied, 'whinnying) —*n.* **2.** gentle neigh

whip (wɪp) *vt.* **1.** strike with whip **2.** thrash **3.** beat (cream, eggs) to a froth **4.** lash **5.** *inf.* pull, remove, insert *etc.* quickly **6.** *inf.* steal —*vi.* **7.** dart (-**pp**-) —*n.* **8.** lash attached to handle for urging or punishing **9.** one who enforces attendance of political party **10.** call made on members of Parliament to attend for important divisions **11.** elastic quality permitting bending in mast, fishing rod *etc.* **12.** whipped dessert —'**whipping** *n.* **1.** thrashing with whip or similar implement **2.** cord used for binding or lashing **3.** binding formed by wrapping rope *etc.* with cord or twine —'**whipcord** *n.* **1.** strong worsted fabric with diagonally ribbed surface **2.** hard twisted cord used for lashes of whips *etc.* —**whip hand** (*usu. with* the) **1.** in driving horses *etc.,* hand holding whip **2.** advantage or dominating position —'**whiplash** *n.* quick lash of whip or like that of whip —**whiplash injury** injury to neck as result of sudden jerking of unsupported head —'**whippersnapper** *n.* insignificant but pretentious or cheeky person, oft. young one. (*also* 'whip**ster**) —**whipping boy** scapegoat —'**whip-round** *n. inf.* collection of money

whippet ('wɪpɪt) *n.* racing dog like small greyhound

whir *or* **whirr** (wɜː) *v.* **1.** (cause to) fly, spin *etc.* with buzzing or whizzing sound —*vi.* **2.** bustle —*n.* **3.** this sound **4.** bustle

whirl (wɜːl) *v.* **1.** swing rapidly round **2.** drive or be driven at high speed —*vi.* **3.** move rapidly in a circular course —*n.* **4.** whirling movement **5.** confusion, bustle, giddiness —'**whirligig** *n.* **1.** spinning toy **2.** merry-go-round —'**whirlpool** *n.* circular current, eddy —'**whirlwind** *n.* **1.** wind whirling round while moving forwards —*a.* **2.** rapid or sudden —'**whirlybird** *n. inf.* helicopter

whisk (wɪsk) *vt.* **1.** brush, sweep, beat lightly **2.** beat to a froth —*v.* **3.** move, remove, quickly —*n.* **4.** light brush **5.** egg-beating implement

whisker ('wɪskə) *n.* **1.** long stiff hair at side of mouth of cat or other animal **2.** any of hairs on a man's face —**by a whisker** *inf.* only just

whisky ('wɪskɪ) *n.* spirit distilled from fermented cereals (*Irish*, **C**, *US* '**whiskey**)

whisper ('wɪspə) *v.* **1.** speak in soft, hushed tones, without vibration of vocal cords **2.** rustle —*n.* **3.** such speech **4.** trace or suspicion **5.** rustle

whist (wɪst) *n.* card game

whistle ('wɪsªl) *vi.* **1.** produce shrill sound by forcing breath through rounded, nearly closed lips —*vt.* **2.** utter, summon *etc.* by whistle —*n.* **3.** such sound **4.** any similar sound **5.** instrument to make it —'**whistler** *n.* —**whistle stop 1.** US minor railway station where trains stop only on signal; small town having such a station **2.** brief appearance in town, *esp.* by political candidate

whit (wɪt) *n.* jot, particle (*esp.* in **not a whit**)

white (waɪt) *a.* **1.** of the colour of snow **2.** pale **3.** light in colour **4.** having a light-coloured skin —*n.* **5.** colour of snow **6.** white pigment **7.** white part **8.** clear fluid round yolk of egg **9.** (**W-**) white person —'**whiten** *v.* —'**whiteness** *n.* —'**whitish** *a.* —**white ant** termite —'**whitebait** *n.* small edible fish —**white blood cell** *see* LEUCOCYTE —'**whitecap** *n.* wave with white broken crest —**white-collar** *a.* denoting nonmanual salaried workers —**white dwarf** one of class of small faint stars of enormous density —**white elephant** useless, unwanted, gift or possession —**white feather** symbol or mark of cowardice —'**whitefish** *n.* **1.** food fish having large silvery scales and small head **2.** in Brit. fishing industry, any edible marine fish or invertebrate excluding herrings but including trout, salmon and all shellfish —**white flag** white banner or cloth used as signal of surrender or truce —'**whitefly** *n.* insect typically having body covered with powdery wax —**white friar** Carmelite friar, so called because of white cloak that forms part of habit of this order —**white gold** white lustrous alloy containing gold together with platinum and palladium and sometimes smaller amounts of silver, nickel, or copper —**white goods 1.** household linen such as sheets, tablecloths *etc.* **2.** large household appliances, such as refrigerators *etc.* —**white heat 1.** intense heat characterized by emission of white light **2.** *inf.* state of intense excitement or activity —**white hope** one expected to bring honour or glory to his group, team *etc.* —**white horse 1.** outline of horse carved into side of chalk hill **2.** wave with white broken crest —**white-hot** *a.* **1.** at such high temperature that white light is emitted **2.** *inf.* in state of intense emotion —**white lead** (lɛd) **1.** white solid usu. regarded as mixture of lead carbonate and lead hydroxide used in paint and in making putty and ointments for treatment of burns **2.** either of two similar white pigments based on lead sulphate or lead silicate —**white lie** minor, unimportant lie —**white matter** whitish tissue of brain and spinal cord, consisting mainly of nerve fibres —**white meat** any meat that is light in colour, such as veal —**white noise** sound or electrical noise that has relatively wide continuous range of frequencies of uniform intensity —**white paper** government report on matter recently investigated —**white pepper** condiment made from husked dried beans of pepper plant —**white sale** sale of household linens at reduced prices —**white sauce** thick sauce made from flour, butter, seasonings, and milk or stock —**white slave** woman, child forced or enticed away for purposes of prostitution —**white spirit** colourless liquid obtained from petroleum, used as substitute for turpentine —**white tie 1.** white bow tie worn as part of man's formal evening dress **2.** formal evening dress for men —'**whitewash** *n.* **1.** substance for whitening walls *etc.* —*vt.* **2.** apply this to **3.** cover up, gloss over, suppress —**white whale** small white toothed whale of northern waters (*also* be'**luga**) —'**whitewood** *n.* **1.** tree with light-coloured wood, such as the tulip tree **2.** its wood —**show the white feather** act in cowardly manner —**the White House 1.** official Washington residence of president of U.S. **2.** U.S. presidency —**White man's burden** supposed duty of White race to bring education and Western culture to non-White inhabitants of their colonies

Whitehall (waɪt'hɔːl) *n.* **1.** street in London where main government offices are situated **2.** British Government

whither ('wɪðə) *adv. Poet.* **1.** to what place **2.** to which

whiting ('waɪtɪŋ) *n.* edible sea fish

whitlow ('wɪtləʊ) *n.* abscess on finger, *esp.* round nail

Whitsun ('wɪtsªn) *n.* week following **Whit Sunday**, seventh Sunday after Easter

whittle ('wɪtªl) *vt.* **1.** cut, carve with knife

2. pare away —**whittle down** reduce gradually, wear (away)

whiz or **whizz** (wɪz) n. **1.** loud hissing sound **2.** inf. person skilful at something —vi. **3.** move with or make such sound **4.** inf. move quickly —**whiz kid, whizz kid,** or **wiz kid** inf. person who is outstandingly successful for his or her age

who (huː) pron. relative and interrogative pronoun, always referring to persons —**whodunit** or **whodunnit** (huːˈdʌnɪt) n. inf. detective story —**who'ever** pron. who, any one or every one that —**whoso'ever** pron. formal whoever

W.H.O. World Health Organization

whoa (wəʊ) interj. command used, esp. to horses, to stop or slow down

whole (həʊl) a. **1.** complete **2.** containing all elements or parts **3.** entire **4.** not defective or imperfect **5.** healthy —n. **6.** complete thing or system —**'wholly** adv. —**'wholesome** a. producing good effect, physically or morally —**whole'hearted** a. **1.** sincere **2.** enthusiastic —**'wholemeal** a. of, pert. to flour which contains the whole of the grain —**whole number 1.** integer **2.** natural number —**'wholesale** n. **1.** sale of goods by large quantities to retailers —a. **2.** dealing by wholesale **3.** extensive —**'wholesaler** n. —**on the whole 1.** taking everything into consideration **2.** in general

whom (huːm) pron. objective case of WHO

whoop (wuːp) n. shout or cry expressing excitement etc.

whoopee (wʊˈpiː) n. inf. gay, riotous time —**make whoopee 1.** participate in wild noisy party **2.** make love

whooping cough (ˈhuːpɪŋ) infectious disease of mucous membrane lining air passages, marked by convulsive coughing with loud whoop or indrawing of breath

whoops (wʊps) interj. exclamation of surprise or of apology

whopper (ˈwɒpə) n. inf. **1.** anything unusually large **2.** monstrous lie —**'whopping** a.

whore (hɔː) n. prostitute —**'whorehouse** n. brothel

whorl (wɜːl) n. **1.** ring of leaves or petals **2.** turn of spiral **3.** anything forming part of circular pattern, eg lines of human fingerprint

whortleberry (ˈwɜːtˀlˌbɛrɪ) n. small Eurasian shrub of erica genus with edible sweet blackish berries (also **'bilberry, 'huckleberry, (UK) 'blaeberry**)

whose (huːz) pron. possessive case of WHO and WHICH

why (waɪ) adv. for what cause or reason

WI Wisconsin

W.I. 1. West Indian **2.** West Indies **3.** UK Women's Institute

wick (wɪk) n. strip of thread feeding flame of lamp or candle with oil, grease etc.

wicked (ˈwɪkɪd) a. **1.** evil, sinful **2.** very bad **3.** mischievous —**'wickedly** adv. —**'wickedness** n.

wicker(work) (ˈwɪkə(wɜːk)) n. woven cane etc., basketwork

wicket (ˈwɪkɪt) n. **1.** small gate **2.** Cricket set of three stumps and bails **3.** cricket pitch —**'wicketkeeper** n. Cricket player on fielding side positioned directly behind wicket

wide (waɪd) a. **1.** having a great extent from side to side, broad **2.** having considerable distance between **3.** spacious **4.** liberal **5.** vast **6.** far from the mark **7.** opened fully —adv. **8.** to the full extent **9.** far from the intended target —n. **10.** Cricket ball bowled out of batsman's reach —**'widely** adv. —**'widen** v. —**'width** (wɪdθ) or **'wideness** n. breadth —**wide-angle lens** lens system on camera that can cover angle of view of 60° or more —**wide-eyed** a. innocent or credulous —**'widespread** a. **1.** extending over a wide area **2.** common

widow (ˈwɪdəʊ) n. **1.** woman whose husband is dead and who has not married again —vt. **2.** make a widow of —**'widower** n. man whose wife is dead and who has not married again —**'widowhood** n.

wield (wiːld) vt. **1.** hold and use **2.** brandish **3.** manage

wife (waɪf) n. a man's partner in marriage, married woman (pl. **wives**) —**'wifely** a.

wig (wɪg) n. artificial hair for the head

wigeon or **widgeon** (ˈwɪdʒən) n. Eurasian duck of marshes, swamps etc.

wigging (ˈwɪgɪŋ) n. UK sl. reprimand

wiggle (ˈwɪgˀl) v. **1.** (cause to) move jerkily from side to side —n. **2.** such movement —**'wiggly** a.

wigwam (ˈwɪgwæm) n. N Amer. Indian's hut or tent

wilco (ˈwɪlkəʊ) interj. expression in telecommunications etc. indicating that message just received will be complied with

wild (waɪld) a. **1.** not tamed or domesticated **2.** not cultivated **3.** savage **4.** stormy **5.** uncontrolled **6.** random **7.** excited **8.** rash **9.** frantic **10.** inf. (of party etc.) rowdy, exciting —**'wildly** adv. —**'wildness** n. —**'wildcat** n. **1.** undomesticated European and Amer. feline animal **2.** inf. wild, savage person —a. **3.** unsound, irresponsible **4.** sudden, unofficial, unauthorized —**wild-goose chase** futile pursuit —**'wildlife** n. wild animals and plants collectively —**wild oats** sl. indiscretions of youth, esp. dissoluteness before settling down (esp. in **sow one's wild oats**) —**Wild West** western U.S., esp. with reference to its frontier lawlessness

wildebeest (ˈwɪldɪbiːst, ˈvɪl-) n. gnu

wilderness (ˈwɪldənɪs) n. **1.** desert, waste place **2.** state of desolation or confusion

wildfire (ˈwaɪldfaɪə) n. **1.** raging, uncontrollable fire **2.** anything spreading, moving fast

wile (waɪl) n. trick —**'wily** a. crafty, sly

wilful or U.S. **willful** (ˈwɪlfʊl) a. **1.**

obstinate, self-willed **2.** intentional —'**wilfully** or U.S. '**willfully** adv.

will (wɪl) v. aux. **1.** forms moods and tenses indicating intention or conditional result (**would** pt.) —vi. **2.** have a wish —vt. **3.** wish **4.** intend **5.** leave as legacy —n. **6.** faculty of deciding what one will do **7.** purpose **8.** volition **9.** determination **10.** wish **11.** directions written for disposal of property after death —'**willing** a. **1.** ready **2.** given cheerfully —'**willingly** adv. —'**willingness** n. —'**willpower** n. ability to control oneself, one's actions, impulses

willies ('wɪlɪz) pl.n. sl. nervousness, jitters, or fright (esp. in **give** (or **get) the willies**)

will-o'-the-wisp (wɪləðə'wɪsp) n. **1.** brief pale flame or phosphorescence sometimes seen over marshes **2.** elusive person or hope

willow ('wɪləʊ) n. **1.** tree, such as the weeping willow with long thin flexible branches **2.** its wood —'**willowy** a. lithe, slender, supple —'**willowherb** n. tall plant with mauve flowers

willy-nilly ('wɪlɪ'nɪlɪ) adv./a. (occurring) whether desired or not

wilt (wɪlt) v. (cause) to become limp, drooping or lose strength etc.

Wilts. (wɪlts) Wiltshire

wimp (wɪmp) n. inf. feeble ineffective person —'**wimpish** or '**wimpy** a.

wimple ('wɪmp'l) n. garment worn by nun, around face

win (wɪn) vi. **1.** be successful, victorious —vt. **2.** get by labour or effort **3.** reach **4.** allure **5.** be successful in **6.** gain the support, consent etc. of (**won, 'winning**) —n. **7.** victory, esp. in games —'**winner** n. —'**winning** a. charming —'**winnings** pl.n. sum won in game, betting etc.

wince (wɪns) vi. **1.** flinch, draw back, as from pain etc. —n. **2.** this act

winceyette (wɪnsɪ'ɛt) n. cotton fabric with raised nap

winch (wɪntʃ) n. **1.** machine for hoisting or hauling using cable wound round drum —vt. **2.** move (something) by using a winch

wind¹ (wɪnd) n. **1.** air in motion **2.** breath **3.** flatulence **4.** idle talk **5.** hint or suggestion **6.** scent borne by air —vt. **7.** render short of breath, esp. by blow etc. **8.** get the scent of —'**windward** n. side against which wind is blowing —'**windy** a. **1.** exposed to wind **2.** flatulent **3.** sl. nervous, scared **4.** inf. talking too much —'**windbag** n. sl. voluble person who has little of interest to communicate —'**windbreak** n. fence, line of trees etc. serving as protection from wind —'**windcheater** n. warm jacket, usu. with close-fitting knitted neck, cuffs and waistband —**wind-chill** n. serious chilling effect of wind and low temperature: measured on scale from hot to fatal to life (esp. in **wind-chill factor**) —'**windfall** n. **1.** unexpected good luck **2.** fallen fruit —**wind gauge 1.** see ANEMOMETER **2.** Mus. device for measuring wind pressure in

bellows of organ —**wind instrument** musical instrument played by blowing or air pressure —'**windjammer** n. large merchant sailing ship —**windmill** ('wɪndmɪl, 'wɪnmɪl) n. wind-driven apparatus with fanlike sails for raising water, crushing grain etc. —'**windpipe** n. passage from throat to lungs —'**windscreen** n. protective sheet of glass etc. in front of driver or pilot —**windscreen wiper** UK electrically operated blade with rubber edge that wipes windscreen clear of rain etc. —'**windsock** n. cone of material flown on mast at airfield to indicate wind direction —**wind tunnel** chamber for testing aerodynamic properties of aircraft etc. in which current of air can be maintained at constant velocity

wind² (waɪnd) vi. **1.** twine **2.** meander —vt. **3.** twist, coil **4.** wrap **5.** make ready for working by tightening spring (**wound, 'winding**) —n. **6.** act of winding **7.** single turn of something wound **8.** a turn, curve —**winding sheet** sheet in which corpse is wrapped for burial; shroud —**wind-up** n. inf., chiefly US **1.** act of concluding **2.** end —**wind down 1.** lower or move down by cranking **2.** (of clock spring) become slack **3.** diminish gradually in force or power —**wind up 1.** bring to or reach a conclusion **2.** tighten spring of (clockwork mechanism) **3.** inf. make nervous, tense etc. **4.** inf. see LIQUIDATE (sense 2) **5.** inf. end up in (specified state)

windlass ('wɪndləs) n. winch, esp. simple one worked by a crank

window ('wɪndəʊ) n. **1.** hole in wall (with glass) to admit light, air etc. **2.** anything similar in appearance or function **3.** area for display of goods behind glass of shop front —**window box** long narrow box, placed on windowsill, in which plants are grown —**window-dressing** n. **1.** arrangement of goods in a shop window **2.** deceptive display —'**windowpane** n. sheet of glass in window —**window-shop** vi. look at goods in shop windows without buying them (-**pp-**) —'**windowsill** n. sill below window

Windsor chair ('wɪnzə) simple wooden chair, usu. having shaped seat, splayed legs, and back of many spindles

wine (waɪn) n. fermented juice of grape etc. —'**wino** n. person who habitually drinks wine as means of getting drunk —'**winepress** n. apparatus for extracting juice from grape —'**wineskin** n. skin of sheep or goat sewn up and used as holder for wine

wing (wɪŋ) n. **1.** feathered limb a bird uses in flying **2.** one of organs of flight of insect or some animals **3.** main lifting surface of aircraft **4.** lateral extension **5.** side portion of building projecting from main central portion **6.** one of sides of a stage **7.** flank corps of army on either side **8.** part of car body that surrounds wheels **9.** Sport (player on) either side of pitch **10.** faction, esp. of political party —pl. **11.** insignia worn by qualified aircraft pilot **12.** sides of stage —*vi.* **13.** fly **14.** move, go very fast —*vt.* **15.** disable, wound slightly —**winged** *a.* having wings —**wing chair** chair having wings on each side of back —**wing commander** officer holding commissioned rank in certain air forces, such as Royal Air Force: junior to group captain and senior to squadron leader —**wing nut** threaded nut tightened by hand by means of two flat wings projecting from central body (*also* **butterfly nut**)

wink (wıŋk) *v.* **1.** close and open (an eye) rapidly, *esp.* to indicate friendliness or as signal —*vi.* **2.** twinkle —*n.* **3.** act of winking

winkle ('wıŋk⁽l⁾) *n.* shellfish, periwinkle —**winkle-pickers** *pl.n.* shoes or boots with very pointed narrow toes —**winkle out** extract

winnow ('wınəʊ) *vt.* **1.** blow free of chaff **2.** sift, examine

winsome ('wınsəm) *a.* charming, winning

winter ('wıntə) *n.* **1.** the coldest season —*vi.* **2.** pass, spend the winter —**'wintry** *or* **'wintery** *a.* **1.** of, like winter **2.** cold —**'wintergreen** *n.* evergreen shrub, *esp.* subshrub of E N Amer., which has white, bell-shaped flowers and edible red berries —**winter solstice** time at which sun is at its southernmost point in sky appearing at noon at its lowest altitude above horizon. It occurs about Dec. 22nd. —**winter sports** sports held in open air on snow or ice —**oil of wintergreen** aromatic compound, formerly made from the shrub but now synthesized: used medicinally and for flavouring

wipe (waıp) *vt.* **1.** rub so as to clean —*n.* **2.** wiping —**'wiper** *n.* **1.** one that wipes **2.** automatic wiping apparatus (*esp.* **windscreen wiper**) —**wipe out 1.** erase **2.** annihilate **3.** *sl.* kill

wire (waıə) *n.* **1.** metal drawn into thin, flexible strand **2.** something made of wire, *eg* fence **3.** telegram —*vt.* **4.** provide, fasten with wire **5.** send by telegraph —**'wiring** *n.* system of wires —**'wiry** *a.* **1.** like wire **2.** lean and tough —**wire-gauge** *n.* **1.** flat plate with slots in which standard wire sizes can be measured **2.** standard system of sizes for measuring diameters of wires —**wire-haired** *a.* (of various breeds of dog) with short stiff hair —**'wiretap** *v.* tap (telephone wire *etc.*) to obtain information secretly —**wire wool** mass of fine wire, used *esp.* to clean kitchen articles

wireless ('waıəlıs) *n.* **1.** *old-fashioned term for* radio, radio set —*a.* **2.** of or for radio

wise¹ (waız) *a.* **1.** having intelligence and knowledge **2.** sensible —**wisdom** ('wızdəm) *n.* **1.** (accumulated) knowledge, learning **2.** erudition —**'wisely** *adv.* —**'wiseacre** *n.* one who wishes to seem wise —**wisdom tooth** third molar usu. cut about 20th year

wise² (waız) *n. obs.* manner

-wise (*comb. form*) **1.** indicating direction or manner, as in *clockwise, likewise* **2.** with reference to, as in *businesswise*

wisecrack ('waızkræk) *n. inf.* flippant, (would-be) clever remark

wish (wıʃ) *vi.* **1.** have a desire —*vt.* **2.** desire —*n.* **3.** desire **4.** thing desired —**'wishful** *a.* **1.** desirous **2.** too optimistic —**'wishbone** *n.* V-shaped bone above breastbone of fowl —**wishful thinking** erroneous belief that one's wishes are in accordance with reality

wishy-washy ('wıʃıwɒʃı) *a. inf.* **1.** lacking in substance, force, colour *etc.* **2.** watery; thin

wisp (wısp) *n.* **1.** light, delicate streak, as of smoke **2.** twisted handful, usu. of straw *etc.* **3.** stray lock of hair —**'wispy** *a.*

wisteria (wı'stıərıə) *n.* climbing shrub with usu. mauve flowers

wistful ('wıstful) *a.* **1.** longing, yearning **2.** sadly pensive —**'wistfully** *adv.*

wit¹ (wıt) *n.* **1.** ingenuity in connecting amusingly incongruous ideas **2.** person gifted with this power **3.** sense **4.** intellect **5.** understanding **6.** ingenuity **7.** humour —**'witless** *a.* foolish —**'witticism** *n.* witty remark —**'wittily** *adv.* —**'wittingly** *adv.* **1.** on purpose **2.** knowingly —**'witty** *a.*

wit² (wıt) *v. obs.* be or become aware of (something) —**to wit** that is to say; namely

witch (wıtʃ) *n.* **1.** person, usu. female, believed to practise, practising, or professing to practise (black) magic, sorcery **2.** ugly, wicked woman **3.** fascinating woman —**'witchery** *n.* —**'witchcraft** *n.* —**witch doctor** in certain societies, man appearing to cure or cause injury, disease by magic —**witch-hunt** *n.* rigorous campaign to expose dissenters on pretext of safeguarding public welfare —**witch-hunting** *n./a.*

witch- (*comb. form*) *see* WYCH-

witch hazel *or* **wych-hazel** *n.* **1.** any of genus of trees and shrubs of N Amer. having medicinal properties **2.** astringent medicinal solution containing extract of bark and leaves of one of these shrubs, applied to treat bruises, *etc.*

with (wıð, wıθ) *prep.* **1.** in company or possession of **2.** against **3.** in relation to **4.** through **5.** by means of —**withal** (wı'ðɔːl) *adv.* also, likewise —**within** (wı'ðın) *prep./adv.* in, inside —**without** (wı'ðaʊt) *prep.* **1.** lacking **2.** *obs.* outside

withdraw (wıð'drɔː) *v.* draw back or out (-'**drew**, -'**drawn**, -'**drawing**) —**with-'drawal** *n.* —**with'drawn** *a.* reserved, unsociable

withe (wıθ, wıð, waıð) *n.* strong flexible twig, *esp.* of willow, suitable for binding things together —*vt.* **2.** bind with withes

wither ('wıðə) *v.* (cause to) wilt, dry up, decline —**'withering** *a.* (of glance *etc.*) scornful

withers ('wıðəz) *pl.n.* ridge between a horse's shoulder blades

withhold (wıð'həʊld) *vt.* **1.** restrain **2.** keep back **3.** refrain from giving (-'**held**, -'**holding**) —**with'holder** *n.*

withstand (wɪð'stænd) vt. oppose, resist, esp. successfully (-'stood, -'standing)

withy ('wɪðɪ) n. 1. see WITHE (sense 1) 2. willow tree

witness ('wɪtnɪs) n. 1. one who sees something 2. testimony 3. one who gives testimony —vi. 4. give testimony —vt. 5. see 6. attest to genuineness of 7. see and sign as having seen —**witness box** or esp. U.S. **stand** place in court of law in which witnesses stand to give evidence

wives (waɪvz) n., pl. of WIFE —**old wives' tale** superstitious tradition

wizard ('wɪzəd) n. 1. sorcerer, magician 2. expert —**'wizardry** n.

wizened ('wɪz'nd) or **wizen** a. shrivelled, wrinkled

wk. 1. week (pl. **wks.**) 2. work

WNW west-northwest

woad (wəud) n. blue dye from plant

wobble ('wɒb'l) vi. 1. move unsteadily, sway —n. 2. an unsteady movement —**'wobbliness** n. —**'wobbly** a. shaky, unstable, unsteady —**throw a wobbly** sl. become very angry or excited

woe (wəu) n. grief —**'woebegone** a. looking sorrowful —**'woeful** a. 1. sorrowful 2. pitiful 3. wretched —**'woefully** adv.

wog (wɒg) n. sl. offens. foreigner, esp. one who is not White

wold (wəuld) n. open downs, moorland

wolf (wulf) n. 1. wild predatory doglike animal of northern countries 2. inf. man who habitually tries to seduce women (pl. **wolves** (wulvz)) —vt. 3. eat ravenously —**'wolfhound** n. largest breed of dog, used formerly to hunt wolves —**wolf whistle** whistle by man expressing admiration for a woman —**cry wolf** raise false alarm

wolfram ('wulfrəm) n. tungsten

wolverine ('wulvəri:n) n. carnivorous mammal inhabiting Arctic regions

woman ('wumən) n. 1. adult human female 2. women collectively (pl. **women** ('wɪmɪn)) —**'womanhood** n. —**'womanish** a. effeminate —**'womanize** or **-ise** vi. inf. (of a man) indulge in many casual affairs with women —**'womanizer** or **-iser** n. —**'womankind** n. —**'womanly** a. of, proper to woman —**Women's Institute** in Commonwealth countries, society for women interested in engaging in craft and cultural activities —**Women's Liberation** movement for removal of attitudes, practices that preserve social, economic etc. inequalities between women and men (also **women's lib**)

womb (wu:m) n. female organ of conception and gestation, uterus

wombat ('wɒmbæt) n. Aust. burrowing marsupial with heavy body, short legs and dense fur

won (wʌn) pt./pp. of WIN

wonder ('wʌndə) n. 1. emotion excited by amazing or unusual thing 2. marvel, miracle —vi. 3. be curious 4. feel amazement —**'wonderful** a. 1. remarkable 2. very fine —**'wonderfully** adv.

—**'wonderment** n. surprise —**'wondrous** a. 1. inspiring wonder 2. strange

wonky ('wɒŋkɪ) a. inf. 1. shaky, unsteady 2. groggy 3. askew 4. unreliable

wont (wəunt) n. 1. custom —a. 2. accustomed —**'wonted** a. habitual, established

woo (wu:) vt. court, seek to marry —**'wooer** n. suitor

wood (wud) n. 1. substance of trees, timber 2. firewood 3. tract of land with growing trees —**'wooded** a. having (many) trees —**'wooden** a. 1. made of wood 2. obstinate 3. without expression —**'woody** a. —**'woodbine** n. honeysuckle —**'woodcarver** n. —**'woodcarving** n. 1. act of carving wood 2. work of art produced by carving wood —**'woodchuck** n. Amer. burrowing marmot —**'woodcock** n. game bird —**'woodcut** n. 1. engraving on wood 2. impression from this —**woodland** ('wudlənd) n. woods, forest —**'woodlark** n. Old World lark similar to skylark —**'woodlouse** n. small grey land crustacean with seven pairs of legs (pl. **-lice**) —**'woodpecker** n. bird which searches tree trunks for insects —**wood pigeon** large Eurasian pigeon —**'woodpile** n. heap of firewood —**wood pulp** finely pulped wood that has been digested by chemical, such as caustic soda, used in making paper —**'woodruff** n. plant, esp. sweet woodruff, which has small sweet-scented white flowers, used to flavour wine and in perfumery —**wood sorrel** Eurasian plant having trefoil leaves, underground creeping stem and white purple-veined flowers —**woodwind** ('wudwɪnd) a./n. (of) wind instruments of orchestra, orig. made of wood —**'woodwork** n. 1. art or craft of making things in wood 2. components made of wood, such as doors etc. —**'woodworm** n. insect larva that bores into wood

woof¹ (wu:f) n. the threads that cross the warp in weaving

woof² (wuf) interj. 1. imitation of bark of dog —vi. 2. (of dog) bark

woofer ('wu:fə) n. loudspeaker for reproducing low-frequency sounds

wool (wul) n. 1. soft hair of sheep, goat etc. 2. yarn spun from this —**'woollen** or U.S. **'woolen** a. —**'woolly** or U.S. (oft.) **'wooly** a. 1. of wool 2. vague, muddled —n. 3. knitted woollen garment —**'woolgathering** a./n. daydreaming —**'woolsack** n. Lord Chancellor's seat in British House of Lords

woozy ('wu:zɪ) a. inf. 1. dazed or confused 2. experiencing dizziness, nausea etc. as result of drink —**'woozily** adv. —**'wooziness** n.

Worcs. (wɜ:ks) Worcestershire

word (wɜ:d) n. 1. unit of speech or writing regarded by users of a language as the smallest separate meaningful unit 2. term 3. message 4. brief remark 5. information 6. promise 7. command —vt. 8. express in words, *esp.* in particular way —'**wordily** *adv.* —'**wording** *n.* choice and arrangement of words —'**wordy** *a.* using more words than necessary, verbose —**word blindness** *see* ALEXIA, DYSLEXIA —**word-perfect** *or* U.S. **letter-perfect** *a.* **1.** correct in every detail **2.** (of speaker *etc.*) knowing one's speech *etc.* perfectly —**word processing** storage and organization of language by electronic means, *esp.* for business purposes —**word processor** installation for word processing, typically consisting of key-board and VDU incorporating microprocessor, storage and processing capabilities —**word wrapping** *Comp.* automatic shifting of word at end of line to new line in order to keep within preset margins

wore (wɔː) *pt. of* WEAR

work (wɜːk) *n.* **1.** labour **2.** employment **3.** occupation **4.** task **5.** toil **6.** something made or accomplished **7.** production of art or science **8.** book **9.** needlework —*pl.* **10.** factory **11.** total of person's deeds, writings *etc.* **12.** *inf.* everything, full or extreme treatment **13.** mechanism of clock *etc.* —*vt.* **14.** cause to operate **15.** make, shape —*vi.* **16.** apply effort **17.** labour **18.** operate **19.** be engaged in trade, profession *etc.* **20.** turn out successfully **21.** ferment —'**workable** *a.* —'**worker** *n.* —'**working** *n.* **1.** operation or mode of operation of something **2.** act or process of moulding something pliable **3.** (*oft. pl.*) part of mine or quarry that is being or has been worked —*a.* **4.** of or concerned with person or thing that works **5.** concerned with, used in, or suitable for work **6.** capable of being operated or used —'**workaday** *a.* **1.** ordinary **2.** suitable for working days —**worka'holic** *n.* person obsessively addicted to work —**work force** *n.* total number of workers employed by company on specific project *etc.* **2.** total number of people who could be employed —'**workhouse** *n. Hist.* institution offering food, lodgings for unpaid menial work —**work-in** *n.* form of industrial action in which factory threatened with closure is occupied and run by its workers —**working class** social class consisting of wage earners, *esp.* manual —**working-class** *a.* —**working party** advisory committee studying specific problem, question —'**workman** *n.* manual worker —'**workmanlike** *or* '**workmanly** *a.* appropriate to or befitting a good workman —'**workmanship** *n.* **1.** skill of workman **2.** way thing is finished **3.** style —**work-out** *n.* session of physical exercise, *esp.* for training or practice —'**workshop** *n.* place where things are made —'**workshy** *a.* not inclined to work —**work station** area in office *etc.* where one person works —**work in 1.** insert or become inserted **2.** find space for —**work of art 1.** piece of fine art, as painting, sculpture **2.** something that may be likened to piece of fine art, *esp.* in beauty *etc.* —**work out 1.**

accomplish by effort **2.** solve by reasoning or calculation **3.** devise or formulate **4.** prove satisfactory **5.** happen as specified **6.** take part in physical exercise, as in training **7.** remove all mineral in (mine *etc.*) that can be profitably exploited —**work to rule** adhere strictly to all working regulations to reduce rate of work as form of protest

world (wɜːld) *n.* **1.** the universe **2.** the planet earth **3.** sphere of existence **4.** mankind, people generally **5.** society —'**worldly** *a.* **1.** earthly **2.** mundane **3.** absorbed in the pursuit of material gain, advantage **4.** carnal —**World Bank** international organization established in 1945 to assist economic development, by advance of loans guaranteed by member governments (official name: **International Bank for Reconstruction and Development**) —**world-beater** *n.* person or thing that surpasses all others in its category; champion —**World Cup** international association football championship competition held every four years between national teams selected through preliminary tournaments —**world-shaking** *a.* of enormous significance; momentous —**world war** war involving many countries

worm (wɜːm) *n.* **1.** small limbless creeping snakelike creature **2.** anything resembling worm in shape or movement **3.** *inf.* weak, despised person —*pl.* **4.** (disorder caused by) infestation of worms, *esp.* in intestines —*vi.* **5.** crawl —*vt.* **6.** work (oneself) in insidiously **7.** extract (secret) craftily **8.** rid of worms —'**wormy** *a.* —'**wormcast** *n.* coil of earth excreted by earthworm —**worm-eaten** *a.* **1.** full of holes gnawed by worms **2.** old, antiquated —**worm gear 1.** device consisting of threaded shaft (**worm**) that mates with gear wheel (**worm wheel**) so that rotary motion can be transferred between two shafts at right angles to each other **2.** gear wheel driven by threaded shaft or worm (*also* **worm wheel**)

wormwood ('wɜːmwʊd) *n.* **1.** bitter herb **2.** bitterness

worn (wɔːn) *pp. of* WEAR —**worn-out** *a.* **1.** worn or used until threadbare, valueless or useless **2.** exhausted

worry ('wʌrɪ) *vi.* **1.** be (unduly) concerned —*vt.* **2.** trouble, pester, harass **3.** (of dog) seize, shake with teeth ('**worried,** '**worrying**) —*n.* **4.** (cause of) anxiety, concern —'**worrier** *n.* —'**worrisome** *a.* **1.** causing worry **2.** tending to worry —**worry beads** string of beads that when played with supposedly relieves nervous tension

worse (wɜːs) *a./adv.* **1.** *comp. of* BAD *or* BADLY —*n.* **2.** inferior or less good person, thing or state —'**worsen** *v.* **1.** make, grow worse —*vt.* **2.** impair —*vi.* **3.** deteriorate —**worst** *a./adv.* **1.** *sup. of* BAD *or* BADLY —*n.* **2.** least good or most inferior person, part or thing

worship ('wɜːʃɪp) *vt.* **1.** show religious

devotion to **2.** adore **3.** love and admire (**-pp-**) —*n.* **4.** act of worshipping **5.** title used to address mayor, magistrate *etc.* —'**worshipful** *a.* —'**worshipper** *n.*

worsted ('wʊstɪd) *n.* **1.** woollen yarn —*a.* **2.** made of woollen yarn **3.** spun from wool

wort (wɜːt) *n.* **1.** *obs.* plant, herb **2.** infusion of malt before fermentation

worth (wɜːθ) *a.* **1.** having or deserving to have value specified **2.** meriting —*n.* **3.** excellence **4.** merit, value **5.** virtue **6.** usefulness **7.** price **8.** quantity to be had for a given sum —'**worthily** ('wɜːðɪlɪ) *adv.* —'**worthiness** ('wɜːðɪnɪs) *n.* —'**worthless** *a.* useless —**worthy** ('wɜːðɪ) *a.* **1.** virtuous **2.** meriting —*n.* **3.** one of eminent worth **4.** (local) notable —**worth'while** *a.* worth the time, effort *etc.* involved

would (wʊd; *unstressed* wəd) *v. aux.* **1.** expressing wish, intention, probability —*v.* **2.** *pt.* of WILL —**would-be** *a.* wishing, pretending to be

wound[1] (wuːnd) *n.* **1.** injury, hurt from cut, stab *etc.* —*vt.* **2.** inflict wound on, injure **3.** pain

wound[2] (waʊnd) *pt./pp.* of WIND[2]

wove (wəʊv) *pt.* of WEAVE

woven ('wəʊv'n) *pp.* of WEAVE

wow (waʊ) *interj.* **1.** exclamation of astonishment, admiration *etc.* —*n.* **2.** *inf.* object of astonishment, admiration *etc.* **3.** variation, distortion in pitch in record player *etc.*

w.p.m. words per minute

W.R.A.C. Women's Royal Army Corps

wrack *or* **rack** (ræk) *n.* seaweed

W.R.A.F. Women's Royal Air Force

wraith (reɪθ) *n.* **1.** apparition of a person seen shortly before or after death **2.** spectre

wrangle ('ræŋg'l) *vi.* **1.** quarrel (noisily) **2.** dispute **3.** *US, C* herd cattle —*n.* **4.** noisy quarrel **5.** dispute —'**wrangler** *n. US, C* cowboy

wrap (ræp) *vt.* **1.** cover, *esp.* by putting something round **2.** put round (**-pp-**) —**wrap** *or* '**wrapper** *n.* **1.** loose garment **2.** covering —'**wrapping** *n.* material used to wrap —'**wrapover**, '**wraparound** *or* '**wrapround** *a.* (of garment, *esp.* skirt) not sewn up at one side, but worn wrapped round body and fastened so that open edges overlap

wrasse (ræs) *n.* type of sea fish

wrath (rɒθ) *n.* anger —'**wrathful** *a.*

wreak (riːk) *vt.* **1.** inflict (vengeance) **2.** cause

wreath (riːθ) *n.* something twisted into ring form, *esp.* band of flowers *etc.* as memorial or tribute on grave *etc.* —**wreathe** *vt.* **1.** form into wreath **2.** surround **3.** wind round

wreck (rɛk) *n.* **1.** destruction of ship **2.** wrecked ship **3.** ruin **4.** something ruined —*vt.* **5.** cause the wreck of —'**wreckage** *n.* —'**wrecker** *n.* **1.** person or thing that destroys, ruins **2.** one whose job is to demolish houses, dismantle old cars *etc.*

wren (rɛn) *n.* kind of small songbird

Wren (rɛn) *n.* member of Women's Royal Naval Service

wrench (rɛntʃ) *vt.* **1.** twist **2.** distort **3.** seize forcibly **4.** sprain —*n.* **5.** violent twist **6.** tool for twisting or screwing **7.** spanner **8.** sudden pain caused *esp.* by parting

wrest (rɛst) *vt.* **1.** take by force **2.** twist violently

wrestle ('rɛs'l) *vi.* **1.** fight (*esp.* as sport) by grappling and trying to throw down **2.** strive **3.** struggle —*n.* **4.** struggle, tussle —'**wrestler** *n.* —'**wrestling** *n.*

wretch (rɛtʃ) *n.* **1.** despicable person **2.** miserable creature —**wretched** ('rɛtʃɪd) *a.* **1.** miserable, unhappy **2.** worthless —**wretchedly** ('rɛtʃɪdlɪ) *adv.* —**wretchedness** ('rɛtʃɪdnɪs) *n.*

wrick (rɪk) *n./vt.* strain; sprain

wriggle ('rɪg'l) *vi.* **1.** move with twisting action, as worm **2.** squirm —*n.* **3.** this action

wright (raɪt) *n. obs.* workman; maker; builder

wring (rɪŋ) *vt.* **1.** twist **2.** extort **3.** pain **4.** squeeze out (**wrung**, '**wringing**) —'**wringer** *n.* machine consisting of two rollers between which wet clothes are run to squeeze out the water

wrinkle ('rɪŋk'l) *n.* **1.** slight ridge or furrow on surface **2.** crease in the skin **3.** fold **4.** pucker **5.** *inf.* (useful) trick, hint —*v.* **6.** make, become wrinkled, pucker —'**wrinklies** *pl.n. inf., offens.* old people —'**wrinkly** *a.*

wrist (rɪst) *n.* joint between hand and arm —'**wristlet** *n.* band worn on wrist

writ (rɪt) *n.* written command from law court or other authority

write (raɪt) *vi.* **1.** mark paper *etc.* with the symbols which are used to represent words or sounds **2.** compose **3.** send a letter —*vt.* **4.** set down in words **5.** compose **6.** communicate in writing (**wrote**, **written** ('rɪt'n), '**writing**) —'**writer** *n.* **1.** one who writes **2.** author —**write-off** *n. inf.* something damaged beyond repair —**write-up** *n.* written (published) account of something

writhe (raɪð) *vi.* **1.** twist, squirm in or as in pain *etc.* **2.** be acutely embarrassed (**writhed** *pt.*, **writhed**, *Poet.* **writhen** ('rɪð'n) *pp.*, '**writhing** *pr.p.*)

W.R.N.S. Women's Royal Naval Service

wrong (rɒŋ) *a.* **1.** not right or good **2.** not suitable **3.** wicked **4.** incorrect **5.** mistaken **6.** not functioning properly —*n.* **7.** that which is wrong **8.** harm **9.** evil —*vt.* **10.** do wrong to **11.** think badly of without justification —'**wrongful** *a.* —'**wrongfully** *adv.* —'**wrongly** *adv.* —'**wrongdoer** *n.* one who acts immorally or illegally —**wrongfoot** *vt. Tennis etc.* play shot in such a way as to cause (one's opponent) to be off balance —**wrong-headed** *a.* **1.** constantly wrong in judgment **2.** foolishly stubborn

wrote (rəʊt) *pt.* of WRITE

wrought (rɔːt) *v.* **1.** *pt./pp.* of WORK —*a.* **2.**

(of metals) shaped by hammering or beating —**wrought iron** pure form of iron used *esp.* in decorative railings *etc.*

wrung (rʌŋ) *pt./pp. of* WRING

W.R.V.S. Women's Royal Voluntary Service

wry (raɪ) *a.* **1.** turned to one side, contorted, askew **2.** sardonic, dryly humorous —**'wryneck** *n.* type of woodpecker

WSW west-southwest

wt. weight

WV West Virginia

WWI World War One

WWII World War Two

WX women's extra (size)

WY Wyoming

wych- *or* **witch-** (*comb. form*) (of tree)

wych-elm *or* **witch-elm** ('wɪtʃɛlm) *n.* **1.** Eurasian elm tree, having rounded shape, longish pointed leaves, clusters of small flowers and winged fruits **2.** wood of this tree

wynd (waɪnd) *n.* in Scotland, narrow lane, alley

X

x *or* **X** (ɛks) *n.* **1.** 24th letter of English alphabet **2.** speech sound sequence represented by this letter, pronounced as *ks* or *gz* or, in initial position, *z*, as in *xylophone* (*pl.* **x's, X's** *or* **Xs**)

x *Maths.* unknown quantity

X 1. Christ **2.** Christian **3.** Cross **4.** Roman numeral, 10 **5.** mark indicating something wrong, a choice, a kiss, signature *etc.* **6.** unknown, mysterious person, factor

xanthine ('zænθiːn, -θaɪn) *n.* **1.** crystalline compound found in urine, blood and certain plants **2.** any of three substituted derivatives of xanthine, which act as stimulants and diuretics

x-axis *n.* reference axis, usu. horizontal, along which *x*-coordinate is measured

X-chromosome *n.* sex-determining chromosome that occurs in pairs in homologically paired cells of females of many animals and as one of pair with Y-chromosome in those of males

Xe *Chem.* xenon

xeno- *or before vowel* **xen-** (*comb. form*) something strange, different or foreign, as in *xenogamy*

xenogamy (zɛ'nɒgəmɪ) *n.* **1.** pollination from another plant **2.** cross-fertilization —**xe'nogamous** *a.*

xenon ('zɛnɒn) *n.* colourless, odourless gas occurring in very small quantities in air

xenophobia (zɛnə'fəʊbɪə) *n.* dislike, hatred, fear, of strangers or aliens

xerography (zɪ'rɒgrəfɪ) *n.* photocopying process —**Xerox** ('zɪərɒks) *n.* **R** xerographic copying process, machine

xi (zaɪ, saɪ, ksaɪ, ksiː) *n.* 14th letter in Gr. alphabet (Ξ, ξ) (*pl.* **-s**)

Xmas ('ɛksməs, 'krɪsməs) Christmas

x-ray *or* **X-ray** *n.* **1.** radiation of very short wavelengths, capable of penetrating solid bodies, and printing on photographic plate shadow picture of objects not permeable by rays —*vt.* **2.** photograph by x-rays

xylem ('zaɪləm, -lɛm) *n.* plant tissue that conducts water and mineral salts from roots to other parts

xylene ('zaɪliːn) *n.* aromatic hydrocarbon existing in three isomeric forms, all three being colourless flammable volatile liquids used as solvents *etc.*

xylograph ('zaɪləgrɑːf) *n.* **1.** wood engraving **2.** impression from wood block

xyloid ('zaɪlɔɪd) *a.* **1.** pert. to wood **2.** woody, ligneous

xylophone ('zaɪləfəʊn) *n.* musical instrument of wooden bars which sound when struck

xylose ('zaɪləʊz, -ləʊs) *n.* white crystalline sugar found in wood and straw and used in dyeing, tanning, diabetic food *etc.*

Y

y *or* **Y** (waɪ) *n.* **1.** 25th letter of English alphabet **2.** speech sound represented by this letter, usu. semivowel, as in *yawn,* or vowel, as in *symbol, shy* **3.** something shaped like Y (*pl.* **y's, Y's** *or* **Ys**)

y *Maths.* **1.** *y*-axis or coordinate measured along *y*-axis in Cartesian coordinate system **2.** algebraic variable

Y 1. any unknown or variable factor, number or thing **2.** *Chem.* yttrium

-y¹ *or* **-ey** (*comb. form*) **1.** characterized by; consisting of; filled with; resembling, as in *sunny, sandy, smoky, classy* **2.** tending to; acting or existing as specified, as in *leaky, shiny*

-y², *or* **-ie,** *or* **-ey** (*comb. form*) *inf.* **1.** denoting smallness and expressing affection and familiarity, as in *doggy, Jamie* **2.** person or thing concerned with or characterized by being, as in *groupie, goalie, fatty*

-y³ (*comb. form*) **1.** act of doing what is indicated by verbal element, as in *inquiry* **2.** state, condition, quality, as in *geography, jealousy*

yacht (jɒt) *n.* vessel propelled by sail or power, used for racing, pleasure *etc.* —**'yachtsman** *n.*

yahoo (jə'huː) *n.* crude, coarse person

yak¹ (jæk) *n.* shaggy-haired, long-horned ox of Central Asia

yak² (jæk) *sl. n.* **1.** noisy, continuous, trivial talk —*vi.* **2.** chatter or talk in this way (**-kk-**)

Yale lock (jeɪl) **R** cylinder lock using flat serrated key

yam (jæm) *n.* large edible tuber, sweet potato

Yang (jæŋ) *n. see* YIN AND YANG

yank (jæŋk) *vt.* **1.** jerk, tug; pull quickly —*n.* **2.** quick tug

Yank (jæŋk) *a./n. sl.* American

yap (jæp) *vi.* **1.** bark (as small dog) **2.** talk idly; gossip (**-pp-**) —*n.* **3.** sharp bark

yarborough ('jɑːbərə, -brə) *n. Bridge, whist* hand of 13 cards with no card higher than nine

yard¹ (jɑːd) *n.* **1.** unit of length, 0.915 metre **2.** spar slung across ship's mast to extend sails —**'yardstick** *n.* formula or standard of measurement or comparison

yard² (jɑːd) *n.* piece of enclosed ground, oft. attached to or adjoining building and used for some specific purpose, as garden, storage, holding livestock *etc.* —**'yardage** *n.* use of yard **2.** charge made for this

yarmulke ('jɑːməlkə) *n. Judaism* man's skullcap worn at prayer, and by strongly religious Jews at all times

yarn (jɑːn) *n.* **1.** spun thread **2.** tale —*vi.* **3.** tell a tale

yarrow ('jærəʊ) *n.* plant with flat white flower clusters

yashmak *or* **yashmac** ('jæʃmæk) *n.* face veil worn by Muslim women

yaw (jɔː) *vi.* **1.** (of aircraft *etc.*) turn about vertical axis **2.** (of ship *etc.*) deviate temporarily from course

yawl (jɔːl) *n.* two-masted sailing vessel

yawn (jɔːn) *vi.* **1.** open mouth wide, *esp.* in sleepiness **2.** gape —*n.* **3.** a yawning

yaws (jɔːz) *pl.n.* contagious tropical skin disease

y-axis *n.* reference axis of graph or two- or three-dimensional Cartesian coordinate system along which *y*-coordinate is measured

Yb *Chem.* ytterbium

Y-chromosome *n.* sex chromosome that occurs as one of pair with X-chromosome in homologically paired cells of males of many animals

yd *or* **yd.** yard (measure)

ye (jiː, *unstressed* jɪ) *pron. obs.* you

yea (jeɪ) *interj. obs.* yes

year (jɪə) *n.* **1.** time taken by one revolution of earth round sun, about 365 days **2.** twelve months —**'yearling** *n.* animal one year old —**'yearly** *adv.* **1.** every year, once a year —*a.* **2.** happening *etc.* once a year —**'yearbook** *n.* reference book published annually and containing details of events of previous year

yearn (jɜːn) *vi.* **1.** feel longing, desire **2.** be filled with pity, tenderness —**'yearning** *n.*

yeast (jiːst) *n.* substance used as fermenting agent, *esp.* in raising bread —**'yeasty** *a.* **1.** of, like yeast **2.** frothy, fermenting

yell (jel) *v.* **1.** cry out in loud shrill tone **2.** *inf.* call —*n.* **3.** loud shrill cry **4.** *inf.* call

yellow ('jeləʊ) *a.* **1.** of the colour of lemons, gold *etc.* **2.** *inf.* cowardly —*n.* **3.** yellow colour —**yellow fever** acute infectious disease of (sub)tropical climates —**'yellowhammer** *n.* small European bunting —**yellow pages** classified telephone directory or section of directory that lists subscribers by business or service provided —**yellow streak** cowardly trait —**'yellowwood** *n.* **SA 1.** type of conifer **2.** its rich yellow wood used *esp.* for furniture and building

yelp (jelp) *vi./n.* (produce) quick, shrill cry

yen¹ (jɛn) *n.* Japanese monetary unit (*pl.* **yen**)

yen² (jɛn) *n. inf.* longing, craving

yeoman ('jəʊmən) *n.* **1.** *Hist.* farmer cultivating his own land **2.** assistant, subordinate —**'yeomanry** *n.* **1.** yeomen collectively **2.** *Brit.* volunteer cavalry force, organized in 1761 for home defence —**yeoman of the guard** member of ceremonial bodyguard (**Yeomen of the Guard**) of British monarch

yes (jɛs) *interj.* affirms or consents, gives

an affirmative answer —**yes man** weak person willing to agree to anything

yesterday ('jɛstədɪ, -deɪ) *n.* **1.** day before today **2.** recent time —*adv.* **3.** on the day before today

yet (jɛt) *adv.* **1.** now **2.** still **3.** besides **4.** hitherto **5.** nevertheless —*conj.* **6.** but, at the same time, nevertheless

yeti ('jɛtɪ) *n. see* **abominable snowman** *at* ABOMINATE

yew (ju:) *n.* **1.** evergreen tree with dark leaves **2.** its wood

Y.H.A. UK Youth Hostels Association

Yiddish ('jɪdɪʃ) *a./n.* (of, in) dialect of mixed German and Hebrew used by many Jews in Europe —*n. sl. offens.* Jew

yield (ji:ld) *vt.* **1.** give or return as food **2.** produce **3.** provide **4.** concede **5.** give up, surrender —*vi.* **6.** submit **7.** (*with* to) comply (with) **8.** surrender, give way —*n.* **9.** amount produced, result **10.** return, profit

Yin and Yang (jɪn) two complementary principles of Chinese philosophy: Yin is negative, dark and feminine; Yang is positive, bright and masculine

Y.M.C.A. Young Men's Christian Association

yob (jɒb) *or* **yobbo** ('jɒbəʊ) *n. sl.* aggressive, surly youth (*pl.* **-s**)

yodel ('jəʊdˀl) *v.* **1.** warble in falsetto tone (**-ll-**) —*n.* **2.** falsetto warbling as practised by Swiss mountaineers

yoga ('jəʊgə) *n.* Hindu philosophical system aiming at spiritual, mental and physical wellbeing by means of certain physical and mental exercises —**yogi** ('jəʊgɪ) *n.* one who practises yoga (*pl.* **-s**, **-gin** (-gɪn))

yoghurt *or* **yogurt** ('jɒgət) *n.* thick, custardlike preparation of curdled milk

yoicks (haɪk; *spelling pron.* jɔɪks) *interj.* cry used by fox-hunters to urge on hounds

yoke (jəʊk) *n.* **1.** wooden bar put across necks of two animals to hold them together and to which plough *etc.* may be attached **2.** various objects like a yoke in shape or use **3.** fitted part of garment, *esp.* round neck, shoulders **4.** bond, tie **5.** domination —*vt.* **6.** put a yoke on **7.** couple, unite

yokel ('jəʊkˀl) *n. disparaging term for* (old-fashioned) country dweller

yolk (jəʊk) *n.* **1.** yellow central part of egg **2.** oily secretion of skin of sheep

Yom Kippur (jɒm 'kɪpə; *Hebrew* jɔm ki'pur) Jewish holiday celebrated as day of fasting, when prayers of penitence are recited in synagogue (*also* **Day of Atonement**)

yon (jɒn) *a. obs., dial.* that or those over there —**'yonder** *a.* **1.** yon —*adv.* **2.** over there, in that direction

yoo-hoo ('ju:hu:) *interj.* call to attract attention

YOP (jɒp) Youth Opportunities Programme

yore (jɔ:) *n. Poet.* the distant past

yorker ('jɔ:kə) *n. Cricket* ball that pitches directly under bat —**york** *vt. Cricket* bowl (batsman) by pitching ball under or just beyond bat

Yorks. (jɔ:ks) Yorkshire

Yorkshire pudding ('jɔ:kʃɪə) savoury baked batter eaten with roast beef —**Yorkshire terrier** very small terrier with long straight coat

you (ju:; *unstressed* ju) *pron.* referring to person(s) addressed, or to unspecified person(s)

young (jʌŋ) *a.* **1.** not far advanced in growth, life or existence **2.** not yet old **3.** immature **4.** junior **5.** recently formed **6.** vigorous —*n.* **7.** offspring —**'youngster** *n.* child

your (jɔ:, jʊə; *unstressed* jə) *a.* belonging to you —**yours** *pron.* —**your'self** *pron.* (*pl.* **your'selves**)

youth (ju:θ) *n.* **1.** state or time of being young **2.** state before adult age **3.** young man **4.** young people —**'youthful** *a.* —**youth hostel** inexpensive lodging place *esp.* for young people travelling cheaply (*also* **'hostel**)

yowl (jaʊl) *vi./n.* (produce) mournful cry

yo-yo ('jəʊjəʊ) *n.* toy consisting of a spool attached to a string, by which it can be spun out and reeled in while attached to the finger (*pl.* **-s**)

Y.S.T. US, C Yukon Standard Time

Y.T. C Yukon Territory

ytterbium (ɪ'tɜːbɪəm) *n.* silvery element of lanthanide series of metals, used to improve mechanical properties of steel

yttrium ('ɪtrɪəm) *n.* silvery metallic element used in various alloys

yucca ('jʌkə) *n.* tropical plant with stiff lancelike leaves

Yugoslav *or* **Jugoslav** ('ju:gəʊslɑːv) *n.* **1.** native of Yugoslavia, federal republic in SE Europe **2.** Serbo-Croatian (language) —*a.* **3.** of Yugoslavia

yule (ju:l) *n.* (*sometimes* Y-) the Christmas festival or season

Yuppie ('jʌpɪ) (*sometimes* y-) *n.* **1.** young urban (*or* upwardly mobile) professional —*a.* **2.** designed for or appealing to Yuppies

Y.W.C.A. Young Women's Christian Association

Z

z or **Z** (zɛd; *U.S.* ziː) *n.* **1.** 26th letter of English alphabet **2.** speech sound represented by this letter **3.** something shaped like Z (*pl.* **z's, Z's** or **Zs**)

z *Maths.* **1.** z-axis or coordinate measured along z-axis in Cartesian or cylindrical coordinate system **2.** algebraic variable

zany ('zeɪnɪ) *a.* comical, funny in unusual way

zeal (ziːl) *n.* **1.** fervour **2.** keenness, enthusiasm —**zealot** ('zɛlət) *n.* **1.** fanatic **2.** enthusiast —**zealous** ('zɛləs) *a.* **1.** ardent **2.** enthusiastic **3.** earnest —**zealously** ('zɛləslɪ) *adv.*

zebra ('zɛbrə, 'ziːbrə) *n.* striped Afr. animal like a horse —**zebra crossing** pedestrian crossing marked by stripes on road

zebu ('ziːbuː) *n.* humped Indian ox or cow

Zen (zɛn) *n. Buddhism* Japanese school teaching contemplation, meditation

zenith ('zɛnɪθ) *n.* **1.** point of the heavens directly above an observer **2.** point opposite nadir **3.** summit, peak **4.** climax —**'zenithal** *a.*

zephyr ('zɛfə) *n.* soft, gentle breeze

zeppelin ('zɛpəlɪn) *n.* large, cylindrical, rigid airship

zero ('zɪərəʊ) *n.* **1.** nothing **2.** figure 0 **3.** point on graduated instrument from which positive and negative quantities are reckoned **4.** the lowest point (*pl.* **-s, -es**) —**zero hour 1.** *Mil.* time set for start of attack *etc.* **2.** *inf.* critical time —**zero option** (in international nuclear arms negotiations) offer to remove all shorter-range nuclear missiles if other side will do same —**zero-rated** *a.* denoting goods on which buyer pays no value-added tax —**zero-zero option** (in international nuclear arms negotiations) offer to remove all intermediate-range nuclear missiles if other side will do same

zest (zɛst) *n.* **1.** enjoyment **2.** excitement, interest, flavour **3.** peel of orange or lemon

zeta ('ziːtə) *n.* sixth letter in Gr. alphabet (Z, ζ)

zigzag ('zɪgzæg) *n.* **1.** line or course characterized by sharp turns in alternating directions —*vi.* **2.** move along in zigzag course (**-zagged** *pt./pp.*, **-zagging** *pr.p.*)

zinc (zɪŋk) *n.* bluish-white metallic element with wide variety of uses, *esp.* in alloys as brass *etc.* —**'zincograph** *n.* —**zin'cographer** *n.* —**zin'cography** *n.* art or process of engraving zinc to form printing plate —**zinc ointment** medicinal ointment of zinc oxide, petrolatum and paraffin —**zinc oxide** white insoluble powder used as pigment in paints, cosmetics, glass *etc.* (*also* **flowers of zinc**)

zing (zɪŋ) *n. inf.* **1.** short high-pitched buzzing sound **2.** vitality; zest —*vi.* **3.** make or move with high-pitched buzzing sound

zinnia ('zɪnɪə) *n.* plant with daisylike, brightly-coloured flowers

Zion ('zaɪən) or **Sion** *n.* **1.** hill on which Jerusalem stands **2.** Judaism **3.** Christian Church **4.** heaven —**'Zionism** *n.* movement to found, support Jewish homeland in Palestine —**'Zionist** *n./a.*

zip (zɪp) *n.* **1.** device for fastening with two rows of flexible metal or nylon teeth, interlocked and opened by a sliding clip (*also* **'zipper, zip fastener**) **2.** short whizzing sound **3.** energy, vigour —*vt.* **4.** fasten with zip —*vi.* **5.** move with zip (**-pp-**)

zircon ('zɜːkɒn) *n.* mineral used as gemstone and in industry —**zir'conium** *n.* greyish-white metallic element, occurring chiefly in zircon, that is exceptionally corrosion-resistant and has low neutron absorption

zither ('zɪðə) *n.* flat stringed instrument

zloty ('zlɒtɪ) *n.* Polish coin (*pl.* **-s, 'zloty**)

Zn *Chem.* zinc

zodiac ('zəʊdɪæk) *n.* imaginary belt of the heavens along which the sun, moon, and chief planets appear to move, divided crosswise into twelve equal areas, called **signs of the zodiac**, each named after a constellation —**zodiacal** (zəʊ'daɪəkəl) *a.*

zombie or **zombi** ('zɒmbɪ) *n.* **1.** person appearing lifeless, apathetic *etc.* **2.** corpse supposedly brought to life by supernatural spirit

zone (zəʊn) *n.* **1.** region with particular characteristics or use **2.** any of the five belts into which tropics and arctic and antarctic circles divide the earth —**'zonal** *a.*

zoo (zuː) *n.* place where wild animals are kept, studied, bred and exhibited (*in full* **zoological gardens**)

zoo- or *before vowel* **zo-** (*comb. form*) animals, as in *zooplankton*

zoogeography (zəʊədʒɪ'ɒgrəfɪ) *n.* science of geographical distribution of animals

zoography (zəʊ'ɒgrəfɪ) *n.* descriptive zoology —**zo'ographer** or **zo'ographist** *n.* —**zoo'graphic(al)** *a.*

zooid ('zəʊɔɪd) *n.* **1.** independent animal body, such as individual of coelenterate colony **2.** cell or body capable of spontaneous motion, produced by organism

zool. 1. zoological **2.** zoology

zoology (zəʊ'ɒlədʒɪ, zuː-) *n.* **1.** scientific study of animals **2.** characteristics of particular animals or of fauna of particular area —**zoo'logical** *a.* —**zo'ologist** *n.*

zoom (zuːm) *v.* **1.** (cause to) make loud buzzing, humming sound **2.** (cause to) go fast or rise, increase sharply —*vi.* **3.** (*with* in *or* out) use camera lens of adjustable focal length to make subject appear closer or further away —**zoom lens** lens used in this way

zoophyte ('zəʊəfaɪt) *n.* plantlike animal, *eg* sponge —**zoophytic** (zəʊə'fɪtɪk) *a.*

Zoroastrianism (zɒrəʊ'æstrɪənɪzəm) *or* **Zoroastrism** *n.* dualistic religion founded by Persian prophet Zoroaster, based on concept of continuous struggle between Ormazd, god of creation, light and goodness, and his archenemy, Ahriman, spirit of evil and darkness

Zr *Chem.* zirconium

Zulu ('zu:lʊ, -lu:) *n.* member, language of native S Afr. tribes

zygote ('zaɪgəʊt, 'zɪg-) *n.* fertilized egg cell

PUNCTUATION MARKS AND OTHER SYMBOLS

,	comma		
;	semicolon		
:	colon		
.	full stop		
—	dash		
!	exclamation mark		
?	interrogation or doubt		
-	hyphen, as in knick-knack		
'	apostrophe, as in *Queen's English*		
( )	parentheses		
[ ]	brackets		
}	brace, to enclose two or more lines		
´	acute accent, as in *blasé*		
`	grave accent } as in		
^	circumflex } *tête-à-tête*		
~	tilde, used over *n* in certain Spanish words to denote the sound of *ny*, as in *señor*		
¸	cedilla, to denote that *c* is pronounced soft, as in *façade*		
" "	quotation marks		
' '	quotation marks, when used within a quotation, as in *"He said, 'I will go at once' and jumped into the car."*		
¯	macron, to mark length of sound, as in *cōbra*		
˘	breve, marking a short sound, as in *lĭnen*		
¨	diaeresis, as in *daïs*		
¨	in German, used to denote modification of the vowel sound, as in *Köln* (Cologne)		
ʌ	caret, marking a word or letter to be inserted in the line		

* *	* .. .. — or - - - - ellipsis to indicate a break in a narrative, or an omission
⁎⁎	or ⁎⁎ asterism, used to call attention to a particular passage
. . .	. . or - - - - leaders, to direct the eye to a certain point
¶	paragraph
*	star, asterisk (1) a reference mark (2) used in philology to denote forms assumed to have existed though not recorded
†	dagger, obelisk (1) a reference mark (2) obsolete or dead
‡	double dagger, a reference mark
²	superior figure, used (1) as a reference mark (2) to indicate a homonym
ᵃ	superior letter
§	section mark
‖	parallel mark
☞	index, hand, fist
#	number; space
„	ditto
&	ampersand, and
&c	et cetera
@	at
℔	per
%	per cent; per hundred
©	copyright
®	registered; registered trademark
♂	male
♀	female.

PUNCTUATION AND THE USE OF CAPITAL LETTERS

apostrophe The sign ('), used to indicate possession. In the singular -'s is used (eg *day's end*); in the plural the apostrophe is added to the end of the word (eg *the neighbours' dog*). Plurals that do not end in -s also take -'s (eg *sheep's eyes*). Except for a few traditional exceptions (like *Jesus', Keats'*) proper names ending in -s take -'s at the end (eg *Thomas's, the Jones's*).

brackets These serve to isolate part of a sentence, which could be omitted and still leave an intelligible statement. Punctuation of the rest of the sentence should run as if the bracketed portion were not there, eg *That house over there (with the blue door) is ours.* Square brackets are used where the writer inserts his own information into a quotation, eg *I knew Pitt [the Younger] as a boy.*

capital letters These are used at the beginning of a sentence or quoted speech, and for proper names and titles of people and organizations, eg *Mr. Robertson, Dr. Smith, South America, British Rail.* They are not used when speaking of a general topic like *the pay of miners, the manufacture of cosmetics.* If an initial *the* is included in a title it has a capital, eg *We went to see The Tempest.*

colons and semicolons The function of these is to provide more of a break than a comma, and less than a full stop. The colon is used to make an abrupt break between two related statements, eg *Take it or leave it: the choice is yours.* It is also used to introduce a list, quotation, or summary and may be followed by a dash if the following matter begins on a separate line. Semicolons can be used instead of conjunctions to link two sentences or parts of them, eg *Two of the lights were working; two were out.*

commas 1. These make divisions or slight pauses in sentences, eg *She stormed out, slamming the door behind her.*

2. Commas are used to divide units in a series of nouns, adjectives, or phrases, eg *The cupboard was full of pots, pans, and crockery.* In such a series the last comma (ie before 'and' or 'or') is optional.

It is not usual to place a comma between the last of a series of adjectives and the noun, eg *It was a long, hot, humid day.*

3. Commas also serve to mark off a word or phrase in a sentence which can stand grammatically complete on its own, as can dashes and brackets. Commas give the lightest degree of separation, dashes produce a jerky effect, and brackets cut off part of a sentence most firmly, eg *He hurried home, taking a short cut, but still arrived too late. It's a long time — over two years — since we last met. They both went to Athens (unaware of each other's plans) and stayed in the same hotel.*

4. When two phrases are linked by a conjunction a comma is used if there is a contrast, eg *She was dark, but her brother was fair.*

5. When addressing a person, commas are used before and after the person's name or title, eg *Well, Mrs. Smith, how are you today?*

exclamation marks These should only be used after genuine exclamations and not after ordinary statements.

full stops These are used at the end of a complete sentence containing a main verb, except in reported speech and where a passage takes the form of an argument, eg *You may think you can get away with it. Not a chance.* Full stops are also often used after abbreviations and initial letters standing for the whole word (as in *fig., a.m., R.C.*) but for abbreviations which include the first and last letters of a word (*Dr., Mr., ft.*) it is equally acceptable to omit the stop (*Dr, Mr, ft*). It is also usual to write titles, like *BBC, USA, TUC,* without stops. As usage varies the above should be taken only as a guide to common practice.

hyphens Compound words, like *lay-by* or *manor house,* or words with a prefix, like *unpick,* may or may not contain a hyphen. It is generally used when the compound is new and dropped as it becomes familiar. When a compound adjective comes before a noun it should be hyphenated to stress that the constituent parts are not to be used independently, eg *He has a half-Italian wife.*

inverted commas (quotation marks, quotes) 1. These are used for direct quotation, not for indirect speech. It is usual to have a comma before and after a quotation if the sentence is resumed, eg *He said, "Follow me", and set off down the street.*

2. Single quotation marks can be used to indicate a title or quotation within a speech, eg *"I loved 'War and Peace'," she said, "but it took so long to read."*

question marks These are used at the end of direct questions, but not after reported ones.

PLURALS OF NOUNS

Plurals are formed by adding -s except in the following cases.

1. When a word ends in -ch, -s, -sh, -ss, or -x the plural is formed by adding -es (eg *benches, gases, dishes, crosses, taxes*).

2. When a word ends in -y preceded by a consonant the plural form is -ies (eg *parties, bodies, policies*). When a word ends in -y preceded by a vowel the plural is formed by adding -s (eg *trays, joys, keys*).

3. When a word ends in -o the more common plural ending is -oes (eg *cargoes, potatoes, heroes, goes*). In many less familiar words when the final -o is preceded by a vowel the plural ending is -os (eg *avocados, armadillos, studios, cameos*).

4. When a word ends in -f the plural is formed either by adding -s (eg *beliefs, cuffs, whiffs*) or by changing the -f to -v and adding -es (eg *wives, thieves, loaves*). Some words may take both forms (eg *scarf, hoof, wharf*).

5. When a word ends in -ex or -ix the more formal plural ending is -ices. In more general contexts -es is used (eg *appendices, appendixes; indices, indexes*).

6. When a word from Latin ends in -is the plural form is -es (eg *crises, analyses*).

With compound words (like *court-martial*) it is usually the most important part which is pluralized (eg *courts-martial, lord-justices, mothers-in-law*).
In certain cases the plural form of a word is the same as the singular (eg *deer, sheep, grouse*) and in some words both forms end in -s (eg *measles, corps, mews*).

There are two main types of plural which take either singular or plural verbs.

a. words like *media* and *data*. These are in common use as singular nouns although, strictly, this is incorrect.

b. words ending in -ics. Generally, these are treated as plural when the word relates to an individual person or thing (eg *his mathematics are poor; the hall's acoustics are good*) and as singular when it is regarded more strictly as a science (eg *mathematics is an important subject*).

GEOLOGICAL TIME CHART

Main Divisions of Geological Time			Principal Physical & Biological Features
Eras	**Periods or Systems**		
		Epochs or Series	
Cainozoic	QUATERNARY	Recent 12,000*	Glaciers restricted to Antarctica and Greenland; development and spread of modern human culture.
		Pleistocene 600,000	Great glaciers covered much of Northern Hemisphere; appearance of modern man late in Pleistocene.
	TERTIARY	Pliocene 10,000,000	W North America uplifted; continued development of mammals; first possible apelike men appeared in Africa.
		Miocene 25,000,000	Renewed uplift of Alpine mountains; mammals began to acquire present-day characters; dogs, solid-hoofed horses, manlike apes appeared.
		Oligocene 35,000,000	Many older types of mammals became extinct; mastodons, first monkeys, and apes appeared.
		Eocene 50,000,000	Alpine mountain building (Himalayas, Alps, Andes, Rockies); expansion of early mammals; primitive horses appeared.
		Palaeocene 65,000,000	Great development of primitive mammals.
Mesozoic	CRETACEOUS 135,000,000		Chalk deposits laid down; dinosaurs reached maximum development & then became extinct; mammals small & very primitive.
	JURASSIC 180,000,000		Rocks of S and C Europe laid down; conifers & cycads dominant among plants; primitive birds appeared.
	TRIASSIC 230,000,000		Modern corals appeared & some insects of present-day types; great expansion of reptiles including earliest dinosaurs.

*Figures indicate approximate number of years since the beginning of each division.

GEOLOGICAL TIME CHART

Main Divisions of Geological Time			Principal Physical & Biological Features
Eras	**Periods or Systems**		**Principal Physical & Biological Features**
Palaeozoic		PERMIAN 280,000,000	Trees of coal-forming forests declined; ferns abundant; conifers present; trilobites became extinct; reptiles surpassed amphibians.
	CARBONIFEROUS	UPPER CARBONIFEROUS 310,000,000	Hercynian mountain building (C Europe, E coast of North America); great coal-forming swamp forests flourished in N Hemisphere; seed-bearing ferns abundant; cockroaches & first reptiles appeared.
		LOWER CARBONIFEROUS 345,000,000	Land plants became diversified; crinoids achieved greatest development; sharks of relatively modern types appeared; land animals little known.
	DEVONIAN 405,000,000		Land plants evolved rapidly, large trees appeared; brachiopods reached maximum development; many kinds of primitive fishes; first sharks, insects, & amphibians appeared.
	SILURIAN 425,000,000		Great mountains formed in NW Europe; first small land plants appeared; shelled cephalopods abundant; trilobites began decline; first jawed fish appeared.
	ORDOVICIAN 500,000,000		Caledonian mountain building; much limestone deposited in shallow seas; many marine invertebrates; first primitive jawless fish appeared.
	CAMBRIAN 600,000,000		Shallow seas covered parts of continents; abundant record of marine life, esp. trilobites & brachiopods; other fossils rare.
Precambrian	LATE PRECAMBRIAN** 2,000,000,000		Metamorphosed sedimentary rocks and granite formed; first evidence of life, calcareous algae & invertebrates.
	EARLY PRECAMBRIAN** 4,500,000,000		Crust formed on molten earth; crystalline rocks much disturbed; history unknown.

**Regarded as separate eras.

NAMES AND SYMBOLS OF METRIC UNITS

Quantity	Name of Unit	Value	Symbol
LENGTH	metre	base unit	m
	centimetre	0.01 m	cm
	millimetre	0.001 m	mm
	micrometre	0.000 001 m	μm (or um)
	kilometre	1 000 m	km
	international nautical mile (for navigation)	1 852 m	n mile
MASS (weight)	kilogram	base unit	kg
	milligram	0.000 001 kg	mg
	gram	0.001 kg	g
	tonne	1 000 kg	t
TIME	second	base unit	s
	minute	60 s	min
	hour	60 min	h
	day	24 h	d
AREA	square metre	SI unit	m^2
	square millimetre	0.000 001 m^2	mm^2
	square centimetre	0.000 1 m^2	cm^2
	hectare	10 000 m^2	ha
	square kilometre	1 000 000 m^2	km^2
VOLUME	cubic metre	SI unit	m^3
	cubic centimetre	0.000 001 m^3	cm^3
VOLUME (for fluids)	litre	0.001 m^3	l
	millilitre	0.001 l	ml
	kilolitre	1 000 l (1 m^3)	kl
VELOCITY	metre per second	SI unit	m/s
	kilometre per hour	0.27 m/s	km/h
	knot	1 n mile/h or o.514 m/s	kn
FORCE	newton	SI unit	N
	kilonewton	1 000 N	kN
	meganewton	1 000 000 N	MN
ENERGY	joule	SI unit	J
	kilojoule	1 000 J	kJ
	megajoule	1 000 000 J	MJ

NAMES AND SYMBOLS OF METRIC UNITS

Quantity	Name of Unit	Value	Symbol
POWER	watt	SI unit	W
	kilowatt	1 000 W	kW
	megawatt	1 000 000 W	MW
DENSITY	kilogram per cubic metre	SI unit	kg/m³
	tonne per cubic metre	1 000 kg/m³	t/m³
	gram per cubic metre	0.001 kg/m³	g/m³
DENSITY (for fluids)	kilogram per litre	1 000 kg/m³	kg/l
PRESSURE	pascal	SI unit (N/m²)	Pa
	kilopascal	1 000 Pa	kPa
	megapascal	1 000 000 Pa	MPa
PRESSURE (for meteorology)	millibar	100 Pa	mb
ELECTRIC CURRENT	ampere	base unit	A
	milliampere	0.001 A	mA
POTENTIAL DIFFERENCE	volt	SI unit	V
	microvolt	0.000 001 V	µV
	millivolt	0.001 V	mV
	kilovolt	1 000 V	kV
	megavolt	1 000 000 V	MV
ELECTRICAL RESISTANCE	ohm	SI unit	Ω
	microhm	0.000 001Ω	µΩ
	megohm	1 000 000Ω	MΩ
FREQUENCY	hertz	SI unit	Hz
	kilohertz	1 000 Hz	kHz
	megahertz	1 000 000 Hz	MHz
	gigahertz	1 000 000 000 Hz	GHz
TEMPERATURE	kelvin	SI unit	K
	degree Celsius	K-273.15	°C

METRIC/IMPERIAL CONVERSION FACTORS

Imperial to Metric Units	Metric to Imperial Units
LENGTH	
1 in = 25.4 mm	1 cm = 0.394 in
1 ft = 30.5 cm	1 m = 3.28 ft
1 yd = 0.914 m	1 m = 1.09 yd
1 mile = 1.61 km	1 km = 0.621 mile
MASS	
1 oz = 28.3 g	1 g = 0.0353 oz
1 lb = 454 g	1 kg = 2.20 lb
1 ton = 1.02 tonne	1 tonne = 0.984 ton
AREA	
1 in^2 = 6.45 cm^2	1 cm^2 = 0.155 in^2
1 ft^2 = 929 cm^2	1 m^2 = 10.8 ft^2
1 yd^2 = 0.836 m^2	1 m^2 = 1.20 yd^2
1 ac = 0.405 ha	1 ha = 2.47 ac
1 sq. mile = 259 ha	1 km^2 = 247 ac
VOLUME	
1 in^3 = 16.4 cm^3	1 cm^3 = 0.0610 in^3
1 ft^3 = 0.0283 m^3	1 m^3 = 35.3 ft^3
1 yd^3 = 0.765 m^3	1 m^3 = 1.31 yd^3
1 bushel = 0.0364 m^3	1 m^3 = 27.5 bushels
VOLUME (fluids)	
1 fl oz = 28.4 ml	1 ml = 0.0352 fl oz
1 pint = 568 ml	1 litre = 1.76 pint
1 gallon = 4.55 litre	1 m^3 = 220 gallons
FORCE	
1 lbf (pound-force) = 4.45 N	1N (newton) = 0.225 lbf
PRESSURE	
1 psi (lb/sq in) = 6.89 kPa	1 kPa (kilo- = 0.145 psi pascal)
VELOCITY	
1 mph = 1.61 km/h	1 km/h = 0.621 mph
TEMPERATURE	
°C = $\dfrac{5}{9}$ (°F − 32)	°F = $\dfrac{9 \times °C}{5}$ + 32
ENERGY	
1 Btu (British = 1.06 kJ thermal unit)	1 kJ (kilo- = 0.948 Btu joule)
POWER	
1 hp = 0.746 kW	1 kW = 1.34 hp
FUEL CONSUMPTION	
mpg = $\dfrac{282}{\text{litres/100 km}}$	litres/100 km = $\dfrac{282}{\text{mpg}}$

TEMPERATURE CONVERSION TABLE

CELSIUS TO FAHRENHEIT

Conversion formulae:

See METRIC/IMPERIAL CONVERSION FACTORS

°C	°F	°C	°F	°C	°F
50	122	20	68	−10	14
49	120.2	19	66.2	−11	12.2
48	118.4	18	64.4	−12	10.4
47	116.6	17	62.6	−13	8.6
46	114.8	16	60.8	−14	6.8
45	113	15	59	−15	5
44	111.2	14	57.2	−16	3.2
43	109.4	13	55.4	−17	1.4
42	107.6	12	53.6	−18	−0.4
41	105.8	11	51.8	−19	−2.2
40	104	10	50	−20	−4
39	102.2	9	48.2	−21	−5.8
38	100.4	8	46.4	−22	−7.6
37	98.6	7	44.6	−23	−9.4
36	96.8	6	42.8	−24	−11.2
35	95	5	41	−25	−13
34	93.2	4	39.2	−26	−14.8
33	91.4	3	37.4	−27	−16.6
32	89.6	2	35.6	−28	−18.4
31	87.8	1	33.8	−29	−20.2
30	86	0	32	−30	−22
29	84.2	−1	30.2	−31	−23.8
28	82.4	−2	28.4	−32	−25.6
27	80.6	−3	26.6	−33	−27.4
26	78.8	−4	24.8	−34	−29.2
25	77	−5	23	−35	−31
24	75.2	−6	21.2	−36	−32.8
23	73.4	−7	19.4	−37	−34.6
22	71.6	−8	17.6	−38	−36.4
21	69.8	−9	15.8	−39	−38.2

MATHEMATICAL SYMBOLS

$+$	1. plus, addition sign 2. positive	$\bigcirc$	circle; circumference
$-$	1. minus, subtraction sign 2. negative	$\frown$	arc of a circle
$\times$	multiplied by	$\triangle$	triangle
$\div$	divided by; also indicated by oblique stroke (8/2) or horizontal line $\frac{8}{2}$	$\square$	square
		$\square$	rectangle
		$\square$	parallelogram
$=$	equals; is equal to	$\sqrt{}$	radical sign (ie square root sign)
$\neq$	is not equal to	$\sum$	sum
$\equiv$	is identical with; is congruent to	$\int$	integral
$\sim$	difference between; is equivalent to	$\cup$	union
$\simeq, \approx$	is approximately equal to	$\cap$	intersection
$>$	is greater than	$\in$	is a member of; is an element of; belongs to
$<$	is less than	$\subseteq$	is contained as subclass within
$\ngtr$	is not greater than	$\supseteq$	contains as subclass
$\nless$	is not less than	$\{\ \}$	set braces
$\leqslant$	less than or equal to	ϕ	the empty set
$\geqslant$	greater than or equal to	$|\ |$	absolute value of; modulus of
$\cong$	is isomorphic to	$\triangleleft$	is a normal subgroup of
$:$	is to; ratio sign	μ	mean (population)
$::$	as : used between ratios	σ	standard deviation (population)
∞	infinity	$\bar{x}$	mean (sample)
$\propto$	varies as, proportional to	s	standard deviation (sample)
$\therefore$	therefore	π	ratio of circumference of any circle to its diameter
$\because$	since, because		
$\angle$	angle	e	base of natural logarithms
$\llcorner$	right angle	$^{\circ}$	degrees of arc or temperature
$\perp$	is perpendicular to	$'$	minutes of arc or time; feet
$\parallel$	is parallel to	$''$	seconds of arc or time; inches

CHEMICAL SYMBOLS

Each element is placed in alphabetical order of its symbol and is followed by its atomic number.

Ac actinium, 89	**Ge** germanium, 32	**Po** polonium, 84
Ag silver, 47	**H** hydrogen, 1	**Pr** praseodymium, 59
Al aluminium, 13	**Ha** hahnium, 105	**Pt** platinum, 78
Am americium, 95	**He** helium, 2	**Pu** plutonium, 94
Ar argon, 18	**Hf** hafnium, 72	**Ra** radium, 88
As arsenic, 33	**Hg** mercury, 80	**Rb** rubidium, 37
At astatine, 85	**Ho** holmium, 67	**Re** rhenium, 75
Au gold, 79	**I** iodine, 53	**Rf** rutherfordium, 104
B boron, 5	**In** indium, 49	**Rh** rhodium, 45
Ba barium, 56	**Ir** iridium, 77	**Rn** radon, 86
Be beryllium, 4	**K** potassium, 19	**Ru** ruthenium, 44
Bi bismuth, 83	**Kr** krypton, 36	**S** sulphur, 16
Bk berkelium, 97	**La** lanthanum, 57	**Sb** antimony, 51
Br bromine, 35	**Li** lithium, 3	**Sc** scandium, 21
C carbon, 6	**Lr** lawrencium, 103	**Se** selenium, 34
Ca calcium, 20	**Lu** lutetium, 71	**Si** silicon, 14
Cd cadmium, 48	**Md** mendelevium, 101	**Sm** samarium, 62
Ce cerium, 58	**Mg** magnesium, 12	**Sn** tin, 50
Cf californium, 98	**Mn** manganese, 25	**Sr** strontium, 38
Cl chlorine, 17	**Mo** molybdenum, 42	**Ta** tantalum, 73
Cm curium, 96	**N** nitrogen, 7	**Tb** terbium, 65
Co cobalt, 27	**Na** sodium, 11	**Tc** technetium, 43
Cr chromium, 24	**Nb** niobium, 41	**Te** tellurium, 52
Cs caesium, 55	**Nd** neodymium, 60	**Th** thorium, 90
Cu copper, 29	**Ne** neon, 10	**Ti** titanium, 22
Dy dysprosium, 66	**Ni** nickel, 28	**Tl** thallium, 81
Er erbium, 68	**No** nobelium, 102	**Tm** thulium, 69
Es einsteinium, 99	**Np** neptunium, 93	**U** uranium, 92
Eu europium, 63	**O** oxygen, 8	**V** vanadium, 23
F fluorine, 9	**Os** osmium, 76	**W** tungsten, 74
Fe iron, 26	**P** phosphorus, 15	**Xe** xenon, 54
Fm fermium, 100	**Pa** protactinium, 91	**Y** yttrium, 39
Fr francium, 87	**Pb** lead, 82	**Yb** ytterbium, 70
Ga gallium, 31	**Pd** palladium, 46	**Zn** zinc, 30
Gd gadolinium, 64	**Pm** promethium, 61	**Zr** zirconium, 40

COUNTRIES, RELATED NOUNS AND ADJECTIVES, CURRENCIES, AND CAPITALS

Country	Noun/ Adjective	Currency Unit	Capital
Afghanistan	Afghan	afghani	Kabul
Albania	Albanian	lek	Tirana
Algeria	Algerian	dinar	Algiers
Andorra	Andorran	franc/ peseta	Andorra la Vella
Angola	Angolan	kwanza	Luanda
Argentina	Argentine or Argentinian	peso	Buenos Aires
Australia	Australian	dollar	Canberra
Austria	Austrian	schilling	Vienna
Bahamas	Bahamian	dollar	Nassau
Bahrain	Bahraini	dinar	Manama
Bangladesh	Bangladeshi	taka	Dhaka
Barbados	Barbadian	dollar	Bridgetown
Belgium	Belgian	franc	Brussels
Benin	Beninese	franc	Porto Novo
Bermuda	Bermudan	dollar	Hamilton
Bolivia	Bolivian	peso	La Paz
Botswana		pula	Gaborone
Brazil	Brazilian	cruzeiro	Brasilia
Bulgaria	Bulgarian	lev	Sofia
Burma	Burmese	kyat	Rangoon
Burundi	Burundian	franc	Bujumbura
Cameroon	Cameroonian	franc	Yaoundé
Canada	Canadian	dollar	Ottawa
Central African Rep.		franc	Bangui
Chad	Chadian	franc	Ndjamena
Chile	Chilean	peso	Santiago
China	Chinese	yuan	Peking
China (Taiwan)	Chinese	dollar	Taipei
Colombia	Colombian	peso	Bogotá
Congo	Congolese	franc	Brazzaville
Costa Rica	Costa Rican	colon	San José
Cuba	Cuban	peso	Havana
Cyprus	Cypriot	pound	Nicosia
Czechoslovakia	Czech. Czechoslovak, or Czechoslovakian	crown	Prague
Denmark	Dane; Danish	krone	Copenhagen
Dominica	Dominican	dollar	Roseau
Dominican Rep.	Dominican	peso	Santo Domingo
Ecuador	Ecuadorean	sucre	Quito
Egypt	Egyptian	pound	Cairo
El Salvador	Salvadorean	colon	San Salvador
Equatorial Guinea		ekpwele	Malabo
Ethiopia	Ethiopian	birr	Addis Ababa
Fiji	Fijian	dollar	Suva
Finland	Finn; Finnish	markka	Helsinki
France	Frenchman, -woman; French	franc	Paris
Gabon	Gabonese	franc	Libreville
Gambia	Gambian	dalasi	Banjul
Germany, East	East German	mark	East Berlin
Germany, West	West German	Deutsche Mark	Bonn
Ghana	Ghanaian	cedi	Accra
Greece	Greek	drachma	Athens
Grenada	Grenadian	dollar	St George's

COUNTRIES, RELATED NOUNS AND ADJECTIVES, CURRENCIES, AND CAPITALS

Country	Noun/ Adjective	Currency Unit	Capital
Guatemala	Guatemalan	quetzal	Guatemala City
Guinea	Guinean	franc	Conakry
Guinea-Bissau		peso	Bissau
Guyana	Guyanese	dollar	Georgetown
Haiti	Haitian	gourde	Port-au-Prince
Honduras	Honduran	lempira	Tegucigalpa
Hungary	Hungarian	forint	Budapest
Iceland	Icelander; Icelandic	krona	Reykjavik
India	Indian	rupee	New Delhi
Indonesia	Indonesian	rupiah	Jakarta
Iran	Iranian	rial	Tehran
Iraq	Iraqi	dinar	Baghdad
Ireland, Republic of	Irishman, -woman; Irish	pound	Dublin
Israel	Israeli	shekel	Jerusalem
Italy	Italian	lira	Rome
Jamaica	Jamaican	dollar	Kingston
Japan	Japanese	yen	Tokyo
Jordan	Jordanian	dinar	Amman
Kampuchea	Kampuchean	riel	Phnom Penh
Kenya	Kenyan	shilling	Nairobi
Korea, North	North Korean	won	Pyongyang
Korea, South	South Korean	won	Seoul
Kuwait	Kuwaiti	dinar	Kuwait
Laos	Laotian	kip	Vientiane
Lebanon	Lebanese	pound	Beirut
Lesotho		rand	Maseru
Liberia	Liberian	dollar	Monrovia
Libya	Libyan	pound	Tripoli
Liechtenstein		franc	Vaduz
Luxembourg		franc	Luxembourg
Madagascar	Madagascan	franc	Antananarivo
Malawi	Malawian	kwacha	Lilongwe
Malaysia	Malaysian	ringgit	Kuala Lumpur
Mali	Malian	franc	Bamako
Malta	Maltese	pound	Valletta
Mauritania	Mauritanian	franc	Nouakchott
Mauritius	Mauritian	rupee	Port Louis
Mexico	Mexican	peso	Mexico City
Monaco	Monegasque	franc	Monaco
Mongolian People's Rep.	Mongolian	tugrik	Ulan Bator
Morocco	Moroccan	dirham	Rabat
Mozambique	Mozambican	escudo	Maputo
Nepal	Nepalese	rupee	Katmandu
Netherlands	Dutchman, -woman; Netherlander; Dutch	guilder	Amsterdam
New Zealand	New Zealander	dollar	Wellington
Nicaragua	Nicaraguan	cordoba	Managua
Niger		franc	Niamey
Nigeria	Nigerian	naira	Lagos
Norway	Norwegian	krone	Oslo
Oman	Omani	rial	Muscat
Pakistan	Pakistani	rupee	Islamabad
Panama	Panamanian	balboa	Panama City

COUNTRIES, RELATED NOUNS AND ADJECTIVES, CURRENCIES, AND CAPITALS

Country	Noun/ Adjective	Currency Unit	Capital
Papua New Guinea	Papuan	kina	Port Moresby
Paraguay	Paraguayan	guarani	Asunción
Peru	Peruvian	sol	Lima
Philippines	Filipino *or* Philippine	peso	Quezon City
Poland	Pole; Polish	zloty	Warsaw
Portugal	Portuguese	escudo	Lisbon
Qatar	Qatari	riyal	Doha
Rumania	Rumanian	leu	Bucharest
Rwanda	Rwandan	franc	Kigali
San Marino	San Marinese *or* Sammarinese	lira	San Marino
Saudi Arabia	Saudi Arabian	riyal	Riyadh
Senegal	Senegalese	franc	Dakar
Sierra Leone	Sierra Leonean	leone	Freetown
Singapore	Singaporean	dollar	Singapore
Somalia	Somalian	shilling	Mogadiscio
South Africa	South African	rand	Cape Town (legislative) Pretoria (administrative)
Spain	Spaniard; Spanish	peseta	Madrid
Sri Lanka	Sri Lankan	rupee	Colombo
Sudan	Sudanese	pound	Khartoum
Surinam	Surinamese	guilder	Paramaribo
Swaziland	Swazi	rand	Mbabane
Sweden	Swede; Swedish	krona	Stockholm
Switzerland	Swiss	franc	Bern
Syria	Syrian	pound	Damascus
Tanzania	Tanzanian	shilling	Dodoma
Thailand	Thai	baht	Bangkok
Togo	Togolese	franc	Lomé
Tonga	Tongan	pa'anga	Nuku'alofa
Trinidad and Tobago	Trinidadian, Tobagan	dollar	Port-of-Spain
Tunisia	Tunisian	dinar	Tunis
Turkey	Turk; Turkish	lira	Ankara
Uganda	Ugandan	shilling	Kampala
USSR	Russian *or* Soviet	rouble	Moscow
United Arab Emirates		dirham	Abu Dhabi
United Kingdom	Briton; British	pound	London
USA	American	dollar	Washington D.C.
Uruguay	Uruguayan	peso	Montevideo
Venezuela	Venezuelan	bolivar	Caracas
Vietnam	Vietnamese	dong	Hanoi
Western Samoa	Samoan	tala	Apia
Yemen, People's Democratic Rep.	Yemeni	dinar	Aden
Yemen Arab Rep.	Yemeni	riyal	Sanaa
Yugoslavia	Yugoslav *or* Yugoslavian	dinar	Belgrade
Zaire	Zairean	zaire	Kinshasa
Zambia	Zambian	kwacha	Lusaka
Zimbabwe	Zimbabwean	dollar	Harare

WORLD STANDARD TIMES

At noon, GMT, 1300 BST

For each degree of longitude, time differs by 4 minutes; west of Greenwich is earlier, east of Greenwich later, than GMT.

Place	Time	Place	Time
Accra	1200	Malta	1300
Adelaide	2130	Melbourne	2200
Aden	1500	Mexico City	0600
Algiers	1300	Montevideo	0830
Amsterdam	1300	Montreal	0700
Athens	1400	Moscow	1500
Auckland	2400	Nairobi	1500
Beirut	1400	New Orleans	0600
Belgrade	1300	New York	0700
Berlin	1300	Oslo	1300
Berne	1300	Ottawa	0700
Bombay	1730	Panama	0700
Brindisi	1300	Paris	1300
Brisbane	2200	Peking	2000
Brussels	1300	Perth, Australia	2000
Bucharest	1400	Prague	1300
Budapest	1300	Quebec	0700
Buenos Aires	0800	Rangoon	1830
Cairo	1400	Rio de Janeiro	0900
Calcutta	1730	Rome	1300
Cape Town	1400	St John's, Newfoundland	0830
Caracas	0800	St Louis	0600
Chicago	0600	San Francisco	0400
Colombo	1730	Santiago	0800
Copenhagen	1300	Singapore	1930
Gibraltar	1300	Sofia	1400
Helsinki	1400	Stockholm	1300
Hobart	2200	Suez	1400
Hong Kong	2000	Sydney	2200
Istanbul	1400	Tehran	1530
Jerusalem	1400	Tokyo	2100
Karachi	1700	Toronto	0700
Lagos	1300	Tunis	1300
Leningrad	1500	Vancouver	0400
Lima	0700	Vienna	1300
Lisbon	1200	Warsaw	1300
Madeira	1100	Winnipeg	0600
Madras	1730	Yokohama	2100
Madrid	1300		

DISTANCES BY AIR

The flight distances shown in the following tables are quoted in kilometres via the shortest normal airline routing from airport to airport. For cities with more than one airport a mean distance is given. An asterisk indicates a maximum distance.

from London

Accra	5086
Algiers	1650
Amsterdam	370
Auckland	24290*
Baghdad	4097
Bahrain	5084
Bangkok	9551
Barcelona	1129
Beirut	3468
Belgrade	1689
Berlin	952
Bombay	7205
Brisbane	23746*
Brussels	340
Budapest	1476
Buenos Aires	13442*
Cairo	3518
Calcutta	11111*
Cape Town	12275*
Casablanca	2062
Chicago	6364
Cologne	525
Colombo	11289*
Copenhagen	984
Dakar	4349
Darwin	18151*
Delhi	6730
Dubrovnik	1715
Geneva	736
Hamburg	745
Harare (Zimbabwe)	10707*
Honolulu	11699*
Istanbul	2502
Jakarta	15208*
Jamaica	7532
Johannesburg	9059
Karachi	8494
Kuwait	4666
Lagos	4988
Lisbon	1555
Madrid	1232
Marseilles	971
Melbourne	25011*
Milan	940
Montreal	5234
Moscow	2507

Nairobi	6825
Naples	1613
New York	5564
Nice	1022
Oslo	1175
Palma	1330
Paris	336
Prague	1037
Rangoon	12255*
Rio de Janeiro	11132*
Rome	1436
San Francisco	10420*
Singapore	14133*
Stockholm	1462
Sydney	24163*
Tehran	4408
Tel Aviv	3577
Tokyo	17518*
Toronto	5727
Tunis	1813
Venice	1135
Vienna	1262
Warsaw	1465
Washington	5889
Wellington	24372

from Montreal

Amsterdam	5509
Auckland	17658*
Berlin	7314*
Bombay	15340*
Cairo	10488*
Moscow	8832*
New York	531
Paris	5527
Rio de Janeiro	9942*
Rome	6601
Vancouver	3684
Zurich	6000

from Sydney

Auckland	2162
Berlin	20940*
Cairo	17475*
Johannesburg	14685*
Moscow	20933*
New York	19407*
Paris	21329*

Rome	20041*
San Francisco	14442*
Singapore	6303
Tokyo	7821
Toronto	18839*

from Auckland

Berlin	23535*
Brisbane	2297
Buenos Aires	15809*
Cairo	20069*
Honolulu	7094
Moscow	24598*
New York	17275*
Paris	23923*
Rome	24588*
San Francisco	13142*
Singapore	10157*
Tokyo	13584*

from Johannesburg

Amsterdam	10848*
Auckland	17161*
Berlin	10930*
Cape Town	1272
Montreal	16061*
Moscow	11162*
Nairobi	2914
New York	15424*
Paris	10600*
Rio de Janeiro	7150
Rome	9507*
Tel Aviv	6506

from Bombay

Auckland	14857*
Berlin	8680*
Cairo	4345
Hong Kong	4303
Johannesburg	8939*
Moscow	8671*
Paris	9068*
Rio de Janeiro	18444*
Rome	6182
San Francisco	19563*
Singapore	3916
Sydney	12262*